DICTIONARY
OF
AFRO-AMERICAN
SLAVERY

DICTIONARY OF AFRO-AMERICAN SLAVERY

Edited by

Randall M. Miller

and

John David Smith

GREENWOOD PRESS

New York • Westport, Connecticut • London

Library of Congress Cataloging-in-Publication Data

Dictionary of Afro-American slavery / edited by Randall M. Miller and
  John David Smith.
     p. cm.
  Includes bibliographies and index.
  ISBN 0–313–23814–6 (lib. bdg. : alk. paper)
    1. Slavery—United States—History—Dictionaries. 2. Afro-
Americans—Dictionaries and encyclopedias. I. Miller, Randall M.
II. Smith, John David, 1949– .
E441.D53   1988
305.5′67′0899607—dc19   87–37543

British Library Cataloguing in Publication Data is available.

Library of Congress Catalog Card Number: 87–37543
ISBN: 0–313–23814–6

First published in 1988

Greenwood Press, Inc.
88 Post Road West, Westport, Connecticut 06881

Printed in the United States of America

The paper used in this book complies with the
Permanent Paper Standard issued by the National
Information Standards Organization (Z39.48–1984).

10 9 8 7 6 5 4 3 2

CONTENTS

INTRODUCTION

Over the past quarter century perhaps no subject of American historical inquiry has commanded so much attention as has Afro-American slavery. Despite warnings issued twenty years ago that the subject was exhausted, important new scholarship continues to appear. It is easy to understand why, for the slavery experience stands at the center of American identity. The South as a region cannot be understood without reference to it, current racial relations in some ways still derive from it, and America's claim to preeminence as the land of liberty must account for it. Slavery helped build the republic and ultimately became the principal cause of a civil war that almost destroyed it. Slavery nagged at the American conscience before and after the slaves' emancipation from bondage. It continues to fascinate our historical imagination.

Though slavery long had been a major subject of historical inquiry, modern slavery scholarship received a major impetus from the civil rights movement of the 1960s. The recent scholarship has increasingly become self-sustaining. Historians discovered new sources and rediscovered old ones in folklore, material culture, music, ex-slave narratives and autobiographies, among others. They also incorporated anthropological, archaeological, demographic, folkloristic, linguistic, musicological, sociological, and other interdisciplinary methodologies into their own research. In doing so, recent scholarship focused increasingly on the social and cultural aspects of slave life and began to assess the slaves on their own terms, not just as victims of bondage. No longer were historians preoccupied with the great antebellum plantations. Scholars instead extended their inquiry backward to look at the colonial origins and evolution of bondage, and also forward, to examine the postemancipation world the ex-slaves and their former masters made. Within the last twenty years prize-winning books have been published on slavery and human progress, the origins of Anglo-American racial beliefs, the slave family, comparative slavery in New World settings, and other topics. These works suggest the sustained intellectual vigor and interest in slavery as a research field. Interest in slavery shows no signs of subsiding in the near future. Indeed, scholars are charting new areas of inquiry and applying new methods of analysis.

The very richness, sophistication, and profusion of scholarship on slavery, however, in some ways has made the subject less accessible to the public, and even to scholars. In his *Black Slavery in the Americas* (1982) John David Smith filled two thick volumes listing the titles of works relating to slavery that had been published between 1865 and 1980, and he no doubt could produce a large companion bibliography simply by covering the period from 1980 to the present. The literature on slavery is so vast and the production so prolific that a scholar can no longer pretend to master it within a lifetime. Nonspecialists and general readers often face confusion and frustration in trying to sort through the many and varied books and articles on slavery. Few attempts at any synthesis of the rich and abundant literature have been made, partly because the literature, by its size and its sophistication, is so intimidating. Thus the dictionary.

In 1982 Greenwood Press invited the editors of the dictionary to prepare a comprehensive reference work on Afro-American slavery. No similar work existed then, and no comparable work has surfaced in the five years it has required to assemble the dictionary. The 1980s seemed an appropriate time to compile an authoritative encyclopedia on slavery in North America. The literature abounded and required synthesis. Also, the studies of slavery had reached a critical turning point away from "macro" investigations of slavery in large regional or national settings, and toward intensive, or "micro," probings of slavery in well-defined localities. At the same time, the emphasis was shifting toward longitudinal studies, tracking communities over time (and sometimes space). Scholars wanted to take stock of the field, to attempt syntheses of past work as they sketched out strategies for new research. The dictionary promised to provide both the occasion and the opportunity for synthesis of the best scholarship on the many and diverse aspects of the slavery experience in North America.

The geographical focus of the dictionary is the United States, though some entries transcend national boundaries when treating such subjects as African and Afro-American cultures, slave resistance, and religion. The time frame for most essays is the period from the first English settlement in North America to Reconstruction after the Civil War. Within those boundaries, the dictionary ranges both widely and plumbs deeply. Readers will find entries on such broad subjects as abolition, the slave trade, and urban slavery, as well as on more self-contained subjects such as the underground railroad, Nat Turner, and slavery in Philadelphia. Appreciating the importance of particular legal, institutional, and political environments in shaping slavery and black-white relations, the editors have included entries on the various regions of the United States, on each of the Southern slave states, and on important cities. Selected biographies of prominent individuals involved in slavery, and of less-known but representative figures in Afro-American history, suggest the variety of individual involvements with and responses to slavery in North America. Important events, such as the American

Revolution and the Civil War, warranted major essays. So, too, did synthetic essays on slave culture, religion, and society, and on the sources for studying slavery and its imagery and historiography.

In selecting subject entries for the dictionary, the editors gave foremost consideration to the broadest potential use of the work. Article topics were selected for their importance to specialists and to lay readers alike. The dictionary was designed to access material on slavery for a wide audience—for patrons of academic as well as public libraries. The editors took special care to include among the almost 300 articles topics that reflected regional and geographic differences within the slave experience and changes in slavery over time. Social, institutional, intellectual, and political aspects of slavery receive considerable attention. The editors chose the contributors on the basis of their special expertise in the study of slavery. Virtually all of the contributors had published on their subjects or showed potential to publish on some aspect of slavery. The editors demanded jargon-free, up-to-date contributions and imposed uniformity and consistency in format and style. The editors did not attempt to reconcile different interpretations or to recast arguments to fit their own beliefs. The worth of the dictionary in part derives from its sometimes contradictory nature, revealing the different approaches, assumptions, and evidence that give the study of slavery its vitality and integrity. Each entry includes bibliographical references to the best published sources on the particular subject.

The picture of Afro-American slavery that emerges from these pages suggests the varied, complex, and contradictory nature of bondage in North America. After years of scholarly debate, historians increasingly have moved away from viewing the slaves or the masters in one-dimensional terms (all good or all bad). No longer do historians defend or excuse slavery. Rather, modern scholarship on slavery seeks to explore the subtleties, the nuances, the dynamic (and syncretic) qualities inherent in a system of unfree labor that evolved over two centuries and that brought together people of different cultures. Quantification, comparative analysis, and sources that reflect the slave's perspective (oral history interviews, slave and ex-slave narratives, and folklore) have opened the slave quarters to scholarly view and understanding. Though many questions about slavery and its effects on all those trapped by it (black and white, slave and master, Southerner and Northerner) remain unanswered, the dictionary promises an essential and convenient starting point for untangling slavery and the racism and injustice that lay at its core.

A NOTE ON USING THE DICTIONARY

Entries to the dictionary are arranged in alphabetical order. To aid in finding related items, most entries include cross-references within the texts. A detailed, comprehensive subject index provides further assistance in identifying both information and issues represented in the dictionary and specific references to them. The bibliographical citations at the end of each entry refer to the best published sources available on the subject of the entry.

The cross-references are designated by an asterisk (*). The asterisk indicates that an individual, issue, event, or term merits an entry of its own. Within each entry, the asterisk follows the first substantive mention of any particular cross-reference. Only substantive cross-references (that is, cross-references bearing on the subject discussed in the text) are noted. Items mentioned only in passing are not marked as cross-references. Thus, for example, every mention of "cotton" does not warrant a cross-reference. States and cities are not specifically cross-referenced, for each slave state and each city in which slavery was significant (that is, Newport, Rhode Island; New York City; Philadelphia; and every large Southern city) has a separate entry. Derivative terms are cross-referenced. Thus, for example, "antislavery" is cross-referenced to the entry on "Abolitionism"; "architecture" to "Housing"; "artisans" to "Craftsmen"; "black churches" to "Religion, Slave"; "herds" to "Livestock"; "hoodoo" to "Voodoo"; "novels and stories" to "Literature, Slavery in"; "slave renting" to "Hiring Out"; "speech" to "Language"; and "white yeomen farmers" to "Nonslaveholding Whites."

ACKNOWLEDGMENTS

Over the course of editing the dictionary we have accumulated debts to many friends and colleagues. We cheerfully and thankfully acknowledge their support, encouragement, and criticism, and we absolve them of any responsibility for errors we might have committed.

James T. Sabin of Greenwood Press invited us to undertake the project and supported us at every stage. History editor Cynthia Harris patiently and carefully handled the editorial management and guided us through the many last-minute changes and improvements she suggested for the book. Production editor Terri Metz skillfully orchestrated the behemoth task of transforming an unwieldly manuscript into a finished book. Maureen Melino assisted us by sorting out administrative details, thereby smoothing the book's path toward completion. The entire book benefited enormously from the careful copyediting by Juanita Lewis at Greenwood Press.

At Saint Joseph's University David Burton and Thomas McFadden provided sustained encouragement and discovered various ways to help underwrite administrative costs. Stephanie McKeller-Auer typed many manuscripts and performed countless other tasks with her usual industry and tact. Margaret Fitzpatrick checked references. At the University of Pennsylvania Gail Farr helped with bibliographical searches and checked citations. At the Temple University Cartographic Laboratory Jeremy Tasch drew the maps for the entry on "African Background." The Saint Joseph's University Board on Faculty Research assisted the project with a grant-in-aid.

At North Carolina State University, in 1982 and 1983, the dictionary received grants from the North Carolina State University Faculty Research and Professional Development Fund. Burton F. Beers, former head of the Department of History, and his successor, Alexander J. De Grand, furnished timely aid, especially support for long-distance telephone calls, postage, office supplies, photocopying, and graduate student assistants. Three generations of North Carolina State history graduate students—Dorothy T. Frye, Alexandra S. Gressitt, Richard W. Hite, Curtis F. Morgan, Jr., and Tyler O. Walters—assisted in the editing of this project. They verified bibliographical citations and quotations, arranged and organized files, and orchestrated mass mailings and photocopying. Amy Hosokawa and Miriam Pond, secretaries in the Department of History, provided essential typing and photocopying. Cynthia Clay Adams, librarian at the University of North Carolina at Chapel Hill, offered encouragement and supplied valuable reference assistance. David P. Gilmartin cheered the dictionary on, even though the office he shared was constantly overrun by our files and seemingly endless conversations about slavery.

DICTIONARY
OF
AFRO-AMERICAN
SLAVERY

A

ABOLITIONISM. Opposition to Afro-American slavery was long-standing, varied, and complex. During the colonial and revolutionary periods slavery had existed in the Northern as well as in the Southern colonies/states and was basic to the fabric of daily life for a great many Americans. Consequently, those who opposed it were quite familiar with the concrete conditions of slaves and focused upon those conditions. They believed that the institution of slavery could only slowly be eradicated. Moreover, they usually offered specific measures for gradual emancipation—particular provisions to curb the African slave trade,* for example, or to manumit the children of bondsmen. Through these measures, there was to be a transition from slave to free labor economies. In contrast to their colonial and revolutionary predecessors, abolitionists of the pre–Civil War decades concentrated efforts in the Northern states where slavery had been eliminated for a generation. Moreover, they rejected gradualism unequivocally; Southern slavery was sin and had to be abolished instantly without compensation to slaveholders. Opposing a slave system that only a few of them had viewed from extensive firsthand experience, they characterized it in abstract moral terms that were often removed from the everyday lives of black bondspeople. Thus, the general presence or absence of slaves in everyday society was what differentiated early American antislavery appeals from antebellum immediatist abolitionism.

Throughout British North America, formal opposition to slavery was rare outside of the Society of Friends (*see* Quakers). Samuel Sewall was one of the few Puritans, for example, who characterized it as wholly incompatible with a Bible commonwealth. But Sewall's emphasis was on the inexpediencies rather than the immoralities of bondage; it retarded the migrations of more efficient European laborers. Similarly, expediency rather than moral propriety explained why the Germans of Ebenezer, Georgia, opposed slavery during the early 1730s. They argued that marauding slaves would force them to abandon their homes and their crops. Claims such as these prompted efforts to limit the importation of blacks from Africa and the Caribbean in diverse locations throughout the American colonies.

The Quakers represented the only group of colonists, however, who advocated emancipation consistently and firmly in the years before the American Revolution. Since all people held the inner light of God within them, Quakers postulated, all were fundamentally equal. Consequently, it was immoral for one man to own another. To be sure, many Quakers departed from this orientation during the first half of the eighteenth century as they sought to emulate prosperous and well-dressed grandee gentlemen. But by the 1750s Pennsylvania and New Jersey Quakers returned to a more devout notion of the inner light and insisted that slavery was antithetical to piety. By 1758 they were disciplining fellow Quakers who purchased blacks by issuing decrees at their Meetings. Anthony Benezet and John Woolman were gaining Quaker adherents in these and even other colonies as they pressed against the morality of slavery and demanded boycotts of slave-produced goods. Woolman even garnered support among Southern Friends in pleas that combined pious admonitions against bondage with practical steps to weaken it.

By the 1780s Quakers throughout the North were forcing members of their Meetings to emancipate their slaves. They were supported by a number of Congregational* and Methodist* clergy. Revolutionary war* fervor also contributed to the spread of antislavery feeling, particularly in New England. The rights of British North American colonists to escape arbitrary rule were frequently analogized to the rights of black slaves against the master class.

Nevertheless, by 1790 there were still 3,763 slaves in New England* and 36,323 in the Middle Atlantic states.* Emancipation in the North was a slow and difficult process; political leaders were intent on gradual and minimally disruptive change. Usually, they enacted laws freeing only the children of slaves who were born after specific dates—1 March 1784 in Connecticut, for example, 4 July 1799 in New York, and 4 July 1804 in New Jersey. Moreover, freeborn children were to serve as unpaid apprentices until their mid or late twenties. To be sure, the prospect of legal emancipation increased voluntary manumissions throughout the North. But it also prompted other Northern slaveholders to sell their bondsmen to Southern slave traders. The more prevalent approach to forestalling this "first emancipation," however, was by curtailing the enforcement of state statutes. Consequently, slaves continued to labor in New York until 1827 and in Connecticut until at least the mid–1850s. Despite an 1804 emancipation statute in New Jersey, the state continued to have slaves (defined as "apprentices") during the Civil War.

While slavery was gradually ending in the North, considerably less change occurred in the South. The invention of the cotton gin* in 1793 augmented profits from enslaved agricultural labor. This helps to explain why attempts by Henry Clay* and others at the 1798 Kentucky constitutional convention to eliminate slavery failed, as efforts were later to fail in Georgia and Virginia. Nevertheless, relatively few Southerners endorsed slavery publicly before the second decade of the nineteenth century. During the revolutionary era, it was regarded with caution and ambiguity in Virginia and Maryland and with general silence in the lower South.

When they commented on "slavery," early Americans were therefore almost always speaking about the black bondage around them. Those who opposed it knew, in very concrete terms, what they sought to eliminate. The Founding Fathers certainly knew it from an immediate vantage point and were troubled by what they saw. Even the Southerners within their ranks regarded it as an evil and impermanent institution. George Washington* made provision within his will to emancipate his bondsmen while Thomas Jefferson* drafted an ordinance in 1784 to prohibit slavery in all western territories. Indeed, the Founding Fathers ratified measures for the eventual elimination of bondage. They forbade traffic in the interoceanic slave trade after 1808, for instance, and their 1787 Northwest Ordinance* outlawed slavery in the Northwest Territory.

But those who founded the new nation would go no further. Acutely aware that republics were frail organisms that lacked the cohesive force of monarchies, they put national political existence over emancipation and were unwilling to engender public hostility by pressing too far down the path toward black freedom. Consequently, they recognized that slaves were property and venerated property rights. Moreover, they warned that any generalized abrogation of property rights could enlarge "the mob" and undermine the republic.

This gradualist, apprehensive, and cautious antislavery tradition, North and South, continued to characterize the crusade against bondage until well into the nineteenth century. By 1827 there were approximately 130 antislavery societies in the new nation and 106 of these operated in the Southern slave states. Indeed, from the end of the Revolution until the 1830s, the most significant antislavery agitation centered in the South. In 1819 Tennessean Elihu Embree published *Manumission Intelligencer*—probably the first American antislavery periodical. The predominantly Quaker North Carolina Manumission Society advocated gradual manumission and colonization. Southerners like John Rankin, Benjamin Lundy,* John Fee, and James Birney* urged gradual emancipation to facilitate a more profitable and moral free labor economy.

By the mid–1820s, however, antislavery agitation in both sections of the country had become linked to the future of the American Colonization Society* (ACS). The ACS was attracting a large and diverse membership—Northerners and Southerners, slaveholders and pious nonslaveholding missionaries, former Federalists and emerging Whigs. Owing to its varied constituency, ACS leaders were consciously vague on how their program of colonizing free Afro-Americans in Liberia would promote voluntary manumissions in the South. Rather, they exalted the Christianization of Africa by American blacks. With this program, the ACS assumed jurisdiction over racial issues within the "Evangelical United Front"—an aggregate of cooperating evangelical reform societies with overlapping memberships and mutually cooperative treasuries. Along with the ACS's program to "uplift" Africa, these societies sought to eliminate liquor trafficking and other sins and to spread Bible truths throughout the world. Thus, ACS ambiguity on the question of emancipation was further diluted by the competing demands of cooperative Bible, tract, and temperance groups in the United Front.

By the late 1820s and early 1830s, several pious white northern missionaries active in the ACS and other United Front societies became suspicious of the Colonization Society's vagueness on the precise road to emancipation. In previous years, a number of these young missionaries had pursued ministerial careers and had made the painful discovery that Northern clergymen tended to temporize with the sins of their congregations. Thus, they sought new moral vocations in missionary endeavors only to encounter similar moral vacillation in the ACS and the larger Evangelical United Front. By 1831 a number of them had come to declare their independence of the "sinful" ACS. They proclaimed immediate and uncompensated emancipation as their new and morally uncontaminated mission. Some, like William Lloyd Garrison,* broke from the entire United Front, declaring it impure owing to its embrace of the ACS. Others, like Lewis and Arthur Tappan, saw only the Colonization Society as the locus of impiety within the United Front; they continued to cooperate with other missionary society affiliates. Thus, though all white immediatist abolitionists were united in rejecting ACS vagueness on emancipation, they differed from the start in their trust of the other evangelical missionary organizations.

The major distinction between white immediatist abolitionists of the 1830s and their gradualist antislavery predecessors, then, was in the intensity of their piety. Launched upon a more sacred vocation than most local clergy, they would not temporize with evil on any front. Consequently, they considered measures for gradual emancipation as no less than acquiescence in the sin of slaveholding. Almost all of these young immediatists resided in Northern communities that had taken legal steps against black bondage nearly half a century before. Many of them had therefore been reared with little or no firsthand knowledge of the peculiar institution. Consequently, they tended to characterize it in far more abstract terms than their antislavery predecessors. Indeed, most at least periodically viewed "slavery" as a metaphor for diverse forms of exploitation—war, gender inequality, impoverishment, and so forth.

Black immediatists rarely evidenced this metaphorical vision of the peculiar institution. Several, like Frederick Douglass,* William Wells Brown,* and James McCune Smith, had been born in Southern bondage while others had family and friends who remained in chains. One has only to peruse the narratives and public lectures of the ex-slaves and their free black colleagues to see how markedly they differed from most white immediatists. For them, slavery was a very concrete racial experience. It had to be eradicated and racial discrimination eased before all other forms of "enslaving" exploitations could be considered. Indeed, freedom from physical bondage and from racial discrimination was the primary plea of national Negro conventions during the 1830s, of black newspapers like *Freedom's Journal*, and of black-authored tracts like *David Walker's Appeal*. To be sure, this difference did not induce black abolitionists from Philadelphia and Boston like William Whipper, Robert Purvis, and William Nell to abrogate cooperation with white Garrisonians. But a number of New York City black abolitionists, particularly Theodore Wright, Charles Ray, and Samuel Cornish, felt that the broader white immediatist vision of "slavery" was rooted in a deep "chord of prejudice" against blacks generally. Consequently, as time passed, they became more receptive to separatist black organizations as well as to integrated antislavery societies. Frederick Douglass himself spoke for many former slaves as well as free blacks when he proclaimed in 1855 that antislavery "is emphatically our battle; no one else can fight it for us."

White or black, however, young immediatist abolitionists represented a hated minority in Northern society. As they launched their crusade in the 1830s, they frequently faced antiabolition mobs and other expressions of contempt. Consequently, most of them drew together to form small friendship circles where they could repair for emotional support. Garrison headed one such informal collectivity in Boston, Lewis Tappan administered another in New York City, and Gerrit Smith led a third in upstate New York. There were dozens of these informal support groups.

Although antebellum antislavery societies were integrated, membership within these support groups tended to be all-white or all-black. Within the all-white groups, the intimacies of interpersonal relations sometimes emerged as more central than the realities of Southern bondage. A provincial rural New England wing of Garrison's Boston Clique, for example, considered the internal power machinations of urbane Clique aristocrats like Edmund Quincy and Maria Weston Chapman as "enslaving." The point, then, is that white immediatists often molded their visions of slavery with both metaphorical abstractions and the emotional relationships of their small support groups. At these times, their concerns were quite remote from Southern racial bondage.

Because black bondage in the South was legally abolished within three and a half decades of the rise of immediatism, it is tempting to postulate that immediatists—like their antislavery predecessors in revolutionary America—had led a successful crusade. In fact, the question of immediatist influence from the 1830s through the Civil War is exceedingly complex.

If immediatists shared a general orientation to life with many other middle-class evangelicals in the North (and even in the South), it does not follow that their antislavery pleas found increasing acceptance as time transpired. To be sure, like most other Northern middle-class evangelical reformers, immediatists espoused cultural voluntarism—the notion that the good society consisted of free individuals who acted on their own initiative while conforming to the society's needs for moral conduct. But this did not mean that other middle-class evangelicals were convinced and willing to act when immediatists went on to insist that slavery contradicted the free individuality and social morality tenets of cultural voluntarism. Based upon immediatists' own private admissions, their scant friendships during the 1830s, and the weak electoral showing of their

Liberty party in the 1840s, they certainly did not command the support of very many other Northern cultural voluntarists.

However, there is considerable evidence to the effect that immediatists induced powerful elements in the South to assume erroneously that they had captured Northern public opinion. Acting on this misperception of an abolitionized North, these Southern elements launched an aggressive anti-Northern defense of the peculiar institution. When this Southern defense accelerated to the point where slaveholders entered Northern communities under the 1850 Fugitive Slave Act* and forcefully recaptured their escaped bondsmen, many Northerners turned against the Southern "invaders." Thus, while failing to win over even the middle-class evangelical segment of Northern public opinion to immediate uncompensated emancipation, abolitionists seem inadvertently to have contributed to the heightened North-South sectional tensions that led to the Civil War.

More than the abolitionists' moral admonitions, then, sectional tensions and the Civil War formed the essential preconditions to the eradication of the South's peculiar institution. Interestingly, President Abraham Lincoln,* the most significant emancipator in the war years, had more in common with the cautious Founding Fathers of the late eighteenth century than he did with pietistic antebellum immediatists. Like the Founding Fathers, Lincoln placed nationhood ahead of emancipation; the perpetuation of the fragile American union was indispensable whereas the elimination of bondage was only desirable. Consequently, he was willing to move against slavery only where it promised to hasten federal military victory without alienating slaveholders in the crucial border states. He watched during 1862 as slavery seemed on the verge of collapse in Virginia and Maryland and as Congress proclaimed the slaves of rebel owners free the moment they crossed Union lines. By 22 September he issued his preliminary Emancipation Proclamation* which threatened to emancipate only the slaves of Confederates on 1 January 1863. But this preliminary proclamation also underscored a plan Lincoln would submit to Congress on 10 December; the plan would ensure compensated emancipation in all Southern states over a thirty-seven-year period to rebel as well as unionist slaveholders.

Like the Founding Fathers, then, Lincoln was a pragmatic gradualist who was willing to let bondage survive for a considerable period but was intent on preserving the republic. Sensing the president's distance from his own moral war against slavery, Oliver Johnson enunciated the opinion of most of his abolitionist colleagues: " 'Old Abe' seems utterly incapable of a really grand action." Johnson was certainly right. On 1 January 1863 Lincoln issued the promised Emancipation Proclamation—the measure that set into motion federal lawmaking and Constitutional amendments that ended the de jure existence of the peculiar institution. But whereas most abolitionists hailed the proclamation as "the dawn of a new era," Lincoln voiced no jubilation. He felt that he was simply responding to grim wartime requirements. His action indicated that bondage was finally ebbing in the South despite, more than because of, the abolitionist crusade.

SELECTED BIBLIOGRAPHY

David B. Davis, "The Emergence of Immediatism in British and American Antislavery Thought," *Mississippi Valley Historical Review*, 49 (1962), 209–230; Duncan MacLeod, "From Gradualism to Immediatism: Another Look," *Slavery & Abolition*, 3 (1982), 140–152; Lewis Perry, *Radical Abolitionism: Anarchy and the Government of God in Antislavery Thought* (1973); James Brewer Stewart, *Holy Warriors: The Abolitionists and American Slavery* (1976); Ronald G. Walters, *The Antislavery Appeal: American Abolitionism after 1830* (1976); and Arthur Zilversmit, *The First Emancipation: The Abolition of Slavery in the North* (1967).

LAWRENCE J. FRIEDMAN

ABSENTEE OWNERSHIP OF SLAVES. The vast majority of plantation owners in the antebellum South lived on their plantations and, with the assistance of overseers* where needed, managed their slave labor forces and agricultural operations. Absenteeism, although on the increase as the plantation regime spread into the lower South and Southwest, nevertheless was limited.

This condition contrasted sharply with plantation operations in the British West Indies. Absenteeism there became widespread by the eighteenth century because British planters, as soon as they accumulated sufficient capital, tended to retire to England. Planters left their estates in the hands of salaried overseers, a situation that often resulted in carelessly managed plantations, mistreatment of slaves, and deterioration of the estates.

Not so in the mainland plantation economy, where the overwhelming majority of slaveholder/planters lived on their plantations. The planters themselves were directly responsible for the treatment of slaves, agricultural operations, and general plantation and financial management. Overseers served in a subordinate capacity. Where absenteeism in the fullest sense did exist—where slaveholders lived so far from the plantation that it was impractical to visit periodically—overseers held more responsibility for the treatment of slaves and agricultural practices.

Such absenteeism occurred infrequently in Virginia and North Carolina. But some planters in tidewater Virginia and Maryland and low-country North Carolina did entrust their plantations to overseers, black drivers,* or foremen for the cultivating season while they vacationed at the Virginia springs. Thus William S. Pettigrew, a Tyrrell County, North Carolina, planter was grateful for two excellent slave foremen: "What a blessing it is to have two such men . . . whose chief desire I think is to relieve me of as much burden as possible, . . . also to add to their own character as men of honesty, faithfulness and success."

Absenteeism appeared more commonly on the rice plantations of low-country South Carolina and Georgia where, during the "sickly season," from May until fall, planters preferred to spend the summers in the mountains. Likewise, planters residing in Savannah, Beaufort, or Charleston were close enough to visit plantations often. Slave owners who plied other businesses or professions, as merchants, financiers, lawyers, or politicians, necessarily spent much of their time absent from the plantations and thus maintained residences in the towns and cities. In such instances of "local absenteeism," the overseers were the only white men having direct impact on the daily life of the slaves.

The expansion of slavery after the 1830s, and the opening up of new lands in the lower South and Southwest, led to the increase of absenteeism. Early in the nineteenth century a number of economic factors contributed to the spread of the plantation system into the lower South, and with it, an increase in the absentee ownership of slaves and plantations. Soil exhaustion, resulting from decades of staple crop cultivation (cotton* and tobacco*), made lands less productive. Moreover, the newly opened rich lands in the lower South were better suited to cotton than the sandy loams of the piedmont in the upper South. Additionally, the increase in the slave population provided large numbers of slaves for transfer to plantations in the Deep South. Thousands of bondsmen were moved with their masters to newly acquired plantations in the lower South.

Some slave owners, however, who neither wished to sell slaves nor move to the Deep South, sought plantations on which they might profitably employ their labor forces. By the 1850s many large slave owners in the upper South had acquired one or more additional plantations in the lower South, entrusting their management to stewards or overseers. Owners of large estates sometimes divided them into several plantations, residing on one of them, the "home plantation," and visiting the others periodically. They left their management to a son and/or overseer. Such "local absenteeism" was not unusual in the lower Mississippi Valley. Slave owners who owned several plantations might choose to live in Natchez, Vicksburg, or New Orleans—close enough to visit regularly and to spend part of the year on the plantation.

It is impossible to determine the exact number of absentee slave owners and the number of slaves who lived and worked under the sole direction of stewards or overseers. However, examination of census data indicates that by the end of the antebellum period, with the exception of the upper South, absenteeism on plantations of fifty slaves or more (much of it "local absenteeism") had reached 50 percent in a few countries in the heart of the staple crop plantation belts. These areas included rice* plantations in low-country South Carolina and Georgia, cotton plantations in Alabama, Mississippi, and Louisiana, and sugar* plantations in Louisiana. Even so, when the total slave population is considered, a very small percentage were held by absentee owners, certainly less than 10 percent.

Absentee slave owners in the upper South generally could have employed their labor forces more profitably on fertile cotton and sugar lands in the lower South. But such absenteeism not only would have separated black slaves from their masters but also would have posed special difficulties in management. If the owner lived in a distant state, visits were necessarily few—rarely more than once a year, sometimes even less frequent. In the absence of the owner, managers had greater responsibilities and more independence in the overseeing of plantation affairs. This, in turn, called for more capable overseers, men who could exercise independence and judgment in agricultural operations, and more importantly, possessed the skills, firmness, and patience to manage a large slave labor force. Managers of absentee estates, commensurate with their abilities and responsibilities, generally received higher salaries and enjoyed longer tenures than the average overseer. But few overseers proved capable of managing on their own large agricultural operations and sizable slave labor forces. As Maunsel White, Louisiana commission merchant and planter, complained in 1860, "From what I can see no man nowadays should own a plantation without being on it all the time."

Controlling slaves without inflicting severe punishment was a problem that plagued virtually all slave owners, but absentee ownership posed special dilemmas. Plantation papers as well as travelers' observations* document occasional instances of excessive physical punishment.* And slaves generally fared worse when supervised solely by overseers. These men, whose tenures usually did not exceed two or three years, had no permanent interest in the slaves, either as persons or as property. And overseers labored under the plantation owner's constant demands for large crops. Clearly, absentee operations minimized paternalism* which, when present, was an important factor in the well-being of the slave population. While the opportunities for mistreatment of slaves and mismanagement were greater on absentee estates, the managers of such estates tended to be abler and more reliable than most overseers.

Roswell King, Jr., Jordan Myrick, and Moore Rawls illustrate typical managers of absentee estates. King served from about 1819 to the mid–1850s as manager of the Pierce Butler holdings on the Georgia rice coast. Careful research has demonstrated that Fanny Kemble's* excoriation of King for his alleged mistreatment of slaves is highly misleading. Perhaps because King was "a rigid disciplinarian," he proved to be "an exceptional overseer." Myrick, described as "the most celebrated overseer in the rice belt during the nineteenth century," superintended thirteen plantations on the Cooper River. And Rawls, after overseeing Lewis Thompson's Bertie County, North Carolina, farms for ten years, managed his Rapides Parish, Louisiana, sugar plantation from 1857 to 1861. Without much formal education, Rawls proved most knowledgeable about agricultural matters, skillful in the management of slaves, and conscientious in the performance of his overseeing responsibilities. Rawls, for example, was careful to inform Thompson whenever he found it necessary to discipline a slave. Thus, in July 1857 he wrote: "Wright has been pretending to be sick several weeks until 8 days ago I caught him in a dirty trick, & I give him a genteel whiping. I think that done him more good than all medicine could have been given to him." Again, in September 1857, he wrote that Old Ben "got so slack" and Rawls had to give the slave "a good whiping." The difficulty of managing bondsmen found expression in Rawls's protest of 6 May 1859: "I don't get time scarcely to eat or sleep. I have not been off the plantation since the 3rd of Oct. . . . The truth is no man can begin to attend to such a business with any set of negros without the strictest vigilance on his part."

In the complex question of miscegenation* in the antebellum South, both slaveholders and overseers no doubt played a part. Most likely sexual relations between overseers and/or planters' sons and slaves occurred more frequently on absentee plantations, where close oversight by a resident slave owner was missing. Although planters occasionally recorded such illicit relations in their diaries and correspondents and visiting travelers took note of them, we do not know their extent.

SELECTED BIBLIOGRAPHY

Eugene D. Genovese, *Roll, Jordan, Roll: The World the Slaves Made* (1974); Ulrich B. Phillips, *Life and Labor in the Old South* (1929); William K. Scarborough, *The Overseer: Plantation Management in the Old South* (1966, reprint ed., 1984); J. Carlyle Sitterson, "Lewis Thompson, A Carolinian and His Louisiana Plantation, 1848–1888: A Study in Absentee Ownership," in Fletcher M. Green, ed., *Essays in Southern History* (1949); J. Carlyle Sitterson, *Sugar Country: The Cane Sugar Industry in the South, 1753–1950* (1953); J. Carlyle Sitterson, "The William J. Minor Plantations: A Study in Antebellum Absentee Ownership," *Journal of Southern History*, 9 (1943), 59–74; and Kenneth M. Stampp, *The Peculiar Institution: Slavery in the Ante-Bellum South* (1956).

J. CARLYLE SITTERSON

THE AFRICAN BACKGROUND. The less than 500,000 Africans brought to mainland North America between 1619 and 1807 derived from an area far more extensive and diverse than that to which they were transported. They came—at least 70 percent by a direct crossing rather than by way of the West Indies— from an African coastal belt as wide as 500 miles, stretching 7,000 miles from Mauritania to northern Mozambique. Even though the great majority of African immigrants to North America hailed from a relatively smaller swathe of West Africa, the range of climatic, geographical, and ecological areas, and ethnic and cultural types, remained at least as great as those from which the non-African Americans derived.

This great variety, coupled with the part-accidental, part-calculated mixing of different Africans, and the comparatively healthy demographic conditions* in North America, guaranteed that the African links would be less continuous than for Caribbean and Latin American slave groups. As a result, the African component of the Afro-American culture was relatively quickly diffused, and progressively more generic. Yet it is still vital to examine and differentiate the African background with as much precision as possible. This will enable us to understand the differences between the Africans transported and the degree to which they shared common and easily transferable features. It also will provide insights into both those cultural elements that could be carried and retained over generations and those that were so intrinsically African that they were left behind forever.

Similar preferences on the part of slave owners, and the same exigencies of trading conditions, determined that the catchment area for North American slaves was very similar to that of the British Atlantic slave trade.* Like the English, the Americans generally preferred slaves from west of Dahomey to those from further east and south (the preference of South Carolinians for Senegambians balancing out the Virginians' preference for Gold Coast slaves). Angolans, however, were preferred to Congolese or any slaves from the Bights of Benin and Biafra, particularly the latter. Americans to a degree, like the English, were constrained by availability and cheaper prices* to take progressively more slaves from trading areas further east and south, and especially from the Bight of Biafra. This trend, though, was offset by other factors. American traders, using mainly smaller ships and without many shore establishments, increasingly took proportionately more captives than the English from the Upper Guinea Coast, from African traders around the mouth of the Congo, and from Portuguese established at Luanda and Benguela.

The number and types of slaves available for transshipment at the African coast were determined by local geographical as well as political, social, and economic conditions. Population densities were largely determined by the means of subsistence. This in turn was mainly decided by climate, soils, and topography. West Africa, broadly, is characterized by latitudinal regions shaped by the amount of rainfall and its seasonal variations. These range from the immense central belt of equatorial rain forest, outward from the equator to north and south through woodland savannas, grassy steppe lands with only seasonal rains, to outright desert with hardly any rain at all. There are, though, significant coastal variations, particularly in the bulge of West Africa north of the equator, affected by elevation, prevailing winds, and offshore currents. These include the summer "monsoonal" belt of Upper Guinea with its interior mountain variants in the Futa Jalon, the relatively dry coastal region of modern Ghana (always relatively healthy for European traders), and the monsoonal-equatorial excess of the Cameroon Mountains, with an annual rainfall as high as 400 inches. The upper slopes of Mount Cameroon may be thirty degrees cooler than the nearby coast, and desert temperatures may fall as much as fifty degrees in the nights, but only at the northern and southern extremes of the coast is there a significant annual variation. Though soils vary (and are not often really good), the critical regime boundaries are formed by the sixty-inch and twenty-inch isoyets. The former delimit the range of tropical forest; the latter, the limit of agriculture without irrigation. A valuable further indicator might be the lines showing the areas that receive at least four inches of rainfall each month, allowing for all types of plant growth throughout the year (and thus several crops), and the considerable area in the savanna and Sahel that receives less than one inch of rain for six or more months each year.

Each region has its distinctive native vegetation and indigenous agriculture, ranging from an almost exclusive reliance on hunting and gathering in the densest equatorial forest, through predominantly root, bean, and tree cultivation in the tropical forest belt, various kinds of cereal in the woodland and savanna areas (including rice in the best irrigated areas), to pure nomadic pastoralism in the Sahel. Only the desert, mountaintops, and substantial areas of coastal mangrove

Table 1
Regional African Sources of American Slaves, 1619–1807 (Percentages)

	Total North America (1619–1807)	South Carolina (1733–1807)	Virginia (1710–1769)	Total English Trade (1690–1807)	Total Atlantic Trade (1701–1807)
Senegambia	13.3	19.5	14.9	5.5	3.6
Sierra Leone	5.5	6.8	5.3	4.3 }	8.7
Windward Coast	11.4	16.3	6.3	11.6 }	
Gold Coast	15.9	13.3	16.0	18.4	12.1
Bight of Benin	4.3	1.6	–*	11.3	22.9
Bight of Biafra	23.3	2.1	37.7	30.1	14.6
Angola/Congo	24.5	39.6	15.7 }	18.2 {	36.8
Mozambique/Madagascar	1.6	0.7	4.1 }		1.3
Unknown	0.2	–	–	0.6	–
	100.0	100.0	100.0	100.0	100.0

Derived from Philip D. Curtin, *The Atlantic Slave Trade*, and Paul E. Lovejoy, *Transformations in Slavery*.
*Included in Angola figure

Figure 1
African Regional Sources of North American Slaves: Estimated Fluctuations (Percentages) with Estimated Annual Total Flow (Thousands), 1700–1800

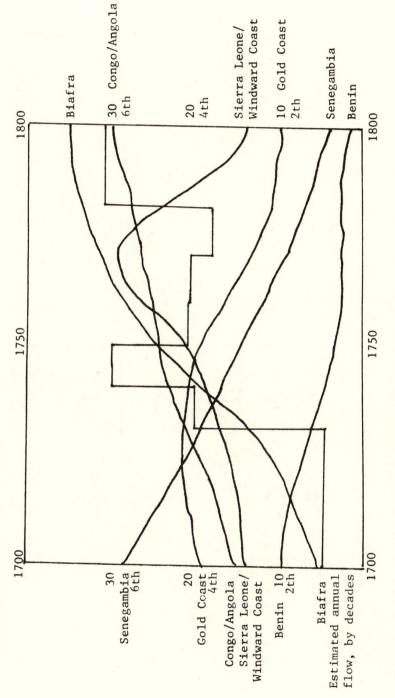

Derived from Paul E. Lovejoy, *Transformations in Slavery;* Philip D. Curtin, *Atlantic Slave Trade;* and James A. Rawley, *The Transatlantic Slave Trade* (1981).
Vertical Scales 10–30% = 2–6,000

Figure 2
Latitudinal Regions of West Africa Shaped by Amount of Rainfall and Seasonal Variations

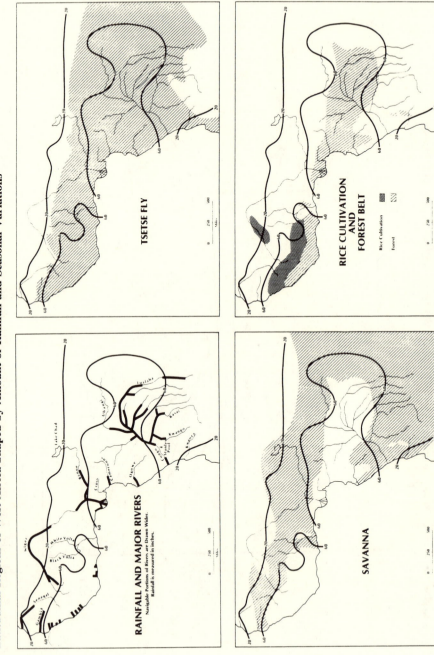

TSETSE FLY

RAINFALL AND MAJOR RIVERS
Navigable Portions of Rivers are Drawn Wider.
Rainfall is measured in inches.

RICE CULTIVATION AND FOREST BELT
Rice Cultivation
Forest

SAVANNA

swamp stand virtually unproductive. One great cultivation boundary was the line between the predominance of the yam and the area where grains provided the chief subsistence. Another was that region, roughly coincident with the forest belt, beyond which the tsetse fly reigned, and raising cattle, save for an inferior dwarf variety, was almost impossible.

As a consequence of these divisions, which were greatly intensified by the introduction, mainly into the coastal and forest belts, of bananas and new forms of yam from Asia, and cassava and maize from America, there was, north of the equator, one belt of dense and increasing population close to the coast. Another stood some 500 miles inland, in the optimal areas for growing grains and raising domestic animals, with an intermediate area of low population density. South of the equator, the coastal region was less populated except around the major settlements and the mouths of the great rivers. The areas of densest population tended to follow the river valleys, particularly those of the Congo River and its southern tributaries, and the Kwanza River, where they traversed the richly diversified area between tropical forest and savanna. In any region, however, there could be local population variations. These depended on the degree of political stability, the stimulus of mining or trade, and the existence of rivers or lakes to provide irrigation or resources of fish. Other factors—the incidence of tribal conflict, religious war, or the disastrous incursions of slave-catching enemies—had negative demographic implications.

Regional variations in traditional African occupations and skills played almost as significant a role in buyer preference as did the age, health, and stereotypical characters of slaves purchased. And such transferable attributes certainly shaped and sustained the Afro-American culture. Farming techniques from the African forest, such as rotational slash-and-burn and swidden agriculture, were of less use in North America than in the American tropics. But the drudgery of hoe cultivation—with its far from simple techniques of breaking, aerating, and irrigating the soil, planting and weeding—became as distinctive a feature of American slave plantations as of much West African farming. Even more direct carryovers were the knowledge of rice cultivation* and cattle herding.* The former made slaves from parts of Upper Guinea and the "Inland Delta" of the Niger vital to the development of South Carolina. Expertise with cattle inclined planters to choose Africans from the pastoral cultures of the northern savanna, such as the Malinke, to manage their stock.

Of almost equal utility on the plantations were the wonderful skills in woodworking found throughout West Africa. Important too were the rarer, quasi-magical crafts* of working in iron and other metals that gave black blacksmiths, even on plantations, mystery and reputation. Other West African crafts—of a sophistication lost upon most whites, and denigrated or ignored by masters because they were not obviously valuable—also influenced the quality of life in the quarters. To different degrees in different places, these included sometimes interrelated skills and styles of carving, pottery, dyeing, weaving, and basketry.

Figure 3
West Africa's Peoples, Population Density and Atlantic Slave Trading Regions

WEST AFRICA'S PEOPLES,
POPULATION DENSITY AND
ATLANTIC SLAVE TRADING REGIONS

WOLOF   Major Peoples
Serer   Minor Peoples
|GOLD COAST| Atlantic Slave Trading Regions

0   250   500
Miles

16

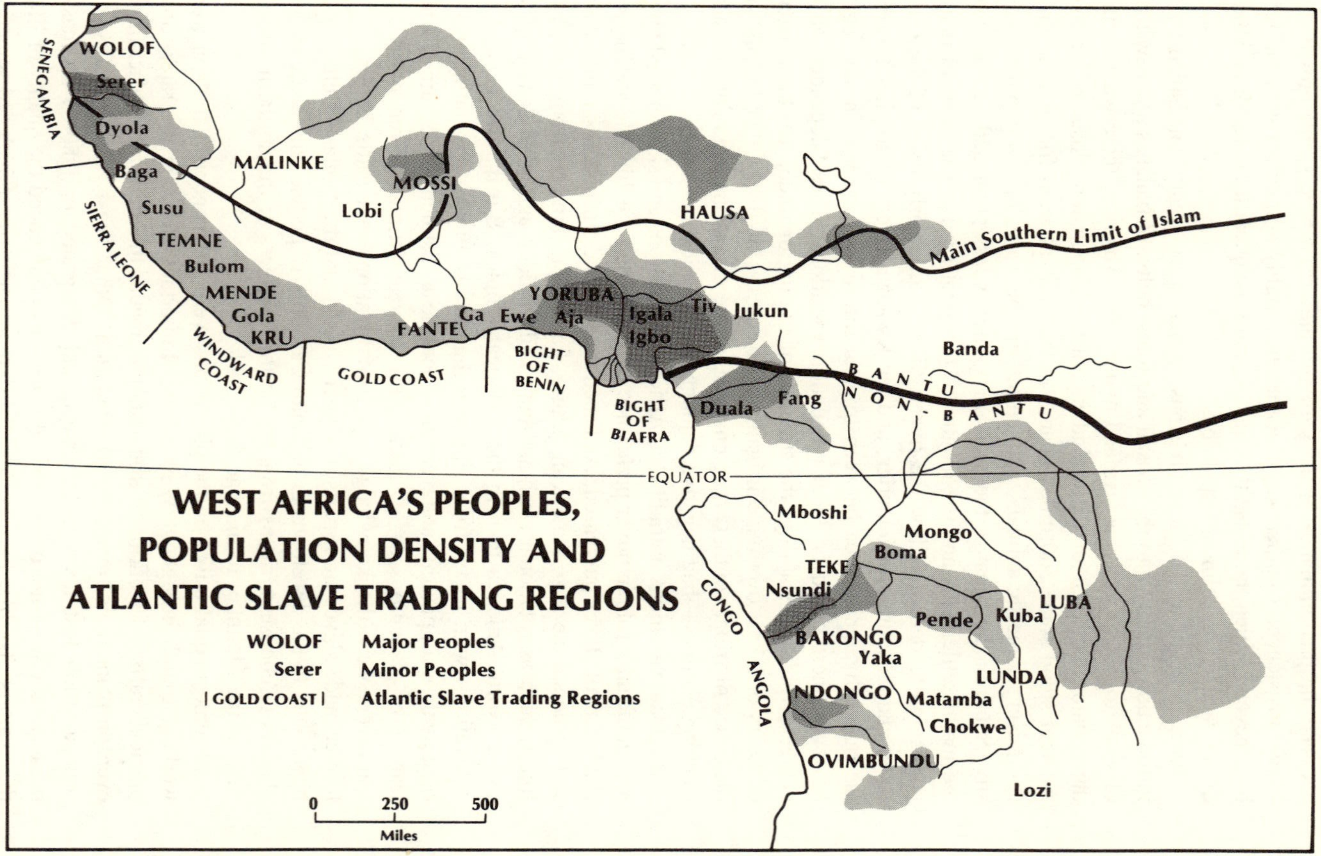

Figure 4
West African States and Principal Trading Towns

WEST AFRICAN STATES
AND
PRINCIPAL TRADING TOWNS

ASANTE   States
Sokoto   Principal Trading Towns

SONGHAI EMPIRE
(to 17th Century)

SOKOTO CALIPHATE
(19th Century)

LIMIT OF
PORTUGUESE CONTROL

0   250   500
Miles

St. Louis
CAYOR
Dakar
FUTA
TORO
JOLOF
BAOL
BONDU
KAARTA
MANDE KINGDOMS
FUTA JALON
SEGU
MANDINKA
CITY STATES
Freetown
Timbuktu
Gao
MOSSI
STATES
ASANTE
Kumasi
Elmina
Cape Coast
Accra
BORGU
OYO
Wydah
Lagos
DAHOMEY
IFE
BENIN
IGALA
OYO
NUPE
Sokoto
HAUSA
STATES
Kano
KANEM
JUKUN
Old Calabar
Bonny
New Calabar
Brass
LOANGO
TEKE
KONGO
Cabinda
San Salvador
Luanda
MATAMBA
LUNDA
KASANSE
NDONGO
Benguela
KONGO
LUBA
Mwata Yamvo
LUNDA
LOZI

17

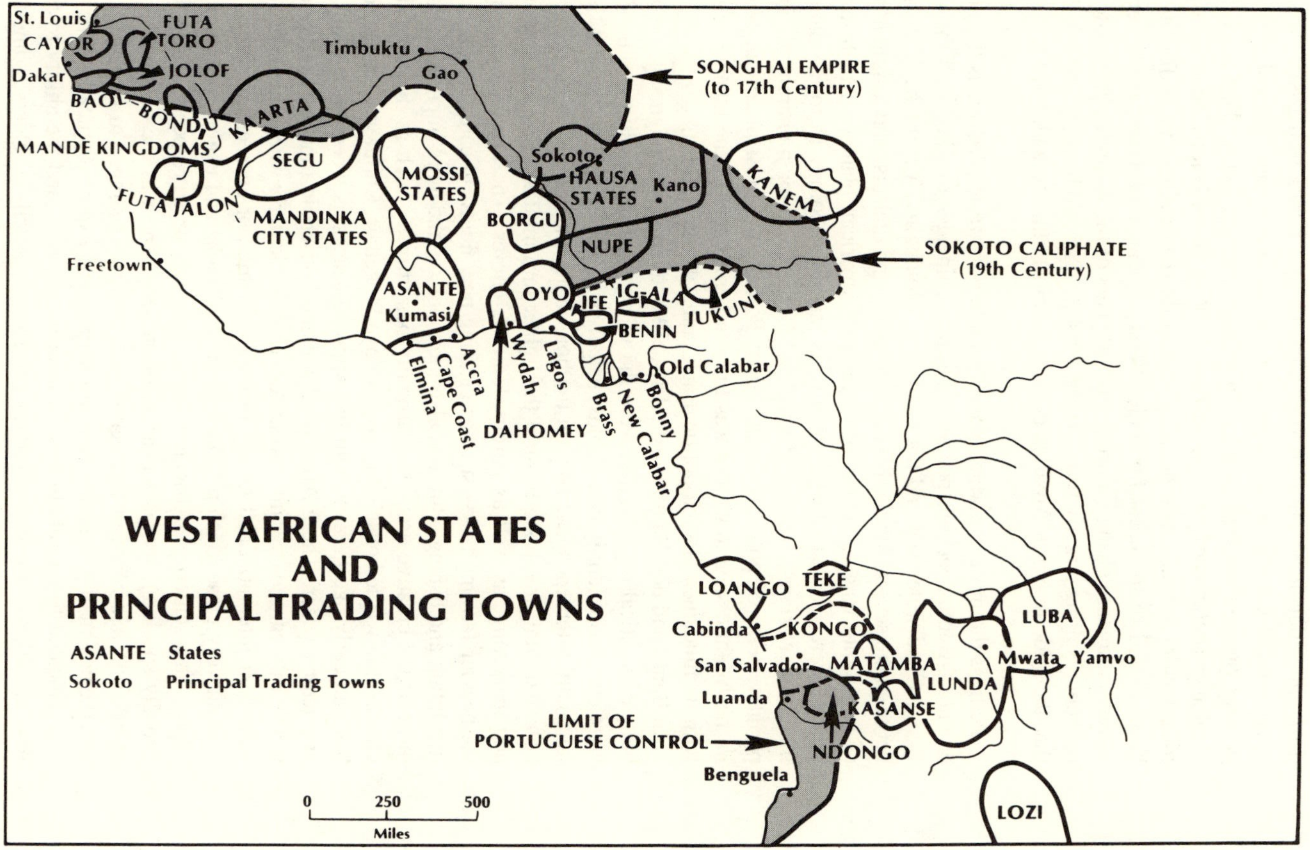

Much the same held true of the richly varied and subtle traditions of music,*
drumming, dancing,* and folklore* carried from Africa to the New World.

Afro-American slaves, however, exhibited an ethnic and cultural diversity far
beyond variations in traditional technical and creative skills. This owed far less
to planter preferences, or even African ecological variations, than to sociopolitical factors that, among other things, helped to determine which Africans should
be delivered to the coast for trade. West African conditions, moreover, went
through immense changes during the 400 years of the Atlantic slave trade, many
of them resulting directly from the trade itself. It should be remembered, though,
that the trade to North America occurred almost entirely within the second half
of the process.

Perhaps the most important ethnic boundary in western Africa is the northern
extent of Bantu-speaking people. This line coincides roughly with the Congo-
Benue-Chad watershed and the Cameroon Mountains. Yet the basic distinction
between the several hundred Bantu languages and dialects, and a similar number
of non-Bantu languages, meant nothing to American planters. Much more important were the distinctions—owing as much to ecology as to the patterns of
trade and warfare—between "stateless," chieftainly or monarchical, and imperial systems of political organization. Perhaps the most important boundary
in the Atlantic slave trade era was the southern extent of the Islamic religion,*
with its fundamental sociopolitical and cultural implications.

In Bantu and non-Bantu West Africa alike, even in sovereign states, the basic
units of political organization were the village and the kinship group. Villages
were clusters of family households, usually polygynous and patriarchal, but also
internally interdependent. Within the household, the roles of women were multiple and vital, involving most of the lighter farming tasks, the tending of stock
and marketing, as well as purely domestic chores. The men were engaged in
the heavier farming tasks, such as clearing new fields, in cattle husbandry, and
in hunting and fishing. But men also monopolized the more important crafts and
most of the creative arts. At seasonally busy times—such as the harvesting of
grains—the whole household was employed together. Children were put to work
from an early age in such light but important tasks as weeding, tending stock,
or fetching water. These African village and household functions and traditions
were easily carried over into North America, particularly where the slave quarters
were well integrated and family life was possible, or even encouraged.

With very close kinship links and internal ranks and canons of honor, reputation, and seniority, African villages were in most respects self-sufficient.
Broadly speaking, it was a peasant existence. Land was the common property
of the folk, and concepts of freehold tenure were as strange to most Africans as
was the notion of producing crops for surplus and export. Typically, village land
was allocated to household heads, according to need and the ability to farm it.
And the village was effectively governed by councils of elders, sometimes in
parallel with quasi-religious "secret societies." Religion,* indeed—contrary to
the ignorant assertions of most European travelers—played an essential part in

all African lives. It provided a satisfying explanation for natural phenomena, a means of intercession, through priests exercising rituals of sorcery and magic, as well as, in most cases, a reinforcement of the social order.

A belief in a universal spirit continuum served as the common denominator in most African religions. This linked persons with the spirits of past kin and folk, as well as with those yet to be born. It also bound the spirits of humankind with all living things, and with numinous objects—rivers, springs, prominent rocks, or certain trees—generally regarded by Europeans as inanimate. Certain objects, locations, or phenomena were sacred, sometimes personified in a pantheon of lesser gods. Such, however, were always subordinate to a supreme spirit-principle, too vast and unimaginable to be easily personified.

The burial sites of kin—often located in the core of the village or even in the household compound—were especially sacred. So too were natural objects vital to the community (such as rivers, springs, or refuge-rocks), or places associated with the origins of the group in folk mythology. Precise structures of belief, pantheons of gods, and forms of ritual extended beyond the narrowest groupings towards ethnic boundaries. These included associations of priests and initiates, and often the existence of a central oracle almost defined some larger ethnic units. Such ethnic entities were sometimes political units too, and imperial rule could even subsume different ethnicities. At the basic sociopolitical level, though, the individual villages were linked to contiguous units, more by concentric bands of wider kinship deriving from common lineage than by the need for trade or common defense. Considerable long-distance trade existed everywhere before the years of European contact. And village markets, concerned with local barter as part of larger commercial networks, served much as social meeting places, just as clannish confederacies were often the limit of political concentration. This was particularly true in areas—such as Iboland before the slave trade intensified—isolated by poor communications, with no shortage of subsistence land, and an absence of external enemies.

Elsewhere, however, more formal states emerged. These existed under dynastic rulers who, despite the often miniscule extent of their sway, were commonly accorded semidivine or at least mythically exotic status—buttressed by the authority of a priestly caste. Debate continues as to whether this system of dynastic monarchy developed from intrinsic forces, or as a result of wars of conquest and cumulative diffusion radiating from across the Sudan. Certainly, the presence of ruling, leisured, warrior and priestly castes, and subordinate classes, including slaves, was usually associated with earlier migrations and wars of conquest. The size and effectiveness of West African states, moreover, related to the importance of trade. Commerce flowed by river or overland caravan, with important market towns at trade crossing places, large capital cities, and in the Niger Delta, even what might be termed commercial city-states.

The extent and power of West African states, at least until the Atlantic trade was underway, also tended to increase from the forest belt northward and westward toward the Sahara and the Sudan, and southward into the savanna. In the north they reached their apogee in the areas of nomadic pastoralism, transhumance, frequent migrations, and long-distance trade. It was here that the earliest known Sudanic kingdoms—Takrur, Ghana, Gao, and Kanem—and their successors developed during the European medieval period. These were centered on Senegambia, the Upper Niger, and Lake Chad. Large and sophisticated states—the sixteenth-century Songhai Empire being as extensive as Western Europe—were created by armies of camel or horse cavalry, with powerful dynastic rulers, nobles, and priests. They were sustained by networks of trade that tapped gold, kola nuts, and slaves from the forest belt partly in exchange for salt. Traders also distributed gold and slaves northward to the Maghrib and Mediterranean, and eastward to the Nile. From the tenth century onward, their power was indissolubly related to the spread of Islam, with its tendency toward holy wars of conquest and the development of literacy and higher education. The Sudanic rulers administered large, dispersed states, and organized long-distance trades with complex credit machinery. They subsumed and refined, if they did not orginate, racial and chattel slavery.

Although there had always been substantial kingdoms in the southern savanna, the coming of the Portuguese, with their Catholic religion,* European weapons, and growing demand for slaves, ushered in rapid political change. Indeed, north and south of the equator alike, the European opening up of the West African coast shifted the directions of trade. It also accelerated political changes—processes, though, that already were well established before the first slave cargo ever left for North America. Except for the Senegambian gateway to the Guinea goldfields and "interior delta" of the Upper Niger, and the Congo-Kwango and Kwanza River routes deep into the interior of south-central Africa, the Atlantic slave trade affected mainly the area within 250 miles of the coast. It reinforced those African states that traded most effectively with the Europeans and, less directly, aided in the development of the more aggressive kingdoms through the importation of firearms.

The chief of these changes south of the equator were the disruption, eclipse, and eventual depopulation of the Bakongo Empire of Kongo. This resulted from pressures from all sides, the absorption of the Ndongo into a Portuguese sphere of influence, and the emergence of the Matamba and Kasenje kingdoms as powerful middlemen between the deep interior and the coast. The Portuguese developed a large-scale slave trade through Luanda, and likewise subverted the Ovimbundu in the service of the port of Benguela. Yet an even more active trade remained in African hands northward of the Congo River—particularly that carried on by Loango with the help of Teke middlemen north of Stanley Pool.

North of the equator, similar processes saw limited European establishments along the coast—notably in Senegambia and on the Gold Coast. These led to the expansion or entrenchment of African polities—such as Benin, the city-states of the Niger Delta, and numerous small states on the Upper Guinea Coast—that functioned as independent middlemen. The most spectacular changes, though, during the seventeenth and eighteenth centuries were the parallel, and partly conflicting, rise of Asante, Dahomey, and Oyo. They expanded at the expense of their neighbors both towards the coast and inland.

In almost all cases, this process of political ferment exacerbated the indigenous system of slavery, whether directly to satisfy the rising Atlantic demand for slaves, or as an incidental by-product of state-building wars. True, as Philip D. Curtin and others have suggested, the Atlantic slave trade as a whole may not have resulted in a net decline in the African population. Nevertheless, much local depopulation and demoralization resulted. Many societies were disrupted by increasing slave raiding from outside. And others, such as the Kingdom of Kongo or the Tio north of Stanley Pool, were dispersed when kings and traders sold their own free peoples to European traders.

Virtually all Africans carried to America were familiar with one form or another of slavery. But very few had experienced the extreme form of hereditary chattel slavery involving intense exploitative labor and social alienation that evolved in the Americas. Exceptions included those mainly Muslim savanna areas where slaves were needed for labor-intensive enterprises such as gold or salt mining, or were shipped as commodities in distant markets themselves, carrying other commodities on their heads. In time there were even some plantations growing crops for export, as in the Sokoto Caliphate of Upper Nigeria, where slaves toiled in the fields in gangs and lived in separate quarters. In an almost exact parallel with plantation America, their masters provided them with one or two days off per week to work their own provision grounds.

Even so, few such Muslim slaves were transported to the Atlantic Coast, and traditional slavery in the areas most tapped was generally of a more "domestic" kind. Nearly all African slaves belonged to a caste whose separate status reflected earlier conquests and subjugations. Almost by definition, slaves belonged outside the tribal lineage. But they were usually valued and protected members of the community nonetheless. They could even rise to wealth and power by fulfilling roles—military, commercial, priestly or administrative—denied to members of the lineage. African slaves, indeed, were rarely sold after the first generation of enslavement. There was a reluctance as well to sell women of any kind because of their value as brides.

Who then were the Africans sold to the Europeans in the Atlantic trade? The best recent estimates conclude that at least half were war captives. Less than one-third were acquired by "normal processes"—through "lawful conviction of crime, indebtedness, dependency and various types of servitude." The remaining one-sixth were made up of "kidnap victims, strangers and unfortunates." The American slave owners' preference for males (which was reflected in slave prices in the Americas) was congruent with the Africans' desire to retain enslaved females (whose value as brides was reflected in their invariably higher prices within Africa itself). As Paul E. Lovejoy has calculated, of all slaves carried to the Americas, 14 percent were children under fourteen years of age, 56 percent were adult males, and only 30 percent were adult females. This resulted in an overall predominance of 63 percent males to 37 percent females. Put in other terms, Lovejoy computed that of those Africans available for enslavement, 46 percent of females between the ages of fourteen and thirty (who represented 25 percent of the total) were retained in Africa. But virtually all men in that age range (mounting to another 25 percent of the total) were exported. Of all children under fourteen (representing 30 percent of the total), only 21 percent were exported. Virtually none of the mature adults (20 percent of those available) were exported.

Clearly, slave traders favored the stronger and healthier elements in the African population. And it is significant to note that many of the least fit failed to survive the rigorous journey to the coast by coffle or canoe. The rigor of their transportation suggests an artificial factor that might have given the Africans an advantage over the more chance-chosen European migrants. Yet there were other physical characteristics of the slaves brought to North America that had important implications for the Afro-American slave population. Recent research shows that African slaves were on the average perceptibly shorter not only than Europeans, but also than their own Creole descendants. African slaves aged between twenty-five and forty imported into the West Indies in the first decade of the nineteenth century, for example, averaged 5 feet 4¼ inches for males, and 5 feet 0¼ inches for females. This was no less than 3¼ inches and 2¼ inches shorter, respectively, than American slaves (Africans as well as Creoles) in the same age range between 1828 and 1860. This differential may have been even greater in the earlier years of the traffic, before new food crops began to improve the West African diet.

The maturation of Africans, moreover, was slower than that of American-born bondsmen. African males apparently reached maximum height around twenty years of age, more than a year later than male Creole slaves. And the age of menarche in African females, at over eighteen years, occurred as much as two years later than for Creole blacks, and even more than that for European females at that time. In addition, the low percentage of females carried to America, the effects of dislocation, the carryover of the common African custom of prolonged lactation, and the fact that female slaves in Africa tended towards a very low fertility rate, explain the comparatively low birthrate of African-born slaves in the Americas. At the same time, though, because the climatic* regime in North America was healthier than elsewhere in the Americas, and indeed, healthier than in Africa itself, these deficiencies were less critical in North America than in the Caribbean and Latin America. As fewer slaves died, the percentage of Africans needed rapidly grew less, and the proportion of African-born slaves in North America fell below 10 percent as early as 1750. Two other demographic factors also contributed significantly to the impact of the African heritage of American slaves. First, throughout the slave-trade period slaves from different African ethnicities were inextricably mixed. And, second, even in the plantation colonies and states, the blacks never outnumbered the white free settlers. Altogether, these forces explain why the African background faded and a distinctive Afro-American identity surfaced more quickly in North America than anywhere else in the hemisphere.

SELECTED BIBLIOGRAPHY

J. F. Ade Ajayi and Michael Crowder, eds., *History of West Africa*, vol. 1 (2nd ed., 1976); Philip D. Curtin, *The Atlantic Slave Trade: A Census* (1969); Philip D. Curtin, *Economic Change in Precolonial Africa: Senegambia in the Era of the Slave Trade* (1975); Philip D. Curtin et al., *African History* (1978); Richard Gray, ed., *The Cambridge History of Africa*, vol. 4: *From c. 1600 to c. 1790* (1975); Ronald James Harrison Church et al., *Africa and the Islands* (3rd ed., 1971); Jean Hiernaux, *The People of Africa* (1975); Ray A. Kea, *Settlements, Trade and Politics in the Seventeenth Century Gold Coast* (1982); Igor Kopytoff and Suzanne Miers, eds., *Slavery in Africa: Historical and Anthropological Perspectives* (1977); M. Kwamena-Poh et al., *African History in Maps* (1982); Robin Law, *The Oyo Empire c. 1600-c. 1836: A West African Imperialism in the Era of the Atlantic Slave Trade* (1977); Paul E. Lovejoy, *Transformations in Slavery: A History of Slavery in Africa* (1983); David Northrup, *Trade without Rulers: Pre-Colonial Economic Development in South-Eastern Nigeria* (1978); and Claire C. Robertson and Martin A. Klein, eds., *Women and Slavery in Africa* (1983).

MICHAEL B. CRATON

AFRICANISMS. In the specialized language of Afro-American studies, the term *Africanisms* (alternatively, *African survivals*; *African retentions*) refers to cultural traits or elements originating in Africa and carried over to the New World, to be manifested in the slave plantation setting as characteristics of emergent Afro-American cultures. The concept is associated primarily with the work of the anthropologist Melville J. Herskovits, who expounded on the term in his ground-breaking study, *The Myth of the Negro Past* (1941). Basing his conclusions on ethnohistorical investigation of certain West African, Afro-Caribbean, and North American black cultures, Herskovits contended that Africa had contributed numerous such Africanisms to the Afro-American cultures of the New World; that those surviving African traits could be measured in terms of their varying "intensities" from region to region within the Western Hemisphere, and that these characteristics were carried forward in time, beyond the age of slavery and into the contemporary Afro-American cultures. Africanisms thus provided an African cultural base which, despite complex processes of acculturation, "syncretism," and "reinterpretation" (cultural blending producing new forms), lent distinction and uniqueness to the various Afro-American populations of the New World.

Upon its appearance, the Herskovits thesis inaugurated a scholarly controversy that has not to date been fully resolved. In general, however, the tendency has been to modify rather than to refute his conclusions, as the ongoing research in the field of Afro-American ethnohistory has confronted their challenges. Yet there can be no doubt that the Herskovits model is beset with conceptual difficulties, deriving for the most part from methodological inadequacies of Herskovits' cross-cultural field investigations. While he was able to show similarities

between contemporary Afro-American cultures and their West African antecedents—similarities in material culture, behavioral tendencies, style and practice
in performance modes, language and folk traditions, belief systems and values—
he was not able to establish historical continuity directly connecting these similarities. Moreover, he was not able to prove his major contentions in ways that
would satisfy most historians. There remained too many hard questions; for
example, how is it possible to establish African provenance for Afro-American
culture elements when the cultural-historical record is so sparse for the early
decades of the transatlantic connection, and indeed for the first century or more
of the existence of the slave system in the Americas? Is much of Herskovits'
methodology not overly impressionistic and based on assumptions simply not
subject to proof? And what of the variables operating on the Afro-American
experiences of, say, Afro-Brazilians, Afro-Caribbeans, and Afro-Americans of
the southern United States, over nearly four centuries?

While such problems have never been completely solved, there are some
conclusions that have come to be generally accepted among the students of the
retention phenomenon, and the remaining differences tend to be those of degree
rather than kind. With regard to Herskovits' "scale of intensity of Africanisms,"
for example, there is a general consensus among Afro-American specialists that
African survivals were significantly more pronounced in certain geographic areas
than in others. Specifically, the African traits carried over from the various slave-
producing cultures did persist, albeit often by way of synthesis with European
or native American equivalents, in those areas where Afro-American blacks
maintained the greatest homogeneity, where blacks substantially outnumbered
whites and functioned relatively free of European supervision within their own
communities, and where there was a longer period during which newly enslaved
Africans were brought into their region. The examples of high-intensity areas
most often cited are those of northern Brazil, Surinam (Dutch Guiana), Trinidad,
Haiti, Cuba, Jamaica, and (to a lesser degree) southern Louisiana and the Sea
Islands off the coast of South Carolina and Georgia in the United States. In such
enclaves the African culture traits that represented no immediate threat to the
master class or to the operations of the plantation system (elements of religious
belief and practice, language, kinship, performance style in music and dance,
folktales, proverbs, and lore) were maintained over the centuries of the slave
experience, though often in relatively attenuated forms.

Conversely, in the areas where slaves fell under more direct European supervision, where black-white ratios were roughly equal, and where the infusion
of new African population elements was minimal, the prevalence of Africanisms
was commensurately of lesser "intensity," and over time diminished and receded
in significance as slaves were afforded greater contact with European Americans
and hence a greater likelihood of acculturation to European norms. Without
question, the least notable evidence of African retentions was to be found among
the black population of the American South, except as noted. There the influence

of carryovers was limited and of lesser significance in the development of the slave subculture, especially after about 1800.

There is equal agreement among the specialists, however, that to some degree the emergent Afro-American subcultures were *all* influenced by certain features of African culture, though in ways that are subtle, often indirect in their influence, and likely to be impossible to prove by the traditional forms of historical evidence, quantitative or literary. The most controversial of these more tenuous areas of influence, and yet one increasingly accepted by ethnohistorians, pertains to the African background of Afro-American religious belief and practice.

West African religious influence was profound in the development of the essentially syncretic religious cults of the Caribbean and Brazil. *Vodun* (Voodoo*) practices are based on reinterpretation and synthesis of certain traditional African religious beliefs, most especially those of Dahomey, with Roman Catholicism.* In *Vodun* (the term means "spirit" in Dahomean), minor African deities are combined with Roman Catholic saints, Catholic sacramentals are supplemented by African rituals and rites, and the Catholic priesthood is augmented by cult priests and priestesses. Though normally associated with Haiti, *Vodun* ritual practices were common throughout the Caribbean and in south Louisiana, and beliefs common to the cult were to be found in attenuated forms throughout the slave community of the antebellum South. Similarly, other Afro-American cults—*Shango* in Trinidad, the Jamaican *Cumina* cult, *Santeria* in Cuba, various *Obeah* cults elsewhere in the Caribbean, *Macumba* and *Candoblé* in Brazil—all represent syncretic forms of African belief systems concerned primarily with ancestor worship and spirit possession.

Far more subtle was the African influence on the development of slave religion* in North America. While there is every likelihood that slaves of the American South maintained vestigial remains of African belief and practice—and possibly of cosmology as well—at least throughout the eighteenth century, some historians have argued that such African influences had been attenuated beyond recognition by the advent of the nineteenth. Current scholarship has come to suggest, however, that in complex but important ways, African retentions were central to slave religion in the United States, and to Afro-American religion after emancipation. Several influential modern historians argue that the African influence is patent if difficult to document. They suggest that, for example, West African traditional religions as practiced in the areas producing most of the Afro-American slaves tend to be life-affirming, present-oriented, this-worldly, eclectic, and pervasive. They presume the existence of a pantheon of gods and lesser deities (under one transcendent God), all of whom require propitiation in the interest of intercession on behalf of the believer. Religious practice is thus a vital part of day-to-day existence. Formal worship tends to be openly emotional, vocally participatory, often accompanied by body movement to drum rhythms and clapping.

Close examination of antebellum slave religion in America reveals that all of these elements were present to some degree in the belief-system and religious practice of American slaves. The highly emotionalized, participatory nature of slave religion, as practiced when the master class permitted unimpeded worship, harked back to African practices. Similarly, the use of music and bodily movement in religious services likely had African antecedents. The African call-and-response patterns were also apparent in slave religion, where the interaction between preacher and congregation was characteristic. And the tendency of slave religion to accept forms of possession and altered states of consciousness reflected African equivalents. More generally, American slave religion manifested a life-affirming quality and promised salvation and redemption through faith. It was, however, little concerned with repentance, sin, or guilt. The same was true of various African traditional religions, and assuredly *not* true of Euro-American Protestantism, or even Catholicism.

At the level of individual belief (as opposed to formal religious practice developed through syncretism) much evidence suggests that American slaves often followed their African forebears in their belief in preternatural powers. Witches and ghosts, spirit possession, conjuring, and other forms of sympathetic magic—all were in evidence among the antebellum slaves. Practitioners of curative techniques were believed to possess special powers, as were the various herbs and roots they employed in their craft ("root magic"), and the historical record suggests that some of them were taught their secrets by Africans. Certain religious symbols and rituals also appear to have carried over in the slave ships: burial practices,* for example, involving burying food with the corpse, and positioning the dead with their heads toward the west. Grave decorations and the celebration of the "homeward" passage of the dead by singing and dancing also suggest African retentions. Even specific African deities appear in the slave pantheon, albeit in highly attenuated versions. What may be a version of the Yoruba trickster god *Elegba*, for example, frequently appears in the form of a shadowy "little man" in slave conversion accounts.

Music* and dance,* so important to the maintenance of any quality of life in the slave community, were powerfully influenced by African survivals. Although the African influence on Afro-American music was clearly relative to time, place, and circumstance, virtually all forms of music produced by slaves in the New World were based on African musical aesthetics, and in some cases instrumentation. Africa provided American slaves with a variety of drums (and drumming techniques), other rhythm instruments (e.g., gourd rattles and rhythm sticks), the one-string fiddle, the *balafo* (a form of xylophone), panpipes, quills, and the banjo. Performance styles developed by the slaves also reflected African antecedents. Rhythm accentuation and polyrhythms, and a certain flexibility in the tonal system, are noteworthy; hand clapping to mark rhythm ("patting Juba") was a common practice among slaves and served to provide dance rhythm when drums were prohibited as potentially dangerous (often the case on Southern plantations). Extemporization in song lyrics and individual improvisation among musicians are important features of African performance style that carried over to the Americas and ultimately came to form the basis of the slave work song tradition as well as the blues, gospel, and later, jazz. Gospel would also involve antiphonal and responsorial techniques (call-and-response patterns), both common in West Africa. The ethnomusicologist Alan Lomax has contended that Afro-American music is in fact a subsystem of the African-style tradition, and has documented his case by utilizing a complex technique for analysis of song performance called "cantometrics." While European folk singing clearly influenced the *content* of slave music, he argues, the *style* of Afro-American performance is near-identical with that of much of West Africa. Slave songs—work songs, folk songs, spirituals, "shouts"—all were indelibly marked by African survivals in America.

As was the case in Africa, all forms of music known to the slave community were related intimately to rhythmic body movement, such that music and dance cannot really be separated. In that African dance features accentuated rhythm and rapid motion, jumping and leaping, sinuous bodily motion, and frequently, pelvic rotation and thrust, Europeans often found it barbaric and lascivious. In the Afro-Caribbean and Brazil, the dance style of Africa nonetheless carried over directly and became the basis of a rich Latin American dance tradition, often closely associated with religious practice. In the American South of the Victorian era, however, slave owners discouraged such uninhibited celebration of the body, and slaves were restricted in their dance style, developing a relatively circumspect tradition, including ring dances and other variants of European folk dance. The exception was in the New Orleans area, where in the *Place Congo*, for example, the slaves gathered to dance on Sundays much in the Afro-Caribbean manner.

Folklore,* folktales, and proverbs provide further evidence of African survivals, though less subject to verification in that much Afro-American folk culture appears to be of European as well as African derivation. While comparative studies have established African antecedents for many tales and proverbs, some of the tales seem to have been shared by Europeans as well. Nonetheless, African animal tales, and more particularly trickster stories, appear to have had special significance for Afro-American slaves. These trickster tales feature the physically weaker, relatively powerless creatures who, through clever ruse and guile, prevail over their more powerful counterparts, winning food, sexual favors, or whatever is at issue. Rabbits, tortoises, and especially spiders ("Anansi") dominate such tales, and so important are spiders to the genre that the Akan-speaking people of coastal West Africa refer to all animal tales as "Anansesem": spider stories. New World equivalents include the "Anansitori" of the Surinam blacks and the "Cuenta de Nansi" of Curaçao. In the slave South of the United States, and especially in Georgia and South Carolina, the Anansi stories were often called "Aunt Nancy" tales, probably suggesting African provenance. It is also notable that in the slave stories that were so popular in the antebellum South, the *slave* as trickster is a standard feature: the clever slave prevails over the gullible master by using his sly cunning to manipulate circumstances in his own interest. There is also evidence to suggest that proverbs originating in Africa served as guides to conduct among Afro-American slaves. The proverbial wisdom that constituted a primary source of West African spiritual and moral guidance thus carried over to influence the values of the emergent slave subcultures.

The matter of language* development suggests another noteworthy (though tentative) connection between the Old World and the New. While African languages were sustained over the lives of first-generation slaves, communication in these mother-tongue languages was difficult among the varying tribal elements present in a given New World location. Hence, necessity compelled the development of pidgins, i.e., forms of basic linguistic communication involving highly simplified elements of languages common to the inhabitants of a given region. In the New World slave plantations these pidgins were based on the European languages of the dominant culture, be it French, Spanish, English, Portuguese, Dutch, or whatever. The loss of African tribal languages was foreordained by the necessities of the slave system: masters had to communicate with slaves and slaves with each other in some language understandable by all. Over time, the vocabulary of the European-based pidgin came to replace that of the original tribal languages (except in the areas of homogeneous concentrations of tribal language speakers, less subject to European influence). As regards the *structure* of the language, however, there is substantial evidence of African retention, as is suggested by the structural similarity of the syncretic, creolized languages that emerged in each of the centers of slavery in the Americas. In reality, though slaves in the New World spoke myriad tribal languages, for the most part mutually unintelligible, their creolized languages based in European lexical material shared substantial structural similarity in that they were all based in two African language families or stocks: the Sudanese and the Bantu. Hence, over time the structural similarity of the African language groups in the Americas provided a shared linguistic base on which the superstructure of vocabulary items could be built. The result was the creation of a group of essentially new, viable Creole languages: the Afro-American languages of Latin America, the Caribbean, and the American South.

Once again, the slaves of the Southern United States were relatively better acculturated to the English of the dominant slave-owning class than was ordinarily the case in the balance of the slave world. But in the cultural enclave of the South Carolina Sea Islands, where such acculturation was less pervasive, the Creole language known as Gullah developed, providing the United States with its best example of African influence on the development of a New World Creole. In a close study of this language, the linguist Lorenzo Turner discovered not only African-based syntactical and grammatical forms but also over 4,000 African words deriving from twenty-one different tribal languages. The Geechee speech of the Georgia coastal blacks developed along similar lines and constitutes a variant of this Bantu-based Creole with its origin in the Congo. The Creole-French-speaking blacks of contemporary south Louisiana constitute yet another language group whose roots lie in Africa: their ancestors arrived from Haiti and Saint-Domingue in the late eighteenth and early nineteenth centuries already speaking Haitian Creole. But whatever the specific example cited, the point is that slave language and linguistic *style* (i.e., the manner in which language is used beyond mere speech, the mode of presentation, the form of expression) are ultimately based in Africa and constitute yet another example of how the Afro-American population of the Americas may look to Africa for its cultural roots.

In certain other respects the African connection is less demonstrable, but a high degree of probability suggests at least indirect African provenance. Extensive kinship systems among the Afro-Americans, for example, while only rarely maintained in the forms associated with West African practice, were likely to have been influenced by such practice in the sense that the slaves produced a kinship structure that incorporated a broad range of familial relationships, surely wider than that of the European whites. Recent scholarship, however, has qualified the notion that the African influence produced matrilineal, matrifocal, polygynous slave families. The nuclear family in the European tradition was the normal form of familial organization among American slaves, and most especially so in the United States, the area most carefully studied to date.

The African influence on agricultural techniques*and work rhythms among American slaves is similarly difficult to establish, as is the case with harvest festival celebrations. While first-generation slaves in the Americas were familiar with the agricultural practices of their homelands (and most of them were agricultural peoples), the plantation system* dictated the *forms* of agricultural labor and planting and harvesting techniques. This occurred despite the fact that African slaves likely brought the techniques of rice planting and cultivation to colonial South Carolina. Work rhythms and the use of work songs to accentuate those rhythms likely had African antecedents, but these too developed according to the dictates of the realities of slave gang labor.* While slaves often introduced improved agricultural techniques sometimes based in African practice, it was in the interest of slave owners to maximize the routinization of labor, and close supervision of the work force was deemed essential; hence, the need for gang labor in simplified work patterns. The African influence, while surely present in the early stages of plantation development, had faded into insignificance by the nineteenth century.

As has been noted on several occasions, the degree and intensity of Africanisms on Afro-American slave culture* were relative to key variables, with the *least* pervasive influence occurring in the American South of the antebellum years. It is thus of considerable importance to note that a microcosmic study of the Georgia coastal blacks carried out in 1940 by the Savannah unit of the WPA Georgia Writers' Project discovered African survivals to have been numerous and influential on the development of local black culture. While this particular population is generally perceived to be atypical, it is nonetheless instructive to note the specific traits of the culture that have identifiable African antecedents. A catalog of these traits would include burial practices, including burial at home and unique forms of funerals and wakes; special attribution of preternatural powers associated with birth circumstances, including birth involving a caul (a facial veil of womb tissue), or the birth of twins; belief in charms ("Mojoes"), sympathetic magic, fetishes, and conjuring powers; root magic and other African medical practices; certain superstitions; certain ritual dances, especially those associated with funerals; belief in diviners and divining; drums, drumming techniques, and signaling by drumbeat; harvest festivals; belief in spirit possession, witches, and witch-riding; substantial lore, tales, and folk beliefs; and certain forms and symbols in woodcarving and weaving. The list is so long and so well documented and the significance of its contents so apparent as to suggest the possibility that similar survival studies among other black American populations might reveal that Africanisms present in the culture of the slaves were even more consequential to the Afro-American experience than is normally claimed to have been the case. Recent studies of Louisiana and southern Mississippi black population isolates would seem to confirm this possibility.

The recitation of lists of African retentions hardly touches the key issue of African *influence*; indeed, such cataloging distorts cultural processes and is misleading as to the real significance of such Africanisms. Culture is by definition in constant process of change; it develops in response to environment, by way of accretion through contact with various stimuli, and by innovation. The cultures of the Afro-American slaves were the products of a creolization process in the New World whereby African cultural elements were blended and shaped to meet the needs and realities of colonial slave societies. In developing the *style* of their respective cultures and in forming their patterns of perception and belief and values, their worldview and their sense of identity, Afro-American slaves produced something essentially new—something that would emerge from the experience of slavery and the plantation unique to them. Without a doubt the cultures of their African homeland, or those of their ancestors, bore heavily on the development of these new cultures, known in all their depth and subtlety only to their practitioners. In this sense, Africanisms were of much greater significance than can possibly be suggested by lists of exotic African traits perceived among the Afro-American slaves. These traits were rather the initial ingredients in a cultural amorphum that ultimately came to produce essentially new peoples and cultures, which would in turn profoundly influence the development of yet other peoples and cultures with whom they came into contact. To the degree that Africanisms in Afro-American slavery contributed to the development of the Afro-American cultures of the Western Hemisphere, Africa made its contribution to the cultural history of the Americas.

SELECTED BIBLIOGRAPHY

Leonard E. Barrett, *Soul-Force: African Heritage in Afro-American Religion* (1974); Dena J. Epstein, *Sinful Tunes and Spirituals: Black Folk Music to the Civil War* (1977); Eugene D. Genovese, *Roll, Jordan, Roll: The World the Slaves Made* (1974); Georgia Writers' Project, *Drums and Shadows: Survival Studies among the Georgia Coastal Negroes* (1940); Melville J. Herskovits, *The Myth of the Negro Past* (1941); Charles

Joyner, *Down by the Riverside: A South Carolina Slave Community* (1984); Lawrence W. Levine, *Black Culture and Black Consciousness: Afro-American Folk Thought from Slavery to Freedom* (1977); Albert J. Raboteau, *Slave Religion: The "Invisible Institution" in the Antebellum South* (1978); and Norman E. Whitten, Jr., and John F. Szwed, eds., *Afro-American Anthropology: Contemporary Perspectives* (1970).

JAMES H. DORMON

AFRICAN METHODIST EPISCOPAL CHURCH. The African Methodist Episcopal (AME) church was organized in 1816 by Northern free Negroes.* Starting with 400 members, the church spread rapidly throughout the North into New York and New England, and westward into Ohio. Before the Civil War, the AME church took a vanguard position on issues affecting free Negroes and slaves. The church, for example, opposed the efforts of the American Colonization Society* to repatriate free blacks to Africa. Colonization, the AME hierarchy thought, was a slaveholders' plot designed to remove free Negroes from America because their presence in American society contributed to slave unrest and undercut the idea that black people could only be "hewers of wood and drawers of water." Believing that Negroes were American and that the peculiar institution contradicted the ideas embodied in the Declaration of Independence* and Constitution,* the AME church took a strong stand against slavery before it was fashionable or politic among other denominations. The Methodist Episcopal church, for example, split into Northern and Southern wings in 1844 over the issue of slave ownership, and other Protestant denominations also divided along sectional lines as slavery, like Banquo's ghost, hovered over the political scene of the 1840s and 1850s. The AME church avoided such issues internally because, as a black institution whose hierarchy and laity included a number of former slaves, it excluded slaveholders as members.

Rejecting the idea that black people were innately suited for slavery because they were biologically inferior to whites, the AME church's first bishop, Richard Allen, in an article entitled "An Address to Those Who Keep Slaves and Approve the Practice," asked slaveholders to try the following experiment. "We believe if you would try the experiment of taking a few black children, and cultivate their minds with the same care and let them have the same prospect in view as to living in the world, as you would wish for your own children, you would find upon trial they were not inferior in mental endowments." In brief, what Allen was telling slaveholders was that black people were not innately suited for slavery, and that slave behavior was a product of conditioning, not of color.

Prior to the Civil War several conferences of the AME church adopted resolutions condemning slavery. In 1856, for example, the General Conference passed a statement which declared that slavery was a "sin of the first degree, and the greatest known in the catalogue of crimes—the highest violation of God's law—a shameful abuse of God's creatures, shocking to enlightened humanity." Words of outrage and protest constituted the AME church's major contribution to the pre–Civil War antislavery movement.* As a consequence of its antislavery posture, the church was banned from the South by slaveholders who feared it would serve as a catalyst for slave revolts.

Although the AME church was excluded from the South, the record indicates that it did cross the Mason-Dixon line before the Civil War. In 1890, commenting on this process Bishop Wesley Gaines wrote, "African Methodism was known to exist in the city of Mobile as early as 1820 but . . . the walls of slavery were towering high, therefore the little band had to bow low again." The church was not established again in Alabama until 1864. Just who established the AME church in Alabama in the pre–Civil War period is not clear, but it may have been founded by slaves from either Baltimore or Charleston who were sold via the slave trade. Before the War between the States, however, the two most conspicuous centers of African Methodism in the South were located in Charleston and New Orleans.

The Charleston church was founded in 1818, when a disagreement developed between the white and black Methodists of that city over control of a burial ground. Until this time, whites and blacks had worshiped together. After seceding, the black "schismatics combined, and after great exertion succeeded in erecting a neat church building. . . . Their organization was called the African Church." This congregation had a short life. In 1822, the church was forced to close because a number of its members were implicated in the Denmark Vesey* plot. The implication in this conspiracy of church members, some of whom were slaves, confirmed the white South's worst fears about independent black churches. Autonomous black institutions were perceived as a threat to slavery and a source of social unrest.

As for the church in New Orleans, it is difficult to discern when it was founded. All that can be said about this church is that it was organized sometime in the 1840s and was harassed by slaveholders. After 1863, the AME church expanded throughout the South as the freedmen flocked to newly established congregations.

SELECTED BIBLIOGRAPHY

Carol V. R. George, *Segregated Sabbaths: Richard Allen and the Emergence of Independent Black Churches, 1760–1840* (1973); Harry V. B. Richardson, *Dark Salvation: The Story of Methodism As It Developed among Blacks in America* (1976); Milton C. Sernett, *Black Religion and American Evangelicalism: White Protestants, Plantation Missions, and the Flowering of Negro Christianity, 1787–1865* (1975); and Clarence E. Walker, *A Rock in a Weary Land: The African Methodist Episcopal Church during the Civil War and Reconstruction* (1982).

CLARENCE E. WALKER

AGRICULTURE. From the introduction of African slaves into Virginia until emancipation, the institution of slavery and Southern agriculture interacted in ways that produced continual change both in labor systems and in methods of cultivating crops. During the seventeenth century the agriculture of the Chesapeake region, based largely on tobacco* and corn, made slavery there different from slavery elsewhere in the New World. Because the cultivation of the staple crop, tobacco, required continuous but not physically taxing labor, women and older children were almost as useful as men in the tobacco fields. Consequently, during the latter half of the seventeenth century tobacco planters purchased a larger percentage of women than did planters in the sugar colonies, approximately two women for each three men.

The black population of the tobacco colonies became the first to reproduce itself. Moreover, tobacco farms and plantations, unlike sugar plantations, were self-sufficient in food, and the tobacco slaves were better fed than slaves elsewhere in the Americas. Tobacco cultivation made less strenuous labor demands on workers than did tropical crops, which meant that slaves in the Chesapeake did not experience so harsh a discipline as slaves on the sugar islands. As a result of these factors, slaves on tobacco plantations enjoyed a measure of family life* that left them more contented and perhaps less rebellious than slaves in the sugar colonies.

Slaves on tobacco plantations cultivated the broad-leaved bushy tobacco plants in hills or rows about four feet apart. They first sprouted the tiny seeds in warm beds of sterilized fertile soil and then transplanted the young plants onto hills in the fields. Throughout the growing season, slaves kept the hills free from grass with frequent plowing and hoeing. About six weeks after the tobacco plants were transplanted, workers cut off the tops of the plants to force the development of the lower leaves. When the plants matured, workers cut them down and placed them on scaffolds to dry in the sun. After the leaves of the plants on the scaffold had yellowed, slaves carefully hung the plants in tobacco barns. There the leaves received a final curing by one of three processes: air curing, fire curing, or flue curing.

So efficient were the eighteenth-century slave-worked tobacco plantations that they first displaced white family-operated farms and then flooded the market with cheap tobacco. Falling prices and increasing indebtedness caused planters of the generation of Washington and Jefferson to lose faith in both the tobacco plantation and the institution of slavery. As a result, they took the lead in abolishing the overseas slave trade after the American Revolution in the mistaken belief that the black population would die out without immigration from Africa. Slavery, however, did not die, and several distinguishing characteristics of slave-worked tobacco plantations were passed on to later generations of slaves engaged in growing rice, indigo, cotton, sugar, and hemp.

In the low country of South Carolina the rice industry* flourished with slave labor from about 1725 until the Civil War. In the mid–1700s planters apparently learned how to cultivate rice on the borders of inland swamps from slaves who had been engaged in growing that cereal in West Africa. Soon afterward, they developed the technology of irrigating rice fields beside tidal rivers with a combination of levees and floodgates. The construction of such works required large capital investments and sizable work forces, factors that effectively limited the rice industry to large planters. Because rice plantations had to be situated along the lower reaches of tidal rivers where fresh water levels rose and fell with the ocean tides, the number of rice plantations was relatively small, and, though efficient, those plantations never saturated the market during the age of slavery.

On the rice plantations of South Carolina and Georgia slaves planted grain in drills in well-prepared soil and then flooded to irrigate the seeds and protect them from birds and rodents. After the plants had grown a couple of inches workers drained off the water and removed weeds from the field with hoes. This process was repeated several times while the rice was growing. When the grain ripened, slaves drained the field to allow it to dry, then cut the stalks close to the ground with rice knives and bound them into bundles. The bundles were carried to a central location for threshing. Having been separated from the stalks, the seeds went through a rice mill, which removed the husks from the grain. The cleaned rice was then packed in barrels and shipped to market.

Slaves on rice plantations lived and worked under vastly different conditions than slaves on tobacco plantations. Flooded rice fields were perfect breeding grounds for mosquitoes carrying malaria and yellow fever. Most whites, having less resistance to these diseases than blacks, could not survive on the rice plantations during the warm months of the year. Because whites could not supervise rice plantations during the sickly season, these enterprises had to be nearly self-operating. Black drivers* directed the day-to-day operations of the plantations, assigning tasks to individual workers. Under the task system* of managing labor developed on the rice coast, incentives more than threats of punishment were used to obtain the cooperation of slaves. The customary tasks of a quarter to a half acre were small enough to be worked by mid-afternoon, and the slaves were encouraged to raise salable products on plots of land assigned to them. Work done by slaves during their "free" time was compensated at the usual rate given free workers. Inasmuch as the rice plantations remained productive for generations, their owners could afford to provide cabins of frame or brick for their workers as well as improved clothing, food, and medical treatment. With minimum interference in their daily lives by whites, the large populations of slaves on rice plantations were able to preserve much of their cultural heritage and develop their own social institutions.

During the 1740s indigo* became a staple crop second in importance only to rice in coastal South Carolina, and from there spread into Georgia and Florida. Indigo, a shrubby annual plant about four feet tall, from which a blue dye was obtained, was cultivated on the barrier islands, on high ground adjacent to rice plantations, and in the interior river valleys. Slaves planted indigo seeds in drills about eighteen inches apart, and kept the growing plants free of grass and weeds by frequent hoeing. When the plants were in full bloom, usually about four months after planting, workers carefully cut down the plants and soaked them in a series of cypress vats to remove the dye from the leaves. The precipitate left in the last vat after the liquid was drawn off was packed in cloth bags to drain and then pressed to remove all remaining moisture. The dried indigo was then cut into small squares and further air-dried before packing for shipment to market.

Because the nearby rice plantations were successfully employing the task system of managing slave labor, indigo planters applied the same system to their plantations both on the coast and in the interior. In the coastal region indigo planters, like rice planters, had to rely upon slave drivers because myriads of flies attracted by the stench of decomposing indigo plants made living conditions untenable for whites during the warm months. As a result, indigo slaves, like rice slaves, were relatively free of white supervision. They also were as exposed to unwholesome working conditions as were slaves on rice plantations.

Independence from Britain and the loss of British subsidies dealt a mortal blow to the American indigo industry, although it lingered on for several decades. By remarkable good fortune American indigo growers found two new crops to replace indigo during the 1790s: a long-staple cotton* that produced well on the Sea Islands, and a hardier short-staple cotton that throve on the uplands. Between 1795 and 1800 all of the indigo plantations on the barrier islands were converted to the black-seeded long-staple cotton, soon known as sea-island cotton, while the river valley plantations shifted to growing green-seeded short-staple cotton. In both cases, slaves worked in their new crops just as they had cultivated indigo, except that they were exempt from the unpleasant and unhealthful task of extracting the dye from the indigo plants.

Restricted to the barrier islands and to coastal lowlands, the sea-island cotton industry prospered until the Civil War. Sea-island cotton, although costly to produce and difficult to prepare for market, brought much higher prices than short-staple cotton. During 1803, for example, sea-island long-staple cotton sold at Charleston for forty-five cents per pound, common upland black-seed short-staple cotton at twenty-five cents, and green-seed short-staple cotton at seventeen cents. As a result, the large planters who cultivated long-staple cotton became one of the wealthiest classes in the South.

On average, slaves on sea-island cotton plantations cultivated only about five acres of cotton and foodstuffs and worked under the task system, permitting them considerable leisure time. They were more isolated than up-country blacks, and did not have the opportunity to develop skills that farm mechanization opened up for workers on short-staple cotton plantations during the late antebellum period.

The short-staple cotton industry, originating simultaneously during the 1795–1800 period in the South Atlantic states and in the lower Mississippi Valley, became the most significant agricultural industry in the Old South. From its dual points of origin the culture of short-staple cotton spread from middle South Carolina through East Texas. It became the principal element in the Southern economy and employed more than half of the region's slaves.

Most of these bondsmen hailed from the upper South, for the cotton industry had developed after the close of the overseas slave trade. Experienced in growing tobacco, these slaves made the transition to cotton without difficulty. Like tobacco, short-staple upland cotton plants, which grew from three to ten feet tall depending upon the fertility of the soil, were cultivated in rows about five feet apart. Similarly, gangs of slaves kept the cotton plants free of grass, weeds, and vines by repeated workings with hoes, plows, and such shallow-running implements as sweeps and cultivators. Nevertheless, working conditions worsened for slaves when they moved southward from established tobacco plantations to new cotton plantations.

During the 1840s and 1850s an agricultural revolution transformed the institution of slavery in the upland cotton belt. Falling cotton prices in the early 1840s compelled cotton growers to increase production of both cotton and foodstuffs by introducing a family of horse-drawn implements devised originally in Pennsylvania and adopted in Virginia and Maryland during the 1820s and 1830s. With the aid of these sweeps, cultivators, double shovels, and seed planters, slaves, on average, were able to cultivate twenty acres in cotton and corn, plus small grains, sweet potatoes, fruits, and garden vegetables. Mechanization with horse-drawn equipment also released women from the fields for spinning, weaving, and garment making. Also during this decade farmers and planters adopted a superior variety of cotton, called Mexican or Petit Gulf cotton, bred by planters in the lower Mississippi Valley. The new variety tripled the amount of fiber that workers could harvest during a picking season. With profits increased and costs reduced, upland cotton growers were able to make significant improvements in their slaves' food, clothing, and shelter, while reducing their hours of labor.

Mechanization of the cotton plantations transformed the slaves from manual laborers into skilled agricultural workers. The increased efficiency of these workers was reflected in rising prices* for slaves during the 1840–1860 period. In order to obtain the best returns from mechanization, planters replaced the old gang system based upon threats of punishment with a modified task system emphasizing incentives for slaves to work diligently. When their individual assignments were completed, workers could leave the fields to work in their own gardens or crops, or simply to amuse themselves. Superior performances were rewarded with goods or money, and work performance during a slave's own time was compensated, often in cash. In this late period, slaves were encouraged to live together as families, with each family provided with a cabin, vegetable garden, and fowl yard, and often with an acre or two upon which to raise cotton or corn. The slaves usually were permitted to sell their surplus produce and spend their earnings as they pleased. By 1860 slaves on some plantations were receiving small cash wages, like hired slaves in industrial establishments.

The tremendous growth of the upland cotton industry between 1830 and 1860 created a strong demand in the lower South for hempen rope and bagging used to pack cotton bales. Most of this material was imported from India, but some was produced in Kentucky and Missouri. Kentuckians cultivated hemp* and manufactured an inferior quality of naval cordage prior to the emergence of the Cotton Kingdom. Their products could not compete with imported Russian rope made by the water-rotted process, but Southern planters found them strong enough for baling purposes. Protected by a tariff, the industry grew rapidly after 1830.

In Kentucky and Missouri hemp was grown on slave-worked plantations much as small grains were cultivated in Virginia. Seeds of the hemp plant were broadcast over fields that had been broken with plows and smoothed with harrows. When the plants ripened, the ten-foot stalks were cut down with special hemp knives by slaves working on the task system. The fibers were separated from the stalks by hemp-breaking machines after the plants had been dew-rotted. Although the hemp growers were often urged to adopt the water-rotted process that produced a stronger and more flexible fiber, they stubbornly refused to do so, largely because their slaves hated to work around the foul-smelling vats. As in other industries that employed slaves, the blacks strongly influenced the development of the American hemp industry.

An important sugar industry* developed in the lower South after 1795, when immigrants from Saint-Dominque introduced improved varieties of sugar cane and techniques for crystallizing the juice. Some sugar cane was grown on plantations in South Carolina, Georgia, and Florida, but most of the American crop was produced in southern Louisiana during the slavery era. In the lower Mississippi Valley sugar plantations were situated on rich alluvial lands of the Mississippi and its tributaries. As these lowlands were subject to flooding, planters erected levees and constructed eleborate drainage systems, in many instances utilizing steam-powered pumps. Establishing large sugar plantations required heavy capital investments in lands, slaves, mules, oxen, and machinery. The sizes of Louisiana sugar plantations varied more than rice plantations, but larger, better-equipped, and more efficient units tended over time to displace less well capitalized competitors. Aided by federal protective tariffs on sugar, some sugar planters became extremely wealthy.

In Louisiana sugar planters employed more labor-saving devices than was usual in the Caribbean (other than in Cuba). When planting, for example, slaves buried sections of cane eighteen inches deep in furrows opened by plows pulled by teams of oxen or mules. They also eliminated much manual labor with hoes by cultivating the six to seven feet between the rows of cane with two-horse implements. As in the older sugar-growing regions, however, slaves harvested ripe canes with knives, and carried the heavy bundles of cane from the field to carts which conveyed the cane to the crushing mill. On large plantations both the mill and the equipment for converting cane juice into crystallized sugar were operated with steam.

Slaves, even on the best-equipped sugar plantations, had to perform exceptionally heavy labor while harvesting the crop and maintaining drainage ditches and levees. The work of ditch-digging and levee-building was so injurious to the health of slaves that planters who could afford to do so employed contractors using Irish laborers to accomplish this heavy construction work. In addition to performing onerous labor, slaves on Louisiana sugar plantations also suffered more from yellow fever, cholera, and other epidemic diseases* than slaves on inland cotton plantations.

In all regions of the South corn* was grown during all periods as a complementary food crop to the staple crop. The grain formed the basis of the diet of humans, and dried leaves of the corn plants fed the horses, mules, oxen, and milk cows. The acreage devoted to the corn crop varied with the fertility of the soil. On the fresh lands of the lower Mississippi Valley during the 1840s and 1850s, one acre of corn was planted for every two acres of cotton, while on the less fertile lands of Georgia as many acres of corn were cultivated as cotton.

Cultivation of the corn crop was done similarly throughout the South. The corn was planted in rows, either on beds or in furrows, and worked mainly with horse-drawn sweeps, shovels, or cultivators. Usually, cowpeas were planted in the corn fields after the corn plants had attained some height. When the corn plants were nearly mature, slaves pulled off some of the leaves from the plants, dried them in the sun, and bound them into bundles of fodder. When the ears had filled out, slaves bent them downward on the stalk so that the shucks would shed rain. Treated in this fashion, the ears could be left to dry in the fields, and the crop could be gathered when laborers could be spared from the commercial crop. In harvesting the crop, slaves pulled the ears with the shuck still on and stored them in well-ventilated, roofed corn cribs. The dried corn was prepared for use by manually stripping off the shucks and shelling the grain from the cob. The grains were then ground in gristmills into meal or grist.

Pulling fodder and shelling corn were among the most laborious tasks performed by slaves. Corn-shelling machines and mills for cutting up fodder came into use in the late antebellum period, but nothing was devised to lighten the labor of pulling fodder under the hot suns of July and August.

In the Southern agricultural industries, slaves became increasingly skilled workers with the passage of time, and as their efficiency improved, so did their living standards tend to rise. As plantations became larger and more complex, many slaves became trained specialists and often skilled craftsmen. Indeed, by the 1850s, most of the South's skilled workmen were slaves.

SELECTED BIBILOGRAPHY

David L. Coon, "Eliza Lucas Pinckney and the Reintroduction of Indigo Culture in South Carolina," *Journal of Southern History*, 42 (1976), 61–76; Lewis C. Gray, *History of Agriculture in the Southern United States to 1860* (2 vols., 1933); Sam B. Hilliard, *Hogmeat and Hoecake: Food Supply in the Old South, 1840–1860* (1972); James F. Hopkins, *A History of the Hemp Industry in Kentucky* (1951); Allan Kulikoff, *Tobacco and Slaves: The Development of Southern Cultures in the Chesapeake, 1680–1800* (1986); Philip D. Morgan, "Work and Culture: The Task System and the World of Lowcountry Blacks, 1700–1800," *William and Mary Quarterly*, 39 (1982), 563–599; and J. Carlyle Sitterson, *Sugar Country: The Cane Sugar Industry in the South, 1753–1950* (1953).

JOHN HEBRON MOORE

ALABAMA, SLAVERY IN. Despite Alabama's rank as the fourth leading slave state in 1860, its institution of slavery began tardily and progressed sluggishly for more than a century. Settled by Europeans in 1702 as a corner of

Table 1

Comparative Table: Population Distribution in Antebellum Alabama

Census Year	Slave			White		
	Number	% of Total	% of Increase	Number	% of Total	% of Increase
1820	41,879	32.74	------	85,451	66.81	------
1830	117,549	37.97	180.68	190,406	61.52	122.82
1840	253,532	42.92	115.68	335,185	56.74	76.03
1850	342,844	44.43	35.22	426,514	55.27	27.24
1860	435,080	45.12	27.18	526,271	54.58	23.39

Census Year	Free People of Color			Total Population	
	Number	% of Total	% of Increase	Number	% of Increase
1820	571	.45	------	127,901	------
1830	1,572	.51	175.30	309,527	142.01
1840	2,039	.34	29.70	590,756	90.86
1850	2,265	.29	11.08	771,623	30.62
1860	2,690	.28	18.76	964,201	24.96

Louisiana, Alabama was sparsely populated, and blacks were scarce. Vague population estimates indicate no more than 6,000 blacks in the entire colony, with Alabamians comprising an almost insignificant portion of the total. Patterns of slaveholding changed little during subsequent British and Spanish colonial administrations. The first American census of Washington County, Mississippi Territory (which, in 1800, included all the settled portions of Alabama except the Mobile district), counted only 494 blacks. Major growth did not occur until after the War of 1812, when a mass migration of settlers flooded Alabama. By 1817, blacks constituted nearly one-third of roughly 30,000 settlers; and from that point, the federal census returns mark phenomenal growth. (See table 1.)

Federal population figures reflect a black increase of nearly 400,000 in just fifty years, a growth rate of 939 percent compared to a much smaller increase of 516 percent for whites and 371 percent for free people of color. In the last antebellum decade, however, growth was more balanced (27 percent for slaves; 24 percent for free population). While the number of slave owners increased by 15.14 percent, their percentage in the free population actually dropped about one-half percentage point (from 6.83 to 6.37), while the average number of slaves per owner rose slightly from 11.70 to 12.90.

Even in the peak years of Alabama's affluence, large-scale slaveholding plantations were not the typical agricultural unit. Masters of twenty or more slaves in 1850 represented only 16 percent of all slave owners and still less than 18 percent in 1860, while the number holding fifty or more increased from 4 to 5 percent, and holders of one hundred or more rose from .80 to 1.03 percent. On the eve of the war, only fifty-one Alabamians owned 172 or more and only nine held at least 300. The 647 slaves of John W. Walton of Greene County represented the extreme example.

Clearly, the insignificant changes in slaveholding patterns do not represent a rapidly expanding slavocracy. Considering that the slave increase was less than

3 percent greater than that of the free population in the same period, the major factors contributing to Alabama's expanding slave population appear to have been natural increase and the westward migration of whites with slave families, rather than wholesale purchases of individual slaves from older states.

Geographically, Alabama's black population was massed principally in the south, with a secondary cluster along the Tennessee River Valley in the extreme north of the state. The highest concentration appeared in the Black Belt, where dark, fertile, limestone and clay soils cut a crescent-shaped swath across Alabama's coastal plain. Significant slaveholdings were also found in the lands radiating out from the Black Belt, in other river valleys, and in the Mobile area.

Even in the two major plantation regions, the most common agricultural units were small to medium-sized farms. The average improved acres per farm in Montgomery County, in 1850, for example, were 211, a figure that included pastures as well as tilled lands. The corresponding average plantation in the "rich" Tennessee Valley county of Madison claimed an even smaller 153 improved acres. Large plantations with stately mansions housing men of great wealth and influence were scarce. The 5 percent of slaveholders who held 50 or more and the 5 percent of planters who owned more than 500 acres, in 1860, must be considered "super planters." Their numbers represented only three-tenths of 1 percent of the state's population, yet they owned 30 percent of its real estate, 30 percent of its slaves, and 27 percent of its personal property— 28 percent of the state's wealth was in their hands.

Economic power in this slave society, however, was not synonymous with political power. At no time did large slaveholding planters hold over 25 percent of the seats in the legislature, and fewer than 10 percent of men owning fifty or more slaves in 1860 had ever served in a legislative body. Significantly, the tax burden was unusually heavy on the planter class, with 70 percent of the state's revenue coming from the levy on land and slaves.

Despite the heavy tax burden of the planter, in a state that produced 23 percent of the nation's cotton* and 5 percent of its corn,* the road to wealth was a rural one. Only a small minority of the population lived in urban areas*: less than 5 percent of the slaves and less than 7 percent of the free population in 1860. Free Negroes,* who were 44 percent urban in that year, were the only group approaching a rural-urban balance.

Within the urban minority, however, blacks were not evenly dispersed. Representing 45 percent of Alabama's population in 1860, blacks comprised 60 percent of the population in Tuscaloosa (west Alabama's trade center), nearly 51 percent in Montgomery (the state capital), 43 percent in Huntsville (trade center of the Tennessee Valley) and only 29 percent in Mobile (whose free Negroes at 3 percent of the city's population represented the largest concentration of that class). Within small urban communities, the black population was drastically smaller.

While a small portion of urban blacks might be considered "drifters," and others were actually agricultural laborers enumerated with a town-dwelling master, many skilled slaves were a vital part of the urban economy. As blacksmiths, carpenters, brick masons, livery stable owners, wagoners, taxi operators, confectionary shop owners, barbers, druggists, and tradesmen of other sorts, some worked directly under white supervision while others lived on their own recognizance. A significant number "hired their time."* Some were simply "turned loose" by their owners. News-hungry editors and outspoken letter writers occasionally complained about the number of unsupervised slaves among them, with scant results. The only keen opposition came from the small class of white urban workers, usually immigrants,* who were in direct competition with skilled slaves for jobs.

As with all aspects of slavery, tremendous variation existed in the nonworking lives of bondsmen. While social and religious activities* usually were subject to the wishes of the master, they were not necessarily confined to Sundays or holidays. While state laws mandated white presence at slave gatherings, such regulations were only loosely enforced in Alabama's lax slave regime. Slaves held socioreligious activities in all-black churches or in interracial churches in which blacks worshiped separately from whites. Some masters permitted slaves to travel to camp meetings on their own accord, despite the accompanying risks such as those evidenced by the slave runaway notice in which a master advertised for a group of his slaves who had gone off to a revival and had not returned. Black preachers,* both ordained and unordained, enjoyed the highest social niche in the slave community; many preached openly while others held clandestine prayer services, depending upon plantation regulations.

Almost universally, religious activities were the center of social life within the slave community; still, many festivities were entirely dissociated from religion. Saturday night social gatherings on plantations were often a reward for, as well as a respite from, the week's labor. Dances* on a larger scale often were scheduled when crops were laid by, and a host of other events varied over time and place—as, for example, the annual barbecue and picnic sponsored by Montgomery businessmen for that city's Draymen's Association, in appreciation of the "honesty and diligence" of the local black draymen.

By law, a slave could not own property (even himself); but, by custom, masters commonly permitted it. Most slaves seemed to have owned such small items as fowls, livestock, and other produce of their after-hours labor. The accomplishments of some under this system (particularly those with skills or trades needed in the local community) phenomenally demonstrated ingenuity and ambition. The economic elite among them owned not merely saddle horses, wagons, and teams, but also real estate, stores, and even other slaves. There appear cases of slaves loaning cash to free men, including whites, and suing when they were not repaid. Making money became easier during the Civil War* when departing masters made sharecropping agreements with trusted slaves who were to look after their property; in some such cases plantations were entirely under black management. Cash also was more readily available when Union forces invaded an area, bringing hardy appetites and unquenchable thirsts for hard liquor that enterprising blacks readily provided.

Statistics on slave runaways* are difficult to interpret with confidence, even when available. Most owners appear not to have advertised in the newspapers, as required by law, or delayed doing so until it became clearly apparent that the slave had absconded and was not merely "taking a vacation." Of the 443 notices involving 562 fugitives published in the Huntsville newspapers between 1820 and 1860, only 182 were placed by owners; the bulk (380) were placed by sheriffs who arrested them. Once found and advertised, slaves were generally claimed; only 24 were sold at public auction, owner unknown.

Newspaper notices also reveal much about the motives and the destinations of runaways. Mobile was almost as attractive as points northward—perhaps due to a combination of the promised excitement of city life, the greater opportunity for jobs, and the increased chance of blending into the urban black population. However, most runaways, because of the migratory westward-moving nature of their owners, attempted to rejoin family members from whom they had been separated.

No major slave insurrections* occurred in Alabama, although alleged conspiracies cropped up occasionally. Personal protests of a criminal nature* were not uncommon, ranging from barn or house burnings to manslaughter or murder. (No special legal charge existed for blacks who took white lives.) Once charged, slaves were tried according to the forms of law.* The accused had a right to legal counsel and a trial by jury. Although black testimony against whites was proscribed, it did occur under various circumstances. Implementors of the law (attorneys, judges, and jurymen) were white; yet extant court records reveal relative justice. Slaves accused of even the more serious crimes of murdering or raping whites were sometimes declared innocent or their actions were deemed "justifiable"; some were freed on legal technicalities; and a significant number appealed convictions with success.

Ironically, the harsh legal system provided more protection, or loopholes, for the oppressed than for the freeman. An influential master could secure the acquittal or pardon of a slave who was clearly guilty but whose crime was not a threat to society. Often, juries felt that the mandatory death sentence was too severe and would actually find innocent an obviously guilty slave rather than have him executed, especially in cases of black-on-black crime. The economic value of the slave criminal to his master surely was a contributing factor in such cases. At the same time, these same "lenient" whites could subvert the legal system, in the case of especially heinous crimes, and mete out extralegal "justice" in the form of lynching.

Once the slave was convicted, the punishment* often differed from that of whites who committed the same crime. Branding and other forms of mutilation gradually declined for both blacks and whites in the 1830s and are rarely found after 1842, when the state penitentiary was constructed. Yet imprisonment and fines were not as effective when applied to the nonfree population. Therefore, slave punishments tended to be physical, with whipping* the usual prescribed measure.

White-on-black crime is also documented by extant court records, of mixed natures and with mixed results. Cases of severe abuse of slaves by their owners were relatively rare and usually decried. Occasional cases of failure to provide adequately for slaves were dealt with more leniently. Cases of assaults against slaves brought conviction more often when the accused was someone other than the owner or his overseer.

Society did display a marked tendency to protect the freedom of those entitled to it. There were no known instances of free Negroes remanded to slavery for violations of the law, even when it was legal to do so. More significantly, in 92 percent of the cases in which slaves sued their owners, alleging to be illegally enslaved, the courts ruled in their favor—and public actions on the part of citizenry often prevented accused owners from spiriting away the slave who claimed to be free.

Public concern for the protection of free blacks apparently was engendered by several factors. To some extent, it might be considered an extension of each freeman's concern that his own rights be forever assured under the law. To a greater degree, probably, white concern for free blacks was influenced by the relatively small size of the latter population. Most such men and women were well known in their community, frequently associated with whites in economic, religious, and even social activities, and usually earned the respect of the dominant population. Moreover, their numbers did not constitute a threat to the political or social system. While politicians were able to play upon white fears with regard to the necessity of keeping black masses in slavery, they were never successful in using the free Negro as a major political issue in Alabama.

While free black numbers climbed noticeably throughout almost all of the antebellum period (to 2,690 in 1860), the percentage of slaves who earned freedom in Alabama peaked early. From the 1830s, manumission laws became more restrictive until the practice was theoretically outlawed in 1860. Nevertheless, masters found ways to circumvent legislation. Some merely "turned loose" the favored slave, granting him de facto freedom, while others bequeathed quasi-freedom by willing their slaves to relatives with the stipulation that they be provided for and not expected to labor. One of the most ingenious circumventions of the law was devised by the slave who purchased himself and thereafter was his own slave and his own master.

Many free Negroes, across the state, were respected members of society. A sizable number were also slave owners, in some cases purchasing nonrelatives for labor. Most free people of color, as did some slaves, supported the Confederacy,* not merely because they may have felt compelled to do so, but also because they stood to lose as much in defeat as would their white neighbors. The propensity of the Union army* to take what it needed from anyone who had it, regardless of color, also alienated both free blacks and slaves who were victimized.

Emancipation* within Alabama was an extended process. As the Union army periodically penetrated the state, beginning in April 1862, some slaves followed in its wake as refugees. Others joined its ranks to serve as body servants, soldiers, guides, wagoners, laborers, and other support personnel. With the defeat of the Confederacy, the final abolition of slavery was foregone, reinforced in Alabama by a provision of the new state constitution of 1865 as well as by the Thirteenth Amendment* to the U.S. Constitution.

SELECTED BIBLIOGRAPHY

Joseph Charles Kiger, "Some Social and Economic Factors Relative to the Alabama Large Planter" (M. A. thesis, University of Alabama, 1947); Gary B. Mills, "Miscegenation and the Free Negro in Antebellum 'Anglo' Alabama: A Reexamination of Southern Race Relations," *Journal of American History*, 68 (1981), 16–34; James B. Sellers, *Slavery in Alabama* (1950); Warren Irving Smith, "Structure of Landholdings and Slaveownership in Antebellum Montgomery County, Alabama" (Ph.D. dissertation, University of Alabama, 1952); and J. Mills Thornton III, *Politics and Power in a Slave Society: Alabama, 1800–1860* (1978).

GARY B. MILLS

AMERICAN COLONIZATION SOCIETY. Organized on 28 December 1816, the American Colonization Society (ACS), or the American Society for Colonizing the Free People of Color of the United States as it was originally called, sought to encourage black Americans to emigrate. The core assumptions were that blacks could never achieve social and economic equality in the United States and that Africa was the only place where they could create a nation free of a dominating white majority. Whites believed, without consultation, that blacks would welcome the opportunity.

There were, however, other motives for colonization. For slaveholders who desired to free their slaves but feared for their future happiness in the United States, the ACS provided a way. Others saw the ACS as a means to remove free blacks,* who stood as symbols for freedom to those who remained in slavery, and those slaves who were deemed worthless and an unnecessary expense. Still others thought black emigrants could create trading networks to tap the assumed riches of the African continent. Finally, some believed the emigrants would serve to attack the paganism of Africa by bringing the blessings of Christianity to the "benighted savages."

Supporters of the movement chose from among these motives as best suited their needs and dispositions. For many, the diverse members of the ACS made for strange bedfellows—Northerners and Southerners, slaveholders and non-slaveholders, merchants and evangelists, to name a few. More importantly for many, both white and black, the ACS represented the antithesis of what they perceived as the rightful solution to the question of blacks and whites living in America. In addition, many free black Americans resented being portrayed as shiftless and worthless. They saw themselves as having as much right to remain and be citizens of the United States as whites.

For many Northerners, the ACS seemed to support the continuation of the institution of slavery. In particular, beginning in the 1830s, abolitionists* led by William Lloyd Garrison* railed loudly and mightily against all that the ACS stood for, and by drawing off antislavery support from the ACS, they had considerable success in eroding the society's weak financial base.

Nevertheless, beginning in 1822, the ACS successfully established Liberia,* a settlement on the coast of Africa. During the course of the nineteenth century approximately 20,000 settlers left America for Liberia under the society's auspices. Prior to the Emancipation Proclamation, about 5,000 were freeborn Americans and 5,500 slaves emancipated on the condition that they emigrate. The total also included about 4,500 Africans who were captured in American slave ships, freed and settled in Liberia.

The society's most intense involvement with Liberia occurred during its formative period, when the society appointed the colony's agents, and subsequently, governors. After the colony gained its independence in 1847, the society's main activity until the Civil War was to continue dispatching settlers. Immediately after the Civil War, large numbers of emigrants left America, but their numbers gradually diminished.

During the latter half of the nineteenth century, the society combined the continued shipment of settlers with an increased interest in supporting Liberian educational activities. With the new century, emigration nearly ceased, and the limited funds which the society received from earlier endowments were channeled solely toward education. Although the society lingered on as a formal institution, in its later years its Liberian involvement was very limited. Finally, in 1963, the society was terminated, and those endowments which remained were transferred to the Phelps-Stokes Fund of New York, an organization chiefly interested in Afro-American and African education.

SELECTED BIBLIOGRAPHY

Penelope Campbell, *Maryland in Africa: The Maryland State Colonization Society, 1831–1857* (1971); Katherine Harris, *African and American Values: Liberia and West Africa* (1985); Floyd J. Miller, *The Search for a Black Nationality: Black Emigration and Colonization, 1787–1863* (1975); Eli Seifman, "The Passing of the American Colonization Society," *Liberian Studies Journal*, 2 (1969), 1–7; Henry N. Sherwood, "The Formation of the American Colonization Society," *Journal of Negro History*, 2 (1917), 209–228; and P. J. Staudenraus, *The African Colonization Movement, 1816–1865* (1961).

SVEND E. HOLSOE

AMERICAN MISSIONARY ASSOCIATION. The nonsectarian American Missionary Association (AMA) was established in 1846. It originated when Christian abolitionists* protested the refusal of American churches and benevolent societies to adopt and implement abolitionist principles. The founders maintained that slaveholding was a personal sin, always and everywhere, regardless of the circumstances that had brought it about or the conditions under which it was continued. They insisted that church discipline, for example, the denial of church fellowship, be applied to slaveholders as it was to other sinners. Christian abolitionists further demanded that churches and benevolent societies not accept "the fruits of unrequited labor" in the form of financial support from slaveholders.

During the antebellum period the AMA emphasized the promotion of Christian abolitionism. The organization believed that the institution of slavery could never survive universal condemnation by American churches. In addition to missions in Africa, Thailand, Hawaii, and Jamaica, the AMA supported scores of home missionaries in the North and West who founded and pastored antislavery churches and circulated antislavery literature. The AMA was also the first missionary* society to support systematic religious and educational work among fugitive slaves in Canada. Closer to home, the organization placed missionaries in Washington, D.C., as well as in three slave states—Kentucky, North Carolina, and Missouri. On the political front, the association lobbied against the Compromise of 1850,* and, after its passage, contended that the Fugitive Slave Act of 1850* violated the U.S. Constitution. All Christians, and particularly AMA missionaries, were urged not to obey the provisions of the act or to cooperate in any way in its enforcement. Even while the compromise was being debated, an AMA missionary was commissioned for New Mexico to preach the advantages of free over slave labor. And following the passage of the Kansas-Nebraska Act* in 1854, the AMA sent nine missionaries to Kansas Territory to work towards making it a free state. Before the Civil War, especially in the slave states, AMA missionaries, with few exceptions, restrained themselves from any personal contact with slaves. They realized that any such contact might jeopardize their efforts to convert whites to abolitionism.

Not until the Civil War began did the AMA labor directly with the South's slaves. The association provided aid, education, and missionary services to escaped slaves and to others who made their way behind Union lines. This work began at Fortress Monroe, Virginia, in August 1861. By 1863 the AMA had established schools not only in Virginia, but in North Carolina, South Carolina, Missouri, Kentucky, Tennessee, Mississippi, and the District of Columbia as well. When the Thirteenth Amendment* was ratified, the AMA was operating schools for freedmen* in every former Confederate state, plus Maryland, Kentucky, Missouri, Illinois, and Washington, D.C.

SELECTED BIBLIOGRAPHY

Augustus Field Beard, *A Crusade of Brotherhood: A History of the American Missionary Association* (1909); Clifton Herman Johnson, "The American Missionary Association, 1846–1861: A Study of Christian Abolitionism" (Ph.D. dissertation, University of North Carolina at Chapel Hill, 1959); John R. McKivigan, *The War against Proslavery Religion: Abolitionism and the Northern Churches, 1930–1865* (1984); and Todd Armstrong Reynolds, "The American Missionary Association's Antislavery Campaign in Kentucky, 1848–1860" (Ph.D. dissertation, Ohio State University, 1979).

CLIFTON H. JOHNSON

AMERICAN REVOLUTION, SLAVERY AND THE. The American Revolution fundamentally altered the development of slavery in the United States. The rhetoric and logic of the Revolution forced Americans to confront slavery in their midst as a violation of natural rights and republican citizenship. In demanding liberty for themselves, white patriots used radical language and frequently claimed that British policies threatened to enslave them. The contradiction of white slaveholders proclaiming the rights of man while holding blacks in bondage was not lost on the revolutionary generation. As early as 1766, when slaves in Charleston paraded through the streets chanting "Liberty, liberty," it became clear the Revolution was breeding a contagion of liberty that never could be wholly contained.

During the revolutionary era slavery came under intense scrutiny by Americans. As early as the seventeenth century various individuals had criticized the institution for its inhumanity, but until the eighteenth century slavery, which was associated with human progress in Western thought, had received no sustained criticism from any group in the British colonies. Indeed, white American colonists took the *institution* of slavery for granted. They perceived slavery as part of the natural order of society, the most degraded status in a world filled with levels of "unfreedom." For them, slavery was hardly unique in its cruelty or debasement in a premodern world where life was cheap. If they thought about slavery at all, prerevolutionary colonists acknowledged its lineage back to the ancients and observed its presence virtually everywhere in the New World. And as the increasingly market-oriented colonists appreciated, much of their prosperity derived from the produce of slave labor and the provisioning of slave societies. Although white colonists might fear the social consequences of black slaves in their midst, they did not much ponder the rightness of slavery itself. During the eighteenth century, however, the same powerful religious and intellectual forces that impelled Americans toward revolution drove them to question the morality and utility of human bondage.

Quakers* took the lead in questioning slavery. In the mid-eighteenth century, such reformers as John Woolman and Benjamin Lay urged fellow Quakers to divest themselves of sinful associations with human bondage, which the critics labeled a species of kidnapping. The slavery question divided the Society of Friends. A large number of Quaker slave owners in Philadelphia and elsewhere resisted calls for manumitting their slaves, but others, such as several North Carolina Friends, freed theirs. Still, once it began to grapple with the issue of human bondage, the Society of Friends moved inexorably against the institution. Turning away from the compromising effects of too much involvement in public affairs and the pursuit of wealth, Quakers were primed for spiritual renewal and moral cleansing. Friends wanting to cultivate their inward spiritual plantations of necessity engaged in a growing and persistent witness against slavery and other social evils. In the midst of the American revolutionary ferment of the 1770s–1780s Quakers extended their witness beyond the Society of Friends by forming the nucleus of early antislavery societies (indeed, organizing the world's first antislavery society in 1775) and petitioning state legislatures and even the First Congress to abolish slavery.

In the case of the Baptists* and Methodists,* the questioning of slavery was a natural concomitant of their challenge to authority generally. The evangelical revivals of the eighteenth century appealed particularly to the lower classes who found the strong, plain preaching invigorating and the egalitarian message of almost universal salvation liberating. The revivals shook the social and political order wherever they occurred, for revival preachers claimed that their authority derived from grace, not learning and social position. The evangelicals welcomed blacks, slave and free, into their meetings and even permitted them to preach if so moved by grace. As large numbers of slaves and free blacks moved into Baptist and Methodist congregations, those churches could not ignore their Christian obligations of fellowship to them. Enthusiastic religion thus closed the social and cultural distance between the races. Under such circumstances, the logic of slavery did not escape criticism. The evangelicals were hardly abolitionists, but their antiauthoritarian attitudes and practices threatened the social and political assumptions undergirding the hierarchical world the planters made. The logic of the American Revolution reinforced the evangelicals' distrust of authority and endorsed their methods of direct appeals to all classes. Soon enough after the American Revolution, the Baptists and Methodists made their accommodations to the planter class in order to gain approval and to carry on evangelization among whites without interruption. Still, the evangelical thrust had put slavery on the moral defensive.

So, too, did the Enlightenment. Virtually every important Enlightenment figure in Europe and America condemned slavery. During the Enlightenment progressive-minded thinkers for the first time recognized that slavery was incompatible with the idea of progress. In accepting the Lockean argument that ideas and knowledge derived from impressions and experience, Enlightenment thinkers assumed an environmentalist logic regarding human behavior. To their minds, the oppressive conditions of bondage stunted the slaves' intellectual and moral growth. Slavery was inefficient as a system of production because it rested on force. Slavery also was wrong as a social institution because it corrupted the master and debased the slave. Imbued with Enlightenment beliefs, many of the leaders of the American Revolution found it difficult to reconcile their statements about natural rights with the reality of human bondage.

By their own actions blacks transformed the discussion of slavery's wrong into social reality. During the Revolutionary war, for example, blacks seized numerous new opportunities for freedom. Thousands of slaves escaped amid the confusion and upheavals caused by rampaging armies. Especially in the upper

South, where many Afro-American slaves were familiar with the countryside and where many towns with free black populations beckoned with the likelihood of anonymity, the periodic collapse of local authority encouraged slaves to flee their masters. Further south slaves sought refuge among the Indians.* Though the Creeks and Cherokees occasionally returned runaways* to their former masters or enslaved them for themselves, these tribes received many fleeing blacks into their own society. The Seminoles offered a more welcome haven for runaways. Meanwhile, military necessity drove both the British and the Americans to recruit black slaves, promising the slaves freedom in exchange for military service.

The British took the lead in mustering blacks. In November 1775 Lord Dunmore, royal governor of Virginia, raised the specter of slave rebellion by declaring that any slaves who willingly bore arms for the British would be freed. Between 500 to 600 slaves responded to Dunmore's proclamation. Dunmore was soon defeated in battle, but other officers made similar appeals to bring slaves into British armies. When the war spread south after 1778 and degenerated into a brutal civil war in the Southern backcountry, Loyalists* encouraged slaves to abandon patriot slaveholders and, in several instances, led them in reprisals against their former masters. Although the British too often reneged on their pledges of freedom, sending fugitive slaves to the West Indies in shackles along with slaves they had captured from patriot planters, many blacks were freed and sent to Canada or Sierra Leone. Thousands of black refugees left with the British armies in 1783.

Reluctantly, the patriots also turned to blacks to fill American regiments. Desperate for soldiers, Washington endorsed proposals to raise black troops. Most Northern states enrolled blacks in military service, and several Southern states followed suit. But in 1779, when merchant John Laurens of South Carolina urged his state to authorize the recruitment of 3,000 black troops, the legislature balked. Georgia also refused to put weapons in black hands—British invasion or not. Among Southern states, only Maryland recruited many slaves and rewarded them with liberty for their military service. Still, about 5,000 blacks served in the American army and navy during the war, helping to reinforce blacks' claim to the revolutionary heritage.

Amid war, social change, and libertarian rhetoric, the revolutionary generation remained profoundly ambivalent about attacking slavery directly. The logic and ideology of the American Revolution condemned slavery as barbaric and tyrannical, but that same logic and ideology recognized slaveholders' property rights in men and women. Amid such a fundamental contradiction, no forthright and full-scale abolition of slavery was politically and economically possible. Emancipation of the slaves required compensation of slaveholders.

The antislavery impulses of the revolutionary generation were further blunted by the demands of building a republic. The principal concern of the age was erecting good government, not social engineering. The experience of the Revolution heightened the concern such political leaders as George Washington,

Thomas Jefferson, and Alexander Hamilton, among others, had over the ability of Americans to establish and maintain a successful republic. During the war, especially, mendacity, cowardice, and avarice were so pervasive that many revolutionary leaders came to believe that Americans lacked the moral character—the virtue—necessary to effect a republic. The loyalism of some, and the indifference and selfishness of many Americans during the dark days of the war, had revealed the weakness of America. Leaders feared that fragmentation would follow the end of the struggle against a common foe. Apprehending disunion, which was predicted by many foreign observers as well, the revolutionary generation made extraordinary efforts to prevent it. Such fears, however, vitiated support for any social reform that threatened political union. The accommodations the Founding Fathers made to the slave interest in drafting the Constitution* in 1787 bespoke their belief that the interests of union superseded those of emancipation.

The widespread distribution of property in the United States forestalled a truly radical revolution anyway. Americans equated property-holding with social and political stability and orderly progress, and they warned that the presence of unpropertied elements unsettled society. As even the friends of antislavery acknowledged, wholesale emancipation of the slaves would introduce a large, dependent class into the body politic and invite demagogues and intriguers to sow political discord among them. Whatever its moral merits, emancipation would have to be gradual and hitched to programs of either apprenticeship or colonization* in order to safeguard the republic from a fatal infusion of propertyless, thus dangerous, citizens.

Concerns about property and political stability were themselves formidable obstacles to emancipation, but antislavery reform bore the additional burden of race.* The revolutionary generation harbored many deep-seated fears about blacks as being bestial, lascivious, and overly passionate. Even such enlightened men as Thomas Jefferson* admitted to ''suspicions'' that blacks had lower intellectual faculties than whites and that blacks and whites could not live together harmoniously, that one would devour the other. Significantly, in that regard, antislavery advocates devoted much effort to explaining the blacks' color, for they recognized that more than anything else the slaves' blackness—what Winthrop Jordan has described as an emotionally charged color to the Western eye—condemned them. Whites' fear of race war and social chaos resulting from black freedom further demanded that colonization accompany any emancipation and slowed antislavery progress during the revolutionary era.

Still, Americans of the revolutionary generation hated slavery. Their evangelical religious or Enlightenment philosophical beliefs hardly tolerated it. The logic of the Revolution contradicted it. Self-conscious about their place in the world, and believing themselves to be a chosen people, Americans keenly felt the sting of Dr. Samuel Johnson's barb upon reading the Declaration of Independence* with its eloquent phrase on liberty and equality: ''How is it,'' asked Dr. Johnson, ''that we hear the loudest *yelps* for liberty among the drivers of negroes?'' How indeed, many Americans asked themselves. The revolutionary generation also hated slavery because it corrupted the slaveholder by giving him absolute power over others. Preoccupied with checking tyranny in government, Americans did not fail to note its insidious influence at home. In addition, critics of slavery observed that the forced labor of slaves enervated free labor. Slavery thus retarded economic progress.

Hating slavery but fearing the consequences of precipitously ending it, the revolutionary generation attacked the institution indirectly, limiting its geographic expansion and its numerical increase by way of the transatlantic slave trade* and pushing it ever southward. Where slavery was weak, late eighteenth-century Americans moved against it; where slavery was deeply rooted, they left it alone, trying only to prevent its growth and spread in the hope that such confinement would lead to its ultimate extinction.

The elimination of slavery in the Northern states revealed the measured progress of antislavery during the revolutionary era. Before the Revolution slavery existed in all the Northern colonies and was of considerable importance in parts of New Jersey, New York, and Pennsylvania. Still, no Northern state's economy hinged on slave labor, thus leaving the institution of slavery there vulnerable to the humanitarian impulses and the liberating ideology of the Revolution. Between 1780 and 1784 Pennsylvania, Massachusetts, Connecticut, and Rhode Island ended slavery. Only in Massachusetts, however, on the basis of a state supreme court ruling in 1783 declaring slavery unconstitutional, did slave owners lose their claim to property in men outright.

Even while freeing blacks from bondage, Northern states maintained boundaries between blacks and whites. In Massachusetts, for example, a law prohibiting interracial marriages followed the state's emancipation legislation. Reflecting the revolutionary generation's respect for property rights and fears of social upheaval, most states adopted plans of compensated and gradual emancipation which provided that slaves born after a certain date would become free upon reaching maturity. In New Jersey and New York slaveholders, who bitterly opposed any antislavery legislation, succeeded in postponing true emancipation. New York's emancipation bill of 1799 only freed the children of slaves, when those children reached twenty-five years of age; slavery existed in New York until the 1820s. In New Jersey, which did not pass an emancipation act until 1804, a few slaves lived in the state into the 1840s.

However slowly, black freedom was secured north of the Mason-Dixon line. In 1810 more than 30,000 slaves (almost 25 percent of the total black population in the Northern states) remained in bondage there; by 1830 fewer than 3,000 slaves (roughly 2 percent of the total black population of over 125,000) served their masters there. Once a national institution, after the Revolution slavery had become a ''peculiar institution'' that would increasingly distinguish the South from the North.

The revolutionary generation's desire to create a republic of independent freeholders helped to keep slavery from expanding. In 1784 Jefferson had drafted a congressional ordinance closing all western territories to slavery, but the bill failed by one vote. In 1787, however, the Continental Congress passed the Northwest Ordinance* which prohibited slavery in the Northwest Territory.* Slavery remained free to enter western territories to the south, but the Northwest Ordinance sealed off an area, above the Ohio River between the Appalachians and the Mississippi River, where slavery likely would have gone. (Both Illinois and Indiana had to beat back powerful efforts to introduce legalized slavery in the early nineteenth century, and in both states long-term indentureships permitted a species of black bondage to thrive until the Civil War.) If the Founding Fathers failed to stop slavery's spread everywhere, they did stop it somewhere. By acting positively to curb slavery's movement into a western territory, the revolutionary generation bequeathed a free soil legacy to the nation that was repeatedly invoked by later opponents of slavery's expansion.

Probably the most important antislavery accomplishment of the revolutionary generation was closing* the African slave trade. The slave trade disgusted Americans who subscribed to Enlightenment and/or Christian beliefs in human dignity; indeed, even slaveholders conceded that the business was brutal. During the revolutionary era the transatlantic slave trade fell victim to politics and war. Colonists protesting parliamentary policies during the 1760s and 1770s included prohibitions on slave importations in their various boycotts of British goods. In 1774 the Continental Congress attacked the trade in its general nonimportation plan. Though the Continental Congress in 1776 deleted Jefferson's passage in the Declaration of Independence condemning the trade, several states had followed the Congress's earlier advice and abolished the trade on their own account. The vicissitudes of war and the uncertainties of the postwar economy effectively halted the traffic during the 1770s and 1780s anyway. South Carolina and Georgia managed to force a clause into the Constitution keeping the slave trade open for at least twenty years, and the two Southern states rushed in over 40,000 African slaves during that period, but in 1807 Congress passed a law, effective January 1808, making it illegal to import slaves into the United States. Though closing the African slave trade did not speed American slavery to a natural death, as many antislavery reformers believed it would, the law saved countless Africans from bondage in the United States.

Closing the African slave trade profoundly affected the lives of the slaves in America. Lacking regular infusions of new Africans, the slave population became increasingly American-born and further removed from direct experience with Africa. The American slaves became Afro-Americans. The spread of cotton production westward in the nineteenth century forced planters to rely on the domestic slave trade* to supply their labor needs. A huge internal migration of blacks from the older eastern seaboard regions, especially the Chesapeake, to the developing Old Southwest disrupted slave families* while extending the older plantation culture westward. Paradoxically, closing the African slave trade also strengthened slavery by forcing slaveholders to protect and care for their slaves sufficiently in order to promote natural increase among them, thereby nurturing a paternalistic ethos* among slaveholders that would later convince them of the "rightness" of their labor system. And the victory over the trans-atlantic slave trade caused many early friends of abolition to lapse into the self-delusion that slavery itself had been conquered, causing them to relax their antislavery vigil at a time when slavery was in fact gathering strength.

The cautious antislavery of the revolutionary generation even made inroads in the Southern states, though the progress was short-lived and limited to the upper South. During the 1780s, for example, antislavery proposals were openly debated in the Virginia and Maryland state legislatures. Several prominent slave-holders acknowledged the contradiction between slavery and republican liberty, and the shift away from a depressed tobacco* economy toward a mixed farming economy made slaves seem less necessary. Both Virginia and Maryland shied away from emancipation, but they nevertheless encouraged individual manu-missions* by passing legislation removing restrictions on the rights of individuals to manumit their slaves. In Virginia alone, between 1782 and 1790, more than 10,000 slaves were freed under the terms of the Manumission Act of 1782. But in South Carolina and Georgia, wherever blacks greatly outnumbered whites, especially in the low country, slavery remained entrenched and few manumis-sions occurred. The rice* and sea-island cotton* economy depended on slave labor, and amid a sea of blacks, whites believed slavery was an essential in-strument of racial control. During the late eighteenth century the Deep Southern states actually tightened local slave codes.*

Meanwhile in the upper South many whites grew increasingly uncomfortable as they surveyed the consequences of generous manumission policies. During the 1780s blacks had seized upon the revolutionary principles and guilty con-sciences of slaveholders to petition for their own freedom. Though many slaves had to purchase* their freedom, rather than having it granted to them outright, the numbers of free blacks* rose dramatically and added to the thousands of "free blacks" who had escaped from bondage during the war. By 1800 more than 10 percent of all blacks in the Chesapeake region were free; by 1810 free blacks comprised more than one-third of Maryland's black population and in Delaware outnumbered slaves three to one.

The rising tide of manumissions seemed likely to threaten the existence of slavery. So, too, did the social character of the free black population. Most of the free black population lived and worked in towns. There they bolstered the development of an autonomous Afro-American culture, making blacks generally more self-confident and assertive. Towns became magnets for runaways. Because slaveholders had manumitted their slaves indiscriminately during the revolu-tionary era, without regard to color or condition as had been the practice earlier, the new free black population consisted of very dark as well as light, unskilled as well as skilled, individuals who could not readily be distinguished from the slave population. Thus, it was easier for runaways to blend unnoticed into the free black communities. In response to slaveholders' complaints about a swelling free black presence loosening their grip on the slaves, the Virginia legislature in 1792 imposed strict new rules to discourage private manumissions. At the same time, during the 1790s the black revolution in Haiti sent shock waves throughout the South, driving whites to reassert their control over blacks. The Gabriel Prosser rebellion* in 1800 further convinced whites in the upper South that the liberalism of the revolutionary era was dangerous. Virginia clamped down on slavery and restricted manumissions. Even before the great cotton boom of the nineteenth century provided an economic incentive to maintain the peculiar institution, Virginia had cast her lot with the slave states rather than the free ones.

Virginia's action signaled a more general Southern retreat from the liberalism of the revolutionary era. Unable to resolve its ambivalence toward slavery, the revolutionary generation let the antislavery initiative slip away. It left to subsequent generations the burden of deciding the fate of human bondage in a republic premised on the inalienable rights of life, liberty, and the pursuit of happiness.

SELECTED BIBLIOGRAPHY

Ira Berlin, "The Revolution in Black Life," in Alfred F. Young, ed., *The American Revolution: Explorations in the History of the American Revolution* (1976); Ira Berlin and Ronald Hoffman, eds., *Slavery and Freedom in the Age of the American Revolution* (1983); David Brion Davis, *The Problem of Slavery in the Age of Revolution, 1770–1823* (1975); William W. Freehling, "The Founding Fathers and Slavery," *American Historical Review*, 77 (1972), 81–93; Winthrop D. Jordan, *White over Black: American Attitudes toward the Negro, 1550–1812* (1968); Robert McColley, *Slavery and Jeffersonian Virginia* (rev. ed., 1973); Duncan J. MacLeod, *Slavery, Race, and the American Revolution* (1974); Benjamin Quarles, *The Negro in the American Revolution* (1961); Donald L. Robinson, *Slavery in the Structure of American Politics, 1765–1820* (1971); and Arthur Zilversmit, *The First Emancipation: The Abolition of Slavery in the North* (1967).

                                                                                  RANDALL M. MILLER

AMISTAD MUTINY. The mutiny on the Spanish slaver *Amistad* occurred in July 1839 as the vessel moved from Havana along the northern coast of Cuba. The previous April, most of the black captives aboard the vessel had been seized in Africa and, contrary to international law, put on a Portuguese slaver for Cuba. At a barracoon in Havana, José Ruiz and Pedro Montes bought fifty-three of the blacks to take to Puerto Príncipe on board the *Amistad*. Two days later, Joseph Cinqué led the revolt, killing the captain and cook and forcing Ruiz and Montes to steer the vessel to Africa. But the two Spaniards deceived the blacks by zigzagging up the North American coast in hopes of rescue. On 26 August 1839, Lieutenant Thomas Gedney of the USS *Washington* seized the *Amistad* off Long Island as salvage.

Lewis Tappan joined Joshua Leavitt, Simeon Jocelyn, and other abolitionists* in establishing the *Amistad* Committee to raise money for the blacks' defense in court and for their needs in jail. Both the district and circuit courts ruled that the blacks had been kidnapped in Africa, in violation of laws against the slave trade. They directed the blacks' delivery to the president of the United States, who would return them to Africa on the basis of a congressional act of 1819. But President Martin Van Buren sought to deliver the blacks to the Spanish minister in accord with Pinckney's Treaty of 1795. The U.S. district attorney appealed to the Supreme Court, where in March 1841 Justice Joseph Story affirmed all of the lower courts' decisions except that he declared the blacks free on the basis of "eternal principles of Justice."

The *Amistad* Committee arranged to send the thirty-five black survivors back to Africa in November 1841. Five years later that committee became the nucleus of the American Missionary Association,* the first Christian mission established in Africa. Until 1860 the Spanish government tried, albeit unsuccessfully, to secure compensation.

SELECTED BIBLIOGRAPHY

Samuel Flagg Bemis, *John Quincy Adams and the Union* (1956); Edwin Palmer Hoyt, *The Amistad Affair* (1970); Howard Jones, *Mutiny on the Amistad: The Saga of a Slave Revolt and Its Impact on American Abolition, Law, and Diplomacy* (1987); R. Earl McClendon, "The *Amistad* Claims: Inconsistencies of Policy," *Political Science Quarterly*, 48 (1933), 386–412; and Bertram Wyatt-Brown, *Lewis Tappan and the Evangelical War against Slavery* (1969).

HOWARD JONES

ANGLICAN CHURCH. Anglicanism grew in the eighteenth century in both the Northern and Southern colonies. It was the official religion of all the Southern colonies, with strong state churches in Virginia, Maryland, and South Carolina. During this period, the conversion of slaves was an important issue for Anglican officials in England, for clergymen in the colonies, and for slaveholding members of the laity.

The Society for the Propagation of the Gospel in Foreign Parts,* chartered in London in 1701, recruited clergymen in England to serve as missionaries in the colonies. Eventually it supported the bulk of the Church of England's ministry in the North and in the South outside of Virginia and Maryland. In addition to spreading Anglicanism among the white colonists, the society's charge to its missionaries included an injunction to bring slaves into the Anglican fold. The bishop of London, who exercised a loose jurisdiction over colonial Anglicanism, endorsed this concept.

The church held that slaves had souls, were potential Christians, and, therefore, that Christian slave owners had a moral duty to expose their bondsmen to Christian teachings. This included providing slaves with the opportunity of joining the church. The Church of England took pains, however, to avoid attacking the institution of slavery. One spokesman stated that the Anglican "Zeal for Religion" extended only to activity that was "reconcileable [*sic*] with Trade and the Nation's Interest." The church made it clear that baptism in no way altered the temporal status of the slave and asserted instead that Christian slaves would make better servants because they would serve out of duty rather than coercion.

Acting under these influences, a large number of clergymen, both missionaries and others, attempted to spread the Gospel to slaves throughout the colonies. In general this consisted of instructing slaves in the rudiments of Christianity and teaching them to memorize the Apostle's Creed, the Ten Commandments, and the Lord's Prayer. Some clergymen also required slaves to refrain from extra-marital sex and to maintain other moral standards. Many Anglican clergymen baptized at least a few slaves, and a few baptized hundreds. Overall, however, the number of conversions was too few to have a significant effect on the religion of American slaves.

Converting the masses of slaves to Christianity in the eighteenth century would have been difficult under the best of circumstances. As it was, missionary activity was hampered particularly by the attitudes of slave owners, who were usually uncooperative and often hostile. Southern laymen believed that a Christian slave would do less work and be more trouble than a non-Christian bondsman. Probably also they feared that the baptism of blacks was a step towards equality between the races. Colonial clergymen in the South were usually slave owners themselves, and many of them shared the prejudices that motivated the laity. Anglican officials were unwilling to confront slave owners in a direct manner, apparently believing, and probably correctly, that the colonists would give up their church before giving up control over their slaves.

SELECTED BIBLIOGRAPHY

S. Charles Bolton, *Southern Anglicanism: The Church of England in Colonial South Carolina* (1982); John Calam, *Parsons and Pedagogues: The S.P.G. Adventure in American Education* (1971); Joan Rezner Gunderson, ''The Anglican Ministry in Virginia, 1723–1776: A Study of a Social Class'' (Ph.D. dissertation, University of Notre Dame, 1972); Winthrop D. Jordan, *White over Black: American Attitudes toward the Negro, 1550–1812* (1968); Frank J. Klingberg, *Anglican Humanitarianism in Colonial New York* (1940); and John Frederick Woolverton, *Colonial Anglicanism in North America* (1984).

S. CHARLES BOLTON

ANTELOPE CASE. On 29 June 1820 a ship carrying 281 Africans in chains was captured off the northern coast of Florida and brought into Savannah, Georgia, by a U.S. Treasury cutter. The U.S. district attorney for Georgia took the position that all these Africans were free and, under the Act in Addition to the Acts prohibiting the slave trade* of 1819, should be transported to Africa by President James Monroe. Agents purporting to represent Spanish and Portuguese slave traders (actually fronts for American slave traders) claimed the Africans as their property unlawfully taken from them by a pirate and brought against their wishes to the Florida coast. The issues were litigated under the name of the ship, the *Antelope*, in a case that was passed on three times by the U.S.

Supreme Court: 10 Wheaton 66 (1825), 11 Wheaton 413 (1826), and 12 Wheaton 545 (1827).

Throughout the case the basic question was whether the Africans were to be recognized as persons or disposed of under the mask of property. Corruption affected their cause in Savannah, and when U.S. district attorney Richard Wylly Habersham appealed, national politics stalled the case in the Supreme Court. Ultimately, John Quincy Adams's maneuvering to be elected president led to the case being argued, and the case for liberty was eloquently presented by Francis Scott Key.

Chief Justice John Marshall attempted a compromise that freed the majority of Africans but left some enslaved. The identity of those to be enslaved—those who came from a "Spanish boat"—was then established in a derisory process. In the end, about 120 of the Africans were sent to Liberia,* where they were among the early settlers; thirty-nine were sold as slaves to a Georgia congressman; the rest had died during the litigation while in the custody of the U.S. marshal. The proceedings were later criticized by Adams as marked by "cold-blooded apathy to human suffering."

SELECTED BIBLIOGRAPHY

John T. Noonan, Jr., *The Antelope: The Ordeal of the Recapture of Africans in the Administrations of James Monroe and John Quincy Adams* (1977).
                                                              JOHN T. NOONAN, JR.

ARCHAEOLOGY, SLAVE HABITATION. Although planters supervised slaves during the day, few slaveholders entered the slave cabins at night to observe the private lives of their servants. Planters may have furnished their slaves with housing,* clothing,* food, and leisure time, but they did not know how the slaves evaluated their living conditions or how they worked to improve the quality of their lives. It was within their cabins that slaves created their own social and cultural world—a black world that whites rarely encountered.

In order to enter the slave cabins and discover this black world, it is necessary to turn to the slave-authored sources. The United States is unique in having a sizable body of slave testimonies*—autobiographies,* narratives,* letters, speeches, and interviews.* Only these slave testimonies permit access to the private world of slave cabins and the thoughts, beliefs, and conversations of their occupants.

By using both slave testimonies and white-authored sources, historians may achieve a more complete and balanced view of slave life. Yet, even so, the written evidence about slave living conditions remains incomplete. Much of human behavior is so patterned that it lies below the level of consciousness and cannot be readily recalled. This is particularly true of the routine household tasks that are overlooked by outsiders and participants alike. Because people take so much of their own behavior for granted, they seldom recognize others' habits and actions. As a result, written descriptions of past household life are always incomplete.

In the case of slaves, these mundane household tasks were not trivial. Rather, they were the essentials of black slave life. In and around their cabins, slaves raised gardens, kept livestock,* cooked meals, fashioned handicrafts, raised children, told stories, sang, slept, and relaxed. In their cabins, between sundown and sunup, the slaves created the foundations of the Afro-American life-style.

Because slave cabin life lacks documentation both in the slave testimonies and in white-authored sources, it is necessary to turn to archaeology. In 1968, Charles H. Fairbanks, an archaeologist at the University of Florida, pioneered this work, excavating a slave cabin on Kingsley plantation, Fort George Island, Florida. The following year, Fairbanks and Robert Ascher, an archaeologist from Cornell University, excavated a second slave cabin on Rayfield plantation, Cumberland Island, Georgia.

By excavating ruined slave cabins, these archaeologists hoped to recover tangible evidence about the housing, foods, utensils, crafts, and recreation* of slaves—aspects of black household life that were only sketchily described in the written record. The slave cabin ruins at Kingsley and Rayfield plantations yielded information about construction materials and building techniques as well as the amount of living space and the amenities available to their occupants. The household refuse at both sites revealed the discarded remains of material possessions as well as the foods that slaves once ate. Material possessions included tools used in work (hoes), food collecting equipment (fishing tackle and firearms), household utensils (cooking pots and ceramics), apparel and adornments (buttons and beads), and items used in recreation and status consumption (tobacco pipes and beverage bottles). Food remains included the bones of domestic and wild animals as well as traces of domestic and wild plant foods.

The archaeological record of slave living conditions, however, was not omniscient. The archaeological evidence was incomplete, because of decay and corrosion. Certain classes of artifacts—clothing, furniture, and plant foods—usually decayed. Others—buttons, ceramics, and food bones—survived.

In spite of losses caused by decay, the archaeological record at the Kingsley and Rayfield cabins yielded qualitative and quantitative evidence—about slave housing, material possessions, and foods—rarely recorded in slave testimonies and white-authored sources. Fairbanks demonstrated that slave cabin archaeology could indeed contribute to the continuing assessment of slave living conditions. Yet Fairbanks recognized the futility of assessing slave life without also considering the lives of lower- and upper-status white people such as overseers and planters.

On many plantations, black slaves and white overseers* and planters lived near one another on the same estate. Such a situation existed on Cannon's Point plantation, Saint Simons Island, Georgia, an antebellum cotton estate where slaves, overseers, and planters resided from 1794 to 1861. The abandoned plantation contained the ruins of at least eight slave cabins and their associated refuse disposal areas. Equally important, the plantation contained the ruins of an over-seer's house and its refuse midden as well as the ruins of a planter's house, kitchen, and refuse dump. Cannon's Point thus offered a unique opportunity to compare the archaeological remains of housing, possessions, and foods at slave, overseer, and planter sites. By comparing the findings from these locations, Fairbanks more accurately assessed slave material living conditions by referring to the material lives of white overseers and planters on the same plantation. Conducting archaeological excavations at Cannon's Point during 1973 and 1974, Fairbanks and other excavators concluded that not surprisingly slave cabins were markedly inferior to the houses of white overseers and planters. But significantly, the possessions and foods of black slaves were remarkably similar to those of white overseers.

Fairbanks's pioneering efforts in slave cabin and plantation archaeology at Cannon's Point, Rayfield, and Kingsley estates have inspired similar archaeo-logical investigations in the United States and the West Indies. As recently as ten years ago, only a handful of publications on slave habitation archaeology were available. But during the past decade an outpouring of theses, dissertations, articles, reports, and books has described slave cabin and plantation excavations in Georgia, South Carolina, Tennessee, Virginia, and elsewhere.

SELECTED BIBLIOGRAPHY

Robert Ascher and Charles H. Fairbanks, "Excavation of a Slave Cabin, Georgia, U.S.A.," *Historical Archaeology*, 5 (1971), 3–17; Charles H. Fairbanks, "The Kingsley Slave Cabins in Duval County, Florida," *Conference on Historical Site Archaeology Papers*, 7 (1974), 62–93; Charles H. Fairbanks, "Historical Archaeological Implications of Recent Investigations," *Geoscience and Man*, 23 (1983), 17–26; Eugene D. Genovese, "The Treatment of Slaves in Different Countries: Problems in the Applications of the Comparative Method," in Laura Foner and Eugene D. Genovese, eds., *Slavery in the New World: A Reader in Comparative History* (1969); William M. Kelso, *Kingsmill Plantations, 1619–1800: Archaeology in Colonial Virginia* (1984); Suzanne S. Mac-Farlane, "The Ethnoarchaeology of a Slave Community: The Couper Plantation Site" (M.A. thesis, University of Florida, 1975); John S. Otto, *Cannon's Point Plantation, 1794–1860: Living Conditions and Status Patterns in the Old South* (1984); John S. Otto and Augustus M. Burns, "Black Folks and Poor Buckras: Archaeological Evidence of Slave and Overseer Living Conditions on an Antebellum Plantation," *Journal of Black Studies*, 14 (1983), 185–200; and Theresa A. Singleton, ed., *The Archaeology of Slavery and Plantation Life* (1985).

JOHN SOLOMON OTTO

ARKANSAS, SLAVERY IN. In 1717 Louis XIV granted financier John Law a vast concession of North American land, including the geographical boundaries of the modern state of Arkansas. Law settled some two thousand Germans and an unknown number of black slaves near the Post of Arkansas. During this pre–black code period (pre–1722), slaveholdings were small and living conditions primitive. In 1771 the entire district contained only thirty-eight white males, thirty white females, nine black males, and seven black females. The blacks appear to have been associated either with the post's business activities or with some facet of agriculture. The post had at least one slave blacksmith. Population in Arkansas increased during the revolutionary war, and more Americans, mostly hunters, continued to enter the region prior to the Louisiana Purchase. By 1803 the post contained 874 inhabitants, including 107 slaves and two "free persons of color."

In 1819, after a heated debate over slavery presaging the Missouri struggle, Congress established the Arkansas Territory. Although Methodists* in the territory objected to the peculiar institution, by the late 1830s Arkansas had emerged as a society committed to slavery. For example, in 1830 the *Arkansas Gazette* refused to print a letter critical of slavery, citing possible "mischievous consequences." Six years later, when statehood was debated, one critic of slavery complained that the need to protect slave property would result in higher taxes for slaveholders and nonslaveholders alike. But the majority agreed that Arkansas's growth rested on luring more slaveholders. As a result, the state's 1836 constitution guaranteed slavery, but permitted emancipation with consent of the owners and guaranteed slaves access to the courts. It further directed equality of punishment of slaves with whites.

Slavery in Arkansas grew slowly and erratically, tied inextricably to the state's haphazard economic development. Not all sections of the state grew at the same time. The Ozark and Ouachita mountain areas developed first. There subsistence farming remained more common than commercial agriculture. Southwest Arkansas's growth was delayed until the opening of the Red River raft in 1838. Plantations developed along all the major rivers, but only Chicot County, in the extreme southeast, matched the richest planting districts of Mississippi or Louisiana. In the eastern counties of Arkansas, where only 10 percent of the land was farmable, expensive levee and drainage projects were needed. Their absence impeded slavery's expansion.

Nevertheless, the yeomen farmers who settled Arkansas brought family slaves with them into the state. In 1830 the upland yeomanry owned 61 percent of Arkansas's slaves. With each successive enumeration that percentage (but not the actual numbers) declined, so that by 1860, 74 percent of the state's slaves lived in the lowlands. Numbers of slaves in 1860 ranged from Newton County's twenty-four slaves to Chicot County's 7,512 slaves. Eighty percent of the latter county's population was composed of blacks. In 1860 Arkansas ranked twelfth among the fifteen slave states with 111,115 slaves. The plantation system never became well established there. Grandiose plantation houses were virtually nonexistent. Planters (slaveholders owning more than twenty slaves) accounted for only 1,363 of the state's 11,481 slave owners. Most were relative newcomers to Arkansas, only in their first or second generation of settlement.

Several factors worked to keep Arkansas's slave population low. Isolated and frontier-like throughout the antebellum period, Arkansas lacked adequate banking and transportation facilities. Its rivers and streams overflowed regularly, contributing to very unhealthy conditions especially in the lowlands. Blacks, exposed to harder working conditions and concentrated in the lowlands, displayed a higher death rate of 1.8 percent compared to 1.32 percent for whites. And the slaves' birthrate, 2.4 percent, compared unfavorably to that of 3.5 percent for whites.

The paucity of bondsmen in Arkansas kept both slave prices* and demand for slaves artificially high. Most farmers and planters started with a low initial investment in slaves and remained active in the marketplace. The rising prices slaves commanded in Arkansas limited opportunity and fostered a spirit of speculation. In 1820 the average value of a bondsman stood at $380. By 1840 the value had risen to $484, and by 1861 a figure of $881 had been reached. A prime young carpenter in early 1860 was inventoried at $2,800. Although the 1836 constitution authorized the legislature to ban the importation of slaves for speculative purposes, no implementing legislation followed. Lacking an organized slave trade in the state, planters used slave trading facilities available at Memphis or New Orleans. In 1836 Little Rock boasted an "Auction Mart" that included slaves among the consigned items. A vigorous local swapping always existed in lands, horses, cattle, and slaves. These transactions often involved dealings with the Indian nations to the west. Agitation for reopening the slave trade became a part of Arkansans' political rhetoric in 1860.

Arkansas's slave laws were shaped to fit a society along the southwestern frontier. The ruling class was careful to guard its slave property because, according to English traveler G. W. Featherstonhaugh, Arkansas was a haven for "all sorts of 'negur runners,' 'counterfeiters,' 'horse stealers,' 'murderers and sich like.' " Much of the slave legislation was aimed at restricting manumission.* The 1836 constitution, for example, placed two restrictions on the slaveholder granting freedom to his slaves. The first preserved the rights of creditors and the second prevented the setting free of elderly* or sick bondsmen. To discourage free blacks,* one law required every county so "damnified by such negro or mulatto" to collect from each a $500 bond. In 1843 another statute prohibited free blacks from immigrating to Arkansas. After the Dred Scott decision* excluded blacks from American citizenship, the Arkansas legislature enacted an expulsion law giving free blacks thirty days to emigrate or be reenslaved. The 1860 census, taken after the new law supposedly went into effect, still showed 144 free Negroes. By 1861, when Arkansas framed a new constitution, the notion that slavery should endure forever was so strongly entrenched that owners were denied the right to free their slaves under any circumstances.

Nevertheless, evidence suggests that Arkansans did free slaves prior to 1861. For example, John Latta of Washington County emancipated his slaves at his death, and not to be inhumane, provided for them by leaving each a bequest of $2,500. James W. Mason, the black son of planter Cyrus Worthington, was sent north to school. And because freedom was often specified in wills, it is not surprising that disgruntled heirs went to court. In an 1860 case, Judge H. F. Fairchild admitted the courts once tended to "lean towards the grant of freedom." But they would do so no longer. As a result, the courts refused to enforce an agreement that had permitted a bondsman to earn his freedom. In another case the judge set aside a will under whose terms free blacks would have inherited slaves. "The ownership of slave[s] by free negroes is directly opposed to the principles upon which slavery exists among us," wrote Judge F. W. Compton in 1859. The most grisly slave case in Arkansas judicial records, *Pyeatt v. Spencer* (1842), concerned a young woman whose owner staked her to the ground, whipped her until she bled, and then rubbed salt into the wounds.

Despite legal hostility, some free blacks nonetheless prospered. Nathan Warren, who worked as a barber and carriage driver, established himself in Little Rock as a pastry cook for social events. In time he was able to buy the freedom of one of his brothers. In Jackson County, Daniel Earls, freed in 1827, acquired 350 acres and the public franchise for a White River ferry. He redeemed his wife and children prior to his death in 1849. In remote Marion County, several blacks acquired estates worth over a thousand dollars. Perhaps the most unusual record of free black activity came from Washington County. In 1834 Elizah Williams, "a free man of color," is identified there on a legal document as "my true and lawful attorney."

Most Arkansas blacks were enslaved, not free blacks. The conditions of slave life tended to be harder in Arkansas than in older areas, primarily because of the extra duties involved in clearing frontier land for cotton cultivation. Slave quarters for Arkansas slaves consisted primarily of log cabins, each housing an average of 5.74 persons. This compared closely to the average for the total population average of 5.72. Slave diet* consisted largely of cornbread, molasses, and pork. One plantation owner reported employing a hunter full-time, although slaves commonly fished* and hunted. Arkansas bondsmen dressed in the manner of most Southern slaves. Early illustrations show Arkansas slave women wearing cloth wrapped around their heads in an African style. By contrast, in 1854 traveler Ida Pfeiffer observed an Arkansas slave ball where the men dressed in black with white neck-cloths and waistcoats. The slave women wore white dresses.

The small size of most Arkansas slaveholdings resulted in many marriages* of bondsmen on distant farms and plantations. This increased the danger of family separation. Slave weddings generally were informal in character, although occasional church weddings were reported. Sexual relations between the races were not uncommon in Arkansas, and the 1850 census classified 15.61 percent of Arkansas's slaves as mulattoes. In one unusual court case (1858), the judge reasoned that it must have taken "at least twenty generations for the black blood to be as white as the complainant," who nevertheless remained a slave. In *Inside Views of Slavery on Southern Plantations* (1864), abolitionist John Roles recounted the flagrant sexual exploitation of a slave cook from Fort Smith.

Unfortunately, little is known of the religious lives* of Arkansas bondsmen. One missionary, Bishop Henry C. Lay, encountered communicants among black cotton factory hands in Pike County who, "although ignorant of the church . . . knew the Creed by transmission from their fathers." Although, in 1853, Arkansas Methodists claimed 2,897 black and 15,665 white members, the majority of blacks were Baptists.* As one black minister allegedly asserted, "If you see a nigger who ain't a Baptist, you know some white man has been triggerin' with him." While other denominations often set aside galleries for the use of slaves, Baptists insisted upon separate facilities. One ex-slave remembered a white minister who preached two sermons simultaneously—one to the whites in the church, and the other to the blacks through an open window. Christian theology aimed at the slaves invariably reinforced the tenets of white supremacy. "Servants obey your masters" was the frequent message, prompting an ex-slave to quip: "Same old thing, all the time." Lest slaves get the idea that religion would bring them freedom, in 1859 the *Arkansas Baptist* published a homily for masters to impress upon the bondsmen slavery's divine origins.

Open slave revolts* were reported in Arkansas, and rumors of insurrections ran rampant throughout the 1850s. The state's slave patrol constituted "a slumbering power," one that justified every manner of extralegal justice and vigilante behavior. Slave treatment was most severe on absentee plantations* along the Red River. But the most common form of slave resistance* was running away. The most publicized bid for freedom came from Fayetteville butler Nelson Hacket, who in 1840 escaped on a stolen race horse. Tracked to Canada, he ultimately was extradited back to Arkansas. Some slave escapes comprised part of organized crime. And the hysteria surrounding the John Murrell gang activities in the 1830s prompted mob violence by whites. Little Rock, with only 3,700 residents, suffered from some of the discipline problems endemic to slavery in cities throughout the South. Fear of slave rebellion there in 1856 prompted an ordinance prohibiting slaves from living "separately and to themselves."

The Civil War* brought about a gradual end to slavery in Arkansas. Although no slave uprisings were reported, the plantation system collapsed as federal armies penetrated the state. Some eastern planters tried sequestering slaves in canebrakes, where they were "found *invariably* through bad faith of some of the negroes." Others relocated hands to remote and safer lands. Some planters hired slaves to the Confederate government, and after August 1862, formal impressment of slaves by the Confederacy* began. Bondsmen hired to the government tended to be employed in the towns. Wartime Little Rock, for example, experienced a large slave population growth. And because owners could not control their slaves from afar, problems of control ensued. By 1863 slaves were reported to be hiring their own time, renting houses for prostitution, selling illegal liquor, and buying horses and firearms. Masters charged the Confederate government not only with failing to discipline their bondsmen but also with failing to provide slaves with proper food or medical care. As a result, many planters hid their bondsmen in Texas. By one estimate 150,000 slaves passed through Arkansas to Texas during the war.

The many slaves who followed the Union army* were quickly put to work building fortifications. Some, poorly fed and housed and also abused by Union troops, returned to the plantations. By 1863 the Union armies had stripped Arkansas farms of most able-bodied bondsmen, leaving very young and old slaves for the Confederacy to feed. Slaves now "hide from us like the dickins," one Union soldier reported in 1863. Late in the war the federal army began arming Arkansas slaves. Eventually 5,000 black Arkansans served in the U.S. Colored Troops.*

Confederates reacted violently to their blacks in Yankee uniforms. At the Battle of Poison Springs (1864), the Confederates took few prisoners, and drivers ran wagon wheels over the skulls of the dead. General Patrick R. Cleburne, a native of Arkansas, first proposed that the Confederacy recruit and arm blacks. Cleburne's proposal was greeted by a storm of opposition and the charge of treason. Late in the war the questions of arming and emancipating the slaves were widely debated in the Trans-Mississippi Department. In 1865 the last Confederate newspaper in Arkansas, the Washington *Telegraph*, asserted that "We owe it to God to sustain" slavery. But common soldiers were far less enthusiastic. The Confederacy's "twenty nigger" law, under which planters' sons often escaped military service, generated much dissension among Arkansas's dominant yeomen class.

The war brought an end to slavery, but not at one time or in one place. In areas of Union occupation wage labor appeared immediately, and leased plantations were established. As a judge during Reconstruction observed, "None questions the fact that all slaves in the State have been emancipated and forever made free, but lawyers and courts do not so well agree as to the sovereign act which gave them freedom." Questions of civil rights, the status of slave marriages, and the validity of antebellum slave purchase contracts were debated in Arkansas courts as late as the 1950s. Post–Civil War racial repression—the convict lease and debt peonage systems, and the Elaine race riot of 1919—served as bitter reminders of slavery to black Arkansas.

SELECTED BIBLIOGRAPHY

S. Charles Bolton, "Inequality on the Southern Frontier: Arkansas County in the Arkansas Territory," *Arkansas Historical Quarterly*, 41 (1982), 51–66; Michael B. Dougan, *Confederate Arkansas: The People and Policies of a Frontier State in Wartime* (1976); Carl H. Moneyhon, "Economic Democracy in Antebellum Arkansas, Phillips County, 1850–1860," *Arkansas Historical Quarterly*, 40 (1981), 154–172; Robert S. Shafer, "White Persons Held to Racial Slavery in Antebellum Arkansas," *Arkansas Historical Quarterly*, 44 (1985), 134–155; and Orville W. Taylor, *Negro Slavery in Arkansas* (1958).

MICHAEL B. DOUGAN

ARTS AND CRAFTS, SLAVE. The standard portrait of slave life commonly presents a view of field hands* engaged in menial tasks requiring much endurance but little creative thought. Even when the slaves are viewed as workers, rather than mere laborers, they are credited with the effort that resulted in bulk commodities—hogsheads of tobacco, bales of cotton, or bushels of rice. But rarely are the bondsmen acknowledged as makers of specific objects. Consequently, they are generally not recognized as craftspersons and never as artists. Yet as early as the eighteenth-century visitors to the Chesapeake region noted that large plantations depended on the special skills of slave artisans. In their accounts, these travelers described scenes resembling industrial villages as well as farms. They observed that a slave's routine could as often include a task in a workshop as a task in a tobacco field.

In the 1830s John Mason of Gunston Hall in Virginia recalled the most explicit statement regarding slave craftsmanship:

... my father had among his slaves carpenters, coopers, sawyers, blacksmiths, tanners, curriers, shoemakers, spinners, weavers, and knitters, and even a distiller. His woods furnished timber and plank for the carpenters and coopers, and charcoal for the blacksmith; his cattle killed for his consumption and for sale supplied skins for the tanners, curriers, and shoemakers, and his sheep gave wool and his fields produced cotton and flax for the weavers and spinners, and his orchards fruit for the distiller. His carpenters and sawyers built and kept in repair all the dwelling-houses, barns, stables, and ploughs, barrows, gates, & c., on the plantations and the outhouses at the home house. His coopers made the hogsheads the tobacco was prised in and the tight casks to hold the cider and other liquors. The tanners and curriers with the proper vats & c., tanned and dressed the skins as well for upper as for lower leather to the full amount of the consumption of the estate, and the shoemakers made them into shoes for the negroes. . . . The blacksmiths did all the ironwork required by the establishment, as making and repairing ploughs, harrow teeth, chains, bolts & c., & c. The spinners, weavers, and knitters made all the coarse cloths and stockings used by the negroes and some of finer texture worn by the white family, nearly all worn by the children of it. . . . All these operations were carried on at the home house, and their results distributed as occasion required to the different plantations.

This description provides both an extensive list of slave skills and a partial inventory of the artifacts they produced. Slaves in the Chesapeake colonies worked with diverse materials—wood, metal, leather, textiles—and competently dominated an array of craft techniques. Slaves practiced a broad range of arts and crafts in a variety of contexts. Only recently have historians come to appreciate the value of Afro-American material culture to our understanding of the slave experience.

Slave artisans played a salient role on the big plantations of Virginia and the Carolinas. Without question they made money for the gentry. Skilled slaves allowed their owners to conserve their cash, enabling planters to produce the goods they otherwise would have had to purchase. And slave artisans also generated income when they were hired out to neighboring planters or to nearby townspeople. Slave artisans, then, both preserved and created capital. But craftsmanship proved valuable to the slaves themselves for other reasons. Skilled work not only gave craftspersons high prestige within the slave community but also provided a means for them to have money of their own, leading ultimately, in some cases, to the purchase of their freedom. Skill thus came to equate with liberty in the minds of the slaves. And it is no mere coincidence that major slave rebellions* were organized by craftsmen or that there were a high number of skilled blacks listed in runaway* notices.

The making of objects is generally regarded as a way for people to gain control of the world around them. Indeed, there is profound therapeutic value for one's self-esteem attached to craft skills. For slaves, who keenly sensed that they were under the control of others, craftsmanship provided a means of regaining or establishing their sense of self-worth, albeit in a manner that often augmented the fortunes of the master class. A slave blacksmith, for example, kept the plantation on its productive schedule by making and repairing the essential tools required for cultivation. But at the same time he frequently also took command of plantation routine and orchestrated completion of the annual work cycle. Consequently, the slave blacksmith could, if he chose, sabotage a year's production. Should he slow down on the repair of the tools, the field tasks would not be completed on schedule, and as a result, the planter might lose a profitable sale. It is crucial, then, to examine slave crafts by identifying the motives of the artisans, which, more often than not, were at cross-purposes with those of their owners. And even if the slaves' goals were shared with their masters, the bondsmen no doubt realized different benefits from their work.

While no written accounts of slave craftsmanship from a slave's point of view have survived, enough evidence exists that offers mute but nonetheless eloquent testimony regarding slave achievements. Such is the case for Dave (1780–1863), a slave from the Edgefield District of west-central South Carolina. Dave, a slave potter, illustrates well the life and experiences of a slave artisan. He is especially important because Dave both wrote on his pieces and made very large, distinctive pots. Most Southern pottery in the eighteenth and nineteenth centuries was made at numerous small, family-run operations owned by whites. But in the Edgefield District, a rather ambitious ceramic industry was founded between 1810 and 1820. Owing to the abundant supply of excellent clays in the area, a number of commercial shops were opened that employed slaves as laborers. They were put to work digging clay, grinding and mixing glazes, cutting wood for fuel, and loading, firing, and unloading kilns. Eventually they were trained to operate kick wheels on which they crafted all manner of jugs, churns, and other containers. As a turner of wares, Dave came to be one of the more highly regarded blacks at the pottery shop at Stoney Bluff plantation near Miles Mill.

But one ability set Dave apart from the other slave potters—he was literate. Trained first as a typesetter at a local Edgefield newspaper before being put to work with clay, Dave showed his earlier talent by writing poems on the sides of his larger pots. Many of his poetic messages, usually rhymed couplets, were comments on the pieces of pottery itself: "Put every bit between / Surely this jar will hold fourteen [gallons]"; "A very large jar which has four handles / pack it full of fresh meat—then light candles"; "This noble jar will hold twenty / fill it with silver then you will have plenty." In one case Dave commented on his own enslavement: "Dave belongs to Mr. Miles / where the oven bakes and the pot biles." He also marked his pieces with the date of manufacture, his name, and the letters "Lm" for Lewis Miles, the owner of the pottery. While enough pots survived with Dave's signature or his distinctive "Lm" mark to show that he made many kinds of wares, the most numerous type left is large storage crocks made for holding ashes or for pickling meat. The largest of these, which Dave labeled "A Great & noble Jar," has an estimated holding capacity of forty-four gallons. One of the largest pieces of stoneware pottery ever made in the South, it stands out as a monument among utilitarian works. Moreover, Dave had a distinctive style of making crocks. They are very narrow at the bottom and flair to their greatest diameter near the top rim. Thus, they seem to teeter precariously as the upper section extends far out over its base. Both scale and shape draw attention to Dave's work.

There are messages embedded in Dave's pots that transcend the life and work of one lone slave artisan. They convey the slave's exceptional mastery of his material. He could work more clay more spectacularly than any potter of his day, white or black. And the poems he composed reveal a marked ability of literary expression.

Slave craft, then, served both as an alternative mode of slave protest and fostered an alternative aesthetic. Moreoever, it is in the aesthetic dimension of an object that we encounter the deepest and most significant layer of meaning that slave-made artifacts held for their makers. Aesthetics, the feeling for form, is inextricably tied to cultural identity. What one senses as beautiful or ugly reflects the learned values of one's culture. These values can be best witnessed in artifacts in which a premium is placed on decoration, artifacts in which material is manipulated expressly for symbolic purposes. While Dave's monumental pots engaged an aesthetic will and served latent symbolic functions, it was a rather different genre of Edgefield ceramics that best illustrates the aesthetic quotient of slave arts and crafts.

Small jugs sculpted to resemble human faces appeared throughout the slave South. They represented the potters' artworks as opposed to their craftworks. These objects were made at the Edgefield potteries as well, but in the style that was quite distinct. By the 1850s it was common for the eyes and teeth of Edgefield face vessels to be made with a white porcelain-like clay that was inserted into the stoneware body of the vessel. These inserts were not glazed so that when completed the white, matte finish eyes and teeth contrasted with the rest of the dark, shiny face. The combination of two clay types in one vessel was a difficult maneuver because the two media shrank at different rates and had different firing temperatures. That the slave potters negotiated this complex decorative ploy so successfully speaks well for their technical ability, but it is not technique that makes these sculptures particularly Afro-American in character. The will to break with precedent and experiment with the potentialities of materials, as in the Edgefield face vessels, reveals evidence of the free-wheeling innovation and improvisation that characterizes so much of Afro-American expressive culture. Slave potters seized an opportunity within the conventions of Anglo-American folk ceramics and made a statement that was theirs alone. No contemporary

Southern white potters are known to have ever combined two different clays in one vessel.

Although the function of Edgefield face vessels is unknown, they almost certainly were not utilitarian objects. Rarely were they more than five inches tall. Yet with all the attention and care that was required in their manufacture, these small jugs must have been important objects. It is tempting to compare these clay sculptures to African sculptures, particularly to those of the Bakongo people of Central Africa, from whence the bulk of South Carolina's slave population was derived. Art historian Robert Farris Thompson, who has made such a comparison, finds

the same pinpoint pupils within white eyes, the same long hooked nose, the same siting of the nose at a point relatively high above the lips, the same open mouth with bared teeth, the same widening of the mouth so that it extends across the width of the jaw.

So many resemblances, Thompson argues, were not mere coincidence, and he suggests that we regard Edgefield face vessels as evidence of the survival of African artistic forms within the experience of slavery.

Further, the mixed-media quality produced by the insertion of white clay into a darker vessel was alien to European artistic canons. Europeans stressed the use of a single, pure material. But the combination of two materials was perfectly consistent with African sculpture. And because such jugs were apparently known among the slaves as "monkey jugs," and because in the Bakongo language clay water carriers are called *mvungi*, the connections between Edgefield and Africa seem quite strong. White potters often referred to their own face vessels as "ugly jugs," thus signaling the spirit of whimsy and tomfoolery in which they were made. No doubt they saw in the works made by slaves simply a black version of the grotesque. But what apparently motivated the slave potters of Edgefield was their own sense of good form, their own cultural preferences derived from a past very much rooted in Africa rather than Europe or America. The work of slave potters showed the black community the potential of the future which they might achieve through action and courage. The face vessels put them in touch with a heritage that was almost lost.

The examples of ceramic skill suggest a broad range of artistic expressions. Some pots—such as the syrup jugs or cream risers—could be very Anglo-American; others, like the face vessels, were very Afro-American. Craftsmanship thus provided a means both of accommodation and resistance, ways to participate in mainstream society and to make a distinct ethnic statement. This same variety existed throughout most black crafts. In textiles, for example, slave women made bolts of cotton or wool cloth to use for tailoring the most usual types of garments. Or they pieced together various scraps to create quilts with geometric designs reminiscent of African patterns. Baskets made in the Carolina low country exhibited African coiling techniques. These were used both to carry produce from the fields and to provide fancy "show baskets" for home use. Slave craftsmen utilized woodworking skills both to make furniture for whites and to fashion furnishings and ornate woodcrafts for themselves. Just as art could spring from craft, black identity could always emerge in the midst of doing a master's bidding.

Because the slave community was a folk society, its artifacts usually combined beauty and utility, and its artifacts were mostly tied to the domestic sphere. Clusters of specialized production craftsmen—such as on a large plantation like Gunston Hall or in an industrial setting like Edgefield—were the exception. Most slaves created within the contexts of the quarters where their skills were directed chiefly at the tasks required for the maintenance of the household. Women patched and mended clothes; men plastered chimneys or shingled roofs. These were mundane but essential chores, but they also exposed the potential for creativity and the display of talent. The routines of daily work provided the context in which the slaves honed their abilities to perfection. House repairs were one way to learn carpentry; mending taught slaves how to tailor or how to do patchwork quilts. From the process of making do the art of living emerged. Afro-American folk art, then, has been focused most closely around the home.

The ex-slave narratives* collected in the 1930s contain numerous recollections of such day-to-day household skills. In one of these accounts, Yach Stringfellow of Brenham, Texas, noted: "In the long winter days the men sit around the fire and whittle wood and make butter paddles and troughs for pigs and such and ax handles and hoe handles and box traps and figure-four traps. They make combs to get wool clean for spinning." Carving skills such as these no doubt gave slaves a sense of self-sufficiency. And their handiwork allowed them to provide for many of their physical needs. Moreover, a smoothly finished and delicately balanced ax handle could be a thing of beauty as well as a useful item. To an important degree, though slaves were owned by others, their crafts enabled them to feel as though they owned themselves.

The nature of the slave community promoted a degree of independence among the bondsmen. Slaves, for example, were encouraged to fend for themselves by growing their own food, making their own clothes,* and building and repairing their own houses.* And slaves all across the South kept their own garden* patches. The spirit of independence that accompanied this modest "landholding" by slaves was augmented by their craft abilities. Once they took claim over the garden plot and its produce, the slaves' expertise in various crafts allowed them to create an environment marked in a way that most judged to be adequate if not suitable. They resided in cabins that they had built with timber felled by the slaves themselves. In their homes they placed homemade beds, stools, tables, blankets, articles of clothing, shoes, baskets, boxes, and numerous utensils carved from wood and gourds. No doubt slaves kept some of their implements and possessions outside in the yard as well, a yard they swept clean and packed hard like those found in African homesteads. It was here in the evenings and on Sundays and holidays that other slaves assembled to visit and sing songs to the accompaniment of African-inspired musical instruments,* including banjos, fiddles, and drums. This was a world, says Eugene D. Genovese, the slaves made. It was a world shaped significantly by the slaves' craft skills.

The importance of slave crafts did not diminish with the abolition of slavery. The skills that blacks acquired in bondage also served them well during Reconstruction and later. They provided the free men and women with a basis for entry into the free-market economy. This succession is explained by Ace Jackson, a contemporary Afro-American mason in Mobile, Alabama, who preserves in his work a family tradition. ''I done all of it,'' explains Jackson. ''I was raised into the trade. My father was a brick mason. My mother's father was a brick mason. My father's father was a full-blood African, and he was a brick mason. He was a slave.'' Such craft skills gave blacks bright moments of inspiration and the encouragement to endure and prevail over their misfortunes. Confidence rooted in a spirit of self-sufficiency never withered, and today we still can find many practitioners of the old crafts. Hundreds of coiled ''sweetgrass'' basket makers ply their craft from South Carolina to Florida. Thousands of black quilters from Virginia to Idaho make distinctive Afro-American patterns. Plenty of whittlers still carve toys and walking sticks, and an occasional blacksmith serves the ironwork needs of a community. These modern craftspersons are not marginal people frozen in time. Rather, they are contemporary citizens who participate fully in the modern world. They do, however, know their history and treasure the lessons of their ancestors. The traditions of skill which they continue to enact are a heritage that they carry forward as a gift of confidence for their children. Slave crafts, then, continue to serve as a source of inspiration instilling the same positive message today that they did in the eighteenth and nineteenth centuries.

SELECTED BIBLIOGRAPHY

William R. Ferris, ed., *Afro-American Folk Arts and Crafts* (1983); Ben Fewel, ''Ace Jackson,'' *Southern Exposure*, 8 (1980), 11–13; Gerald W. Mullin, *Flight and Rebellion: Slave Resistance in Eighteenth-Century Virginia* (1972); George P. Rawick, ed., *The American Slave: A Composite Autobiography* (19 vols., 1972); Leonard Price Stavisky, ''Negro Craftsmanship in Early America,'' *American Historical Review*, 54 (1948), 315–325; Robert Farris Thompson, ''African Influence on the Art of the United States,'' in Armstead L. Robinson, Craig C. Foster, and Donald H. Ogilvie, eds., *Black Studies in the University: A Symposium* (1969); John M. Vlach, *The Afro-American Tradition in Decorative Arts* (1978); and Peter H. Wood, '' 'It Was a Negro Taught Them': A New Look at Labor in Early South Carolina,'' in Roger D. Abrahams and John F. Szwed, eds., *Discovering Afro-America* (1975).

JOHN MICHAEL VLACH

AUTOBIOGRAPHIES. In 1855 John Little, a fugitive slave, uttered this commentary on attempts to portray the existence that he had fled: ''Tisn't he who has stood and looked on, that can tell you what slavery is—'tis he who has endured.'' From the eighteenth to the twentieth century a voluminous number of autobiographies, personal testimonies, and interviews with those who had ''endured'' were published or recorded. These autobiographical accounts constitute an illuminating source of information about antebellum Southern life, about the institution of slavery, and, most importantly, about the experiences and perspectives of those who had been enslaved. Moreover, slave autobiographies and the oral tradition on which they were based have had an extraordinary impact on Afro-American culture. As the works of Frederick Douglass,* Booker T. Washington,* W.E.B. Du Bois, James Weldon Johnson, Richard Wright, and Malcolm X attest, the autobiography has been one of the most distinctive features of Afro-American literature and has affected the entire Afro-American literary tradition.

The literary tradition of the slave autobiography extends back to the eighteenth century. Since 1776 more than 200 book-length autobiographies of former slaves have been published in the United States and England. Several thousand stenographically recorded speeches, depositions, and interviews with slaves and former slaves have been obtained by journalists, scholars, and government officials. When compared to the dearth of such publications in other slaveholding societies, these autobiographical accounts represent a unique historical record.

The greatest vogue of the slave autobiography occurred during the three decades preceding the Civil War. These autobiographies performed the political function of challenging the benign view of slavery advanced by its apologists. The proslavery justification* of the peculiar institution alleged that it was a benevolent system and that the position of the slave was more secure than that of the Northern wage earner.

But the stereotype of the contented slave was contradicted by the many fugitive slaves* who sought refuge from bondage in the North and in Canada. Their graphic depictions of slave life were a persuasive challenge to Southern justifications of slavery. During the antebellum period several thousand autobiographical and biographical accounts of slave experiences, generally promoted and distributed by abolitionist propagandists,* enjoyed immense popularity and were widely published—in book form and in newspapers and magazines.

Interest in slave autobiographies waned after the Civil War. Since one of the primary functions of slave autobiographies was to undermine the legitimacy of human bondage, such literary forms had little appeal once slavery had been legally abolished. Moreover, whites intent upon sectional reconciliation expressed little desire to be reminded of the realities of antebellum slave life. The autobiographies of former slaves that were published in media intended for white audiences were used as a nostalgic and sentimental reaffirmation of the "plantation legend." However, as the number of former slaves began to dwindle during the late nineteenth and early twentieth centuries, there was a dramatic increase in interest among blacks in their stories of bondage and freedom. Their accounts became, in John Blassingame's words, "deeply embedded in the black folk tradition, engendering communal respect for those who had endured the privations of slavery."

The late 1920s and 1930s witnessed a revival of interest in slave autobiographies. During the twenties black scholars at Fisk University and at Southern

University initiated projects to interview surviving ex-slaves. The most ambitious of such efforts was undertaken by the Federal Writers' Project* of the Works Progress Administration during the thirties. The result was the Slave Narrative Collection,* a group of autobiographical accounts of former slaves that stands as one of the most enduring and noteworthy achievements of the Writers' Project. Compiled in seventeen states during the years 1936–1938, the collection consists of over 3,000 interviews with former slaves. These interviews, almost exclusively verbatim testimonies concerning antebellum life and the respondents' personal reactions to bondage, afforded aged ex-slaves an unparalleled opportunity to give their personal account of life under the peculiar institution, to describe in their own words what it felt like to be a slave.

The availability in published form of an abundance of slave autobiographies was one of the major turning points in the post–World War II historiography* of American slavery. Until the 1960s historians of slavery had generally been reluctant to use slave autobiographies. However, evidence from slave sources has been a crucial ingredient in the surge of scholarship on slavery during the past quarter century. As scholars began to explore the nature of slave culture and the dynamics of the slave community, the personal accounts of those who experienced slavery became essential data. As a consequence, slave autobiographies in general and the Slave Narrative Collection interviews in particular have been used extensively.

In addition to being used to develop general historical portraits of slavery, emancipation, and Reconstruction, slave autobiographies have been invaluable in efforts to comprehend qualitatively many specific dimensions of slave culture* and the slave community. Religion,* funeral and burial practices,* marriage rites,* family patterns,* children's play,* folklore,* folktales, folk songs and music,* work habits, and social relations in the slave community are among the many topics for which the autobiographies have been a primary source* of data. Moreover, because of the substantial number of autobiographies, historians have attempted to use them for quantitative studies that undertake more precise, systematic—even computer-assisted—studies of various facets of slavery.

Slave autobiographies are not the only sources with which to reconstruct American slavery. But if one wishes to fully understand the nature of slavery from the perspective of the slave, to reconstruct the cultural characteristics and social milieu of the slave community, or to analyze the social structural dynamics of the slave system, slave autobiographies are sources of essential information. As their extensive use on a wide range of topics has recently demonstrated, comprehension of American slavery has been enhanced immeasurably by the availability of slave autobiographies.

SELECTED BIBLIOGRAPHY

John W. Blassingame, ed., *Slave Testimony: Two Centuries of Letters, Speeches, Interviews, and Autobiographies* (1977); Charles T. Davis and Henry Louis Gates, Jr., eds., *The Slave's Narrative* (1984); George P. Rawick, ed., *The American Slave: A Composite*

Autobiography (19 vols., 1972; supplement, series 1, 12 vols., 1977; supplement, series 2, 10 vols., 1979); Marion W. Starling, *The Slave Narrative: Its Place in American Literary History* (1981); and Norman R. Yetman, "Ex-Slave Interviews and the Historiography of Slavery," *American Quarterly*, 36 (1984), 181–210.

NORMAN R. YETMAN

B

BALL, CHARLES (1780–?). Raised a slave in eastern Maryland, Ball cultivated corn and tobacco and was hired out for two years to work in a shipyard in Washington, D.C. Not long after marrying Judah and beginning a family, he was torn away from all of his acquaintances and marched south to Columbia, South Carolina, where he became the property of a wealthy planter around 1805. Soon he learned the harsh routine of life and labor on a cotton plantation. Later he accompanied a new master to Morgan County in piedmont Georgia, but after more years of labor he ran away and retraced his path back to his home in Maryland. There he settled down with his second wife Lucy and worked a small farm.

About ten years later, around 1830, he was seized again and returned to slavery near Milledgeville, the capital of Georgia. He escaped again and stowed away on a vessel in Savannah, which brought him to freedom in Philadelphia. After discovering that his wife and children had been carried away into slavery, he settled in rural Pennsylvania, dictated his autobiography to a sympathetic white lawyer named Isaac Fisher, and faded into obscurity, fearful of again being seized as a fugitive slave.*

Slavery in the United States: A Narrative of the Life and Adventures of Charles Ball, a Black Man appeared in 1836, and several revisions followed. A thirty-two-page abridgement in a magazine drew heavy criticism from a Southern white and caused considerable skepticism. Even the full account is difficult to evaluate because the crucial years in South Carolina and Georgia are described in very general terms almost entirely lacking in specific names. Yet the conservative historian Ulrich B. Phillips included an excerpt from Ball's narrative in his *Plantation and Frontier* in 1909, so Ball's story may well be an authentic description of slavery from the black perspective, and along with Solomon Northup* (Louisiana) and John Brown* (Georgia), Ball furnishes one of the few black narratives of slavery in the Deep South.

SELECTED BIBLIOGRAPHY

Charles Ball, *Slavery in the United States: A Narrative of the Life and Adventures of Charles Ball, a Black Man* (1836); John W. Blassingame, ed., *Slave Testimony: Two Centuries of Letters, Speeches, Interviews, and Autobiographies* (1977); and Ulrich B. Phillips, ed., *Plantation and Frontier, 1649–1863* (1909).

F. N. BONEY

BALTIMORE, MD, SLAVERY IN. Springing from a modest town, Baltimore had become the largest seaport on the Chesapeake Bay by 1770. During the generation following the War of 1812, it supplanted St. Michael's as Maryland's leading shipbuilding center. By 1860 it was the largest city in the South and the fourth largest in the nation. Though not dependent upon slave labor, Baltimore had a slave population and performed various services linked with slave society. Most of the slaves were domestic workers. European visitors penetrating no farther south than Baltimore, remarked E. T. Coke after his 1832 visit, "will certainly return under the impression that the situation of a slave is far from degrading." The young slave Frederick Douglass,* upon being sent there to live during the 1820s, recognized "a marked difference in the treatment of slaves from that which I had witnessed in the country. A city slave is almost a freeman compared with a slave on the plantation." Baltimore's free blacks had organized a vast network of churches, schools, and benevolent societies. Urban slaves sometimes hired their own time, often lived apart from their masters, and usually joined with free blacks in their separate community life. Douglass, for example, joined the East Baltimore Mental Improvement Society where he met his future wife, Anna Murray, a free black housemaid.

Over 130,000 European immigrants* (mostly Irish and German) who arrived between 1820 and 1850 increasingly supplied Maryland's labor needs. A few Baltimore ships illegally imported slaves directly from Africa and reaped handsome profits, but the city loomed more important as an established seat of a large domestic slave trade.* Such firms as Franklin and Armfield maintained offices there and sold slaves not only to the sugar parishes of Louisiana but also to the cotton-cultivating states. Consequently, many slaves from Maryland's rural counties, like the 208 individuals shipped to New Orleans in 1836, were taken to Baltimore to be sold. Others, like the Eastern Shore field hand John Boggs, were relocated within the state. Sold "five or six times" before escaping to Canada in 1854, Boggs was once sold in Baltimore and detained for a month before being resold for $550 to someone living thirty miles away.

The city's slave population declined from an all-time high of 4,672 in 1810. The wide geographical dispersion of slaves, found during the 1820s, persisted into the 1850s—with all twelve of the city's wards having a scattering of slaves. Between 1820 and 1860, as its free black population* grew from 10,326 to 25,680, Baltimore's slave population dwindled from 4,357 to 2,218 (2.7 percent of the state's slaves and 7.9 percent of all blacks in Baltimore). That women outnumbered men among slaves in 1860 (1,541 to 677) underscores the predominantly domestic use of slaves. Given the size of Baltimore's free black population, none should be surprised that a small handful of them owned slaves (ninety-four in Baltimore city in 1830). Thus, although slavery persisted until emancipation in 1864, Baltimore's dominant economic and population tendencies pulled it increasingly away from the orbit of the slave economy as the Civil War approached.

SELECTED BIBLIOGRAPHY

John W. Blassingame, ed., *Slave Testimony: Two Centuries of Letters, Speeches, Interviews, and Autobiographies* (1977); William Calderhead, "How Extensive Was the Border State Slave Trade? A New Look," *Civil War History*, 18 (1972), 42–55; Edward T. Coke, *A Subaltern's Furlough: Descriptive of Scenes in Various Parts of the United States, Upper and Lower Canada . . .* (1833); Barbara Jeanne Fields, *Slavery and Freedom on the Middle Ground: Maryland during the Nineteenth Century* (1985); Thomas Hamilton, *Men and Manners in America* (1843; repr. 1968); Michael Meyer, ed., *Frederick Douglass: The Narrative and Selected Writings* (1984); and Richard C. Wade, *Slavery in the Cities: The South, 1820–1860* (1964).

ROBERT L. HALL

BAPTIST CHURCH. The first Baptist churches in America were established in Rhode Island in the 1630s; by the close of the seventeenth century Baptist congregations had been formed in the Middle and Southern colonies. On the eve of the American Revolution there were more than 150 Baptist churches in the thirteen colonies. Perhaps one-half of them were in New England.

Africans were in America before the Baptists, and by the time of the American Revolution they constituted approximately 18 percent of the colonial population. Most of the black Baptists (ca. 92 percent) were slaves, and although slavery existed in all of the colonies, perhaps 89 percent of the slaves lived south of the Mason-Dixon line.

At the close of the colonial era some Baptists in all areas of British America owned slaves, and the membership of Baptist churches from Massachusetts to Georgia included slaves. The family of the most prominent Baptist in America, the New England patriarch Isaac Backus, owned slaves. By the eighteenth century probably as many as 40 percent of the Baptist preachers in South Carolina owned slaves; and in one Virginia county in the late antebellum era 80 percent of the Baptist clergymen in the county owned slaves.

Although Africans had been in America since 1619, efforts by churchmen to bring them into the church were meager and converts were few. The religious enthusiasm associated with the Great Awakening (ca. 1735 +), however, stimulated the growth of Baptist churches and also aroused the conscience of white Christians in all churches to minister to the spiritual needs of the blacks. The humanitarian impulse associated with the Great Awakening together with the rights-of-man ideology as expressed in the Declaration of Independence* had an ameliorating influence on the status of blacks in American society. In the revolutionary era all of the states north of Maryland abolished slavery. Although slavery was not abolished in the Southern states, the churches in the region maintained a keen interest in the spiritual care of the blacks. Spokesmen in no denomination expressed more concern for the religious care of the blacks than the Baptist.

In the century before the Civil War thousands of slaves became members of Baptist churches. Indeed, by 1860 they numbered 157,000 or approximately 26 percent of the membership of Southern Baptist churches. Slaves were accepted for membership in the same manner as whites. After expressing a desire to join a church, one was required to relate his or her religious experience. If the congregation was favorably impressed by one's testimony, the applicant was accepted into the fellowship and was baptized. When black church members moved from one community to another, they were given letters of dismissal which they might place with another Baptist church. Black church members worshiped in the sanctuary with whites, participated in the service of Holy Communion, and contributed to help support the various programs of the denomination. Still blacks and females in antebellum Baptist churches held a membership status subordinate to that of white adult males, since that group determined denominational policies and procedures.

Slave members of Baptist churches were subject to the same disciplinary rules and procedures as other members of the congregation. Much time was consumed in the monthly business meetings of some antebellum congregations with slave discipline. Lying, stealing, fornication, fighting, and adultery, the sins for which most whites were disciplined, were the offenses most frequently committed by the blacks.

Occasionally a congregation would discipline one of its slave-owning members for mistreating a slave. The Black Creek Baptist Church in Virginia, for example, once excommunicated a member for beating his Negro. Baptist associational gatherings and newspapers advised slaveholding Baptists to avoid severe or improper treatment of their slaves. If masters refused this injunction, congregations were advised to deal with them as they would "offenders of other crimes."

Black Baptist preachers were not uncommon in the South, although in some states such as Virginia and South Carolina they were more restricted than in other areas. Most black Baptists were members of mixed congregations, but others joined black or African Baptist churches, which existed throughout the South by 1860. In practically all instances these churches were branch organizations of a parent white congregation. The black deacons, exhorters, overlookers, and pastors for the black churches were often chosen by the white members of the parent church, after some consultation with black members. In some states statutes required that the pastor of a black congregation be a white clergyman. But in others black congregations seemed to be free to choose their own pastors, and a number of black Baptist churches were affiliated in local associations with churches of white or mixed membership.

Although some black Baptists attended Sunday school classes and were taught from catechisms prepared by white Baptist preachers, all instruction was oral and slaves remained illiterate. All states except Tennessee had laws that prohibited the teaching of blacks to read and write.

The teachings given to blacks in Sunday schools and the message dispensed to them by white Baptist preachers stressed the virtues of docility, obedience, hard work, honesty, and truthfulness. What the slaves received was a form of indoctrination designed to make them satisfied with their status, and also to be more conscientious servants of their masters.

The attacks upon slavery and slave owners by a new generation of abolitionists* from the 1830s on elicited a response from Baptist spokesmen and others in the South, which defended slavery as an institution sanctioned by Holy Scripture and ordained by God. One of the most ardent proslavery apologists* was the Virginia Baptist clergyman, Thornton Stringfellow. In 1841 he published *A Brief Examination of Scripture Testimony on the Institution of Slavery*. Although this booklet was widely disseminated, it probably reinforced the views of more people than it converted.

A number of prominent Baptists in the South were outspoken defenders of slavery, but they were almost equally outspoken opponents of the slave trade.* From the early years of the nineteenth century various Baptist associations went on record denouncing slave trading and advocated that congregations should expel any church member who engaged in this activity. The Baptist press described the slave traffic as a disreputable business and claimed that any congregation that retained a slave dealer among its members would lose its reputation, influence, and usefulness. In the closing years of the antebellum era Baptist spokesmen firmly opposed all efforts to reopen the African slave trade; they termed such trade brutal and inhumane.

Although antislavery sentiment had persisted among some Baptists since the time of the American Revolution, it was not until the 1830s that scattered Baptist groups in New England and the Old Northwest questioned the propriety of holding fellowship with slaveholders, and adopted resolutions which urged their coreligionists in the South to emancipate their slaves. In 1840 a number of antislavery Baptists formed the American Anti-Slavery Baptist Convention. This convention was designed to promote missionary activities without associating with slaveholding Baptists. The growth of antislavery sentiment among Baptists outside the South resulted, in the mid–1840s, in the withdrawal of Baptists in the Southern states from cooperative programs in home and foreign missions— enterprises that Baptist churches throughout the nation had cooperated in since 1814. In 1845 Baptist leaders in the slave states formed the Southern Baptist Convention and terminated their relationship with the Triennial Convention, which dated from 1814.

At the same time that the Baptists in the slave states formed a sectional organization they accelerated their efforts to convert the slaves to Christianity. Various associations in all of the states appointed "Committees on the Instruction of the Colored People'' and counseled slave owners of their Christian duty to provide religious instruction for their blacks and to encourage their slaves to attend worship services.

Although Southern Baptist spokesmen were apologists for slavery, they also recognized that the institution needed reform to correct certain abuses. Baptists in various states urged legislative bodies to legalize slave marriage* and to repeal the laws that prohibited the teaching of slaves to read and write, or a slave to conduct worship service and preach, and that required the presence of whites at black worship services.

Prior to 1800 some Baptist leaders in the South sought to have religious and civil authorities in the area abolish slavery. However, fear, economic interest, racist ideology, and a literal and limited reading and interpretation of Scripture negated all efforts by churchmen for emancipation of the slaves. By 1800 the principal concern of Southern Baptists was to evangelize the Negro and ''win him for Christ.'' This approach received a favorable response from many blacks. Apparently they believed that the white Baptists who expressed a concern for their souls were sincere. The degree of ''rough equality'' among Baptist church members, all addressed as brother and sister, appealed to the black person's sense of dignity and worth. In Baptist churches blacks were given a degree of leadership which was not common in other groups. Slaves might be deacons, overlookers, exhorters, and preachers,* and be permitted to attend meetings of the local association. Perhaps many blacks found the informal atmosphere and worship service of Baptist churches more appealing than the more formal and decorous service in some other churches. The form of baptism (immersion) in Baptist churches, which symbolized death to an old way of life and resurrection to a new life, was especially meaningful to countless antebellum blacks—and whites. It was a shared experience that both slave and master found meaningful.

SELECTED BIBLIOGRAPHY

W. Harrison Daniel, ''Virginia Baptists and the Negro in the Early Republic,'' *Virginia Magazine of History and Biography*, 80 (1972), 60–69; W. Harrison Daniel, ''Virginia Baptists and the Negro in the Antebellum Era,'' *Journal of Negro History*, 56 (1971), 1–16; William G. McLoughlin, *Isaac Backus and the American Pietistic Tradition* (1967); Norman H. Maring, *Baptists in New Jersey: A Study in Transition* (1964); Donald G. Mathews, *Religion in the Old South* (1977); Mechal Sobel, *Trabelin' On: The Slave Journey to an Afro-Baptist Faith* (1979); and Robert G. Torbet, *A History of the Baptists* (rev. ed., 1952).

W. HARRISON DANIEL

BIBB, HENRY WALTON (1815–1854). Henry Bibb was the child of Mildred Jackson, a slave, and James Bibb, a slaveholding planter and politician of Shelby County, Kentucky. While still in his teens, Bibb wed, fathered a daughter, and began to plot to free himself and his family. After several foiled attempts, Bibb escaped to Ohio in 1837 but was recaptured the next year when he returned to

Kentucky to rescue his wife and child. Reenslaved and sold away from his family, Bibb successfully fled his new owner after being taken to the Southwestern frontier. He settled in Detroit in January 1842 and became a paid lecturer for Michigan abolitionist groups* and an agent for the Raisin Institute, a manual labor school for blacks. Later in the 1840s, Bibb lectured throughout the North and participated in numerous black and abolitionist conventions. Although largely self-educated, he published a stirring autobiography, *Narrative of the Life and Adventures of Henry Bibb, an American Slave*, in 1849. The same year, the abolitionist American Missionary Association* engaged Bibb as its principal fund-raiser for a campaign to distribute Bibles to slaves. Following passage of the Fugitive Slave Act of 1850,* Bibb resettled in Windsor, Ontario, and founded Canada's first black newspaper, the *Voice of the Fugitive*. In September 1851, he presided over the North American Convention of Colored People at Toronto, which endorsed black migration to Canada. In his last years, Bibb helped organize the Refuge Home Society, which purchased Canadian farmland for resale to blacks, and defended that body against charges of mismanagement and financial malfeasance.

SELECTED BIBLIOGRAPHY

Henry Bibb, *Narrative of the Life and Adventures of Henry Bibb, an American Slave* (1849); David M. Katzman, *Before the Ghetto: Black Detroit in the Nineteenth Century* (1973); John R. McKivigan, "The Gospel Will Burst the Bonds of the Slave: The Abolitionists' Bibles for Slaves Campaign," *Negro History Bulletin*, 45 (1982), 62–64, 77; William H. Pease and Jane H. Pease, *Black Utopia: Negro Communal Experiments in America* (1963); Benjamin Quarles, *Black Abolitionists* (1969); and Jason H. Silverman, *Unwelcome Guests: Canada West's Response to American Fugitive Slaves, 1800–1865* (1985).

JOHN R. MCKIVIGAN

BIRNEY, JAMES GILLESPIE (1792–1857). James Gillespie Birney was the Liberty party candidate for the presidency of the United States in 1840 and 1844. Born on 4 February 1792, to James and Martha Reed Birney of Danville, Kentucky, he became a slaveholder when he was given a slave on his sixth birthday. Yet several influences in his youth planted antislavery opinions in his mind. His father and the aunt who raised him decried the system and at Transylvania and Princeton, and in Philadelphia where he studied law, he heard vigorous debates over slavery. In Philadelphia he developed a friendship with the free black leader, James Forten, and with Abraham L. Pennock, an antislavery Quaker.

Yet Birney returned to Kentucky, married Agatha McDowell (1816), and became a slaveholding planter and lawyer. He began a career in state politics, but the lure of the frontier led him to Alabama in 1818. There he was instrumental in inserting a clause in the state constitution which forbade the bringing of slaves into the state for sale and empowered the legislature to allow emancipation provided owners consented or were compensated. He was elected to the first state legislature, and was a founder of the University of Alabama.

Converted in a Presbyterian revival, Birney felt increased responsibility to devote his life to humanitarian causes, particularly on behalf of the Cherokee Indians and the slaves. For a time he served as an agent of the American Colonization Society,* but convinced that it was based on racial prejudice, he turned instead to plans for gradual emancipation, and finally embraced full-fledged abolition. Encountering opposition in both Alabama and Kentucky, in 1835 he freed the slaves he held and moved to Ohio to publish an antislavery newspaper, *The Philanthropist*.

Destruction of his press by a mob in 1836 only cemented Birney's determination to devote full time to the abolitionist cause and led to his appointment as corresponding secretary for the American Anti-Slavery Society in New York City. When the split in the Society came in 1840, he was a leader of the anti-Garrisonians who had moved to the advocacy of direct political action via a third party as the most effective means of fighting the "peculiar institution." With the demise of the Liberty party, and because of an accident which took him out of active service, Birney became a bitter recluse on the Michigan frontier, mellowing only when he and his second wife, Elizabeth Fitzburgh, joined Theodore Dwight Weld* and Angelina Grimké Weld* in a community of the Raritan Bay Union in New Jersey. He died there on 18 November 1857. With his first wife Birney had six children: James, William, Dion, David, Arthur, Martha, George and Florence; and with his second wife, one son, Fitzhugh.

In addition to his political leadership, Birney authored numerous antislavery pamphlets and articles. Never an agitator or demagogue, he put his hopes in constitutional interpretation and legal measures, but by the time of his death he foresaw that emancipation would come through war and bloodshed.

SELECTED BIBLIOGRAPHY

William Birney, *James G. Birney and His Times: The Genesis of the Republican Party* . . . (1890); Dwight L. Dumond, ed., *Letters of James Gillespie Birney, 1831–1857* (2 vols., 1938); and Betty Fladeland, *James Gillespie Birney: Slaveholder to Abolitionist* (1955).

BETTY FLADELAND

BREEDING, SLAVE. Contemporary opponents of Afro-American slavery accused Southern slave owners, particularly those of the upper South, of deliberately breeding slaves for the market. The charge was often intended to arouse outrage at the ethics of slaveholders, but it also served to counter the oft-repeated proslavery argument that the rapid growth of the black population proved slaves were being treated humanely. The response of slave owners as a group was muted and mixed. A few bitterly dismissed the charge, particularly the lurid comparisons to cattle breeding and the accusations of forced matings made by some abolitionists.* But others privately boasted of their "breeders" and of the profit to be made in selling slaves.

Historical evaluation of the issue has been difficult. In part this has resulted from the nature of the primary evidence. Some scholars have suggested that planters most likely would have been unwilling to keep written records of such activities. In addition, the subject of slave breeding has an almost unique capacity to arouse strong emotions, feelings that have sometimes interfered with the objectivity of the investigation. The first histories of slavery, for example, were written by those who reflected the perspectives of the slave owners. Most often they ignored the issue of slave breeding, but if the subject was mentioned, these historians took the position that the practice did not exist. Winfield H. Collins, writing in 1904, was the first historian to discuss the subject in any detail. He rejected the idea that planters intentionally raised slaves for sale. Instead, he suggested that most slave sales were forced by such exigencies as the bankruptcy of the slaves' owners. Collins also presented a calculation designed to show that raising slaves would not have been a profitable business given the price of slaves and the cost of maintaining them. Ulrich B. Phillips, the historian who did so much to influence subsequent scholarship on slavery, reported in 1918 that he could find "no shred of supporting evidence" for slave breeding.

Other historians, however, soon took an opposite view and the evidence that they accumulated began gradually to establish a different picture. Frederic Bancroft, in a well-researched study of the domestic trade in slaves, amassed evidence drawn largely from Southern newspapers establishing that slave owners had been greatly concerned with the number of children* born to their slaves, that they placed a high value on fertile women,* and that slave mothers received various incentives to encourage reproduction. In some cases, women were punished when they failed to produce sufficient numbers of children. More recently, historian Kenneth Stampp reached the same conclusions and extended the evidence significantly through extensive research in plantation manuscripts.

Histories of slavery that reflected the perspective of the slaves themselves presented evidence that at least some slave owners actively interfered in the sexual life of their slaves in the interests of increasing the number of children born. E. Franklin Frazier, in his classic history of *The Negro Family* (1948), maintained that "there were masters who, without any regard for the preferences of their slaves, mated their human chattel as they did their stock." Subsequent research in the narratives of ex-slaves produced testimony from a significant number of those interviewed that slave women were subjected to arranged marriages,* forced matings, and other forms of sexual abuse. There were reports of the use of slave men, rented for the purpose, to impregnate slave women. For example ex-slave Maggie Stenhouse explained: "Durin' slavery there were stockmen. They was weighed and tested. A man would rent the stockman and put him in a room with some young women he wanted to raise children from." Other ex-slaves reported that slave owners systematically offered rewards and threatened punishment in an effort to increase the birthrate among the slave women.

Any historical dispute that remains over the question no longer concerns the existence of slave breeding, but rather the matter of degree. Was slave rearing so common and so widespread that it had a significant impact on the profitability of slavery?* Did breeding practices affect the rate of growth of the slave population? Were the majority of slave women subjected to systematic and repeated sexual abuse? Although the research on these questions continues, answers have begun to emerge in the scholarly literature.

Research on the profitability of slavery suggests that the slave market and the practice of slave breeding fit naturally into the context of nineteenth-century American capitalism. Slave plantations were businesses, established and managed to make money for their owners. Because the growth of the slave population of the upper South produced a surplus of labor in those regions, owners who did not sell off unneeded slaves found their fortunes declining as the burden of maintaining a larger than optimal labor force cut into their profits. As a consequence, most slave owners either sold slaves or purchased land as necessary to maintain an efficient balance between the labor supply and the land under cultivation. The sale of slaves produced a substantial increment of income, one that supplemented the proceeds from tobacco, cotton, and other crops.

Historian Lewis C. Gray, in his monumental history of Southern agriculture, rejected Collins's arguments that slave breeding and subsequent sale lacked profit and argued that "the rearing of slaves constituted an important element in the agricultural economy of the South." Calculations in the 1950s by economists Alfred Conrad and John Meyer established that gains generated by the growing slave population were important components of slave owners' income. In fact, the steady sale of slaves by owners located in the upper South proved necessary to maintain the profitability of slave agriculture in those regions at levels comparable to the returns on alternative investments. These results, confirmed in numerous studies of the profitability of slavery, lend a strong element of plausibility to the slave-breeding hypothesis.

The term *slave breeding* itself suggests the deliberate and routine interference by owners in the sexual life of their slaves in order to increase the number of slaves born. Some economic historians, however, have argued that the profitability of slave rearing need not imply the widespread practice of slave breeding. No doubt many slave owners simply let nature take its course and found they were satisfied with the increase in their slaveholdings without the need to resort to overt acts of forced coupling. Stanley L. Engerman has even suggested that a policy of noninterference might have been the best way to increase the birthrate, "given the natural tendencies of men and women." On some plantations this might have been the case. On those where it was not, however, economic considerations would have induced masters to take measures to increase the birthrate. For owners located on poorer land where crop productivity was low, such steps would have been a matter of economic survival. In that situation, competitive pressures would have overwhelmed the restraining influence of moral or ethical considerations, ruling out policies incompatible with maximum economic efficiency. The question then becomes whether or not the overall slave birthrate was higher than it would have been had these slave owners not bred slaves.

Demographic* studies of the slave population have established that the fertility of slave women was extraordinarily high. Indeed, during the antebellum period slave fertility* was close to the biological maximum. After the close of the African slave trade in 1808, the American slave population grew at a phenomenal rate—well in excess of 2 percent per annum. This high rate of increase was maintained despite very high infant mortality rates. Richard Steckel has estimated that infant mortality among slave children exceeded that observed among the poorest populations of the world today.

The demographic mechanisms of high fertility were an early start on child-bearing, short intervals between births, and a low rate of childlessness. The median age of slave women at the birth of their first child was comparatively low, only two or three years after the onset of fertility and about two years earlier than Southern white women. These findings corroborate the direct evidence that slave owners actively encouraged early marriages for slave women. Child spacing was unusually short, perhaps because slave owners encouraged early weaning of infants in order to speed their mother's return to field labor after the birth. Because lactation tends to inhibit the postpartum return of fecundity, these practices should have increased fertility. Evidence also suggests that masters sometimes broke up slave marriages that failed to produce children or forced new partners on childless women.

Perhaps the most startling evidence of slave breeding to emerge from the demographic studies concerns the sex distribution on slave plantations. Richard Sutch undertook a study of 2,588 separate slave farms examining the age-sex distribution of their slaveholdings as reported in the census of 1860. He found on slaveholdings with at least one woman that the average ratio of women to men exceeded 1.2. The imbalance between the sexes was even more dramatic in the ''selling states''—the states of the upper South that supplied slaves to the newer states of the South and West. There the excess of women over men exceeded 300 per thousand. The missing men were located on holdings with only one slave. The unbalanced sex ratios suggest that slaveholders with large holdings wished to maximize the number of children produced by a given number of adults. The adults constituted the work force available for crop production (the size of the labor force required would be determined by the amount of acreage under cultivation), and the children born represented the potential gains from slave breeding. The more women in the labor force, the higher would be the potential number of children produced on a given farm. The maximum child-to-adult ratio was achieved on farms where women outnumbered men by between two and three to one. In the selling states the ratio of children to adults on such farms exceeded that on farms with balanced sex ratios by more than one-third.

Unbalanced sex ratios and high fertility, however, do not prove that forced matings, multiple sexual partners, or other forms of sexual abuse were common.

Nor does the surplus of women over men on some holdings prove that many women did not have stable relationships with men they considered their husbands. Slave women often were allowed to have husbands who resided on nearby farms. Historical studies of the slave family suggest that while master-directed interferences in the family and sexual life of slaves occurred with alarming frequency, most slave women nevertheless escaped such degradations. But those who escaped abuse were by no means left unaffected. All slave women lived with the knowledge that what was sometimes forced on others could at any time legally be forced on them. The best insurance against such abuse was for a woman to marry early and to produce many children within that marriage. Most slave women followed this pattern. It resulted in a steady increase in the net worth of their owner as measured either by the size of his slaveholding or by the returns from selling surplus slaves to others.

SELECTED BIBLIOGRAPHY

Frederic Bancroft, *Slave-Trading in the Old South* (1931); Alfred H. Conrad and John R. Meyer, "The Economics of Slavery in the Ante-Bellum South," *Journal of Political Economy*, 66 (1958), 95–130; E. Franklin Frazier, *The Negro Family in the United States* (rev. ed., 1948); Lewis C. Gray, *History of Agriculture in the Southern United States to 1860* (2 vols., 1933); Herbert G. Gutman and Richard Sutch, "Victorians All? The Sexual Mores and Conduct of Slaves and Their Masters," in Paul A. David et al., *Reckoning with Slavery: A Critical Study in the Quantitative History of American Negro Slavery* (1976); Richard Steckel, "The Health and Mortality of Slave Children Reconsidered: Were the Abolitionists Right?" *Explorations in Economic History*, 23 (1986), 173–198; and Richard Sutch, "The Breeding of Slaves for Sale and the Westward Expansion of Slavery, 1850–1860," and Stanley L. Engerman, "Comments on the Study of Race and Slavery," in Stanley L. Engerman and Eugene D. Genovese, eds., *Race and Slavery in the Western Hemisphere: Quantitative Studies* (1975).

RICHARD C. SUTCH

BROWN, JOHN (1800–1859). Holding that Afro-American slavery would not die peacefully, John Brown was the foremost figure in advocating its militant overthrow. Though born in Torrington, Connecticut, Brown grew up in an abolitionist environment in Hudson, Ohio. His home was a station on the underground railroad.* By the mid–1850s, with his own twenty children no longer so fully dependent on him, Brown devoted himself to striking a direct blow at slavery. Locating in "bleeding Kansas," in May 1858, Brown headed a party of eight who murdered five unarmed proslavery men at Pottawatomie Creek. This incident evoked widespread discussion and threw Brown into the national limelight.

By the fall of 1859, Brown was ready to spring his long-cherished plan of striking at slavery in the South itself. On 16 October 1859, with twenty-one followers, Brown launched an attack on the government arsenal at Harpers Ferry, Virginia (now West Virgina). In the ill-fated assault, ten of his men were killed and seven were captured, Brown among them. Brought to trial for murder and treason, he was hanged on 2 December 1859. The Harpers Ferry raid aroused deep and mixed emotions throughout the country. Some people regarded Brown as a martyr; others viewed him as a crazed, cold-blooded murderer. Brown's raid helped spark the Civil War, and his name would be kept alive by the stirring ''John Brown Song,'' used as a war cry by Union soldiers.

SELECTED BIBLIOGRAPHY

Stephen B. Oates, *To Purge This Land with Blood: A Biography of John Brown* (1970); Benjamin Quarles, *Allies for Freedom: Blacks and John Brown* (1974); and Jeffery S. Rossbach, *Ambivalent Conspirators: John Brown, The Secret Six, and a Theory of Slave Violence* (1982).

BENJAMIN QUARLES

BROWN, JOHN (ca. 1810–1876). Born in Virginia around 1810, the young slave named Fed also spent some time on a tobacco farm in North Carolina before he was separated from his mother around 1820 and sent to Georgia. There he labored on Thomas Stevens's growing farm near Milledgeville. Fed grew to manhood under a harsh master, but he was also influenced by John Glasgow, a slave who had once been a free black British sailor, and several times Fed tried to escape without success. He accompanied Stevens who moved first to Decatur and then into northwest Georgia as the Cherokees departed.

His master died in 1839, willing Fed to a son, Decatur Stevens. In the mid–1840s Fed escaped from Georgia but was recaptured in New Orleans and sold to Theodoric J. (''Jepsey'') James, a big planter in Mississippi. Soon Fed fled to the North where he assumed the name John Brown. He lived awhile in Michigan and briefly at Dawn Institute in Canada, and in 1850 he sailed for England, his friend Glasgow's homeland.

Brown settled in London and contacted the British and Foreign Anti-Slavery Society. He lectured frequently on the evils of slavery and dictated his memoirs to Louis Alexis Chamerovzow, the society's secretary. *Slave Life in Georgia* was published in 1855, and it remains today one of the few authentic fugitive slave narratives* from the Deep South. Brown married an Englishwoman, became an herb doctor in London, and died there in 1876, poor but free.

SELECTED BIBLIOGRAPHY

F. N. Boney, *Southerners All* (1984); and John Brown, *Slave Life in Georgia: A Narrative of the Life, Sufferings, and Escape of John Brown, a Fugitive Slave, Now in England* (1855, rev. ed., 1972).

F. N. BONEY

BROWN, WILLIAM WELLS (1815–1884). William Wells Brown was born into slavery near Lexington, Kentucky, in 1815, the biological nephew of his owner. Moved to Saint Louis where he was hired out to various merchants, Brown eventually worked on a steamboat. In 1834, aided by an Ohio Quaker named Wells Brown, he escaped to Cleveland and freedom.

Brown wrote the first black American novel, *Clotel*, in 1853, and its revised version, *Clotelle*, in 1864. He also is remembered for writing the first black play, *The Escape* (1858), as well as travel books and histories. Less well known were Brown's literary activities in England during his flight from fugitive slave laws in 1849. To support himself, Brown wrote *Panoramic Views* (1849), *Three Years in Europe* (1852), and *Clotel*. He also delivered numerous addresses before English audiences, describing America and its peculiar institution. In the process Brown not only retained and enhanced his independence, but also expanded and perfected his literary craft.

Brown was a tireless social crusader and public speaker. Before the Civil War he assisted runaway slaves on the underground railroad* and lectured widely against slavery. After the war he worked to gain civil rights for the freedmen* and labored in the temperance crusade. Brown also wrote several historical works aimed at destroying the myth of inherent black inferiority.

"Necessity" proved to be the strongest influence on Brown's life and work. He commands our respect as writer, public speaker, and self-reliant social crusader.

SELECTED BIBLIOGRAPHY

Josephine Brown, *Biography of an American Bondsman, by His Daughter* (1856); W. Edward Farrison, "William Wells Brown, Social Reformer," *Journal of Negro Education*, 18 (1949), 29–39; and J. Noel Heermance, *William Wells Brown and "Clotelle"* (1969).

J. NOEL HEERMANCE

BURIAL PRACTICES. Slaves on Southern and Caribbean plantations followed their African ancestors in attaching great significance to what they called "a good burial." The funeral was considered life's true climax. At once a religious ritual, a major social event, and a community pageant, the slave funeral drew upon cherished tradition. Slave funerals celebrated the African belief that upon dying the deceased went "home." Some believed their spirits were literally transported back to their African homeland. Thus, the slaves sang, danced, and drank the departed one "home." An appropriate funeral also helped guard against the return of a restless spirit.

Tradition and custom were carefully observed upon the death of a slave, but New World equivalents often had to be improvised in the preparation of the body. While a coffin was being made, the body was laid out on a cooling board. Most commonly coffins were constructed by skilled slave carpenters or purchased by the masters. Sometimes the body was simply wrapped in a blanket to be carried to the burial ground in a handbarrow. In the cities coffins were often furnished by the burial lodges to which some slaves belonged. The completed coffin was lined with straw, and perhaps the body was wrapped in winding sheets. Occasionally the coffins were more ornate, lined with cambric and lace and personal objects of the departed.

In the semitropical heat of Southern and Caribbean plantations, corpses quickly decayed, and the slave community had to protect the dead from prowling cats and other animals. From Virginia to Louisiana, from South Carolina to Barbados, the slaves would "sit up" all night with the dead, singing and praying through the night.

Some masters refused to allow their slaves time off to attend funerals. More commonly, however, masters gave the slaves a day off for the burial. Typically, the whole plantation—every man, woman, and child who could walk—turned out for the funeral. Slaves who were able to obtain passes came from nearby plantations. The funerals of urban slaves in Richmond, Charleston, Savannah, and New Orleans were attended by gatherings sometimes numbering more than a thousand. Whites frequently attended plantation funerals; they attended urban ones less often.

White ministers conducted slave funerals with some frequency, but even more frequently black preachers themselves officiated, owing something both to white indifference to the souls of their bondsmen and black preference for their own preachers. After the insurrectionary scares of Denmark Vesey* and Nat Turner,* however, whites grew alarmed at the growing influence of slave preachers.

Night funerals were the norm on the plantations of the Old South, and in the Caribbean until laws in Jamaica in 1816 and Barbados in 1826 put an end to the practice. Night funerals also came in for special criticism from urban slaveholders. Night funerals for slaves were forbidden in New York in 1772 and in New Orleans in 1808, and they were perennial subjects of white concern. Despite urban fears, however, the night funeral persisted in the countryside, partly because of plantation labor requirements and partly because of the slaves' cultural preference.

After the slave community had a last look at the deceased brother or sister, the coffin would be nailed shut and transported to the burial ground. Pallbearers in Antigua, Barbados, and Jamaica, following Akan and Ga tradition, reeled and staggered about, zigzagging from one side of the street to the other. On Southern plantations the slow procession of mourners carried pine torches to light the way to the burial ground. The coffin and pallbearers led off, followed by the family of the deceased and the master's household, with the slave community and visitors bringing up the rear. Urban funerals were sometimes quite elaborate. Whether urban or rural, the processions to the graveyard were always accompanied by slow, mournful spirituals.

When the procession arrived at the burial site, the slaves marched around the grave. From the South Carolina Sea Islands to Barbados, graves were dug east-west. The body was buried with its head to the west, its eyes facing Africa. This positioning followed both African and European tradition, although the cultural meaning of the practice varied. After the body was lowered into the ground, the mourners threw clods of dirt into the grave.

Throughout the New World, from Haiti and Guadeloupe to Mississippi, Georgia, and South Carolina, the graves were decorated with the last objects used by the departed, and especially with broken bits of earthenware, colored glass, and sea shells—a continuation of the Kongo-Angolan belief in the grave as a charm for the persistence of the spirit. Sometimes carved wooden figures or patchwork quilts were laid upon the grave.

On the return from the gravesite, the slaves' songs* became more rhythmic and spirited, accompanied by hand clapping and body movements. Funeral processions were accompanied by drums in the Caribbean and in the South Carolina Sea Islands after Union occupation in 1862. After the funeral, the slave community visited the departed's family to express their condolences. Sociable feasts—considered boisterous by whites for their singing, and dancing, and drinking—celebrated the spirit's trip "home" and distracted the family from moping over their loss.

According to West African tradition, however, a period of time had to elapse after interment before the deceased's spirit could be at rest. As in West Africa, on Southern and Caribbean plantations the "first burial" was considered temporary; and a "second burial"—a memorial service at which the entire slave community gathered—was held weeks later. This "two-burial" custom was often denigrated by white observers who did not understand the religious tradition behind it.

Of course not all slave deaths were accorded what the slave community considered an appropriate funeral. By African standards, that was slavery's ultimate degradation.

SELECTED BIBLIOGRAPHY

Roger D. Abrahams and John F. Szwed, eds., *After Africa: Extracts from British Travel Accounts and Journals . . .* (1983); Eugene D. Genovese, *Roll, Jordan, Roll: The World the Slaves Made* (1974); Charles Joyner, *Down by the Riverside: A South Carolina Slave Community* (1984); and George P. Rawick, ed., *The American Slave: A Composite Autobiography* (19 vols., 1972; supplement, series 1, 12 vols., 1977; supplement, series 2, 10 vols., 1979).

CHARLES JOYNER

BURNS, ANTHONY (1834–1862). Anthony Burns was born a slave in Stafford County, Virginia, on 31 May 1834. His was to become perhaps the most famous fugitive slave* case in the entire pre–Civil War period.

Young Anthony exhibited an independent streak from the beginning, learning to read and write very early. As a young man he was converted to the Baptist faith and began to preach. Because Burns was hired out by his owner, he gained a high degree of autonomy. In February 1854 he escaped by stowing away on a vessel bound from Richmond to Boston. Although Burns obtained employment in Boston, his literacy ironically soon betrayed him. A letter he wrote to his brother was intercepted by his master, who thus located Burns and followed him to Boston to secure his return. In May Burns was arrested on a bogus theft charge and jailed. This obviously was a means of holding Burns so that he might be returned to slavery by the court. Burns's case led an antislavery mob to attempt to remove him from jail. They failed, though one policeman was killed in the fray. U.S. soldiers, the state militia, and Boston police prevented a crowd of some 50,000 antislavery agitators from interfering when Burns was shipped back to Virginia in June. Estimates of the cost of returning this one fugitive to slavery run as high as $100,000.

The Burns case occurred in 1854, amid heightened agitation over slavery and its expansion into the territories in general, and the Kansas-Nebraska Act* in particular. The case probably contributed as much to crystallize Northern sentiment against slavery as any other single event in the fiery decade, save John Brown's* raid in 1859. Never again was a fugitive slave removed from Boston.

Burns was subsequently sold to a different owner. He was freed when a group of Bostonians, mostly blacks, raised the money to purchase his freedom. Burns attended Oberlin College and then became the minister of a small Baptist church in Canada, where he died on 27 July 1862.

SELECTED BIBLIOGRAPHY

Jane H. Pease and William H. Pease, *The Fugitive Slave Law and Anthony Burns: A Problem in Law Enforcement* (1975); and Charles Emery Stevens, *Anthony Burns: A History* (1856).

DAVIS D. JOYCE

C

CALHOUN, JOHN CALDWELL (1782–1850). John Caldwell Calhoun was born near Abbeville, South Carolina, 18 March 1782 and died in Washington, D.C., 31 March 1850. Descended from early settlers of the Carolina up-country, Calhoun employed 154 slaves on his cotton plantations near Pendleton, South Carolina, and in Marengo County, Alabama. He also utilized slave workmen at his gold mine near Dahlonega, Georgia. As U.S. representative, secretary of war and state, vice president, and senator, and as a political thinker, Calhoun ranked among the half dozen major national figures during the years 1811–1850.

Calhoun left his mark on every major issue of his day—tariff, banking, internal improvements, foreign relations. But he is best remembered for his ingenious defense of the minority South and for marshaling the Southern strategy against abolitionism.

Prior to the mid–1830s, Calhoun showed only a perfunctory interest in anti-slavery, supporting the Missouri Compromise.* But about 1836 he began the counterattack that occupied the rest of his career. In defending slavery, Calhoun was in large company, but he led the ideological shift from the "necessary evil" stance to the "positive good" defense. Calhoun's insistence on meeting every abolitionist challenge at the threshold created a new school of proslavery strategy,* united the South, and aroused the sectional antagonism of many Northerners who had hitherto been indifferent to slavery.

Calhoun never stated his defense of slavery systematically or in one place; rather, he articulated it in occasional statements on particular legislative issues. Calhoun's defense was predominantly based upon the unconstitutionality and impropriety of Northern interference with Southern rights. Philosophically, his position represented a transition between the Old Republican defenders of slavery in the early nineteenth century and the "organicists" of the late antebellum period.

SELECTED BIBLIOGRAPHY

Margaret L. Coit, *John C. Calhoun: American Portrait* (1950); Ernest M. Lander, Jr., *The Calhoun Family and Thomas Green Clemson: The Decline of a Southern Patriarchy*

(1983); August O. Spain, *The Political Theory of John C. Calhoun* (1951); and Charles M. Wiltse, *John C. Calhoun* (3 vols., 1944–1951).

CLYDE N. WILSON

CATHOLIC CHURCH. Whereas slavery was truly national during the colonial and early national periods, Catholicism was largely confined to the South. Until the 1820s the largest concentrations of Catholics were in Maryland, Kentucky, and Louisiana. The two greatest churchmen within American Catholicism in the pre–Civil War era were Southern bishops, John Carroll of Baltimore and John England of Charleston. As late as 1840 the majority of Catholic episcopal sees were located in the South. However, at the very time slavery was being abolished in the Northern states mass immigration was shifting the center of the Catholic church in America from Southern plantations and farms to Northern cities. In 1860 fewer than one in ten slaves were held by Catholics.

Catholics easily accommodated themselves to the peculiar institution. The traditional moral theology of the church held that slavery was not in itself evil so long as the mutual rights and duties of slaveholder and slave were respected. Even before the discovery of America, however, Pope Pius II denounced the enslavement of African natives. His successor, Leo X, in the early sixteenth century condemned the attempts of the Spanish and Portuguese to enslave the Indians as something "not only the Christian religion, but Nature herself cried out against." By the seventeenth century the papal strictures were in no common memory of French or English Catholics settling in Louisiana and Maryland. Catholic slaveholders included prelates and religious orders. The Jesuits by 1820 had nearly 400 slaves on their Maryland plantations.

Catholics in general were no better or worse as slaveholders than were Protestants. Personality, economics, and community custom rather than religious ideals tended to determine the individual treatment of slaves. Some Catholic slaveholders were very conscientious about providing for the spiritual and material needs of the blacks under them. Slaves of the religious orders often had more freedom than those of secular owners. They also had the advantage of an appeal to a superior beyond their local master. At least one religious order, the Vincentians, gave their slaves in Missouri the right to veto their sale. But, even with the religious orders, economic expediency often prevailed over religious ideals, as when the Maryland Jesuits sold their slaves to Louisiana in 1838.

Most masters allowed their slaves to be baptized. Far fewer did much more. The indifference of Catholic slaveholders to the faith and morals of their slaves that Carroll decried in 1785 was still all too true in the 1850s. A reflection of the low quality of the slaveholders' own religion, this indifference hampered the efforts of the church to minister to Catholic slaves, as did the shortage of priests and religious and the pressing needs of an increasingly immigrant church. Religious such as Mother Elizabeth Ann Seton and the Jesuit John McElroy conducted classes for free blacks. Another Jesuit, Thomas Lilly, started a Sunday school in Frederick, Maryland, for slaves. But Lilly's apostolate was almost unique.

Opportunities for blacks, free or slave, to minister within the church were highly limited. An exception was the Healys of Georgia, common-law children of a slave and an Irish planter. Three brothers were ordained to the priesthood in the 1850s and 1860s and rose to high positions in the Archdiocese of Boston and the Society of Jesus. Their sister, Eliza, became a Mother Superior of the Congregation of Notre Dame. Two religious communities of black women were formed in the antebellum period, the Oblate Sisters of Providence (1829) and the Sisters of the Holy Family (1842), to work with free blacks.

Like their neighbors, many Southern Catholics before the 1820s regarded slavery as a social and economic affliction. Roger B. Taney in 1818 characterized it as "a blot on our national character." Taney and Charles Carroll of Carrollton were both officers of the American Colonization Society. Catholics like Taney and the Carrolls favored gradual emancipation. A month before his death in 1815, Archbishop Carroll was "surprised and mortified" to learn that the Jesuits had abandoned their policy of deferred emancipation.

As late as 1832, William Gaston, a justice of the supreme court of North Carolina, termed slavery "the worst evil that afflicts the Southern part of our confederacy." By that time Gaston, who even supported voting rights for free blacks, was dangerously out of step in the South. John England, an immigrant bishop from Ireland who privately shared Gaston's abhorrence of slavery, nonetheless defended it publicly in response to allegations that Pope Gregory XVI, in his encyclical on the slave trade in 1839, had endorsed abolitionism. Catholics North and South opposed the abolition movement* on several grounds. They identified it with nativism, perfectionism, and Great Britain. The immediate abolition of slavery, Catholic spokesmen like Orestes Brownson argued, would be an injustice to the slaveholder and a disaster for the freedman. Then, too, they feared that the assertion of federal power that abolition involved would be a dangerous precedent for the federal government's interference in other areas, including religion. Many of the foreign-born clergy found the lot of the American slave a favorable one in comparison with that of the European serf.

American church leaders as a group maintained silence on the issue, despite Gregory XVI's condemnation, at least implicitly, of not only the slave trade but the institution itself. All too conscious of the Catholic status as an alien minority in America, the bishops concentrated on private behavior rather than social ethics. Except for public education, the bishops foreswore any activity that could be deemed political. When the prelates held their first plenary council in Baltimore in 1852, they limited their remarks about slavery to the need to provide for the spiritual needs of the individual slaves. Francis Kenrick, bishop of Philadelphia and the leading moral theologian in the American church, lamented the regressive developments regarding the condition of slaves in the United States since the rise of the antislavery movement, but concluded that "such is the state of things, nothing should be attempted against the laws." In the Catholic press only the

Cincinnati *Catholic Telegraph* vigorously opposed slavery. Such a rigid separation between the private and public orders might explain why Roger Taney could free his own slaves and treat blacks as equals within the church, yet still issue the Dred Scott decision* in 1857.

Ironically, a Southern bishop, Augustin Verot of Saint Augustine, was the first prelate to preach publicly on the morality of slavery. In January 1861 Verot defended the institution but called for its significant reform if the new Confederacy was to endure. When the war came, Catholic prelates with few exceptions supported the cause of their section. Some Northern Catholic leaders, such as Brownson and Archbishop John Purcell of Cincinnati, became early supporters of emancipation as a war aim.

With emancipation came new opportunities and responsibilities for the church. The first parish for black Catholics was established in Baltimore in 1863. At the prodding of Verot the prelates at the Second Plenary Council of Baltimore in 1866 committed themselves to evangelizing and meeting the needs of the freedmen, both Catholic and non-Catholic. Some schools were begun for blacks by Verot and others. The Mill Hill Fathers were secured from England to work exclusively with blacks. But in general the performance of the church fell far short of the goal set by the Council fathers. As the mass immigration of German and Irish Catholics had preoccupied the American church in the 1840s and 1850s, so a new wave of Catholic immigrants from central and southern Europe ensured a new failure for the church's mission to the blacks.

SELECTED BIBLIOGRAPHY

Peter Finn, "The Slaves of the Jesuits in Maryland" (M.A. thesis, Georgetown University, 1974); Gerald P. Fogarty, "Public Patriotism and Private Politics: The Tradition of American Catholicism," *U.S. Catholic Historian*, 4 (1984), 1–48; Michael V. Gannon, *Rebel Bishop: The Life and Era of Augustin Verot* (1964); John T. Gillard, *Colored Catholics in the United States* (1941); Thomas O'Brien Hanley, ed., *The John Carroll Papers* (3 vols., 1976); James Hennesey, S.J., *American Catholics: A History of the Roman Catholic Community in the United States* (1981); Randall M. Miller, "Black Catholics in the Slave South: Some Needs and Opportunities for Study," *Records of the American Catholic Historical Society*, 86 (1975), 93–106; Randall M. Miller and Jon L. Wakelyn, eds., *Catholics in the Old South: Essays on Church and Culture* (1983); Madeleine Hooke Rice, *American Catholic Opinion in the Slavery Controversy* (1944); Walter G. Sharrow, "John Hughes and a Catholic Response to Slavery in Antebellum America," *Journal of Negro History*, 57 (1972), 254–269; Walter G. Sharrow, "Northern Catholic Intellectuals and the Coming of the Civil War," *New-York Historical Society Quarterly*, 58 (1974), 35–56.

ROBERT EMMETT CURRAN, S. J.

CHARLESTON, SC, SLAVERY IN. Unofficially, Charleston reigned as the capital of slavery in the United States. For almost two centuries—from 1680 to 1865—slavery dominated the economy, society, and politics of Charleston as it did in no other city in North America.

Enslaved Africans funneled into Charleston by the tens of thousands during the eighteenth century. More than 40 percent of the slaves brought to North America between 1700 and 1776 passed through Charleston. They arrived in the city after a quarantine stop at nearby Sullivans Island, what one historian has aptly termed the Ellis Island of Afro-Americans. Following the American Revolution, African slaves again streamed through the city. Between 1804 and 1807 slave traders rushed 40,000 Africans to Charleston harbor before the African trade officially closed in 1808.

White Charlestonians made fortunes from slaves, selling them to rural planters, supplying them and their masters with provisions and services, and exporting the rice, indigo, and cotton they produced. Most slaves in the city worked as laborers or domestic servants, but slave fishermen* (and women), boatmen, carpenters, blacksmiths, coopers, tailors, bakers, masons, and draymen were common. A few slaves even plied such highly specialized trades as printers, bookbinders, cabinetmakers, and locksmiths. Although only a minority of Charleston's residents actually owned slaves, the profits derived from slave labor and the accompanying Atlantic slave trade gave the city 150 years of prosperity. During the colonial period white South Carolinians enjoyed the highest per capita wealth and income in North America. After 1820, when the cotton boom moved west, Charleston's economy suffered. But slavery remained the bedrock of the city's economic life until emancipation.

In Charleston, unlike every other city in the United States, slaves comprised an absolute or near majority of the population. Between 1790 and 1850 the slave population ranged between 45 and 54 percent of the city's inhabitants. In addition, an anomalous caste of free Negroes* was wedged between the slaves and the whites. These free Afro-Americans, predominantly mulattoes, grew from 4 to 8 percent of Charleston's population during the first half of the nineteenth century. Together with slaves they gave the city a solid Afro-American majority. Only during the 1850s, when many city slaves were sold away to rural planters, did the number of slaves in Charleston significantly decline. By 1860 slaves comprised 34 percent of all Charlestonians, still more than in any other Southern city.

Slaves in Charleston contributed to a distinctive Afro-American culture. More than 80 percent of the slaves imported to Charleston came directly from Africa, giving African languages, customs, and traditions greater weight in Charleston and the South Carolina low country than elsewhere in the South. From the babel of English, French, Spanish, and numerous West African tongues, Charleston's bondsmen crafted Gullah, a Creole language reflecting both the extent and limits of acculturation. In the homes and workshops of white Charlestonians slaves learned habits of obedience and deference. But the bustle of city life loosened white supervision and allowed many slaves to affirm their humanity and self-control. They formed families, socialized with each other, celebrated births, weddings, and funerals, and, in general, refused to act like stunted, irresponsible beings. These activities constituted day-to-day resistance to the dehumanizing pressures of slavery. Those pressures exploded in 1739 just outside Charleston with the Stono Rebellion*—the largest slave rebellion in colonial North America. In 1822 resistance once again verged on rebellion when free black Denmark Vesey* and his conspirators planned a large-scale slave uprising in Charleston. Although their planned revolt was crushed by white authorities, the intricate plot jolted white Charlestonians, reminding them of the omnipresent problem of slave control.

To maintain control of both slaves and slavery, white Charlestonians manned the vanguard of the secession movement, itself the culmination of slaveholders' political dominance. The firing on Fort Sumter in Charleston harbor precipitated full-scale civil war that ultimately ended slavery. Late in March 1865, just a month after Charleston fell to Union troops, Afro-American men, women, and children organized a victory parade that stretched for two and a half miles along city streets. Led by a regiment of U.S. Colored Troops,* the parade included representatives from virtually every segment of the city's former slave population. One of the parade banners proclaimed an aspiration that bridged the slave past of Charleston's Afro-Americans to their future as free men and women: "We know no master but ourselves."

SELECTED BIBLIOGRAPHY

W. Robert Higgins, "Charleston: Terminus and Entrepôt of the Colonial Slave Trade," in Martin L. Kilson and Robert I. Rotberg, eds., *The African Diaspora: Interpretive Essays* (1976); Michael P. Johnson and James L. Roark, *Black Masters: A Free Family of Color in the Old South* (1984); Michael P. Johnson and James L. Roark, eds., *No Chariot Let Down: Charleston's Free People of Color on the Eve of the Civil War* (1984); Ulrich B. Phillips, "The Slave Labor Problem in the Charleston District," *Political Science Quarterly*, 22 (1907), 416–439; Bernard Edward Powers, Jr., "Black Charleston: A Social History, 1822–1885" (Ph.D. dissertation, Northwestern University, 1982); Leonard Price Stavisky, "The Negro Artisan in the South Atlantic States, 1800–1860: A Study of Status and Economic Opportunity with Special Reference to Charleston" (Ph.D. dissertation, Columbia University, 1958); and Peter H. Wood, *Black Majority: Negroes in Colonial South Carolina from 1670 through the Stono Rebellion* (1974).

MICHAEL P. JOHNSON

CHAVIS, JOHN (1763?–1838). John Chavis, a free black educator, minister, and soldier, was born in either the West Indies or near Oxford, North Carolina. The precise place of his birth is still questionable. In fact, little is known about his formative years. Most sources agree that he married a woman named Frances and that he had a brother named Anthony. He said that he fought in the Revolutionary war in 1778, and shortly after became a minister. Chavis attended Princeton University during the mid–1780s and later enrolled at Washington Academy (now Washington and Lee University) in Lexington, Virginia.

During the late 1780s, he served the Hanover, Virginia, Presbytery* as a riding missionary to the slaves. He moved to North Carolina from Maryland, and was admitted to the Orange Presbytery in 1809. By 1808 Chavis had opened a school for whites and blacks. Among his white students were the children of North Carolina's chief justice and two students who later became prominent in politics and the professions. He taught whites during the day, and blacks at night. His curriculum for both races focused on the three R's and included a strong emphasis on Christianity. Chavis was an idealist who believed that each individual could improve his or her own condition through hard work. By his own example, he showed that, with education and good character, a black man might find some social space and prestige in a racist society.

He also participated in state politics. He considered himself a Federalist and opposed the presidency of Andrew Jackson in 1828. He also favored the tariff of 1828. He advised, and sometimes criticized, his friend U.S. Senator Willie P. Mangum, and commented on public affairs. Chavis denounced abolitionism, but in the white blacklash after the Nat Turner rebellion* in 1831, his teaching and ministerial careers ended because whites opposed any teaching of blacks.

During the time of his retirement in 1832, he and his wife received support for life by the Orange Presbytery in North Carolina, even though he had been forced to resign from the presbytery. By the time of his death in June 1838, he had published a pamphlet entitled *Chavis' Letters upon the Atonement of Christ*. As a result of his achievements and the contributions of both blacks and whites in North Carolina, a federal housing project and recreation park were named in his honor. Chavis's true significance, however, was how his life revealed the contradictory, but eventually destructive, race relations in antebellum Southern society.

SELECTED BIBLIOGRAPHY

William K. Boyd, *History of North Carolina* (1919); John Hope Franklin, *The Free Negro in North Carolina, 1790–1860* (rev. ed., 1982); Edgar W. Knight, "Notes on John Chavis," *North Carolina Historical Review*, 7 (1930), 326–345; and Stephen B. Weeks, "John Chavis: Antebellum Negro Preacher and Teacher," *Southern Workman*, 43 (1914), 101–106.

LARRY E. RIVERS

CHILDREN, SLAVE. We have virtually no concept of what life was like for children born into slavery in the seventeenth century, and very little more insight into their lives during the early colonial period. We do know that the family* was very important to West Africans, and almost all African societies represented in the American colonies had specific rituals attached to childhood. Presumably, many West Africans brought their rituals and values with them when they arrived in North America.

What emerges is a composite picture, but we must keep in mind that we are faced with specific attitudes and behaviors on large plantations, small farms with only a few slaves, and cities where slave fathers were primarily artisans and slave mothers were primarily house servants. Further complications arise in analyzing behavior and attitudes over time. This means that, from the West

African background to the Civil War, life for slave children undoubtedly changed a great deal. In addition, we must create a synthesis which includes piedmont, tidewater, Deep South, old colonies, and new states. Slaves worked in labor-intensive areas, such as rice fields in coastal South Carolina and cotton fields in Mississippi. The gradual spread of slavery to the west involved children in migrations and in resettling new, uncultivated areas.

After the Revolutionary war, between 1790 and 1810, 15,000 Africans were imported into South Carolina; 48,000 into Georgia; and 18,000 into Mississippi and Louisiana. In those decades (and earlier) a constant influx of African traditions was mixed with the ongoing culture formed by slaves who had long been in those states. This same mixture of old slaves and new Africans occurred elsewhere, although in ever lessening numbers by the nineteenth century. The African concept of kinship—close family ties between grandparents, uncles, aunts, and the extended family—came with Africans and stayed with them as slaves. Children growing up in slave families were part of a loving and close family group unless members of their family were sold away. As time went on, families were broken up most often by selling members to the south and the west where the demand was great. In this case, children lost not only distant kin, but sometimes their own mothers and fathers. Slave owners, however, did often make an attempt to sell mothers and small children together. Some slave men begged to be sold with their wives and children, but if sale occurred, most often fathers were sold away separately. Owners like Thomas Jefferson* believed that slaves were more productive when families were intact; they made an effort to keep them together. But sometimes slave women* married men on distant plantations, and then the concept of family was an impossibility—unless one or the other owner bought the spouse.

On large plantations slave mothers returned to the fields soon after their babies were born. Nurseries for these babies and younger children were run by old slave women who were no longer able to go to the fields themselves. Some nurseries contained as many as sixty children with ages ranging from a few weeks up to eight or twelve years old. Mothers usually came from the fields four times a day to nurse their babies; when babies were weaned they saw their mothers and fathers only in the early hours of the morning before they went to the nursery, and late at night after their parents returned exhausted from the fields. Sundays and holidays were the only time families were together, and even then, parents were often involved in working private plots of land, family laundry, and housekeeping chores. Wintertime meant more time for the family on some plantations. On small farms, where there were few slaves, year-round activity was the norm. Children also grew into sources of labor more quickly on small farms, learning early to do chores for their masters and mistresses.

In the plantation nursery young children were frequently involved in child care themselves. It was not uncommon for children aged seven and older to have almost total supervision over two or three tots. The nurseries were located in the slave quarters and featured crowded facilities with no games or toys, as we know them. In the worst places, it has been reported that babies and children were fed in troughs two times a day. In the best, children ate off tin plates. Most slave children seemed to have diets consisting of corn-meal mixed with scraps or meat and whatever vegetables, if any, the old women could get. Standard childhood diseases*—measles, whooping cough, and diphtheria—made periodic appearances in the nursery. Some old women treated children with local herbs or boiled roots. On other plantations, doctors attended sick children, but death rates were frequently high among them no matter the treatment.

Education* was limited. Perhaps a few children learned Bible stories in the nursery. On some plantations, mistresses* taught their slave children Bible stories on Sundays. The rare plantation mistress taught slave children to read and write— but as the decades passed, education was equated with troublesome slaves and was all but prohibited. Slave children often played with masters' children when they were very young; at school age, the white children went off by day and the slave children began to learn the rudiments of work. Some whites shared their early learning with their slave counterparts, usually beyond sight of their parents. The education slave children received came from their own families and consisted of lessons which prepared them for adulthood. They were taught respect for both black and white elders. They were forced to obey family members so that when they grew up they would obey masters and overseers and stay out of trouble.

Discipline was strict in the slave quarters. On large plantations masters did not generally interfere with slave life there, but on smaller farms some slaves remembered being whipped by their mistresses when they were small. Most mothers, and fathers if they were present, switched their children for minor infractions of rules. If a child was rebellious or difficult, he received a severe beating from one or both of his parents. If a child was especially difficult and his behavior came to the attention of his master, he could be punished—or worse. Parents were aware of this possibility and did all they could to instill personal discipline in their children.

Slave children had few items of clothing.* Some little boys wore dresses— the same as worn by girls—until they were about ten years old. In hot climates, slave children often went naked until they reached seven or eight. Most wore homespun clothes which were heavy and uncomfortable. Those who lived on big plantations might have a Sunday outfit which they wore to church or to the Big House, where they visited their masters and mistresses. Sundays were almost always free days for slaves, and it was on those days that slave children played the few games that were available to them.

"Swingin' in de corner" was played in Georgia. "Hide the Switch" and "Hide and Seek" were played by slave and free children—often together. Almost all children had a few marbles and some pitched horseshoes. Little girls liked to jump rope. At Christmas and Easter there were likely to be celebrations and maybe a toy from owners. Fathers taught their sons to trap, hunt, and if a lake or stream was available, to fish. House servants* often gave their children special treats from the kitchen, and an occasional master brought a few sweets to slave children after a provisioning trip to town. For most slave children, life was relatively carefree, if impoverished, until they went to work.

By the age of eleven or twelve slave children began learning to work. Boys often started out in the stables, or were sent as messengers between plantations. Girls began helping in the Big House, waiting tables, or caring for a young mistress from the age of ten and older. One woman remembered "totin water to de fields" when she was but a tot. If fathers were artisans, they taught their skills to their sons. Slave children's indoctrination into the plantation regime varied according to the crop being produced. On sugar plantations, for example, children were less useful in the fields than on tobacco or cotton farms, where they could help with the picking at the busiest time.

Values placed on slave children give some indication of their skills at a certain age. One master valued his fourteen-year-old slave girl at the same price as a forty-year-old woman. Another valued his sixteen-year-old blacksmith apprentice at half the value of a senior smith. But even very young children had a value: one master in the 1850s placed one hundred dollars on his seven-year-old female slave. She was "alright, but a great liar." Babes in arms, if in good health, were then worth about the same price.

If children had a sale value, it was because on occasion they were sold. One little girl of seven was burned by her youthful mistress, and because of her rebellious spirit, was sold south alone. In 1834 a North Carolina dealer advertised children from the age of ten and up for sale. Sale of children from thirteen to sixteen was common, and a few young girls were sold as concubines. In the domestic slave trade,* when children were moved to the south or west, and during migrations with families, small children rode in wagons while men and women walked alongside. Many little bodies were packed together, and rations were even more limited on the road. When a move took place, or if fathers were sold away, mothers usually maintained care over their children until they were old enough to be sold or begin families on their own. Girls married (or cohabited) when they were young—usually in their midteens—and they soon began bearing children, reestablishing the circle of bondage which was common to all.

SELECTED BIBLIOGRAPHY

John W. Blassingame, *The Slave Community: Plantation Life in the Antebellum South* (1972, rev. ed., 1979); Eugene D. Genovese, *Roll, Jordan, Roll: The World the Slaves Made* (1974); Herbert G. Gutman, *The Black Family in Slavery and Freedom, 1750–1925* (1976); Ulrich B. Phillips, *American Negro Slavery: A Survey of the Supply, Employment and Control of Negro Labor as Determined by the Plantation Regime* (1918); Willie Lee Rose, *Slavery and Freedom*, edited by William W. Freehling (1982); Kenneth

M. Stampp, *The Peculiar Institution: Slavery in the Ante-Bellum South* (1956); Thomas L. Webber, *Deep Like the Rivers: Education in the Slave Quarter Community, 1831–1865* (1978); and Norman R. Yetman, ed., *Life under the Peculiar Institution: Selections from the Slave Narrative Collection* (1970).

PATRICIA ROMERO CURTIN

CHRISTIANA RIOT. The major episode of armed fugitive slave resistance to enforcement of the Fugitive Slave Act of 1850* occurred on 11 September 1851 near the village of Christiana, in southeastern Pennsylvania. That morning, Maryland slave owner Edward Gorsuch and a party of slave catchers bearing federal warrants surrounded the house of William Parker, a local black leader, and demanded the surrender of four of Gorsuch's slaves, who were inside. Parker and his guests refused and sounded an alarm to which local citizens responded. As a segment of Gorsuch's party retreated, blacks inside the house fired on Gorsuch, killing him and wounding three others. News of the violence soon reached Washington, and President Millard Fillmore urged immediate action to apprehend and punish the blacks involved. A company of U.S. Marines and two civil posses reached Christiana on 13 September. But the five blacks most responsible for Gorsuch's death escaped; three—including Parker—fled to Canada. Thirty-six blacks and two whites with tenuous links to the incident were eventually arrested, indicted for treason, and imprisoned pending trial before the U.S. Circuit Court. The federal prosecuting attorney used the trial of Castner Hanway, a local white, as a test case upon which to decide the fate of the other thirty-seven. After Hanway's acquittal in early December, the Christiana prisoners were released without further charges. The outcome of the Christiana incident outraged Southerners, but heightened black determination to resist the Fugitive Slave Act.

SELECTED BIBLIOGRAPHY

W. U. Hensel, *The Christiana Riot and Treason Trials of 1851: An Historical Sketch* (2nd & rev. ed., 1911); Jonathan Katz, *Resistance at Christiana: The Fugitive Slave Rebellion, Christiana, Pennsylvania, September 11, 1851: A Documentary Account* (1974); and Roderick W. Nash, "William Parker and the Christiana Riot," *Journal of Negro History*, 46 (1961), 24–31.

ROY E. FINKENBINE

CHURCH OF ENGLAND. *See* ANGLICAN CHURCH.

CHURCH OF JESUS CHRIST OF THE LATTER-DAY SAINTS. *See* MORMON CHURCH.

CIVIL WAR, SLAVERY AND THE. Slavery played an integral role in the cause, prosecution, and results of the Civil War. In 1860, just before the war, the United States had 3,953,760 slaves, practically all residing in the South. Eighty-nine percent of the nation's blacks were slaves, forming 13 percent of the country's population and 33 percent of the South's population. As property, as laborers, and as a controlled class of people, slaves held much economic and social significance.

Slavery's presence in the South set it apart from the rest of the nation. The institution also affected differences in culture, class systems, economics, and values. Long before the war slavery had entered political debates mostly over its extension into the territories. These prewar conflicts accentuated sectional differences, intensified separate identities, and heightened concern about the sectional balance of power. Extreme partisans, North and South, espoused divergent views of the Constitution, morality, and economic development. Slavery undeniably had a part in causing the Civil War, though historians have argued and will continue to argue over how much weight it carried and how it influenced events.

Sectional conflict climaxed after Abraham Lincoln's* election to the presidency in 1860. The Republican party,* which he led, was composed mostly of Northerners who criticized slavery and opposed its expansion. Although they did not advocate the abolition of Southern slavery, Southern sectionalists nevertheless distrusted them and considered their party a direct threat to the peculiar institution. Subsequently, during 1860–1861, South Carolina, Mississippi, Florida, Alabama, Georgia, Louisiana, Texas, Arkansas, North Carolina, Virginia, and Tennessee declared their independence and joined together as the Confederate States of America.* Secessionist pamphlets emphasized the liberty to hold slave property, and the Confederacy's vice president proclaimed slavery the new nation's "cornerstone." These states contained 89 percent of the slaves in the United States. After Lincoln's inauguration in March 1861, the Republicans dominated the federal government and refused to accept secession. When war began during the next month, Lincoln defined preservation of the Union as the aim for his side. Both he and Congress declared slavery irrelevant to the conflict.

Though the Lincoln administration sought to keep the issue of slavery apart from secession, slaves nevertheless provided a major manpower resource for the new Confederacy. Much of their agricultural production, transportation services, and industrial output went into the war effort. The government hired or impressed many slaves to build fortifications, haul supplies, cook, manufacture military equipment, and perform hospital duties. Numerous slaves accompanied their masters to war as body servants.

Whether at the front or at home, the war brought new stresses to the slaves. Most bondsmen suffered at some time or another from the scarcity of food and clothes that plagued the Confederacy. Rough-hewn, homemade clothes and shoes quickly replaced the manufactured items that previously had come from the North. Economic necessity often ended the small material benefits that some slaves had gained from paternalistic owners; financial hardship on the part of whites may have increased slave sales. Prices appeared to soar due to the depreciation of Confederate currencies. Actually, though, the gold value of slaves probably fell as the cause lost ground and as refugees flooded interior markets with their surplus slaves.

Slaves responded to the chaos of war in several ways. Genuine affection, isolation, or a sense of dependency kept some slaves obedient to their masters. Other slaves performed unusual acts to aid owners, even participating in their masters' battles. Still other slaves, having heard whites say that the war was over slavery, simply bided their time behind a mask of faithfulness.

Many slaveholders feared that the slaves knew too much and might, as a consequence, rise in revolution. During the secession crisis a wave of insurrection panics swept through the South. These fears probably affected troop stations and arms allocations at the beginning of the war. Every Confederate state expanded its patrol system by establishing home guard units for maintaining order in rural areas. Various states also tightened laws governing the slaves' using boats, living alone, possessing weapons, procuring liquor, and selling goods. Enlistment, conscription, and militia duty eventually devitalized many patrols. As a result, slave rebellion panics continued throughout the war.

As the number of whites declined in most neighborhoods, some slaves exhibited more independence. They openly criticized their owners, disobeyed, and reduced their work. Some slaves quietly aided federal escapees from prisoner-of-war camps. Others ran away and formed maroon* villages in swamps and forests. A few slaves openly attacked whites, but no major rebellion occurred.

Other factors contributed to the weakening of institutional control behind Confederate lines. Mistresses,* lacking experience in managing farms, often found themselves disregarded by their bondsmen and unable to hire effective overseers. If an owner decided to move all his slaves to a safer interior area, the slaves might refuse to go or escape unnoticed during travel. Impressments separated master and slave, in some instances, permanently, when poor living conditions killed the slave or when he took advantage of being at the front to flee to the enemy. Other slaves were exposed to new ideas when hired out* in cities booming with wartime work. In many cases the masters allowed them to live on their own. These slaves gained a reputation for boldness in their dealings with whites.

The presence of Confederate troops provided the best means of maintaining slave subservience. Disobedience could not go too far when soldiers backed up the slaveholders. Military patrols disciplined unruly slaves and captured runaways. In 1863 the army established central depots that held and advertised the recaptured slaves.

Even so, masters generally carried the greater burden of slave control. Some relied upon psychological tactics. As in the past, ministers preached obedience to masters. Some owners emphasized the paternalistic ideal* of reciprocal obligations between master and slave. Many owners tried to make slaves fear the federals through tales about the enemy's cruelty toward blacks. Some slaveholders kept rigidly to old routines to stress that things would never change. When psychological tactics failed, forceful methods remained. Troublemakers could be sold or severely punished. In some instances entire work forces were shipped away from the front.

Efforts to control slaves varied in effectiveness. Many slaves had never trusted their masters' word and so were not easily deluded. Long before the war a theme in the slaves' secret religious meetings had been a belief that God would soon deliver them from slavery and punish masters, much as in the biblical story of the Israelites' escape from Egyptian bondage. While not all slaves accepted this belief, the institution's evils had provoked a general desire for liberation.

In the war's last months the Confederate government considered liberating slaves who would fight for its side. In 1865 the Confederate Congress finally passed an enlistment law with provisions that limited the black soldier's numbers and left the decision about their emancipation up to the states. President Davis allowed the army to accept only slaves volunteered by their owners. By the war's end a few companies had enrolled, mostly in Virginia.

Slaves gained the opportunity to overthrow their bondage when federal forces approached their area. Behavior varied in this circumstance too. Common choices were continuing to serve a master loyally, staying home but covertly passing information to federals, striking for compensation and new work conditions, or running away in search of a new life. Violence against masters occurred infrequently, because it rarely was needed in order to escape to the federals. Some individuals carried out acts of personal retribution. Group violence most often took place in Louisiana, where slaves comprised almost half of the population and the institution had a reputation as particularly cruel. All slaves touched by federal occupation quickly realized the military might of the invaders and the comparative weakness of slaveholders.

The flight began as early as the second month of the war when three slaves appeared at Fortress Monroe, Virginia, and offered to serve the federals rather than their Confederate owners. General Benjamin Butler called these people ''contraband''* classifying them as goods used in the enemy's war effort. With the War Department's approval, Butler appropriated these slaves on the grounds of military necessity. Later, in the First Confiscation Act, Congress permitted the seizure of slaves who worked for the Confederate army. Some of those slaves as well as many others fled to the federals, either believing the invaders were God's agents for their deliverance or calculating that their lives would be better on the other side.

A cross section of the slave community fled. Some went in organized, even armed, groups; others traveled as families or alone. They came on foot, on horseback, by wagon, or by boat. The transition could take just a few steps or many difficult and dangerous miles. They came with valuable goods stolen from the master, or with small bags containing all their worldly possessions, or with nothing but a few rags wrapped around their bodies. Some had to fight to escape; others left quietly with ingenuity or luck. In May 1862 Robert Smalls,* the most celebrated runaway, fled with friends and family through Charleston's harbor defenses on his owner's boat carrying a load of Confederate military supplies. He turned these over to the federal ships blockading South Carolina's coast.

But most slaves found the path to freedom encumbered with roadblocks. Early in the war most federal commanders outside the occupied part of the southeastern coast refused to accept runaways. They argued that use of the slaves was not a military necessity. Some officers even returned runaways* to owners, a practice which Congress prohibited in early 1862. Later the same year Congress passed the Second Confiscation Act, which freed all slaves who entered federal lines except those belonging to unionists. On 1 January 1863, Lincoln issued the Emancipation Proclamation,* freeing all slaves in Confederate states except Tennessee and parts of Louisiana and Virginia. Later that year the new state of West Virginia, most of which had been in the exempted part of Virginia, enacted a gradual emancipation program. During 1864 and 1865 new state governments established by unionists in Tennessee, Louisiana, Arkansas, and Virginia declared slavery abolished. The implementation of these policy decisions, though, came slowly.

The trend toward emancipation forced Union officers to accept contrabands into their lines, but did not guarantee the runaways a positive experience of federal power. Unscrupulous soldiers robbed, raped, and beat blacks. The army sometimes forced slaves to leave masters against their will, either directly through impressment as laborers or indirectly through appropriation of food supplies. Such actions and the open expression of racial bias by the troops might have discouraged slaves from supporting the Union cause. On the other hand, blacks knew that the Confederacy represented slavery's preservation. Whenever the federals retreated, numerous slaves followed.

Federal occupation created great frustrations for slaveholders. A few realized that slavery was doomed and honorably entered into compensatory agreements with their slaves. Some made only minimal concessions in order to keep slaves working and immediately restored the old relationship when federal troops left the area. Others formed vigilante groups and employed violent means to keep the bondsmen in check. Some slave owners simply gave up, deserting their slaves and fleeing behind Confederate lines.

In the federal occupation zone abandoned slaves frequently took over their owners' farms. This provided the blacks with a sure subsistence. But it also exposed them to the ravages of war. Most contrabands preferred to move into towns and cities. Black shantytowns arose in these urban settings with overcrowded housing, poor or nonexistent water and sanitation facilities, rampant disease, much poverty, and a high crime rate. At the same time, the black neighborhoods developed their own schools, churches, social organizations, and businesses.

A minority of contrabands lived in camps maintained by the army. Federal officials provided shelter, clothes, rations, and medical care, though often in inadequate quantity. Freedmen's aid societies, established by sympathetic Northerners and by Southern blacks, sent additional supplies plus teachers and missionaries.* Most camps experienced periods of great human misery. Occupants sometimes participated in governance, as at Davis Bend, a very successful operation which included Jefferson Davis's plantation in Mississippi.

The contrabands came seeking freedom. They sought the rights of compensation for work, choice of employers or business activities, security from physical punishment on the job, unrestricted movement, reunification of families, religious independence, education, and bearing arms. Some also felt that freedom should be followed by the right to vote. The disruptions caused by the war opened the door to change. But every gain required black self-assertion. Few whites eagerly granted them new privileges.

The war remolded the black community. Free black ministers and businessmen joined slave drivers,* preachers,* and craftsmen* in leadership roles. In 1863 the new communities began articulating a desire for civil and political rights through mass meetings and marches. In October 1864 delegates from occupied towns in Virginia, North Carolina, Florida, Missouri, Tennessee, Mississippi, Louisiana, the District of Columbia, and eleven Northern states formed the National Convention of Colored Men in Syracuse, New York. They unanimously demanded the end of slavery, no forced colonization* of blacks outside the country, and fully equal rights. The meeting founded the Equal Rights League, the first national organization for civil rights.

To implement this agenda, however, contrabands had to lean heavily on the army for support. Employing many contrabands as laborers, the military commonly interfered with enforcement of the various slave codes. The degree of interference varied widely through the occupied regions but included permission to assemble, sell merchandise, attend school, lawfully marry, hold property, testify in court, and bear arms.

Most regions of federal occupation had a superintendent of contrabands' affairs. These officers eventually directed contract labor programs for contrabands. Previously private employers had sometimes failed to pay contraband workers, and the army had impressed black laborers without compensation. All of the new programs required blacks to work, written contracts to be filed, and army officials to enforce the contract on both sides. Most programs involved low, fixed wages paid at the year's end. Because the army viewed contrabands as being in transition from slavery, most programs restricted the laborers with behavioral rules, partly borrowed from the slave codes. For example, in the Mississippi Valley during 1864, black workers could not leave their employer's premises, sell merchandise, purchase liquor, or possess guns without federal permission. From 1863 to the war's end the army absorbed most male contrabands as military laborers or soldiers, leaving the contract labor force predominantly composed of women and children. Some of them worked on plantations operated by the War, Navy, and Treasury departments for government profit. Most found jobs with Southern planters and Northern lessees of federally appropriated land.

In occupied regions the government frequently leased some appropriated land to contrabands. On the South Carolina Sea Islands, where all masters had fled, contrabands in 1864 bought part of the land auctioned for unpaid taxes. In early 1865 General William T. Sherman set aside a thirty-mile-wide coastal strip from Charleston, South Carolina, to the St. John's River in Florida for black colonization. The contrabands who managed to farm on their own were a fortunate minority.

Contract laborers sometimes wondered if they had escaped bondage after all. On occasion they bargained for better work conditions, but employers had the advantage of summoning troops to punish those blacks who refused to follow the original contract. Military officials had to sort through numerous allegations, often true, of wage defrauding. Some employers simply fled the area and took the harvest's profits. Confederate guerrillas relished whipping contract laborers on the more isolated farms. Few contraband workers ended the war with much in the way of savings.

Superintendents of contrabands' affairs were also concerned about education.* Soon after federal occupation of an area local blacks or sympathetic Northerners established schools. Most superintendents organized and standardized school systems to prevent friction between sponsoring groups. The superintendent in Louisiana relied primarily upon local white teachers in order to make the program less controversial. The army tried to protect the schools, but teachers still incurred much verbal and physical abuse from angry whites. Contrabands supported the schools with enthusiasm and small donations.

Contrabands' superintendents encouraged couples to formalize their unions, and several established marriage training programs. While the war created opportunities for contrabands to reunite with separated family members, it also divided many couples during refugee movements and military roundups of laborers or draftees. A little education helped greatly to reopen or maintain contact through the mail. In such ways cooperation between Northern reformers and contrabands had a constructive effect on social change.

The greatest opening for change seemed to come when the federal government decided to enlist black troops. The navy had long permitted black enlistments, and thousands of contrabands performed a variety of functions in it during the war. Prior to 1862 federal law excluded blacks from the army, though many served as spies, scouts, cooks, teamsters, officers' servants, and laborers. In 1862 the federal commander in the Sea Islands conscripted a number of contrabands into military service but had to release them under War Department orders. Later that year contraband volunteers were accepted in the Sea Islands, Louisiana, and Kansas. Not until 1863 did the federal government enter wholeheartedly into black recruitment*—both by soliciting volunteers and by conscripting. The majority of the 186,017 black soldiers were probably contrabands.

Black troops failed to receive equal treatment in the army. At first the government paid them less than white soldiers and denied them an enlistment bounty. Their medical care was often inferior and contributed to a high death rate from disease. Commanders mostly gave black troops labor and garrison assignments, not combat duty. Few blacks received promotion above the rank of sergeant.

Congress remedied the pay and bounty discrepancies in 1864 and decreed slaves free upon enlistment.

The Confederacy never officially recognized U.S. Colored Troops* as soldiers, but rather as runaway chattels or as insurrectionary slaves. In several battles, most notably at Fort Pillow, Tennessee, in 1864, some Confederates refused to take black prisoners, but massacred them instead. South Carolina tried captured blacks for rebellion, but no convictions resulted. The Confederate army returned some prisoners to their owners and forced a number of others to perform military labor. The Confederates' refusal to exchange captured black troops formed a major obstacle in prisoner exchange negotiations.

Becoming a trained and armed soldier in a powerful military machine profoundly affected contraband volunteers, especially by heightening their self-esteem. Several regiments refused to accept less than equal pay. One mutinied over the issue. Others mutinied when white officers imposed what the blacks considered excessive discipline—whipping or prohibiting passes to visit families. Some of the units became very skilled at precision drilling and took great pride in exhibiting their dexterity. Black troops participated in brave and futile charges at Port Hudson, Battery Wagner, Olustee, Cold Harbor, and the Crater. Their combat efforts were more successful at Millikin's Bend, Nashville, and the fall 1864 assaults on Petersburg's defenses. In helping to destroy the Confederacy, contrabands were also helping to end slavery.

As the institution came under massive strain in the Confederate states, the bonds of slavery weakened where it existed elsewhere in the United States. In 1862 Congress abolished slavery in the territories and in the District of Columbia. In the loyal states—Missouri, Kentucky, Maryland, and Delaware—some federals returned fugitive slaves, but others impressed or hid runaways. The army established contraband camps near Confederate states and unavoidably had trouble distinguishing between runaways from those states and those from the border states, who were exempt from emancipation policies. Slave values declined in the border states, especially after the Emancipation Proclamation.

The recruitment of blacks posed a major challenge to loyal-state slavery. Although Kentucky politicians first won a ban on black recruitment in their state, fugitive slaves flocked to enlist in neighboring states. Kentucky's exemption ended in 1864 when Lincoln agreed to send all the state's black enlistees elsewhere for their service. In that same year Congress explicitly made slaves in the loyal states subject to the military draft. Huge enlistments in Kentucky and Maryland greatly damaged the institution there.

Maryland's Unionists voted to abolish slavery in an 1864 constitutional referendum. In the same year Missouri enacted a gradual emancipation program, then, in 1865, switched to immediate abolition. An 1865 congressional law freeing the families of black soldiers primarily affected Kentucky. The army inflicted further damage to the institution there by issuing travel passes to all blacks seeking work regardless of their legal status. That forced some slaveholders to compensate their bondsmen. By the war's end in the spring of 1865, slavery remained fully legal only in Kentucky and Delaware. West Virginia and possibly New Jersey still had some slaves due to gradual emancipation programs. However, court challenges to emancipation seemed likely on constitutional grounds. In January 1865, to head off that possibility, Congress proposed a Thirteenth Amendment* ending slavery throughout the country.

After the Confederacy's collapse a few white Southerners quickly conceded slavery's end in hopes of smoothing the way to a new labor system. But many refused to believe that such a big change would really occur. Everywhere returning veterans and refugees increased the white side of the racial balance of power. As the federal army occupied all of the ex-Confederate states, it and a new Freedmen's Bureau* announced and enforced emancipation. Owners either acknowledged the institution's end, preserved their slaves' bondage by force, or kept silent. Slaves either requested recognition of their freedom, waited for it, remained ignorant of the news, or left on their own. When masters finally accepted emancipation, many slave communities held special celebrations.

The economic consequences of slavery's end immediately touched ex-master and ex-slave alike. Angry or impoverished ex-masters might force slaves off their farms, hire a few select hands, or allow all to work for just room and board. In some states children were apprenticed as farmhands without their parents' consent. To keep the work going, some ex-masters promised freedmen a fair but indefinite compensation, often just room and board. Some freedmen gladly left an abusive owner. But others clung to their old masters fearing the uncertainties of the future. Relatively few masters helped freedmen get a new start in life. When both sides recognized their interdependence, smooth bargaining was possible. Sometimes the Freedmen's Bureau intervened to pressure one or both sides into a quick agreement. Such contracts often required bureau enforcement, however.

Wages ranged widely because the bureau refused to set them. Compensation also took the forms of shares of crop, goods, or the use of some land. All contracts worked within an economy which had suffered serious setbacks. Billions of dollars had been lost in slavery's destruction and other costs of the war. Now laborers required a compensation that exceeded the slave's subsistence. Postwar state legislatures heard many pleas for laws to control black laborers. Southern states already had laws restricting free blacks, and some quickly passed new, tougher ones.

On most farms the freedmen occupied the weaker economic position. As communal services, like child care and cooking, disappeared from plantations, some black wives reduced their work time in order to give more attention to children and the household. Demobilization of the army decreased job opportunities and protection. The Freedmen's Bureau quickly shut down contraband camps, land leasing programs, and General Sherman's colony on the southeast coast.

The fact that the bureau had the power to rent forty-acre plots of confiscatable land convinced some freedmen that the government would give them the land

and means to start small farms. Others, who proved prescient, found the rumor unbelievable. Ex-masters, fearful of such a program's consequences, loudly criticized freedmen as lazy. Some succumbed partially to black hopes by renting small farms to them. But for most freedmen the future brought only poverty.

The major benefits blacks gained from emancipation were social. They reunited families, received education, established their own churches, and gained freedom of movement and gathering. Liberty encouraged assertive efforts for more rights and dignified treatment from whites. Whites responded with resistance and violence.

In December 1865 the Thirteenth Amendment finally became a part of the U.S. Constitution.* Because the amendment required approval from three-fourths of the states, several ex-Confederate states had to ratify it in acknowledgment of their military defeat. Ratification ended most hopes for a reversal of emancipation and forced most white Southerners to resign themselves to a new era in race relations. A few whites preserved slavery for several more years, but most began to pay freedmen laborers. Freedom's meaning varied from state to state as the full legal impact of the Thirteenth Amendment remained to be seen. Much of the conflict of Reconstruction would revolve around this issue.

SELECTED BIBLIOGRAPHY

Ira Berlin et al., eds., *Freedom: A Documentary History of Emancipation, 1861–1867* (2 vols. to date, 1982-); John Cimprich, *Slavery's End in Tennessee, 1861–1865* (1985); Louis S. Gerteis, *From Contraband to Freedman: Federal Policy toward Southern Blacks, 1861–1865* (1973); Victor B. Howard, *Black Liberation in Kentucky: Emancipation and Freedom, 1862–1884* (1983); Leon F. Litwack, *Been in the Storm So Long: The Aftermath of Slavery* (1979); Clarence L. Mohr, *On the Threshold of Freedom: Masters and Slaves in Civil War Georgia* (1986); Benjamin Quarles, *The Negro in the Civil War* (1953); and Bell I. Wiley, *Southern Negroes, 1861–1865* (1938).

                                                                    JOHN CIMPRICH

CLAY, HENRY (1777–1852). Henry Clay was born in Hanover County, Virginia, 12 April 1777, and died in Washington, D.C., 29 June 1852. After reading law in Richmond, in November 1797, Clay was licensed to practice, and moved to Lexington, Kentucky, where he was admitted to the bar, 20 March 1798. His ardent Jeffersonian Republicanism pleased the state's dominant political faction, which sent him repeatedly to the Commonwealth's legislature, to the U.S. Senate, and to the U.S. House of Representatives. A leader in the National Republican and Whig parties, Clay ran unsuccessfully for the presidency in 1824, 1832, and 1844.

Clay inherited two slaves in 1782 but owned only one bondsman when he settled in Kentucky. By the 1840s, however, he held sixty slaves and ranked among the Commonwealth's largest slaveholders. Yet Clay also was an emancipationist who believed, as he said in 1799, that existing slaves were not prepared for freedom but "their posterity" might be qualified by education to "exercise . . . the rights of a citizen." In 1816, having concluded that the two races "never could amalgamate," he was a founder of the American Colonization Society,* formed to transport free Negroes to a colony in Africa. Although Clay served as president of the society, 1836–1849, none of his slaves freed during his lifetime was required to emigrate. His last will apportioned among his family all slaves except the children born after 1 January 1850. These slaves were to receive a basic education, and, upon reaching their twenties, were to be emancipated and sent to Liberia.*

Much of Clay's reputation rests on his being a skilled politician who hammered out compromises over the troublesome slavery crises of his day. Deploring the escalating sectional bitterness after the War of 1812,* Clay criticized both aggressive antislavery agitation and threats of secession. His labors in Congress helped to resolve the three great political crises of his time. In 1820–1821 Clay's efforts to gain admission of Missouri as a slave state succeeded with the Missouri Compromise,* although he had to accept a restriction on slavery above the line 36°30'. The Nullification Crisis* of 1832–1833 ended after enactment, under Clay's leadership, of a tariff measure to replace one that South Carolina considered unacceptable. And in Clay's last senate term he offered proposals that, first defeated, were altered and adopted, during his absence, as the Compromise of 1850.* Owing largely to Clay's leadership, the ultimate sectional confrontation was postponed until he had passed from the scene.

SELECTED BIBLIOGRAPHY

Calvin Colton, ed., *The Works of Henry Clay, Comprising His Life, Correspondence, and Speeches* (6 vols., 1904); Clement Eaton, *Henry Clay and the Art of American Politics* (1957); James F. Hopkins, Mary W. M. Hargreaves, Robert Seager II, et al. eds., *The Papers of Henry Clay* (8 vols. to date, 1959-); Lonnie E. Maness, "Henry Clay and the Problem of Slavery" (Ph.D. dissertation, Memphis State University, 1980); P. J. Staudenraus, *The African Colonization Movement, 1816–1865* (1961); and Glyndon G. Van Deusen, *The Life of Henry Clay* (1937).

                                                                      JAMES F. HOPKINS

CLIMATE. Climate often has been put forth as an explanation for why the "sunny" South has ways that differ from those of the rest of the nation. According to this view, the Mason-Dixon line separated lands where warm weather fostered sloth, poverty, and slavery from lands where an invigorating climate encouraged a commendable attitude toward labor and the accumulation of capital. Yet surely the differences between the two regions have been greater than those that may be directly attributed to climate. The West Coast has milder winters than the South, while higher summer temperatures are recorded in New York, Chicago, and Bismarck, North Dakota, than in Miami, New Orleans, and Galveston. While climate is indeed relevant to North-South differences, the relationship is no simple one.

When planning their colonial enterprises, seventeenth-century Englishmen were influenced by climatic considerations in deciding where to locate particular

kinds of colonies. Mercantile theorists, for example, saw little value in establishing colonies in an area that would produce commodities that would compete
with those in England. Sectarian leaders, on the other hand, wanted to create
"new Englands" in America and generally favored areas where climate was
similar to that at home. Thus, with few exceptions, the sectarian experiments
were located north of the Chesapeake, while colonies that developed a plantation
pattern of society were distributed southward from Maryland to Barbados.

But if tobacco,* rice,* indigo,* and sugar cane* flourished in the warm lands,
seventeenth-century Englishmen did not. The plantation colonies suffered an
appalling death rate, and, as a result, a chronic labor shortage. These colonies
attracted or retained insufficient free immigrants* and might have disappeared
altogether had not the planters experimented with various forms of coerced labor.
By 1700 they had settled upon black slavery. In this development, health conditions,* resulting from climate, appear to have been decisive. In the Mediterranean countries, where health conditions were approximately the same for blacks
and whites, slavery continued to be a racially mixed institution. But, though the
American plantations generally proved unhealthy for blacks as well as whites,
the death rate of blacks in the New World was about one-third that for European
newcomers. Therefore, as European servants became increasingly difficult to
recruit, shippers expanded the traffic in African slaves.

Thus the plantation labor system* molded in the English colonies was influenced strongly by the deadly disease environment* of the seventeenth century.
As a result, fully free labor and eventually even the half-free labor of European
indentured servants* were in extremely short supply. Heavy-handed coercion
was used to bring in and to retain workers. The plantation system became strictly
defined by race, first as a custom, then by law. And few, if any, slaveholders
in history proved more grudging about manumitting slaves than those in English-
speaking America.

Yet, if the Southern colonies had been able to attract few white immigrants
in the seventeenth century, such was not true of the eighteenth century. Even
the pestilent Southern low country became less a land of death, as whites adjusted
to their new disease environment. There the white as well as the black population
stabilized and both groups began to increase at about the same rate. But it was
the higher and better-drained Southern piedmont that attracted immigrants. Although even in this Southern "backcountry" health conditions were not as
favorable as in certain parts to the north, especially New England, conditions
for raising livestock* were a great deal better.

In the Northern colonies the size of a farmer's herd was limited by the feed
he could grow in summer to nourish his animals in winter. But in the Southern
colonies, so long as population density remained low, little or no winter feed
was necessary. Southern cattle fed on frost-resistant reeds along the banks of
streams, hogs on the acorns and pine mast in the forest. Thus the Southern farmer
could allow his animals to multiply prodigiously. These growing herds gave rise
to a crude, backwoods prosperity. They provided a ladder of upward mobility.

At first the vigorous development of a farming-herding economy on the Southern frontier fostered the growth of free labor, not slavery. Indeed, the prevalence of a free-market labor system, North and South, helped to unite the regions against Great Britain during the American Revolution* and encouraged the sharing of common political ideals. Yet this North-South unity of the late eighteenth century is deceptive. The dynamics of upward mobility were different in the two regions. In the Northern region, a free laborer, working in competition with slaves, often saw slavery as an obstacle to his self-improvement. There, when the Revolution weakened traditional power relationships, slaveholders were forced to accept emancipation plans. But in the Southern region, so long as livestock range remained unlimited and the price of plantation lands and the price of slaves stayed low, the farmer could hope that his promiscuously multiplying herds would generate the capital or the credit that he would need to become a planter. As a result, within a single generation, plantation slavery spread from the Atlantic states to Texas.

In the nineteenth century, as problems arising from incompatible labor systems became more apparent, as Northern and Southern elites developed conflicting objectives, and as the struggle for the control of the federal government and the western territories became more menacing, leaders of both sides tried to defuse the explosiveness of this antagonism. They described it not as a conflict of classes, but rather one of regional interests. Each of the regions was said to have adopted a labor system appropriate to its own climate and soil. Regional loyalties thus began to take on a fetish-like intensity, as they subsumed the tensions of rival labor systems. People began to write the terms ''North'' and ''South'' with capital letters.

But if ''nature'' and ''climate'' had really established a clear boundary between the ''North'' and the ''South,'' as people argued, antebellum politics would have been considerably less tempestuous. In the northern Chesapeake area, for example, the boundary seemed uncertain. Continuous cropping of tobacco had exhausted the soil and forced a conversion to mixed farming. Plantation gang labor* was now less effective. In mixed farming close supervision of labor was more difficult. Stronger motivation and more skill were required. Planters adjusted to the new situation in two ways. They made greater use of hired labor, opening a slot that was soon filled by free workers from the North or from Europe. They also increased the motivation and skill of slaves, as had long been done in household slavery, by a system of rewards, the most important being the prospect of freedom for the slave himself or for his children. By 1860 half the slaves in Maryland had been set free. Without any change in climate or location, the northern Chesapeake was becoming less ''Southern.''

In the 1850s certain political leaders, especially Stephen A. Douglas,* attempted to reduce North-South tension over the control of the western territories. The climatic geography* of plantation crops, especially tobacco, hemp* and cotton,* said Douglas, already had determined the limits of slavery. But this optimistic view failed to consider that one of the most important activities of

the Far West* was mining,* an industry in which the profitability of slave labor*
long had been demonstrated, from the silver working of Laurium in ancient
Greece to the gold fields of nineteenth-century Georgia. Furthermore, entrepreneurs of the Far West, like seventeenth-century English colonial planters, suffered a severe labor shortage and had begun experimenting with half-free Chinese
labor. What inhibited the westward spread of slavery, as Douglas himself was
later forced to acknowledge, was the absence of slave patrols,* slave codes,*
and sympathetic local governments—all the elaborate protective machinery that
slavery required. By the late 1850s many Southern leaders and their Northern
rivals alike recognized that if geography had set the western limits of plantation
agriculture, it was the power struggle in Washington, not climate, that set the
western limits of slavery.

SELECTED BIBLIOGRAPHY

Avery O. Craven, *Soil Exhaustion as a Factor in the Agricultural History of Virginia
and Maryland, 1606–1860* (1926); Philip D. Curtin, "Epidemiology and the Slave
Trade," *Political Science Quarterly*, 83 (1968), 190–216; Eugene D. Genovese, *The
Political Economy of Slavery: Studies in the Economy and Society of the Slave South*
(1965); Lewis C. Gray, *History of Agriculture in the Southern United States to 1860* (2
vols., 1933); Allan Nevins, *Ordeal of the Union*, vol. 2: *A House Dividing, 1852–1857*
(1947); Orlando Patterson, *Slavery and Social Death: A Comparative Study* (1982); and
Charles W. Ramsdell, "The Natural Limits of Slavery Expansion," *Mississippi Valley
Historical Review*, 16 (1929), 151–171.

                                                                    WILLIAM MCKEE EVANS

CLOSING OF THE AFRICAN SLAVE TRADE. The closing of the African
slave trade found few advocates as late as the American Revolution,* but it
became an important transatlantic political issue by the time of the Federal
Convention at Philadelphia in 1787. Here antislavery zealots joined Virginia
planters in an uneasy alliance. Whereas the former opposed the trade on religious
and philosophical grounds, the latter were eager to secure a good market for
their surplus slaves on the rapidly developing southwestern frontier. Together
they attempted unsuccessfully to insert into the new Constitution* a national ban
on the importation of slaves. The opposition, representing both New England
shipping interests and their prospective customers in the Deep South, won instead
a twenty-year moratorium on any federal interference with the overseas slave
trade to the United States. The trade was finally outlawed by Congress on 1
January 1808.

   Nevertheless, by 1800 American participation in the international slave trade
already was *legally* impossible. As early as 1794, federal law prohibited the
outfitting in American ports of ships destined to carry slaves to any *foreign*
country. Six years later this prohibition was extended to American citizens
serving on slave ships under foreign flags. And by 1799 every American state
(even those of the Deep South, where there was fear both of rising debts and
of "contagion" from the great slave revolt in Santo Domingo) had enacted

statutes banning the importation of slaves. In practice, however, neither state nor federal laws were immediately effective in stopping the slave trade. Slavers apprehended at sea found sympathetic local prosecutors and juries when taken into American ports for trial. Overland smuggling ran rampant along the borders with Spanish Florida and Louisiana.

Rapid development of cotton plantations in the Deep South and Southwest stimulated not only smuggling but also the reopening of the legal slave trade by South Carolina in 1803. Almost 40,000 African slaves entered the South through this state's ports before the national ban on imports took effect on 1 January 1808. In defiance of American law and the British navy—England also outlawed the slave trade in 1808—slavers continued to bring thousands of Africans into the United States, especially during the boom years of 1815–1819. By the mid–1820s, however, American slave buyers depended far more on the remarkable fecundity of their own country's slaves, and on a flourishing domestic trade, than on illegal African imports to meet their demand for bondsmen.

Still, in spite of an 1820 federal law making slaving punishable by death as piracy, Americans' participation in the illicit transatlantic trade continued throughout the antebellum years. This was aided by the refusal of the U.S. government to allow British search and seizure of American vessels and by the failure of American courts to invoke the death penalty until 1862. Most of the slaves carried by this illicit traffic were taken to Cuba or Brazil, not the United States. From 1810 to 1860, as the slave population of the United States increased by two and one-half million, probably fewer than 60,000 slaves were illegally brought into the country.

SELECTED BIBLIOGRAPHY

Philip D. Curtin, *The Atlantic Slave Trade: A Census* (1969); David Brion Davis, *The Problem of Slavery in the Age of Revolution, 1770–1823* (1975); W.E.B. Du Bois, *The Suppression of the African Slave-Trade to the United States of America, 1638–1870* (1896); Peter Duignan and Clarence Clendenen, *The United States and the African Slave Trade, 1619–1862* (1963); Warren S. Howard, *American Slavers and the Federal Law, 1837–1862* (1963); James A. Rawley, *The Transatlantic Slave Trade: A History* (1981); and Donald L. Robinson, *Slavery in the Structure of American Politics, 1765–1820* (1971).
JAMES E. CRISP

CLOTHING. Although the planter's family enjoyed a finer and more extensive wardrobe, special clothing was unnecessary to set apart slave from master because of obvious racial distinctions. From the master's perspective, slave clothing was functional. Slaves exercised little control over the cuts and fabrics of their apparel, but clothes helped distinguish them by sex, age, and status. Women* dressed differently than men, children* more simply than adults, and house slaves* more elaborately than field-workers.* In both North and South America most owners recognized the significance of clothing to both the health and morale of their slaves and hoped that personal pride would carry over into other areas including work.

Indications are that the sparsity of slave clothing often cited in colonial times had been alleviated by the eve of the Civil War. The primary cause was the mushrooming cotton acreage which resulted in locally manufactured inexpensive cloth. Slave narratives concur that clothing received less criticism as the nineteenth century unfolded.

By the third decade of the 1800s, slaves generally were receiving clothing allotments every spring and fall. On plantations, men received two shirts and two pairs of trousers and women two dresses each per season. These two basic outfits allowed for changes and facilitated weekly laundering. Gifts, secondhand, or especially made clothes supplemented the slave family's wardrobe.

Among field slaves, only the drivers* received extra allotments and finer grades of clothing, including even broadcoats, shoes with buckles, and hats. Such distinctions in dress marked status and authority as defined by the master. Skilled slaves and artisans* might also wear special clothes befitting their work and status and, in some instances, their ability to purchase items from their "earnings."

Work clothes for household slaves on large plantations were understandably more elaborate than those of their field counterparts, although not necessarily so. It was in the owner's interest to have well-dressed personal servants since such an appearance reflected a generally well-run household. Travelers' accounts testify that wealthy planters bedecked slave butlers and coachmen in high style. House servants were also most likely to receive secondhand clothing from the Big House.

Little is recorded concerning the clothing allotment for small children. Many simply ran around naked in warm weather. Since owners were primarily concerned with providing work clothes, juvenile clothing probably merited scant attention. Clothing or cloth for youngsters may have been issued as needed without regard to seasonal work conditions.

On most plantations, boys up to the age of eight, and sometimes up to twelve, received only shirttails, a one-piece garment usually reaching the knees. In the winter small boys apparently wore britches. Young girls up to the age of puberty generally dressed solely in a one-piece frock. In several instances, grown men also worked in the fields wearing only shirttails. Reportedly, it was easier to whip a man in only shirttails because all the assailant had to do was to lift up the tails.

Clothing for slaves past their working years was probably handled like clothing for children, that is, at the discretion of the master. Contemporary records suggest, however, that elderly slaves* were adequately clothed. Wills occasionally specified that "Old Ben" or "Old Mary" be issued a hat, coat, or other designated items of clothing at least once a year.

Proper clothing was especially important during the winter months for health reasons. Men's winter wear included jackets and often woolen caps. Coats, cloaks, and capes served as the women's outer garments. Slave women wore kerchiefs as standard head covering throughout the year. Headkerchiefs appeared wherever black women were held in bondage throughout North and South America, the brightly colored material covering women's hair revealing cultural ties to West African tradition. Slave testimony further suggests that sunbonnets were occasionally issued to women in the Southeast in the mid-nineteenth century.

Although several agricultural reformers advocated rainwear for slaves, few slaves likely got such protection. Raincoats, for example, are seldom mentioned in testimonies or plantation records, although boots appear in occasional listings of slave clothing. Blankets, which served as both bedding and occasional clothing, were issued every two years to each household member. Owners tried to stagger distributions so that every family received at least one new blanket annually. If blankets were not issued or were in short supply, slave women sewed scrap materials together to make two large pieces, often creating their own designs with the scraps and thereby interlacing their own artistic and cultural values into the cloth. In between the pieces they stuffed cotton to form a warm quilt. Slave women occasionally held quilting parties to help each other make bed coverings. Slaves prized fancy clothing, which they wore to church and on special occasions. Through the generosity of their owners or personal ingenuity, many slaves acquired special garments and other finery. Some owners regularly furnished all their slaves with Sunday clothes. Slave women often supplemented family wardrobes by making garments, sometimes from materials they had spun and woven themselves. Discarded clothes from the owner's family were the chief source of ornate slave clothing. Runaway slave* advertisements describe such fancy wear as pumps with buckles for both men and women, and fur hats. When escaping, slaves usually took along their favorite wear. Advertisements describing the dress of runaway slaves suggest that slaves often owned choice pieces of clothing. Changes of clothing also helped escapees in preventing detection and starting a new life.

Ironically, slave sales were also occasions for slaves to be well-dressed. After the sale, however, the slaves discarded their fine clothes as soon as possible, for they viewed their sale as an occasion of shame and sought to divest themselves immediately of all conspicuous reminders. Conversely, some slaves tried to look their best on the auction block, hoping that a good appearance would attract a kindly owner.

No general rule apparently existed for the issuing of stockings and underwear. Only a few plantations apparently provided such comparative luxuries. By the late antebellum period slaves on plantations commonly had at least one pair of stockings for the winter months. The plantation mistresses* did the knitting or supervised the work.

Many runaway slave advertisements mention petticoats, which suggests that slaves prized petticoats or trimmed underskirts, or that many slaves owned them. Slaves no doubt welcomed their warmth during the winter. Aprons were another item common to the female wardrobe, but not included as part of the regular clothing allowance. Field slaves probably made their aprons, while house slaves received theirs from the mistress. Only the most generous owners supplied dress hats for either men or women.

Since store-bought shirts and dresses were a luxury, slave clothing was usually constructed on individual plantations. For this purpose, slave owners in the nineteenth century imported coarse, durable, low-grade materials advertised as "Negro cloth." Calico and homespun, for example, comprised staple materials for women's garments and headpieces. Testimony of former slaves details the discomfort they endured when breaking in their scratchy new garments. Some ex-slaves compared the rough "Negro cloth" to needles sticking one all the time.

Responsibility for making wearing apparel for slaves varied with the size and circumstances of the plantation. On some plantations the plantation mistresses made the slave clothing themselves, or hired seamstresses to do the work. On other large plantations specially appointed slaves made the garments under supervision. Often the slave mother constructed her family's clothes from material furnished by the owner. The owner usually provided heavy coats, but the slaves made or adapted the regular clothing. As with other family projects, sewing took place after other chores ceased. When the owner furnished cloth, he also provided needles, buttons, and thread.

Indigo, sumac, walnut hulls or leaves, red clay, and bark were among the items slaves used for dyeing materials. They made starch from wheat bran, and crafted buttons from dried gourds and rams' and cows' horns.

Patterns for slave garments indicate that masters gave little consideration to style and size. Cut full and with baggy legs, men's pants could accommodate a variety of bodily sizes and shapes. Slave clothes were usually made in only two sizes, small and large. Dresses usually hung loose from the shoulders and were referred to as frocks, shifts, or chemises, but they could be belted to give the appearance of a better fit.

Slaves received shoes only for the winter months. In the summer slaves went barefoot. In Brazil, where the wearing of shoes was a mark of freedom, slave owners only issued sandals. During the winter, North American slaves wore "Negro brogans," heavy, ill-fitting shoes with nails all around. They were usually purchased ready-made or produced by shoemakers on large plantations. In order to reduce repairs and replacements, many owners withheld shoe allotments until late November or early December.

Brogans were made from hard, red leather, often with steel tips at the toes. In addition to the hardness of the leather, the clumsy uncomfortable fit partially explains why slaves preferred to walk long distances barefoot. In addition, men and women apparently shared the same shoe sizes, which came in lengths only, with one standard width. A few lucky slaves obtained dress shoes as cast-offs from the owner's family. Children's shoes were usually hand-downs, although on large plantations shoemakers constructed lighter weight shoes for their use.

If clothes make the man or woman, slave clothing made enslaved men and women appear at least partly as the masters wanted them to be—dependent. But the slaves adapted the materials and clothes they received from the master to suit their own needs too. By adding color or wearing headkerchiefs, by using scraps to make quilts and blankets, or whatever, the slaves established their own individual, and community, standard of style. Like so much of slave life, slave clothing was a blend of the master's and the slave's contributions.

SELECTED BIBLIOGRAPHY

Eugene D. Genovese, *Roll, Jordan, Roll: The World the Slaves Made* (1974); Charles Joyner, *Down by the Riverside: A South Carolina Slave Community* (1984); George P. Rawick, ed., *The American Slave: A Composite Autobiography* (19 vols., 1972); Kenneth M. Stampp, *The Peculiar Institution: Slavery in the Ante-Bellum South* (1956); Gerilyn Tandberg, "Fieldhand Clothing in Louisiana and Mississippi During the Slavery Period," *Dress*, 60 (1980), 89–103; and Lathan A. Windley, comp., *Runaway Slave Advertisements: A Documentary History from the 1730's to 1799* (1983).

MARTHA H. BROWN

COLONIZATION. Colonization was a movement based on the belief that free blacks and whites could not live together successfully in the United States. This concept arose at the time of the American Revolution* and persisted until emancipation and beyond. Although it was opposed by most blacks and by white abolitionists,* some blacks and many whites endorsed the idea. Colonizationists tried a number of experiments in Africa, Haiti, Canada, and elsewhere before slavery ended.

The primary motive for colonization was the belief that racial differences made it impossible for blacks to gain equality with American whites, who considered blacks fundamentally inferior. Most reasoned that the appropriate status for blacks was slavery. They perceived free blacks* as threats to racial purity and as agitators against slavery. Consequently, colonizationists concluded that only the removal of free blacks from the United States would protect the racial status quo. Even those who were friendly to blacks or who opposed slavery believed that American society at large would never allow blacks full equality. Therefore, for their own good, blacks should leave to find better opportunities. Other rationales for colonization included evangelizing Africans, opening trade, fighting the slave trade, showing the superiority of free labor, and pursuing black nationalism.

Serious thought about colonization began in 1773 when Rev. Samuel Hopkins, of Newport, R.I., helped train two African-born slaves for missionary service in their homeland. Thomas Jefferson,* then governor of Virginia, wrote in 1777 that because slavery degraded both blacks and whites, slaves should be freed and settled in the remote West, where they could gain strength and independence. As emancipation swept the Northern states between 1783 and 1804, Virginia's leaders, anticipating the end of slavery there, actively sought ways to rid the state of blacks in order to avoid racial problems.

Meanwhile, British reformers had founded a colony at Sierra Leone, West Africa, in 1787 as a refuge for impoverished Africans from London, and later from Nova Scotia, Jamaica, and the United States. Despite difficulties, Sierra Leone survived and attracted the attention of American Quakers, particularly Captain Paul Cuffe, a black shipowner from Westport, Massachusetts. A devout man and a civil rights activist, Cuffe conceived a plan to settle skilled Afro-Americans in Africa, where they could become an inspiration to blacks everywhere. In 1811 Cuffe visited Sierra Leone and England to work out arrangements for his Afro-American settlers, and in 1815 he sailed to Sierra Leone with thirty-eight colonists. Cuffe's motives started with evangelism and commerce as means to civilize Africa, but by 1815 he also saw colonization as a way to escape American racism.

In 1816 Robert Finley, a white clergyman, organized the American Colonization Society* to reform and help the quarter-million free blacks then living in the United States. Finley's new organization sought to settle blacks in Africa and hoped that colonization would eventually lead to the end of slavery. But when the American Colonization Society quickly won support from prominent slave owners, free blacks in Philadelphia and elsewhere soundly opposed it. In their opinion, colonization would lead to their forced deportation. Although the American Colonization Society outlived American slavery (it ceased operations in 1892), and although its African colony, Liberia,* attracted more than 10,000 colonists before 1865, most free blacks strongly opposed its work. Nevertheless, several prominent free blacks, including Lott Cary, Joseph J. Roberts, John B. Russwurm, and Edward W. Blyden, emigrated to Liberia and served there as leaders. Many of Liberia's colonists were former slaves whose owners had freed them provided that they go to Africa.

The Fugitive Slave Act of 1850,* with its severe threats to both escaped slaves and to free Negroes incited many blacks to flee to Canada, long a haven for American blacks. During the 1850s several all-black communities, including Dawn, Wilberforce, and Elgin, attracted black American refugees, while others settled elsewhere in Upper Canada (Ontario). Perhaps as many as 30,000 fugitives lived in Canada in 1860. Among the Americans who lived there for a time were Henry Bibb,* Josiah Henson,* Mary Ann Shadd, and Martin R. Delany.

Delany, a black physician, editor, and abolitionist, had more ambitious colonization plans. As a young man he had dreamed of settling in East Africa, but by 1854 he campaigned for Latin America as the best place for a proud, self-reliant black nation. Delany bitterly criticized the American Colonization Society and what he considered its weak offspring, Liberia. In 1859 Delany visited present-day Nigeria and planned for Afro-American emigrants to settle there to grow cotton. Despite his persistent black nationalism, Delany failed to establish any colonies.

Haiti, after winning its independence from France in 1804, attracted Afro-American colonists as early as 1824. Interest in emigration to Haiti arose mostly among free blacks as an alternative to Liberia. That interest languished, however, until the passage of the Fugitive Slave Act. During the 1850s James Theodore Holly, a black clergyman from New Haven, Connecticut, persistently advocated emigration to Haiti. By 1861 many blacks and whites saw emigration to Haiti as the best escape from increasing persecution of free blacks in the United States. And the Haitian government hired agents to attract American colonists. Even Frederick Douglass,* who had consistently opposed any form of colonization lest the emigrants forget the plight of the slaves, announced early in 1861 that he would visit Haiti to report on conditions there. Douglass changed his mind, however, when the Civil War began. He and many other blacks sensed that the war would make emigration unnecessary.

Abraham Lincoln,* long an advocate of colonization, viewed the repatriation of blacks as a solution to racial questions created early in the Civil War. Convinced that blacks and whites could never live together as equals, Lincoln hoped to colonize the slaves who flocked to U.S. army camps. Lincoln won congressional approval for a colonization scheme to settle black volunteers in Panama. There they would mine coal, build a railroad, and perhaps hinder French intrigues in Mexico. But the plan collapsed because it rested on false land claims, because Central American governments feared American meddling, and because most blacks objected to leaving the United States. Lincoln then endorsed a project to settle blacks on Île-à-Vache, an island off Haiti. Although 500 settlers went there in 1863, fraud, disease, and death drove the survivors back to the United States a year later.

The Reconstruction amendments to the Constitution ended slavery, giving blacks their freedom, citizenship, and the franchise. These changes gave Afro-Americans new hope and virtually ended serious attempts at wholesale resettlement. Although few blacks ever emigrated from the United States, the idea of mass colonization or deportation lingered well into the twentieth century to keep the permanent status of black Americans in question.

SELECTED BIBLIOGRAPHY

David M. Dean, *Defender of the Race: James Theodore Holly, Black Nationalist Bishop* (1979); Sheldon H. Harris, *Paul Cuffe: Black America and the African Return* (1972); Floyd John Miller, *The Search for a Black Nationality: Black Emigration and Colonization, 1787–1863* (1975); P. J. Staudenraus, *The African Colonization Movement, 1816–1865* (1961); and Robin W. Winks, *The Blacks in Canada: A History* (1971).

EDWIN S. REDKEY

COMPARATIVE SLAVERY IN THE AMERICAS. Comparisons between slavery in the United States and systems of bonded labor in other nations began in the nineteenth century when Northern abolitionists* noted the peculiarity of the Southern institution. Beyond the fundamental distinction they made between enslavement and freedom, the abolitionists contrasted the harshness of life and labor in the Old South with apparently less trying conditions that slaves and blacks endured in other parts of the New World. Opponents used such critical depictions of U.S. slavery as one means of accenting the South's special cruelties, particularly in contrast with Brazil.

Southern slaveholders also invoked comparisons to defend themselves. From the 1830s to the Civil War, proslavery apologists* insisted that a paternalistic ethic undergirded Southern slavery and made bondage in the American South less harsh and human relations there less violent than in other slave regimes or in the wage labor system in the North and Great Britain. They coupled the notion of race* to that of slavery to justify the servility in which they held a black labor force adapted, they argued, to the sheltered environment of paternalistic enslavement. From the very beginning of self-conscious reflections on slavery in the United States, then, its supporters and detractors alike based their cases in part on contrasts selectively chosen to present themselves in the most positive possible terms.

Similarly, comparative treatments have continued to inform historical interpretations* of U.S. slavery down to the present. While striving toward a less charged understanding of the institution, modern comparisons of the South's slave labor system have only slowly dropped the emotional tones underlying the participants' first formulations of these contrasts. Their use of slavery as a window on the recent American dilemmas of race, rights, and responsibility, and a tendency to attribute any and all aspects of the multifaceted history of blacks in the United States to the single institution of slavery, have thus preserved the confusion introduced at the start between race and civil status.

Anthropological studies by Melville and Frances Herskovits published in the 1930s anticipated the tenor of this recent debate over the nature and meaning of slavery in a comparative framework. Drawing on extensive field research in Africa and among people of African descent in Haiti, Surinam, Trinidad, and elsewhere, the Herskovitses emphasized the differing cultural consequences of three to four centuries of black life in various parts of the Americas. Among modern North American blacks the relative rarity of customs and words derived from African sources was striking. The Herskovitses explained this unusual loss of the African heritage* at least in part by comparing the history of American blacks elsewhere and finding the experience of slavery in the South especially harsh. Though the Herskovitses also addressed a wide range of factors other than slavery that had contributed to the observed differences, and in fact emphasized the residue of Africanisms* remaining in North American black culture as a tribute to the tenacity of people who had lived under severe duress, the much greater richness of the African flavor among Caribbean and South American blacks suggested that slavery in the United States had exerted a distinctively stressful influence on the people who had survived it. Not only did this implication revive comparison as an analytical technique, of the type critical of the Old South, but it also identified culture as a key benchmark of oppression. This definition of the field set the stage for much of the liberal and neo-abolitionist comparative scholarship that flourished in the context of antitotalitarian impulses after World War II and during the civil rights movement of the 1960s and early 1970s.

In 1946 Frank Tannenbaum's famous *Slave and Citizen* took a long first stride toward more explicit and more historical comparison along these lines. Tannenbaum's seminal study reinforced suspicions of the uniquely harsh quality of slavery in the Old South that, with at least implicit support from the Herskovitses, liberals inherited from nineteenth-century abolitionist propaganda. Like them, Tannenbaum was an American scholar sensitive to his country's modern racial agony but, as a specialist in Latin America, he was also positioned to observe the contrast between Latin American and U.S. race relations from a vantage point outside the conventional bounds of U.S. historiography.

Tannenbaum's book interpreted slavery to proclaim a liberal message of hope for eased relations between the races at some future time in the United States. For the historical examples that inspired his optimism, Tannenbaum compared the U.S. experience with race relations to the allegedly less troubled history of the Indo-African-European nations of Latin America. Compared to the English who settled the North American mainland, the Portuguese and Spanish colonizers of South America, he pointed out, had a long history of slavery reaching back to Roman times and also centuries more familiarity with people of dark complexion, the neighboring Moors of North Africa. Brazil, the focus of the nineteenth-century abolitionists' invidious contrast, provided the principal demonstration of the benefits of such intimacy. Extensive historical interaction, however hostile at the time, had eventually led to racial toleration and hence to legal codes protective of black slaves, to Catholic* religious institutions open to all races and conditions, and to a toleration of manumission that together acknowledged the "moral personality" of both enslaved and freed blacks. English settlers, lacking not only the Iberians' familiarity with interracial contact but also prior experience with slavery itself, created a slave system so rigid that it left even the emancipated freedmen and their twentieth-century black descendants in "the shadow of slavery."

The ray of hope in Tannenbaum's linkage of slavery to modern race relations beamed from the element of time: given long enough to familiarize themselves with the blacks among them, white North Americans of English descent, too, would overcome the burdens of their slave past and welcome Afro-American citizens into the national community. Still more reassuring was Tannenbaum's expectation that the famed flexibility of the North Americans would allow them to create the necessary political and social institutions in less than the millennium that the Spaniards and the Portuguese had required to achieve racial toleration.

Slavery served well as a scapegoat for American liberals who sought to explain the strained race relations of the present. By displacing the sources of the modern problem of race to a vanished institution of the past, activists were freed to work for reconciliation in the future. But Tannenbaum's complex comparison left blurred the vital distinctions between race and institutions, past and present, moral judgment and dispassionate analysis, and legal prescript and daily behavior that have required two generations of subsequent scholarship to clarify.

Stanley M. Elkins amplified Tannenbaum's attribution of distinctively harsh qualities to slavery in the United States in his controversial and immensely influential book, *Slavery*, published in 1959. This book brought a postwar abhorrence of totalitarianism to the comparative debate over the effects of slavery on the slaves. Elkins looked to the dehumanizing experiences in Nazi concentration camps and to the American encounter with brainwashing in Korea to analyze human psychological responses to enormous duress. According to Elkins, the planters of the Southern states, lacking the protective plurality of legal and religious institutions that had inhibited masters in Latin America, had given themselves over to unrestrained pursuit of the capitalist profits particularly characteristic of the United States. Thus freed, they had made their plantations into "total institutions" that had reduced their slaves to a helpless infantilized passivity. Domination had even converted some of them into willing collaborators in their own degradation, analogous to the submissive inmates reported from the concentration camps of Nazi Germany. In the stock figure of Sambo*—a stupidly grinning, childlike victim who appeared in many accounts of the Old South— Elkins found evidence of the ultimate human destructiveness of a system of slavery there that seemed uniquely damaging.

Elkins's strong contrast between slavery in the United States and elsewhere stimulated Herbert Klein's more detailed and systematic 1967 comparison between church, state, economy, and manumission in colonies of Iberian and English background, in which Klein confirmed the contrasting harsh and mild qualities of the two systems. Winthrop Jordan modified Tannenbaum's derivation of racism from slavery by contrasting the classification of mulattoes as "blacks" on the mainland with the clear differentiation of mixed offspring among very similar English masters in the West Indies. Drawing on Freudian psychology, Jordan argued that the presence of blacks aroused fears of losing the English cultural heritage uniquely in the continental colonies, causing American whites to reject the fruits of their own passions.

In spite of these scattered extensions of the Tannenbaum-Elkins thesis, in general critics looked beyond Tannenbaum's portrait of the friendly Latin American master to emphasize the real hardships of slavery south of the border. They also discovered the presence of racial hostilities among the Portuguese and Spanish. Anglo and Iberian institutions and national cultural heritages may have differed, but what they had to do with the day-to-day lives of the slaves seemed much less certain. Enslavement in the United States began to appear hardly more abusive than its counterparts in other parts of the Americas.

In the United States, much of the initial criticism of Elkins's *Slavery* implicitly accepted the comparative judgment he rendered on the general harshness of the American plantation regime and centered instead on his related allegation that Southern slaves had not risen above its oppressiveness, instead succumbing to passive Sambo-like acquiescence in their captivity. In this effort to restore initiative, pride, and autonomy to the slaves the comparative method was summoned to demonstrate that the Sambo stereotype had not appeared uniquely in the United States. It could therefore indicate neither any special duress nor black collaboration in North America. At the least, Sambo had been only a rationalization of the masters to bury their guilt. At best, it had been a cunning slave strategy to preserve a measure of dignity and privacy behind the falsity of a stereotype they perpetrated. Slavery for the masters may have differed, it seemed, but for the slaves, comparison showed that suffering and challenge had hardly varied.

Contradictorily, other studies quickly accumulated evidence that slaves in the United States had rebelled less violently against the harshness of their lives than had other captives in Latin and Caribbean America. Though slaves everywhere had also devised an imaginative repertoire of subtle ways to resist white social, political, and psychological domination, the comparison suggested, something had muted the form of the struggle on the North American mainland. This comparative documentation of pan-American slave initiatives begged the question of why so few North American slaves had resorted to large-scale outbursts of violence to express their rage, particularly if they had suffered more than their counterparts elsewhere.

With culture, institutions, and racial attitudes all withering as indexes of difference between systems of slavery, and with attention turning from the masters' backgrounds to the daily lives of the slaves, conventional comparisons on the level of nations—Brazil, the United States, Spain, England, the French Antilles, or the Dutch West Indies—seemed about to yield to contrasts defined in terms of other units: regions, different crops, or in terms of the urban, plantation, proto-industrial, or mining bases of particular forms of slavery. But the old focus died hard, particularly among U.S. historians, who seemed unable to shed completely their deep commitment to the exceptionalism of U.S. history, and hence of the slavery of the Old South.

In 1969 Eugene D. Genovese distinguished American slave systems in terms of the varying positions that different master classes—including the Dutch and French, as well as the Spaniards, Portuguese, and English—had held in the huge integrated capitalist economy developing on both shores of the Atlantic Ocean in the seventeenth, eighteenth, and nineteenth centuries. He thus replaced the old, essentially bilateral contrasts between slavery in the United States and other slave systems with a systematic multilateral comparison. Rather than differentiating isolated features, he proposed a comprehensive comparison of systems. Genovese's method scored clear gains in adding change and history to hypotheses that had previously rested on mostly static typological contrasts. He also clearly separated slavery from race, broke the national units of analysis into the often conflicting regional classes of masters who had in fact existed, most successfully in the case of Brazil, and distinguished further between divergent metropolitan and colonial interests in slavery. Still, even in this view, slaveholders in the

U.S. South emerged as *sui generis*, a uniquely seigneurial regime in the context of buoyant capitalist expansion.

In the same year, Philip D. Curtin's thoroughly comparative quantitative study of the Atlantic slave trade from Africa to all regions of the Americas added powerful demographic* explanations for differences between slavery in the United States and slave systems elsewhere. Curtin's work consolidated the victory of critics intending to reduce the distinctive harshness of Southern slavery as interpreted by Tannenbaum and Elkins. Systematically counting the numbers of slaves reaching the New World showed that only a small minority had landed on the North American mainland. These few had somehow reproduced to account for more than a third of recent black populations in the Americas. This fact forced historians to ask how, if U.S. slavery had been so abusive, had North American slaves multiplied many times over while the slave populations of nearly all other importing regions, including Brazil, had declined.

In 1971 an initial answer came in Carl N. Degler's reasoning that slavery had been equally oppressive everywhere in the Americas but that in underpopulated Brazil the demographic necessity of filling positions of social respectability by promoting freedmen had opened a "hatch" through which acculturated mulattoes in particular escaped to acceptance through manumission. Other elements of Degler's explanation covered free groups other than the masters to propose that North American white women had objected to the mulatto offspring of their husbands. In their absence elsewhere, "colored" people had achieved a modest acceptance. In addition, the relatively large poor white yeomanry and working classes of the United States had supported this racist hostility to colored citizens of the republic to protect their own humble positions on the ladder of success.

Degler added ideological and political contrasts as well. The absolute freedom accorded citizens in the United States moved voters there to a more jealous defense of their liberties than had the limited rights accorded subjects of the Brazilian emperors or to residents in Spain's South American colonies. Mass democracy translated these fears of the underclasses into harsh laws in the United States, while in Latin America more authoritarian political institutions reflected the benevolent ideals of entrenched masters and patrons. This reinterpretation of the old institutional factors—now as products of contrasting demographic circumstances in the New World rather than sources of difference inherited from Europe, and carefully distinguished as influences on race relations rather than on slavery itself—neatly brought the initial cycle of comparative debate over New World slavery to a close. The hardships of slavery in the United States conformed to larger New World patterns, but the United States stood alone in defining its "black" population more inclusively than most other societies and in the extreme racialist marginalization of its freedpeople.

Unlike the comparisons derived from Tannenbaum, profoundly historical in the sense that they essentially debated the uniqueness of slavery in the American South, social science methods sought to explain when and where the general phenomenon of slavery—as opposed to other forms of labor—occurred at all, whether in the United States, in the West Indies, or, for that matter, in ancient Rome or nineteenth-century Africa. Marvin Harris's *Patterns of Race in the Americas* (1964) had contrasted Afro-American slavery anywhere in the New World with corvée, debt peonage, and other methods of forcing labor from Amerindian populations by examining the environmental distinction between lowland slave plantations and alternative forms of coercion in the highland regions. In monographic studies of the U.S. South, a parallel distinction appeared in a growing appreciation of the differences between lowland counties that grew cotton,* rice,* or sugar* and had large gangs* of plantation slaves and upland areas inhabited mainly by smaller farmers working their fields with family labor sometimes assisted by a few slaves. The basis of comparison thus implicitly shifted toward economic and regional distinctions within the United States. Judgments on the implications of these contrasts for the enduring issue of harshness divided scholars. Some scholars lamented the loss of African or Afro-American culture among slaves Americanized by their intimate contact with their masters on family farms, while others decried the physical rigors of the gang system employed in the cotton fields of large plantations.

The great volume of monographic research on North American slavery stimulated in the 1970s by debate over the old Tannenbaum-Elkins comparisons continued to break down the original conception of an undifferentiated brutal "U.S. slavery." Though these studies documented a wide range of distinct types within the South, few of them pushed the contrasts implicit in their descriptions to the explicitly comparative analyses that had seemed to flow so naturally from differences drawn at the national level. The past diversity historians detected there seemed for a while to sink beneath the unity of black nationalism and of the "mind of the South"—concepts without which study of the subject lost much of its appeal in the present.

Only one of the contrasts featured in the post–Tannenbaum-Elkins generation touched the sensitive issues that had erupted in the earlier scholarly debate over Sambo. Two economic historians, Robert W. Fogel and Stanley L. Engerman, employed economic theory and quantitative techniques to supplement ordinary historical methodologies. The resulting study, *Time on the Cross* (1974), offered reconstructions of the material conditions under which slaves had lived in the U.S. South and compared them favorably not only with the food, shelter, punishments, and (imputed) income given slaves elsewhere in the Americas but also with the hardships of life for wage laborers in the northern United States at the same time. Their application of quantitative techniques struck other historians as neglecting the established abuses that Southern slaves had endured. Equally alarming was what many took to be the book's economic transmogrification of the Sambo thesis into the proposition that slaves had cooperated in their captivity, even if only by responding as self-interested rational "optimizers" to incentives that the masters had built into slavery. A comparison that appeared to lessen the ideological resistance mounted by the slaves aroused criticism no less intense than had Elkins's concentration camp analogy.

Time on the Cross also addressed the long-standing comparative issue of slavery's economic efficiency relative to free wage labor. Though the discussion arose in part from debates purely internal to U.S. historiography on whether the use of slaves had doomed the South to technological backwardness, economic stagnation, and ultimately to armed conflict with a progressive and growing North, it at least implicitly paralleled the agenda of the established social science inquiry into the circumstances under which specific types of labor systems occurred worldwide. At the turn of the century the Dutch sociologist, H. J. Nieboer, had concluded in his *Slavery as an Industrial System* (1900, rev. ed., 1910) that bound labor tended to appear in export-producing regions adjacent to open frontier lands, into which free workers would otherwise flee. This theory fit well with the contrasting free and slave regimes of the Northern and Southern parts of the United States. Other economists, in part looking in comparative terms at the regional contrasts within the United States, identified the importance of the differing annual cycles of labor requirements among various crops in explaining why slavery became a fixture only in the South. Northern crops with sharp seasonal peaks in labor input, like wheat,* could not cover the high expenses of maintaining slaves through a long period of relative idleness each year. Crops like maize* or cotton, with more evenly distributed applications of labor throughout the months, were better able to absorb these costs, especially when grown by large multifunctional units capable of applying slave labor time to other ends during the off season. The lengthy growing season of southerly latitudes thus favored plantations and slavery, while Northern farms relied on a skeleton crew of family labor assisted for the few brief weeks of the harvest by hired hands.

Other comparatively structured reflections on the specific reasons for slavery in the continental colonies centered on the differences between indentured servants* and slaves. These studies posed the question in the more historical form of asking why American mainland and island planters had switched in the seventeenth century from contracted British labor to purchased Africans. Rising wages in Britain, a possible lowering of the delivered costs of slaves from Africa, agricultural skills Africans possessed for certain types of crops, and the relative immunity to tropical diseases* enjoyed by Africans figured among the factors favoring the use of blacks in the warmer parts of the New World. This discussion risked drifting back toward confusing race and labor economics, since it derived the reasons for slavery in part from the physical characteristics of the slaves, thus explaining "why Africans" as much as it explained "why slaves." A particularly complex and historical analysis of this type cited rising demand for American crops in seventeenth-century Europe, the consequent availability of credit to finance rapid growth of a capitalized (slave) labor force in the export sectors, low requirements for (indentured) European agricultural skills for certain crops, and the tendency of slaves, once introduced, to displace indentured labor from skilled job categories as a locally born acculturated slave population began to grow.

Comparison of slavery as a labor system with the alternatives—mostly indentured servants and free wage workers in the United States—dovetailed with an increasingly prominent effort to place slavery in the United States and elsewhere within the context of an integrated global history, particularly in relation to the emergence of modern capitalism. One possible route to this end lay through disciplined application of Marxist-derived theories of the "mode of production." Theorists of this bent expanded the comparative framework to include the ancient Mediterranean but could not agree on whether slavery constituted a mode distinct from the social and economic matrices surrounding it. The formal debate did not strongly influence studies on slavery in the United States, though Genovese's more supple historical materialism produced a rich interpretation of "the world the slaves made" in *Roll, Jordan, Roll* (1974).

More influential were the ramifications of several types of world-systems analysis. These attempted to position slavery in relation to other forms of labor organization (or "modes of production") throughout a worldwide economic system composed of complementing functional zones and focused on the capitalist wage labor relations simultaneously emerging in northwestern Europe. For those who emphasized exchange among the system's complementing parts, slavery in the American South formed part of a larger range of thoroughly capitalist forms of coerced labor systems that contributed minerals and agricultural commodities from the periphery of this world system to its industrializing core in Europe. For others more concerned with specific local class structures, merchant capitalism in Europe allowed masters and other sorts of ruling classes elsewhere to consolidate regimes based on entirely noncapitalist relations of production, including slavery. By the early 1980s, comparisons in this vein were moving logically forward in time to examine local conditions that influenced the labor forms that succeeded slavery in the nineteenth century and that bore more than a passing resemblance in practice to the chattel bondage ended by emancipation of the slaves—tenancy, sharecropping, debt peonage, and recruitment of contract laborers from Asia. From whichever point of view, slavery and postemancipation labor arrangements in the United States were at last losing some of their apparently exceptional qualities and becoming structurally comparable to labor systems elsewhere in the world.

As macrohistorical analyses broadened their comparative scope and embedded slavery in the context of world capitalism, other scholars refined comparisons of specific aspects of slave systems in the United States and the Caribbean. They focused on the one remaining clear distinction in the history of North American slaves: their rapid growth in numbers. Had slaves in the South managed to reproduce because their masters promoted family living and child rearing or because the lactation practices of slave mothers reduced the mortality of their infant offspring? How did the foods that slaves grew on West Indian islands compare to the rations that planters imported for slave labor forces on mainland farms and plantations? Did the common immunological and genetic heritage of Africans affect their chances for survival differently in temperate as opposed to tropical latitudes of the New World? What inferences could be drawn from comparing statistical data on mortality, or heights? The air of scientific objectivity surrounding quasi-medical and scientific studies that compared demographically defined cohorts of slaves, infants, nursing mothers, or malnourished field hands was moving the units of analysis far beyond the nationalities of the masters, or of the historians.

The history of North American slavery has thereby broken decisively through the original stereotype of a peculiarly national dilemma, tinged with racial and other peripheral issues. Formal comparisons of all three main types—(1) historical contrasts with other slave systems in terms of culture, agricultural systems and other occupational categories, or demography and the biological sciences, (2) multilateral testing of general social science propositions and the delineation of general typologies, and (3) insertion of the slave experience in the United States into a changing world economic context—now allow historians to address enslavement itself in the regionally specific and historically changing forms which in fact marked the American past. Comparing the numbers of the slaves among the masters, and in particular the rate of growth in recent arrivals and hence also the proportion of raw African recruits in the slave population, revealed how the basic demography influenced both the lives of the slaves (their ability to reproduce, their propensities to revolt, the balance of African and American elements in the culture they shared) and the severity with which the masters attempted to control the behavior of the misunderstood aliens living among them. The same internal contrasts showed how the sociology of slavery and its varying legal and police environments resembled treatment accorded other numerous and unruly groups of nonslave immigrant workers at later periods of U.S. history. Technological innovations, price changes for American commodities in Europe, delivered costs of alternative forms of labor, and the availability of merchant capital to finance the rapid economic growth that expanding gangs of new slaves made possible—all contributed to the varying rates at which slave populations increased. Slaves and masters in the subtropical colonies of North America (South Carolina in particular), in the tobacco regions of the Chesapeake, and in the cities and occasionally even on the farms of the Middle colonies and New England had distinctly different experiences owing to varying timing and intensity of these factors in each region.

With the spread of cotton cultivation early in the nineteenth century, new regional contrasts of the same sort emerged to divide the old slave-breeding areas near the Chesapeake from newer slave-buying plantation zones in the Cotton Kingdom to the south and west, with tendencies toward urban and industrial slavery emerging in the larger cities of the Old South, and still other innovations in the border states or in antebellum rice- and sugar-producing areas. Long after imports from Africa had declined to a marginal source of dislocated and pliable new laborers, a dynamic slave trade* within the borders of the United States continued to convert settled slaves born in the eastern states into relatively isolated newcomers on recently established cotton plantations. In older areas like Virginia and South Carolina, the institution had acquired overtones of peasantry, hiring out,* and other forms of labor organization suited to acculturated populations of native-born laborers. Thus, lessons applied from the world-systems style of comparison showed not only the diversity of slavery within the South but also its continuing changes and relocation and the extent to which each type depended on the others for its viability.

The logic of comparing slavery had moved from treating the phenomenon as a reified and undifferentiated object of study, largely static and defined at the national level, to a supple and changing dialectic among slaves of varying backgrounds and masters of differing needs and objectives, all of whom lived in much more complicated worlds than the chanceries, or plantations, or concentration camps posited in the first studies of the subject. Comparison now shows that nearly all of the conclusions overstated by the unwieldy early comparisons have turned out to apply to one phase or another of these nuanced slave systems, as they consolidated or broke down, or to apply to one regional or economic context if not some other. Even Elkins's disoriented Sambo had a limited place as emphasizing the helplessness of some isolated and dependent Africans just off the boat, while the objections of Elkins's critics referred even more clearly to the cunning with which assimilated survivors of the first baffling months hid behind a stereotype that played on the inability, or unwillingness, of masters anywhere to accept the humanity, or as Tannenbaum had put it, the "moral personality" of people they insisted on treating as incomprehensible and dangerous aliens in their midst.

The most recent generation of comparisons has also extended the range of comparisons to retest some of the propositions originally drawn in terms of narrow intra-American contrasts. George Fredrickson's *White Supremacy* (1981) qualified Tannenbaum's linkage between colonial slavery and later white racial dominance in a carefully controlled comparison between two contemporaneous northwestern European Protestant frontier settlement societies in the United States and South Africa. While slavery in both instances may have left a general presumption of white mastery over dark-skinned races, North America's greater economic potential allowed a system of racial segregation, however rigid in comparison to Latin America, that was flexible compared to the systematic total separation (apartheid) practiced in South Africa. Orlando Patterson's brilliant and erudite *Slavery and Social Death* (1982) sketched the Old South's conformity to a universal conceptualization of slavery as total denial of honor to uprooted newcomers but noted the unique contradictions of its refusal to allow acculturated native-born antebellum slave populations access to freedom through manumission as masters nearly everywhere else had done. Eric Foner (*Nothing But Freedom*, 1983) added the colonial experience of southern and eastern Africa to American examples of the transition from slavery to subsequent forms of labor organization. The comparison revealed the general weakness imposed on former slaves lacking access to credit in a modern capitalist economy, but it also emphasized the distinctive strength that U.S. freedpeople gained from even the ephemeral franchise they were given.

One new bilateral contrast, between slaves in the antebellum South and the slave-like serfs of contemporaneous Muscovy, held up still another mirror in which to view the image of U.S. slavery. Taking its departure from the issues of demography and community developed in earlier comparisons, but focusing clearly on the sociology of labor systems by framing the contrast at a level that transcended the distracting factor of race, the American-Russian comparison suggested that the dispersal of North American slaves among numerous small holdings, often as a minority among their masters, hindered the development of an autonomous slave culture and promoted greater economic dependence than experienced by the huge populations of serfs on the estates of absentee Russian landowners. This contrast assessed the damage done by the peculiarities of slavery in the United States in cultural terms reminiscent of the Herskovitses.

Comparisons, broadened by a growing range of linguistic and methodological skills and reaching into new times and places, continue to reveal additional aspects of slavery in the United States with a power as undiminished after forty years of creative application as American exceptionalism remains a resilient strain in the national historiography.

SELECTED BIBLIOGRAPHY

Ira Berlin, "Time, Space, and the Evolution of Afro-American Society in British Mainland North America," *American Historical Review*, 85 (1980), 44–78; Philip D. Curtin, *The Atlantic Slave Trade: A Census* (1969); Carl N. Degler, *Neither Black nor White: Slavery and Race Relations in Brazil and the United States* (1971); Stanley M. Elkins, *Slavery: A Problem in American Institutional and Intellectual Life* (1959, rev. eds., 1968, 1976); Laura Foner and Eugene D. Genovese, eds., *Slavery in the New World: A Reader in Comparative History* (1969); Eugene D. Genovese, *The World the Slaveholders Made: Two Essays in Interpretation* (1969); Orlando Patterson, *Slavery and Social Death: A Comparative Study* (1982); and Frank Tannenbaum, *Slave and Citizen: The Negro in the Americas* (1946).

JOSEPH C. MILLER

COMPROMISE OF 1850. The Compromise of 1850 was a congressional attempt to settle the issue of slavery in the territories—an issue agitated ceaselessly since the introduction of the Wilmot Proviso in 1846. By the time the Thirty-first Congress convened in December 1849, many observers believed that civil war was possible, even imminent. Asserting leadership among politicians anxious to preserve the Union, Henry Clay* put forward a legislative settlement of outstanding sectional grievances. He successfully imposed an agenda on Congress, and his "amicable arrangement" was eventually embodied in five laws. Collectively they provided for admission of California as a free state, organization of Utah and New Mexico as territories, adjustment of the boundary between Texas and New Mexico coupled with partial federal assumption of Texas's public debt, a new fugitive slave act,* and suppression of interstate slave trading based in the District of Columbia.

The failure of the compromise to solve the issues it addressed was foreshadowed by the parliamentary maneuvers necessary to enact it. When combined into a single package the compromise was rejected; in the end each component was passed by a different coalition of supporters. The territorial provisions on Utah and New Mexico were acceptable to a majority in Congress only because the question of slavery's legality in the territories was ultimately reserved for judicial decision. Federal action against the slave trade,* however limited, was taken as a fearful precedent by Southern fireaters, who called for disunion in defense of slavery. Obversely, enforcement of the fugitive slave act outraged abolitionists* and produced thousands of new converts to the antislavery cause.

SELECTED BIBLIOGRAPHY

Stanley W. Campbell, *The Slave Catchers: Enforcement of the Fugitive Slave Law, 1850–1860* (1968); Larry Gara, *The Liberty Line: The Legend of the Underground Railroad* (1961); Holman Hamilton, *Prologue to Conflict: The Crisis and Compromise of 1850* (1964); Thomas D. Morris, *Free Men All: The Personal Liberty Laws of the North, 1780–1861* (1974); David M. Potter, *The Impending Crisis, 1848–1861* (1976); Robert R. Russel, "Constitutional Doctrines with Regard to Slavery in the Territories," *Journal of Southern History*, 32 (1966), 466–486; and Robert R. Russel, "What Was the Compromise of 1850?" *Journal of Southern History*, 22 (1956), 292–309.

JOHN D. BARNWELL

CONFEDERACY, SLAVERY IN THE. During the brief life of the Confederate States of America, 1861–1865, white Southerners fought a desperate and eventually disastrous war for what they perceived as their "way of life." Certainly Afro-American slavery was a crucial component in that way of life. Indeed, in 1861 Vice President Alexander H. Stephens pronounced slavery the Confederate "cornerstone." During the Confederate period, most white Southerners hoped that nothing would disturb the slave status quo. They feared the demise of the slave system—as a result of the Republican administration in the United States or through slave insurrections within the Confederate States.

Black Southerners, on the other hand, hoped the Confederacy and its war with the Union would end in freedom. They did not rise in massive rebellion as many whites feared they would. But neither did they remain passive. Whenever possible, the Afro-American slaves fled their masters and sought refuge within federal battle lines. Ultimately about 180,000 black men fought for freedom as Union soldiers.

Initially, however, the slave population in the Southern states made a significant contribution to the Confederate war effort. Because a black labor force existed on Southern farms and plantations, white Southerners joined the Confederate armies in large numbers without sacrificing productive capacity. So the slaveholders marched off to war, and in theory at least, their land did not lie fallow.

Perhaps of even greater significance was the contribution of industrial slavery*
to the Confederate war. The antebellum South had a very small base from which
to conduct what became an industrial war. Nevertheless, slaves composed an
important portion of the labor force, skilled and unskilled, in Southern mills and
factories. And when the demands of wartime provoked expansion in both private
and public sectors of the Southern industrial economy, slaves provided much of
the labor. In Selma, Alabama, for example, 310 of 400 workers at the Confederate navy's ordnance works were black.

At the beginning of the war, some free black men from New Orleans formed
a regiment, the "Native Guards," and notified the Confederate secretary of war
that they were ready to fight for the South. The Confederate government declined
the offer, however, and the "Native Guards" ultimately fought for the Union.
At issue here was the concept of war and military service as an exalted expression
of manhood. Most Southern whites were committed to notions of black racial
inferiority and justified slavery itself on that basis. If they admitted Afro-American slaves into the fraternity of warriors, they also admitted that black manhood
was equal to white manhood. And this they were loath to do.

Southern slaves did march off to war, though, albeit in technically noncombatant roles. Many officers and a few enlisted soldiers in Confederate armies
took body servants with them to military camps. These men performed chores
for their masters. They cooked, cleaned, polished, groomed horses, and generally
made military life easier for the men they served by doing more than the duties
of enlisted orderlies in the Union armies. Some Southern officers employed
talented slaves as entertainers. General J.E.B. Stuart, for example, enlivened
his headquarters with black men who danced and played the fiddle and banjo.
Body servants also went into battle with their masters. Some of these slaves
even became combatants when circumstances demanded it.

Although the Confederates did not sanction active black participation in the
war, the Richmond government did employ slaves in many facets of the war
effort. For example, black men served as nurses, often more than half the staff,
in government hospitals. They drove supply wagons and ambulances and served
as cooks for Southern troops. The Confederate War Department had the authority
to impress (arbitrarily seize) as many as 20,000 slaves to fill its needs for laborers.
Most often Southern armies used black labor to construct earthen fortifications
around cities and on critical military terrain (rivers, harbors, and railroads). From
time to time, state and municipal governments borrowed, hired, or impressed
slaves to work on forts and defense lines which lay in the anticipated path of
federal invasion. In some cases these governments hired slaves from their masters; at other times they "borrowed" laborers; and they also impressed slaves
from their owners. There was more than some irony in the fact that a government
formed to protect the sanctity of property in slaves resorted to the confiscation
of slaves in order to protect itself.

An irony more crucial was the significant contribution of slaves to the war
cause of the slaveholders. Yet the very existence of the South's peculiar institution

limited the Confederacy's military options and, to an extent, conditioned Southern strategy. The Richmond government believed, with reason, that it had to protect as much Southern soil as possible in order to protect the slave-plantation system which occupied that soil. The system by definition required land area; consequently, the Confederate high command had to adopt a strategic posture which disturbed as little land area as possible. Initially, Jefferson Davis and his generals attempted to fortify frontiers and defend every square inch of Southern soil. When, during the first year of the war, this policy proved to be folly, the Confederacy developed a strategy of offensive defense (allowing the enemy to penetrate Southern land area and then, at an opportune moment, attacking and destroying the invaders). But because of slavery, there had to be limits to the amount of land area the Confederates would surrender while seeking the moment to attack. And as long as slavery was a vital element in the Southern way of life, the Confederates could never wage a full-scale guerrilla war in which control of land area was not a factor. The slave system required absolute control of Southern farms and plantations by slaveholders.

Slavery also conditioned Confederate military thinking, because the maintenance of a large captive population required a large emphasis upon internal security. Surely the Davis government resorted to the imposition of martial law so early and so often during the war in part because of the necessity to ensure the home front against slave insurrections. And every Southern soldier stationed behind the battle lines was one less available to face the federals.

When the Richmond government imposed conscription upon the Southern people, slavery and its internal security played no small part in the policy adopted by the Confederate Congress. Among the categories of people exempted from liability for military service were those men who oversaw or owned a prescribed number (eventually twenty) of slaves. Although the number of men excused from the draft on this basis was relatively small, the exemption policy provoked conflict within the broad Southern white population. The so-called Twenty Negro Law offended many in the South's nonslaveholding majority, divided people and classes, and encouraged the idea that this was a "rich man's war and a poor man's fight."

It should not be too surprising that slaves and slavery should play roles in the nature and extent of the Confederate war for national survival. What is often overlooked, however, is the impact of the Confederate experience upon the slave system and slaves themselves. To the degree that slavery was, at base, a relationship between master and slave, the war worked to upset that essential relationship. In vital ways the Confederate experience challenged the stability of the slave system and generated considerable ferment among both slaves and slaveholders.

When a master, for example, left his farm or plantation to join the Southern army, he left behind his slaves. Someone—a wife, teenaged son, aging family member, or hired overseer—ostensibly assumed the role of master. But the new arrangement did not always work. And the effect of this was to subtract the master from the master-slave relationship.* Very seldom did the slaves launch any open revolt.* But the results of fundamental strains in the slave system manifested themselves nonetheless.

Similar strains upon the system, and especially the master-slave relationship, occurred when federal troops threatened to occupy the region in which master and slave lived. In these circumstances slaveholders usually moved their slaves to some safer locale—another plantation or the home of a relative. Such flights, known at the time as "refugeeing," produced disruptions in the master-slave relationship and also offered slaves the unflattering view of the master class in disarray.

One way in which absent masters or masters in flight tried to cope with what in effect was an excess of slaves during wartime was to hire* them out. Renting slaves to someone or some institution that required more laborers seemed a sensible solution to a slaveholder who had to abandon his plantation or who chose to curtail his planting while he performed military duties. Yet hiring out on any sizable scale also added stresses in the system. The slave left a stable situation and entered a fluid environment that might involve multiple or institutional masters as well as transient quarters.

Wartime tended to swell the size of Southern cities as centers of manufacturing, transportation, hospitals, and troop concentrations. Slaves composed a significant portion of this increase in urban population, and to this extent they increased the volatility in their lives. Many urban slaves* "lived-out"—in shanties or predominantly black sectors of town. They remained slaves; but they were often free to find housing and food for themselves and were given an allowance with which to pay for their maintenance. Urban slaves could achieve anonymity if they lived out and to some extent if they hired out. As a consequence, cities and towns passed "Negro Ordinances" in an effort to act as surrogate masters for their black populations. Such regulations (many of which applied to free as well as bonded black people) regulated conduct, limited assembly, and imposed curfews. The fact of these laws, rules, and ordinances indicates some degree of anxiety on the part of white Southern city-dwellers. And these fears were well-founded. Within the urban Confederacy, slaves often lived beyond the observation and control of their masters. Such slaves were much less likely to act like slaves than their brothers and sisters who lived in a stable, rural environment.

Certainly slaves who were impressed for government work for any length of time shared the unsettling experiences of those whose masters transported them, hired them out, or allowed them to live out. In essence, the slaveholders asked their bondsmen to act more like slaves at the same time that they, the masters, were acting less like traditional masters.

It is impossible to calculate with precision the results of these rifts in the master-slave relationship. Ample evidence exists, however, of ferment and friction within the slave system of the Confederate South.

In letters and diaries white Southerners complained of shiftlessness, neglect, arrogance, and hostility on the part of their slaves. What the whites interpreted in these pejorative ways was the response of slaves learning to be less servile. Amid the instability of wartime, Afro-Americans began to act out varying degrees of freedom, even while they were still slaves. They embraced Unionist invaders even though some whites tried to make them believe that Yankees were monsters. They assisted fellow slaves in escape attempts. They ignored rules and orders even at the cost of punishment and reduced rations. They abused livestock* and slowed down planting, cultivating, and harvesting.

Examples abound of black behavior that white Southerners described as "treacherous" or "ungrateful," but which was more accurately assertive or independent. The instability of wartime with attendant privation all but compelled many slaves to begin to think for and of themselves and their families. So, by 1864, slavery was a very sick institution, one in many ways undermined by the war fought to save it. And the slaves themselves were a major part in the process.

White Confederates, too, played an ironic role in the decline and demise of the South's peculiar institution. As the war wore on and hopes of victory dimmed, many white Southerners became collectively introspective. By 1863 Confederate church leaders were preaching that military reverses and wartime adversity were God's ways of testing the people, calling white Christians to repentance, and challenging them to virtue. And prominent among the sins that the clerics denounced was the failure of slaveholders to behave as proper masters toward their slaves. Consequently, the church, which had traditionally supported slaveholding in the South, began preaching reform to the slaveholders.

The reformers asked that masters not separate slave mothers and children by sale, that slave testimony be potentially valid evidence in courts of law, and that the law sanction religious gatherings among slaves. Neither the Confederate Congress nor state legislatures enacted these reform measures, however. Georgia did authorize black men to receive licenses to preach, and Alabama required slaveholders to provide legal counsel for slaves indicted for criminal offenses. But otherwise the clamor for reform of the slave system remained merely the cries of a relatively few Southern whites.

However, as Confederate military fortunes continued to fail, more and more pragmatic white Southerners began to contemplate changes in the slave system more radical than even the reformers proposed. They considered using slaves as Confederate soldiers, and such considerations compelled them to confront the prospect of massive emancipation.

Early in January of 1864, Confederate General Patrick R. Cleburne offered a written argument for the employment of black troops to the officer corps of the Army of Tennessee. Cleburne contended that the South had mobilized about as many white men as possible and still faced heavier enemy battalions. Thus the time had come to tap the last source of soldiers available to the Confederacy— black men. Cleburne proposed that the War Department organize and arm male slaves in large numbers and that these men receive freedom in exchange for faithful military service. "Cleburne's Memorial," as the paper was known, received a mixed reaction from his fellow officers, and Jefferson Davis himself ordered the document and attendant debate squelched.

As Confederate armies encountered repeated defeats during the campaigns of 1864, Cleburne's idea resurfaced in several places. In September Governor Henry W. Allen of Louisiana wrote, "The time has come for us to put into the army every able-bodied negro man as a soldier." In October the governors of North Carolina, South Carolina, Georgia, Alabama, and Mississippi met in conference and adopted a resolution in favor of using black troops. In November President Davis greeted a new session of the Confederate Congress with a request for authority and funds to purchase 40,000 slaves for noncombatant military tasks. And, in what Davis admitted was a "radical modification," the president proposed freedom for these men upon satisfactory completion of their service. This amounted to compensated emancipation for at least 40,000 Afro-Americans. About the prospect of black troops, Davis stated, "Should the alternative ever be presented of subjugation or of the employment of the slave as a soldier, there seems no reason to doubt what should then be our decision."

Of course, by November 1864, the Confederacy was staring "subjugation" squarely in the face, and many Southern whites were ready to arm the slaves. Yet many, perhaps the majority, of white Southerners, preferred defeat to the radical social changes that arming the slaves entailed. In press, pulpits, and political forums during the waning months of 1864 and early 1865, white Confederates debated the question of resorting to black soldiers.

Although they argued about a military expedient, the issue ultimately centered on emancipation, and most Confederates knew it. Georgia politician Howell Cobb opposed arming slaves. "The day you make soldiers of them," he wrote, "is the beginning of the end of the revolution. If slaves will make good soldiers our whole theory of slavery is wrong." However wrong Cobb's racial assumptions were, he saw clearly the implications of arming the slaves. Once white Southerners admitted that black men were capable of being soldiers, they could never logically claim that those black soldiers were less than men.

The debate attracted spirited editorial exchanges in Southern newspapers. The Confederate press, like Howell Cobb, grasped the fundamental questions at issue. In Jackson, Mississippi, the *News* called slavery "the chief object of this war" and asked "why fight one moment longer, if the object and occasion of the fight is dying, dead, or damned?" But the *Mississippian*, published in the same city, stated, "Let not slavery prove a barrier to our independence. If it is found in the way—if it proves an insurmountable object of the achievement of our liberty and separate nationality, away with it! Let it perish!"

When the Confederate Congress carried on a protracted wrangle over an administration bill to arm slaves (and eventually free those armed), the military, too, entered the debate. Officers and entire units in Southern armies wrote open letters to senators and congressmen, usually in support of employing black troops.

Finally General Robert E. Lee made public his enthusiasm for arming and freeing the slaves. Still Congress delayed, while the war went very badly.

At long last, on 13 March 1865, the Confederate Congress authorized the Davis administration to recruit as many as 300,000 black men for Confederate armies. However, this radical act concluded with a reactionary clause: "nothing in this act shall be construed to authorize a change in the relation which the said slaves shall bear toward their owners." The Davis War Department, though, countered with regulations implementing the law that required all black recruits to be free men as a condition of their service. Other army regulations prescribed "provident, considerate, and humane" treatment for black troops and protection from "injustice and oppression." By late March a company of black Confederate soldiers was drilling on Capitol Square in Richmond.

Also in late March, Davis sent Louisiana politician Duncan F. Kenner on a mission to London and Paris. Kenner offered, in the name of the Confederate government, to emancipate all Southern slaves if Britain and France would recognize the Confederacy.

All of this was too little too late to influence the outcome of the war. Richmond fell within a week of the first formation of black troops in the Confederate capital, and the Kenner mission came to naught. Yet the white Confederates who seemed so willing, even eager, to undo the slave system spoke and acted for the nation supposedly founded to protect the status quo in regard to slavery. That they waited until their war was all but lost, and perhaps did not represent the sentiments of the majority of Southern whites, is some measure of their fatal attachment to a heinous institution. That they acted at all is a measure of their capacity to respond to the desperate demands of a war for national survival.

Confederate slaves responded to wartime, too, albeit in ways even less clearly defined than the response of white Southerners. The war unsettled their lives and strained the institution which bound them as chattels. On a farm in Georgia in 1863, a slave named Willes assumed leadership of the black work force and answered the orders of the teenaged white boy who was supposedly in charge, "What's the matter with you? What the reason you can't do it?" And soon after the war ended, a freedman informed his former master, "When you'all had de power you was good to me, and I'll protect you now. No niggers nor Yankees, shall touch you. If you want anything, call for Sambo. I mean, call for Mr. Samuel—that's my name now." Willes and Mr. Samuel expressed themselves in different ways. But they both spoke to freedom.

SELECTED BIBLIOGRAPHY

Robert F. Durden, *The Gray and the Black: The Confederate Debate on Emancipation* (1972); Eugene D. Genovese, *Roll, Jordan, Roll: The World the Slaves Made* (1974); Leon F. Litwack, *Been in the Storm So Long: The Aftermath of Slavery* (1979); Clarence L. Mohr, *On the Threshold of Freedom: Masters and Slaves in Civil War Georgia* (1986);

Emory M. Thomas, *The Confederate Nation, 1861–1865* (1979); and Bell I. Wiley, *Southern Negroes, 1861–1865* (1938).

EMORY M. THOMAS

CONGREGATIONAL CHURCH. Congregationalism came to America with the Pilgrims and dominated religious life in New England. The Reformation and the turmoils of the sixteenth and seventeenth centuries in England established Congregationalism's foundations—a Calvinistic theology, and a polity based upon the independence of the local congregation. Before 1871, when a National Council was first organized, individual Congregationalist churches were held together by associations or conferences, or by common support of missionary societies.

Several churches with a "New England polity and theology" were established in the Old South. But of the dozen such churches, all but two failed, suffering extinction, or converting to Presbyterianism during the days of the Plan of Union, 1801–1852. One of these surviving Congregational churches, Circular Church in Charleston, South Carolina, was founded in 1691. The other, Midway Church in Liberty County, Georgia, was established in 1752.

Both of these churches played significant roles in Southern history. Circular Church was the first non-Anglican congregation in Charleston, and frequently drew its ministers from New England. Circular Church had a number of black members, both slaves and free Negroes. They participated in most church activities, including singing, reading from the scripture, and even exhorting. Blacks, however, could not preach.

Midway Church, in rural Liberty County, was located thirty miles from Savannah. From its very origins, this church had an overwhelming majority of black members. When the large frame building was built to house the congregation, an ample balcony was provided for the church's black members. The Reverend Charles Colcock Jones* led Midway Church's efforts to bring religion to the slaves. Jones established the Liberty County Association for Religious Instruction, a massive mission* between 1830 and 1848 that preached the Gospel to the bondsmen. Yet Jones was ever careful to train slaves in a creed that bolstered, not threatened, the peculiar institution. Jones reached 4,500 slaves on over one hundred plantations. He organized them into eight Sunday schools, each led by black "Watchmen" trained in the catechism which Jones himself had developed. Although the Civil War decimated Midway Church, several black churches, two of them Congregational, resulted from the breakup of the old Midway community.

Congregationalism also took another form in the antebellum South. The denomination was influenced strongly by abolitionists* at Oberlin College, whose disciples carried their antislavery message into Missouri and Kentucky. Financed by the American Missionary Association,* in the 1840s and 1850s antislavery missionaries penetrated Missouri as well as Kentucky. They established antislavery churches that welcomed blacks on an equal basis with whites, and were essentially Congregational in polity and theology. In 1855 the Reverend John G. Fee founded Kentucky's Berea College, dedicated to antislavery ideology and biracial education.

SELECTED BIBLIOGRAPHY

Gaius Glenn Atkins and Frederick L. Fagley, *History of American Congregationalism* (1942); Erskine Clarke, *Wrestlin' Jacob: A Portrait of Religion in the Old South* (1979); Clifton H. Johnson, "The American Missionary Association, 1846–1861: A Study of Christian Abolitionism" (Ph.D. dissertation, University of North Carolina, 1959); Robert Manson Myers, ed., *The Children of Pride: A True Story of Georgia and the Civil War* (1972); Elisabeth S. Peck, *Berea's First Century, 1855–1955* (1955); and James Stacey, *History of Midway Congregational Church, Liberty County, Georgia* (1899).

RICHARD B. DRAKE

CONTRABAND CAMPS. Eager to encourage slave defections from the Confederacy,* but initially uncertain about the status of slaves under federal control, Union forces sanctioned the confiscation of fugitive and refugee slaves as "contraband of war." General Benjamin F. Butler first applied the term *contraband* to slaves confiscated at Fortress Monroe, Virginia, in May 1861. Wherever Union armies occupied Southern territory, contraband camps offered escaping and displaced slaves refuge and relief, and provided protection from masters and from rebel forces. By 1865, approximately one million blacks—a quarter of the 1860 slave population—lived within Union lines and more than two hundred thousand (in addition to an equal number of black soldiers) lived and labored under direct U.S. Army control. Contraband laborers raised fortifications, constructed roads, built railroads, and repaired levees. In the Mississippi Valley, General Ulysses S. Grant located contraband camps from New Madrid, Missouri, to Millikin's Bend, Louisiana, to supply cordwood for the Union gunboats, troop carriers, and supply ships engaged in the campaign against Vicksburg. During the last year of the war, Grant similarly assembled hundreds of contraband laborers at City Point, Virginia, as stevedores supplying federal forces (including black troops) during the siege of Petersburg. From Virginia to Louisiana, from Nashville to New Orleans, contraband camps accompanied the advance of Union arms and contraband labor hastened Union victory.

Like all military encampments of their day, contraband camps raised serious problems of administration, especially regarding sanitation and disease. Considerations of public health as well as fears of civil disturbances encouraged federal authorities to isolate contrabands from towns and cities and, in the absence of military need, to disperse the contraband population from the camps to the countryside as quickly as circumstances permitted. Most camps functioned in part as labor depots supplying contract labor to loyal planters and to Northern lessees of abandoned lands. Unemployed contrabands (including the aged and infirm and thousands of women and children) lived as wards of the federal government on contraband farms. Several hundred contrabands, notably in the

Vicksburg district, left the camps as independent farmers leasing five to forty acres of abandoned lands from the Treasury Department. Guerrilla attacks against loyal planters and freedmen farmers produced fresh waves of black refugees, however, and Union advances added to their number. Not until the last months of the war did federal authorities succeed in closing the contraband camps.

Life in the camps varied with the vicissitudes of war, with the character of the contraband populations, and with shifting federal policies regarding land reform and wage labor. At Port Royal, South Carolina, and at Davis Bend, Mississippi, antebellum slave communities remained intact within areas of secure federal control. Here, the administration of federal land and labor policies revealed the optimism of Northern free labor principles as well as their uncertain application to the Southern freedmen.* Here, too, with contraband slaves occupying land abandoned by their masters, the freedmen's responses to free labor "experiments," particularly their tenacious hold on the land, revealed concerns at variance with the stated goals of the Lincoln administration.

Divided administrative responsibility for contraband affairs compounded the uncertainties of federal policy. While the Treasury Department administered abandoned lands and contraband labor, the U.S. Army controlled the contraband camps. Treasury agents sought able-bodied laborers to raise cotton on abandoned plantations. Union officers employed contrabands on military projects and, after the issuance of the Emancipation Proclamation, enlisted thousands more as soldiers. In March 1865, the Bureau of Refugees, Freedmen, and Abandoned Lands (the Freedmen's Bureau*) became an independent agency within the War Department. This resolved administrative rivalry and recognized the army's primary responsibility in the administration of freedmen policies.

Throughout the South, contraband camps provided a focus for a massive infusion of Northern humanitarian sentiments and free labor values. Eager to bring material aid, education, and moral guidance to the former slaves, scores of relief societies emerged in the North to send supplies to the camps and to sponsor black and white missionaries among the contrabands. Out of these efforts emerged the earliest Negro schools and colleges in the South and much of the impetus for future civil rights struggles. Eager not to promote idleness or dependency among the former slaves, Northern philanthropists also encouraged federal authorities to move resolutely to close the contraband camps and farms at the end of the war. Although the freedmen resisted the return to plantation labor and pressed where possible for independence as self-sufficient producers, the closing of the contraband camps coincided with the collapse of leasing arrangements and land reform. Federal policy regarding the freedmen smoothed the way for the restoration of plantation production and the rise of the postwar sharecropping system.

SELECTED BIBLIOGRAPHY

Ira Berlin et al., eds., *Freedom: A Documentary History of Emancipation, 1861–1867* (2 vols. to date, 1982-); James T. Currie, *Enclave: Vicksburg and Her Plantations, 1863–*

1870 (1980); Louis S. Gerteis, *From Contraband to Freedman: Federal Policy toward Southern Blacks, 1861–1865* (1973); Willie Lee Rose, *Rehearsal for Reconstruction: The Port Royal Experiment* (1964); Steven Joseph Ross, "Freed Soil, Freed Labor, Freed Men: John Eaton and the Davis Bend Experiment," *Journal of Southern History*, 44 (1978), 213–232; Cam Walker, "Corinth: The Story of a Contraband Camp," *Civil War History*, 20 (1974), 5–22; and Bell I. Wiley, *Southern Negroes, 1861–1865* (1938).

LOUIS S. GERTEIS

CORN. The army of Afro-American slaves marched to and from its fields of labor on corn-fed stomachs. Maize, or Indian corn, was the primary food base from the earliest years of American slavery to abolition. It served directly as sustenance in many forms and indirectly as the principal feed crop for the production of animal and poultry products that the slaves consumed. But this versatile grain was far more than an energy base for the slaves' production of cash crops such as cotton,* tobacco,* rice,* and indigo.* It met a multitude of nonfood needs, and contributed significantly to slave culture, recreation, and preparation for eventual economic freedom.

A given number of laborers could raise far more cotton than they could harvest. Thus corn, which was planted either before or after cotton and harvested as long as necessary after cotton picking, was compatible with cash crop production. It was also indispensable to the feeding of humans and domestic animals throughout the South. Corn acreage exceeded that of any other crop in the slave era. Unlike the cash crops, it was both a field and home garden commodity. And because of lack of any measurement of the garden-grown increment, its production has been much underestimated and ignored.

Working from dawn until dark, slaves were intensively involved in every phase of corn culture. Both on undeveloped parts of established plantations and in frontier areas, they followed practices adopted from the Indians: girdling trees to bring new acres into production, cropping the seed in holes poked with sharpened sticks, and chopping weeds and "hilling up" the corn plants with crude hoes. After the first year's crop was in, slaves cleared the deadened trees from the new ground for future years of cultivation.

By the eighteenth and nineteenth centuries, improved plows and harrows changed and mechanized the ways slaves prepared the seedbed, but planting remained primitive into the late nineteenth century. Despite the development of wheeled and animal-drawn mechanical planters, slaves for the most part dug holes with the hoe, "drapped" corn by hand, and covered by hoe. A major reason for the tenacity of the primitive method of planting was its suitability to the abundance of women* and child labor. Except for some of the heavy plowing, female slaves and, to a considerable extent, children* performed much the same corn work as did men, from planting and early thinning and cultivating to harvesting, shelling, grinding, and cooking.

The use of the double shovel and other animal-drawn cultivators largely banished the hoe from many of the country's corn fields, but hoeing persisted widely where gangs* of slaves were available. The workers were expected to keep pace with the driver,* bending, chopping weeds, mulching, and hilling through each field—three and sometimes four times during the growing season until the corn was "laid by," or left to mature on its own. But still other corn work remained. Insects, birds, wild and domestic animals, and sometimes human thieves were interested in harvesting corn from the day of planting to the final act of consuming. Slaves, particularly women, children, and the elderly, were habitually assigned the chore of fending off the crop's enemies by shouting, waving, calling dogs, or using a variety of noisemakers. Owing to fear of insurrections, however, planters generally did not permit the slaves to use the most effective firearms to drive off or kill the corn "thieves."

Slaves engaged in all stages of the corn harvest. They picked baby ears for eating, and tore off many ears at the green or roasting-ear stage for immediate consumption or for parching and preserving. Because of its layered, weather-resistant husk, mature corn was the most flexible of all crops in terms of scheduling the harvest. It could be "hogged down," or left standing in the field, cut and shocked in the field (a practice widely followed after the 1780s), or hauled to the barn or corn crib and stored in the husk until cotton, wheat, turnips, potatoes, and other more vulnerable crops were safely harvested and stored. Shucking time could be any time when other work was slack.

By a wide margin, the most frequently mentioned form of corn-related activity in slave accounts was the "shucking," or husking frolic. It combined work and play and was one of the most common and popular kinds of recreation* in America during the slave era. The shucking bee was a harvest festival at each farm or plantation. Each slave might attend many such work frolics each autumn. The activity involved competitive work—singing, feasting, dancing*—and the consuming of corn liquor or cider from the jug at the bottom of each corn pile. Blacks and whites commonly participated together in the shucking contests, and some slaves recalled that the "patterolers" (slave patrollers) did not bother them at such gatherings. But shucking was by no means all play. It was drudgery, especially hard on the hands, despite the universal use of an old and simple Indian device, the shucking peg, throughout the slave era. Husking was often done indoors on rainy days in order to get more work from slaves.

Just as the hard, mature corn could be kept indefinitely before shucking, it could be stored for long periods in carefully roofed and well-aerated cribs before shelling and grinding. Shelling by hand with the aid of a piece of iron or a corn cob was typical until after the first third of the nineteenth century. Then the hand-cranked mechanical sheller spread with unparalleled swiftness throughout the farm country. A sizable part of the slaves' toil was thus made easier, freeing them for other tasks.

Grinding, like shelling, was a job commonly performed by slaves, who often accomplished this task with primitive hand tools. These included the gritter (or grater) for semihard kernels, stone or wood mortar and pestle, and quern. Another implement, the hominy block, a hollowed stump under a suspended wood plunger, could be heard pounding over such distances that planters feared the slaves would use it to signal one another (in the absence of drums, which were banned). Owners of large plantations often built animal- or water-powered mills for grinding their own grain and that of neighboring farmers. It was customary to send a slave boy to the mill with corn to be ground on a "shares" basis.

Approximately half of the South's corn crop was consumed by humans. Each person ate an estimated two pounds of corn daily, or thirteen bushels annually. A typical food ration given to each slave was one peck of corn meal and three or four pounds of meat per week. Field-workers often received, in addition, an ear of green corn at midday. Unlike cotton choppers and pickers, workers in fields of immature corn were able to eat unnoticed on the job. At the barn or house, masters suspecting their slaves of stealing from the corn meal barrel would write on the meal with their fingers, and the slaves, deliberately kept in an illiterate state, could not duplicate the writing.

Of the many references to food in the slave narratives,* corn was clearly the main item, the common denominator. Slaves prepared and ate the full range of corn foods of the era—hominy grits, roasting ears, dodgers, corn bread, hoe cake, fritters, mush, parched corn, porridge, pone, spoon bread, pudding, succotash, "Hoppin' John" (corn with peas), ash cake, coosh-coosh, popcorn, and batter for frying fish and alligator tails. Because many families had only one cooking pot, corn was commonly cooked together with other vegetables and meat. Much of the meat and animal products (pork, beef, poultry, eggs, milk, and butter), which comprised an important part of slave diets, was produced by corn, since it also served as the principal crop fed to livestock. Corn was long blamed for the high incidence of pellagra in the South, but the cause was lack of foods containing niacin, or vitamin B.

Corn supplied the slaves with much more than mere food. It provided whiskey, which served both as a drink and as the almost universal home medicine. Remedies for hives, fever, and other ailments were fashioned from steeping the shucks to produce tea. Shredded corn shucks afforded the most common paddings for horse collars and slaves' mattresses. Corn cobs became smoking pipe bowls, corn shellers, handles for files and other tools, fishing corks, litter, back scratchers, imitation baking soda, substitutes for hickory in smoking meat and, above all, kindling and fuel. There were countless other nonfood uses of corn as well.

Indian corn, then, constituted a prime ingredient in the culture of the slaves, a major element in their work, sustenance, and recreation. The bondsmen, women, and children played numerous corn games, sang corn songs, and hid in shocks or among corn rows to escape from masters or to make love. They engaged in friendly corncob fights or hunted wild game in the corn fields. Corn also was an economic bridge to freedom. In order to cut costs, many planters allocated plots of land to the slaves so that the latter could grow their own corn between plantation tasks and on Sundays. More than their experiences with cotton and tobacco, the slaves' intimate familiarity with corn production provided, however unintentionally, their essential schooling for survival as freed men and women.

SELECTED BIBLIOGRAPHY

Lewis C. Gray, *History of Agriculture in the Southern United States to 1860* (2 vols., 1933); Nicholas P. Hardeman, *Shucks, Shocks, and Hominy Blocks: Corn as a Way of Life in Pioneer America* (1981); Sam B. Hilliard, *Hog Meat and Hoe Cake: Food Supply in the Old South, 1840–1860* (1972); George P. Rawick, ed., *The American Slave: A Composite Autobiography* (19 vols., 1972); and Joe Gray Taylor, *Eating, Drinking, and Visiting in the South: An Informal History* (1982).

                                                                                    NICHOLAS P. HARDEMAN

COTTON. Sea-island cotton entered the American South from the Bahamas near the end of the American Revolution. Its production was confined to a small area along the southeastern coast. Its smooth black seed did not adhere to the lint so that cleaning presented no problem. Another type of cotton, known as "green seed cotton," had a much shorter staple than sea island, but since it had the ability to thrive in the up-country, it became known as upland cotton. Because of the tenacity with which the lint adhered to the seed, it could be separated only by laborious hand-cleaning. Thus the short-staple variety achieved no commercial importance until after 1793, when Eli Whitney invented the mechanical gin.*

The rapid expansion of upland cotton soon brought complete eclipse to the commercial importance of the sea-island variety. While the latter continued to be grown throughout the antebellum period, when it sold for four times as much as the short-staple upland cotton, its restricted area of production made it non-competitive in the world market.

The invention of the cotton gin was soon followed by the opening of vast areas of rich cotton lands throughout the lower South. Thus occurred a rapid development of the Cotton Kingdom where labor was exceedingly scarce in proportion to the vast wilderness which beckoned prospective growers. In Missouri and Florida cotton growing made slight headway, and in Virginia and Kentucky practically none at all. The expansion of cotton production continued throughout the antebellum era. In 1850 almost 2.5 million bales of 400 pounds each were produced. This figure had more than doubled by the beginning of the Civil War.

The growth of cotton production revitalized the faltering slave economy and fixed its significance in Southern culture. In 1860 there were approximately 400,000 slave owners in the South, the majority of whom owned five or fewer slaves. Roughly three-fourths of the white population owned no slaves at all. Slaveless farmers as well as small slaveholders produced great quantities of cotton, and both groups joined planters to defend the institution of slavery against abolitionist attacks.

Of the 2.5 million slaves of all ages employed in agriculture in 1860, only 1,815,000 were in cotton production, and these slaves also produced considerable quantities of corn* and other foodstuffs. Corn was the only grain crop that was coexistent with cotton, but its overcover and the hilly land on which much of it was grown prevented close supervision of laborers.

Indeed, maximum effort by slaves was seldom achieved even under the most favorable circumstances. Understandably, the slave was adept at killing time and was quick to take advantage of any opportunity to do so. In an effort to speed up the slave's work, overseers* and drivers* often attempted to force fast-tempo songs on the slave, but the slave successfully resisted such hastening devices. The Negro spiritual may have had its origin here, where the slow tempo and dreamy lilt of the blacks' own work song added an element of eternal poetry to such lowly tasks as hoeing cotton.

Soil exhaustion and erosion ran like a thread throughout the history of slavery in the South. These problems were largely inherent in the combination of cheap and abundant land with scarce and expensive labor. The absence of cover crops and animal manure further compounded the problems of soil management. Throughout the cotton South soil was sacrificed in the interest of conserving labor.

While slavery was fundamentally the same throughout the South, it was conditioned in certain areas by a greater fertility of the soil, particularly in the Alabama Black Belt and in the Mississippi Delta. Here also the greater closeness to the frontier made black thralldom a much harsher institution than it was on the old settled estates of the Atlantic seaboard.

Despite the slaves' considerable employment in the production of food crops and tobacco,* slavery came to be most closely identified with cotton growing. This cheek-by-jowl companionship was reflected in the value which the market assigned to slaves, which was closely geared to the price of cotton. A rule of thumb dictated $800 as the value of a full hand when cotton sold for eight cents a pound. To this figure was added $100 with each increase of one cent in the price of cotton. Throughout the first half of the nineteenth century cotton prices ranged from five to thirty cents. When the price fell to five cents a pound, as it did following the Panic of 1837, the slave market collapsed.

During the 1850s the price* of slaves became proportionately much greater than that of cotton. The staple brought an average of a little more than ten cents during this period, while the price of slaves increased to $1,800 under a growing demand for labor. Yet the average slaveholder appeared to be earning a satisfactory income from this type of investment, and slavery as an institution seemed more firmly established than ever.

Despite the apparent prosperity of the 1850s, numerous economic historians agree that, except on the very fertile lands of the Old Southwest, slavery had all but ceased to be profitable* by the beginning of the Civil War. Yet some planters made large profits in spite of it. They have been described as mining the soil of its fertility and selling it in the form of lint at the marketplace. The most fabulous profits—as much as $250 a hand—were achieved on lands of the Mississippi Delta, the Louisiana bayous, and the Red River and Arkansas River valleys.

These were areas of level topography and great plantations where cotton could be grown at a cost of five cents in the mid–1850s, when the staple brought eleven cents at New Orleans. On small farming units the production cost was eight cents. More effective organization and supervision of workers on the large plantations as well as soil fertility and unbroken topography accounted for this difference in production costs. The yearly outlay for the support of an adult slave seldom exceeded $30, including his food at $15 a year.

The high degree of adaptability of slave labor to cotton growing on small farms as well as on large plantations was somewhat unique. While no great amount of skill was required to grow cotton, it demanded an immense output of physical labor under a hot sun. Unlike most grain crops which could be left alone between planting and harvesting, cotton demanded constant attention from April to July when the fields were cleared of grass and the soil around the plants kept loose. This attention usually required four plowings and three close hoeings during a three-month period. After the crop was "laid by" in July, the labor force took up harvesting peas, fodder, and corn, although in an emergency the last might be delayed indefinitely without much injury to the crop.

Then in early September cotton harvesting (picking) began, when as much as fifty pounds could be gathered in one day by a single hand. Picking might last into January or even February, after which laborers were engaged in clearing additional land. This was also the season for cutting down corn and cotton stalks and plowing under the litter in anticipation of a new planting.

The harvesting of cotton utilized the labor of all available hands, including children. On very large plantations house servants and other specialized groups also went into the fields, particularly if some danger threatened damage to the crop. When cotton had a high degree of thickness, adults might gather 200 pounds in one day. During the picking season planters might substitute the task system* of labor for the gang system,* but planters never agreed on which of these systems was more productive.

Improved techniques of cotton production got under way in the 1850s. They included the use of fertilizers and improved tools. Contour plowing and primitive terracing were slowly coming into use as well. Most significant were the slave-holders' efforts to improve the skills of operatives and to provide them with more adequate clothing, food, and housing. A few plantation managers recognized that a law of diminishing returns made it desirable to limit working hours and to grant frequent holidays and long rest periods in the middle of the day when the sun was hottest. Southern slavery on "modern" cotton plantations steadily grew more temperate in the waning years of its life.

During the Civil War* cotton production declined from 4,491,000 bales in 1860 to 299,000 bales three years later. Production of food crops increased to a point that enabled the South to feed itself, although with little margin. Exemptions from Confederate conscription known as the "twenty Negro provision" assured widespread use of slaves on plantations. Throughout the war cotton was the basis of Confederate diplomacy, but largely because of its association with slavery, Southern diplomacy proved unsuccessful. Slavery died with the South's defeat in the war, but cotton production under various new labor arrangements continued throughout the South in the postwar era.

SELECTED BIBLIOGRAPHY

James C. Bonner, *A History of Georgia Agriculture, 1732–1860* (1964); David L. Cohn, *The Life and Times of King Cotton* (1956); Lewis C. Gray, *History of Agriculture in the Southern United States to 1860* (2 vols., 1933); John H. Moore, *Agriculture in Ante-Bellum Mississippi* (1958); James Oakes, *The Ruling Race: A History of American Slave-holders* (1982); James B. Sellers, *Slavery in Alabama* (1950); and Joseph Addison Turner, *The Cotton Planter's Manual: Being a Compilation of Facts from the Best Authorities on the Culture of Cotton . . .* (1857).

JAMES C. BONNER

COTTON GIN. Devices for separating the seed of cotton* from the lint date from antiquity. The *charkha*, a wooden instrument consisting of a pair of wooden rollers placed horizontally on a frame, originated in India centuries ago. As the rollers were turned, seeds were squeezed from cotton as it passed between them. Devices that employed the principle of the *charkha* were used in colonial North America and were known as "gins."

Commercial cotton production began in the United States in the late 1700s. The increased demand for cotton in Great Britain, in response to the Industrial Revolution, caused a commercial cotton region to begin to emerge along the South Carolina–Georgia coast. Long-staple "black seed" cotton was grown and prepared for market using hand- and foot-propelled gins and larger animal-powered gins. A slave using a small machine with iron rollers could gin from 25 to 100 pounds of cotton in a day.

But production of black seed cotton was confined by climate to the subtropical coastal region. In the piedmont, or "Upper Country," short-staple "green seed" cotton could be grown. Because the seed of this variety adhered tightly to the fiber, the lint could not be cleaned satisfactorily with roller gins, a factor that limited commercial cotton production. When Eli Whitney arrived in Georgia in 1792, a number of persons already were attempting to perfect the gin for green seed cotton. Whitney developed a new principle of ginning, one based in part on modification of the existing gin.

Rows of wire teeth were fitted into a cylinder. The teeth pulled the cotton through a breastwork of slots that were too small for seed to pass through. The ginned lint was then removed from the teeth with brushes on a second revolving cylinder. Other persons modified Whitney's new gin concept by substituting circular saws for the rows of wire teeth, giving the name "saw gin" to the Whitney principle. The Whitney principle of ginning was adopted in the piedmont and throughout the other upland cotton regions of the South. Saw gins were never accepted in the long-staple coastal, or sea-island, cotton region. Roller gins continued to be used until the demise of the region in the twentieth century.

Whitney and his gin quickly passed into legend. Textbooks commonly purport that Whitney invented a device for removal of seed from cotton where none previously existed. This device, *the* cotton gin, was the factor that caused the production of cotton in the South, which in turn led to the revival of the dying institution of slavery. Such a simplistic interpretation fails to consider the fundamental role of soaring demand for cotton and ignores the importance of the roller gin in the emergence of commercial production. Even after the introduction of the Whitney gin, others worked to perfect the roller principle for upland cotton because saw gins shortened the staple. The major breakthrough in roller ginning came in 1840, when Fones McCarthy of Demopolis, Alabama, patented his principle. Though never adopted in the upland cotton regions of the South, in Egypt, India, and China, the McCarthy machine became the accepted cotton gin.

SELECTED BIBLIOGRAPHY

Charles S. Aiken, "An Examination of the Role of the Eli Whitney Cotton Gin in the Origin of the United States Cotton Regions," *Proceedings of the Association of American Geographers*, 3 (1971), 5–9; Charles S. Aiken, "The Evolution of Cotton Ginning in the Southeastern United States," *Geographical Review*, 63 (1973), 196–224; Charles A. Bennett, *Roller Cotton Ginning Developments* (1960); Jeannette Mirsky and Allan Nevins, *The World of Eli Whitney* (1958); and Daniel H. Thomas, "Pre-Whitney Cotton Gins in French Louisiana," *Journal of Southern History*, 31 (1965), 135–148.

CHARLES S. AIKEN

COWBOYS. Given the position of colonial South Carolina, both as the major center of early Anglo-American open-range cattle herding and as the most important place of entry of African slaves, it is not surprising that blacks served as cowhands in the Southern colonies. Some of the Carolina blacks perhaps had African experience in cattle herding,* for Charleston slave dealers expressed a preference for Gambians, many of whom were cattle nomads. Blacks tended South Carolina herds as early as the 1670s, and a 1741 inventory mentioned "a Stock of Cattle . . . from Five Hundred to One Thousand Head . . . [and] a Man used to a Cow Pen." Other colonial documents referred to "2 negroes, excellent cattle hunters, used to the stock," and "negroes to look after the . . . kine." Even the word *cowboy* possibly originated as a term for a slave herder, just as *buckaroo* and *corral* perhaps entered the American ranching vocabulary by way of Gullah* *buckra* and Angolan-Portuguese *kraal* (*crawl*).

In light of recent research documenting a spatial and temporal continuity between colonial Carolina cattle herding and nineteenth-century ranching on the Great Plains, the African slave component in Southern livestock raising takes on added significance. The Carolina herding system spread westward via several routes, the most important of which followed the belt of infertile pine barrens paralleling the Gulf Coast. All along that route, from Carolina to Texas, slave cowboys plied their trade, and some free blacks even became large-scale cattle raisers.

In postbellum times, blacks remained active as cowboys and participated in the spread of cattle ranching into the Great Plains. In 1880 sixty-eight black cowhands worked in the western counties of Texas. The rodeo event "bulldogging" was first performed by Bill Pickett, a black cowboy of South Carolina ancestry.

SELECTED BIBLIOGRAPHY

Gary S. Dunbar, "Colonial Carolina Cowpens," *Agricultural History*, 35 (1961), 125–130; Philip C. Durham and Everett L. Jones, *The Negro Cowboys* (1965); Bailey C. Hanes, *Bill Pickett, Bulldogger: The Biography of a Black Cowboy* (1977); Terry G. Jordan, *Trails to Texas: Southern Roots of Western Cattle Ranching* (1981); and Peter H. Wood, " 'It Was a Negro Taught Them': A New Look at African Labor in Early South Carolina," *Journal of Asian and African Studies*, 9 (1974), 160–189.

TERRY G. JORDAN

CRAFT, WILLIAM (1827–1900), and ELLEN (ca. 1826–ca. 1890). William Craft and his wife Ellen Craft won considerable renown for their daring escape from slavery in 1848. Born in different parts of Georgia, the Crafts met and married after their masters both settled near Macon. They fled slavery during the Christmas holidays when the light-skinned Ellen disguised herself as an ailing young white man traveling north for medical treatment in the company of her servant, William. The Crafts settled in Boston where William worked as a carpenter and Ellen as a seamstress. Soon after passage of the Fugitive Slave Act of 1850,* two agents arrived in Boston to arrest and return them to slavery. Constant harassment from the Boston Vigilance Committee and the local black community forced the slave catchers to depart empty-handed, but the Crafts were persuaded by friends to seek a safer refuge abroad. Together with another fugitive slave,* William Wells Brown,* the Crafts toured England and Scotland delivering antislavery and temperance lectures. During the mid–1850s, British abolitionists* paid the tuition for the Crafts to attend the Ockham agricultural school in Surrey where they studied academic subjects while teaching carpentry and sewing. The Crafts continued their antislavery lecturing in Great Britain and published an autobiography, *Running a Thousand Miles for Freedom*, in 1860. From 1862 to 1867, William made several extended visits to Africa to promote cotton production and trade with Britain. In 1869 the Crafts returned to the United States and later established a cooperative farm and school in Bryan County, Georgia.

SELECTED BIBLIOGRAPHY

R.J.M. Blackett, "Fugitive Slaves in Britain: The Odyssey of William and Ellen Craft," *Journal of American Studies*, 12 (1978), 41–62; R.J.M. Blackett, *Building An Anti-*

slavery Wall: Black Americans in the Atlantic Abolitionist Movement, 1830–1860 (1983); William Craft, *Running a Thousand Miles for Freedom; Or, The Escape of William and Ellen Craft from Slavery* (1860); Jane H. Pease and William H. Pease, *They Who Would Be Free: Blacks' Search for Freedom, 1830–1861* (1974); Benjamin Quarles, *Black Abolitionists* (1969); William Still, *The Underground Rail Road: A Record of Facts, Authentic Narratives, Letters, Ex. . . .* (1872).

                                                                              JOHN R. MCKIVIGAN

CRAFTSMEN. Traveling through the South in 1835, J. H. Ingraham observed that "slaves are trained to every kind of manual labor. The blacksmith, cabinet-maker, carpenter, builder, wheelright [*sic*]—all have one or more slaves laboring in their trades. The negro is a third arm to every working man who can possibly save money to purchase one." Even though Ingraham was unaware of it, this large representation of Southern blacks in the skilled crafts had deep roots in the American experience already by 1835. Some scholars have suggested that those roots stretched back to West Africa. African culture probably exerted little influence on the work of Afro-American artisans, however, because slavery and the Atlantic Ocean severed contact with the traditional source of those skills. Moreover, colonists gave little thought to the possibility that newly arrived Africans could be used for anything other than brute field work. The origins of slave craftsmanship, therefore, are to be found in the material needs of the American colonies.

During the first decades of American settlement, craftsmen were in critically short supply. As the colonial population expanded, and home industries developed, an ever larger number of artisans were required, and wages demanded by tradesmen became exorbitant and unpredictable. Occasionally, severe shortages forced communities to advertise for badly needed skilled labor. Even after the American Revolution some states were still actively recruiting tradesmen. Virginia, for example, offered a five-year exemption from taxes to craftsmen who settled in the state. Because fertile land was readily available at reasonable rates, craftsmen were constantly lured away from their trades by the prospect of becoming independent property owners. Therefore, in countless forced choices, colonists turned to black slaves as a solution to the problems of scarcity, costliness, and high turnover of skilled labor.

Black artisans were utilized in all of the American colonies from an early period, although craftsmanship was not the predominant form of slave service in any of them. Even in the Northern colonies where the conditions for staple crop production did not exist, slaves worked along with their masters as shopkeepers, silversmiths, blacksmiths, tanners, shipbuilders, and in a host of other trades. The largest proportion of black artisans were clustered in the Middle colonies, particularly in New York and Philadelphia. In New England, where the black population was always very small, Boston had the largest population of Afro-American craftsmen. The vast majority of slaves were concentrated in the Southern colonies, of course, and slave craftsmen were found in significant numbers in all of the Southern towns, including Baltimore, Williamsburg, Charleston, and Savannah. The pages of the *South Carolina Gazette*, for example, are filled with advertisements for a wide variety of slave artisans, including the various specialized trades associated with metalworking, woodworking, textiles, leather, shipbuilding, and construction.

On the Southern plantations where most slaves were concentrated, the crafts were ancillary to the production of crops. Initially, the isolated plantations and farms employed slaves only in the fields. It is likely that the first Negro field hand to become an artisan learned the cooper's trade, since casks had to be made to ship agricultural products to market, and the supply was never dependable. As the plantation economy grew in complexity, more and more slaves were taught those skills necessary to operate the plantations on a self-sufficient basis. Eventually, the larger plantations came to resemble independent economic units with slaves in all occupations from making shoes and clothing, to building and repairing iron implements. Some plantations virtually were "factories in the field." Robert Carter, the prominent Virginia planter, for example, operated textile factories, flour mills, bakeries, saltworks, blacksmith shops, and iron forges on his vast landholdings.

During the colonial period there was little division of labor, and artisans conceived, designed, and finished their own products. Moreover, craftsmen had to be thoroughly competent in several related trades in order to perform their own. Even though slave owners frequently questioned the ability of slaves to learn the more complex aspects of a trade, slave artisans sometimes earned recognition for the excellence of their craftsmanship. Such was the case with those Afro-American bondsmen who made the name Andover synonymous with quality iron ware, those carpenter-architects who built Southern mansions, and those who fashioned the handwrought grills decorating the famous balconies of Charleston and New Orleans.

Not every slave was capable of becoming an artisan. Native intelligence, age, sex, health, personality, and other factors entered into the master's decision to select a particular slave for training. Normally, "country born" Negroes were chosen to serve under the supervision of an experienced craftsman who was usually brought to the plantation for a specified period to work and teach a slave his trade. Few served formal apprenticeships, and those instances usually were found in the cities. Some manufactories and shops purchased slaves to train for the business, for example, as did James Hunter, who purchased and trained slaves for numerous crafts at his Virginia iron foundry.

Four basic master-slave artisan relationships evolved during the eighteenth century and prevailed until slavery was abolished. Most slave artisans were owned and employed by their masters. In other cases, masters placed their slaves under free craftsmen and relinquished any immediate financial benefits to the craftsmen as compensation for the training. Many slave artisans were hired out* to a third party for a stipulated period and amount of money. In some cases, masters granted slave craftsmen the privilege of hiring their own time to employers of their own choice. Necessity and profit motivated masters to train slaves in the skilled trades, but they were also aware that the practice contained an inherent threat to slave control. A little learning could be dangerous, and the relatively high percentage of slave tradesmen implicated in servile uprisings and conspiracies presented whites with sound evidence for linking slave discontent with intelligence and training. Practicing a craft exercised the mind, forced it to conceptualize and make decisions, and taught self-discipline and elevated personal pride. Slave artisans also worked with little or no supervision, enjoyed considerable freedom of movement, and gained a limited measure of control over their own lives.

This diminution of social control over slave craftsmen assured that there would always be some level of resistance to the training of slaves in the crafts, even among some owners. It was the white tradesmen, however, who objected to slave training most forcefully. As early as 1744 white shipwrights in South Carolina petitioned the general assembly to prohibit Negro slaves from becoming artisans and competing against free labor. They were ignored, as were subsequent appeals, because masters derived significant financial advantages from the practice, and it was their will which prevailed.

Slavery was gradually abolished in the Northern states in the late eighteenth and early nineteenth centuries, but in the South, where it was firmly entrenched, reliance on slave artisans grew in importance and scale. On small Southern plantations labor specialization continued to be slight with a slave or two trained in a craft useful to farm work. These slaves still might divide their labor between field and craft as necessity dictated. Labor specialization increased with the size of the unit, however, and substantial numbers of slave artisans were found on large plantations where their skills usually exempted them from fieldwork.

As Southern cities expanded in population during the nineteenth century, the importance of urban slave* craftsmen grew apace. In 1860, the South's largest cities were about 20 percent black, and in Charleston, Richmond, and Savannah, one-third of the population was composed of slaves, a significant percentage of whom were craftsmen. In Charleston, for example, slave carpenters outnumbered free Negro and white carpenters, and the same was true for coopers. In fact, a profusion of slaves were found in virtually every trade known to the region's cities.

The basic master-slave relationships* established in the eighteenth century were refined during the antebellum era. From the colonial period to the Civil War, slave prices* followed a nearly constant upward spiral, with the exception of a few temporary downturns, such as the Panic of 1837. Under these pricing conditions businessmen and planters, who always seemed to be strapped for capital, increasingly came to rely on slave hiring, rather than ownership, as a more effective adaptation to the growing needs of manufacturing and business. Owners, therefore, commanded substantial rates for hiring a skilled slave, but employers found this method less expensive than purchasing their own tradesmen. Between 5 and 10 percent of the slaves in the South were hired out in any given year during the antebellum period, and artisans represented a large percentage of them.

Even though masters benefited from this economic arrangement, slaves gained a degree of freedom which many whites continued to find disquieting, especially when slave artisans were permitted to hire their own time. If they worked hard, and their skills were in demand, slave craftsmen could negotiate favorable terms with employers and retain substantial sums of money for themselves. This opportunity to save money enabled them to better their standard of living, or even purchase their own freedom. At the very least these privileged slaves achieved a level of individual freedom unique among the slave population. Frederick Douglass,* who was permitted to hire his own time as a caulker in the Baltimore shipyards, summed up his privileges and responsibilities succinctly: ''I was to be allowed all my time; to make all bargains for work; to find my own employment, and to collect my own wages; and, in return for this liberty, I was required, or obliged, to pay . . . three dollars at the end of each week, and to board and clothe myself, and buy my own calking [sic] tools.'' A failure to carry out any of these terms, however, would bring an end to the arrangement.

This increasing independence, and the elevation of self-esteem that whites detected in slave craftsmen, prompted sporadic, although abortive, efforts to prohibit self-hire in most Southern states. Undoubtedly, competition with slaves threatened the self-respect of white artisans, and frequently they attempted to drive away their slave competitors by physical force. The ship-caulker Frederick Douglass, for example, was brutally assaulted by white artisans and driven away from his work at the Baltimore shipyards. Being a slave craftsman had its advantages, but obviously it was not without its hardships.

The role of the slave craftsmen presents one of the more illuminating paradoxes of Afro-American slavery. Even as the ideology of racial inferiority was being embroidered into ever more intricate patterns, slave owners continued to rely on black bondsmen to perform even the most complex tasks in the Southern economy, tasks which many refused to entrust to white tradesmen.

SELECTED BIBLIOGRAPHY

Frederick Douglass, *Narrative of the Life of Frederick Douglass, an American Slave, Written by Himself* (1845); Philip S. Foner and Ronald L. Lewis, eds., *The Black Worker: A Documentary History from Colonial Times to the Present*, vol. 1: *The Black Worker to 1869* (1978); James E. Newton and Ronald L. Lewis, eds., *The Other Slaves: Mechanics, Artisans, and Craftsmen* (1978); and Kenneth M. Stampp, *The Peculiar Institution: Slavery in the Ante-Bellum South* (1956).

RONALD L. LEWIS

CREOLE SLAVE REVOLT. The slave revolt* on the American brig *Creole* occurred outside the Bahamas on 7 November 1841 as the vessel was engaged in the domestic slave trade* between Virginia and Louisiana. The *Creole*, carrying 135 slaves and several white passengers, was overtaken by Madison Washington and eighteen others in a mutiny that resulted in two deaths, those of a white slave owner and one of the mutineers. Because the *Creole* was unable to make the long trip to Liberia,* Washington and his cohorts sailed for Nassau, where two days later they appealed to the mercy of British authorities. After considerable discussion, the attorney general on the island declared the blacks free on the basis of the British government's laws prohibiting slavery.

Even before the *Creole* reached New Orleans on 2 December, white Southerners were already angry with the British. Their visit-and-search practices had attempted to halt the illicit African slave trade.* And now the Americans demanded compensation for the freed *Creole* slaves on the ground that they were part of the *legal* American insterstate slave trade. President John Tyler, himself a Virginia slaveholder, could not insist upon extradition, because not since the expiration of Jay's Treaty of 1795 had such an arrangement existed between the United States and England. Secretary of State Daniel Webster, only moderately antislavery, declared that the *Creole* was forced into Nassau by "disaster and distress" and, as a result, on the basis of "comity," or hospitality among friendly nations, the British should return the slaves. But British Prime Minister Sir Robert Peel could not comply without causing a furious outcry throughout England.

Excitement over the *Creole* lingered on both sides of the Atlantic. The issue remained an irritant during the Webster-Ashburton negotiations of 1842 until Lord Ashburton promised no more "officious interference" with vessels forced into British ports. But while the treaty authorized the extradition of individuals charged with any of seven nonpolitical crimes, the list of offenses did not include mutiny. The *Creole* case was finally closed in 1853, when an Anglo-American claims commission ruled that the British had indeed violated international law. It awarded compensation to the owners of the slaves.

SELECTED BIBLIOGRAPHY

Howard Jones, "The Peculiar Institution and National Honor: The Case of the *Creole* Slave Revolt," *Civil War History*, 21 (1975), 28–50; and Howard Jones, *To the Webster-Ashburton Treaty: A Study in Anglo-American Relations, 1783–1843* (1977).

HOWARD JONES

CRIME. The term *slave crime* is ambiguous, especially since it probably had diametrically opposite meanings for slaveholders and slaves. Although some convicted slaves may have acted just for themselves, many of the Africans and Afro-Americans who violated the criminal code when trying to survive or to surmount the rigors of slavery conformed to their own ethic or set of social and moral values. This "customary law" of slaves came into dramatic conflict with the statutory, criminal law of the slave owners.

Slaves were, by definition, under duress. Recognizing the implications of their lifetime servitude, many slaves consciously defied slave owners' laws and courts; some others acted in fury or for reasons unrelated to slavery. Slave owners in turn accused a considerable number of them of stealing, assault, murder, rape, arson, poisoning, and other common-law or statutory crimes. On the basis of laws passed to create penalties particularly for slaves, the courts often sentenced them to whipping,* execution, transportation, or other such punishments* as castration, to which sixteen North Carolina slaves and at least four Virginia slaves were subjected in the eighteenth century.

Both lawbreaking slaves and lawmaking whites faced the same reality. The continuation of slavery as well as the safety of the slave owners depended upon the maintenance of the owners' dominant status. If laws or persuasion failed, owners and public authorities were quick to use private or governmental force. Slaves who wished to contest slave owners' domination or who threatened that domination in the course of seeking other objectives had to use covert or openly violent methods. Research on this subject is incomplete, but available evidence does suggest certain patterns.

Many slaves "took" meat, clothing, and other necessities from whites, while some others occasionally stole goods from fellow slaves or free blacks. Some slaves struck back when whipped or threatened with a whipping; others killed fellow slaves out of jealousy or for some other reason only indirectly related to their status. It is evident, however, from the small percentage of slaves convicted of felonies or misdemeanors, especially more than once, that both private and public methods of punishment effectively reinforced and upheld slavery. Most slaves chose not to challenge openly the overwhelming power of slave laws and courts.

The nature of the behavior of slaves convicted of crimes differed significantly in various places and times, depended profoundly upon the distinct motives of individual slaves, and met with inconsistent, sometimes conflicting, responses in the same or different periods, places, or courts. The history of the relationship between Afro-American slaves and crime usually reflects the general history of slave societies. In times of war or internal discord, for example, prosecutions could increase. But prosecutions resulted from more than white people's anxieties. Some slaves took advantage of the ruling group's weaknesses, defeats, or divisions in order to improve their own position; others sought to compensate for deprivation or devastation heightened by general economic reversals such as the Panic of 1819 or overwhelming dislocation such as that caused by the Civil War.

Burglary or stealing was the felony charge slaves faced the most often. Thus in Virginia, more than 60 percent of felony convictions of slaves between 1706 and 1785 were for theft or actions related to theft, and just over 35 percent of Old Dominion slaves transported or executed between 1785 and 1865 had been found guilty of theft, robbery, or burglary. Similar patterns existed in such locations as New York between 1750 and 1776 and the Anderson and Spartanburg districts of South Carolina between 1818 and 1860. The necessities of food and clothing predominated among articles listed as stolen, indicating the motives leading many slaves to take high risks. Only a small number of slaves violently confronted property owners in robberies. Because slave courts across the South fairly uniformly treated the use of force or violence against persons in the commission of any crime as a capital offense, the risk was apparently too high for most slaves.

The most powerful challenge a single slave or a small group of slaves could openly make to the power of white owners, overseers, or other authorities was to kill one or more of them. In spite of all the insurrection convictions in North American slave societies, homicides by one or a few slaves took the greatest toll of whites. While some colonies or states occasionally allowed slaves to plead provocation or self-defense even when the victim was white, others rarely did so. In either case, available court testimony often reveals motivation. For example, slaves killed whites who had repeatedly whipped or otherwise abused them. No slave court admitted that a "corrective" whipping as such could be abusive; lawmakers and judges regarded such corporal punishment as a necessary means of coercing obedience or forcing slaves to work. A large number of slaves obviously saw it as intolerable, however. Many slaves also faced capital charges for assault with intent to kill. In Virginia and South Carolina, the purpose of this charge was clearly control more than retribution. It never was used against a slave suspected of trying to kill another slave; it resulted in execution in only about one-quarter of convictions even though it was a capital offense.

Some slaves killed whites whose only authority over them derived from the generalized claim of white supremacy. Such cases did not appear frequently in the courts, raising the possibility that retaliation in such instances was often private. There is little conclusive evidence on these deadly encounters. It is easier, but by no means easy, to learn why some slaves killed other slaves. Court testimony is particularly helpful since judges often did search for a motive in order to determine whether the verdict should be for manslaughter rather than first-degree murder. Such inquiries uncovered tragic stories of jealousy over men or women, provocation or insult, sometimes related to the harsh circumstances of slavery and sometimes not, or cases of contested honor, in which one slave refused to submit to challenges of any sort by another.

As might be expected, slaves convicted of murdering a white person faced a very high risk of hanging. It is impossible, however, to measure the chances that slaves who actually killed a white would be tried in court. Circumstances do indicate that secret attacks were much harder to detect and even more difficult to prove in court than were open attacks. This made poisoning a particularly appropriate weapon for slaves in North American slave societies, and in other Western Hemisphere slave societies as well, to use against white or black enemies. In addition, knowledge of herbs, roots, and natural substances handed down from African ancestors, acquired from Native Americans, or even developed independently, allowed Afro-American slave doctors, obeahmen, medicine men, or conjurers to claim and apparently sometimes exercise great power over other people.

During the eighteenth century, whites sometimes misunderstood such behavior, prosecuting slaves for malicious poisoning when they may only have been dispensing "love potions," protective powders, or similar mixtures. The extent of whites' fear of poisoning accounts in part for the fact that in eighteenth-century Virginia, the largest North American slave society, judges found slaves guilty of poisoning or illegally administering medicine more often than for any other offense, with the exception of theft and burglary. But both whites and slaves did sometimes die or suffer long illnesses at the hands of slave poisoners. At least one ex-slave dismissed conjurers as frauds, yet in the last decades of slavery doctors testified in court that the cause of victims' deaths was everything from rat poison to ground glass. It is clear that slaves found effective means of secretly killing whites or other slaves, probably in many instances without ever being detected. In eighteenth-century New York and nineteenth-century Tennessee, however, slave courts appear not to have paid special attention to poisoning, regarding it as little more than another kind of homicide.

A particularly effective weapon for slaves to use exclusively against whites was arson. Like poisoning, it was hard to prove and could cause extensive damage to a slave owner. White "barn burners" did sometimes force or persuade slaves to attack their enemies for them, resting assured that the inability of slaves to testify in trials of whites would provide protection. But slaves could and did frequently act on their own. Like slaves who relied on killing, slave arsonists sought to control their owners, to retaliate for cruelty or abuse, or even hoped to gain a new owner as a result of the financial losses of the person whose property they burned. Less able than slave men to overpower masters and overseers, some slave women found arson a particularly useful means of attack.

Slave owners' fear of arson by slaves was sometimes high. Lack of evidence often prevented conviction, hence judicial authorities could not demonstrate strong control over slave arsonists. At particularly tense times, many whites associated arson with slave rebellion. Reports of arson after the trial of John Brown* in 1859, especially against some of the jurors in that trial, uniformly blamed slaves. Three slaves and one free black in a county next to the one in which Harpers Ferry is located stood trial for arson and insurrection after Brown's raid.

While slaves were convicted of insurrection only periodically, there were always some slaves willing to act together against overwhelming odds. Many colonial or state laws concerning conspiracy and insurrection tended to identify the crime of insurrection with the collaboration of one slave with one or more other slaves in violence against whites, giving rise to fears that temporary increases in slave crime showed an insurrectionary spirit among slaves. This could happen even after noticeable increases in convictions of slaves for property crimes. Many whites also perceived a connection between outlawed and insurrectionary slaves. Outlawed slaves were those whose long-term "lying out" and living off the land and property of many people made them resemble maroons.* That is why white leaders placed them in the special status of outlaws, subject to capture or death at the hands of designated pursuers or, in many cases, of any whites who could corner them. These marauding runaways* frequently caused as much anxiety among whites as did insurrectionaries, yet the courts could not usually deal directly with them. The weakness of the courts had a great deal to do with both whites' anxiety and the extraordinary means allowed by law to suppress persistent runaways.

Rape or attempted rape of a white female by a slave was a status offense— i.e., one which only a slave could commit—and therefore was subject to the same kind of fears or misperceptions as poisoning or insurrection. The common law and legislative enactments concerning rape included any male's rape of any female—regardless of race. White fear and racism, perceptions of white honor, and the circumstances of slavery, however, assured that besides whites alleged to have assaulted white females, only slaves suspected of raping free black or white females would regularly stand trial. The same factors also make it probable that the relatively very high conviction rate of slaves in rape and attempted rape trials cannot be taken as evidence of accuracy or fairness in such trials.

It is not at all clear whether slaves regarded sexual attacks as a means of resistance to slavery. Rape probably had greater emotional, social, and political meaning for slave owners and other whites than it did for slaves. On the other hand, the consequences of rape trials, including the mandated sentences of castration or execution in varying jurisdictions or times, contained high signif- icance for slaves. An antebellum ex-slave once claimed that more slaves went to the gallows upon being convicted for sexual offenses than for any other kind of conviction. Statistics for Virginia reveal that he was only slightly exaggerating, since the eighty-four slave men who swung from a noose for attempted rape and rape between 1785 and 1865 were outnumbered only by slaves convicted of murder and executed. Between 1800 and 1855, South Carolina slaves went to the gallows for rape less often than those executed, respectively, for assault, burglary, insurrection, or murder. Convicted rapists constituted 9.4 percent of executed slaves in South Carolina, 1800–1854, while they were 12.9 percent of the slaves executed in Virginia between 1800 and 1854. (Eleven percent of slaves tried for capital offenses in several representative counties of Tennessee between 1825 and 1861 faced the charge of rape or attempted rape.) There are also some indications that lynchings or other kinds of extralegal retribution occurred in rape cases, as in insurrection episodes.

Some published primary sources provide insights into slave crime, yet they are usually neither random samples nor comprehensive. Various narratives and some pamphlets or broadsides in the "dying words of a convict" genre contain scattered references to slaves' illegal behavior. But there is no substitute for systematic collection of lower court records as a base for evidence concerning changes over time and differences among the convicted and from region to region. Because some trials resulted in inaccurate identification of the person responsible for particular actions, they must be used carefully as evidence concerning slaves' behavior. Moreover, what criminologists call the "dark figure" of unrecorded crimes must also be kept in mind. Slaveholders created a special kind of unrecorded crime, for example. The slaves who successfully ran away, thereby "stealing themselves," obviously were unlikely to appear in judicial proceedings. Court records do, however, yield occasional convictions of slaves for aiding runaways or forging passes.

There is a greater opportunity for comparing the incidence of felonies in different colonies or states than for comparing misdemeanors because of differences among the separate slave codes. Some jurisdictions singled out certain kinds of slave behavior for public prosecution and punishment, but other jurisdictions neglected or ignored similar conduct, presumably permitting owners to act at their discretion in such matters. Prosecutions for gambling, swearing, insulting language, or even fighting and rioting were delegated to the judiciary in Georgia and South Carolina and in most towns and cities of any size, such as Richmond, Charleston, Memphis, and New Orleans, but county courts in Virginia and some other colonies or states ignored such behavior. Urban officials convicted slaves of violating Sabbath or curfew regulations, public smoking, or membership in secret societies; antebellum Memphis authorities punished slaves for traffic violations; and a few courts in Virginia even made self-contradictory attempts to convict slaves of treason.

But the existence of different punishments for the same felonies as well as the changing atmosphere in various jurisdictions over time necessitates caution even when comparing behavior classified as felonious. The prosecution of slave women for infanticide* was sporadic, for instance. Much more analysis of slave crimes within most of the colonies and states of North America is necessary before satisfactory conclusions concerning slave crime in North American slave societies can be reached.

SELECTED BIBLIOGRAPHY

Douglas Greenberg, *Crime and Law Enforcement in the Colony of New York, 1691–1776* (1976); Michael S. Hindus, *Prison and Plantation: Crime, Justice, and Authority in Massachusetts and South Carolina, 1767–1878* (1980); Arthur F. Howington III, "The Treatment of Slaves and Free Blacks in the State and Local Courts of Tennessee" (Ph.D. dissertation, Vanderbilt University, 1982); James H. Johnston, *Race Relations in Virginia and Miscegenation in the South, 1776–1860* (1970); and Philip J. Schwarz, *Slaves and Crime in Virginia* (1988).

PHILIP J. SCHWARZ

CULTURE, SLAVE. Only twenty-five years ago scholars debated whether slaves in the southern United States had an identifiable culture, much less whether aspects of African culture persisted in this country. Phrases like "cultural amnesia" were bandied about, and it was widely assumed that the horrors of the Middle Passage—the trip from Africa to America—combined with the harshness of plantation life in the South, dehumanized and infantilized slaves to such an extent that they became whatever whites wanted them to become. The search for "survivalisms," or Africanisms,* was almost entirely confined to vestigial words whose origins could be traced back to African roots. The scholarship of the last twenty-five years has transformed the debate and changed the terms of discussion, so much so that Afro-American slave culture is now a given whose origins and richness are explored in ever more sophisticated interdisciplinary studies.

The origins of Afro-American culture are to be found in Africa, in Europe, and in the New World, and the blend and relative strength of the diverse components changed over time, varied from place to place, and were dependent on factors ranging from birthrates and death rates to plantation size. There was no one African culture; instead, West Africa, from which most slaves came, supported a wide diversity of cultures separated from one another by geography and language.

Those people most able to transmit African ways to America—ritual specialists, mostly old people—were least likely to be brought here, and those most apt to come—young males—were least knowledgeable about African culture. Not only did white slaveholders actively discourage overt Africanisms when they could recognize them and gauge their importance, but language and cultural barriers among the slaves themselves slowed the sharing and fusion of folkways. Nature, too, presented difficulties. The rituals and ceremonies that gave form and substance to many aspects of African culture depended on a multiplicity of ingredients—feathers, shells, the sap from certain trees, animal parts—all chosen because some feature of the ingredient represented a precise value or trait. In this land, with different flora and fauna, it was impossible to transmit African rituals exactly even if ritual specialists had been available and given freedom by the white authorities to practice their arts.

Nevertheless, despite the difficulties involved, a wide variety of African cultural traits were transported to America, took root, merged with European and Indian folkways and beliefs, and evolved into a distinct Afro-American culture that incorporated features of the mix of cultures present in the colonies. Generally speaking, those African traits that bore some resemblance to European or Indian traits, and hence were reinforced by the similarities, were most apt to survive, albeit often in a hybrid or syncretic form, in the New World. The evolutionary process by which an Afro-American culture developed in the American South is time-specific, for the institution of slavery itself changed significantly over time and the temporal perspective must constantly be kept in mind.

Some twenty-odd Negroes arrived in Virginia in 1619, having been bartered for provisions by sailors on a Dutch vessel. The ultimate fate of these Africans is unknown, and a decade later only several dozen blacks lived in the colony. Most of them seem to have been slaves, but others were apparently servants (whose labor, but not person, was owned for several years), and at least a handful were free blacks* who themselves owned property (including servants and slaves), served on juries, and may even have voted. By as late as mid-century there were still only a couple of hundred blacks in the Chesapeake region; the labor force remained overwhelmingly composed of white indentured servants. The few hundred blacks, most having been transported from the West Indies and hence relatively acculturated, lived interspersed with the much larger white work force. With one or two blacks on scattered plantations often miles apart, with the settlements separated by trackless forests and divided by unbridged rivers and estuaries, with language barriers as uncrossable as the terrain, individual African slaves found themselves isolated culturally and geographically, with practically no sense of black community to nurture their fragile memories of Old World folkways.

Culture is best sustained and legitimated in a social framework; in the absence of a supportive community, old ways are shuffled aside and new ways grafted on. This is exactly what happened to African culture among blacks in the first two generations of their experience in the mainland colonies. This tendency was exacerbated by the small numbers of blacks and the degree of acceptance they found among the white indentured servants.* As long as there were few blacks and those relatively acculturated from the West Indies, they seemed neither shockingly strange nor threatening to the white majority. In fact, from the planter perspective they hardly seemed distinguishable from the larger working-class population with whom they lived, toiled, and died. Correspondingly, from the perspective of white indentured servants, black slaves seemed more like fellow workers than frightful heathens. As long as there were only a few blacks, there was remarkable biracial harmony, and white and black laborers socialized together in the first half century of the African experience in the British mainland colonies. In this environment of white hegemony and numerical dominance, overt African cultural traits faded as Africans adapted European attitudes; blacks during the period from about 1625 to 1675 became more Europeanized than at any other period perhaps before 1808. But forces were at work that would change this situation.

Almost imperceptibly the number and concentration of blacks continued to increase, and simultaneously with population growth in general came better roads, ferries, and bridges—improving communication among plantations. Blacks, sprinkled in ones and twos across the vast countryside, not only became aware of the presence of other blacks but were increasingly coming into contact with them. African-based language* barriers slowly were overcome as slaves developed a pidgin language composed of bits of various African dialects as well as snatches of English and Spanish. Underlying African grammatical principles incorporated new vocabularies that facilitated communication between slaves and masters and, more importantly, between slaves from different language groups. Breaking these language barriers was the first step toward the creation of a black community in the American South. Increased contact made it easier for blacks to find spouses of the requisite age, and slowly a second generation of American-born slaves developed. These "country-born" slaves were healthier than their parents, reached menarche earlier, and found it easier— as one result of population growth—to find spouses. The result was even greater population growth, and these American-born slaves, with an equal sex ratio (unlike the imported population of slaves who were mostly male), made possible the formation of slave families* and increases in population on a scale unknown before or anywhere else in the Americas.

American-born slaves used the pidgin language of their parents as their native tongue, so it became for them their native language, or, as linguists say, the pidgin language was "creolized." While certain underlying African grammatical principles remained constant, the vocabulary became increasingly Europeanized. Through the process of creolization the surrounding English words were incorporated into a linguistic structure that retained recognizable African patterns—although neither slaves nor masters may have been aware of the complexities involved. The growth of the slave population in the last decades of the seventeenth and the early decades of the eighteenth centuries not only made possible but made necessary the development of an Afro-American culture whose process of evolution parallels the shift from pidgin to creole language. So long as young, unattached males were the majority of slaves, with very limited family formation and few children,* there was little sense of a separate slave or African culture—these slaves were being culturally incorporated into the white, lower-class society. But with demographic changes making marriage and the growth of families possible and even probable, a shift occurred. With wives and children, young males now had reason to recover at least portions of their cultural heritage. The presence of children especially made desirable the rediscovery and practice of rituals, for births, adolescence, marriage, and death demanded ritual and ceremonial acknowledgment. The increasing frequency of slaves living in family groups provided not only the necessity for certain rites of passage but an arena in which such cultural phenomena could develop.

By the second quarter of the eighteenth century this process was underway, and various types of borrowings and blendings from several African cultures as well as the surrounding white and Indian cultures occurred. A slave man and wife from different African cultures, for example, might have both acknowledged that a certain stage of life required ritual celebration, but their backgrounds would have prescribed different rites, and neither being a ritual specialist, they would not have known precisely the correct ingredients or phrases, and even if they had, the prerequisite flora and fauna did not exist in the New World. What occurred, then, was a makeshift adaptation of hybrid African ceremonies in America, with the actual rituals more African in concept than in performance. American ingredients, even words, were drafted for duty as African cultural instruments, with the result neither truly African nor American but a new syncretistic creation, an *Afro-American* cultural invention. This process of cultural blending became possible and necessary at approximately the same time, and because the age cohort of slaves most involved was overwhelmingly American-born, the emerging Afro-American culture was more European than that elsewhere in the Americas, where the white presence was numerically so minimal as to make almost no impress on the black culture. Yet just at this moment of culture formation in the Southern colonies, roughly the period 1725–1775, came the high point of African arrivals in the slave trade.

Thus, the creole culture in the process of development received, at the most critical phase, a fresh infusion of African influences. The result was that the culture of American Negro slaves was both more African and more European than scholars once realized. Slavery scholarship has long emphasized the last generation before the Civil War, but it may well be that the fifty years before the American Revolution were more important in shaping the slave culture. Certainly in the decades after 1790 the American slave population was mostly American-born, and gradually African influences became more covert, operating as a kind of underlying grammar through which white European styles were expressed. Those who saw the obvious European trappings of the slave culture seldom understood the African patterns that determined how particular white cultural components were utilized. To employ a linguistic metaphor, an African grammar dictated the use of a white vocabulary, and this white vocabulary has made recognition of the underlying principles of construction more difficult.

With this linguistic metaphor in mind as the model for slave culture, and remembering the cultural changes over time—first a nearly Europeanized black slave force, then one with a syncretistic Afro-American culture that gradually saw its vocabulary components become increasingly Europeanized even while the underlying African grammatical principles helped shape the resulting folk-ways—it becomes possible to understand black history on the North American mainland. African models of the extended family reemerged in the South, with naming patterns* and quasi-kinship practices surviving as reminders of African ways. Slave women made quilts using available cloths, but the patterns sewed into the quilts maintained continuities with African uses of irregular rectangles.

Likewise, slaves in the rice-growing sea-island districts wove baskets out of American materials for use in winnowing their master's rice, but the patterns woven into the baskets bore clear resemblance to African styles. Pottery remnants discovered in South Carolina, showing sparse use of colors and the sometimes physiognomic shape, have definite African parallels. Slave folktales, especially the Brer Rabbit stories, are populated with animal characters common to the American South, but the genre of animal trickster tales was carried over from many African cultures.

In the realms of music* and song, dance,* body language, food preparation (even when much was borrowed, for example, from American Indians), housing styles* (the small size of slave cabins may have been as much a result of African conceptions of appropriate housing space as the parsimony of the planters, and the shotgun house and even the idea of a verandah may have come from Africa via Haiti), agricultural techniques* (almost certainly the manner of planting rice in the Carolinas was brought from the African grain coast, and some herding practices appear to have African antecedents), carving and metalworking styles, some aspects of religious expression, all have an identifiable African cultural heritage.

The survival and evolution of an Afro-American style was especially noteworthy in those aspects of slave culture that seemed irrelevant to the masters.
For example, whites little noticed or cared what patterns were woven into the
winnowing baskets as long as the winnowing was done, nor did they attach
significance to the patterns slave women sewed into their quilts. In such incon-
spicuous ways a rich panoply of Afro-American cultural and artistic styles persisted, an achievement that helped slaves hold on to a spark of automony and
survive their bondage without being completely enslaved psychologically. Masters were often only partially if at all aware of what was occurring right under
their noses.

Developments in slave religion* were different, however, and require special
discussion, for masters often *did* care what kind of religious practices their slaves
performed. Slave folklore* and folktales were considered heathenish, naive, and
of little import by whites; because they were ''harmless,'' planters did not bother
to control or even monitor such beliefs. Since folk beliefs were discussed almost
entirely within the confines of the slave community, there was little occasion
for interaction between whites and blacks; consequently, while slaves often
incorporated concepts from white folk beliefs (various superstitions, for example)
that reinforced their own, the black folkloric experience was more African than
any other aspect of slave life. Slave religion was a wholly different issue, for
here—most whites agreed—it *did* matter what slaves believed and practiced,
and the normative slave religious experience was biracial. In many respects the
development of slave religion was analogous to other cultural developments.
Beginning in the mid-eighteenth century, slaves adopted those aspects of Christianity that bore some resemblance to African religion, and slave Christianity
provided blacks with a sense of purpose and a context of meaning for their lives.
In other respects slave Christianity was a unique aspect of black culture, for
nowhere else in the black experience was the impact of white values as influential.

Before about 1750 no appreciable slave Christianity existed in the Southern
colonies, but this was primarily because of the weakness of institutional religion
in the region. During the second quarter of the century especially, in the face
of heavy African importation, churchmen questioned the ability of slaves to
understand the Christian message. Such racist assumptions misled many whites,
for this period was also a time when the slave population was enjoying rapid
indigenous population growth with a corresponding increase in slave family life,
which also meant that the emerging slave community increasingly desired the
ritualistic and legitimating functions of religion. After about 1750 a powerful
surge of evangelical Protestantism developed in the Southern colonies, with
several series of small revivals (a Presbyterian, Baptist, then Methodist phase
of church growth) that eventually resulted in a Great Revival (1800–1805) that
ensured the dominance of evangelical Christianity in the region. These evangelical groups, especially in their formative stages, welcomed black participation
and indeed sought out black converts and members. Moreover, the style of
religious expression in the evangelical churches was similar in important ways

to African traditional religion, easing the transition of Africans from an African religious orientation to a Christian one. The African background preconditioned slaves to be receptive to the kind of overtly emotional religion they found within the evangelical sects.

In West Africa, from which most Southern slaves came, there was a great diversity of cultures, languages, and religions, but there were also certain underlying cultural similarities, especially in religion. Despite the variety of titles, rituals, and beliefs, most West Africans had three types of gods—ancestral spirits, nature spirits, and an omnipotent creator god. Moreover, a common method of experiencing religion was called spirit possession, a transforming emotional state wherein one was "seized" by the spirit. Religion incorporated the believers into a larger community, joining contemporary believers with each other and also with their ancestors, who were thought to be still present. Worshipers often participated actively in the religious ceremonies, with voice and body expression part of the communal experience of the holy. Finally, water was involved in a number of African religious rites, often being symbolic of life. This range of beliefs and practices predisposed many Afro-Americans, torn from their comfortable spiritual world inhabited by ancestral and nature gods, to seek reincorporation into a larger sphere of meaning and existence in the context of evangelical churches. The intense emotionalism of the revival sects, with their "felt," as opposed to abstract, worship—baptism by immersion, laying on of hands, foot washings, the right hand of fellowship, for example—and their often trancelike enthusiasm, seemed to validate their worship experience in African terms. Most West Africans had considered the less immediate but more powerful creator god to be the One turned to when all else had failed, and certainly the trauma of capture and transferral to the New World as a slave would be the kind of desperate situation that would incline one toward a deliverer. When such slaves came into contact with warmly enthusiastic evangelists, whose proffered God the father, God the son, and God the holy spirit seemed to parallel the African trinity, whose spiritual intensity seemed related to African spiritual possession, whose rites made potent use of water, and whose leaders reached out to the bondsmen and sought to unite them with the family of God—the ancestral God of Abraham and the church fathers—they found it easy to accept the religious invitation offered.

Beginning with the mid-eighteenth century, when evangelical churches were being founded in the South, they had substantial black membership. After 1800 the earlier emancipationist reputation associated with the Baptist and Methodist churches in particular had been moderated as the churches made a conscious decision to adjust their policies to the economic and racial realities of the South, justifying themselves on the grounds that only by so doing would they be able to bring the Gospel to the slaves. Now that religion was made "safe" for the slaves, increasing numbers of planters allowed and even promoted evangelical membership for their bondsmen. This movement was enhanced after the 1830s as planters and churchmen desired to refute the Northern abolitionist charge that

Southerners left their slaves in a heathen state. Slave membership in the evangelical churches throughout the Old South was substantial, with blacks sometimes constituting the majority of members in individual churches. Blacks heard the same sermons, took communion with whites, were buried in the same cemeteries, and participated in church disciplinary proceedings with a degree of equality unmatched anywhere else in the society.

Clearly slaves found in the evangelical churches a sense of belonging to a larger group, an arena for leadership skills, a method of enhancing their self-worth, and a theology that provided meaning and a feeling of moral superiority. Religion helped slaves avoid the kind of self-abasement that slavery otherwise could promote. But precisely because slaves typically worshiped in the presence of whites, and whites deemed what slaves believed and how they practiced their faith important, whites *did* monitor slave Christianity. Whites, both lay and clerical, attempted to teach religious precepts to slaves; chapels were sometimes provided, though more often slaves attended church with whites. White supervision was required at most black religious services. There is evidence, especially in isolated regions where the black-to-white ratio was very high, of secret, underground slave religious practices—ranging from so-called brush arbor meetings to voodoo,* but these were by no means typical. The normative slave religious experience was biracial, and though slaves probably preferred the more openly emotional, participatory services of the Baptists* and Methodists,* and by their presence helped characterize those denominational services, slave religion in general was more influenced by white attitudes than was any other aspect of slave culture.

Even to consider such a topic as the culture of slaves suggests the historiographical revolution in slavery scholarship that has occurred since 1960. Despite the obvious harsh features of bondage, an oppressive system that at the most profound level deprived bondspeople of freedom, the enslaved men and women discovered various ways to hold on to and multiply at least a degree of autonomy. Every opportunity they gained or created to control a portion of their lives— mental and physical—represented an aspect of slave culture. This culture that allowed them a modicum of psychological independence drew both from African roots and New World (European and Indian) influences, and the result was a panoply of beliefs, practices, and artistic expressions that clearly show that slaves were not merely human property or childlike Sambos. While much of this culture had survival value, it was more than functional in a mechanistic sense. Slave culture gave meaning, purpose, and depth to slave existence, and allowed the slaves to find even joy and a sense of victory in the midst of their travail in bondage. From this inner strength blacks gained the resilience to survive slavery, then sharecropping, poverty, and racism; and much of the poetry, the music, the religion of their slavery-time culture has flowered in freedom to enrich the whole of American culture.

SELECTED BIBLIOGRAPHY

Ira Berlin, "Time, Space, and the Evolution of Afro-American Society on British Mainland North America," *American Historical Review*, 85 (1980), 44–78; John W. Blassingame, *The Slave Community: Plantation Life in the Antebellum South* (1972); John B. Boles, *Black Southerners, 1619–1869* (1983); Dena J. Epstein, *Sinful Tunes and Spirituals: Black Folk Music to the Civil War* (1977); Eugene D. Genovese, *Roll, Jordan, Roll: The World the Slaves Made* (1974); Charles Joyner, *Down by the Riverside: A South Carolina Slave Community* (1984); Lawrence W. Levine, *Black Culture and Black Consciousness: Afro-American Folk Thought from Slavery to Freedom* (1977); Sidney W. Mintz and Richard Price, *An Anthropological Approach to the Afro-American Past: A Caribbean Perspective* (1976); Willie Lee Rose, *Slavery and Freedom*, edited by William W. Freehling (1982); John M. Vlach, *The Afro-American Tradition in Decorative Arts* (1978); and Peter H. Wood, *Black Majority: Negroes in Colonial South Carolina from 1670 through the Stono Rebellion* (1974).

JOHN B. BOLES

D

DANCE. Under slavery, dance played a vital role in the lives of Afro-Americans and served three functions. In an attempt to "civilize" their workers, owners forced slaves to adopt a new language* and religion.* Dance remained as one of the few uniquely African cultural traditions left to the bondsmen. And it was through this medium that blacks celebrated their rich African heritage.

Dance served as an extremely important cultural element in Africa. Life, death, hunting or crop-raising success, birth, puberty, marriage,* or recovery from illness—all were celebrated through dance. As Africans were transported to the Americas their movement traditions traveled with them; several dances performed on Southern plantations had direct African counterparts. Among these were dances that imitated animals, including the buck, pigeon wing, buzzard lope, turkey trot, snake hips, fish tail, and camel walk.

A second group of dances with African parallels was the challenge dances. These were competitive dances in which one dancer would attempt fancier, more difficult steps than his opponent. Sometimes a glass of water was placed on each dancer's head, and the fanciest stepper spilling the least amount of water was declared the winner. Challenge dances included the jig, buck, pigeon wing, and sometimes the juba.

The final dance type that the slaves brought directly from Africa was a circular shuffling sacred dance called the ring shout. This was performed by a group of people circling an ill person or a grave. Most frequently the shout accompanied a Protestant prayer meeting or church service and was performed to hymns or spirituals. The ultimate aim of the shout was possession, achieved through continuous, hypnotic movement.

Relief from the frustration of their subject status, their inferior caste position, was the second basic function of dance among Afro-American slaves. The bondsmen accomplished this in two ways. First, by physically outperforming the whites, the slaves gained a feeling of superiority based on the belief that Afro-Americans were better, more innovative dancers. Second, the slaves' frustrations were relieved when they poked fun at their masters unbeknownst to their captors.

They accomplished this type of role reversal by imitating and exaggerating such white dances as cotillions, quadrilles, and the Virginia reel. The most popular of the imitative dances, however, was the cakewalk, a satirized version of the grand march. This high-stepping, prancing-couple dance became so popular that whites eventually held cakewalk contests, never suspecting that they were indeed performing a satirization of their own dance.

Finally, dance functioned as a tool of socialization. The bondsmen achieved group cohesiveness and identity through dancing. Put another way, dance provided a mechanism for the slave to learn society's expectancies of his or her sex role. It enabled the slaves to become acquainted and provided a means for individual blacks to demonstrate their movement virtuosity. Further, dance served as entertainment within the slave community for fellow slaves and white onlookers alike. Finally, dancing was the most popular and widely practiced pastime of Afro-American slaves. If for no other reason than the momentary relief it provided from the drudgery and harshness of enslavement, dance played a unique, important, and vital role in Afro-American lives.

SELECTED BIBLIOGRAPHY

Lynne Fauley Emery, *Black Dance in the United States from 1619 to 1970* (1972); Federal Writers' Project, *Slave Narratives: A Folk History of Slavery in the United States from Interviews with Former Slaves* (1936–1938); Georgia Writers' Project, *Drums and Shadows: Survival Studies among the Georgia Coastal Negroes* (1940); and David K. Wiggins, "Sport and Popular Pastimes: Shadow of the Slavequarter," *Canadian Journal of History of Sport and Physical Education*, 11 (1980), 61–88.

LYNNE FAULEY EMERY

DECLARATION OF INDEPENDENCE, SLAVERY AND THE. The word *slavery* fails to appear in the Declaration of Independence as it was finally adopted on 4 July 1776. Nevertheless, the document served primarily as a protest against what the North American colonists regarded as a form of political slavery by Great Britain. The Declaration was the last in a long line of eighteenth-century American polemics that employed slavery as a metaphor. Throughout the Enlightenment, slavery was considered the ultimate political evil, and references to it appeared commonly in almost every American revolutionary pamphlet published at the time. *Tyranny*, a term that did appear in the Declaration, was defined as the act of rendering a loyal subject a slave to his ruler by "oblig[ing him] to act or not to act, according to the arbitrary will . . . of another."

In the Declaration of Independence Thomas Jefferson* accused England's George III of enslaving the American colonists under British tyranny. Not content simply with declaring the colonies independent, Jefferson sought to alter by revolutionary means what he deemed the outmoded social order that had been maintained by the British. Black slavery lay at the core of that social order. Though himself a slave owner, Jefferson argued that it would be both inconsistent and hypocritical to condemn political slavery without denouncing black slavery.

As a result, Jefferson included specific denunciations of slavery and the slave trade in an early draft of the Declaration.

The king, Jefferson wrote, "has waged cruel war against human nature itself, violating it's [*sic*] most sacred right of life and liberty in the persons of a distant people who never offended him, captivating & carrying them into slavery in another hemisphere or to incur miserable death in their transportation thither." Jefferson went on to charge that the English monarch was "Determined to keep open a market where *Men* should be bought & sold" and "suppress[ed] every legislative attempt to prohibit or to restrain this execrable commerce." In this draft of the Declaration, Jefferson openly attacked slavery and alleged that not only had George III forced slavery and the slave trade on the colonists, but that he had prevented colonial governments from banning the trade as well. Jefferson even accused the king of inciting slave revolts against the colonists.

Much to Jefferson's diasppointment, his entire passage on slavery was struck out by the Continental Congress. Delegates from South Carolina and Georgia sought to protect slavery at all costs, as did Northerners who profited from the transatlantic slave trade. Other members of Congress objected to Jefferson's references to slavery, not because they favored the institution, but because they believed that the allegations were false. The king had never coerced the colonists to purchase slaves, they said. And it was the royal governors, not the crown, who had vetoed slave trade bans on mercantilist grounds. Few delegates to the Congress took seriously Jefferson's charge that George III had incited blacks to revolt.

Although Jefferson argued that the omission of references to slavery seriously weakened his document, Congress retained what in its day constituted a most revolutionary notion: "that all men are created equal." Slaveholders and slave traders alike accepted this phrase because they believed it to be true. Historian Carl Becker has concluded that although Jefferson and his colleagues "apprehended the injustice of slavery; . . . one is inclined to ask how deeply [they] felt it." It was left to a later generation to grapple with the Declaration's social and political consequences.

SELECTED BIBLIOGRAPHY

Bernard Bailyn, *The Ideological Origins of the American Revolution* (1967); Carl Becker, *The Declaration of Independence: A Study in the History of Political Ideas* (1942); Frederick M. Binder, *The Color Problem in Early National America as Viewed by John Adams, Jefferson and Jackson* (1967); Edwin Gittleman, "Jefferson's Slave Narrative: The Declaration of Independence as a Literary Text," *Early American Literature*, 8 (1974), 239–256; and John Chester Miller, *The Wolf by the Ears: Thomas Jefferson and Slavery* (1977).

CURTIS F. MORGAN, JR.

DELAWARE, SLAVERY IN. The history of slavery in Delaware is conditioned by two important factors. First, it was a border state, the inhabitants of which in the two southern counties, Kent and Sussex, had close ties with their neighbors on Maryland's Eastern Shore, while in the northern county of New Castle the influence of nearby Pennsylvania and Philadelphia was strong. Second, the state never developed a crop such as tobacco or cotton involving the use of large numbers of slaves throughout the year.

During its early history the colony on the Delaware River changed hands several times. The Swedes established the first permanent settlement at Fort Christina (Wilmington), but lost control to the Dutch in 1655. The English defeated the Dutch in 1664. The new owner was the Duke of York, brother of King Charles II, but in 1682 he surrendered control to William Penn, in order that the access route up the Delaware River to Pennsylvania would be safer.

At no time before Penn acquired the colony was the black population numerous. The first black inhabitant was named Anthony, who came to New Sweden on a Swedish ship from the West Indies in 1639. It is uncertain whether he was then slave or free, but in later life he became free. In 1664 one-fourth of 300 slaves arriving at New Amsterdam were assigned to New Amstel (New Castle) on the Delaware River, but most of them ended up in English hands as part of the spoils of war and were sold in Virginia. A census of 1677 revealed only eight slaves of each sex living under the jurisdiction of the New Castle Court.

Under William Penn the area in the colony south of New Castle became more thickly settled, and Kent and Sussex counties were developed. Demand for labor increased greatly. When indentured servants* from Europe proved insufficient in number to supply the need for labor, the settlers turned to slaves. Many settlers who came from Maryland's Eastern Shore brought slaves with them. Other slaves were imported from overseas. Figures from reports of ministers of the Church of England indicate that slaves and free blacks* were numerous in the Three Lower Counties by 1728. The number of slaves and free blacks in Sussex County in that year totaled 241, and, by some accounts, comprised one-third of the total population in southern New Castle County. About twenty-five years later they numbered 364 in the parish of Appoquinimink in southern New Castle County and were "very numerous" in Kent County, the Church of England minister there having baptized 100 black adults and 17 children. On the basis of these figures, perhaps a minimum of 1,000 free blacks and slaves lived in the Lower Counties by 1750. At least 2,000 blacks lived in the colony in 1775, and according to the federal census of 1790, the total was 8,887 slaves and 3,899 free blacks.

Most of the slaves and free blacks in the Lower Counties worked as farm laborers or domestic servants. Inventories of deceased persons from the colonial period indicate that most families owned no slaves, some owned one or two or a family, and a small number owned ten or more slaves. For example, when Nicholas Loockerman, a wealthy farmer of Dutch descent, died in Kent County in 1770, he owned twelve slaves. A friend who died in the same year, John Vining of Dover, owned seventeen slaves.

A few slaves were trained for other jobs than farming or domestic service. In 1764 John Dickinson advertised for rent his Kent County plantation. He mentioned that the renter might also secure the services of slaves trained as tanners, shoemakers, carpenters, and tailors as well as for farm work, provided that they would be treated kindly. Advertisements for runaways occasionally point out that the missing slave could play the violin or read and write.

By 1700 the increasing number of slaves attracted the attention of the assembly representing both the Lower Counties and three Pennsylvania counties. An act passed in that year setting up special courts "for the trial of Negroes" marked the beginning of discriminatory legislation against blacks in Delaware. During the colonial period other laws provided for more severe penalties for blacks than for white persons and prohibited them from carrying weapons and assembling in large numbers. Especially severe was the punishment* of sexual relations between white females and black males, occasional examples of which are presented in county records. Both were placed in the pillory and whipped,* but the ear of the black male offender was nailed to the pillory and cropped off. Intermarriage of black and white persons was forbidden. Laws in the 1760s permitted owners to free slaves, provided that a bond had been posted, as free blacks were suspected of being "slothful" and an evil example to slaves. Lawmakers also feared that free blacks might become dependent for relief upon counties.

The Anglican church expressed interest in the spiritual welfare of the black inhabitants, both free and slave. Upon orders from the Society for the Propagation of the Gospel* in London, Anglican missionaries in the Lower Counties in the eighteenth century held special services for blacks and performed baptisms with mixed results. In 1748, for example, the Reverend Philip Reading of Appoquinimy in New Castle County reported that converting blacks to Christianity was not easy, partly because their African religions assured them that at death they would return to their native country. The Reverend Hugh Neill of Dover in Kent County, however, had considerable success in attracting attendance at services on Sunday evening. In 1752, within six months, he had baptized thirtysix black adults, each of whom could recite the creed, Lord's Prayer, the Ten Commandments, and part of the catechism, though few could read. A special study of the Anglican church* in colonial Delaware estimates that 500 black persons received instruction and were baptized.

The number of slaves in Delaware was rapidly growing, and the assembly on the eve of the American Revolution* tried to exercise some control. In 1775 the assembly passed a bill to prohibit both the importation and exportation of slaves, but Governor John Penn vetoed the proposal. When the first constitution was drawn up for the state in 1776, one provision provided that "no person hereafter imported into this state from Africa ought to be held in slavery under any pretence whatever, and no Negro, Indian or mulatto slave ought to be brought into this state for slavery from any part of the world." But upon application to the legislature farmers who owned land along the Maryland-Delaware border could receive permission to transport slaves into and out of the state to work on their land. Court records reveal that slaves continued to be sold out of the state and that sometimes freedmen were kidnapped for this purpose.

During the American Revolution the black inhabitants of the state made important contributions to American victory as toilers of the soil and in general service. Slaves and free blacks sometimes served as express riders, hostlers, and teamsters. Free blacks, like their white neighors, paid taxes, sometimes in grain, for the support of the common cause. The labor of slaves and free blacks on Delaware plantations produced provisions for the American army. State laws forbade the recruiting of black soldiers; consequently, few blacks likely served as soldiers.

At the time of the American Revolution Quakers* in the state, inspired by the example and teachings of Warner Mifflin of Kent County, began to free their slaves. He submitted petitions urging abolition to the general assembly and later to Congress. Perhaps his example influenced John Dickinson in 1777 to manumit twenty-two of his slaves in Kent County. The Methodists,* who began to grow rapidly after the Revolution, also urged their members to free their slaves. Although a large number of slaves were manumitted during and after the Revolution, the census of 1790 revealed that there were still three slaves for every free black in the state.

Influenced perhaps by the example in nearby Pennsylvania, some Delawareans, mostly Quakers, established in 1788 the Delaware Society for Promoting the Abolition of Slavery. In the same year the Delaware Society for the Gradual Abolition of Slavery also began meeting. These were the first of several "gradualist antislavery" societies that were organized in the state. The members protected free blacks from kidnapping and encouraged slave owners to free their slaves. In 1823 a branch of the American Colonization Society* was formed in Wilmington to sponsor sending free blacks to Africa, but the free blacks in the city held a public meeting of protest. The Wilmington society gathered money for the support of Liberia* and continued to be active for at least twenty-five years.

Some Delawareans were bitterly opposed to slavery. The most prominent leader was Thomas Garrett, a Wilmington businessman and Quaker, who claimed that by 1858 he had aided the escape of 2,152 slaves. Free blacks were also conductors on the underground railroad.* Abraham D. Shadd, a Wilmington shoemaker, was active in this capacity and was also a community leader. Samuel Burris of Kent County served as a conductor. Jailed upon one occasion, he had his services sold from the courthouse steps and found that his friends had bought his time. One of the most prominent black conductors in the nation, Harriet Tubman,* sometimes led runaways to freedom through Delaware from the Eastern Shore of Maryland.

The number of slaves in Delaware decreased rapidly, from almost 9,000 in 1790 to half that number in 1820 and to 1,798 in 1860, most of the latter number being confined to Sussex County. The work of Quakers and Methodists, the activities of abolitionist societies, running away, and the example of nearby northern states contributed to the decrease in the number of slaves. So too did the exhaustion of the soil and the year-round cost of keeping slaves. Also the industrialization of the Wilmington-Brandywine area made slavery unattractive in northern Delaware. By 1860 slavery was almost extinct in Wilmington and rapidly disappearing in New Castle County. Due to the efforts of Quakers and Methodists, aided by soil exhaustion, the number of slaves in Kent County was reduced to 203, the smallest number of any county in the state. Even in Sussex County, the ratio of slaves to free blacks was one to three.

Delaware, like other border states, experienced a dramatic rise in its free black population during the nineteenth century and responded by constraining free blacks wherever possible. Prior to the Civil War free blacks faced many legal discriminations. When the Reverend William Yates visited the state in 1837, he found that free blacks could not vote, hold office, serve on juries, or testify freely in cases involving white persons. Free blacks needed passes to leave the state, and if they were absent more than six months, they were not permitted to return. Free blacks were not taxed for the support of schools, but neither could their children attend public schools.

Laws became noticeably stricter after the Nat Turner insurrection* of 1831 in Virginia. Rumors circulated that such an uprising might occur in southern Delaware. At the time of an election in October 1831, some "evil-disposed" white men, with black handkerchiefs across their faces, engaged in a mock "shootout" on the south bank of the Nanticoke River across from the town of Seaford. An express rider with news of the "insurrection" was sent to Dover for aid. Although it soon became known that the incident was just a prank, several petitions thereafter asked the general assembly to provide for stricter control of the activities of slaves and free blacks. The assembly obliged by passing laws limiting the hours of religious meetings for blacks, requiring black preachers from out of state to secure licenses, and placing limitations on blacks' ownership of firearms. Every decade up to the Civil War saw additions to these restrictions, which increased in number as the number of free blacks grew.

Free blacks in the decades before the Civil War worked at many occupations, and some became prosperous. This was especially true in Wilmington. A city directory of 1845 listed twenty-six occupations in which free persons were engaged. In 1839 the number paying taxes on property worth more than $500 totaled fifty-two, and five of that number owned more than $1,000 worth of property. Some free blacks in the state became tenant farmers, and others owned small farms. In 1860 free blacks owned $638,657 worth of property in the state.

Free blacks in Wilmington usually assumed leadership in pushing for advances and improvements for members of their race. In that city appeared the first black church, the first African school, and the first black lodge. Petitions in the general assembly over such grievances as the need to have passes to leave the state, restrictions on firearms, and the licensing of out-of-state preachers originated in Wilmington.

Among organized religions, the Methodist church enjoyed the largest following among blacks in Delaware. The lively services of the Methodists appealed to blacks, as did the excellent sermons of preachers such as Harry Hosier, known as "Black Harry," a traveling companion of Francis Asbury noted for his rousing delivery. Methodism among Delaware's blacks also spilled over into Pennsylvania. Richard Allen, a former slave in Kent County, became a Methodist, and later founded the African Methodist Episcopal Church in Philadelphia.

The first black church in Delaware was Ezion Methodist Episcopal Church, which began in Wilmington in 1805 following the withdrawal of many black members from Asbury Methodist Episcopal Church. Later, under the leadership of the Reverend Peter Spencer, the Union African Methodist Episcopal Church began. In 1814 Spencer originated Big Quarterly, a homecoming occasion when free blacks and slaves from far and near gathered for religious services and socializing. This event still takes place annually in Wilmington. In rural areas slaves and free blacks attended Methodist services, sitting in the balcony as at Barratt's Chapel near Frederica in Kent County.

During the Civil War* a large number of the black inhabitants served in the Union forces. In 1862 President Abraham Lincoln* proposed an experiment of compensated emancipation in the state, in the hope that its success would spread, but he abandoned the attempt when he learned that the general assembly would defeat his proposal. A key member of the House of Representatives who had been elected as a "Lincoln man" and was supposed to favor the proposal decided against it. Probably at that time the majority of Delawareans were not yet prepared psychologically for the freeing of all the slaves in the state. The slaves in Delaware, as in the other border states, were not freed until the Thirteenth Amendment was ratified in December 1865, but blacks discovered that legal emancipation did not bring complete freedom. The Democratic politicians who controlled the general assembly found ways to restrict the blacks' economic and social freedom during the next twenty-five years and to remind them that they were only second-class citizens.

SELECTED BIBLIOGRAPHY

John Gary Dean, "The Free Negro in Delaware: A Demographic and Economic Study, 1790–1860" (M.A. thesis, University of Delaware, 1970); Harold B. Hancock, "Not Quite Men: The Free Negroes in Delaware in the 1830's," *Civil War History*, 17 (1971), 320–331; Harold B. Hancock, ed., "William Yates's Letter of 1837: Slavery and Colored People in Delaware," *Delaware History*, 14 (1971), 205–216; John A. Munroe, "The Negro in Delaware," *South Atlantic Quarterly*, 56 (1957), 428–444; H. Clay Reed, "The Negro in Delaware: Legal Status," in Reed, ed., *Delaware, A History of the First State* (2 vols., 1947), 2: 571–580; and Pauline A. Young, "The Negro in Delaware: Past and Present," in H. Clay Reed, ed., *Delaware, A History of the First State*, 2: 581–607.

HAROLD B. HANCOCK

DEMOCRATIC PARTY. The politics of slavery shaped much of the antebellum Democratic party's history from its inception in the 1820s to its disruption in 1860. The party's origins stemmed partially from the crisis in 1819–1820 over the admission of Missouri as a slave state. Leading politicians in the North and South hoped that a national party would focus attention on issues other than slavery and thus ease sectional tensions. And throughout the antebellum period the Democratic party remained staunchly antiabolitionist. For this and other important social and economic reasons, white Southerners overwhelmingly supported the Democrats until the mid–1830s, rendering the South the most important cog in the national Democratic machine. Throughout the 1830s, the South's concerns coincided with those of the party. For example, united Democrats in Congress imposed the "gag rule" that suppressed abolitionist petitions. And Andrew Jackson's Democratic administration encouraged the exclusion of abolitionist pamphlets from the mails.

In the 1840s, the political focus shifted from slavery to its expansion. Democrats from all regions favored territorial expansion, whether or not Southerners took their slaves into the new territories. But when Northern Whigs denounced the annexation of Texas and the Mexican War* as proslavery plots, portraying Northern Democrats as lackeys of the South, some defensive Northerners sought to prove themselves defenders both of Northern rights and of expansion. They introduced in Congress in 1846 the Wilmot Proviso, prohibiting slavery in territories acquired from Mexico as a result of the war. After the proviso's rejection, and despite the bolt of some Northeasterners to the antislavery Free-Soil party, Democrats coalesced around a compromise on the slavery expansion issue. The compromise, called "popular sovereignty," allowed the people of a territory to determine for themselves whether or not they wanted slavery. That seemingly straightforward proposal was actually ambiguous, and both Southerners and Northerners interpreted it in ways most beneficial to their regions. The party applied its popular sovereignty solution to the Kansas-Nebraska Act,* which made possible slavery's expansion into territories from which it had been excluded. The act helped to drive many Northern Democrats into the Republican party; nevertheless, the party maintained its support for popular sovereignty until 1857, when the U.S. Supreme Court issued the *Dred Scott v. Sanford** decision. By declaring that Congress could not exclude any property, including slaves, from the territories, the court raised doubts about whether a congressional creature—the territorial governments—could do it. Democrats throughout the South concluded that because slaves were property, the federal government was responsible for slavery's protection in the territories. They therefore demanded that the Democratic party include in its platform a call for a federal slave code. When Northern Democrats rejected that demand, delegates from the lower South (and some from the upper South) walked out of the 1860 national convention. Although Democrats tried unsuccessfully to patch up the sectional rift, not until the 1870s and 1880s would the party be fully reunited.

During the Civil War, Northern Democrats denounced emancipation and raised the banner of white supremacy. After the war, the Democrats, though accepting emancipation as a fait accompli, remained the party of white supremacy.

SELECTED BIBLIOGRAPHY

Richard H. Brown, "The Missouri Crisis, Slavery, and the Politics of Jacksonianism," *South Atlantic Quarterly*, 65 (1966), 55–72; William J. Cooper, Jr., *The South and the Politics of Slavery* (1978); Eric Foner, "The Wilmot Proviso Revisited," *Journal of American History*, 56 (1969), 262–279; Michael F. Holt, *The Political Crisis of the 1850s* (1978); David M. Potter, *The Impending Crisis, 1848–1861* (1976); Leonard L. Richards, "The Jacksonians and Slavery," in Lewis Perry and Michael Fellman, eds., *Antislavery Reconsidered: New Perspectives on the Abolitionists* (1979); and Joel H. Silbey, " 'There Are Other Questions Beside That of Slavery Merely": The Democratic Party and Anti-slavery Politics," in Alan M. Kraut, ed., *Crusaders and Compromisers: Essays on the Relationship of the Antislavery Struggle to the American Party System* (1983).

MARC W. KRUMAN

DEMOGRAPHY. The slave population of the North American mainland had a unique demographic pattern—a high and sustained natural increase for more than a century and a half. While contemporaries comparing slavery on the mainland with slavery in the Caribbean islands recognized this, it was only with the work of Philip D. Curtin on the magnitude of the Atlantic slave trade that the dimensions became clear. The mainland received only about 6 percent of the slaves brought from Africa to the Americas. But the rate of natural increase was so high that by 1825 the United States had about one-quarter of all blacks (and over one-third of all slaves) residing in the New World. The total imports of about 600,000 expanded into a black population of over 2.3 million in 1830, and over 4.4 million in 1860. This rate of natural increase—unique for a large slave society and unusual even for free societies outside of North America—has major implications for understanding U.S. slavery and slave culture.

Explanations of the differences in slave demographic patterns between the United States and elsewhere have pointed to several possible factors. Climate, crops grown, size of plantations, the cultural implications of different black-white ratios in settlement, and differences in the material treatment of slaves—all are significant. The availability of slaves from the international slave trade was never a critical explanatory factor. The United States and the British Caribbean islands ended the slave trade* in the same year (1808), and after the closing of the slave trade,* most Caribbean areas still suffered from natural decrease, while the U.S. black population grew at rates of over 2 percent per annum. The onset of a high rate of natural increase on the mainland preceded the closing of the international slave trade by about three-quarters of a century. Recent estimates show that in the Chesapeake, where large-scale slave arrivals began in the last decade of the seventeenth century, the slave population was self-sustaining by about the second decade of the eighteenth century. In South Carolina, where slave imports accelerated after the first quarter of the eighteenth century, sustained measured natural increase began after mid-century.

Several problems confound measurement of the rate of natural increase of the slave population. The desired measure of natural increase—the excess of births over deaths for the population resident in the region—is a difficult measure to calculate for several reasons. First, while the slave trade was open, population could increase by new arrivals, and among new arrivals there were often high rates (up to one-third according to some estimates) of mortality in the first year of arrival. To measure accurately the rate of natural increase of the slave population, it is necessary to eliminate deaths to, and births from, these new arrivals. The presence of the slave trade poses a further measurement problem because, unlike the native-born population, the sex composition among new arrivals was uneven (generally 60 to 70 percent male). The skewed sex and age pattern of new arrivals makes comparisons of birth rates and death rates difficult. Further, the slave population could decline as a result of manumission,* outmigration, and runaways,* not just deaths. Nevertheless, given the number of slaves imported into the mainland colonies and the United States in the international slave trade, the infrequency of manumission, the unimportance of outmigration, and the high percentage of U.S. blacks enslaved, the basic measurement of the rate of increase of the black population on the mainland should provide a good indication of the rate of natural increase of North American slaves (particularly after the middle of the eighteenth century).

The most unusual characteristic of the demographic performance of U.S. slaves was the extremely high rate of fertility. At a time when European birthrates were about thirty-five per thousand, the Afro-American population had a crude birthrate (the ratio of births to population) of fifty to fifty-five per thousand. This meant that each female who completed her childbearing years bore between seven and eight children. Rates that high were achieved by the free white settlers of North America, but not by slave populations elsewhere in the Americas. By the mid-nineteenth century, because there had been sharper decreases in the fertility of the free population than of the slaves, the fertility rate for slaves exceeded that of white Southerners. The positive price of slave children, the relatively higher measured fertility among slaves in the older than in the newer areas of the South (a pattern different from that of whites), the movement of slaves towards the South and West, and the argument that slave mothers would not voluntarily wish to have children, led to a frequent charge of "slave breeding,"* implying a deliberate and direct interference in the sexual activity and family life of slaves to foster high fertility. Masters did set constraints influencing slave life, within which the slave cultural and demographic patterns developed. Nevertheless, it now seems generally accepted that there was no pattern of deliberate "breeding." Even so, masters influenced the sustained high fertility of U.S. slaves by encouraging and accepting slave marriages, by providing health care* for the slaves, and by providing relatively better nutrition to slaves on the mainland than was available to those in the Caribbean. The better nutrition of U.S. slaves is suggested by their greater height compared with slaves in the Caribbean and blacks in Africa.

Richard H. Steckel has provided the most systematic analysis of U.S. slave fertility patterns in the late antebellum period. He presents a decomposition of the number of children* per female into the percentage bearing children, the ages at first and at last birth, and child spacing. He uses this to analyze important questions about the impact of culture, nutrition, and economics (as influenced by crops grown and size of farms). Much work continues on both the measurement and interpretation of these variables, but some of the basic contours now are clear. While there were some variations across crops and plantation size, the basic findings are that most (about four-fifths) slave females bore children, the start of childbearing began several years after the onset of fecundity (although childbearing began for slaves at younger ages than it did for the white American population), childbearing ended at an age comparable with that of the white population, and child spacing was relatively short (about two and one-half years between surviving children). The period of lactation among U.S. slaves was about one year, shorter than the lengths observed among Caribbean slaves and blacks in Africa. Several studies of the pre-nineteenth-century years suggest that the age of the mothers at the birth of their first child may have increased over time. Less is known about fertility among antebellum free blacks, although the slow growth of that population suggests that birthrates may have been lower and/or death rates higher than among slaves. Among Southern blacks, the birthrate in 1880 was at about the 1860 level, and it was only after 1880 that the black birthrate began a sharp decline.

The mortality rate of Southern slaves was above that of Southern whites, with both having a higher mortality rate than whites in the Northern states. In the early years of settlement, Southern slave death rates were apparently higher, particularly when there were large numbers of slave imports who suffered from the initial impact of seasoning (the exposure to a different climate* and disease* environment). The estimated crude death rates in the late eighteenth and nineteenth centuries, about twenty-five to thirty per thousand, were below those of slaves in the Caribbean and were comparable to rates found in Western Europe at this time. The charges made that slaves were worked to death in a short period (usually seven years) are not accurate as applied to the North American slave population (or any other New World slave population), and, consistent with recent scholarship on nutrition, medical care, and physiology, differences in mortality and material treatment between the slave and free populations in the South were not as sharp as earlier argued. Differences in mortality existed among crop types and by size of farm. Death rates were apparently higher in rice- and sugar-producing regions of the South, reflecting the nature of crop production as well as the nature of the areas in which production was most profitable.

Some differences existed in the effects of various diseases and in causes of death between black slaves and free whites in the South. These differences related to varying patterns of disease immunities and played an important role in settlement patterns and in explaining the relative importance of slavery. The high death rates of whites due to malaria and the relatively lower mortality from malaria of blacks (due to the presence of the sickle-cell trait) had been used to buttress a climatic theory of slavery. While such an explanation is no longer held sufficient, there were, nevertheless, important differences in the mortality and morbidity experiences of blacks and whites, and the unwillingness of whites to settle in unhealthy regions did spur the development of slavery. Blacks died relatively less frequently from malaria and yellow fever than did whites, but suffered more from other diseases, such as cholera, tetanus, and what is now called Sudden Infant Death Syndrome. Southern black death rates rose after emancipation, and while they began to fall after about 1880, it was not until early in the twentieth century that the antebellum rates were again achieved.

In addition to natural increase, before 1808 the slave population also grew as a result of the importation of slaves from the Caribbean and from Africa. At first, with small numbers arriving, slaves were brought from the Caribbean, but by the end of the seventeenth century most bondsmen came direct from Africa. Slave imports were highest in the period 1730–1770 and then 1780–1810, the last three decades accounting for about one-half of all slave arrivals. Recent studies suggest that there was relatively little smuggling of slaves into the United States between 1808 and 1860.

There was, however, an extensive internal movement of the slave population, particularly in the nineteenth century. In terms of location and crops, North American slavery differed quite dramatically in its first two centuries from its last half-century. At the time of the Revolution almost all slaves still resided within the original colonies of settlement. While some movement into newer areas of the South (e.g., Kentucky, Tennessee, Alabama) occurred after the war, it was only with the rise of short-staple cotton* that the massive westward movement of the slave (and white) population began in the South. The move westward and into the lower South was greatest during the great cotton booms of the 1830s and 1850s. Over 800,000 slaves were involved in the interregional movement of slaves between 1800 and 1860, although the relative numbers moved by the slave trade and by migration with masters remain a source of historical controversy. By 1860 the southern states outside of the original colonies held roughly one-half of all slaves. Nevertheless, the movement westward and southward did not mean absolute declines in the slave populations of the older areas of the South. As late as 1860 more slaves resided in Virginia than in any other state.

The unusually high rate of natural increase of the North American slave population had important cultural and economic implications. The high rate of natural increase meant that in the United States, Afro-Americans had a higher percentage of their population native-born than did whites. There were also fewer native Africans in the South than in the slave populations elsewhere in the Americas. In addition, the much lower ratio of blacks to whites in the United States than in most Caribbean slave societies suggests a different pattern of social and cultural adaptations by slaves on the mainland than elsewhere. The high rates of population growth contributed to the profitability of slavery. The high fertility enhanced the value of females, although most of the value of slave females came from crop production. The relative healthiness of the mainland, at least as compared to the Caribbean, also made it more probable that slaves would have more productive years. The very high rates of natural increase made it possible for slaves to be moved into newer, more productive areas of the South, while not reducing the absolute numbers in the older areas. The high rate of natural population increase meant that the United States, the recipient of a relatively small share of those slaves brought across the Atlantic in the international slave trade, became the largest American slave power of the mid-nineteenth century.

SELECTED BIBLIOGRAPHY

Philip D. Curtin, *The Atlantic Slave Trade: A Census* (1969); Robert W. Fogel and Stanley L. Engerman, *Time on the Cross: The Economics of American Negro Slavery* (1974); Robert W. Fogel and Stanley L. Engerman, "Recent Findings in the Study of Slave Demography and Family Structure," *Sociology and Social Research*, 63 (1979), 566–589; Kenneth F. Kiple and Virginia H. King, *Another Dimension to the Black Diaspora: Diet, Disease, and Racism* (1981); Allan Kulikoff, "A 'Prolifick' People: Black Population Growth in the Chesapeake Colonies, 1700–1790," *Southern Studies*, 16 (1977), 391–428; Richard H. Steckel, *The Economics of U.S. Slave and Southern White Fertility* (1985); and Richard H. Steckel, "Slave Mortality: Analysis of Evidence from Plantation Records," *Social Science History*, 3 (1979), 86–114.

STANLEY L. ENGERMAN

DIET. Questions regarding the adequacy of the slaves' diet have become increasingly interesting to historians as more and more has been learned about the importance of food nutrition. These questions have focused largely both on the quantities of the nutrients consumed and on the quality of the nutrients contained in the nutriments.

Today most scholars agree that by the nineteenth century the majority of slaves enjoyed a sufficient intake of calories. There was neither hunger in the slave cabins nor outright starvation as slaves sometimes experienced in the West Indies. Nevertheless, researchers have been embroiled in an ongoing debate over the quality of the slave diet. (Compare the arguments in Robert W. Fogel and Stanley L. Engerman, *Time on the Cross* [2 vols., 1974] with those set forth here.) Recently a related question has been raised regarding the ability of the slaves' bodies to utilize properly many of the nutrients delivered by that diet.

A principal cereal comprised the basic energy fuel for the slaves. For some in coastal South Carolina, Georgia, and Louisiana that cereal was rice.* For a few in the wheat belt to the north, it was wheat.* But for the overwhelming majority of the slaves in the South, corn* was the single most important supplier of calories. The average daily ration amounted to about a pound of cornmeal for each adult slave.

Animal protein comprised the other major component in the slaves' core diet. Again, for a relatively few slaves residing in coastal regions, that protein was often fish.* For some it was beef. For most bondsmen the chief source of their animal protein was salted or pickled pork. This was issued in the amount of about a half pound daily per adult slave.

This core diet of meat and cereal was supplemented to a greater or lesser extent by molasses or sorghum, red peppers, and, for much of the year, sweet potatoes. Seasonal items such as field peas, black-eyed peas, crowder peas, cowpeas, and greens (spinach, collard, mustard, poke salad) also found their way on to slave tables, often in a soup. Milk and milk products never were important items of slave consumption in the South. This resulted in part because of low milk production, and in part because slaves from an early age would have suffered from lactose intolerance. They, like their modern-day descendants, had difficulty in digesting milk sugars.

To measure the adequacy of the slave diet, one must first determine the extent to which slaves were able to provide food for themselves. Fishing and hunting doubtless supplemented the diets of many slaves. And many slave families raised poultry and hogs and tended their own truck gardens. Even so, the realities of slavery—physical labor from sunup to sundown—afforded little leisure time for fishing, hunting, and gardening. Much literature exists to indicate that the slaves became habituated to a "hog and hominy" diet and generally experienced little variety of viands. The bondsmen actually sold much of the foodstuffs that they raised and grew to purchase such "luxury" items as tobacco, alcohol, and clothing for special occasions.

For these reasons, then, masters furnished most of the slaves' comestibles, a diet largely of corn, pork, and supplements. The half pound of pork, although generally of a medium fat variety, combined with cornmeal and sweet potatoes to deliver enough protein to the adult slave to provide reasonably good health. Even so, much of the protein was of the incomplete variety—one or more of the essential amino acids were inadequately supplied. The pork in the diet, however, would have been enough to protect the adult slave from protein deficiency.

That pork, with assistance from the cereal and vegetable supplements, also probably delivered enough vitamin B_2 (riboflavin) and vitamin B_1 (thiamine) to most slaves to keep deficiency diseases at bay. Corn, however, without special processing, is peculiarly deficient in usable vitamin B_3 (niacin) and high in leucine (an amino acid) that acts adversely on the ability of the body to produce a niacin substitute. Thus many slaves were probably niacin deficient. Because the B-complex vitamins must be in balance to function efficiently, this deficiency would have meant that many slaves became somewhat riboflavin deficient and perhaps even thiamine deficient.

Because the corn consumed by the slaves was mostly of the white variety, and because many of the varieties of sweet potatoes and yams in the South were also white (as opposed to orange) many slaves doubtless suffered a vitamin A deficiency. This problem occurred particularly during those months when green leafy vegetables did not find their way into slave cooking pots. Rancid lard—frequently used by slaves in cooking—added another complication to the slaves' difficulty with vitamin A. A fat soluble vitamin, it is rendered usable by fatty acids. However, if that fat is rancid, it will not facilitate the utilization of the vitamin, but rather will destroy it.

Heat destroys vitamin C, and the slaves' habit of extensively boiling or simmering the vegetables they consumed would have considerably reduced the vitamin-C yield of those vegetables. Oxidation, another enemy of vitamin C, would have been precipitated by the slaves' iron cooking pots. During those spring and summer months when high yielding vitamin-C foods such as cowpeas and greens went into those pots, probably enough of the vitamin survived the heat and oxidation to supply the slaves. For the remainder of the year, however, it is quite likely that the slaves were somewhat vitamin-C deficient.

If iron cookingware exerted a pernicious effect on vitamin C, there was compensation in the fact that these utensils would have supplied the slaves with some badly needed iron. Exactly why blacks of West African origin tend to have higher frequencies of iron deficiency anemia than other peoples is not known. Some scholars speculate that part of the difficulty may lie in the blood anomalies developed as a protection against malaria. Others believe that blacks may utilize iron somewhat differently than whites. Regardless of the ultimate resolution of the problem, without question the slaves' genetic makeup played an important role in shaping their nutritional status in utilization of iron as well as other minerals. For example, lactose intolerance, in militating against the slaves' consumption of milk products, would have robbed them not only of a valuable source of complete protein, but of a crucial source of calcium as well. Moreover, the slaves' dark skin would have made it difficult for them to absorb calcium from other sources during the winter months. Darker skins are considerably less able than lighter skins to utilize the ultraviolet rays of the sun to stimulate bodily vitamin-D production. And vitamin D is essential for the absorption of calcium and magnesium.

The slaves' low intake of vitamin C further exacerbated their difficulties with calcium, for vitamin C facilitates the absorption of calcium. Indeed, the slaves' lowest vitamin-C intake would have occurred during the winter months—those same months when overcast skies and indoor work would have sharply reduced the ability of the slaves' bodies to produce vitamin D. And the slaves' diet was quite high in phosphorous relative to the calcium intake. This imbalance would have also served to hinder the absorption of calcium. The fate of magnesium, and other minerals as well, would have been much the same as calcium as far as the slaves were concerned. But the point is that although the diet of the slaves differed little from that of many white Southerners, because of genetic factors the slaves would have suffered much more than whites from deficiencies in that diet.

Evidence, however, is accumulating to indicate that by virtue of their West African ancestry, the slaves may have had some defenses against nutritional hardship. For example, many scholars argue that blacks have a heavier bone structure than whites—precisely because of a long-standing problem of a calcium-deficient diet. The heavier bone structure, they contend, results from an ability to store calcium in those bones during early life while still on the breast against a lifetime of deprivation. Or again, research has shown that blacks of West African origin can be quite tolerant of anemias that other peoples would find devastating.

Yet even if adult slaves were able to "live" with various kinds of malnutrition better than other peoples, their youngsters were not, and slaves of all ages revealed symptoms of deficiency diseases. The high frequency of bleeding gums among them suggests a low yield of vitamin C from the diet. The prevalence of eye afflictions indicates a serious problem with vitamin-A intakes and quite possibly riboflavin as well. Pellagra-like symptoms that appeared in both endemic and epidemic form confirm a diet dangerously low in niacin.

There is no question, however, that it was the young bondsmen who suffered most from the inadequacy of the slave diet. For some, nutritional difficulties began even before birth. Those whose mothers were seriously calcium, mag-nesium, or iron deficient were likely to be born (often prematurely) with these deficiencies. A year or more of breast feeding by a nutritionally depleted mother, with little or no dietary supplementation, added minimal nutritional succor.

Slave children who developed calcium or magnesium deficiency, or who received an inadequate supply of vitamin D, frequently fell victim to nutritional tetany (then a usually fatal disease) whose symptoms in the very young resemble those of tetanus. Rickets, the penalty for these deficiencies in later life, is not so severe and seldom became a fatal illness. Nonetheless, physical descriptions of slaves mention bowed legs and bossed skulls with sufficient regularity to leave little doubt that numerous slave children suffered from rickets.

Perhaps the most dangerous time for the young slave was shortly after weaning. Planters commonly believed that hominy and fat comprised a proper diet for slave children and that vegetables and meat (as opposed to fat) were not good for them. Thus, often until puberty, slave children were subjected to a diet even higher in carbohydrates and lower in good-quality protein than that of their parents.

On farms and plantations where milk was available to children for at least a portion of the year, the slave young probably escaped severe physical harm. But where little milk was served to the young, or for those children who suffered from the early onset of lactose intolerance, the nutritional consequences were often devastating. Without the injection of at least some complete protein into the diet, a child quickly becomes a candidate for what modern researchers call protein calorie malnutrition (PCM).

Ample evidence suggests that many slave children fell victim to this tragic disease. Of these, some succumbed to marasmus—symptomatic extreme of PCM that is outright starvation—and simply wasted away. Most, however, developed symptoms of kwashiorkor—on the opposite symptomatic pole from marasmus. In the case of kwashiorkor, the child has a more or less adequate intake of calories, but calories that derive almost exclusively from carbohydrates, as opposed to good-quality protein sources. Kwashiorkor, of course, is too frequently seen today throughout much of the developing world with its most prominent outward symptom, the distended stomachs of toddlers. Ironically, planters took pride in the potbellies of their slave youngsters, believing that they represented the wisdom of feeding the young as they did. The brain and liver damage that results from the illness is generally manifested in later life.

For the slave youngster who escaped tetany and PCM, other nutritional hazards loomed ahead. Many consumed earth—often a sign of iron or calcium deficiency. While the use of pica is seldom fatal, it introduces worms into the body. Worms proved exceptionally fatal to slave children (as they are to the malnourished young everywhere) because growing bodies very often simply cannot stand this additional nutritional burden.

Slave children died of poor nutrition at a significantly higher rate than their white counterparts. Even so, the diet of the slave children and adults in North America surpassed that of slaves in the Caribbean and Brazil. In the latter two regions, the death rates of slave children—attributable largely to severe nutritional deprivation—were consistently so high as to undercut the natural growth of the slave populations. Thiamine deficiency, an antecedent of beriberi, ranked among the serious deficiencies within these slave populations. It was a deficiency passed along to the children through the milk of a mother. The result for slave infants and toddlers in the Caribbean and Brazil was widespread infantile beriberi, an almost always fatal malady. In addition, slave children in these regions suffered considerably more from PCM than did their North American counterparts.

A final piece of evidence that the slave diet in the United States contained more high-quality protein than slave diets elsewhere in the hemisphere can be found in studies of the heights that adult slaves achieved. Slaves in the United States grew to a significantly greater height than creole-born slaves in islands throughout the Caribbean. These data on slave heights will doubtless suggest to some that the North American slave diet was nutritionally adequate after all. Yet hurricanes, wars, and the circumstances of sugar slavery on islands with limited useful land all combined to make Caribbean slave populations the most nutritionally deprived slave populations of the hemisphere. Therefore, while it is true that North American slaves consumed a relatively much better diet than did their Caribbean counterparts, that diet, as we have seen, was still far from adequate.

SELECTED BIBLIOGRAPHY

Robert W. Fogel and Stanley L. Engerman, *Time on the Cross: The Economics of American Negro Slavery* (1974); Eugene D. Genovese, *Roll, Jordan, Roll: The World the Slaves Made* (1974); Sam B. Hilliard, *Hog Meat and Hoe Cake: Food Supply in the Old South, 1840–1860* (1972); Kenneth F. Kiple, *The Caribbean Slave: A Biological History* (1985); Kenneth F. Kiple and Virginia H. King, *Another Dimension to the Black Diaspora: Diet, Disease, and Racism* (1981); Todd L. Savitt, *Medicine and Slavery: The*

Diseases and Health Care of Blacks in Antebellum Virginia (1978); and Richard Sutch, "The Treatment Received by American Slaves: A Critical Review of the Evidence Presented in *Time on the Cross*," *Explorations in Economic History*, 12 (1975), 335–438.

KENNETH F. KIPLE

DISCIPLES OF CHRIST. The Disciples of Christ began in 1832 with the merging of the Christian movement led by Barton Stone in Kentucky and a group of Reforming Baptists led by Alexander Campbell in western Virginia. The new church grew rapidly in the decades before the Civil War and claimed about 200,000 members in 1860. The center of the church's strength lay in the Midwest and in the border states of Kentucky and Missouri. While the Disciples also had considerable strength in Tennessee, Arkansas, and Texas, the movement gained fewer numbers in the lower South.

According to *The Eleventh Annual Report of the American and Foreign Anti-Slavery Society*, published in 1851, "Campbellites" owned over 100,000 slaves. While that estimate seems excessively high, by 1860 there were about 800 Disciples churches in slaveholding territory. And some of the older, most distinguished families of Kentucky and Missouri belonged to the church. Disciples congregations generally followed the same patterns of black church membership found in the other evangelical churches of the South. Although church record books listed black members along with whites, blacks were segregated during worship. Only a handful of independent black Disciples churches existed before the Civil War, largely in Kentucky or the North. The most celebrated black preacher in the church was Alexander Cross. A Kentucky slave, Cross was purchased and freed by the churches of Christian County, Kentucky. In 1853 he was sent to Liberia* by the church's missionary society.

The roots of the Disciples of Christ movement reached into the early nineteenth century revivalism in the American West. The religious ferment at the turn of the century stirred considerable sentiment for the abolition of slavery, and early Disciples shared that enthusiasm. The most widely known leader of the movement, Alexander Campbell, criticized slavery openly and advocated the colonization* of the freed blacks. A member of the Virginia Constitutional Convention of 1829–1830, he favored the constitutional enactment of a colonization scheme.

As the antislavery debate turned more bitter in the 1830s and 1840s, Campbell and other Disciples leaders withdrew to a more moderate course. Although most of the church's leaders continued to deprecate slavery, they ultimately lost hope of any practical solution. Most found the abolitionist movement distasteful in spirit and unscriptural in argument. Furthermore, the Disciples churches were almost totally located in those areas of the nation that took a moderate middle course during the antislavery debate. In a series of eight articles beginning in January 1845 entitled "Our Position to American Slavery," Campbell argued that slavery was biblically permissible and called for an end to debate on the subject.

Nevertheless, the Disciples of Christ contained a small abolitionist movement.* Led by Ovid Butler, an Indianapolis businessman and patron of North-Western Christian University (later Butler University), the abolitionist wing objected to the moderate stance of the Disciples missionary society. In 1859 they established a rival Christian Missionary Society. Three years later, however, it was dissolved when the war pushed other Northern Disciples into a stronger antislavery posture.

SELECTED BIBLIOGRAPHY

Robert Oldham Fife, "Alexander Campbell and the Christian Church in the Slavery Controversy" (Ph.D. dissertation, Indiana University, 1960); David Edwin Harrell, Jr., *Quest for a Christian America: The Disciples of Christ and American Society to 1866* (1966); and *Preliminary Guide to Black Materials in the Disciples of Christ Historical Society* (1971).

DAVID E. HARRELL, JR.

DISTRICT OF COLUMBIA, SLAVERY IN THE. From its origins in 1791 by an act of Congress, to April 1862, the District of Columbia contained a substantial slave community. The federal census of 1800 reported 3,244 slaves in the District, a slave population that grew to 6,277 bondsmen in the 1820 enumeration. The slave schedules of 1850 and 1860 indicate that Washington masters owned an average of five slaves. Those masters holding more than fifteen bondsmen lived primarily on farms in the county of Washington. Most slaves in the District, however, labored at skilled or semi-skilled jobs—as domestic servants, upholsterers, nurses, chamber maids, carpenters, houseboys and room servants, teamsters, carriage drivers, and cooks. Some lived apart from their masters and hired their own time.

By 1860 the District's slave population had declined to 3,185 bondsmen. This reduction resulted largely from private manumissions. Abolitionists* and colonizationists* long had targeted the District as fertile ground for emancipation. How, they asked, could the United States profess democratic values to the world, all the while trading slaves within earshot of the nation's capital buildings? In the 1840s Whigs, most notably Congressman Abraham Lincoln,* introduced legislation aimed at the gradual freeing of Washington slaves. It failed. The Compromise of 1850* restricted—but did not outlaw—the slave trade in the District. Unlike slave states in the lower South, manumission by will or deed never was outlawed in the District.

As a result of these forces, the free Negro population of the District rose from 783 in 1800, to 11,131 in 1860. Some free blacks purchased and, subsequently, manumitted their relatives. Absalom Shadd, for example, emerged as a prominent free black businessman, owning three bondsmen in 1850. Compensated emancipation in the District finally was enacted by Congress on 16 April 1862. It allocated a maximum of $1 million to compensate loyal slaveholders in the District. The Lincoln administration hoped to resettle these blacks beyond the

United States. Over 3,000 blacks ultimately were freed in the nation's capital. Compensations per slave averaged $300.

SELECTED BIBLIOGRAPHY

James Borchert, *Alley Life in Washington: Family, Community, Religion, and Folklife in the City, 1850–1970* (1980); Letitia W. Brown, *Free Negroes in the District of Columbia, 1790–1846* (1972); Constance McLaughlin Green, *The Secret City: A History of Race Relations in the Nation's Capital* (1967); Michael J. Kurtz, "Emancipation in the Federal City," *Civil War History*, 24 (1978), 250–267; and Page Milburn, "The Emancipation of the Slaves in the District of Columbia," *Records of the Columbia Historical Society*, 16 (1913), 96–119.

HENRY S. ROBINSON

DOUGLAS, STEPHEN A. (1813–1861). U.S. Representative (1843–1847) and Senator (1847–1861) from Illinois, presidential candidate, and Democratic party leader, Douglas was the most prominent and controversial figure in the political struggle over slavery in the territories during the 1850s. He chaired the committee on territories in both House and Senate and consequently played a central role in congressional debates over the Wilmot Proviso, the Compromise of 1850,* the Kansas-Nebraska Act* (which he wrote and sponsored), and the Lecompton crisis. Douglas took a middle-of-the-road, moderate position, rejecting both the antislavery and proslavery extremes as dangerous to the Union. He argued instead for "popular sovereignty," the doctrine with which his name became most closely identified. Slavery, declared Douglas, must be treated as a local, domestic institution, to be determined by the people in the territories without interference from Congress. He remained convinced that allowing the people to decide the slavery question for themselves would result in an increase of free territory. In his debates with Abraham Lincoln* (1858), Douglas argued that the agitation of the slavery question as a moral issue was both inexpedient and dangerous. There was no "tribunal on earth," he insisted, that could decide between the two conflicting positions on slavery's morality. To interject the moral question into political discussion was to court disunion and civil war. Douglas never advocated slavery. The peculiar institution, he said, was a "curse beyond computation, to both white and black" races. And he hoped the border slave states would soon adopt plans for gradual emancipation. Although he shared his generation's belief in the racial inferiority of blacks, Douglas rejected the argument that blacks should therefore be slaves. In the 1860 election, his concern was for the Union; the question of slavery was of secondary importance. Douglas blamed the outbreak of civil war on the extremists on both sides: the abolitionists and the southern radicals. He died while trying to mobilize Democratic popular support for Lincoln's effort to suppress the rebellion when it came.

SELECTED BIBLIOGRAPHY

Harry V. Jaffa, *Crisis of the House Divided: An Interpretation of the Issues in the Lincoln-Douglas Debates* (1959; paperback 1973); and Robert W. Johannsen, *Stephen A. Douglas* (1973).

ROBERT W. JOHANNSEN

DOUGLASS, FREDERICK (1818–1895). The fourth child of a slave mother, Frederick Douglass was born in Tuckahoe Creek on Maryland's Eastern Shore. At age seven he was sent to Baltimore, a turning point in his life. Here he learned to read and write, grew accustomed to the less restrictive life of a town slave, and mingled with a free black population that had a communal life of its own through its churches and secular organizations. Psychologically then ready to become his own master, Douglass escaped in September 1838, making his way to New York. By prearrangement he was soon joined by his fiancée, Anna Murray, a free black from Baltimore. Assisted by well-wishers, the newlyweds went to New Bedford, Massachusetts. While working to support his wife and growing family, Douglass found time to attend antislavery meetings. After making a spontaneous speech at the Massachusetts Anti-Slavery Society in 1841 at Nantucket, he was hired as an agent by the society. Thus began his twenty-year career as the major black figure in the abolitionist* crusade.

In Douglass slavery faced a formidable foe. His background as a slave gave a dramatic personal touch to his denunciations of the peculiar institution. Of equal importance, however, was the eloquence that marked his testimony. Douglass was a public speaker par excellence; his rich baritone voice sounded every degree of light and shade and gave an emotional vitality to every phrase. His communication skills, though, were not confined to the spoken word. Douglass wielded a vigorous and effective pen, as his three autobiographies and numerous speeches and letters attest.

In addition to condemning slavery, Douglass sought to undermine it by constantly exhorting his fellow blacks to be industrious, reliable, and thrifty, thereby refuting the charge that blacks were improvident and childlike, destined for slavery by their innate inferiority. Douglass led the organized movements for black self-help and racial advancement during the 1850s. His was the loudest and most insistent voice urging blacks to vote, electing candidates opposed to slavery. Striking more directly at the institution, he gave financial assistance to fugitive slaves and used his home in Rochester, New York (where he lived from 1847 to 1872), as the headquarters of the local underground railroad.* Over a ten-year span no fewer than 400 Canada-bound runaways found refuge under Douglass's roof.

Douglass hailed the coming of the Civil War,* certain that it would lead to slavery's downfall. "Men of color, to arms," ran his urgent and repeated calls for black enlistments. He aggressively recruited Negroes for the Union armies, Douglass's first signees being his own two eligible sons. His war-related activities included two interviews with President Abraham Lincoln,* these White House visits giving Douglass a lift of spirit. As Douglass had foretold, the Civil War brought an end to slavery. But the racial stereotypes and patterns of racial discrimination that it had spawned did not die. Douglass trained his guns on these twin relics of slavery until his death in 1895.

SELECTED BIBLIOGRAPHY

Philip S. Foner, ed., *The Life and Writings of Frederick Douglass* (5 vols., 1950–1955); Nathan Irvin Huggins, *Slave and Citizen; The Life of Frederick Douglass* (1980); Waldo E. Martin, Jr., *The Mind of Frederick Douglass* (1984); Dickson J. Preston, *Young Frederick Douglass: The Maryland Years* (1980); and Benjamin Quarles, *Frederick Douglass* (1948).

BENJAMIN QUARLES

DRED SCOTT CASE. The Dred Scott case began in St. Louis in 1846 as *Dred Scott v. Irene Emerson*, a slave suing his mistress for freedom. Scott had lived in free territory before returning to Missouri, and, by Missouri law, was thereby entitled to freedom. Unforeseen developments delayed the litigation for several years. Then, through no intention of either party, the case became enmeshed in Missouri and national political debates involving slavery. In 1850 Missouri's lower court declared Scott free. But in 1852, in a dramatically partisan pronouncement, the Missouri Supreme Court reversed that decision, overturned numerous legal precedents, and proclaimed controversial proslavery rhetoric to be law.

To enable the U.S. Supreme Court to clarify that law, St. Louis lawyers instituted a new case, *Dred Scott v. John F. A. Sanford*, in the federal courts. Specifically at issue was the "once free always free" doctrine—whether a slave once emancipated could lose freedom by returning to a slave state. During argument, though, counsel introduced additional issues involving slavery and race. The Supreme Court could have simply dismissed the suit on noncontroversial procedural grounds. Instead, the Court's Southern proslavery majority chose to deal with volatile, substantive issues, thereby hoping to settle them permanently by judicial authority.

Chief Justice Roger Brooke Taney delivered the opinion of the Court on 6 March 1857. "Negroes of African descent," he decreed, could not be citizens of the United States. The Missouri Compromise, which in 1820 had prohibited slavery in the territories, above the 36° 30′ line, was unconstitutional, Taney explained, because slaves were property protected by the Fifth Amendment of the Constitution. Finally, the chief justice declared that an erstwhile emancipated slave who returned to a slave state was restored to slavery if that was the law of the state. In other words, "once free" no longer meant "always free."

With this decision the Supreme Court seemingly had finally placed the weight of the law behind the proslavery argument.* And many feared the next step would be to legalize slavery in the states as well as in the territories. Antislavery forces thus launched an unprecedented assault on the Dred Scott decision, denouncing it as obiter dictum and invalid, and attacking Taney and his colleagues in singularly vitriolic terms. Proslavery forces countered with equally bitter defenses.

With the country dividing along sectional and slavery lines, the Dred Scott decision figured prominently in political debates, especially in the famous Lincoln-Douglas debates of 1858. Douglas's suggestions on how to circumvent the decision not only lost him the presidency two years later, but it led Southerners to demand an explicit slave code that would unequivocally protect slavery everywhere. In the 1860 presidential election, the Democratic party* split over that code and over conflicting interpretations of the Dred Scott decision. That split resulted in the election of Abraham Lincoln* as president, with secession following immediately thereafter.

Only after the Civil War was it possible to redefine the status of blacks as declared in the Dred Scott decision. The Thirteenth Amendment* (1865) abolished slavery completely. The Fourteenth Amendment (1868) overthrew the rest of the Dred Scott decision, declaring that "all persons born or naturalized in the United States," which included former slaves, now were citizens of this nation. After eleven years and a bloody civil war, the Dred Scott decision finally was overturned.

SELECTED BIBLIOGRAPHY

Walter Ehrlich, *They Have No Rights: Dred Scott's Struggle for Freedom* (1979); Don E. Fehrenbacher, *The Dred Scott Case: Its Significance in American Law and Politics* (1978); and David M. Potter, *The Impending Crisis, 1848–1861* (1976).

WALTER EHRLICH

DRIVERS, SLAVE. Slave drivers were agricultural bondsmen with diverse responsibilities in field production and labor supervision on large plantations or small farm enterprises. In the management structure of large plantations, the slave driver ranked below the overseer,* steward, and/or planter. In the slave hierarchy, the driver's status was comparable to that of the slave artisans and household slaves. The position of driver originated in seventeenth-century South Carolina, where seasoned slaves supervised the field labor of new slaves by standing behind and "driving," or coercing, them to perform their new duties. By the nineteenth century, the position and responsibilities of the slave driver had expanded. Depending on the size of the agricultural unit, several occupational levels could exist: the head driver, also known as the the overdriver; the underdriver; and the foreman, who directed field task gangs.*

Most drivers were men, although there were some slave women who worked in the capacity of drivers when supervising "trash gangs" of young children, superannuated slaves, and women in an advanced stage of pregnancy. The male slave driver was usually in his thirties or forties. In some instances drivers were younger, and some managed to retain their positions into their sixties. Most slave drivers were intelligent individuals with forceful personalities and physical power or presence who also possessed leadership and management skills. Their major responsibility was to maintain a highly disciplined, efficient, and well-coordinated productive agricultural slave labor force.

The commercial agricultural South was dominated by a single crop economy. High productivity required an extremely regimented work force, specialization of field labor, and a high degree of labor interdependence and cooperation. Rigid discipline was required to maintain assembly-line fieldwork to meet production goals. In fulfilling these responsibilities of his position, the slave driver has often been compared to a shop foreman. His major purpose was to "drive" the slaves to maintain efficiency and discipline. Given authority to punish field hands, the driver historically was often called "whipping man" or "whipping boss."

But the slave driver was more than a "straw boss" whipping man or foreman who supervised field hands from sunup to sundown. Drivers collected information on field production, which they analyzed, interpreted, and passed on to the overseer, steward, or planter. In the absence of an overseer and often the owners, the driver had to schedule production and to plan how to deploy limited resources. In fulfilling these diverse responsibilities, the slave driver in this management capacity thus provides an example of slave "intrapreneurship." Possessed of both practical and specialized knowledge of crop production, the slave driver could come to dominate field operations in the production of cotton, sugar, tobacco, and rice that brought in the plantation dollars. The slave driver James Pemberton, who managed Jefferson Davis's Brierfield plantation, was representative of the slave driver as "intrapreneur."

Slave drivers were both generalists and specialists in the performance of their management duties, but more than anything else perhaps they had to be "people managers" who knew how to set goals and to motivate the field laborers. Their expertise was invaluable in contributing to the agricultural productivity of the antebellum South. Given the high rate of periodic absentee ownership, and that only 30 percent of plantations and farms had white overseers, as Eugene D. Genovese explains, "Probably, at least two-thirds of the slaves in the South worked under a black man who had direct access to the master with no white overseer between them—probably at least two-thirds, that is, experienced responsible and direct black leadership in their everyday work life."

Planter compensation for the success of slave drivers varied. High-top leather boots, greatcoats, and top hats in addition to the whip were often symbols of the driver's status and position. Since drivers were seldom "bred," opportunities existed for the slave driver to groom a promising son for this "privileged" position. Often the driver was rewarded with better housing and more abundant food rations. The position could also be used to mitigate punishment* of family members and friends; it could also be abused, to mete out punishment to enemies as well as to obtain sexual favors. Sometimes, planters provided drivers with extra land for their personal use with permission to use other slaves to cultivate the plot. Produce raised could be taken to town by the driver and sold for cash. Some drivers received money incentives in wages and bonuses, amounting in some instances to hundreds of dollars, for their efficiency in labor management and field production.

The management styles developed by drivers to maintain their position have become the source of great historical controversy. Historians, however, have been reluctant to accept the neo-abolitionist description of the cruel, sadistic, and brutal slave driver portrayed by Sambo and Quimbo in Harriet Beecher Stowe's 1852 *Uncle Tom's Cabin*. Rather, most historians tend to agree with Robert S. Starobin, who admits that, "Sometimes drivers punished slaves more severely than whites did; their ambiguous position thus could express itself in vicious cruelty. But most slave drivers bent the other way, and they often used their position to protect the slaves and ease the burdens of bondage."

The management operations of a capital-extensive, labor-intensive, single-crop agricultural unit encouraged development of a performance-oriented business culture as opposed to that of a paternalistic profit-sharing business culture. Even privileged slaves with specialized skills were inadequately compensated, despite the perquisites that could be derived from their positions. Yet most slave drivers attempted to retain their often unenviable positions as field managers. The duration of their tenure required that they push for optimum labor productivity and efficiency to meet the production goals and profit expectations of their masters. In doing so, drivers often found it difficult to act in the best interests of the slave community. John W. Blassingame speaks to that fact: "Using the self-serving testimony of a few remarkable drivers, historians have tried to demonstrate that he was the classic man caught in the middle who went to unusual lengths to protect his fellows. . . . The evidence from the blacks themselves contradicts this portrait."

After freedom, some drivers were able to use their knowledge of field production and farm management, and their personal ties to former masters, to become successful owners of small farms. A few continued working for their former owners as sharecroppers or tenant farmers: others took whatever job they could find. White hostility, racism, and discrimination prevented most former slave drivers from using their management skills developed during slavery to their own advantage after the Civil War.

SELECTED BIBLIOGRAPHY

John W. Blassingame, *The Slave Community: Plantation Life in the Antebellum South* (rev. ed., 1979); Eugene D. Genovese, *Roll, Jordan, Roll: The World the Slaves Made* (1974); Randall M. Miller, "The Man in the Middle: The Black Slave Driver," *American Heritage*, 30 (1979), 40–49; Randall M. Miller, ed., *"Dear Master": Letters of a Slave Family* (1978); Leslie Howard Owens, *This Species of Property: Slave Life and Culture in the Old South* (1976); Robert S. Starobin, ed., *Blacks in Bondage: Letters of American Slaves* (1974); and William L. Van DeBurg, *The Slave Drivers: Black Agricultural Labor Supervisors in the Antebellum South* (1979).

JULIET E. K. WALKER

DUBOIS, SILVIA (ca. 1768–1884?). Silvia Dubois, born into slavery in New Jersey about 1768, was the daughter of a black Revolutionary war veteran and a woman who unsuccessfully attempted several times to buy her freedom by mortgaging herself against loans. Growing to a formidable size, five feet ten inches tall and over 200 pounds, Dubois remained with her parents' first owner, moving with him to a small farm in Pennsylvania. There she performed work usually allotted to men and gained a reputation as intractable.

Although reasonably content with her master, Dubois hated her unusually cruel and bad-tempered mistress. Eventually the slave retaliated, striking her mistress with a fierce blow and immediately fleeing. When her master caught Dubois, he decided to free her instead of punishing her. On foot and with an infant child, she left to find her mother. When challenged for a pass, she replied that she belonged to God alone, put down her baby, put up her fists, and was left alone.

Years later, when over one hundred years old, Dubois was interviewed by a physician, C. Wilson Larison, who published the interview as *Silvia Dubois (Now 116 Years Old) A Biografy of the Slav Who Whipt Her Mistres and Gand Her Fredom* (1883). Printed in "diacritic type following phonic orthography," the book is difficult to read and reflects a neo-abolitionist's bias. But it remains valuable for its insights into slavery and the persistence and courage of individuals forced to live under it.

SELECTED BIBLIOGRAPHY

Cornelius Wilson Larison, *Silvia Dubois (Now 116 Years Old) A Biografy of the Slav Who Whipt Her Mistres and Gand Her Fredom* (1883); and Bert James Loewenberg and Ruth Bogin, eds., *Black Women in Nineteenth-Century American Life: Their Words, Their Thoughts, and Their Feelings* (1976).

LINDA O. MCMURRY

DURNFORD, ANDREW (1800–1859). Andrew Durnford, a free man of color, was born in New Orleans, Louisiana, in 1800 to Rosaline Mercier, a free woman of color, and Thomas Durnford, an Englishman. John McDonogh, a white merchant of New Orleans, was a friend, factor, creditor, and advisor to both Thomas Durnford and his son. Letters exchanged between McDonogh and Andrew Durnford provide information on Durnford, who became one of America's few black, slave-owning sugar planters.*

In 1828 Andrew Durnford established St. Rosalie plantation on a bend in the Mississippi River in Plaquemines Parish, Louisiana. Durnford planted and manufactured sugar cane with his slaves, a force that numbered seventy-six at his death. A mortgage to McDonogh funded Durnford's land and slaves. At McDonogh's death twenty-two years later the mortgage, increased by additional land purchases, was not paid off. Careful studies of Durnford's planting activities suggest that he was not a financially successful planter.

Durnford's slave-buying trip to Virginia in 1835 produced letters that reveal rare aspects of the business of marketing and transporting human slaves. The travels apparently persuaded Durnford to educate his son, Thomas McDonogh Durnford (McDonogh's godson), at a Northern school. Durnford mingled freely with whites, free blacks, and slaves. He apparently regarded slavery as a condition of man without regard to human quality. He personally provided medical care for his slaves, and he wrote of grief when one of them was injured or died. He did not approve of slavery, but he did not think it could be abolished without governmental interference. (He did not think, for example, that colonization was the answer to so large a question.) Surviving papers suggest that Durnford did not provide an easy or comfortable life for his slaves. Although he reported lashing but one slave, frequent runaways* suggest harsh treatment.

Durnford married Marie Charlotte Remy, a free woman of color. Their children were Thomas, Rosema, and Andrew, Jr. Andrew Durnford died on his plantation in 1859.

SELECTED BIBLIOGRAPHY

David O. Whitten, *Andrew Durnford: A Black Sugar Planter in Antebellum Louisiana* (1981); David O. Whitten, "A Black Entrepreneur in Antebellum Louisiana," *Business History Review*, 45 (1971), 201–219; David O. Whitten, "Rural Life along the Mississippi: Plaquemines Parish, Louisiana, 1830–1850," *Agricultural History*, 58 (1984), 477–487; and David O. Whitten, "Slave Buying in 1835 Virginia as Revealed by Letters of a Louisiana Negro Sugar Planter," *Louisiana History*, 11 (1970), 231–244.

DAVID O. WHITTEN

E

ECONOMICS OF SLAVERY. The "economics of slavery" might be defined broadly enough to cover almost every aspect of every historical experience with slavery. Of central concern to historians of slavery in the United States, however, are four economic issues. These issues are (1) the origins of slavery in North America; (2) the functioning of slave markets and the profitability of slavery; (3) the effects of slavery on economic efficiency and resource allocation; (4) the relationship between slavery and economic development in the American South.

A venerable tradition in economic thought associates slavery with free land or "open" resources. If land is available to all comers, and if cultivation may be practiced at any scale without major loss of efficiency, then there will be no way for an entrepreneur to achieve a large absolute profit except with unfree labor. Under a free labor system in these circumstances, wages would rise to exhaust all land rents, and large-scale agriculture would not persist. Broadly construed, this line of argument helps to explain why the European powers presided over expanding slave empires in the New World, at the same time that slavery, serfdom, and related forms of unfree labor were dying out in Europe itself. But within North America, "free land" cannot explain why slavery became concentrated in the Southern rather than in the Northern colonies. Throughout the eighteenth century, between 80 and 90 percent of the Negro population of continental North America was in Maryland, Virginia, and colonies farther south.

There is a deeper reason why the free land tradition is not the appropriate vehicle for explaining the early economic geography of American slavery. African slavery was not an institution created in North America. Far larger volumes of slaves were carried from Africa to the Caribbean and to South America, long before and long after the slave trade to the North American mainland became significant. Because slavery was a preexisting institution to which the North American colonies tapped in as a relatively minor and peripheral extension, slave *prices** were essentially determined in wider markets and were thus given (exogenous) to North America. In a legal sense, slavery developed in both the Northern and Southern colonies. But since they both faced a common externally determined price, a price which reflected the high profits of slave labor in the sugar islands, slaves were imported only where the value of the (marginal) product of labor was unusually high, as it was in the tobacco areas of the Chesapeake and later in the rice districts of Georgia and South Carolina. In other words, the "origins of slavery" are not part of North American history; instead, the geographic distribution of the slave population was "economic," reflecting the interaction of supply and demand. "Supply" took the form of an exogenous price, and "demand" was mainly determined by the availability of profitable export staples. The timing of this development, however, depended on the interaction between these elements and a third factor, the supply of alternative forms of unfree labor, primarily indentured servants.

The analysis is depicted in figure 1, adapted from David Galenson. Labor supply in each colony had three potential components: (1) natural growth of domestic population (S_D), assumed to be independent of the price of labor; (2) white indentured servants* (S_W), the supply of which was a positive function of the local price; (3) slaves (S_S), available at the given world price. The aggregate supply of labor (S_T) is the horizontal sum of these three curves. The major groups of colonies were each characterized by different relative positions of demand relative to this supply curve: New England had a high rate of domestic increase and low demand; the Middle colonies had a higher demand, but larger inflows of both free and servant labor, plus some slaves; the rice colonies were so unattractive to white settlers that virtually all of the growth of labor was slave labor (S_W above S_S at all points); and in the Chesapeake, slavery and servitude coexisted until the 1690s, by which time the growth of demand outran the supply of servants (which had already begun to contract in any case). The supply-side basis for the Chesapeake transition may be seen in the sharp rise in the price of servants relative to slaves (as much as 40 percent from the 1670s to 1690). The main forces behind this change in relative costs include rising real wages in England, the decline of landowning opportunities in the Chesapeake, the end of the Royal African Company's slave trade monopoly in 1698, and (on the demand side) the beginning of the great eighteenth-century expansion of tobacco demand.

Tobacco* was at the core of American slavery before the nineteenth century, and it provides the example which refutes most of the other ad hoc explanations for slavery. There were no significant scale economies in tobacco cultivation, and it was a crop which required delicate handling rather than brute physical force. Neither of these facts prevented slavery from becoming the dominant labor system. Nor was tobacco grown in areas which were fatal or even inhospitable to free settlers. Like cotton in the nineteenth century, tobacco was a good small-farm crop, and hence raises the question how the Southern regions might have developed differently, had slavery been abolished everywhere in the United States (as it was in the Northern states) shortly after the American Revolution.

For many years American historians entertained the idea that antebellum slavery was "unprofitable." Loosely based on the observation that slave prices had tripled between 1807 and 1860, while cotton prices drifted downward, the notion

Figure 1
Supply and Demand of Labor in Colonial Era (adapted from David Galenson,
White Servitude in Colonial America, **p. 148)**

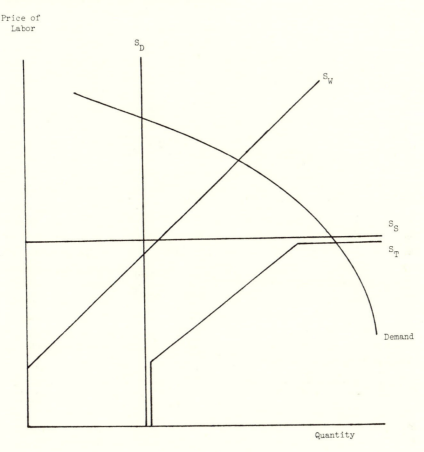

of unprofitability was also associated with the view that the slave system was
in a state of economic decline at the time of secession. (These doctrines are
linked with the name of Ulrich B. Phillips, though in fact his position was more
subtle than that of many of his followers.) In 1958 two Harvard economists,
Alfred H. Conrad and John R. Meyer, published calculations intended to refute
this doctrine, showing that at prevailing prices, yields, and life expectancies,
investments in slaves would have paid rates of return about equal to those
available from alternative investments, such as railroad bonds.

Subsequent research revealed, however, that Conrad and Meyer had merely
confused the underlying issue. If rates of return based on market prices were
too high or low, this imbalance could readily be corrected in the market for

Figure 2
Supply and Demand for Slaves in the Antebellum Era (Gavin Wright, *Political Economy of the Cotton South*, p. 140)

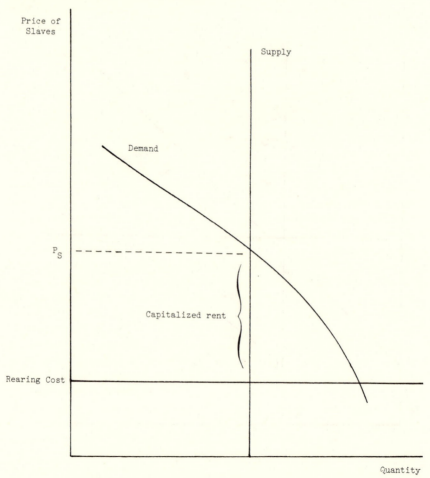

slaves, and would in fact be corrected by the normal operation of market forces. The more fundamental question was how these prices were determined. The analysis first presented in 1961 by Yasukichi Yasuba has since then become generally accepted, and is depicted in figure 2. The crucial point is that after the closing of the African slave trade* in 1808, the size of the aggregate slave population was fixed in the short run, independent of price. The slave population did, of course, grow over time, but only through the slow process of natural population growth; there was no short-run mechanism of elastic supply, in response to changes in demand. The implication is that the observed rise in slave prices must have been a result of increases in *demand*, and hence it could not very well be the basis for an "unprofitability" that would cause the decline of slavery. Indeed, the high profitability of slavery is itself reflected in the rising slave prices, the bulk of which are "capitalized rent" captured by owners at the time of birth or at the time of the price increase in the form of capital gains. In prosperous decades like the 1830s and the 1850s, capital gains were a major component of the profitability of slavery,* and they were enjoyed by every owner, whether efficient in production or not.

This analysis helps to explain a number of the distinctive features of slavery in the United States, such as the high rate of natural population growth, the infrequency of manumission, the absence of intermediate color categories, and the relatively good level of material welfare by comparison with Latin America. (The purely demographic* indicators, however, seem to predate the closing of the slave trade and to be equally rooted in dimensions of North American climate and epidemiology.) The high prices of slaves, for example, made self-purchase extremely difficult, even if the promise of freedom had a positive incentive effect on productivity. Apart from problems of contract enforcement and borrowing, a slave couple attempting to purchase their own freedom had to buy out not just the value of their own labor for years into the future, but the expected value of their children's labor for the indefinite future. The difficulty involved may be measured by the fact that rising slave prices were placing the status of slave ownership out of reach for a steadily increasing fraction of the *free* population. The percentage of all Southern families who were slave owners declined from 36 in 1830 to 31 in 1850 to 25 in 1860.

The now-accepted finding of vigorous profitability during the antebellum era does not necessarily imply that this profitability was firmly rooted in sustainable sources of growth, such as productivity. There is reason to believe that the two-generation history of rising slave prices was *not* sustainable, because with the aid of hindsight it appears that the antebellum era was unique in its growth rate of demand for cotton,* a crop for which the South had a strong geographic advantage. Cotton demand grew at 5 percent per year from 1820 to 1860; but the rate fell to between 1.5 and 2 percent per year from 1866 to 1895. This development seems to have been largely independent of the American Civil War, but reflects the fact that the first great wave of the Industrial Revolution in cotton textiles eventually had to slow down. The census year 1860 was at the very crest of this wave: a season in which cotton yields were far above normal combined with a year of record demand to produce the most prosperous year in Southern history, and the highest slave prices. But these extremes of performance and price would surely not have continued, even if there had been no secession and Civil War.

Another ancient tradition in Western thought holds that slave labor is inherently inefficient because it is reluctantly supplied. At most, slaves might perform simple repetitive tasks under close supervision and threats of physical punishment, but they could not do work requiring care, thought, or skill. The profitability evidence does not address this issue: slavery might have been profitable though inefficient, if a higher ratio of expropriation made up for a lower level of output per worker. Antebellum Northerners, including those who visited the South, were convinced that the inefficiency of slave labor was obvious and virtually self-evident. But productivity measurements by Robert W. Fogel and Stanley L. Engerman, published in their 1974 book *Time on the Cross*, indicated that slave plantations were as much as 30 percent more efficient than free family farms in the North or South. The subsequent debate has clustered around two interpretive positions: that of Fogel and Engerman, who attribute the productivity advantage to scale economies, gang labor methods, and the intensity of labor time; and that of Gavin Wright and others, who attribute the differential to the allocation of labor time between production for the market, on the one hand, and food production, household activities, and leisure time on the other.

As Fogel and Engerman approach the issue, scale economies and labor intensity are inferences drawn directly from the statistical data. The productivity differential is largest on large plantations, while slaves do not seem to have worked significantly more days or hours per year than Northern family farmers. The alternative view rests on certain regularities in the economic structure. The main points are (1) that slave-using operations planted a substantially larger share of their acreage in cash crops as opposed to food crops (mainly cotton versus corn), and (2) that a larger share of the labor time of slave households was allocated to market production than was true for free families (mainly women doing fieldwork instead of housework). Direct tests indicate that cotton was a more profitable choice than corn* for farms at all levels, but for a variety of reasons smaller farms chose to grow smaller amounts. Some were too far from markets or transportation facilities. Others were simply cautious. Production of cotton for the market at the expense of self-sufficiency was a risky choice for a small farmer with little in reserve. The rule of thumb they followed is known as "safety first": plant enough corn to meet the farm's requirements (with a reasonable margin for error), then plant the remainder in cotton, treating it "as a surplus crop."

Concerning the intrafamily division of labor and the length of the work year, comparisons with Northern farmers are not necessarily germane, because the seasonality of agriculture was so different in the two regions. But slavery increased the number of fieldwork hours per family, or so adjustments after emancipation suggest. Black women withdrew from fieldwork in large numbers after emancipation, while hours per day and per week declined across a wide range of margins. Roger Ransom and Richard Sutch estimate the decline in black labor supply at 28 to 37 percent per capita.

If these two effects, crop mix and family labor, are both valid, the crucial productivity effect comes from the interaction between them. A number of studies have shown that both large and small Southern farms were self-sufficient in foods, at about the same levels of consumption per person, per hog, per mule. Because of its ability to "collectivize" such household duties as food preparation and child care, however, the slave plantation was able to put additional labor into the fields. In effect, all of this additional labor went into the high-payoff cash crop. Thus, the two effects jointly had an impact substantially greater than the sum of their separate effects would have been.

The plausibility of this view of things is enhanced by two additional observations: (1) The sizes of cotton farming operations did not cluster around a large "optimal" scale, as they did in crops like sugar and rice, where technological scale economies were important. Farm sizes remained widely diffused, as they typically do in a constant-returns-to-scale industry. (2) In other economic activities with homogeneous outputs and inputs, such as mining, manufacturing, and grain farming, there is no evidence of a productivity differential between free and slave labor.

Slavery did, however, affect the allocation of land and labor. In an analysis advanced by Ralph V. Anderson and Robert E. Gallman, slaves had the character of fixed capital to owners, who therefore attempted to spread slave labor across as many acres as possible, and to fill in the work year as fully as possible. Here, too, the effect of slavery on the allocation of land and labor became apparent in the radical change at the time of emancipation, which produced a decline in the land-labor ratio (reversing previous trends) and an intensification of land use. The argument also helps to explain why plantations exhibited a strong impulse toward self-sufficiency and tried to minimize their interaction with local sellers of commodities and services.

Strictly speaking, the Anderson-Gallman analysis assumes that slaves could not be rented, an assumption which was not literally true. Especially in the towns of the upper South, slave rentals* were relatively common. But rental markets were not well-developed over most of the cotton belt. Even in the towns, slave rentals involved significant "transactions costs," precisely because slaves were so valuable that any owner had to be concerned about responsibility for health, safety, and escape. Thus, the mere fact that rental markets existed in some places does not imply that these were convenient and inexpensive to use (from either the demand or supply side), or that the slave economy could readily have developed rental markets as a means of adapting to changing economic conditions, in the manner of a wage labor economy.

If slave labor was productive, mobile, and allocated efficiently according to market principles, and if production and wealth were growing rapidly in the South under the slave regime (albeit with the aid of strong cotton demand), the question arises as to why so many Northern observers (and some Southerners) felt so strongly that both slavery and the South were economically backward. It is possible, as some argue, that such views reflected only bias, ignorance, racism, or lack of economic sophistication. A more plausible interpretation is that these perceptions arose from the objective fact that patterns of Southern economic development under slavery were indeed quite different from those in the North. Most of these differences may be traced back to a key distinction between forms of wealth: slaves were movable personal property, whereas Northern wealth was primarily held as land or fixed capital, both of which were effectively fixed in place. This contrast was at the heart of the peculiar economics of slavery, because it created a different set of incentives regarding such enterprises as transportation, town building, mineral exploration, and recruitment of immigrant labor. In 1860 the average slaveholder held more than three-fourths of his wealth in a form which was completely independent of local developments, wherever he might be at a particular moment. Instead, slave values were determined in a broad but fundamentally efficient market encompassing the entire Southern region. Within the region, slave owners were economically "footloose." Geographical turnover among wealthy planters was extremely high, as high as that of the poorest classes of unskilled workers in Northern cities. Their ability to leapfrog directly to the best cotton lands of the Old Southwest left many "backwater" areas behind in the Southeast, largely unaffected by the national trend toward commercialization.

The contrast in economic geography between North and South illustrates some of the effects of this incentive structure. The South invested far less in transportation facilities relative to its area than did the North. The canal boom of the 1830s almost completely bypassed the South, and the density of railroad mileage even in 1860 was only about one-third that of the North. Urbanization rates were markedly lower, and this difference was steadily widening over time. Even more notable was the contrast in numbers of small towns; crossroads communities with stores, post offices, libraries, and schools dotted the countryside across the Northern states, but were few and far between in the South. Because towns, railroads, and factories were the most visible manifestations of progress, it is not hard to see why Northerners thought the South was "backward"; but the sustained economic pressure for canals, railroads, and towns in the North was coming from *landowners* hoping for a capital gain on their holdings. In the South, land wealth was dwarfed by slave wealth, which was unaffected by such developments.

Perhaps more important was the difference in population growth, almost entirely the result of the fact that foreign immigration went overwhelmingly to the North. Immigrants* were actively recruited by Northern landowners, as well as by owners of fixed manufacturing capital looking for cheap labor. These motivations were virtually reversed under slavery. Slave values would not be enhanced by immigration; under any reasonable assumptions, slave values would decline. Indeed, slave owners in all parts of the South actively opposed the campaign to reopen the African slave trade. They may have had many reasons for doing so, but an aspect which was not lost on them was that such a proposal would instantly wipe out a large fraction of their accumulated wealth (by reducing slave prices). Thus, the incentives intrinsic to slave ownership led the South to remain isolated from outside labor flows, and for this reason the South was "falling behind" in the specific sense that the Southern share of the total national population or economy was steadily declining.

Slower population growth was directly related to Southern backwardness in manufacturing. Numerous studies have now confirmed that slaves could and did work effectively in factories, including skilled jobs. But their value was still greater in the cotton fields, especially in the rich new lands of the Old Southwest. The ability to tap into an elastic supply of foreign labor was crucial to the survival and growth of manufacturing in the North, even while opportunities in farming were expanding. But the slave South could not choose this option (for reasons given above), and hence manufacturing languished during times of agricultural prosperity. A specific example is textiles,* which grew at a 6 percent annual rate during the 1840s, only to find its further progress stifled in the 1850s.

A second way in which the economic effects of slavery may be ascertained is by noting the changes in economic structure which began immediately after emancipation. A reorientation toward land-intensity occurred on many fronts. Railroad investment accelerated, and interior towns began to spring up. A new interest in mineral exploration led to a wave of discoveries and development schemes, from the phosphorous deposits of South Carolina to the coal and iron ores of Alabama and Tennessee. Phosphorous mining was associated with another striking new development, the fertilizer revolution which revived or initiated commercial cotton growing in many parts of the Southeast which had been abandoned or previously passed over. In both the Southeast and Old Southwest, town-building efforts were closely linked to new progress in manufacturing, especially in the textiles and iron industries.

These departures make it clear that the institution of slavery did have a major influence on the pattern and structure of the Southern economy. Emancipation did not, of course, immediately bring the South into the mainstream of national economic development. But that is a chapter in the economic history of the postslavery era. Exactly what shape the slave economy might have taken had it survived into the twentieth century will always be a matter for speculation. But slavery did not create an economy well suited for rapid integration into the capitalist world as we know it.

SELECTED BIBLIOGRAPHY

Hugh Aitken, ed., *Did Slavery Pay? Readings in the Economics of Black Slavery in the United States* (1971); Ralph V. Anderson and Robert E. Gallman, "Slaves as Fixed Capital: Slave Labor and Southern Economic Development," *Journal of American History*, 64 (1977), 24–46; Paul A. David et al., *Reckoning with Slavery: A Critical Study in the Quantitative History of American Negro Slavery* (1976); Robert W. Fogel and Stanley L. Engerman, *Time on the Cross: The Economics of American Negro Slavery* (1974); David W. Galenson, *White Servitude in Colonial America: An Economic Analysis* (1981); Russell Menard, "From Servants to Slaves: The Transformation of the Chesapeake Labor System," *Southern Studies*, 16 (1977), 355–390; and Gavin Wright, *The Political Economy of the Cotton South: Households, Markets, and Wealth in the Nineteenth Century* (1978).

GAVIN WRIGHT

EDUCATION. Education is a process of cultural transmission and transformation. The two basic cultures taught or transmitted to first-generation African slaves in the British North American colonies were African culture,* which they learned from their relatives and friends, and European culture, which their captors forced upon them. The American environment (social, political, economic, and physical); the rise of staple-crop, plantation agriculture; the passage of time; succeeding generations of masters and slaves; and the interaction of African and European cultures slowly transformed them into Euro-American and Afro-American cultures. These two cultures were the content of slave education, their interaction, transformation, and transmission its method.

African and Afro-American slaves learned the English language, Christian religion,* and many values and practices from whites. Early twentieth-century racist scholars (e.g., Ulrich B. Phillips) viewed slavery as moral, a school for civilization and Christianity for African savages. A later generation of scholars, most notably Stanley Elkins, described slavery as an immoral process that taught Africans to become infantilized, obsequious Sambos who internalized their masters' dehumanizing views of slaves. Both schools of thought, however, basically agreed that slave education was primarily the imposition of white culture upon Afro-Americans.

In the 1960s a new generation of scholars began to counterbalance the white masters' writings and records with black primary sources (e.g., Afro-American history and folklore, autobiographies of escaped slaves, and interviews with former slaves), and discovered that white-training was neither totally effective nor one-sided. Rejecting the view that Africans brought no culture to or lost their culture in slavery, John W. Blassingame and others described the elements of African culture that slaves retained and the viable institutions (family and underground church) and folklore that Afro-American slaves developed, and also shared with and taught to their children. Learning and teaching this Afro-American culture allowed slaves partially to resist the dominance of white culture, and permitted them to transmit elements of their culture to whites. Scholars such as Blassingame and Eugene D. Genovese have described how the interaction of slaves and masters produced plantation society in the South. Ironically, even racist historians such as Phillips, who so long found "The Central Theme of Southern History" in white Southerners' determination to maintain white supremacy, recognized that the very existence of blacks in the South shaped the essence of Southerners, or, in educational terms, blacks taught whites to be Southerners.

Most studies of North American slavery discuss education only in terms of formal (schools) or informal (tutoring or self-instruction) teaching of reading-writing-arithmetic. A few slaves did, in fact, learn to read, write, and compute. During the colonial period there were few restrictions on slave education. Especially in the Middle and New England colonies, some masters and religious groups provided literacy training for slaves. Phillis Wheatley,* the noted poet, was the best example of a slave tutored by her master's family. Such organizations as the Anglican Society for the Propagation of the Gospel in Foreign Parts* and the Society of Friends (Quakers*) founded a few schools (usually in cities) for free and slave Afro-Americans. Later, even after most Southern states had passed laws in the 1830s forbidding slave education, Presbyterians* and Southern Methodists* established carefully supervised plantation missions and schools which taught religion and, sometimes, enough literacy to permit slaves to read the Bible. From the late 1700s on, free urban blacks began schools for their children. Some urban slaves attended these schools; others received secret instruction from the black teachers.

Formal (school) literacy training for slaves, even when it was available, remained limited, as it also was for most middle- and lower-income Americans, black and white, before the Civil War. Most slaves who could read and write learned from their masters (as they taught the slaves to do jobs which required some literacy) or, more often, from the masters' wives or children. Even after teaching slaves to read and write became illegal in the South (except in Maryland, Kentucky, and Tennessee) in the 1830s, many planters' wives still taught favored slaves the rudiments. Slave children* who carried the master's children's books to and from school learned by listening outside the school. When planters' children wished to "play school," they literally had a captive class in the plantation's slave children. Slaves sometimes traded their skills or possessions to whites for education or books, a practice especially common in cities. While it is impossible to document precisely how much of this literacy training occurred, laws against teaching slaves to read and write, laws punishing slaves who wrote passes, and the testimony of ex-slave interviews and fugitive slave narratives all suggest that some slave literacy training continued until the arrival of Union troops and Northern, black and white, missionary-teachers during and after the Civil War allowed these underground streams to bubble up and flow freely.

By focusing on literacy training, scholars have tended to overlook or slight another type of education which was even more important in most slaves' daily lives, namely, vocational training. The primary education most Americans received before the Civil War (as children, apprentices, or slaves) was job training. In this area, as Booker T. Washington* and others have noted, the plantation was a school for slaves. Slaves, who did most of the work on the antebellum Southern plantations (and much of the work in towns), received careful, continuous training in all aspects of domestic service, farming, dairying, care of livestock, construction and repair of fences and buildings, and all the other jobs on plantations (even, in some cases, overseeing the operation of the entire plantation), as well as most jobs in the South's few mines, factories, and towns. Indeed, Washington frequently stated that his emphasis on vocational training at Tuskegee Institute was, in part, an attempt to regain for Afro-Americans the level of vocational education many had acquired under slavery.

While forced contact with white culture from the 1660s through the 1860s was teaching Africans to be Afro-Americans (as, simultaneously, these Africans and Afro-Americans were teaching Europeans, then white Americans, in the South to be Southerners), a distinctive Afro-American culture remained the essence of the slave education that succeeding generations of slaves received, reworked, and remitted to their descendants. Although this Afro-American slave culture differed discernibly from Euro-American Southern culture, slave education varied by time and location. Purely African education virtually stopped when the external slave trade became illegal in 1808, but elements of African culture continued to be taught for decades (even into the twentieth century) on isolated Georgia and South Carolina Sea Islands after slavery ended in 1865. Where as well as when slaves lived influenced their education. Because of their continuous contact with whites and relative isolation from slave quarters, slaves on farms and small plantations, and yard slaves (artisans) and house servants on large plantations had the least distinctively Afro-American education. Urban and industrial slaves' education included both white and free black influences. Afro-American education developed most fully among field slaves in the slave quarters of large plantations.

Education in plantation slave quarters was distinctive in content and method, although the overlap of the two frequently made the medium the message. Older slaves, for example, taught youngsters to resist white values and to trick whites both by doing so and by rewarding such behavior, just as life in the community taught the value of community. Young slaves learned how their elders perceived black superiority to whites, the unity of the quarter community, the importance of the family and freedom, the reality and significance of the spirit world, the difference between true, black Christianity and the false religion (subservience and obedience) their masters sought to teach, and both antipathy-distrust of whites and the necessity for constant vigilance and care in dealing with such powerful adversaries. By example, precept, and participation the slave quarter taught these lessons through the community, extended family, peer group, and secret slave congregation, and through songs (secular and spirituals) and religious, heroic, historic, and trickster myths, folktales, and stories.

Emancipation and the dispersion of the slave quarters after the Civil War ended slave education in its unique form. Continued segregation and discrimination, however, insured the continuous teaching-transmission of Afro-American culture through Afro-American education to the present, even as the "great migration" to cities and the North, the modern civil rights movement, and other economic, political, and social forces have shaped and continue to transform Afro-American education and culture.

SELECTED BIBLIOGRAPHY

John W. Blassingame, *The Slave Community: Plantation Life in the Antebellum South* (rev. ed., 1979); Henry Allen Bullock, *A History of Negro Education in the South: From 1619 to the Present* (1970); Eugene D. Genovese, *Roll, Jordan, Roll: The World the Slaves Made* (1974); Lawrence W. Levine, *Black Culture and Black Consciousness: Afro-American Folk Thought from Slavery to Freedom* (1977); Ulrich B. Phillips, *American Negro Slavery: A Survey of the Supply, Employment and Control of Negro Labor as Determined by the Plantation Regime* (1918); Robert G. Sherer, *Subordination or Liberation?: The Development and Conflicting Theories of Black Education in Nineteenth-*

Century Alabama (1977); and Thomas L. Webber, *Deep Like the Rivers: Education in the Slave Quarter Community, 1831–1865* (1978).

ROBERT G. SHERER

ELDERLY SLAVES. In the antebellum American South, where the life expectancy of slaves ranged from the low thirties for males to the mid-thirties for females, few blacks reached old age. In 1860 less than 10 percent of the slave population was over fifty and only 3.5 percent was above age sixty. But those who did reach old age faced a precarious existence in a production-based economic system. While paternalism* could be the reward for a slave's long and faithful service under one master, many slaveholders linked work expectation to physical capacity rather than chronology. They failed or refused to acknowledge the aging of their bondsmen. Ultimately, the fate of most elderly slaves depended upon the personality of the master and the financial exigencies of the plantation.

Most slaveholders regarded the senescent slave as an economic liability, but many found ways to maintain elderly slaves and keep costs to a minimum. For example, to prevent the health care of a chronically ill slave from draining off plantation funds, masters employed black healers. Slaves often preferred their herbal prescriptions to the treatments of white doctors. Also, the capitation or head tax on slaves was eliminated at age fifty or sixty, thus relieving the burden of maintaining old slaves. Even so, masters often pursued more drastic means to offset or remove the economic liabilities of aged slaves. Masters sometimes sold their slaves to unsuspecting buyers by dyeing or plucking out gray strands of hair or falsifying documents. In some cases slave masters isolated old slaves in out-of-the-way huts. Frederick Douglass recalled bitterly the fate of his grandmother, given a hut in the woods and "made . . . welcome to the privilege of supporting herself there in perfect loneliness; thus virtually turning her out to die." Such, charged Douglass, was the "base ingratitude and fiendish barbarity" of the master class. In spite of laws designed to protect white society from pauperized slaves, masters freed senescent slaves to beg morsels of food from neighbors, to spend their last days in the poorhouses, or to become public charges. In spite of the planters' proslavery argument, few elderly slaves were "retired" or maintained as pensioners at the master's expense.

Notwithstanding the variations of slave treatment, slavery was primarily an economic system that valued slaves, young as well as old, in accordance with their economic worth and productivity. The usefulness of slaves could be maintained into old age because the agricultural unit was well-suited for a myriad of abilities and strengths. Useful employment meant not only intrinsically profitable tasks, but also the performance of jobs that freed the more robust to perform duties that were more physically demanding. The jobs of old men included watering and feeding animals, hunting game, shucking corn,* sharpening, polishing and repairing tools, and gardening.* Elderly women cooked food, cleaned houses, attended the sick, cared for plantation children, sewed, and knitted.

Although these gender distinctions generally prevailed, the parity of strength in old age rendered few jobs the exclusive province of a particular sex. And both sexes continued to be utilized by the plantation economy in their later years.

The care and status of old or superannuated slaves did not rest entirely on the attitude and treatment of individual owners. Within the slave community the elderly held a special position and filled diverse roles. It was here that the old found care, respect, and a ''place'' to live as well as the opportunity to practice religious tenets that sustained them in their belief in the hereafter. According to Eugene D. Genovese: ''The slaves themselves did everything possible to allow their old people to end their lives with dignity.''

Reverence for the old harked back to the West African tradition, survived the trauma of enslavement, and persisted in relationships between young and old slaves. The elderly slave generally was respected for his age, wisdom, and rarity, as well as for the performance of valuable functions similar to those performed by senior members of West African communities. Elderly slaves socialized children, acted as intermediaries between parents and children, advised on religious matters and love affairs, served as doctors-midwives, told stories of Africa and America that linked past and present, and served as conduits of the cultural heritage. Consonant with West African tradition, grandparents frequently named slave children, particularly boys, after ancestors—a practice that gave continuity to families in a society where family separation was a likely occurrence.

Thus it was in the slave community that the old and superannuated found dignity, respect, and usefulness. Paradoxically, old age earned the slave respect in the quarters at the very time that its accompanying infirmities jeopardized his existence in an economic system that valued only his productive capacity. This dynamic contributed in no small measure to the ambivalence and anxiety characteristic of the aging process.

SELECTED BIBLIOGRAPHY

John W. Blassingame, *The Slave Community: Plantation Life in the Antebellum South* (1972); Frederick Douglass, *Narrative of the Life of Frederick Douglass, an American Slave, Written by Himself* (1845); Eugene D. Genovese, *Roll, Jordan, Roll: The World the Slaves Made* (1974); Herbert G. Gutman, *The Black Family in Slavery and Freedom, 1750–1925* (1976); Benjamin Klebaner, ''American Manumission Laws and the Responsibility for Supporting Slaves,'' *Virginia Magazine of History and Biography*, 63 (1955), 443–453; Todd L. Savitt, *Medicine and Slavery: The Diseases and Health Care of Blacks in Antebellum Virginia* (1978); and Kenneth M. Stampp, *The Peculiar Institution: Slavery in the Ante-Bellum South* (1956).

LESLIE J. POLLARD

EMANCIPATION. Ultimately, emancipation was the fruit of the Civil War, but more than a year after the fighting had begun, President Abraham Lincoln* still insisted that he sought only to preserve the Union. As he said in an August 1862 letter to Horace Greeley, he would maintain slavery if it saved the Union; he would end it if emancipation guaranteed the future of the republic.

Lincoln's policies toward slavery and the question of emancipation were always shaped by his sensitivity to the loyalty of the border states. The Confiscation Act of 6 August 1861 did give army officers the authority to seize and free the slaves of Confederates, but it had no effect upon the fate of more than 800,000 slaves who were the "property" of Unionists in the border states and it left open the possibility that an end to the "insurrection" might allow the continuation of slavery. Whatever his own views—and Lincoln insisted that he remained personally committed to ending slavery—as president of a divided nation he moved cautiously through 1861 and into 1862. In the spring of 1862 he successfully pushed through the Congress a plan for compensated emancipation in the District of Columbia. (Owners were, however, paid $300 or less—a price far below antebellum "market" value.) At the same time, Lincoln failed in his effort to persuade the border states to adopt a policy of gradual, compensated emancipation. Only with the rejection of his proposal by the border states and the improvement of Union military fortunes in September of 1862 did Lincoln announce his intention to issue the Emancipation Proclamation,* still carefully excluding the border states from the impact of its provisions.

International politics were an additional, though unacknowledged, factor in Lincoln's decision. In 1862, Confederate diplomats were desperately seeking recognition from the European powers. The American government's decision to begin the process of emancipation transformed the Civil War into a moral struggle between slavery and freedom and probably doomed Confederate attempts to achieve international recognition from England and France.

On 1 January 1863, Abraham Lincoln issued his anxiously awaited Emancipation Proclamation. All persons held as slaves within any portion of the South still in rebellion were "henceforward and forever free." While Lincoln described the Emancipation Proclamation as an "act of justice" for which he invoked divine approval, he justified the proclamation as a "fit and necessary war measure for suppressing [the] . . . rebellion." No wonder one historian has described it as a revolutionary document with all the "moral grandeur of a bill of lading."

Such a jaundiced view of the Emancipation Proclamation is reinforced by the document's limitations. Lincoln, still concerned over the loyalty of the border states, had signed a measure which left slavery intact in those areas where the federal government could act while he abolished the peculiar institution in those regions (for the most part) beyond the reach of federal authority. The majority of the four million black men, women, and children of the South and border states remained enslaved until the final collapse of the military forces of the Confederacy. The Thirteenth Amendment* to the Constitution finally ratified in 1865, not the Emancipation Proclamation, was to be the final nail in the coffin of human bondage in North America.

But if the Emancipation Proclamation was not the final end of slavery, it was, in legal terms, the turning point in a revolutionary historical process well underway by the fall and winter of 1862. Afro-American abolitionists* and their white allies who had spent a lifetime fighting for unconditional emancipation were convinced that the commitment of the federal government to ending slavery outweighed the limitations of Lincoln's action. Frederick Douglass,* who had gathered in Boston's Tremont Hall with hundreds of black and white abolitionists on New Year's Day 1863, described the explosion of joy when the telegraphed confirmation of Lincoln's action arrived and the packed audience stood to sing the nineteenth-century anthem, "Sound the loud timbrel o'er Egypt's dark sea, Jehovah Hath triumphed, his people are free."

And the word moved through the Afro-American communities of the slave South on the invisible wires of the black "grapevine telegraph." Even before 1863, thousands of black Southerners had refused to wait for a cautious national government to act. As the war had begun in earnest in the late spring and summer of 1861, every movement of federal troops into the South acted as a magnet for slaves who were either abandoned by their masters or who had slipped away from bondage and fled toward the Union armies.

Well before such policy had been stabilized, the first significant number of freed slaves reached the federal lines in west Tennessee in late 1861 and 1862. There General Ulysses Grant named John Eaton to organize a refugee camp at Grand Junction, Tennessee. By the winter of 1862–1863 more than 20,000 slave refugees were crowded into a string of federal camps from Cairo, Illinois, south to Vicksburg. After the Emancipation Proclamation, the slave system disintegrated ever more rapidly. In the spring of 1863 a single military expedition into nine Louisiana parishes returned with more than 8,000 slaves who had seized the chance to gain their freedom.

Their reception was by no means uniformly friendly. They encountered confusion and, in some cases, hostility by individual army commanders who were left without decisive guidance from the Lincoln administration. During the first wartime summer of 1861, some officers such as General Henry W. Halleck (operating in the West) and General Winfield Scott (claiming Lincoln's approval) insisted that slave owners—even Confederate slave owners—should be allowed to recover their "property."

Such policies ended with the Confiscation Act of 1861. But most army officers were far less interested in emancipation than maintaining "order" and "discipline" and protecting the rights of loyalist slave owners. In those areas of Louisiana freed from Confederate control, Generals Benjamin Butler and Nathaniel Banks initiated a wage-labor, later a contract-labor, system, in which the army theoretically guaranteed wages for black slave runaways. In many cases, this meant forcible removal from the refugee camps. "Loyal" masters who swore allegiance to the federal government were often able to obtain their former slaves as laborers.

The former slaves who had gathered in these camps thus often suffered deprivation and extraordinary hardships, but almost none were willing to return to slavery. Freedom, once grasped, was not voluntarily relinquished. And the war itself seemed to serve as a corrosive solvent to the institution of slavery—nowhere more so than in the federal government's decision in August 1862 to recruit black soldiers.* Placing a rifle in the hands of former slaves may have, in itself, sounded the death knell of slavery. There was first of all the incongruity of asking black Americans to give their life for a society which sanctioned their bondage. But, more than that, the act of soldiering stripped away any vestiges of the so-called slave mentality. Shouldering a gun for the republic (as 186,000 black Americans did) marked another step along a path toward freedom from which there was no exit.

In one sense, slave owners were the last to grasp the revolution through which they lived. Although they insisted that they had absolute confidence in their "servants," an English visitor to the Civil War South found something "suspicious" in white Southerners' "constant never-ending statement that 'we are not afraid of our slaves.' " The worst nightmares of white Southerners—midnight murders, insurrections, and sabotage—seldom came true. But neither did their public professions of slave loyalty stand the test of experience. Even as they insisted that the black men and women in their midst were contented, slavery eroded, as one historian has observed, "plantation by plantation, often slave by slave, like slabs of earth slipping into a Southern stream."

There were the runaways,* a reality reflected in slave owners' desperate attempts to move their "property" away from the incursions of federal troops. (White Southerners sent more than 100,000 slaves to Texas as the war progressed.) Equally unsettling to masters was the gradual deterioration of the complex web of psychological controls which surrounded slavery. Whites had always been supersensitive to "uppity" behavior, but the war triggered subtle, but widespread acts of self-assertiveness and independence. As wartime upheavals disrupted the disciplined routine of plantation society, Afro-Americans remained legally slaves, but they increasingly grasped at freedom within the widening crevices of a collapsing system.

However much they raged against the ingratitude and "treachery" of their slaves, Southern slave owners were often last to recognize that the peculiar institution was dying. The acrimonious and (by that time) irrelevant debate by Confederates in the winter and spring of 1865 over arming their slaves reflects the reluctance of white Southerners to come to grips with reality.

Thus, in the late spring of 1865 hundreds of thousands of black and white Southerners gathered in farm yards, plantations, and dusty town streets across the South to hear the official news. At times the word was read by a former slave owner, at times by representatives of the victorious Union army. Slavery had ended.

Emancipation marked the end of the slavery, but the first few years after the war were critical in defining the limits of that freedom. White Southerners (and a surprisingly large number of white Northerners) were reconciled to the death of the peculiar institution, but they envisioned a postwar world in which the former slave would occupy indefinitely a halfway house between absolute servitude and legal equality. Blinded by their own proslavery argument,* most Southern whites anticipated economic disintegration in the region. The more pessimistic whites forecast a race war in the absence of rigid controls and limitations over the freed population. Rigid controls were the only solutions, they argued. Not only would the freedmen of the South be denied political rights, their economic status and their everyday life would be tightly circumscribed by stringently enforced vagrancy codes and race-specific laws. This vision of emancipation was reflected in the infamous "black codes" adopted or proposed in many Southern states during presidential Reconstruction.

For Afro-Americans—and particularly the former slaves—emancipation meant something quite different. It meant, as a convention of freedmen* argued in late 1865, absolute equality before the law; it meant the right to vote; and it meant the ownership of land to give concrete meaning to the rhetoric of freedom.

The first three years after the Civil War were critical ones for testing the meaning of emancipation, and the results were mixed. During the Civil War the U.S. Congress had proposed confiscating the land of white Confederates, and in January of 1865, General William T. Sherman's Field Order Number 15 provided for the distribution of abandoned land to 40,000 black refugees in forty-acre tracts. But the commitment to the sanctity of private property ran deep, even among angry Northerners. The Congress refused to confirm the freedmen's title to the abandoned plantations. By 1868, ex-Confederates had, for the most part, succeeded in regaining control of their property. The great majority of former slaves moved from slavery to some form of tenancy in the years after Appomattox.

But if the dream of land for the landless remained unfulfilled, the issue of freedom was, by no means, resolved entirely against black Southerners. In the latter part of the twentieth century we are inclined to focus upon lost opportunities of the post–Civil War generation, to see the shortcomings of the policies that followed in the wake of emancipation, and to bemoan the timidity of a nation crippled by racism and wedded to restrictive notions of states' rights and limited government. But there were other, even bleaker alternatives in 1865. Emancipation in other parts of the Western Hemisphere was often followed precisely by the kind of restrictions envisioned by white Southerners. When the British ended slavery in the West Indies in 1833, for example, the government specified a six-year interim apprenticeship for all agricultural slaves.

Even though widespread opposition by West Indian blacks (including riots in St. Kitts and Montserrat) led to the abandonment of the apprentice system, the freed population of the West Indies confronted a broad range of coercive and discriminatory legislation. Politically, the great majority of former slaves remained powerless. Sixty-five years after emancipation, less than 1 percent of the black male voting-age population in the British West Indies could cast a ballot.

In part because of the political ineptitude and inflexibility of Southern whites, the Congress moved with increasing sternness in 1866 and 1867 against the plans of these ex-Confederate Southerners—first by granting full civil equality to the freed population and then by giving the right to vote to the freedmen. The

Thirteenth, Fourteenth, and Fifteenth Amendments to the U.S. Constitution were imperfect, incomplete, and (in the case of the Fourteenth and Fifteenth Amendments) increasingly violated by white Southerners. But they remained a part of the organic law of the United States, a powerful legal legacy and moral commitment to future generations.

"In giving freedom to the slave, we assure freedom to the free," Lincoln had told the Congress in December of 1862. But many abolitionists who had fought for a generation to end slavery recognized that emancipation was a beginning as well as an end. As the Afro-American abolitionist Henry Highland Garnet observed in an 1863 sermon preached in the House of Representatives, the nation had "begun its exodus from worse than Egyptian bondage." But only when "caste and prejudice" were completely destroyed would the "good work which God has assigned for the ages to come . . . be finished."

SELECTED BIBLIOGRAPHY

Dan T. Carter, *When the War Was Over: The Failure of Self-Reconstruction in the South, 1865–1867* (1985); Eric Foner, *Nothing But Freedom: Emancipation and Its Legacy* (1983); John Hope Franklin, *The Emancipation Proclamation* (1963); Leon F. Litwack, *Been in the Storm So Long: The Aftermath of Slavery* (1979); and Armstead L. Robinson, "Day of Jubilo: Civil War and the Demise of Slavery in the Mississippi Valley, 1861–1865" (Ph.D. dissertation, University of Rochester, 1977).

DAN T. CARTER

EMANCIPATION PROCLAMATION. The Emancipation Proclamation, a document that declared most slaves in the United States free, was issued 1 January 1863, after almost a year of drafting alternate plans, waiting for the proper moment, and issuing warnings to Southern slaveholders.

Early in 1862, Union military failures led President Abraham Lincoln* to see his only alternatives as "either surrendering the Union . . . or . . . laying a strong hand upon the colored element." His early hopes of avoiding military emancipation by inducing slave states still in the Union to initiate gradual, compensated emancipation schemes were crushed by uncooperative border state members of Congress.

In June or July Lincoln decided, alone, to issue an emancipation proclamation. He read a draft to his cabinet on 22 July. Lincoln ignored Postmaster General Montgomery Blair's warning that the document would doom Republicans in next fall's elections. But he heeded Secretary of State William H. Seward's advice that, if issued in the wake of continuing federal military reverses, the proclamation would be regarded as the desperation measure of a defeated government. The president waited for a military victory.

In the meantime Lincoln answered public pleas for emancipation with enigmatic responses that suggested the impotence of paper proclamations. He stressed the secondary importance of emancipation vis-à-vis saving the Union.

Nevertheless, after the Battle of Antietam, Lincoln issued on 22 September 1862 a preliminary emancipation proclamation. This warned Southern insurgents that persons living in areas of the country still in rebellion on 1 January would lose their slave property. True to his word, and much to the relief of black people everywhere, Lincoln signed the final proclamation on New Year's Day 1863.

The final proclamation incorporated numerous revisions added since July. Lincoln stated the government's willingness to accept blacks in Union military service. He toned down a passage stating that the fugitive slave law would no longer be obeyed so that it would not sound, as it had to British ears especially, like an invitation to slave insurrection. And he exempted Tennessee, Louisiana parishes around New Orleans, and certain Virginia counties because, as he explained later, they were under federal control and therefore could not justifiably be touched on grounds of military necessity. Lincoln estimated that by February 1865 the document had freed perhaps 200,000 slaves.

SELECTED BIBLIOGRAPHY

John Hope Franklin, *The Emancipation Proclamation* (1963).

MARK E. NEELY, JR.

ENTREPRENEURS, SLAVE. Slave entrepreneurs were bondsmen who established their own business enterprises. Usually, the enterprises were in occupational areas where regular work supervision was impractical and unprofitable. Or slave entrepreneurs established enterprises along occupational lines shunned by many Southern whites as demeaning, particularly in the food and personal services industries. Most slave entrepreneurs were urban slaves who hired* their own time, using their wages as the start-up capital to enter business. As business proprietors, slave entrepreneurs worked only for themselves. Management was independent of the master's direction, control, or supervision.

As initiators and directors of production, a substantial number of self-hired slaves who risked establishing their own businesses were highly proficient craftsmen.* The carpentry, blacksmith, wheelwright, cabinetmaking, and coopering trades were promising areas for slave business development. In the building trades, skilled self-hired slave painters, masons, bricklayers, and glaziers also found their services in high demand in growing Southern cities. Attractive opportunities existed for the development of independent enterprises. The personal services industries also afforded lucrative areas for business development for self-hired slave barbers and tailors. Many slave women who hired their own time also enjoyed success in establishing laundry, dressmaking, millinery, hair dressing, and, as nurses, health care enterprises.

Unskilled occupations were also translated into profitable enterprises by innovative self-hired vendors, peddlers, and hawkers, who established catering enterprises, restaurants, retail secondhand clothing stores, grocery shops,* and underground, but profitable, grog shops.* In transportation, occupations such as teamster, drayman, liveryman, and boatman, carrying cargo or passengers, also provided business opportunities for enterprising self-hired slaves. In the wholesale and retail food industry, truck farming and fishing offered opportunities for slaves with highly developed marketing skills.

As independent business proprietors, slave entrepreneurs assumed the risk and responsibility for the production and/or distribution of their goods and services. Their commercial transactions, marketing, and management operations differed little from those of their free counterparts. Slave entrepreneurs also advertised, negotiated contracts, extended credit, and assumed debts. Their earnings depended as much on customer demand as on the extent of their business acumen, expertise, initiative, productivity, and propriety as businesspeople. Among the more successful antebellum self-hired slave entrepreneurs, annual profits in the hundreds of dollars were realized. Included in their business expenses were owner's fees, payments made by those slaves granted permission to hire their own time.

In operation, the self-hire system provided greater capitalization of the value of the slave's labor for the owner. While employers of hired, rented, or leased slaves paid owners annual fees ranging from $80 to $100, payments made by self-hired slaves averaged from $150 to over $200 annually, in the thirty-year period before the Civil War. But for the self-hired slave, the system offered greater freedom and mobility within the societal constraints of the institution, and, perhaps, the only opportunity for a slave to capitalize profitably on his skills and initiative. With its entrepreneurial dimension, the self-hire slave system in the United States was akin to the *obrok* system in tsarist Russia, where serfs were allowed to pay a yearly fee, also in exchange for "freedom," to develop their own enterprises.

The pattern of slave entrepreneurship rested more on a subtle process of mutual compromise between the owner and the slave than it did on the owner's coercion or the slave's accommodation. The process by which a slave craftsman, initially hired out by his owner, became a slave who hired his own time and, subsequently, established his own business reveals the dynamics of slave entrepreneurship. In one such instance, a slave blacksmith, who worked in a county different from that where his owner lived, asked his master for authorization to open up his own shop, explaining: "I am satisfied that I can do well and that my profits will amount to a great deal more than any one would be willing to pay for my hire."

Considering institutional constraints that limited full expression of their business acumen, self-hired slaves were distinguished, however, by their ability to make unusual amounts of money using commonly available resources or highly developed skills. Accumulated profits were used primarily as venture capital by slave entrepreneurs to purchase freedom for themselves, family members, or friends. Several case histories make the point. With the crude niter he mined on the Kentucky frontier, the self-hired slave Free Frank McWhorter (1777–1854) established a manufactory for the production of saltpeter during the War of 1812. With profits earned from this enterprise, the slave purchased first his wife's freedom in 1817 and then his own two years later. The total amount paid for their manumission was $1,600. Richard Allen, founder of the African Methodist Episcopal church,* purchased his freedom with earnings from his enterprise as an independent self-hired slave teamster. Elizabeth Keckley,* dressmaker for Mary Todd Lincoln, was a self-hired slave in St. Louis who purchased her freedom with money earned from her designer dressmaking business in that city.

Slave "intrapreneurship" also provided the basis for entrepreneurial activities among slaves granted decision-making authority in managing their owners' business enterprises. The slave riverboat captain, Simon Gray,* who was owned by a Mississippi lumber company, had complete control of the firm's shipping vessels along with bookkeeping responsibilities. Other company-owned slaves worked under Gray's supervision, as did the white crewmen whom Gray had authority to hire. He also paid their salaries. In the course of delivering lumber,* as John H. Moore found, Gray "solicited orders for the lumber mill, quoted prices, extended credit to customers, and collected money owed to the lumber company." Using this experience, Gray, while still a company slave, established his own independent lumber shipping business, even hiring a slave to assist him.

With business expansion, it was not unusual for slave entrepreneurs to hire other slaves. Charles Ball,* while a slave who hired his own time, was employed by a slave entrepreneur who had established a successful "odd jobs" enterprise. At that time, Ball was one of seven or eight black men hired by this enterprising bondsman to help him remove cotton in wheelbarrows. In addition to paying the salaries of his black employees, the slave entrepreneur also paid his owner $250 annually, in monthly installments, all from the profits of his "odd jobs" enterprise.

The participation of slaves in the American business community began during the colonial period and was a well-established practice before the American revolutionary era. Either to discourage competition from self-hired slaves or to limit their "freedom," laws were passed in Southern states, beginning in the late eighteenth century, which made it illegal for slaves "to go at large and trade as freemen." These laws were easily circumvented, particularly in urban areas where many self-hired slaves established businesses. Whether in urban places or rural areas, the self-hire slave system was, as Ulrich B. Phillips emphasizes, "too great a public and private convenience to suppress." Southern judicial records, contemporary travelers' accounts, private papers, autobiographies, and family oral histories attest to the extensiveness of the self-hire slave system. And as Richard Wade has concluded: "The extent to which each town struggled to stop this practice is a good indication of how widespread it was."

A large number of slave entrepreneurs and slave "intrapreneurs" who purchased their freedom continued business participation after manumission, emerging as prominent leaders of the antebellum black community. Their enterprise, experience, and leadership also helped build the economic and social infrastructure of postemancipation black life.

SELECTED BIBLIOGRAPHY

Clement Eaton, "Slave-Hiring in the Upper South: A Step toward Freedom," *Mississippi Valley Historical Review*, 46 (1960), 663–678; John Hope Franklin, "Slaves Virtually Free in Ante-Bellum North Carolina," *Journal of Negro History*, 28 (1943), 284–310; Edna Chappel McKenzie, "Self-Hire among Slaves, 1820–1860: Institutional Variation or Aberration?" (Ph.D. dissertation, University of Pittsburgh, 1973); Sumner E. Matison, "Manumission by Purchase," *Journal of Negro History*, 33 (1948), 146–167; John Hebron Moore, "Simon Gray, Riverman: A Slave Who Was Almost Free," *Mississippi Valley Historical Review*, 49 (1962), 472–484; Richard B. Morris, "The Measure of Bondage in the Slave States," *Mississippi Valley Historical Review*, 41 (1954), 219–240; and Juliet E. K. Walker, *Free Frank: A Black Pioneer on the Antebellum Frontier* (1983).

JULIET E. K. WALKER

EPISCOPAL CHURCH. After the American Revolution* the Episcopal church continued the same attitudes and policies toward slavery that had been formed in the parent colonial Anglican church.* It accepted the principle of racial slavery and worked within—not against—the peculiar institution. The Protestant Episcopal Church held considerable strength and influence in the Old South, where it had previously enjoyed the privileges of being an established or state church. The invention of the cotton gin in 1793 gave renewed importance to plantation slave society, with which the church was closely identified, and set the stage for continuation of the colonial accommodation to slavery into the antebellum period.

Like the Anglican Society for the Propagation of the Gospel* founded in 1701, Episcopal bishops and clergy ministered to both the masters and their slaves. Resistance to converting and giving religious instruction to the African then centered on the belief that no Christian could hold another Christian in bondage. But the Anglicans rejected this view, arguing that Christianity in no way altered the "civil relations" between master and slave. In fact, they said, the church served to bolster the South's racial status quo. Following Denmark Vesey's* 1822 abortive slave revolt, an Episcopal minister in Charleston denied charges that educated slaves, especially slave ministers, had participated in the plot. Black Episcopalians, he explained, "were not allowed to exhort or expound scripture in words of their own, to use extempore prayer, or to utter, at such times, whatever nonsense or profanity might happen to come into their minds." The Episcopal church, then, saw its role as acculturating the bondsmen to the white hegemony of slave society.

There is more evidence on how the church reached the slaves than on how many bondsmen were reached. Bishops repeatedly urged slaveholders to provide religious instruction and services of worship, and their records show visitations to plantations to administer the sacraments and to preach. Parish clergy in the towns had both free and slave in their congregations. They enumerated the baptisms, weddings, and funerals of blacks, although oftentimes failing to record them on parish roles as communicants. Separate black Episcopal congregations existed throughout the South, for example, in Baltimore; Charleston; Fayetteville, N.C.; Petersburg, Virginia; and Savannah. In the towns, blacks and whites generally used the same building, but with separate sections and at different hours. In rural areas, slaveholders frequently built chapels on their plantations both for their own use and for that of their bondsmen. Dr. William Mercer, a Mississippi planter, endowed and constructed a chapel and parsonage at St. Mary's on his Laurel Hill plantation near Natchez. He sought, Mercer recalled in 1851, "to provide religious instruction and the ordinances of our church for my slaves, and the consolations of religious worship to my family."

Like Dr. Mercer, the Episcopal church accepted Christianity as an essential prop of the peculiar institution. The denomination in fact took no decisive stance on the slavery issue except to accept, indeed support, the South's racial status quo. At the start of the century the church was preoccupied with rebuilding and expanding westward. At mid-century, when other denominations were splitting into Northern and Southern Baptists,* Methodists,* and Presbyterians,* the Episcopal church was debating the effects of the English Oxford Movement upon its liturgical life. Indeed, during the Civil War, Confederate Episcopal bishops sat apart from their Union opposites only to rejoin them with the cessation of hostilities. Throughout the antebellum period the church attempted with varying degrees of success to minister concomitantly to both master and slave. Never challenging the slave system, at best it attempted to ameliorate the worst aspects of slaveholding. White Episcopalians' insensitivity to the horrors of slavery led the freedmen to abandon the church in the postbellum decades.

SELECTED BIBLIOGRAPHY

Robert A. Bennett, "Black Episcopalians: A History from the Colonial Period to the Present," *Historical Magazine of the Protestant Episcopal Church*, 43 (1974), 231–246; George F. Bragg, *History of the Afro-American Group of the Episcopal Church* (1922); Denzil T. Clifton, "Anglicanism and Negro Slavery in Colonial America," *Historical Magazine of the Protestant Episcopal Church*, 39 (1970), 29–70; Albert J. Raboteau, *Slave Religion: The "Invisible Institution" in the Antebellum South* (1978); Lester B. Scherer, *Slavery and the Churches in Early America, 1619–1819* (1975); and Carter G. Woodson, *The History of the Negro Church* (3rd ed., 1972).

ROBERT A. BENNETT

EQUIANO, OLAUDAH (1745?–1797). Olaudah Equiano—slave, sailor, trader, freeman, abolitionist, and author—is best known for his autobiography,* first published in England in 1789. According to Equiano, the book refutes "the notion of European cultural superiority." Despite his reliance on other eighteenth-century travel writers, the work contains graphic descriptions of slave communities in England and the Americas.

Born about 1745 in what is today Nigeria, Equiano was kidnapped by slavers when he was about ten years old. During the following year he was sold several times, eventually to a planter in Virginia. In 1757 a British naval officer purchased the slave, renaming him Gustavus Vassa. The skills Equiano acquired on his voyage to England launched him on a long career as a seaman and during the next thirty years he visited ports in Italy, Turkey, Spain, Portugal, North and South America, and the Caribbean. He also served on an expedition which attempted unsuccessfully to reach the North Pole.

Equiano often engaged in petty trading during his travels, and by 1766 he had amassed enough money to purchase his freedom. He returned to England the following year and apprenticed himself to a hairdresser but soon returned to sailing, which he found more lucrative and exciting. In 1785, a group of British abolitionists invited Equiano to serve on a committee established to repatriate Africans to Sierra Leone. Although disillusioned by governmental corruption, Equiano continued to work for the improved treatment of blacks. Before his death in 1797, Equiano saw eight editions of his autobiography published.

SELECTED BIBLIOGRAPHY

Francis D. Adams and Barry Sanders, eds., *Three Black Writers in Eighteenth-Century England* (1971); Paul Edwards, ed., *Equiano's Travels: The Interesting Narrative of the Life of Olaudah Equiano, or Gustavus Vassa, the African* (1977); Olaudah Equiano, *The Life of Olaudah Equiano, or Gustavus Vassa, the African* (reprint ed., 1969); G. I. Jones, "Olaudah Equiano of the Niger Ibo," in Philip D. Curtin, ed., *Africa Remembered: Narratives by West Africans from the Era of the Slave Trade* (1967); S. E. Ogude, "Facts into Fiction: Equiano's Narrative Reconsidered," *Research in African Literature*, 13 (1982), 31–43.

                                                        SUZANNE AUSTIN BROWNE

F

FAMILY, SLAVE. The slave family in mainland North America has a history extending over nearly two centuries. The history of the slave family can be divided into three phases: the enslavement of Africans (stretching from the late seventeenth century to 1807), the development of slave families and kinship networks (mid-eighteenth to early nineteenth centuries), and the spread of slave family networks resulting from the settlement of the Southwest and the internal slave trade (roughly 1810 to 1865). The kind of families slaves established and the ability of slave families to mitigate the destabilizing impact of chattel slavery varied greatly over time and in response to local circumstance.

Africans forced into chattel slavery in America lived in a remarkable variety of family systems—monogamous and polygamous, matriarchal and patriarchal—but they shared several common characteristics. West Africans gained identity in their communities through a complex set of genealogical links that united every living member of the tribe as kindred and traced their genealogies* back to the "living-dead" who helped unify their living descendants. Although few Africans, other than tribal chiefs, could expect to head polygamous households, the institution of polygamy accentuated the role of the mother in child nurture and child development and often increased the role of the mother's brother in childrearing.

Enslaved Africans bound for America came from societies where slavery was common, but its characteristics were far different from the chattel slavery found in the New World. Captured in African wars or kidnapped by other Africans from their homes, slaves in Africa stood outside the system of kinship that bound members of tribes together. Their masters possessed some rights in their persons, including the right to sell them. Sometimes the slaves worked in separate villages, producing food; at other times they served as personal servants. Unlike chattel slaves, however, they or—more likely—their children could hope for partial incorporation into a kin group. The status of slave, adopted outsider, and full tribal member merged into one another, and the specific rights a slave might have (to start a family, join a kin group, bear free children) varied from place to place. West Africans, then, had little experience with the absolute dichotomy of free persons and slaves they would discover as chattels in North America.

As the Atlantic slave trade* increased, however, the position of slaves in Africa deteriorated. Rather than being incorporated into the kinship groups of their captors, they were increasingly sold to European slave traders. Africans destined for America lost their communal identity. Kindred, both alive and dead, were left behind, and the slaves had to build new identities and families. As many as a fifth (but more typically about a tenth) of the Africans died during the Middle Passage to America because of unsanitary conditions and poor diets. Shackled together, these men and women (who came from different tribes and spoke different languages) began to develop shipboard friendships and to establish fictive kinship ties with those nearby. These fragile friendships inevitably were severed when they reached Virginia or South Carolina. Put on sale each day until they were sold, these new friends were split among many planters.

The period of a substantial Atlantic slave trade to mainland British North America and the United States stretched from 1700 to 1807, but Africans dominated the slave population of particular regions for only short periods of time. Although black people had lived in Virginia since the outset of settlement, shiploads of Africans first landed in that colony late in the seventeenth century. The number of Africans imported into the region rose from 1700 to 1740 but declined after 1740. As a result, the proportion of Africans in the adult population declined from nearly two-thirds in 1728 to just a quarter in 1755. A similar pattern was evident in South Carolina. There, the slave trade began early in the eighteenth century but rose from the late 1720s to the 1770s. Half the adult slaves in South Carolina had been born in Africa in the 1770s, but less than a third were African-born by 1790. The brief resurgence of the African slave trade between 1790 and 1807, when more Africans entered the United States than had been forced to come to the colonies in any similar period of time, probably created a similar society on the Southwest frontier, where most Africans now worked.

African slaves in the Chesapeake region and the Carolinas created families and kinship groups with great difficulty. In the first place, the cultural differences between slaves on the same plantation were great. With few exceptions, slaves on Chesapeake and Carolina plantations came from different West African regions. Even if they came from the same region, they infrequently shared particular dialects, religions, or kinship systems and had to forge new kinship systems from common attitudes about kindred, causality, religion, and historical change. Moreover, Africans had to contend with the demands made by masters. They had to adopt English names* (which destroyed the rich meaning that their names had held) and such European mores as monogamy (which demeaned elite African men forced into slavery).

The demographic* circumstances of their new lives made the development of such a syncretistic family system difficult. Two men were exported for every woman, thereby making polygamous marriages nearly impossible and preventing some slave men from mating until they had been in the country for years, if even then. Given the very high death rates of newly imported Africans (perhaps half died within a decade of arrival), many African men had to create fictive ties or live entirely outside the bonds of family. The problems Africans had of creating effective families were heightened by the small size of plantations in the Chesapeake colonies; Africans there typically lived on farms with just ten or fifteen slaves. (The largest planters placed their slaves on different quarters.) Slave couples often lived on different plantations, thereby reducing the role of husband and father to weekly visits. Even in South Carolina, where slaves lived on units with twenty-five or thirty other blacks, marriage opportunities were constrained by the unwillingness of native-born slave women to marry Africans. Nevertheless, Africans who survived their captivity usually formed conjugal families, even if husbands and wives had to live on different plantations.

Although African women enslaved in the Chesapeake bore few children, some of their daughters survived. The high fertility of these native-born women diminished the proportion of Africans in the population, thereby reducing the surplus of men in the adult slave population. By the mid-eighteenth century in the Chesapeake and by century's end in South Carolina, there were roughly equal numbers of men and women, and the women among them usually married and bore their first child before reaching age twenty. Even with high infant mortality, sufficient numbers of children* survived to provide the raw material for family formation and the development of kinship networks.

While African slaves formed families with difficulty, their native-born children created extensive family networks. The family culture that eighteenth-century Afro-American slaves devised persisted until after the end of slavery. Native-born slaves not only began families but created a peculiar Afro-American kinship system. On larger plantations (where increasing numbers of slaves lived in both the Chesapeake region and in South Carolina), husbands and wives often cohabited. Kindred worked in the fields during the day, and cooperated in cultivating what gardens masters permitted them to have. They taught each other craft skills and ways to ''put massa on'' and socialized at their quarters outside their small cabins once work was done. Men from smaller units visited families on larger plantations in the evenings. Families, however, never could achieve security, for parents, spouses, and children at any time might be sold or transferred. Slaves therefore took advantage of other resident kindred, relying on uncles, aunts, cousins, and grandparents to help with childrearing and to harbor runaways.*

Slaves who lived on units with fewer than twenty slaves—where half of all late eighteenth- and nineteenth-century slaves resided—had few opportunities to establish such family networks. Women on small plantations usually resided with their small children, but their husbands lived elsewhere in the neighborhood. These women had to rear their children alone or seek help from whatever kinfolk lived on their plantation. Lacking husbands and often other kindred, these women often created female slave networks and called on other women to help with child care and other tasks. Slaves on small plantations could participate in a fuller family life only by visiting large plantations or running away from them.

The sale or transfer of slaves by masters disrupted slave families and kin networks, often separating men from day-to-day family life, but these transfers sometimes permitted slaves to establish complex cross-plantation social and kin networks. When slaves were forced to move short distances, kindred spread across neighborhoods. They and their friends visited one another in the evenings or weekends and, even more important, provided temporary refuge and support for slave runaways.

The family culture of Afro-American slaves combined elements from West African culture (especially their wide definitions of family and kin connections) with needs mandated by chattel slavery and the behavior of masters. This culture is perhaps most clearly seen in the ways slaves named their children. Almost as soon as slaves accepted English names, they began to name their children for kin. Naming served crucial symbolic functions: it linked the child to his close and extended kindred, especially absent kinfolk or those likely to be sold. Slaves rarely named daughters for mothers, for mothers usually lived with their children, but frequently named sons for fathers who either lived off the plantation or could be sold or bequeathed away from their children. On plantations where two generations of slave families remained, naming for fathers might decline but name exchanges (e.g., brothers naming sons for one another) became common.

Within the slave family the role of fathers was particularly ambivalent. Wealthy Southern white men prided themselves on establishing strong patriarchal families, but they prevented slave men from creating similar units. Most slave men who resided on large plantations lived with their wives and children. These men headed their families, but their authority was undermined by the demands of masters. Slave husbands could rarely protect their wives and children from beatings. Even on plantations where the master permitted slaves to cultivate their own gardens and left food distribution up to slave fathers, masters kept ultimate control over the material well-being of slave families.

Given these power relations, the role of slave women* within slave families cannot be overestimated. Masters recognized only mothers and children as legitimate slave families and took some pains to keep them together. Slave women looked forward to childbearing, for it provided them both with a new family and the possibility of some independence. A new mother on a small unit lived in her own hut and headed her own family, creating a small matriarchy. On large plantations, mothers resided with husbands, and they reared small children, leaving them in the hands of an older woman or young girl when they worked in the fields beside their husbands. If their husbands were sold or transferred, slave women assumed control over their families.

Such familial arrangements undermined the strict Victorian morality that characterized white West European cultures in the nineteenth century. Neither slave marriages* nor their kin ties were recognized by any law except the custom of the plantation. The insecurity of slave families (and the master's encouragement

of fertility) led numerous late adolescent slaves to experiment. Premarital intercourse was common on Southern plantations, despite attempts by slave mothers
to keep daughters chaste. But once slaves married, promiscuity ended and husbands and wives expected their spouses to remain faithful. Slaves kept together
by masters, of course, might become incompatible. Separation in those cases
was relatively simple and far more common than among whites. For example,
about one Mississippi slave in twelve born before 1825 reported to the Freedmen's
Bureau in 1865 a marriage broken by mutual consent or desertion.

Masters understood that the domestic happiness of their slaves raised plantation
productivity and reduced the likelihood of slaves' running away. They did attempt
to keep slave families together. But the needs of a master's own conjugal family
took precedence over the desires of slaves. Planter fathers sought to set up each
of their children with stocked farms and therefore either gave them slaves when
their children married or, when planter fathers died, distributed slaves to them.
Slave owners faced this contradiction by pretending that slave families consisted
(in reality as well as law) of only mothers and their small children and claimed
to respect slave families by keeping mothers united with children under age six
or seven.

Partible inheritance, however, destroyed the integrity of slave families (defined
narrowly as parents and minor children) everywhere except on rice and sugar
plantations and on the largest cotton plantations of the Black Belt. Even in these
areas, extended kinship networks were likely to be broken when the master died.
While sons and daughters of slaveholders often lived near the paternal home in
the eighteenth century, making visits between separated slave kindred possible,
the great migration to the Southwest in the nineteenth century increased the
probability that slaves bequeathed to different family members never would see
one another again.

The security of slave family life thus was entwined closely with the life cycle
of the master. A wealthy young man constructed a slave labor force through
inheritance, gift, marriage, and purchase of slaves—acts that destroyed earlier
slave family networks. If he prospered, new slave kinship networks developed
through slave marriages (both on the plantation and between plantations) and
natural increase. If the master fell on hard times, he might sell his slaves,
endangering the security of slave families. The stability of slave families was
greatest on the farm of a prosperous middle-aged master. But when the master
reached old age, or died, he distributed his slaves to his children or ordered that
his slaves be sold to pay his debts, thereby again separating slave families and
breaking up fragile slave kinship networks.

While these contradictions in slave family persisted from the mid-eighteenth
century to the end of the slave regime, a noticeable change occurred after 1807
when the African slave trade* was legally abolished. As a result, the internal
slave trade* increased, disrupting the fragile security some slave families had
enjoyed. Between 1810 and 1860 nearly a million slaves were forced to move
with masters to the Southwest or were sold to interstate slave traders. The level

of the trade rose dramatically after 1810, peaked in the 1830s (a time of high cotton prices), diminished in the 1840s, and rebounded in the 1850s (another boom period in the cotton trade). Given the youthfulness of slaves sold to the traders and the propensity of masters to leave older slaves behind, slaves born early in the nineteenth century were far more frequently forced to leave parents and kindred than those born in the eighteenth century or during the last generation before the end of slavery.

These internal movements disrupted the family lives of nearly every slave who lived in the nineteenth-century South. Slaves fortunate enough to stay their entire lives near their birthplace saw children, siblings, and other kindred forced to move vast distances. Slaves sold to slave traders, mostly young men and women, left parents and siblings behind. Masters often carried all their slaves when they moved to the Southwest, but because many slaves established marriages with slaves off the plantation, these slaves often left spouses behind. Young white families, among the most common migrants, frequently took slaves given them by their parents. These slaves already had been torn from their extended families and moved to the Southwest with only a small portion of their families.

Marriage registers compiled in Mississippi by the Freedmen's Bureau in 1865 (and analyzed by Herbert G. Gutman) show the devastating impact of the sale and migration of slaves upon slave families. Prior marriages of over a third of men and women older than forty (mostly born between 1800 and 1825 and therefore mostly migrants) had been broken by force. Half of all marriages in which both spouses were still alive in 1865 were ended by the actions of the master. The vast majority of marriages destroyed by masters had been relatively stable unions; two-thirds of them had lasted more than five years; and one in seven had endured for more than fifteen years when ended by sale or forced transfer.

Once slave migrants arrived in the Southwest, they began to reestablish extended family networks. Married adults who had been separated from spouses, knowing they would never see their mates again, remarried (often encouraged and on occasion forced to do so by the master). Marriages on the plantation, followed by numerous births, led to the creation of new conjugal families, and when children born on the plantation began to marry a generation later, new family networks formed. Of course, slaves in the Southwest, like slaves in the Old South, never formed wholly secure families. White migration, sale, or the master's death could always force slaves to move further to the Southwest, which would undermine new and fragile kinship networks.

Slave families and kinship networks were the most important social institution that eighteenth-century slaves devised. Family and kin ties provided slaves with an identity somewhat independent of the master and his rules. But because masters owned the bodies of slaves, family life was always insecure and precarious, and became increasingly less secure in the nineteenth century. When evangelical religion* spread among slaves at the end of the eighteenth century, they gained a second independent identity as Christians, an identity sustained by slave preachers. Christian doctrine and fellowship, with its insistence upon spiritual quality, was carried by antebellum slaves from the Old to the New South.

Even more important, evangelical religion helped slaves strengthen family bonds. Some masters permitted slaves to marry or have their children baptized in church, which regularized the ties of matrimony and family responsibility. Slave women and men could take complaints about spouses or other kindred to their congregation and gain relief from family violence or alcohol abuse. Sinners often changed their ways, for those who did not comply with church discipline could lose church fellowship. Church discipline did not prevent masters from selling slaves or moving to the Southwest, but, on occasion, disciplinary committees criticized masters for violence to slaves or requested them to purchase spouses who lived on other plantations when they carried slaves to the Southwest.

The emancipation* of slaves during the Civil War allowed slaves to strengthen their family bonds. During the war, the proximity of the Union army* emboldened many slaves to gather their families and run away to army camps. After the war, freed slaves took to the road all over the South searching for spouses and families torn from them by force. To legitimate their families, they rushed to register slave marriages with the Freedmen's Bureau. While freedmen and women never fully adapted to white marital norms (women still had to work part-time in the fields if the family was to survive), they did create strong two-parent unions. Almost 90 percent of rural black families in 1870 and 1880 were headed by men and were nuclear in structure, including husband, wife, and children. The strength of the postemancipation black family derived in many ways from the bonds of marriage, family, and kinship slaves had forged during two centuries of slavery.

SELECTED BIBLIOGRAPHY

Ira Berlin and Ronald Hoffman, eds., *Slavery and Freedom in the Age of the American Revolution* (1983); Orville Vernon Burton, *In My Father's House Are Many Mansions: Family and Community in Edgefield, South Carolina* (1985); Eugene D. Genovese, *Roll, Jordan, Roll: The World the Slaves Made* (1974); Herbert G. Gutman, *The Black Family in Slavery and Freedom, 1750–1925* (1976); Allan Kulikoff, *Tobacco and Slaves: The Development of Southern Cultures in the Chesapeake, 1680–1800* (1986); and Deborah Gray White, *Ar'n't I a Woman?: Female Slaves in the Plantation South* (1985).

ALLAN KULIKOFF

FEDERAL WRITERS' PROJECT (FWP). This New Deal white-collar relief program, established in 1935 under the aegis of the Works Progress Administration, made significant contributions to the study of Afro-American slavery by conducting interviews* with ex-slaves and by related projects. While the FWP was nationally administered, it was made up of separate state units that often initiated their own projects. The first FWP effort to interview former slaves was begun in Georgia in July 1936; however, it was a group of ex-slave narratives* submitted by the Florida FWP in March 1937 that led to the establishment of a nationally directed regional study. In April 1937, John Lomax, the FWP folklore editor, issued instructions to Southern and border state units on interviewing former slaves. Lomax's instructions emphasized how "to get the Negro talking about the days of slavery."

Until the publication of *The American Slave: A Composite Autobiography* in 1972 (and subsequent supplemental volumes) under the editorship of George P. Rawick, most of the ex-slave narratives had been available only in manuscript form at the Library of Congress. Historian David Brion Davis has called the publication of the FWP ex-slave testimony one of the major turning points in the post–World War II historiography of slavery. Although national FWP officials intended that the slave narratives collected reach a general audience, they were not able to fulfill that goal largely because the conservative reaction to the New Deal in the late 1930s and the coming of World War II curtailed FWP activities. The Virginia Writers' Project's *The Negro in Virginia* (1940), which drew on ex-slave interviews conducted in that state, and the anthology of slave narratives, *Lay My Burden Down: A Folk History of Slavery* (1945), edited by B. A. Botkin, who succeeded John Lomax as FWP folklore editor, indicate the direction and unfulfilled potential of the FWP program. In addition, other state-initiated projects collected material pertaining to slavery, some of it published in Georgia Writers' Project, *Drums and Shadows: Survival Studies among the Georgia Coastal Negroes* (1940); Louisiana Writers' Project, *Gumbo-Ya-Ya: A Collection of Louisiana Folk Tales* (1945); and Roi Ottley and William J. Weatherby, eds., *The Negro in New York: An Informal Social History* (1969).

Although the FWP ex-slave narrative collection represented all types of slave occupations and all sizes of plantations, the sample was not collected on a scientifically random basis. Interviewers often selected interviewees on the basis of previous contact or proximity. The sample greatly underrepresents the slave experience in the upper South and border states. Only a small portion of the interviewees were fifteen years old or older when the Civil War began. The great majority had experienced the life of a slave as children and only during the last two decades of slavery. Two-thirds were over eighty years old when interviewed, and because such a long life span was unusual for a former slave, it is possible that these interviewees had been better fed and treated than most slaves. It has been estimated that only 2 percent of the ex-slave population in the United States at the time were interviewed by Federal Writers.

Scholars have pointed out the challenges in learning how to read and interpret the FWP ex-slave interviews. Key questions center around the circumstances surrounding the interview, the role of the interviewer in shaping the interview, and the ways in which these materials were edited. Answers to questions about conditions in slavery also could have been influenced by the period in which the questions were asked. Many ex-slaves compared slavery with conditions during the Great Depression. Some of the exchanges between interviewees and interviewers indicate the ex-slaves viewed the interviewers as individuals who could help them obtain old age pensions. Many of the ex-slaves resided in the same areas as their master's descendants and were economically dependent on whites. Most often the interviewers were members of the local white community and sometimes were descendants of the interviewee's former owners. A careful reading of the interviews demonstrates that the former slaves were often guarded in their remarks to white interviewees and tried not to violate the etiquette of Southern race relations in the 1930s.

Few blacks served on the Writers' Project outside of Virginia, Louisiana, and Florida. Scholars have discovered significant differences between interviews conducted by white and black interviewers. Interviewees clearly talked more openly with black interviewers than they did with whites about attitudes toward slavery, their former masters, punishments, family customs, and other topics. Furthermore, white women interviewers received more open responses than did white men. Material dealing with kinship relations and slave culture appears to be less affected by the race of the interviewer than other topics.

The abilities of the FWP interviewers varied greatly. Few possessed any previous experience relevant to interviewing. Many failed to pursue important topics. Many asked leading questions. They most often were uninformed about interview techniques and the way that interviewers helped shape the interview. In numerous cases they compulsively strove to have the interviewee confirm their preconceptions about slavery and race relations. Because the Federal Writers did not use tape recorders, there is no way of being certain that the interviews are verbatim accounts; in many cases, evidence clearly shows that they are not. In addition, several versions of some interviews exist, and while these different versions may be similar in content, they do reveal that someone—the interviewer or an editor—either deleted or added material, rewrote passages, and sometimes changed the wording of quotes attributed to the former slave. Finally, white editors tended to regard interviews that contained accounts of cruel treatment as untrustworthy. In several instances they deleted such material from interviews conducted by black interviewers.

Notwithstanding these weaknesses, ex-slave narratives represent one of the earliest attempts to obtain an oral history of anonymous Americans. Recent research in oral history has been accompanied by the development of a theoretical sophistication about what goes on in an interview and the nature of the document that results from the collaboration between interviewer and interviewee. Questions scholars ask about the ex-slave narratives are similar to questions that they ask about memoirs, diaries, and the work of other historians. A key difference is that the interviews were the result of a collaboration that produced the conversational narrative other researchers consult. The linguistic, grammatical, and literary structure of the interview offers key evidence regarding the relationship, the interaction between interviewer and interviewee, and the way the interviewees presented their life and history to the interviewer, to themselves, and to the larger community.

Although today it would be impossible to write a history of American slavery without using the narratives of the former slaves, scholars ignored them for a long time. Even before the slave narrative collection was published, these interviews deposited at the Library of Congress were no more inaccessible than other primary sources historians used. Scholars remained distrustful of these sources and uncertain how to use them. Recent work on the history of slavery, however, draws heavily on the FWP slave narrative collection and echoes B. A. Botkin's call for a history "from the bottom up," a cultural history that used folklore to help reconstruct the history of a folk culture. Increasingly, the FWP ex-slave narratives have been used not only to describe slave culture, but also to gain a sense of the dynamics of an oral culture, to understand the slaves as both bearers of tradition and creators of culture.

As early as 1939 B. A. Botkin recognized the value of oral testimony to understand the role of tradition and adaptation—culture as a historical process, the product of the interaction between past and present. During the Depression era Botkin and other officials asked questions about black history and culture that would not again become central issues of historical inquiry until the 1960s and 1970s. They advocated going directly to the former slaves to obtain a black perspective on slavery. The many historians today who are trying to answer questions about the life of the slaves guarantee that there will be a continuing exploration of the uses of the FWP materials.

SELECTED BIBLIOGRAPHY

David T. Bailey, "A Divided Prism: Two Sources of Black Testimony on Slavery," *Journal of Southern History*, 46 (1980), 381–404; John W. Blassingame, "Using the Testimony of Ex-Slaves: Approaches and Problems," *Journal of Southern History*, 41 (1975), 473–492; Paul D. Escott, *Slavery Remembered: A Record of Twentieth-Century Slave Narratives* (1979); Jerrold Hirsch, "Portrait of America: The Federal Writers' Project in an Intellectual and Cultural Context" (Ph.D. dissertation, University of North Carolina at Chapel Hill, 1984); Jerrold Hirsch, "Reading and Counting," *Reviews in American History*, 8 (1980), 312–317; C. Vann Woodward, "History from Slave Sources," *American Historical Review*, 79 (1974), 470–481; and Norman R. Yetman, "Ex-Slave Interviews and the Historiography of Slavery," *American Quarterly*, 36 (1984), 181–210.

JERROLD HIRSCH

FERTILITY. The levels of fertility maintained by different slave populations of the Western Hemisphere pose one of the more complicated questions concerning the demographic history of the slaves. Even in the case of the United States, where for the last few decades of the antebellum period, at least, relatively good data are available, those data remain sufficiently incomplete. Researchers thus have been forced to generate estimates based on sometimes tenuous assumptions.

Much of the difficulty stems from an underreporting of slave births and infant deaths. This complicates the problem of judging slave fertility in terms of performance. A dearth of stillbirth data makes it even more difficult to judge fecundity.

Despite these obstacles, a consensus exists on some of the broader aspects of the question. Most would agree that black slaves married somewhat earlier than free whites, that the average age of a slave woman at first birth was somewhere around twenty, that child spacing was probably at about two-year intervals, and, consequently, that North American slave fertility was very high, higher in fact than that of the white population. Researchers also agree that slave fertility declined during the last few decades of the antebellum period.

Yet even during this period of decline, the slave population increased from approximately one million at the turn of the nineteenth century, to roughly four million on the eve of the Civil War. Because most students of slavery today do not believe the slave population was augmented significantly by illicit slave imports—or by slave breeding*—it follows that the increase was a natural increase. Slave fertility, then, ranked sufficiently high enough to outstrip high infant and child mortality rates. Most scholars place the crude birthrate for slaves during the nineteenth century at somewhere between fifty to fifty-five per thousand, and the infant mortality rate at about a quarter of all slave infants born. After the remainder of slave mortality is deducted, it appears that the annual average net natural increase of the slave population was about twenty-five per thousand, or 2.5 percent for the last six decades of slavery.

Unquestionably, this rate of growth from natural means makes the North American slave population seem unique in the hemisphere. Other slave populations normally recorded net natural decreases annually, but were augmented only due to a continuing slave trade* that provided fresh imports from Africa. Many who have studied the problem find the answer in the significantly lower fertility in these slave societies, particularly among the newly imported African women. Possible cultural reasons include prolonged lactation and sexual taboos while the female was lactating. Biological reasons include poor nutrition and a new disease environment. Yet evidence also points to significantly higher rates of infant and child mortality than those suffered by the North American slave population. Thus the extent to which low fertility or high mortality among the young can explain the net natural decrease of slave populations elsewhere in the Americas remains unclear at present.

SELECTED BIBLIOGRAPHY

Jack E. Eblen, "New Estimates of the Vital Rates of the United States Black Population during the Nineteenth Century," *Demography*, 11 (1974), 301–319; Reynolds Farley, "The Demographic Rates and Social Institutions of the Nineteenth-Century Negro Population: A Stable Population Analysis," *Demography*, 2 (1965), 386–398; Robert W. Fogel and Stanley L. Engerman, *Time on the Cross: The Economics of American Negro Slavery* (1974); Allan Kulikoff, "A 'Prolifick' People: Black Population Growth in the Chesapeake Colonies, 1700–1790," *Southern Studies*, 16 (1977), 391–428; Richard Steckel, "The Fertility of American Slaves," *Research in Economic History*, 7 (1982),

229–286; James Trussell and Richard Steckel, "The Age of Slaves at Menarche and Their First Birth," *Journal of Interdisciplinary History*, 8 (1978), 477–505; and Melvin Zelnick, "The Fertility of the American Negro in 1830 and 1850," *Population Studies*, 20 (1966), 77–83.

KENNETH F. KIPLE

FIELD HANDS. The rhythm of work in a plantation economy followed seasonal fluctuations. Extraordinary exertions at critical points of the year alternated with more leisurely activity during slack periods. Working in spurts rather than steadily characterizes much agricultural labor, and enslaved plantation labor was no different. Indeed, slavery reinforced this traditional agricultural work cycle, for field hands seem to have embraced irregular work habits, working with great energy and spirit at peak periods in the year, doing as little as possible at slack times. A preference for irregular work, however, is not the same as avoidance of hard work, and indeed slaves were well known for their disciplined and intense labor at key points in the crop cycle.

Within this general pattern, slave work habits varied considerably, according to different staple crops, time periods, planter management principles, and plantation sizes. Sugar workers, for example, experienced the most arduous work regimen of any plantation staple. Over time, significant developments in the type of crops cultivated and in the nature of the slaves' work patterns occurred. In North America most field hands in the eighteenth century grew tobacco,* whereas, by the middle of the nineteenth century, about three-quarters of the field hands in the United States cultivated cotton.* Planters became more businesslike over time, as the proliferation of agricultural journals in the early nineteenth century attests. The degree to which planters realized economies of scale in large production units remains a controversial subject, but there can be no doubt that field hands on large estates were organized into highly disciplined and interdependent teams. Furthermore, less intimate and more impersonal relations* between master and slaves undoubtedly characterized the larger units.

More than anything else, staples determined the variations in slave work patterns. Sugar cane* had the longest crop cycle of any plantation staple; "holing" or trenching as well as cane-harvesting were extremely onerous tasks; and since sugar had to be processed on the plantation, many field hands worked at night in the factory after cutting cane during the day. Because of these extreme labor demands, sugar estates generally had higher mortality rates than other staple-producing units. Indeed, first-gang field laborers in early nineteenth-century Jamaica worked an average of 4,000 hours during the year, almost three times the amount worked by a modern factory worker.

If sugar was the most demanding plantation staple, tobacco imposed the lightest work load. The tobacco cycle could generally be completed within a year; tobacco units were small; and processing requirements were minimal. Tobacco growing consequently had little need for high levels of regimentation. Indeed, tobacco became known as a "free man's crop" because of the nicety of judgment it required and the small scale of its operations. Although the tobacco regime was monotonous and painstaking, it was not backbreaking. Tobacco cultivation moved with slow and measured tread, not at the breakneck and killing speed of a crop like sugar.

Rice* and short-staple cotton lay somewhere between these two extremes. The rice cycle generally extended beyond a calendar year and many of its operations were extremely strenuous, not to say unhealthy. The length and laboriousness of the rice production schedule thus approximated that of sugar. Cotton, on the other hand, was closer to tobacco in its industrial requirements, its suitability for family farms (though, over time, large holdings became common in alluvial districts), and in the relatively short duration of its crop cycle. It has been calculated that slaves in the cotton fields of the antebellum South worked about 3,000 hours during the year, considerably less than sugar workers.

Despite these staple crop variations, the commonalities existed in the labor patterns of slave field hands. On virtually all mainland plantations field hands devoted more of their labor time to subsistence activities than to the growing of the respective staples. Second, while plowing became more prevalent over time, particularly on cotton plantations, hoe agriculture remained central to the lives of almost all field hands. Third, since skilled opportunities were more available to slave men than to women, and since plantation labor was characterized by an extremely high labor-force participation rate, women and to some extent children often composed the majority of a plantation's field hands. Fourth, the life cycle of a field hand was much the same from region to region. Put into the field as a half hand at or before the age of ten, the field worker became a full hand in his or her late teens and was considered most productive in his or her early twenties, when field hand prices were generally at their highest. Those field hands fortunate enough to survive into their forties were often "retired" from the field and put to less onerous work.

Finally, important as the lash was to plantation labor, positive incentives were generally held out to field hands. Slave field hands therefore shared many of the same experiences even though there were considerable variations from one region to another, even from one plantation to another.

Slave field hands played a central role in the development of these various laboring patterns. They set limits to what could be imposed, they struggled to improve their own working conditions, and they molded many aspects of the plantation work regime. Slaves exerted some control, for instance, over their pace of work. At some tasks, and particularly under a task system,* field hands hurried to complete their work assignments. They generally and genuinely responded with extraordinary bursts of energy whenever collective work was required. Conversely, some operations and the gang system* as a whole encouraged slaves to find ways to work slowly, to shirk, to feign illness, to abuse both equipment and livestock, and even to engage in sabotage. Moreover, wherever an overseer* was employed, the field hands rarely missed an opportunity to undermine his position. Slaves exerted some control over their work routines in another way—by cooperating with another. Young field hands might help respected elderly slaves in their work, a husband might come to the aid of his wife, and family members might unite to complete a task. A sense of collective and family solidarity could be forged in many a plantation field.

SELECTED BIBLIOGRAPHY

Paul A. David et al., *Reckoning with Slavery: A Critical Study in the Quantitative History of American Negro Slavery* (1976); Robert W. Fogel and Stanley L. Engerman, *Time on the Cross: The Economics of American Negro Slavery* (1974); Eugene D. Genovese, *Roll, Jordan, Roll: The World the Slaves Made* (1974); Lewis C. Gray, *History of Agriculture in the Southern United States to 1860* (2 vols., 1933); B. W. Higman, *Slave Population and Economy in Jamaica, 1807–1834* (1976); B. W. Higman, *Slave Populations of the British Caribbean, 1807–1834* (1984); and Ulrich B. Phillips, *American Negro Slavery: A Survey of the Supply, Employment and Control of Negro Labor as Determined by the Plantation Regime* (1918).

PHILIP D. MORGAN

FILM, SLAVERY IN. Pictured against a backdrop of vast, riverfront cotton fields and laboring under spreading trees laden with Spanish moss, white actors in blackface portrayed hardworking slaves. The scene was from the silent movie *Uncle Tom's Cabin*, released in 1903 by Thomas Edison's film company. Directed by Edwin S. Porter, it was a landmark: it heralded the use of narrative "cards" to explain the action; it was also intended to provide a story line rather than just a sample of cinematic tricks. Just as significantly though, it brought to the screen the already popular myth of plantation slavery, already popular because in the post–Civil War years there had emerged a general fascination with local color. It was not long after 1865 that writers such as Thomas Nelson Page, John Esten Cooke, or Joel Chandler Harris with his Uncle Remus tales were regular features of the prestigious periodicals, such as *Cosmopolitan, Century, Harper's,* or *Munsey's.*

Praise of things Southern made for good reading in an era of reconciliation and curiosity about the nation's various regions, and that the Southern tales were also almost invariably racist reflected national, not merely sectional, biases. Novels and stories* were actually only part of a larger general celebration of the South. For example, on the minstrel stage the tale of Uncle Tom was reworked to comport with the growing romance and contemporary racial views; Currier and Ives published for their New York shop several immensely popular Southern rural scenes. By 1900, then, the images of the plantation and slavery were established and favored subjects. The South thus seemed a natural subject for the new medium of film.

Lured to predominantly urban theaters, ticket buyers craved excitement and escape in the new motion pictures. Though only a few minutes long, those first films spirited the audiences away to other places, other times, hence the early popularity of productions set in a grand South supported by plantation slave labor. The very short films presented instantly recognizable characters already so familiar from literature, popular art, and the theater.

The earliest silent movies fostered an image with little variation. *Uncle Tom's Cabin* alone was remade at least a dozen times by 1920, and as was usual in early film, the black parts were taken by white actors in blackface. It was not until the 1914 production that a black finally played the lead. Even as late as 1927 in *Topsy and Eva* whites still sometimes played the role of slaves. The slave in silent film was invariably devoted to both the labor system and his master. Even the Confederacy drew the support of the workers. David Wark Griffith's early production, *In Old Kentucky* (1909), included a black butler loyal to "the cause." The common theme running throughout three 1911 produc- tions—*A Special Messenger, Mammy's Ghost,* and *Uncle Peter's Ruse*—is the slave's effort to conceal wounded Confederates. In *The Old Oak's Secret* (1914), Old Mose is emotionally unable to leave the plantation and so hides his master's will with its manumission clause; in *For Massa's Sake* a devoted black attempts to sell himself so as to raise money to pay off his owner's gambling debts.

Even the studios' publicity bore out the filmmakers' and the audiences' racial assumptions. A press release for *His Trust Fulfilled* (1911) described a slave character overcome with joy, with tears "streaming down his black *but* [italics added] honest cheeks." D. W. Griffith's *Birth of a Nation* (1915) is the most remembered of the silent "Southern" films, but it was but one of hundreds which with smaller budgets and less directorial flair presented the same outlook.

Finally, both the need for more escapist entertainment during the Depression and the advent of sound recording technology brought about change in Hollywood and further adaptation of the slave character. Southern films became even more exaggerated in their romanticism. At first, the movie industry generally believed that silent film would continue to dominate and that sound productions were better suited for short subjects. The technical shortcomings of early sound re- cording were such that the black voice was both easier to record and clearer, and so among the first sound productions were brief pictures set in the South and featuring black music and dance. In films such as *Dixie Days* (1928), *Slave Days* (1929), and *Cotton Pickin' Days* (1930), there followed a wave of stylized shorts in which the Hall Johnson Choir, the Forbes Randolph Kentucky Jubilee Singers, and other groups cavorted about the quarters joyfully singing of slavery times.

Soon enough, though, Hollywood productions throughout the 1930s empha- sized the planters and their families, but the views of slavery remained frequent and benign. Bill "Bojangles" Robinson danced with Shirley Temple to save her imprisoned Confederate father in *The Littlest Rebel* (1935). Two more child stars, Jane Withers in *Can This Be Dixie?* (1936) and Bobby Breen in *Way Down South* (1939), likewise led attentive black workers on their various escapades. Such black comics, dancers, and actors as Willie Best, Stepin Fetchit, and Clarence Muse were relegated to comic relief in musical comedies such as *Dixiana* (1930) and *Mississippi* (1935). More serious roles were no different in romanticizing the slave's life. Daniel Haynes in *So Red the Rose* (1935) promised to maintain the plantation while his master went off to war; Eddie "Rochester" Anderson in *Jezebel* (1938) repeatedly risked his life for his mistress. And while lecturing Miss Scarlett that she had "no mo' manners than a field hand," Hattie McDaniel as Mammy in *Gone with the Wind* (1939) demonstrated that slave characters even exhibited the class consciousness of their owners.

The advent of World War II, however, brought significant change. The Office of War Information's Motion Picture Section pressured Hollywood that if the United States was indeed fighting a war for freedom, then in the best interests of the Allied war effort, productions should refrain from flagrant celebrations of the plantation. As a result, images of slavery were greatly altered. For example, slave characterizations were essentially eliminated from the 1943 musical *Dixie*, popular with troops overseas. In others, such as *The Flame of New Orleans* (1941) with Teresa Harris, slaves became as much confidantes as servants.

The end of the war ratified many changes, and by the 1950s the myriad court decisions such as *Brown v. The Board of Education*, integration of the armed services, and federal legislation aimed at fair hiring guidelines, all signaled a tentative Hollywood that further change was in order. Films involving depictions of slavery were fewer but at last demonstrated a new depth. Elizabeth Taylor in *Raintree County* (1957) is haunted by the possibility her mother was a slave; Sidney Poitier in *Band of Angels* (1957) escapes to join the Union army. By 1965, film seemed in step with general audiences. Made to observe the Civil War Centennial, *Shenandoah* (1965) includes a farmer's daughter actually advising a local slave to run to freedom.

By the late 1960s, the Hollywood studio system, audiences, and the standard plot formulas had all declined. Freed from traditional constraints, some producers found the theme of slavery a fertile means of attacking contemporary society. Black separatist politics, racial violence, and the height of the civil rights movement all contributed to productions filled with racial violence and revenge such as *Slaves* (1969) with Ossie Davis, *The Quadroon* (1971), and Dino De-Laurentis's *Mandingo* (1975) and its sequel *Drum* (1976). More recent years have brought blaxploitation pictures, *Passion Plantation* (1978) for example, produced expressly for inner-city audiences, relieved only occasionally by such films as *Skin Game* (1971), a comic, picaresque tale with Louis Gossett, Jr., playing a free black.

Such films contributed to a new awareness of black history and white racism but did not draw broad, general audiences. It was television that attracted those viewers to the most recent interpretation. Though sometimes the television premiere of a film such as *Beulah Land* (1978) represented a step back, other television films—*The Autobiography of Miss Jane Pittman* (1974), *Roots* (1977, 1979), or *Freedom Road* (1979)—presented the new themes in a palatable, even attractive, fashion.

SELECTED BIBLIOGRAPHY

Donald Bogle, *Toms, Coons, Mulattoes, Mammies, and Bucks: An Interpretive History of Blacks in American Films* (1973); Edward D. C. Campbell, Jr., *The Celluloid South: Hollywood and the Southern Myth* (1981); Thomas J. Cripps, *Slow Fade to Black: The Negro in American Film, 1900–1942* (1977); Jack T. Kirby, *Media-Made Dixie: The South in the American Imagination* (1978); Jim Pines, *Blacks in Films: A Survey of Racial Themes and Images in the American Film* (1977); and Allen Woll and Randall M. Miller, *Ethnic and Racial Images in American Film and Television* (1987).

EDWARD D. C. CAMPBELL, JR.

FISHERMEN, SLAVE. Across the South slaves supplemented bland diets* of hog and hominy with a rich variety of fish and other seafood, meshing African skills and dietary norms with New World abundance. Along the Eastern Shore of Virginia and Maryland, for example, slaves crabbed; on the Sea Islands of Georgia and South Carolina, they gathered oysters and assisted masters in the more adventurous sport of drumfishing. In port cities like Savannah or Charleston slaves put out to sea in huge flotillas, gathering flounder and mullet in dragnets. Shad, mackerel, croaker, weakfish, channel bass, and striped bass were caught in the South's numerous bays and tidal rivers. Catfish was the most popular catch for slaves in interior lakes and rivers. Virtually any slave who could haul a net, bait a hook line, or wield a shovel, trap, or basket was, in some measure, a fisherman. According to historian Joe Gray Taylor, "Many plantations had one or more slaves whose primary duty in summer and fall was to keep the table at the big house supplied with fish."

Fishing enriched monotonous diets, for blacks and whites alike. In coastal areas, particularly where rice* and sea-island cotton* flourished and livestock* production languished, fish provided a crucial source of protein and vitamin D. In these regions, dominated by the task system,* large slaveholders commonly trained a few hands to work full time as fishermen, or allowed them to hire their own time at the trade in port cities. Where water flowed nearby, however, slaves who worked under the task system* could supplement diets with little extra labor—a fact many masters relied upon in trimming food allowances. Though slaves working under the gang system* had fewer licit opportunities to fish, their diets were probably more varied and better balanced. Nevertheless, they also fished in ponds and streams when opportunities presented themselves. While slaves preferred catfish, they also consumed bowfin and garfish, species not generally eaten by whites.

Beyond supplementing slave nutrition and serving as the basis of a delectable regional cuisine, fishing provided bondsmen with an important recreational activity and conferred economic power within the slave community. Fishing sometimes opened an important avenue of market involvement for the slaves. Though Charles Ball's* South Carolina master collected the shad his fishermen netted, the rest of the catch was theirs to enjoy or distribute at will. The clever Ball doubled the opportunities fishing offered, secreting some of the shad he caught to sell to boats traveling downriver. By 1865, fishing had become so economically important in the Sea Islands that U.S. Army officers complained that the freedmen* would never turn back to cotton production unless the army destroyed their boats.

Planters had learned long before fishing's most important attraction to slaves: it provided the bondsmen with a measure of independence, a mode of resisting authority. Fishing enabled black men and women at least partially to feed themselves and thereby to produce and trade in the marketplace. Slave fishermen, then, were not the shiftless dependents pictured by slavery's defenders. If only unwittingly, the slave who set out to catch a fish often hooked old Massa too.

SELECTED BIBLIOGRAPHY

Charles Ball, *Slavery in the United States: A Narrative of the Life and Adventures of Charles Ball, a Black Man* (1836); Sam B. Hilliard, *Hog Meat and Hoe Cake: Food Supply in the Old South, 1840–1860* (1972); Charles W. Joyner, *Down by the Riverside: A South Carolina Slave Community* (1984); and Joe Gray Taylor, *Eating, Drinking, and Visiting in the South: An Informal History* (1982).

LAWRENCE T. MCDONNELL

FITZHUGH, GEORGE (1806–1881). George Fitzhugh, born in Prince William County, Virginia, emerged in the 1850s as one of the most articulate Southern voices in the defense of slavery.* Fitzhugh, a member of a prominent family, was largely self-educated. As a lawyer he never held elected office but did serve as a law clerk in the office of the attorney general of the United States under President James Buchanan. During Reconstruction he served as an agent of the Freedmen's Bureau* and as an associate judge of the Freedmen's court.

In the decade prior to the Civil War he came into prominence as a writer for a number of newspapers and journals. His most significant articles appeared in *De Bow's Review*. Fitzhugh rejected the philosophic thrust of the Enlightenment, preferring Robert Filmer to John Locke and Thomas Jefferson. Opposing the Manchester school, Fitzhugh, in his *Sociology for the South* (1854), attacked capitalism and laissez-faire economics as exploitive. He believed that the conditions of free labor were "worse than slavery." In contrast, Fitzhugh pictured the South's peculiar institution as benevolent and paternalistic. Despite his unorthodox economic ideas, he won Southern acclaim in his praise of slavery in *Cannibals All!* (1857). Southerners, uncomfortably ignoring his socialism, enthusiastically greeted his defense of the South and the justification of its social and economic systems. For William Lloyd Garrison* and other abolitionists,* however, he became a symbol of Southern militancy. Actually, he opposed nullification* and secession and feared their consequences. Following Reconstruction he moved to Kentucky in 1877 and then to Texas, where he died in 1881.

SELECTED BIBLIOGRAPHY

George Fitzhugh, *Cannibals All! Or, Slaves Without Masters*, edited by C. Vann Woodward (1960); Eugene D. Genovese, *The World the Slaveholders Made: Two Essays
in Interpretation* (1969); and Harvey Wish, *George Fitzhugh, Propagandist of the Old
South* (1943).

RICHARD DUNCAN

FLORIDA, SLAVERY IN. Slaves were introduced into Florida when the area
was claimed by Spain as part of her vast New World colonial empire. As early
as 1580, colonial officials had requested permission to import Negro slaves to
work in the St. Augustine area. Several years later a small group was brought
in to help reinforce the fort there and to clear the woods for planting. The number
of black slaves in Spanish Florida did not increase in any significant way,
however, because the Spanish Crown prohibited the use of slave labor in Florida
on a scale comparable to that of the labor forces used to develop the sugar
plantations of the Spanish West Indies. Thus, a labor shortage prevailed in Florida
during the period of Spanish control, between 1565 and 1763. This greatly
hampered the development of crop production, and the colony was never self-
sustaining, having to rely upon staples imported from Havana, Cuba, and abroad.

With the cession of Florida to Great Britain in 1763, at the close of the Seven
Years' War, the Spanish population withdrew. Even before this war ended,
wealthy planters and merchants of South Carolina had become interested in east
Florida along the St. Johns River for cultivating rice* and indigo.* Some of
them moved to the area, imported black slaves, and developed large plantations
with the use of this labor force. During the American Revolution,* many Tories
from Georgia and South Carolina fled to Florida, taking their slaves with them.
Approximately 5,000 whites and 8,000 slaves had fled to Florida by the close
of the Revolution to escape the penalties of their pro-British sympathies.

Unlike the Spanish period, Florida under English colonization was relatively
self-sufficient. The British government offered bounties for indigo and naval
stores,* which soon became the principal staples of the region. The progress of
agriculture and slavery in British Florida, however, proved temporary. At the
close of the Revolutionary war in 1783, Florida receded to Spain, and most of
the British inhabitants, with their slaves, left the country. Under this period of
Spanish control, from 1783 to 1821, Florida relapsed into the economic stalemate
of her earlier days under Spanish rule. Such were the conditions when Florida
was acquired from Spain by the United States in 1821 to become a frontier
development for slaveholding cotton planters from the older states of the South.

It was already known that the lands called middle Florida, lying just below
the thirty-first parallel of latitude between the Apalachicola and Suwannee rivers,
and the lands bordering those rivers were extremely fertile and desirable for
growing cotton.* As early as 1773, the botanist William Bartram had described
the country as exceptionally fertile for the cultivation of cotton and other agricultural products. The area is well defined geographically, as its soil type differs

from that of the rest of the state. In this relatively small and isolated region, between 1821 and 1860, a cotton economy emerged that compared favorably in output with that of the Georgia piedmont or the Black Belt of Alabama and Mississippi.

The rapid expansion and increase of cotton culture in Florida would not have happened without slavery. Abundant cheap labor made possible the process of winning new lands from a wilderness. The plantation was a frontier institution, and its development in Florida exemplified the manner in which settlers pushed into virgin lands to create new slaveholding societies based upon an enforced labor system. The Cotton Belt in Florida, when it became fully developed, extended from Jackson County, west of the Apalachicola River, into Alachua and Marion counties, southeast of the Suwannee River. The heaviest concentrations of plantations, slave populations, and cotton production were located in Jackson, Gadsden, Leon, Jefferson, and Madison counties. It was only after 1840 that settlers with their slaves spilled over into Alachua and Marion counties to develop new cotton lands. In south Florida, sugar* plantations, developed as early as the 1820s, had been completely destroyed during the Seminole Wars of the 1830s. After 1840, a new migration to south Florida along the Manatee River resulted in the rise of a few large sugar plantations, but sugar in Florida compared in no way to cotton as a money crop, and after 1850 its importance declined.

Much of the slave trade* in Florida centered in Tallahassee, since this capital city was in the heart of the Cotton Belt. "Negro-traders" purchased slaves there "from the block" at public outcry, then proceeded with them to various areas for resale. A large part of the supply for Florida planters was brought in by these traders. They came to St. Marks by ship, then went on to Tallahassee to dispose of their cargoes. Slaves were kept in the public jail or in "slave pens" until time of sale. The latter were buildings especially designed with cells. The sale of slaves was widely advertised in advance, and as they were presented at auction, bidding was often spirited.

The mania for buying slaves that seized Florida planters is evidenced by the fact that the black slave population increased from 7,587 in 1830 to 26,526 in 1840, a growth rate far in excess of the normal increase. This rapid growth continued during the 1840s, though it was not as pronounced. By 1850, there were 39,310 Negro slaves in the state, and 61,750 by 1860, nearly half of the state's total population of 140,500. The slave population remained concentrated in the Cotton Belt.

Various classifications determined individual prices* for slaves. For instance, blacksmiths, carpenters, seamstresses, prime field hands, brick masons, and house servants commanded higher prices than other slaves. Sex, age, temperament, physical condition, skill, and experience were also determining factors. Blacks recently imported from Africa were considered less valuable than "country" Negroes from an older state like Virginia, because the Africans were not yet acclimated or acculturated.

Field hands between eighteen and thirty years of age brought more than older slaves, and male hands brought higher prices than female hands. Children were often priced according to height and weight, and infants were valued by the pound. Attractive females and skilled workers sometimes sold for triple the value, and in some instances the buyer would pay more for a group of Negroes upon agreement that the old and infirm would be excluded.

At the time of William Bellamy's death in 1846, for example, most of the 108 slaves on his "home" plantation in Jefferson County were appraised and classified as nineteen family groups, with the value of each family given. "Moses, Molly, Parris, in a family" were valued at $1,000, while another family, consisting of eleven Negroes, some of whom were small children, was valued at $2,750. "Hannah," who was old, was "of no value." In 1851, Reddin W. Parramore's slaves were valued separately: "Wash, a man about 30 yrs. $600; Cherry, a young woman 16 yrs. $600; Amanda, a woman 19, unhealthy, $400." Mary, who was thirty years old and blind, had no value.

Closely allied with slave trading was the practice common throughout the plantation belt in Florida of owners hiring out* their slaves. In certain instances, when planters died and left a wife and minor children, they directed in their wills that their slaves be hired out, the proceeds to be used for education and maintenance of a child or for partial support of their families. In other instances, administrators or guardians, legally responsible for estates, hired out slaves belonging to the estate as a form of investment and income for the heirs. Slaves were also hired from owners to do construction work on roads or railways, and skilled slaves were sometimes hired individually for a certain period during the year to work as carpenters or blacksmiths.

The usual period of hire was for a year, and the person hiring was expected to furnish the slave with at least two suits of clothing, a hat, shoes, and a blanket. The rate of hire varied with the type of labor. The average annual rate of hire in Florida prior to 1850 was less than $100. During the 1850s the average rate increased, and yearly slave hire ranged from $100 to $400.

Many persons in Florida (also in the other slave states) were opposed to the system of hiring out because it encouraged a certain amount of freedom for the slave, especially as the system developed in the cities, where slaves were allowed to hire themselves out for wages, paying to the owner a stipulated amount and keeping the rest for themselves. Though the amount retained was very small, it gave the slave some independence. Under this system, the slave located his own job, agreed upon the amount of the wages, and gave to the owner a certain amount monthly or weekly. Opposition to this type of hire became especially sharp after 1850. Several white residents of Quincy, Tallahassee, and St. Augustine, for example, sent memorials to the Florida legislature and to the governors petitioning for laws to prevent hiring and to restrict the Negro in other ways. The petitioners complained that it had "become a common practice for owners, guardians, and agents to allow slaves to hire their own time." More than this, it was "getting common for slaves to own horses and buggies, and to go to and fro of nights and of Sundays as they may desire. . . . Allowing some slaves such latitude is calculated to create dissatisfaction among others.'' White Floridians' fears that the hiring system in the cities was eroding the very foundation of slavery were well founded. City slaves were free of the restrictions and police regulations put upon plantation slaves, and their time was their own when they were not working.

Slavery was first of all a labor system, and the slaveholders' primary concern was getting work out of their slaves. As the work was basically agricultural, the vast majority of slaves toiled on cotton plantations. Many plantations were small units using only a few slaves, where slaves and owners worked together in the fields at various tasks, but when the number of slaves owned included thirty or more field hands, an overseer was usually employed. (There has been a tendency to identify slaveholders as planters when they owned this number or more working hands and employed an overseer to direct the work.) One overseer* directing fifty or more Negroes was thought to be a good balance. If the number reached one hundred or more, the planter might engage another overseer and divide the force to operate more than one plantation.

The federal census returns for 1860 list 468 overseers directing the work of slaves on Florida plantations. It is fairly certain that most of the plantations of average size (1,500–2,500 acres) using thirty or more field laborers, and certainly the larger ones, were managed by overseers. Nearly half of the slave population of the South was owned by slaveholders operating plantations of these dimensions. Many planters believed that a force of less than thirty slaves could not be worked profitably.

The large plantations were elaborate organizations, resembling somewhat the modern factory system, with extensive supervision by the owner or his overseer or both. The tendency of Florida planters, and those in other cotton states, was to develop more than one plantation as ownership in land and slaves increased sufficiently to warrant profitable returns.

Edward Bradford's two plantations, Pine Hill and Horseshoe, not far distant from one another north of Tallahassee in Leon County, serve as examples of large units under efficient management. Bradford owned more than one hundred slaves and was a successful cotton planter. He also operated a gristmill, sawmill, shingle mill, and brickyard. He employed an overseer to manage his labor force and four other white men—an engineer, miller, and sawyer to operate his mills, and a bookkeeper to account for these various enterprises. His skilled laborers included a blacksmith, three carpenters, three coopers, two wheelwrights, and other craftsmen. Four slave foremen or drivers supervised the field hands. Bradford also had numerous house servants, including a butler, cooks, a housekeeper, housemaids, houseboys, laundresses, and seamstresses. Pine Hill was a large, self-sufficient plantation that, because of its size, required much labor and strict enforcement of many necessary regulations to ensure successful operation and production.

Another type of plantation was the frontier unit, where the owner's relationship with his slaves was rather informal and where few or no formal regulations operated. The owner of this unit was not of the "high-bred" society described by Solon Robinson in his travels in Florida, although his wealth in acreage and slaves was considerable. He often occupied a dilapidated, one-story structure, built several feet off the ground, and lived a crude sort of life, enjoying few luxuries except his artful loafing and hunting, and in several instances, seeking only the company, and sometimes the sexual contact, of his slaves.

Owners were well aware of the importance of providing the necessities of life to ensure profitable returns from investments in slaves and, more especially, to sustain a labor force. And so, if for no other reason, self-interest prompted most planters to care "properly" for their slaves. To provide them with adequate food and clothing was the first consideration. Although the food for slaves varied somewhat from plantation to plantation, the chief staples of their diet were pork and corn meal. Provisions were issued once a week, on Saturday, Sunday, or Monday. At such time, three-and-a-half to four pounds of pork and a pack of meal were provided each hand. Children ten years old or over received the same amount as adults. Molasses and sweet potatoes were often dispensed from time to time as supplemental foods. Slaveholders allowed, and sometimes encouraged, their slaves to have small gardens* near their cabins where they could grow greens and other vegetables for their own use. They kept chickens and hogs in small plots near the gardens.

To ensure the health of slaves, planters carefully supervised their clothing.* At least three separate outfits of clothing and one pair of shoes a year were considered necessary. Negro seamstresses generally made the clothing, but the planter's wife supervised the work. Ellen Call Long observed that it was the planter's wife who was directly concerned with the welfare of the slaves on the plantation: "The clothing of a plantation of negroes is in itself a great care; the cutting, fitting and sewing, by several seamstresses for both sexes, must be superintended the year round, and when they weave the cloth, there is the carding, the spinning, the reeling, warping, etc., also to be directed."

Housing* for slaves varied in construction and adequacy, depending on the area of settlement, size of the plantation, and efficiency and success of its management. The houses on John Finlayson's plantation in Jefferson County, for example, were constructed of logs notched together at the corners, with pine straw and mud to close the cracks. The roofs were covered with wooden shingles and shutters were hung on the windows. The chimney, exterior to the house, was made of brick or, more frequently, of split sticks, laid horizontally and plastered with mud, and the fireplace opening inside was covered with clay. The slave houses on Edward Bradford's plantation were single-frame units, each housing a family. They were whitewashed and had brick chimneys, and they were built well off the ground, with windows for ventilation and overhanging roofs to protect against rain. Many slave houses did not come up to these standards. As revealed in the slave schedules of the unpublished federal census returns for 1860, the ratio of slaves to slave houses on various Florida plantations was an average of five slaves in each house.

Many planters recognized the importance of cleanliness and proper hygiene in preventing illness among their slaves and usually employed a physician, at an annual fee, to care for and treat them. Even with the strict attention given to what planters considered proper food and adequate clothing and shelter, slaves suffered "a good deal of sickness." The slaves' diet,* which planters thought to be healthful, was deficient in many ways, and, as a result, left slaves susceptible to many diseases. The mortality rate for slaves in Florida was greater than that for whites. Slave children suffered an especially high mortality rate. Of the 122 deaths in Leon County in 1850, for example, 97 were slaves; of the slaves who died, 62 were children aged six years or younger. In Jefferson County 85 deaths occurred in 1850, 51 of them slaves (33 of whom were children). A similar ratio existed in other counties in Florida where large slave populations resided.

Many planters engaged ministers to preach to their slaves, believing that religious instruction was a way to inculate obedience in the slaves and also to give them some contentment. A group of planters often hired a minister to preach to the whole neighborhood. Ellen Call Long wrote, "It is important to look after the negro's morals; to instruct him religiously, which is done by hiring preachers. Neighborhoods unite in this, so that they have preaching and prayer meetings on one or the other plantation every Sunday. They are usually white men of the Methodist or Baptist persuasion, but they (the negro) prefer them to be of their own color." Slaves preferred a black preacher,* licensed or unlicensed, to conduct their services because they wanted to practice their own form of religion, away from the view of whites, where they could express a ritualistic style of singing and dancing, reminiscent of their African origins. This was especially true of plantation slaves who had to stifle these expressions when attending the white man's church on Sunday mornings.

In the 1830s and 1840s, Southern churchmen launched a movement to create plantation missions* to bring Christianity to the large majority of rural slaves who remained outside the institutional church's reach. The plantation movement, centered in the Carolina and Georgia low country, eventually spread to all the slave states. The success of the plantation mission in Florida, as elsewhere, was due in a large way to the appointment of Negro preachers, exhorters, and watchmen. These appointees more meaningfully communicated Christianity to slaves than did white preachers, whose doctrine centered upon docility, obedience, and subservience to the white man's rules. Black slave preachers remained cautious and seemingly preached doctrines approved by whites—in public. But they understood the slaves' secret longings for freedom and their desires to sublimate emotionally through dancing, shouting, and singing—to escape temporarily the demands of plantation routine exacted under the slave regime.

Negro slaves were aware that whites used religion* as a form of social control. Although many slaves were encouraged to attend the services of the whites and to become members of the whites' churches, most slaves preferred the less formal services held by members of their own race, at which they could assert themselves while singing and shouting to express their African religious forms and to seek relief from their oppression. The plantations of middle Florida provided praise houses at which slaves met to pray and sing on Sunday evenings and hold prayer meetings during the week. If the owner deprived the slaves of evening prayer meetings, they met together secretly in a cabin or brush arbor to hold their services, at which they were careful not to sing and shout too loud. The Negro spiritual "Steal Away to Jesus" was originally composed and sung to inform neighbors in the slave community of a secret prayer meeting to be held. The traditional custom, mentioned several times in Florida slave narratives, of turning the iron pot or wash tub upside down to muffle the noise at these secret meetings derived from a West African religious form associated with the gods. The iron pot did not muffle the noise but symbolized the African gods who gave divine protection. The custom of worshiping in brush arbors also was an African tradition, for the African ancestors of slaves reserved sacred groves for their religious meetings. In these, as in other ways, slaves in Florida built a religious world on African cultural foundations and their New World experiences and needs.

Of all the African traits retained by slaves in Florida and throughout the slave South, perhaps the family* concept was the strongest. Family solidarity grew from within the slave culture and was not dependent upon prescribed civil and religious norms. Over the years, expanded slave kin and quasi-kin networks characterized slave family linkages, and these linkages were tremendously significant in providing social security within the slave community. Within the family, the young slave learned behavioral patterns and was taught traditional values (quite different from those upheld by whites) that fostered self-esteem. The slave family was "far more than an owner-sponsored device designed to reproduce the labor force" and served as a form of social control. Traditionally, the family was monogamous, and even though it was frequently broken through separation by sale, extended kinship helped to ease the heartbreak and trauma of such an experience. Family solidarity acted as a survival mechanism for Florida slaves.

Negro literature in the form of autobiographies,* letters, and speeches of slaves who escaped to freedom to record their experiences while in bondage, and WPA interviews* made with former Florida slaves are a rich source for knowledge of the slaves' attitudes. In their work songs* and spirituals, the underlying themes manifest hope for freedom, for a better day, for relief from the burden of forced labor, and they express subtle attitudes toward the owner and his treatment of them. Throughout their literature and music the slaves bespoke their tenacious struggle to preserve as much of African culture as they could and to transform it into a weapon to repel the worst aspects of the slave system. Their art, dance, folk literature, language, music, and social traditions all manifested, to one or another degree, their African origins. Blacks retained their cultural heritage in Florida, and in America, as a means of survival in a world where white ideals were superimposed as a condition for acceptable behavior. Blacks took their enslavement stoically, though they never admitted inwardly that it was right or permanent. They practiced diplomacy and showed marked expertise in misleading whites with their use of parables and symbols.

Although slaves resisted their bondage directly, most frequently by running away, they also resisted in more subtle ways. They destroyed property, stole, slowed down on the job, hid out as maroons,* feigned illness, and created their own *volksunde* to preserve their traditional customs, beliefs, dances, songs, and tales, often impregnating them with undetected allegory to express their hidden feelings of resentment and rebelliousness.

Slaves did not always comply with their owners' demands, for which they suffered. The usual form of punishment* for slaves was whipping.* Owners instructed overseers to whip slaves when necessary, and some owners specified the number of lashes to be given for certain offenses. Slaveholders generally regarded whipping as the most effective form of punishment, but this method was sometimes flagrantly abused, accounting for the many runaways* from overseers and planters.

In Florida, statutory law* protected the slaveholders' interests as well as the vast agricultural economy that was the mainstay of the Cotton Belt. Only in a small measure did the law protect the slaves, in that owners were required to treat slaves with humanity and to provide them with necessary clothing, food, housing, and medical care. Slaves accused of crimes* were tried in the territorial court and, after 1845, the state court at Tallahassee. Court proceedings under the law were the same for slaves as for free persons, but the trials* were different. In only two instances was the Negro allowed to give testimony as a witness: when the territory or the state issued a suit against persons or concerns, and in civil cases between blacks and mulattoes, where no white persons were involved. Before the slave appeared as a witness, he was usually threatened with punishment to make sure he testified truthfully. These restrictions quite probably resulted in many unfair trials.

Evidence concludes that the standard of slave life in Florida was no better or worse than the standard provided on cotton plantations elsewhere in the antebellum South. Legally, slaves were chattel. Gradually, to regulate slaves in Florida, whites enacted laws based upon slave codes in the older Southern states. The critical point is not whether slave life in Florida, in terms of physical adequacy, was more or less harsh than in other areas of the South, but that the slave system, by controlling the individual's life, denied him the basic right to human dignity. That the slave retained his humanity and overcame the dehumanizing process of the slave system is his most signal achievement.

At the end of the Civil War, after emancipation, many blacks already had left the plantations to escape to Union lines or had gone into the towns. The majority of blacks, however, remained on the land, for they had no place else to go. Native white Floridians opposed the federal legislation implemented under the Reconstruction program that granted civil and political rights to the new freedmen.* They believed that granting equality to Negroes was unconstitutional—indeed, so much so that their opposition often erupted into violent crimes against the freedmen and white Republicans who controlled Florida's Reconstruction government and sought to enforce the law. Patriarchal members of the planter class, who at first had responded favorably to the freedmen's civil liberties, angrily opposed any black political activity in support of the Republican party,* and so joined forces with other native whites to drive the Negro out of politics. Determined to reestablish white supremacy in Florida, they resorted to various acts of physical violence against blacks. The blacks left politics, and the Republican party in the state disintegrated. Democratic party* solidarity and white supremacy once again held sway, and, after the Compromise of 1877, blacks were forced into a role of public accommodation that accorded with their poverty in postwar Florida.

SELECTED BIBLIOGRAPHY

John B. Boles, *Black Southerners, 1619–1869* (1983); Eugene D. Genovese, *Roll, Jordan, Roll: The World the Slaves Made* (1974); Herbert G. Gutman, *The Black Family in Slavery and Freedom, 1750–1925* (1976); Albert J. Raboteau, *Slave Religion: The "Invisible Institution" in the Antebellum South* (1978); Todd L. Savitt, *Medicine and Slavery: The Diseases and Health Care of Blacks in Antebellum Virginia* (1978); Jerrell H. Shofner, *Nor Is It Over Yet: Florida in the Era of Reconstruction, 1863–1877* (1974); Julia Floyd Smith, *Slavery and Plantation Growth in Antebellum Florida, 1821–1860* (1973); and Julia Floyd Smith, *Slavery and Rice Culture in Low Country Georgia, 1750–1860* (1985).

JULIA FLOYD SMITH

FOLKLORE. Folklore is a process of communication through the use of artistic forms which arise in recurring performances. These forms may consist of oral traditions (folk speech,* proverbs, legends, folk songs, etc.), customs (folk beliefs or "superstitions," rituals, dances, folk games, etc.), and material culture* (folk architecture, arts and crafts, foodways, etc.). The term *folklore* refers not to a collection of things but to patterns of behavior. For folklore to exist, these forms must be performed. Such performances are necessary to cultural continuity.

The folk speech of the slaves included a wide variety of folk linguistic phenomena, ranging from full-blown Creole languages such as Gullah* to lexical, syntactical, or phonological variations from standard speech. Their folk expressions made colorful and explicit comments on the experience of slavery. The slaves worked "from can to can't." They had to "root like a pig or die." The master "didn't give me sweat off de black cat's eye." But slavery made the slave tough: the "buzzards laid me and de sun hatch me." A significant aspect of slave folk speech had to do with onomastics, or naming practices.* Not only were Akan day names still found among slaves as late as the 1860s, but African *patterns* of naming persisted to an even greater extent. Kin-names were passed on in families, and surnames (or "titles") were in wide use within the slave community before emancipation.

The African penchant for proverbial ways of speaking—that is, speaking by indirection—was reflected in slave proverbs, which served as metaphors of social experience. Some African proverbs survived almost unchanged: the Hausa "Chattering doesn't cook the rice" continued in the South Carolina low country as "Promisin' talk don' cook rice." But others underwent local changes. The Bantu "Every beast roars in its own den" became the Gullah "Every frog praise its own pond [even] if it dry." Some spoke directly to the experiences of the plantation: "Ol' Massa take keer o' himself, but de niggah got to go ter God." Others could take on heightened meaning in the context of slavery. "Dere's a fambly coolness twixt de mule an' de singletree" could be employed as a comment on master-slave relations. "Yuh mought as well die wid de chills ez wid de feber" could be employed as a comment on the relative merits of trying to escape or remaining in bondage.

Across the South, slaves narrated legends (folk narratives set in historical time which are told *as though* true) of "Ole Nat" (Nat Turner*), "Moses" (Harriet Tubman*), Frederick Douglass,* John Brown,* and Abraham Lincoln.* According to one such legend, "I was looking right in Lincoln's mouth when he said, 'The colored man is turned loose without anything. I am going to give a dollar a day to every Negro born before Emancipation until his death—a pension of a dollar a day.' That's the reason they killed him." Another form of legend purports to explain how things came to be. Many such legends persisted as humorous stories—or etiological tales—even after belief had eroded.

The folktales of the slaves included tall tales (or improvements on reality, with smart slaves smarter, bad weather worse, and big crops bigger), outrageous falsehoods narrated with a straight face in the sober tones of truth. But trickster tales, with their theme of the struggle for mastery between the trickster (usually a small but sly, weak but wily animal such as Buh Rabbit) and his bigger and more powerful adversary, were the most popular tales on the plantations. The trickster defeats his rival by outwitting him. The slaves also narrated a cycle of human trickster stories featuring the slave John and his never-ending contest with the master. In such tales the slaves used language as symbolic action. By manipulating the words that defined their world, they verbally rearranged it and turned it symbolically upside down.

Singing* and making music were especially significant performances on the slave plantations. An Alabama slave remembered, "I'se can hear them darkies now, going to the cotton patch 'way 'fore day a-singing." The slaves sang while they plowed and hoed under the broiling sun and came in singing from the fields. After the day's work was done, slaves entertained their children with play songs and at night sang them to sleep with lullabies.

Religious services were especially marked by music. Whether they slipped away into the woods on Sunday evenings or had general prayer meetings on Wednesday nights at slave chapels, the slaves often "turn de wash pot bottom upwards so de sound of our voices would go under de pot.'' They ''would have a good time shouting, singing, and praying just like we pleased.'' At baptizings they would sing appropriate spirituals, such as ''Roll, Jordan, Roll'' or ''Going to the Water.'' After evening services slaves would sing on the way home. ''As the wagon be creeping along in the late hours of moonlight,'' a slave recalled, someone would raise a tune. ''Then the air soon be filled with the sweetest tune as us rid on home and sung all the old hymns that us loved.'' As they rode through the quarters, slaves who had not been to church would ''come out to the cabin door and jine in the refrain. From that we'd swing on into all the old spirituals that us love so well and that us knowed how to sing.''

On Saturday nights, from Virginia and the Carolinas through Alabama and Mississippi to Louisiana and Texas, the slaves held dances* and frolics. Talented slave ''musicianers''* played such old-time songs as ''Arkansas Traveler,'' ''Black Eyed Susie,'' ''Jimmy Long Josey,'' ''Soldier's Joy,'' and ''Old Dan Tucker.'' According to a Mississippi slave, when the fiddler played the old reels, ''you couldn't keep your foots still.'' ''Oh, Lord,'' recalled a North Carolina slave, ''that fiddle could almost talk.''

Some of the slave songs commented directly on the world of the plantation:

> Run nigger, run
> De Patteroll [patrol] get you!
> Run nigger, run,
> De Patteroll come!

A North Carolina slave said, ''Dat one of the songs de slaves all knowed.'' In Virginia the slaves sang a song when the master was shipping them to market: ''Massa's Gwine Sell Us Tomorrow.'' Other songs were satirical. Texas slaves sang

> Fool my master seven years,
> Going to fool him seven more.
> Hey diddle, de diddle, de diddle, de do.

When Sherman's troops marched through South Carolina and many masters fled their plantations for safer ground, slaves sang

> Master gone away
> But darkies stay at home.
> The year of jubilee is come
> And freedom will begun.

And in the aftermath of emancipation, they sang

> Now dat overseer want to give trouble
> And trot us 'round a spell,

But we lock him up in de smokehouse cellar
With de key done throwed in de well.

There was considerable continuity with African patterns of folk belief on the slave plantations of the New World. Ghosts or haunts—the spirits of the dead—returned to trouble the living. "I knows dere is ghosts," recalled an Alabama slave, because "dis spirit like an angel come to my mammy and told her to tell de white lady to read de Bible backwards three times." Various charms—a rabbit foot or coon foot—could ward off their unwelcome visits. Other slave folk beliefs included signs—if "a screech owl lit on your chimney and hollered," it signified that "somebody in dat house was goin' to die."

African spirit possession was incorporated into slave Christianity, but many slaves took their problems to plantation conjurers. The conjurers, assisted by various substances which were held to be magical, were relied upon for protection against "ruin or cripplin' or dry up de blood" (all misfortunes were regarded as emanating from magic) and for casting spells upon enemies. On the Sea Islands of South Carolina conjurers were known to "put bad mouth on you." Not all slaves believed in conjure. "Dem conjure-folks can't hurt you lessen you believe in 'em," one slave contended. Another said, "Ma told us chillen voodoo was a no 'count doin' of de devil, and Christians was never to pay it no attention." But others took no chances. "I been a good Christian ever since I was baptized," an Oklahoma slave said, "but I keep a little charm here on my neck anyways."

As in peasant cultures, the slaves' long days of toil in the cotton,* sugar,* and rice* fields alternated with periods of ritual celebration. Harvest time was such an occasion. "After the cotton was picked dey would eat barbecue, and dance, and have a big time," a Georgia slave remembered. In the South Carolina up-country on the Fourth of July "us went to barbecues after morning chores was done." There were also corn shuckings, wedding parties, and festivities on various holidays. Slaves typically celebrated Christmas and Easter. Some Virginia slaves also had a Whitsun holiday. "On dem days we would play ring plays, jump rope, and dance. Then nights we'd dance juba." Christmas was the most popular holiday. A Missouri slave reported that "during Christmas time and de whole month of January, it was de rulin' to give de slaves a holiday in our part of de country. A whole month to go and come as much as we pleased and go for miles as far as we wanted to, but we had better be back by de first of February." A two- or three-day holiday was more typical elsewhere. In Georgia,

A tree am fix, and some present for everyone. The white preacher talk 'bout Christ. Us have singing and 'joyment all day. Then at night, the big fire builded, and all of us sot round it. There am 'bout hundred hog bladders save from hog killing. So, on Christmas night, the children takes them and puts them on the stick. First they is all blowed full of air and tied tight and dry. Then the children holds the bladder in the fire and pretty soon, "BANG!" they goes. That am the fireworks.

In North Carolina (as in Jamaica) the John Canoe festival was an exotic part of the Christmas celebration in which bands of dancers, keeping time to the beat of the "gumbo box," triangles, and jawbones begged donations from spectators.

Slave children* played various folk games in the quarters, ranging from pastimes (running, jumping, skipping, jumping poles, walking on stilts, riding stick horses, etc.) to games of skill (jump rope, ball, marbles—"with marbles us make"—horseshoes, etc.). Games of concealment, such as "I Spy," "Blindfold and Tag," "Peep Squirrel Peep," and "You Can't Catch Me," taught young slaves potentially useful skills. "Sometimes us made bows and arrows. Us could shoot 'em, too, jus' like de little Injuns." For older children, there was the "well game." "De gal or boy set in de chair and lean way back and pretend like dey in de well. Dey say dey is so many feet down and say, 'Who you want pull you out?' And de one you want pull you out, dey s'posed to kiss you."

Folk architecture was strikingly exemplified in the slave cabins, varying from slave quarters built of stone (reported in Kentucky) to "old ragged huts made out of poles" (in Alabama). Some slave cabins were described by ex-slaves as "good houses, weatherboarden with cypress and had brick chimneys," but more commonly they were built of logs, perhaps covered with slabs. On some plantations, "dey wasn't fitten for nobody to live in. We just had to put up with 'em." The cracks between the logs were chinked with mud or clay, not always successfully. A Texas slave reported that "the cold winds in the winter go through the logs like the walls was somewhere else." Some cabins were large; a Missouri slave claimed that "de hewed log house we lived in was very big, about five or six rooms." Far more typical was the one- or two-room cabin in which as many as a dozen people might live. The chimneys were usually built of sticks, clay, and mud, with a coat of clay daubed over them. All too often they caught fire. "Many the time we have to get up at midnight and push the chimney away from the house to keep the house from burnin' up." Some cabins had plank floors, but others had none. A Georgia slave lamented, "Dey no floor in dem houses, 'cept what God put in dem." According to a Mississippi slave, "My ma never would have no board floor like de rest of 'em, on 'count she was a African."

Talented slave artisans* created beautiful arts and crafts. On the rice plantations of the South Carolina low country, women made wide fanner baskets with low sloping sides after the African method of coiled basketry. In Georgia slave basketmakers made plaited baskets and mats. Throughout the South slave women made quilts—often in strip patterns—both to keep their families warm and to provide a beautiful object in the cabin. A North Carolina slave described how "the womenfolks carded and spun and wove cloth, then they dyed it and made clothes. And we knit all the stockings we wore." Slave blacksmiths not only shod horses and other livestock but also made the striking wrought-iron gates that were especially prized in South Carolina and Louisiana. And slave craftsmen were adept at making musical instruments which were beautiful both to see and to hear. There were fiddles made from gourds, banjoes made from sheep hides, bones from beef ribs, and quills made from willow stalks: "You takes de stick and pounds de bark loose and slips it off, den split de wood in one end and down one side, puts holes in de bark and put it back on de stick. De quill plays like de flute."

Folk cultural expression was also exemplified in slave foodways. At sunset in the slave quarters one could smell the aromas of cornbread, peas and rice, and pork or fish cooking over wood fires. Typically, each slave family had its own garden plot from which the family supplemented its weekly allocation of rations. Hunting and fishing added additional variety to the cuisine. On some plantations, "we always made at least one barrel of peach brandy and one of cider. That would be vinegar 'nough by spring. 'Simmon beer was good in the cold freezing weather too. We make much as we have barrels if we could get the persimmons." Slaves ate the foodstuffs of the plantation environment; but slave cooks applied to them African methods of cooking and spicing, remembered recipes, ancestral tastes. They thus not only maintained cultural continuity with African foodways but also creatively adapted African traditions to the New World.

The folklore of the slaves was thus a pattern of learned behavior that functioned both to express and to shape the attitudes of the slave community. Its forms and style were social rather than individual, denoting in a very direct way the ranges of behavior appropriate to various contexts. Slave folklore was not peripheral to slave life. On the contrary, through their folklore the slaves proclaimed their sense of community and molded individuals into a common culture.

SELECTED BIBLIOGRAPHY

J. Mason Brewer, "Old Time Negro Proverbs," *Publications of the Texas Folklore Society*, 11 (1933), 101–105; Paul A. Cimbala, "Fortunate Bondsmen: Black 'Musicianers' and Their Role as an Antebellum Southern Plantation Slave Elite," *Southern Studies*, 18 (1979), 291–303; Dena J. Epstein, *Sinful Tunes and Spirituals: Black Folk Music to the Civil War* (1977); Gladys-Marie Fry, *Night Riders in Black Folk History* (1975); Herbert G. Gutman, *The Black Family in Slavery and Freedom, 1750–1925* (1976); Charles Joyner, *Down by the Riverside: A South Carolina Slave Community* (1984); Lawrence W. Levine, *Black Culture and Black Consciousness: Afro-American Folk Thought from Slavery to Freedom* (1977); Charles Perdue et al., eds., *Weevils in the Wheat: Interviews with Virginia Ex-Slaves* (1976); George P. Rawick, ed., *The American Slave: A Composite Autobiography* (19 vols., 1972; supplement, series 1, 12 vols., 1977); Sterling Stuckey, "Through the Prism of Folklore: The Black Ethos in Slavery," *Massachusetts Review*, 9 (1968), 417–437; and Robert F. Thompson, *The Flash of the Spirit: African and Afro-American Art and Philosophy* (1981).

CHARLES JOYNER

FREE BLACKS. Within a generation after the arrival of the first Africans at Jamestown, Virginia, in 1619, free blacks had emerged as a discrete group in the American colonies. In some locales they comprised a large percentage of the total black population. Among the approximately 144 Negroes in Northamp-

Table 1
Population of Free Negroes in the United States, 1820–1860

	1820	1830	1840	1850	1860
North	99,281	137,529	170,728	196,262	226,152
South	134,223	182,070	215,575	238,187	261,918
	-------	-------	-------	-------	-------
total	233,504	319,599	386,303	434,449	488,070

ton County, Virginia, in 1662, about 44 were listed as free persons, and several among them, including tobacco farmer Anthony Longo, had acquired small tracts of land. During the seventeenth century, small enclaves of free Negroes established themselves as laborers and farmers along the Eastern Shore of Virginia and Maryland, and in Boston, New York, Philadelphia, and Charleston. But with the influx of slaves toward the end of the century, blacks found it increasingly difficult to secure their freedom. By 1750, there were probably no more than a few thousand free Negroes in the thirteen colonies. A 1755 census in Maryland, the single enumeration of this group in the colonial South, counted 1,800 Negro freemen, 2 percent of the colony's nonslave population. Yet, through self-purchase, manumission, and running away (or being born of a free Negro mother), a few slaves continued to move out of bondage.

The American Revolution* ushered in a new era. Some slaves fled to British lines after being offered their freedom by Lord Dunmore, the governor of Virginia. Others were promised their liberty if they fought for the colonists. Still others received their freedom as a result of the gradual abolition of slavery in the Northern states. In 1775, Pennsylvania Quakers* organized the first antislavery society* in America, followed by similar organizations in New York, Massachusetts, and New Jersey. Even in the Southern states, inspired by the ideals of liberty and equality in the Declaration of Independence, slave owners manumitted increasing numbers of slaves.

Following the Revolution, slavery was outlawed in the Northwest Territory (1787),* and several thousand French-speaking mulattoes from the Caribbean immigrated to ports along the Gulf Coast in the wake of the slave revolt in Saint-Domingue led by Toussaint L'Ouverture. (They were persecuted in Haiti because of their white ancestry and in Cuba because of their loyalty to France.) By 1790, the year of the first decennial census, there were 59,466 free Negroes in the United States, 27,109 in the North and 32,357 in the South. A decade later the total had increased to 108,395, with 47,154 and 61,241 in each section; and by 1810, to 186,446, with 78,181 and 108,265. This rapid expansion slowed considerably in subsequent decades, but each census recorded at least 48,000 more

free blacks than its predecessor. By 1860, free Negroes comprised 9 percent of
the black population in the United States.

For a variety of reasons—employment opportunities, social and cultural advantages, the need for anonymity—free blacks migrated to towns and cities.*
Between 1800 and 1850, the free Negro population in the nation's fifteen major
cities increased sixfold (compared to a threefold increase for the entire population). In Baltimore, the number of free blacks rose from 2,771 to 25,442 (and
from 10 percent to 15 percent of the city's total); in New Orleans from 800 to
9,905 (remaining at about 9 percent of the total); in New York City from 3,499
to 13,815 (declining from 6 percent to 3 percent); and in Washington, D.C.,
from 123 to 8,158 (4 percent to 20 percent). By the eve of the Civil War, despite
population declines in a few urban areas, nearly half of the free blacks in the
United States (47 percent) lived in towns and cities (compared to a third for
whites), while in the North, the proportion was nearly two-thirds (61 percent,
compared to 41 percent for whites) and in the South slightly more than one-
third (35 percent, compared to 15 percent for whites and 5 percent for slaves).
Free Negroes were, in this broad comparison, the most urban group in the nation.

A demographic profile of free persons of color reveals several other unique
features. By mid-century the average female-to-male ratio in towns and cities
was 125 to 100, half way between the nearly normal proportion for urban whites
(97 to 100) and the extremely skewed ratio for city slaves (151 to 100). This
was primarily a result of white men taking black women as their wives and
mistresses and eventually providing them with their freedom. In addition, urban
free Negroes had a lower fertility (and/or higher infant mortality) rate than other
groups.

Whether living in towns and cities, or in rural areas, free blacks confronted
a web of legal restrictions. In the colonial period they were barred from testifying
in certain court cases, prohibited from engaging in sexual relations with whites,
and sometimes included in certain provisions of the slave codes. In 1705, the
Virginia assembly prohibited any Negro, mulatto, or Indian, "bond or free,"
from lifting his hand in opposition to a white colonist. During the early national
and antebellum periods, free Negroes encountered a growing body of laws specifically designed to keep them in a subordinate position. In some states, they
could not own real estate; in others, including those carved out of the Northwest
Territory, they could not enter the state, or upon entry, were required to post a
substantial bond ($500 to $1,000). Except in six states (Massachusetts, New
Hampshire, Vermont, and Maine; Tennessee and North Carolina prior to 1834–
1835), they were not allowed to vote (nor, of course, hold political office); in
most states they were prohibited from testifying in court cases involving whites.
Even in the absence of specific statutes governing their actions, custom and
prejudice made it impossible for them to serve on juries, or travel next to whites
on railroad cars, omnibuses, stagecoaches, and steamboats. Nor could they gain
equal access to theaters, restaurants, museums, and resorts. In the North, historian Leon F. Litwack writes, free blacks were "often educated in segregated

Table 2
Free Negro Population Distribution in Fifteen Cities, 1800–1850

Cities	1800	1810	1820	1830	1840	1850
Albany	156	*	645	1,050	886	860
Baltimore	2,771	3,973	10,326	14,790	17,967	25,442
Boston	1,174	1,464	1,687	1,875	*	1,999
Brooklyn	196	*	657	973	1,772	2,424
Buffalo	*	*	24	219	503	675
Charleston	951	1,472	1,475	2,107	1,558	3,441
Cincinnati	*	82	433	1,090	2,240	3,237
Louisville	1	11	93	232	619	1,538
New Orleans	800**	4,950	6,237	11,562	15,072	9,905
New York	3,499	8,137	10,368	13,960	16,358	13,815
Philadelphia	4,210	6,352	7,579	9,795	10,507	10,736
Pittsburgh	92	185	285	473	710	1,959
Providence	656	865	975	1,206	1,301	1,499
St. Louis	70	*	*	*	531	1,398
Washington	123	867	1,696	3,129	4,808	8,158

*missing data   **estimate

Source: Leonard P. Curry, *The Free Black in Urban America, 1800–1850: The Shadow of the Dream* (1981), p. 250.

schools, punished in segregated prisons, nursed in segregated hospitals, and buried in segregated cemeteries." The famous Dred Scott* decision in 1857 declared that no descendant of a slave could claim the right of citizenship.

In the face of these oppressive and discriminatory laws, free Negroes reacted in several ways. One response was to turn inward, to seek friends and acquaintances among others in their group, to join churches and form societies with other free blacks. Another response was to separate themselves as much as possible from blacks who had not attained as high an economic or social standing. Thus, prosperous free persons of color tried to separate themselves from those living in poverty; mulattoes sometimes refused to associate with blacks. But these class and color prejudices have probably been overemphasized by historians. Most free Negroes, living and working in close proximity with whites and other blacks, sought to maintain friendly and productive relationships with a wide variety of people—slaveholders and nonslaveholders, other free blacks and slaves.

The occupational skills of free blacks varied considerably in different sections of the country. In the Deep South, where whites sometimes emancipated highly skilled slaves, a large number of free Negroes were carpenters, masons, wrights, engineers, merchants, mechanics, and tailors. In Charleston, South Carolina, in 1860, for example, they comprised 75 percent of the city's millwrights, 40 percent of its tailors, and 25 percent of its carpenters. In New Orleans, at mid-century, there were 355 free black carpenters, 278 masons, 156 cigarmakers, 92 shoemakers, 82 tailors, 64 merchants, 61 clerks, 52 mechanics, as well as several physicians, cotton factors, real estate brokers, and teachers. At the same time, free women of color found employment as hairdressers, nurses, midwives, and boardinghouse keepers. In the North, free blacks worked primarily as day laborers, domestic servants, or subsistence farmers, with only a small percentage becoming skilled artisans and tradesmen. In antebellum Philadelphia, 81 percent of the men who could find employment toiled as laborers, porters, waiters, seamen, carters, and manual workers. Similar patterns prevailed in the border states of the South, although the skill level was higher than in the North. In Virginia, in 1860, there were 4,224 free Negro blacksmiths, 236 barbers, 1,895 coopers, and 3,728 shoemakers, but farm laborers numbered 30,518 and servants 11,053. Among the latter two groups, some fared little better than slaves. Several hundred farm workers in Westmoreland County, Virginia, for instance, signed long-term indentures (up to twenty years) in return for food, clothing, and shelter.

Quasi-free slaves in the South were sometimes more highly skilled than the mass of free blacks. Visitors to Savannah, Georgia, were constantly struck by the large numbers of slaves who, in the words of Charles C. Jones, Sr., "go about from house to house—some carpenters, some house servants, etc.—who never see their masters except at pay day, live out of their yards, hire themselves without written permit, etc." The city's slave population included cotton factor Monday Habersham, hostler John Butler, livery keeper Henry Wane, butcher Abram Steward, and cotton farmer Prince Kendy. It was well known that Steward was the largest and most successful butcher in the city, and that Kendy's father, worth thousands of dollars, had been "the richest slave in Georgia." It took an unusual slave to "pay wages" and secure such an estate, but nearly free bondsmen could be found in various towns and cities as well as rural areas.

Regional contrasts were also apparent among free black property owners. By far the most prosperous group of free persons of color was located in the Deep South. Propertied blacks in Louisiana actually accumulated more property than the average Northern white. In 1860, for example, free Negroes—mostly Creoles of color, *gens de couleur libre* as they were called, who had descended from French-slave ancestry—controlled approximately $9 million worth of property. According to the U.S. census, the average free Negro property owner (total number = 2,116, excluding 145 Negro women cohabiting with white men) controlled $3,800 worth of real and personal property. This was nearly the same as the average Southern white ($4,000), almost twice the amount of the average Northern white ($2,000), and three times the amount of the average foreign-born ($1,300) property holder. According to the 1850 census returns, in Charleston County, South Carolina, free blacks (total number = 59) controlled about $122,000 worth of real estate. Their average holding was $2,100, more than twice that of the average white American. Nine years later, as shown in a tax assessment list, 355 free blacks in the city alone owned $755,000 worth of property. Elsewhere, free Negroes were not able to acquire such large estates. In 1860, black farmers in Virginia (total = 1,200) controlled 60,000 acres worth only about $370,000; in Tennessee free blacks acquired $750,000 worth of property; in North Carolina, $1 million; in Maryland, $1.2 million. Their average estate was considerably less than in Louisiana and South Carolina. Blacks fared worst in the North. Their combined real property holdings in the cities of Boston, Brooklyn, Buffalo, Cincinnati, New York City, Philadelphia, and Pittsburgh, in 1850, was only $1.2 million.

A number of the wealthiest free Negroes in the United States were slave owners.* While the great majority of the 3,775 free blacks who possessed bondsmen in 1830 owned only a few slaves—sometimes a husband or wife or relative who could not legally secure freedom papers—forty-four free persons of color (.01 percent of the total) in eight Louisiana parishes (Iberville, Natchitoches, Pointe Coupée, St. John the Baptist, St. Landry, St. Martin, Ouachita, West Baton Rouge) owned 1,335 blacks, or nearly one out of ten slaves owned by Negroes. In St. John the Baptist Parish, three plantation owners held 139 blacks in bondage—an average of 46 slaves each; in St. Landry Parish, Jean Baptiste Meullion, a sugar planter on Bayou Teche, owned fifty-two blacks; in Plaquemines Parish, Andrew Durnford,* owner of St. Rosalie plantation, acquired a similarly large black labor force.

The racial attitudes of these rich blacks differed only slightly from those of their white neighbors. "He was good to all de slaves on de place, but he mean for dem to wuk w'en he say wuk," the nephew of St. Mary Parish, Louisiana, rice planter Romaine Verdun recalled. "He ain' never 'low non of them to be famil'ar wid him." But during periods of political and economic unrest, even

Negro slave owners could feel threatened. Few among them failed to realize that their future might be jeopardized by the fears and hatreds of whites. The well-to-do merchant Louis Sheridan, a slave owner and farmer in Bladen County, North Carolina, worth an estimated $20,000, became so concerned about white hostility against free blacks during the 1830s that he left the country and settled in Liberia.

Blacks who felt the same as Sheridan but lived in the North could speak out against racial injustice. In 1830, a group of twenty-six prominent Negroes from Pennsylvania and neighboring states, including Richard Allen and Austin Steward,* organized the American Society of Free Persons of Color. This led to a series of national Negro conventions. Meeting annually between 1831 and 1835, and periodically thereafter (1843, 1847, 1848, 1853, 1855), these gatherings brought together such outstanding leaders as Frederick Douglass,* clergyman Henry Highland Garnet, colonizationist Martin R. Delany, as well as white abolitionists Arthur Tappan and William Lloyd Garrison.* Although concerned primarily with the abolition of slavery and equal rights for blacks, they discussed temperance, how to improve educational opportunities, and the need for economic advancement.

Among the most important institutions in free Negro communities was the church. Excluded from or segregated within white institutions, free blacks formed large Baptist and Methodist congregations in Boston, New York, Philadelphia, Cleveland, and Cincinnati. Those who were more affluent often joined the African Methodist Episcopal,* or the AME Zion church. Beginning in 1847, the AME church published the *Christian Herald*. In the South, slave owners opposed separate congregations, especially following the Denmark Vesey* conspiracy (1822) in South Carolina, but free Negro preachers often defied the various restrictive laws and preached to all-black congregations. Free blacks also became Presbyterians.* During the 1840s, separate Presbyterian churches were established in Baltimore, Brooklyn, Buffalo, Cincinnati, Louisville, and Pittsburgh. In Washington, D.C., in 1843, John Francis Cook, pastor of the Fifteenth Street Church, became the District's first ordained Presbyterian minister. In Louisiana, and other areas of French and Spanish influence, free Negroes joined the Catholic church.*

Although often illiterate, or semiliterate, free Negroes struggled desperately to educate their children. Excluded from public schools (until Boston permitted them to attend the city's schools in 1855), they sent their children to private schools sponsored by churches or philanthropic organizations. The Bethel African Methodist Church in Philadelphia, the African Baptist Church in Boston, the Sharp Street Methodist Church in Baltimore, and the Manumission Society of New York City sponsored such schools. In New York City, the African Free School enrolled about 1,500 students during the 1840s. A few institutions were founded by private philanthropists. Gilmore High School in Cincinnati, established in 1844 by Hiram S. Gilmore, a wealthy British clergyman, offered its 300 students courses in Latin, Greek, art, music, and English. In the South, many whites believed that educated free blacks were dangerous, but even in the slave states a few free Negro schools survived the winds of political and ideological change. In 1816, Daniel Coker founded the Bethel Charity School in Baltimore, and during the next decade other free Negro schools were established in Virginia, South Carolina, Tennessee, and North Carolina. For nearly thirty years John Chavis* ran a night school in Raleigh, North Carolina. The resourceful Mary Peake secretly taught as many as fifty slaves and free blacks in her Norfolk home during the 1850s. Free persons of color in Louisiana established more than a dozen schools. During the 1849–1850 academic year, 43 percent of the free black children in New Orleans attended school.

Besides churches and schools, free Negroes associated with one another in various other ways. To provide death and burial benefits as well as offer assistance in time of need, they organized mutual aid societies. Among the oldest were the Free African Society in Philadelphia (1778), the Brown Fellowship Society in Charleston (1790), and the Boston African Society (1796). By the 1830s, there were hundreds of these organizations in the United States. In Philadelphia, in 1838, seventy-nine benefit associations boasted a membership of 7,372; a decade later about half the adult Negro population in the city belonged to one mutual aid organization or another. Free blacks also formed literary clubs, debating societies, and poetry groups, and joined secret fraternal societies (Freemasons and Odd Fellows). The Prince Hall Freemasons (named after the founder of black freemasonry in America) attracted members notable for their economic achievements—Absalom Jones and James Forten of Philadelphia, William Wormley and William C. Costin of Washington, D.C., and William H. Gibson of Louisville.

White attitudes toward free Negroes varied considerably during different periods and in different locations. Prior to 1830, especially in the border states, a number of white Southerners held genuinely liberal views toward free blacks, praising them as industrious, hardworking, and trustworthy, assisting them in obtaining freedom papers, and serving as their guardians when the law required it. In some instances they offered them financial assistance. But following the publication of David Walker's* *Appeal* (a pamphlet written by a free Negro urging slaves to revolt), the Nat Turner insurrection* in Virginia, and a severe economic depression during the 1830s, Southern whites launched an attack on free blacks, castigating them as indolent, thieving, and ungovernable, and accusing them of inciting a spirit of insubordination and rebelliousness among slaves. These attitudes were reflected in the comprehensive legal codes which restricted or completely outlawed manumissions, prohibited free blacks from visiting slaves, and denied them the right to travel in certain areas. By the late 1850s, Southerners proposed laws to resettle free Negroes in Africa or remand them to slavery.

Many Northern whites felt equally hostile toward blacks. Sometimes their enmity erupted in violence. Race riots occurred in Cincinnati (1829, 1841), Providence (1831), Philadelphia (1834), New York City (1834), Washington,

D.C. (1835), Boston (1843), and other cities. The 1841 riot in Cincinnati was among the worst of the prewar era. A mob of 1,500 whites moved into a black neighborhood, and in the burning, looting, and pillaging that followed, four people were killed and twenty wounded. Such confrontations prompted Southerners to contend that white hatred of free Negroes was more pronounced in "the Promised Land" than in the slave states. Whatever the validity of this contention, most Northern whites looked upon free Negroes as a degraded and inferior caste, without motive for virtuous conduct.

Except during periods of economic or political crisis, free blacks in the South probably felt more secure than their brethren in the North. Despite the anti-free Negro sentiment and legal restrictions, they traveled through different regions, moved about without passes, and engaged in various economic pursuits. They were sometimes assisted by whites who rejected the prevailing notions of free Negro depravity. Those who were especially industrious could depend on white allies and found the legal barriers relatively easy to surmount. The law against property ownership in Georgia, for instance, did not deter free Negroes like Anthony Odingsells, who, according to the 1860 census, owned thirteen slaves, two thousand acres of farm and timber land, thirty-five head of cattle, fifty sheep, and seventy-five hogs.

At the same time, paradoxically, many Southerners believed that America should rid itself of its free black population. In 1817, John Randolph and Henry Clay* helped organize the American Colonization Society* (ACS). Seeking to establish a colony for free Negroes in West Africa, the Society's officers included William Crawford, James Monroe, James Madison, and Andrew Jackson. During the 1820s and 1830s, the ACS established affiliates in every Southern state except South Carolina and Arkansas, and raised several hundred thousand dollars to achieve its goal. Southerners supported emigration for several reasons: to solve the "race problem" in the United States, to Christianize "the heathens" in Africa, and to rid the country of "the menace" of free blacks. Only a few thousand Negroes, including many emancipated slaves, however, were actually transported to Africa, though the Society did help establish the country of Liberia.

Most free Negroes were skeptical about the motives of whites who supported the back-to-Africa movement. They hoped to improve economic, social, and political conditions within the United States. Indeed, their values and attitudes were often similar to those of the vast majority of whites. This could be seen not only in their determination to acquire property, and, whenever possible, assert their legal rights, but also in their social and religious activities.

The decade of the 1850s was especially trying for free Negroes. Struggling to improve their situation in the midst of a nation moving ever closer to the abyss of civil war, they found themselves confronting new oppressive laws and at times mass hysteria among slave owners who felt their civilization was under attack, even in jeopardy. As a result, they made every effort to live quiet, unobtrusive lives, devoting their energies to improving their economic lot. Ironically, during these troublesome years, they made substantial progress in just about every index of advancement—increased literacy, growing church membership, burgeoning associations, and marked improvement in ownership of property. While many would find the Civil War and its aftermath a wrenching experience, others accepted the challenges of the new era and became leaders in the first generation of freedom.

SELECTED BIBLIOGRAPHY

Ira Berlin, *Slaves without Masters: The Free Negro in the Antebellum South* (1974); T. H. Breen and Stephen Innes, *"Myne Owne Ground": Race and Freedom on Virginia's Eastern Shore, 1640–1676* (1980); Letitia W. Brown, *Free Negroes in the District of Columbia, 1790–1846* (1972); Leonard P. Curry, *The Free Black in Urban America, 1800–1850: The Shadow of the Dream* (1981); John Hope Franklin, *The Free Negro in North Carolina, 1790–1860* (1943); Theodore Hershberg, "Free Blacks in Antebellum Philadelphia: A Study of Ex-Slaves, Freeborn, and Socioeconomic Decline," *Journal of Social History* 5 (1971–2), 183–209; William Ransom Hogan and Edwin Adams Davis, eds., *William Johnson's Natchez: The Ante-Bellum Diary of a Free Negro* (1951); Luther Porter Jackson, *Free Negro Labor and Property Holding in Virginia, 1830–1860* (1942); Michael P. Johnson and James L. Roark, *Black Masters: A Free Family of Color in the Old South* (1984); Michael P. Johnson and James L. Roark, eds., *No Chariot Let Down: Charleston's Free People of Color on the Eve of the Civil War* (1984); Leon F. Litwack, *North of Slavery: The Negro in the Free States, 1790–1860* (1961); Gary B. Mills, *The Forgotten People: Cane River's Creoles of Color* (1977); Loren Schweninger, ed., *From Tennessee Slave to St. Louis Entrepreneur: The Autobiography of James Thomas* (1984); Herbert E. Sterkx, *The Free Negro in Ante-Bellum Louisiana* (1972); Juliet E. K. Walker, *Free Frank: A Black Pioneer on the Antebellum Frontier* (1983); Marina Wikramanayake, *A World in Shadow: The Free Black in Antebellum South Carolina* (1973); David O. Whitten, *Andrew Durnford: A Black Sugar Planter in Antebellum Louisiana* (1981); Carter G. Woodson, *Free Negro Owners of Slaves in the United States in 1830* (1924); and Arthur Zilversmit, *The First Emancipation: The Abolition of Slavery in the North* (1967).

LOREN SCHWENINGER

FREEDMEN. The Civil War* gave America's slave population of just under four million the opportunity to emancipate themselves and become freemen. Although there were no major slave uprisings and but one-quarter of the slaves actually made it behind Union lines before the war's end, major chunks of slavery disintegrated with an irreversible momentum during the war. By seizing freedom whenever the opportunity presented itself, Afro-Americans began a process of self-emancipation which they extended into all spheres of their lives after the war. Reconstruction, to a much greater extent than whites could admit, was a response to black demands and actions.

Lincoln's Emancipation Proclamation* of 1 January 1863 converted the black quest for freedom into an official war aim of the Union. The proclamation, consistent with Lincoln's constitutional scruples that he could act only under his war powers as commander in chief, applied only to slaves within areas still controlled by the Confederacy. Nonetheless, it became fixed in the public mind as a general call for a moral crusade against slavery.

No later than 1863 the slaves sensed, as one Union officer reported, "that it was a war for their liberation; that the cause of the war was their being in slavery; and that the aim and result would be their freedom." Even before then, the presence of federal forces acted like a magnet in attracting slave families from surrounding areas. This first occurred on a large scale in the low country of rice and sea-island plantations between Charleston, South Carolina, and Savannah, Georgia. As blacks hurried into Union enclaves established after a successful amphibious assault in the fall of 1861, slavery collapsed all along the coast.

The same flight to freedom was repeated in a ripple effect wherever the Union armies* pushed into new areas. In the spring of 1862 Union forces seized New Orleans. As a result, the foundations of slavery throughout the lower Mississippi Valley cracked. Thousands of blacks streamed into Union camps set up on the outskirts of New Orleans. In the river parishes above and below the city the comforting Southern myths of black docility were blown away when the slaves saw their chance to release their accumulated anger and hostility. The slaves stopped working, drove off overseers, seized land they wanted for their own use, or fled to the Union lines. Up-river, Grant's Vicksburg campaign between the fall of 1862 and the summer of 1863 had the same effect.

The black refugees poured into contraband camps,* holding centers set aside by the Union army for these "contrabands" of war. The mortality rate in these camps, filled as they were with sick, the poor, and the uprooted, averaged 25 percent. By the spring of 1863 a consistent Union policy towards the refugees began to emerge. The goal was to employ the refugees in whatever capacity promised useful service to the Union war effort. In practice, this meant the military imposition of forced-labor controls that differed little from open exploitation. The army and navy organized labor battalions of the refugees for work as cooks, teamsters, laundresses, construction hands, and so on. Wages were paid, but at rates far below what whites were paid or what blacks could command in the open market. A greater number of the freedmen were leased out by the army to work on plantations seized by the invading Union forces. Annual contracts, drawn up in conferences between the federal commanders and local planters or, where there were none, superintendents who represented Northern freedmen's aid societies, regulated the terms of employment. After deductions were made for clothing, medical care, and any missed work, most of the blacks wound up working for little more than room and board.

The recruitment of soldiers* from among the ex-slaves was the most revolutionary use made of the fugitive population. In a major policy shift the Union began an active program of enlisting black soldiers in early 1863. This was a bold step by Lincoln, almost as bold as emancipation itself. The insecurities of the white supremacist majority in the North were immediately aroused by the thought that the Union would be somehow tainted if the blood of black soldiers were shed in its defense or in the liberation of the remaining slaves. Despite the political risks of a white backlash and the military danger of a drop in troop morale, Lincoln successfully implemented his new policy. The need for additional manpower in the Union armies was a compelling one. Eventually some 200,000 Afro-Americans served in the Union military.

Four-fifths of the black soldiers came from the slave states of 1860, and nearly half were recruited in the lower Mississippi Valley. Although the numbers involved were smaller, the impact of military recruitment was also revolutionary in the loyal slave states of the border South. As noted earlier, the Emancipation Proclamation did not touch slavery in these states. Nonetheless, the institution was but a shell of its former self by 1863. An Englishman traveling on the Eastern Shore of Maryland in the autumn of 1863 immediately saw why. "The government is revolutionizing this district by recruiting all negroes who will go, slave or free." Union steamboats picked up runaways along the Eastern Shore of the Chesapeake and transported them to the training camps in Baltimore. Taught in childhood by their parents to mask their intentions from whites, the slaves gave all signs of docile loyalty up to the moment they fled.

In the interior of the Confederacy,* where Union armies did not penetrate and slaves remained under the nominal control of their masters, slavery still underwent fundamental changes during the war. The institution lost much of its rigidity as the iron rod of physical coercion softened with so many white males drawn off into the Confederate armies. Women and their young sons stood in as replacements for the departed masters, but they were no match for the guile and determination of the slaves. The letters and diaries of those left in charge of the slaves in the countryside indicate a steady decline in the amount of work that could be extracted from the slaves and a corresponding increase in the independence claimed by the slaves. As the war progressed, slaves not conscripted for Confederate labor details were more likely to roam off plantations without passes, ignore work assignments, and test the expanding limits of the liberties they could now enjoy.

At the war's end the emancipated slaves needed no whites to give them an agenda for freedom. They immediately seized freedom as the opportunity to build an autonomous black community anchored in the values and institutions that had sustained them under slavery. The core institution was the family.* As the fugitives had shown so strikingly during the war, when they organized their escapes along family lines, the first objective under freedom was the achievement of domestic security. Despite the prime importance of family ties under slavery, thousands of black families had to reconstitute themselves in 1865. Many had already been broken up before the war. Throughout the South one-fifth to one-third of slave marriages ended with the sale or forced removal of one of the partners. The war years then brought on massive family disruptions as masters relocated their slaves to keep them away from the Yankees, and as Union and Confederate officials competed for able-bodied black labor. All during 1865 countless blacks left the plantations in a search for family members.

By physically moving around in an effort to reunite their family units, the freedmen were also attempting to remove themselves psychologically from that direct white supervision that had been so integral to the slavery experience. They demonstrated this desire for their own cultural space by laying claim to full control over the key community institution of slave society, the black church.*

Driven by racial pride and their own sense of community, the freedmen pushed for separate black churches once deliverance came. The religion that had sustained them as slaves was now drawn on to inform the blacks' self-definition as a freed people. Blacks used the disciplinary structure of their churches as a community-controlled judiciary system which operated like a small-claims court in moral and economic matters. Here, free from white interference and prejudice, the freedmen set down and enforced the behavior they expected of each other. Here, organizational skills were learned, family disputes were settled, social gatherings were planned, labor meetings were held, and lessons in literacy were offered for children and adults. In the rural South the freedmen made their churches synonymous with their communities.

Another key institution for the freedmen was the school. The basic black demand of education for their children was registered by the actions of the freedmen during the war. They quickly grasped the importance of their labor to the Union war effort, as well as the urgency with which federal officials wanted to establish that free black labor could be as profitable and disciplined as slave labor. Using the only weapon at their disposal—their labor—the freedmen often refused to work until they were assured that their children would receive an education. The Union army responded by establishing an organized system of black elementary education, notably in southern Louisiana in 1864.

Because, as one black Mississippian put it in 1869, ''I considers education the next best ting to liberty,'' the freedmen were eager for education after the war. They equated ignorance with a continuation of their bondage, and they prized education as being essential for self-advancement. White Protestant denominations in the North, such black denominations as the African Methodist Episcopal church,* and the Freedmen's Bureau,* a federal relief agency, combined their resources to launch a mixed system of private and public schooling. Then, despite the bitter opposition of whites, the reconstructed state governments in the postwar South provided the tax dollars for a public system of schools open to both races. These governments were overturned in the mid–1870s, but in their most enduring accomplishment, they were instrumental in reducing black illiteracy from 80 percent in 1870 to 45 percent by 1900.

The freedmen, by knitting together family ties separated by slavery and the war, sending their children to schools, and regulating their own affairs with their own institutions, largely reconstructed their own lives in the aftermath of emancipation. As eager as the freedmen were for domestic security and cultural independence, they also realized that the full measure of freedom could come only with economic independence. Possession of land offered the surest path to such independence, both for the freedman and his family.

When the Confederacy surrendered, the freedmen immediately pressed their moral claims to a share of the land they had always worked against the legal claims of their former masters. In the moral economy of the freedmen, the land was already theirs by virtue of their uncompensated labor under slavery. "We has a right to the land where we are located," proclaimed one Virginia freedman in 1866. Other blacks agreed, but their claims were denied. Expectations that were high in the spring and summer of 1865 were soon dashed when President Andrew Johnson ordered that confiscated and abandoned lands being administered by the Freedmen's Bureau would not be distributed to the freedmen, but instead were to be returned to the pardoned ex-Confederate owners. Then, in the winter of 1865–1866, Congress decisively rejected a bill sponsored by Thaddeus Stevens of Pennsylvania which would have confiscated the large estates of rebels and distributed the land in forty-acre plots to the freedmen and their families.

Barred from claiming the land, often at the point of federal bayonets, the freedmen nonetheless forced basic changes in plantation agriculture. The planters immediately attempted to structure working conditions under freedom as closely as possible to the labor regime under slavery. The Southern black codes of 1865, state legislative enactments necessitated by the need to define the legal rights of the now emancipated blacks, catered to the wishes of the planters. Sweeping vagrancy, apprenticeship, and contractual provisions in the codes left the blacks with virtually no economic freedom save that of agreeing to work as a landless peasantry under labor terms set by their former owners. The planters wanted the centralized control of the prewar years. The freedmen were organized into labor gangs, directly supervised by an overseer or resident planter, provided rations from the employer, and housed in the old slave quarters. The only difference now was the contractual obligation to pay fixed wages for the blacks' labor. This wage system of 1865 and 1866 soon broke down. The Freedmen's Bureau suspended the most discriminatory sections of the black codes, but above all, it was the determination of the freedmen to achieve greater control over their own lives that frustrated the intentions of the planters.

The freedmen rejected the personal dependency and coercive controls of the old system that had reemerged in the guise of wage labor. They hated being treated like slaves all over again. Declaring that the entire family would no longer work like slaves, they pulled their women and children from the fields. They flooded the local agents of the Freedmen's Bureau with complaints of being cheated by employers who dismissed them without their annual wages once the harvest was in. Capitalizing on the mobility that came with emancipation, they moved in search of better working conditions. Many sought out jobs in the towns and cities, but most of the moves were local rural ones. They forced the planters to bid for their services by creating temporary shortages of labor which they then exploited for a better contract. By 1870 the typical contract was not for cash wages but for a share of the crop. Under this arrangement the planters divided their estates into small family plots which were worked by the cropper.

Depending upon the amount of food and farm supplies provided by the planter, the cropper turned over one-third to one-half of the crop as rent.

Sharecropping became an economic trap that ensnared the freedmen in a form of semipeonage. But when first instituted, sharecropping offered blacks real advantages over what the planters had originally tried to fix upon them. Unable to acquire land of their own, blacks still sought the economic independence and social autonomy which they associated with the ownership of land. In their quest blacks did transform the plantation. Sharecropping eliminated overseers, gang labor, and the daily supervision of whites. The freedmen now had more control over their time, working conditions, and family life. They had more freedom to choose between work and leisure, and in common with other emancipated labor forces and the white yeomanry of the antebellum South, they opted, wherever possible, for self-sufficiency, a reduced work load for the family, and more leisure time for hunting and fishing.

Sharecropping was in place by the end of the 1860s because blacks wanted it. The planters gave in to black demands. Most of them were strapped for capital after the war, and the failure of the plantation economy to revive quickly left them scrambling for credit. Despite their concerns that sharecropping left the freedmen with too much independence, planters recognized the advantages for them in an economic arrangement which conserved their scarce capital by not requiring that it be spent on wages.

By the time that congressional Reconstruction got underway in 1867, blacks had already made significant gains since emancipation. The earnest enthusiasm with which the freedmen registered to vote and the speed with which a new political class of blacks arose were the best evidence that the freedmen realized that these gains could ultimately be protected and extended only through political mobilization. If land could not be acquired, then the legal protection of their right to a share in the crops they produced became an even more vital political objective. Agricultural credit in the postwar South took the form of advances secured by a lien upon the crops. In order to ensure that the sale of the crop would cover their advances, plus interest, planters and merchants vied with one another to establish a superior legal claim on the crops. The freedmen insisted that their claims for wages or shares should take precedence. This struggle to gain economic justice by establishing their rights under the crop-lien system shaped much of the freedmen's political experience. Other major goals included public support for schools and the recognition by Southern courts of black equality under the law.

Although the freedmen supplied 80 percent of the vote for the Southern Republican parties,* they held only 15 to 20 percent of the political offices. At the upper echelon of leadership, federal offices, black politicians were well-educated men drawn primarily from a Northern-born professional class of ministers, lawyers, and teachers. State and local offices were filled predominantly by ex-slave ministers and artisans,* those who had held positions of leadership and trust in the slave community. We still know little of the blacks who did the grass-roots organizing, those who mobilized the plantation workers, spoke at meetings of the local Republican clubs, the Union Leagues, got out the vote, and led protests against white economic pressure. Here, the leadership probably came straight from the ranks of the field hands.

The freedmen supplied the votes, but white politicians held the power. With the exception of South Carolina, and less so in Mississippi, blacks did not come close to filling offices in proportion to their numbers in the population. This imbalance between black voting power and officeholding meant that the attainment of black political goals was dependent on the Northern and Southern whites who monopolized the key leadership posts within the new Republican parties. Once the unstable alliance between the Northern whites, stigmatized by the pejorative label of carpetbaggers, and the Southern whites, scornfully referred to as scalawags, broke down by the mid–1870s, a major casualty was not just these black goals, but the very reality of meaningful black political participation in Southern civic life.

Political Reconstruction was over by 1877. Nonetheless, black accomplishments in the first generation of freedom were nothing short of remarkable. For every 100 blacks in 1860 only 2 were enrolled in school; by 1880 that number had risen to 34. Black illiteracy, over 90 percent in 1865, had fallen to under 30 percent by 1910. Although cropping and tenancy were the norm in 1900, one-quarter of black farmers were still successful enough to own the land they worked. Above all, despite the unrelenting and often violent opposition of Southern whites, the blacks persevered in their ongoing effort to make themselves free.

SELECTED BIBLIOGRAPHY

Ira Berlin et al., eds., *Freedom: A Documentary History of Emancipation, 1861–1867* (2 vols. to date, 1982-); W.E.B. Du Bois, *Black Reconstruction . . . 1860–1880* (1935); Louis S. Gerteis, *From Contraband to Freedman: Federal Policy toward Southern Blacks, 1861–1865* (1973); Peter Kolchin, *First Freedom: The Responses of Alabama's Blacks to Emancipation and Reconstruction* (1972); Leon F. Litwack, *Been in the Storm So Long: The Aftermath of Slavery* (1979); and Willie Lee Rose, *Rehearsal for Reconstruction: The Port Royal Experiment* (1964).

WILLIAM L. BARNEY

FREEDMEN'S BUREAU. Slave self-emancipation, radical abolitionist agitation, ostensible military needs, and burgeoning industrialism hastened the passage of such Reconstruction legislation as the Freedmen's Bureau bill in 1865. The Bureau became the first large-scale U.S. government venture into social welfare and intervention in economic and social change. The Bureau was intended to be an umbrella under which slaves could pass unhindered to freedom, citizenship, and self-determination. Although created only for a one-year term, the Bureau's tenure was extended to four years by acts of Congress.

The first one, passed on 3 March 1865 and signed that day by President Abraham Lincoln, established the Bureau of Refugees, Freedmen and Abandoned Lands in the War Department. The president was authorized to appoint a commissioner headquartered in Washington and nine assistant commissioners (ten were named) in the seceded states. No special funds were appropriated for the Bureau.

General Oliver Otis Howard became commissioner in May 1865. He and the assistant commissioners were responsible for distributing rations, clothing, and fuel to destitute freedmen and to "refugees," a euphemism for uprooted whites in the seceded states; supervising and managing 800,000 acres of abandoned and confiscated land of former Confederates; and generally controlling all matters relative to freedmen* and refugees. The law provided for assignment to every male freedman or refugee of up to forty acres of land, which they could rent for three years at the 1860 appraised value. However, President Andrew Johnson's restoration of land to former owners in mid–1865 left scarcely any for distribution. The Bureau did succeed in relieving hunger, exposure to cold, and illness, but failed to provide an equitable economic base for the freed people. The Bureau's one-year term became palpably inadequate for the tremendous task it faced. The black codes, the president's amnesty and restoration of ex-Confederates, and the reign of terror against freedmen, e.g., the Memphis and New Orleans riots in 1866, called for a more durable and more rigorous agency.

The act of 16 July 1866 over President Johnson's veto gave the Bureau national jurisdiction over freedmen's affairs up to 1868. Two more assistant commissioners were authorized (for Kentucky and Maryland). Congress appropriated $6.9 million, more than half of it for rations and clothing and half a million for renting and repairing schools and asylums. The act provided for freedmen's courts to take up race discrimination cases and to adjudicate labor contract disputes between freedmen and planters. Eventually, 900 agents, largely ex-army personnel, served in the South "ruling, directly and indirectly, many millions of men." The Bureau's active role ended in 1869 after a congressional act in 1868 granted it a final one-year term. Total Bureau expenditures were estimated at almost $18 million in four years.

W.E.B. Du Bois called Reconstruction a "splendid failure," and the Bureau reflected the basic mix of failure and success. Most freedmen were denied economic opportunities. Their civil rights were made hollow by their frustrations. But public school systems and black colleges such as Howard, Fisk, and Atlanta owed their establishment to the Bureau's efforts, freedmen's initiatives, and freedmen's aid societies. A permanent Bureau staffed by civilians, in Du Bois's view, could have avoided the decades of segregation, economic bondage, and second-class citizenship that became the black people's legacy of "benign neglect" policies.

SELECTED BIBLIOGRAPHY

George R. Bentley, *A History of the Freedmen's Bureau* (1955); W.E.B. Du Bois, *Black Reconstruction . . . 1860–1880* (1935); W.E.B. Du Bois, "Of the Dawn of Freedom," in Du Bois, *The Souls of Black Folk: Essays and Sketches* (rev. ed., 1953); James M. McPherson, *The Struggle for Equality: Abolitionists and the Negro in the Civil War and Reconstruction* (1965); Edward Magdol, *A Right to the Land: Essays on the Freedmen's Community* (1977); and Claude F. Oubre, *Forty Acres and a Mule: The Freedmen's Bureau and Black Land Ownership* (1978).

EDWARD MAGDOL

FUGITIVE SLAVE ACT OF 1793. The Fugitive Slave Act of 1793 was the popular name for a U.S. statute that established procedures for the extradition of fugitives from justice and from labor (hence including criminals, apprentices, and indentured servants as well as slaves) who had fled into another state or territory. The fugitive-slave provisions empowered the owner or his agent to seize the fugitive and take him or her before a federal judge or local magistrate. Proof that the accused was a fugitive could be by oral testimony or by an affidavit of a magistrate in the state of origin. The penalty for concealing a fugitive or obstructing his arrest was $500.

Article IV, Section 2 of the U.S. Constitution* obligated states to return both criminal fugitives and fugitives from labor, but the Constitution did not specifically require a federal statute and at first some believed state laws would suffice. In 1791, however, Pennsylvania's governor twice asked Virginia to turn over criminal fugitives; one request, made at the behest of the Pennsylvania Society for Promoting the Abolition of Slavery, was for the kidnappers of a free black who had been taken to Virginia. Virginia declined, citing among other reasons the lack of a positive federal law. Pennsylvania sent the correspondence to President Washington, who laid it before Congress. In drafting the law, Congress did not address the criminal-fugitive issue in isolation but linked the two categories of fugitives just as the Constitutional Convention had done.

After its passage, sporadic attempts were made to amend the law. Abolitionists* tried to protect free blacks, while Southerners attempted to strengthen its provisions. In the 1820s and 1830s, Northern states, notably Pennsylvania, enacted legislation impeding its operation. Then, in 1842, a U.S. Supreme Court decision, *Prigg v. Pennsylvania*, sharply limited its effectiveness by declaring that federal authorities alone must carry out the law, since the national government could not compel states and states' magistrates to act. Thereafter, Northern states passed "personal liberty" laws,* forbidding officers to aid a claimant in a fugitive-slave case. Infuriated Southerners pressed for congressional action, and a stronger law was passed as a part of the Compromise of 1850.*

SELECTED BIBLIOGRAPHY

William R. Leslie, "A Study in the Origins of Interstate Rendition: The Big Beaver Creek Murders," *American Historical Review*, 59 (1951–1952), 63–76; Marion Gleason

McDougall, *Fugitive Slaves, 1619–1865* (1891); and U.S. *Statutes at Large*, 1: 302–305 (12 February 1793).

                                                                                  JOAN WELLS COWARD

FUGITIVE SLAVE ACT OF 1850. The Fugitive Slave Act of 1850, enacted as part of the Compromise of 1850,* was designed to make it easier for Southern slave owners to recapture slaves who had escaped to the North. Enforcement of the Fugitive Slave Act of 1793,* which the 1850 act replaced, had become increasingly difficult, as abolitionist sentiment* rose in the North, as Northern states enacted personal liberty laws protecting the interests of blacks claimed by Southerners to be fugitive slaves,* and, after 1842, as those states prohibited their own officials from assisting in the capture of fugitive slaves. By creating a new position of "commissioner," the act increased the number of federal officials who were authorized to issue warrants for the arrest of fugitives and certificates entitling the captor to remove the slave to the South. The commissioners received $10 each time they authorized the removal of a fugitive, and only $5 when they found that the person seized was not a fugitive slave. The act prohibited physical obstruction of recapture and legal interference with the rendition process. Northern opposition to the act centered on its creation of a body of federal officials to enforce the property rights of Southern slave owners, the inherent bias in the compensation of the commissioners, and the threat that easier recapture procedures posed to free blacks living in border states.

Although enforcement of the 1850 act probably made it slightly easier for slave owners to recapture fugitive slaves, the act did not appreciably reduce the rate of successful escapes from slavery. In *Ableman v. Booth* (1859), the Supreme Court held that state courts had no power to direct federal officials to release from their custody a person convicted of aiding a fugitive slave to escape. Dictum in the opinion stated that the 1850 act was constitutional. In the eyes of opponents of slavery, the Court's decision confirmed the commitment to slavery that the Dred Scott* decision had shown. It thus exacerbated those already deep divisions in the nation over the constitutional status of slavery.

SELECTED BIBLIOGRAPHY

Stanley W. Campbell, *The Slave Catchers: Enforcement of the Fugitive Slave Law, 1850–1860* (1968); and David M. Potter, *The Impending Crisis, 1848–1861* (1976).

                                                                                  MARK V. TUSHNET

FUGITIVE SLAVES. Fugitive slaves were slaves who ran away to escape from bondage altogether. They are not to be confused with the many short-term runaways* who plagued every slaveholder.

Temporary runaways usually had good reason to leave their homes. They fled to avoid punishment, sometimes to return to a former, less cruel owner; to avoid heavy work assignments; to join their spouses or other family members; or simply to take a break from their monotonous routine. Slaves who acquired reputations as habitual runaways lowered their value on the market. At times, such short-term escapes constituted a control mechanism similar to work stoppages in the free labor market place.

Fugitive slaves, in contrast, posed a much more serious threat to the slave system. Their destination was usually the Northern states or Canada, though some fled to Mexico and others joined colonies of former slaves hiding out in the Southern swamps or mountains. Others found refuge among the Seminoles and other Indian peoples. Their objective was freedom from bondage. At the time that apologists for slavery were arguing that slaves had no desire for freedom, and that blacks were especially adapted to slavery, evidence to the contrary accumulated. Those few travelers in the Southern states who had an opportunity to speak with slaves and gain their confidence found them to be obsessed with the idea of someday living in freedom. The narratives* or autobiographies* written by former slaves underscore the same point. Slaves understood the meaning of freedom. They observed the way whites and some blacks lived outside slavery, and could not understand why they were forced to live in servitude. The slaves' religious observances, secular songs, spirituals, and much of their oral folk literature, all were obsessed with achieving freedom—if not in this life, then in the next. Yet relatively few slaves—perhaps a few thousand a year—decided to make the break from bondage.

Masters fantasized that their slaves were happy and therefore had little cause to run away. But the answer for the paucity of runaways lies elsewhere. A major deterrent was the odds against success. Masters were determined that those who escaped must be caught and punished, even though an escaped slave was a constant source of trouble and discontent in the slave labor force. White Southerners assumed that slave discontent resulted from abolition agitation from the North. Masters looked upon slave escapes as personal insults, and runaway bondsmen as ingrates. When captured, fugitive slaves were most often sold to the Deep South or Southwest, sometimes under false pretenses. When slaves escaped for any lengthy period of time, their owners advertised in newspapers, hired slave catchers to bring them back, and, occasionally, took the time and trouble to pursue them personally. One master, Edward Gorsuch, was killed at Christiana, Pennsylvania, in 1851 when he tried to remove several fugitives from a building where they were hiding. Gorsuch's presence resulted in a large gathering of supporters of the fugitives. Someone fired several shots, killing Gorsuch and wounding his son. The incident, known as the Christiana Riot,* led to a number of treason trials in which all the defendants were acquitted. The fugitive slaves ultimately reached Canada.

In addition to information useful to those pursuing fugitives, newspaper advertisements of slave runaways revealed much about slavery itself. Advertisements exposed the double personalities that some slaves assumed, such as pretending to be unusually stupid while at the same time devising schemes to gain more privileges or to escape. Advertisements also provided data for those who rejected the concept of the peculiar institution as a benevolent system.

Planters occasionally asked that a slave be captured dead or alive. The fugitives described had missing teeth, wounds from being shot, brandings, scars from whippings, cropped ears, iron collars and leg chains, and other evidence of cruel treatment. These, along with other material from Southern newspapers, were included in Theodore Dwight Weld's* book, *Slavery As It Is* (1839), an indictment of the institution by those who knew it firsthand.

Some planters owned "nigger hounds" to track down runaway slaves. These vicious animals were trained to locate and then maul their prey. Runaways often carried pepper or other substances to throw bloodhounds off the scent. Most masters, however, commissioned a professional slave catcher (some of whom were not above kidnapping free blacks) to reclaim their bondsmen. Slave catchers also employed trained dogs.

Another deterrent to slave escapes was the slaves' lack of information about distance, geography, the weather, and conditions in the Northern states. Masters deliberately spread stories about bitter cold winters, the great distances from the South to Canada, and the alleged brutality of abolitionists. Accurate knowledge of geography was especially hard to come by. Masters also threatened slaves and promised severe punishment to any bondsman who contemplated escape. Captured fugitives were lashed without mercy, brutalized by overseers who specialized in breaking the spirit of rebellious blacks, or sold to distant points far away from friends and relatives. Every slave who succeeded in reaching freedom undermined the security of the whole system and provided an example which even the most benevolent owner could not tolerate.

Given the odds against their success, it is no wonder that the majority of fugitives were young men from the border states. What is amazing is that some couples and even groups as large as fifty managed to escape. These determined and courageous bondsmen came from every possible station within slavery. Very often it was the most privileged slaves who escaped. Their "privileged" conditions produced higher expectations in them, including the possibility of freedom. And there were successful escapes from the Deep South. One slave walked from Louisiana to New England. Another fugitive took a year to travel from Alabama to Ohio.

Canada offered the safest northern haven, but for those who headed south, Mexico, too, promised a land without slavery. Those escapees who chose to settle in the nominally free Northern states encountered a multitude of discriminatory practices and laws. They also faced the very real possibility of being returned to slavery either by being kidnapped or by the legal procedure under the Fugitive Slave Act of 1793* or by the even more severe Fugitive Slave Act of 1850.*

Fugitive slaves tended to be self-reliant individuals who planned and carried out their own escapes. Sometimes several attempts were required before they achieved their objective. A St. Louis slave, William Wells Brown,* for example, thought long and hard about various escape methods and made one abortive flight before his successful bid for freedom in 1834. He seized the opportunity to run when the steamer on which he worked reached an Ohio port. Like many bondsmen, Brown preferred to rely on his own resources rather than on the help of others. He later wrote, "Supposing every person to be my enemy, I was afraid to appeal to anyone, even for a little food, to keep body and soul together." Brown existed on corn taken from cribs and turnips and other vegetables growing in roadside fields. He slept in barns along the way. Eventually, even Brown found it necessary to ask for directions, and he was fortunate to meet a sympathetic Quaker who provided clothes, shoes, and two weeks lodging. Brown's journey finally brought him his hard-earned freedom. He went on to become an important lecturer in the antislavery movement and in 1853 published a novel, *Clotel*, about the slave daughter of an American president. He also wrote his autobiography, several books on European travel, and an early history of the black people.

Other slaves also took off on their own, resting by day and traveling by the North Star at night. To avoid being recognized from advertised descriptions, fugitive slaves frequently resorted to disguises. One of the most ingenious escape plans was that of Ellen and William Craft,* who escaped from Georgia in 1848. William, a skilled slave cabinet maker, saved up money for their escape from extra work. Ellen, the daughter of her master, was nearly white. In the Crafts' escape she played the part of a deaf and ailing master. Her disguise included wearing dark glasses and a muffler on her face and carrying her arm in a sling. William acted as her faithful servant. They traveled north by train and steamboat. Except for one incident in Baltimore, the Crafts had no trouble with their plans. They settled first in Boston, but were forced to flee to Nova Scotia when two agents of their Georgia masters appeared in Boston. The Crafts ultimately moved to England, where they recorded their daring escape in a pamphlet, *Running a Thousand Miles for Freedom* (1860).

Steamboats running from Southern ports often carried fugitives who either passed as white passengers, stowed away, or became clandestine passengers. Many paid the steamboat captains with money they had earned or stolen. Other fugitives carried borrowed passes, free papers given them or forged for them by a free black, or an American sailor's protection papers. Group escapes by ship were very risky, as Captain Edward Sayres of the *Pearl* discovered in 1848 when he agreed to transport seventy-seven slaves from Washington, D.C., for a hundred dollars a slave. When the small craft was apprehended, both Daniel Drayton, who had planned the escape, and Captain Sayres spent nearly four and a half years in prison before they were pardoned by President Millard Fillmore. Jonathan Walker, another sea captain, was apprehended while attempting to transport slaves in 1844 off the Florida coast. Walker was imprisoned and branded on his hand with the letters "S.S." for "slave stealer."

The escape plan devised by Henry Brown necessarily involved the cooperation of another person. Brown, who worked in a Richmond, Virginia, tobacco factory, long had pondered escaping from slavery. One day in 1849, as he prayed, Brown heard a voice say, "Go get a box, and put yourself in it." He had a carpenter construct the largest shipping crate that could be transported and had himself shipped to Philadelphia. After a twenty-six-hour trip Brown arrived safely at the office of the Philadelphia Anti-Slavery Society whose officers had been warned of his imminent arrival. As Henry ''Box'' Brown, the fugitive gained immediate fame, reaching many audiences with the story of his life and escape. A number of other slaves also escaped in boxes, though Brown's accomplice, who shipped him from Richmond, later was arrested and convicted when he tried to repeat the ruse.

Henry Bibb's* escape from slavery involved a variety of tactics. Bibb first contemplated escape in the 1830s and made six unsuccessful attempts. In 1842, following one of his failed bids for freedom, he was sold to speculators who agreed to give him part of the sale money and directions for getting to Canada if he would cooperate in getting himself sold for a high price. When Bibb completed his part of the bargain, the original owners gave him some of the purchase money and directions as promised. Traveling on a stolen horse, and posing as a free black, Bibb used his own purchase money to stay at first-class hotels along the way. Commenting on his escape, Bibb explained: ''No man ever asked me whether I was bond or free . . . but I always presented a bold front and showed the best side out, which was all the pass I had.'' Bibb finally arrived at Detroit without difficulty. After 1850 Bibb lived in Canada, publishing an antislavery, emigrationist newspaper, the *Voice of the Fugitive*.

Although the fleeing slaves generally had to rely on their own resources, assistance sometimes was available in the Southern states. Mostly, fugitives could depend on other slaves or free blacks for food, supplies, and shelter while they were making their way north. Some whites, including a few planters, took pity on the escapees and assisted the runaways in their quest for freedom. These whites believed that in order for a slave to run away the bondsman must have been abused by his owner. Other whites provided aid for a fee. The more fortunate of the fugitives who reached the free states received help from antislavery activists or the various vigilance committees of the legendary underground railroad.* While some fugitives settled in the North, more went on to Canada where they were joined by others who were threatened by the Fugitive Slave Act of 1850. Several Northern states passed laws discouraging the settling of blacks within their borders, forbidding blacks to vote or hold office, and providing for seg-regated schools and other kinds of public facilities. In Canada the refugees encountered no legal discrimination, but where they settled in large numbers the blacks suffered from discrimination and harassment by private citizens.

While virtually all of the slaves who made their way to freedom sympathized with the abolition movement, only a few became active participants. Some were simply exhibited at antislavery gatherings. Others became speakers. Frederick Douglass* began his renowned speaking career in 1841 by addressing an abo-litionist* gathering with his satirical version of a slaveholder's sermon based on the text ''Servants, obey in all things your master.'' William Wells Brown read antislavery dramas to numerous Northern audiences; Bibb gave dramatic readings of his personal narrative for several nights in a city, always leaving his audience guessing as to how he would escape from the latest difficulty. Anthony Burns,* Josiah Henson,* Lewis and Milton Clarke, Samuel Ringgold Ward, and Henry "Box" Brown also provided valuable services to the antislavery cause. While these fugitives from slavery often differed with their white co-workers in the antislavery cause over tactics, they nevertheless added an important element, authenticity. The escaped slaves also insisted on civil rights for blacks in the North. Whites frequently came to hear a fugitive slave out of curiosity and often went away convinced that slavery was indeed far worse than they had imagined. The eyewitness accounts of these former slaves had more impact in the antislavery cause than hundreds of theoretical speeches and pamphlets.

While it was impressive to hear a former slave's personal account, the next best thing was to read about it. Abolitionists published slave narratives both in newspapers and in inexpensive pamphlet form. These ex-slave narratives found a receptive audience and circulated in large numbers. By 1849 William Wells Brown's narrative had sold 8,000 copies, and two years after its publication in 1853 Solomon Northup's* narrative had sold 27,000 copies. Douglass's 1845 *Narrative of the Life of Frederick Douglass*, published in several editions, has become a classic of American literature. Because most slaves were kept illiterate by their masters, the narratives were usually recorded by a white abolitionist. Some of the best-known slave autobiographies, however, were generally written wholly by their authors, including those of Douglass, William Wells Brown, Bibb, and Ward.

Former slaves made many significant contributions to American life. As speakers and writers they revealed the horror of slavery. Their personal accounts underscored slavery's brutalities for thousands who otherwise would have been ignorant of the peculiar institution. Their speaking and writing ability and their bearing gave the lie to the concept of black inferiority. Their demand for full civil rights answered those who proposed colonizing blacks outside the United States. And their insistence on being independent in their views, even when these opinions clashed with those of their white co-workers, further testified to blacks' demand for full equality in a land that boasted of its freedom. In short, the fugitive slaves were a remarkable lot, one that earned an important niche in American history.

SELECTED BIBLIOGRAPHY

John W. Blassingame, *The Slave Community: Plantation Life in the Antebellum South* (rev. ed., 1979); Stanley W. Campbell, *The Slave Catchers: Enforcement of the Fugitive Slave Law, 1850–1860* (1968); Larry Gara, *The Liberty Line: The Legend of the Underground Railroad* (1961); Eugene D. Genovese, *Roll, Jordan, Roll: The World the Slaves Made* (1974); and Kenneth M. Stampp, *The Peculiar Institution: Slavery in the Ante-Bellum South* (1956).

LARRY GARA

G

GANG SYSTEM. The gang system of slave labor was one of the two favorite means of production on plantations of the Old South that were large enough to justify such a formal organization. The gang system and its alternative, the task system,* often occurred side by side on the same plantation. In the gang system the slaves were divided into groups (or, as the name suggests, gangs) of varying sizes, each with a daily assignment of work, and each under the supervision of a slave who was designated as the "driver."* His function was to set the pace of work, and, through a combination of example, cajolery, rewards, and punishments, including, if necessary, laying on the whip, to see that the job was accomplished. The entire operation was conducted under the control of an overseer,* usually a hired white man, or on smaller places under the direct management of the owner.

The gang and task systems originated early in the history of African slavery in the West Indies and spread to the American mainland where both forms survived as long as slavery itself lasted. Preference between the two systems depended largely on the kind of work involved. The gang system prevailed for the primary production on most cotton* plantations throughout the South, on the tobacco* plantations of the upper South, and on the sugar* plantations of the Gulf coastal area.

The nature and amount of work assigned the gangs varied with the nature of the gangs themselves, whether made up of "full hands," "three-quarter hands," "half hands," or "quarter hands." These classifications were determined according to the strength, age, or sex of the slave laborer. For example, plowing, cutting wood, or digging drainage canals were usually done by adult men (full hands). Other work—hoeing and picking cotton—was performed by women and teenage children (ranging from three-quarter to quarter hands), as well as by men.

Masters who preferred the gang system argued that it created superior organization by delegating responsibility and authority to the drivers. They in turn received special privileges as incentives to exact the optimum amount of effort from the laborers. Frederick Law Olmsted* viewed the gang system as the more burdensome of the two, but at least in some instances, it afforded relief to the weaker slaves by allowing the stronger ones to shoulder a heavier part of the load. The gang system also enabled compassionate drivers to shield their subordinates from overwork. On the other hand, though, it encouraged callous drivers to play the tyrant.

While the preference of the slaves themselves between the two systems is perhaps impossible to determine, after emancipation most freedmen clearly favored working as tenants on individual plots of land to working in gangs as wage laborers. Yet in parts of the South, especially the Louisiana sugar country, a form of the gang system endured in plantation agriculture until the twentieth century, when the advent of modern machinery made it inapplicable.

SELECTED BIBLIOGRAPHY

Walter L. Fleming, "The Slave-Labor System in the Ante-Bellum South," in Julian A. C. Chandler et al., eds., *The South in the Building of the Nation* (12 vols., 1909), 5:104–120; Lewis C. Gray, *History of Agriculture in the Southern United States to 1860* (2 vols., 1933); Ulrich B. Phillips, *American Negro Slavery: A Survey of the Supply, Employment and Control of Negro Labor as Determined by the Plantation Regime* (1918); and Ulrich B. Phillips, "The Origin and Growth of the Southern Black Belts," *American Historical Review*, 6 (1906), 798–816.

CHARLES P. ROLAND

GARDENS. Slaves who tended gardens lived in the Big House as well as in the quarters. Usually, slaves were part-time gardeners or were appointed by the planters. They grew vegetables and raised crops because they were directed to do so, either out of necessity for their own subsistence or to earn money.

Numerous gardens of many varieties appeared in the Southern region. Flowers grew in profusion everywhere in the South, sometimes known as the "land of flowers." Flower gardens were common on plantations, and, in several instances, stood in front of slave cabins or brightened the slave quarters. In the more settled areas of the Old South, the grounds around the main plantation house were often adorned with shrubbery and flower beds. On the frontier some planters and farmers maintained small flower gardens, when cotton prices did not drive them to tear up the flower beds and plant them in cotton.

Much of the growth, production, and arrangement of flowers on the Southern plantations depended on the horticultural skills of slaves. A part of the slaves' work, too, included trimming the hedges and shrubbery. Slaves also planted, and sometimes arranged, orchards, herb gardens, and trees.

Most, if not all, plantations maintained vegetable gardens for general use. The master or overseer assigned small patches of land on which to grow cereals (wheat, rye, and oats) and legumes. Peas were planted between the rows of corn. Cabbage and yams (large sweet potatoes, coarser than the kind generally used by the slaveholder and not so delicate in flavor) were also raised for the servants in liberal quantities. The garden vegetables and cereals supplemented the corn crop,* which remained the staple for virtually everybody in the South.

Throughout the South, by the nineteenth century, most slaveholders allowed slaves to maintain their own gardens. Each slave might cultivate his own plot independently, the husband often leading his wife and children in the undertaking, or slaves on a particular plantation might work a larger plot collectively and divide the harvest among themselves. The slaves tended their gardens at night and in their free time on Saturdays and Sundays, raising vegetables and tobacco or cotton for home consumption or for sale to obtain cash for clothes, adornments, entertainment, or even freedom. Sometimes the slaveholder purchased the slaves' garden produce—thereby controlling the market, minimizing theft, and limiting the slaves' access to the local market economy. In many cases, however, slaveholders let their slaves sell their garden produce to local farmers or carry it to town for sale. Slave marketing of garden surpluses in the South never approached the level and sophistication of such activity among slaves in the Caribbean, but it did introduce Southern slaves to the petit bourgeois economy. The production and sale of garden crops thus prepared slaves to function in freedom.

In developing areas of the South, it was not uncommon for slaveholders to encourage their slaves to locate their gardens in woods or on barrens. The slaves thereby cleared the land for later staple crop cultivation. After the harvest, the slaveholders pushed the slaves off the garden clearings and sent them to uncleared land to continue the process.

Slave gardens allowed bondsmen to increase their minimum diet,* to provide somewhat for themselves, and to enter the market economy. In their gardens the slaves thus learned to work for themselves, even as they outwardly served their masters' interest.

SELECTED BIBLIOGRAPHY

John W. Blassingame, *The Slave Community: Plantation Life in the Antebellum South* (rev. ed., 1979); John B. Boles, *Black Southerners, 1619–1869* (1983); Eugene D. Genovese, *Roll, Jordan, Roll: The World the Slaves Made* (1974); and Kenneth M. Stampp, *The Peculiar Institution: Slavery in the Ante-Bellum South* (1956).

GOSSIE HAROLD HUDSON

GARRISON, WILLIAM LLOYD (1805–1879). William Lloyd Garrison was born in Newburyport, Massachusetts, to poverty and a pious mother. Reared in New England conservatism, amid revivalist benevolence, Garrison found work as a newspaperman, first with local papers and, in the 1820s, with Nathaniel White's reform-minded *National Philanthropist*, then, in 1829, in Baltimore with Benjamin Lundy's* antislavery *Genius of Universal Emancipation*. Returning to New England in 1830, Garrison pledged himself to abolitionism.* In September 1834, Garrison married Helen Eliza Benson of Brooklyn, Connecticut, daughter of abolitionist George Benson. The couple had seven children.

The Garrisons lived frugally and moved often; the expense of Garrison's reform activities and a large family often tested the generosity of Boston abolitionists.

Throughout his life Garrison remained an uncompromising foe of slavery. Through his own weekly journal, *The Liberator*, which he launched in 1831, Garrison battled the sin of slavery and advocated moral uplift and social change. Garrison founded the New England Antislavery Society in 1831, and served as a paid agent of the society. A year later he published *Thoughts on African Colonization*, attacking those who would colonize slaves abroad rather than liberate them and guarantee their rights as free men and women—a position that Garrison himself had abondoned only a few years earlier. In 1833, at a gathering of abolitionists in Philadelphia, Garrison formed the American Anti-Slavery Society (AAS), and wrote its *Declaration of Sentiments*. The AAS became the institutional base for his "immediate" abolitionism. Garrison and his followers called on Americans to immediately cease their support of slavery and all who held slaves. They demanded that churches, political parties, and even the federal government sever all ties with the South's sinful, immoral, un-Christian labor system.

Throughout the antebellum period, Garrison was the single most visible antislavery radical. Positive that he could change society solely by using moral suasion to convince others to "come-out" from evil and reject slavery as sinful, Garrison and his followers reminded the American people that slavery contradicted the nation's religious and republican values. The Garrisonians' agitation and condemnations helped fracture religious denominations and destabilize national political coalitions. Garrison labeled churchmen who were apathetic or apologists for slavery the custodians of "cages of unclean birds, Augean stables of pollution." A "nonresistant" who scoffed at human pretensions to govern in place of the government of God, Garrison condemned the Constitution, the federal government, and both major parties as proslavery. In 1843, he used his influence in the Massachusetts Anti-Slavery Society to pass a denunciation of the Constitution as a "covenant with death and an agreement with hell" that "should be annulled." When he ascended to the presidency of the AAS later that year, he engineered the passage of a similar resolution. Garrison did not call for armed rescue of the slaves or encourage slave uprisings, but his constant agitation helped to transform the mild Northern objection to slavery into a more widespread anti-Southernism during the 1850s.

Garrison's uncompromising radicalism made him enemies within the antislavery movement. In 1840, the AAS split over the proper role of women in reform and whether or not abolitionists should participate in partisan politics. Garrison opposed the formation of the Liberty party and all political initiatives requiring compromise. Supporting an active, public role for Sarah and Angelina Grimké,* Garrison insisted upon equal participation for women in the antislavery movement. His opponents bolted, forming the American and Foreign Anti-Slavery Society in 1840.

The volatility that Garrison generated himself, he often had to prevent from completely undermining his support. Always the radical, he yet managed to hold together the potentially divisive AAS until the Civil War, frequently rejuvenating the crusade with his own passion for reform. With the passage of the Thirteenth Amendment,* Garrison turned to other reforms, including women's suffrage, temperance, and Indian rights, though none captured his imagination as had abolitionism.

SELECTED BIBLIOGRAPHY

Aileen S. Kraditor, *Means and Ends in American Abolitionism: Garrison and His Critics on Strategy and Tactics, 1834–1850* (1967); Walter M. Merrill, *Against Wind and Tide: A Biography of William Lloyd Garrison* (1963); Walter M. Merrill and Louis Ruchames, eds., *The Letters of William Lloyd Garrison* (6 vols., 1971–1981); Russel B. Nye, *William Lloyd Garrison and the Humanitarian Reformers* (1955); and John L. Thomas, *The Liberator, William Lloyd Garrison: A Biography* (1963).

ALAN KRAUT

GENEALOGY. Throughout two centuries and more of enslavement, powerful familial ties nurtured both the individual Afro-American and his developing culture. Sometimes real and sometimes fictive, an intricate kin network often developed on large plantations or within small, isolated, and close-knit communities to provide the slave with a source of identity and a sense of place that transcended forced uprootings, as well as a peer moiety (distinctive from the dominant white society) through which African mores could be transmitted.

However, current historical and genealogical scholarship indicates that the familial bonds which united slaves reflected more the characteristics of clan membership than those of genealogy—as the latter is universally defined. While evidence of the strength of the nuclear slave family* is indisputable, while current studies indicate a previously unknown degree of grandparental-child associations, and while individual knowledge of closer family relationships within contemporary generations is clear from slave taboos against first-cousin marriages, there has yet to emerge evidence that the transmission of ancestral lineages (oral or written) was an integral part of slave life.

The traditionally limited exercise of genealogy among Afro-Americans is expressed, historically, in a variety of ways. The most advanced studies of slave family life, for example, reveal exceedingly limited transmission (in comparison with other societies) of ancestral given names antedating the mother's or father's own parents. The family knowledge of twentieth-century blacks rarely extends past great-grandparents, and recorded evidence suggests that the same pattern prevailed within slave society. Even on occasions when the very freedom or enslavement of an individual black rested upon his or her knowledge of ancestry, that knowledge was prone to be limited. Of 163 studied slaves, for example, who sued for their freedom in Virginia and Alabama courts between 1770 and 1860 on the grounds that their maternal lineage was free, none were able to identify ancestors past their grandparents, and most who spoke of grandparents could not supply names. Mastin Murphy of Shelby County, Alabama, typically stated in 1832 that he had "been informed [his father] was the child of a white woman," although he did not know her name. John Hudson of Tuscaloosa, Alabama, in 1829, chronicled the removal of his grandmother from the West Indies to Maryland, but of her ancestry his family tradition related only that she "was of German de[s]cent." In other cases, as with Rachel Finley of Powhatan and Amelia counties, Virginia, in 1819, aged whites who were called as witnesses were able to extend the slave's lineage to great-grandparents although Rachel herself could not.

The limited degree to which slaves transmitted definite knowledge of ancestral lineages, the invariable tendency of oral tradition among all peoples (when it exists) to deify ancestors so that they might serve as role models, the degree to which oral accounts are invariably mutated by the passage of time and lapses of memory, and the adoption of a host of fictive kin by slaves who were forcibly removed from the clan or kinship network of their birth, all serve to complicate present attempts to document the history of any individual slave family. Success in this endeavor, however, is far more possible than has been previously assumed.

For Afro-Americans in search of roots, standards and initial procedures parallel those of any ethnic group arriving in America before the Civil War. From living relatives and family papers, genealogists identify known antecedents, gather personal detail on each, and then use the data as *clues* to the documentary evidence that must be found for every identity, relationship, or detail within the pedigree. Like all genealogists, Afro-Americans must accept the fallibility of family tradition and acquaint themselves with inherent flaws within all types of records. They must search out all extant documents, analyze the results with discretion, and correlate evidence carefully in order to reach valid conclusions.

Post-Civil War documentation is most often found in censuses, birth and death records, county courthouses, city halls, state archives, churches, and cemeteries. Researchers with access to the Salt Lake City headquarters or regional branches of the Church of Jesus Christ of the Latter-Day Saints (LDS) find some (but by no means all) of these localized records on microfilm, although such LDS-compiled collections as indexes and family groups sheets are presently of minimum value to Afro-Americans.

The character (but not standards) of black genealogical research varies substantially beyond the Civil War period. The 1860 federal census identifies some one-half million free blacks, their numbers almost equally divided between Northern and Southern states. Statistically, therefore, Afro-Americans may expect one of eight antebellum black ancestors to be free,* and their research on this minority should proceed in those records created by the free population. For enslaved lines, the backward transition from freedom to slavery is the most difficult challenge that Afro-American genealogists face, since owners must be identified before records can be found. Traditionally it was assumed that freedmen* routinely took the name* of their last owner; recent scholarship, however, questions the assumption with inconclusive results. One statistical analysis of Louisiana and Alabama ex-slaves reveals that 71 percent of freedmen used the name of their last master, 2 percent reverted to using the name of an earlier master, and 27 percent used the name of no known owner, while another study of South Carolina blacks found 17 percent using the name of last owner, 46 percent using a surname different from that of the last owner, and 37 percent for whom evidence is said to be unclear. Clues to the identity of owners may also be found in unusual given names within the manumitted family or through a study of white census neighbors, courthouse mortgage and sharecropping records, and the National Archives files of Civil War claims commissions and the Freedmen's Bureau.

Tracking enslaved lineages requires not only the identification of ancestors, but also the ferreting out and studying of all documents created by the white, free black, or Indian owner-family. Invariably, genealogists must reconstitute the various branches of the owner-family and track their migrations, since the transfer of slave property between individuals and locales more commonly resulted from interfamily donations, inheritances, and owner migration than from the activities of slave traders. In addition to those records routinely used for postbellum research, Afro-American genealogists may (but do not usually) find plantation records maintained by descendants of the owner-family or deposited in university archives. A major neglected source is the minutes maintained by Southern churches, particularly Baptists, whose slave members moved their letters of membership from one locale to another just as white and free black churchgoers did.

The identification of African names and tribal origins for immigrant ancestors is entirely possible. In many locales, particularly Louisiana, imported slaves were officially identified by their African names throughout their lives. However, odds weigh heavily against success in extending lineages into Africa, despite the prevalence of tribal *griots*, since their oral narratives rarely contain valid information on real people living before 1800.

For assistance in research, Afro-American genealogists may turn to any of several organizations—most notably the Afro-American Historical and Genealogical Society and the National Genealogical Society—or to professionals certified by the National Board for the Certification of Genealogists or accredited by the Genealogical Society of Utah.

SELECTED BIBLIOGRAPHY

John W. Blassingame, *The Slave Community: Plantation Life in the Antebellum South* (rev. ed., 1979); Alice Eichholz and James Rose, *Black Genesis* (1978); Herbert G. Gutman, *The Black Family in Slavery and Freedom, 1750–1925* (1976); Elizabeth Shown Mills, "Ethnicity and the Southern Genealogist: Myths and Misconceptions, Resources and Opportunities," in Ralph J. Crandall and Robert M. Taylor, eds., *Generations and Change: Genealogical Perspectives in Social History* (1985); Elizabeth Shown Mills and Gary B. Mills, "The Genealogist's Assessment of Alex Haley's *Roots*," *National Ge-*

nealogical Society Quarterly, 72 (1984), 35–49; James D. Walker, *Black Genealogy— How To Begin* (1977); and Donald R. Wright, "Uprooting Kunta Kinte: On the Perils of Relying on Encyclopedic Informants," *History in Africa*, 8 (1981), 205–217.

ELIZABETH SHOWN MILLS

GEOGRAPHIC INFLUENCES ON SLAVES. Within the Old South slavery was universal, but the distribution of bondsmen was far from uniform. Slaves became numerous enough to account for more than 80 percent of the population in some counties and parishes, but were virtually absent in others. The greatest numbers lived in Virginia, North Carolina, South Carolina, Georgia, Alabama, Mississippi, and Louisiana, but remarkable variation existed even within those states. Considering such a striking distribution, it is pertinent to ask what factors were responsible for its occurrence. Why were slaves concentrated in certain places and virtually absent in others?

Tradition holds that the African evolved in a tropical environment and was best suited to labor in warmer places. Europeans, on the other hand, were much disadvantaged under such conditions, especially when employed in strenuous labor. Yet experience over the past three centuries demonstrates no such environmental selectivity. White laborers survive quite well within the tropics (both humid and arid) as do blacks in the upper mid-latitudes, such as those in New York, Chicago, and Detroit. Even if such environmental explanations are granted, the spatial variation of slaves in the South remains a puzzle. Clearly, other factors must have been at work during the development period.

Though slaves were first imported in numbers to the Chesapeake tidewater area in the seventeenth and eighteenth centuries, slavery expanded inland in all directions in response to the demand for labor. Long experienced in using slave labor in the Caribbean, Spanish, French, and English entrepreneurs imported slaves in large numbers, almost always in response to opportunities in labor-intensive agricultural activities. Initially, tobacco culture provided the greatest impetus, but with the development of indigo, rice, and cotton along the South Atlantic coast, slavery expanded southward as well. The development of the sugar cane industry in the nineteenth century along the Gulf Coast, especially Louisiana, provided another impetus for slavery's expansion. By 1860 the institution had reached its greatest areal extent, stretching from Virginia to Texas and northward to include Missouri (figure 1). Slaves were ubiquitous in the Old South—only a handful of counties reported no slaves in 1860. But bondsmen appeared most numerous in several places: in eastern Virginia and parts of adjacent Maryland and North Carolina; in central Georgia and most of South Carolina including the Georgia tidewater counties; in the Alabama Black Belt; and in the lower Mississippi Valley including the Red River Valley in Louisiana. Small outliers of slave concentrations existed in Kentucky, Tennessee, northern Alabama, Florida, and Texas (figure 2).

Slave occupation patterns explain this distribution. Each of these areas produced one or more of the basic Southern staple crops—cotton,* rice,* sugar

Figure 1
The Slavery Frontier Areas with Significant Slave Numbers, 1800–1860

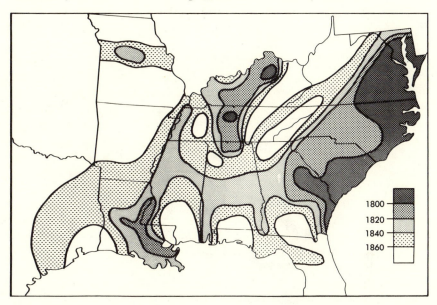

Figure 2
Slave Concentration Areas Where Slaves Were in the Majority, 1860

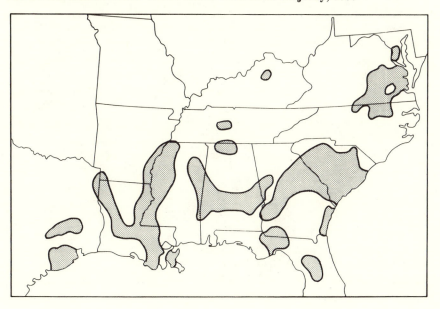

Figure 3
Slaveholders with 100 or More Slaves in 1860

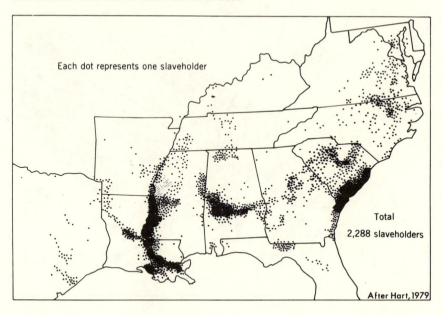

Each dot represents one slaveholder

Total
2,288 slaveholders

After Hart, 1979

Figure 4
Farms of 1,000 Acres or More in 1860

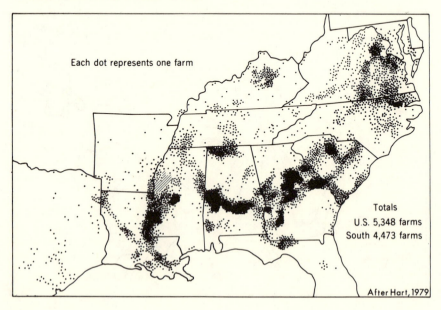

Each dot represents one farm

Totals
U.S. 5,348 farms
South 4,473 farms

After Hart, 1979

cane,* and tobacco.* All four crops were labor-intensive and were sold for cash. They thus provided the capital necessary for the purchase of slaves.

Another important feature of North American slavery was its association with the plantation.* Most slaveholders owned fewer than five slaves, but the average number of slaves per slaveholding was somewhat higher, indicating the importance of large slaveholders.* A mapping of both large slaveholdings and large landholdings reveals similar patterns (figures 3 and 4). Moreover, both distributions bear striking similarities to figure 2, which shows the areas where slaves amounted to more than half the population. The existence of abundant productive agricultural land, and the opportunity to produce and market on a large scale the agricultural commodities in demand at the time, were the most important determinants in the distribution of slaves in the South.

SELECTED BIBLIOGRAPHY

John Fraser Hart, "The Role of the Plantation in Southern Agriculture," *Proceedings of the Tall Timbers Ecology and Management Conference*, No. 16, Thomasville, Georgia (February 1979), 1–19; Sam B. Hilliard, *Atlas of Antebellum Southern Agriculture* (1984); and Charles O. Paullin, *Atlas of the Historical Geography of the United States* (1932).

SAM B. HILLIARD

GEORGIA, SLAVERY IN. During the 1730s, when England's other South Atlantic colonies had irrevocably committed themselves to black bondage and plantation agriculture, British philanthropists founded Georgia as an experiment in diversified small-scale enterprise through free white labor. Having banned both slavery and large landholdings, the Georgia Trustees waged an abortive seventeen-year struggle to create a wilderness utopia where indigent Englishmen could become tradesmen or thrifty yeomen, producing raw materials for the mother country and defending nearby South Carolina against the Spanish and Indians. Although the plan defied conventional wisdom, it was not entirely implausible. Virginia had prospered without slavery during its initial stages of development, and viable, town-oriented societies of artisans and small farmers existed elsewhere in eighteenth-century North America. Certain individuals and groups did, in fact, achieve modest prosperity under trustee rule, but in comparison to the older plantation colonies, Georgia languished. Population grew slowly and lucrative export commerce failed to materialize. Mounting domestic criticism caused the trustees to drop landholding restrictions during the 1740s, and finally in 1750, to permit slavery, subject to various humanitarian restrictions that were quickly brushed aside.

One recent scholar has characterized the repudiation of trustee period antislavery policy as the "great tragedy" of Georgia's early history. Certainly the decision had tragic implications for the approximately 15,000 black people born or brought into the colony during the quarter century before the American Revolution. Overwhelmingly, they were destined for lives of drudgery on coastal rice* plantations, producing the staple exports that would stimulate Georgia's economy while concentrating wealth and power into the hands of an emerging planter elite. For fifteen years after slavery's legalization the black population grew slowly. In July 1750 Governor James Wright reported the presence of some 349 adult "working negroes" plus an unspecified number of young children. Between that year and 1765 some 637 slaves arrived in Georgia ports from Jamaica, St. Christopher, and other West Indian islands. A much larger slave influx of more than 1,200 came from neighboring South Carolina, which also supplied many white migrants anxious for new opportunities in rice planting. After 1765 the pace of slave importation quickened as nearly 11,000 slaves poured into Georgia from various sources. Nearly half came directly from Africa into the ports of Savannah and Sunbury, while another 3,000 more or less were purchased from South Carolina. As had been true before 1765, many if not most of the slaves obtained from South Carolina were newly arrived Africans reexported by Charleston merchants to Georgia customers.

The demography* of the African slave trade* had a major impact on black life and culture in prerevolutionary Georgia. When the first statistics on slave population were reported in 1750, adult black men outnumbered women by roughly 25 percent, and for at least a generation the unbalanced sex ratio persisted. Responding to the labor demands of Georgia's emerging plantation system, local merchants sought African cargoes containing approximately two adult males for each female between the ages of fourteen and twenty-five. The resulting scarcity of black women had a blighting effect on slave family life and probably inhibited the preservation of African cultural norms, particularly those religious concepts most directly related to ancestor worship and a belief in reincarnation. Low rates of black population growth during the early decades can be attributed largely to the predominance of men in the work force, although the long period of breast feeding and the consequent child spacing common to some West African polygamous societies also helped depress slave birthrates.

Ethnographic generalizations about Georgia's eighteenth-century Africans are risky at best, but available evidence suggests that most bondsmen came from Gambia, Sierra Leone, and other locations along the Windward and Gold Coast. Angolans, who had comprised the bulk of black immigrants to South Carolina prior to the 1739 Stono Rebellion, entered Georgia only in small numbers. Common geographic origins may have facilitated communication among the first generation of Georgia slaves, and it is likely that overlapping cultural practices from West Africa provided an element of social continuity that helped offset the effects of shattered family or tribal bonds. Whites contributed unwittingly to African cultural persistence by resorting to task labor as the principal means of plantation management. Introduced to Georgia during the 1750s by migrants from South Carolina, the task system* required each slave to complete a fixed amount of work, such as hoeing a quarter acre of rice or planting a half acre of corn, in the course of a single day. White overseers* or black drivers* (often called "headmen") normally supervised the field hands, who were allowed to move at their own pace so long as the stipulated labor assignment was completed and the work performed in a satisfactory manner. Built around visible and easily measured units of productivity, the task system required little direct interaction between blacks and whites. Georgia rice planters saw tasking as a practical method of extracting systematic toil from a largely unassimilated slave work force.

Contemporary witnesses showed little surprise when a full decade after slavery's legalization most Africans remained "new Negroes," possessing little knowledge of their oppressors' language, mores, or religion. The half dozen white clergymen who evangelized slaves in colonial Georgia reached only a tiny fragment of the black population and often made little lasting impression on the bondsmen who heard their preaching. During the late 1750s, for example, the Reverend John Solomon Ottolenghe complained that Georgia slaves were "mostly Africans" who were "as Ignorant of our Language, as we are of theirs." Since no one could be found to translate white preaching, the blacks had difficulty "understanding what it is that is offer'd to them in order to forsake Paganism and embrace Christianity." As a group, the slaves appeared "nurs'd in extravagant Idolatry," with the "old Superstition of a false Religion . . . riveted by Time" on their consciousness.

While clinging tenaciously to African belief systems, many colonial bondsmen also tried to reclaim the personal freedom that whites had taken away. Between 1763 and 1775 some 160 different slave owners sought to recover 453 black runaways* through newspaper advertisements. Native Africans accounted for 75 percent of the fugitives, most of whom were unskilled young male field-workers. The few skilled and acculturated slaves tended to converge on Savannah where they might find employment or pass as free. Their behavior contrasted sharply with that of most absconding Africans who tried to avoid contact with whites by fleeing toward the coast or backcountry. In the mid-1770s four men and a woman owned by Governor James Wright actually set out "in a small paddling boat . . . to look for their own country." Apparently Florida held little attraction for local runaways after the end of the French and Indian War, although prior to 1763 Georgia authorities took extraordinary measures to prevent black fugitives from joining the Spanish near St. Augustine. Anyone capturing and returning an adult male slave could collect five pounds sterling, and the scalp of a dead bondsman would bring one-fifth of that sum, provided both ears were still attached. In the circumstances, some desperate and resourceful escapees joined the semipermanent runaway bands that emerged periodically from the swamps north and east of Savannah to pillage outlying plantations.

The context of black resistance* changed appreciably during the turbulent years of the American Revolution.* Opportunities for freedom expanded and took new forms, familiar authority structures weakened or collapsed, and at times, slaves played an active role in the military struggle between Tories and Whigs. Agriculture was among the war's first casualties, laid low by the early departure of many loyalist planters and the subsequent chaos of armed conflict along the seaboard and in the backcountry. When royal governor Wright fled the province in February 1776, he met several hundred black runaways outside

Savannah and arranged for their departure on British vessels. For the next several years Georgia's slave population dwindled as bondsmen slipped away from poorly supervised plantations or accompanied their owners to other colonies. By 1780 a combination of physical damage and labor scarcity had eliminated the colony's annual rice exports (estimated at 20,000–25,000 barrels before the war), and left local residents with only one-tenth that amount for domestic consumption.

As the plantation system ground to a halt, both the British and Americans mobilized Georgia blacks to build fortifications and perform other kinds of military labor. Each side confiscated slaves owned by "the enemy" and impressed bondsmen belonging to friendly masters. Probably most black Georgians felt little true attachment to whites on either side of the conflict, although two dramatic instances of slave assistance to the redcoats suggest a tendency (however unwarranted) to identify Britain with the cause of emancipation. In the winter of 1778–1779 an elderly black man named Quamino (or Quash) Dolly guided Colonel Archibald Campbell's 3,500 British troops through the coastal swamps as part of a successful surprise attack on the rebel garrison in Savannah. Nine months later when French and American forces tried to retake the city, the British armed some 200 local blacks to help repel the attack. Although Georgia's colonial militia laws authorized arming slaves and freeing them for acts of valor, most white loyalists had no intention of liberating Savannah's black defenders. On the contrary, local authorities moved quickly to disband the Negro company as soon as the emergency had passed. Whether because of the black soldiers' example or simply as a result of prevailing social disorder, armed gangs of slaves refused to give up their weapons after the siege was raised and continued to terrorize Savannah and its outskirts for several months. After the war ended, moreover, a group of 200–300 armed blacks calling themselves the "King of England's soldiers" established a fortified village in Belle Isle Swamp where they remained until 1786 when their camp was destroyed by state militia.

If the war bequeathed a legacy of maroon* communities to coastal Georgia, it also created an acute labor shortage for white plantation owners. The number of slaves removed during the British evacuation of Savannah in 1782 has been variously estimated at between 3,500 and 6,000, or some 25 percent of the state's prerevolutionary black population. When this figure is added to previous wartime slave losses resulting from theft, desertion, escape, death, and removal, the Revolution's demographic impact on the plantation system takes on an ironic significance. In Georgia, at least, the outcome of a war fought in the name of liberty and republican values all but ensured that victorious white patriots would proceed to negate human freedom by reopening the African slave trade. Between 1784 and 1799 almost 7,600 slaves entered Georgia from foreign sources, with all but 638 arriving during the 1790s. At first they came in small groups including many "seasoned" bondsmen from the West Indies, but in 1793 the black uprising in Saint-Domingue caused state lawmakers to ban further imports from the islands. For the next five years Rhode Island slave traders like James D'Wolf and Cyprian Sterry sold white Georgians nearly 4,800 black men and women form Sierra Leone, the Gold Coast, and other portions of West Africa. Even after Georgia closed the foreign slave trade* in 1798, Africans continued to enter the state from South Carolina, where slave ships made regular stops for the next eight years. Taking note of the influx in 1799, a Georgia grand jury concluded that the "narrow channel of the Savannah River will never, like the Chinese wall, be found an ample barrier" against illegal African importation.

Georgia's postwar resumption of the African trade occurred at a time when slavery as an institution was entering upon a period of geographic expansion, economic reorientation, and sociocultural change. On the eve of the Revolution chattel bondage had been confined almost entirely to the seaboard, with only a handful of black laborers dispersed among interior farms and plantations as far north as Augusta. Colonial era up-country slaves lived in small, isolated units and performed a variety of jobs associated with the production of corn, small grains, livestock, tobacco, and indigo. Yeomen subsistence farms predominated in more remote interior regions during the early years of settlement, although a few slaves were present in even the newest frontier areas. When occupation of Georgia's western lands resumed after independence, slave-owning planters, including many immigrants from the upper South, played a conspicuous pioneer role. Arriving early with slaves, capital, and valuable political connections, such Virginia newcomers as the Gilmers, Lewises, Harvies, Meriwethers, Markses, Mathewses, Crawfords, Taliaferros, and others vied with Scotch-Irish plain folk from the Carolina backcountry for control of choice farmland north and west of Augusta. For more than a decade moderate size tobacco* plantations coexisted with a prevailing system of family-based subsistence agriculture in what would later become the eastern counties of Georgia's lower piedmont. After 1800, however, cotton* rapidly displaced tobacco as the chief staple crop, yielding profits that invigorated the plantation system and propelled its steady advance. During the next three decades recurrent waves of Indian removal and white expansion carried cotton and slavery southwestward across a broad swath of central Georgia between the northern hill region and the pine barrens and wire-grass land to the south. Black majorities became common in the new plantation belt, and by 1840 the state's slave population had risen to over 280,000, more than a fourfold increase since the turn of the century. Growth slowed in percentage terms as the base of calculation became larger, but more than 180,000 additional bondsmen were present in Georgia when the antebellum era ended. Representing 44 percent of the state's total population by 1860, slaves were concentrated along the seaboard and in the interior cotton counties where a newly arisen planter elite shaped the economic and political destiny of Georgia's 41,000 white families, nearly two-thirds of whom owned no slaves.

By enlarging Georgia's planter class and broadening its social base, the rise of the Cotton Kingdom helped legitimate slavery among less affluent whites, thereby sealing the fate of at least three generations of antebellum blacks. At the same time, however, the spread of plantations from tidewater to up-country wrought profound changes in Afro-American life and established new contexts for master-slave relations.* By the 1820s, if not sooner, the numerically typical Georgia slave ceased to be a young, unassimilated male African engaged in rice production, and became instead an American-born man or woman of African descent, whose attachments to family and fellow bondsmen lent a certain coherence to daily life in the Cotton Belt. What took place in the older sections of the Georgia piedmont during the decades following the Revolution was a complex process of social interaction between survivors of the Middle Passage, native-born slaves from the upper South, and white masters or overseers. Standing as crucial intermediaries between local planters and newly enslaved Africans were the thousands of bondsmen from other states who arrived in Georgia bearing the hyphenated Afro-American cultural forms which had taken shape in the Chesapeake hearth area during the mid-eighteenth century. These thoroughly acculturated black immigrants affected and were in turn influenced by the Africans with whom they came in contact.

Cultural formation occurred through a series of syncretic borrowings and face-to-face encounters like those which took place in Oglethorpe County during the 1820s on the plantation of William H. Crawford. A white neighbor recalled that Crawford owned four native Africans who frequently kept company with a fifth "rather more Americanized" countryman on an adjoining farm. Still bearing tribal scars upon their faces, the aging bondsmen would talk for hours of the "fierce wars which had raged between hostile princes in their native country." Groups of American-born slaves listened to the stories with "staring eyes, open mouths, and peculiarly respectful attitudes." Unschooled in the rituals of paternalist deference, the Africans had evolved a pragmatic modus vivendi with their Georgia masters. As captives, the men accepted the obligation to serve their captors, so long as white demands did not appear capricious. Only when a "misunderstanding" arose about "some matter of business betwixt them and the overseer" did they become "refractory." Punishment in such instances was of no avail because rather than fleeing or submitting, the Africans stood their ground doggedly, "like Roman or British soldiers." Hardly subservient figures, they remained "exclusive and somewhat unapproachable" at the personal level, and were treated with "marked respect by all the other negroes for miles and miles around."

It was partly through the melding of African and Anglo-European folkways into hybrid forms of music,* dance,* speech,* religion,* and group ethics that black Georgians defined themselves as a people. But specific labor needs and structural features of the state's economy also helped determine what it meant to be a slave. Along the coast where geography and specialized agricultural skills discouraged population interchange with the Cotton Belt, the cultural legacy of Africa and the Afro-Caribbean gave a distinctive ambience to slave life. Planter absenteeism slowed the pace of acculturation, while the extension of task labor to nearly all agricultural operations allowed blacks the "free" time to raise livestock and provision crops for domestic consumption or local sale. By the late antebellum era de facto ownership (and even inheritance) of personal property had developed among low-country bondsmen, whose limited commercial activities fostered a social outlook with certain peasant-like overtones.

Greater regimentation and closer white supervision were central features of the gang system of labor organization that prevailed throughout the Cotton Belt where the vast majority of black Georgians spent their lives. In this typical antebellum setting slavery became an institution that simultaneously forced human beings together and drove them apart. For whites, a combination of ethnic chauvinism and paternalist dogma created the mental distance that made physical intimacy with slaves acceptable. Blacks, on the other hand, found exposure to whites hazardous and personally humiliating. The ritualized deference exacted by members of the ruling race impelled most blacks to a kind of self-segregation. Negroes routinely sought psychological refuge by withdrawing to rural slave quarters, urban fringe areas, and emerging "African" churches or less formal religious gatherings. In the process they fostered a kind of racial separation as profound in some ways as any later imposed from above by white supremacist Jim Crow legislation.

By choice and through necessity, black Georgians became a people apart during the years of slavery. Vulnerability quickened the pace of their strategic retreat from the white world and bequeathed a legacy of ambiguous ethnocentrism to the generation that would make the transition from slavery to freedom. By adopting a posture of outward subservience and defensive racial exclusiveness, bondsmen minimized the inner damage of slavery, but they could not escape its pain. Instead of infantile personalities, Afro-Americans developed a fine sensitivity to human limits. Through a supple expressive culture* they were able to dispel anger and frustration, articulate forbidden aspirations, and sustain a rich fantasy life. Yet, for all its vitality, slave culture exhibited a deep ambivalence, an unstable dualism growing out of the tension between what blacks felt justified in desiring and the much different reality that slavery forced them to accept. The message conveyed through music, folktales, and other oral lore was complex but on some points remarkably consistent. The weak might confound the strong through cunning or artifice. The rabbit might win a skirmish with the fox, but the antagonists would retain their respective roles of prey and hunter. A degraded and scorned member of the animal kingdom could harbor secret longings and, at times, even aspire to greatness. But to stray too far from the conservative folk norm—to "get above" one's self—was to invite disaster. The portrait of life drawn in black folklore was, on the whole, quite uncompromising. Frequently its honesty was chilling. Happy endings were a luxury those at the bottom could not afford.

The growth of cities and industries introduced a new element in Georgia's racial equation during the generation preceding the Civil War. By 1860 over 37,000 bondsmen lived in towns or villages whose population exceeded 1,000 residents. More than half the nonrural slaves could be found in Georgia's five largest towns—Savannah, Augusta, Columbus, Atlanta, and Macon—which ranged in size from 22,299 to 8,247 inhabitants. Slavery did not break down in an urban environment, but it did become a different kind of institution, less master-oriented and paternalistic and more bureaucratic and cosmopolitan than in the countryside. As town slaves interacted with literate free Negroes* and black artisans* and entrepreneurs,* or when they attended semiautonomous black churches with "colored" ministers in the pulpit, their mental universe expanded to include new strategies and aspirations. Bondage weighed heavily on the human spirit in any setting, but if the plantation world emphasized slavery's restrictions, urban life exposed its possibilities.

In almost any crossroads hamlet during the 1840s and 1850s one might routinely have encountered quasi-independent town slaves who lived apart from white owners and "hired their own time."* After remitting a stipulated sum to masters, the blacks thus situated could keep any additional income derived from day labor or other employment. Similar economic opportunities were available to Georgia's 12,000–24,000 "industrial" slaves,* a diverse group of manual laborers, skilled and semiskilled factory hands, plantation craftsmen, urban artisans, and workers in crop processing or extractive enterprises. Whatever their specific job or skill level, nonagricultural bondsmen usually had some access to a system of task labor that included incentive payments for extra work. A minority of black Georgians hoped eventually to purchase their freedom through "overwork" and self-hire arrangements, but tragically few succeeded in the all-but-impossible quest. Most bondsmen settled for more immediate and limited financial rewards within a framework of continuing servitude, perhaps nurturing dreams of freedom that were made more vivid by the exploits of successful black fugitives like John Brown* (formerly "Fed" owned by Thomas J. Stevens) and William and Ellen Craft* of Macon, who reached the North and attacked Georgia slavery in book-length autobiographies.*

More than rising slave prices and white pursuers stood between Georgia's black folk and liberty. There were legal obstacles even to acts of manumission by individual masters. Responding to the pressures of militant proslavery sectionalism and pseudoscientific racialist dogma, antebellum politicians closed off all avenues to domestic emancipation in a series of laws* and court decisions between 1818 and the Civil War. When Georgia adopted its first separate penal code in 1833, slaves received virtually no civil rights but labored under a long and growing list of racially discriminatory criminal statutes and restrictions on personal conduct. Anticipated slave uprisings in each antebellum decade triggered periods of fierce repression that juxtaposed mob violence with zealous law enforcement, and frequently resulted in still more restrictive state legislation and municipal ordinances. The 1831 Nat Turner insurrection* in Virginia shook white Georgians badly, but the 1859 abolitionist attack on Harpers Ferry, Virginia, convinced many slave owners that a black uprising was imminent. In the two-year nightmare of racial terrorism which followed, dozens of Georgia slaves were killed or tortured while the liberty of the state's miniscule free Negro population was placed in jeopardy.

As limits of acceptable dissent over slavery grew narrower, antebellum whites who questioned black servitude or sympathized with bondsmen had little choice but to direct their humanitarian impulses into channels which followed the political contours of plantation society. Between 1817 and 1860 more than seventy Georgia slave owners freed nearly 1,200 slaves and sent them to Liberia under the auspices of the American Colonization Society* (ACS). In Georgia and other Deep South states, advocates of colonization labored against mounting odds to preserve the eroding middle ground of antislavery gradualism. While offering whites like Richard Hoff and Alfred Cuthbert a way to free their bondsmen without threatening the rights of other slave owners, the ACS sought black support by depicting emigration as a route to racial equality. Attracted by the egalitarian themes in colonization writing, Georgia slaves like William Moss and Harrison Berry drew upon ACS accounts of the African past for a sense of hope, racial pride, and historical identity.

From at least the mid-1840s onward organized religion became a vehicle for ameliorative reform as clergymen like Charles Colcock Jones* expounded an elaborate biblical rationale for slavery, rooted in doctrines of paternalist reciprocity and Christian stewardship. By embracing proslavery theology, many masters convinced themselves that ownership of human beings was ethically defensible (if not actually "right"), but the price for such moral validation was an enlarged concept of paternalism's self-imposed obligations. In Georgia, as elsewhere, the religious defense of slavery* gradually filled the void created by the stillbirth of Southern abolitionism. In time, a substantial minority of white ministers and laymen came to view themselves as benevolent agents working for the spiritual and cultural uplift of inferior black dependents. The evangelical program to legalize black education, protect slave families, and foster participatory Negro church membership produced more rhetoric than action, and did not imply a larger commitment to racial equality. It did, however, constitute an affirmation of the common humanity of blacks and whites, as well as a conscious rejection of the slave regime's most callous and destructive tendencies.

The latent contradictions within Georgia's slave system became manifest only during the bloody struggle for southern independence. In the postsecession euphoria of 1861 white Georgians seemed ready to put aside philosophical differences and unite in defense of the peculiar institution. For a brief moment the future of slavery appeared secure, but wartime circumstances gradually undermined the foundations of black subordination and shattered the illusion of master-class solidarity. From 1862 onward the diversion of slave labor from agriculture to industry, the removal of bondsmen from invaded regions to inland farms and cities, the conscription of masters or overseers, and the growing reliance upon women to supervise planting operations, all helped redefine the context of black-white interaction. With a consistency apropos to a democratic revolution led by slave-owning conservatives, the struggle for Confederate nationhood pulled domestic race relations in opposite directions. Between 1859 and 1865 campaigns of racial repression and acts of unparalleled barbarity toward blacks went hand in hand with religiously motivated efforts to ameliorate slavery and expand the legal rights of bondsmen. In a similar fashion, the changes associated with wartime urbanization, industrialization, and refugee life produced both benefits and disadvantages for the black people involved. Opportunities to alter plantation routine, to escape white surveillance, and to gain economic bargaining power were often achieved at the expense of family separation and loss of direct access to free territory. Hard-pressed masters became more tolerant of independent behavior among blacks but they also abandoned an increasing number of paternalism's self-imposed obligations.

For some black Georgians the war did, of course, bring escape from slavery, but the freedom obtained behind Union lines was often less complete and more exploitive than justice would have dictated. Ambiguity also surrounded the triumph of Northern arms during the 1864 Sherman invasion. Blacks had reason to look askance at Yankee liberators who often appeared as hostile to Negroes as to slavery itself. The obvious bigotry of some federal troops helped dampen the enthusiasm of slaves for the Union cause and may, in the long run, have reinforced the already profound alienation that many freedmen felt toward white society. During the summer of 1865 Georgians of both races stood astride the boundary of Confederate defeat as they faced an uncertain future amid vivid reminders of the past. Instead of seeking revenge, most freedmen seemed anxious to put the past behind them and make a new start. Postwar magnanimity toward former masters grew out of deeply felt religious values, buttressed by the knowledge that Southern whites would probably retain control of local affairs when the Yankees had come and gone. Acutely aware of their long-term vulnerability, black Georgians looked first to obtaining physical security, family stability, economic independence, and, when possible, literacy—tangible elements of freedom that might be preserved in the midst of political defeat and adversity. For future generations these priorities would become a crucial antidote to despair.

SELECTED BIBLIOGRAPHY

Ralph B. Flanders, *Plantation Slavery in Georgia* (1933); Clarence L. Mohr, *On the Threshold of Freedom: Masters and Slaves in Civil War Georgia* (1986); Julia Floyd Smith, *Slavery and Rice Culture in Low Country Georgia, 1750–1860* (1985); Darold D. Wax, "New Negroes Are Always in Demand: The Slave Trade in Eighteenth-Century Georgia," *Georgia Historical Quarterly*, 68 (1984), 193–220; and Betty Wood, *Slavery in Colonial Georgia, 1730–1775* (1984).

CLARENCE L. MOHR

GRAY, SIMON (1800–?).   Simon Gray, a mulatto slave of Natchez, Mississippi, became a minor executive in the large lumber firm of Andrew Brown and Company of Natchez and New Orleans. Born around 1800, Gray belonged to Andrew Donnan, a blacksmith and merchant of Natchez. In 1835 Donnan hired Gray to Andrew Brown, who retained the slave in his employ until 1863.

After working as a carpenter for three years, Gray was made a flatboat captain. In that capacity he transported lumber from the sawmill to customers between Natchez and New Orleans. Gray commanded mixed crews of slaves and white riverboatmen,* hiring and firing white crewmen. The slave handled large sums of money, maintained records, and wrote reports to his employer.

After 1853 Donnan permitted Gray to live virtually as a free black. With Brown's assistance Gray purchased his wife and children. In 1856 Brown placed Gray in charge of purchasing timber and lumber* from lumbermen in the Yazoo–Mississippi Delta, in addition to handling the transportation of lumber from Brown's large sawmill at Natchez to his lumber yard in New Orleans. By 1860 Gray was acting as superintendent of all of the company's logging and lumbering enterprises in the Delta. He continued in this position after the outbreak of the Civil War, serving until Vicksburg was captured by the Union army in July 1863. After this event, Gray left the region with his family, presumably going to the North. Nothing is known of his subsequent career.

SELECTED BIBLIOGRAPHY

Andrew Brown Papers, University of Mississippi Library, Oxford; Harnett T. Kane, *Natchez on the Mississippi* (1947); John H. Moore, *Andrew Brown and Cypress Lumbering in the Old Southwest* (1967); and John Hebron Moore, "Simon Gray, Riverman: A Slave Who Was Almost Free," *Mississippi Valley Historical Review*, 49 (1962), 472–484.

JOHN HEBRON MOORE

GRIMKÉ, SARAH MOORE (1792–1873), and GRIMKÉ, ANGELINA EMILY (1805–1879). The Grimké sisters were born the sixth and fourteenth of fourteen children to John Faucheraud Grimké, who was of French Huguenot descent, educated at Cambridge University, and a prominent member of the South Carolina judiciary, and Mary (Smith) Grimké, who belonged to a leading South Carolina family. Raised in Charleston, where they socialized with families who engaged in brutal punishments of slaves, Sarah and Angelina moved north in the 1820s and became the most popular antislavery* speakers in the mid-1830s because their testimony about the horrors of slavery was based on personal experience.

Sarah, the elder by twelve years, led the way out of South Carolina, when, on a trip with her father to Philadelphia in 1819, she first encountered antislavery sentiments and found them congenial to her own views. Two years later at the age of twenty-eight, she emigrated permanently to Philadelphia. In 1829 Angelina followed her at the age of twenty-four. Both joined the Society of Friends (*see* Quakers), leaving their family's Episcopal faith.

Angelina, more confident and outgoing than Sarah, in 1835 joined the Philadelphia Female Anti-Slavery Society, and decided to speak out publicly, writing *An Appeal to the Christian Women of the South* (1836), a pamphlet that called upon its readers to "*overthrow* [her emphasis] this horrible system of oppression and cruelty, licentiousness and wrong." Southern postmasters destroyed copies of the pamphlet, and Angelina was warned not to return to Charleston. That year Angelina, as a paid agent of the American Anti-Slavery Society, began to speak before small groups of women in New York City.

Sarah soon joined her there, writing *Epistle to the Clergy of the Southern States* (1836), which refuted the biblical basis for slavery. Angelina's second pamphlet, *Appeal to the Women of the Nominally Free States* (1837), emphasized the ties between Northern institutions and the slave system of the South.

In 1837–1838 Angelina and Sarah Grimké toured New England, attracting throngs of listeners and earning the condemnation of the Congregational ministerial association for discussing "things which ought not to be named," presumably meaning the abuse of women slaves. At their tour's conclusion in Boston, thousands heard them speak in Odeon Hall.

The sisters' leadership within the antislavery movement challenged assumptions about the role of women in the public domain, and Angelina and Sarah each wrote treatises on the equality of the sexes and the right of women to engage in all the reform activities that men pursue. The issue of women's rights ultimately split the antislavery movement in 1839–1840, when conservatives left the American Anti-Slavery Society to form the American and Foreign Anti-Slavery Society.

After her marriage to Theodore Weld* in 1838, Angelina Grimké retired from public life, Sarah joining them on their farm near Belleville, New Jersey, and helping to raise the Weld's three children—Charles Stuart (b. 1839), Theodore Grimké (b. 1841), and Sarah Grimké (b. 1844). The Welds and Sarah Grimké later left Belleville to open progressive schools, first in New Jersey and then in Massachusetts, where they remained from 1863 until their deaths. In 1868 the sisters adopted two mulatto nephews, Archibald Henry and Francis James Grimké, sons of their brother Henry by a slave mother. Both nephews pursued distinguished professional careers.

SELECTED BIBLIOGRAPHY

Catherine H. Birney, *The Grimké Sisters: Sarah and Angelina Grimké, the First Women Advocates of Abolition and Woman's Rights* (1885); Aileen S. Kraditor, *Means and Ends in American Abolitionism: Garrison and His Critics on Strategy and Tactics, 1834–1850* (1967); Gerda Lerner, *The Grimké Sisters from South Carolina: Rebels Against Slavery* (1967); and Gerda Lerner, "The Political Activities of Antislavery Women," in Lerner, ed., *The Majority Finds Its Past: Placing Women in History* (1979).

                                                                        KATHRYN KISH SKLAR

GROG AND GROCERY SHOPS. Grog and grocery shops were places where alcoholic beverages were sold. They also were known as doggeries, dram shops, fruit and pop shops, punch houses, tippling houses, and by numerous other names. Grog shops sold liquor only, while grocery shops sold food products. Usually operating on the fringe of social and legal control, the shops attracted customers whose economic, social, and legal conditions tended to exclude them from more respectable and socially controlled taverns. The shops existed in all states but played a special role in the slaveholding South.

Consumption of liquor was never a significant problem among slaves in rural areas. In villages, towns, and cities, however, slaves had little difficulty purchasing liquor from grog and grocery shops. Shop owners often discreetly encouraged slaves to trade their products and other items of value for liquor. The shops also provided a place where slaves could relax and engage in limited social intercourse with fellow blacks and a few whites in a relatively unrestrained manner.

These shops were an abomination to slave owners and community leaders who believed they contributed to loud and disorderly conduct, thievery, and rebelliousness among the slaves. Numerous state and local laws were passed to govern such shops and their dealings with slaves. To sell or give liquor to a slave without the owner's permission was a crime.* In many places the mere presence of a slave in a shop without the owner's permission was prima facie evidence of the operator's guilt. Despite these laws and urgent demands for vigorous enforcement, and even an occasional resort to vigilante tactics, the grog and grocery shops continued to operate in their traditional manner, which is to say that many served as havens where slaves could enjoy brief interludes of freedom from the usual restraints of the slave system.

SELECTED BIBLIOGRAPHY

Henry G. Crowgey, *Kentuckey Bourbon: The Early Years of Whiskey-making* (1971); Charles C. Pearson and J. Edwin Hendricks, *Liquor and Anti-Liquor in Virginia, 1619–1919* (1967); Deets Pickett, ed., *The Cyclopedia of Temperance, Prohibition and Public Morals* (1917); and Ian R. Tyrrell, *Sobering Up: From Temperance to Prohibition in Antebellum America, 1800–1860* (1979).

KENNETH R. JOHNSON

GULLAH. Gullah was the language* of the slaves along the coast of South Carolina and Georgia. There, enslaved Africans, torn from family and friends whose languages and folkways they had shared, could understand neither one another nor their white masters. Out of two overwhelming needs—to comprehend their masters and to comprehend one another—these Africans through trial and error increasingly became aware of common elements in their diverse tongues.

Perhaps the most conspicuous source of Gullah was Wolof, but there were also important influences from Fante, Ga, Kikongo, Kimbundu, Mandinka, Twi, Ewe, Ibo, and Yoruba. The complex process through which a language based on the convergence of other languages expands both in use and form is called *creolization*. Creole languages developed and became widespread among slaves in the New World. Afro-Portuguese creoles evolved in Brazil and Curaçao; Afro-Spanish creoles in Cuba, Puerto Rico, and Colombia; Afro-French creoles in Louisiana, French Guiana, Haiti, Guadeloupe, and Grenada; an Afro-Dutch creole in the Virgin Islands; an Afro-English creoles in Barbados, Antigua, Guyana, Jamaica, Surinam, South Carolina, and Georgia.

While the vocabulary of Gullah was largely (but not exclusively) English, its grammatical rules were different. Gullah pronouns were no respecters of person, but used an all-purpose pronoun (*e* and later *he*) for masculine, feminine, and neuter forms. Neither did Gullah speakers distinguish between location and approach in their prepositions ("One boat stop *to* Sandy Island"). They did not add *'s* to their nouns to denote pluralization ("John play for *all de dance*") but did employ a distinctive form of the second-person pronoun (*yinnah* or *unna*) to express plurality. They indicated possession by juxtaposition ("Sam he *husband name*"). They usually omitted equating verbs in present tense ("*I glad* for freedom"), but they combined other verbs in distinctive ways ("e *tell me say* he Messus broder" [he told me that he was Mistress's brother]). In both verbs and negators they distinguished between ongoing and momentary actions rather than when those actions might have taken place. Moreover, they intensified negation by the use of multiple negators. Verbs that take complements in English did not necessarily do so in Gullah ("I ain't *wuth!*" [I am not worth (anything), i.e., I am not feeling very good]). Not only did Gullah speakers follow a different set of grammatical rules, they also manifested different gestures and intonation patterns, they defined eloquence differently, and they put a higher value on the role of the man-of-words than did English speakers. All of these manifested continuities with African linguistic patterns creatively adapted to a new social and linguistic environment.

Those commentators who considered Gullah to be an imperfect imitation of English were mistaken. It is now clear that Gullah-speaking slaves did not "fail" to adopt their masters' language; they succeeded in creating a creole language. A speech community, even more than a political community, implies shared culture and worldview. It was through Gullah that Africans from diverse backgrounds communicated with one another, entertained one another, gave shape to a common culture, and handed down that culture to their posterity.

SELECTED BIBLIOGRAPHY

Dell Hymes, ed., *Pidginization and Creolization of Languages* (1971); Charles Joyner, *Down by the Riverside: A South Carolina Slave Community* (1984); Loreto Todd, *Pidgins and Creoles* (1974); and Peter H. Wood, *Black Majority: Negroes in Colonial South Carolina from 1670 through the Stono Rebellion* (1974).

                                                                    CHARLES JOYNER

H

HAMMON, JUPITER (1711–1806?). Jupiter Hammon has been recognized by scholars as "the first American Negro to publish poetry." As the favorite slave to three generations of the Lloyd family of Lloyd's Neck, Long Island, New York, where he was born in 1711, Hammon received some rudimentary education. His exact duties at Lloyd Manor, however, remain unclear.

Assisted by his master, Jupiter, at the age of forty-nine, published *An Evening Thought: Salvation by Christ, with Penitential Cries* (1760), an eighty-eight line "spontaneous and chaotic effort" combining Calvinism with metrical rhymes common to Wesleyan hymnals. Rhythmic repetition of "Salvation comes by Jesus Christ alone" suggests traits common to Negro folk poetry. This work antedates the poetry of Phillis Wheatley.*

During the American Revolution the Lloyd family fled to Hartford, Connecticut, where Hammon published other poems, notably, *An Address to Miss Phillis Weatly* [*sic*] ... (1778); "Poem for Children, with Thoughts of Death" (1782); and "The Kind Master and Dutiful Servant" (1782). His prose works include *A Winter Piece* (1782); *An Evening's Improvement* (1782); and *An Address to the Negroes, in the State of New-York* (1787).

While conceding his privileged status, Hammon, at age seventy-six, was ambivalent about slavery. He urged blacks to be obedient, honest, and faithful to their masters "in all their lawful commands," but he still hoped that "young Negroes" would soon be free. "For my own part I do not wish to be free," he said, doubting as he did that slaves without masters would "know how to take care" of themselves.

As a precursor of the Negro spiritual, Jupiter Hammon's achievement as preacher-poet merits wider recognition. He died sometime between 1790 and 1806.

SELECTED BIBLIOGRAPHY

Stanley A. Ranson, Jr., ed., *America's First Negro Poet: The Complete Works of Jupiter Hammon of Long Island* (1970); and Oscar Wegelin, *Jupiter Hammon, American Negro Poet: Selections from His Writings, and a Bibliography* (1915).

ROBERT E. QUIGLEY

HEALTH AND DISEASE.   Morbidity and mortality data suggest that the health of adult slaves in the antebellum Southern United States was almost as good (or bad) as that of their white masters. By contrast, the health of young slaves was considerably worse than that of their white counterparts. This having been said, it should be quickly added that comparisons of this nature frequently can be more misleading than illuminating.

For example, the much higher death rates of the slave young suggest that those reaching adulthood had survived a significantly more rigorous "weeding out" process than whites. Thus one might reasonably expect to discover that slave adults enjoyed substantially better health than whites. Moreover, blacks and whites suffered from and died of different diseases at different rates. Almost all slaves possessed resistance to vivax malaria, while upwards of half carried blood traits that afforded them protection against deadly falciparum malaria. Blacks also proved remarkably resistant to the ravages of yellow fever, which paid regular epidemic visits to the coastal cities. Thus it was the Southern whites who dominated the death rolls generated by "fevers." Had blacks not possessed the ability to survive these diseases that destroyed so many white lives, or conversely, had there been no yellow fever and malaria in the South, then the death rates of adult slaves would have been substantially higher than those of whites.

In the case of the high morbidity and mortality levels of the slave young, while some of the causes were environmental, others harked back to their West African heritage. A black skin, which may have evolved as a defense against the rays of the sun, lacks the ability to reflect those rays as well as a white skin. As a result, a black body receives far less stimulation than a white for vitamin D production. In West Africa, which receives abundant sunshine for most of the year, pigment should have caused persons few problems with vitamin D production. But West Africans transplanted from the tropics to the temperate Southern United States historically have suffered vitamin D deficiency during the winter months of overcast skies, or whenever they have spent an excessive amount of time indoors.

This deficiency itself could have crippled many slave youngsters, but when combined with lactose intolerance, it frequently resulted in cases of full-blown rickets. Most adults of West African ancestry are lactose intolerant, lacking the lactase enzyme necessary to break down milk sugars. For them, consumption of even small amounts of milk can cause cramps, bloating, and diarrhea. As the conditon develops the victim learns to avoid milk consumption.

With those of West African descent the frequency of lactose intolerance increases with age. It begins in some cases with the very young and today approximately 40 percent of black school-age children are lactose intolerant. Because there is no reason to believe that the frequency of lactose intolerance among slaves would have been lower, it is clear that even on those plantations where milk was available, a substantial percentage of the slave youngsters could not have consumed it. This deprived them of an important source of protein and a crucial source of calcium as well. Vitamin D is essential for the absorption of calcium and magnesium. And with lactose intolerance denying many slaves a good source of calcium, no wonder descriptions of slaves frequently mentioned bowed and crooked legs, evidence of a childhood bout with rickets.

Unfortunately, wherever rickets appears, tetany usually prevails as well (it also is caused by an insufficient or poorly absorbed intake of calcium, or by calcium and magnesium imbalances). While rickets seldom proved fatal, nutritional tetany in children invariably was. Its symptoms in a youngster resemble those of tetanus, and it would appear that the slave young suffered excessively from both diseases. Tetanus was especially prevalent among the newborn, when midwives employed unclean instruments to sever the umbilical cord, or unclean materials to dress the umbilical stump. In this case the disease usually revealed itself within the first nine days of life, and was called the "nine day fits." Slave adults also suffered from tetanus to a greater degree than whites. This resulted in part because slaves' work exposed them more to injury, but mostly because habit or circumstances kept the slaves barefoot throughout much of the year.

Many slave infants died from what Southern physicians and masters believed was smothering—parents accidentally rolling over on the babies while asleep at night. Recently, however, historians have come to suspect that the infants supposedly smothered actually were victims of sudden infant death syndrome (SIDS). In the United States today SIDS tends to seek out a much higher percentage of its victims among black, as opposed to white, babies.

A particularly tragic disease among slave toddlers was protein calorie malnutrition (PCM). This disease, widespread in much of the developing world today, strikes the child soon after it is weaned from breast milk to diets that provide too few calories to support life or that prove adequate in calories but deficient in high quality protein. Most slave children developed the latter form of the disease, today called kwashiorkor, which is manifested by the characteristic distended stomach. Yet cases with such overt symptoms as potbellies form only a small portion of the whole. Generally, the disease remains without outward signs until prominent symptoms are summoned by an added nutritional burden.

Worm infection frequently provided such a burden, and "worms" ranked high as a killer of slave, as opposed to white, children. Blacks do not suffer from hookworm disease to the extent that whites do. They consistently reveal lighter loads of the worms and generally do not develop severe cases of hookworm anemia of the sort that rendered poor whites in the South so apathetic and listless. But blacks do seem to succumb more than whites to infections by *ascaris* and *trichuris*. Both kinds of worms have been credited with precipitating a PCM crisis for innumerable youngsters in the developing world.

Dirt eating, which many slave children reportedly engaged in, would have been an important factor in the introduction of worms. Dirt eating was also a widespread practice of adults, especially women.* Planters, however, were mistaken in their belief that dirt eating was an important cause of death, for it rarely killed anybody. On the other hand, dirt eating was symptomatic of mineral deficiencies—particularly of calcium and iron—the chief deficiencies suffered by the slaves. Dirt eaters, then, would already have been in a weakened condition and thus more likely than healthy individuals to die of an intercurrent illness. Moreover, if coupled with the introduction of worms, which can trigger a PCM crisis in children, dirt eating easily could have been indirectly lethal.

Infectious diseases can also intertwine in deadly fashion with PCM. This doubtless helps to explain the extraordinary deadliness of whooping cough among slave children.* Indeed, the disease was credited with killing almost as many of them as worms.

Slaves of all ages suffered more from lung-related ailments than whites. To some extent this resulted from cramped quarters and outdoor work in inclement weather. But, in addition, the slaves were descended from a people with little opportunity to build resistance to some of these illnesses. Bacterial pneumonia, for example, was nonexistent in West Africa prior to the arrival of the Europeans. Tuberculosis seems to have arrived at an earlier date via the Arabs, but because tuberculosis would have spread very slowly in the essentially nonurban West African environment where there was often little contact among peoples, most slaves brought to North America probably arrived with no resistance to the illness. This is supported by the high frequency of the lymphatic form of tuberculosis that many slaves acquired. Antebellum physicians, unfamiliar with this form, thought it a different disease entirely, calling it "struma africana" or "negro scrofula."

Slaves throughout the Western Hemisphere suffered greatly from periodic smallpox epidemics, despite knowledge of the techniques of inoculation and, after the turn of the nineteenth century, vaccination. Yet at least from the time of the American Revolution* onward, smallpox only occasionally visited the plantations of the South. This resulted because the African slave trade, which so frequently introduced smallpox to other slave societies in the hemisphere, declined to the United States for the last quarter of the eighteenth century, and became virtually extinct after the first decade of the nineteenth century.

The diminishing volume of the slave trade and a temperate climate served to spare North American slaves other diseases that reached out from African reservoirs. Yaws, leprosy, and filariasis—although not unknown in the South—were nonetheless relatively uncommon when compared with their incidence in other New World slave societies.

West Africa affected slave health in other ways as well. Genetic defenses developed against falciparum malaria, such as sickle trait and glucose-6-dehydrogenase deficiency, tend to leave some carriers of these traits more prone to anemia, more susceptible to certain diseases and, in the case of sickle trait in women, more likely to have a premature infant. Moreover, a quarter of those who inherit sickle trait from both parents develop deadly sickle cell anemia. This was yet another disease that would have contributed to the high mortality rates of slave children.

Slaves of all ages suffered from what appears to have been a high frequency of eye, skin, and dental complaints. Many of these doubtless had nutritional causes. Certainly the periodic outbreaks of what apparently was pellagra stemmed from the slaves' unbalanced diet.

Poor slave nutrition also probably contributed to the terrible susceptibility that slaves displayed to the epidemics of Asiatic cholera that began in the years 1832 and 1848. Because cholera tended to follow major transportation arteries (then mostly water routes), slaves in coastal cities and on plantations clustered along the rivers of the South often constituted a demographic* majority in the path of the disease. And once the illness was acquired, slaves had a much greater chance of dying from it than whites. This phenomenon cannot be explained by differential and discriminatory medical care. Prior to the age of modern medicine the accepted treatment of cholera patients was more likely to kill than to cure them.

To a certain extent, however, it can be explained by poor nutrition. Both the badly nourished and the undernourished tend to have substantially lower levels of hydrochloric acid in the stomach than the well-nourished. And hydrochloric acid, which kills ingested cholera vibrios, constitutes the body's first line of defense against cholera. Similarly, large gulps of water can temporarily dilute stomach acid and consequently hot and thirsty field hands who drank from contaminated ponds quite likely developed severe and life-threatening cases of cholera.

Blacks in the antebellum South, then, were subjected by genetics, nutrition, their past relationship with disease, and their immediate environment to a disease experience that differed considerably from that of whites in the region. Unfortunately, this experience played a prominent role in their exploitation by whites. The blacks' ability to resist malaria and yellow fever convinced whites that only blacks could perform hard work in hot climates. And the slaves' disease susceptibilities, coupled with their immunities to other diseases, persuaded antebellum doctors that blacks constituted both a different and inferior species of man. Their medical and pseudoscientific doctrines in turn bolstered the proslavery argument.*

Yet bad as the slaves' disease experience was in the South, it was not nearly so disastrous as it was for slaves elsewhere in the Americas. For despite the high death rates of its young, the North American slave population sustained a substantial rate of natural growth. Due in large part to phenomenally high levels of infant and child mortality, other slave societies in the Americas generally witnessed a net annual natural decrease of their numbers.

SELECTED BIBLIOGRAPHY

Philip D. Curtin, "Epidemiology and the Slave Trade," *Political Science Quarterly*, 83 (1968), 190–216; John Duffy, "A Note on Ante-Bellum Southern Nationalism and Medical Practice," *Journal of Southern History*, 34 (1968), 266–276; Kenneth F. Kiple, *The Caribbean Slave: A Biological History* (1985); Kenneth F. Kiple and Virginia H. King, *Another Dimension to the Black Diaspora: Diet, Disease, and Racism* (1981); William D. Postell, *The Health of Slaves on Southern Plantations* (1951); Todd L. Savitt, *Medicine and Slavery: The Diseases and Health Care of Blacks in Antebellum Virginia* (1978); and Richard Allen Williams, ed., *Textbook of Black-Related Diseases* (1975).

KENNETH F. KIPLE

HEALTH CARE. Sickness and death were constant worries of nineteenth-century Americans, especially in the disease-ridden antebellum South. Whether one lived in a crowded city or on a large, isolated plantation, whether one was white or black, one could not totally escape the ravages of endemic and epidemic disease.

For whites in the South this problem of sickness and health was often compounded by the fact that they were overseers not only of their own and their family's well-being, but also of that of their black slaves. Slave owners and hirers met their responsibilities with varying degrees of enthusiasm, for despite the monetary investment represented by each slave, not all those in charge of the slaves' care fulfilled their obligations adequately or humanely. Furthermore, medical knowledge was at such a state in the early and mid-nineteenth century that helpful medical intervention was, in many cases, a questionable matter.

Health care for slaves was more than the actual ministrations to ailing blacks. It included those variables that promoted, maintained, or destroyed good health, i.e., living and working conditions. Housing,* sanitation, clothing,* diet,* work hours, whipping,* exposure to heat and cold, and severity of labor all contributed to the slave's state of well-being, and so properly belong in a discussion of health care. Because each of these subjects is already fully discussed in this volume, no reference will be made here to such matters or, for similar reasons, to specific disease immunities and susceptibilities or real or imagined other medical differences between blacks and whites. (*See* Clothing, Diet, Health and Disease, Housing, Punishments, and Seasoning.)

Bondage placed blacks in a difficult position with regard to health care. When taken ill they had a limited range of choices. Masters usually insisted that their slaves, legally an article of property, immediately inform the person in charge of any sickness so the malady might be treated before it worsened. But some bondsmen, as people, felt reluctant to submit to the often harsh prescriptions and remedies of eighteenth- and nineteenth-century white medical practice. They preferred self-treatment or reliance on cures recommended by friends and older relatives. They depended on black herb and root doctors, or on influential conjurers among the local black population. This desire to treat oneself, or at least to have the freedom to choose one's mode of care, sometimes came into direct conflict with the demands and wishes of white masters, whose trust in black medicine was usually slight and whose main concern was keeping the slave force intact.

To compound the problem further, unannounced illnesses did not entitle bondsmen to time off from work. To treat their own illnesses slaves had to conceal them or pass them off to the master as less serious than they actually were. Masters who complained that blacks tended to report sickness only after the disease had progressed to a serious stage often discovered that slaves had treated illnesses at home first. The blacks' dilemma, then, was whether to delay reporting illnesses and treat those diseases at home, risking white reprisal, or to submit at once to the medicines of white America and, in a sense, surrender their bodies to their masters. The result was a dual system in which some slaves received treatment both from whites and blacks.

When illness afflicted a slave, white Southerners responded in several ways. They almost always applied treatments derived from the Euro-American experience. Most often the master, mistress, or overseer first attempted to treat the ailment with home remedies. If the patient failed to respond to these home ministrations, the family physician was summoned. Some slave owners distrusted "regular" doctors and used instead "irregular" medical systems such as Thomsonianism (botanic) remedies, homeopathy, and hydropathy. Masters who hired out their bondsmen to others for a period of time arranged for medical care when signing the hiring bond. Whatever the situation, whites often displayed concern for the health of blacks in bondage. The reasons were threefold: slaves represented a financial investment which required protection; many masters felt a true humanitarian commitment toward their slaves; and whites realized that certain illnesses could easily spread to their own families if not properly treated and contained.

Those responsible for the care of sick slaves made home treatment the first step in the restorative process. White Southerners recognized that physicians, though possessed of knowledge of the human body and the effects of certain medicines on it, were severely limited in the amount of good they could perform. Because no one understood the etiology of most diseases, no one could effectively cure them. Astute nonmedical observers could make diagnoses as well as doctors, and could even treat patients just as effectively. Physicians played their most crucial roles in executing certain surgical procedures, assisting mothers at childbirth, and instilling confidence in sick patients through an effective bedside manner. At other times their excessive use of drugs, overready cups and leeches, and ever-present lancets produced positive harm in depleting the body of blood and nourishment and exhausting the already weakened patient with frequent purges, vomits, sweats, and diuretics. Laypeople often merely followed the same course of treatment that they had observed their physicians using or that they had read about in one of the ubiquitous domestic medical guides. Anyone could do bloodletting or dosing with a little practice. And a physician's services cost money, even when no treatment or cure resulted from the consultation.

Self-care stemmed from people's natural instincts to relieve their own or their family's illnesses as quickly as possible. The unavailability of physicians, the inaccessibility of many farms to main highways, and the lack of good roads and speedy means of transportation reinforced such thinking among rural Southerners. Even when a physician was summoned, hours or even a day passed before his arrival, during which time something had to be done to ease the patient's discomfort. People learned to tolerate pain and to cope with death, but the mitigation of suffering was still a primary goal. To that end most Southerners stocked their cabinets with favorite remedies (or the ingredients required for their preparation) in order to be well equipped when relief was demanded. On large plantations with many slaves this was a necessity. Some physicians made a living selling medicine chests and domestic health guides designed specifically for use on Southern plantations. Self-sufficiency in medical care was desirable on farms and even in urban households, especially when financial considerations were important.

An additional feature of home medical care for slaves was the plantation hospital or infirmary. Its form varied from farm to farm and existed primarily on the larger slaveholdings. It was quicker and more efficient to place ailing slaves in one building, where care could be tendered with a minimum amount of wasted movement and where all medicines, special equipment, and other necessary stores could be maintained. Of course, infectious diseases could spread quite rapidly through a hospital, exposing those present to further sickness.

Armed with drugs from the plantation or home dispensary, one person, usually white, had the responsibility of dosing and treating ill slaves. The master, mistress,* or overseer* spent time each day with those claiming bodily disorders and soon developed a certain facility in handling both patients and drugs. The approach was empirical—if a particular medication or combination of drugs succeeded in arresting symptoms, it became the standard treatment for that malady in that household until a better one came along. Overseers and owners entered useful medical recipes into their diaries or journals and clipped suggestions from newspapers, almanacs, and books.

An overseer's or owner's incompetence or negligence was the slave's loss. New and inexperienced farm managers, unskilled in the treatment of illness, necessarily used bondsmen as guinea pigs for their "on-the-job" training. As a consequence of living on the wrong plantation at the wrong time, some slaves probably lost their lives or became invalids at the hands of new, poorly trained, or simply inhumane overseers or masters.

Despite many masters' policy of delaying a call to the physician until late in the course of a slave's disease, there were times when owners desperately wished for the doctor's presence, for physicians did play important roles, both physiological and psychological, in the treatment of illness. Dr. Charles Brown of Charlottesville, Virginia, for instance, had a thriving country practice during the early nineteenth century. He handled many types of problems: James Old wanted him to determine whether his slave woman, then "in a strange way," was pregnant or not; Bezaleel Brown needed his opinion "if I must bleed her [Jane, who had a pain in her side and suppression of urine] either large or small in quantity"; and Jemina Fretwell wished Brown to "cutt of [f] the arm" of a four-month-old slave which had been "so very badly burnt" that "the [elbow] joint appears like it will drap of[f]." Sometimes physicians made daily visits to dress slaves' wounds or to keep track of household epidemics. In emergencies some owners panicked and fretted away many hours after learning of their physician's temporary absence.

Between the remedies of the household and the standard treatments of the physicians stood "irregular" medicine. Most slave owners either treated with conventional medicines or called in regular doctors, rejecting the new sects as quackery; but a sizable minority of Southerners, difficult to estimate, became enthusiastic proponents of at least one self-help system—Thomsonianism. This movement, based on restoring lost heat to the body through herbals and steam treatments, appealed to masters who were fed up with the ineffective and expensive treatments of their regular physicians. With adherents to the sect so widely diffused throughout the South, the success stories of practitioners no doubt reached at least a portion of the slaveholding class and influenced its thinking. Homeopathy and hydropathy received less attention from slave masters.

Beyond the master's and overseer's eyes, back in the slaves' cabins, some Southern blacks took medical matters into their own hands. When under the surveillance of whites, slaves usually (but not always) accepted their treatments. Some even administered them in the name of the master. But others developed or retained from their African heritage a different brand of care, complete with special remedies, medical practitioners, and rituals. The result was a dual system of health care, the two parts of which sometimes conflicted with each other.

Masters did not appreciate slaves' overusing the plantation infirmary, medicines, or the family doctor, but they preferred this to black self-care for several reasons. Their quarrel with slaves was the same as physicians' with masters: blacks waited too long before seeking medical assistance and often misdiagnosed illnesses. Most owners permitted slaves a small amount of freedom in treating minor ailments at home, but lost their patience when sickness got out of hand. Whites further accused slaves of irresponsibility, ignorance, slovenliness, and indifference in the management of their own and other blacks' illnesses. "They will never do right, left to themselves," declared one Franklin County, Virginia planter.

Left to themselves, however, blacks did try self medical care. Perhaps to offset the failures and harshness of white remedies or the negligence of masters, or to exert some control over their lives, some slaves treated their own diseases and disorders or turned to other trusted blacks for medical assistance, with or without the master's knowledge. Black home remedies circulated through the slave quarters and were passed down privately from generation to generation. Most of these cures were derived from local plants, though some medicines contained ingredients that had magical value only. Occasionally whites would learn of a particularly effective medicine and adopt it, as when Dr. Richard S. Cauthorn announced in the [Richmond] *Monthly Stethoscope* (1857) that an old folk remedy (milk week or silk weed, *Asclepias syriaca* in the U.S. Dispensatory) which had been used for years by blacks in the counties north of Richmond worked almost as well as quinine for agues and fevers. Otherwise, most whites simply ignored or tolerated the black medical world until something occurred to bring their attention to it—either a great medical discovery or a slave death caused by abuse.

Because blacks practiced medicine in virtually every portion of the Old South and because their methods were based partially on magic, problems occasionally arose. The main source of trouble was usually not the misuse of home remedies, but the "prescriptions" and activities of so-called conjure doctors. These men and women used trickery, violence, persuasion, and medical proficiency to gain their reputations among local black communities. They were viewed as healers of illness that white doctors could not touch with their medicines, and as perpetrators of sicknesses on any person they wished—all through "spells."

Folk beliefs were a powerful force within the slave community, and a difficult one for white nonadherents to understand or overcome. For instance, the older brother of a slave patient of Dr. A. D. Galt of Williamsburg, Virginia, observed to the physician that his medicines were useless because Gabriel "had been tricked" and "must have a Negro Doctor" to reverse the progress of the illness. Galt soon claimed to have cured the man, though he did admit that Gabriel suffered frequent relapses, "probably from intemperance in drink." In another case, a slave woman took sick and eventually died on a plantation near Petersburg, Virginia, from what her fellow bondsmen believed were the effects of a conjurer. Some slaves speculated that the young man whom she had refused to marry "poisoned or tricked" her, though the overseer attributed her death to consumption.

Old South whites did permit blacks to fulfill certain medical functions. Some planters assigned trusted slaves to the task of rendering medical assistance to all those ailing on the farm. In most cases, these blacks simply dispensed white remedies and performed venesection and cupping as learned from the master. Though not complete black self-care, this activity did represent a transitional stage in which slaves had the opportunity to apply some of their own knowledge of herbs, gained from elders, in addition to white remedies. These nurses, predominantly women, usually won the respect of both blacks and whites for their curative skills.

To black women often fell another task: prenatal and obstetrical care, especially in rural areas. At least one slave on most large plantations learned and practiced the art of midwifery, not only at home but also throughout the neighborhood. Masters preferred to employ these accoucheurs in uncomplicated cases rather than pay the relatively high fees of trained physicians. An antebellum Virginia physician estimated that nine-tenths of all deliveries among the black population (another physician set it at five-sixths) were conducted by midwives, most of whom were also black. He further asserted that midwives attended half the white women. Physicians often saw obstetrical cases only when problems arose.

Blacks did play a significant role in the health care system of the Old South. They assisted whites and blacks in delivering children, letting blood, pulling teeth, administering medicines, and nursing the sick. The techniques and drugs they used were overtly derived from white medical practices. But blacks also resorted to their own treatments derived from their own heritage and experience. Occasionally the white and black medical worlds merged or openly clashed, but usually they remained silently separate.

SELECTED BIBLIOGRAPHY

James O. Breeden, ed., *Advice among Masters: The Ideal in Slave Management in the Old South* (1980); Kenneth F. Kiple and Virginia H. King, *Another Dimension to the Black Disapora: Diet, Disease, and Racism* (1981); William D. Postell, *The Health of Slaves on Southern Plantations* (1951); and Todd L. Savitt, *Medicine and Slavery: The Diseases and Health Care of Blacks in Antebellum Virginia* (1978).

TODD L. SAVITT

HELPER, HINTON ROWAN (1829–1909). Hinton Rowan Helper was born 27 December 1829, near Salisbury, North Carolina. Following indenture to a storekeeper (1851–1854), Helper unsuccessfully sought wealth in the gold fields of California, an experience that he denounced in *The Land of the Gold: Reality Versus Fiction* (1855). Two years later Helper published his best-known and most controversial work, *The Impending Crisis of the South: How to Meet It.* By invoking numerous statistics and quotations from contemporary authorities, Helper attacked slavery on two essential grounds. First, he asserted that the peculiar institution kept the slave states inferior—socially, culturally, and economically—to the free states. Second, Helper charged that the "slavocracy" used slavery to maintain class dominance over lower-class white Southerners. On the one hand, Helper advocated abolitionism, but on the other, he denounced blacks as savage inferiors. He predicted that blacks ultimately would become extinct.

The Impending Crisis became a best-seller in the North where it was endorsed by Republicans* in the Congress and engendered a bitter contest for Speaker of the House in 1859–1860. Its *Compendium of the Impending Crisis* (1859) was used as a Republican campaign document in 1860. As a reward, Helper served as consul to Buenos Aires from 1861 to 1866. Afterwards, he produced three militantly antiblack books: *Nojoque* (1867), *The Negroes in Negroland . . .* (1868), and *Noonday Exigencies in America* (1871). In the 1870s Helper returned to Latin America as a claims agent, which he described in *Oddment of Andean Diplomacy . . .* (1879). In later years he used his journalistic talents to promote an inter-American railway, most effectively in *The Three Americas Railway* (1881). Helper committed suicide in Washington, D.C., on 8 March 1909.

SELECTED BIBLIOGRAPHY

Hugh C. Bailey, *Hinton Rowan Helper: Abolitionist-Racist,* (1965); Clement Eaton, *The Freedom-of-Thought Struggle in the Old South* (1964); and Hinton Rowan Helper, *The Impending Crisis of the South: How to Meet it,* edited by George M. Fredrickson (1968 ed.).

HUGH C. BAILEY

HEMINGS, SALLY (1773–1835). Sally Hemings was one of several quadroon slave children of the Virginia planter John Wayles and his mulatto concubine Betty Hemings. In 1773 Wayles's will left the Hemingses to his daughter Martha, wife of Thomas Jefferson.* When Martha Jefferson died in 1782, all the Hemings slaves passed to her husband and stayed at Monticello. In 1787, at age fourteen, Sally accompanied Jefferson's younger daughter Maria ("Polly") to Paris, where Jefferson served as American minister (1784–1789). French law did not recognize slavery; consequently, during the Paris sojourn Jefferson paid Sally small wages and granted her many special favors.

In 1789 she returned to Monticello and slavery as a high-ranking house hand. Soon after she may have given birth to her first child. Subsequently (1795– 1808), she bore six children, two of whom died in infancy. Jefferson was present at Monticello nine months before each birth. Two of the surviving children were permitted to leave Monticello during his lifetime. He freed the two others in his will.

In 1802 Jefferson was accused of keeping Sally Hemings as his concubine and of siring her children. The story created a national scandal and was indignantly denied by his friends and allies. Jefferson himself remained silent.

After Jefferson's death in 1826, Sally was freed by his daughter and lived with her two sons near Monticello. Census returns in 1830 recorded her as white. She died in 1835. The "scandal" remains neither proven nor disproven and a continuing source of controversy.

SELECTED BIBLIOGRAPHY

Douglass Adair, *Fame and the Founding Fathers: Essays* (1974); Fawn M. Brodie, *Thomas Jefferson, An Intimate History* (1974); Virginius Dabney, *The Jefferson Scandals: A Rebuttal* (1981); Winthrop D. Jordan, *White over Black: American Attitudes toward the Negro, 1550–1812* (1968); Dumas Malone, *Jefferson the President: First Term, 1801– 1805* (1970); Merrill Peterson, *The Jefferson Image in the American Mind* (1960); and Page Smith, *Jefferson, A Revealing Biography* (1976).

BERNARD W. WISHY

HEMP. Hemp (*Cannablis sativa*), a tall, annual dioecious herb native to Asia, produces oil-rich seed, leaves and blossoms containing a narcotic drug, and long strands of bast fiber that resembles flax fiber. Hemp culture was introduced into Europe before the modern era and into the Western Hemisphere with the establishment of European colonies there. On both continents hemp became an agricultural staple, valued for its fiber. Hemp was the basic raw material for a variety of cordage and textiles ranging from those useful in the home, to the strong rope and heavy canvas needed by seagoing sailing vessels.

Hemp cultivation began in the English colonies when Sir Thomas Dale brought seed to Jamestown in 1611. The plant thrived, but the American colonies never became a reliable source of fiber for England's naval and merchant fleets. Though some shipments were made over the years, only a relatively small amount of fiber produced in the colonies proved suitable for making sailcloth and rigging. The New England shipping industry consumed American hemp in the eighteenth century, but most American hemp was intended for domestic use. By the end of the American Revolution, hemp cultivation extended to the Ohio and Cumberland River valleys.

Eli Whitney's gin,* invented in 1793, made possible the large-scale production of cotton,* a versatile fiber that supplanted hemp in many uses. But Whitney's invention also opened a new market to hemp and ushered in a brief, though somewhat turbulent era in its history.

For ease of transportation, ginned cotton was packed into bales, each wrapped in coarse cloth and bound by strong rope, two articles that the hemp industry hastened to supply. Expansion of cotton production after the War of 1812 brought prosperity, for a time at least, to hemp growers and manufacturers of bale rope and bagging. These were located principally in Kentucky, Missouri, and Tennessee.

Resentful of the tariff protection enjoyed by hemp and the products made from it, cotton planters complained often of the poor quality of bale rope and bagging sold to them, and experimented with other baling materials. After the Civil War, their adoption of jute bagging and metal bands ended their reliance on hempen goods. Left with limited market opportunities, the hemp industry declined, revived briefly during each World War, and then expired.

Labor involved in growing hemp was heavy, sometimes unpleasant, and at one stage unhealthful. In Europe it was performed by serfs and peasants. In America subsistence farmers, hired hands, and slaves cultivated it. Increasingly in the nineteenth century whites concluded that hemp production was "Negro work." A Kentuckian, for example, noted in 1836 the reluctance of white men to work at breaking hemp to extract the fiber. Another, citing in 1849 the concentration of hemp production in his state and Missouri, called it a monopoly that would last as long as their states retained slavery.

Yet slavery never was essential to the production of hemp. This was demonstrated in the late nineteenth and early twentieth centuries by the farmers in Kentucky, Missouri, and the Midwest who found markets for their hemp in the binder twine industry. And even though the largest concentration of slaves in Kentucky and Missouri resided in these states' hemp-growing regions, hemp never became a year-round crop. It was grown on farms of varying sizes, the largest rarely covering more than five or six hundred acres altogether. The farmers practiced diversification: hemp was a money crop but took up only part of the acreage, the remainder of which was devoted to grain, livestock, and other uses as the farmer might choose. Meanwhile, as early as the 1830s, manufacturers of bale rope and bagging adopted machinery that replaced the old rope walks and hand looms that once had depended so heavily on slave labor.

The failure of hemp to return after the Civil War even to its status as a minor crop in the South had little to do with the abolition of slavery. Rather, it resulted from the diminishing world market for the ancient fiber. Not only was hemp gradually replaced by other fibers and wire rope, but it lost an important market when the shipping industry adopted steam power instead of sails.

SELECTED BIBLIOGRAPHY

Miles W. Eaton, "The Development and Later Decline of the Hemp Industry in Missouri," *Missouri Historical Review*, 43 (1949), 344–359; Lewis C. Gray, *History of Agriculture in the Southern United States to 1860* (2 vols., 1933); G. Melvin Herndon, "Hemp in Colonial Virginia," *Agricultural History*, 37 (1963), 86–93; James F. Hopkins, *A History of the Hemp Industry in Kentucky* (1951); Brent Moore, *A Study of the Past, the Present and the Possibilities of the Hemp Industry in Kentucky* (1905); and Richard L. Troutman, "Plantation Life in the Ante-Bellum Bluegrass Region of Kentucky" (M.A. thesis, University of Kentucky, 1955).

JAMES F. HOPKINS

HENSON, JOSIAH (1789–1883). Josiah Henson, frequently taken to be the model for Harriet Beecher Stowe's* Uncle Tom, was born at Port Tobacco, Charles County, Maryland, 15 June 1789. During his lifetime and since, contemporaries and scholars have continued to debate whether Henson did, in fact, inspire Mrs. Stowe to create the figure of Uncle Tom in her widely acclaimed *Uncle Tom's Cabin*, published in 1852. Some scholars have argued that Lewis Clarke actually served as Stowe's model. Others contended that if Henson inspired Stowe, it was in the figure of Will Clayton. Nevertheless, Josiah Henson's name remains closely linked with the original Uncle Tom.

Passing through the hands of three owners, Henson married when he was twenty-two, fathered twelve children over forty years, and labored loyally for his owners in Maryland and Kentucky. In 1830, realizing that as a Christian he could not ethically kill his owner, Henson determined that he no longer would sustain moral mistreatment and fled to Canada with his wife and four children. An early fugitive slave who reached "freedom under the lion's paw," well ahead of the larger influx of escapees, Henson always marked 28 October as the anniversary of his first reaching Canadian soil.

Henson devoted much thought to the problems of fugitive adjustment to life in Upper Canada. Beginning in 1836 he worked with Hiram Wilson to establish the British-American Institute, in effect a resettlement institute. In 1842 Henson moved to Dawn, a community of fugitive slaves,* though in the end he proved to be an ineffective leader for the community. Henson nevertheless was an able public speaker, and he came to be in great demand at antislavery rallies.

Henson's famous autobiography appeared in Boston in 1849. The first edition was written for Henson by Samuel A. Eliot, a former mayor of Boston known for his moderate antislavery stand. In part because of its unblemished simplicity, the book was an immediate success. A second edition, greatly revised, and retitled *Truth Stranger than Fiction: Father Henson's Story of His Own Life*, appeared in 1858. This and subsequent revisions were prepared by John Lobb, and it was Lobb who promoted Henson's autobiography into the best-seller that it became.

Though Henson's initial story was remarkable, fresh, and without self-serving guile, fame came to him largely because he soon was identified with the figure of Uncle Tom. Mrs. Stowe was accused by some reviewers of having allowed zeal to outrun discretion, and in 1853 she prepared *A Key to Uncle Tom's Cabin: Presenting the Original Facts and Documents upon Which the Story Is Founded* to refute her critics. It was while preparing the *Key* that Mrs. Stowe apparently first encountered Henson's narrative. In one instance she related Henson to the figure of George Harris in her novel, and on another occasion she found an "instance parallel" in Henson's book to Uncle Tom's Christian forebearance. But she never unequivocally associated Henson with Uncle Tom.

Nor did Henson ever unequivocally make such a claim, though Lobb did so for him in 1877. As a result, Henson's fame grew, and he and Lobb were received by Queen Victoria. Ultimately, legend and fact merged, and after his death in Dresden, Ontario, in 1883, Henson's home became the site of an annual celebration and "the real Uncle Tom's grave" was marked as a tourist attraction. Henson remained to his death proud, intelligent, and quick-witted. Throughout his life he had exhibited resourcefulness and independence, and though he permitted abolitionist* writers to press fictitious claims for him, he never pressed them himself. In no way, then, did he qualify for the later pejorative meaning of "an Uncle Tom."

SELECTED BIBLIOGRAPHY

John F. Bayliss, *Black Slave Narratives* (1970); Jessie L. Beattie, *Black Moses, The Real Uncle Tom* (1957); Leo W. Bertley, *Canada and Its People of African Descent* (1972); Charles H. Foster, *The Rungless Ladder: Harriet Beecher Stowe and New England Puritanism* (1954); Brion Gysin, *To Master—A Long Good Night: The Story of Uncle Tom, a Historical Narrative* (1946); Josiah Henson, *Life of Josiah Henson, Formerly a Slave, Now an Inhabitant of Canada, as Narrated by Himself* (1849); Charles Nichols, "The Origins of *Uncle Tom's Cabin*," *Phylon*, 19 (1958), 328–334; Headley Tulloch, *Black Canadians: A Long Line of Fighters* (1979); Robin W. Winks, *The Blacks in Canada: A History* (1971); and Robin W. Winks, ed., *An Autobiography of the Reverend Josiah Henson* (1969).

                                                                    ROBIN W. WINKS

HIRING OUT. The practice of slave renting reveals the elasticity and adaptability of slavery in the American South. Hiring out slaves allowed some internal flexibility in the system of slavery that may have prevented its extinction from within, while at the same time, renting and the additional freedom it brought to the slaves may have undermined the system itself.

Renting indentured servants* in the English colonies probably antedated the institution of Afro-American bondage itself. Slave hiring has been common in other cultures and at other times, such as fifth and fourth century B.C. in Athens. A slave represented a major capital investment, and when a slave's services were no longer needed by the owner, renting the slave to someone else ensured an economic return. Slave rental was present in the early eighteenth century throughout the British mainland colonies and was pervasive by the time of the American Revolutionary war. Some scholars estimate that hiring transactions occurred five to six times more frequently than did sales. The practice continued and prospered in the antebellum South and proved vital to the Confederate war effort.

Although slave rental was widespread, estimates of its extent vary. Estimates range from 5 to 10 percent of all slaves to nearly a third of urban slaves* being rented in the late antebellum period. In Richmond, the figure approached half of all slaves. Sarah S. Hughes, in a study of a rural Virginia county, estimated that at least 60 percent of the area's slaves were hired in a three-year period.

The jobs that rented slaves performed were the same as those of other slaves. One could rent field hands,* domestic servants,* miners,* or construction workers for railroads, canals, highways, and roads. Most public works were done by slaves hired out to the county or municipal government. Then, too, slave artisans* were hired to work as blacksmiths, carpenters, sawyers, coopers, wheelwrights, masons, and wagon makers. Hired slaves worked as teamsters, drovers, and stevedores; they worked in mines, iron foundries,* tobacco factories, and cotton mills.* Slave hiring was so common on the frontier that pioneers anticipated renting slaves to help open newly settled areas where the hired slaves cut timber, broke land, and drained swamps. Teenage slave children were sometimes engaged as nurses to tend children or help some elderly white person. During the Civil War, many nurses in Confederate hospitals were hired slaves. On ships and riverboats—albeit with some reluctance on the part of the slave owners who perceived these jobs as opportunities for escape—hired slaves served as sailors, crewmen, stewards, and cooks.

Slaveholders had mixed emotions about slave hiring. Frederick Law Olmsted* reported the dilemma of a Virginia planter in 1852 who had rented slaves to work at an iron furnace in Petersburg. The planter had been offered $200 for the best workers, but he pondered that hired slaves "were worked hard, and had too much liberty, and were acquiring bad habits. They earned money by overwork, and spent it for whiskey, and got a habit of roaming about and *taking care of themselves*; because when they were not at work in the furnace, nobody looked out for them." When Thomas Green Clemson, John C. Calhoun's* son-in-law, planned to rent his slave force, Calhoun thought that renting slaves was so wrong that he offered to buy them. This great defender of slavery felt that a renter had no reason to "take good care of them." Calhoun said, "The object of him who hires, is generally to make the most he can out of them, without regard to their comfort or health."

Yet many slave owners did rent out their slaves. For one thing, it was profitable. Specific profits need to be analyzed on a regional basis, but generally slave owners could expect a return of 10 to 20 percent of the local value of a male slave per year. Challenging Frederic Bancroft's thesis that vast numbers of slaves flowed from the border states to the Old Southwest, one historian suggests that it was more profitable annually to rent slaves in Maryland at a rental rate of from one-fifth to one-fourth the local sales value than to sell the slaves. Women, children, and aged slaves brought less return, while skilled hands brought more. A famed potter, such as Lewis Miles's slave, Dave Potter of Edgefield, or a noted lumberman, such as Andrew Donnan's slave, Simon Gray* of Natchez, received yearly wages that equaled the price of a slave.

Rental prices were closely tied to the fluctuations of the sale price of slaves; high slave prices* increased the demand for slave rental. Prices rose during the revolutionary period and during the 1850s and 1860s. Wars created male labor shortages and rental demands increased. During both the American Revolution* and the Civil War* the slave buyer was threatened with emancipation, so hiring a slave seemed less risky than purchasing one. Competition drove prices even higher. Even at lower rates, the master's return for "hiring out" replaced his initial investment for the slave. Thought to be a more stable investment than stocks or other items, slaves were often left to widows and orphans in wills. The beneficiary would then receive income from the rental fees.

Profit was the major motive for slaveholders to rent out their slaves, but hiring out also served social purposes. Some owners rented slaves to escape the social stigma attached to selling slaves. Others chose to rent rather than sell in order to maintain the prestigious rank of slave owner. Then, too, some slaveholders hired out slaves they considered unruly. A few planters wanted special training for a favored slave, sometimes a relative. Thus, "hiring out" served as apprenticeship to learn a trade, such as gin maker or viticulturist, to assure the rented slave higher status, some independence, and possibly eventual freedom. "Hiring out" of slaves extended the traditional boundaries of the slave community and legalized within slavery an interplantation community and network.

Renting a slave was often a prelude to purchase; the rental period could be a time of "testing" by both prospective buyer and slave. Just as selling a slave disrupted slave families,* so did renting since slaves generally were hired out as individuals. Some slaves, however, particularly children* and the elderly,* rented as a "family package," and in some circumstances owners rented slaves so that they could be with their families. It was also common to rent out the slaves belonging to estates that were being settled, the rental continuing until the legal process was completed.

Since the wealthy owned slaves, it was generally the less wealthy who rented them. Tenants and small farmers who could not afford the capital or credit to buy a slave could rent one. Rich as well as poor rented slaves with specialized skills. Horse enthusiasts rented jockeys. City and town dwellers hired slaves as domestic servants. Doctors and lawyers hired slaves to help in their offices. Southern industries* hired large numbers of slaves.

In return for hiring a slave, the employer paid a fee and promised to furnish the slave with food, clothing, and often medical care. Renters were responsible if slaves escaped, but not if slaves died, unless the renter had been negligent. Contracts specifying the details of the rental agreement were either written or spoken. Slaves were hired for various time periods; about two-thirds were hired out from 1 January to the Christmas holidays, or for one year. Often these slaves were rented at mass hirings at or around 1 January. Slave rental in the rural South is less well-documented than in the urban South, although plantation records suggest regular patterns of hiring out particular slaves for days, weeks, or months. Sometimes, in the upper South especially, ''agents'' took care of all the details of hiring in return for 5 to 8 percent of the rental fee. Some agents also received bribes from the renter and even the slave who wanted to be appointed a particular worker or employer. Richmond, Virginia, had eighteen such agents and nine commercial hiring agencies in 1860. Rental agents apparently escaped the stigma attached to slave traders.

The growth of Southern industry in the late antebellum period, primarily in the processing fields, brought the need for more and better transportation, warehouses, and other related services. This opened more opportunities for slave rental. It also bred white opposition to slave hiring. White urban workers vehemently opposed the use of rented slaves for urban industrial work; they wanted those jobs for themselves.

Planters usually were reluctant to rent their slaves to factories or lease them for other kinds of urban employment. They feared that the freer life of the towns would destroy the supposed submissiveness of their slaves, and they felt that town blacks tended to be more independent and presumptuous than rural bondsmen. Many whites opposed the practice of hiring out any slaves because they felt it gave the slaves a degree of freedom that resulted in ''bad habits.'' White opponents of slave hiring especially criticized the practice of owners permitting their slaves to ''hire their own time.''

Slaves who ''hired out their own time'' found their own employers and made their own arrangements, turning back a set fee or a percentage to their owner. Frequently these slaves found their own living quarters entirely independent of and removed from any control of a slave owner. Slaves who hired out their own time sometimes were motivated to do so in order to live with or near their families from whom they had been separated. Slaves who hired themselves out were frequently indistinguishable from the free blacks with whom they often worked and socialized. In urban areas, there was complete confusion between who was a legally free black and who was a slave hiring out his/her own time. Hirers even insisted on the same rules for governing free blacks* as those that governed the slaves they rented. Many urban whites complained about this practice. Typical of complaints was an 1846 Wakulla County, Florida, Grand

Jury report that "The subject of negroes hiring their own time, is a source of much trouble and vexation, and calculated materially to injure that species of property." Since those Afro-American slaves who hired out their own time created a place of relative freedom within the peculiar institution, opponents passed laws* that made this practice illegal; owners faced fines if not the loss of the slave. Other laws made any hiring more difficult. These laws, however, were generally ignored. Slave hiring was too profitable.

In reaction to slaves' hiring their own time, many cities instituted a badge system to control the renting of slaves. In these cities each slave hired out had to wear a badge purchased from the city government. The badge system provided revenue for municipalities, placated the white working class (especially artisans), and extended the rights of the master class to every white who came into contact with the designated rented slave.

One of the biggest controversies in the meager literature on slave renting concerns the effect of hiring on slaves and on the institution. Supported by frequent references in the WPA ex-slave narratives on the poor conditions rented slaves labored under, one group of historians argues that hired slaves were often mistreated, neglected, poorly fed and clothed, and overworked by employers who had no long-term interest in the slaves' welfare. A second group of scholars insists that being rented away from the owner was a step toward freedom. Citing many examples of concerned owners and reasonable employers, this group stresses the lessening rigidity of slavery, incentive wages, and extra money paid to the slave for "overwork."

The two historiographical viewpoints on slavery are not mutually exclusive, for the hiring out of slaves involved a paradox. Hiring out could be used as a step for freedom for individuals, as was the case of Frederick Douglass,* yet it also further entrenched slavery as an institution by providing flexibility and alternatives within the system of slavery. In addition, because an owner could rent a slave, he had less incentive for manumission.* With some additional freedom by being hired out, a slave, too, may have had less incentive for escape or sabotage. The hiring of slaves also had a practical aspect for the acceptance of the social and economic system by those who were not slave owners. By being able to hire a slave, non–slave-owning whites participated and had a stake in the slave system.

The study of slave rental provides insight into the historiographical debate* on the system of slavery. How slaves were treated as rental property, for example, sheds light on arguments about slavery's profitability and inflexibility. Eugene D. Genovese, who has argued that slavery was not a capitalistic system, framed his arguments in terms of slavery's economic irrationality. For example, he has argued that a slave owner could not adjust the size of his labor force in response to business fluctuations, that the initial capital outlay was much greater and much riskier for slave labor than for free labor, and that there was little task differentiation in the selection of slaves to match planters' needs. Yet the extent of "hiring out" suggests that slavery was never as inflexible as Genovese and some historians or economists have suggested. Furthermore, the renting of slaves is just one of several options planters had. Slaves could be sold, overworked, freed, starved, or whatever, depending on the fixed needs of the planter.

Slavery and slave renting in America lasted for over two hundred years, and former slave owners attempted to reconstitute the peculiar institution in other forms after the Civil War. In some ways, hiring out had been a rehearsal for the labor relationships following the Civil War. When whites hired or contracted with former slaves during the postbellum years, their model had been the relationships that laborer and employer had with antebellum free blacks and slaves that had been rented.

SELECTED BIBLIOGRAPHY

Frederic Bancroft, *Slave-Trading in the Old South* (1931); Charles B. Dew, "Disciplining Slave Ironworkers in the Antebellum South: Coercion, Conciliation, and Accommodation," *American Historical Review*, 79 (1974), 393–418; Clement Eaton, "Slave-Hiring in the Upper South: A Step toward Freedom," *Mississippi Valley Historical Review*, 46 (1960), 663–678; Eugene D. Genovese, *Roll, Jordan, Roll: The World the Slaves Made* (1974); Claudia Dale Goldin, *Urban Slavery in the American South, 1820–1860: A Quantitative History* (1976); Sarah S. Hughes, "Slaves for Hire: The Allocation of Black Labor in Elizabeth City County, Virginia, 1782–1820," *William and Mary Quarterly*, 3rd ser., 35 (1978), 260–286; Clarence L. Mohr, *On the Threshold of Freedom: Masters and Slaves in Civil War Georgia* (1986); Richard B. Morris, "The Measure of Bondage in the Slave States," *Mississippi Valley Historical Review*, 41 (1954), 219–240; and Richard C. Wade, *Slavery in the Cities: The South, 1820–1860* (1964).

ORVILLE VERNON BURTON

HISTORIOGRAPHY OF SLAVERY. No sooner had General Robert E. Lee's army stacked its guns at Appomattox than a new battle front emerged: the postwar polemical and historical conflict over Afro-American slavery. For much of the next century, in fact, writings on slavery fell roughly into either the old proslavery* or antislavery* camps. Following emancipation there was no loss of interest in slavery by Americans, North and South, black and white. Well over 600 books and articles on slavery were published in the years 1865–1889. Slavery also ran like a leitmotif through postbellum writings on the "Negro problem" and race relations.

Most whites, especially Southerners, revived elements of the old proslavery argument. They described slavery in genial terms and remained convinced that some variant of the old institution held the key to racial order in the postwar South. While few openly advanced the actual return to chattel slavery, one writer after another described slavery as a beneficent school where, unlike under freedom, the blacks lived in harmony with the whites. In return for the fruits of their labor, the bondsmen received adequate food, clothing, and housing. According to this new proslavery argument, slaves reaped humane treatment from their paternalistic masters. Cruel, abusive slaveholders were rare. The domestic slave trade only occasionally divided slave families. Writing in 1876, for example, novelist John Esten Cooke remarked that the Virginia slave was "well fed, and rarely overtaxed." He "was a merry, jovial musical being," who, "when his day's work was over, played the banjo in front of his cabin, and laughed and jested and danced by the light of the moon." According to Cooke, the blacks "were slaves in nothing but the word." Such statements dominated popular and polemical writings on slavery. The new proslavery argument comforted the defeated South and won many converts among conservative Northerners.

Other Northerners—especially former abolitionists, blacks, and friends of the freedmen—took exception to this rhetoric and met the proslavery barrage head on. These "neo-abolitionists" condemned slavery as a blot on American civilization and identified vestiges of the institution in the black codes of Reconstruction, and later, in sharecropping, convict labor, peonage, and the Jim Crow laws. Writing in 1883, for instance, Parker Pillsbury, an ex-abolitionist, assailed slavery as "the sublimest scourge and curse that ever afflicted the human race." He concluded that slavery "was wholesale, legalized, sanctified concubinage, or adultery, from first to last." Ex-slaves and their descendants likened the racial discrimination and proscription that surrounded them to the old peculiar institution. In 1894 Frederick Douglass* concluded that "The sentiment left by slavery is still with us and the moral vision of the American people is still darkened by its presence." Indeed, the neo-abolitionists accurately described the long-lasting influence of slavery on American racial thought. The spirit of slavery, of white domination, remained very much alive in the New South. Slavery as metaphor helped to fuel the racist reaction that enveloped the nation in the 1890s.

It was within this context that slavery emerged as a leading topic of historical inquiry. More than 2,000 slavery items, including many theses and dissertations, appeared in the period 1890–1920. Influenced strongly by the forces of nationalism, scientism, and the development of graduate training in history, scholars sought to examine the peculiar institution impartially and objectively. The so-called Nationalist historians—including Hermann E. von Holst, James Schouler, John Bach McMaster, James Ford Rhodes, and Albert Bushnell Hart—dominated historical writing on slavery at the turn of the century. They served as a bridge between the postwar polemicists and the "scientific" historians of slavery trained in these years at the Johns Hopkins University and other graduate schools.

The Nationalist historians, especially Rhodes and Hart, popularized the scholarly study of slavery and focused on the institutional features of slavery that scores of later historians would examine in more minute detail. Determined to chart a truly national history, they interpreted slavery and the Civil War* as national tragedies. While restrained in blaming the South for slavery and the Civil War, the Nationalist historians criticized slavery with the moral fervor of the abolitionists. They underscored, for example, the evils of the domestic slave trade* and the inadequate conditions of slave life. In several ways the Nationalist historians pioneered the "scientific" study of slavery. Their outrage with slavery, though couched in moral terms, was largely constitutional and theoretical in nature. Sharing the pervasive white racism of their day, they distanced themselves from the plight of the slaves as persons. Nonetheless, the Nationalist historians' obvious antislavery bias clashed with the ideal of "scientific" history. In the end, their histories served polemical ends: to counter the pro-Southern and pro-slavery polemics of their day. In doing so, the Nationalist historians were no more impartial or dispassionate than the old abolitionists or the postbellum neo-abolitionists.

"Scientific" historians at Johns Hopkins University believed that their brand of legalistic, factual history would provide the necessary antidote to partisan, sectional history once and for all. Dedicated to producing detached, unemotional studies, in 1876 Herbert Baxter Adams imported German "scientific" history to Johns Hopkins. This approach—utilizing primary sources to trace the evolution of institutions over time—seemed especially well-suited to slavery. From 1889 to 1914 students at Johns Hopkins completed fifteen monographs on slavery, seven dealing specifically with slavery in the South. In important studies, Jeffrey R. Brackett, John Spencer Bassett, James C. Ballagh, John H. Russell, and Harrison A. Trexler evaluated slavery systematically on the colonial and state level. Employing new sources, government records, manuscripts, and newspapers, the Johns Hopkins students asked fresh questions about the origins of slavery and race in North America. And breaking with previous writers, they described, not judged, the evolution of slavery's various institutional features. In sheer volume and in detail these studies brought a new scholarly dimension to the study of slavery. Graduate students at other institutions conducted state and local studies using the Johns Hopkins model.

Even so, the Johns Hopkins monographs smacked of the old proslavery rationale, contributing significantly to the image of slavery as a patriarchal, benevolent institution. Like the vast majority of whites of their generation, they agreed that blacks benefited from slavery's tutelage. Despite their dedication to "scientific" methodology, the authors ultimately failed to distance themselves from their own biases and preconceptions. Overtly legal in their emphasis, the studies tended to view blacks as things, not people, and generally interpreted slave laws as humane. Although they described these laws, the Johns Hopkins authors failed to assess or analyze whether or not the statutes were enforced. Though less moralistic in tone than the Nationalist historians, they nonetheless felt obliged to pass judgment on slavery, almost always portraying the masters as fair and generous in their treatment of the bondsmen. And significantly, the Johns Hopkins students virtually excluded economic questions from their consideration. In short, they too fell short in their quest of an objective, "scientific" history of slavery.

Among those influenced by the early Johns Hopkins studies was Ulrich Bonnell Phillips (1877–1934), who dominated North American slavery studies until the mid-1950s. In the first two decades of the twentieth century Phillips, a Georgian who earned his doctorate at Columbia University in 1902, filled the pages of scholarly journals with pathbreaking articles on slavery. Like the Johns Hopkins authors, Phillips objected to the neo-abolitionism of Rhodes and Hart. Writing in 1903, he remarked that "The history of the United States has been written by Boston and largely written wrong." But while Phillips found no fault with the proslavery bias of the Johns Hopkins studies, he nevertheless judged their narrow focus too limited and lifeless. Phillips, alone among his generation, went on to interpret slavery for the entire South as a broadly based economic and social institution.

Slavery, Phillips explained again and again, enabled white Southerners to employ the profitable plantation system, in his opinion, the agricultural equivalent of the factory of the industrial age. But slavery also provided whites with a crucial system of police control over blacks, a race that Phillips deemed backward and inert, culturally and genetically inferior. Phillips argued that slavery served as a positive force on blacks, schooling and civilizing them. He described black-white relations on the plantation as harmonious and praised slaveholders for their firm but indulgent treatment of their bondsmen. Phillips was quick to note, however, that for all its advantages for blacks, slavery saddled his beloved region with long-term economic liabilities.

In 1918, in *American Negro Slavery*, Phillips summarized his ideas regarding slavery. The product of twenty years of original research—principally in a previously unmined source material,* plantation records—Phillips depicted slavery as a benign, yet dynamic, evolving institution, one shaped largely by social and economic influences. Surpassing any previous investigator, Phillips focused on the workaday world of master, overseer, and slave. He emphasized changes in the peculiar institution over time and underscored variations in slavery from locale to locale. Unlike his contemporaries, Phillips played down the importance of slave law as a force in the plantation community. "The government of slaves was for the ninety and nine by men," he wrote, "and only for the hundredth by laws." Blacks and whites lived together in a plantation community predicated upon respect and mutual dependency. Slavery, insisted Phillips, proved unprofitable as a labor system but succeeded admirably as a social system. It "was less a business than a life; it made fewer fortunes than it made men."

Phillips added to his portrait of slavery as a humane and civilizing experience for blacks in his award-winning social history, *Life and Labor in the Old South* (1929). In both books Phillips adhered to a pro-Southern, proslavery interpretation—one that received little criticism during the age of rigid de jure segregation in the South and de facto segregation in the North. Despite his prodigious research and brilliant insights, Phillips was blinded by his racism. Because he never recognized blacks as people with human needs and feelings, he failed to appreciate that blacks suffered from slavery's harmful effects and thirsted for freedom. Phillips glossed over slavery's cruelties and indignities and ignored the significant accomplishments of the bondsmen. Though he raised important questions about slave economics, Phillips miscalculated slavery's profitability* and virtually ignored slavery on small farms.

Nevertheless, Phillips's writings, especially *American Negro Slavery*, dominated the historiography of slavery for over three decades. As the literature on slavery mushroomed (almost 13,000 slavery items were published in the period 1921–1980) Phillips's reputation remained largely intact. From the 1920s up to the post–World War II years, white scholars, despite the loud protests of black historians, turned to Phillips and *American Negro Slavery* for the definitive account of the peculiar institution. A number of historians, dubbed ''the Phillips school,'' applied Phillips's organization, sources, and interpretive model to studies of slavery on the local level. Phillips continued to reign as the master of slave historiography from 1918 until the publication of Kenneth M. Stampp's highly revisionist *The Peculiar Institution* in 1956. Even later, Phillips's interpretations continued to find their way into textbooks and lectures. The persistence of Phillips's ideas signifies both the conservative, racist climate of these decades, and the willingness of historians to define slavery in outmoded, simplistic, proslavery-versus-antislavery terms. Ultimately, the civil rights revolution of the 1950s and 1960s dethroned Phillips and ushered in the return of the neo-abolitionist approach to slavery. Phillips's blatant racism and disregard for blacks as people joined Jim Crow waiting rooms and segregated schools as discarded vestiges of an unfortunate earlier day.

Stampp's *The Peculiar Institution* appeared in the racially tense 1950s, an era when Phillips's racial and social values were under siege in every quarter of American life. Stampp acknowledged that he approached the study of slavery ''with different assumptions and from a different perspective'' than Phillips. Armed with twentieth-century advancements in the social and natural sciences, Stampp prefaced his book by saying: ''I have assumed that the slaves were merely ordinary human beings, that innately Negroes *are*, after all, only white men with black skins, nothing more, nothing less.'' Clearly declaring himself in the neo-abolitionist camp, Stampp, like Rhodes before him, described slavery in tragic terms. He challenged Phillips's interpretation point by point.

In marked contrast to Phillips, Stampp described slavery as a dehumanizing, exploitative, but highly profitable labor system. While not all masters overworked their bondsmen, Stampp insisted that the blacks themselves perceived slavery ''as a system of labor extortion.'' Slavery, he said, depended on rigid discipline to function and demanded unconditional submission by blacks to the wishes of the whites. It was a social system that continually impressed upon the slave his innate inferiority and one that sought to ''develop in him a paralyzing fear of white men.'' Far from a school, according to Stampp, slavery trained the slave to adopt the master's ''code of good behavior'' and sought to ''instill in him a sense of complete dependence.'' Under slave law ''the slave was less a person than a thing.'' Challenging Phillips's point that masters and slaves shared a paternalistic relationship, Stampp remarked that ''the predominant and overpowering emotion that whites aroused in the majority of the slaves was neither love nor hate but fear.'' Again unlike Phillips, Stampp argued that the blacks ''longed for liberty and resisted bondage as much as any people could have done in their circumstances." For all the oppression to which they were subjected, the bondsmen remained "a troublesome property," capable of both enduring and resisting. In sum, Stampp argued that "slavery had no philosophical defense worthy of the name—that it had nothing to commend it to posterity, except that it paid."

By the early 1960s Stampp's *The Peculiar Institution* clearly had nudged Phillips's *American Negro Slavery* aside. Carefully researched and deeply critical of slavery's cruelties, it became a mainstay of sorts for white liberal historians who were conscious of battling racism in every avenue of American life. But for all of his advances over Phillips, Stampp nonetheless allowed the pioneer historian to set the terms of the debate and he still approached slavery from the same ideological perspective as had the Nationalist historians. According to historian Stanley M. Elkins, "Stampp, locked in his struggle with Ulrich Phillips," failed "to disengage his mind from the debate of which he, Phillips, and Rhodes, were all a part and which they had taken over from the proslavery and antislavery debaters of ante-bellum times." In his provocative *Slavery: A Problem in American Institutional and Intellectual Life* (1959), Elkins set out to offer a new viewpoint, one free of the old debate over slavery's morality, one that focused on the slaves, not their masters, and one that assumed the equality of the races. Elkins hoped to raise new questions and draw conclusions that would hold special meaning for the post–World War II generation.

Drawing heavily on interdisciplinary insights—from comparative history, role psychology, and interpersonal theory—Elkins made two major points. First, he argued that owing to the persistence of Catholic-hierarchical traditions in Spanish and Portuguese America, slavery there was more mild, that race relations were more "open" than in British America. In contrast, Elkins said, an especially harsh, "closed" system of slavery evolved in Protestant, locally autonomous, capitalist British America. As a result, Elkins asserted that North American slavery was so oppressive that it reduced a majority of the South's slaves to childlike, docile, dependent Sambos.* He identified this stereotype in "Southern lore," which reportedly described the typical plantation slave as "docile but irresponsible, loyal but lazy, humble but chronically given to lying and stealing; his behavior was full of infantile silliness and his talk inflated with childish exaggeration." Elkins went on to claim that the Sambo personality type was analogous to the behavior of survivors of the Nazi concentration camps of World War II. He concluded that slavery so brutalized Afro-Americans that they indeed exhibited characteristics identified with Sambo.

Elkins's controversial theses, and an increased interest in the lives of the obscure and oppressed, redirected North American slavery studies in the 1960s and 1970s. For almost a century black writers and a handful of whites had stressed the Afro-American origins of black culture and slave resistance. By the 1960s, however, white mainstream historians increasingly emphasized the importance of Africanisms, slave rebelliousness, and subtle forms of day-to-day resistance. These themes, according to historian Peter Kolchin, "received fresh emphasis as early critics of Elkins sought to rebut the notion of slave docility, and in the process found it necessary to focus on the slaves more as subjects in their own right than as objects of white treatment. The effort to test—and usually to repudiate—the Sambo thesis thus brought the slaves themselves to center stage in the drama of slavery.'' In addition, historians of slavery finally liberated themselves from an outlook and from sources that viewed the slave experience through the eyes of the white master.

Increasingly, historians of the 1970s employed source materials—ex-slave autobiographies,* interviews* with former slaves, black folklore*—that placed the bondsmen, not their masters, at the focal point of the discussion. Their common focus was the lives of the slaves themselves. The new slavery scholarship examined slave family patterns, religious beliefs, folklore, resistance, and slave community behavior. In 1972, for example, in *The Slave Community: Plantation Life in the Antebellum South*, John W. Blassingame drew heavily on ex-slave autobiographies and other black testimony ''to show what it was like to be a slave.'' Penetrating the psychology of the slave quarters like no previous scholar, Blassingame challenged Elkins's simplistic typology. He argued that instead of just Sambo, slaves displayed a full range of personality types. He portrayed the typical bondsman as a resourceful, multidimensional human being. Skilled at masking his true feelings, the slave feigned humility, simulated deference, and ''used his wits to escape from work and punishment.'' As occasion demanded, he could be ''hostilely submissive and . . . obstinate, ungovernable, and rebellious.'' In the slave quarters and in stolen moments of respite, freed from the supervision of their masters, slaves emulated positive role models from within the slave community itself. They drew heavily, Blassingame explained, upon a wide variety of Afro-American cultural traditions to withstand their oppression.

The slave family,* according to Herbert G. Gutman, ranked high among those factors that enabled slaves to weather the shocks of enslavement. In *The Black Family in Slavery and Freedom, 1750–1925* (1976) Gutman revised numerous previous studies that discredited the stability of the black family. Slave familial arrangements were not nearly as fragile as previous historians and others had assumed, said Gutman. Reconstructing slave familial and kinship patterns and practices, he credited the slaves with an ''adaptive capacity'' to the troubles confronting them. Gutman concluded that the ''slaves made limited but highly significant choices affecting their social and sexual being.'' Familial norms were transmitted from one slave generation to another. The bondsmen, Gutman insisted, were deeply attached to their nuclear families. In Virginia, for example, two-parent households were most common under slavery; upon emancipation most older couples had lived together in enduring unions. Slaves, both unskilled and skilled, had long-lasting marriages.* As a result, ''young slaves everywhere learned from other slaves about marital and familial obligations and about managing difficult social realities.'' Group pressures within the slave family often enforced dominant slave patterns of courtship, sexual behavior, and mating. According to Gutman, these practices continued into the early twentieth century.

In *Roll, Jordan, Roll: The World the Slaves Made* (1974) Eugene D. Genovese identified two forces—paternalism* and Christianity—that enabled the slaves not only to persevere but "to make a livable world for themselves . . . within the narrowest living space and harshest adversity." According to Genovese, both masters and slaves accepted paternalism as the normal and proper form of class relations. Masters understood paternalism to mean "reciprocal duties within which the master had a duty to provide for his people and to treat them with humanity, and the slaves had a duty to work properly and to do as they were told." The bondsmen accepted paternalism as a dual system of reciprocal duties and reciprocal rights. "To the tendency to make them creatures of another's will," however, "they counterposed a tendency to assert themselves as autonomous human beings." In reality, says Genovese, while the masters congratulated themselves for the slaves' apparent acceptance of slavery, at most the bondsmen "had only accepted the limited protection that even slavery had to offer, while acknowledging the reality of the power over them." Throughout their captivity the slaves asserted their rights and maintained their self-respect. Significantly, explained Genovese, the slaves transformed paternalism "into a doctrine different from that understood by their masters and . . . forge[d] it into a weapon of resistance to assertions that slavery was a natural condition for blacks, that blacks were racially inferior, and that blacks had no rights or legitimate claims of their own."

Slave religion,* however, argued Genovese, was the real force that the masters had to fear. The blacks reshaped white Christianity to meet their own psychological needs. Religion promised the slaves "collective deliverance as a people and redemption from their terrible personal sufferings." Guided by their preachers, the bondsmen resisted slavery's assault and learned to value themselves, to love their fellows, and to have faith in their deliverance. In Christianity the slaves "achieved a degree of psychological and cultural autonomy and therefore successfully resisted becoming extensions of their masters' wills—the one thing they were supposed to become." Nonetheless, slave religion fell short of providing slaves with a revolutionary ideology. "It left them free," concluded Genovese, "to hate slavery but not necessarily their individual masters." Slave Christianity armed the blacks to fight a defensive struggle within the world that the slaveholders had made; "offensively, it proved a poor instrument."

The works of Elkins, Blassingame, Gutman, and Genovese clearly signaled a major redirection of slavery scholarship in the two decades following the publication of Stampp's landmark book. No longer did scholars, black or white, feel compelled to attack slavery as morally repugnant or denounce theories of black racial inferiority. Slavery's horrors and racial equality were now common assumptions. The new scholarship stressed black strength, creativity, adaptability, and survival. Reflecting, however, in 1977 upon what he termed "the new consensus" among slavery studies, historian Bertram Wyatt-Brown observed a marked trend toward deemphasizing slavery's essential brutality. Peter Kolchin reached a similar conclusion in his appraisal of slave historiography in 1985. Calling for a better balanced view of slave life, Kolchin urged historians "to take account more fully of *slavery*, which after all did impose certain constraints on those whom it touched—including the slaves." The new slave studies, explained Wyatt-Brown, focused so minutely on blacks that whites were virtually eliminated from the story. "As a result," he complained, "black bondage itself has become increasingly benign and psychologically neutral." Commenting on Gutman's account of order and stability within the slave family, Wyatt-Brown charged that the author did little more than "romanticize, to rewrite *Gone with the Wind* with black heroes and heroines instead of white." Critiquing Genovese's paternalism thesis, Wyatt-Brown remarked that plantation life in *Roll, Jordan, Roll* "seems softened in the glow of cabin hearths and roasting yams, while Simon Legree fades to the edge of the shadows."

Although slavery scholarship finally had gone beyond the confines of the old debate, critics in the 1970s faulted historians who softened slavery's harsh sides or who argued that the institution's impact on the South was minimal. They objected most stridently to a controversial two-volume work—*Time on the Cross: The Economics of American Negro Slavery* (1974) by Robert W. Fogel and Stanley L. Engerman. This highly publicized economic study denied slavery's harmful effects on the slaves and on Southern economic growth. Over the years many historians, including Phillips and Stampp, had examined the economics of slavery. But it was not until 1958, when Alfred H. Conrad and John R. Meyer employed economic models to assess slavery's profitability, that the modern study of the subject began. Building upon Conrad and Meyer's work, Fogel and Engerman studied the Southern economy by employing sophisticated econometric models, computer technology, teams of researchers, and statistics gleaned from census reports and plantation records.

Fogel and Engerman concluded that the material conditions of slave life compared favorably with those of contemporary free industrial workers. Admitting that the bondsmen were exploited by their masters, the authors argued nevertheless that "Over the course of his lifetime, the typical slave field hand received about 90 percent of the income he produced." Correcting the stereotype of Sambo, Fogel and Engerman described the average field hand as "harder-working and more efficient than his white counterpart." They also deemphasized slave breeding, sexual exploitation, and promiscuity. Instead Fogel and Engerman credited the planters with instilling in the slaves the Protestant work ethic and Victorian attitudes toward family life. Economically, Fogel and Engerman judged slaves a highly profitable investment, one from which slave owners could earn as much as a 10 percent annual return. They argued that far from leaving the South economically moribund, between 1840 and 1860 the slave-based economy grew at a faster rate than the free labor economy of the North. Fogel and Engerman went on to claim that "Economics of large-scale operation, effective management, and intensive utilization of labor and capital made southern slave agriculture 35 percent more efficient than the northern system of family farming."

While some historians in the 1980s set out to test Fogel and Engerman's conclusions, the most common recent trend has been toward detailed, microscopic case studies. Works such as Charles Joyner's *Down by the Riverside: A South Carolina Slave Community* (1984) and Orville Vernon Burton's *In My Father's House Are Many Mansions: Family and Community in Edgefield, South Carolina* (1985) have added richness and texture to the more broadly based slave studies of the last three decades. Integrating the methodologies of the historian and the folklorist, Joyner investigated slave culture on the local level, in All Saints Parish, Georgetown District, in the South Carolina low country. He concluded that the slaves creatively adapted African customs and beliefs—in crafts,* foodways, housing,* language,* naming patterns,* off times, and work patterns—to New World conditions. Burton's heavily quantified and detailed study of slave, free black, and white family life in the Edgefield District supported Gutman's earlier findings. Both before and after emancipation, Burton argued, both races were committed to the family ideal—"to the patriarchal values of the nineteenth century." The family, he wrote, "provided Edgefield blacks with the strength and confidence to cope successfully with slave conditions and to emerge from bondage after the Civil War eager to influence the course of Reconstruction." Upon their liberation, "blacks went to great lengths to solidify their families in large households and to form kinship communities of closely knit families."

These works and others have filled in considerable gaps in our knowledge of the lives of the bondsmen. Largely interdisciplinary in approach, the new slavery scholarship interprets the bondsmen as active, not passive, in shaping their own destinies. It underscores a broad and influential Afro-American cultural nexus and draws heavily on black sources (ex-slave autobiographies, oral history interviews, and folklore) and census data to document the contributions of the slaves themselves. Today's historians are especially interested in studying variations within the slave experience—differences based on changes in time and place, on varying size of slaveholdings, and on slave occupation patterns. Future research promises to illumine such questions as the varieties of slave resistance, stratification within the slave community, and differences between American slavery and other systems of unfree labor.

SELECTED BIBLIOGRAPHY

David Brion Davis, "Slavery and the Post–World War II Historians," *Daedalus*, 103 (1974), 1–16; Charles B. Dew, "The Slavery Experience," in John B. Boles and Evelyn Thomas Nolen, eds., *Interpreting Southern History: Historiographical Essays in Honor of Sanford W. Higginbotham* (1987); Stanley M. Elkins, *Slavery: A Problem in American Institutional and Intellectual Life* (1959); Peter Kolchin, "American Historians and Antebellum Southern Slavery," in William J. Cooper, Jr., Michael F. Holt, and John McCardell, eds., *A Master's Due: Essays in Honor of David Herbert Donald* (1985);

Orlando Patterson, "Slavery," *Annual Review of Sociology*, 3 (1977), 407–449; John David Smith, *An Old Creed for the New South: Proslavery Ideology and Historiography, 1865–1918* (1985); John David Smith, ed., *Black Slavery in the Americas: An Interdisciplinary Bibliography, 1865–1980* (2 vols., 1982); William L. Van Deburg, *Slavery and Race in American Popular Culture* (1984); Bennett H. Wall, "African Slavery," in Arthur S. Link and Rembert W. Patrick, eds., *Writing Southern History: Essays in Historiography in Honor of Fletcher M. Green* (1965); Peter H. Wood, " 'I Did the Best I Could for My Day': The Study of Early Black History during the Second Reconstruction, 1960 to 1976," *William and Mary Quarterly*, 3rd ser., 35 (1978), 185–225; and Bertram Wyatt-Brown, "The New Consensus," *Commentary*, 63 (1977), 76–78.

JOHN DAVID SMITH

HOLBROOK, FELIX (ca. 1743–ca. 1794). Felix Holbrook was born in Africa about 1743. Enslaved before his tenth birthday, and delivered to a Boston auction block from a Massachusetts slaver around 1750, he served schoolmaster Abiah Holbrook's family for "upwards of twenty-five years." In the 1770s, the well-educated servant who did day labor for a living, unsuccessfully petitioned both royal and revolutionary Massachusetts governments to obtain freedom for the state's 5,000 slaves. Soon after Abiah Holbrook's widow freed him early in the American Revolutionary war, he removed to Providence, Rhode Island. He completed a six-month enlistment in the Rhode Island Regiment. Later he joined like-minded black nationalists in founding the Providence African Union Society, a mutual aid/emigrationist organization that planned an expedition to Sierra Leone. The expedition failed to get off.

Felix Holbrook's name on a petition to the Massachusetts government dated 6 January 1773 requesting emancipation for himself and the "many slaves, living in the Town of Boston, and other Towns in the Province" secures his place in history, for the Boston slave transformed black protest in America by giving it a political dimension. Studded with screaming punctuation marks, Holbrook's indictment blasted the regional conceit that held New England slavery to be "mild," and revealed its essence—social death. He wrote: "Neither [slaves], nor their Children to all Generations, shall ever be able to possess and enjoy any Thing, no not even *Life itself*, but in a Manner as the *Beasts that Perish*. We have no property! We have no Wives! No children! We have no city! No Country!"

This first black collective plea for freedom to an American legislature demonstrates with rage and irony that during the American Revolution* Boston bondsmen had successfully appropriated their patriot masters' political tools, the ad hoc committee and the petition, as well as their political rhetoric. Holbrook, for example, compared unfavorably chattel bondage with the gentler yoke of colonial subordination, couching the analogy in strict Lockean language. The ambitious agenda that followed included compensated emancipation and state funding for a free black Christian commonwealth, either in Massachusetts or Africa. Although rejected at the time by white officialdom, Holbrook's analysis and prescription were enthusiastically embraced in numerous black urban New

England strongholds during the "first emancipation" of the late eighteenth century, and his program survived as the foundation for future incarnations of American black nationalism.

SELECTED BIBLIOGRAPHY

Herbert Aptheker, ed., *A Documentary History of the Negro People in the United States* (1951); and Jay Coughtry, "Creative Survival: The Providence Black Community in the 19th Century," in *Creative Survival: The Providence Black Community in the 19th Century* (1984).

JAY COUGHTRY

HORTON, GEORGE MOSES (1797?–1883?). George Moses Horton, born in Northampton County, North Carolina, was the only slave to publish volumes of poetry while in bondage and the first black man to publish any book in the South. Owned by William Horton and his heirs, George taught himself to read, and in 1817 he began a career as the "Colored Bard of North Carolina" at the university in Chapel Hill. Students paid Horton to compose love verses for their ladies; then, from the early 1830s until his emancipation in 1865, Horton hired his time* and worked full-time as poet, handyman, hotel waiter, and servant at Chapel Hill. In the 1830s he married a slave of Franklin Snipes and had a son, Free Snipes, and a daughter, Rhody.

For thirty years, Horton's patrons conducted several futile campaigns for his manumission, while his poems and letters also pleaded for freedom. The twenty-one poems in *The Hope of Liberty* (1829) were transcribed for him—he learned to write only in 1833; later he published *The Poetical Works of George M. Horton, The Colored Bard of North Carolina* (1845) and *Naked Genius* (1865) with over 150 new poems. Horton's poems on his bondage, poetic art, religion, love, nature, and everyday events vary in quality; the best show skillful use of meter and rhyme, firm control over content, sensitivity to language, and hearty enthusiasm for life.

In 1866, Horton left his family to live for seventeen difficult and lonely years in Philadelphia, where he died at age eighty-five.

SELECTED BIBLIOGRAPHY

M. A. Richmond, *Bid the Vassal Soar: Interpretive Essays on the Life and Poetry of Phillis Wheatley (ca. 1753–1784) and George Moses Horton (ca. 1797–1883)* (1974); Joan R. Sherman, *Invisible Poets: Afro-Americans of the Nineteenth Century* (1974); and Richard Walser, *The Black Poet: Being the Remarkable Story (Partly Told My [sic] Himself) of George Moses Horton, a North Carolina Slave* (1966).

JOAN R. SHERMAN

HOUSE SERVANTS. It is difficult to particularize about slave house servants before the abolition of indentured servitude* and Northern slavery in the early nineteenth century. One problem is terminology. Eighteenth-century Americans usually referred to both indentured servants and house slaves as "servants," which makes it difficult to distinguish one from the other in surviving records. Africans served infrequently as house servants in English colonies before the mid-seventeenth century. Only as indentured servitude for blacks came to mean slavery, and as more blacks gained a knowledge of English customs, manners, and language, did the number of black domestics increase. Black house servants proved equally popular in Northern and Southern colonies, even though the numbers of blacks in the former could not compare with those in the latter. By 1700, for example, New York claimed the largest black population in the Northern colonies (2,256), with blacks representing 12 percent of the colony's total population. Virginia, by comparison, had seven times that number (16,390), representing 30 percent of its population. Still, the proportion of slaves who resided in Northern towns, where the majority of slaves labored as house servants, grew steadily during the eighteenth century. This suggests that a higher proportion of Northern slaves worked as house servants, the larger Southern black population being more heavily engaged in agriculture.

By the nineteenth century, house servants accounted for approximately 20 percent of the slave population, but the geographic distribution of house slaves is difficult to determine. The largest numbers were found in areas with the highest concentrations of slaves, but with some exceptions. Towns and cities always had higher proportions of house slaves than nearby plantations. A large town-house usually had three to six servants, nearly as many as a plantation with fifty to a hundred slaves. Cities like Charleston, Louisville, Mobile, New Orleans, Norfolk, Richmond, and Savannah accounted for large numbers of the house servant population in their respective states. Likewise, parts of the rural South with uncharacteristic clusters of large plantations, such as the Natchez district, tidewater Virginia, and the low country of South Carolina and Georgia, had large concentrations of house servants.

The work of house servants varied. Few colonial or antebellum slaves could claim the degree of specialization (front parlor maid, upstairs chambermaid, and so on) found in large retinues of post–Civil War house servants. Household staffs of a dozen or more servants existed, but the wide range of chores and lack of labor-saving machines required that all servants perform numerous tasks. In any case, most nineteenth-century servants, black or white, slave or free, labored singly or in pairs. Most females, even when three or four labored in the same household, were "maids-of-all-work," a very descriptive title, for these women could be called upon to do anything remotely associated with the house, including gardening, milking, and tending chickens. They even worked in the fields during the peak seasons of planting and harvesting. Men, too, filled numerous roles. A butler might double as coachman or gardener; a waiter labored not only at table but as a footman, handyman, and errand boy. The only true specialist might be the cook, whose special skills required training and practice.

Housework was not as grueling as life in a canebrake or a cotton field, but its unceasing nature took a toll on the slaves in the Big House. House servants were perpetually "on call." They might be summoned from meals or awakened in the night to serve. Sundays, when most field hands* could relax, found domestics dressing the white family for church, greeting visitors, and washing dishes. Moreover, domestics worked under the ever-vigilant eye of masters and mistresses. They labored under a psychological pressure unknown to other slaves. This contrasted sharply with the fairly regular hours, privacy, and even horseplay that characterized life in the fields. As one slave woman, who gave up housework for the fields, explained, "I was tired livin' in de house where dey wasn't no fun." No other member of the slave community experienced so many daily reminders of his or her subservient status.

The demands on their time, the nature of their work, and their proximity to the white family created a unique and controversial relationship between house servants and masters. Tradition has it that masters treated house servants more tolerantly and accorded them more privileges than other slaves. In this view, the rough edges of slavery were worn down by personal bonds of respect, concern, and affection between maid and mistress, valet and master. In truth, the relationship between house servants and masters could be warm and affectionate. Domestics lived in the midst of the white family. No overseers or drivers interpreted the master's orders, whims, and desires. No intermediaries diminished personal contact. Kindly masters could gain respect by this arrangement, just as petty, tyrannical masters might be identified by their behavior. Yet the slave's personality* also affected relations. Even considerate masters could not win the devotion of naturally bumptious, rebellious types. Likewise, slaves predisposed to passivity and meekness would only be further intimidated by tyrannical masters. They might give the appearance of perfect service without feeling a particle of genuine attachment.

Regardless of their relationship with masters, regardless of the pressure of their environment, house servants could receive benefits for their labor unknown to other slaves. House servants generally obtained better food,* clothing,* and housing* than other slaves. Even when not provided these benefits, house servants enjoyed excellent opportunities to obtain things like food and clothing surreptitiously. "Good" servants—that is, those slaves whom whites identified as people of moderate intelligence who learned white ways, remained unobtrusive, performed their functions without constant scolding, and acquired what one Georgian vaguely referred to as "a house look"—gained additional advantages. They could occasionally be impertinent without suffering punishment.* They were the slaves least likely to be sold or separated from their families. Good house servants were rare finds, and masters did not sell them or brutalize them on whim. Servants in large households also had opportunities for upward mobility. Where some specialization of tasks was recognized and a marked hierarchy of occupations existed, servants could gain "promotion" from waitress to cook, chambermaid to nurse, or footman to valet.

The size of a farm, plantation, or household could affect treatment of house slaves. Masters with small numbers of slaves (and nearly half of all slave owners in 1850 owned fewer than five slaves) perhaps tended to treat their slaves more leniently than large slave owners, mainly because masters with two or three slaves rarely felt threatened by violence at the hands of their own slaves. Moreover, because of the inconvenience of establishing a separate "community" for two or three workers, slaves in small households, whether in town or country, generally ate the same food as the white family and received tolerant treatment. Such advantages were less likely on a large plantation, where order and discipline stood as primary concerns. On the other hand, large households and slave communities promised greater material benefits plus the advantages of family security and identification with a prominent family.

The status of house servants within the slave community and their relations with other slaves are other controversial issues. Traditionally, both masters and slaves recognized house servants as an upper class in the slave world. However, recent interpretations modify this impression of rigid class lines by stressing camaraderie, a "sense of brotherhood," between field hands and domestics. They suggest that the lack of sharp divisions between household labor and outdoor labor, the desire of slaves to escape the psychological pressure and constant supervision of the Big House, and extensive communication between house servants and non–house servants often encouraged close ties between house and field. It is also true that criteria other than occupation determined status. Proof of loyalty to the slave community, rather than to the white family, was important. Opportunities for geographic mobility were desirable. So, too, were the chance to make money, the ability to read and write, and freedom from white supervision. House servants fared better in some of these categories than in others. Lack of freedom from white supervision obviously put them at a disadvantage. House servants might also have a hard time proving their loyalty to the black community, their close association with the white family being a natural cause for suspicion. On the other hand, many house servants could read and write, and some categories of servants, especially valets and ladies' maids, enjoyed trips away from the household.

One must bear in mind, too, that a large portion of house servants were in no position to put on airs. A house servant on a farm or small plantation with only a handful of other slaves would not react in the same manner towards her fellow bondsmen as a cook on a plantation with a hundred or more hands. Even on a large plantation, where a slave community of fifty or more people would contain only about five house servants, the issue of "class" would be important only on rare occasions. More to the point, tens of thousands of house servants worked in towns and cities,* where they formed the bulk of the slave population, and where they had little contact with field hands or other unskilled or common laborers. All in all, the question of status remains elusive.

The Civil War* revolutionized black-white relationships, but it changed the world of the Southern household worker only slightly. When slaves became free servants and masters became employers, both blacks and whites had to adjust. Yet the nature of household labor and the employer-servant relationship kept servants in a subservient position less removed from slavery than any other occupation. Workers even retained the name "servant," a word Southerners had used traditionally in place of "slave." Whites and free blacks had always despised household service as a lowly occupation. Freed slaves, even those who had once recognized certain advantages to life in the Big House, soon adopted the same attitude. Domestic service became a last resort for blacks who could not obtain other employment.

Still, the new regime did not please white Southerners, who had lost a serious degree of control over their servants. They began to imagine the antebellum years as a golden age of household service. Southern authors and politicians incorporated their fancy into a mythologized, stereotyped "Old South," in which nearly all slaves—discounting an occasional Nat Turner—responded to universally benevolent masters with affection and loyalty. House servants were remembered as the most affectionate and loyal of all, and the finest examples of black-white relationships during slavery. This image prospered in Southern legend and literature for over a century. Even historians accepted the largest part of the myth for nearly a half century, and wholesale revision did not begin until the 1960s.

SELECTED BIBLIOGRAPHY

John W. Blassingame, "Status and Social Structure in the Slave Community: Evidence from New Sources," in Harry P. Owens, ed., *Perspectives and Irony in American Slavery* (1976); Paul D. Escott, *Slavery Remembered: A Record of Twentieth-Century Slave Narratives* (1979); Eugene D. Genovese, *Roll, Jordan, Roll: The World the Slaves Made* (1974); Lorenzo J. Greene, *The Negro in Colonial New England, 1620–1776* (1942); C. W. Harper, "House Servants and Field Hands: Fragmentation in the Antebellum Slave Community," *North Carolina Historical Review*, 55 (1978), 42–59; Edgar J. McManus, *A History of Negro Slavery in New York* (1966); Randall M. Miller, ed., *"Dear Master": Letters of a Slave Family* (1978); Julia Cherry Spruill, *Women's Life and Work in the Southern Colonies* (1938); Robert S. Starobin, ed., *Blacks in Bondage: Letters of American Slaves* (1974); Daniel E. Sutherland, "The Servant Problem: An Index to Antebellum Americanism," *Southern Studies*, 18 (Winter 1979), 488–503; Daniel E. Sutherland, "A Special Kind of Problem: The Response of Household Slaves and Their Masters to Freedom," *Southern Studies*, 20 (1981), 151–166; Edward R. Turner, *The Negro in Pennsylvania: Slavery-Servitude-Freedom, 1639–1861* (1911); Richard C. Wade, *Slavery in the Cities: The South, 1820–1860* (1964); and Arthur Zilversmit, *The First Emancipation: The Abolition of Slavery in the North* (1967).

DANIEL E. SUTHERLAND

HOUSING. Slave houses were once an integral part of the Southern rural landscape. In such houses lived the majority of the population of many plantations, and frequently the majority of entire counties. It is, however, now difficult to imagine slave homes with historical accuracy, for they were typically built of impermanent construction, were rarely preserved, and were inadequately documented in manuscripts, drawings, or photographs.

When Africans arrived in America, they did not enter an alien world in which their traditions of construction and design had no use. Instead, the preindustrial cultures of Europe, Africa, and native America shared similar forms of building construction and design, thereby permitting Africans to continue to utilize their own traditions, albeit in a new and often hostile environment. With only a limited supply of white labor in the colonial South, it often became the job of the slaves to construct the houses, public structures, and farm buildings. Yet, as slaves, they were under pressure to build in ways compatible with their masters' tastes and interests, and they blended their own traditions with European skills and designs, passing on the synthesis to the next generation.

Afro-American housing evolved over the years, the product of Afro-American creativity, on the one hand, and the forcible constraints of a dominant culture, on the other. As a result, the few nineteenth-century slave houses that survived hardly exhibit overt African characteristics. Yet an examination of African traditions* suggests that these later-built survivals did spring from less visible, African-derived traditions and were not as foreign to their inhabitants as they might appear.

Because construction was a cooperative endeavor in traditional African societies, involving the labor of entire villages or extended families, most Africans who came to America had considerable experience in design and construction. As one eighteenth-century African declared in regard to the traditional construction of his homeland, "Every man is a sufficient architect for the purpose." Among the building skills Africans brought to America were brick and stone masonry, thatching, and variations of wattle and daub, frame, and log construction. Women participated as well, being especially skilled in the application of decorative finishes on the interior and exterior.

Traditional house forms in West Africa exhibited a rich diversity—round, oval, square, rectangular—with rooms varying in size, usually from ten to twenty feet or more in length or diameter. Some houses were freestanding; others were joined or clustered in a compound. There was no standard type or size of dwelling across all West Africa. But there was a strong degree of uniformity within the same ethnic group and more or less within the same geographical or environmental region. As a result, if large numbers of the same ethnic group or region arrived in the same area in America, the prospect of their continuing their customs in some form was enhanced. Such was the case in the coastal region of the lower South, where slaves apparently modeled floor plans after ones in their homeland. On the other hand, if Africans from different backgrounds arrived and were dispersed in small lots, the opportunities for the retention of distinct African housing traditions were more tenuous, as was the case in the colonial Chesapeake region and in the Northern colonies.

In most cases during the seventeenth and early eighteenth centuries, slaves in British North America tended to live in quarters dispersed about the farm, rather than in a slave community. The preponderance of adult males in the slave population prevented the recreation of African communal patterns. Their quarters were typically lofts of barns, farm buildings, or extra rooms in the main house, or perhaps the attic or basement. But with the increase in the native slave population over the eighteenth century, the male-female ratio equalized and two-parent slave households developed. These developments required the construction of specific houses as slave quarters.

Slave quarters became an integral component of the plantation complex in the Southern low country. Typically, the quarters were located behind the planter's house. On farms with only a few slave households, slave dwellings were usually within a short distance of the "main house." On large plantations, house servants* and artisans* tended to live near the main house or their workplace in separate quarters from field hands. Their quarters were often aligned with other outbuildings or dependencies, forming a design element of the plantation complex. They were also more likely to be of frame or brick construction and more finished inside and out than were slave quarters. Field hands* generally lived near the fields where they worked. A stable or barn, a corn crib, and perhaps a granary also formed part of the quarters complex. The field hands' houses were typically aligned along a lane or "street" more or less equidistantly spaced. Nearby or along the lane was the house of the overseer or slave foreman. Field hand houses typically had a swept dirt yard, and also might have a chicken coop, hog pen, and/or vegetable garden enclosed by paling fences a short distance behind the houses.

In design, slave houses were typically small, plain, freestanding dwellings, one story in height, with a gable roof and chimney exterior to one gable end. Their floor plan usually consisted of one room down and a loft above, with one door centered in the long wall, and perhaps one or two windows on either side of the door, one in a gable end, or no windows at all. There were some examples of two-unit (double-pen) houses that consisted of two identical rooms on either side of a central chimney with back-to-back fireplaces, each room having its own front door. In coastal South Carolina such houses had dimensions similar to Yoruba houses in Nigeria, indicating the retention of distinct African house forms in a region with a strong black majority.

Another type of double-pen dwelling common to the lower South was the dog-trot house. This design consisted of two rooms of equal size divided by a wide passageway open at each end for cross ventilation and joined by a common roof. Yet another type found especially in the lower South was the shotgun house, which was at least two rooms in depth, with the gable end serving as the facade. Such houses may have been derived from Yoruba floor plans. Two-story houses or dormitories for slaves in rural areas were quite rare, though there are extant examples at Stagville plantation near Durham, North Carolina, featuring two rooms down and two up, each room heated by a gable-end fireplace and presumably housing one family each.

In keeping with African traditions, slaves used the yards around the house as additional "rooms." Especially in hot weather, they cooked and washed laundry in the backyard, and in the front engaged in such social activities as playing music and games, dancing, and swapping stories and the news among family and neighbors. Often a shade tree provided a "roof" for this outside "room."

Slaves customarily constructed their own houses and frequently built the main houses of plantations. They usually built the slave quarters of logs, but there were numerous frame examples, especially towards the end of the antebellum era, and a few examples of stone or brick. In the coastal South slaves built houses of tabby, a composite of equal parts of sand, lime, shell, and water. The word *tabby* is African in origin, and the technique was presumably introduced by Africans.

On both large and small plantations, from the mid-eighteenth century onward, the most common type of slave house was the single-unit log cabin. Its design and floor plan, in general, were similar to those of the houses of antebellum white tenants and landowners of limited means, the home of Abraham Lincoln being the most celebrated. Indeed, it is ironic that the log cabin, the house type associated in American iconography with the frontier and the rise of democracy, served also as the principal house type of slaves.

Log cabin construction proliferated in the slave South because the housing was made from locally available material at practically no cost, was quick and relatively easy to build, and was durable. Its thick walls, if properly chinked with cohesive mud daubing (a technique well practiced in Africa), provided insulation from cold weather, and its thick log walls made it less flammable than the frame houses.

To construct the log houses, slaves used skills transmitted from one generation to the next. Slaves learned to "read the woods just like a book" and knew the types and forms most appropriate for construction. Among the types found in surviving houses are chestnut, pine, poplar, and oak. Using a pole ax, broad ax, and/or adze, they hewed the logs, removing the sapwood to expose the resilient heart wood, and notched the logs at the corners to join them. With the aid of family and friends, the builders raised the logs into place, often joining them with vertical pegs passing from one log to another. Interstices between the logs were in-filled with stones or boards and thickly plastered inside and out with a wet clay mixture. Inside, the floor was typically of dirt, which was made as hard as cement by pounding or molding a claylike mixture, a technique developed in Africa. If the site was not properly drained, the floor could become quite damp, and in some cases as "miry as a pig sty." Windows might be cut into the walls and covered with wood shutters, rarely with glass panes. Typical chimneys were built of wood and clay (hewn logs, boards, or wattle and daub, depending upon the builder) and plastered thickly with clay to insulate the wood from heat, with a firebox lined with stones. Chimney fires were common, and rain barrels were kept nearby as a result. Construction materials for roofs varied and included wood shingles, planks, and thatch. In many houses a loft was created by laying planks over the upper joists; this room, accessible by ladder or corner stairs, served as sleeping quarters for children. To finish out the house, many slaves whitewashed their house inside and out, brightening the interior and protecting the wood from insect infestation and decay.

Frame, stone, and brick houses represented the "top of the line" in housing for slaves. Such houses were usually occupied by house servants or artisans and rarely by field hands, except on larger and wealthier plantations. Like log houses, brick, stone, and frame dwellings were typically single-unit, one-story structures with a chimney exterior to one gable end. Though of one room, they usually had more floor space, were more "finished" in appearance, and were more likely to have brick or stone chimneys, and plank floors rather than earthen ones, and customarily had larger windows with glass panes that provided more light inside and more control over ventilation than wood shutters. In general, they provided more comfortable living conditions than log quarters. Like log houses, these dwellings were usually constructed by slave carpenters or masons.

Housing for slaves in urban areas* differed substantially from that in rural areas. Most slaves in towns and cities were domestic servants living in the houses of their masters or in outbuildings or single or multiunit dwellings of wood or brick construction behind the main house. Slaves working as artisans or laborers lived in or near their workplace, often inhabiting tenement-style quarters. Towards the late antebellum era the practice of boarding slaves in rented rooms increased, sometimes with free blacks, and contributed to the establishment of predominantly urban communities.

Furnishings in slave houses on plantations were sparse and, for the most part, utilitarian. They were generally made on the plantation by the families themselves, slave artisans, or even the overseers. In slaves' houses on late antebellum plantations the principal furnishings would likely include bedsteads, usually made by slaves, typically consisting of a plank frame with a plank or rope bottom. Quilts commonly served as bedcovers over cornshuck mattresses and as pallets for children, who frequently slept on the floor. Around the hearth were found cooking utensils for open hearth cooking, such as Dutch ovens, skillets, skewers, and heavy pots suspended from cranes. Nearby were barrels or crockery pots used for storage of water, molasses, weekly rations (typically corn meal and smoked pork), as well as dried or pickled vegetables or meat procured by slaves to supplement their diet. Hanging from the ceiling joists or stored in crocks were dried herbs and roots used for cooking and medicinal purposes. In the middle of the room stood a dining table, usually of plank, typically with benches for the children and chairs for the parents at each end. A simply designed pie safe or homemade chest cabinet served for storage of dinner and kitchen ware. A rocking chair, bureau, or trunk, homemade or second hand from the main house, would complete the principal furnishings. Everyday clothes typically hung from nails on the walls. Furnishings for slaves on isolated farms or in newly developed regions were invariably less abundant and more crude than those described.

Though sparse in appearance, slave houses were enlivened as places for family entertainment, and this was reflected in the furnishings. Children's playthings included marbles, tops, "mumble pegs" and handmade dolls. Musical instruments* included the African-derived banjo, the fiddle, or mouth harp. Hand-crafted artifacts of special significance or beauty might also be present, especially in low-country settings, for slaves wove baskets, produced clay pots and face jugs, braided colorful rag rugs, carved wooden figures and walking canes, and created other examples of folk* art that expressed their creativity and personalized their homes.

Artifacts of ordinary appearance were also used in special ways and endowed with unique qualities. For example, to bar evil spirits, a conjurer's horseshoe, root, or other device might be hung over the door or placed elsewhere. A washpot was central to clandestine religious services throughout the South. Inside the house or out, slaves turned the washpot upside down and gathered around, for it allegedly "caught the sound" so the master could not hear them as they worshiped.

Slaves lived in a variety of quarters: from crudely built shacks to well-crafted log or frame houses, from lofts of farm buildings and rooms in the main houses to urban tenements. For many slaves, cramped, uncomfortable, and unhealthy living conditions resulted in severe strain on personal and family life. But slaves did not simply submit to a completely passive role; rather, they used their repertoire of traditional skills—a synthesis of African, European, and American techniques—to construct or furnish houses in ways that required a considerable measure of expertise. Using primarily materials at hand and techniques passed down from generation to generation, slaves "made do." Indeed, slave houses, like black music, decorative arts, and dance, reflect the improvisational nature of Afro-American culture. Slaves used creatively what was at hand to make their houses into more than just structures. The slaves created homes, thereby enabling themselves to survive the rigors of bondage.

SELECTED BIBLIOGRAPHY

Carl Anthony, "The Big House and Slave Quarters: Part II, African Contributions to the New World," *Landscape*, 21 (1976), 9–15; John W. Blassingame, *The Slave Community: Plantation Life in the Antebellum South* (rev. ed., 1979); Eugene D. Genovese, *Roll, Jordan, Roll: The World the Slaves Made* (1974); Charles Joyner, *Down by the Riverside: A South Carolina Slave Community* (1984); George W. McDaniel, *Hearth & Home: Preserving a People's Culture* (1982); John S. Otto, *Cannon's Point Plantation, 1794–1860: Living Conditions and Status Patterns in the Old South* (1984); and John M. Vlach, *The Afro-American Tradition in Decorative Arts* (1978).

GEORGE W. MCDANIEL

HUGUENOTS. Between 1680 and 1695 some 2,000 French Protestants—"Huguenots"—arrived in America fleeing religious persecution in France and dismal futures in European exile centers like London. They arrived in the same decades that large numbers of English mainland colonists first acquired slaves. As young tradesmen, artisans, and unskilled laborers, Huguenot refugees had no previous experience with slavery. Yet they vigorously embraced this newly developing American institution.

Like English colonists, Huguenots used slavery for personal economic gain. Between 1685 and 1710, Huguenots purchased captured Africans to bring them headrights to thousands of acres of land in South Carolina. As a result, 90 percent of Huguenot estates there contained slaves; average estates contained some 25 slaves and large ones counted upwards of 400 slaves. Huguenots also supported slavery in New York. By 1703 half of New York's Huguenot households contained slaves. Huguenots purchased enough slaves to make New Rochelle 18.9 percent black by 1698, and they held these slaves even past 1800, despite slavery's general decline in the colony after 1740.

Huguenot slaveholding outlasted knowledge of its harm to Africans. A New York City layman, Elie Neau, founded the first slave school in British America, but, like other humanitarians, never demanded slavery's abolition, and Huguenot owners suffered retribution from angry slaves during New York City's slave disturbances in 1712 and 1741* and South Carolina's 1739 Stono Rebellion.* In all its features, then, slaveholding became a major feature of rapid Huguenot Americanization and a telling sign of slavery's extraordinary appeal in late seventeenth-century America.

SELECTED BIBILIOGRAPHY

Jon Butler, *The Huguenots in America: A Refugee People in New World Society* (1983); Jon Butler, ed., "Les 'hymnes ou cantiques sacrez' d'Elie Neau: un nouveau manuscrit de 'grand mystique des galères,' " *Bulletin de la société de l'histoire du protestantisme français*, 124 (1978), 416–423; Sheldon Cohen, "Elias Neau, Instructor to New York's Slaves," *New-York Historical Society Quarterly*, 55 (1971), 7–27; David Brion Davis, *The Problem of Slavery in Western Culture* (1966); Peter H. Wood, *Black Majority: Negroes in Colonial South Carolina from 1670 through the Stono Rebellion* (1974).

JON BUTLER

HUMOR. Humor helped to make life in slavery liveable. It was prominent in the essentially serious Brer Rabbit and other animal tales and, in varying degrees, it pervaded the entire body of black folklore*—songs, sayings, proverbs, rhymes, and riddles. Its most familiar vehicles were anecdotes, "lies" (tall tales), and stories about the quasi-mythical John, the black superman who could confound not only the white man but the Devil himself; he personified the idea of "making a way out of no way." In nonmythic stories, John was often the name of the central black character, portrayed as trickster or simpleton.

In the master's presence, slave humor was defensive and ingratiating—an instrument of appeasement or appeal. In the confidentiality of the slave quarter, humor was suffused with a spirit of resistance. Slaves could laugh sincerely at the foibles, posturings, hypocrisies, and vulnerability of their masters, and they could laugh critically at themselves and each other. Whatever its artful pretext or genuine cause, laughter was an effective palliative for the injuries to body and psyche which bondage inflicted, and a medium for articulating hopes and fantasies of freedom.

The content of slave humor grew directly from the material conditions and social relationships of the peculiar institution. Its dominant theme—that of the powerless but nimble-minded overcoming the merely powerful—was expressed in stories running a wide gamut of situations and behavior which involved lying, stealing, sabotage, malingering, or running (from punishment or toward freedom).

The slaves in many stories were motivated by a chronic yearning for food, not merely to add substance and savor to their limited rations but to recapture, in small part at least, the fruits of their ill-rewarded labor. Stories also abound in which slaves obliquely but effectively rebuked their masters. Such indirection is still described as "hitting a straight lick with a crooked stick." Religion was a subject for humorous consideration in an extensive repertory of stories about slaves and, on occasion, masters, whose prayers produced ironic or ludicrous results. A related category of anecdotes made indulgent fun of preachers and believers and derided the religious pretensions of the slave owners.

As a group to which literacy was forbidden, slaves placed high value on skillful, imaginative use of the spoken word. This ability, characteristic of the Afro-American culture as a whole, is especially evident in the telling of "lies" and in the specialized form of humor known as "the dozens." The latter, of African origin, is a contest in which two adversaries exchange slanders, mostly sexual, about each other and about each other's relatives. It has been well known since emancipation, but no doubt it also was practiced in slavery.

No sharp dividing line separates slave humor from black humor of subsequent periods. Analogous situations and relationships have produced analogous humor. New events have generated new subjects and new treatments. In the present, as in the past, Afro-American humor remains a creatively expressed perception of the difference between things as they are and things as they ought to be.

SELECTED BIBLIOGRAPHY

B. A. Botkin, *A Treasury of Southern Folklore* (1949); J. Mason Brewer, "John Tales," in *Mexican Border Ballads and Other Lore* (1946); Langston Hughes and Arna Bontemps, eds., *The Book of Negro Folklore* (1953); Zora Neale Hurston, *Mules and Men* (1935); Lawrence W. Levine, *Black Culture and Black Consciousness: Afro-American Folk Thought from Slavery to Freedom* (1977); William Pickens, *American Aesop, Negro and Other Humor* (1926); and Philip Sterling, *Laughing on the Outside* (1965).

PHILIP STERLING

I

IMMIGRANTS. Americans usually associate the term *immigrant* with Europeans who lived and labored in Northern urban areas and the term *slave* with Africans who toiled on Southern plantations. Initially, however, both white and black newcomers engaged in unskilled agricultural labor as indentured servants,* predominantly in what became the American South. They often worked side by side in the fields and in the coal, iron, and other industries. Both groups were abused by their masters and experienced devastating death rates. While indentured whites and Africans constituted the bulk of the labor force throughout the colonial period and represented the majority of unskilled workers in many areas of the nation until the Civil War, starting in the seventeenth century distinctions related to race divided the labor force. By the end of the colonial era the Southern work force was predominantly black and slave and that of the North overwhelmingly white and free.

In the past scholars focused on the role of white attitudes in relegating people of African descent to perpetual bondage. Contemporary scholarship, however, stresses the importance of the profit motive in the creation of a caste-based labor system in the Southern colonies. Improved wages and living conditions for unskilled workers in England along with decreasing opportunities for freed servants in the New World made the decision to migrate less and less attractive to whites. By the mid-seventeenth century in Virginia and thereafter in all the British North American colonies, Negroes were held in servitude for unlimited terms, and there was no means by which word of harsh or arbitrary treatment could reach their homelands or affect the future flow of labor. Even though white planters and others preferred to have Europeans work with and under them, by 1690 slaves outnumbered servants among unfree workers in the Chesapeake colonies, and as early as 1710 in some regions slaves dominated the labor force. Where slavery became widespread, blacks were assigned to unskilled field labor and whites to skilled and supervisory positions. As the indentured system declined in the eighteenth century, American-born slaves were trained, often by white servants, to do tasks once performed by Europeans. The gradual transformation of the Southern labor force from a biracial, to a racially stratified, and eventually to a predominantly black one made the South proportionately less appealing to immigrants.

Slavery and indentured servitude existed in the Middle and New England colonies, but the relatively low level of marginal productivity of labor in most of these areas resulted in primary reliance on free domestic labor. In the colonial and early national periods white immigrant and black workers tended to engage in similar productive activities, although free blacks* were typically paid less than native and foreign-born whites. With the resumption of immigration after the Napoleonic Wars, however, white newcomers began to displace Northern blacks from occupations they had previously shared and even from those which blacks had dominated. Competition between Afro-Americans and Irish and German immigrants led some aliens to join native white workers in opposing the spread of slavery in the 1840s and 1850s. Likewise, during the Civil War many criticized the Lincoln administration and participated in draft riots. The hostility of many white newcomers, combined with black suspicion of those with alien ways and resentment at being displaced from jobs and housing, fostered a disposition among Afro-Americans to distrust and fear immigrants, especially the Irish.

In the antebellum South, as in the North, contact between blacks, free and enslaved, and immigrants was increasingly an urban phenomenon. By the 1850s in many Southern cities Northern-born workers and blacks made up over 90 percent of the working class. The willingness of immigrants to do tasks viewed as "nigger work" by native whites and the high price for bondsmen in rural areas stifled the expansion of urban slavery* but did not undermine it. Even though Europeans pushed blacks out of some occupations, they often saw slavery as an impediment to improved wages and working conditions. Consequently, some foreign-born workers supported the largely unsuccessful attempts of native white artisans to secure legislation which would exclude blacks from access to higher paid trades.

Although rivalry between blacks and immigrants exacerbated race relations in early America, it is easy to exaggerate the extent and importance of conflict between Afro-Americans and recently arrived whites. Since early in the eighteenth century slaves and immigrants typically lived in quite separate worlds. The relatively few who came into direct contact often labored and lived together without friction. Much of the angry rhetoric from each group regarding the other was directed in part to native whites who had created and maintained racial and class divisions which contributed to the subjugation of black Americans and immigrants. Furthermore, some immigrants befriended blacks and condemned the institution of slavery. Likewise, Afro-Americans found qualities in the experiences of Jews and to a lesser extent of all immigrant groups that inspired them in their struggles.

SELECTED BIBLIOGRAPHY

Richard N. Bean and Robert P. Thomas, "The Adoption of Slave Labor in British America," in Henry A. Gemery and Jan S. Hogendorn, eds., *The Uncommon Market: Essays in the Economic History of the Atlantic Slave Trade* (1979); Ira Berlin and Herbert G. Gutman, "Natives and Immigrants, Free Men and Slaves: Urban Workingmen in the Antebellum American South," *American Historical Review*, 88 (1983), 1175–1200; David W. Galenson, *White Servitude in Colonial America: An Economic Analysis* (1981); Claudia Dale Goldin, *Urban Slavery in the American South, 1820–1860: A Quantitative History* (1976); Randall M. Miller, "The Enemy Within: Some Effects of Foreign Immigrants on Antebellum Southern Cities," *Southern Studies*, 24 (1985), 30–53; Jay Rubin, "Black Nativism: The European Immigrant in Negro Thought, 1830–1860," *Phylon*, 39 (1978), 193–202; and Fred Siegel, "Artisans and Immigrants in the Politics of Late Antebellum Georgia," *Civil War History*, 27 (1981), 221–230.

DAVID J. HELLWIG

INDENTURED SERVITUDE. Indentured servitude first appeared in use in mainland North America by 1620. The system, which was developed by the Virginia Company as a solution to the problem of how colonial planters could obtain a hired labor force, effectively allowed English workers unable to afford the cost of passage to America to borrow the necessary funds. In return for transportation to the colonies the migrants signed "indentures," or contracts, that bound them to repay their debts by working for colonial planters for specified periods of years. Servitude soon became a central institution in the economy and society of many parts of colonial British America; it has been estimated that between one-half and two-thirds of all white immigrants to the British colonies between the Puritan migration of the 1630s and the American Revolution came under indenture. During the colonial period, indentured servitude therefore enabled between 300,000 and 400,000 Europeans to migrate to the New World.

Men predominated among the servants throughout the colonial period. The age group most heavily represented among both sexes in the servant population was that of the late teens and early twenties. In the seventeenth century most of the servants bound for British America were English. Few came in families. Analysis of their occupations suggests that they were drawn quite evenly from a broad cross-section of English society, including significant numbers from all major economic groups below the gentry. In the eighteenth century large components of the servant population came to be made up of Scottish, Irish, and German immigrants.* Many of the Germans came as redemptioners. Rather than signing an indenture in Europe, redemptioners would promise to reimburse a ship's captain for their passage; if they were unable to raise this amount within two weeks of arrival in America, they would be sold as indentured servants for the necessary sum. This system was often used by families of German immigrants. During the eighteenth century approximately 30,000 British convicts were also sentenced to transportation to the colonies, and were sold to colonial planters as indentured servants.

In addition to passage to the colonies, servants were provided maintenance during their terms and were given specified freedom dues at their conclusion. The contract, which stated the length of the servant's term and his colony of destination, was typically signed by the servant and a merchant in a European port; the contract was then sold to a colonial planter upon the servant's arrival in America. The duration of the contracts varied considerably, from a normal minimum of four years for adults to terms as long as ten or more years for minors. All servants incurred debts of similar value in emigrating to the colonies and sold claims on their future labor to repay these debts. Servants whose labor was more valuable could repay these debts more quickly, and individual characteristics that raised the expected productivity of a servant in the colonies therefore shortened the term for which the servant was bound. Surviving collections of servant contracts reveal that older servants tended to receive shorter terms than younger ones, and that skilled and literate servants received shorter terms than the unskilled and illiterate. Servants who agreed to serve in the West Indies received shorter terms than those bound for the mainland colonies. Mortality rates were generally higher in the islands than on the mainland, the gang labor of sugar cultivation was harsh, and the densely populated islands offered relatively little opportunity for former servants to obtain land of their own after the conclusion of their terms; consequently servants had to be given an inducement to travel to these less desirable destinations.

The presence of active markets for indentured servants both in Europe and in the colonies provided a consistent link between European labor supply and the labor demands of colonial planters from the 1620s through the time of the American Revolution. The economic role of indentured labor changed considerably during the course of the colonial period, however, and in many places the evolution of the functions of servants was closely related to the growth of black slavery.

Indentured servants were quantitatively most important in the early history of those colonies that produced staple crops for export. The primary demand was for unskilled laborers to grow the staple, and initially sugar planters in the West Indies and tobacco* planters in the Chesapeake Bay region relied on white indentured labor to grow their crops. In addition, as colonial output and wealth increased, there was a growing demand for skilled workers to build houses and farm buildings, to make the hogsheads to ship the crops, and to perform a variety of other crafts, and skilled servants were imported to do these jobs.

Over time, as conditions for bound workers deteriorated in some colonies and economic conditions improved in Europe, it became more expensive to attract indentured workers to the colonies. By the middle of the seventeenth century, planters in Barbados found African slaves a less expensive source of unskilled agricultural labor than additional indentured Europeans, and the same became true throughout the English West Indies and the southern mainland colonies by the end of the century. Planters responded by substituting slaves for servants, and the majority of the bound labor forces in these regions changed from white to black.

The transition from servants to slaves was initially only partial, however. Although blacks were substituted for whites in field labor, colonial planters continued to import skilled white servants to perform skilled crafts, and in many cases to act as plantation managers and supervisors of the slaves. A racial division of labor by skill therefore characterized an intermediate period in the growth of the labor forces of staple-producing colonies during the late seventeenth and early eighteenth centuries.

Yet this was not the final phase of development. Further increases in the cost of white labor prompted colonial planters to have their slaves trained in skilled trades, often by white servants. Although the timing of this process differed across colonies, by the middle of the eighteenth century most large plantations throughout the staple colonies relied almost exclusively on slave labor. By the time of the American Revolution the English West Indies had ceased to import white servants, and indentured labor had dwindled to only marginal importance on the mainland.

Indentured servitude finally disappeared from the United States in the early nineteenth century. The use of indentures to facilitate migration to the Americas had not ended, however. The abolition of slavery in the English West Indies in the 1830s produced a renewed demand for indentured labor. Whereas the indenture system had earlier involved the immigration of Europeans to the Americas, in the nineteenth century it was Asia that furnished American planters with a supply of bound labor. An estimated total of 775,000 Indians and Chinese arrived in the West Indies and parts of South America between the 1830s and 1917, when the legal use of indentured servitude in the Americas came to an end.

Entry into an indenture involved a substantial sacrifice of freedom for a migrant. In colonial America a master normally had an unrestricted right to determine the work his servant was to do, and local courts would enforce this right. Servants' living conditions were similarly controlled by their masters, and servants could marry during their terms only with their masters' permission. The treatment of servants varied considerably, depending on factors including the attitudes and wealth of their masters, the sizes of the plantations they worked on, the kind of work they did, and their region of destination. Servants on small farms in the early colonial period might live under the same relatively meager conditions as the families of their masters, whereas skilled servants on large plantations in the eighteenth century were often paid wages and treated substantially better than the many slaves who made up the bulk of their master's labor forces.

Unlike slaves, servants had important basic legal rights. Servants could bring suit in colonial courts, their testimony was accepted on the same basis as that of free men, and they were legally entitled to hold property. Colonial courts were concerned with upholding the conditions of servants' indentures against abuses by masters. Colonial laws protected servants from excessive corporal punishment, and masters who killed their servants would be tried for murder, although masters were permitted considerable latitude in beating their servants.

Servants normally appear to have been provided for and treated decently by their masters, in large part because their labor was a valuable asset. Yet servants had little control over their conditions of work during the years of their terms, and their ability to make decisions about most aspects of their lives in that time was severely circumscribed. As a result, even many migrants accustomed to societies in which the rights of workers were limited relative to those of their employers might have been reluctant to enter into the long-term indentures. Yet one of the major consequences of the settlement of North America, and the use of the continent's natural resources, was the promise of extraordinary economic opportunity for workers. This promise provided an attraction sufficiently powerful to encourage hundreds of thousands of prospective settlers from Europe and Asia over the course of three centuries to enter indentures, voluntarily giving up much of their freedom for a term of years in the hope of improving their economic and social condition in the New World.

SELECTED BIBLIOGRAPHY

David W. Galenson, "The Rise and Fall of Indentured Servitude in the Americas: An Economic Analysis," *Journal of Economic History*, 44 (1984), 1–26; David W. Galenson, *White Servitude in Colonial America: An Economic Analysis* (1981); and Abbot Emerson Smith, *Colonists in Bondage: White Servitude and Convict Labor in America, 1607–1776* (1947).

DAVID W. GALENSON

INDIANS. The history of Indians who lived in the southeastern United States is intimately linked to that of Afro-American slavery. Indians suffered enslavement and worked alongside slaves of African ancestry on Southern plantations. The westward expansion of the Cotton Kingdom precipitated the eviction of Indian nations from their homelands and removal west of the Mississippi. Furthermore, some native Americans became planters and masters of black slaves.

At the time of European contact, a few people whom whites called "slaves" lived in most Indian societies. These slaves were war captives who had escaped the usual fate of torture and death. Unlike some captives, the slaves were not adopted into clans but lived instead on the fringe of society. They worked with their captors in clearing and planting fields or scraping and tanning deerskins. They did not, however, form the bulk of the labor force. Most southeastern Indian societies lived at the subsistence level. Every person had to work to survive, and as a consumer, the slave promised little economic reward.

The arrival of Europeans and, in particular, the demand for labor in the Southern British colonies dramatically changed aboriginal slavery. Indians began to sell war captives instead of torturing, adopting, or keeping them. Whites also began enslaving Indian prisoners for use in the tobacco* and rice* fields or for export to the West Indies. Exactly how many Indians were enslaved is unknown, but in a recent work, J. Leitch Wright, Jr., speculated that the number reached "tens of thousands." Wright also suggested that the enslavement of so many Indians had a significant genetic and cultural impact on American slavery. Because the number of Indians enslaved was so great, it is inaccurate to think of slaves as overwhelmingly African in ancestry. Crafts,* music,* folktales,* and other aspects of slave culture* may have had native American origins. In addition, Indian captives, who came from matrilineal societies, may have been responsible in part for the position of women* in slave families.

By the mid-eighteenth century, however, Indians began to distance themselves from Afro-Americans. Southern society was becoming strictly biracial, and Indians avoided, if possible, classification as black. Whites usually concurred. The Indian population had been so depleted that it no longer provided many slaves. Furthermore, a number of white traders had married Indian women, and their descendants began to play a significant role in white and Indian society.

The Indian offspring of white traders as well as some prominent Indian hunters and warriors began to emulate the life-style of wealthy whites in the late eighteenth century. Such a life-style provided an opportunity for achievement at a time when the traditional male avenues to success—hunting and war—were being closed by encroaching colonists and the U.S. native pacification policy. These men began to produce and market an agricultural surplus or to engage in other lucrative enterprises. They prohibited their wives and daughters from laboring in the fields, as was traditional in Indian culture; instead, they purchased black slaves to cultivate their fields and perform other manual labor. In the early nineteenth century, four Southern Indian nations—the Cherokee, Chickasaw, Choctaw, and Creek—came to be dominated by these native slaveholders, who also promoted other aspects of Anglo-American culture including centralized government and formal law codes largely to protect property rights. These nations became known as the "civilized tribes" because they were so adept at imitating Anglo-American culture, a culture whose hallmark in the South was plantation slavery.

Anglo-American culture did not have as great an impact on the Seminole, the fifth of the "civilized tribes." The Seminole were Creek refugees from the War of 1812* who had fought against the United States and its Creek ally. They fled to Florida where they joined with other native peoples to resist the United States. With the Seminole were many slaves who had been seized during the war from white and Indian masters. In Florida, these bondsmen acquired considerable autonomy. Runaway slaves* augmented their number, and these Seminole blacks fought valiantly on the Indian side in the Second Seminole War (1835–1842),* a conflict caused by the federal government's attempt to relocate the Florida Indians and their slaves west of the Mississippi.

In the 1830s, the United States did succeed in removing the "civilized tribes" to territory in what is today the state of Oklahoma. Most Indian planters took their bondsmen with them to their new homes, but a few, such as the Choctaw

Greenwood LeFlore who went on to a successful career in Mississippi politics, remained on their plantations in the East. When they arrived in the West, the Indian nations reestablished their governments and laws. Legislative councils enacted slaves codes which varied in severity.

When the federal government finally managed to remove the majority of the Seminole from Florida, a major problem developed. The government reasoned that since Seminole and Creek had been one people before the War of 1812, they could share territory in the West. The Seminole refused because they feared for the safety of their blacks. The Creek had paid whites for the loss of slave property during the war, but the Seminole had taken many of these slaves with them to Florida. Because they had paid for the slaves, the Creek believed that they were entitled to them. The Seminole disagreed, and they worried that the Creek would seize their blacks as soon as they entered the Creek Nation. Consequently, they refused to leave the Cherokee Nation where they had disembarked. The Cherokee complained that the freedom enjoyed by the Seminole blacks had an adverse effect on their own bondsmen and attributed a slave revolt in the early 1840s in part to Seminole influence. Finally, the United States arranged for a separate Seminole Nation.

Among all the Southern Indian nations, some people opposed the adoption of Anglo-American culture, including plantation slavery. These factions were particularly strong among the Creek and Cherokee in the decade before the Civil War. With encouragement of the white Baptist missionary Evan Jones, Cherokee traditionalists organized the Keetowah society. While its general aim was cultural revitalization, the Keetowahs had strong abolitionist and unionist sentiments. Proslavery Confederate sympathizers among the Cherokee organized the Knights of the Golden Circle and began recruiting troops even before the Cherokee Nation negotiated a Confederate alliance. These activities compelled chief John Ross to abrogate treaties with the United States and become a Confederate ally. The other Southern Indian nations pursued a similar course.

One of the initial tasks assigned Cherokee soldiers was the capture of the Creek traditionalist Opothleyohola and his followers who were attempting to flee the Confederate Creek government and take refuge in Kansas. Many Cherokee traditionalists refused to battle Opothleyohola and instead joined his flight to Kansas.

The Civil War* produced internecine warfare among the Southern Indians. In some respects, the factions went back to the removal era, but slavery also was an issue. Slaves, after all, were a sizable proportion of the population, and their fate rested on the outcome of the war. In 1860, 8,376 slaves lived in Indian territory and comprised 14 percent of the total population.

Following the Civil War, the United States negotiated treaties with the five Southern Indian nations which provided for the abolition of slavery and the extension of citizenship to freedmen. The latter provision was particularly important for freedmen because Indians held their territory in common, and any citizen was permitted to use unoccupied land. Indian freedmen, therefore, automatically had an economic base denied most former slaves in the white South. When the Indian nations were dissolved and their land allotted to individuals at the turn of the twentieth century, Afro-Americans received titles to their property.

The aboriginal landholding pattern which endured among Southern Indians until the late nineteenth century is only one example of how traditional native culture tended to ameliorate some aspects of the slave experience. Race* was not a native American concept; racism was learned from Europeans and only gradually permeated Indian culture. Furthermore, an egalitarian, nonacquisitive way of life characterized Southern Indian societies into the eighteenth century and was still widespread in the twentieth century. The harshness of slavery among the Indians, therefore, tended to depend on how acculturated the master was, that is, how thoroughly he had adopted the values of the white South. The persistence of native culture probably explains why the former slave Henry Bibb,* who had belonged to both Cherokee and white masters, insisted: "If I must be a slave, I had by far, rather be a slave to an Indian than to a white man."

SELECTED BIBLIOGRAPHY

Annie Heloise Abel, *The American Indian as Slaveholder and Secessionist* (1915); Michael F. Doran, "Negro Slaves of the Five Civilized Tribes," *Annals of the Association of American Geographers*, 68 (1978), 335–50; Daniel F. Littlefield, Jr., *Africans and Creeks: From the Colonial Period to the Civil War* (1979); Daniel F. Littlefield, Jr., *Africans and Seminoles: From Removal to Emancipation* (1976); Daniel F. Littlefield, Jr., *The Cherokee Freedmen: From Emancipation to American Citizenship* (1978); Daniel F. Littlefield, Jr., *The Chickasaw Freedmen: A People without a Country* (1980); William G. McLoughlin, "Red Indians, Black Slavery and White Racism: America's Slaveholding Indians," *American Quarterly*, 26 (1974), 367–385; Theda Perdue, *Slavery and the Evolution of Cherokee Society, 1540–1866* (1979); and J. Leitch Wright, Jr., *The Only Land They Knew: The Tragic Story of the American Indians in the Old South* (1981).

THEDA PERDUE

INDIGO. Because the indigo plant (*Indiofera*) never was cultivated in Europe, until the beginning of the sixteenth century European dyers were forced to rely upon domestic woad (*Isatis tinctoria*) as a source of blue coloring matter. After 1500, however, indigo became available to Europeans through trade with the East Indies, and by 1670 it had replaced woad. The Spanish introduced indigo culture to America, and in the 1650s both the French and English developed indigo plantations in the West Indies. A little more than a century later commercial production of indigo had shifted almost entirely to the Western Hemisphere.

Towards the end of the seventeenth century indigo production in the British West Indies declined, due largely to displacement by the more profitable sugar industry. England thus was compelled to rely largely upon the French West Indies for its supply of the dye. Attempts at indigo culture were made in several of England's mainland colonies. A small amount was first produced in South

Carolina in the 1670s; the Huguenots there marketed some in the 1690s; and evidence suggests that small amounts were still being grown in the 1720s. Finally, in the 1740s, indigo emerged as an important export staple in South Carolina. Indigo became a commerical staple in Georgia in the 1750s and spread to British Florida after the French and Indian War. But neither Georgia nor Florida ever came close to rivaling South Carolina's production.

The rapid growth of the indigo industry in South Carolina resulted from several factors. From 1739 to 1748 war cut off England's indigo supply from the West Indies. George Lucas, lieutenant-governor of Antigua and owner of plantations in South Carolina, was among the first to see the possibilities of indigo as a great agricultural staple for South Carolina. He sent seed and encouraged his daughter Eliza (the future Mrs. Charles Pinckney) to experiment with the growth of indigo. After several years of experimentation, Eliza demonstrated that the Bahama, or Guatemala, variety of indigo adapted well to the climate and soil of South Carolina. In 1744 Patrick Cromwell, an indigo maker sent by Lucas from Montserrat, made a small quantity (seventeen pounds) of good dye from that year's crop. By then others also had become interested in indigo culture. In 1744 South Carolina merchant Robert Pringle wrote from Charleston that "a pritty many Persons are going upon it to make it [indigo]." A large supply of native seed was also harvested and the *South Carolina Gazette* soon was filled with advertisements of seed for sale and instructions on how to grow and manufacture indigo.

Depression in South Carolina's rice industry* caused planters to search for a new staple, and after 1748 a parliamentary bounty on indigo provided an additional stimulus to the infant industry. In 1749–1750 South Carolina exported over 138,000 pounds of indigo, and by 1775 exports from Charleston exceeded one million pounds. Significantly, rice and indigo complemented one another. Where soils were suitable for both, indigo could be cultivated and manufactured during slack periods in rice culture. And because planting and harvest periods for the two crops were different, a planter could grow both rice and indigo at the same time. Indigo also thrived on marginal land that proved unsuitable for rice.

Blacks from some regions of Africa, such as the Gold Coast, were long familiar with several crops later grown in South Carolina, including indigo. Many Africans were imported from those parts of Africa principally for that reason. Indeed, blacks were among the first to grow and manufacture indigo in South Carolina. In 1744, when Cromwell made seventeen pounds of dye from the indigo grown by Eliza Lucas, another South Carolinian, Andrew Deveaux, reported the sale of "a hundred weight . . . made by one of his own Negroes." In July 1745 George Lucas contracted to send Nicholas and Patrick Cromwell back to South Carolina. Nicholas was assigned to the Lucas plantation as "Indigo Planter or Overseer, obliging himself to directly and fully Instruct Two Negroes . . . in the manner of planting and making Indigo and in the Building of such [indigo] Works" for a period of three years. Charles Pinckney immediately wrote Lucas, saying that he had "ordered 15 of the hands to go under his [Cromwell's] direction to make Corn and Indigo." Without the labor of blacks neither rice nor indigo would have become major staples in South Carolina.

Indigo culture in South Carolina declined sharply during the American Revolution.* The embargo on exports to England, the loss of the British bounty, destruction resulting from military action, and the flight of thousands of blacks contributed to the decline of indigo production during the Revolution. Production slowly recovered after the war due primarily to the reopening of the British market. England imported almost two million pounds of indigo in 1792.

Despite this recovery, America's indigo industry virtually collapsed by 1796, due largely to competition from India. In 1779 the East India Company initiated indigo production in Bengal with phenomenal success. Employing Bengali labor, and aided by British bounties and tariffs, British-Indian planters produced vast amounts of indigo both higher in quality and lower in price than the American product. With a broken market and strong competition from British East Indian indigo, South Carolina and Georgia planters turned their attention to cotton, a crop that grew especially well on former indigo lands.

SELECTED BIBLIOGRAPHY

David L. Coon, "Eliza Lucas Pinckney and the Reintroduction of Indigo Culture in South Carolina," *Journal of Southern History*, 42 (1976), 61–76; Lewis C. Gray, *History of Agriculture in the Southern United States to 1860* (2 vols., 1933); Daniel C. Littlefield, *Rice and Slaves; Ethnicity and the Slave Trade in Colonial South Carolina* (1981); G. Terry Sharrer, "Indigo in Carolina, 1671–1796," *South Carolina Historical Magazine*, 72 (1971), 94–103; Peter H. Wood, *Black Majority: Negroes in Colonial South Carolina from 1670 through the Stono Rebellion* (1974); and C[harles] W[oodmason], "The Art of Manufacturing Indigo in Carolina: General Observations on the Quality of Indigo, with Rules to Know the Best," *Gentleman's Magazine*, 25 (1755), 256–258.

G. MELVIN HERNDON

INDUSTRIAL SLAVERY. The colonial period in American history preceded the accelerating impact of the industrial revolution in the United States, but industrial slavery existed in the American colonies. Chronic scarcity of labor, both skilled and unskilled, was a characteristic of the United States until the late nineteenth century. Slavery was one means of resolving this problem of economic development (which is not to say that advocacy of slavery did not have other motives as well). By the 1830s and 1840s, when the industrial revolution began having a marked impact upon the Northern United States, other factors were confining slavery to the antebellum South, where it was more applicable in supplying labor to an agricultural setting.

Even though the antebellum South's economy and the system of slavery associated with it were predominantly agricultural, by the 1850s about 200,000 bondsmen, or 5 percent of the total slave population, worked in industry. Most slaves employed in industry were men, although women and children also worked in nonagricultural positions. The textile,* hemp,* and tobacco* industries were most likely to use children and women in the slave labor force, but both were used in a wider variety of demanding industrial jobs. The nature of antebellum Southern industry was such that most industrial slaves lived in rural or small-town environments rather than in larger Southern cities. As Southern industry developed, however, more of it moved from rural beginnings to cities such as Richmond.

The depression in the cotton economy of the late 1830s and through the 1840s spurred Southern industrial development and the record of that development is, with some exceptions, the source material for current understanding of the use of slave labor in industry. An important exception to this general statement is the development of industry in the South that accompanied the conduct of the Civil War. A history of industrial slavery in the Old South is therefore best seen as the application of an available labor institution to incipient industrial devel-opment rather than a conscious extension of the institution itself. Indeed, as Clement Eaton observed, "the development of cotton mills in the ante-bellum South was socially more significant than the rise of any other industry, for it pointed the way to utilizing the labor of the poor whites in factories."

The Southern effort to bring the cotton mills to the cotton fields was under-standable, given the importance of cotton to the Southern economy. Entrepre-neurs established Southern mills in three waves: in the 1790s, following the War of 1812, and in the 1840s. The latter period was the most significant, occurring at a time when cotton was selling at the lowest price in American history. North Carolina initially led the development of this industry in the South. As the textile mill boom leveled off in the 1850s, Georgia became the leading Southern textile state. William Gregg of North Carolina and others who promoted the develop-ment of textile mills did so primarily with an eye toward the employment of poor whites, especially women and children. The geographical location of mills on the fall line of the piedmont away from the largest concentrations of slave population reinforced the tendency of the mills to employ whites. However, many mills employed slave labor exclusively or combinations of free and slave workers. By 1860 Southern cotton and woolen mills together employed more than 5,000 slaves.

Unlike the textile industry, the tobacco factories of the South employed slaves as their principal labor force. Tobacco manufacturing was centered in Virginia and North Carolina and expanded into Kentucky and Missouri in the 1850s. Most tobacco factories worked fewer than fifty hands, but a trend toward larger labor forces continued throughout the antebellum period. One Richmond man-ufacturer employed 150 slaves. By 1860 Richmond housed over fifty factories, Lynchburg nearly as many, and Petersburg some twenty establishments. By the outbreak of the Civil War, the tobacco industry included some 15,000 slaves.

Another industry that made great use of slave labor was the manufacture of iron.* The Southern iron industry consisted mostly of small companies operating charcoal-burning furnaces and forges in the rural areas of the piedmont and mountains of Virginia, South Carolina, Alabama, Tennessee, Kentucky, and

Missouri. Northern competitors outstripped Southern pig iron production by the 1850s, but the Southern industry remained important in its local impact. The Tredegar works in Richmond had even broader importance. By 1860 this firm had the third largest ironworking labor force in the United States and the largest labor force in Richmond. Many iron-making establishments worked large numbers of slaves. Tredegar employed some 450 slaves in 1861, half of its total labor force. In the 1840s Senator John Bell of Tennessee had 365 bondsmen at work in his business. Other firms employed more than 100 black workers. An estimated 10,000 slaves worked in ironworks in the South by the close of the antebellum period.

Various mining* enterprises also employed slaves. The Southern coal industry was widespread in the Appalachian and Cumberland mountains but small in total volume. Mining concerns extracted gold in North Carolina and Georgia, copper in southeast Tennessee, lead in Virginia and Missouri, and salt* in Virginia and Louisiana. In 1854 Virginia, the South's largest producer of salt, employed 1,230 male and 67 female salt boilers, most of whom were slaves.

Other industrial concerns that employed slaves were lumbering and turpentine extractors, sugar refineries, rice and gristmills, hemp and cordage manufacturers, agricultural machinery producers (especially cotton gins), steamboat, canal, and railroad companies, and shipbuilders. In addition, slaves held almost every conceivable unskilled or semiskilled job in the antebellum economy, as well as numerous skilled positions.

Industrial concerns employed slaves in these nonagricultural pursuits in two basic ways: direct ownership and hiring.* Robert S. Starobin, who made the first extensive analysis of industrial slavery, estimated that about 80 percent of all industrial slaves were owned directly by employers with the remainder rented from masters by the month or by the year. Which pattern of employment predominated in a given instance appears to be the result of local factors, not clear patterns of preference within a particular industry. Generalizations about recruitment practices, working conditions, mobility, and productivity and profits across a broad range of industries over a span of over fifty years are difficult. The reader should consult articles on specific industries elsewhere in this volume for further information.

The principal question about employment practices is the extent to which the hiring out of slaves worsened work conditions surrounding their existence. Slavery as a labor practice had many psychological incentives for being an inhumane institution, counterbalanced by an owner's profit motive invested in slaves as property. Slave owners were impelled by their investment in slave property to protect that property's life and limb. Hiring out distanced that concern one further step and contributed to employers' seeing slaves even more as a factor of production than as human beings. Slave owners, of course, sometimes resorted to legal agreements with industrial employers, specifying terms of employment and working conditions for hirelings. Most hiring agreements, however, lacked detail, specifying only length of employment and amount and terms of payment. Case studies reveal mixed evidence of cruelty and marginal accommodation.

Industrial slaves no doubt endured worse working conditions than agricultural slaves. Nature imposes some annual, cyclical conditions on agriculture that cannot be pressed, a fact less true in industry. The push for profits in industry led to twelve- to sixteen-hour days, six—sometimes seven—days a week. Some industries—sugar milling and large-scale fishing, for example—were seasonal, with extremely harsh working conditions for concentrated periods of time. Other industries—mining and iron production, for example—were less seasonal and demanded long hours and round-the-clock shiftwork for over 300 days a year. Primitive machinery and the yet physically intensive nature of industrial development of the antebellum period added to the already harsh, subsistence-level conditions of slavery as an institution. Exposure to weather, wild animals, and poisonous reptiles were everyday dangers in such industries as lumbering, mining, and construction work. Fires and explosions were threats in mines, mills, distilleries, and steam-powered operations. Unless an industrial slave worked in a business that processed food, access to more than a basic diet of corn, pork, and molasses was limited. Long work hours limited relief through seasonal gardening, as did the urban locales of some industries. Clothing, housing, and medical care also tended to be minimal. Conditions could vary widely, however, depending upon locale, industry, owner/employer, and economic conditions in a given year.

The extent to which slaves resisted such adverse conditions and the incentives used to motivate them to produce in spite of adversity are controversial issues. The former is more difficult to measure than the latter. Slave resistance* varied from subtle measures, such as "carelessness," feigned illness, slowdown, and theft, to active measures, such as refusal to work, vandalism, arson, and escape. All forms of such resistance are documented but difficult to assess quantitatively. A little noticed fact is that leaders of the few slave insurrections—Gabriel Prosser,* Denmark Vesey,* Nat Turner,* and others—had been trained as skilled laborers.

The basic measures for disciplining slave workers resembled those used in agricultural settings: routinization of daily work; religious indoctrination; badge and pass systems; allotment of food, clothing, and housing; and close supervision by employers and foremen. Restrictions, whippings, and worse beatings were more extreme measures. In addition, employers used incentives such as holidays and cash or in-kind payments for extra work to promote increased, or at least timely, production. The use of holidays varied by industry. The seasonal nature of sugar refining often eliminated even Christmas celebrations. Masters/employers completely controlled payment systems, which functioned as additions to work demanded as a condition of slavery, not as a substitute for it. There is little, if any, evidence to suggest that payment systems were progressively replacing slavery as an institution.

The chronic labor shortage affecting antebellum economic development that contributed to the maintenance of slavery also contributed to the use of slaves in skilled labor positions. The extent to which slaves were used as skilled laborers is difficult to quantify, but abundant examples of such use may be found. Slave artisans and craftsmen* generally enjoyed privileges: better clothes, more food, greater freedom. Slave artisans worked directly for masters, were hired out, or, in some cases, had freedom to work when and where they could by returning all or a portion of their earnings to their masters. The latter case illustrates that limited upward mobility existed within the industrial slavery system. Skills gave slaves some bargaining position with masters. On the whole, of course, mobility decisions were in the hands of masters, who could assign duties and promote as they chose. Some slaves became managers of labor forces. Some became trusted lieutenants of their owners. Some operated with virtual independence in such matters as buying, rafting, and selling lumber and building bridges and performing other construction work.

White workers often resisted such slave advances, since the latter threatened the former both economically and socially. But one example of white resistance to skilled slaves occurred in 1847 at the Tredegar Iron Works in Richmond, when white puddlers refused to work with blacks. The Tredegar labor force, however, was successfully integrated after this incident. In areas where white artisans were well-organized, such as Charleston, resistance to slave labor was recurrent. Free white resistance to slave labor, however, was most common during periods of economic stagnation when wages were depressed and available jobs were less numerous.

Determining the profitability* of firms employing slave labor and the productivity, or effectiveness, of that labor is extremely difficult due to the fragmentary survival of records and the infancy of antebellum concepts of cost-accounting. Starobin, whose study of industrial slavery dominates the field, drew several conclusions about these questions. Starobin believed that industries and transportation projects employing slaves could expect under normal operating conditions to earn reasonable profits. He also concluded that available evidence indicated that slave labor ''was not less efficient'' than the free labor that was available in the antebellum South and that the maintenance of slave labor cost much less than payment of wages to free workers. The use of women and the elderly and young of both sexes in a variety of tasks helped the slave owner/ employer hold down labor costs in order to compete with older, more efficient industrial locales in the Northern United States and in Europe. The use of slaves rather than free supervisors also lowered the cost of that important function. Business managers often applied the costs saved on slave labor to securing skilled foreign or Northern technical expertise in such industries as textiles, mining, iron production, and heavy construction. Entrepreneurs also used slave property as investment capital. Planters, for example, could supply labor to fledgling industrial enterprises in exchange for stock in those enterprises.

The reader should remember that industrial slavery, as interesting a topic as it is, represented a very small part of the total slave economy of the Old South. For the most part, the industry it served was incipient, local, and lacking in both transportation outlets and markets. The onset of the Civil War pointed out the backwardness of manufacturing in the South. New industries, many sponsored by the Confederate government, sprang forth to meet the needs for iron, small arms and ordnance, powder, and textiles. Ironically, those firms that employed slave labor suffered a double blow at the end of the war, when the Fourteenth Amendment cancelled the Confederate war debt to its suppliers but left them with private debts for purchases and rentals of slaves and for food, clothing, and shelter for that labor force.

SELECTED BIBLIOGRAPHY

Paul A. David et al., *Reckoning with Slavery: A Critical Study in the Quantitative History of American Negro Slavery* (1976); Charles B. Dew, "Disciplining Slave Ironworkers in the Antebellum South: Coercion, Conciliation, and Accommodation," *American Historical Review*, 79 (1974), 393–418; Clement Eaton, *The Growth of Southern Civilization, 1790–1860* (1961); Ronald L. Lewis, *Coal, Iron, and Slaves: Industrial Slavery in Maryland and Virginia, 1715–1865* (1979); Randall M. Miller, "The Fabric of Control: Slavery in Antebellum Southern Textile Mills," *Business History Review*, 55 (1981), 471–490; James E. Newton and Ronald L. Lewis, eds., *The Other Slaves: Mechanics, Artisans, and Craftsmen* (1978); and Robert S. Starobin, *Industrial Slavery in the Old South* (1970).

ROBERT H. MCKENZIE

INFANTICIDE. Knowledge about Afro-American slaves and the conditions of slavery would lead one to conclude that some black parents must have intentionally murdered their offspring rather than watch them grow up in bondage. In fact, various records document instances of slave infanticide dating back to colonial days. Between 1670 and 1780 Massachusetts and Connecticut courts tried eleven cases of black (not necessarily slave) infanticide, and found five of the defendants guilty. Both the rate of accusation (15 percent of all infanticides, when the black population comprised 3 to 4 percent of the total population) and the rate of conviction (one-and-a half times the white) may have reflected, according to two historians of American infanticide, black "despair or anger, or a selective application [by whites] of the [infanticide] laws against them."

As in the cases of a Massachusetts slave, Flora, accused in the late 1750s of drowning her newborn in a privy well, and, about one hundred years later, of a Georgia slave, charged with leaving her newborn baby in the grass and bushes until it died, all too often the records fail to provide a motive for the killing. Thus, though clearly slave infanticide did occur, the reasons are not always known. Evidence presented in several Virginia court hearings and petitions to the governor in the 1850s provides explanations for at least some of the murders. Parental influence and fear of discovery of an illegitimate child by the couple's parents or owners were given as reasons in four of the six slave infanticide cases reported. Seventeen-year-old Charlotte, hired in Richmond, murdered her new-born at least partially out of a desire to conceal the birth from her employers. Fourteen-year-old Lucy destroyed her infant "to hide her shame," while the mother of another Lucy acted in a similar manner "to hide the shame of the [unmarried] daughter." Most masters vouched for the previous "good character" of the women who perpetrated such brutal acts (one mother struck her child's head with a blow "sufficient to drive in the skull," and another murdered by "strangling and suffocating" the infant). Though the underlying motives in these cases may have been humanitarian (saving the child from slavery), available evidence points to the contrary.

Legend and early scholarship attributed slave infant deaths to mothers "over-laying"—accidentally or intentionally smothering their children—or to careless mothers allowing children to strangle or suffocate in their bed clothes. Recent studies indicate that many of these slave infant deaths may have been actually instances of "crib death" (Sudden Infant Death Syndrome).

SELECTED BIBLIOGRAPHY

Eugene D. Genovese, *Roll, Jordan, Roll: The World the Slaves Made* (1974); Peter C. Hoffer and N.E.H. Hull, *Murdering Mothers: Infanticide in England and New England, 1558–1803* (1981); Michael P. Johnson, "Smothered Slave Infants: Were Slave Mothers at Fault?" *Journal of Southern History*, 47 (1981), 493–520; Kenneth F. Kiple and Virginia H. King, *Another Dimension to the Black Diaspora: Diet, Disease, and Racism* (1981); and Todd L. Savitt, *Medicine and Slavery: The Diseases and Health Care of Blacks in Antebellum Virginia* (1978).

TODD L. SAVITT

INTERVIEWS, SLAVE. Slave interviews constitute a very large and valuable part of the surviving evidence in which Afro-Americans speak about their ex-periences in bondage. Although many interviews remain little-known and vir-tually unused by scholars, the most familiar have provided revealing and oft-quoted statements about what it was like to be a slave in the American South.

Interviews with slaves or former slaves have diverse origins and span a con-siderable period of time. The principal kinds of slave interviews include inter-views printed (or described) by antebellum newspapers and magazines; interviews that appeared in newspapers and magazines during and after the Civil War; interviews conducted by the American Freedmen's Inquiry Commission in 1863; the Federal Writers' Project Slave Narratives* of the Depression era Works Progress Administration; and interviews conducted by scholars in the late nine-teenth or early twentieth century.

According to John W. Blassingame, hundreds of slave interviews were pub-lished in antebellum newspapers, magazines, and books, beginning in the eigh-teenth century. Although various journals in Canada, the United States, and England published slave interviews, the overwhelming majority appeared in antislavery publications. Usually the subject of the interview was a fugitive slave who had only recently escaped from bondage. As a result, his story frequently had the directness and immediacy of recent experience. But, as was the case with other types of slave interviews, many editors or publishers selected from, rearranged, or otherwise altered the text of the interview. The resulting articles, though varying in length, tend to be fairly substantial, probably because newspaper editors viewed them as interesting features.

During and immediately after the Civil War, interviews with former slaves continued to interest the Northern public. The pressing issues of Reconstruction, however, drove them from the pages of most publications, and they did not return in quantity until around the turn of the century. Then, for three or four decades in both North and South, the ex-slave was a subject of great interest to a new generation of Afro-Americans, to readers in an increasingly urban, industrial society, and to residents curious about their local community's history. Newspapers often marked centennials or anniversaries by publishing historical articles and interviews with ex-slaves. These postbellum interviews, some fairly lengthy, usually were conducted by trained reporters. Despite editors' cuts and condensations and the interjection of opinions and comments by interviewers, some of the interviews unearthed keen insights into the lives and experiences of the former slaves.

The American Freedmen's Inquiry Commission conducted interviews notable for their circumstances and their form. Established in 1863, the commission reported to the Secretary of War and investigated the freedmen's past in order to make recommendations about their future. In addition to gathering depositions and written answers to questions, the commission sought out some informants in their homes or workplaces and made verbatim transcripts of interviews. The former slaves interviewed had only recently gained their freedom and came mostly from states of the upper South. Exact records of what was said in an interview, these documents are almost unique, but unfortunately the commission interviewed only forty-eight ex-slaves.

By contrast, the Federal Writers' Project of the Works Progress Administration generated the largest single collection of slave interviews. Its field-workers reached approximately 3,000 former slaves, and the project's staff and editors assembled written, revised, and edited reports on most of the interviews. Thanks to the painstaking work of historian George P. Rawick and others, virtually all of these records are available to scholars in printed form. Although most reports on interviews are brief and run to no more than four or five pages, they contain much information, many eloquent statements, and have been judged "incomparable" among interviews as a source on religious and secular songs, genealogical data, and black speech patterns. The Federal Writers' Project narratives are, by far, the most familiar and best studied of all the slave interviews. The valuable perspective they have provided suggests that additional insights may await the systematic examination of the other types of slave interviews.

For example, only a few of the numerous interviews conducted by scholars have been studied. John B. Cade published an article based on his interviews in the 1920s, and scholars have used the accounts compiled in the same decade by A. P. Watson, Paul Radin, and Ophelia Settle Egypt at Fisk University. Scholars are acquainted with, but have not used the approximately 250 interviews directed by Lawrence D. Reddick in 1934. Before the publication of John W. Blassingame's *Slave Testimony* in 1977, few historians even were aware of the slave interviews conducted by both amateur and professional historians, including Tuskegee Institute's Thomas Monroe Campbell, the Tennessee State Library's John Trotwood Moore, and Florida's Orland Kay Armstrong. Anthropologists and folklorists created a significant portion of these slave interviews. Their work generally used only excerpts of them to illustrate points made in scholarly articles.

In sum, a large number of slave interviews of all types are available for study. But because most types are located in scattered sources, a majority of the slave interviews still have not been systematically examined. Future use of slave interviews requires sensitivity, care, common sense, and the application of scrupulous methods that have been developed thus far. The challenge of these documents derives from their complex nature: they are the product of interviews but typically are *not* actual transcriptions of interviews. Because of this historians must deal with two types of potential distortion.

First, because they originated as interviews, all the factors that go into an interview had a shaping, and possibly distorting, influence. Judicious use of slave interviews requires that historians consider the race of the interviewer; the social status, attitudes, skill, and other characteristics of the interviewer; the age of the subject; the physical, economic, and social condition of the subject; political, economic, and social conditions of the time; the degree of rapport between the interviewer and the subject; and the perceived purpose of the interview.

Second, the scholar has no easy way, in most cases, to discover shortcomings that these factors produced. Original records of most interviews do not exist, and the surviving record is not a transcript but rather something closer to a story or a narrative report. In addition, many editors revised or altered the original form of these reports. As a result, the slave interviews contain layers of potential distortion to consider, detect, and counter.

This task requires a high degree of skill in the traditional work of historical research. In evaluating slave interviews scholars need to be alert for internal evidence, nuances of expression, forms of address, words that reveal the tone of the encounter, and changes in the slave's degree of responsiveness. More systematic analysis of word choice, symbols, or the pattern of information offered may also be useful. As always in oral history methodology, there is no substitute for thorough grounding in all the facts relating to the background of the interview.

Much may be gained from newer quantitative methods as well. These can greatly facilitate the compilation of data from slave interviews. Key facts collected from a large number of brief interviews may add up to new or additional pieces of information. Similarly, quantitative methods make comparison of data possible and work to systematically restrain impressionistic thinking. In some cases it is also possible to utilize quantification to measure causal relationships more accurately and to assess the weight of different factors.

The future study of slave interviews could lead in interesting directions. Painstaking editorial research would improve the usefulness of many slave interviews, for little or nothing is known about the slave or the interviewer in many sources. Slave interviews might offer a way to illuminate differences in slave experience over time or in a variety of specific situations. To date scholars have used interviews mainly to document generalizations regarding slavery, not to illustrate changes within the institution over time and place. Many approaches are now visible, due to the editorial work of Blassingame and Rawick. Continued discovery, compilation, and indexing of slave interviews will open new avenues for research in the history of slavery.

SELECTED BIBLIOGRAPHY

John W. Blassingame, ed., *Slave Testimony: Two Centuries of Letters, Speeches, Interviews, and Autobiographies* (1977); Charles T. Davis and Henry Louis Gates, Jr., eds., *The Slave's Narrative* (1984); Paul D. Escott, *Slavery Remembered: A Record of Twentieth-Century Slave Narratives* (1979); Charles L. Perdue, Jr. et al., eds., *Weevils in the Wheat: Interviews with Virginia Ex-Slaves* (1976); George P. Rawick, ed., *The American Slave: A Composite Autobiography* (19 vols., 1972; Supplement, Series 1, 12 vols., 1977).

PAUL D. ESCOTT

IRONWORKERS. Slaves provided the backbone of the work force in the Southern iron industry from its inception in the first decades of the eighteenth century. By the time of the American Revolution the colonies were the world's third largest producer of crude iron, and the vast bulk of that production came from the slave-operated furnaces and forges in Maryland and Virginia. These two colonies contained 25 percent of the 257 ironworks erected in the colonies prior to the Revolution. The Principio Iron Works and the Baltimore Iron Company, both primarily operated with slaves, were two of the earliest and largest of all industrial establishments in colonial America. Following independence the industry expanded and so did the slave labor force. The average colonial ironworks required about 70 workers, and with sixty-five ironworks in the Chesapeake region, about 4,500 hands were required at the peak of the industry's development in the eighteenth century. By the nineteenth century, the number of slave-operated ironworks increased to about eighty, and the average work force grew to about 90, for an average of 7,000 slaves. The Oxford Iron Works of Virginia, the new nation's largest iron manufacturer, owned 220 slaves in 1812. On the eve of the Civil War, the Tredegar Iron Works of Richmond, Virginia, the South's leading iron company, employed 900 workers, one-half of whom were slaves.

Although Virginia dominated the Southern iron industry, and the largest number of bondsmen were concentrated there, local iron-producing centers developed in other Southern states by the 1840s and 1850s. The Nesbitt Manufacturing Company and the Aera and Aetna Iron Works of South Carolina also were significant iron manufacturers, employing 140 and 90 bondsmen respectively. Similarly, the Shelby Iron Company of Alabama, which expanded during the Civil War and became a major supplier of iron for the Confederacy, was almost completely dependent on slave labor. Another local center for iron production was the Cumberland River district of Tennessee. Senator John Bell's iron company owned 365 slaves, and the other twenty ironworks in the district controlled an additional 1,800 black bondsmen. The Maramec Iron Works in Missouri also became an important Southern producer by the end of the slave era, and following the common pattern, employed numerous slaves in its operations.

Throughout the entire slave era bondsmen filled every occupational category in the Southern iron industry from common laborer to the highly skilled positions. Ironmasters attempted to protect themselves from the vicissitudes of the slave market by owning those hands that were most crucial to the production process, while hiring* unskilled laborers whenever that was possible. This practice ensured stability at the critical points of production without saddling owners with the expense of maintaining less critical unskilled workers during economic downturns. Since skilled slaves exercised considerable control over each step of the production process, Southern ironmasters preferred to rely on positive incentives, such as cash bonuses, to stimulate their bondsmen, rather than brute force.

SELECTED BIBLIOGRAPHY

Kathleen Bruce, *Virginia Iron Manufacture in the Slave Era* (reprint ed., 1960); Charles B. Dew, "Disciplining Slave Ironworkers in the Antebellum South: Coercion, Conciliation, and Accommodation," *American Historical Review*, 79 (1974), 393–418; Charles B. Dew, *Ironmaker to the Confederacy: Joseph R. Anderson and the Tredegar Iron Works* (1966); Ronald L. Lewis, *Coal, Iron, and Slaves: Industrial Slavery in Maryland and Virginia, 1715–1865* (1979); and James D. Norris, *Frontier Iron: The Maramec Iron Works, 1826–1876* (1964).

RONALD L. LEWIS

ISLAM. Islam, spreading southward along Saharan trade routes, came slowly into West Africa from the eleventh to the seventeenth centuries. Merchants and clerics introduced Islam in their trading villages and the commercial quarters of Sudanese cities where ruling families often made it an imperial cult of their court and circle. The peaceful introduction of the faith, attendant trade, and profound impact of literacy and Islamic culture won the religion numerous African adherents. Equally important in the process was Islam's accommodation, at least for many centuries, of much that was traditional in African life. Islamic legal elements were often complementary to preexisting African ones, notably polygamy. Hence, although Islam was an immigrant, it was adaptable and quickly became a native religion, not a foreign sect.

In the eighteenth century African Muslims resided throughout West Africa, from Senegal on the Atlantic Ocean to Chad and Cameroon 2,000 miles eastward. Muslim influence was dominant or substantial among (from east to west) the Wolof and Tokolor, the sedentary Fulbe (or Fulani), various Mande-speakers (the Soninke, Dyula, and Mandinka), certain Niger River peoples, and many of the Hausa and Kanuri. Muslim penetration even spread into upper Guinea and the upper Ivory Coast. In many places, however, Islamic influence was partial, or even superficial, and was confined to urban areas and dominant social classes.

Islam put a distinctive stamp on its believers, one that set them apart from neighboring "pagans." Acceptance of Islamic social and personal law reflected itself in a Muslim's daily life by attention to the five "Pillars of Faith"—belief in only one God and in Muhammad as His Prophet, prayer, charity, fasting, and pilgrimage. Concomitant rites and customs included abandonment of idolatry and witchcraft, prohibition of alcoholic drinks, adoption of the Islamic calendar, and alteration in diet and dress. African Muslims wore Islamic amulets and adopted sundry taboos and even new burial rites. In Muslim communities Quranic schools flourished. These spread literacy in Arabic and in native languages written in Arabic characters, disseminated powerful religious values, and introduced Islamic law and institutions. The cultural prestige of Islam enhanced the feeling of superiority its followers felt over animists and local cultists.

Some African Muslims were carried into New World slavery as early as the sixteenth century. Regulations enacted in that era prohibited Berber and black slaves of the Muslim faith from being imported into colonial Mexico. Most Muslim slaves seem to have arrived in the Americas during the eighteenth and early nineteenth centuries, when militant Islamic reformers began a revolutionary series of religious and state-building wars that shook the Sudan. The first *jihad* occurred in Futa Jalon in the 1720s. Others followed in Futa Toro and Bondu (1776), Hausaland (1804), Bornu (1808), Adamawa (1809), and Macina (1810). These struggles, some short but others protracted, unsettled all of West Africa and produced many prisoners of war for the slave trade, Muslims among them. Other Muslims were sent into slavery from such non-Islamic states as Bambara and Ashanti. Lack of exact ethnographic data makes it impossible to state with accuracy the number of these Muslim emigrants. One recent estimate suggests that 10 percent of the West Africans sent to the United States from 1711 to 1808 were, to some degree, Muslims—perhaps 30,000 total. Substantial numbers went to the West Indies and Brazil as well.

Several noteworthy Muslims served as slaves in the United States. Ayuba Suleiman of Bondu (ca. 1701–1773) was a merchant trading to the Gambia River when enslaved in 1731 and taken to Maryland. His extraordinary abilities ("he could say the whole Alcoran by heart") led to his being freed and returned to Africa in 1734. Abd al-Rahman (1762–1829), another Muslim who returned to Africa, a warrior son of one of Futa Jalon's founders, endured forty years of slavery in Mississippi. Bilali of Futa Jalon (fl. 1814–1859), a Georgia slave, left a manuscript (a portion of the *Risala* of Ibn Abi Zaid), that demonstrates the high level of legal study in his homeland.

Other Muslims whose lives are documented include Abu Bakr al-Siddiq of Timbuktu (fl. 1790–1841), a slave for nearly thirty years in Jamaica; Salih Bilali of Macina (fl. 1770–1830), a Georgia slave; Lamine Kebe (fl. 1775–1835), a Sononke teacher from southern Futa Jalon and a slave in various Southern states; Omar Ibn Said (ca. 1770–1864), a Tokolor from Futa Toro and a slave in North Carolina; and Muhammad Gardo Baquaqua (fl. 1820s–1850s), a native of Borgu, a Brazilian slave and an American college student.

Historians have not yet fully assessed the role of Islam and its adherents in American slavery. Islam, a universalist religion, was mobile. As a personal faith it traveled to the New World as easily as did Christianity. Evidence of that is found in the fact that none of the Muslim slaves whose American lives are known in detail can be said to have made a voluntary and wholehearted conversion to Christianity. Brief correspondences in Arabic between Muslim slaves in Georgia, and also in Jamaica, exist in English translation. An admonitory letter of 1786 from Guinea, enjoining believers to faithfulness, circulated to some extent in Jamaica. But in countries other than Brazil, where the largest number of Muslims resided, contact between individual Muslims was limited. Muslim slaves, cut off from fellow believers, religious texts, and services, struggled to practice their faith in the Americas.

Whites frequently appointed Muslim slaves as drivers,* farm managers, or to similar positions of trust. Planters regarded them as more civilized than other Africans, much as European colonial administrators in West Africa who later employed Muslims as subordinates there. But slave owners, especially in Brazil, where after 1807 Islam provided a wellspring for revolts by Hausa and others, discovered something else that European colonists in Africa also learned: that Islam provided a potent source of anti-Western opposition.

The true importance of a religion* lies in its personal significance in the life of a believer. Islam's spiritual consolation sustained those thrown into a difficult foreign bondage. As Abu Bakr al-Siddiq put it, "As God Almighty Himself has said, 'Nothing can befall us unless it be written for us.' He is our Master. In God, therefore, let all the faithful put their trust!"

SELECTED BIBLIOGRAPHY

Terry Alford, *Prince among Slaves* (1977); Allan D. Austin, *African Muslims in Antebellum Slavery: A Sourcebook* (1984); Philip D. Curtin, ed., *Africa Remembered: Narratives by West Africans from the Era of the Slave Trade* (1967); Douglas Grant, *The Fortunate Slave: An Illustration of African Slavery in the Early Eighteenth Century* (1968); and J. Spencer Trimingham, *A History of Islam in West Africa* (1962).

TERRY ALFORD

J

JACKSON, ANDREW (1767–1845). Andrew Jackson's rise to national prominence closely paralleled the increase in the number of slaves that he owned in Tennessee: 10 in 1794, 15 in 1798, 44 in 1820, 95 in 1829, and 150 in 1842. A large slaveholder, Jackson expressed no moral or ideological objections to slavery. By local planters' standards, he reportedly treated his bondsmen well. He rarely had his slaves whipped because, he said, the practice was "humiliating." Chains were only placed on runaways* who, because of their actions, were quickly sold. Jackson dismissed overly zealous overseers and slave drivers. Such leniency not surprisingly elicited complaints from his overseers.

Jackson viewed slaves as economic units, investments crucial for agricultural success and social standing. In his early years Jackson sold slaves for a profit. As a soldier he protected slave traders from hostile Indians. In 1812, when he was an inactive partner in a slave-trading firm, Jackson set out to destroy Silas Dinsmore, a Choctaw agent in Mississippi Territory who aided runaway Negroes and confiscated slaves from masters lacking proof of ownership. Dinsmore, after successfully evading Jackson's raids into the agency, ultimately was removed from his position as agent by the general's friends in Congress. In 1816 Jackson ordered General Edmund P. Gaines to destroy "Negro Fort," an abandoned British outpost in Florida, and to execute the escaped slaves who occupied it. Jackson justified his actions in the First Seminole War (1818) both as punitive measures against the Seminoles and as a means to recapture and punish fugitive slaves hiding among the Indians.

As president, Jackson struggled with his personal commitment to slavery on the one hand, and its divisive effect on the Union on the other. First and foremost a nationalist, Jackson was disturbed by the Missouri Compromise,* which he believed encouraged Northern abolitionists to attack the South's constitutional right to hold slaves, while, at the same time, forcing Southerners to adopt a defensive and potentially destructive states' rights stance. The slavery issue intruded in Jackson's presidency in several ways. He met the Nullification movement* forthrightly in 1832, but acquiesced in other states' rights controversies affecting Southern interests. He sided with Georgia in its effort to remove the Cherokee Indians in the face of a Supreme Court decision to protect Cherokee rights. In 1835 Jackson ordered Postmaster General Amos Kendall to stop delivery of abolitionist* literature to nonsubscribers in the South because it incensed slaveholders. He privately supported the efforts of slaveholders in Texas to break free from Mexican rule when their slaveholding interests were threatened by Mexican law, and he wanted the United States to annex Texas. But Jackson backed off from Texas annexation when abolitionists made the issue politically dangerous. Later in life Jackson concluded that if slavery continued to threaten the Union, then it must go. Jackson considered slavery the most problematical issue facing the country. As president he walked a moderate line, resisting the arguments of abolitionists and slavery expansionists alike.

SELECTED BIBLIOGRAPHY

Frederick M. Binder, *The Color Problem in Early National America As Viewed by John Adams, Jefferson and Jackson* (1968); Stanley F. Horn, *The Hermitage: Home of Old Hickory* (1938); Marquis James, *The Life of Andrew Jackson* (1938); and Robert V. Remini, *Andrew Jackson and the Course of American Empire, 1767–1821* (1977).

CURTIS F. MORGAN, JR.

JASPER, JOHN (1812–1901). John Jasper was a noted slave preacher who became a significant community leader in Richmond, Virginia, following the Civil War. Born and raised on a plantation in Fluvanna County, Virginia, Jasper at the age of thirteen was hired out to work in tobacco factories in Richmond and later in the coal mines of Chesterfield County. Self-educated and devoutly Christian, Jasper became a very popular slave preacher,* in great demand particularly for his funeral orations. Frequently, he filled the pulpit of Richmond's First African Baptist Church, and for several years before the Civil War he served the Third African Baptist Church of Petersburg. Jasper became the first black minister to form a church in postwar Richmond when he organized the Sixth Mount Zion Baptist Church in 1867. The church initially was housed in a decrepit stable once belonging to the Confederate government, but by 1887 his congregation constructed a large Norman-Gothic edifice that became the center of religious life in the section of Richmond known as Jackson Ward. In 1878 Jasper first delivered the sermon that created for him a national reputation, and guaranteed capacity crowds whenever he preached in Richmond, Washington, Baltimore, and Philadelphia. "The Sun Do Move," billed as an ecclesiastical challenge to Galileo, was actually not so much a discourse on astronomy as it was a testimony of the Lord as a defender of His people. Of even greater significance than Jasper's preaching was his enduring impact upon Richmond's black community during the pivotal years of transition from slavery to freedom.

SELECTED BIBLIOGRAPHY

Mary Jo Bratton, "John Jasper of Richmond: From Slave Preacher to Community Leader," *Virginia Cavalcade*, 29 (1979), 32–39; W. Asbury Christian, *Richmond: Her*

Past and Present (1912); William Elridge Hatcher, *John Jasper, The Unmatched Negro Philosopher and Preacher* (1908); and Edwin Archer Randolph, *The Life of the Rev. John Jasper, Pastor of Sixth Mt. Zion Baptist Church, Richmond, Va.; From His Birth to the Present Time, with His Theory on the Rotation of the Sun* (1884).

MARY JO BRATTON

JEFFERSON, THOMAS (1743–1826). Thomas Jefferson, perhaps more than anyone else, was intellectually trapped by American slavery. He regarded the institution as an unjustifiable moral wrong. At the same time, he could see no way to end it short of massive bloodshed. After the American Revolution* he grew deeply pessimistic about this burden on the republic. Having hailed the great West as "an empire for liberty," he called the controversy about slavery there "a firebell in the night."

Jefferson viewed slavery in terms of eighteenth-century ideas about natural rights. By reason of their natural endowments, all men possessed the natural right of liberty. In common with his contemporaries, Jefferson regarded liberty and slavery as logical and actual antitheses. Jefferson eloquently enshrined these ideas in one of the great founding documents of his nation.

Throughout his life, Jefferson never wavered from his conviction that American slaves ought to be freed. He expressed this conviction most openly in his early years, in his draft of the Declaration of Independence,* in the revisal of Virginia's laws, and in his *Notes on the State of Virginia* written in 1781–1782. As time went on and his pessimism grew deeper, he refused requests to make further public pronouncements lest they exacerbate tensions on the matter.

While his political theory and indeed his entire worldview declared slavery to be wrong, Jefferson's social views greatly complicated and compromised his thinking about the institution. He was always more concerned with the damaging effects of slavery upon whites than with its impact upon slaves themselves. American slavery was based on a racial distinction. Despite his emphasis on the importance of physical differences between the races, Jefferson remained convinced that blacks were equal to whites in one important sphere, the moral sense. Otherwise, Jefferson regarded blacks as mentally inferior to whites, innately so.

Jefferson also stressed the deep-seated animosities that had accumulated on both sides, the "deep rooted prejudices" of the whites and the "ten thousand recollections . . . of the injuries they have sustained" on the part of blacks. He viewed the forthcoming conflict in apocalyptic terms and wrote of an eventual bloodbath in which the Almighty could not possibly side with the whites.

As a Virginia slaveholder, Jefferson's life and livelihood were enmeshed in the institution. He toyed with the idea of freeing his more than one hundred slaves and making them tenant farmers, but he always found his financial debts a higher obligation. During the presidential campaign of 1800, a notorious scandalmonger accused Jefferson of fathering mulatto bastards by his own slave, Sally Hemings.* Such paternity has been neither proved nor disproved. Historians have taken great interest in the matter, though they have usually neglected its real historical importance, which lies in the fact that the charge itself has greatly fascinated Americans.

Jefferson's statements about Negro inferiority reflected widespread views on the part of American whites, but they were vigorously attacked then and since. His antislavery pronouncements also represented a strong strain of thought in revolutionary America. As time went on, however, his antislavery and natural rights ideology became an embarrassment to white Southerners as they turned to endorsement of slavery in the years before the Civil War. In the long run Jefferson provided an ambiguous legacy concerning slavery. His combination of antislavery and antiblack pronouncements capsulated a tendency that has been remarkably enduring in American culture.

SELECTED BIBLIOGRAPHY

William W. Freehling, "The Founding Fathers and Slavery," *American Historical Review*, 77 (1972), 81–93; Winthrop D. Jordan, *White over Black: American Attitudes toward the Negro, 1550–1812* (1968); John Chester Miller, *The Wolf by the Ears: Thomas Jefferson and Slavery* (1977).

WINTHROP D. JORDAN

JEWS. "Slavery," wrote Solomon Cohen, a prominent Jewish leader of Savannah in 1861, "is the only human institution that could elevate the Negro from barbarianism and develop the small amount of intellect with which he is endowed." His words indicate that not all American Jews possessed, as the abolitionist Rabbi Bernard Felsenthal of Chicago had wrongly asserted several years earlier, a "heart and soul" moral aversion to slavery. In fact, Felsenthal probably would have been horrified to know that during the colonial period Jewish shippers throughout the colonies, like others, had ventured into the profitable slave trade*; that Jewish colonists had owned slaves; and that as the newly established country began to divide over the issue of slavery, so did American Jewry. To be sure, Jews were culturally and religiously distinctive from their Christian neighbors. They, nevertheless, experienced serious sectional, ethnic, cultural, and even religious differences among themselves. This diversity, in turn, mitigated against the emergence of an authoritative nationwide governing body capable of coalescing the ancient traditions, biblical ideals, and European experiences into a common American Jewish social conscience and sense of social responsibility. Consequently, the Jews exhibited highly individualized attitudes toward slavery that were no more lofty or less diverse and sectional than those of the rest of the American population.

The boldest Jewish voices against slavery resounded in the free states of the North where many of the more recent and numerous immigrants, who arrived during the 1830s and through the 1850s, brought the libertarian ideals of the recent European revolutions. Those Jews who were abolitionists* and Republicans,* however, expressed a sentiment that was usually a product of a varied recipe of self-serving Jewish, antislave, and pro-Union ingredients. At one extreme were the fiery Kansas abolitionist editor Moritz Pinner and the Jews who rode with John Brown. At the other end of the spectrum was Rabbi Morris Raphall of New York, who defended the biblical sanction of slavery and merely called for a humanization of slavery from the Roman chattel model to the Hebraic humanistic model, that is, from a system that callously treated the slave as an animated tool to one that looked compassionately upon the slave as a bonded human being endowed with protections against ill-treatment. In between these two poles was a diverse group of spokesmen, including the ardent abolitionist Max Lilienthal of Cincinnati, the staunch Democrat Isaac Wise, and the silent Isaac Leeser who had many Southern Jewish friends. There were Rabbi David Einhorn of Baltimore and Rabbi Sabato Morais of Philadelphia who, contrary to the wishes of their nervous or opposing congregants, attacked slavery as a menace to the rights of Jews and all other minorities and preached support of the Union as the sole bastion of liberty.

In the South, being Jewish had a much lesser influence on any aspect of the relationship between Jews and slaves. Wanting to participate fully as equals in the slave-based Southern society, almost all Jewish residents completely and unhesitatingly acclimated themselves to Southern values. Their acceptance of slavery as a normal aspect of life also was fostered by a varied combination of other factors not present in the North. Jews feared that disagreeing with Southerners would arouse anti-Semitic prejudice. They also understood that, as peddlers and merchants, their physical survival rested in the hands of Southern customers whose opinions could not be challenged. They further realized that they enjoyed the protective coloration of being white, which offered them greater opportunity for status and recognition than possible in the North, where religion and ethnicity, not color, had a greater influence. Jews comforted themselves and removed any feelings of guilt in holding slaves by rationalizing that they were applying the lofty tradition of the Mosaic code toward slavery. "The institution of slavery as it existed in the South was not so great a wrong as people believe," said Aaron Hirsch of Mississippi. "The Negroes were brought here in a savage state; they captured and ate each other in their African home. Here they were instructed to work, were civilized and got religion, and were perfectly happy." Finally, among the Jews were many who, rather than being newly arrived immigrants in the South, were native Southerners who happened to be Jewish, who were imbued with Southern traditions, and who readily embraced the Southern cause.

The Jews' involvement in the slave system, therefore, was not appreciably different from that of their Christian neighbors. Those Jews who could afford to own slaves and who had need for their services participated in the buying, bartering, owning, and selling of slaves. The potentially lucrative slave-dealing business attracted such Jews as the Monsanto brothers of Natchez and the Davis brothers of Petersburg. Some Jews, particularly those living in the larger towns and cities, owned slaves as status symbols. The few Jewish planters and more numerous Jewish owners of farm stores worked as many as 150 slaves or as few as one in the fields. It was not uncommon for small Jewish merchants to see little difference between a slave and other kinds of merchandise. They bought slaves for speculative purposes, accepted them as payment of debts, and offered them as collateral for loans. And if Jewish peddlers and merchants were more inclined than others to have both legal and illegal business dealings with slaves, it probably was a consequence of both a sense of pity for the slave's plight and a marginal merchant's need for trade.

In conforming to Southern slave society, the Jews also adopted attitudes toward slavery that were compatible with their actions and indistinguishable from those of other Southerners. None were abolitionists. At best, some Jews exhibited a private conviction that slavery was wrong by either refusing to buy slaves or treating slaves as human beings rather than as beasts of burden. Others, such as Judah Touro of New Orleans, manumitted their slaves prior to the 1840s when it was legal in the South to do so. Similar attitudes and acts of emancipation by Southerners as a whole, however, were not rare during the same period. Among the thoughtful Southerners were Samuel Myers of Virginia and Solomon Heydenfelt and Philip Phillips of Alabama, who all felt slavery ultimately would prove to be an economic and psychological threat to Southerners. Neither they, however, nor such leading Jewish political figures as David Levy Yulee of Florida and Judah P. Benjamin of Louisiana publicly expressed any reservations about slavery. No Southern Jewish intellectual—such as the Texas newspaper editor Jacob De Cordova, or the South Carolina dramatist and political essayist Isaac Harby, or the Virginia journalist Samuel Mordecai—questioned the justice of slavery. To the contrary, in speeches, articles, novels, and editorials, these Jews not only accepted the doctrines about slavery, they contributed, proportional to their small numbers, to the formulation and circulation of the various defenses of slavery.

On the issue of slavery, then, no clear-cut and universal "Jewish position" emerged. The Jews neither acted nor thought differently from the rest of the American population. In the process of becoming a part of American society, the Jews adopted in various degrees the values of the regions in which they lived. Because of their small numbers, they played a relatively insignificant role in the establishment, maintenance, and opposition of slavery.

SELECTED BIBLIOGRAPHY

Special issue on slavery, *American Jewish Archives*, 13 (1961), 149–170; Nathan M. Kaganoff and Melvin Urofsky, eds., *Turn to the South: Essays on Southern Jewry* (1979); Bertram W. Korn, *American Jewry and the Civil War* (1951); Bertram W. Korn, *Jews and Negro Slavery in the Old South, 1789–1865* (1961); Jacob R. Marcus, *Early American Jewry* (2 vols., 1951–1953); Jacob R. Marcus, ed., *Memoirs of American Jews, 1775–1865* (3 vols., 1955–1956); Ralph Melnick, "Billy Simons: The Black Jew of Charleston," *American Jewish Archives*, 32 (1980), 3–8; Abraham J. Peck, "That Other 'Peculiar Institution': Jews and Judaism in the Nineteenth-Century South," *Modern Judaism*, 7

(1987), 99–114; and Samuel Proctor and Louis Schmier, eds., *Jews of the South: Selected Essays from the Southern Jewish Historical Society* (1984).

LOUIS D. SCHMIER

JONES, CHARLES COLCOCK (1804–1863). Charles Colcock Jones was both a missionary* to slaves and a slave owner whose life represented the moral dilemma that surrounded the institution of slavery. Born in Georgia's Liberty County in December 1804, he had among his forebears the rice planters of the Georgia coast. Educated at Exeter Academy, Andover Theological Seminary and Princeton Theological Seminary, he demonstrated an interest in the American Colonization Society,* and helped found the Society of Inquiry Concerning Africans. After ordination, he returned to Liberty County where he organized the Liberty County Association for Religious Instruction of Negroes (1831). For the next two decades, although with interruptions, he promoted slave involvement in church life. He established mission churches, regularized plantation preaching, and used blacks as watchmen in the church. He wrote a *Catechism of Scripture Doctrine, and Practice, . . . Designed Also for the Oral Instruction of Colored Persons* (1837) and *The Religious Instruction of the Negroes in the United States* (1842). Jones's message alarmed those who feared the implications of Christian teaching for slaves. Sensitive to that, and representing the planters, Jones's sermons stressed duty, obedience, and morality. He succeeded in developing a basis for Christian salvation among the blacks. Slaves, however, resented the class implications of his preaching, and in 1841 a sermon which discussed the sinfulness of runaway behavior produced a walkout on the part of slaves. Caught between a desire to uphold plantation traditions and the need for a black church experience that would produce both moral behavior and salvation, Jones issued only a mild challenge to slavery. His importance lies in his attempt to humanize slavery through religion. His legacy of a biracial Christian community has provided a model of an integrated religious experience. Exhausted by his labors, Charles Jones retired from preaching in 1847 and served from 1850 to 1853 with the Board of Domestic Missions of the Presbyterian Church. His increasingly poor health left him a semi-invalid before his death in 1863.

SELECTED BIBLIOGRAPHY

Janet Duitsman Cornelius, "God's Schoolmasters: Southern Evangelists to the Slaves, 1830–1860" (Ph.D. dissertation, University of Illinois, 1977); Eduard N. Loring, "Charles C. Jones: Missionary to Plantation Slaves, 1831–1847" (Ph.D. dissertation, Vanderbilt University, 1976); Donald G. Mathews, "Charles Colcock Jones and the Southern Evangelical Crusade to Form a Biracial Community," *Journal of Southern History*, 41 (1975), 299–320; Randall Miller, "Charles Colcock Jones," in Kenneth Coleman and Charles Stephen Gurr, eds., *Dictionary of Georgia Biography* (1983); and Robert Manson Myers, ed., *The Children of Pride: A True Story of Georgia and the Civil War* (1972).

THOMAS F. ARMSTRONG

K

KANSAS-NEBRASKA ACT. The Kansas-Nebraska Act was signed into law by President Franklin Pierce in May 1854, following a bitter debate in Congress. The act accelerated and expanded the national struggle over slavery in the territories and was one of the most significant political issues in the decade preceding the Civil War. This act called for the organization of the new territories of Kansas and Nebraska from the remaining unorganized portion of the 1803 Louisiana Purchase territory. Although the Missouri Compromise of 1820 had specifically outlawed slavery north of the 36° 30' line in the region (except for Missouri), proslavery advocates raised the issue in the 1854 congressional debate. Senator Stephen A. Douglas* of Illinois, author of the bill, sought to avoid a congressional crisis over the issue by a compromise that would repeal the Missouri Compromise prohibition and permit the matter to be determined by the people who lived there, the principle of "popular sovereignty."

The idea that slavery might be allowed in an area in which it had previously been banned, and which conceivably was the last region in the United States open to slavery expansion, substantially altered the American political scene. Antislavery spokesmen interpreted the act as an outrage. The proslavery ideologues* defended the right to carry slaves into the territories as an inherent right. Ultimately, the act divided the Democratic party,* destroyed the Whig party, and created an all-new, all-Northern, antislavery Republican party.*

In order to determine the destiny of Kansas as "free" or "slave" in accordance with popular sovereignty, proslavery and antislavery groups raced to the region, contributing to its image as "Bleeding Kansas" in the 1854–1859 period.

SELECTED BIBLIOGRAPHY

Robert W. Johannsen, *Stephen A. Douglas* (1973); James C. Malin, *The Nebraska Question, 1852–1854* (1953); Roy F. Nichols, "The Kansas-Nebraska Act: A Century of Historiography," *Mississippi Valley Historical Review*, 43 (1956), 187–212; David M.

Potter, *The Impending Crisis, 1848–1861* (1976); and James A. Rawley, *Race and Politics: "Bleeding Kansas" and the Coming of the Civil War* (1969).

FRANKLIN D. NICKELL

KECKLEY, ELIZABETH (ca. 1818–1907). Elizabeth Keckley was born a slave at Dinwiddie Court House in Virginia around 1818. Her earliest recollections of slave life came at age four, when she began taking care of her owner's child. At about age eighteen Keckley was sold to a North Carolinian, who fathered her son. Later, when her master moved to Saint Louis, Missouri, her skills as a seamstress provided much needed income for the entire household. After a disastrous marriage to James Keckley, who falsely purported to be free and successful, Elizabeth decided to use her own considerable talents to provide a better life for herself and her son. Borrowing money from customers, in 1855 she purchased her and her son's freedom. She also learned to read and write. Finally settling in Washington, D.C., she established a flourishing dressmaking business with such prominent customers as Mrs. Jefferson Davis. Eventually Keckley became dressmaker and confidante to Mary Todd Lincoln, thereby gaining an intimate view of the Lincoln household. She made a personal contribution to the war effort, in 1862, when she helped establish, and became first president of, the Contraband Relief Association.

Believing Mrs. Lincoln to be unfairly misunderstood, in 1868 Keckley published *Behind the Scenes; or Thirty Years a Slave, and Four Years in the White House*, probably with the help of James Redpath. Keckley had hoped the book would provide much needed funds for Mrs. Lincoln, but the appendix contained personal letters that angered Robert Lincoln, who prevailed upon the publisher to suppress the book. Although the authorship was later questioned, the book nevertheless became generally accepted as accurate and useful. Keckley died on 26 May 1907, after spending her last years in the Home for Destitute Women and Children, an institution that she had helped to found.

SELECTED BIBLIOGRAPHY

Elizabeth Keckley, *Behind the Scenes; or Thirty Years a Slave, and Four Years in the White House* (reprint, 1968); Bert James Loewenberg and Ruth Bogin, eds., *Black Women in Nineteenth-Century American Life: Their Words, Their Thoughts, Their Feelings* (1976); and John E. Washington, *They Knew Lincoln* (1942).

LINDA O. MCMURRY

KEMBLE, FRANCES ANNE (1809–1893). Frances Anne Kemble was born in London, England, the second daughter of Charles Kemble and Marie Thérèse de Camp. By 1832 she was both a famed Shakespearean actress and a woman of intense antislavery convictions. After an American tour (1832–1834) Kemble married Pierce Mease Butler of Philadelphia, and quit the stage. Two years later Butler inherited a Georgia estate and 700 slaves. Kemble paid a single visit to this property—Butler Island, and Hampton Point on St. Simons Island—for a three-month period in 1838–1839.

Kemble kept a close record of slavery and subjected plantation life and organization to detailed scrutiny. Her *Journal of a Residence on a Georgian Plantation in 1838–1839*, published in 1863, went out of print after a brief wartime notoriety and remained unavailable to the public for nearly one century. Early historians recoiled from Kemble's Dantesque vision of slavery and dismissed her book as fiction. She wrote, they asserted, to avenge herself upon Butler for the humiliation of a divorce suit that, in 1849, had been the sensation of the day.

The authenticity and factual truth of Kemble's book have been corroborated by archival and cartographic research, by the narratives* of ex-slaves, and by site excavations. Kemble's *Journal* now is viewed as an important source for the study of slavery and as a contribution to the literary heritage of the antislavery movement.

SELECTED BIBLIOGRAPHY

Frances Anne Kemble, *Journal of a Residence on a Georgian Plantation in 1838–1839*, edited by John Anthony Scott (1961, 1984); John Anthony Scott, *Fanny Kemble's America* (1973); Theresa A. Singleton, "The Archaeology of Afro-American Slavery in Coastal Georgia: A Regional Perception of Slave Household and Community Patterns" (Ph.D. dissertation, University of Florida, 1980); Paul Wagret, *Les Polders* (1959); and Constance Wright, *Fanny Kemble and the Lovely Land* (1972).

JOHN ANTHONY SCOTT

KENTUCKY, SLAVERY IN. Slaves entered Kentucky with the first white settlers. Slaves explored the Ohio River valley with Christopher Gist in 1751 and crossed the mountains with Daniel Boone in 1760. They led the wagons of the first settlers, carried their supplies, and tended their livestock. When attacked by Indians, Kentucky's slave pioneers fought bravely, lining up side by side with their masters, sharing their victories and defeats.

It is difficult to ascertain the number of slaves in Kentucky during the pioneer period, but the earliest census at Fort Harrod in 1777 indicated that 9.6 percent of its inhabitants were blacks. By 1800 Kentucky's slaves were 18.3 percent of the population and continued to grow until 1830, when 165,213 slaves comprised 24 percent of the Commonwealth's inhabitants. Thereafter, the percentage of slaves declined steadily, and in 1860 only 19.5 percent of the state's population were slaves although the absolute number increased to 225,483. Most of Kentucky's bondsmen lived in the Bluegrass region, where, by the 1850s, a number of counties were more than 40 percent slave. The other centers of slave population lay along the Ohio River and the tier of counties of south central Kentucky from the Ohio River to the Tennessee border. Almost all the counties in the latter area experienced a steady growth in their slave population during the forty years before the Civil War. The counties of eastern and southeastern Kentucky had the smallest slave populations.

A surprisingly large percentage of Kentucky's slaves resided in towns and villages. In the Bluegrass area, where the largest farms existed, the percentage of slaves living in towns was about the same as, or slightly greater than, the percentage living in the counties. The same held true for the other large slave-holding areas. The percentage of slaves living in towns in small slaveholding counties often was higher than the percentage for the entire county. The total urban population for the state, however, never was large.

The relationship between Kentucky slaves and masters was uniquely personal, though one clearly was in bondage and the other free. Slaves and their masters cleared the forests together, built their homes together, and reared their families together. The vast majority of Kentucky's slaves toiled in agriculture, and many worked alongside their masters, helping to transform the Kentucky wilderness into a civilized community. The average slaveholder in the Commonwealth owned about five slaves, and only 12 percent owned more than twenty. Nevertheless, profits were higher throughout the state on farms where larger numbers of slaves labored. Fewer than 30 percent of white Kentucky families held slaves.

Kentucky's slaves were more than just farm laborers or domestic servants. The predominance of small farms and the unsuitability of Kentucky soil for the labor-intensive crops of the Deep South freed Kentucky slaves for various types of work. Males worked as handymen, carpenters, brick masons, factory workers, longshoremen, waiters, and cattlemen. Slave women wove and dyed cloth, sewed clothes, and nursed the sick. Possessing such skills often led to a slave's being hired out* for a short period of time or even annually. Though open to potential abuse, the hiring-out system also provided hired slaves a measure of independence. They usually gained leverage with their employer, who stood to lose if the slave's work was interrupted. And hiring out often brought slaves bonuses or opportunities to earn extra money. Slave hiring increased steadily in the late antebellum period and sometimes provided Kentucky bondsmen a step toward freedom.

Living conditions for Kentucky slaves depended largely upon the prosperity of their owners and their willingness to share with their bondsmen, but some of the slave's comfort in life depended upon his own initiative. Most slaves lived in a one-room, dirt floor log cabin with a single window. Furniture often consisted of a slab of lumber across boxes to make a table or a wall peg for a closet. Children* usually slept on a trundle bed or in the loft on a shuck mattress or a pile of straw. Cover consisted of old, ragged clothes or a worn-out quilt. Slaves received no luxuries, few conveniences, and very little privacy. Urban slaves* often lived in the home of their owners or resided in servants' quarters on the alley behind their master's house.

Slaves cooked over an open fireplace that also served as their source of heat in winter. The food provided by their owners frequently was repetitious—meat, meal, and molasses. Such standard rations were monotonous but usually whole-some. Most slaves supplemented their diet* from their own vegetable gardens where they grew beans, potatoes, greens, cabbage, and corn. Additional variety came from hunting, fishing,* and picking wild berries or other fruit from the woods. Though some slaves complained in their memoirs of a "mush and milk" diet, most described their sustenance as good. This fact was confirmed by the Civil War physical examinations that revealed remarkably healthy Kentucky black recruits.

The vast majority of Kentucky slaves wore homespun clothes* made from coarse woolen, cotton, linen, or flaxen material colored by dye extracted from sassafras bark or wild berries. Though the quality of clothes varied from farm to farm, in general Kentucky slaves were poorly clothed, especially children, who usually wore little more than a "tow-cloth" shirt until they were six or seven years old. Many slave owners doled out clothes annually, often at Christmas, and most slaves went without shoes from spring to late fall. Slaves frequently supplemented their wardrobe with extra money earned working at odd jobs at night or on weekends.

The family* was the central institution in slave society. Slaves fell in love and married just as their owners did, but there the similarity ended. Bondsmen had to have permission of their owners to live together because Kentucky law did not recognize slave marriages.* Owners could sell either partner or the offspring of the marriage at any time, and frequently did. The easiest slave marriage occurred when two slaves on the same farm united, but a large number of partners lived on separate farms. Though on isolated farms cohabitation marriages were the norm, most Kentucky slaves preferred standing before a slave minister when they married. Slave wedding ceremonies were often the biggest and most meaningful events in the slave community, and occasionally slave owners provided elaborate celebrations for the couple and their friends. The slave family proved to be remarkably resilient.

In their recollections many former slaves remembered a home where no male was present. For others, fathers often lived on nearby farms and visited their family one or two nights a week or on weekends. Still others wrote of their mothers and fathers as the strongest personalities in their lives. Alexander Walters, who rose from slavery to become a renowned Methodist minister, wrote that his mother taught him the meaning of justice and his father gave him a hopeful spirit in spite of slavery. Many slaves grew up in a stable slave community where they regularly saw their grandparents, aunts, and uncles. They often told of a childhood during which they played happily with their brothers, sisters, cousins, their owner's children, and visited other relatives in the neighborhood. Henry Bibb,* one of Kentucky's most famous fugitives, exaggerated when he wrote that it was "almost impossible" for a Kentucky slave to trace his or her ancestry.

There was, however, a darker side for the Kentucky slave family. Slavery remained, after all, a capitalistic system of labor predicated upon profits, and separation of families by owners for financial gain or to relieve economic pressure was an ever-present possibility. For many slaves the destruction of their families constituted the most devastating aspect of Kentucky slavery. Slaveholders sold children only six years old and advertised the sale of children even younger. Newspapers regularly carried advertisements for mothers and their young children to be sold together, and on occasion separately. Elisha Green, one of Kentucky's most famous post–Civil War Baptist ministers, described in his memoirs the agony he and his wife suffered when they witnessed the sale of their teenage son "down the river." Isaac Johnson, after being auctioned off at age eleven, stood hitched to a post and watched as one buyer purchased his mother and another his four-year-old brother.

Though most slaves were sold regionally, Kentuckians carried on a growing slave trade with the Deep South. An 1833 law prohibiting the importation of slaves into Kentucky for resale probably diminished Kentucky's slave traffic. But declining profits from slave labor in the Commonwealth and rising prices* for slaves in the Cotton Belt led to the law's repeal in 1849. Thereafter, Kentucky became a slave emporium. Slave traders in Louisville and Lexington, who regularly advertised their need for slaves for the Southern market, maintained large jails where they held their purchases until they were taken south. Smaller traders went from town to village purchasing slaves to fill their orders. Most white Kentuckians felt a need to denounce slave traders, their slave "pens," and the Southern trade, but without significant effect. Slave coffles moving southward on Kentucky roads and rivers were a frequent sight throughout slavery's existence.

As harsh as the system seemed, the nature of bondage in Kentucky occasionally allowed slaves to affect their own destiny. Some slaves received permission to find someone to purchase them rather than face the uncertainty of auction. Others occasionally donated their life's savings to a neighborhood white to be applied toward the purchase of a loved one to prevent his or her being sold south. In the case of George Dupee, a Lexington Baptist minister, the members of his church persuaded the white pastor of the First Baptist Church to buy Dupee when he was placed at auction, preventing his being sold away from his church and family. For years thereafter, the treasurer of the black church paid installments to Dupee's benefactor until the debt was erased. Other slaves were less fortunate. In 1860 Nancy Lee scoured Lexington unsuccessfully to find local buyers for her teenage granddaughters whose "freedom papers" had been lost or stolen. No one in Lexington intervened as slave traders purchased the girls and carried them off to the Deep South.

The strength of the slave family also can be seen in efforts of slaves to maintain contact with loved ones from whom they were separated. Slaves freed to emigrate to Liberia* often wrote their Kentucky relatives, and occasionally slaves sold to the Deep South sent letters inquiring about their family. More frequently, Kentucky slaves ran away to return to their friends and family. Even Kentucky fugitives* in Canada occasionally corresponded with their relatives or former masters. The desire to see relatives was the major cause of running away. Other slaves, when allowed, visited their kinsmen who lived in various parts of Kentucky or even in the Deep South, and at least one Kentucky slave ran away to New Orleans in search of his wife.

State and local laws strictly regulated the movement of slaves, and the vast majority of slave owners attempted to enforce the system rigidly. Slaves could not be away from their homes for more than four hours without a pass. Common carriers were under threat of a fine for allowing a slave to travel illegally. Passes usually described the holder, the task he was attending to for his owner, and the time he was to be home. Some masters, however, gave their slaves open-ended passes, allowing them to go and come as they pleased.

The local slave patrol* served as the primary agency for enforcing restrictions on slaves, and much of the harshness associated with that system can be attributed to the unscrupulous whites who too often constituted the majority of its members. Blacks viewed the patrol as less a system of law and order than an instrument of harassment or even sadistic abuse. Several factors, however, made it very difficult for white Kentuckians to control the mobility of slaves. The laws aimed at limiting mobility were loosely applied and unevenly enforced. Some slaves claimed that they were never stopped by patrols though they traveled extensively. The rural nature of Kentucky society and the absence of adequate roads, along with the fact that most slaves knew their neighborhood as well as the patrollers, made it difficult to police the counties thoroughly. Many slaves thus found it relatively easy to travel in their neighborhoods, with or without their owner's approval, especially at night.

Slavery in Kentucky never was so harsh as to prevent recreation* from being an important part of the lives of the bondsmen. Slaves used their voices and their physical dexterity, and, on occasion, made their work a social event. Children played hide-and-seek around the cabins in the evening while their parents pitched horseshoes, played musical instruments,* danced,* and sang songs.* Most Kentucky slaves, after finishing their tasks on Saturday afternoon, were free to use the remainder of the day and Sunday as they pleased. Men hunted or fished while the women visited neighbors or participated in quilting bees. Weekends also provided slaves an opportunity to "resort to the woods" where they held such athletic contests as boxing and wrestling, and dancing "frolics" where liquor sometimes flowed. In many parts of Kentucky slave frolics occurred simultaneously with those of their white owners. Former slave Robert Anderson, however, remembered preferring the separate, secret slave dances of his "own particular race" where slaves expressed their innermost feelings. Slaves who lived near towns frequently spent their Sunday afternoons riding around in rented carriages or buying ice cream or sodas at local stores. Christmas to New Year was the longest holiday period slaves enjoyed. Bondsmen usually received special food allotments from their owners. Slave children looked forward to a stick of hard candy in addition to Christmas gifts their parents provided.

To preserve his labor force, it was in the owner's best interest to provide for the health care* of his slaves. The rural nature of Kentucky society required that someone on the farm, usually the farmer's wife, administer health care for whites and blacks alike. Farmers depended on patent medicines as a first line of defense against illness, but when these failed, slaveholders usually called in a physician. Many slaves also utilized folk remedies when they or their children were ill. State law required that slave owners provide for the infirm, aged, and insane. While it is clear that most did, there is some evidence that masters occasionally sold seriously ill slaves in order to evade responsibility. The fact that the percentage of slaves who lived past age fifty was smaller than the corresponding figure for Kentucky whites suggests the effect not only of a harsher life but also of inferior health care.

Most slaves and slaveholders believed that bondage was less harsh in Kentucky than in the Deep South, a view reinforced by the testimony of foreign visitors to the Commonwealth. This idea arose partially from Kentucky's low owner-slave ratio, which reportedly made the master-slave relationship* more personal than that generally present in the lower South. But the proximity of Kentucky to free territory also served to ameliorate slave treatment by offering slaves faced with unreasonable treatment the option of running away. Kentucky law promised punishment for slaveholders who engaged in abusive or inhumane behavior toward their slaves. Most masters treated their bondsmen, as Lexington fugitive slave Jonathan Thomas phrased it, "as well as the nature and condition of servitude permits." The character and personality of the slave owner, the accommodation of the slave to bondage, the slave's expectations in life—all were important variables regarding treatment. But the economic value of slaves provided their best protection against abuse. Most slaves quickly learned that the key to good treatment, as a Tompkinsville slave explained, was for slaves to "do what their masters told them to do." Slaves usually developed a good working relationship with their masters, and as a result, most survived and a few even prospered.

As benign as Kentuckians, black and white, believed slavery to be, there were, nevertheless, famous instances of severe abuse. Violations of farm rules typically meant punishment, and many slaves reported severe whippings that left their backs cut and bleeding. The body of a female Lexington slave examined at the workhouse after her owner was charged with abuse revealed abrasions, contusions, and burns. In 1855 a Bourbon County court confiscated and sold the slaves of a couple who severely beat and tortured a slave and her daughter. And in 1837 in Lexington the wife of a judge pushed a slave from a second-story window, resulting in a broken arm, leg, and a severe spinal injury.

Justice administered to slaves by the state was separate and unequal. Conviction for a misdemeanor led to thirty-nine stripes, with death the punishment for a felony. Slaves charged with crimes frequently were subjected to pressure to confess and were convicted on hearsay evidence, mere suspicion, or the fact that testimony against them originated from whites. Nevertheless, on paper at least a Kentucky slave had a right to an informal defense by his master in a court of law.

Many slaves accepted their condition, believing it could be changed only by degrees. They engaged in passive resistance to their owner's will, destroyed property, or even engaged in violence. Others, however, rejected bondage outright. They agitated for voluntary emancipation by their owners, worked nights and weekends to purchase their freedom, or fled to free territory.

Deciding to run away to the North and freedom posed an extremely difficult decision for Kentucky bondsmen, one that only a small number made. It meant leaving the security of family and friends for the unknown, possibly even death. Those slaves who fled generally did so during a period of uncertainty in their lives. They resented changing work rules, objected to unusually harsh punishment, or feared being sold to the Deep South. Successful escape often depended on the sophistication of the runaway*; the more thoughtful the plan, the greater the possibility of acquiring freedom. Most fugitives made the difficult part of the escape—traversing Kentucky and crossing the Ohio River—without outside assistance. They fled on their own, followed unfamiliar roads, sometimes lived off wild berries and stolen food, and almost always experienced hardships. When fugitives arrived north of the Ohio River, they inevitably sought out the assistance of their free black* brethren. For most Kentucky fugitives, the underground railroad* began north of the Ohio River. Once securely free, many fugitives initiated efforts to purchase the freedom of loved ones left behind in the Commonwealth. And some even returned to Kentucky clandestinely to rescue members of their family.

For slaves who spent their lives in Kentucky, the church constituted the single most important institution outside the home. Most slaves attended white churches—a slave minister sometimes pastored the black flock with a white man present—where they were second-class members and where the religious message urged obedience to their masters. Though religious services represented the most integrated aspect of slave life, blacks preferred to form separate churches that became the center of their social activities and educational opportunities. Their churches provided black Kentuckians a refuge from white domination. Beginning with the First African Baptist Church in Lexington in 1801, separate black congregations increased until they were common by the 1840s in Kentucky's larger towns.

Black churches provided a valuable leadership training ground that made antebellum black preachers the strongest leaders in the slave community. Though never totally free from white interference and oversight, black preachers and their congregations objected to white domination of their church affairs and demanded the right to govern their churches and to determine their own spiritual values. Strong personalities—such as Henry Adams, the pastor of Fifth Street Baptist Church in Louisville, and Elisha Green of the African Baptist Church of Paris—often dominated the thinking of the black community and won the respect of the whites.

Black churches engaged in numerous self-help benefits for the black community. Some of the larger churches established day schools that provided a small number of their children a rudimentary education. Others opened their doors for night schools, built church libraries, or used their Sunday schools to teach their pupils to read the Bible. Churches also provided singing classes, concerts, and lectures for their members. In addition, they held fairs and benefits to raise money for church projects, the poor, and the infirm.

The growth of emancipation,* the increasing tendency to hire out slaves, and the acceleration of the Southern slave trade* diminished the importance of slavery in Kentucky during the 1850s. By the outbreak of the Civil War, Kentucky's slaves, many of whom had been aware of the rising sectional controversy, exhibited a spirit of unrest. Though a time of tremendous trial for most Kentucky blacks, the Civil War* afforded many slaves their first opportunity to protest their condition. They became, slaveholders noticed, less malleable and more independent. Many of the most trusted male servants were the first to run off to join the Union army, followed soon after by their wives and children who sought the protection of Union refugee camps such as the one established at Camp Nelson. Kentucky's black soldiers helped impress other slaves, and eventually over 28,000 Kentucky slaves served in the Union army. By war's end they, and 75,000 of their family members, had been freed by the federal government. The Civil War essentially doomed slavery in Kentucky, but its official demise came with the ratification of the Thirteenth Amendment, 18 December 1865.

SELECTED BIBLIOGRAPHY

J. Winston Coleman, Jr., *Slavery Times in Kentucky* (1940); Lowell H. Harrison, *The Antislavery Movement in Kentucky* (1978); and George P. Rawick, ed., *The American Slave: A Composite Autobiography*, vol. 16: *Kentucky* (1972).

MARION B. LUCAS

L

LANGUAGE, SLAVE. Among the commonplaces of the history of slavery is the observation that slave ship captains practiced separation of tribal, and therefore language, groups for purposes of control. Although some African languages survived in places like Cuba and Trinidad, no wholesale importation of African languages into the New World occurred. For purposes of comparison only, it would be safe to say that African languages probably played a much smaller role in the communicative strategies of slaves brought to the Americas than did European languages for immigrants to those continents. What was the primary factor in communication by Afro-American slaves, is, however, of great importance in work on language contact phenomena.

Beginning perhaps as early as the sixteenth century on the west coast of Africa, a class of special languages, conventionally referred to as ''pidgins,'' played a central role in cultural and social adaptation between different people. Almost every pidgin shows evidence of having been through a rudimentary stage that can be termed a ship's jargon (in which it was used perhaps even more by European sailors than by slaves) and a shore jargon (often so Africanized or otherwise nativized in other parts of the world that it became virtually inaccessible to Europeans). The earliest special contact languages were Romance. The earliest on the west coast of Africa showed great lexical influence, at least, from Portuguese—or, perhaps more accurately, Iberian. Linguists differ in their assessment of the situation. Some claim that Pidgin English developed from the Iberian pidgin. Others assert that Pidgin English was primarily a domestic development, one that simply happened to follow the Iberian pidgin in place and time.

The ship's jargon was not a purely African development. The Portuguese-, or Iberian-, based creole languages of Guinea, Senegal, and the islands of São Thomé and Annabon, spoken by Africans, resemble the Papiamentu of Aruba, Curaçao, and Bonaire of the West Indies, spoken by descendants of Africans. But both are strikingly similar to Papia Kristang (Malacca Portuguese Creole), a language that has no discernible component of African speakers. Indian Ocean

French Creole, with virtually no African influence, is grammatically very like the varieties of Martinique, Guadeloupe, Haiti, and Louisiana.

The preverbal system of tense, modal, and aspect is the common characteristic of these languages. This is an unusual development because European languages are marked by suffix morphology. The English-based varieties tend to have aspect as the obligatory verbal component, although Standard English accords that status to tense. The issue hardly arises in the English pidgins and creoles, but the Romance-based varieties notably have the order subject, verb, pronoun object unlike the standard Romance languages and their European dialects. A number of other structural characteristics, most of them consistent with the notion of "simplification," are shared by Iberian, English, and French pidgins and creoles, whether or not the speakers are of African ancestry.

The primary African contribution to Afro-American languages, apart from phonological features like imploded (injective) consonants and (marginally) lexical tone, was vocabulary. Most of the Afro-creoles have some reflex of *nyam nyam hoodoo/voodoo* or *obiah*. The Ashanti day names, along with attributive adjectival use of similar forms from other West African languages, are still widespread and were strikingly so in the eighteenth and nineteenth centuries. Phrasal compounds like *eye water* (tears), *big eye* (greed), and *day clean* (dawn) often have analogues in creole languages based on different European languages.

The term *creole* applies to these languages when they have passed from the pidgin stage by the process of nativization. Significantly, this last process is social more than linguistic; it operates on the expanded shore jargon stage. The process by which the language becomes the "only" variety of a speech community within one generation is complex. In the West Cameroon, for example, Pidgin English has creolized—for at least some of its speakers—without the African languages of the area being lost. In many places, as for example in the use of a pidgin version of a Surinam creole with Trio Indians, a "reconnaissance" version (about the same as a ship's jargon) remains in use by part of the speech community, with the great majority of its members speaking the creolized variety. Repatriation of freed slaves to Liberia* introduced New World varieties, further complicating a situation that probably already included the creolization process.

When the standard dialect, or other more traditional varieties, remains as a model—English in Jamaica, the Sea Islands of Georgia and South Carolina, most of the Caribbean, and the coast of Central America—change in the direction of the standard variety takes place. One theory holds that this same process produced the "nonstandard" varieties spoken by blacks in the continental United States, now known as Black English. The relatively low socioeconomic status of the slaves and their descendants has virtually assured low prestige for their language varieties. Movements to give them prestige through such expedients as literary creation have been quite recent and only partly successful. About 20 percent of black Americans either do not speak Black English at all or know it primarily as the source of ethnic slang terminology. Nevertheless, Black English has strongly affected the vocabulary of the blues, jazz, and rock music.

Nearly four hundred years after the first slaves were brought to Virginia, the linguistic aftermath of slavery remains, even in areas that hardly participated in the plantation system. These linguistic consequences will last at least as long as the social consequences.

SELECTED BIBLIOGRAPHY

David Dalby, ''The African Element in American English,'' in Thomas Kochman, ed., *Rappin' and Stylin' Out: Communication in Urban Black America* (1972); J. L. Dillard, *Black English: Its History and Usage in the United States* (1972); J. L. Dillard, *Black Names* (1976); J. L. Dillard, *Lexicon of Black English* (1977); and Lorenzo Dow Turner, *Africanisms in the Gullah Dialect* (1949).

J. L. DILLARD

LAW. American slavery's growth, development, political potency, and day-to-day workings were all affected by statutes, court cases, and constitutions. The earliest roots of slavery in Virginia and Maryland are connected to laws, court cases, and legal documents. Legal records suggest that in the 1620s blacks received treatment similar to whites. Blacks testified in courts, owned property (including white and black servants), and if indentured servants, they became free when their indentures ended. This treatment gradually changed between 1630 and 1660 as Virginia courts upheld wills and contracts that bequeathed or sold black servants and their children ''for life.'' Similarly, Virginia courts began to impose harsher criminal sentences on blacks than on whites.

The case of John Punch illustrates how criminal punishments, especially for running away, helped create slavery in Virginia. In 1640 Punch, a black indentured servant,* and two white servants were punished for running away from their master. The two whites were whipped and had four years added to the terms of their indentures. This was a common form of punishment for running away. However, the court ordered that the ''negro named *John Punch* shall serve his said master or his assigns for the time of his natural Life here or elsewhere.'' No whites ever received a similar punishment.

Before 1659 there were no formal statutes creating slavery in Virginia. A 1659–1660 statute explicitly encouraged Dutch traders to bring ''negro slaves'' into the colony. A 1661–62 statute referred to ''negroes who are incapable of making satisfaction by addition of time.'' These laws both recognized the existence of slavery and supported the development of the institution. In 1662 a Virginia law declared that all children* born in the colony would inherit the status of their mother. This was the first explicit recognition and support of the concept that children could be slaves from birth. This statute was also an explicit rejection of English law, which held that a child inherited the status of the father. Eventually all American slave jurisdictions would adopt this rule, based on Roman law, known as *partus sequitur ventrem* (the offspring follows the dam [mother]). Later statutes prohibited free blacks from owning white servants, declared that baptism would not affect the status of slaves, and prohibited interracial marriages. Other laws designed to control slaves modified the common law to prevent the prosecution of masters and other whites who might kill slaves. In 1723 Virginia adopted what might be considered the first comprehensive American slave code. The act contained twenty-four sections and covered nine pages of William W. Hening, ed., *The Statutes at Large . . . of . . . Virginia.*

In the seventeenth and eighteenth centuries the other mainland colonies adopted slavery and passed laws to maintain and control the institution. Most of these colonies adopted strict laws for punishing such infractions by slaves as running away, unlawful assembly, battery on a white, arson, or rebellion. The most common penalties for such crimes were whipping,* transportation out of the colony, dismemberment, or death. While criminal penalties for slaves were quite similiar throughout the Southern colonies, several variations in the laws regulating slavery existed. For example, in 1663 Maryland adopted the English common-law rule that the status of a child followed the father (*partus sequitur partem*). But by 1715 all vestiges of this English rule had been eliminated in Maryland. While Virginia prohibited blacks from carrying guns and marrying whites in the seventeenth century, South Carolina did not pass such legislation until the eighteenth century.

Although blacks were considered property as early as the 1640s, none of the colonies were certain what *kind* of property slaves were. Initially, under Virginia common law, slaves were treated as personal property, or chattel property. However, a 1705 law declared slaves to be real estate. Despite subsequent attempts to change this law, slaves remained real estate in Virginia until 1792. Other slave jurisdictions experimented with slaves as real property in the eighteenth century, but gradually most enacted laws making slaves personal property. The distinction between personal and real property affected inheritance, mortgages, and other financial aspects of slavery, but did not affect the growth or development of the institution in other ways.

Court decisions affected the law of slavery in two major ways during the colonial period. First, courts in Virginia helped establish slavery by ignoring English law and allowing blacks to be enslaved through inheritance or sale, even though no statutes had created slavery. Criminal courts sentenced free blacks to lifetime servitude, and later supported the institution by punishing slaves, especially after rebellions such as the New York Slave Conspiracy (1712)* and the Stono Rebellion (1739).* By the time of the American Revolution slavery was firmly established as an integral part of the colonies' legal system.

The ideology of the Revolution* undermined the intellectual and moral basis for slavery, especially in the North. During and after the Revolution, Massachusetts (1780), New Hampshire (1784), and Vermont (1791) ended slavery through constitutional provisions and judicial interpretation. In 1781 the Massachusetts courts interpreted the state's constitution to have ended slavery in a series of cases involving the slave Quock Walker. Gradual emancipation statutes in Pennsylvania (1780), Rhode Island (1784), Connecticut (1784), New York (1799), and New Jersey (1804) provided that all existing slaves would remain in lifetime servitude, but that their children would be born free. Under the gradual emancipation statutes these children were held as indentured servants by their parents' masters until they reached a statutory age of complete emancipation. That age varied from eighteen to twenty-eight years, depending upon the sex of the child and the state in which he or she lived.

Revolutionary ideology also led to some changes in Southern law. All of the slave states prohibited the African slave trade* during and immediately after the Revolution. In Virginia private manumission* was legalized in 1782. In North Carolina a 1791 statute which reflected revolutionary liberalism declared that the murder of a slave was a crime at common law. This statute was so poorly drafted, however, that the North Carolina Supreme Court, in *State v. Boon* (1801), felt it could not be applied to a convicted murderer.

In order to "create a more perfect Union" the framers of the Constitution* were forced to make compromises over slavery. James Madison asserted that the states at the convention "were divided into different interests not by their difference of size, but by other circumstances, the most material of which resulted partly from climate, but principally from the effects of their having or not having slaves." This division led to passionate debates over slavery, and particularly over the continuation of the slave trade. In exchange for South Carolina's support for the commerce clause (Art. I, Sec. 8) New Englanders supported an un-amendable prohibition on congressional interference with the slave trade until 1808 (Art. I, Sec. 9, and Art. V). Slave state delegates won protection and political influence for their peculiar institution in other parts of the Constitution as well. In the three-fifths clause the South gained a supplement to its congressional delegation (Art. I, Sec. 2); the fugitive slave clause provided for the return of runaway slaves and led to two federal enforcement statutes (Art. IV, Sec. 2); and the domestic violence clause committed the national government to providing federal troops to combat slave rebellions (Art. IV, Sec. 4).

Federal courts heard relatively few slave cases. Most concerned slavery in the District of Columbia (where all cases were federal), violations of laws prohibiting the African slave trade (after 1808), and the fugitive slave laws of 1793* and 1850.* Few such cases were heard by the U.S. Supreme Court. The federal courts, particularly the U.S. Supreme Court, generally tended to support slavery and the claims of slave owners. The Supreme Court issued especially proslavery opinions in *Prigg v. Pennsylvania* (1842), *Jones v. Van Zandt* (1847), *Strader v. Graham* (1850), *Moore v. Illinois* (1852), *Dred Scott v. Sandford* (1857), and *Ableman v. Booth* (1859). The Taney Court set a proslavery tone on questions of fugitive slaves, the rights of free blacks,* slavery in the territories, and interstate comity, and thereby exacerbated sectional conflicts in the 1850s.

By 1860 common-law precedents and statutes had combined to create a distinct slave law in each of the fifteen slave states. While there were important variations among the slave states, some general propositions about slave law can be applied to most of the slave South.

By the 1850s most slave states discouraged or prohibited private manumission, even when it would take effect outside of the state. With a few exceptions, slave state hostility toward free blacks made it impossible for manumitted slaves to remain in their home states. Furthermore, wills were usually construed to defeat attempts by masters to free their slaves, even when the slaves were to be sent out of the state or out of the country. *Bailey v. Poindexter* (Va., 1858) offers a striking example of this. Poindexter had directed his executor to ask his slaves if they wished to go to Liberia,* and to accommodate their wishes. Those who did not choose freedom in Liberia were to be sold for the benefit of Poindexter's heirs. In a split decision the Virginia Court of Appeals ruled that to ask the slaves what they wanted would violate the laws of Virginia, and thus they had to remain slaves. While the Georgia Supreme Court upheld an out-of-state man-umission in *Cleland v. Waters* (1854), Chief Justice Joseph Lumpkin made it clear to the legislature that he believed all postmortem manumissions should be prohibited. The legislature complied with Lumpkin's dictum in 1859 with ''An Act to prohibit the post mortem manumission of slaves.'' In *Mitchell v. Wells* (1859) the Mississippi High Court of Errors and Appeals refused to recognize an out-of-state manumission executed by a master while he was alive.

While manumission became increasingly difficult in the nineteenth century, the legal protections of slaves involved in criminal cases grew. At the time of the Revolution slaves were not considered within the protection of the common law in most states. The Georgia Supreme Court, in *Neal v. Farmer* (1851), provided a detailed discussion of why, with the exception of an early Mississippi case and an early Tennessee case, Southern courts had held that there was no crime at common law for the murder of a slave. In *Neal* the Georgia court held that there was in fact no common-law crime of murdering a slave because slaves were unknown to the English common law.

By 1860 all the slave states gave slaves statutory legal protections to the extent that some crimes against them by whites or other slaves could be prosecuted. These statutes punished not only the murder of a slave, but batteries by strangers, inhumane cruelty, and even the rape of one slave by another. Whites could of course not be prosecuted for the rape of a slave, although a white might be prosecuted *for trespass* if he raped another man's slave. While whites might be prosecuted for the murder or maiming of a slave, such prosecutions were rare, and capital punishment for such cases even rarer. In *State v. Hoover* (1839) the North Carolina Supreme Court upheld a death sentence for a master who had viciously tortured and murdered his slave. More common, however, was the outcome in *Souther v. Commonwealth* (1851), where a Virginia master received only a five-year sentence for a similarly barbaric killing.

Short of killing a slave, a master faced few restraints when punishing slaves,* even though some laws proscribed cruel treatment. The classic statement on the power of masters was Judge Thomas Ruffin's of North Carolina. In *State v.*

Mann (1829) Ruffin asserted that the state could not question the authority of the master over his slave: "The power of the master must be absolute to render the submission of the slave perfect. . . . We cannot allow the right of the master to be brought into discussion in the courts of justice. The slave, to remain a slave, must be made sensible that there is no appeal from his master; that his power is in no instance usurped; but is conferred by the laws of man at least, if not by the law of God."

While masters were virtually immune from the legal consequences of harming a slave, third parties were not. Those who harmed the slaves of others were prosecuted for battery or murder. They were also sued by masters for the damages caused to their property. Most Southern courts also recognized that slaves had some minimal right to defend themselves against the batteries caused by whites other than their owners. However, slave state courts used different standards of provocation and evidence when trying slaves. Similarly, courts used very different standards when trying a white who had harmed a slave. For example, behavior by a slave could be considered provocative, and thus mitigate a white's crime against that slave, even though similar behavior by a white would not have been considered sufficient provocation to mitigate the crime. In trials slaves were usually granted counsel and often protected from self-incrimination through forced confessions and from double jeopardy. However, because blacks could *never* testify against whites in the antebellum South, prosecutions for batteries on or murders of slaves were difficult when the defendant was white. The leading Southern expert on slave law Thomas R. R. Cobb admitted in his treatise, *An Inquiry into the Law of Negro Slavery* (1858), that the slave's "mouth being closed as a witness in a court of justice" did diminish the quality of Southern criminal justice.

Noncriminal law raised enormous problems for the Southern legal system. As property, slaves could be bought, sold, devised, inherited, rented, and loaned. Contracts for rented slaves often limited the work slaves could do. But because slaves were human beings, it was sometimes impossible to prevent individual slaves from doing things they were forbidden to do. If death or injury resulted, courts were often asked to determine if the renter was responsible. Hard-and-fast rules were difficult for courts to establish and are virtually impossible to generalize about. In industrial situations some Southern courts tried, with great difficulty, to apply such doctrines as the "fellow servant rule" to slaves. Whatever sense the "fellow servant rule" may have made for industrial workplaces in mid-nineteenth-century America, an application of the rule to slaves would have undermined the institution of slavery. To cite just one problem, the fellow servant rule implied that a contract existed between the "fellow servant" and the hirer; but, of course, slaves could not make contracts. The contract existed between the hirer and the slave owner. Similarly, slaves could not be "fellow servants" of white workers because that would have elevated them to a status equal to whites.

The dual status of slaves as both property and persons raised enormous problems for Southern jurists and legislatures. Most Southern lawmakers tried to protect the humanity of slaves, but they were never completely successful. An example of the difficulty of balancing these needs is a Georgia statute of 1854, designed to prevent the unnecessary separation of mothers and young children. The law directed executors and other fiduciaries when dividing estates *not* to separate mothers from children who were not yet five years old. This statute recognized the human needs of mothers and infants (although allowing the separation of five-year-olds from their mothers was hardly humane). However, the statute concluded with an escape clause ''unless such division [of the estate] cannot in any wise be effected without such separation.'' Whatever the legislature's humanitarian goals were, the property interest in the slaves, even in slave babies, became the highest priority of the legal system.

The nineteenth century witnessed an explosion in legal literature. During this period American law came into its own, as such eminent jurists and legal scholars as Joseph Story, James Kent, St. George Tucker, and Samuel Livermore produced treatises on nearly every imaginable subject of law. Curiously, very few treatises were written on slave law, despite its importance to the political stability and economy of the nation. Kent, Story, Tucker, and others naturally mentioned slavery in their treatises on other aspects of law, but did not offer either detailed analyses of the legal problems it generated or a practical survey of the laws and decisions affecting it. Many works were written on constitutional aspects of slavery, particularly by those opposed to the institution. Only five works appeared on the non-constitutional law aspects of slavery. Jacob Wheeler's relatively short *Practical Treatise on the Law of Slavery* (1837) organized case law by subject and would have been useful to a lawyer seeking precedents for particular legal problems. George M. Stroud, *A Sketch of the Laws Relating to Slavery* (1827, 2d ed., 1856), and William Goodell, *American Slave Code in Theory and Practice* (1853), were antislavery in character and were organized more for the use of a polemicist or politician than a lawyer. Other antislavery writers, such as Theodore Dwight Weld* in *Slavery As It Is* (1853) and Harriet Beecher Stowe* in *A Key to Uncle Tom's Cabin* (1853), also exploited Southern case law and statutes for antislavery purposes. These and many other antislavery writers reflected the sentiments of Goodell as stated in the first chapter of his book: ''*We Propose, then, by an exhibition of the American Slave Code, to test the moral character of American slaveholding.* The practice (in the absence of mere abuses) cannot be better than the code, or rule of conduct, that gives it license and sanction.''

More comprehensive, although equally biased, was the aggressively proslavery* treatise by Thomas R. R. Cobb, *An Inquiry into the Law of Negro Slavery in the United States of America* (1858). John Codman Hurd's *The Law of Freedom and Bondage in the United States* (2 vols., 1858, 2nd ed., 1862) is a moderately proslavery treatise written by a Bostonian. Hurd's volumes contain exhaustive analysis of some major cases, including *Dred Scott*, and short summaries of the statutory law concerning slavery in all of the American states. Hurd's volumes are the only ones that offer any systematic analysis of the statutory law of slavery; however, Hurd's work is not comprehensive and must be used with caution.

For American judges, particularly those in the antebellum South, slavery posed difficult problems. The dual status of the slave—as a person and a "thing"—challenged jurists and lawmakers, especially when the "thing" acted like a person. Southern jurists often complained when certain types of cases were brought before them. They did not want to grapple with the contradictions created by the peculiar institution. When slaves were pushed to the limit and struck back with deadly force, Southern jurists had to balance the needs of the slave system with the obviously human characteristics of slaves. Similarly, when masters or other whites harmed slaves, judges were forced to support either racial solidarity and the stern necessities of the system or abstract concepts of justice. The results were mixed. In *Ford v. Ford*, an 1846 manumission case, the Tennessee Supreme Court concluded that slaves were "not in the condition of a horse or an ox." In that case the slaves gained their freedom. But in *State v. Mann* (1829) the North Carolina Supreme Court refused to allow the prosecution of a man who deliberately shot and wounded a slave he was renting. There Judge Thomas Ruffin asserted, "The end" of slavery was "the profit of the master, his security and the public safety." The slave was "one doomed in his own person, and his posterity, to live without knowledge, and without the capacity to make any thing his own, and to toil that another may reap the fruits." Ruffin realized that "such service" could "only be expected from one who has no will of his own; who surrenders his will in implicit obedience to that of another." Ruffin logically concluded that "Such obedience is the consequence of uncontrolled authority over the body. . . . The power of the master must be absolute, to render the submission of the slave perfect." Ruffin acknowledged his "sense of the harshness of this proposition" and that "as a principle of moral right, every person in his retirement must repudiate it." However, "in the actual conditions of things, it must be so. . . . This discipline belongs to the state of slavery."

The law of slavery ultimately relied on force to smooth over the contradictions between the liberal values of the Anglo-American legal heritage and the obvious tyranny that slavery produced. The tensions between the necessity to protect slavery and the legal training of the jurists and legislators were never fully resolved. Thus, there was never a "law of slavery," but rather, there were many "laws of slavery" competing with each other to preserve the peculiar institution and yet at the same time to prevent its corrupting influences from undermining the entire legal system of the South and the nation.

SELECTED BIBLIOGRAPHY

Robert Cover, *Justice Accused: Antislavery and the Judicial Process* (1975); Paul Finkelman, *An Imperfect Union: Slavery, Federalism, and Comity* (1981); Daniel J. Flanigan, "Criminal Procedure in Slave Trials in the Antebellum South," *Journal of Southern History*, 40 (1974), 537–64; A. Leon Higginbotham, Jr., *In the Matter of Color: Race and the American Legal Process: The Colonial Period* (1978); Thomas D. Morris, " 'Society is not marked by punctuality in the payment of debts': The Chattel Mortgages of Slaves," in David J. Bodenhamer and James W. Ely, Jr., eds., *Ambivalent Legacy: A Legal History of the South* (1984): A. E. Keir Nash, "Reason of Slavery: Understanding the Judicial Role in the Peculiar Institution," *Vanderbilt Law Review*, 32 (January 1979), 7–218; and Mark V. Tushnet, *The American Law of Slavery, 1810–1860: Considerations of Humanity and Interest* (1981).

PAUL FINKELMAN

LIBERIA. Liberia, the oldest republic on the African continent, has its historical roots in the controversy that raged in antebellum America over the domestic institution of slavery and the destiny of Afro-Americans, both chattel and free. Deeply troubled by free black population growth and unable, or perhaps unwilling, to envision interracial harmony in American society should slavery end, early nineteenth-century conservative reformers began urging physical separation of the races as the necessary panacea. Their position rested, in part, on the premise that Afro-Americans were racially inferior to Euro-Americans, thus making their continued presence in the country inimical to the development of an orderly, civilized society. Other sentiments, including missionary zeal and paternalism, fused with racial prejudice to form the foundation of the African colonization movement.*

In 1816 prominent religious and political supporters of colonization assembled in the nation's capital, where they formed the American Colonization Society.* The organization's principal aim was to sponsor a colony in Africa as a haven for repatriated Afro-Americans. By 1822 agents, acting on the society's behalf, secured land for the enterprise at Cape Mesurado on the coast of West Africa and named the first settlement, Monrovia, in honor of President James Monroe. The Liberian colony grew slowly as the society and its state auxiliaries established other settlements along the coast between Sierra Leone and the Ivory Coast. Direct control of the fledgling colony's administrative affairs passed from the American Colonization Society in 1847, when the settlers proclaimed their political independence, electing Joseph Jenkins Roberts, a freedman from Petersburg, Virginia, as the first president of the Republic of Liberia.

The pattern of American emigration did much to shape the texture of Liberia's settler society. Constant financial uncertainty, the by-product of domestic opposition to colonization that intensified over time, sharply limited the total number of emigrants sent to Liberia by the society. Less than 5,000 "free people of color" and slaves manumitted by their masters reached Liberia under the society's auspices by 1843, and thereafter the annual emigration rate did not grow appreciably. Those that did make Liberia their new home generally came in family units from both Northern and Southern states and lived in small, scattered enclaves such as Bassa Cove, Marshall, Millsburg, Monrovia, Sinoe, and Cape Palmas. Liberia also received thousands of recaptured Africans taken from slave ships seized by the U.S. naval squadron.

Motivated by the desire to escape bondage and racial discrimination yet clinging tenaciously to American values and tastes, the settlers resisted absorption
by Liberia's more numerous indigenous people. Instead, they tried to fashion a
more insular existence that quickly became internally stratified along economic
and social lines. At the outset a small elite of leading citizens from among the
free black emigrants set the tone and pace. They brought to Africa the advantages
of literacy and personal property and found success engaging in mercantile
commerce. They also used their relative prosperity to dominate settler politics
and establish prevailing social standards by founding churches, benevolent and
temperance societies, fraternal orders, and other community institutions. Moreover, they consolidated their status position through the bonds of marriage,
making proper family ties an enduring feature of settler political and social
dynamics.

The experience of slaves emancipated on the condition that they emigrate to
Liberia, however, was far more typical than that of the elite. They arrived with
meager resources, usually not extending beyond enough provisions for the first
twelve months. Necessity led the majority of them into farming and petty trade
with Africans—important economic activities avoided by the elite because they
were both arduous and painfully reminiscent of the past. Some former slaves
who had artisan skills were able to find work in the building trades as an
alternative to working the land, but generally their lives were no less precarious.
Perhaps the most devastating factor was the tropical disease environment that
exacted a fearsome mortality among the settler population. The frequent death
of adults, succumbing to malaria and other infectious diseases, left many or-
phaned children who, along with the aged and disabled, composed a dependent
class within each settlement. Even with the blessings of good health, settlers
faced hardships and difficult adjustments at every turn. Still the settlers, both
free blacks and emancipated slaves, cleared the land, built their homes, and
persevered on the belief that by their labors conditions would improve for themselves and those that would follow. Under adverse circumstances, remarkably
few settlers returned to America or abandoned Liberia for other locations.

The settlers, regardless of individual background or status, were united in
their determination that Christianity and Western civilization would be Liberia's
cultural foundation. By never doubting that their life-style was superior, they
assumed the dubious mission of trying to impose their values on Africans.
Inevitably, conflicts ensued, many of which might otherwise have been avoided.
When peaceful means failed to resolve disputes, neither group hesitated to resort
to military force in advancing their perceived interests. The settlers organized
militia companies for self-defense but also used them as instruments of territorial
expansion and to make punitive raids on local slave traders. Thus, relations
between settlers and Africans, forged in a climate of mutual suspicions, evolved
into a pattern of uneasy coexistence punctuated by intermittent warfare.

In spite of its obvious flaws and weaknesses, most settlers staunchly defended
their adopted homeland and urged other Afro-Americans to help them with the

task of nation-building. In letters sent back to America, emancipated slaves took pride in reporting every sign of progress, no matter how modest. They seemed to welcome the opportunity Liberia afforded them to demonstrate their self-reliance. The rhetoric of racial nationalism, imbued with the spirit of religious conviction, deepened their sense of unity and higher purpose. And yet sustained, large-scale immigration from America never materialized in the nineteenth century. Liberia was destined to remain a symbol of colonization's futility.

SELECTED BIBLIOGRAPHY

Randall M. Miller, " 'Home as Found': Ex-Slaves and Liberia," *Liberian Studies Journal*, 6 (1975), 92–108; Randall M. Miller, ed., *"Dear Master": Letters of a Slave Family* (1978); Tom W. Shick, *Behold the Promised Land: A History of Afro-American Settler Society in Nineteenth-Century Liberia* (1980); and Bell I. Wiley, ed., *Slaves No More: Letters from Liberia, 1833–1869* (1980).

TOM W. SHICK

LIELE, GEORGE (ca. 1750–ca. 1826). George Liele was the first independent black Baptist minister and founder of one of the earliest independent black Baptist churches* in America. He also was instrumental in spreading the Baptist faith to blacks in Jamaica. Born a slave in Virginia about 1750, he and his master(s) traveled throughout the colonies and by 1777 (some accounts put this date earlier) he was living in Burke County, Georgia. Liele was early inspired by his religious father, and later under the influence of his master, Henry Sharp, a deacon in the Big Buckhead Baptist Church, and Matthew Moore, Big Buckhead's minister, he was converted and baptized around 1773. Showing a gift for public speaking, he was invited to address a quarterly meeting, and he so impressed the congregation that he was licensed to preach. Emancipated in 1777, Liele began preaching to blacks in Georgia and South Carolina, and by the end of the year had established at least two churches. One of these continues today as the First African Baptist Church of Savannah. Like Moore and Sharp, Liele was a Loyalist,* and when the British occupied Savannah he took refuge there, although he still kept contact with his congregations outside the city. In 1782, when the British evacuated Savannah, Liele indentured himself to a Loyalist officer in return for passage to Jamaica. By the end of 1783 Liele was again free and at work organizing a church in Kingston. Despite initial opposition from officials, his movement grew, even after his death, about 1826. Indeed, by the 1830s, 10 percent of the black population of the island was Baptist. At that time there were twenty-one black Baptist churches in Jamaica, along with twenty-seven Negro schools serving some 4,000 students. Liele's efforts to spread the Baptist faith place him among the most important early Afro-American religious leaders.

SELECTED BIBLIOGRAPHY

Beverly Brown, "George Liele: Black Baptist and Pan-Africanist, 1750–1826," *Savacou*, 9–11 (1975), 58–67; Robert S. Davis, Jr., "The Other Side of the Coin: Georgia Baptists

Who Fought for the King,'' *Georgia Baptist Viewpoints*, 7 (1980), 47–57; ''Letters Showing the Rise and Progress of the Early Negro Churches of Georgia and the West Indies,'' *Journal of Negro History*, 1 (1916), 69–92; Donald G. Mathews, *Religion in the Old South* (1977); Albert J. Raboteau, *Slave Religion: The ''Invisible Institution'' in the Antebellum South* (1978); and Reba Carolyn Strickland, *Religion and the State of Georgia in the Eighteenth Century* (1939).

HARVEY H. JACKSON

LIFE INSURANCE. In the late antebellum period slave masters began to demonstrate interest in slave life insurance. Blacks were frequently employed on dangerous jobs in public-works construction, coal mining,* iron manufacturing,* and railroad and steamboat operations. A number of industrial concerns* that owned slave workers protected their large investments by purchasing life insurance. Similarly, masters who hired out* their bondsmen to industry bought life insurance or insisted that the lessee do so; and a few slave owners took out policies on valuable or favorite servants not hired out.

This form of insurance had existed for some time prior to the 1840s, but mainly as a protection to slave traders transporting blacks from Africa to the New World or from one domestic slave market to another. Few, if any, Northern or Southern companies insured plantation, industrial, or urban bondsmen on a regular basis until the 1840s, when life insurance began gaining in sales and in the number of new firms. But even after the introduction of slave life insurance, owners of bondsmen did not flock to the doors of agents. Only about 3 percent of all industrial slaves and a substantially smaller number of plantation slaves employed during any year in the 1850s were covered by life insurance. The problem of cost was undoubtedly a major factor. Owners were probably reluctant to lay out an extra five to fifteen dollars annually for every laborer, even if the number insured was limited to prime hands. Though agents advertised frequently in local newspapers, the concept of slave insurance was still so new that many masters must have simply ignored the publicity or put off inquiries for a future time. Too, there was the confusion in the Old South between slaves as people and slaves as property. The situation was more clear-cut when a master hired out his slave or purchased one for dangerous industrial labor. Then the slave was obviously a piece of property, and the investment required financial protection. But on a large plantation, for instance, the bondsman was still treated ambiguously as both person and property.

Some white Southerners disapproved of the whole concept of slave life insurance. Dr. Josiah Clark Nott of Mobile, Alabama, was probably the best-known and most vocal opponent. Nott feared that bondsmen would be the sufferers in the long run, as masters and mistresses succumbed to temptation and permitted insured sick or injured slaves to die.

Nott's dire predictions did not prevent the formation of companies to insure slaves in the South during the late 1840s and the 1850s. But these firms did heed Nott's caveats in several ways. They limited the amount for which a slave could be insured, required a medical examination before approving a policy, restricted the term of a slave insurance policy, prohibited the free movement of insured bondsmen from place to place, charged extra premiums for dangerous jobs, and insisted on proof of proper treatment in health and of medical attention in sickness.

The available evidence does not substantiate Nott's predictions of inhumanity to slaves whose lives were insured. In a representative sample, the proportion of deaths among one North Carolina company's white and black clients remained about equal for the years 1857, 1858, and 1860. Companies attempted to safeguard their investments by establishing guidelines and rules and in so doing served to protect the lives of black servants.

SELECTED BIBLIOGRAPHY

Eugene D. Genovese, "The Medical and Insurance Costs of Slaveholding in the Cotton Belt," *Journal of Negro History*, 45 (1960), 141–155; Josiah C. Nott, "Statistics of Southern Slave Population, with Especial Reference to Life Insurance," *De Bow's Review*, 4 (November 1847), 275, 286–287; Todd L. Savitt, "Slave Life Insurance," *Journal of Southern History*, 43 (1977), 583–600; and Robert S. Starobin, *Industrial Slavery in the Old South* (1970).

                                                                         TODD L. SAVITT

LINCOLN, ABRAHAM (1809–1865). Although born in a slave state, Kentucky (in 1809, Hardin County, where, two years later, there were 1,007 slaves and 1,627 white males over the age of sixteen), Abraham Lincoln probably inherited antislavery views from his father, a member of a Baptist congregation that had withdrawn from another church in a dispute over slavery. In 1860 Lincoln claimed that his family left Kentucky for the North in 1816 "partly on account of slavery," but he admitted that the move was due mostly to difficulties with land titles.

While serving in the Illinois House of Representatives in 1836, Lincoln was among six of eighty-three members who voted against a proslavery resolution. He and fellow Whig Dan Stone wrote a protest, stating that "the institution of slavery is founded in both injustice and bad policy." True, they said, abolitionism was more likely to make things worse than better, but they asserted the right of Congress to abolish slavery in the District of Columbia (with the consent of the District's citizens). In 1860 Lincoln could state truthfully that this early resolution "briefly defined his position on the slavery question; and so far as it goes, it was then the same as it is now." He favored gradual emancipation, ending perhaps in 1900, and compensation to slave owners.

In the 1830s and 1840s Lincoln thought slavery "a minor question," and he optimistically "rested in the hope and belief that it was in course of ultimate extinction." American institutions operated benignly, he thought, and were ever approaching the equalitarian ideals of the Declaration of Independence.* The Texas question never interested him much because slavery already existed there.

But as a member of the U.S. House of Representatives during the Mexican War,* Lincoln supported the Wilmot Proviso because he feared the spread of slavery to other untainted soil.

The Southern proslavery argument, with its shocking denunciations of the ideals of the Declaration of Independence, unsettled Lincoln in the early 1850s. But he seems to have attributed such denunciations to selfish economic interests, always more powerful in politics than mere sentiments. The Kansas-Nebraska Act* of 1854 startled Lincoln into action, for it offered an opportunity for slavery to spread and the offer was made by a Northerner, Stephen A. Douglas,* with no powerful economic interest in the peculiar institution. Lincoln began to fear that the ability to recognize the immorality of slavery was declining in America, and after violence erupted in Kansas Territory and the U.S. Supreme Court issued the Dred Scott decision* in 1857, he argued that the Kansas-Nebraska Act marked the beginning of a conspiracy to make slavery perpetual and national. In his famous series of debates with Douglas in the 1858 campaign for one of Illinois's seats in the U.S. Senate, Lincoln, the Republican candidate, accused Douglas of being a party to this conspiracy. He also stressed the gulf that separated moral opposition to slavery from Douglas's "popular sovereignty" platform, which would indifferently allow voters in each territory to choose or reject slavery according to their local interests and needs.

As this opposition to local options on slavery perhaps suggests, Lincoln was a nationalist. He had always assumed that saving the Union was more important than abolishing slavery. Such a position seemed more sensible when that Union embodied the ideals of the Declaration of Independence, but Lincoln's growing perception that the country might not be approaching that ideal confused his thinking. In 1854 he admitted, "Much as I hate slavery, I would consent to the extension of it rather than see the Union dissolved, just as I would consent to any GREAT evil, to avoid a GREATER one." By the secession crisis of 1860–1861, however, Lincoln increasingly hinted at the primacy of liberty over Union. "There is nothing," he said on 20 February 1861, "that can ever bring me willingly to consent to the destruction of this Union, . . . unless it were to be that thing for which the Union itself was made"—liberty.

As president during the Civil War,* Lincoln at first adhered to his traditional Republican constitutional delicacy in regard to slavery. In 1861 he revoked General John C. Frémont's proclamation freeing the slaves of Missouri rebels on the grounds that such edicts, "making permanent rules of property by proclamation," whether issued by generals or presidents, were "simply 'dictatorship.' " Meanwhile, however, Lincoln himself already had violated and stretched the Constitution for the sake of saving the Union. He soon changed his mind in regard to slavery too, and within less than a year of the Frémont incident, wrote the Emancipation Proclamation.* In short, slavery also caused Lincoln to handle the Constitution* in a way inconceivable to him in 1861.

SELECTED BIBLIOGRAPHY

Roy P. Basler et al., eds., *The Collected Works of Abraham Lincoln* (9 vols., 1953–1955).

                                                                        MARK E. NEELY, JR.

LITERATURE, SLAVERY IN. Creative literary expression is both a source and a product of national attitudes, opinions, and popular myths. Literature not only reflects a society's social judgments, but also initiates and shapes them. In effect, the creators of a national literature serve as cultural historians who simultaneously formulate, record, and sanction national values. As such, their views are important indexes of opinion on topics of historical interest.

Literary depictions of the Old South have been enormously influential in shaping Americans' perceptions of the Southern slave system. They have contributed greatly to characterizations of plantation life which have appeared in stage, film,* and television productions and in both popular and academic history texts. Although early literary impressions of black slavery often were vague, incomplete, or internally contradictory, the degree to which they approximated later, more carefully considered descriptions is itself a significant commentary on American culture.

America's first novelists, poets, and short fiction writers worked in an intellectual atmosphere which owed much to British precedent. Colonists who had both the time and the taste for literature favored works that were mannered, didactic, and sentimental. This moralistic sentimentality was evident in depictions of New World slavery written by British authors such as Aphra Behn, whose *Oroonoko: Or, The Royal Slave* (1688) hastened the development of a noble savage tradition in literature. This tale of an African prince who was kidnapped and forced to labor as a slave in Surinam described blacks as unspoiled children of nature whose unfortunate descent into bondage could only serve to awaken humanitarian sympathies.

American authors created similar backdrops for their gentle, sensitive noble savages. *A Poetical Epistle to the Enslaved Africans* (1790), *The American in Algiers* (1797), and Thomas Branagan's *Avenia* (1805) encouraged the notion that African-Americans were either weak-willed or psychologically ill-adapted to the demands of an ordered life. Noble and contented while in Africa, wretched, melancholy, and suicidal in America, fictionalized slaves were shown to be easily cowed and defeated by bondage. Such characters stood in stark contrast to literary portrayals of Anglo-American champions of faith and freedom.

Fictional portraits of slaves, unable to help themselves when confronted with powerful whites, were well suited for use as sentimental props in the early antislavery campaign. Although perpetuating the suspicion that blacks were a different and inferior type of humankind, poets and short story writers of the late eighteenth and early nineteenth centuries angered slaveholding interests by picturing white Southerners as greedy exploiters of a labor system based upon blood and rapine. Well suited to this context in which slave imagery had not yet hardened into stereotype, works such as James Fenimore Cooper's *The Spy* (1821)—which contained the first detailed portrait of an Afro-American slave to appear in an American novel—and George Tucker's *The Valley of Shenandoah* (1824)—the first American novel to employ a plantation setting in any important way—provided remarkably restrained, balanced treatments of slave society and of the slave personality.

Buffeted by abolitionist* invective, writers of the 1830–60 period were compelled to abandon their tentative and ambiguous portrayals of the slave South. Increasingly, they directed their efforts to creating literary portraits suitable for use in either the proslavery or antislavery campaigns. Reformers lashed out against the harmful effects of slavery upon cherished institutions such as marriage, the family, democratic government, and the Christian church, while proslavery writers* contrasted the harsh treatment of Northern blacks with the sheltering care provided by benevolent Southern planters.

To antislavery writers such as Harriet Beecher Stowe,* author of the widely read *Uncle Tom's Cabin* (1852), black bondage was evil personified. Having no saving grace, the institution was shown to be so cruel and debasing that the slave's personality often was perverted or destroyed. Constitutionally prone to innocence, gaiety, and docility, a bondsman might find shelter in the promises of the Anglo-Saxon's Christian religion, but this appropriation from white culture only highlighted the slave's impressionable, dependent nature.

Most Southern authors were hostile toward *Uncle Tom's Cabin*. By 1861 more than thirty novel-length replies had been published. Anti-Stowe works such as Mary Eastman's *Aunt Phillis's Cabin* (1852) and William Grayson's *The Hireling and the Slave* (1854) were said to be based upon a strict adherence to truth gained through close personal observation. Their portrayals of the Southern way of life combined antiabolitionist rhetoric with a romantic vision of aristocratic chivalry borrowed both from Sir Walter Scott and from the works of antebellum writers such as John Pendleton Kennedy, William Alexander Caruthers, and Caroline Lee Hentz. In novels like Kennedy's *Swallow Barn* (1832, 1851), the English baron became the genteel Virginia planter; faithful slaves were substituted for loyal vassals; and the South was transformed into one great, romantic jousting field. When turned to proslavery purposes, these panoramas became politically potent inversions of Stowe's wicked South.

While white writers from both North and South practiced a literary paternalism which denied childlike slave characters the will and ability to direct their own lives, early works by black authors developed contrasting themes of strength, self-definition, and survival. These Afro-American writers often defined strength as rebelliousness, self-definition as purposeful pride, and survival as the ability to understand the oppressors without being understood by them. When slaves endowed with these qualities appeared in William Wells Brown's* *Clotel* (1853), Frederick Douglass's* "The Heroic Slave" (1853), or Martin Delany's *Blake* (1859), they illustrated the dramatic differences between black and white conceptions of slave life.

Although wartime novels such as J. T. Trowbridge's *Cudjo's Cave* (1863) and Epes Sargent's *Peculiar* (1864) revealed that white authors could, on occasion, join in celebrating the slaves' intelligence and bravado, most postbellum literary portrayals of the Old South retained a determined allegiance to romanticized visions of Southern gentility and slave loyalty. Encouraged by the postwar movement toward sectional reconciliation as well as by a nationwide enthusiasm for Southern local color writing, Thomas Nelson Page, Joel Chandler Harris, and other late nineteenth-century authors employed Afro-American dialect and "genuine folk-lore tales" to further establish the notion that black Southerners were simple-hearted peasants who always had enjoyed the affectionate indulgence of paternalistic whites. The pervasiveness of this literary convention was so great that only the boldest of black authors dared break with popular expectations.

Twentieth-century literary depictions of slavery reveal that the black writers' race pride could not long be concealed by the dialect mask. Eventually, white proponents of a new literary realism joined in stripping the cloak of benevolent paternalism from the master-slave relationship. Still, at the opening of the present decade, much remained to be done by those who would disown, discredit, and abolish popular stereotypes.

Buoyed by the ethos of cultural pluralism that was so evident in the Harlem Renaissance writings of the 1920s, black authors reshaped literary history with interpretations of slave life which they hoped would provide inspiration and encouragement for their own and future generations. Novels such as Arna Bontemps's *Black Thunder* (1936), Margaret Walker's *Jubilee* (1966), Ernest J. Gaines's *The Autobiography of Miss Jane Pittman* (1971), Alex Haley's *Roots* (1976), and Frank Yerby's *A Darkness at Ingraham's Crest* (1979) recounted the horrors of the Atlantic slave trade and detailed the institutionalized denial of human rights that afflicted black plantation labors. These works denigrated slaveholders and described slaves who nurtured a deep hatred toward whites. At the same time, they boosted black pride through descriptions of the slaves' spirit, endurance, and group solidarity.

Motivated by harsh Depression-era social and economic conditions, white authors of the realist school also rejected the dialect/local color norms of an earlier generation and began to echo the sentiments of slavery's black critics. Concerned that their literary productions accurately depicted rural southern life, writers such as William Faulkner, Allen Tate, T. S. Stribling, and Evelyn Scott modified popular plantation stereotypes by revealing the financial underpinnings of the antebellum market economy, scrutinizing the personal weaknesses of slaveholders, and describing both the nature and extent of the slaves' purposeful deceptiveness. These modifications are evident in later white-authored works such as Frances Gaither's *The Red Cock Crows* (1944), Robert Penn Warren's *Band of Angels* (1955), and Daniel Panger's *Ol' Prophet Nat* (1967).

Although accounts of slaveholding brutality and determined black resistance have been introduced to a wider and increasingly diverse audience, mainstream literary culture continues to promote many of the traditional stereotypes. From

Margaret Mitchell's immensely popular *Gone with the Wind* (1936) to William Styron's Pulitzer Prize–winning *The Confessions of Nat Turner* (1967) to the pulp fiction of Kyle Onstott's, Lance Horner's, and Ashley Carter's Falconhurst series (1957–83), white-authored fiction has depicted comically blundering, primitive, psychologically tranquilized bondsmen whose lives have meaning only in and through their subservient relationships with whites. In comparing these images with the noble slave heroes created by contemporary black authors, one gains new perspective on the segmented nature of American culture and a new respect for literature as both formulator and index of national values.

SELECTED BIBLIOGRAPHY

Jay B. Hubbell, *The South in American Literature, 1607–1900* (1954); Francis Pendleton Gaines, *The Southern Plantation: A Study in the Development and the Accuracy of a Tradition* (1924); Catherine Juanita Starke, *Black Portraiture in American Fiction: Stock Characters, Archetypes, and Individuals* (1971); William R. Taylor, *Cavalier and Yankee: The Old South and American National Character* (1961); William L. Van Deburg, *Slavery & Race in American Popular Culture* (1984); and Jean F. Yellin, *The Intricate Knot: Black Figures in American Literature, 1776–1863* (1972).

WILLIAM L. VAN DEBURG

LIVESTOCK. Slaves tended cattle throughout the history of the South in both time and place—from the earliest settlements along the Atlantic seaboard to beyond the Sabine, probably to the Rio Grande. Whether under the domain of Great Britain, France, or Spain, the slave cowboy* was as ubiquitous as his bovine charges. During the colonial era, blacks undoubtedly watched over livestock in the Middle and New England colonies as well, but their presence in those areas was the exception rather than the rule.

The earliest English settlers in the Carolinas quickly noted the suitability of the region for the raising of stock, particularly cattle, horses, and hogs. Because the terrain and climate* there were ideal for running animals on the open range, grazing soon became an important business activity—so important that many herds belonged to absentee owners. Regardless of where the owners lived, those directly supervising the herds quickly recognized that Africans, particularly those from along the Gambia River, were excellent herdsmen and horsemen. Their descendants cared for the cattle and hogs as the culture of their masters spread westward across the Old South into Texas. Some scholars contend that cowboy lingo, such as the word *buckaroo*, has Gullah rather than Spanish origins. Not all Afro-American herding tradition stemmed from the Carolinas, however. Spanish, French, and British settlers relied on black slaves as stock raisers in Florida and Louisiana as well. From several directions a black herding culture spread throughout the Old South.

Because the cotton culture overshadowed every aspect of Southern history, historians generally have ignored the prevalence of livestock on plantations—a curious fact in light of the significant number of valuable cattle owned by planters.

Prior to the War of 1812, many plantations in fact were ranches by another name. Cliometricians in the 1970s calculated that slaves on large plantations expended roughly 25 percent of their labor time on the rearing of livestock. No wonder that travelers in the antebellum South observed a number of expert horsemen among the slave population. Had scholars paid more attention to the cis-Mississippi roots of the post–Civil War black cowboys, they would not have been surprised in recent years to discover how many of them were riding the trails and ranges west of the Mississippi. Neither they nor their ancestors were owned exclusively by Euro-Americans. Many had tended the stock belonging to the Indians of the American Southeast who took thousands of their African slaves with them to the Indian Territory, where their ranching practices continued. Much remains unknown about the links between the plains of Africa and those of the Great Plains of North America. Black herdsmen played a significant role in that agricultural and cultural nexus.

SELECTED BIBLIOGRAPHY

Joe A. Akerman, Jr., *Florida Cowman: A History of Florida Cattle Raising* (1976); Gary S. Dunbar, "Colonial Carolina Cowpens," *Agricultural History*, 35 (1961), 125–130; Estwick Evans, *A Pedestrious Tour* (1819); Robert W. Fogel and Stanley L. Engerman, *Time on the Cross: The Economics of American Negro Slavery* (1974); Lewis C. Gray, *History of Agriculture in the Southern United States to 1860* (2 vols., 1933); John D. W. Guice, "Cattle Raisers of the Old Southwest: A Reinterpretation," *Western Historical Quarterly*, 8 (1977), 167–187; Terry G. Jordan, *Trails to Texas: Southern Roots of Western Cattle Ranching* (1981); and Peter H. Wood, *Black Majority: Negroes in Colonial South Carolina from 1670 through the Stono Rebellion* (1974).

JOHN D. W. GUICE

LOUISIANA, SLAVERY IN. The French brought enslaved Africans into their new colony of Louisiana in the early eighteenth century. During these final years of the reign of Louis XIV, France experienced financial troubles and a decline from preeminence in Europe. Mercantile authorities hoped to recoup French fortunes by exploiting the presumed riches of the lower Mississippi River valley. However, they experienced perennial difficulties recruiting and maintaining settlers, especially ones willing to till the rich soil in the area's subtropical climate. Enslaving Indians* proved as ineffectual as it had been in the British North American colonies. The French, therefore, imported black slaves like those who were already producing great wealth in the French West Indies.

Antoine Crozat, a wealthy merchant and slave trader, became proprietor of Louisiana in 1712; his patent from the crown required that he settle his colony with white Catholics and black slaves. In 1717, John Law's Company of the West succeeded the disillusioned and bankrupt Crozat. This chartered company promised to send 3,000 Negroes to Louisiana within ten years. When Law's reorganized Company of the Indies nearly collapsed in 1721, the struggling colony had a population of only 684 whites and 565 blacks. Although over 2,000 slaves had entered Louisiana, an appalling death rate, attributable mostly to disease, killed off immigrants to its unhealthy lowlands. Acclimation—surviving for two years—was a vital concern for both masters and slaves.

Bourbon officials adapted the slave codes of the French West Indies to the situation in Louisiana, issuing a *Code Noir* in 1724. Unlike British slave codes but akin to those of Spain and Portugal, it recognized slaves as persons who had certain, limited rights. For instance, the code prohibited masters from selling slave children away from their mothers and from inflicting certain severe punishments; it required that slaves be baptized, catechized, married, and buried as Roman Catholics. It also obligated masters to provide their servants with adequate food, clothing, and shelter. In practice, individual masters ignored this code with impunity.

Latin masters usually lived in closer familial intimacy with their slaves than did Anglo-Americans. Yet such domestic patterns did not ameliorate French and Spanish slavery. Instead, they probably increased the tension between blacks and whites because slaves knew their masters' human frailties and were in close enough contact with them to pose a constant threat. Fearing violence, slave-holders maintained dominance through intimidation and sometimes violent repression. Furthermore, colonial planters expected to earn a good return on investments in human flesh; they typically followed the West Indian pattern of overworking slaves, who were predominantly young males, and replacing the many who died with newly imported stock. Despite the code, few cases to protect slave "rights" reached court, and very few slaves became practicing Catholics in the colonial era.

While Louisiana was a large, neglected French colony and later from the 1760s to 1803 a geographically smaller Spanish colony, some slaves were artisans or personal servants, but the majority worked in plantation agriculture.* Their numbers grew from 4,519 out of a total population of 11,224 in 1771 to 16,544 of 32,062 in 1785. A limited number of politically influential concessionaires were the only masters to acquire sizable slaveholdings under Bourbon France and Bourbon Spain. These individuals prospered as their slaves produced rice,* indigo,* tobacco,* and lumber* for export, but because of mercantile trade restrictions and difficulties developing staple crops truly suited to Louisiana conditions, the colony foundered.

Several developments at the end of the eighteenth and the beginning of the nineteenth centuries infused new life and new direction into Louisiana's economy and its system of slavery. The invention of the cotton gin* and the spread of mechanized spinning and weaving rewarded those who grew cotton,* a staple crop well suited to production by forced labor. Meanwhile, in 1795, an innovative planter, Étienne de Boré, profitably produced granulated sugar* from Tahitian cane grown near New Orleans. In these same years, numerous planters and slaves who were familiar with cultivating and processing sugar fled the revolt against French authority on Saint-Domingue and ultimately settled in south Louisiana. By 1812, another technological innovation, the steamboat, began traversing the many waterways of Louisiana; it was soon adapted to transporting these bulky staple crops to New Orleans for export. Given sufficient planters and farm laborers, a stable government as part of the United States, and the industrializing world's growing markets for cotton and sugar, Louisiana was poised to reap the prosperity which had bypassed it in the colonial era.

The Spanish had brought to Louisiana their slave code, *Las Siete Partidas*. By emphasizing the moral and reciprocal aspects of the master-slave relationship, by trying to curtail the slave trade from Africa and the West Indies, and by requiring government officials to enforce these laws, the new regime attempted, with little success, to protect Louisiana bondsmen.

Both the French and the Spanish slave codes contained specific provisions for manumitting slaves. Several factors caused the numbers of freed blacks* to increase dramatically during the Spanish colonial and American territorial periods. The paucity of marriageable white women combined with lenient Latin attitudes conduced many white men to cohabit with black women; they often freed the children of these unions. Moreover, the Spanish authorities saw the free people of color as a stabilizing influence in a colony thinly populated by headstrong Frenchmen and restive slaves. Free Negroes not only occupied an important economic niche as skilled craftsmen, but they also filled out the ranks of the militia in this military outpost on the edge of the Spanish empire. Finally, large numbers of free people of color entered Louisiana, along with the other refugees from the tumult in Saint-Domingue.

Ever-present fears of slave insurrections date from the colonial era. Rumors and plots abounded, and authorities actually thwarted well-documented conspiracies in 1791 and 1795. Friction persisted between slaveholders, who wanted tight control over their slaves, and Spanish authorities, who sought just treatment for blacks under the law. Simultaneously, conflict arose between planters, who wanted to buy more slaves in order to produce more wealth, and the Spanish regime, which tried to close off slave trade so as to keep out troublemakers and revolutionary ideas. After the Louisiana Purchase, the territorial legislature addressed the first problem in 1806 with one of the nation's most comprehensive slave codes. It reinforced the autonomy of the master over his own servants. The other controversy was exacerbated under American control because Congress stopped Louisiana's foreign slave trade* in 1804 and the U.S. Constitution prohibited any further importation of slaves into the country as of 1808. Considerable pressure from French Creole planters did, however, convince Congress to approve a temporary exception. It allowed some 2,700 white Saint-Domingan refugees, recently expelled from asylum in Cuba, to enter Louisiana with more than 3,000 of their slaves.

Frequently repeated concerns that the blacks, both slave and free, who migrated from Saint-Domingue, would bring dangerous ideas into Louisiana materialized in the great slave revolt of 1811—the United States's largest slave uprising.* Between 150 and 500 blacks took farm tools as weapons and marched in ranks from their plantations down river towards New Orleans. They killed two whites and destroyed considerable property. The civil and military authorities quickly killed at least sixty-six blacks in a one-sided battle. A hastily convened court tried some thirty others; twenty-one of these were found guilty and executed. To forestall other revolts, the whites displayed the severed heads of the insurrection's leaders on pikes erected along the river road and kept this alarming incident out of the newspapers.

This revolt substantiated the whites' worst fears. Thereafter, as part of the United States, Louisiana repeatedly tightened its slave code, making it more like that of the other Southern states and requiring documents which proved the place of origin and warranted the good behavior of all slaves offered for sale. Unlike its sister states, however, Louisiana law continued to assert that slaves were people and were not merely chattel property.

Interest in reviving the foreign slave trade persisted. A tide of Anglo-American immigrants surged into the Territory of Orleans, giving it sufficient population for statehood in 1812. Some settlers brought slaves with them from the older states where exhausted soil devalued labor. All of the aspiring planters wanted low-cost slave labor to help them make their fortunes growing sugar and cotton in Louisiana's rich alluvial soil. Slaveholders already settled in Louisiana were loath to part with seasoned slaves; they, too, wanted more. Others in the state always feared that the continued influx of slaves encouraged social unrest. Following Nat Turner's revolt,* the state legislature briefly curtailed the domestic slave trade.* Yet the economic and political interests of the powerful planters were still clearly evident in the 1850s when the legislature approved several bills to reopen the external slave trade; these efforts never secured national approval.

Slave smugglers, including the famous privateer Jean Lafitte and the knife-wielding frontiersman James Bowie, did successfully import new bondsmen because policing Louisiana's myriad coastal waterways was virtually impossible. Illegal importation of thousands of enslaved blacks continued into the 1850s.

As Louisiana prospered in the antebellum years and the demand for slaves increased, the price of slaves* rose. Slaves in Louisiana often sold for more than twice their cost in Virginia, Maryland, Tennessee, and Kentucky. Therefore, a vast, legal, internal slave trade arose. Thousands of slaves traveled overland, marching in coffles, downriver on flatboats and steamboats, and locked in the holds of ships sailing from Atlantic ports. Traders occasionally sold their movable property in the smaller towns, but New Orleans became the largest slave market in the United States. By 1860, when prime male field hands brought $2,000, thirty-four slave dealers at twenty-five exchanges sold six to eight thousand slaves a year for the highest prices in America. In his book *Twelve Years a Slave*, Solomon Northup,* a freeman kidnapped in New York and sold into slavery, wrote a vivid account of such an exchange and the demeaning experience of being examined and purchased in the Crescent City in 1841. Northup believed that Louisiana slavery was the "the most abject and cruel form" of bondage found in the United States. Blacks from other states dreaded being "sold down the river" to New Orleans.

Table 1
Population of Louisiana, 1810–1860

Year	Slaves	Free Coloreds	Whites	Total
1810	34,660	7,585	34,311	76,556
1820	69,064	10,476	73,383	152,923
1830	109,588	16,710	89,441	215,739
1840	168,452	25,502	158,457	352,411
1850	244,809	17,462	255,491	517,762
1860	331,726	18,647	357,456	707,829

Historians still debate the accuracy of this reputation. Several factors un-doubtedly contributed to its existence and persistence: harsh conditions had definitely prevailed in colonial Louisiana. The mortality rate in the state remained very high. Blacks sent to distant Louisiana could seldom maintain contact with the family and friends they left behind. Some masters elicited cooperative be-havior by threatening to ship slaves to the markets of New Orleans; the most unruly and difficult slaves were probably the first ones offered to traders. Making a handsome profit, not having contented slaves, was the paramount concern of managers on Louisiana's many large and impersonal plantations. And finally, sugar plantations used an onerous gang labor system.* Whatever the reasons, the bad reputation endured; Harriet Beecher Stowe's cruel slave driver Simon Legree cracked his whip in Louisiana.

Other authorities have noted that the antebellum Louisiana slave's burden was heavy, yet bearable. They have found slave diets to be adequate, though mo-notonous, and clothing and shelter to be rough, but functional. In his book *Negro Slavery in Louisiana,* Joe Gray Taylor wrote of Virginia bondsmen who actually wanted to be sent to Louisiana because they understood that masters there could afford better care for their slaves. The morbidity rates of blacks and whites in Louisiana were quite similar and, other than the high mortality attributable to disease, correspond to data from neighboring Southern states. Furthermore, re-cent studies indicate that after the demise of the foreign slave trade, conditions became sufficiently temperate and stable to allow for a sizable natural increase in the state's slave population. Although the internal slave trade was extensive, the more than 3,000 bondsmen brought in each year from 1830 to 1860 cannot account for the 300 percent increase in the state's slave population during this period.

These figures also indicate that the number of slaves remained roughly equal to the white population in this growing state. However, in those areas with the richest soil, along the Mississippi River, the lower Red River, and the bayous in the south central region of the state, the slave population greatly outnumbered the free people. Consider, for example, the ratio of slaves to free inhabitants in some parishes (counties): in 1860, over 90 percent of Concordia and Tensas parishes' inhabitants were slaves, while slaves constituted well over 70 percent of the population in seven other parishes where intensive cotton and sugar cultivation prevailed.

Louisiana slaves were not only geographically concentrated in certain areas, they were also concentrated in the possession of a small percentage of the free population. According to the 1860 census, only 29 percent of the free families in the state actually owned slaves; only 2.2 percent of the free families owned fifty or more slaves. Yet these 1,640 large planters who owned fifty or more slaves held 48.4 percent of the state's bondsmen, planted 42.7 percent of the state's improved acreage, and produced 48.5 percent of the state's cotton crop and 76.2 percent of its sugar. Between 1850 and 1860 the size of the average slaveholding in the state increased 20 percent, while the number of owners grew only 5 percent. By 1860, Louisiana ranked first among the states in the number of families owning 70 or more, 100 or more, and 200 or more slaves. The state's median average slaveholding in 1860 was 49.3, while that of South Carolina, the lower South, and the border states stood at 38.9, 32.5, and 15.6 slaves, respectively. At this time, the median slaveholding in the sugar-growing parish of Ascension reached an astounding 175.

Not only were Louisiana plantations usually larger than those in other states, they were also more productive. They typically harvested more cotton and sugar per acre and per hand than was the case in other states. Therefore, return on capital investments, including slaves, was among the highest in the South. Joe Gray Taylor estimates that cotton growers in Louisiana reaped net profits averaging 7 percent on their investments. Sugar planters, protected by a tariff from cheaper West Indian imports, could expect a return of about 10 percent on their sizable investments in slaves, land, and equipment.

This proclivity for large plantations and the opportunity for considerable profits undoubtedly affected the lives of Louisiana's rural slave population. The many Louisiana slaves who lived on large plantations had less contact with whites than their typical counterparts elsewhere. Owners tended to view them as entries on ledgers. Their daily routines, like those of slaves throughout the South, closely followed the pattern of the seasons and the requirements of the crops. Solomon Northup's account of slave life on both cotton and sugar plantations, as well as cutting timber and milling lumber, provides a clear and accurate description from the point of view of a slave who was also a remarkably objective outside observer. He recounted diverse slave-driving techniques, the details of daily toil, the ways slaves adjusted to a dehumanizing system, and the merriment savored during occasional respites.

Several things made plantation slavery in south Louisiana distinctive. Sugar produced there required special harvesting and processing methods. The longer it grew, the higher its sugar content, but a hard frost would ruin the whole crop.

After waiting as long as possible in the fall to cut and grind the crop, all hands worked in shifts around the clock, seven days a week, to complete the task. Often Christmas had to be postponed until the job was finished. The whole process involved very hard work with huge knives, steam-driven machinery, and a series of boiling kettles. It was truly industrial in nature and was quite dangerous, but the slaves typically labored with alacrity. Here, as elsewhere in the South, everyone joined in the harvest, knowing its importance to their livelihood; most of the states' sugar and cotton planters paid their hands small amounts for working on Sunday to bring in the year's crop. Few problems in slave control arose at such times.

Slave unrest more typically developed in the summer after slaves had chopped the last weeds. At this time slave owners attempted to keep their hands productively occupied clearing land, mending fences, raising levees, repairing tools, and constructing buildings. Sugar growers used this season for cutting the firewood required at grinding time and for digging the canals which drained low-lying fields into the backswamps. Disgruntled slaves often chose these hot, slack days to slow down, feign sickness, or run away. Only a small portion of runaways* really attempted to reach freedom outside the South; most were shirking work, avoiding punishment, or moving nearer to loved ones. Numerous newspaper advertisements for runaways testify to the extent of this problem in slave control. Runaways were usually captured, returned, and punished, but occasionally they managed to live for some time in the state's dense thickets and swamps.

Although most Louisiana slaves spent their lives on plantations, others labored on smaller farms, on steamboats and railway lines, in towns, or in the big city of New Orleans. The farm and town slaves* led lives similar to their counterparts elsewhere in the South. Although they had close contact with a limited group of whites, they usually remained sheltered from the wider world. However, those slaves who worked in transportation or in the Crescent City encountered something quite different: exposure to disparate jobs, people, and ideas. Owned by individuals, by businesses, and even by the municipality, they performed many tasks. They were personal servants, barbers, seamstresses, longshoremen, draymen, street cleaners, lumberjacks, mechanics, and skilled artisans in the building trades. They also served diverse patrons in hotels, restaurants, and steamboats; built roads, railways, and levees; tended boats, ferries, and streetcars; toiled in factories, cotton presses, and graveyards.

Successful performance of these varied tasks demonstrated the flexibility of slavery, especially in an urban setting. But in a city as large, diverse, and tolerant as New Orleans, authorities could not closely police all aspects of slave life. Slaves hired out* their own services, met with strangers, drank intoxicating spirits, attended the theater, and gathered in groups without white supervision. Contradicting conventional opinions about slavery in Louisiana, blacks familiar with New Orleans asserted that it was the best place in the country to be held in bondage.

Slaves in New Orleans observed large numbers of free people of color. In the 1820s and 1830s slaves and free people of color each constituted about one-fourth of the growing metropolis's population (thereafter, these percentages steadily declined). This situation clearly showed these slaves the possibilities of freedom. It was, therefore, an ongoing concern of whites.

The many free people of color who held slaves was another distinctive aspect of Louisiana slavery. The free coloreds of Louisiana were predominantly French-speaking, Catholic mulattoes. They usually held themselves apart from slaves and in turn found themselves assigned by whites to a separate caste. Many of them prospered enough to purchase slaves, sometimes members of their own family. The 1830 census indicated that over 1,000 free colored households in Louisiana held slaves; this constituted one-third of the free colored slaveholdings in the nation. The great majority of these slaveholdings consisted of less than five slaves and were located in New Orleans. However, about fifty free people of color were planters. Andrew Durnford* was a fascinating example of a "black" sugar planter who concomitantly bought more slaves and supported the African colonization movement.*

Durnford's close friend and patron, John McDonogh, was a unique white Louisiana slaveholder. He amassed a huge fortune as a merchant, planter, and land speculator. The industry of McDonogh's slaves amazed observers. They were so hardworking because they had literally bought their master's ingenious scheme. Over the course of fifteen years (1825–1840), they gradually purchased their freedom. McDonogh, a strong supporter of African colonization, also had them earn one-way tickets to Liberia. The wealth this plan brought to one eccentric slaveholder was insufficient evidence to convince others of its efficacy.

McDonogh strongly supported another, much more popular activity for slaves: religious instruction. The Christian mission to slaves* grew throughout the South in the 1840s and 1850s. By this time, the Louisiana clergy and their Southern compatriots began defending slavery with religious arguments and supporting this biblically ordained, patriarchal institution. The Reverend Holland N. McTyeire, the Reverend Benjamin M. Palmer, and Bishop Leonidas Polk, state leaders in the Methodist, Presbyterian, and Episcopal churches, respectively, were in the vanguard of this movement which Christianized most Louisiana slaves.

The slaves readily saw through the white gospel that taught them to be obedient to their masters and to wait for the rewards of their earthly labors until the life hereafter. They, nevertheless, found something in the Christian message that was comforting and communal and that offered a type of release from their oppressive bonds. Because faith in the supernatural helped them to endure slavery together, fully 55 percent of the narratives of former Louisiana slaves collected in the Federal Writers' Project mentioned religious activities.* Interestingly, the average for the rest of the Deep South was closer to 70 percent, and former slaves from Louisiana noted more cases of masters who tried to prohibit religious activities. Louisiana slaveholders worried especially about the black preachers* and root doctors, who were leaders in the slave community and who sometimes conjured or invoked voodoo* powers.

Whites in Louisiana developed several defenses of slavery besides the widely accepted religious justification. New Orleansian J.D.B. De Bow argued persuasively in *De Bow's Review* that slavery was the best labor system for ensuring Southern prosperity. His widely read journal contained almost as many articles on the proper care of slaves as on the latest agricultural techniques. Another respected periodical, the *New Orleans Medical and Surgical Journal*, contained articles by Samuel A. Cartwright, a physician who claimed that blacks were so physiologically different from whites that they required a different diet, different medical care, and enslavement. Although Cartwright's views were a curiosity, those of De Bow and the Southern clergy clearly indicated the economic and social significance of slavery in antebellum Louisiana.

By 1860, Louisiana had enjoyed four decades of growth and prosperity based primarily upon slave labor. Nearly half of the state's population lived in bondage; the rest accepted or supported the economic and social structure of slavery while fearing a slave revolt. Slavery in Louisiana had grown quite similar to the peculiar institution in the other Deep South states, yet a few characteristics set it apart. The average slaveholdings were larger, the profits from slave labor were greater, the cost of slaves was higher, and the ascendancy of the large planters was more complete than in any other state. These economic and social conditions were of far greater importance in determining the characteristics of slavery in Louisiana than were the remnants of Latin-Catholic law and custom. Some Latin sentiments did persist, especially in the large, lax city of New Orleans. Also, the Latin acceptance of blacks as individuals survived, though waned, in tolerant attitudes toward free people of color. Finally, Negrophobia was stronger in the newer settlements of north Louisiana than in the older French and Spanish communities to the south where many slaves and masters still spoke French.

In the spring of 1862, the Civil War* split Louisiana into Confederate and Union states. Whenever the federal forces moved through the countryside, the slaves abandoned their plantations in droves and cooperated with the invaders, but only one small revolt occurred. The federals still considered them property, called contraband of war, and continued to acknowledge the existence of slavery in areas occupied before the Emancipation Proclamation took effect. Beginning in 1863, the federals recruited Louisiana blacks into the Union army*; many thousands eventually served. An 1864 Unionist constitutional convention exhibited strong proslavery sentiments, but after much debate, ended the peculiar institution without compensating masters. The final Confederate defeat in 1865 freed Louisiana's remaining slaves.

SELECTED BIBLIOGRAPHY

James H. Dormon, "The Persistent Specter: Slave Rebellion in Territorial Louisiana," *Louisiana History*, 18 (1977), 389–404; Paul F. Lachance, "The Politics of Fear: French Louisiana and the Slave Trade, 1786–1809," *Plantation Society in the Americas*, 1 (1979),

162–197; Robert R. Macdonald, et al., eds., *Louisiana's Black Heritage* (1979); Joseph Karl Menn, *The Large Slaveholders of Louisiana—1860* (1968); Solomon Northup, *Twelve Years a Slave*, edited by Sue Eakin and Joseph Logsdon (1968); David C. Rankin, "The Tannenbaum Thesis Reconsidered: Slavery and Race Relations in Antebellum Louisiana," *Southern Studies*, 18 (1979) 5–31; and Joe Gray Taylor, *Negro Slavery in Louisiana* (1963).

BLAKE TOUCHSTONE

LOUISVILLE, KY, SLAVERY IN. Slavery in Louisville differed little from that in other Southern urban areas. At the same time, however, it varied enough so that the peculiar institution found a sometimes peculiar home in the border state metropolis.

In numbers, the story of slavery in Louisville is a familiar one of initial growth, then stagnation, and, finally, decline. In 1820, when the Falls City was just beginning the growth that would make it the nation's twelfth largest city on the eve of the Civil War, the 1,031 bondsmen in the population represented 25.7 percent of the city's total population. While the numbers rose through 1850, the percentages declined—23.3 in 1830, 16.2 in 1840, and 12.6 at mid-century. By 1860 Louisville's 4,914 slaves comprised only 7.8 percent of the city's population.

Statistics reveal only a part of the forces that shaped the daily lives of the bondsmen. Few slaves would have agreed with an 1835 editorial that asserted that in Louisville, blacks "scarcely realize the fact that they are slaves" or with an 1848 observation that "slavery exists in Louisville . . . only in name." The 1781 hanging of the first slave in Louisville, the city's slave patrol* begun in 1809, the local ordinance that set a 10:00 P.M. curfew for slaves—all reminded slaves that theirs was a life controlled in large part by others. Until 1850 Kentucky slaves remained both real estate and personal property. But perhaps the clearest voices that proclaimed slavery's existence came from the slave stalls in the city. Louisville ranked as a major center for slave sales, and men such as the Arteburn brothers engaged in large-scale buying and selling of slaves.

Despite the controls on their lives, slaves in Louisville—as in other urban areas*—moved in ways that limited those restraints, weakened the laws, and, in the end, strengthened their independence. Extensive slave-hiring* provided one way to do this. As early as 1820 a local paper reported that "at least 150 slaves"—almost one-third of those in the city—were being hired out—"some of whom pay their 'owners' twenty dollars per month." In 1833 some 20 percent and in 1860 about one-quarter of the city's slave population engaged in slave-hiring. The freedom of movement such practices often gave, the virtual breakdown of the pass system in the city, and the fact that for most of the antebellum period in Kentucky no laws restricted slaves in being taught to read or write— all meant that Louisville slaves gained a fair amount of latitude within the bounds of the system. That freedom reached its strongest institutional apex in the black church. There, pastors, such as Henry Adams, operated schools and ministered to congregations that approached a thousand in number. Even if limited and otherworldly in emphasis, the city's halls of worship provided yet another urban avenue to freedom.

In Louisville, the peculiar institution showed its flexibility, but that adaptability did not always please slave owners or the white population at large. Nor did slavery in the city prove resilient and attractive enough to resist the wave of immigrants that challenged it in the workplace in the 1840s and 1850s. In the end, slaves in Louisville may have found fewer barriers than did slaves in other settings, but the declining numbers meant that they faced a darkening future in which fewer and fewer of them would enjoy even such limited freedoms.

SELECTED BIBLIOGRAPHY

Claudia Dale Goldin, *Urban Slavery in the American South, 1820–1860: A Quantitative History* (1976); Mary Lawrence O'Brien, "Slavery in Louisville during the Antebellum Period, 1820–1860" (M.A. thesis, University of Louisville, 1979); and Hanford Dozier Stafford, "Slavery in a Border City: Louisville, 1790–1860" (Ph.D. dissertation, University of Kentucky, 1982).

JAMES C. KLOTTER

LOYALISTS. Historians have often remarked on the paradox that white Americans fought against Britain under the banner of universal liberty during the American Revolution,* while at the same time they held black Americans in slavery. During the revolutionary era the slaves recognized this paradox and sought the application of those inalienable rights to themselves. Even before the outbreak of hostilities between Britain and the American colonies, several groups of slaves petitioned their colonial assemblies for their freedom on the grounds of natural rights, and then during the Revolutionary war many thousands of slaves acted to secure the liberty which they believed to be their birthright. Ideologically, therefore, these slaves were committed to the revolutionary concepts which moved white patriots to declare independence from Britain. But because they perceived the oppressor as the local slave owner, and the Continental Congress as the sustainer of the racial status quo, the vast majority of slaves who took action did so as allies of the British.

As early as September 1774 a group of Boston slaves offered to fight for the British, and the following summer some North Carolina slaves plotted to rebel and join the Loyalists. These incidents suggest an almost immediate identification of Britain with the interests of the slaves, an identification that was articulated and broadly disseminated by Lord Dunmore's Proclamation of 7 November 1775. In this statement the royal governor of Virginia promised freedom to any slave who deserted a patriot master to help restore British authority. Organizing his slave recruits into an "Ethiopian Regiment," Dunmore gave them uniforms with the inscription "Liberty to Slaves" across their chests and led them into battle. Though fever decimated the black troops and the survivors were forced to retreat from Virginia with their commander, Britain had gained the slaves' faith that a

Loyalist victory would result in freedom for all blacks in America. This principle was apparently confirmed by the Philipsburg Proclamation issued by British Commander in Chief Sir Henry Clinton in June 1779, offering freedom to any patriot-owned slave who sought British protection. Clinton's offer included all slaves, not just those capable of bearing arms, and after joining the British they would be free to follow any occupation.

Inspired by the proclamations, tens of thousands of slaves fled to the British whenever an opportunity occurred. Some created their own opportunity by revolting against their masters and encouraging British or Loyalist forces to occupy their district; others risked escape through patriot-occupied territory; most took advantage of a friendly army's presence in their neighborhood and went out to claim their protection.

Although not required to do so, practical circumstances or Loyalist fervor led most of the runaways* to offer their services to the royal war effort. Probably the most significant contribution was made in the construction and maintenance of fortifications. Both Savannah and Charleston, when under siege, depended on black laborers for their defense. Lord Cornwallis had two thousand blacks working in shifts on the earthworks at Yorktown and wished for more. Many blacks plied their skills as cooks, laundresses, teamsters, blacksmiths, and carpenters in the royal regiments. Others became waiters and orderlies or were assigned as personal servants to the officers. Forage and fatigue duties were frequently carried out by the runaways; black marauding parties raiding for food and for general harassment purposes were common. Several Black Pioneer Corps were formed, with their own noncommissioned officers, and each infantry regiment could enlist three or four blacks as pioneers. In addition, almost every regiment had a black drummer or fifer, often teenagers who might be reassigned to combat duty as they matured. A favorite function of the blacks was to act as guides and intelligence agents for invading British armies. Instructions were sent out to use ex-slaves as informants concerning their former home districts; some were sent on deliberate spying expeditions, and delivered messages through enemy lines. Several thousand saw action as sailors and soldiers, attached to British, American Loyalist, and even mercenary Hessian corps. They served as ordinary seamen, river pilots, military policemen, and musketeers. In 1782 a black cavalry troop was created. Very few Loyalist endeavors lacked the presence of at least some blacks.

British gratitude, however, was not always apparent. Conditions in the camps were horrible, with thousands of blacks dying of disease. There were numerous instances of runaways being sold back into slavery, or being kept by white officers as personal slaves despite their promised freedom. Although these acts were not legal—at least two British officers were court-martialed in New York for enslaving Loyalist blacks—they were relatively easy to do since slaves owned by white Loyalists were not included in the proclamations and the original ownership could be difficult for a runaway to prove. The fact was that the slaves were mistaken in their understanding of British motives, for the British Empire was not committed to the general abolition of slavery or to the equality of black citizens. The proclamations were a desperate attempt to bring the rebellious colonies to their knees, intended as much to induce the patriots to lay down their arms as to attract runaway slaves. The British command had no explicit policy concerning the status and disposition of the black Loyalists. As long as the war continued this could be afforded, but in defeat and retreat decisions had to be made. Deprived Patriot owners expected the restoration of their property; indeed, Article VII of the Provisional Peace Agreement, which was carried unaltered into the final Treaty, obliged the British to withdraw "without Causing any destruction or carrying away any Negroes or other Property of the American Inhabitants." In the end, British honor prevailed, and British Commander in Chief Sir Guy Carleton insisted that the runaways were not in fact American property at the time of the agreement and that they must be allowed to evacuate with other Loyalists. Compensation was offered to those patriots who could prove a claim against a departing former slave.

Detailed records were not kept, but an estimate of about 15,000 blacks evacuated seems realistic: 4,000 from Savannah, 6,000 from Charleston, 3,500 from New York, others from Boston, the Floridas, and elsewhere. Policy dictated that black Loyalists were to be given priority over Loyalist-owned slaves, but many white Loyalists pretended their slaves were free in order to win passage for them in the evacuations. The exact numbers of free black Loyalists to escape from the United States cannot therefore be known with precision. Furthermore, many thousands were left behind, some to be reclaimed and some to continue a guerrilla warfare against the Americans until finally defeated in 1786. Those who did manage to secure a safe retreat were shipped to the Bahamas, Jamaica, Barbados, and other British territories in the Caribbean, to London, and probably the largest single group, about 3,500, to Nova Scotia. A small number actually accompanied the Hessians to Germany. British officials generally continued to ignore the black Loyalists in their new homes. Most of the blacks presenting petitions before the Loyalist Claims Commission in London were dismissed on the grounds that they had gained their freedom from the war and could expect no further compensation. Black Loyalists in the Caribbean, it was reported in 1786, were cruelly used and frequently sold to the French islands as slaves. Even in Nova Scotia, where the best treatment was received, conditions fell far short of the equality they had been led to expect.

But just as the British were consistent in their ambivalence, so were the black Loyalists consistent in their pursuit of the ideals which had drawn them to the British during the war. Those in Nova Scotia campaigned vigorously against slavery, though they themselves were now free, and in favor of black equality. When equality was not achieved, about 1,200 of them migrated once again in 1792 to the colony of Sierra Leone in West Africa. Continued disappointment caused them to rebel against their white-led government in 1800, leading to the ironic yet accurate charge that the black Loyalists were imbued with the ideals of revolutionary America.

The American Revolution was a civil war as well as a rebellion, with many Americans remaining loyal to Britain and participating in the war against independence. People who joined each side were moved by both ideology and self-interest, and by a vision of the kind of America they wanted to emerge from the war. Historians' tendency to see the white Patriots as the sole proprietors of an ideology of freedom has led to the assumption that freedom-seeking blacks must naturally have cast their lot with the cause of American independence. At the time, however, many slaves were convinced that a British America would secure black independence, whereas an independent America would perpetuate their enslavement. The slaves' war for independence was another paradox.

SELECTED BIBLIOGRAPHY

Sylvia R. Frey, "The British and the Black: A New Perspective," *Historian*, 38 (1976), 225–238; Mary Beth Norton, "The Fate of Some Black Loyalists of the American Revolution," *Journal of Negro History*, 58 (1973), 402–426; Benjamin Quarles, *The Negro in the American Revolution* (1961); James W. St. G. Walker, "Blacks as American Loyalists: The Slaves' War for Independence," *Historical Reflections*, 2 (1975), 51–67; and James W. St. G. Walker, *The Black Loyalists: The Search for a Promised Land in Nova Scotia and Sierra Leone, 1783–1870* (1976).

JAMES W. ST.G. WALKER

LUMBER. Lumber production constituted one of the most important branches of Southern industry by 1860. More than $10 million was invested in Southern saw and planing mills by that date, comprising the greatest concentration of capital in any Southern manufacturing enterprise. By 1860 Southern mills were producing nearly $23 million worth of lumber, a 100 percent gain over the value of lumber produced in 1850. Over 16,000 white Southerners owed their jobs directly to employment in saw and planing mills, and their wages totaled over $1,750,000 by 1860. No other branch of Southern industry so nearly approximated the rate of Northern industrial growth during the antebellum period as did the South's lumber industry.

Labor played a vital role in this growth. In a region that was heavily black in many areas, it was inevitable that slaves and free blacks* would complement and compete with white labor. During the fall and winter, when slaves could not be profitably utilized on farms and plantations, masters found it much to their advantage to hire their slaves out to sawmill or lumberyard owners. Although whites dominated management and most skilled positions in the Old South's lumber industry, slaves and free blacks commonly served as sawyers, engineers. and raft captains in all areas of the region. Whether hired* or owned by the mill owners, slaves were unlikely to desert their job. Free blacks also found positions in the lumber industry that offered relatively high wages and allowed them to live with a measure of dignity. Because white workers tended to be more transient than black laborers, mill owners increasingly preferred black lumbermen. Blacks introduced an element of stability into the labor force employed in the Southern lumber industry.

The great majority of blacks who labored in the antebellum South's lumber industry worked not in cities but in the interior. Rarely did blacks work full-time as lumbermen. They typically were agricultural laborers who worked in the production of staple crops during the cultivating and harvesting seasons. In slack periods, when the master sought ways to maximize his income and to utilize his labor force more fully, slaves often were dispatched to the forests as "timber getters." While rough timber commonly was rafted to communities for finishing in mills, many plantations* possessed small mills of their own. Production beyond the needs of the plantation would be sold commercially. In keeping with the objective of self-sufficiency, the system inevitably produced slaves who were skilled as sawyers, coopers, and smiths. Excesses of skilled laborers often led planters to "hire out" their skilled bondsmen to neighboring planters or to commercial sawmills located in or near cities.

Simon Gray,* a slave hired out at first only as a semiskilled laborer, offers an excellent example of how a Southern slave rose in skill and status in the lumber industry. Intelligent and diligent, Gray earned the esteem of his employer, Andrew Brown, in the 1830s by performing skilled jobs. Eventually, he was elevated to the position of raft captain. Gray's skills were such that, in 1845, he made regular trips on the Mississippi River and purchased the bulk of the timber for Brown's sawmill. Gray received a regular salary that was supplemented by extra compensation each time he took a raft to New Orleans. He eventually saved enough money to begin a small business of his own, despite being a slave. He purchased his son's freedom even though Gray himself remained a slave until the fall of Vicksburg in 1863.

While Simon Gray was the exception rather than the rule, the important role blacks played in the development of the South's lumber industry was crucial. They provided the manpower, and often the skills, that made the industry competitive with that of the North. No accurate count of the total number of slaves and free blacks who engaged in the lumber industry, full-time or part-time, is possible. It can be safely estimated, however, that, by 1860, it ran into the several tens of thousands.

SELECTED BIBLIOGRAPHY

John H. Moore, *Andrew Brown and Cypress Lumbering in the Old Southwest* (1967); and Richard C. Wade, *Slavery in the Cities: The South, 1820–1860* (1964).

JOHN A. EISTERHOLD

LUNDY, BENJAMIN (1789–1839). Benjamin Lundy, antislavery editor, was born 4 January 1789 at Greensville, New Jersey, the only child of Joseph and Elizabeth (Shotwell) Lundy, and died 22 August 1839 at Lowell, Illinois. In

February 1815 he married Esther Lewis, by whom he had five children: Elizabeth, Susan, Charles, Esther, and Benjamin.

As a birthright Quaker* young Lundy had ample occasion to imbibe the humanitarianism that then characterized the sect. From such perspective he viewed with revulsion the cruelties of the internal slave trade as he witnessed them while laboring as an apprentice saddler in Wheeling, Virginia. Thenceforth, antislavery* was his preoccupation.

A trip to St. Louis in 1818 acquainted him with persons ambitious to extend slavery into the Western territories. This experience destroyed his illusion that slavery was a dying institution and that owners sincerely sought means for ending it. Deciding that slavery must be opposed by political action, he spent many months in Missouri futilely attempting to organize opposition to the territory's admission as a slave state.

In January 1821, upon returning to Ohio, he founded the *Genius of Universal Emancipation*, a journal dedicated almost exclusively to exposing the iniquities of slavery and promoting antislavery programs. For a decade it remained the principal American antislavery journal. In comparison with most of his abolitionist successors, Lundy had an eclectic editorial policy. Thus, the *Genius* served as an organ for Quaker and evangelical opponents of slavery (most of them resident in the upper South) who castigated the institution for its cruelty and its violation of God's writ and who predicted the imminent visitation of divine wrath, most probably in the form of slave rebellion. But the *Genius* also publicized secular antislavery arguments. Lundy charged slavery with being a wasteful, inefficient labor system. He particularly criticized its reputed tendency to generate aristocratic attitudes and despotic behavior among masters, thereby subverting the wholesome republic of simplicity and virtue projected by the Founding Fathers.

Lundy was similarly eclectic in his receptivity to proposals for ending slavery. He would endorse almost any antislavery means, except the use of violence. He publicized demands for both gradual and immediate emancipation, did not categorically condemn projects for colonization,* and, more enthusiastically than most of his immediate successors, urged the utility of antislavery political action.

One of his favorite plans embraced efforts to establish a free labor colony in Haiti, Canada, or Mexico. Such an establishment, he believed, would allow blacks to escape American prejudice, would encourage manumissions by removing some of the allegedly dangerous free blacks, and, by demonstrating the economic superiority of free over slave labor, would lead to a general emancipation. While in Mexico on this mission, Lundy witnessed the early stages of the Texas Revolution. His account of that event, emphasizing a purported "slaveholders' conspiracy," supplied both data and an interpretation invaluable to politicians bent upon preventing the annexation of Texas.

SELECTED BIBLIOGRAPHY

Merton L. Dillon, *Benjamin Lundy and the Struggle for Negro Freedom* (1966); and [Thomas Earle], *The Life, Travels, and Opinions of Benjamin Lundy; Including His Journeys to Texas and Mexico* . . . (1847).

MERTON L. DILLON

LUTHERAN CHURCH. Martin Luther once reminded peasant rebels in his country that the New Testament taught that the slave, in spite of his slavery, could still be a Christian. His view, when transported to America by his followers, dictated that a slave, in spite of his slavery, could still be a good Lutheran. To be a good Lutheran required both the slave and the free person to obey authority and maintain the status quo. Lutheranism was a conservative, quietist denomination, disinclined to tamper with social and political controversies.

The Lutheran church in antebellum America included mainly German, Dutch, and Swedish immigrant groups. Its strongest representation was in the Middle Atlantic states. By 1713, in New York, it had baptized its first slave. To encourage additional such baptisms, Wilhelm Christopher Berkenmeyer (1686–1751), a prominent slave-owning minister, executed a church constitution that specified clearly that baptism into Lutheran Christianity did not bring with it emancipation. Other Lutherans followed Berkenmeyer's lead. In Georgia, Lutheran pastors, after an initial reluctance, purchased and baptized slaves. In Virginia, the Hebron Lutheran Church in Madison County paid its pastors' salaries and other congregational costs by hiring out the slaves it owned.

When Henry Melchior Muhlenberg (1711–1787) arrived in America from Germany in 1742 to inspect, to organize, and to unify the Lutheran church, he confronted the widespread use of slaves by his coreligionists. In his journals Muhlenberg carefully noted that his fellow Lutherans diligently pursued the spiritual welfare of their black slaves (including teaching them German hymns), that they were more humane to their slaves than were their English-American neighbors, and that they feared black insurrections would be the consequence of slave emancipation. Muhlenberg had no appreciative word for slavery, but neither did he issue a public resolution against it. Indeed, no public protest of slavery emerged from any Lutheran before the nineteenth century.

The chief Lutheran spokesman for slavery during the nineteenth century was John Bachman (1790–1874). A native of New York, where his family had owned slaves, Bachman accepted a call in 1815 to the prestigious St. John's Church in Charleston, South Carolina. He helped to establish, and served as president of, the General Synod, which represented two-thirds of the Lutherans in antebellum America. As a slave owner, ministering to slave owners, Bachman devotedly carried on a mission to the blacks. By 1860, the year he delivered the prayer at South Carolina's secession convention, Bachman had performed 1,835 baptisms, 800 confirmations, and 300 marriages among the blacks.

Bachman's ministry might well have been guided by a protocol issued by the Evangelical Lutheran Synod of North Carolina in 1816. That protocol instructed

Lutheran ministers to baptize and confirm slaves, and to provide them with a place to worship. In regard to marriage,* it advised ministers to warn the slaves that if they were separated from their spouse through the sale or division of property, the slaves had to obtain the combined consent of their minister and master and mistress to remarry. Later the Synod of South Carolina added the suggestion to the protocol that Lutherans employ the *Catechism . . . for the Oral Instruction of Colored Persons* by the Presbyterian minister, Charles Colcock Jones.* Substituting a Presbyterian catechism for *Luther's Small Catechism* signified a major theological concession, but Lutherans appreciated the proper questions and answers on the master-slave relationship that Jones, unlike Luther, had provided.

Bachman, as the most successful Lutheran minister to reach the blacks, felt compelled to define for his denomination and for the South their personality and place in humankind. A gifted naturalist who had collaborated with John James Audubon in publication, Bachman combined his scientific knowledge and biblical training to affirm the ''one-ness'' of humanity. In 1850, in his *The Doctrine of the Unity of the Human Race Examined on the Principles of Science*, Bachman argued that the anatomical, psychological, and physiological structures of both Negroes and Caucasians were the same. But the Negroes as a ''degenerate'' race needed the superior Caucasians to educate and to support them. This need, Bachman maintained, could best be met in a society at whose center was a ''benevolent slavery.''

In the nineteenth century Lutherans marshaled few attacks upon the slavery that Bachman called benevolent. In 1822, the German Evangelical Lutheran Synod of Tennessee resolved that slavery was ''a great evil'' in America. But after 1831 this lonely statement was overwhelmed by the anti-abolitionist rhetoric from the South Carolina Synod that characterized abolitionists as ''rotten hearted benefactors'' of the Negro race. Most Lutherans however, were colonizationists rather than abolitionists and saw the American Colonization Society* (ACS) as the proper agency to deal with slavery. Many of their regional synods commended its work (the influential New York Ministerium did so as late as 1857), and the ACS was the darling project of two presidents of the General Synod, Dr. Benjamin Kurtz (1795–1865) and Dr. David Frederick Schaeffer (1787–1837). Kurtz praised its activities in his widely circulated newspaper, the *Lutheran Observer*, and Schaeffer did the same in his *Evangelical Lutheran Intelligencer*. Owing to his fear of slave insurrections, Schaeffer felt it incumbent upon him to prod Lutherans to support the return of the ''degraded'' blacks to Africa in order to spare white sons and daughters ''scenes of desolation and human carnage.'' But most Lutherans aided the ACS as the kind of conservative organization that appealed to them as conservative Christians.

One prominent Lutheran who moved beyond colonization to a moderate antislavery position was Samuel Simon Schmucker (1799–1873), yet another president of the General Synod and founder of the Lutheran Theological Seminary in Gettysburg. Influenced by the antislavery writings of William Ellery Channing,

Schmucker refused to join the American Anti-Slavery Society because of its abuse of Southern Christian slaveholders. He argued for a gradual abolition of slavery legislated by the slave states themselves and financed by federal funds. Schmucker's student, William A. Passavant (1821–1894), published a newspaper, the *Missionary*, in which he adopted a similar moderate antislavery position, once in a celebrated debate with John Bachman.

The only Lutherans to style themselves abolitionists were members of the small Franckean Synod located on the fringes of the "burned over district" of New York State. Abolitionists after the mode of the Tappan brothers, they used appeals, petitions, synodical declarations, and the publication of their journal, the *Lutheran Herald*, to inspire Lutherans to oppose slavery. Yet the Franckeans failed to persuade the General Synod to produce an antislavery resolution before the Civil War. They were a curious anomaly in a conservative denomination. They even were suspected of not being true Lutherans at all, and in a property dispute with another Lutheran synod they were judged by a New York court to be similar to the Church of God denomination. If the skepticism over the Franckeans' Lutheran credentials is added to the suspicion that Schmucker and Passavant, in their social action, were pseudo-Presbyterians, then the Lutheran church could be said to have lacked an authentic abolitionist witness. Not surprisingly, the Lutheran church saw its black membership in the South evaporate immediately following the Civil War.

SELECTED BIBLIOGRAPHY

Raymond M. Bost, "The Reverend John Bachman and the Development of Southern Lutheranism" (Ph.D. dissertation, Yale University, 1963); Robert Fortenbaugh, "American Lutheran Synods and Slavery, 1830–1860," *Journal of Religion*, 13 (1933), 71–92; Douglas C. Stange, "A Compassionate Mother to Her Poor Negro Slaves: The Lutheran Church and Negro Slavery in Early America," *Phylon*, 29 (1968), 272–281; Douglas C. Stange, "Lutheran Involvement in the American Colonization Society," *Mid-America*, 49 (1967), 140–151; Douglas C. Stange, "Our Duty to Preach the Gospel to Negroes: Southern Lutherans and American Slavery," *Concordia Historical Institute Quarterly*, 42 (1969), 171–182; Douglas C. Stange, *Radicalism for Humanity: A Study of Lutheran Abolitionism* (1970); and Willis D. Weatherford, *American Churches and the Negro: An Historical Study from Early Slavery Days to the Present* (1957).

DOUGLAS C. STANGE

M

MAMMIES. The vision of the black mammy, enshrined in the hearts of white Southerners after the Civil War as a loyal, capable, forthright house servant* devoted to the white children of her master, appears to be an invention of the postwar period, rather than a reflection of antebellum reality. It ranks, then, with other stereotypes that arose from the way in which whites rationalized the slaves' oppression and produced such figures as Sambo* and Uncle Tom.

The female house servant, and the mammy in particular, have received very little attention, and commentators have rarely analyzed in any depth the exact nature or numbers of the mammy, perhaps because she smacked of the over-weaning matriarchal figurehead in the black family* whose existence has been disputed. But even with this relative lack of information some broad outlines emerge.

The mammy was not universal, even among wealthy white families. Few black slave women escaped field tasks altogether. Indeed, relatively few planters had a sufficient labor force to afford segregating a cadre of house servants. On most plantations, even the care of young children was entrusted to a range of slaves rather than a slave nurse-cum-housekeeper, or mammy. Slaveholders as parents generally preferred not to leave control of their children to others anyway. The slave nurse was constantly under supervision, wet-nursing was only em-ployed when the white mother could not herself nurse, and often the mammy might be a young girl who would act more as a youthful companion rather than a mother-substitute. In families where men were widowed, it was more likely that a single slave would become housekeeper, nursemaid, and source of moral and physical comfort. Under these conditions, the female slave might provide the roots of the later image of the loyal servant.

This does not mean that there were not numbers of black women who formed close attachments to the white children under their care, or that the white children who were raised by black slaves did not retain some sort of relationship with these women that transcended the usual master-slave relationship.* But huge barriers remained. Until more is known about the lives of antebellum slave women,* it is not possible to judge the extent that white men or women listened to, or heeded, the advice of the black mammy after they had left the nursery. Whether many freed black women who had been mammies remained as family retainers after the war also remains unclear.

After 1865 *mammy* and *aunty* were simply terms of relative respect used for elderly black women who were house servants, midwives, or nurses in some capacity. As the century wore on, the terms referred to the black domestic also, who took on the numerous tasks of running a household without the support of other servants that had been usual on the large plantations. It is from this context that the image of Aunt Jemima or Aunt Sally arose, and it was this vision that provided the source for the successful effort to have a statute to the black mammy erected in Washington, D.C., in the 1920s. The suggestion itself simply reveals the extent to which the Old South had come to provide myths to fuel the race relations of the present.

The black mammy was an image carved out of a mixture of myth and reality that would become a symbol of subservience and would be used by whites to recall a golden age that had never been as bright as memory gilded it.

SELECTED BIBLIOGRAPHY

Jane Turner Censer, *North Carolina Planters and Their Children, 1800–1860* (1984); Jacqueline Jones, "My Mother Was Much of a Woman: Black Women, Work, and the Family under Slavery," *Feminist Studies*, 2 (1982), 235–269; Jessie Parkhurst, "The Role of the Black Mammy in the Plantation Household," *Journal of Negro History*, 23 (1938), 349–369; and Deborah Gray White, *Ar'n't I a Woman? Female Slaves in the Plantation South* (1985).

                                                                  MARION ROYDHOUSE

MANUMISSION. Manumission is the formal release from slavery or servitude. During the colonial period few restrictions were placed on the slaveholder wishing to free his slave, and manumission was usually construed as a matter of individual preference. In 1670, Virginia permitted the manumission of black and Indian male slaves, who were allowed to have black servants but prohibited from having white servants. No other laws restricting manumissions were enacted in that colony until 1723, when, in the wake of insurrections, meritorious service became the basis for manumission, and permission had to be obtained from the governor and his council.

In Maryland, the other Chesapeake colony, verbal order, or promise of freedom, was the simplest form of manumission. Evidently, concern over slaveholders' abandoning old, perhaps in some instances senile, slaves prompted the enactment in 1752 of a law prohibiting manumission by word of mouth and by last will and testament; manumission by deed subsequently became the chief means of freeing slaves in that colony.

In the Southern colonies manumission was most commonly granted for meritorious service. In North Carolina the county courts customarily determined the merits of the manumission application, a practice that was codified by the assembly in 1777. Only South Carolina in 1722, required manumitted blacks by law to leave the colony. Other than this law, which expired after several years and was not reenacted, no restrictions were placed upon manumissions, which generally were regarded as a private matter. Georgia slaveholders freed their slaves for meritorious service as well as for faithful service, without answering to any governmental body.

Manumission laws of the Northern colonies reflect concern about manumitted blacks becoming a burden on the community. Early laws of New York and New Jersey required sufficient bond to pay each manumitted black £20 sterling annually for the rest of his life. The New York law required a flat sum of £200 sterling as bond, while New Jersey's required an annual payment of £20 sterling for every slave freed. In 1717 New York eliminated the annual payment requirement to the freed black, but still required the former master to post bond. New Jersey did not revise its law until 1769, when it adopted one similar to the 1717 New York law. Pennsylvania required posting of a £30 sterling bond for each slave freed, but any slave freed before he or she was twenty-one could be bound out to service.

In 1702 Connecticut enacted legislation requiring slaveholders to assume responsibility for the support of their former slaves. The following year Massachusetts passed a similar law, but required the posting of a £50 sterling bond. Rhode Island required a £100 sterling bond.

Between 1780 and 1865 the Northern states and some of the border states (including the West) emancipated their slaves, through legislation, constitutional provisions, or judicial rulings, while the South went in a different direction. There, with a few exceptions, the generally liberal manumission laws of the colonial period became either restrictive or, in some instances, proscriptive.

Most manumission laws in the South contained a clause requiring the manumitted party to leave the state. An 1852 Louisiana law required manumitted blacks to leave the United States and masters to post $150 to pay for transporting those blacks to Africa. Manumission laws of the region commonly vested legislatures with sole authority to grant manumissions. A majority of the states proscribed manumission by last will and testament. By 1860 Louisiana, Georgia, Mississippi, and Alabama had enacted legislation prohibiting emancipation in any form.

Kentucky required the master to give a bond assuring the manumitted party's departure from the state, and North Carolina required a $1,000 bond for good conduct. The major change in North Carolina's law, enacted in 1830, was the provision for a bond. The major change in Virginia's law was the requirement that the manumitted party leave the state. Kentucky revised its law only slightly after 1794. Kentucky, Virginia, and North Carolina did not stray far from their original positions on manumission laws.

Manumissions declined in the nineteenth century because the increase of free blacks alarmed many whites and the Southern economy sustained a long period of prosperity that led to greater reliance on slave labor, which, with its consequent increase in slave prices, tended to discourage manumissions. Antislavery agitation and sectionalism also strengthened the slaveholders' resolve to protect the peculiar institution, and stiffened manumission laws ensued. Moreover, in South Carolina the assembly tightened legislative loopholes to prevent further acts of "judicial legislation" by the highest court, which tended to be somewhat liberal when interpreting the slave codes. This may not have been unique to South Carolina's state judiciary.

The upper South and what subsequently became the border states reacted less harshly to these circumstances than did the lower South. Although Virginia's free black population was larger than that of any other slave state, Maryland excepted, and the most violent slave uprising of the nineteenth century occurred there, its manumission laws were less restrictive than Alabama's. States in the upper South and border states marched to the beat of a different drummer. Their economies had a high slave visibility, but they did not rely on slave labor as heavily as the lower South and their political leadership appears to have been more responsible. These factors doubtless influenced manumission laws there.

By comparing the manumission laws of the colonial period with those of the national period one can conclude that (1) the major differences in positions on manumission between North and South came after the American Revolution, and (2) there were subregional differences in manumission laws, with those of the upper South being relatively liberal, while those of the lower South were not.

SELECTED BIBLIOGRAPHY

James C. Ballagh, *A History of Slavery in Virginia* (1902); Ralph B. Flanders, *Plantation Slavery in Georgia* (1933); John Hope Franklin, *The Free Negro in North Carolina, 1790–1860* (1943); Howell M. Henry, *The Police Control of the Slave in South Carolina* (1914); Willie Lee Rose, ed., *A Documentary History of Slavery in North America* (1976); James B. Sellers, *Slavery in Alabama* (1950); Joe Gray Taylor, *Negro Slavery in Louisiana* (1963); and Arthur Zilversmit, *The First Emancipation: The Abolition of Slavery in the North* (1967).

WHITTINGTON B. JOHNSON

MAROONS. Though the term *maroon* sometimes is applied to individual fugitive slaves,* it is applied here to independent communities, or variously, *cumbes*, *cimarrones*, *palenques*, and *quilombos*, of such people. These communities—which ranged from a few members and survived for a brief time, to thousands of members and survived for decades—existed in the Americas virtually everywhere that plantation slavery existed. They were, however, more common where particular conditions prevailed.

Among these conditions certain ratios are most salient. First, the greater the slaves' suffering, for example, from inadequate plantation food supplies or exploitation by absentee owners demanding high returns, the greater the spur to flee to maroons. Second, the higher the ratio of slaves of African to non-African birth the more likelihood of maroon development. Many maroons were founded by Africans who, still possessing ethnocultural identity, looked to replicate native societies. Third, the higher the ratio of blacks to whites, the more opportunity for slaves to escape to maroons. Fourth, the more mountainous, forested, swampy, and unexplored the hinterland, the better the chances for maroons to remain secreted or to defend themselves. Fifth, the more tropical the climate,* the easier for maroons to produce food and the less protection they required against the elements. Finally, the more unstable the government of the master class, or the more frequent the conflicts among governments of master classes, the less the threat to maroon survival.

Broadly construed, the ratios favorable to maroons were less characteristic of slave society in North America than in the Caribbean and Latin America. In North America, adequate food supplies, permanently domiciled masters, large numbers of Creole blacks, numerous white people, less rugged hinterland, colder climate, and stable government were common. Nevertheless, maroons were not unknown or even uncommon in North American slave society.

Certain regions of the Old South contained the demographic,* geographic,* and climatic conditions advantageous to maroons. In fact, from the genesis of slavery in the seventeenth century until its death in the nineteenth, North American slaveholders were seldom entirely free of harassment by maroons. Even as white settlers were establishing the institution in Virginia, small maroons became active in the colony. By the end of the seventeenth century, threats from more vigorous maroons in the Dismal Swamp along the Virginia-Carolina border aroused white fears of a general slave uprising. Once established, these maroons—whose combined populations sometimes numbered hundreds, perhaps even several thousand—sought to lead a settled life of farming and raising livestock.* Military forays against them notwithstanding, they persisted, albeit sometimes equivocally, into the nineteenth century.

In the eighteenth century, again despite efforts to suppress them, maroons appeared from time to time in South Carolina and Georgia. By the 1760s maroon activity in South Carolina once more instilled fears of slave rebellion. After the defeat of the British in Georgia during the American Revolutionary war, fugitives whom they had armed continued to harry settlers along the Savannah River. The next century saw the rise of maroons in the Southwest. For example, a maroon community in Mobile County, Alabama, sustained itself by raiding local plantations until armed whites destroyed it in 1827. In the early 1840s, white Alabamians again marched against a maroon north of Mobile. In those decades maroon inhabitants of Mississippi and of the bayous of Louisiana also plundered white settlements.

Florida, sparsely settled, semitropical, often politically unstable, proved especially well-suited for the establishment of maroons. There, not only had the relaxed rule of Spain been beckoning fugitives from the Carolinas and Georgia since the colonial period, but since the mid-eighteenth century the Seminole

Indians had been offering runaways support and opportunity to establish maroons. Encouraged first by the Spanish, and during the American Revolution* by the British, blacks and Seminoles raided the frontiers of South Carolina and Georgia. In the 1740s, British troops and colonial militia began making counter forays into Florida against the Spanish. Later these attacks also were leveled against the maroon blacks and their Seminole allies. At times, for example during the First Seminole War (1816–1818),* blacks and the Seminoles became the Americans' primary targets. And the invaders' testimony frequently described the blacks as their fiercest opponents. After the annexation of Florida to the United States in 1819, the Seminole-maroon alliance continued to trouble slave owners in Georgia and the Carolinas. Correspondence from American officials in Florida testifies to its determination to resist white encroachments. Not until the Second Seminole War (1837–1843) was the federal government able to defeat the Florida maroons and the Seminoles and remove them to the American West.* Yet relocating rather than reenslaving the blacks itself acknowledged their continued strength.

Throughout the antebellum period maroon guerrilla activity continued in the Carolinas, Georgia, and Gulf states. Once the Civil War* began, it became especially prominent in Confederate* territory invaded by federal troops, particularly in Virginia, the Carolinas, Florida, and Louisiana. At one time, Confederate military authorities in Florida considered the situation sufficiently critical to ask the governor to declare martial law in six counties. Southern whites charged black maroons with cooperating with white brigands, outlaws, and traitors. Not until the war ended slavery did maroon life end in the South.

Although maroons were not unimportant features of slave society in North America, their presence paled in contrast to that of other Western slave cultures. Except for those of the Dismal Swamp and Florida, maroon communities in the United States never reached the magnitude and duration nor had the impact on slave society of the most vigorous maroons in Latin America and the Caribbean. There a few—Palmares in Brazil, San Basilio in Colombia, and Nirgua in Venezuela—endured for a century or more. And in Brazil, Colombia, Cuba, Dominica, Equador, Hispaniola, Jamaica, Mexico, and Surinam, maroons actually obliged white authorities to recognize their autonomy in return for a cessation of marauding and for cooperation in apprehending future fugitives. Even here, writes one historian, such modi vivendi "merely postponed the final conflict and resolution."

Throughout the Americas, maroons frequently evinced common characteristics. To subsist, their people raided neighboring plantations for food, arms, animals, cloth, and metal tools. They traded with nearby white settlers and pursued horticulture, hunting, and fishing. To defend themselves against whites, they waged guerrilla warfare and extablished armed camps. Though their leaders often were African-born, after 1700 Creoles increasingly assumed their role in Latin America and the West Indies and, after the end of the slave trade, in North America. Some isolated maroon societies, notably the Bush Negroes from Guyana, retained the customs of their African forebears. But the culture of most maroon societies was a syncretism of cultural characteristics derived from Africa, Europe, native America, and the slave quarters.

Whenever feasible, maroons formed alliances of opportunity. Often they were with slaves who provided them with supplies. Sometimes they were with European enemies of their former masters—the British against the Spanish on the Mosquito Coast; the French against the Spanish in Hispaniola; and the Spanish and British against the Americans in Florida. One might assume that maroon alliances with Indians, as with the Natchez in Mississippi, the Seminoles in Florida, and the Sumus in Central America, would have been natural. But in fact, maroons and Indians, separated by culture and by white machinations, frequently became antagonists. Indians sometimes assisted whites in subduing maroons, and conversely, maroons occasionally joined whites in subduing Indians. In order to survive, maroons even established temporary alliances with their former masters and worked with them against the interests of the slaves.

Nevertheless, the existence of maroons always was a serious inconvenience and an acute embarrassment to the slaveholders. Maroons offered an opportunity for slaves to escape to a life-style that, however much it posed problems of food, shelter, and defense, was an alternative to servitude. Too well, according to Eugene D. Genovese, the "authorities understood that unchecked maroons presented a constant temptation to the slaves to rise in revolt or to desert *en masse.*" As a result whites passed severe laws aimed at suppressing maroon communities. In Virginia, for example, a 1672 law promised a reward for killing runaways associated with maroons. In colonial South Carolina authorities paid £20 for a captured maroon associate, or £10 for his scalp. Maroons contradicted both the master's portrayal of slavery as benign and of the slave as docile. They were, explains anthropologist Richard Price, "living proof of the existence of a slave consciousness that refused to be limited by the whites' conception or manipulation of it."

SELECTED BIBLIOGRAPHY

Herbert Aptheker, "Maroons within the Present Limits of the United States," *Journal of Negro History*, 24 (1939), 167–184; Michael Craton, *Testing the Chains: Resistance to Slavery in the British West Indies* (1982); Eugene D. Genovese, *From Rebellion to Revolution: Afro-American Slave Revolts in the Making of the Modern World* (1979); John D. Milligan, "Slave Rebelliousness and the Florida Maroon," *Prologue*, 6 (1974), 4–18; Richard Price, ed., *Maroon Societies: Rebel Slave Communities in the Americas* (2nd ed., 1979); Leslie B. Rout, Jr., *The African Experience in Spanish America, 1502 to the Present Day* (1976); and Vera Rubin and Arthur Tuden, eds., *Comparative Perspectives on Slavery in New World Plantation Societies* (1977).

JOHN D. MILLIGAN

MARRIAGE. In the United States, unlike the Latin American countries, marriage between slaves had no legal foundation. The absence of legal bonds and the reluctance of national and state church organizations to endorse motions against the separation of slave spouses have encouraged the view that slave marriages were unstable and subject to the whim of slaveholders and slaves alike. Slave owners could, if they chose, select mates and break unions whenever their financial calculus dictated. According to this formulation, which received scholarly impetus from the writings of sociologist E. Franklin Frazier and public currency in the Moynihan Report on the status of black families in the 1960s, slaves, as victims of this system, had little influence in the shaping of their own family lives and fell into a pattern of serial marriage at best, and promiscuity at worst.

Most scholars have been uncomfortable with this simplistic assessment of slave marriage and family life* and offer several competing hypotheses about the attitudes and behavior of slaves and the relative influence of owners in determining slave experience. They have focused on four interrelated questions. What direct role did owners play in the selection of mates and in the stability of unions once formed? Did slaves adopt the attitudes and roles of owners in creating their own familial structures or did they retain some cultural autonomy? How successful were slaves in achieving the norms they established? Did the usurpation of the traditional male role of provider affect the quality of husband-wife relations?

To a large extent the scholarly debate has been shaped by the problem of evidence. Travelers' accounts,* planters' correspondence and farm manuals, and the slave narratives* provide descriptions of rituals of courtship and marriage and some insight into the attitudes of slave spouses. But these sources describe a myriad of life experiences and offer powerful testimony to the variety of unions, both marital and nonmarital, formed by slaves. Systematic documentation of slave marriages is rare. Unlike the births and deaths that were regularly recorded by many owners, the marriages of slaves escaped notation. Among the most valuable sources for historians are the postemancipation records of the Freedmen's Bureau,* which register tens of thousands of slave marriages.

The single factor that most shaped the quality of a marriage was the ability of slaves to find mates on the same plantation or farm. Unbalanced sex ratios, the size of plantation populations, the degree of kin embeddedness at a particular site, and the relative geographic isolation of the community all affected the size of the pool of potential mates for slaves. Bondsmen on plantations with an imbalance between the sexes or a very small population could not expect to find a mate on the same plantation and searched "abroad" for a partner.

In unions between spouses owned by two individuals, or located at two separate sites, the frequency of contact between spouses and between a father and his children depended upon the policies of the owners and the geographic distance between partners. Since the children of such unions resided with their mother, for most of the week she served as both father and mother, particularly in fulfilling the role of provider. Historians differ, as slaves and slave owners probably differed, on the relative advantages and disadvantages of "broad" unions. On the one hand, a slave husband would not be subjected to the stress of seeing his spouse suffer physical or sexual abuse at the hands of the owner or overseer. At the same time, the separation encouraged independence for slave women* who by necessity provided for their families. Spouses who belonged to different owners were more likely to be separated by sale or inheritance dispersals. From the perspective of the husband's owner, a marriage "abroad" would not contribute to his slave population and may have contributed to problems of control of the slave man who traveled between plantations.

In the selection of a mate, slaves were further limited by the cultural rules defining appropriate partners. Unlike their owners, slaves avoided marriage between first cousins and may have practiced taboos against marriage between other kin. This avoidance of first-cousin marriage has been seen by some historians as an indication of the autonomy slaves exercised in mate selection, as well as a sign that slaves did not merely imitate the marital practices of their owners.

Though evidence on slave courtship is sparse, some slave narratives recount a romantic ritual of courtship, with young men competing for the attention of young women. The crowding of slave cabins and the narrow confines of the quarter must have limited the opportunities for young people to court. And in situations where the potential partners resided on separate farms or plantations, these instances may have been even more rare. Nonetheless, many slave marriages were not formalized until after the woman had borne her first child. Illegitimacy apparently carried no stigma in the slave quarter and most women went on after the birth to form stable and monogamous unions. Though many women had intercourse prior to marriage, this in no way proves that slave women were promiscuous. Evidence on the age at which women bore their first child, by several estimates between age nineteen and twenty-one, suggests that they delayed intercourse at least three years after menarche. Once united, slaves placed a great value on fidelity. Adultery was considered a serious offense in the slave quarter.

Normally, slave parents, not masters, supervised marriages, and with the owner's consent, unions were formalized by a variety of rituals. One common practice was "jumping the broomstick." Other slaves, particularly household servants, were wed in the Big House, some in the hand-me-down wedding dress of the mistress. Some slave owners performed marriages themselves, other delegated this task to the churches. Black and white ministers of all Southern Christian congregations regularly encouraged and performed marriages.

Unlike most marriages in other societies, and certainly in contrast to the marriages of their owners, property played little role in the choice of slave partners. Slave women brought to their marriages about as much material goods as their husbands and by virtue of their ability to contribute to the family economy had as much influence in family decisions as men. Both men and women acted as providers who supplemented the family's food supply. This produced greater equality in the marriage. Because slave women needed always to be prepared for the possibility that they might lose their spouses, slave women may have developed an independence that made them more willing to separate from husbands who were incompatible.

Marriage vows for slaves were occasionally modified to recognize the vulnerability of slaves to sale. "Until death or distance do you part" acknowledged that slave spouses could indeed be sold. Slaves who resided in the slave-exporting states in the upper South were those most likely to face this separation. One measure of the impact of the westward expansion of cotton on slaves' marriages was derived by Herbert G. Gutman from the Freedmen's Bureau marriage registers. Slaves in the upper South in 1865 reported long-lasting unions, and Gutman suggests that these marriages provided a model of "marital, familial, and kin obligation" that was transmitted by each generation of slaves. Bondsmen in the lower South who registered marriages in 1864 and 1865, however, provided a grim testimony of the impact of westward expansion. One in four of these unions involved at least one partner who had been forcibly separated from a spouse.

A variety of circumstances, demographic* and geographic,* affected slave marriages and significantly determined their form and stability. Unions between spouses who belonged to different owners clearly had a different quality than those between coresident spouses. Both slaves and slave owners probably held stable two-parent families as the desired norm, but again, circumstances could intervene to break up spouses and separate parents from their children. Most devastating to unions was the internal migration of slaves to the cotton Southwest. Limited evidence on slave unions has restricted the work of scholars to the domestic lives of bondsmen in the nineteenth century. Much remains to be learned about marriage practices of newly arrived Africans and the first generation of American-born slaves. Such information would provide valuable insights into the evolution of the institution of slave marriages.

SELECTED BIBLIOGRAPHY

Janet Cornelius, "Slave Marriages in a Georgia Congregation," in O. Vernon Burton and Robert McMath, eds., *Class, Conflict, and Consensus: Antebellum Southern Community Studies* (1982); Eugene D. Genovese, *Roll, Jordan, Roll: The World the Slaves Made* (1974); Herbert G. Gutman, *The Black Family in Slavery and Freedom, 1750–1925* (1976); Richard H. Steckel, "Slave Marriage and the Family," *Journal of Family History*, 5 (1980), 406–421; and Deborah Gray White, *Ar'n't I a Woman?: Female Slaves in the Plantation South* (1985).

                                                            CHERYLL ANN CODY

MARSHALL, ANDREW COX (ca. 1755–1856). Andrew Cox Marshall was born on a plantation in South Carolina. His mother was a slave; his father was a white overseer, an Englishman who intended to manumit his slave family but died before effecting their emancipation. At various times Marshall was the property of John Houstoun, a colonial governor of Georgia; of Joseph Clay, a member of Congress from Georgia; and of Robert Bolton, a prominent Savannah businessman. Houstoun had freed Marshall in his will, but the executors of Houstoun's estate refused to honor the provision and sold Marshall. While a slave of Houstoun, Marshall had married.

When he was in his forties, Marshall became a convert to Christianity and joined a Baptist church.* Shortly thereafter, he began to preach. For several years he was an assistant to his uncle, Andrew Bryan, pastor of the First African Baptist Church in Savannah. After Bryan's death in 1812, the congregation asked Marshall to be their minister. He accepted and served until his death in 1856.

About the time of his conversion Marshall was encouraged and assisted by Richard Richardson, a white merchant who was Marshall's last master, to pursue his freedom and also that of his family (his second wife Rachel and their four children and a stepson). At the time Marshall was engaged in the draying business, and throughout his lifetime he combined the career of minister with that of entrepreneur.* He operated a successful portage and drying business and was patronized and respected by some of the most influential white merchants in Savannah. Marshall lived in a two-story brick home and at one time owned several teams of horses and a few slaves.

Although Marshall had no formal education, he learned to read and accumulated a small library, including a set of Bible commentaries. Cognizant of the value of education, in 1826 he was assisted by white Presbyterian friends in forming a Sunday school for his parishioners; this school functioned throughout the antebellum area. Marshall was also an ardent supporter of the temperance movement in the area.

We have no collection of Marshall's sermons, but witnesses claim that he spoke without notes and was a powerful expository preacher. In his preaching he probably focused attention on the same themes as most Baptist preachers: sin, redemption, and salvation, and the importance of Christian conduct in daily living. One white clergyman who knew Marshall well stated that his preaching was purely textual and abounded in numerous quotations from the Scriptures. Throughout the years a number of white persons visited Marshall's church; there was a segregated section reserved for them at the front and center of the building, near the pulpit.

Although the local Baptist association tried to discipline Marshall and his congregation for alleged "Campbellism" in the early 1830s, the association did not interfere with the policy of open communication at the First African Baptist Church. This practice was unusual for Baptist churches at that time, and it made Marshall's possibly one of the most ecumenical congregations of Baptists in the country.

SELECTED BIBLIOGRAPHY

Whittington B. Johnson, "Andrew C. Marshall: A Black Religious Leader of Antebellum Savannah," *Georgia Historical Quarterly*, 64 (1985), 173–192; Emmanuel King Love, *History of the First African Baptist Church, from Its Organization, January 20, 1788 to*

July 1, 1888 (1888); James M. Simms, *The First Colored Baptist Church in North America* (1888); Albert J. Raboteau, *Slave Religion: The "Invisible Institution" in the Antebellum South* (1978); and Edgar G. Thomas, *The First African Baptist Church of North America* (1925).

W. HARRISON DANIEL

MARYLAND, SLAVERY IN. The first slaves in Maryland probably came from Virginia, but soon most new arrivals were coming directly from Africa, with occasional small shipments from Barbados and the Caribbean. Early statistics are incomplete and probably misleading because seventeenth-century Maryland did not include blacks, Indians, and mulattoes in its vital records.

If, as some have argued, slavery evolved from indentured servitude,* the transition in Maryland took less than five years. In 1639 black servants were stripped of their rights as Englishmen and required to serve for life. Only Christians (slaves excepted) were to have the rights of Englishmen. In 1644, when the total recorded population was still less than 400, the assembly decreed that slaves could no longer seek manumission on the grounds of faith in Christianity. Obviously, the Africans had quickly discovered the material as well as the spiritual advantages of Christianity. The 1644 law also declared that a white woman who married a black servant would serve as a slave until her husband's death, and their children would be slaves until the age of thirty. Since these laws were passed when the African population was infinitesimal and before tobacco* had become an economic mainstay, they were probably generated primarily by racial prejudice and fears and probably drew heavily upon the experience of Virginia. Also, of course, the early Maryland settlers probably considered Virginia their future economic model. Once the fate of Maryland as a tobacco colony had been determined, the economic advantages of a permanent slave labor force over the more expensive short-term use of indentured white servants became obvious. Tobacco was a labor-intensive crop, and the wealth it produced was directly proportionate to the number of workers employed.

Still, however, white indenture remained the primary source of labor for both Virginia and Maryland until the final years of the seventeenth century, and until 1660 or so the white servants enjoyed considerable upward mobility. Of 160 white men who came as servants by 1642, more than 90 percent of the survivors became landowners, and twenty-two of the men became political leaders. After 1660, however, rising land prices and falling tobacco prices kept most white servants from becoming more than landless laborers. In this status, as Bacon's Rebellion in Virginia showed, they were more likely to become a troublesome political element.

For reasons still debated by historians, the planters after 1680 expanded African slavery dramatically. Edmund S. Morgan attributes this primarily to the shock of Bacon's Rebellion, in which numerous white servants participated. Winthrop D. Jordan suggests that the planters resisted the advantages of slavery as long as they did only because they wished to keep Virginia and Maryland a "white man's world." Ultimately, however, economic and political pressures overcame this objective, and slavery triumphed. Richard Dunn offers a simpler explanation. Slaves were hard to get before 1680 because the traders found the West Indies a more profitable and accessible market. In 1698, however, Parliament abolished the monopoly of the inefficient Royal African Company and thereby expanded the number of Africans available just as the planters were feeling a greater need for them. Also, King William's War, 1689–1697, reduced white immigration while enlisting white laborers already in the colonies. Paradoxically, the war created an economic boom for Maryland as the planters compensated for lower tobacco prices by buying more slaves and producing bigger crops. For all of these reasons, more than 1,500 slaves were imported in the years 1697–1703, and the total number had reached 9,000 by 1715. By 1718 the black population exceeded the white servant population by more than 1,000. Nonslaveholding whites always outnumbered slaveholders by a wide margin, but by mid-eighteenth century, when the slave population reached a plateau, the institution had achieved a status over and beyond its economic value. It provided great wealth for some people and was the society's most distinctive mark of prestige. It also kept the blacks inferior to the ever-growing poorer white population, and the devotion of all classes of whites to its preservation was further strengthened by often reiterated fears of slave rebellion.

Ironically, the institution expanded most while its long-range economic value was steadily declining. Tobacco exhausted the soils and the price of the crop fell more often than it rose. In bad times, however, the demand for slaves increased as the planters tried to compensate by increasing production, and this in turn increased slave prices.* A male slave aged sixteen to forty brought from £16 to £30 in 1715, but his value had reached £56 to £60 by the American Revolution.

The Maryland slavery laws* underwent considerable tampering through the seventeenth century, but were essentially completed by 1715. Judging by the laws, the chief problems were racial intermarriage, interbreeding, and religion.

During Maryland's first three decades unmarried white males outnumbered the females by some four to one, but a noticeable number of unions between white women and black men still occurred. That is why the 1644 law, which decreed that a white woman who married a black servant would become a slave until her husband's death and their children would be slaves until the age of thirty, was passed. Similar laws with slight variations were enacted in 1664, 1681, and 1692. Ironically, until 1681 the laws' purpose was occasionally nullified by unscrupulous masters who would marry white women servants to blacks to get more slave children and extend the services of the women. This practice ended after 1681, when Governor Charles Calvert sold an Irish servant named Nell to a planter who married her to a slave to produce more slaves. The angry Calvert got new laws passed that nullified all such marriages and penalized heavily anyone henceforth connected with any such marriage. The earlier laws, however, had already created numerous free mulattoes and white slaves, and confusion reigned over the status of children born after 1681 of parents married before 1681. In 1770 the grandchildren of Calvert's Irish Nell unsuccessfully sued for freedom on the grounds that their grandmother had been a free white woman. In 1787, however, Nell's great-granddaughter won her freedom on those grounds. Under the laws of 1692 and 1715, which endured until emancipation, the white fathers of mulatto children were not penalized, but their children were slaves. Any white woman, free or servant, who married or had illegitimate children by a black father, slave or free, would serve her county for seven years. If her husband was a black freeman, he became a slave for life and the marriage would be voided. The children would be slaves until the age of thirty-one.

Another apparent problem was the reconciliation of slavery with Christianity. As early as 1644 slaves were denied the right to seek manumission on the grounds of conversion to Christianity, and this was reaffirmed in 1671. In 1671 legislators argued that the question was causing masters to deny their slaves Christian education or opportunities for fear it might result in manumission. Presumably, the elimination of Christian status as an argument for freedom would send more slaves to heaven as well as reassure the masters hoping to go with them.

Various historians have argued that the Catholic theology in Latin America made the slave codes there more humane than those in North America on such questions as manumission, marriage, separation of families, and religious activity. The Maryland Catholic* leaders did urge humane practices, and this probably did affect at least some individual slaveholders. Manumission could not have become a religious issue without being argued as such by whites. The priesthood, however, was careful to avoid questioning the morality of slavery itself, and the Jesuits became large landowners and slaveholders whose practices varied with the fortunes of their enterprises. In 1819 a Jesuit supervisor found many Jesuit slaves in quarters "almost universally unfit for human beings to live in." Slaves, he reported, were underfed and often whipped, while the practice of religion was almost nonexistent. There was improvement when times improved after 1830, but in 1838, the Jesuits sold 272 slaves for $115,000, with most of them shipped to Louisiana and a number of families separated despite promises to the contrary.

By mid-eighteenth century, the expansion of Maryland's slave population had virtually halted. White concern over black population growth produced import duties designed to restrict black immigration, and by 1783 these taxes had almost stopped the foreign slave trade in Maryland. The pattern of births and their distribution indicates that black women were not held as concubines among the male slaves and that deliberate slave breeding* was not practiced. By 1775, however, from natural developments, the slave children were as numerous as the adults, and the institution was clearly reproducing itself. Meanwhile, the overall population was increasing at the rate of 25 percent, and the ratio of black to white was steadily declining.

The ideology of the America Revolution* and the effective military participation of a significant number of blacks, both slave and free, ended slavery in the Northern states. The Southern states, however, were reluctant to arm the blacks and faced a major problem in keeping slaves from running away to join the British, who promised freedom to all black recruits. The numerous tributaries of Chesapeake Bay provided escape routes for a considerable number of Maryland slaves, as attested by constant formal complaints, warnings, laws, and preventive actions. Perhaps in response and certainly from need, Maryland alone of the Southern states authorized slave enlistments. By 1778 both free blacks and slaves were occasionally being used as substitutes for white draftees, and in October 1780, the legislature decreed that any slave between sixteen and forty could be voluntarily enlisted with the consent of his master. In May 1781 the lawmakers decided further that all free men, including blacks, were eligible for the draft. For more than a month the legislature debated a bill for raising a regiment of 750 slaves to serve as a unit. All owners of six or more slaves between the ages of fourteen and sixty-five would be required to furnish one slave if he consented to enlist for the duration. The promise of ultimate freedom was implicit in all of this. The regimental bill was finally defeated, but the able service of the blacks, particularly as pilots on Chesapeake Bay, contributed to a strong anti-slavery movement led primarily by the Quakers* and Methodists.*

Maryland's flexibility toward slave enlistment and manumission* reflected profound economic changes. The Revolution almost stopped the export of tobacco and badly damaged the Maryland economy. In response many people turned to other activities less dependent upon slavery. Farmers in northern Maryland increased their production of grain, fruits, and vegetables, and wealthier people began investing in urban pursuits. Soil exhaustion, low tobacco prices, and marketing problems sent more and more of the planters' children into banking, commerce, real estate speculation, and industries like shipbuilding. Military exigencies and philanthropic impulses, therefore, struck Maryland when slavery was in a weakened economic status.

This declining importance of tobacco and growth of a rich economy independent of slavery, when combined with the revolutionary ideology and events, put Maryland slavery into a downhill slide. In 1785 the legislature rejected abolition petitions by a vote of only thirty-two to twenty-two. A surge of manumissions accompanied the Revolution, and between 1790 and 1810 the Maryland slave population increased less than 10 percent, while the number of free blacks* almost quadrupled. By 1850 only 54.7 percent of Maryland's black population were slaves, as compared to 89.7 percent in Virginia and 99.7 percent in Mississippi. The slave population, one-third of the population in 1790, was only one-sixth by 1850. The white percentage, meanwhile, grew from 62 percent in 1810 to 72 percent in 1850. By 1860 the 1800 slave population of 100,000 had declined to 87,000, while the free blacks numbered 84,000.

In 1831, reacting to the Nat Turner rebellion* in Virginia, Maryland forbade, with certain limited exceptions, any further importation of slaves into the state. Slaves involved in violations would be confiscated and freed if they would consent to go to Liberia* or leave the state forever. Otherwise they would be sold to the

American Colonization Society* for five dollars and be sent to Liberia anyway. Step by step, however, the law was relaxed, and in 1849 it was repealed except for slaves being imported for resale, and in 1860 even this prohibition was removed.

The Colonization Society was popular with Marylanders eager to expel free blacks, but the reluctance of blacks to go and the expense involved limited the movement's success. In 1841 a committee reported that the state had spent over $66,000 sending 627 emigrants to Africa and 25 to Haiti. After 1807, free blacks could not immigrate to Maryland under pain of heavy fines and the imposition of slave status if the fines were not paid. After 1831 the fine was $50 a week. Meanwhile, of course, the state's growing free black population suffered from serious legal and economic discrimination.

In Baltimore by 1860 the free blacks outnumbered the slaves by eleven to one, and the whites outnumbered them by eighty-three to one. In Maryland white workers were available to perform numerous tasks often done by blacks in other areas, and this meant competition for jobs between blacks and whites as well as between foreign-born and native-born workers. Baltimore endured a long period of strife and violence between native and immigrant workers,* and the prejudices of the Know-Nothing movement against white Catholics were equally virulent against the blacks. Frederick Douglass,* as a slave hired out by his master, was almost beaten to death by four fellow shipyard workers, while more than a hundred witnesses cheered his attackers and refused to testify when Douglass's master sought redress for this damage to his valuable property.

In 1860 a legislative committee made a last stand for slavery by recommending an elaborate program for the reenslavement of all blacks who refused to leave the state. This failed, but a new law did prohibit all future manumissions and authorized free blacks over eighteen to return to slavery voluntarily. No such returnees were ever recorded. In the same year a free black minister was sentenced to six years in prison for owning a copy of *Uncle Tom's Cabin*.

In many ways nineteenth-century Maryland resembled the United States as a whole. A static and sometimes declining slave society in southern and Eastern Shore Maryland was both competing and cooperating with a dynamic northern region marked by expanding commerce, technology, and industry, supplemented by prosperous agriculture based on grain, vegetables, fruits, and dairying. Baltimore, with 212,418 people, became a great city of cotton mills, clothing factories, shipbuilding, ship docks, merchants, and bankers. Its cigar-makers still used tobacco from the South, but the industry was becoming relatively less important. By 1860 the average farm value in northern Maryland was $44.21 per acre, as compared to $24.93 in the south and $24.35 on the Eastern Shore. Sixty percent of Maryland's population lived in the north, with 25 percent in Baltimore alone. The white population in southern Maryland actually declined by 10 percent between 1790 and 1850, while that of northern Maryland grew by 231 percent.

Similarly, just as the leaders of the slave states dominated national politics until 1860, the leaders of southern and Eastern Shore Maryland held the northern farmers and Baltimore at bay with a constitution and laws that denied the northern areas proportional representation in the state government. Like the nation, also, the Maryland sections shared much economic interdependence and a common racial prejudice that made any practical threat to slavery extremely unlikely unless the question should become entwined with some larger question like nationalism. During Maryland's earlier history, the political conflicts had been east versus west, with Chesapeake Bay the natural divider. In the nineteenth century, however, the struggles over matters like taxation, the judiciary, land policies, and representation shifted to a north-versus-south pattern with the slavery-dominated Eastern Shore aligned with the south and with Baltimore the wicked northern symbol for both. The Eastern Shore had virtually abandoned tobacco by 1830, but just as several divergent Southern states were united only by their concern for slavery, Eastern Maryland, with an economy based upon food crops, adhered to southern Maryland because of its equally large black population. Thus, when secession and the Civil War came, the Union-Confederate division with a significant Union majority was a natural development in Maryland.

The acceptance of abolition, however, was much more difficult. In 1861–1862 the Maryland legislature firmly rejected Lincoln's offer of emancipation with compensation. Maryland slavery was difficult to defend on economic grounds, however, and the Emancipation Proclamation, Lincoln's 1864 reelection (he won in Maryland), the impending defeat of the Confederacy, and the proposed Thirteenth Amendment* persuaded Maryland's leaders to accept the inevitable. After two years of confusion, hesitation, and angry debates, Maryland in 1864 wrote a new constitution that freed all slaves, established an "iron-clad" loyalty oath for voters, established a new public school system, and greatly increased the representation of the northern counties in the state legislature. Perhaps ironically, a major advocate of what the South considered "harsh reconstruction" was the former Know-Nothing and later Republican congressman from Maryland, Henry Winter Davis.

The Marylanders seriously affected economically by abolition were a distinct minority, and the change therefore brought no serious upheavals. The new freedmen assumed the liberties, uncertainties, dangers, threats, risks, and blessings long enjoyed and endured by the existing free black population. The adjustment was far less painful and violent than in some other states, but the heritage of slavery and prejudice remained.

Coming directly from Africa, most of Maryland's first generation of slaves missed the West Indian "break-in" experience, but the effects of this are difficult to measure. A slave's initial ignorance of the English language and the white settlers' customs may have made the prejudice against him come easier. The ease or difficulty with which a slave adjusted to Maryland, however, probably depended more upon the character of the individual slave and his master than upon whether or not the slave had first been broken to hard labor in the West

Indies. The ocean passage itself was usually a barbaric experience, and a cruel apprenticeship in the Caribbean would not make a cruel Maryland master any easier to take. Likewise, the speed with which a slave acquired the simple but laborious skills required for tobacco cultivation would depend more upon his attitudes and physical strength than upon an earlier experience in the Caribbean sugar cane fields. In any case, the slave usually found that acceptance and where possible the imitation of his master's ways were his best hope for any of life's amenities if not for survival itself. Also, of course, the early white settlers were themselves adapting to a strange and perilous world in which their own survival was threatened by crop failures, disease, and Indians. While both white and black settlers came with strong memories of the recent past, the earlier cultures of both groups met powerful assaults. The whites, however, maintained their physical ties with Europe, while the blacks were largely cut off from Africa as well as denied the white man's dreams of material progress in a world of freedom.

Like most slave codes, that of Maryland was extremely harsh. Whipping,* branding, and cropping were the usual punishments* for minor infractions, with hanging, quartering, or beheading reserved for major crimes. In law, slaves were forbidden to carry guns or other offensive weapons, to testify in cases involving whites, to marry without the master's permission, to meet in unsupervised gatherings on Sundays or other holy days, or to go anywhere without written permission. They were prohibited from keeping hogs or other animals except for the master's use. Families could be separated at the whim or from the economic needs of the master. By law slaves were to be kept illiterate, although this rule was occasionally violated in Maryland as well as in other states. Here and there a few whites, usually women, surreptitiously taught bright slave children on an individual basis.

Certain laws were designed to protect the slaves. The law of 1715 gave the courts authority to free any slave whose master was guilty three times of denying him food, shelter, and rest, or who punished him by dismemberment or cauterization. No provision was made for the slave who might not survive the first two infractions. In 1752 a law provided that masters could free only those slaves who were sound in mind and body, capable of labor, and under fifty years of age. The philanthropy that would free the master from obligations to a disabled or worn-out elderly slave was illegal.

Actually, the laws against physical abuse were impossible to enforce in any Southern slave area. Since slaves could not testify against whites in court, the laws protected them only when other whites were willing to stand up on their behalf. When Frederick Douglass was badly beaten before a large crowd, his angry master could not find a single witness to name his attackers. In turn, the master himself could beat or have any slave, male or female, beaten with impunity. The quality of a slave's life depended upon the character of his master rather than upon the laws. The debates over religion and the periodic reenactment or refinement of the more restrictive laws indicate that humane masters did exist.

The laws, after all, were aimed at masters suspected of being too lax with their discipline and too prone to use religion as an excuse for manumission.

Many variables affected the individual slave. On a well-managed and profitable plantation owned by a happy master, a slave might take at least some satisfaction with his work, feel some loyalty to his master's family, find solace in religion, find a satisfactory mate, enjoy meeting with others (even under white supervision) on Sundays and other holidays, and acquire a certain status within the slave community. Even under these ideal circumstances, however, his potential talents would be smothered, he would enjoy no freedom to make his own decisions, and with the passing years he might live in dread of his master's death. The death of a master all too often meant that debts had to be paid and that slave families* had to be divided or sometimes sold. The loud sobbing of slaves as Old Massa lay dying was not always based upon deep affection for his person.

In contrast, the slaves on Maryland's many marginal farms and plantations shared the masters' ups and downs in every way. In times of frustration and failure the slave was a convenient scapegoat for masters unable to vent their anger against their economic and social superiors. The lot of the average slave was in close proportion to the economic, social, and psychic successes and failures of his master. Tobacco, unfortunately, was a capricious crop that rapidly depleted the soils and suffered from frequent fluctuations in price and transportation costs. When economies became necessary and production had to be expanded to avoid failure, it meant harsher living conditions and longer hours of hard work for everyone, and even kind masters would sell slaves as a last resort. Soil depletion also meant frequent land sales and much movement from area to area. This, too, often meant that slaves had to be sold and thereby separated, and the movement itself was away from friends and perhaps relatives on neighboring farms and estates. While a slight majority of the slaves lived on the larger estates, most of the slaveholders owned estates valued at £100 to £500, which were obviously the ones most likely to become marginal in hard times.

Music provided slaves with a release and a means of expressing deep frustration and sorrow. Religion promised relief and freedom in a life after death. Like everything else, however, these experiences varied from master to master. Some wanted singing. Some did not. Some allowed or encouraged religion. Others did not. In 1700, Dr. Thomas Bray, the Anglican clergyman who later helped found Georgia, launched a movement to get all of Maryland's slaves baptized, but his efforts were defeated by opposition and indifference. Frederick Douglass always remembered the constant singing during one period of his childhood, and realized only later that the songs "breathed the prayer and complaint of souls overflowing with the bitterest anguish." The legislative debates over religion illustrated the ambivalence of the slaveholders. Some wanted the slaves to be religious, but feared it might become an excuse for manumission. Others recognized that a religious slave might be more willing to accept his lot. Still others, particularly after the Nat Turner rebellion, feared the religious slave as a potential firebrand. Frederick Douglass imbibed deep religious principles from an elderly free black in Baltimore, and the experience enabled him to forgive his tormentors and recognize the evil impact of slavery upon white and black alike. His master, however, forbade him to visit the old man, and when he later tried to start a Sunday school for young slaves on a plantation, he was beaten for this effrontery and threatened with the same punishment given Nat Turner. Douglass was also painfully aware of the hypocrisy of an outwardly pious master who overworked, underfed, and whipped his slaves for the slightest infraction, real or imagined.

If Maryland offered any advantage over other states to its slaves, it was that while escape was very difficult, it was easier than in most places. Pennsylvania abolished slavery in 1780, and the Quaker influence there provided a congenial reception and important assistance to a great many runaways. In 1851 a Maryland slaveholder and his son invaded the free black section of Lancaster, Pennsylvania, in search of a runaway.* An angry crowd killed the father and badly wounded the son. Several blacks and two whites were indicted for murder and treason, but all were acquitted. Only Maryland produced a Harriet Tubman,* an extraordinarily clever slave who after escaping herself returned again and again to organize runaway groups and guide them to freedom.

Perhaps the best original source for studying slave life in nineteenth-century Maryland is the brilliant memoir of Frederick Douglass. The son of an unknown white father and a slave mother whom he rarely saw, Douglass was passed back and forth among members of the same family. His legal owner was kind and generous on occasion, but capable of terrible cruelty when unhappy. In Douglass's childhood, a kind mistress in Baltimore taught him to read until her husband discovered this crime and stopped it immediately. When the older master died, Douglass lived in terror for weeks lest he be inherited by a drunken relative noted for cruelty. Luckily, he was returned to Baltimore where he found both comfort and inspiration in the religious teachings of an elderly black friend. Sent back to the plantation because of a capricious quarrel between family members, he incurred white wrath by trying to start a Sunday school, and by regularly allowing a horse to escape to a neighboring plantation, where Douglass, badly underfed at home, would get a full meal when he went for the horse. To crush his spirit, his master leased him to a notorious "slave-breaker," who overworked and underfed him while beating him terribly on a regular basis. After six months Douglass could take no more and defeated his tormentor in a physical combat. For this he expected death, but the master remained silent rather than risk his lucrative reputation for being able to handle unruly slaves.

Douglass then went to a genuinely religious, kind, and generous master. Instead of feeling gratitude toward slavery at its best, however, Douglass was encouraged by the lax discipline to organize an escape attempt with several other slaves. One of them betrayed the plot and all spent several weeks in jail expecting to be sold to the Deep South, but they were valuable, they had not actually run away, and their denials were ultimately accepted. Douglass was again sent to the family branch in Baltimore, where he was hired out to a shipyard and earned good wages for his master.

In Baltimore, Douglass was caught up in the city's angry ethnic and racial animosities triggered by job competition, and was terribly beaten by four white fellow workers. After his recovery he worked overtime and concealed the extra wages from his master. Finally, he borrowed a free black sailor's identity card, dressed as a sailor, and made his way without incident by train and ferry boat to Philadelphia, where Quakers sent him on to safety in New Bedford, Massachusetts.

Frederick Douglass ultimately became a famous abolitionist and a post–Civil War political power in Washington, D.C. For most Maryland slaves, however, emancipation did not bring legal justice or equality of opportunity, whether economic or political. The racial prejudice and fear that had nurtured slavery for almost two and a half centuries continued to motivate Maryland's large white majority for many decades after emancipation and became one of slavery's most enduring legacies.

SELECTED BIBLIOGRAPHY

Ira Berlin and Ronald Hoffman, eds., *Slavery and Freedom in the Age of the American Revolution* (1983); Jeffrey R. Brackett, *The Negro in Maryland: A Study of the Institution of Slavery* (1889); Ralph Cassimere, Jr., "The Origins and Early Development of Slavery in Maryland, 1633–1715" (Ph.D. dissertation, Lehigh University, 1971); Lois G. Carr and David Jordan, *Maryland's Revolution of Government, 1689–1692* (1974); Avery O. Craven, *Soil Exhaustion as a Factor in the Agricultural History of Virginia and Maryland, 1606–1860* (1926); Frederick Douglass, *Life and Times of Frederick Douglass* (reprint ed., 1962); Barbara J. Fields, "The Maryland Way from Slavery to Freedom" (Ph.D. dissertation, Yale University, 1978); Allan Kulikoff, *Tobacco and Slaves: The Development of Southern Cultures in the Chesapeake, 1680–1800* (1986); Aubrey Land, "Economic Base and Social Structure: The Northern Chesapeake in the Eighteenth Century," *Journal of Economic History*, 25 (1965), 639–654; Aubrey Land, "Economic Behavior in a Planting Society: The Eighteenth-Century Chesapeake," *Journal of Southern History*, 35 (1967), 469–485; Russell R. Menard, "From Servant to Freeholder: Status Mobility and Property Accumulation in Seventeenth-Century Maryland," *William and Mary Quarterly*, 3rd ser., 30 (1973), 37–64; Randall M. Miller and Jon L. Wakelyn, eds., *Catholics in the Old South: Essays on Church and Culture* (1983); Benjamin Quarles, *The Negro in the American Revolution* (1961); David B. Quinn, ed., *Early Maryland in a Wider World* (1982); and George T. Sharrer, "Slaveholding in Maryland, 1695–1775" (M.A. thesis, University of Maryland, 1968).

ELBERT B. SMITH

MASTER-SLAVE RELATIONS. In the Old South, as elsewhere, master-slave relations varied according to the size of farm or plantation, the roughness of frontier conditions, the nature of the process of production, and much else, especially the respective personalities* of masters and slaves. Despite such innumerable variables master-slave relations developed within common boundaries and manifested some common patterns. The law established basic rules that overwhelmingly favored the masters but guaranteed minimal protection to the slaves, if only to restrain irresponsible masters from provoking widespread disaffection and dangerous forms of resistance. Legal norms notwithstanding, the master-slave relation remained essentially a system of social relations derived from discrete personal relations that were anchored in a political economy in which some lived off the labor of those whom they owned as chattel.

Everywhere and always the master-slave relation depended upon violence.* Slavery's principal object of permitting some to live off others—socially and psychologically as well as economically—has normally led masters to attempt to hold that violence to a minimum. In the Old South, religion and community sentiment strongly reinforced the economic incentive to restrict violence. But even when masters sought to avoid the indiscriminate practice of violence, they relied heavily on the constant threat of its use to keep the slaves, if not docile, at least orderly.

Essays on slave treatment abounded in the Old South and were widely circulated. Almost invariably they insisted that a good (efficient, successful) master rarely had to resort to physical violence. Good masters combined material incentives, appeals to pride, shaming, withdrawal of privileges, and other ostensibly benign techniques of control. These essays, together with the feeble constraints imposed at law and, much more important, the exhortations of an influential ministry, did have an impact. After all, the model of the good master and the specifics of the advice corresponded with common sense. But, as often happens, common sense and the everyday experience of personal relations between discrete human beings failed to correspond.

Too many slaves refused to be sensible and chose to risk punishment* rather than submit to real or perceived demands for excessive labor, insults and verbal abuse, or a thousand and one indignities and provocations. Some were notoriously unwilling to take orders from anyone. Some slave women* resisted the sexual abuse that the relations of power invited. Some slave men interceded to protect or avenge their women. And what was even the most saintly of masters to do with those who, by his standards, proved incorrigibly lazy or destructively stupid or prone to be sullen and ''impudent''? What especially was he to do with those who took to the woods? Not only must the guilty be punished, they had to serve as examples to others. No matter how kind the master, how exemplary a Christian gentleman, either he went to his whip periodically or he lost control of ''the people.'' And every master knew it.

Formal punishment did not exhaust the violence and may not have been the most psychologically dangerous form of it. The slaves usually knew the rules of the farm or plantation and could steel themselves to the expectation of specific punishments for specific acts of error or insubordination. Less harsh physically, but perhaps more scarring emotionally, were the casual blows designed to step up the work pace, correct fooling around on the job, or answer the ubiquitous ''impertinence'' and ''impudence.'' Such blows fell often and were by no means readily predictable. House servants* took their share, probably a disproportionately high share, in a society in which parents and teachers beat children, public officials caned and pistol-whipped critics on the streets, judges and defendants exchanged blows in courtrooms, and just about everyone reserved the right to beat someone for offenses against dignity or honor. If the lady of the house quarreled with her husband, the house servants would do well to stay out of her way if they possibly could, and the field hands would do well to try to avoid being noticed at all. We may assume that the ownership of human beings inspired haughtiness and an oppressive touchiness in masters and mistresses, but even if we were to drop that assumption, not much would change. People who get up "on the wrong side of the bed" and are out of sorts are quick to take their miseries out on others, and these people had only their individual powers of self-restraint to keep them from venting their spleen on dependents who, as a matter of course, could not but disappoint impossible expectations.

The peculiar development of the Old South generated especially strong paternalist tendencies,* even relative to the other slave societies that somehow managed to acquire better reputations. Plantations* were small—on the average hardly more than farms of twenty slaves. Masters lived on them or, if rich, in nearby villages, where they were accompanied by house servants. The Southern states, fearful of the spur to slave insurrection provided by high black-white ratios, moved individually to close the foreign slave trade* even before the trauma of Saint-Domingue, and they joined the national effort at closure in 1808. Yet at that very moment the plantation system was spreading westward, the Cotton Kingdom was emerging, and the demand for slave labor was rising sharply. Also at that very moment, evangelical Christianity was sweeping the South and instilling a greater sense of responsibility in the masters.

In consequence, the Old South, alone among the slave societies of the ancient and modern worlds, had to grow its own labor force. In order to do so slaveholders had to guarantee at least a minimal level of material comfort and personal attention for their slaves. In doing so, the Old South alone displayed positive, indeed high, reproduction rates for slaves. And the master-slave relation matured into a compromise between the parties—an uneven, unstable, unjust compromise, but a compromise nonetheless.

Proslavery theorists* especially celebrated the master-slave relation as paternalistic, and in so doing echoed the sentiments of the typical slaveholders, the ministers, and, increasingly, the jurists. They sought, with indifferent results, to identify paternalism with kindness, affection, and the Golden Rule. Yet ordinary masters and theorists alike rarely deceived themselves about their ultimate dependence upon the raw powers of coercion or about the absolute necessity for the superordinate class to maintain a monopoly of the weapons of violence. For the most that might be said of paternalism is that under the most favorable conditions it ought to encourage a humane attitude toward subordinates. Strictly speaking and in common execution, the upholders of paternalism as a system of human relations and as an attendant ideology did not necessarily mean more than that the master-slave relation was organic—that one person related to another directly and not through the mediation of the market.

Some proslavery theorists often went so far as to deny that the Southern social system was slavery at all since, in their reading, masters had no claims to the bodies, much less the souls, of their laborers, but only had claims to their labor and social subordination. The abolitionists* had little trouble in exposing such sophistry and in demonstrating that the master's power not only included but required control of his slaves' bodies. Thomas Ruffin, North Carolina's most distinguished jurist and a fierce opponent of self-serving cant, spoke bluntly. He asked in what ways the master-slave relation was analogous to the parent-child relation, and concluded that there was no likeness between the cases. With slavery, wrote Ruffin, "the end is the profit of the master, his security and public safety; the subject, one doomed in his own person, and his posterity, to live without knowledge, and without the capacity to make anything his own, and to toil that another may reap the fruits." Ruffin continued: "Such obedience is the consequence only of uncontrolled authority over the body. There is nothing else which can operate to produce the effect. The power of the master must be absolute to render the submission of the slave perfect."

Ruffin's remarks underscored a fundamental tenet of Southern law—that, to the fullest extent possible, masters, not the courts, ought to have responsibility for slave discipline and that, therefore, they ought to be permitted the widest possible discretion. The laws did stipulate, subject to variations of time and place, that masters must provide adequate material comfort, and Louisiana forbade the sale of children under the age of ten away from the mother. In time the law set limits to the physical power of the masters to the extent that if they willfully killed a slave, they could be indicted for murder. But blacks could not testify against whites, and willfulness was hard to prove when masters claimed death as a result of normal "correction." Thus, the courts could barely protect the slaves' right to life, and the law remained primarily symbolic, as an ethical guide to the proper conduct of responsible Christian masters. Its significance lay primarily in the admission by the masters themselves that their slaves did have human rights and could not, except for specified purposes, be treated as things— treated as other than dependent human beings.

Once the ideological special pleading of the slaveholders is set aside—and, with it, the obtuseness of those historians who continue to confuse paternalism with kindness and "good treatment"—the authentic historical nature of paternalism emerges as a system of hierarchically structured mutual rights, duties, and responsibilities. Masters owed their slaves cradle-to-grave material security and spiritual and moral guidance; slaves owed their masters work and obedience. The masters arrogated to themselves the right to define the terms, and to the surprise of no one, they defined those terms to their every advantage.

All might have ended well for the masters if their slaves had proven to be the docile, obedient, submissive, and grateful creatures they were expected to be. Of docility, obedience, and submissiveness the slaves had their share. The prospect of a whipping or, worse, sale away from loved ones no doubt concentrates the mind wonderfully, and fear of pain is hardly race, class, or gender specific. But bold spirits abounded, and even the timid knew how to frustrate their masters' grand schemes. Like the colonial bureaucrats of the Spanish Empire in its great days, they proclaimed ¡*Obedsco, pero no cumplo*! [I obey, but I do not comply!] And of gratitude they knew little.

In the slaves' view, paternalism merely offered them the care and security to which they were entitled and for which, in any case, they worked hard. They viewed food, shelter, clothing, Christmas and other holidays, a six (or in some cases a five-and-a-half) day week, and much more not as privileges from on high, but as rights earned by their labor in a system of reciprocal duties. Much of the fiercest individual violence, in the Big House as well as in the fields, arose from this misunderstanding. For the most "loyal" slaves could turn bitter and aggressive when their "rights" were violated, and the sweetest of masters could turn savage when confronted by disobedience. But because masters and slaves defined rights and privileges in radically different, often opposite, ways, confrontation threatened to emerge at any time and over almost any issue, however trivial it might seem to outsiders.

The masters struggled with the problem but never could resolve it satisfactorily. In their characteristically self-defeating manner they excused their inability to cope with their slaves' behavior by complimenting themselves on their own racial superiority. What, after all, could you expect from a degraded black race? As Frances Butler Leigh, daughter of Fanny Kemble* and Pierce Butler, fumed after the Civil War: If you want a Negro to do something, first tell him what to do, then show him how to do it, and then do it yourself.

The masters imposed paternalism, and the slaves accepted it—after their fashion. They hardly had a choice, for notwithstanding their deep longing for freedom and their irrepressible resistance, the blacks knew that they were outnumbered and outgunned. Besides, slaves, like other human beings, normally craved security and order and feared the consequences of rebellion against a ruthless constituted authority. Yet they did rebel, and those moments, not the long periods of quiescence, compel wonder and awe. Had Gabriel Prosser,* Denmark Vesey,* Nat Turner,* and many anonymous souls not taken up arms, the masters would never have been struck with fear and never would have had to make the larger concessions inspired by a respect born of fear. In spite of themselves and against their own self-serving propaganda, the master class did make concessions, did extend "privileges," did do everything possible to raise the conditions of life just high enough to keep their slaves from rebelling out of sheer desperation. They thereby recognized by actions that belied their words their slaves' subjectivity—recognized them as historical actors with wills of their own.

For if the slaves accepted paternalism after their fashion, that fashion had much less in common with their masters' understanding than their masters knew. Only when the Civil War came, and the most trusted, loyal, and friendly slaves joined their less placid brothers and sisters in striking for freedom, did the masters finally come face to face with their self-deception. The slaves had never accepted their enslavement and had firmly rejected its religious rationale. Their accommodation to the web of compromises and dependencies that marked paternalism never implied an acceptance of the legitimacy of slavery itself. The slaves made a distinction that their masters had no way to fathom.

According to the plantation legend, masters and slaves generally lived together affectionately in an atmosphere of mutual kindness and concern. Masters often, indeed normally, referred to "my family, white and black." The obviously romantic, self-deceiving, sometimes flagrantly dishonest features of the legend have long inspired anger and ridicule in modern critics, and deservedly so. Yet intimacy and mutual concern, even affection, were by no means absent or even rare. Living at close quarters in the isolation of plantation districts and villages, masters and slaves drew upon each other for emotional and physical support. Both black and white sources reveal deep and lasting bonds across class, racial, and gender lines.

Those who created and sustained the plantation legend missed the tragedy. For to the extent that it had its large kernel of truth—to the extent that the finest potential of the master-slave relation as an organic relation was realized—the fundamentally violent and intrinsically unjust nature of the relation itself was thrown into bold relief. Nothing, in the end, could compensate the slaves for the freedom they craved. Nothing, at given moments, could restrain even the kindest and most responsible of masters from abusive, self-corrupting, and cruel behavior. Whatever virtues may be credited to paternalism, they were inseparable from the process of domination inherent in a relation not merely unequal but unjust. Under the most favorable of circumstances slavery remained an enormity.

SELECTED BIBLIOGRAPHY

Drew Gilpin Faust, *James Henry Hammond and the Old South: A Design for Mastery* (1982); Eugene D. Genovese, *Roll, Jordan, Roll: The World the Slaves Made* (1974); Charles W. Joyner, *Down by the Riverside: A South Carolina Slave Community* (1984); Leslie Howard Owens, *This Species of Property: Slave Life and Culture in the Old South* (1976); Willie Lee Rose, *Slavery and Freedom* (1982); Kenneth M. Stampp, *The Peculiar Institution: Slavery in the Ante-Bellum South* (1956); and Mark V. Tushnet, *The American Law of Slavery, 1810–1860: Considerations of Humanity and Interest* (1981).

EUGENE D. GENOVESE

MATERIAL CULTURE. Until the early nineteenth century, African culture in the South was being constantly renewed and strengthened by frequent shiploads of new arrivals from Africa. As a result, the slaves developed a new Afro-American culture, one that was neither purely African, nor Euro-American, but rather a synthesis of the two. The acculturation process was reciprocal. Each race absorbed something of the other's culture, and sometimes the results were synergistic; sometimes each culture was retained in a pure form.

Although the masters usually supplied the raw materials for most material objects, the blacks provided the labor to make them. Slaves generally had considerable latitude in the techniques and tools employed, and their African cultural background* influenced the result in many subtle ways. Geographical factors,* tribal origins of the slaves, and the economic status of the slave owners resulted in wide variations in the slaves' material culture. Still, some common elements existed.

Housing* was one of the most important material objects the master provided to the slaves. On large plantations in the lower South the house servants* and craftsmen* often lived on what was called "the street," a row of cabins or quarters near the master's house. The field hands also might live on the street, or they might occupy a group of cabins nearer the fields where they were to work under the supervision of a black boss, known as a "driver."* Such slaves had little personal contact with white people and retained more of their African culture than did those who lived nearer to their masters or who were supervised by a white overseer.*

The quality of the slave cabins varied greatly. Those on larger plantations generally were more ample than those on smaller farms where the master himself might live in a crude log cabin. During the nineteenth century, at least, most planters tried to care for the health* of their slaves by providing them with adequate housing. As a rule, slaves lived in one-family households, though occasionally single men were quartered in dormitories. The buildings were similar in size and style: a rectangular, gable-roofed house of one or two rooms, or "pens" as they were called, of identical size and shape. Often they had a narrow front porch, called a veranda, that ran across the width of the cabin. The materials varied. They were of wood, brick, rammed earth, or "wattle-and-daub" (twigs or cornstalks, daubed over with clay or mud). Roofs were most often composed of handmade cedar or cypress shingles, but occasionally were of thatch or tile. Most slave cabins had large fireplaces with brick or wattle-and-daub chimneys. Plank floors were often provided but some were of dirt. Although poorly ventilated and crowded by modern standards, these cabins compared favorably with free white workers' housing of the antebellum period.

European construction and design was bound to influence slave cabin architecture. Indeed, many slave cabins were clearly of European origin in design, like those at Arundel plantation, near Georgetown, South Carolina, with their gothic-arched windows, and the brick slave quarters at Boone Hall plantation, with their European-style "pantiles." But closer observation of extant slave housing shows that while some architectural features of slave quarters could have arisen from either European or African culture, others definitely are African in nature. The well-proportioned, rectangular, gable-roofed house appears equally throughout West Africa and Europe, so the style in fact reveals little of its cultural origin. Similiarly, primitive looking thatched roofs and wattle-and-daub construction were as common to Europe as to Africa. Many features of slave housing, previously interpreted as signs of shame and dishonor, actually appealed to the slaves because of their African character. The small size of the average slave cabin closely approximated the ten-by-ten-foot norm of African dwellings. The Anglo-American buildings averaged between sixteen-by-sixteen feet and eighteen-by-eighteen feet. And unlike the Europeans, who objected to dirt floors, some Afro-American slaves preferred them. Susan Snow, for example, raised as a slave in Alabama, said: "Every nigger had a house o' his own. My ma never would have no board floor like the rest of 'em, on 'count she was a African—only dirt."

Several examples of pure African architecture in slave quarters are known: the eighteenth-century, conical-roofed quarters at Mulberry plantation near Charleston, South Carolina; the circular slave houses of rammed earth in Virginia; and the famous Metoyer slave house at Natchitoches, Louisiana, which has been likened to the Bamileke houses of the Cameroons. Some slaves, like "ole man Okra," a slave near St. Simons Island, Georgia, built their own houses to suit themselves. These cabins tended to be small, like African houses, and usually featured thatched roofs, dirt floors, one door, and no windows, like so many African houses.

The front porch was probably an African importation. Though Europeans usually built their front entrance right on the street, their passion for privacy prompted them to position their gardens at the back of the house or hidden within a courtyard. While Europeans disliked being viewed by the public, Africans were accustomed to a communal life, one that revolved around the compound and the outdoor activities there. Both African and Afro-American slaves utilized their houses primarily for sleeping, for shelter from the weather, or sometimes for cooking (though much cooking was done outdoors in communal pots). The veranda was a well-known feature in both Africa and the Caribbean, and blacks knew its value in a hot, semitropical climate. In the shade of the porch roof, slaves carried out small tasks while enjoying the companionship of the busy life on "the street." Porches also adorned not only many of their cabins but the houses of the masters.

While slave mechanics constructed much of the housing "provided" by the master, their contributions did not end there. Expert black craftsmen, with skills brought over from Africa, enriched both their master's lives and their own in innumerable ways. Urban slave craftsmen produced much of the material culture of Southern cities. On the plantations slave artisans' contributions were even more important because of the difficulty of obtaining manufactured and imported goods so far from ports.

The plantation* was actually a factory where almost all the necessities of life were produced by slave craftsmen. But whereas most of the crafts practiced in the cities could also be found on the plantations (except for the luxury crafts such as silversmithing or gilding) the main difference between urban* and plantation slaves lay in the fact that the plantation slave rarely specialized. The leatherworker, for example, acted as saddler and harnessmaker, and often made pouches, boots, dancing slippers, or mule shoes. He obtained his leather from both wild and domestic animals on the plantation, including pigs and alligators. The blacksmith doubled as tinsmith, farrier, and wheelwright and also made tools, nails, and screws. He was an artist who made wrought-iron gates and balconies, and was called upon to produce virtually any metal object required by his master, from bathtubs to syllabub churns. Slave smiths made such household items as candle molds, pot trammels, kitchen utensils, and even andirons for the master's house. They also commonly produced such agricultural tools as shears, steelyards, or a "pee" (weight for cotton bales).

The slave carpenter was another important craftsman who performed a variety of tasks. He built both the slave cabins and the master's plantation house, often incorporating in the latter such fine details as joinery and delicate putty work. He often made the elegant furniture to put into the house as well, using walnut, pine, and other wood from trees grown on the plantation. The slave carpenter also fashioned his own furnishings and household utensils. According to one ex-slave, "we make most uh duh house needs sech as cheahs an tables, baskets an buckets an stools an sometimes spoons an beds an cubbuds."

Slave carpenters produced all the cooperage needed on the plantation as well as many wooden objects that today would be manufactured from plastic or metal. Bowls, buckets, trenchers, washtubs, ladles, spoons, and mortars—all were carved out of wood. Carpenters rived out the handmade shingles that covered plantation buildings. Such woodworking skill also was applied to the construction of boats. Like their African forebears, Afro-American slaves were superb boatmen and fishermen.* They built and manned both single- and multiple-log boats quite similar to African ones. These boats were indispensable on many plantations, especially in the riverine areas of the Georgia and South Carolina low country and the tidewater sections of Virginia. Occasionally, slave carpenters doubled as manufacturers and layers of brick.

Significantly, the tools and containers crafted by American slaves were closely modeled after those used in the agricultural societies of West Africa. Gracefully hollowed-out logs for rice mortars, large, well-balanced pestles, and flat winnowing baskets made of palmetto and marsh grass appeared on the rice* plantations of the Carolina low country with the same materials, shapes, and techniques that had been used in Africa. Hoes also closely resembled African ones, but with longer handles. Copper, wooden-handled rice scoops were very like the all-wood examples of Africa.

Much like their African forebears, Afro-American slaves improvised from materials at hand. Door and chair seats were fashioned of cornshucks. A tree branch was ingeniously adapted to make a rake or a pitchfork. Fishnets identical to those in Africa were knitted and given a marrow bone for a slide. Hemp* and flax grown on the plantations augmented the native grasses, bulrushes, pine straw, and palmetto fronds used for making fishnets, baskets, brooms, and other articles. Gourds served as dippers, ladles, and bird houses. As in any agricultural society, baskets served many purposes: as hampers for cotton,* rice, or other crops; as containers for eggs or vegetables in the kitchen gardens; as cages for small fowl; as fish traps; and as receptacles for washcloths and sewing materials. On upland plantations slaves used white oak and other woods to make twilled and twined baskets. Coiled baskets made of marsh grass, long-leaf pinestraw, and palmetto fronds were crafted on the plantations of the South Carolina Sea Islands. These are identical—both as to materials and techniques of manufacture—to those made in the Senegambia region of Africa.

Though some slave pottery may have been made by the African methods of coiling or moulding, most pieces were thrown on a wheel, a technique not employed in West Africa. Nevertheless, slaves utilized ceramics, both glazed and unglazed, for dining, for storage, and for transporting foodstuffs and liquids.

Many slave potters, like those who operated in the Edgefield district of South Carolina, plied the same trade as their masters. The most famous of these is "Dave," who crafted large stoneware open-mouthed storage jars with slab handles round the rim. One of his jars stood about twenty-nine inches high and held at least forty gallons of liquids. Some other very uncommon pottery was made in this area as well. These include face jugs—similar in general shape to "Toby" jugs and other face vessels of European origin—but which exhibit a striking resemblance to African effigy pots. They were used to carry water to thirsty field hands. Called variously "ugly jugs," "voodoo pots," and "monkey jugs," the latter is the name by which they were known to the slaves. Field hands reportedly exclaimed "I see a monkey" when dizzied by the heat.

In contrast to those slave crafts produced commercially, or at the behest of the master, some of the most interesting examples of slave handwork were done during leisure time, for the bondsmen's own use or amusement. In their free time the slaves wove fishnets, "sewed" baskets, and carved a wide variety of objects. Significantly, in carving, slaves used an adze, the tool common to African woodworking, rather than a knife. Like their African forebears, the slaves carved images that held broad cultural meaning. Closely in touch with nature, they carved birds, animals, and reptiles. But bondsmen also made such diverse items as toys, eating utensils, and canes. Among the most beautiful and unique of the slaves' material culture, canes served roles both in traditional slave dance* and in the folk conjure ritual. Slave canes were decorated with snakes, alligators, and other animals, intricately carved with great skill and attention to details. Some employed the common West African device of using blue heads, or nails, to simulate eyes.

The slaves also used their native craftsmanship to fashion musical instruments.* Although slave musicians played European-style fiddles and other instruments, they also developed the banjo from African chordophones and made single-stringed instruments and others much like the African sanza, or finger piano. Slave musicians played a variety of instruments traditional in West Africa, including "the bones" (quite literally beef ribs held in the hand and clicked together), fifes, flutes (made of canes), quills (pan pipes of reeds fastened together), rattles made of gourds, and belt bells. Drums and other percussion instruments dominated slave music, and those made in America were indistinguishable from their African models. Drums were used to beat the rhythm for slave dances, to announce deaths and funerals, and to send all sorts of messages.

Although slave men performed most of the carving and woodworking, slave women* excelled at such tasks as basket making, soap and candle making, quilt making, and spinning, weaving, and dyeing cloth. Slave women perfected plain sewing as well as such fancy needlework as knitting, tatting, and lace making.

While some slave owners bought ready-made clothing* for their slaves, most depended on their female slaves to produce the garments worn by the bondsmen. Except for shoes, and men's straw hats, the wardrobes of the slaves (including kerchiefs for women) were fashioned from coarse, cheap fabric known as "Negro cloth" which was imported from Great Britain throughout the eighteenth century and from American textile mills during the nineteenth century. The task of making the garments was done under the direction of the plantation mistress.* Kate Stone Holmes, raised on a cotton plantation in Louisiana, described the clothes making process: " . . . when the time came to have everything cut out; a room would be cleared out and great bolts of white woolen jeans, Osnabergs, and linseys, with bolt after bolt of red flannel for the little ones, would be rolled in and the women with great shears would commence their work." This Negro cloth was sturdy and durable but rough. Slaves complained about its texture as readily as about the sparse quantity of the clothing they received. "Dat ole nigger cloth," protested an ex-slave from Virginia, "wus jus' like needles when it was new. Never did have to scratch our back. Jus' wriggle yo' shoulders an' yo' back was scratched." Shoes also came in for much criticism from the slaves. Children received no shoes, and as a result, adults adjusted slowly and painfully to wearing shoes. Many slaves worked barefoot, partly from habit or preference, but mostly because of dissatisfaction with their shoes, which were stiff and fitted poorly.

Although a great deal of the material used for slave garments was manufactured, much of it was also homespun and handwoven from raw materials that were products of the plantation. Africans arriving in the New World were already familiar with the art of weaving and may have brought their skills with them. Nearly every plantation of any size had its weaving room where slaves wove cotton, linen, wool, and even silk with great dexterity. They also practiced the art of dyeing, using local plants and bark which they transformed into glowing color. Indigo,* popular in Africa, was a money crop on some eighteenth-century plantations and frequently was used for Negro cloth, coverlets, and quilts.

The art of quilting had been known and practiced in Africa since the Crusades, and the appliqué banners of Dahomey are made today in much the same way as were slave-made patchwork quilts. Homegrown cotton was used to pad the quilt between the patterned top and the simpler bottom piece of fabric, stretched on a frame and hand-quilted. Quilts were either patchwork or piecework. In the former, a rather plain background had a pattern, usually floral, appliquéd on top. The latter was made by sewing many small pieces together in a pattern. Quilts and woven coverlets made for the Big House were usually of well-known

Anglo-European designs. Sometimes, however, slaves managed to introduce innovations of their own.

Quilts made by blacks for their own use were probably quilted while held on the lap, without the aid of a quilting frame, much as they are by Gullah Negroes today. Many Afro-American quilts and coverlets, whether made by slaves or contemporary blacks, leave no doubt as to their ethnic origin. Euro-American quilts are very symmetrical, with uniform repetition and balanced color. Afro-American quilts, in contrast, are often random-patterned with uneven, asymmetrical pieces of different sizes, colors, and shapes juxtaposed to each other. Many Afro-American quilts have been closely compared to African strip weaving. To what extent this irregularity of pattern was by design, and how much of it was accidental, may never be known. Surely those quilts made by the slaves for their own use must have been made with difficulty—at night in candle light and after a long day of fieldwork. They were intended primarily for warmth, not appearance, yet the results were attractive. As in much of the slaves' handcrafts, their quilts demonstrate the blacks' artistic heritage from Africa.

SELECTED BIBLIOGRAPHY

Boston Afro-American National Historic Site, *Negro Cloth: Northern Industry and Southern Slavery* (1982); Judith Wragg Chase, *Afro-American Art and Craft* (1971); Judith Wragg Chase, "American Heritage from Ante-Bellum Black Craftsmen," *Southern Folklore Quarterly*, 42 (1978), 135–158; William R. Ferris, ed., *Afro-American Folk Arts and Crafts* (1983); Melville J. Herskovits, *The Myth of the Negro Past* (1941); and John M. Vlach, *The Afro-American Tradition in Decorative Arts* (1978).

JUDITH WRAGG CHASE

MEMPHIS, TN, SLAVERY IN. Memphis began in the 1820s as a biracial river town. In 1820 Shelby County, which contains Memphis, had a total population of only 364 (251 whites, 113 slaves); two decades later the population stood in round numbers, at 14,700 (7,600 whites, 7,000 slaves, 70 free blacks*). At first a frontier-like informality characterized relations between slaves and white citizens. A branch of the American Colonization Society* suggested some public sentiment for emancipation.

Indicative of the loose racial boundaries in early Memphis was the experience of Marcus B. Winchester, the city's first mayor, who married a free person of color. Acting as town banker, he opened accounts for his slaves and credited them for their work so they could purchase their freedom. During the 1820s most Memphis slaves hired themselves out for money, which they entrusted to Winchester's safekeeping. He also supported the famous Scotswoman, Frances Wright, who founded Nashoba* colony in 1825 outside Memphis to prepare slaves for emancipation and equal participation in society. For three years, she conducted a Brook Farm–type cooperative community. In town, she used Winchester's house as a lecture hall, and in an 1828 issue of the Memphis *Advocate* published her manifesto advocating racial amalgamation. Most white Memphians accepted her with tolerant amusement.

Blacks and whites cooperated in bringing Christianity to Memphis. The town's first preacher was a Negro Methodist* who appeared before racially mixed gatherings. During the 1830s and 1840s Baptist,* Methodist, and Presbyterian* congregations admitted slave members. Although confined to special galleries and separate Sunday school rooms, some slaves learned to read as part of their religious instruction. By the 1850s black Methodist members of Wesley Chapel numbered 500 and held their own separate services in the basement under the leadership of Reverend Daniel H. Jones, a slave. Meanwhile, blacks worshiped in an independent Baptist church built for them by a white mechanic in 1837. Known as the African Church after 1847, this imposing structure at Main and Overton streets was used by blacks exclusively.

Unfortunately, such early racial harmony as existed disappeared because planters, who controlled the state government in Nashville, felt threatened by the abolitionists'* assaults on slavery. The Tennessee Constitution of 1834, for example, disfranchised free blacks. Memphis, with a relatively small black population, had always been an anomaly, but in the 1830s began to shed its earlier racial tolerance. In 1837 the city passed an ordinance against "Citizens keeping colored wives." Memphis, like other Southern cities, also passed ordinances restricting the activities of its blacks. The laws imposed curfews and bans on blacks' gathering, preaching, and learning to read.

The large-scale selling of slaves in the Memphis marts also altered the early frontier informality in race relations. Advantageously located on major river and rail routes, and positioned in the midst of an expanding area of cotton plantations, Memphis by the 1850s became the most important slave-trading center in the central South. A dozen slave traders imported surplus slaves from eastern states and sold them to planters in west Tennessee, Arkansas, Mississippi, and northern Louisiana. By the late 1850s Nathan B. Forrest used large profits from slave trading to rise from his humble estate as a farmer to become a planter aristocrat. Forrest energetically combed six states gathering slaves for his Memphis market. Like other successful traders, he pretended no humanitarian concern for slaves and built his reputation on dealing honestly and maintaining a safe and clean slave pen. Selling about 1,000 slaves annually, Forrest became one of the South's richest slave traders. Indicative, perhaps, of slavery's importance to the city's economy, Memphians seemingly did not find Forrest's occupation offensive. In 1858, for example, they elected the popular Forrest alderman.

Surprisingly, the permanent black population of Memphis remained relatively small during the 1850s. In 1850 slaves and free blacks comprised only 28 percent of the city's population. Slaves suitable for urban use cost too much. In the 1840s and 1850s sufficient Irish immigrants* came to Memphis to meet the city's growing labor needs. They competed successfully with free blacks and slaves for skilled and unskilled jobs. City growth caused the average prices of Memphis slaves to soar: carpenters sold for $2,500, blacksmiths' helpers sold for $1,114, and painters sold for $1,005. The cost of field hands ranged from only $750 to $1,000. In 1860 Memphis contained 3,882 Negroes—17 percent of the total city population of 22,623. The 1860 tax report counted 1,875 bondsmen. Evidently, the remaining 1,809 slaves were considered transients awaiting sale because free Negroes in 1860 numbered only 198. By comparison, Nashville contained 719 free Negroes the same year. Local ordinances restricting the movement and · activities of free blacks discouraged free black population growth in Memphis. Perhaps large-scale slave trading in Memphis further reduced the presence of free Negroes, who were always vulnerable to kidnapping.

The Civil War* ended slavery in Memphis but not the problem of racial tensions. During Union occupation fugitive slaves* flocked to the city. They did not find the Union military forces necessarily more congenial than their former masters. General William T. Sherman, for example, forced 6,000 fugitive slaves to work on city fortifications for mere subsistence. After the war, as thousands of freedmen* flooded into Memphis, racial tensions surfaced anew. A major race riot in 1866 revealed the continued rivalry between immigrant, poor white workers, and blacks, which the unsettled status of the freedmen only exacerbated.

SELECTED BIBLIOGRAPHY

Frederic Bancroft, *Slave-Trading in the Old South* (1931); Kathleen C. Berkeley, " 'Like a Plague of Locust': Immigration and Social Change in Memphis, Tennessee, 1850–1880" (Ph.D. dissertation, University of California at Los Angeles, 1980); Gerald M. Capers, *The Biography of a River Town: Memphis—Its Heroic Age* (rev. ed., 1966); James D. Davis, *History of the City of Memphis* (facsimile ed., 1972); Leigh Fraser, "A Demographic Analysis of Memphis and Shelby County, Tennessee, 1820–1972" (M.A. thesis, Memphis State University, 1974); Carolyn Pittman, "Memphis in the Mid-1840s," *West Tennessee Historical Society Papers*, 23 (1969), 30–44; James E. Roper, "Marcus B. Winchester, First Mayor of Memphis: His Later Years," *West Tennessee Historical Society Papers*, 13 (1959), 5–37; and David M. Tucker, *Black Pastors and Leaders: Memphis, 1819–1972* (1975).

JAMES R. CHUMNEY

METHODIST CHURCH. American Methodism shaped and represented the major religious patterns of slavery characteristic of mainstream Protestantism. Formed as an evangelical renewal within the Church of England by John and Charles Wesley, the movement remained under British authority until 1784. Numbering slaveholders and slaves in its first societies, it also earned an early antislavery reputation, dramatized by John Wesley's writings and the commitments of its first two superintendents, Thomas Coke and Francis Asbury. In 1780, before organizing to become the Methodist Episcopal (ME) church, the American preachers officially declared slavery "contrary to the laws of God, man, and nature, and hurtful to society" and "contrary to the dictates of conscience and pure religion."

Despite its antislavery beginnings,* the ME church failed, in 1784–1785 and in 1800, to implement a slaveholding prohibition in its standards for membership and ministry. Eschewing a sectarian option like the Quaker purge of slave owners, the Methodists became popular by adapting to the customs of each region. Having published successive editions of the *Discipline* for the South in 1804 and 1808, excising all references to slavery, Bishop Asbury and the preachers abandoned efforts to regulate the slaveholding laity. Itinerant clergy in the annual conferences were still required to manumit their slaves, but only if state laws legalized emancipation.

Formal attempts to urge secular legislation against slavery were not much more successful in early Methodism. General Conference petitions in 1800 calling for state abolition laws fomented Southern mobs and aroused legislators to restrict religious meetings among the slaves. After 1816, the denomination surrendered its efforts to extirpate slavery as a social institution until Methodist abolitionists in the 1830s renewed the attack on the relationship of master and slave as evil per se. Some churchmen advocated African colonization,* while the General Conference, first in 1824, promoted a missionary program* to slaves, substituting evangelization for abolition.

The mission to the slaves inculcated conversion and provided pastoral care to those in bondage. The same idealistic paternalism which marked the foreign mission enterprise combined with white self-interest and need for social control to promote the scheme. Missionaries insisted that blacks had souls and that the slaves deserved Christian instruction. They also assured owners that their message did not encourage liberation resembling the religiously inspired revolt of the black Methodist, Denmark Vesey.* Their catechisms for and sermons to the slaves, therefore, sanctioned a religion devoid of overt emphases on freedom and equality, while their appeals to planters pointed to the advantages of evangelization for better discipline and improved morality among the slaves.

In practice, American Methodism's relationship to slavery bore contradictory outcomes. First, the church's antislavery effort in the North harmonized with legal actions which outlawed bondage, immediately or gradually, in eleven states between 1777 and 1817. On the border, especially in Maryland, Methodist antislavery success developed by tying religious conversion of masters to the manumission of their chattels. After 1830, a new generation of antislavery Methodists recollected this earlier achievement and urged its replication. Encouraged by British Wesleyan support for emancipation in the West Indies (1834), they called for abolitionist reform in church and state. They were joined by independent African Methodists, like ex-slave Richard Allen, Daniel Coker, David Walker,* Hosea Easton, and Christopher Rush, who openly advocated abolition.

Second, both enslaved and free blacks rallied to Methodist revivalism during the Second Great Awakening. They joined and maintained a significant presence in the churches, North and South. Between 1789 and 1815, they represented one-fifth of the membership in the ME church. With the rise of black Methodist denominations and an expanding white membership in the Midwest, the ratio declined between 1820 and 1844, but in the latter year black membership was still 12.5 percent, 145,409 of 1.2 million adherents in the nation's largest ecclesiastical body. Most free black Methodists, many of whom were manumitted or fugitive slaves, organized separately in the African Union (1813), African Methodist Episcopal (1816),* and African Methodist Episcopal, Zion (1821) denominations in the North.

Third, with one major exception, every division in the ME church that created new denominations between 1792 and 1860 perpetuated distinctive aspects of the tradition's paradoxical legacy over slavery. The secessions that formed the Republican Methodists (1792) and the Reform Methodists (1814), the three black schisms, the Wesleyan Methodist withdrawal (1842–1843), and the Free Methodist movement (1860) all sought to maintain the original antislavery reputation of the founders. The largest rupture of episcopal Methodism incorporated the other side of the ambivalent heritage.

Defending the slaveholding of Bishop James O. Andrew of Georgia, Southerners at the ME General Conference of 1844 refused to accept the Northern majority's order that he "desist from the exercise of his office" as long as he was "connected with slavery." Since three-fourths of the Southern delegation, all ministers, were slave owners themselves, Andrew's case precipitated the sectional break of the ME church. Constituted in 1845, the ME Church, South, unapologetically embraced the historic accommodations over slavery and celebrated the success of plantation missions. It also contributed, through the writings of eminent pastors and educators like William A. Smith, Augustus B. Longstreet, and Holland N. McTyeire, to the regional justification of slavery as morally acceptable and biblically based.

Declaring the church's mission to be spiritual and neither social nor political, Southern Methodists rescinded all reference to slavery in their *Discipline* by 1858. The changes might have come earlier, as anticipated by an unauthorized version of the *Discipline* expurgating the rules on slavery, which was published in Charleston in 1850. It was, however, legally necessary to retain an unaltered church government to secure the denomination's claims to a portion of the financial interests of the old ME church. With that adjudication in 1853–1854, the ME Church, South, first struck out the chapter on slavery dating back thirty years. Then, four years later, the preachers repealed Wesley's historic General Rule against buying or selling slaves. Confident that they stood "upon a scriptural basis" on the issue, the Southern bishops rejoiced, "We have surrendered to Caesar the things that are his."

Ironically, the Southern secession did not settle church policy on slavery for the ME church. Before 1844, it had lost its most fervent abolitionists—Orange Scott, Lucius C. Matlack, and Luther Lee—to the Wesleyan Methodists. After 1844, Northern Methodism still counted white slaveholders and 30,000 black members, many of whom were slaves, in its Philadelphia and Baltimore conferences. That fact precipitated renewed antislavery activism in the church, led by William Hosmer, Hiram Mattison, J. S. Lame, and John D. Long. A conservative corps of bishops, editors, and leading preachers, however, staved off the abolitionist attack until 1864, when revised legislation removed slaveholders from the membership and ministry.

Border missions to slaves in the ME church struggled to remain stable after 1844. Statistics for 1851 showed about 4 percent of the membership as "colored," some of whom were free blacks. In contrast, slave missions in the South thrived. Black membership in the ME Church, South, grew by two-thirds, or 82,955, between 1845 and 1860 to represent 27.9 percent of the biracial total for laity. In conferences in the Deep South, blacks comprised between 30 and 55 percent of the members, and their entire number in 1860 equaled 5 percent of the chattel population nationally. A network of annual conference missionary societies, begun under the inspiration of William Capers, produced $1.7 million in contributions between 1844 and 1864 to make Southern Methodism the leading church in the region in its outreach to slaves.

Accompanied by an undetermined number of blacks who came under Methodist influence without joining the church, slave members were attracted to the denomination's passionate preaching and the sung theology of Wesleyan hymnody. Partly within the shared world of white paternalism, partly within the exclusive world of black life with its echoes of Africa, Methodist slaves molded a religious life of their own. Like free blacks who had separated from whites but remained Methodist, they affirmed that their Methodism was neither created nor controlled by whites but by an ultimate divine reality which they experienced within it. In not a few instances, their spirituality became the occasion for white conversion.

When black Methodists got the call to preach or exhort, the white ecclesiastical system had to respond. Some slaves but more free blacks were licensed local preachers.* Less frequently, they were ordained with sacramental authority for a local ministry, though they were rarely given professional equality in the conferences of itinerating clergy. Black laity became class leaders or assumed informal roles as praying mothers, spiritual teachers, and fathers in the faith. In urban settings, slaves sometimes belonged to quasi-independent "colored charges" with black local preachers functioning within white-dominated Methodism, or to independent African Methodist congregations in New Orleans and along the border.

The final testimony to Methodism's concern for slaves was its popularity after emancipation among the freedpeople. Four organizations reaped the results of ecclesiastical reconstruction: the old ME church, returning to the South, the two African Methodist bodies, and a newly formed black denomination out of the ME Church, South, called the Colored Methodist Episcopal church (1870). Of the three black organizations, at least twenty-eight of their nineteenth-century bishops were born in slavery, demonstrating that the religious tradition of Wesley accompanied them and their followers on the pilgrimage to freedom.

SELECTED BIBLIOGRAPHY

Kenneth K. Bailey, "Protestantism and Afro-Americans in the Old South: Another Look," *Journal of Southern History*, 41 (1975), 451–472; William B. Gravely, "Meth-

odist Preachers, Slavery and Caste: Types of Social Concern in Antebellum America,''
Duke Divinity School Review, 34 (1969), 209–229; W. P. Harrison, *The Gospel among
the Slaves: A Short Account of Missionary Operations Among the African Slaves of the
Southern States* (1893); Donald G. Mathews, *Slavery and Methodism: A Chapter in
American Morality, 1780–1845* (1965); Joseph Mitchell, ''Travelling Preacher and Settled
Farmer,'' *Methodist History*, 5 (1967), 3–14; Milton B. Powell, ''The Abolitionist Controversy in the Methodist Episcopal Church, 1840–1864'' (Ph.D. dissertation, University
of Iowa, 1963); Lewis M. Purifoy, Jr., ''The Methodist Episcopal Church, South, and
Slavery, 1844–1865'' (Ph.D. dissertation, University of North Carolina at Chapel Hill,
1965); and H. Shelton Smith, *In His Image, But . . . . : Racism in Southern Religion, 1780–
1910* (1972).

WILL B. GRAVELY

MEXICAN WAR. The Mexican War concluded a protracted dispute for control
of the American Southwest. In the sixteenth century Texas, New Mexico, and
California were claimed by Spain, but isolation and sparse settlement required
only slight supervision there. Although French and British intruders called forth
military entratas and missions, generally the Spanish and their Mexican successors left the territory alone. American filibusters caused some difficulty, but in
1819 the United States renounced claims west of the Sabine River. During the
1820s the Mexican government allowed Americans to settle in Texas, hoping
to raise tax revenues and to block U.S. expansion by requiring the settlers to
become Mexican citizens. Many Southerners moved to Texas, accompanied by
their slaves.

The Mexican government's opposition to slavery contributed to strained relations between Texans and their rulers. In 1824 the Mexican Congress outlawed
the slave trade.* The constitution of Coahuila y Texas prohibited the importation
of slaves and emancipated all children born to slaves. In 1828, however, the
Mexicans reversed their policy and permitted American settlers to import slaves
as servants under lifetime contract. A year later, President Vicente Guerrero
decreed an end to slavery, except in Tehuantepec, and on 6 April 1830 the
Mexican Congress prohibited the immigration of slaves. Although the Texans
were excluded from this provision, they vigorously protested the intent of the
law.

Mexico's official ban on slavery frustrated Southern slaveholders and contributed to tensions between the Texans and the Mexican government. In 1835–
1836 Texans revolted and formed the Republic of Texas. This revolt developed
in the context of a larger civil war in Mexico in which the issue of state rights
versus centralization was paramount and had critical implications for the future
of the peculiar institution in Texas. After Texas won its independence in 1836,
many Texans hoped for immediate annexation by the United States. Politicians
in Congress blocked it, hoping to avoid the issue of slavery expansion and worried
about the consequences of America inheriting the continuing dispute over the
Texas-Mexican border. The Texans claimed that the Treaty of Velasco (1836)
had set their southern border at the Rio Grande; the Mexicans, who never

recognized Texas independence anyway, insisted that their boundary was the Sabine River, but acknowledged that the Nueces River had been a boundary between Coahuila and Texas.

President James K. Polk, elected in 1844 on an expansionist program, was determined to annex Texas and acquire New Mexico and California. Following Polk's election, the Tyler administration obtained from Congress a joint resolution for the annexation of Texas. In the summer of 1845, as Texans accepted the American terms of annexation, they requested the protective presence of U.S. troops on their southern frontier. President Polk ordered General Zachary Taylor to the Nueces River and sent John Slidell to Mexico to purchase New Mexico and California. When the Mexican government refused to discuss the matter, Polk ordered Taylor to the Rio Grande. Resulting military clashes produced a declaration of war on 13 May 1846. Less than two years later American military forces defeated the Mexicans. The Treaty of Guadalupe Hidalgo (2 February 1848) ended the war. Mexico ceded California and New Mexico to the United States, acknowledged the Rio Grande boundary, and received $15 million in return.

The Mexican War added to the growing sectional schism within the United States over slavery. Southerners supported the war, partly from nationalism and partly from a desire to expand their peculiar institution and a desire for the land itself. Antislavery forces* denounced the war as a Southern attempt to expand slave territory. In August 1846, Representative David Wilmot, a Democrat from Pennsylvania, unsuccessfully attempted to block the acquisition of territory open to slavery with an amendment to legislation requested by Polk for funds with which to negotiate an end to the war. The Wilmot Proviso would have permitted "neither slavery nor involuntary servitude" in any territory acquired from Mexico. The proviso passed the House, but was defeated in the Senate. Its introduction, however, made slavery's expansion a matter of sustained public debate thereafter, ending the relative silence in Congress regarding slavery's expansion that had persisted since the Missouri Compromise* had "resolved" the issue in 1820.

The Mexican War left the question of slavery in the territories unresolved. Not until 1850, after a major congressional compromise, would the framework be established by which the status of slaves in the Mexican Cession could be "settled"—but at the cost of abandoning the Missouri Compromise, arousing antislavery and proslavery forces* to fight for control of the western territories, and disrupting the American political system.

SELECTED BIBLIOGRAPHY

K. Jack Bauer, *The Mexican War, 1846–1848* (1974); Seymour V. Connor and Odie B. Faulk, *North America Divided: The Mexican War, 1846–1848* (1971); Odie B. Faulk and Joseph A. Stout, Jr., eds., *The Mexican War, Changing Interpretations* (1973); Paul D. Lack, "Slavery and the Texas Revolution," *Southwestern Historical Quarterly*, 89 (1985), 181–202; Archie P. McDonald, ed., *The Mexican War: Crisis for American*

Democracy (1969); and John Edward Weems, *To Conquer a Peace: The War between the United States and Mexico* (1974).

ARCHIE P. MCDONALD

MIDDLE ATLANTIC STATES, SLAVERY IN THE. Slavery in the Middle Atlantic states (New York, New Jersey, Pennsylvania, and Delaware) never rivaled in scope or significance the institution in the plantation South. Still, slavery came early to the region, before it had established a firm presence in the Chesapeake area, and continued into the nineteenth century. It flourished especially in the large urban centers* of New York City and Philadelphia, as well as in selected agricultural subregions. Slavery in the Middle Atlantic states assumed a variety of forms and appearances, though everywhere in the region slaves constituted only a small percentage of the total population.

Slavery began during the period of Dutch control. The Dutch West India Company recognized slavery in New Netherland as early as 1626. About 600 slaves resided there at the time of the English conquest in 1664. They performed labor for the company as well as for the local government and individual owners. The Dutch considered slavery a satisfactory and acceptable mode of labor exploitation.

Slavery experienced a slow growth in the Middle Atlantic region during the remainder of the seventeenth century. Conflict with the French and Indians, as well as internal strife aggravated by domestic upheaval in England, slowed population growth and economic expansion. Still, an influx of settlers from the British islands and the Continent had swelled the region's population to 53,000 by 1700. The residents included about 3,600 black slaves transported to meet the pressing demand for laborers.

By the time of the American Revolution the slave population had increased nearly tenfold, to roughly 35,000. Natural increase accounted for most of the expansion, though the overseas slave trade also brought new African arrivals to the region. Until the 1730s slaves were transported in small lots from the West Indies. As time progressed, larger slave cargoes shipped directly from Africa became more common. Altogether, 6,800 slaves entered New York from 1700 to 1774, 2,800 of these arriving directly from Africa. Pennsylvania's slave trade peaked between 1759 and 1765, with the delivery of about 1,243 slaves, three-fourths of whom were brought from Africa. Neither New Jersey nor Delaware sustained a trade in slaves; both relied instead on shipments from New York and Pennsylvania. Nevertheless, New Jersey contained over 8,000 slaves in 1775, ranking second only to New York's slave population among the colonies north of Maryland.

The colonies of the Middle Atlantic region developed the most complex economies in British North America. Possessed of excellent soil, residents practiced a diversified and highly productive agriculture. The export of farm goods as well as lumber products contributed to thriving commercial centers at Philadelphia and New York City. Such industrial pursuits as iron manufacturing, shipbuilding, and related subsidiary activities added to the varied character of the regional economy. The slave system that emerged reflected the great range of labor demands.

Tax lists and newspaper advertisements reveal the varied occupations that blacks had. Most worked in agriculture, serving masters who owned farms. Rarely did masters hold more than three or four bondsmen, and then often in the form of a slave family.* Some owners, however, had a labor force that totaled dozens of slaves. Both the ironworks scattered throughout the region and the shipbuilding industry employed slaves. Other slaves were trained as craftsmen* and artisans, holding such posts as coopers, tailors, bakers, tanners, weavers, shoemakers, candlemakers, and masons. A select few were highly skilled clockmakers, goldsmiths, and silversmiths.

The distribution of slaves and ownership patterns imposed major barriers that inhibited the formation of Afro-American communities. Living among whites, often as members of white households, slaves had difficulty forging an independent cultural existence. They soon learned the English language along with other skills that enabled them to survive in a hostile environment.

Even so, other forces encouraged a sense of identity and community among the blacks. Urban settings weakened the chains of bondage by opening avenues of social intercourse and creating opportunities for independent black action. Furthermore, whatever the nature of their employment and wherever they resided, slaves were bound together by a shared status. Recognizing their common burden as members of an exploited minority, they created support systems and furtive mutual aid societies. Native-born and fully acculturated slaves, for example, often assisted newly arrived Africans as they adjusted to their altered circumstances.

Slaves were outsiders whose position in society had been determined by the white majority. Laws* known collectively as slave codes, enforced throughout the Middle Atlantic region, detailed the legal dimensions of the institution. Such laws were first enacted in New York during Dutch rule and were elaborated on by English colonists. Pennsylvania and Delaware began scaffolding their slave codes in 1700, while in New Jersey the basic code was passed in 1714. Though they differed in details, all of the codes circumscribed the freedoms of slaves, regulated their behavior, and imposed penalties for violations. Social practice resting on alleged black inferiority filled in wherever the law left gaps. Most of these laws and customs sought to discourage recalcitrant and rebellious behavior.

Slave runaways* posed a persistent challenge to black bondage in the Middle Atlantic region. Running away could be a means of underlining a grievance or displaying dissatisfaction with conditions—a short-term device used to make a direct point. Sometimes, however, runaways intended to achieve a permanent victory: they hoped to win their freedom. Conspiracies and rebellions were the most feared of all forms of resistance* to slavery. Whites watched uneasily for signs of collective action. As early as 1693 Pennsylvania leaders noted with alarm "the tumultuous gatherings of the negroes in the towne of philadelphia, on the first dayes of the weeke.'' Rumors of slave rebellion were seldom followed by actual uprisings. A singular exception was the slave rebellion in New York City* on the night of 6 April 1712. A group of heavily armed slaves first committed arson and then killed and wounded more than a dozen whites before being overpowered. Retaliation was swift and brutal. As reported by Governor Hunter, twenty-one slaves ''were executed. . . . Some were burnt, others hanged, one broke on ye wheele, and one hung alive in chaines in the town, soe that there has beene the most exemplary punishment inflicted that cold [*sic*] be possibly thought of.'' Generally wanting to avoid direct physical confrontation with the white community, slaves proceeded in more subtle ways, locating and applying pressure at the soft points of slavery.

Many white residents similarly were uneasy with the institution. Members of the Society of Friends (*see* Quakers) had inherited from George Fox a concern over the inhumane treatment of blacks, and they persisted in their criticism of slavery in America. With few exceptions the earliest American protests against slavery and the slave trade were composed by Friends, most of whom were residents of the Middle Atlantic region. George Keith, William Southby, Ralph Sandiford, and Benjamin Lay all had spoken out against slavery by 1750. Their efforts helped to force the issue of black bondage onto the Quaker agenda. The Philadelphia Yearly Meeting, whose membership and influence extended into New Jersey and Delaware, became increasingly firm in its directives, urging that Friends should no longer buy, sell, or keep slaves. Between 1750 and 1775 John Woolman and Anthony Benezet added their voices to the growing anti-slavery movement.

Abolitionist sentiment* gained further strength from the emerging conflict between the colonies and England. Americans who employed the natural rights argument in their debates with the mother country found it awkward to claim liberty for themselves while simultaneously enslaving blacks. As an anonymous writer declared in 1768 in the *Pennsylvania Chronicle*: ''How suits it with the glorious cause of Liberty, to keep your fellowmen in bondage, men equally the work of your great Creator, men formed for freedom as yourselves.'' Such sentiment mirrored a broader public concern. In 1767 the Delaware legislature made an unsuccessful attempt to prohibit further importations of slaves. In 1774 New York City distillers agreed that they would no longer distill molasses intended for the slave trade.

Events of the revolutionary era significantly weakened the institution of slavery in the Middle Atlantic region. Manumissions* increased sharply after 1774. The free black population was further enlarged by the social and political upheaval that accompanied the American Revolution.* Marching armies, intense fighting, and the British occupation of territory, including New York City and Philadelphia, created new opportunities for slaves, among them the prospect of acquiring their freedom through enlistment in the military.

The new state legislatures soon moved to restrict the slave trade and to question the future of slavery. Pennsylvania took the lead, with serious public discussion beginning in 1778. Two years later it passed "An Act for the Gradual Abolition of Slavery," outlining a strategy that would eradicate slavery over a period of several decades. While retaining slaves in bondage, the act provided for freeing yet unborn children after they had reached the age of twenty-eight. Subsequent legislation passed in 1788 addressed weaknesses in the law and also ended the slave trade. But the gradual approach to abolition was not abandoned.

The other states followed the same pattern and approach. New York, New Jersey, and Delaware all had prohibited the further importation of slaves by 1788. New York passed an emancipation act in 1799 that followed the gradualist approach pioneered in Pennsylvania. New Jersey implemented a similar plan in 1804.

The combination of widespread manumission and legislative emancipation programs led to a steady decline of the slave population and a corresponding rise in the number of free blacks. By 1810 New York, New Jersey, and Pennsylvania together had fewer than 27,000 slaves, less than 2 percent of the total population. Still, slavery died a slow death. Both New York and Pennsylvania listed slaves in their 1840 census returns. A small number of blacks were held as slaves in New Jersey as late as 1860.

But it was Delaware that stood as a stark reminder of slavery's past in the Middle Atlantic region. Although Delaware ended the slave trade in 1787, antislavery forces were unable to mount a successful drive against slavery there, and the institution survived without legislative interference until the Civil War. Nearly 1,800 blacks remained enslaved in Delaware when Abraham Lincoln was elected president of the United States. Full freedom came only with the adoption of the Thirteenth Amendment in 1865.

Slavery survived in the Middle Atlantic region for over two centuries. Its presence and its powers of preservation testify to the force it exercised over the minds of men and women. As John Woolman observed, "the ideas of Negroes and Slaves" were "interwoven in the Mind."

SELECTED BIBLIOGRAPHY

Edgar J. McManus, *Black Bondage in the North* (1973); Edgar J. McManus, *A History of Negro Slavery in New York* (1966); Benjamin Quarles, *The Negro in the American Revolution* (1961); Edward R. Turner, *The Negro in Pennsylvania, Slavery-Servitude-Freedom, 1639–1861* (1911); and Arthur Zilversmit, *The First Emancipation: The Abolition of Slavery in the North* (1967).

DAROLD D. WAX

MINERS. Mining was an important component of Southern industry,* and, like other sectors of the region's economy, relied upon the labor of Afro-American slaves. Coal probably was the most widely mined mineral resource in the South. Most of the vast deposits of the "Great Allegheny Coal Field" lay buried beneath the western watershed of the Appalachian Mountains in Tennessee, Kentucky, and West Virginia. Important deposits also were found in northwestern Alabama, and, in conjunction with the rich iron deposits, spawned a mighty steel industry near Birmingham. For most of the slave era, however, these two coal districts remained relatively unimportant because of their remoteness from the population centers and transportation difficulties. Prior to the decade before the Civil War, only the eastern Virginia coal district played a significant role in the Southern economy.

Coal was being mined regularly in the eastern Virginia field near Richmond and Petersburg at least by 1760, and transported to the towns and cities along the Atlantic Coast increasingly during the eighteenth century. In fact, slave-mined Virginia coal dominated the coastal trade until the 1830s when Pennsylvania began to assert its dominance. Virginia's mines varied in size and importance, but a few were extensive operations employing 150 or more slaves. The average mine, however, employed between fifty and sixty slaves. The number of mines varied over time from ten to twelve between the American Revolution and 1820, twenty-five to thirty during the 1830s and 1840s, and then declined to about ten at the time of secession. During those same respective periods, the coal companies utilized a total of nearly 700 slaves, 2,000 during the peak years, and between 1,600 to 1,900 just prior to the Civil War.

The number of slaves in western Virginia increased between 1810 and 1860 with the rise in salt* manufacturing along the Kanawha River. The exact number of slave miners in the salt industry is uncertain, but a contemporary observed in 1836 that 995 slave miners were digging coal for the salt companies. By 1850, 3,140 slaves labored in the Kanawha saltworks, and many of these mined the coal which fired the saline kilns. By 1860, twenty-five independent coal mines also produced coal in western Virginia, and many of the hands working in these pits were slaves.

Gold mining held a small but significant position in Southern mining, and slaves dug most of the precious metal for the U.S. Mint. Until 1828, when gold was discovered in Georgia, most of the metal was mined in North Carolina. After 1848 California dominated gold production in the United States, and many Southern masters took their slaves with them to mine claims in the West. By 1850, several hundred slaves were in the California gold fields. Even though California entered the Union as a free state, the law prohibiting slavery was not strictly enforced, and throughout most of the 1850s bondsmen continued to labor in the Western fields.

Lead mining was another small, but important, segment of the Southern mining industry. During the colonial and antebellum periods lead was mined in southwestern Virginia for the military and for home industries. By 1819, another center of production had developed in Missouri where, along with their counterparts in Virginia, hundreds of slaves toiled.

Most mine operators owned a core of experienced bondsmen in order to ensure continuity of production, and hired the remainder of their slave work force. Because miners worked more or less on their own, operators used a variety of positive incentives to stimulate production, such as cash for work performed in excess of the required quotas. If such incentives failed, the operator could apply sterner measures. Labor was difficult and hazardous for all underground miners, including slaves. Explosions, rockfalls, fire, and watery inundations were constant threats, and numerous slaves were killed or maimed in Southern pits. Naturally, some rebelled against these conditions, normally by running away. So many slave miners fled when federal troops laid siege to Richmond and Petersburg in 1865 that the eastern Virginia coal companies were forced to stop production.

SELECTED BIBLIOGRAPHY

Brent D. Glass, " 'Poor Men with Rude Machinery': The Formative Years of the Gold Hill Mining District, 1842–1853," *North Carolina Historical Review*, 61 (1984), 1–35; Ronald L. Lewis, *Coal, Iron, and Slaves: Industrial Slavery in Maryland and Virginia, 1715–1865* (1979); Robert S. Starobin, *Industrial Slavery in the Old South* (1970); and John Edmund Stealey III, "Slavery and the West Virginia Salt Industry," *Journal of Negro History*, 59 (1974), 105–131.

RONALD L. LEWIS

MINSTRELSY. The blackface minstrel show was America's first national entertainment form, and it remained the nation's most popular entertainment from the 1840s to the 1890s. As an aspect of mass culture, minstrelsy reflected white perceptions and expectations of Afro-Americans and helped to perpetuate Negro stereotypes. Minstrel images were so powerful that blacks who sought to enter the theatrical world in the late nineteenth century had to conform to the minstrel caricatures.

The two stock characters of minstrel shows were Jim Crow and Zip Coon. Jim Crow represented the happy-go-lucky, childlike plantation darky who loved to entertain whites. Zip Coon was the pretentious Northern black dandy whose pompous speech was filled with malapropisms. While such figures bore little relationship to real people, blackface characters were so popular that *Jim Crow* passed into the language as a synonym for segregation; and Zip Coon's name fixed *coon* as a general epithet for blacks. (The origin of the term *coon* as applied to blacks is obscure, and in the 1840s the word was popularly used when referring to a member of the Whig party. The political reference derived from the view that the Whig mascot, the raccoon, was a clever, wily "critter." In the 1850s with the fall of the Whigs and the triumph of minstrelsy, competing uses disappeared and Zip Coon nailed the label to blacks.)

The principal feature of the minstrel show—blackface characters—had its origins in blackface actors and performers who appeared back in the eighteenth century. Nearly all of the early characterizations were of slaves who were ignorant, foolish, and fond of drink. The stage slaves exhibited nearly every stereotype that would later be invested in Jim Crow and Zip Coon. They danced and sang, put on airs, unsuccessfully mimicked their white masters, spoke in fractured English, and got into trouble because of wenching, drinking, gambling, and petty thievery. These loyal but intellectually inferior Negroes presented no threat; and white audiences readily accepted blacks in this form. By the 1820s and 1830s, these joke-book versions of blacks were a stock part of popular entertainments. Some blacked-up actors specialized as "Ethiopian Delineators" and performed in circuses, medicine shows, showboats, menageries, museums (such as P. T. Barnum's museum in New York), and between acts of regular plays. The delineators claimed to present authentic Afro-American music and characters; but much of the music was of British origin, and characterizations stressed the "oddities, peculiarities, eccentricities, and comicalities of that Sable Genus of Humanity." Still, most early burnt-cork performers toured with circuses, showboats, or drama troupes, and some consciously sought material and borrowed black folk tunes and dances. For example, Thomas D. Rice, described as the "father of minstrelsy . . . the first real prince of the burnt cork," invented Jim Crow around 1828–1831. He saw an old, deformed slave doing an odd dance while singing a tune which ended with "Weel about, turn about, Do jis so / An' ebery time I weel about, I jump Jim Crow." Already a popular Ethiopian delineator, Rice became a sensation by dancing "Jim Crow" in his routine.

The first minstrel show was created when four unemployed burnt-cork specialists banded together, styled themselves as the Virginia Minstrels, and presented a show in February 1843 at the Bowery Amphitheater in New York. This was the first time that a troupe of players had presented an entire evening of blackface music and humor. They were an instant success.

Innumerable minstrel troupes sprang up across the country, and within a year the Ethiopian Serenaders performed at the White House. American companies toured abroad, even performing before Queen Victoria, and soon English troupes began imitating the Americans, singing "plantation songs" and speaking in Negro dialects which they learned from touring American actors. One of the most amazing cultural transferences occurred when an American minstrel company toured South Africa in the 1880s; for decades afterwards, the Coloureds in Cape Colony presented blackface minstrels and "coon shows."

In the first decade of minstrel shows, troupes traveled widely, and performers sought new material from black and white folk music and dance, and especially appropriated black dance steps and rhythms. However, during the height of the minstrel craze from the 1850s to the 1870s, the companies resided for long periods in Northern cities, adopted a standardized show format, and became increasingly remote from folk sources. Until the Gilded Age, all minstrels were white men, and most were Northerners or foreign-born immigrants who had little or no firsthand knowledge of Afro-Americans. The great centers of minstrelsy were the northeastern cities such as Philadelphia, Boston, and New York. Providence, Rhode Island, a thoroughly minstrel-mad city, spawned many troupes, invented the minstrel parade, and even named a street after a local lad who became one of the nation's leading endmen and "Champion Clog Dancer of the World."

The minstrel show evolved a stylized, three-part format. The first part presented the entire company, seated in a semicircle, singing and joking, and ended with a grand "walk-around." The second part, called the olio, was a kind of variety show which presented individual acts and featured a hilarious stump speech. The third part was a comic opera, burlesque, or farce. The setting for these farces was usually a Southern plantation. As such, the minstrel show had to deal with the institution of slavery and black life. In the first decade of minstrelsy, Northern audiences saw an ambivalent picture of slavery because minstrels presented both positive images of happy plantation darkies and negative statements about cruelty and the inhumanity of slavery. While the happy image predominated, the minstrels attacked heartless masters who separated black lovers, broke up families to maximize profit, or whipped or abused slaves. Although sympathetic to the runaway slave,* the ministrels never portrayed a happy or successful fugitive.* Instead, homesickness or ignorant dandyism was the lot of the black outside the South. In the 1850s, as the issue of slavery became more threatening to national unity, the objections to slavery disappeared from minstrels, leaving only images of happy slaves and the unhappy Northern black ignoramus.

Minstrels constantly commented on current events, and the Civil War* affected them profoundly. They unequivocally supported the Union, but were vehemently antiabolitionist. The carnage of battles and the lengthening war produced a flood of sad and sentimental songs about the suffering of Northern white women and bereaved families. In another example, a singer without blackface makeup, dressed as a Union soldier, stood alone in a spotlight and sang the haunting song, "Tenting Tonight on the Old Campground," in every show for over two years. After the Emancipation Proclamation* went into effect in January 1863 and blacks were enlisted in the army, the minstrel shows presented them as uniformed Jim Crows and Zip Coons.

One effect of the war on minstrelsy was to accelerate the shift from "Negro subjects" to social commentary on the problems of whites. Consequently, the Southern plantation as the setting for the comic opera segment became less frequent. As the popularity of minstrelsy declined in the 1880s and 1890s, promoters introduced more and more gimmickry, gargantuan troupes, all-female or all-black companies, and constant touring. After minstrelsy decayed into its local, amateur form, its central images endured, passing into the blackface acts in vaudeville, the movies of Al Jolson and Eddie Cantor, and the hit radio show of the 1930s, "Amos 'n' Andy."

SELECTED BIBLIOGRAPHY

Alan W. C. Green, " 'Jim Crow,' 'Zip Coon': The Northern Origins of Negro Minstrelsy," *Massachusetts Review*, 11 (1970), 385–397; Hans Nathan, *Dan Emmett and the Rise of Early Minstrelsy* (1962); Richard Orton, "Black Folk Entertainments and the Evolution of American Minstrelsy," *Negro History Bulletin*, 41 (1981), 885–887; Orrin Clayton Suthern, "Minstrelsy and Popular Culture," *Journal of Popular Culture*, 4

(1971), 658–673; Robert C. Toll, *Blacking Up: The Minstrel Show in Nineteenth-Century America* (1974); William L. Van Deburg, *Slavery & Race in American Popular Culture* (1984); and Carl Wittke, *Tambo and Bones: A History of the American Minstrel Stage* (1930).

                                                               J. STANLEY LEMONS

MISCEGENATION. Miscegenation has deeply affected American society and culture. The practice of interracial mating began soon after the arrival of the first Africans in the colonies, and was particularly widespread during the slavery era. Especially under conditions of slavery, but even after slavery was abolished, it provoked extensive prohibitory legislation and spawned a mulatto[1] population whose members both benefited and suffered from the contradictory ways in which they were perceived and treated.

Today, even a casual observer would notice the hybrid nature of the Afro-American population, but as early as the 1920s Melville Herskovits estimated that over 70 percent of black Americans had non-African ancestry. Recent genetic studies have calculated the range of "white" genes in the Afro-American population at 5 percent in a Deep South community like Charleston, South Carolina, 20 percent in a border city like Washington, D.C., and 49 percent in a Northern city like Seattle, Washington.

Interracial sexual contact was probably more prevalent early in the nation's history than at any time since. Especially in colonial Virginia and Maryland it was widespread among white indentured servants*—both male and female— who labored alongside blacks. The demise of indentured servitude resulted in fewer mulattoes being born to white women; by the middle of the eighteenth century, such births were largely the product of white men mating with black women. Miscegenation was also common in the lower South, but because slaves in that region were fairly isolated from the bulk of the white population, the practice was not as widespread. Most racially mixed children there probably were fathered by planters, sons of planters, and overseers.

These distinctive regional patterns of Southern miscegenation, plus a different pattern in the North and West—namely, black men married to white women— combined to produce a mixed population that, by the end of the slavery era, comprised 13 percent of all Negroes in the United States. Of the 588,352 persons classified by the 1860 census as mulattoes, 260,823 lived in the upper South, 233,938 in the lower South, and 93,591 in the North and West.[2] They comprised respectively 16, 10, and 27 percent of the total Negro population in those regions. Following emancipation, sexual contact between blacks and whites declined sharply, but the "browning" of the Afro-American population continued, as blacks and mulattoes married and mated with one another.

Although miscegenation between whites and Indians—and between blacks and Indians—was extensive enough to arouse concern, miscegenation between whites and blacks provoked by far the greatest anxieties. According to Winthrop D. Jordan, interracial sex was second only to slave revolts as a source of tension in areas of plantation slavery, and prompted vigorous efforts to suppress it. As early as 1630 a certain Hugh Davis was sentenced by a Virginia court to be publicly whipped for the act of "defiling his body in lying with a Negro." Ten years later the fruits of such activity became evident when Robert Sweat was made to do public penance because he had "begotten with child a negro woman," and the woman was "whipt at the whipping post." In 1700 a Pennsylvania court ordered a black man "never more to meddle with any white woman more uppon paine of his life."

In the 1660s colonies with plantation slavery—plus Massachusetts and Pennsylvania—reinforced local efforts by enacting laws* prohibiting miscegenation and interracial marriage. It is indicative of white opposition to interracial sexual contact that as late as 1967, when the Supreme Court declared antimiscegenation laws unconstitutional, interracial marriage was still banned in sixteen states.

Such laws had little effect. During the slavery era black men and white women did not need them to realize the dangers of interracial liaisons. And, despite the above-mentioned court decisions, white men were seldom prosecuted for sexual transgressions. The laws did, however, cause great inequities, first by denying black women and their mulatto children legal or financial claims on the father, and second by specifying that such children would remain the property of the woman's owner.

Although such laws, along with social pressure, caused much miscegenation to be of a temporary, fleeting nature, it would be wrong to think of interracial mating as involving nothing more than the use of brute force by men to satisfy their sexual urges. Owners, along with their sons and overseers, sometimes exerted coercion over women in their charge, but this seems not to have been the norm. In interviews conducted in the 1930s, half the slaves from the upper South and three-fourths from the lower South reported having been whipped, but only 1 percent mentioned forced sex. Moreover, because much miscegenation involved household servants,* it occurred in the context of intimate, daily contact and included varying degrees of seduction and mutual attraction, as well as coercion.

Despite hostile laws and rhetoric, attitudes toward miscegenation were relatively mild in two states. South Carolina did not outlaw interracial marriage until after the Civil War, and during the colonial period, one of its leading newspapers carried a humorous exchange on the delights of interracial sex. Louisiana, in addition, developed a system of concubinage, called *placage*, in which wealthy whites could meet young women at elegant "quadroon balls," the intent being to establish long-term, semipublic relationships with these "free people of color" by "placing" them in apartments and rearing a second family. This more tolerant attitude toward miscegenation somewhat resembled that of the West Indies; significantly, South Carolina and Louisiana were originally settled by slave owners from those islands.

Even though the law gave them no legal claims on the father, children* who were the products of interracial mating could benefit in several ways from having a white parent. In some instances they might have been judged white. South Carolina and Louisiana, for example, supplemented the almost universally accepted "one-drop" rule—whereby one drop of African blood makes one a Negro—and used criteria such as color, personal character, and community acceptance to decide the race of specific individuals.

The children of interracial unions were more likely to be manumitted. Even though family relationships were seldom acknowledged publicly, the historical record is not lacking in instances of men and/or their families manumitting the women and their natural offspring. Manumission* was rare in the United States, where the ratio of free to slave was lower than almost anywhere else in the New World. Because of the difficulty in obtaining freedom, it is significant that mulattoes were substantially more likely than blacks to be free. By 1860 they made up only 12 percent of the Southern Negro population but, in the upper South, comprised 35 percent of all free Negroes* and, in the lower South, 76 percent.

After being manumitted, mulatto children sometimes were aided or sponsored by their white fathers. The history of Wilberforce University is an instructive example of this. Founded in the mid-1850s as one of the first universities dedicated to the education of Negroes, most of its early students were mulatto children who had been emancipated—often along with their mothers—and brought to Ohio, where their fathers either enrolled them in the university or settled them on nearby farms.

Although such benefits help explain why mulattoes were more likely to be educated, to own property, and to constitute the core of the free Negro elite, the extent of such benefits should not be exaggerated. Most mulatto children were neither manumitted nor aided by their fathers. In the upper South, only 30 percent were free, and in the lower South only 12 percent. Mulattoes appear privileged only because the situation for blacks was even more grim.

In no state were mulattoes *as a class* granted special privileges. Social status in the United States did not depend on the degree of one's white ancestry, and mulattoes, who were legally lumped with Negroes, did not benefit from an elaborate system of racial classification and color stratification like that which prevailed in Latin America. The only special terms, other than *mulatto*, used to describe black-white mixtures in the United States were *quadroon* and *octoroon*—one-fourth and one-eighth, respectively, black ancestry. But outside Louisiana and South Carolina those terms were rarely used. Nor, except to some extent in South Carolina and Louisiana, did mulattoes benefit from the more simplified "three-tier" system of the West Indies, in which racially mixed persons occupied an intermediate position between whites and blacks.

Mulattoes who remained slaves—which was the condition of 70 to 88 percent—fared no better than their black counterparts. Interviews with ex-slaves in the 1930s show that those with white fathers were less likely than others to have had their families broken and, in the upper South, to have been house servants.

But in both regions they were *more* likely to have been whipped and to have left their masters right after emancipation.

Despite the ambiguities in their treatment and social status, brown- and light-complexioned Negroes had a highly stereotyped image in the public mind. They were almost universally portrayed as "tragic mulattoes"—rejected by the white world whose acceptance they supposedly craved, and too proud or refined to be comfortable around blacks. George Harris and Cassy in Harriet B. Stowe's* novel, *Uncle Tom's Cabin*, are examples of such characters in antebellum white fiction; the heroine of William Wells Brown's* *Clotel* is an example in black fiction.

The stereotype of the tragic mulatto persisted well into the twentieth century. While perhaps accurate for some, it certainly caricatured others, and failed to account for the very active role they played in the political, economic, social, and intellectual life of black America. It was society more than the mulatto that was tragic. A more accurate characterization of mulattoes could be based on the life of Frederick Douglass,* rumored to be his master's son. Douglass's tragedy was not that he was a mulatto, but that he was a man of talent, sensitivity, and ambition living in a racist society.

NOTES

1. A *mulatto* is defined as a person whose parents are of unmixed black and white ancestry. In common usage the term referred to any brown- or light-skinned Afro-American, but often no such distinction was made, and the terms *Negro* and *black* were used interchangeably to describe anyone of African ancestry. Not infrequently persons who tried to make such distinctions—census takers, for example—differed in their judgment of who should be considered a mulatto. As a result, references to mulattoes should be considered tentative and approximate. In the present essay, *mulatto* will refer both to light- and brown-skinned Afro-Americans, as well as to Afro-Americans with one white parent. The context will make clear which definition is being used.

2. Not until the census of 1870 were census takers given instructions on how to determine whether a person was a mulatto. Hence, these figures should be considered suggestive rather than definitive. The prevailing usage, however, was to call anyone a mulatto who had a noticeable degree of white physical characteristics.

SELECTED BIBLIOGRAPHY

Carl N. Degler, *Neither Black nor White: Slavery and Race Relations in Brazil and the United States* (1971); Melville J. Herskovits, *The American Negro: A Study in Racial Crossing* (1928); A. Leon Higginbotham, Jr., *In the Matter of Color: Race and the American Legal Process: The Colonial Period* (1978); James H. Johnston, *Race Relations in Virginia and Miscegenation in the South, 1776–1860* (1970); Winthrop D. Jordan, *White over Black: American Attitudes toward the Negro, 1550–1812* (1968); Robert B. Toplin, "Between Black and White: Attitudes toward Southern Mulattoes, 1830–1861,"

Journal of Southern History, 45 (1979), 185–200; and Joel Williamson, *New People: Miscegenation and Mulattoes in the United States* (1980).

LAURENCE GLASCO

MISSIONARIES TO SLAVES. Missionaries to the slave community engaged in a labor that spanned nearly three centuries and involved individuals with commitments as diverse as full-time field agents, local pastors, itinerant revivalists, and slave preachers.* For white missionaries, work among Afro-Americans represented one part of an effort to Christianize society by bringing slaves as well as masters under the spiritual care of the church. To obtain slave converts, missionaries first had to obtain access to slaves, but across this threshold fell the shadow of the master. Most white missionaries sought to acquire access by underscoring the compatability of slavery and Christianity. By the eighteenth century, however, some white missionaries began to see the intrusive authority of the master as one example of an irredeemably evil institution.

The difficulty of obtaining the master's cooperation became apparent to the first white missionaries in the seventeenth century. George Fox, the founder of Quakerism,* provoked strenuous opposition from Barbadian planters during a preaching tour in 1671. Agents dispatched by the Society for the Propagation of the Gospel in Foreign Parts (SPGFP),* an official arm of the Anglican church,* fared no better than the despised Quakers. In the Caribbean and around the Chesapeake, the society's missionaries heard a similar refrain from masters: religious instruction of slaves disrupted work schedules and spoiled good servants by filling their heads with exalted notions about their worth before God. Worse yet, religious meetings might furnish slaves with a cover to ripen insurrectionary plots. Masters therefore responded to missionary overtures with suspicion mixed with hostility.

To dispel such suspicions, Anglo-American preachers struggled to prove that Christianity would enhance the slave system, not destroy it. In the first half of the eighteenth century, agents for the SPGFP attempted to establish model Christian plantations on the Codrington estates of Barbados. The endeavor failed when the society assigned a higher priority to profit-making than soul-winning. Leaders of the colonial revival of religion known as the Great Awakening (1740–1743) stressed themes similar to those of the society's missionaries. The preeminent revivalist George Whitefield argued that Christianity would make slaves more loyal and productive servants by reconciling them to their station. Samuel Davies, an evangelical Presbyterian in Virginia, insisted that spiritual deliverance from the bondage of sin involved no change in temporal status and provided slaves with an inestimable reward for their earthly toils.

The Great Awakening had two major consequences for American slavery. First, Afro-Americans responded warmly to evangelical preaching, for they associated conversion with the experience of "possession" in African religion, and they viewed the dynamic rapport between preacher and audience as reminiscent of their own worship forms. Second, the Awakening generated a militance about converting slaves that masters had seldom seen before. When white evangelicals of the late eighteenth century encountered opposition from masters, they endured threats, whippings, and mob activity with defiance rather than surrender the mission field. The experience of persecution led some white missionaries to launch an attack on the entire slave system.

Realizing that antislavery protests* would undermine religious gains in the South, moderate and conservative Protestants forcefully reasserted the old idea that Christianization would neutralize the evils of slavery. In the early years of the nineteenth century Northern and Southern whites joined hands in such nationally organized ventures as the American Sunday School Union (1824) and the American Home Mission Society (1826), two benevolent societies which devoted at least part of their time to slave evangelism. For Southern whites, the "mission" to the slaves provided an ideological weapon against a growing number of Northern abolitionists who portrayed the South as a hotbed of cruelty, wickedness, and ignorance; it also allowed slaveholding Christians to reassure themselves about their essential decency. With the heightening of sectional tensions in the 1840s and 1850s, white Southerners began to look on Northern missionaries to slaves as double-agents who covertly worked for the destruction of the regime. Their mistrust of Yankees led them to withdraw from national missionary societies and to set up regional organizations that could ensure the orthodoxy of both missionary and literature.

The "missionaries" who conducted the most fruitful, and unfailingly devoted ministry came from among the slaves themselves. At times the slave preachers worked with white missionaries, but ultimately they adapted Christianity to the slaves' needs and created a communal experience that whites could not share. Slave preachers enabled their people to endure the system as "more than conquerors" by encouraging them to remember God's love, bear one another's burdens, and hold fast until the Almighty delivered them from their bondage. When emancipation did come, black preachers led their people forward to realize the meaning of freedom.

SELECTED BIBLIOGRAPHY

David Brion Davis, *The Problem of Slavery in Western Culture* (1966); James D. Essig, *The Bonds of Wickedness: American Evangelicals Against Slavery, 1770–1808* (1982); John W. Kuykendall, *Southern Enterprize: The Work of National Evangelical Societies in the Antebellum South* (1982); and Donald G. Mathews, *Religion in the Old South* (1977).

JAMES D. ESSIG

MISSISSIPPI, SLAVERY IN. In 1540 the Spanish explorer Hernando De Soto led the first European expedition into the wilderness of what would later comprise the state of Mississippi, reaching the Mississippi River the following year and bequeathing his name to the county which today lies just south of Memphis. But it was not until 1699 that a Frenchman, Pierre Le Moyne, Sieur d'Iberville, constructed Fort Maurepas on Biloxi Bay, thus establishing the first permanent European settlement in the lower Mississippi Valley. During the following century three European powers—France, England, and Spain—competed for supremacy in the area.

Under the leadership of Iberville's younger brother, Bienville, the French moved rapidly to consolidate their position. During the first two decades of the eighteenth century they founded settlements at Mobile and New Orleans and, in 1716, erected Fort Rosalie on the bluffs of the Mississippi River at Natchez. Three years later, the first significant number of slaves entered French Louisiana—a number which increased to nearly 6,000 by the end of the French period. Few of these slaves, however, were situated east of the Mississippi River within the boundaries of present-day Mississippi. As the French ventured further into the interior, they encountered the three great Indian tribes—the Choctaw, Chickasaw, and Natchez—that inhabited Mississippi before the Europeans' instrusion. Most powerful were the Choctaws, numbering some 20,000, who controlled the central portion of Mississippi until well into the nineteenth century. The Chickasaws and Natchez, each numbering about 4,500, occupied the northern and southwestern areas respectively. Least congenial were the Natchez who massacred the garrison at Fort Rosalie in 1729, thereby precipitating retaliatory action by the French that resulted in the virtual extermination of the Natchez Nation two years later. However, intermittent campaigns against the Chickasaws, who had incurred French wrath by establishing close commerical ties with the English, ended in failure. As a consequence of inveterate misrule, emphasis upon commerce rather than settlement, and chronic warfare with the Indians, Mississippi was still sparsely populated when it passed under English control in 1763 at the conclusion of the French and Indian War.

The British period was marked by relative tranquility in Indian-white relations and by vigorous efforts to promote settlement of the Natchez area, particularly after 1770. Following the outbreak of the American Revolution, Natchez received an influx of Loyalist refugees from the Atlantic colonies, thus reinforcing its rapidly developing Anglo-American, Protestant character. Somewhat surprisingly, this ethnocultural orientation did not change when Spain, following France's lead, entered the war against Great Britain and occupied Natchez in September 1779. Despite a counterclaim by the United States after 1783, Spain retained control of the Natchez District until 1798. Under the loose, benevolent rule of the Spanish, the colony prospered. Spanish authorities confirmed land grants made during the British period and stimulated economic growth by encouraging tobacco and indigo production. When the indigo boom faltered in 1795, the fortuitous introduction of the cotton gin brought the promise of enduring prosperity to the region. Thus, by the end of the Spanish period, a population which in 1784 numbered but 1,619, of whom 498 were slaves, had increased more than fourfold to 4,500 whites and 2,400 blacks.

The Mississippi Territory, as created by Congress in 1798, included those lands extending from the thirty-first parallel northward to Tennessee and bounded by the Mississippi and Chattahoochee rivers. During the War of 1812 the area south of the thirty-first parallel between the Pearl and Perdido rivers, previously a part of Spanish West Florida, was annexed to the territory. Initially, settlement was confined almost exclusively to the Natchez District along the lower Mississippi and to a small colony on the Tombigbee River in what is now Alabama. However, the eastern area experienced modest growth during the first decade and a half of the territorial period. Then, following Andrew Jackson's decisive victory over the Creeks in 1814, twenty million acres in the eastern part of the territory were opened to white settlement.

Apprehensive lest they lose political control to the horde of white farmers who poured into the eastern settlements after the war, the conservative planters of the Natchez region campaigned successfully for a partition of the burgeoning territory. On 1 March 1817, President James Madison signed the enabling act which provided for admission of the western half to statehood and reorganization of the eastern portion as the Alabama Territory. Mississippi, with a population already more than 40 percent slave, entered the Union as the twentieth state on 10 December 1817.

The first two decades of statehood were years of unparalleled growth and prosperity for Mississippi. It was during this period that cotton* assumed its dominant position in the state's economy. Facilitated by uniformly favorable prices, the introduction of improved varieties from Mexico, and the cession of Indian lands in the northern two-thirds of the state, cotton culture spread rapidly across Mississippi. As the state's forests gave way to cotton fields, a heavy tide of Afro-Americans poured in from the older slave states to till the newly cleared lands and harvest the white gold. The cotton-slavery boom reached a climax in the 1830s, when cotton output quadrupled and the slave population increased by nearly 200 percent to constitute, for the first time, a majority of the state's total population. Thus, by the end of the decade, Mississippi had established itself as the leading cotton-producing state in the nation and, along with South Carolina, as one of only two black majority states in the South. Both distinctions were to have profound implications for the future.

When Mississippi became a state, white settlement was concentrated in three areas: the Natchez District, extending from the mouth of the Yazoo River southward along the Mississippi to the Louisiana line and comprising 60 percent of the total population and 75 percent of the slaves; the infertile piney woods region in the southeast, where whites outnumbered blacks by four to one; and a small, isolated enclave east of the Tombigbee River on the Alabama border. In 1820 the Choctaws, who had previously surrendered title to the piney woods area, ceded a substantial bloc of territory in west-central Mississippi. This New Purchase area, as it was called, developed rapidly during the 1820s, soon rivaling the Natchez District in population and political influence. Finally, the huge Choctaw and Chickasaw cessions of 1830 and 1832, respectively, extinguished Indian title to the remaining land in Mississippi and inaugurated the ''flush times'' of that decade. As land-hungry immigrants from the older states surged in to settle the vacated Indian lands, thirty new counties—half of the antebellum total—were organized in just two years, 1833 and 1836.

This influx of new settlers brought far-reaching political as well as economic changes to Mississippi. Predominantly small farmers who owned few if any slaves, the newcomers exhibited more democratic propensities than did the planter aristocrats of the Natchez region. Their hero was Andrew Jackson,* chastiser of Indians and champion of the common man. They began to flex their political muscles as early as 1822 when they forced a removal of the capital from Natchez to a new site in central Mississippi, appropriately named Jackson. A decade later, they secured a new and much more democratic state constitution which provided, among other features, for universal manhood suffrage and popular election of all judges. In the 1830s party divisions, based largely on a conjunction of economic interests and intrastate sectionalism, began to emerge. The plantation areas—the old Natchez District augmented by the newer Yazoo and upper Pearl River regions—became Whig strongholds, while Democratic* strength was greatest in the former Choctaw and Chickasaw lands of east-central and north Mississippi. Capitalizing on both the personal popularity of Jackson and the population base engendered by settlement of the Indian cession lands, the Democrats gradually established their ascendancy in Mississippi politics. Although the Whig presidential candidate, William Henry Harrison, carried the state in 1840 and Whig principles persisted in the river counties until the time of disunion, the party of Jackson was clearly the dominant political faction in Mississippi throughout the late antebellum period.

The topography of Mississippi profoundly affected agricultural and demographic patterns as well as political alignments. Although ten distinct soil regions are discernible within the state, they may be consolidated into four major ones. The most fertile of these areas, and thus the most propitious for the development of slave plantations, was the Delta-Loess region which encompasses the western part of the state from just below Memphis to the Louisiana line and includes two subregions: a flat, elliptical expanse of alluvial soil between the Mississippi and Yazoo rivers north of Vicksburg and a narrow strip of brown loam soil, perhaps thirty miles wide, bordering the Delta on the east and proceeding thence along the Mississippi River to the southwestern tip of the state. It was the southern part of the Delta-Loess, the Natchez District, which was the first to be settled. However, an inadequate levee system precluded development of the northern portion, or Yazoo Delta, until after 1840, and it was not until the postbellum period that the Delta became the heart of Mississippi's Cotton Kingdom. Fertile soil also characterized two extensions of the Alabama Black Belt into Mississippi—the Northeast Prairie, a strip varying from ten to twenty-five miles in width, which extends southward from Corinth through Lowndes and Noxubee counties to the Alabama line; and the Central Prairie, a slightly wider belt of black calcareous earth, which runs from Madison County in a southeasterly direction to the Alabama border. The other two soil regions, which may be defined broadly as the red clay hill country of east-central and northeast Mississippi and the long-leaf pine barrens of the southeast, were too poor to support slave plantations. Consequently, most inhabitants of these areas were small slaveholders and yeomen farmers who practiced subsistence agriculture, supplemented in the piney woods with open-range cattle grazing.

The salubrious soils of western Mississippi and the black prairie belts provided the basis for a dramatic expansion of cotton culture during the 1830s. The spread of cotton was also promoted by the appearance of a new variety, christened Petit Gulf, which was developed by Dr. Rush Nutt and other planters in the Natchez-Vicksburg area. Superior to its predecessors in yield, quality of fiber, resistance to disease, adaptability to various soils, and ease of picking, this hybrid was first marketed in 1833 and soon spread to other cotton-producing states, where it became the ancestor of all later American breeds. Under these and other favorable circumstances, including easy credit from state banks and a sustained demand for cotton on the world market, Mississippi agriculturists cleared thousands of acres of fertile land and concentrated their resources almost exclusively on cotton production. The results were impressive. More than a million acres were planted in cotton in 1836, when the price reached 20¢ per pound in the New Orleans market, and cotton production mushroomed from 100,000 bales in 1830 to 386,803 by the end of the decade.

This impressive growth was arrested sharply by the Panic of 1837, which produced acute distress throughout the state, especially after 1840. As cotton prices plummeted to an all-time low of 5¢ per pound in the mid-1840s, Mississippi planters began to heed the pleas of reformers such as Martin W. Philips, who stressed crop diversification, selective breeding of livestock,* and more intensive methods of husbandry in order to promote self-sufficiency and increase per-acre yields. Propagated through agricultural societies, fairs, and journals, such practices enabled the state to attain a degree of diversity and self-sufficiency which would not be approached again for nearly a century. Nevertheless, rising cotton prices in the last decade of the antebellum period induced a return to the emphasis upon cotton. In 1859 Yazoo County led the state in the production of that fleecy white staple with 64,075 bales of ginned cotton, a figure exceeded by only two other counties in the United States. With the rich alluvial lands of the Yazoo Delta yielding as much as 3,000 pounds of seed cotton per acre, compared to the South-wide average of 530 pounds, Mississippi cotton growers enjoyed a decided competitive cost advantage by the time of the Civil War.

The spectacular expansion of Mississippi's agricultural economy during the antebellum years was based on the exploitation of slave labor. As the profitability of cotton increased, so too did the importation of slaves. Table 1 indicates the magnitude of this increase during each of the five decades preceding the Civil War. Following a rise of approximately 100 percent in both the second and third decades of the century, the state's slave population soared to nearly 200,000 during the boom period of the 1830s; then, in the wake of the agricultural depression, the rate of increase slowed appreciably in the final two decades of the antebellum period. Only in the depression-ridden 1840s did Mississippi's

Table 1
Rate of Growth of Slave Population Relative to White Population, 1810–1860

Year	Number of Whites	Percent Increase	Number of Slaves	Percent Increase
1810	23,024	---	17,088	---
1820	42,176	83.18	32,814	92.02
1830	70,443	67.02	65,659	100.09
1840	179,074	154.21	195,211	197.31
1850	295,718	65.13	309,878	58.74
1860	353,901	19.67	436,631	40.90

white population increase more rapidly than its blacks. Consequently, by 1860 slaves constituted 55.2 percent of the total population—a figure exceeded only by South Carolina among all the slave states.

Blacks became most heavily concentrated in those areas best suited to large-scale cotton production—the Natchez region initially, and, after 1840, west-central Mississippi and the Yazoo Delta. The density of slave population in selected Mississippi districts during the half century preceding the Civil War is depicted in table 2. In the last two decades of the antebellum period slaves constituted approximately 75 percent of the population in the five leading cotton-producing counties but only 20–40 percent of the population in the nonplantation areas. The proportion of slaves was highest in the Delta counties of Issaquena and Washington, where, in both 1850 and 1860, blacks outnumbered whites by more than nine to one. By contrast, slaves constituted only 12 percent of the population in the piney woods county of Jones, where disaffection toward the slaveholders and the Confederacy* became so intense during the Civil War that stories of the legendary "Free State of Jones" persist to this day.

Much of the huge increase in Mississippi's slave population can be attributed to importations from the older slave states, particularly those of the upper South. More than 200,000 Negroes were imported into the state by immigrant masters and professional traders during the period 1830–1860. Most slaves made the journey to Mississippi on foot, departing the upper South in the fall and traveling in slave coffles at the rate of about twenty-five miles per day. Franklin and Armfield, the largest domestic slave-trading firm in the nation, operated a major selling depot at Natchez, and there were smaller slave markets in Vicksburg, Woodville, Aberdeen, and Crystal Springs. Periodic legal and constitutional efforts to limit or prohibit the importation of blacks for sale proved abortive in the face of a mounting demand for slaves after the opening of the Indian cession lands.

The presence of a large slave population in Mississippi obviously necessitated strong measures of control by public authorities. As in other Southern states, slaves were subject to special legal codes* which severely restricted their freedom of movement and imposed upon them unique occupational, educational, and commercial limitations. Slaves were also liable to prosecution under the general criminal laws of the state, although trial procedures differed from those established for whites. Thus, slaves charged with minor offenses were tried before an informal court consisting of a justice of the peace assisted by two or more slaveholders. Those convicted of misdemeanors received corporal punishment ranging from ten to thirty-nine lashes. Under both antebellum state constitutions slaves accused of felonies were accorded jury trials. The jury was drawn from a panel of twenty-four men, half of whom were required to be slaveholders. Those adjudged guilty of noncapital felonies were usually punished by burning in the hand, executed by the sheriff in open court. Some twenty offenses—including malicious assault with intent to kill, manslaughter of whites, rape, arson, insurrection, and conspiracy—were deemed capital crimes* when com-

Table 2

Percentage of Slave Population to Total Population in Selected Mississippi Districts, 1810–1860

District	Counties	1810	1820	1830	1840	1850	1860
Yazoo Delta	Bolivar, Issaquena	---	---	---	71.6	89.1	89.2
West Central	Carroll, Yazoo, Warren	42.5	47.8	48.2	63.0	63.2	68.0
West Central	Hinds, Madison	---	---	39.4	68.8	70.0	74.0
Old Natchez Region	Claiborne, Jefferson, Adams Wilkinson	52.5	59.1	68.6	75.5	77.9	77.6
N.E. Prairie	Lowndes, Monroe, Noxubee	---	19.2	28.5	56.3	63.2	68.6
Short-leaf Pine Uplands	Attala, Choctaw Lafayette, Yalobusha	---	---	---	38.1	38.5	41.1
S.E. Pine Barrens	Greene, Jones, Perry	---	25.0	27.0	21.9	25.1	22.7

mitted by slaves. The patrol system* was also an important agency in controlling the slave population of Mississippi. Originally tied to the militia, the patrol apparatus was placed under the jurisdiction of local units of civil government in the 1830s. Charged primarily with the tasks of apprehending Negroes found at large after curfew and of dispersing unlawful assemblies of blacks, slave patrols, which generally consisted of four men in each patrol, were effective instruments of control over the large black population in some parts of the state. The vast majority of slave transgressions, however, were relatively minor infractions of plantation discipline which were handled privately by masters and overseers without state intervention.

Despite the array of public and private restrictions imposed upon Mississippi's slave population, blacks did not submit willingly or passively to the system which oppressed them. As recent scholarship has demonstrated, slaves could and did play a major role in defining the complex set of rules and relationships which governed the slave society of the Old South. If they could not challenge successfully the condition of enslavement itself, they at least could ameliorate the quality of life within slavery. Thus, in the constant struggle to preserve their self-esteem and to resist personal degradation, slaves found solace in such African cultural survivals* as music,* dancing,* folktales,* and conjurism. They took the religion * forced upon them by their masters and shaped it to meet their own emotional needs. On the more practical level, slaves exploited the natural antipathies between planter and overseer and between overseer and driver to win important concessions on work requirements and disciplinary parameters.

Mississippi planters constantly complained of the slow pace set by their field hands, but, as with the chronic problem of runaways, they accepted these "leisurely" work habits with relative equanimity, attributing them to the racial peculiarities of the Negro. Nor did masters object too strenuously when slaves converted such benefits as garden plots,* holidays, and nuptial and burial ceremonies* from privileges into rights. If slaveholders proved obdurate, their black charges resorted to subtle means of resistance*—breaking implements, feigning sickness, mishandling livestock—to effect desired changes.

Only rarely did the pent-up frustrations of Mississippi's black majority flare into open violence,* though whites were acutely aware of that potential. White fears were manifested most vividly during the summer of 1835 when sensational revelations concerning an alleged slave conspiracy purportedly engineered by the notorious outlaw, John A. Murrell, resulted in the execution or summary killing of more than a score of supposed conspirators in the west-central portion of the state. Thus, by relying upon a variety of cultural mechanisms and striking a delicate balance between accommodation and resistance, Mississippi blacks protected themselves from the most dehumanizing features of slavery.

In the absence of specialized studies on the subject, one can only speculate on the degree to which slave life and culture in Mississippi were distinctive. Certainly, the long presence of a large Indian population* added an ethnographic dimension not found in most other slave states. Introduced into Choctaw and

Chickasaw villages as early as the 1750s, slaves acted as interpreters between whites and Indians and played a vital role in tribal acculturation. During the territorial and early statehood periods there was considerable social and commercial intercourse between blacks and Indians, leading inevitably to miscegenation.* As mixed-blood families and tribal leaders themselves became slave owners, slaves in adjacent areas sought refuge in Indian territory and exploited in other ways the confusion resulting from the movement of blacks between white and Indian jurisdictions. Gradually, however, by means of legislation and military patrols, white authorities moved to discourage communication between the two subordinate racial groups. Consequently, by the 1820s, such measures, together with the accelerated pace of Indian removal and a substantial increase in slave ownership by the remaining Indians, had combined to produce a greater separation between blacks and Indians. Indicative perhaps of the new order is the fact that Greenwood LeFlore, chief of the Choctaw Nation, was one of the largest planters in the state on the eve of the Civil War.

Other factors influenced the characteristics of Mississippi's slave population. It is likely that the migratory origins of that population had a deleterious effect upon the integrity of the slave family* in Mississippi, although a distinction should be made between those who emigrated with their masters and those introduced into the state by professional traders. The former probably replicated familial and demographic patterns* prevalent in the older slave states, whereas the latter included a preponderance of young male slaves, many of whom had been separated by sale from their families. The substantial number of absentee estates, particularly in the heavily black Yazoo Delta, facilitated greater cultural autonomy and promoted a sense of group solidarity among blacks in that environment. Because of the large pool of potential marriage* partners on large Mississippi plantations, the practice of taking "broad wives"—mates owned by neighboring slaveholders—was less common than in such predominantly farm states as Virginia, North Carolina, and Tennessee. Finally, the paucity of urban sites reduced social contacts between whites and blacks with the result that Mississippi had a relatively small proportion of mulattoes in its slave population.

It is doubtful that living conditions of plantation slaves in Mississippi differed significantly from those in other states. Perhaps the best that can be said is that they were tolerable. The standard food ration was three and one-half to four pounds of pork and a peck of corn meal per week, supplemented on many plantations by poultry and garden produce. Slave housing* was rustic but adequate. Typical were the accommodations on Martin W. Philips's Log Hall plantation, where each family was quartered in a sixteen-by-eighteen-foot frame dwelling with a brick chimney. These houses were furnished with bedsteads and bedding, crude chairs, and chests or trunks in which clothing could be stored. It was customary to dispense clothing* twice annually, usually in May and November. Each hand received two summer outfits and a straw hat, two winter outfits and a wool hat, and two pairs of shoes. Blankets were distributed less frequently, perhaps every other year to each family. For both humanitarian and economic reasons, owners evinced genuine concern for the physical well-being of their slaves. Minor ailments were usually treated by the master or overseer, but trained physicians were called in to diagnose more serious cases of slave illness. There was less unanimity among planters in making provision for the spiritual welfare of their black charges. Some discouraged any kind of religious observance, others refused to permit their slaves to worship off the plantation, but most allowed blacks some form of Christian worship. Integrated services were the norm in regular churches, although blacks were seated in special galleries and subjected to sermons pitched toward the white communicants. In terms of church membership, blacks constituted more than a third of Mississippi's 41,500 Baptists* and one-sixth of the 66,000 Methodists* in the state in 1860. Despite their long hours of labor—as many as sixteen hours a day during the summer—slaves were accorded a generous allotment of holidays. Except in the most unusual circumstances, Sundays were days of rest, and most planters gave occasional whole or half holidays on Saturdays. In addition to customary holidays like Christmas, when three to seven days were normally given, and the Fourth of July, blacks also received a respite from labor on such special occasions as the end of cotton harvest or the day of a slave wedding. In the final analysis, the general treatment of slaves in Mississippi, as elsewhere, depended largely on the character of the individual master. And that, of course, was the greatest iniquity of slavery—placing the life of one human being completely at the mercy of another.

From the beginning of statehood lawmakers sought to minimize the number of free blacks* in Mississippi. Private emancipation was permitted only with the consent of the legislature and for some meritorious service to the master or to the state. Even these limited grounds for manumission were abrogated by the Revised Code of 1857, which prohibited private emancipation under any circumstances. In the 1830s, doubtless because of changing attitudes toward slavery, attempts were made to eradicate altogether the free Negro element in Mississippi, which numbered little more than 500 at the beginning of that decade. Thus, an 1831 statute compelled all free blacks between the ages of sixteen and fifty to leave the state unless they could furnish proof of "good character and honest deportment" to their county probate court.

Simultaneously with this action by the state, the Mississippi Colonization Society was organized in Natchez to promote the same goal. Supported by some of the wealthiest planters in the state, this society labored assiduously during the 1830s to resettle freed blacks in the African colony of Liberia,* but in the end its efforts proved as ineffectual as those of its parent organization on the national level. Although the Mississippi Colonization Society received nearly $100,000 in contributions, it managed to send to Liberia only 571 blacks—most of them ex-slaves freed for the specific purpose of being colonized—before becoming virtually defunct by 1840.

Despite its early demise, the free Negro element in Mississippi remained one of the smallest in any Southern state, numbering only 1,775 in 1860. One of

Mississippi's free blacks, the celebrated barber of Natchez, William Tiler Johnson, acquired considerable property and social standing before falling victim in 1851 to the system of white domination. His murder at the hand of a white neighbor went unpunished because the only witness, a Negro boy, was prohibited by state law from testifying against a white person.

In Mississippi, as in other slave states, there was a pronounced change in public attitudes toward slavery during the 1830s. Prior to that time most Mississippians had been apologetic about the institution, viewing it as a necessary evil. By 1835, however, largely as a consequence of the increasing profitability of cotton and popular revulsion against the radical abolition crusade, politicians and writers began to defend slavery* as a positive good and to extol its virtues for both blacks and whites. One of those who made a significant contribution to the proslavery literature of the period was Henry Hughes, a lawyer from Port Gibson. Credited with being the first American writer to use the word *sociology* in the title of a book, Hughes presented a novel defense of slavery in an 1854 work, entitled *A Treatise on Sociology*. According to Hughes, slavery had evolved over time into something which he termed *warranteeism*, a near-utopian condition in which the master merely exercised a trusteeship over the slave, owning his labor but not his body. Also a warm advocate of reopening the African slave trade, Hughes was more extreme than most of his contemporaries. By the 1850s most white Mississippians had become convinced of the inherent rectitude of the slave system and were determined to preserve it at any cost.

Slave labor was employed most efficiently and profitably on the plantation, which may be defined as an agricultural unit containing at least 200 acres of improved land and a minimum of twenty slaves. Using this definition, about 20 percent of the agricultural operators in Mississippi on the eve of the Civil War could be classified as planters, thus making Mississippi one of the major plantation states in the South. In the Delta-Loess section of west Mississippi nearly half of the heads of agricultural families were planters. Moreover, Mississippi had a greater number of large planters*—those owning 100 or more slaves—than any other cotton state except Alabama. In 1850 some 216 Mississippi proprietors were listed in that category—a number which rose to 316 by the end of the decade. Similarly, reflecting a general trend toward consolidation of slaveholdings during the 1850s, the number of owners holding 300 or more slaves in the state increased nearly threefold during the same decade. Data on the twenty-four Mississippi slaveholders making up this elite group are presented in table 3. It should be noted that these figures do not include holdings in other states, chiefly Louisiana, where a number of Natchez planters had extensive slave parcels by 1860. Table 4 indicates the magnitude of such multistate holdings by Natchez area slave owners.

These Natchez nabobs constituted the aristocracy of Mississippi slaveholders. Heterogeneous in background and cosmopolitan in outlook, they were far from typical representatives of their class, either in Mississippi or elsewhere in the South. Some, like William J. Minor and brothers Alfred Vidal and Samuel

Table 3
Planters Owning 300 or More Slaves in Mississippi, 1860*

Name	Age	Birth-place	County	No. of Planta.	No. of Slaves
Wade Hampton III	(S.C. absentee)		Issaquena, Washington	5+	899+
John H. Horne	58	N.C.	Wayne	2	751
Stephen Duncan	73	Pa.	Adams(R), Issaquena	5	717
Benjamin Roach	40	Va.	Adams, Warren, Washing-ton, Yazoo(R)	3	552+
John Robinson	39	Miss.	Madison	5	550
Gerard Brandon	43	Miss.	Adams	4	512
J.D. Hill	40	Miss.	Issaquena	4	502
Elgee & Chambers	(absentee owners)		Wilkinson	?	501
John A. Miller	50	Ky.	Washington	4	500+
Edward McGehee	74	Ga.	Wilkinson	6	471
David Hunt	82	N.J.	Issaquena, Jefferson(R)	4	468
John D. McLemore	(absentee)		Carroll, Tallahatchie	3	462
William N. Mercer	70	Md.	Adams	3	452
Levin R. Marshall	60	Va.	Adams(R), Claiborne, Wilkinson	3	448
John C. Jenkins Est.	--	Pa.	Wilkinson	2	424
Robert J. Turnbull Est.	--		Issaquena	4	401
Chris. F. Hampton	(S.C. absentee)		Issaquena, Washington	2	388+
Philip St. Geo. Cocke	(Va. absentee)		Lowndes, Yazoo	6	375
Joseph E. Davis	65	Ga.	Warren	1	355
George W. Humphreys	40	Miss.	Bolivar, Claiborne(R), Lafayette	5	323
James Metcalfe	62	Miss.	Adams	1	315
Evan S. Jefferies	47	Miss.	Claiborne(R), Jefferson	3	314
Adam L. Bingaman	60	Miss.	Adams	1	310
Henry Turner & John A. Quitman Est,	50	Miss.	Warren	1	308

*indicates county of residence. Washington County census records for 1860 have been destroyed; hence figures for that county are estimates.

Table 4
Natchez-Area Residents with Combined Mississippi-Louisiana Slaveholdings of More Than 300 in 1860

Name	No. of Slaves in Miss.	La. Parish	No. of Slaves in La.	Total Slaves
Levin R. Marshall	448	Concordia, Jefferson, Madison	610	1,058
Gerard Brandon	512	Concordia, Tensas	194	706
Alfred Vidal Davis	14	Concordia	637	651
William J. Minor	42	Ascension, Terrebonne	580	622
David Hunt	468	Concordia	99	567
Samuel Manuel Davis	174	Concordia	386	560
Edward McGehee	471	West Feliciana	74	545
Francis Surget	147	Concordia, Madison	309	456
Anna F. Elliott	12	Concordia, Tensas	437	449
Gabe B. Shields	91	Concordia	353	444
George W. Humphreys	323	Madison	85	408
James Railey	78	Carroll	324	402
Rice C. Ballard & F.F. Boyd	120	Carroll, Madison	265	385
James Surget	13	Concordia	349	362
John Murdock	166	Tensas	195	361
John Helm	170	Tensas	189	359
Alexander C. Henderson	77	Concordia	260	337
Alexander K. Farrar	238	Catahoula	84	322
Smith C. Daniell	150	Tensas	164	314
James A. Ventress	222	Ascension	88	310

Manuel Davis, were descended from former Spanish governors; others, like Henry Chotard and the Surgets, were of French ancestry; still others, most notably Stephen Duncan, David Hunt, John Carmichael Jenkins, and William Newton Mercer, were natives of Northern or border states. Most entered the area during the Spanish or territorial periods and, through fortunate marriage alliances and shrewd capitalistic entrepreneurship, accumulated great wealth. Two of them, Stephen Duncan and Levin R. Marshall, amassed multistate slaveholdings in excess of 1,000 each, placing them among the half-dozen largest slaveholders in the entire South. The palatial homes of the Natchez planters stand today as monuments to the opulent society which they created in the mid-nineteenth century—an opulence which enabled Adams County to lead the nation in per capita wealth on the eve of the Civil War.

Ironically, the Natchez nabobs, those with the greatest vested interest in the peculiar institution, manifested the least inclination to sever the ties of union when secession fever struck Mississippi in the wake of the Mexican War. There were, of course, exceptions. Governor John A. Quitman, a hero of that war and a political maverick among the traditionally conservative Natchez planter-aristocrats, brought the state to the brink of secession in 1851 before cooler heads prevailed. Thereafter, the only significant political question in Mississippi was whether slavery, the very cornerstone of the state's socioeconomic system, could best be preserved by remaining in the Union or separating from it. Prodded by rural editors, provincial lawyer-politicians, and petty slaveholders, the state gradually but inexorably moved toward the latter option. The Mississippi convention, by a vote of 84–15, with token opposition primarily from delegates representing the river counties and the northeast hill country, adopted an ordinance of secession on 9 January 1861. Only South Carolina, the other black majority state, had acted with greater celerity.

During the ensuing Civil War,* Mississippi contributed to the Confederacy not only its president, Jefferson Davis, but also nearly 80,000 soldiers. More than a third of the latter paid with their lives—a death toll exceeded only by North Carolina among the Confederate states. The plantation-slave system, which secessionist leaders had sought desperately to preserve, disintegrated before their eyes as the Union launched its onslaught against Vicksburg during the early months of 1863. By war's end the state had suffered incalculable human and material losses. Once a wealthy state, Mississippi has never recovered from the economic consequences of the war and emancipation. At the close of hostilities, with freedmen classified as population rather than property, Mississippi dropped from fifth among thirty-three states in per capita wealth to last—a distinction which the state has yet to relinquish. Saddled with a one-crop agricultural economy until well into this century and plagued for more than a century by racial problems, perhaps no state has been more profoundly affected by the legacies of the antebellum era than Mississippi.

SELECTED BIBLIOGRAPHY

Richard A. McLemore, ed., *A History of Mississippi* (2 vols., 1973); Robert E. May, *John A. Quitman: Old South Crusader* (1985); Edwin A. Miles, *Jacksonian Democracy in Mississippi* (1960); John H. Moore, *Agriculture in Ante-Bellum Mississippi* (1958); Percy Lee Rainwater, *Mississippi: Storm Center of Secession, 1856–1861* (1938); Charles S. Sydnor, *Slavery in Mississippi* (1933); and Daniel H. Usner, Jr., "American Indians on the Cotton Frontier: Changing Economic Relations with Citizens and Slaves in the Mississippi Territory," *Journal of American History*, 62 (1985), 297–317.

WILLIAM K. SCARBOROUGH

MISSOURI, SLAVERY IN. Black slavery figured significantly in Missouri's history from the era of French and Spanish rule and settlement in the early eighteenth century, rapidly replacing Indians as the nonfree labor force in the territory. Blacks were first brought to Missouri to help meet the labor needs of the territory in 1719. During that year, Sieur Philip Renault, son of the celebrated iron founder of France, purchased about 500 blacks on the island of Santo Domingo to work as lead miners in Missouri. Another French explorer, Des Ursins, in search of silver mines in the territory, also imported slaves to Missouri.

In addition to mining lead, slaves in territorial Missouri labored in diversified industries. For example, Monsieur Valet, regarded as the wealthiest planter on the upper Mississippi in 1770, engaged his 100 black laborers in lumbering and maize production. The maize was ground by the water-driven mill on his Sainte Genevieve plantation located on the western bank of the Mississippi River. Other slaves were employed in Missouri's saltworks.* The salt trade was an important factor in the commercial life of early Sainte Genevieve. Jean La Grange, owner of La Saline saltworks until 1766, worked his ten black slaves in the production of salt. When Daniel Blouin purchased the slaves and the saltworks in 1766, the slaves were probably the primary labor force at the works. During the 1770s, black slaves largely made up the population of the vicinity of the saltworks. Documents also indicate that black slaves cultivated the lands in the vicinity of the saltworks.

Because profitable uses were found for black slaves in Missouri, and because of the fertile valleys of the Mississippi and Missouri rivers, slaveholders and settlers who expected to own slaves were attracted to the territory and state. The first American emigrants, largely Southerners, brought to Missouri not only their livestock* and other personal property, but their black slaves as well. When the first big wave of Southern Americans began to rush into Missouri after the Louisiana Purchase of 1803, they found the best land along the rivers already occupied. The older settlers, however, readily sold their landholdings to the newcomers for a few dollars. These land transfers enabled the slavery economy of the Missouri Territory and later state to develop in the river valleys.

The second big wave of Southerners to enter Missouri followed the War of 1812. The years between 1815 and 1825 constituted the period of the most intensive migration of American fortune seekers to Missouri. During this period slaveholders from both the upper and lower South began to dominate the economic and social affairs of the territory and frontier state. According to one keen observer of the evolution of Missouri's society, "nearly all of the first settlers [during the 1815–1825 period] owned negro slaves."

A study of the growth of Missouri's population between 1803 and 1860 provides insights concerning the demand for slave labor during both the territorial and statehood years. The data in table 1 show that the slave population increased numerically during the entire period. The percent of slaves in the total population also showed a steady increase from 1803 to 1830. Until 1830 the percentage increase of the slave population started to decline in ratio to the percentage of white inhabitants. Nevertheless, these statistics must not be construed to mean that by 1830, or 1860 for that matter, slavery in Missouri had reached its natural limits of expansion. During the 1840s and 1850s, nonslaveholding Germans and Irish came to the state in droves to escape conditions in their native lands. Other developments in Missouri also lead to the conclusion that slavery was not dying in Missouri by 1860.

Furthermore, a careful study of federal census data for Missouri for the years 1850 and 1860 reveals a significant pattern. The Missouri River counties, from Callaway County west to the Kansas border, showed substantial growth in slave population during the decade, while several of the counties in the eastern section of the state from St. Louis southward along the Mississippi River, witnessed either a decline in their slave populations or a relatively small increase. Slaveholders in Callaway County, located in east central Missouri, for example, represented roughly 50 percent of the state's slaveholding families in 1850. During the 1850s, when slaves brought very high prices in the lower South, the slave population of Missouri increased 24 percent.

In 1860 Missouri ranked eleventh among the slave states and the District of Columbia. As the data in table 2 reveal, however, Missouri was a state of small slaveholders. According to the federal census, the average number of slaves per slaveholding family in the state in 1850 was 4.6, or about one-half of the national average. Of the 19,185 slaveholding families in 1850, 12,604 or 65.6 percent of them held less than five slaves. One slaveholding family, however, was listed as owning at least 200 bondsmen. By 1860 the number of slave owners in Missouri had increased to 24,320, and the average number of slaves per owner had increased to 4.7. An analysis of the data in table 2 also shows that by 1860, not only had the number of slaveholders increased about 21 percent over the 1850 number of slaveholding families, but that the number of slaveholders in each classification of owners represented in the table increased significantly from one decade to the next. Even the number of slaveholders with 100 or more slaves was four times greater in 1860 than the number in that category ten years earlier. These figures suggest that in 1860 slavery was firmly entrenched in Missouri.

During the antebellum era, St. Louis was Missouri's largest urban center. The border city was first settled by French traders about 1764. The growth of the settlement, situated along two great rivers, was influenced by imperial com-

Table 1
Population Trends in Missouri, 1803–1860

Year	White	Free Black	Slave	Percent Slave
1803	9,020		1,320*	12.7
1810	17,227	607	3,011	14.5
1820	59,988	376	10,222	15.4
1830	114,795	569	25,091	17.8
1840	323,888	1,478	58,240	15.5
1850	592,004	2,618	87,422	12.8
1860	1,067,081	3,572	114,941	9.8

Table 2
Classification of Slaveholders in Missouri in 1850 and 1860

Census Year				Number of Slaves				
	1	2-4	5-9	10-19	20-49	50-99	100-199	
1850	5,762	6,878	4,370	1,810	345	19		
1860	6,893	8,770	5,737	2,400	402	34	4	

Table 3
Population Trends in St. Louis, 1840–1860

Census Year	White	Free Black	Slave	Percent Slave
1840	14,407	531	1,531	9
1850	73,806	1,398	2,656	3
1860	57,476	1,755	1,542	1

mercial activities and the coming of the steamboat. Table 3 shows the growth of the city's population from 1840 to 1860. Although the slave population witnessed a decline of more than 1,100 persons between 1850 and 1860, the number of bondsmen in the city in 1860 was eleven more than the number for 1840. Nevertheless, the slave population of St. Louis declined from about 9 percent of the city's total number of residents in 1840 to about 1 percent twenty years later.

The increased number of free blacks* in St. Louis in 1860 does not suggest that the 1,114 fewer slaves in the city's population were freed, hence increasing the free black population. The increase of free black residents from 1,398 in 1850 to 1,755 by 1860 "was not more than the natural increase," noted historian Frederic Bancroft in 1931. Federal census figures show that only 139 slaves were manumitted in the whole state between 1840 and 1860. Evidently the slave population in St. Louis was not becoming freer as the nation was drawn closer to civil war.

Several factors contributed to the declining slave population in St. Louis during the 1850s. The slave-trading* business in the city during the decade only partly explains the situation. Bancroft asserted in 1931 that the frontier town was "one of the six cities that sent the most negroes to the insatiable 'Southern Market.' " Undoubtedly some of St. Louis's slaves were sold "down the river," but the number sold rarely included prime field hands. In 1860 St. Louis County had 4,346 slaves. Of that number 3,605, or about 83 percent, were under forty years of age. Before his escape from bondage in St. Louis in 1835, William Wells Brown* was hired out for a year to "Mr. Walker," a slave dealer. In his autobiography Brown wrote, "I am sure that some of those who purchased slaves of Mr. Walker were dreadfully cheated, especially in the ages of the slaves which they bought." Doubtlessly, Walker was typical of the slave trader in St. Louis.

Moreover, in 1861 slave auctions in St. Louis were abruptly halted by a crowd of about 2,000 young white men who dominated bidding in January with what were deemed ridiculously low bids, thereby forcing the auction to stop. St. Louis never again held slave auctions. The rush for gold in California also affected the slave population in St. Louis as well as the whole state. Jesse Hubbard, a St. Louis slave, accompanied his master to California and returned with $15,000. Upon his return to St. Louis, Hubbard purchased his freedom and bought a farm in St. Louis County. Regarding St. Louis City and County, J. Thomas Scharf maintained that a large proportion of the emigrants to California were men of substance, including farmers, mechanics and merchants, classes well-represented among slave owners.

Missouri's emancipation movement,* starting in St. Louis during the 1850s, also worked to undermine slavery in the river city. A group of St. Louis politicians, who were known as radicals, advocated emancipation and subsequent colonization* of Missouri's slaves. The battle cry of the movement was voiced by one of its leaders in a March 1857 speech in St. Louis. Benjamin G. Brown, an astute lawyer and state representative, explained the philosophy of the emerging movement in these words: "Agitate the emancipation of slaves? No! Let us agitate the emancipation of ourselves—our brothers and sisters—our children and those who are come after us, from competition with serfdom, and conflict with bondsmen, and bondswomen." This movement on behalf of the white laboring class in Missouri probably proved more successful in controlling the growth of slavery in St. Louis than in any other part of the state. Aided by this white labor movement, many of the black slave domestic workers in St. Louis were replaced by unskilled Germans and Irishmen who had migrated to St. Louis in droves during the late 1830s and after. Nevertheless, a St. Louis clergyman observed that as late as 1860, the proslavery spirit* remained very much alive. Although he noted that many businessmen recognized the debilitating impact slavery had upon the city's business interest, clergyman Galusha Anderson insisted that the advocates of slavocracy still remained firmly in control. The defenders of black slavery in St. Louis, wrote Anderson, controlled the entire city as late as 1860. Thus, as historian Claudia Dale Goldin found, "slavery and Southern cities were not incompatible during the period 1820–1860." Slavery was slavery in St. Louis until it was abolished by state law in 1865. Above all, slavery in Missouri was an important economic system. Missouri's slaveholders, as one contemporary of Marion County remarked, "worked their slaves for profit. Slavery to them was not only social power and supremacy, but it was wealth and a source of wealth. . . . Men and women worked in the fields here, as they did in the cotton fields of Mississippi." Foremost in the minds of Missouri's slaveholders was wealth, and the labor needs of the frontier state caused slaves to be valuable investments.

Doubtlessly, the largest number of slaves in Missouri during the antebellum era served as agricultural laborers in the state's chief cash products, hemp, tobacco, and livestock. During the statehood period, the vast majority of Missouri slaves were employed in the production of hemp. In 1850, for example, those counties that proportionally had the largest number of slaves were the state's largest hemp,* tobacco,* and livestock producing counties. Accounting for 34 of the state's 101 counties, in 1850 these counties produced 13,216 of the state's 16,028 pounds of hemp, 1,859,115 of 3,523,632 head of livestock, and 15,218,721 of 17,113,784 pounds of tobacco. For the general farmer as well as for those who engaged their slaves in the cultivation of hemp, tobacco, and raising livestock, Missouri by the 1840s was a "new agriculture paradise," according to a North Carolinian who moved to Jackson County in western Missouri in 1842. Throughout the slavery era, black slaves fulfilled the multifaceted duties of farmhands.

Missouri's slaves also were used extensively as domestic servants. Before the 1850s only a few of the household servants* in St. Louis were not slaves. Black slaves were engaged on a large scale as servants in households throughout the state. Christian College, a women's school located in Columbia, employed female slaves to work as cooks, washwomen, and servants to the students. The institution also permitted families to contribute the labor of their slaves in lieu of tuition. In 1860 another school, Saint Louis University, employed six slaves as domestic servants.

Moreover, the continued labor needs of the lead mines of Missouri and Illinois added to the economic significance of slavery in Missouri. The Maramec Iron Works of Missouri, according to one scholar, "quickly resorted to slave labor for the difficult but routine tasks of mining ore, quarrying flux, and chopping timber." From 1828 until the Civil War the company regularly used between fifteen and twenty-five slaves, both hired slaves and those owned by the firm. Among the slave mine laborers were blacksmiths, carpenters, and furnace keepers.

Missouri's bondsmen also were engaged in a variety of other occupations, both skilled and unskilled. Slaves were used in forestry industries and in tobacco and cotton* cultivation as well. Although cotton never became a major crop in Missouri, it nevertheless flourished with slave labor in some of the more southern counties of the state. Slaves also labored in the construction of railroads and served widely aboard steamboats in all capacities. Many slaves labored in Missouri's brickyards.

Many of Missouri's businesspeople owned slaves, and evidence suggests that most of the nonfree blacks were used for nonagricultural purposes. These slaves quite often were hired out or employed as saddle shop workers, blacksmiths, shoemakers, and in other occupations. These slaves were used to enhance their masters' social status as well as to supplement their masters' family income.

The early and steady hiring practices* in Missouri indicated how valuable slaves were as investments and for helping to meet labor needs in the state. Slaves always could be hired out in antebellum Missouri, and their labor brought comfortable sums to masters. Throughout the antebellum period, farmers, industrialists, and merchants competed to hire surplus slaves. Because of the state's labor needs and the profits from slave hire, domestic and interstate slave traders doing business in pre–Civil War Missouri found it hard to purchase good-quality slaves in the state. These factors made Missouri something less than a buyer's market for the frontier slave trader. According to a student of slavery in Boone County, a large number of Missouri's slaveholders "found it quite profitable and preferable to hire their excess slaves rather than to sell them."

Although it is difficult to determine the value of Missouri's human property during the slavery era, historian Harrison A. Trexler correctly observed in 1914 that "in general it can be said that a gradual rise in slave values is apparent [in Missouri] up to the Civil War." In his inaugural address of 3 January 1861, Governor Claiborne F. Jackson estimated the slaves in Missouri to be worth $100 million. In 1862 Congressman John W. Noell of Bollinger County introduced a bill in the House of Representatives to compensate Missouri's slaveholders $10 million for their total slave property. A year later the state auditor reported 73,811 slaves of 67 of the state's 113 counties were appraised for tax* purposes at $11,704,809. Using the governor's figures, one can conclude that in 1861 the average Missouri slave was valued at about $700. Two years later a slave in Missouri was still valued at more than $150. While the governor's estimate was probably too high, the tax assessor's valuation too low, and Congressman Noell probably was uninformed of the value of slaves in his state, Missouri's slave property nonetheless was quite valuable socially as well as economically on the eve of the Civil War.* A slave's real worth was determined not only by his monetary value because a bondsman gave his master a social status that could not be measured in terms of dollars and cents.

The slaves of Missouri provided not only the labor system upon which the economy was built, but the foundation of the state's social order as well. The numerical ratio between slaveholder and nonslaveholder in Missouri always was very wide. Though seven out of eight white Missouri families never owned slaves, the authors of a recent study conclude that "whites of all classes were encouraged to believe that they would some day enhance their social status by becoming slaveowners."

Although few white Missourians depended directly on slavery for their economic livelihood, nevertheless a large number of the outright defenders of slavery were nonslaveholders. Proslavery nonslaveholders held considerable political and social power in even so small a slaveholding area as Cole County. As one prominent Missourian remarked, it seemed that "slavery had been woven into [the] warp and woof of the social web." Slavery's social significance in Missouri helps to explain why the institution survived so long in the state and why it was not dying on the eve of the American Civil War. Socially as well as economically, slavery was alive and doing well in Missouri in 1860.

Indeed, after more than one and a half centuries of slavery in Missouri, there was no substantial evidence to indicate that the peculiar institution was breaking down anywhere in the state by 1860. Black slaves, integrated into almost every phase of the state's economy, showed that they could be employed profitably in a variety of labor pursuits. The elasticity of the demands for slave labor in Missouri and the versatility of the slave gave lasting viability to the peculiar institution in the territory and state. Not until 11 January 1865, when Missouri's governor signed into law the Ordinance of Emancipation, was slavery in Missouri abolished.

SELECTED BIBLIOGRAPHY

Donnie D. Bellamy, "Slavery, Emancipation, and Racism in Missouri, 1850–1865" (Ph.D. dissertation, University of Missouri–Columbia, 1971); Robert William Duffner, "Slavery in Missouri River Counties 1820–1865" (Ph.D. dissertation, University of Missouri–Columbia, 1974); Lloyd A. Hunter, "Slavery in St. Louis, 1804–1860," *Bulletin of the Missouri Historical Society*, 30 (1974), 233–265; and Harrison A. Trexler, *Slavery in Missouri, 1804–1865* (1914).

                                                        DONNIE D. BELLAMY

MISSOURI COMPROMISE. The debate over the application of Missouri Territory for statehood in 1819 raised, for the first time, the issue of slavery to the center of national politics. From the founding of the republic, both Northern and Southern political leaders had realized that slavery could jeopardize the existence of the Union and had labored to keep the issue under wraps. By 1820, however, rapid population growth in the North and the westward expansion of slavery undermined past concessions and constitutional understandings. The South held a minority of seats in the House of Representatives, but free and slave states were equally balanced in the Senate. Missouri's request for admission as a slave state threatened this political equilibrium.

The House, on a sectional split, voted to admit Missouri only if it agreed to prohibit further introduction of slaves and to provide gradual emancipation of those already there. The Senate rejected the measure and neither chamber seemed willing to yield. A bitter congressional debate ensued, reflecting every moral and constitutional argument concerning the future of slavery that would be used over the next forty years.

The immediate issue was resolved by a compromise worked out largely through Henry Clay's* efforts. Congress voted to admit Missouri as a slave state while granting Maine admission as a free state. It dealt with the future expansion of slavery by prohibiting the institution in the remaining portions of the Louisiana Purchase north of latitude 36° 30′. A major sectional crisis had been resolved, but with ominous implications for the future of the Union.

SELECTED BIBLIOGRAPHY

George Dangerfield, *The Awakening of American Nationalism, 1815–1828* (1965); Harold M. Hyman and William M. Wiecek, *Equal Justice under Law: Constitutional Development, 1835–1875* (1982); and Glover Moore, *The Missouri Compromise, 1819–1821* (1953).

WILLIAM F. WILLINGHAM

MORAVIANS. The Moravian experience with slavery reflected a broad trend in which individual ownership of property replaced community control. This experience represented an American phenomenon, occurring in Moravian settlements in Pennsylvania and North Carolina but not in Hernnhut, Saxony. The American experience signaled the overall decline in church control within the community.

Officially, the *Aufseher Collegium*, or Board of Supervisors, in North Carolina always opposed the use of slave labor, especially in Salem, the religious and commercial center of the Wachovia tract. From Gottlieb Krause's purchase of a slave in 1785 against the *Collegium*'s advice, until the abolition of all restrictions on buying, hiring,* and selling slaves in 1847, North Carolina Moravians resisted prohibitions on the peculiar institution. Economic forces—a chronic shortage of labor, a desire for help in laborious duties such as domestic chores, an unwillingness by whites to serve in certain jobs—simply proved too much for the *Collegium* to thwart.

The Moravians' adaptation to slavery revealed ambivalence on the part of the Brethren and resistance, along with considerable autonomy, on the part of the slaves. Zealous missionaries* who expressed an interest in the spiritual salvation of slaves from their first contact in 1762, the Brethren nevertheless wavered between treating blacks as people and as property. For example, on Easter Sunday, 1776, a slave was beaten so badly by Br. Vogler and John Hein that the bondsman could not work for several days. The *Collegium* reprimanded the Brethren for being "too friendly with the Negroes." A slave grew confused, they explained, when one day a Brother joined him in "a joke or some other amusement," and the next day "beat him 'like a dog.'"

The Moravians, unlike their Quaker* neighbors, held no moral strictures against the peculiar institution, but they feared its impact on whites and worried about the behavior of the slaves themselves. Slaves, the *Collegium* maintained, "inspired idleness and harshness in their owners and employers." The board concerned itself most with the institution's possible ill effects on young people and women.

In deciding whether or not to grant an exception to the rules on slaveholding, the Brethren always considered the character of the individual slave. Even so, they generalized enough regarding blacks to express concern frequently about theft by bondsmen and, from the mid-1820s on, to fear slave uprisings.

On the important matter of religion,* North Carolina Moravians noted that blacks demonstrated decidedly independent views. For example, as deliberations regarding the construction of a black church commenced in the 1820s, blacks indicated that they did not feel at ease among whites and would prefer worshiping by themselves. At some of the early meetings with Br. Steiner, a "missionary" to the blacks appointed by the Provincial Elders Conference at the behest of the Female Missionary Society, slaves interjected their own observations and prayers and, at one point, several "who did not have the best character" got up and left. Once the church was established, Br. Steiner was forced to cancel services on occasion because of "unruly conduct" by members of his congregation or because of rumors of slave revolts. At times, the bitterness of slaves bubbled more overtly, as reflected in comments by a pastor who noted that a fellow Moravian's slave "cursed and did such godless things and said drily that all Negroes curse."

Traditionally, the Moravian experience with slavery has been viewed as atypical, with the implication being that the Brethren accepted slavery more reluctantly and treated slaves more kindly than other white Southerners. Observers did sometimes comment that Moravians "spoiled" their slaves, allowing them more freedom and spending more money on their upkeep than was necessary. Still, the ambivalence, fear, and perplexity of the Moravians on the one hand, and the resistance and autonomy of their slaves on the other, reflected an evolving, dynamic black-white relationship that prevailed in much of the South, or at least in the southern piedmont where land- and slaveholdings were relatively small. In the end, perhaps the biggest difference between the Moravians' experience with slavery and that of their neighbors lies in the Brethren's better documentation of this regretful episode in America's history.

SELECTED BIBLIOGRAPHY

Philip Africa, "Slaveholding in the Salem Community, 1771–1851," *North Carolina Historical Review*, 54 (1977), 271–307; Norma Taylor Mitchell, "Freedom and Authority in the Moravian Community of North Carolina, 1753–1837" (M.A. thesis, Duke University, 1961); Nora Lea Rogers Reese, "The Moravian Attitude toward the Negro and Slavery" (unpublished paper, Duke University, 1966); and Jerry L. Surrat, "The Role of Dissent in Community Evolution among Moravians in Salem, 1772–1860," *North Carolina Historical Review*, 52 (1975), 235–255.

GAIL W. O'BRIEN

MORMON CHURCH. The Church of Jesus Christ of Latter-day Saints (Mormon) began in upstate New York in 1830. Prophet-founder Joseph Smith and most early converts had New England roots. In 1831 the Mormons moved to Ohio and created settlements in Missouri. By 1839 persecutions forced them to move en masse to Illinois.

At first the church had "no special rule" regarding blacks. But in order to reside in Missouri, a slave state, Mormons were forced to condone slavery. Missourians feared slave insurrections, and Mormons did too, after Smith's 1832 revelation that soon "slaves shall rise up against their masters." Three years later the Mormons adopted a policy that declared it unlawful, unjust, and dangerous to interfere with slaves or to preach to them without their owners' permission. In 1836 the Mormon newspaper in Ohio rebutted abolition, in part because, biblically, God cursed the sons of Canaan with servitude that only He could rescind. Nevertheless, Mormons believed that the Gospel was for men "both bond and free."

After the Mormons moved to Nauvoo, Illinois, Smith in 1842 reversed the church's position and endorsed antislavery sentiment but not abolitionism. He advocated equal rights for all men, including blacks, but opposed miscegenation. Smith urged Mormon slaveholders to move to Nauvoo and to free their slaves, although he considered creating a southwestern colony for Mormon slaveholders. When Smith ran for president in 1844, he proposed to eliminate slavery within six years through federal compensation of slaveholders.

Driven from Illinois in 1847, the Mormons moved to Utah (then under Mexican control), led by Smith's successor, Brigham Young. The Compromise of 1850* made Utah Territory a "popular sovereignty" zone, neither slave nor free. Quickly, Southern Mormon slaveholders moved with their slaves to Utah. Among the original 148 Mormon pioneers to enter Salt Lake valley in 1847 were three black "servants." Perhaps 100 blacks reached Utah by 1850, two-thirds as slaves, but many owners and slaves soon moved to Mormon colonies in California, a free state. Utah was the only Western territory in 1850 with black slaves; the 1850 Utah census listed twenty-six.

In 1851 the church reported that "There is no law in Utah to authorize Slavery, neither any to prohibit it. If the slave is disposed to leave his master, no power exists there, either legal or moral, that will prevent him. But if the slave choose to remain with his master [and move to Utah], none are allowed to interfere.'' A year later Utah legalized slavery, mainly so that Mormons could buy and raise Indian children sold by Indian slave traders. The 1860 Utah census listed twenty-nine black slaves.

During the Civil War* the church favored the Union. Brigham Young, however, remained convinced that blacks were destined to be servants, not the equal of whites. He disliked Lincoln's Emancipation Proclamation* because, Young said, man cannot ''destroy the decrees of the Almighty.'' Church policy from Young's time until 1978 barred black Mormons from ordination to priesthood offices.

SELECTED BIBLIOGRAPHY

Newell G. Bringhurst, *Saints, Slaves, and Blacks: The Changing Place of Black People within Mormonism* (1981); Lester E. Bush, Jr., ''Mormonism's Negro Doctrine: An Historical Overview,'' *Dialogue: A Journal of Mormon Thought*, 8 (1973), 11–68; Lester E. Bush, Jr., and Armand L. Mauss, eds., *Neither White nor Black: Mormon Scholars Confront the Race Issue in a Universal Church* (1984); Dennis L. Lythgoe, ''Negro Slavery in Utah,'' *Utah Historical Quarterly*, 39 (1971), 40–54; and ''Joseph Smith's Presidential Platform,'' *Dialogue: A Journal of Mormon Thought*, 3 (1968), 17–36.

WILLIAM G. HARTLEY

MUSICAL INSTRUMENTS. Slave musicians exhibited their talents on every type of instrument that was available to their white counterparts. From colonial New York to colonial Virginia and throughout the antebellum South, Afro-American bondsmen entertained audiences with tunes played on German flutes, French horns, mandolins, accordions, and pianos. This diversity, however, should not obscure the prominent place that string instruments played in the slaves' musical arsenal. The musicians' practical concerns, personal tastes, and West African heritage,* adapted to the new environment produced by American slavery, made string instruments, especially the violin, the most desirable and prominent of all.

During the colonial and antebellum eras, masters attempted to suppress the use of traditional African drums for fear that slaves would use them to relay calls of insurrection. For the same reason, some masters also prohibited the recreational use of horns, which were familiar to Africans in the form of elephant tusks and other animal horns. Despite these restrictions, slaves continued to play drums and ''windjammers'' while serving their masters at colonial and antebellum militia musters and in sophisticated marching bands of the antebellum urban South. In fact, in scattered areas of the South, African-style drums existed down to the end of the nineteenth century.

The absence of traditional drums on most of the South's nineteenth-century plantations did not deprive slave music of a percussive base. Slaves filled the void with all sorts of ordinary materials from cooking pots to animal bones. Not the least effective percussion instrument was the slave's own body. ''Jubba patting,'' which consisted of syncopated hand-clapping, body-slapping, and foot-tapping, was a widespread method of producing an accompaniment to songs and instrumental music whereby slaves preserved the complex rhythms of West African percussionists.

Slaves added to this rhythmic base tunes played on wind instruments that also had African counterparts. In America flutes (often made of reeds and also used at militia musters) and pan's pipes or ''quills'' (an assortment of one-note reed flutes of various lengths tied together to provide the musician with an instrument capable of producing a range of notes) were commonly found on antebellum plantations. By the nineteenth century, however, the banjo, an instrument of African origin, and the violin, an instrument with African counterparts, generally carried the melodies at plantation frolics.

A convenient overlapping of African and Scottish and English instrumental folk forms further assured the predominance of string instruments, which were versatile, portable, and aesthetically appealing to both masters and slaves. Ambitious musicians fashioned effective instruments from gourds, pine boards, wooden boxes, tanned skins, animal gut, and horse hair. But even within the select group of string instruments, one instrument, the fiddle, was the most favored. True, nineteenth-century white minstrels* popularized the notion of the ubiquitous plantation banjo picker in their burlesques of black life, but in actuality, the fiddle surpassed the banjo in popularity. The store-bought violin became the coveted possession of many a talented slave.

Neither the fiddle's nor the banjo's popularity survived emancipation intact. During the twentieth century some black folk musicians continued to use the fiddle, but the banjo became almost completely identified with white folk forms. The guitar, piano, and harmonica were more suited to the emerging blues repertoire of black America. Further displacing the slave musician's favorite tools were the brass and reed instruments that became the ''front line'' of the modern jazz ensemble.

SELECTED BIBLIOGRAPHY

Paul A. Cimbala, ''Fortunate Bondsmen: Slave 'Musicianers' in the Antebellum Southern United States'' (M.A. thesis, Emory University, 1977); Harold Courlander, *Negro Folk Music, U.S.A.* (1963); Dena J. Epstein, *Sinful Tunes and Spirituals: Black Folk Music to the Civil War* (1977); David Evans, *Big Road Blues: Tradition and Creativity in Folk Blues* (1982); and Eileen Southern, *The Music of Black Americans: A History* (2nd ed., 1983).

PAUL A. CIMBALA

MUSICIANS. During the antebellum period, slave instrumentalists, or ''musicianers'' as their fellow bondsmen dubbed them, served as useful additions to their masters' chattel property. Consequently, they were common fixtures on plantations and in cities throughout the Southern United States. More important than their service to their masters, however, were their social and cultural contributions to black life that earned for them a special, honored position in the slave community. Rooted in their West African heritage* and the development of Afro-American culture during the colonial era, the accomplishments of "musicianers" placed them squarely in the ranks of the slave elite.

By the eighteenth century, slave musicians were sufficiently common in the North American colonies to appear regularly in reports of militia musters, white social gatherings, and black celebrations. By the mid-nineteenth century, however, they were the most common source of music in the Southern United States. One ex-slave claimed that nearly every farm in his old neighborhood had a resident fiddler. He might have been exaggerating, but the record reveals "plenty of colored folk fiddlers," as another ex-slave reminisced, living and playing on large farms and small. Cities, too, had their share of black musicians. During the two decades preceding the Civil War, for example, Savannah, Georgia, residents enjoyed the music of marching bands composed of slaves and the people of Columbia, South Carolina, contributed to the incomes of Andrew, James, and George, three musician brothers who were "almost free" slaves. In fact, so noticeable was the black monopoly on music that one traveler who rode the well-worn path between Washington, D.C., and Charleston, South Carolina, claimed he had not seen one white orchestra south of the Potomac.

White Americans had never hesitated to appropriate for their own purposes the talents of their black slaves and those of the slave musicians proved to be no exception. During the seventeenth century, when the North American colonies' black population was not large, black musicians learned to play European tunes on European instruments. Their musical ability earned them popularity in the white community and by the 1690s white Virginians, for example, considered the slave fiddler a valuable commodity. During the eighteenth century, slave musicians continued to prove their usefulness by performing at white functions throughout the colonies.

In the antebellum South, slave musicians found themselves entertaining in the Big Houses and other places frequented by their masters. Southerners still employed slave musicians at their dances, parties, and informal gatherings. Owners of fashionable resorts had them entertain their guests during the watering season. Even proprietors of the more common roadhouses used their musically inclined black servants to help travelers relax after a hard day's journey. Slave musicians were also on hand for their masters' militia musters and parades, a practice that continued down through the outbreak of the Civil War. As late as April 1861, black field musicians—probably slaves, given past practice—fell into formation to be photographed in uniform with the Sumter, Georgia, Light Guards.

Plantation owners had reasons other than simple entertainment for valuing their slave musicians. Musicians, like any other kind of skilled slave, could earn their owners extra cash when planters not fortunate enough to have a fiddler on the farm hired their services. Planters also considered musicians to be useful instruments of slave control. By encouraging music and dancing, they hoped to keep moody slaves happy, lazy slaves productive, and idle slaves out of mischief.

Given the usefulness of slave musicians, it should not be surprising to learn that some masters encouraged their talented chattels by supplying them with instruments* and formal training. The South Carolina master of Ben Horry's father and two uncles, for example, provided some formal tutoring for the three musicians, and another slaveholder permitted, if not openly encouraged, a white man to teach one of his slaves the fiddle and another the banjo. Black initiative also played a critical part in slaves' musical education. Indeed, the slaves who received formal training probably exhibited some signs of ability which attracted their masters' attention in the first place. The slave Robin, for example, received music lessons only after his owner, John Lawrence Manning of South Carolina, discovered the boy playing on a makeshift fiddle. But Robin, in turn, became the principal instructor of three other slaves, including his brother.

Most ''musicianers'' probably developed their skills either on their own, as did Robin initially, or with the assistance of other members of the slave community, as did Robin's students. Ex-slave William Grant, for example, ''learned to fiddle after the fiddler on the place.'' Another fiddler impressed a Yankee governess with a tune he had learned from his father. If the postwar experiences of some ex-slave musicians and their sons are any indication of what occurred during slavery, the family was a nurturing place for the musical talents of other slaves, too. Both ragtime composer Scott Joplin and Texas bluesman Mance Lipscomb received musical guidance from their fathers, former slave musicians.

Black initiative was also apparent in the way many ''musicianers'' acquired their instruments. While some received the tools of their trade from their masters, probably the majority acquired them on their own, either making them from ordinary materials available on any farm or purchasing a coveted professionally crafted violin. In the process they exhibited characteristics incongruous with those supposedly held by the stereotypical docile slave. The slave Isaac Williams exhibited determination and thrift when he accumulated and sold over a hundred muskrat skins in order to purchase a fine violin. And some slaves on a plantation near LaGrange, Georgia, ignored plantation rules, risked punishment, and stole into town to sell chickens they had raised so that they could buy instruments. Undoubtedly, these ''musicianers'' understood that in the long run the returns in pleasure and profit reaped from performing on their instruments would far surpass their initial investment in time and money, for even the harshest master had to make some concessions if he wished to exploit his slave musician to the fullest.

The role of entertainer, as both master and slave understood, required some freedom of movement not normally given to ordinary hands. Solomon Northup* traveled to engagements as far away as ten miles from his Louisiana plantation, and Texas slave Pete Robinson ''played de fiddle all over de country.'' Traveling about the countryside, musicians expanded their circle of friends and became aware of a world much larger than their masters' plantations.

Calls to perform also broke the dull plantation routine and provided musicians with a relatively independent source of income. Northup's mistress of ten years interrupted the slave's monotonous day by requiring him to entertain in her home. Another slave's difficult master not only provided him with a horse to speed him off to his engagements but allowed him to leave the fields well in advance of the appointed hour of his performance and to keep half of what he earned playing. Other slaves made enough money to allow them to enjoy a relatively comfortable existence by adding furniture, clothing, pipes, tobacco, and pocket knives to their meager possessions.

Some masters even tolerated disobedience from their musicians as the slaves tested the limits of their personal bondage. South Carolina slave John Drayton audaciously ignored his owner's command to mend a fence one Friday and slipped away to entertain at a slave soiree. When he returned on the following Monday, he offered his angry but obliging master not one word of explanation.

Such treatment along with the other privileges and perquisites did not go unnoticed by the slave community. Solomon Northup's acquaintances acknowledged his position as the wealthiest slave on Bayou Beouf. It was an ex-slave who recounted old John Drayton's escapade. Other ex-slaves recalled aged or sick musicians being excused from work and attributed the treatment not to planter paternalism but to the slaves' musical skill. And there is sufficient evidence to suggest that the musicians' relationship with their white masters and audiences generally raised their status among their peers. Nonetheless, that relationship was not essential for securing the musicians' prestige in their own community.

In West Africa musicians had enjoyed the esteem of their fellow villagers and tribesmen because they enriched all celebrations and many ordinary occasions with their music. The collective memory of the importance of music and the role of the musician probably withstood the ravages of enslavement, the Middle Passage, and the process of acculturation better than many other elements of African life. After the development of a strong Afro-American community during the eighteenth century, musicians again assumed a central role in the black community. As entertainers, teachers, and transmitters of Afro-American folk culture, they provided useful services to their community, something that was more important to slaves than the privileges they earned from their white masters. As entertainers, the "musicianers" were the physical and symbolic center of the "frolic," one of the few gatherings that allowed slaves to identify themselves as a community. Because of their contributions to life in the quarters, "musicianers" earned the respect of their community, a community that recognized the special role of the entertainers and willingly rewarded the comfort and pleasure its members received from the musicians' songs.

During slavery time, most ordinary bondsmen were not in a position to exchange money for the services provided by their musicians, but they did not hesitate to bestow small favors and special treatment on them. Popped corn, candy, or a bucket of hard cider were rewards sufficient to keep a musician playing into the night. Indeed, many a "musicianer" probably found the pleasures of playing and being the center of attention significant rewards in themselves.

At frolics, audiences obliged them by giving them hearty greetings, and at feasts, the honored seats. And once they set aside their instruments, they had the status and the opportunity necessary to monopolize the company of the most desirable ladies. Slaves also recognized their instrumentalists by verbally acknowledging their position with the title "musicianer," by awarding individuals the sobriquet "fiddler" to be carried as part of their names, and by identifying them as musicians despite the fact that most players were burdened with other jobs.

The musicians' own perceptions of their special role, reinforced by their fellow bondsmen, reveal slaves who nurtured a sense of accomplishment and worth that flowed from the mastery of their instruments. Musicians took pride in their talent, boasted about their community standing, and never seemed to fail to flaunt their accomplishments. Charles Anderson, for example, claimed to have been "a great hand at fiddlin'." "Anything I heard once," he proclaimed, "I could play." And James Davis, a banjoist during "Civil War time," was also certain of his skill. He simply stated, "I use to be one of the best banjo pickers. I was good." Men such as these did not hesitate to identify themselves by their favored skill, even though the majority of them probably served their masters most of their days in the fields. When Jeptha Choice told an interviewer that his fellow slaves had a band on their Texas plantation, he added, "and I was one of the players."

Musicians clearly enjoyed a special place in the black community. Furthermore, they exhibited a sense of self-worth that surpassed any stereotyped notions of obsequious behavior. It is unclear, however, whether "musicianers" used their confidence and status to shape the events of the slave community in what their white contemporaries would have considered conventional ways. Still, despite the restrictions of slavery, they did influence the cultural and social fabric of black life, helped to ease the burden of slavery for their fellow bondsmen, and loosened their own chains with their music.

SELECTED BIBLIOGRAPHY

John W. Blassingame, "Status and Social Structure in the Slave Community: Evidence from New Sources," in Harry P. Owens, ed., *Perspectives and Irony in American Slavery* (1976); Paul A. Cimbala, "Fortunate Bondsmen: Black 'Musicianers' and Their Role as an Antebellum Southern Plantation Slave Elite," *Southern Studies*, 18 (1979), 291–303; Paul A. Cimbala, "Fortunate Bondsmen: Slave 'Musicianers' in the Antebellum Southern United States" (M.A. thesis, Emory University, 1977); Dena J. Epstein, *Sinful Tunes and Spirituals: Black Folk Music to the Civil War* (1977); Solomon Northup, *Twelve Years a Slave* (1854); Eileen Southern, *The Music of Black Americans: A History* (2nd ed., 1983).

PAUL A. CIMBALA

N

NAMES. " 'Give it up, Toby, you hear?' Kunta's face flushed with anger. 'Kunta Kinte!' 'I'm tellin' you, boy, you got to forgit all dat African talk. Make white folks mad an' scare niggers. Yo' name Toby.' "

One suspects that few of the millions of Americans who saw this scene acted out a decade ago in the television adaptation of Alex Haley's *Roots: The Saga of an American Family*, attached much significance to the refusal of an enslaved African to give up his African name. But this should not surprise since American historians were themselves just beginning to appreciate and write about slave names and naming practices in the mid-1970s. In the intervening decade, they have come to appreciate the overlooked significance of this complex subject. The names given to slaves, the extent to which slave parents named their own children,* the origins of the names given slaves or those they selected for themselves, the extent to which slaves had surnames, the impact of emancipation* on the names of the newly freed slaves—these and related questions speak directly to the larger and ongoing debate concerning the integrity and cohesiveness of the underground culture* slaves fashioned for their own psychic and physical well-being.

Notwithstanding their legal status as nonpersons, slaves had names, and they cared about their names and about the attitudes of whites to them. Many slaves brought to the colonies in the seventeenth and eighteenth centuries came from Spanish territories in the Caribbean. This area of recruitment accounts for the preponderance of Spanish (and to a lesser degree Portuguese) names given slaves, for example, Pedro, Francisco, Maria, and even "pickanniny," after the Portuguese or similar Spanish phrase, *pequeño-niño*, meaning "very little one." Conversely, when slaves were imported from an English colony—Jamaica or Barbados—they would have been given common English names like Jack, Kate, Peg, Tom, and Barbados-Mary. In South Carolina, which had a sizeable French Huguenot settlement,* slaves acquired French names like Pierot, François, and Espérance.

It would be misleading to draw hard and fast conclusions about slave place of origin, or even the places from which slaves had come, solely on the basis of their names. The names of slaves often tell us as much about the individuals who gave them as they do about the slaves themselves. The crude humor which led shipmasters, traders, and owners to draw upon ancient and modern history or mythology for names (Caesar, Hannibal, Jupiter, Cromwell, Robin Hood, for example), and the use, more than once, of Ape or Monkey for a name reveals an all too prevalent racist attitude of whites toward blacks. Biblical names were common, while other slaves were named after their occupation—cook, smith, miller—and still others after the area in which they resided—York, Warwick, Accoumac-Jack.

Whim, expediency, and the places from which slaves had come or were living, then, accounted for the names of many slaves imported in the seventeenth and eighteenth centuries. But white input in the naming of slaves—whatever the degree of involvement—does not reveal how slaves reacted to these given names, nor the extent to which slave parents named their children or used African names for them, nor even the number of slaves who took or were given family names. Herbert G. Gutman's observation about not making too much of the fact that most mid-nineteenth-century slaves had common Anglo-American given names is a sensible caveat if applied sensibly. Like a society's laws, which seldom reflect actual practice, public lists of given names leave unanswered the extent to which slaves developed an identity independent of the names they may have been given. Nor do such lists say much about the origins of these cognomens or of the number of slaves who took on family names.

The extent to which slaves named their children has been obscured by the powerful acculturative pressures exerted on them to adopt English, or English-sounding, names. Slaves reacted to this pressure by what may be described as creative compromise: they settled upon, or suitably modified, an English name whose *sound* was very nearly identical to an original African name. A man named Quack or Quock had probably been so named by his parents who had simply adopted the African Quaco, meaning a male born on Wednesday. Another slave accommodation was to adopt a direct English translation of a common African day-name. In place of Cuffee, from the Ashanti Kofi, the name given a male born on Friday, the slave would simply have been called Friday. There is no way to calculate how many of the English and English-sounding names had an African origin, but the number of African adaptations was much larger than previously suspected.

The same was true of slaves with surnames. Throughout the slavery period, considerable numbers of slaves had surnames—some with, many without, their masters' consent or knowledge. In taking a family name, slaves consciously went back in time to take the name of the first master they had had, or took the name of whites who had owned their parents or grandparents. What was important, as Eugene D. Genovese notes, is that "the name had to be 'real'; it had to embody a living history without which genuine identity could not have become possible.''

In many instances, the ex-slaves' choice of family names after emancipation revealed the ongoing concern for symbolic ties to older blood kin; alternatively, expediency and prudence prevailed. Ex-slaves wishing to apply for relief at the Freedmen's Bureau office needed to ''get a name,'' while others believed changing their family name—sometimes repeatedly—provided a margin of safety against possible reenslavement in the event, as one slave put it, ''the white folks get together and change their minds.''

As was true for so many other aspects of slave life—religion, language, and others—slave names were shaped in the crucible of black-white interaction out of which has been forged the single social chain we call American culture.

SELECTED BIBLIOGRAPHY

Wesley F. Craven, *White, Red, and Black: The Seventeenth-Century Virginian* (1971); Eugene D. Genovese, *Roll, Jordan, Roll: The World the Slaves Made* (1974); Herbert G. Gutman, *The Black Family in Slavery and Freedom, 1750–1925* (1976); Leon F. Litwack, *Been in the Storm So Long: The Aftermath of Slavery* (1979); Newbell Niles Puckett, *Black Names in America: Origins and Usage*, edited by Murray Heller (1975); George P. Rawick, ed., *The American Slave: A Composite Autobiography* (19 vols., 1972); and Peter H. Wood, *Black Majority: Negroes in Colonial South Carolina from 1670 through the Stono Rebellion* (1974).

                                                                  GEORGE A. LEVESQUE

NARRATIVES, SLAVE. The slave narrative occupies a special place in the evolution of nineteenth-century American literature and Afro-American ''high culture.'' It fastens upon black history and culture a unitary theme, joining the slave heritage to the American literary mainstream. The slave's personal account of his escape to freedom became a key literary metaphor—a paradigm of self-contradictory ideology. The genre underscores the constant tension in a slave society, where freedom for some is contingent on the bondage of others.

More than 6,000 slave narratives exist, ranging from full-length autobiography* to half-page interviews.* They appeared in three phases: 1760–1807, 1831–1865, and 1920–1930. These were periods of keen public interest in Afro-Americana, coinciding with the emergence of European antislavery, American antislavery,* and the Harlem Renaissance–Négritude movement, respectively. American slave narrative is a phenomenon somewhat unique in hemispheric slaveholding societies where, with few exceptions, even white autobiography is scant.

The bulk of narratives separate into two essential forms. First, conventional published autobiographies, numbering more than 135 accounts, date from the early eighteenth century. They extend from John Saffin's *Adam Negro's Tryall* (1703) to Booker T. Washington's* *Up from Slavery* (1901). The second category includes interviews given by ex-slaves in this century. About half the autobiographies appeared before, and half after, the Civil War. The former frequently were prepared with the assistance of white patrons, while most postbellum autobiographies were the products of unmediated ex-slave authorship. As many as ninety-three such accounts may be considered "authentic." They stress the themes of freedom, identity, and assimilation. Though righteous and moralistic, but not radical literature, they mirror the Western preoccupation with mobility, civic success, and the autonomous self.

In all, these works did well, both as genre and publishing venture, several having exceeded half a dozen editions. Unfortunately, only a handful of the earliest ones deal at all with the authors' African background and experiences.

The largest grouping of narratives consists of over 3,000 interviews with ex-slaves. These were initiated in 1929 by black researchers at Hampton and Tuskegee institutes and Southern and Fisk universities, and culminated in the Federal Writers' Project* of the Work Progress Administration (WPA). This agency dispatched a corps of "frankly amateur," mostly white male interviewers to collect 2,194 testimonies from ex-slaves in the 1930s. Most of the WPA interviews were edited and sent to the project's Washington office and then housed in the special collections division of the Library of Congress, where they languished thereafter, except for occasional perusal by folklorists.

A few writers excerpted and edited portions of the typescripts to convey some idea of their scope, flavor, and potential uses. Conspicuous among these were the project folklore director Benjamin Botkin's *Lay My Burden Down* (1945), Norman R. Yetman's *Life under the "Peculiar Institution"* (1970), and Julius Lester's *To Be a Slave* (1968). State historical studies were developed from the WPA efforts of the Virginia Writers' Project in *The Negro in Virginia* (1940) and by the Georgia Writers' Project in *Drums and Shadows* (1940), preparing the way for more comprehensive works such as Charles L. Perdue, Jr., et al., *Weevils in the Wheat* (1976) and Ronald Killion and Charles Waller's *Slavery Times When I Was Chillun* (1973), which deal with Virginia and Georgia, respectively.

Curiously, the WPA material drew little attention for nearly four decades—until the social ferment of the 1960s generated the necessary conditions for a corollary "democratization" of historical writing. Testimony from the "underside" of American history achieved scholarly validity, as the leading lights of slavery scholarship turned to the WPA narrative collection for fresh insights and evidence to support more radical hypotheses. With the publication of Eugene D. Genovese's *Roll, Jordan, Roll* (1974) and Paul D. Escott's *Slavery Remembered* (1979), the WPA material finally served as the basis for a comprehensive social history.

These works were facilitated by the editing achievement of George P. Rawick et al., who between 1972 and 1979 rendered the WPA typescripts into forty volumes in three series. Volumes 18 and 19 contain much of the material gathered by graduate students at Fisk University during the 1920s into some 200 interviews with ex-slaves in Tennessee and Kentucky. These had been partially issued in

1945 by Ophelia S. Egypt et al. as *The Unwritten History of Slavery* and by
A. B. Watson et al. as *God Struck Me Dead*.

The first supplement of twelve volumes, published in 1977, represents glean-
ings from regional archive and library holdings, including interviews and me-
morabilia of ex-slaves in local papers and other publications and manuscripts.
These materials derive from states generally unrepresented in the first nineteen
volumes and tend to compensate for the shortage of data from the border states
and Mississippi, where some WPA narratives may have been suppressed for
their unfavorable portrayal of slave masters.

Many of the accounts in the second and third sets, or supplements, of the
Rawick volumes are more disparate and fragmentary than those in the first set.
Given the notoriety of Louisiana's slave regime and the demographic and cultural
impact of Africans in the lower Mississippi–Gulf Coast region, the paucity of
Louisiana accounts that found their way into the WPA collection poses a significant lacuna, compensated only partly by an examination of the WPA materials
at the Louisiana State Library, Louisiana State University, Northwestern Louisiana State University, and Southern University. Virginia's WPA material likewise remained at home.

Recent studies have yet to exhaust the possibilities of the WPA narratives,
now accessible in the Rawick edition. They include a wide assortment of secular
and religious songs,* together with copious data on black genealogy,* regional
dialect,* and folk practice.* The collection reveals details of the social structure
and internal dynamics of American "slave society," the slaves' perceptions of
Reconstruction, and information concerning the nature of black-Indian relations
on the moving frontier.

The Rawick volumes lend themselves to myriad disciplinary and interpretive
schemata, though a wide sampling is often required to discern socioeconomic
patterns and trends that commonly interest researchers. Due to the primitive
methods applied in many of the interview situations and the varying quality of
responses elicited, the uneven character of the interviews is predictable. But at
the very minimum they serve to communicate a sense of the verve and immediacy
of a defunct idiom. They allow us to listen in, at least, on the "left" side of a
historical dialogue—the bottom half of the master-slave conversation.

Both the nineteenth-century ex-slave autobiographies and the Rawick volumes
present methodological problems to researchers. The former tend to overrepresent
the upper South and to underrepresent female slaves. Nor is it easy to dismiss
idiosyncracies following from the anomalous position of an ex-slave who was
at the same time a published author, a celebrity, and a member of society's
lowest caste. Though far more representative, the WPA-Rawick materials also
contain potentially misleading impressions. Two-thirds of the informants, for
instance, were at least eighty years old when queried. Their recollections of
slavery were drawn from childhood experiences, and their advanced age perhaps
inclined them to recall only the milder aspects of the slave condition.

Distortions also result from the skewed geographical distribution. For example, while only 7 percent of all slaves in 1860 lived in Arkansas and Texas, the 985 informants from those states make up 45 percent of the WPA interviews.

The interviewer's race seems also to have been a factor in conditioning responses. In WPA materials collected in Florida and in Tennessee and Kentucky (the Fisk interviews)—mostly by black researchers—informants spoke openly of their negative sentiments. The frequently uncritical posture of the generality of WPA informants, on the other hand, may suggest that slavery in childhood did not compare badly with the experience of abandonment and destitution among the aged poor during the Depression.

Although the two narrative variants—autobiography and interview—complement each other, scholars approach them with contrary methodological assumptions and disagree as to their proper utilization. As abolitionist reformers of the past century regarded the slave autobiography as proof of the sensibility and capacity for human perfection that blacks shared with whites, so today's critics of the American past point to the WPA narratives as prime evidence of a coherent "community" within the structures of slavery. There follows by implication the validity and indeed the centrality of Afro-American culture in the larger American experience. There remains, however, little consensus regarding either the exact contours of the "slave community" or what it is the ex-slaves' accounts really tell about it.

Next to African influences on American music, folklore, and humor, the slave narrative is Afro-America's most enduring contribution to the national culture. Due to the florid polemicizing in the narratives and such stylistic deficiencies as lengthy digression and stilted sentimentality, critics have generally regarded the autobiographies as a subliterature.* Whatever their aesthetic merits, they nevertheless stimulated the countergenre of the "plantation romance," and inspired major writers from Herman Melville through Mark Twain to Richard Wright and James Baldwin. Both narrative types make us mindful that a cogent representation of man's inhumanity cannot be realized without inclusion of the personal, subjective, even folklorist expression of that experience from the vantage point of the victims themselves.

SELECTED BIBLIOGRAPHY

John W. Blassingame, ed., *Slave Testimony: Two Centuries of Letters, Speeches, Interviews, and Autobiographies* (1977); Stephen Butterfield, *Black Autobiography in America* (1974); Stanley Feldstein, *Once a Slave: The Slave's View of Slavery* (1970); Frances Smith Foster, *Witnessing Slavery: The Development of Ante-bellum Slave Narratives* (1979); George P. Rawick, ed., *The American Slave: A Composite Autobiography* (19 vols., 1972; supplement, series 1, 12 vols., 1977; supplement, series 2, 10 vols., 1979); Marion W. Starling, *The Slave Narrative: Its Place in American Literary History* (1949); Robert B. Stepto, *From Behind the Veil: A Study of Afro-American Narratives* (1979);

and C. Vann Woodward, "History from Slave Sources," *American Historical Review*, 79 (1974), 470–481.

THOMAS FIEHRER

NASHOBA EXPERIMENT. Frances Wright (1795–1852), an upper-class Scotswoman with a passion for social reform, founded Nashoba in 1826 as an experimental alternative to slavery. The interracial colony was established on 2,000 acres of wilderness land twelve miles east of present-day Memphis, Tennessee. Among supporters of the experiment were the Marquis de Lafayette, Thomas Jefferson,* and Andrew Jackson.* Jackson helped Wright find the site for the colony.

Wright's basic scheme was to buy slaves, bring them into the new community, train them for freedom and self-sufficiency, and resettle them in a colony outside the United States. She hoped to demonstrate that slavery could be abolished without causing economic collapse, and also that well-intentioned whites and former slaves could enjoy freedom and equality in cooperative communities.

Nine whites and fifteen blacks made up the population of Nashoba when it was formally launched in the spring of 1826. A year later, when Wright went to Europe to seek financial support, the community was torn internally by inexperience, dissension, and lingering racial and social bias. It also was under attack from the outside as a radical threat to prevailing customs.

Frances Wright returned to defend the colony in 1828, but by June of that year most of the whites had departed. Wright herself soon followed, leaving thirty blacks there, uncertain of their status. She returned late in 1829 and, with Lafayette's help, escorted the blacks to the new nation of Haiti, where they were promised land and jobs. Three years after its founding, Nashoba was dead.

SELECTED BIBLIOGRAPHY

John Egerton, *Visions of Utopia: Nashoba, Rugby, Ruskin, and the "New Communities" in Tennessee's Past* (1977); and William H. Pease and Jane H. Pease, "A New View of Nashoba," *Tennessee Historical Quarterly*, 19 (1960), 99–109.

JOHN EGERTON

NAVAL STORES INDUSTRY. Slaves labored in a little-known aspect of Southern history—the naval stores industry—the production of tar, pitch, and turpentine. These were essential commodities for waterproofing wooden sailing vessels in colonial times. To achieve independence from Baltic sources, the British government paid bounties to colonial producers from 1705 until the American Revolution. The industry centered in the Carolinas because the long-leaf pine, native to the South, was the most prolific yielder of oleoresin.

Tar was the principal product, produced by gathering fragments of long-leaf pines from the ground, stacking them in a circular kiln thirty feet wide by ten feet high, covering the kiln with green pine boughs and earth, and by controlled burning forcing out the resinous matter which was barreled for market.

During the first three decades of the eighteenth century, naval stores production centered in the region between North Carolina's Cape Fear River and Charleston, South Carolina. Planters used slaves productively in winter in preparing and burning tar kilns. Overproduction caused a reduction of bounties in 1729, and South Carolina planters accordingly shifted their labor force to rice* and indigo* cultivation. Tar became principally a North Carolina product, produced primarily by small white farmers who lived in the pine barrens and worked unassisted.

For a generation after the American Revolution, production of naval stores declined, due to the loss of bounties and the introduction of cotton. In the 1830s the industry had a remarkable revival based upon the discovery of new uses for turpentine and more extensive use of slave labor. Crude turpentine, when distilled, yielded two valuable products: spirits of turpentine which was used as an illuminant to replace whale oil and as a solvent in the new rubber industry; and rosin, a by-product, which was used in the manufacture of fine soap and as a lubricant. Improvements in distilling in 1834 increased the yield, and repeal of British tariffs on turpentine in 1846 boosted prices. By the decade of the 1850s, naval stores had emerged as the South's third largest export crop.

With these inducements planters entered the business, buying or leasing thousands of acres of pine land, and using slave labor—either owned or hired* from neighboring planters—to conduct large-scale operations. In the early 1850s from four to five thousand laborers (not all slaves) were engaged in turpentine operations in North Carolina and perhaps three times that many were supported by the proceeds of the industry. In 1859–1860 100 slaves on the James R. Grist plantation near Mobile, Alabama, produced over 26,000 barrels of crude turpentine, yielding over 3,000 barrels of spirits of turpentine and 15,000 barrels of rosin, worth about $70,000. By 1860 the total value of crude and distilled turpentine produced in the United States was almost $7.5 million, over $5 million of which was produced in North Carolina. Derivative products brought the total value of the industry to almost $12 million.

In opening a turpentine plantation, a laborer was assigned a task* of trees to contain approximately 10,000 boxes and occupying from 50 to 100 acres of land. From October to March, "boxers" were busy cutting elliptical holes in the base of the trees that would hold a quart of turpentine. Above the box the tree was "cornered" by removing two triangular chips to form a V face. The flow of resin into the box then began. From April to October "chippers" returned each ten days to "chip" the face and reopen the wound to maintain the flow. "Dippers" visited the tree at intervals of two weeks to dip the turpentine from the box, using a flat, iron paddle. The turpentine was placed in wooden buckets that were emptied into barrels stationed throughout the woods. They were transported in two-wheeled carts to a distillery, located near a stream, for distillation into spirits of turpentine and rosin in the same manner in which whiskey was distilled. Nearby was a cooperage shop for making barrels. Boxing, coopering, and distilling were the most important aspects of the business, and each commanded a high wage. White distillers were always in demand, usually receiving $25 to $30 per month.

In 1860 a partnership of Grist and Stickney in eastern North Carolina hired thirty-five slaves from John W. Grist for turpentine production. Among these slaves were one distiller, an assistant distiller, two coopers for making barrels, fifteen hands engaged in chipping, a driver, two wagoners—all men—and eight dippers, including four men and four women. In addition there were four small boys, three of whom helped about the still, and one who assisted about the house. There was a woman cook and two elderly women who sewed when able or, according to the contract, did "Nothing."

When slaves were hired, the owner usually specified that the slave should be furnished three suits of clothes (one of which was to be woolen), one pair of stockings, one hat and blanket, one pair of shoes, "and Two if worked in Turpentine. . . . All to be well made." In the 1850s the average price for hiring slaves for turpentine production was about $125 annually, plus board and clothing, but by 1860 the price had doubled.

Because of the skill of North Carolina slaves trained in turpentine operations, they were sometimes hired and transported to other parts of the state, even to Florida and Alabama, to open new turpentine plantations. Owners usually sought the consent of their slaves to be sent to another area to work turpentine before committing them to a planter.

Some planters encouraged their slaves to do good work by giving them an honorarium for a crop well attended, or by giving them a task and paying for the additional work after the task had been completed. Some permitted them to build a tar kiln on their own time and to sell the tar.

The turpentine business was considered extremely favorable to health* and long life. The pure air of the pine forest was considered salubrious for pulmonary diseases.* Slaves engaged in turpentine operations were said to be healthier, happier, and more intelligent than those engaged in other pursuits. Turpentine plantation slaves worked as part of a production team, yet at an individual task, rather than in gang labor.* This may have contributed to a sense of independence, responsibility, and greater contentment. One writer noted, " . . . it is equally as healthy, and no set of hands have ever been known to willingly leave it and go back to cotton."

SELECTED BIBLIOGRAPHY

C. C. Crittenden, *The Commerce of North Carolina, 1763–1789* (1936); Lewis C. Gray, *History of Agriculture in the Southern United States to 1860* (2 vols., 1933); John Macleod, "The Tar and Turpentine Business of North Carolina," *Journal of Agriculture*, 2 (1846), 13–19; Frederick Law Olmsted, *A Journey in the Seaboard Slave States with Remarks on Their Economy* (1856); Percival Perry, ''The Naval Stores Industry in the Ante-bellum South, 1789–1861'' (Ph.D. dissertation, Duke University, 1947).

PERCIVAL PERRY

NEW ENGLAND, SLAVERY IN. New England slavery was something of a paradox, a series of paradoxes, in fact. The international slave trade* increased the fortunes of many local merchants, but the region's black population was never very large. Slavery was insignificant in the overall New England economy, but it was crucial in certain trades and establishments. It was characterized by more freedoms and milder conditions than elsewhere, but under the surface of life slavery in New England was a bubbling cauldron of violence and retribution.

Even the words *slave* and *slavery* had confusing applications in colonial New England. When used as a description of the status of criminals and war prisoners, as an indictment of government and authority, or as socially derogatory terms, *slave* and *slavery* applied to whites as well as blacks. *Slave* was also employed interchangeably with *servant*, and in reference to all blacks regardless of status, making it difficult to know just who among the seventeenth- and eighteenth-century population was bound, to what extent, or was a free person.

Several censuses and population estimates prior to the American Revolution establish that blacks never were more than 2.5 percent of the New England population. By the 1770s there were nineteen blacks in Vermont, .04 percent of the total population. New Hampshire had 519, or 1.1 percent; Massachusetts (including Maine) 5,249, or 1.8 percent; Connecticut 6,464, or 3.2 percent; and Rhode Island 3,761, or 6.3 percent.

The comparatively high figures for Connecticut and Rhode Island suggest that had their topography and climate* resembled the South's, slavery might have taken firmer hold in these colonies. Its relative importance in Rhode Island can be explained by three principal factors: the slave-trading and commercial significance of Newport, the rum distilling industry, and large-scale agriculture around Narragansett Bay. Reliance on rum as a medium of exchange in the international slave trade and as a popular domestic drink made it especially ironic that Rhode Island Africans engaged in its manufacture played an unwilling role in the capture of their overseas brethren.

Extensive farms in the Connecticut River valley, in the eastern portion of the colony, and in the Narragansett country of southern Rhode Island—averaging 300 acres in the mid-eighteenth century—account for the densest African populations in New England. Dairying and cattle raising were the major slave activities, but sheep, horse, vegetable, and tobacco* production were also important. Some wealthy whites on the largest farms owned up to fifty slaves. Robert Hazard, a South Kingston, Rhode Island, dairy farmer, for example, employed twenty-four slave women* in his creamery alone.

Elsewhere in New England Africans worked at almost every occupation. After agriculture, domestic service seems to have been their most common occupation, followed by skilled and unskilled labor in manufactures and trades. Positioned between the slave metalworkers employed on Newport's Touro Synagogue at the upper end of the ladder, and the Boston chimney sweeps and lemon sellers at the bottom, were coopers, tailors, carpenters, printers, ship caulkers, and other artisans that formed a complex occupational slave hierarchy. Slavery as an institution might not have been essential to the New England economy, but individual slaves proved vitally important in its every nook and cranny.

Except on some large farms where they were grouped separately after the Southern fashion, most slaves lived in their owners' homes, often sharing their tables. Many bondsmen attended and were members of the Puritan churches. By all accounts—contemporary and modern—slavery in New England was less brutal than elsewhere. One indication was the slaves' relative equity in the judicial system. New England slaves convicted of crimes generally were given the same punishments* as whites for the same offenses, and in court slaves had full legal rights except the right to serve on juries. Indeed, after 1701 slave plaintiffs won almost every manumission suit they initiated, culminating with the 1783 judicial declaration ending slavery in Massachusetts. Other New England states soon emulated this abolition decree.

Despite these comparatively liberal arrangements, tension and terror lurked near the surface of slave life in New England. As elsewhere, resistance* to slavery in New England took many forms, from violent retaliation against individual whites to organized efforts to end the peculiar institution itself. An incident recorded in the *Boston News-Letter*, 9 June 1763, illustrates a number of important points:

A most shocking Murder was committed last Saturday at Taunton [Mass.], by a Negro Fellow belonging to Dr. McKinstry;—a Sister of the Doctor's getting up early in the Morning to iron Cloaths, the Negro (after making a Fire) got his Master's horse, and left him at the Door, and finding an Opportunity took up a hot Flat Iron, with which he struck the Woman on the Back of her Head, and stunned her, he repeated the Blow, then dragged her down in the Cellar, and there with an old Ax, struck her several times; he then took the hot Iron and rubb'd over her Face, flicking the Point of it into her Eyes, whereby she was scorch'd considerably; after he had done this, he took the Horse and rode off— The Family soon got up and found the Woman in the above Condition; she continued till the Evening of the next Day; and then died: the Negro was pursued, and taken up at Newport [R.I.], and confessed the Fact,—What induced the Fellow to perpetrate this Crime is not known, as he was always treated well, and there had been no Difference with him in the Family.

Episodes like these were common: poisoning, arson, murder, and assault revealed profound discontent among blacks, and equally profound fear and incomprehension among whites, illustrated when another newspaper, commenting on the above-mentioned affair, staunchly maintained that most blacks had no complaints against their owners. Retaliation and protest were simply "the bad Effects of Negroes too freely consorting together."

New England slaves did indeed consort together in an effort to escape constant white control. So-called alley society existed wherever there was an appreciable community of free people, slaves, free blacks, and white servants. Pleasure seeking such as eating and drinking together in out-of-the-way places—in water-side warehouses and isolated mid-block buildings, for example—was common. More solemn occasions such as funerals and burials,* on the other hand, demonstrated in singing and dancing a lingering West African commitment to the continuation of life after death. Blacks of varying status mingled freely on these occasions, revealing a degree of social cohesion surprising to whites.

In southern New England blacks in certain towns, sometimes of an entire colony, banded together on Election Day at the end of May each year to choose a "governor" or "king" at an inaugural festival featuring games, singing, dancing, and storytelling. The governor and his appointed advisors adjudicated minor disputes among blacks and even on occasion between blacks and whites. The principal function of these activities, however, was to perpetuate African cultural traditions in a rough approximation of West African political and judicial rule by a chief and council of elders. Surviving from about 1750 into the 1830s, Election Day was a ceremonial assertion of black ethnic pride.

Blacks also consorted together to petition for their freedom. In the revolutionary era* particularly, and especially in and around Boston, bound and free blacks approached the colonial government at least a dozen times using the libertarian rhetoric of the independence movement. One 1773 appeal was particularly telling. After outlining the detrimental effects of slavery on family ties, morality, and freedom of worship, the petitioners claimed as their own the "natural rights" of white people, pointing out correctly that no local laws had ever legalized their bondage. Foregoing any claims to financial compensation, they made two demands: "some part of the unimproved land, belonging to the province, for a settlement," or, failing that, transportation "to our native country within a short time."

The impulse toward separation—on an American land grant or home in Africa—ran through the entire slavery period in New England. Blacks utilized other less spectacular ways—alley society, funerals, Election Day, and more—to gain as much independence from whites as possible. Despite the relatively mild facade of New England slavery, the impulse toward self-determination always was present.

And when this was difficult, as it usually was, blacks resorted to violence, sometimes, to affirm their humanity. From individual retaliations to collective action in pursuit of freedom, New England's slaves, servants, and free people never acquiesced to the peculiar institution.

SELECTED BIBLIOGRAPHY

Lorenzo J. Greene, *The Negro in Colonial New England, 1620–1776* (1942); Edgar J. McManus, *Black Bondage in the North* (1973); William D. Piersen, "Afro-American Culture in Eighteenth-Century New England" (Ph.D. dissertation, Indiana University,

1975); Joseph P. Reidy, " 'Negro Election Day' & Black Community Life in New England, 1750–1860," *Marxist Perspectives*, 1 (1978), 102–117; Richard Slotkin, "Narratives of Negro Crime in New England, 1675–1800," *American Quarterly*, 25 (1973), 3–31; and Arthur Zilversmit, *The First Emancipation: The Abolition of Slavery in the North* (1967).

ROBERT TWOMBLY

NEW ORLEANS, LA, SLAVERY IN. Slaves lived in New Orleans from its very beginning. In 1721, just three years after the city was founded on a broad curve in the Mississippi River, there were nearly a hundred slaves in New Orleans, a quarter of whom were Indians.* Fifty years later some Indians were still among the city's slaves, but the vast majority of the 1,300 bondsmen living on the "Island of New Orleans" were now Africans who had come directly from Africa, particularly the Senegambia hinterland, or from the French West Indies. Natural reproduction accounted for some increase in the city's slave population, but throughout the colonial period of French and Spanish rule the number of slaves remained relatively small as the fledgling colony struggled along with tobacco,* rice,* and indigo* in its search for a viable cash crop. At the time of the Louisiana Purchase in 1803, less than 3,000 slaves lived in New Orleans.

Slavery expanded dramatically in New Orleans during the nineteenth century. The successful cultivation of sugar* and cotton* allowed New Orleans to grow as a service and administrative center as well as the major entrepôt for the entire Mississippi Valley. In the first twenty years of American rule the city's slave population doubled, and by 1840 more slaves lived in New Orleans than in any other Southern city at any time prior to the Civil War. But 1840 also marked the first time since 1721 that slaves accounted for less than a quarter of the city's total population; indeed, nearly half of the city's inhabitants had been slaves in 1806. After 1840 the number of slaves declined steadily, and in 1860 slaves constituted only 8 percent of the city's total population. Despite this numerical decline, which was largely the result of tremendous demand for slave labor on rural plantations, slavery remained a vital institution in the Crescent City. In 1859 the conservatively assessed value of the city's slaves was over $6 million. A year later Orleans Parish was the third largest slaveholding parish in Louisiana, and only a hundred slaves away from being the second largest.

The slaves of Orleans Parish were distributed among a large number of slaveholders. Although slaveholders as a percentage of the total free population declined after 1830 because of the dramatic growth of the white population, the total number of slaveholders increased during the nineteenth century. In 1860 there were 4,169 slaveholders in Orleans Parish. A handful of them—often slave traders who contributed to making New Orleans the greatest slave market in the antebellum South—owned twenty or more slaves. A third of them owned only one slave, half owned two or fewer, and over

Table 1
Population of New Orleans

Year	Slaves	Free Negroes	Whites	Total
1721	94	--	278	372
1771	1,288	99	1,803	3,190
1785	1,631	563	2,826	5,020
1791	1,589	862	2,065	4,516
1805	3,105	1,566	3,551	8,222
1806	8,378	2,312	6,311	17,001
1810	5,961	4,950	6,331	17,242
1820	7,355	6,237	13,584	27,176
1830	9,462	8,018	12,214	29,694
1840	23,448	19,226	59,519	102,193
1850	17,011	9,905	89,459	116,375
1860	13,385	10,689	144,601	168,675

two-thirds owned three or fewer. Most slave owners were white, but the city's large free Negro* population—slaves and free Negroes joined to make New Orleans a black city from 1790 until 1840—also produced a significant number of slave owners. In 1805 free Negroes constituted 15 percent of the city's slaveholders, and they owned 10 percent of the city's slaves. In 1830, 752 free Negroes held 2,354 slaves, and like the predominantly white slave-holders of Orleans Parish in 1860, over two-thirds of them owned three or fewer slaves.

During the eighteenth century slaves resided primarily in the European section of the city below Canal Street. In the nineteenth century this pattern gradually changed as the American section of the city expanded and increasing numbers of slaves were taken uptown. Wherever they lived, most slaves tended to be housed within the master's compound. Within these compounds, however, treatment varied considerably from master to master, and there is little evidence that the city's Latin heritage significantly tempered slavery or improved race relations. What made slavery in New Orleans relatively mild compared to slavery in rural Louisiana was the variety, density, fluidity, and opportunity of urban life. As valets, butlers, carriage drivers, stevedores, draymen, domestics (the great majority of the city's slaves were women), and so forth, slaves traveled well beyond the master's compound. They carved out a unique existence that included speaking Creole French, singing African songs, dancing in Congo Square, practicing Vodun,* hiring out* their own labor, purchasing their own freedom, and absconding. It was this liberating dimension of urban bondage that provoked a slave from rural Louisiana to confide to Frederick Law Olmsted that he "would rather live in New Orleans than any other place in the world."

But the city's urban environment could only partially ameliorate the physical and psychological oppression inherent in a labor system based upon one man owning another. A New Orleans slave was still the property of his master and generally subject to his whims and wishes. Although he undoubtedly fared better than his country cousin, he typically remained illiterate, unskilled, impoverished, sickly, and dependent. To the famed architect Benjamin Henry Latrobe, slavery in New Orleans was a perverse system where one found "cruelty & confidence, cowhiding & caressing perfectly in accord with one another."

SELECTED BIBLIOGRAPHY

Claudia Dale Goldin, *Urban Slavery in the American South, 1820–1860: A Quantitative History* (1976); John S. Kendall, "New Orleans' 'Peculiar Institution,' " *Louisiana Historical Quarterly*, 23 (1940), 864–886; David C. Rankin, "The Tannenbaum Thesis Reconsidered: Slavery and Race Relations in Antebellum Louisiana," *Southern Studies*, 18 (1979), 5–31; Robert C. Reinders, "Slavery in New Orleans in the Decade before the Civil War," *Mid-America*, 44 (1962), 211–221; Judith Kelleher Schafer, "New Orleans Slavery in 1850 as Seen in Advertisements," *Journal of Southern History*, 47

(1981), 33–56; Richard C. Wade, *Slavery in the Cities: The South, 1820–1860* (1964); and Charles Herman Woessner, "New Orleans, 1840–1860: A Study in Urban Slavery" (M.A. thesis, Louisiana State University, 1967).

DAVID C. RANKIN

NEWPORT, RI, SLAVERY IN. In all likelihood, slavery was first introduced into the colony of Rhode Island at Newport, principal port of the province. The institution's genesis occurred without dire economic warrant and despite a 1652 statute that excluded men of Roger Williams's generation from the "common course practised amongst English men to buy negers," by limiting bonded service to ten years. Twenty-four years later, Williams himself undermined that act by prescribing enslavement and sale for Indians* captured in King Philip's War.

Aware of this legal wedge or not, some Newport merchants trading to the West Indies soon began sporadically to include a slave or two in their return cargoes of sugar and molasses. By default the latter item had become the colony's surrogate staple, an economic "engine" sold locally and exported along the Atlantic littoral either as raw syrup or distilled rum.

For the Caribbean slaves arriving in Newport on the sugar shuttles, slavery most often meant domestic service. By 1708, a Newport census enumerated 220 "blacks." Two years later, in response to news that the town was 10 percent black, critics surfaced with the cry that slavery would discourage "the importing of white servants." A succession of import duties on slaves quickly followed.

Undeterred by taxes or racist propaganda from nonslaveholders, leading merchants again looked to the West Indies where they saw a trading strategy that simultaneously offered a vast new market for rum and a new source for slaves. Caribbean "separate traders" who shuttled rum to England's West African forts provided the model, and Newport's mercantile elite—the Vernons, Thurstons, Scotts, and Malbones—began mimicking them. Because the Newporters embarked from Rhode Island, their trade in rum, slaves, and molasses necessarily assumed a triangular configuration. From the 1720s until federal statute outlawed the trade on 1 January 1808, Newport "rum-men" navigated the "notorious triangle" more often than any American competitor.

A new source brought a new kind of slave to Newport. For forty years, slaves coming through the Newport customhouse arrived "raw" from Africa, and thereby avoided the subtle process of assimilation undergone by their Caribbean predecessors. The result of this infusion of African stock was a revitalization of the African component of local black culture.

Obviously bicultural, Newport slaves at mid-century had accomplished assimilation in both parallel and syncretic fashion. Bilingualism illustrates the former, customs such as Negro Election Day, the June role reversal celebration with African antecedents, the latter. While a conspicuous few practiced a maritime trade, received a rudimentary education or a new religion, most slaves continued to work as domestics or unskilled laborers, learned fluent English but remained illiterate, and never became Christians.

Not surprisingly, when highly acculturated ex-slaves founded their first free black institution in the wake of the Revolution, the long-standing cultural duality persisted. The Newport African Union Society (1780) therefore simultaneously espoused mutual aid, Protestant values, and a return to Africa. Occasionally, one of their number, such as longtime leader Newport Gardner, who retained his African dialect so that "he might return to Africa, and find a people with whom he might converse with intelligibly," realized that lifetime goal. In 1826, at eighty, Gardner (aka Occramer Marycoo) sailed for Liberia.*

SELECTED BIBLIOGRAPHY

Charles Battle, *Negroes on the Island of Rhode Island* (1932); Jay Coughtry, *The Notorious Triangle: Rhode Island and the African Slave Trade, 1700–1807* (1981); Lorenzo Greene, *The Negro in Colonial New England, 1620–1776* (1942); William D. Johnston, "Slavery in Rhode Island, 1755–1776," *Publications of the Rhode Island Historical Society* (1894), 113–164; and Edgar J. McManus, *Black Bondage in the North* (1973).

JAY COUGHTRY

NEW YORK CITY, NY, SLAVERY IN. For two centuries New York City exploited the labor of blacks under a slave system that did not legally end until 1827. The first African slaves were brought in by the Dutch in 1629, when New York was still New Amsterdam, and they continued to be imported throughout the New Netherland period. Because the free Dutch settlers preferred the fur trade to the harder and less profitable tasks of farming and basic economic development, the Dutch West India Company, the governing colonial body, turned to slavery as an alternative form of labor. The company was involved in slave trading* as well as colonizing, and it was hoped that blacks imported from Angola and Curaçao would provide the labor needed for economic progress and increase the company's trading profits. The slaves brought to New Amsterdam performed many essential tasks for which free workers were generally unavailable. They raised food for the local garrison and kept the military works guarding the town in repair. Their labor helped transform what had been a shaky trading outpost into a permanent settlement.

Slavery in New Amsterdam was not characterized by the corrosive racism that embittered relations between whites and blacks in other places. The pragmatic Dutch regarded it as an economic expedient, not a system of social organization, and they enacted no laws* derogating slaves racially or setting them apart as a special subgroup in the population. Slaves had full legal standing to testify in the courts not only against one another but against free whites. The West India Company granted a status known as "half-freedom" to some of its slaves in return for goods and services. Half-free blacks had legal obligations to the company, but they also had the same rights and liberties of other free people. The arrangement relieved the company of the costs and problems of managing slaves full-time without giving up the benefits of their labor.

When New Amsterdam passed to English control and became New York City in 1664, the new government strongly supported the importation of slaves. The use of black labor increased under the English until by the middle of the eighteenth century New York City and its surrounding counties had the largest slave force of any colony north of Maryland. Slaves were advertised in all the city newspapers, and public sales were held weekly, sometimes daily in the principal markets. There was a wide diffusion of small-scale slaveholding, typically one or two slaves per owner, that promoted the adaptation of slavery to virtually every economic activity. Slaves acquired proficiency in most occupations, and some of them matched the skills of the best white artisans. They worked as tailors, bakers, coopers, tanners, masons, carpenters, blacksmiths, weavers, sailmakers, tobacconists, brushmakers, glaziers, and goldsmiths. Nothing would have distinguished them from free workers except for the fact that they worked for the benefit of others. They were so integrated in the work force that some were hired out* for wages by their owners, a practice bitterly resented by whites with whom they successfully competed for employment.

Highly skilled slaves usually had considerable bargaining power. Their skills could not be exploited efficiently by coercion alone, so various concessions were made in order to obtain their cooperation. Not every slave could bargain effectively, for the ability to do so depended on many things, but enough privileges were won to bring a spirit of give-and-take to the slave system generally. Slaves were usually allowed to work for their own benefit during time off, and some used the opportunity to buy their way out of slavery. Their everyday treatment was probably no worse than that of white indentured servants.* The latter, because their indentures were limited, often had to work a full seven-day week, while the slaves generally had one day off for rest and relaxation.

New York City blacks resisted slavery from the beginning, and their resistance cut deeply into the profitability of the system. Slave owners had to contend with everything from malingering and running away to plots and armed revolt.* An uprising in 1712 (*see* New York Negro Plots) cost a number of white lives and left no illusions about the true feelings of the slaves. A suspected conspiracy in 1741 (*see* New York Negro Plots) threw the city into a panic that did not end until over thirty persons, including four whites, had been executed. Seventy-two slaves suspected of complicity in the plot were deported to other colonies. There is no credible evidence that a conspiracy in fact existed, but the affair cast a permanent pall over slave relations. By the time the process of legal abolition began in the late eighteenth century, most New Yorkers realized that slavery for blacks meant fear and insecurity for whites.

SELECTED BIBLIOGRAPHY

Thomas J. Davis, *A Rumor of Revolt: The "Great Negro Plot" in Colonial New York* (1985); Samuel McKee, *Labor in Colonial New York, 1664–1776* (1935); Edgar J.

McManus, *A History of Negro Slavery in New York* (1966); Edgar J. McManus, *Black Bondage in the North* (1973); and Ansel Judd Northup, *Slavery in New York* (1900).

EDGAR J. MCMANUS

NEW YORK NEGRO PLOTS. Shortly after midnight on 6 April 1712, at least twenty-five blacks set fire to a building in New York City's east ward. Armed with a few pistols, knives, axes, and staves, they ambushed whites who rushed into the night to fight the fire. Eight white men died on the spot, and about two dozen white men in all became casualties in the surprise attack that ended when Governor Robert Hunter dispatched troops to the scene. The blacks fled northward under cover of darkness, but at dawn whites scoured the island's woods and brought back six blacks dead and nineteen others who were tried and executed: fourteen were hanged, two were burned at the stake, one was roasted alive for eight to ten hours, another was broken on the wheel, and the last was strung up and starved to death over three days.

Muttering citizens blamed the uprising in part on the Reverend Elias Neau, who ran a school for blacks which allegedly made them surly. But more substantial tensions lay in the fact that between 1703 and 1712 the number of blacks had increased significantly and that all 185 slaves imported to the city in 1710–1712 came directly from Africa, contrasting with the period 1701–1704 when the 225 imports had slaved elsewhere and thus been seasoned before arriving in the city. The captured rebels in 1712 proved to have been imported directly from Africa, and by 1714 the city shifted back to importing seasoned slaves—at least none of the fifty-three imported that year came directly from Africa.

By the time of what became known as the "Great Slave Plot" or the "New York Conspiracy" of 1741, almost one in every five of the city's 11,000 residents was black, as at least 1,429 slaves were imported to the city between 1730 and 1740. White workingmen complained about competition from the increasing number of slaves, and the tensions of King George's War (1739–1748) also heightened popular insecurities in 1741, as Queen Anne's War (1702–1713) had in 1712.

When the governor's residence and all of Fort George burned to the ground in New York City on 18 March 1741, and a three-week rash of fires followed, citizens suspicious of slaves began to shout, "the negroes are rising!" A five-month long investigation spearheaded by New York Supreme Court Justice Daniel Horsmanden linked the fires to an illicit ring of blacks and whites that officials alleged had plotted to plunder the city. Although the officials' evidence and logic were fundamentally flawed, during a series of trials—including that of John Ury, a schoolteacher accused of being a Roman Catholic priest—they convinced the jurors that there was a grand conspiracy. Wholesale convictions and executions followed: thirteen blacks were burned at the stake, and seventeen more were hanged, along with Ury and three other whites. Seventy-two blacks were banished.

Underlying the tensions in 1712 and 1741 was the fact that colonial New York City, which occupied only lower Manhattan Island with its total area of twenty-two square miles, had the highest slave population density of any major urban area in the British colonies in North America. Indeed, on the eve of the American Revolution, the city's black population ranked second in size to that of Charleston, South Carolina, where there were 5,833 blacks in a total population of 10,863 in 1770. New York City had 3,137 blacks in its total population of 21,863 in 1771. The proportion of blacks in New York City in 1771 (14.3 percent) was about equal to what it was in 1703 (14.4 percent) but was significantly lower than it was in 1746, when 20.8 percent of the city's population was black.

SELECTED BIBLIOGRAPHY

Thomas J. Davis, *A Rumor of Revolt: The "Great Negro Plot" in Colonial New York* (1985); Thomas J. Davis, "The New York Slave Conspiracy of 1741 as Black Protest," *Journal of Negro History*, 56 (1971), 17–30; Thomas J. Davis, "New York's Long Black Line: A Note on the Growing Slave Population, 1626–1790," *Afro-Americans in New York Life and History*, 2 (1978), 41–59; Daniel Horsmanden, *The New York Conspiracy, or A History of the Negro Plot*, edited by Thomas J. Davis (1971); and Kenneth Scott, "The Slave Insurrection in New York in 1712," *New-York Historical Society Quarterly*, 45 (1961), 43–74.

THOMAS J. DAVIS

NONSLAVEHOLDING WHITES. For those who view Afro-American slavery fundamentally as a system of race oppression, nonslaveholders in the free white population raise knotty problems that cannot easily be explained away. Not only were nonslaveholding whites to be found in every slave society in the Western Hemisphere, but they always constituted the majority of whites, whether on dense sugar plantation islands such as Barbados and Saint-Domingue or in more demographically and economically diverse lands such as Brazil and Cuba. Their very presence highlights the complex social relations that shaped the formation and maturation of New World slavery: almost everywhere black slavery emerged from an array of forced labor arrangements that pressed upon poor whites as well as Indians and Africans, and that derived from European precedents owing nothing to race. If the consolidation of racial bondage ultimately served to secure whites who did not own slaves from legal servitude, and, in some cases, to strengthen their claims to the liberties enjoyed by their social betters, the early origins and struggles of nonslaveholders left a deep and lasting imprint.

Nowhere were the origins and struggles of nonslaveholders of greater consequence or their role in slave society of greater importance than in the American South. As English indentured servants,* they comprised the bulk of the labor force in the seventeenth-century Chesapeake and, to a lesser extent, contributed to the settlement and early development of South Carolina. By the 1670s they had stirred all manner of unrest in Virginia and then, together with white freemen, swelled the ranks of the most serious popular rebellion in colonial history. As Scots-Irish and German migrants, they filled much of the eighteenth-century

Southern backcountry and, fired by the Quaker* or evangelical Baptist* faiths, some challenged the institutions and pretensions of the tidewater gentry. In the nineteenth century, nonslaveholders helped carry through sweeping democratic reforms in the lower South, inspired the Virginia slavery debates of 1831–32,* wrote the few Southern antislavery tracts of the 1840s and 1850s, and generally made their presence felt on political life in all parts of the South. On the eve of the Civil War,* their numbers nearly equaled those of the slaveholders and slaves combined and their unclear loyalties gave secessionist leaders cause for concern. During the war itself, their growing disaffection served to hasten the Confederacy's* collapse.

Southern nonslaveholders were by no means uniform and perpetual antagonists of the slaveholders and slave regime, however. They were, in fact, a diverse lot in occupation, fortune, experience, and sensibility, and even as a group their numerical significance changed over time. As slavery took hold in the Southern colonies and the slave population began to reproduce itself naturally during the eighteenth century, large numbers of white households passed into the status of slave ownership, particularly in the plantation regions of Maryland, Virginia, Georgia, and the Carolinas. By the turn of the nineteenth century perhaps one-third of the white families throughout the South owned slaves. Indeed, in the early national period slave ownership appears most firmly to have linked whites in countryside and town, as geographical* expansion thrust the chattel system deep into the interior and a substantial portion of urban artisans either owned or hired* slaves. Thereafter, the steady rise in slave prices* and the influx of European immigrants* into Southern cities reversed the trend. By 1860, slaveholders accounted for only one-quarter of all white families.

But if nonslaveholders composed a growing portion of the Southern white population as the nineteenth century wore on, a good many had some experience as slave masters, derived direct benefits from slave labor, or carved out an economically and socially viable niche in the slaveholding order. More than a few white household heads began their adult lives without slaves but eventually succeeded in purchasing or inheriting them. Others owned slaves for a time and then, due to personal or financial misfortune, had to sell out. Still others moved into and out of the relation of slave owning on more than one occasion. That most slaveholders owned only a slave or two suggests considerable fluidity.

To be sure, the majority of Southern whites who started out in life as nonslaveholders remained nonslaveholders. And yet, in a variety of ways, slavery defined the boundaries of their social worlds. In the plantation districts, for example, nonslaveholders often were tied by kinship to members of the master class or, at minimum, commonly relied on slaveholders and their slaves for a range of services and opportunities, if not for their very livelihoods. Farmers carried on numerous exchanges with slave-owning neighbors, whether in small quantities of foodstuffs and livestock, in the ginning and marketing of cotton, or in seasonal swap work when slaves would be borrowed or hired. Rural artisans and country storekeepers depended on slave-based farms and plantations for much of their trade, even if the more substantial slaveholders made large purchases from Northern and European suppliers. Landless whites did odd jobs for slave owners or perhaps rented tracts of land from them. In nearby towns and in more distant port cities, furthermore, merchants, factors, and lawyers staked their fortunes on the slaveholders' business if they did not make their way into the slaveholding class themselves. It was the very availability of white nonslaveholders to perform such functions essential to the slave economy that accounts, in large part, for the limited size and precarious status of the free black population in the South. In most other New World slave societies, where blacks heavily outnumbered whites, free blacks* found a real foothold in the service sector.

As might be expected, nonslaveholders occupied the middling and lower reaches of the Southern social structure. The vast majority could be found in the countryside working small farms that they owned or leased, or, less frequently, hiring on as overseers* and farm laborers for the year, month, week, or stint. Others had small shops, livery stables, or inns at crossroads hamlets and interior market towns. And in the larger towns and cities there were, particularly during the antebellum decades, growing numbers of artisans and mechanics as well as a floating class of day laborers whose rough and tumble plebeian world included urban slaves and free people of color. Relatively few nonslaveholders, especially in the rural districts, matched the stereotype of declassé "poor white trash," for if they did not own land they usually had close connections to landowning families. Even so, their lives were generally governed by long hours of labor, fairly rude conditions of shelter and diet, widespread economic uncertainty, and the ever-present threat of real hardship.

Exceptions, of course, there were: an occasional large landowner who had no slaves and, more likely, some prosperous commission merchants, professionals, politicians, and master craftsmen who resided in urban areas and chose not to invest in slaves. But the route to prosperity normally demanded slave ownership and, thus, nonslaveholders, almost by definition, had not proceeded very far along it.

The divisions among nonslaveholders were not only occupational. To understand their class experiences and the ways in which slavery shaped the dynamics of Southern society as a whole, it is necessary to distinguish between plantation and nonplantation regions and between the upper and lower South. For although nonslaveholders in the plantation districts were drawn most tightly into the orbit of the dominant slaveholding culture, the great majority of them lived in areas in which slaves and plantations were rather scarce: in areas ranging from the pine lands of Mississippi, South Carolina, and Georgia to the hill country of Alabama, Texas, and Louisiana, to the mountains and valleys of western North Carolina and Virginia and eastern Kentucky and Tennessee. Even in the plantation regions, nonslaveholders often clustered in upland settlements set off from the larger aggregations of slaveholders and slaves.

The locales in which nonslaveholders predominated normally were characterized by less skewed distributions of wealth, less involvement in the market economy, and more of an egalitarian ethos than was true in the plantation districts. Whether in the upper or lower South, such locales welcomed planters and slaves without much enthusiasm, less because of any moral or political opposition to slavery than because of the mix of extreme domination and dependency associated with that relationship; antiplanter, antiaristocratic rhetoric struck responsive chords. Whether in the upper or lower South, too, such locales tended to place strong emphasis on semisubsistence agriculture and local exchanges of goods and services. But in the upper South, and notably in the border states, economic activity either created ties—at times rather intricate—to the North or proved less reliant on the slave regime, so that Whiggish politics and Unionism came to establish a substantial base.

The traditions of independence and political truculence that were apparent among nonslaveholding whites in the seventeenth century thus continued to ripple through the South. As late as the 1850s, Charleston artisans could burn proslavery theorist George Fitzhugh* in effigy. Yet, in point of fact, few nonslaveholders ever challenged the institution of slavery directly, and by the nineteenth century, what little organized opposition had existed simply dissipated. It is not surprising that the isolated antislavery voices* came chiefly from the upper South, but even there they met hostile receptions: one of them provoked mob violence in the streets of Louisville. Indeed, although slave ownership sharpened social divisions among whites, slavery as a system served to limit the trajectory of white social antagonisms.

The racial dimensions of slavery, of course, created a certain cohesiveness among Southern whites. The democratization of the political process not only brought all adult white males into the political community but also very much strengthened the notion that slavery gave nonslaveholders and slaveholders alike greater power in the national government. After all, counting slaves as three-fifths of a white person for the purpose of federal apportionment provided Southern whites with more representation than any other group of Americans. Equally as important, if not more so, slavery mitigated the development of directly exploitative economic relations between different classes of whites while reinforcing the decentralization of Southern society at large. With black slavery as the foundation of commercial agriculture,* planters and substantial farmers had no need to accumulate and discipline a white labor force; market relations grew slowly and land remained cheap, so that nonslaveholders found room to establish an economically independent footing, either in the quest for slave ownership or in the relative security of semisubsistence farming. While the 1850s did see increasing stratification, outside of the cities a substantial class of whites depending on wages of some sort for their livelihood had yet to emerge. In the cities* such a class had emerged, but it was strongly immigrant and Catholic,* and thereby very much apart from the nonslaveholders in the countryside. Only in the border states and in the most isolated nonplantation enclaves did the social webs of the slave regime loosen considerably.

Nonetheless, slave owners never rested comfortably. It is true, of course, that nonslaveholders earned a reputation for nastiness toward the slaves and that more than a few rode patrols and carried out other duties necessary to the maintenance of order in a slave society. But there were always occasions when poorer whites, in town and country, could be found trading, drinking, gambling, and perhaps cohabiting with slaves, and they conjured the most dreaded images of a rising by the disadvantaged and dispossessed of both races. Planters sought, at times, to buy out neighboring nonslaveholders so as to avoid possible intermingling, and strangers were often looked upon with suspicion. As the sectional crisis intensified, the suspicions and anxieties rose, fueling secessionist sentiments among many slaveholders: should the South remain in the Union, a Republican president might use his patronage to build an antislavery party in the region, and nonslaveholders seemed the most promising constituency for such an undertaking.

When the moment of reckoning did arrive, a good many nonslaveholders opposed immediate secession, favoring either Unionism (more likely in the upper South) or Cooperationism (more likely in the lower South), but they closed ranks with slaveholders once Lincoln called for troops and set out to crush the rebellion. In the early stages of the war, they fought enthusiastically to resist the Yankee invaders and to defend their homes and families. Only when the demands of protecting slavery forced nonslaveholders to shoulder the disproportionately heavy burdens of war did that enthusiasm flag and discontent begin to smolder. Especially among the soldiers from nonplantation areas, whose families faced increasingly severe hardships, disaffection eventually ran rampant and desertion rates soared. Whether such wounds ultimately proved fatal to the Confederacy is a matter of debate, but they surely contributed to the Confederacy's final death throes.

Thus, just as free blacks continually reminded the slaveholders that blacks were not naturally slaves, nonslaveholders continually demonstrated that Afro-American slavery was not simply a system of white over black, that the relations between slaveholders and nonslaveholders were shaped by, and in turn shaped, the relations between slaveholders and slaves. The legacy would be felt in the South for decades after emancipation.

SELECTED BIBLIOGRAPHY

Steven Hahn, *The Roots of Southern Populism: Yeoman Farmers and the Transformation of the Georgia Upcountry, 1850–1890* (1983); J. William Harris, *Plain Folk and Gentry in a Slave Society: White Liberty and Black Slavery in Augusta's Hinterlands* (1985); Michael P. Johnson, *Toward a Patriarchal Republic: The Secession of Georgia* (1977); Robert C. McMath, Jr., and Orville V. Burton, eds., *Class, Conflict, and Consensus: Antebellum Southern Community Studies* (1982); Edward Magdol and Jon Wakelyn, eds., *The Southern Common People: Studies in Nineteenth-Century Social History* (1980); Frank L. Owsley, *Plain Folk of the Old South* (1949); Roger W. Shugg, *Origins of Class Struggle in Louisiana: A Social History of White Farmers and Laborers during Slavery and After, 1840–1875* (1939); Bell I. Wiley, *The Life of Johnny Reb: The Common*

Soldier of the Confederacy (1943); Gavin Wright, *The Political Economy of the Cotton South: Households, Markets, and Wealth in the Nineteenth Century* (1978); and Bertram Wyatt-Brown, *Southern Honor: Ethics and Behavior in the Old South* (1982).

STEVEN HAHN

NORTH CAROLINA, SLAVERY IN. The origins of slavery in North Carolina were consciously commercial. The eight Lords Proprietors who received the Carolina Charter from Charles II in 1663 hoped to accumulate huge profits from colonists who rented land, raised a wide variety of commodities, and employed slave labor. Barbadians were among the first colonists to invest in Carolina, and they persuaded the Lords Proprietors to institute a headright system under which a certain amount of acreage was apportioned to a colonist for each "Negro-Man or Slave" and "Woman-Negro or Slave" brought to Carolina. Moreover, Carolina's Fundamental Constitutions, drafted in 1669, reinforced the slave status of Africans.

Though Africans were being imported directly into North Carolina as early as the 1680s, slavery, in comparison with South Carolina, expanded slowly. North Carolina's treacherous coastline and poor harbor facilities forced slaveholders to purchase Africans in Virginia or South Carolina and bring them via overland or inland water routes. In 1710 there were 308 blacks reported living in Pasquotank and Currituck counties on the Albemarle Sound, and two years later the entire black population of North Carolina was estimated to be only 800. By 1730 that number had grown to perhaps 6,000. The most dramatic growth of the black population occurred between 1755 and 1767 when the number more than doubled, from approximately 19,000 to nearly 41,000, a yearly rate of increase of over 6 percent. About 2.5 percent of the growth can be attributed to natural increase, but over half of the population surge resulted from the importation of slaves from Africa* and the West Indies or the forcible immigration of slaves from neighboring colonies. On the eve of the American Revolution slaves made up about one-fourth of the colony's population.

By 1790 there were 100,572 slaves in North Carolina, composing approximately 25.5 percent of the total population. Twenty years later slaves composed 30.4 percent of North Carolina's population. From 1820 to 1860 the slave population stabilized at between 32 and 33 percent of the aggregate population. In 1860 slaves numbered 331,059, almost precisely one-third of North Carolina's total population.

Among whites, slaveholding families accounted for 31 percent of the population in 1790; 26.8 percent in 1850; and 27.7 percent in 1860. By the 1850s only 3 percent of North Carolina's slave owners could be considered planters (twenty or more slaves), and only 2 percent owned more than fifty slaves. Indeed, 70.8 percent of the Tar Heel slaveholders in 1860 owned fewer than ten slaves.

The distribution of slaves in North Carolina followed agricultural patterns. The lower Cape Fear region was settled in the 1720s by South Carolina planters who brought slaves to cultivate rice and naval stores. Slavery also expanded along a northern tier of counties bordering Virginia where the production of tobacco played an increasingly important part in the eighteenth century. By 1860 slaveholding remained concentrated in the coastal plain and piedmont and was tied closely to the commercial production of such crops as cotton,* tobacco,* and rice* and to industries (turpentine, lumber) associated with naval stores.* Of the sixteen counties that had more slaves than whites, eleven relied heavily on cotton production. In the mountain counties slaves ranged from as few as 2 percent of the population to over one-fourth. In the southern Appalachians the black population tended to swell during the summer months, when slaveholders and their bondsmen moved up to the cooler mountain resort areas of North Carolina from South Carolina and Georgia.

In 1795, fearing the spread of slave insurrections from the Caribbean, North Carolina prohibited the importation of slaves from the West Indies. However, state and, later, federal laws closing the foreign slave trade* received lax enforcement. In 1825 the North Carolina Manumission Society reported the persistence of illegal smuggling in African flesh. The interstate slave trade* from the upper South to the lower South streamed through North Carolina during the antebellum period. Apparently, North Carolina contributed its share to this interregional migration. The decade of the 1830s was especially critical. Growth of the slave population came to a virtual standstill between 1830 and 1840, and the white population grew only 2.4 percent. According to one estimate, 84 percent of the approximately 835,000 slaves who participated in the migration from upper to lower South, 1790–1860, accompanied their owners. Fully two-thirds of that migration occurred after 1830.

The testimony of several former slaves in the 1930s suggested that Tar Heel masters engaged in slave breeding.* If so, the practice may have been less pronounced in the mountains, where the sale of slaves was often kept within white families, the community, and the region of the state. Between 1840 and 1860 North Carolina's slave population resumed its growth, increasing by 34.6 percent in absolute terms, or 1.47 percent annually. In the same two decades the remainder of the population expanded at a rate of 30.3 percent, or 1.31 percent annually. In the southern highlands, however, the growth rate of the slave population was 62 percent in absolute terms—from 7,519 in 1840 to 12,182 in 1860—or 2.36 percent annually. Mountain masters clearly were expanding their holdings, which made the sale of slaves outside the region or migration with owners less prevalent.

The price of slaves* at the time of the French and Indian War was approximately £60 to £80, the amount the General Assembly compensated slaveholders for each slave executed. (An estimated eighteen slaves were castrated in lieu of execution in capital cases between 1758 and 1772.) During the 1780s slaves brought between £120 and £180. In 1804 an African slave in Charleston, bound for North Carolina, cost $300. By 1840 a prime field hand cost about $800. In mountainous western North Carolina the average price of a slave in 1860 was

$835, but in other parts of the state slave artisans commanded as much as $2,000; field hands, $1,500 to $1,700; and women, $1,300 to $1,500.

These figures were comparable to slave prices elsewhere in the South, which fluctuated with labor demands, crop prices, and regional economic trends. For example, a prime field hand in Virginia or South Carolina in 1810 cost around $500. The average price for a field hand in the South in 1848 was approximately $900; female slaves usually were $100 to $150 cheaper. The average price of a slave reached $1,221 in 1859 as slave prices rose by 72 percent across the South in the 1850s. In western North Carolina during the same decade, slave prices rose even faster—108 percent.

The basic slave codes* defining the social, economic, and physical place of bondsmen were enacted in 1715 and 1741, with only slight modifications thereafter. In 1753, for instance, a system of slave patrols* was instituted. During the eighteenth century special slave courts consisting of two magistrates and four slave-owning freeholders tried slaves for criminal offenses.* In 1793 the county courts assumed jurisdiction over slaves; in 1816 superior courts began trying slaves as freemen except in the case of conspiracy. It was not murder to kill a slave until 1791, and that law was ruled too vague by the state supreme court in 1801. This defect in Tar Heel jurisprudence was not remedied by the legislature until 1817. Particularly harsh restrictions were enacted in the period 1830–1833 in the wake of abolitionist agitation and the Nat Turner rebellion.* By 1855 the slave code forbade slaves to engage in a variety of activities: insolence to white persons; trespass against whites; intermarrying or cohabiting with free blacks; running away; producing forged papers (passes, certificates of freedom); hiring* their own time; raising horses, cattle, hogs, or sheep; selling spirits; gambling; hunting with a gun; setting fire to woods; preaching at a prayer meeting where slaves of different masters were assembled; and trafficking articles of property with slaves or whites except by written permission. The code also forbade whites to teach a slave or free black to read or write (math skills were excepted).

The living and working conditions of North Carolina slaves ranged from execrable to tolerable. In a society where planters composed only 3 percent of the population, those bondsmen owned by small farmers may have experienced conditions not too different from those of their masters in terms of diet, housing, and clothing. The "sawbuck equality" that characterized much of the colonial South's race relations may have persisted well into nineteenth-century North Carolina. However, a recent analysis of slave narratives in the 1930s revealed that less than one-fourth of the slaves on small holdings ate the same food as their masters. On larger plantations conditions also varied widely.

During the eighteenth century most observers portrayed slaves in North Carolina as ill fed, ill housed, and ill clothed. According to a German traveler in the 1780s, the largest planters kept blacks "the worst, let them run naked mostly or in rags, and accustom them as much as possible to hunger, but exact of them steady work." By the nineteenth century planters had refined the management of slaves in accordance with custom, the demands of black laborers, and the maximization of profits. Masters issued clothes* twice a year, in the spring and autumn. In the winter men wore shoes, a jacket, trousers, and a shirt; women wore shoes, a chemise, petticoat, and dress. Men might also receive wool caps and women head cloths. Summer clothes were scantier. "Negro cloth"—cotton for summer, wool for winter—was often made on the plantation and dyed blue or brown. Planters also occasionally purchased osnaburg and linen. In addition, each slave received a blanket. Both white and black women spent much of their time spinning, sewing, and weaving.

The rations for slaves consisted of meat, meal, molasses, and potatoes. In 1853 the *Farmers' Journal* (Raleigh) recommended giving men five pounds of boneless pork and a peck of meal per week in the winter; women four pounds of meat and a peck of meal. These rations were increased by one pound of meat and a quart of molasses in the summer. In the winter of 1854–1855 one Brunswick County planter who owned 150 slaves slaughtered 150 hogs and as many cattle as needed. Slaves supplemented their diet by keeping their own gardens,* hunting, and fishing.* Planters also offered incentives for slaves to earn money by producing more than required. On the Pettigrew plantations in Washington County slaves were permitted to trade various commodities at the plantation commissary, which enabled them to buy needed items or a few luxuries. Pettigrew slaves, on their own time, collected honey; made shingles, staves, and fence rails; cured coonskins; and grew rice, corn, flax, and wheat. On other plantations masters bought vegetables, butter, cheese, milk, eggs, and chickens from their slaves. Some slaves even raised cattle or hogs, though the law forbade such practices.

Most slave housing* was constructed poorly with inferior materials. One Cumberland County slaveholder recommended that slave houses be replaced every five to seven years to prevent the serious outbreak of disease. A visitor to the rice-growing district of the lower Cape Fear in 1809 commented on the "rich nabobs" who lived "amidst large villages of negroe huts." On rice plantations slaves lived in double houses of wooden boards or shingles with a chimney in the middle; two families occupied the double house. Most slave dwellings were built from timber and stone found nearby. The slave huts in Halifax County were described as "small, crowded, and smoky . . . and very filthy." These dwellings were "built of round pine or cypress logs." Log slave houses usually had stick and dirt chimneys, one door, and one window that lacked glazing. There were exceptions. The Pettigrew slaves lived in two-room houses. The Roanoke River plantations of Henry and Thomas Burgwyn featured "good frame buildings" for slaves, and the state's largest planter in 1860, Paul Cameron, erected solid one- and two-story frame houses on his Stagville and Fairntosh plantations that are still standing.

Though most slaves lived and worked in an agricultural setting, their labor was not tied strictly to the production of crops. By the 1840s a task system* had become fairly standardized in the rice-growing district. Most work could be accomplished by two or three o'clock in the afternoon. During the harvest season, however, slaves often labored from dawn to dusk seven days a week. On tobacco plantations slaves sometimes had to strip tobacco leaves at night after working all day in the fields. Slaves usually worked in gangs* under black drivers.* On the Pettigrew plantations slaves cleared new ground, rolled logs into heaps, planted crops, hoed, harvested, threshed, and loaded crops on vessels, cleared vines and underbrush, repaired ditches, built dikes, rived staves and shingles, and cut down and sawed trees. Other slaves had more specialized tasks such as coachman, house servant, cook, blacksmith, and herdsman of cattle and hogs.

The hiring-out process assured that slaves could be busily employed at all seasons of the year. Though slave artisans* were not allowed to hire out their own time, the practice was prevalent in such urban areas as Wilmington and New Bern. Moreover, the skill of slave artisans was widely recognized by planters who hired them to build stately mansions and by white workingmen such as the Wilmington mechanics who rioted in 1857 to protest unfair competition from slave labor.

In western North Carolina, where commercial crops were impractical, slaveholders raised livestock* and relied on slaves as herdsmen. Mountain slaves also became involved in various mercantile, industrial, and manufacturing enterprises, including hotel resorts, mining, railroad construction, public works (constructing roads and courthouses), and the production of cloth and hats.

Despite varied and disruptive work routines, the slave family* proved remarkably sturdy. In the eighteenth century the sex imbalance ratio between male and female slaves on individual plantations was wide enough that in the colony's eastern region as many as 39 percent of the slaves could not form marriages* on their plantations. The percentages ranged as high as 62 percent in western counties. Slaves overcame this disparity by finding marriage partners on other plantations, which extended the slave kinship pattern and therefore the slave community far beyond the immediate plantation. Women tended to have their first children before the age of nineteen. Naming patterns* among slaves showed strong family ties, with slaves named for fathers, grandfathers, aunts, and uncles. Slave children* grew up among siblings, even if they did not always share the same father. On small farms it was to the master's benefit to allow slave women to marry men on adjoining farms or plantations; any children that resulted from such unions became the property of the master. Consequently, by the mid-nineteenth century long slave marriages and naming patterns rooted in consanguineous and affinal relationships were not unusual. To be sure, slave marriages were not recognized by law, but masters were sometimes reluctant to separate families. The precarious condition of the slave family remained deeply etched in the memories of former slaves who in the 1930s described in moving terms the breakup of families.

Slaves were especially vulnerable to changes in the planter family's life cycle. Marriage, death, or migration posed the greatest threats to a slave family's stability. Planters made presents of slaves to newly married children, in wills and estate settlements divided slaveholdings among white family members, and sold slaves to pay off debts or to dispose of troublesome property. Moreover, older children and unmarried young adults were especially susceptible to sale. Thus, any break in the planter family's routine usually brought dramatic and unwelcome change for slave families.

Religion* deeply affected slave life and slaves' perception of society. Conversion of Africans to Christianity began slowly in the eighteenth century partly because of the planters' resistance to it. Indeed, certain Islamic practices* and African folk rituals persisted well into the nineteenth century. After the First Great Awakening in the 1740s, however, the Anglican* baptism of slaves accelerated. Presbyterians,* Quakers,* and Moravians* also took an active part in teaching Christianity to slaves in the eighteenth century. The Baptists* and Methodists,* however, proved most successful in proselytizing Africans and Creoles. Both denominations conducted services in a democratic atmosphere, stressed fellowship, and addressed members, no matter what color, as "brother" and "sister." In the 1780s the Methodists were openly abolitionist.* Baptists allowed black preachers* to sermonize mixed congregations, and Henry Evans, a free black shoemaker, organized the first Methodist church in Fayetteville in the 1790s.

Baptists and Moravians showed especial concern for the plight of slave families, with mixed success. In 1824 a Moravian minister who had married slaves with the *Book of Common Prayer* had to suspend the practice. "It is not within the power of Negroes to promise that they will live together as married people," the Moravians noted, "for it often happens that one or the other is sold by the owner. . . . " Henceforth, the Moravians concluded, slave marriages "shall simply be announced . . . and the blessing of God shall be wished for them." By 1830 most religious services in North Carolina were conducted on a rigidly segregated basis, and churches that earlier had debated the morality of slavery were now defending it with biblical justification.

Such segregated practices were not without advantages, however. By 1810 separate African churches had been established in Wilmington, New Bern, Fayetteville, and Edenton. In the slave quarters black preachers rejected the masters' institutionalized religion—with its emphasis on the theme "servants obey your masters"—and expounded freedom, dignity, hope, and sometimes rebellion. The 1802 slave insurrection scare had its inception and inspiration at religious gatherings, where at least one black preacher reportedly carried a gun.

Of all the religious denominations only the Society of Friends steadfastly contested the morality of slavery. The Quakers declared slavery an evil in 1776 and urged Friends to give it up. Quakers fought hard to abolish slavery and to loosen extremely restrictive manumission laws. Emancipation was permitted only for "meritorious Services" to be judged by the courts. Quakers circumvented the law by giving some slaves the "full Benefit of their labour" and assigning other slaves to agents who delivered the liberated blacks to Haiti, Liberia, and the free-soil North. By 1830 Quakers had sent 652 blacks out of North Carolina and still had under their charge another 402.

North Carolina slaves engaged in various types of resistance* to bondage including running away, sabotage, stealing, feigning illness, malingering, and poisoning. Fear of slave insurrections* was evident as early as 1715. The first instance of collective revolt may have occurred in the winter of 1752–1753. With the coming of the American Revolution* in 1775, Whigs feared a slave revolt in Wilmington, but an actual uprising seems to have taken place in the coastal plain counties of Beaufort, Pitt, and Craven. Slave unrest persisted throughout the Revolutionary war and was especially acute when British forces were present off the Cape Fear coast in 1776 and along Lord Cornwallis's line of march in 1781. In 1802 a full-scale slave insurrection scare gripped northeastern North Carolina, where slaves, encouraged by the Gabriel Prosser revolt* of 1800 in Richmond and inflamed with a religious zeal ignited by the Second Great Awakening, plotted a racial cataclysm. The last-minute discovery of a written message being circulated among the conspirators interdicted the rising and resulted in the execution of twenty-four slaves. Three years later a series of poisonings in Wayne, Sampson, and Johnston counties ended with a slave woman being burned at the stake and three other slaves being hanged. In 1821 a contingent of 200 militiamen spent twenty-six days in the field subduing a band of eighty runaways in Onslow County. Four years later Edgecombe County whites suspected slave preachers of agitating blacks with rumors that the federal government would free them in October and of plotting a Christmas eve rebellion. The appearance of David Walker's* *Appeal* in North Carolina in 1830 set off a panic in several southeastern counties where slaves were said to be uncontrollable. White hysteria, perhaps only matched in 1802, followed in the wake of the Nat Turner rebellion* in 1831 in neighboring Southampton County, Virginia, but it was the last major slave scare in antebellum North Carolina.

The conditions of slavery changed dramatically with the outbreak of the Civil War.* The Confederate government* used black labor to operate railroads, to dig wells, to construct earth works and fortifications, and to perform fatigue duty for the Southern army. Blacks were lent by masters, hired by the Confederacy, or often simply impressed. Defection of slaves began as early as 1861–1862 when the Union army* invaded and occupied much of coastal North Carolina. The former slaves soon performed the same chores for Union forces they had for the Confederacy, with the significant new role as soldier. Slaves also acted the part of spies and guides for Union operations in eastern North Carolina.

By war's end major encampments of freedmen on Roanoke Island and at James City across the river from New Bern established a black presence that would lead to greater political and economic power in postbellum society than anyone could have envisioned at the outset of the war. In September 1865, 117 delegates representing forty-two of North Carolina's counties convened in Raleigh for the first freedmen's convention in the South. Scarcely one-fourth of them could read and write. They urged freedmen to avoid cities and to strive for ownership of land, for education, for amicable relations with whites, and for the normalization of marriage. To the constitutional convention assembled across town they appealed for the protection of the law to their persons and property, for Negro education, for the regulation of hours of labor, and for the abolition of all laws that discriminated "on account of race or color." Black Reconstruction was under way.

That the nature of antebellum slavery shaped the postemancipation experience of blacks is a truism. Primarily an agricultural people, propertyless blacks quickly became ensnared in the sharecropping and tenant system of the postbellum economy. Sixteen counties in the piedmont and east continued to hold black majorities before the turn of the twentieth century. Though many blacks migrated to eastern towns such as Raleigh, New Bern, and Wilmington, they did not participate to any large extent in the industrialization that spread principally across the piedmont. Mill work remained for whites only.

The concentration of black population in certain eastern counties and cities, however, enabled Tar Heel blacks to wield sizable political power before disfranchisement in 1900. In places where blacks enjoyed numerical and political strength, such as the lower Cape Fear region, the Ku Klux Klan failed to exercise much influence during Reconstruction. Black voters, sometimes with the assistance of white Republicans* and Populists, elected numerous black politicians to local offices, more than 100 to the legislature, and 4 to Congress. A profile of black politicians who rose to power in the postbellum decades might suggest that, whether former slaves or antebellum free blacks, they shared similar characteristics. Black politicians were normally natives of North Carolina; they were usually literate, despite antebellum prohibitions; they ordinarily possessed a specialized skill or practiced a profession; and they were overwhelmingly Republican.

The agenda blacks established for living in postemancipation society reflected precisely those rights and freedoms denied them under slavery: normalization of marriage; equal political and civil rights; education; and the right to own property, especially land. Ironically, after a promising start under Reconstruction, blacks faced reversals in nearly every area by 1900 as the age of segregation descended.

SELECTED BIBLIOGRAPHY

James M. Clifton, "Golden Grains of White: Rice Planting on the Lower Cape Fear," *North Carolina Historical Review*, 50 (1973), 365–393; Jeffrey J. Crow, *The Black Experience in Revolutionary North Carolina* (1977); Herbert G. Gutman, *The Black Family in Slavery and Freedom, 1750–1925* (1976); John C. Inscoe, "Mountain Masters: Slaveholding in Western North Carolina," *North Carolina Historical Review*, 61 (1984), 143–173; Guion Griffis Johnson, *Ante-Bellum North Carolina: A Social History* (1937); Marvin L. Michael Kay and Lorin Lee Cary, "A Demographic Analysis of Colonial North Carolina with Special Emphasis upon the Slave and Black Populations," in Jeffrey J. Crow and Flora J. Hatley, eds., *Black Americans in North Carolina and the South*

(1984); and Bennett H. Wall, "The Founding of the Pettigrew Plantations," *North Carolina Historical Review*, 27 (1950), 395–418.

JEFFREY J. CROW

NORTHUP, SOLOMON (ca. 1808–1863). Solomon Northup was the author of a popular and sensational slave narrative. Born free about 1808 in Minerva, New York, he was the son of a former Rhode Island slave who was moved to New York by his owners and subsequently manumitted. Like his father (Mintus), Solomon Northup became a literate, landowning farmer in upstate New York near Saratoga Springs. He lived there uneventfully with his wife (Ann Hampton) and three children (Elizabeth, Margaret, and Alonzo) until he fell victim in March 1841 to kidnappers who sold him into slavery.

Northup was shipped to New Orleans and sold there to a cotton planter from the Red River region of central Louisiana. For the next twelve years Northup worked in that area under three different owners. Although he tried to escape several times, each attempt failed until an itinerant Canadian carpenter helped to gain his release.

After Northup returned to his family in January 1853, he began to write his narrative* with the assistance of David Wilson, a local author. The remarkable similarity of Northup's experience in Louisiana to the fictional account of *Uncle Tom's Cabin*, which had just appeared in 1852, boosted the sales potential of his story. The eventual book, *Twelve Years a Slave*, appeared in 1853 and sold over 30,000 copies. Widespread publicity about the book enabled Northup to find and apprehend his kidnappers, but legal technicalities made it impossible to convict them. Northup used income from the book to buy a home in Glens Falls, New York, where he lived until his death in 1863.

SELECTED BIBLIOGRAPHY

John W. Blassingame, *The Slave Community: Plantation Life in the Antebellum South* (1972); Solomon Northup, *Twelve Years a Slave*, edited by Sue Eakin and Joseph Logsdon (1968); Gilbert Osofsky, ed., *Puttin' on Ole Massa: The Slave Narratives of Henry Bibb, William Wells Brown, and Solomon Northup* (1969).

JOSEPH LOGSDON

NORTHWEST ORDINANCE. On 13 July 1787, the Continental Congress, meeting in New York City, passed the famed Northwest Ordinance. It provided for temporary government in the wilderness, the protection of civil liberties, and an orderly transition to statehood. Moreover, the Ordinance's sixth article prohibited slavery northwest of the Ohio River.

Historians have had difficulty explaining why the Southern-controlled Congress approved this antislavery proviso. The Founding Fathers were notably ambivalent on the question of human bondage. They may have acted pragmatically in this instance by attacking the peculiar institution at its weakest link (in the territories where its influence was still negligible) and leaving it alone where it was already firmly entrenched. Other evidence suggests a compromise. In return for a ban on slavery in the Old Northwest, Southern interests received the protection of the fugitive slave law and a tacit endorsement of slavery in the Southwest territory. This might even have been linked to events at the Constitutional Convention in Philadelphia.

Although the Ordinance did not free slaves already in the region, it did prevent further importation. This in effect precluded any large buildup of a slave population. It also gained time for antislavery migrants from New England and the Middle states to become a majority. With the opening of new lands in the lower Mississippi Valley, and the increased profitability of cotton and sugar production, more and more slaveholders migrated to the Southwest. The Northwest Ordinance in the long run helped channel the expansion of slavery, by directing its flow toward the Deep South.

SELECTED BIBLIOGRAPHY

Robert F. Berkhofer, Jr., "Jefferson, the Ordinance of 1784, and the Origins of the American Territorial System," *William and Mary Quarterly*, 3rd ser., 29 (1972), 231–262; Paul Finkelman, "Slavery and the Northwest Ordinance: A Study in Ambiguity," *Journal of the Early Republic*, 6 (1986), 343–370; William W. Freehling, "The Founding Fathers and Slavery," *American Historical Review*, 77 (1972), 81–93; J. David Griffin, "Historians and the Sixth Article of the Ordinance of 1787," *Ohio History*, 78 (1969), 252–260; Merrill Jensen, *The New Nation: A History of the United States during the Confederation, 1781–1789* (1950); Staughton Lynd, "The Compromise of 1787," *Political Science Quarterly*, 81 (1966), 225–250; Duncan J. MacLeod, *Slavery, Race, and the American Revolution* (1974); and Francis S. Philbrick, *The Rise of the West, 1754–1830* (1965).

STEVEN E. ANDERS

NORTHWEST TERRITORY, SLAVERY IN. Early French settlers brought the first black slaves to the Old Northwest. They used these blacks, and some Indian slaves, as farm laborers or lead miners. While the original black slaves came from French lower Mississippi outposts, Indians soon carried in and sold blacks captured from other colonies. Great Britain took over the Northwest in 1763, and British merchants promptly brought in more slaves; James Rumsey, for example, sold thirty Jamaicans to the French villages in 1763. Other slaves were imported by Virginians after Virginia's Revolutionary war occupation of the Northwest. France, Britain, and Virginia all recognized the legitimacy of African slavery.

When the U.S. government acquired formal responsibility for the Northwest in the 1780s, a number of prominent men urged that slavery be kept out of the region. Some, like Timothy Pickering or Thomas Jefferson, genuinely hoped to stop the spread of slavery. It is probable that many Southern congressmen saw the Northwest as a potential tobacco-growing rival, and for that reason agreed that slavery should be barred there. Article Six of the Northwest Ordinance of

1787* therefore forbade the introduction of slavery into the new Northwest Territory.

Article Six seemed to completely rule out slavery in the Northwest. However, territorial governor Arthur St. Clair decided to accept the existing French slavery system. He was influenced above all by a fear that many Frenchmen, to protect their property, would leave the Northwest and move to Spanish St. Louis. Such an exodus would gravely weaken the territory in case of Indian or foreign wars. In 1794, when territorial judge George Turner tried to free slaves owned by Vincennes probate judge Henry Vanderburgh, St. Clair ruled that all pre-1787 slaves must remain in slavery.

Some of the Northwest's settlers and land speculators who wanted to promote rapid Southern settlement called for repealing Article Six and opening the territory to slavery. Most of the early pioneer settlers, however, opposed this idea. The Northwest attracted many Southern Quakers* and Methodist* converts, at a time when both faiths condemned slavery. Indeed, some of these antislavery Southerners moved to the Northwest precisely because it forbade slavery. Many other pioneers simply had no desire to compete against planters and slave labor, or to live amidst planters and blacks. When Congress created Indiana Territory in 1800, and removed the Ohio Valley French villages from the Northwest's jurisdiction, support for slavery declined further. Most northwestern leaders—whether Federalist Yankees like Ephraim Cutler or ex-planters like Thomas Worthington—condemned the institution. At the 1802 Ohio state constitutional convention, Cutler bottled up in committee a proposal by Cincinnati publisher John Browne to permit adult slavery, while Worthington's Republicans would clearly have defeated such a proposal on the convention floor. Ohio entered the Union in 1803 as a free state.

Ohio acquired a growing free black population. Many freedmen moved to the state, while some former planters like Worthington brought in their ex-bondsmen as farm tenants. Most Ohioans had no desire to grant these freedmen full rights as citizens, and many feared that a lenient state racial code would lead to a heavy in-migration by Southern blacks. Ohio's assemblies therefore forbade black voting, militia service, jury duty, testimony against whites, and public school attendance. An 1807 law required new black settlers to post a $500 bond. Since many laws were only sporadically enforced in a frontier state, several thousand blacks moved into Ohio by the late 1820s without registering or posting bond. This growing black presence was met by increasing white hostility. Major antiblack riots swept Cincinnati in 1829, 1836, and 1841, forcing many blacks to leave the state.

Given this hostile atmosphere, Ohio's blacks turned to their own communities for support. A network of black Masonic lodges, African Methodist Episcopal churches,* and private schools (backed by white philanthropists) helped blacks develop a community life. Yankee settlers, who flooded northern Ohio after 1830, gave blacks some tolerance and support. Such Yankees allowed black public school attendance, and at Oberlin College let them attend college. Ohio's

Free Soil movement also flourished in the north. Accounts agree that the state's large free black community—which, thanks to migration from the South, numbered 25,279 in 1860—led a relatively relaxed life only in the Lake Erie settlements.

The Indiana-Illinois settlements attracted more slavery supporters than early Ohio. Indiana territorial governors William Henry Harrison and Thomas Posey favored slavery, and while the assembly hesitated to challenge Article Six of the Ordinance, it passed a law permitting men to import blacks as indentured servants. Indiana's laws placed some limits on indentured slavery. Masters had to give their indentures adequate food, clothing, and shelter, while servants under fifteen, or newborn children, owed service only until their late twenties or thirties. Still, indentured slavery flourished, and masters brought in hundreds of blacks. Both the old French slaves and newer indentures were freely bought and sold. When Illinois became a separate territory, it too allowed indentured black servitude, and by 1820 it had 917 slaves and servants.

While a slavery system thus developed north of the Ohio River, it was a weak system. Many pioneers disliked slavery, and masters preferred to move to such regions as Kentucky or Missouri where their property seemed more secure. That in turn further reduced support for slavery. Indiana's 1816 constitutional convention forbade both slavery and future indentures. Many owners promptly sold their blacks southwards. Still, the state's antislavery laws were laxly enforced, and as late as 1820 a census formally listed 190 slaves. Indiana's courts began to act against slavery only when a Vermont settler, lawyer Amory Kinney, launched a series of suits on behalf of slaves and servants. Despite his energy, some slaves remained in bondage; an 1832 Vincennes town census recorded thirty-two slaves.

In Illinois, many Southern settlers favored summoning a state constitutional convention that would officially open the new state to slavery. Such a movement in Indiana got weak support, and a constitutional referendum there failed in 1823, by 2,601 to 11,991. But the stronger Illinois proslavery voters came much closer to getting their convention. Their drive failed in 1824 by a relatively narrow margin, 4,950 to 6,822. Despite the general backwoods antipathy to plantations, Illinois contained a large number of proslavery settlers. Indentured servitude remained strong there for years, and as late as 1830 Illinois counted 746 indentured blacks among a total of 1,637 blacks.

In both states the white community felt strong hostility towards free blacks. An 1813 Illinois territorial law—fortunately not enforced—penalized new black settlers with thirty-nine lashes every fifteen days until they left the region. A more moderate 1829 state law required black settlers to post a $1,000 bond. Indiana's 1851 constitution, upheld by a huge voting majority, banned future black settlement, fined whites who employed new black settlers, and mandated that the fines be used to send existing free black residents out of the country. Both states enforced a full set of discriminatory laws on voting, trials, and schools. Blacks in these states found tolerant treatment only in Yankee-settled northern regions and in the Quaker communities of eastern Indiana.

Published sources tell us relatively little about individual slaves and free blacks in Illinois and Indiana, but they do suggest that most of them worked as farm laborers growing grain or cotton or labored in southern Illinois saltworks. Local laws, while restricting the activities of slaves, required their masters to give them sufficient food, clothing, and shelter, and probably those slaves enjoyed marginally better health than many of the free blacks. Free blacks moved fairly quickly out of the Southern-settled counties and into such Quaker areas as Richmond, Indiana, or into such cities as Indianapolis and Chicago. A few prospered—Chicago tailor and real estate owner John Jones being a good example—but most remained poor. As in Ohio, the blacks turned to their own community institutions, with religion playing a crucial role in their lives. The African Methodist Episcopal (AME) church expanded rapidly in Indiana and Illinois. The national church created an Indiana Conference for those states (and two territories) in 1840, and by 1854 the AME church officially enrolled one-third of Indiana's adult blacks. Others became Baptists, or in a few cases Quakers, and most community leaders in this region were ministers.

Wisconsin and Michigan, in the upper Great Lakes, were later communities with a largely Yankee and European population. Perhaps this explains their relative moderation on racial issues. While a few slaves labored in early Detroit and the southwest Wisconsin lead region, slavery never developed strong roots in these states. Still, both states showed the antiblack prejudices common to nineteenth-century Americans. Michigan's constitutions barred black voting, with one referring to blacks as "a degraded caste." In Wisconsin, interracial marriage was not forbidden, and the state displayed strong opposition to the enforcement of fugitive slave laws. Still, Wisconsin's citizens defeated referenda to allow black voting, by three to two margins.

In sum, the Old Northwest developed a weak slavery system, which grew either openly or in an indentured form only in the areas near the Ohio River. Some pioneers—Yankees, Quakers, Methodist converts, and others—condemned the whole institution, while many other frontiersmen displayed no desire to live in a plantation culture. Northwestern slavery, a weak system, slowly eroded. Yet antiblack attitudes remained very strong in most of the Northwest, and for most free blacks in that vast region, life was difficult at best. Only the Yankee-settled communities along the Great Lakes and the Quaker counties of eastern Ohio and eastern Indiana showed any tolerance for the Northwest's free blacks.

SELECTED BIBLIOGRAPHY

John D. Barnhart, *Valley of Democracy: The Frontier versus the Plantation in the Ohio Valley, 1775–1818* (1953); Eugene Berwanger, *The Frontier against Slavery: Western Anti-Negro Prejudice and the Slavery Extension Controversy* (1967); Leonard P. Curry, *The Free Black in Urban America, 1800–1850: The Shadow of the Dream* (1981); Philip

S. Foner, *History of Black Americans: From the Emergence of the Cotton Kingdom to the Eve of the Compromise of 1850* (1983); Lulu Merle Johnson, "The Problem of Slavery in the Old Northwest, 1787–1858" (Ph.D. dissertation, State University of Iowa, 1941); Leon F. Litwack, *North of Slavery: The Negro in the Free States, 1790–1860* (1961); and Emma Lou Thornbrough, *The Negro in Indiana: A Study of a Minority* (1975).

JEFFREY P. BROWN

NULLIFICATION CONTROVERSY. The idea of nullification, formulated by John C. Calhoun* in 1828, reposed on an extreme doctrine of states' rights. Each state, in this view, possessed the power to veto—to nullify—a federal law; the veto by one state accordingly meant that the federal government would cease to enforce the law in any of the states. On 19 November 1832 a convention in South Carolina put theory into practice, fixing 1 February 1833 as the day when tariff laws ceased to operate. President Andrew Jackson* responded with a proclamation condemning nullification as subversion and reaffirming his constitutional duty to enforce all laws. This action rallied the nation; and his call in mid-January for added force compelled the Nullifiers to back down. Henry Clay,* with Calhoun's support, then pushed through Congress a compromise tariff which resolved the crisis.

South Carolinians, hit hard by depression in the 1820s, blamed the high tariff for their problems. But, more profoundly, nullification expressed a pervasive anxiety about slavery. Slaves constituted a higher proportion of the population in South Carolina than in any other state; and four incidents in the years before nullification increased the anxiety. In 1822 the Denmark Vesey plot* for a slave uprising in Charleston was narrowly averted; four years later widespread arson in the city created the "Great Fire Scare"; in 1829 a conspiracy of slaves was uncovered in Georgetown; and the Nat Turner insurrection* in Virginia two years later brought fears to a new peak. Framing these mounting concerns were the debates over Missouri in 1820–1821 and the rising voice of abolitionism a decade later trumpeted by William Lloyd Garrison.* State laws against "incendiary" publications, manumission, and the right of free Negroes to enter the state constituted one political response. Nullification was another. Ostensibly a tactic for securing economic interests, it pointed to the more vital interest of social order and anticipated South Carolina's later leadership in the secession movement.

SELECTED BIBLIOGRAPHY

John Barnwell, *Love of Order: South Carolina's First Secession Crisis* (1982); William W. Freehling, *Prelude to Civil War: The Nullification Controversy in South Carolina, 1816–1836* (1965); Richard B. Latner, "The Nullification Crisis and Republican Subversion," *Journal of Southern History*, 63 (1977), 19–38; and Merrill D. Peterson, *Olive Branch and Sword: The Compromise of 1833* (1982).

MAJOR L. WILSON

O

OBEAH. Obeah is a set of supernatural beliefs and practices among blacks in the British West Indies. Also sometimes referred to as shadow-catching, the term *obeah* probably comes from one of several Twi words, most likely including *obeye* (the power used by witches) or *obeyifo* (he who takes a child away). Among Africans, the closest analogy to West Indian obeah practice appears to have been among the Papaw, where witches used hair cuttings and other artifacts to manipulate the spirit world for clients.

The origins of obeah in Jamaica and Barbados cannot be pinpointed. The settlement patterns of slaves, in which they were left largely in their own communities, allowed the development of slave culture to a degree unique in British-American slavery. It is likely that those slaves who had practiced witchcraft in Africa used the terrifying conditions of the New World plantation system* to impress upon the other slaves their power and importance. At least until the late eighteenth century, obeah practitioners were invariably born in Africa, often misshapen or deformed, most often elderly and primarily male, although women tended to work as obeah practitioners in such matters as betrothals.

Obeah was, in the simplest terms, one of the earliest businesses in the slave communities of the British colonies. A practitioner was hired for both positive and negative reasons. Some slaves would request protection against evil spirits, from theft, or from ill health. In this sense, obeah was similar to myalism, a public, religious worship of the spirits, which in part provided protection against obeah. More noteworthy, though, were the negative purposes for which the use of obeah was hired, from ending a love affair to bringing about the death of a client's enemy. The fundamental concept of obeah was to manipulate spirits, termed *duppies*. To guard against evil, an obeah man would summon up the spirit of an ancestor; for evil purposes, the duppies of dead obeah men or other malefactors could be called upon. Among the most feared duppies were those of infants, who could not be identified and who had no human knowledge. Duppies could be summoned up through a variety of techniques usually using such artifacts as grave dirt and, later, tobacco pipes or pieces of glass. Although duppies were manipulated in a variety of ways as well, two frequently cited techniques were catching the spirit in a bowl and stabbing it through the heart, or tying it under the silk-cotton tree.

These practices served a variety of purposes in the slave community. To be sure, they brought a special, African-based meaning to the slave experience. Moreover, at times they served as lightning rods for slave society. Anger toward the continually cruel and harsh treatment of the bondsmen could be displaced in the slave community upon the obeah man, who could be seen as the source of all misery. In a few instances, resistance* to the system also coalesced around obeah. In Barbados, some whites worried for their safety from such "black magic." In Jamaica, obeah men may have been directly involved in the rebellion of 1760. Although whites may not have fully understood obeah, they universally disapproved of its practice. In 1806, for example, Barbados made the practice of obeah a felony punishable by death.

Little specific practice of obeah seems to have moved to the American South. Although the sources report none of the details of shadow-catching in North American slavery, conjuring nevertheless did serve some of the same purposes, in a less routinized fashion. Again artifacts were used in a mysterious way to bring about good or evil results. Conjuring, best thought of as a second-generation supernatural activity, was too distanced from its African roots to include the quasi-theological concept of the duppy. Instead, it joined bits of obeah, vudon, and perhaps Christian concepts of a spirit world together to serve the same functions for the much less independent slave communities of the South.

SELECTED BIBLIOGRAPHY

Jerome S. Handler and Frederick Lange, *Plantation Slavery in Barbados: An Archaeological and Historical Investigation* (1978); Orlando Patterson, *The Sociology of Slavery: An Analysis of the Origins, Development, and Structure of Negro Slave Society in Jamaica* (1967); Albert J. Raboteau, *Slave Religion: The "Invisible Institution" in the Antebellum South* (1978); and George E. Simpson, *Religious Cults of the Caribbean: Trinidad, Jamaica and Haiti* (1970).

DAVID T. BAILEY

OLMSTED, FREDERICK LAW (1822–1903). Born 2 April 1822 in Hartford, Connecticut, Frederick Law Olmsted distinguished himself as a keen social analyst and one of the most influential prewar critics of slavery in the South. In 1852 this gentleman farmer and author agreed to make a Southern tour and record his observations of day-to-day life in the pages of the New York *Daily-Times*. Between December 1852 and August 1854 Olmsted made two lengthy trips. This assignment resulted in a trilogy—*A Journey in the Seaboard Slave States* (1856), *A Journey Through Texas* (1857), and *A Journey in the Back Country* (1860). A revised two-volume condensation, *The Cotton Kingdom* (1861), summarized the sweep of Olmsted's experiences and observations in the South.

Although his writings reflect his New England background, Olmsted distanced himself from the sectional passions of his day. He deliberately concentrated on the economic and social side of slavery in hopes of convincing masters that slavery was too costly, less profitable than free labor. Stressing that the peculiar institution harmed blacks and whites alike, Olmsted emphasized that a slave could be taught to become a worthwhile citizen. Today Olmsted's careful observations of Southern life are recognized as among the most insightful and comprehensive of the antebellum travel* accounts. According to Edmund Wilson, Olmsted "talked to everybody and he sized up everything, and he wrote it all down."

The outbreak of the Civil War* dashed the journalist's hopes for a peaceful and gradual end to slavery. After wartime service as secretary of the U.S. Sanitary Commission, Olmstead designed, among other parks and gardens, Central Park in New York City. He ranked as the nation's foremost landscape architect until his death 28 August 1903 in Waverly, Massachusetts.

SELECTED BIBLIOGRAPHY

Laura W. Roper, *FLO: a Biography of Frederick Law Olmsted* (1973); Arthur M. Schlesinger, ed., *The Cotton Kingdom by Frederick Law Olmsted* (1953); and Elizabeth Stevenson, *Park Maker: A Life of Frederick Law Olmsted* (1977).

DAVID M. DEAN

OVERSEERS. Overseers played an indispensable role in the management of Southern slave plantations. Most commonly utilized on units with twenty or more working field hands, the overseer occupied a position subordinate to the proprietor or his agent and superior to black drivers* in the managerial structure of the plantation. The primary responsibilities of the overseer, charged principally with executing policies formulated by his employer, were slave discipline and crop production. More specifically, he assigned gangs* to work, apportioned tasks,* supervised field labor, administered punishment,* treated minor ailments, distributed food* and clothing,* inspected slave cabins,* and maintained various record and account books. In many areas, overseers afforded the sparse white population its only security against possible slave uprisings. The degree of success enjoyed by individual plantation proprietors depended largely upon the skill and energy exhibited by their managerial subordinates.

Modeled after English bailiffs who managed the great landed estates of the island kingdom, the overseer system was introduced into America by the Virginia Company early in the seventeenth century. As the black tide of African slaves inexorably swept across the fields of the Southern colonies, the use of overseers expanded accordingly until it became a cardinal feature of the plantation system.* With few exceptions, most notably the common practice during the colonial period of paying overseers in crop shares rather than cash wages, the broad outlines of the overseer system remained essentially unchanged until the demise of slavery.

By the mid-nineteenth century there were approximately 18,000 overseers in the slave South, most of them concentrated in the seven leading plantation states of Alabama, Georgia, Louisiana, Mississippi, the two Carolinas, and Virginia. As a consequence of the continued expansion of the plantation system into the Southwest together with the consolidation of existing holdings, this number doubled during the last decade of the antebellum period. By far the greatest number were employed on cotton plantations, although the incidence of overseer employment was highest on the huge rice* and sugar* estates of South Carolina and Louisiana, respectively.

The overwhelming majority of Southern overseers were white. Occasionally, planters disenchanted with hired managers dispensed with them in favor of slave foremen or relied exclusively upon Negro drivers to manage their properties. Among those who did so were such prominent Southerners as Jefferson Davis, John McDonogh, Edmund Ruffin, and Thomas Spalding; but they were the exceptions. Despite numerous complaints, the white overseer remained an almost ubiquitous figure on large plantations of the slave South.

Recruited primarily through written or oral contacts with fellow planters and, less frequently, through newspaper advertisements, overseers were normally engaged at the beginning of each calendar year for a term of one year. The mutual obligations governing the relationship between planter and overseer were usually formalized in a written contract, signed at the outset of the overseer's term. In addition to a stipulated monetary payment, it was the general practice to furnish overseers with lodging, provisions, and often a servant and other privileges. Overseer salaries were determined by a number of variable factors. Chief among these were the size and geographic location of the agricultural unit, the length of tenure and experience of the overseer, and the type of plantation (i.e., absentee or resident). In general, average annual wages in the mid-nineteenth century ranged from $200 to $250 in the tobacco* grain region of the upper South to $1,500-$2,000 on the great rice and sugar estates. The average for overseers of cotton plantations was about $450. Some planters offered added inducements in the form of bonuses tied to production quotas. This practice, particularly common in the Gulf South, had the unfortunate effect of encouraging overseers to maximize production at the expense of the welfare of slaves, land, and livestock. Many slave owners manifested a distressing propensity to change overseers frequently and often capriciously. Like the bonus provision, this tendency was most pronounced in the cotton states of the Deep South, where proprietors sought a rapid return on their investment and consequently measured managerial performance almost exclusively by the number of cotton bales produced. By contrast, continuous terms of ten, fifteen, and even twenty years or longer were not uncommon in the Atlantic seaboard states. Taking the region as a whole, however, insecurity of tenure coupled with inadequate pay militated against the perpetuation of a more capable group of overseers.

Those who pursued the calling of overseer in the slave South may be divided into three general categories. The first and smallest consisted of young men from planter families who managed the properties of their fathers or neighboring proprietors in preparation for later careers as planters. A floating population of youthful, unmarried, poorly educated, inexperienced, propertyless amateurs comprised the second group. Most numerous in the cotton and sugar regions of the Southwest, they drifted from one plantation to another, offering their services at exceedingly low rates and tarnishing the reputation of their more skilled counterparts. The third body of overseers—perhaps the most typical—was composed of conscientious, professional managers, drawn primarily from the yeoman farmer segment of Southern society, who entered the business in order to accumulate sufficient capital to purchase some land and perhaps a few slaves and thus to establish themselves as independent farmers. That many attained this goal is evident from the fact that only 20 percent of Southern overseers were more than forty years of age. It is apparent that most overseers abandoned their socially distasteful profession to enter more desirable occupations when their means permitted.

In view of the isolation and vulnerability of the overseer post, it is little wonder that few chose to pursue the calling as a permanent vocation. Virtually ostracized by his employer, forbidden to fraternize with the slaves, discouraged from entertaining company, and compelled to remain constantly at his post, the overseer was doomed to a lonely and Spartan existence. Moreover, as the man in the middle of the plantation establishment, he was hated intensely by the slaves and berated by his superiors for a variety of transgressions, both real and imagined. Some of the criticism was justified, but planters exacerbated the deficiencies in the system by castigating their subordinates at every opportunity, failing to accord them proper respect, refusing to pay fair and equitable wages, and constantly and capriciously changing managers.

Because their self-interests were in part antithetical, a certain degree of friction was inherent in the owner-manager relationship. Lacking a proprietary interest in either slaves or plantation equipment and often under intense pressure to harvest bountiful crops, the overseer found it difficult to appreciate the concern manifested by owners for the property which constituted the bulk of their capital investment. Even more fundamental as a source of discord was the question of division of authority between overseer and employer. Chafing under regulations which they found excessively constrictive, overseers argued that they should be granted greater control over routine plantation operations if they were to be held accountable for the results. On the other hand, plantation owners understandably were reluctant to entrust to hired subordinates complete authority over costly agricultural enterprises.

Cognizant of such conflicts between owner and manager, the slaves exploited them to their own advantage, thereby rendering the overseer's position even more untenable. Whenever a new overseer was installed, there was invariably a period of testing as the slaves sought to determine the disciplinary parameters of the new regime. If those limits proved unacceptable, the disgruntled slaves might seek to oust the overseer by massive acts of disobedience or, if circumstances did not warrant such extreme action, to undermine his authority and mitigate the harshness of his administration by carrying complaints directly to the owner. Much to the consternation of plantation managers, most slaveholders permitted—and some explicitly encouraged—such direct appeals. Once again, the explanation is to be found in the essentially antithetical roles of proprietor and overseer. The latter represented the most odious features of slavery. The planter, on the other hand, precisely because of the presence of a hired inter-mediary who could serve as a scapegoat, was enabled to assume the guise of benevolent patriarch. Thus, the practice of affording dissatisfied slaves a direct avenue of appeal to their masters served as a safety valve, rendering the system more flexible and alleviating potentially explosive frustrations.

Whatever his deficiencies, the overseer remained a key figure on slave plan-tations until the end of the Civil War. Indeed, so great was the outcry from planters when Confederate* authorities sought to enlist overseers during that conflict that they were one of the privileged groups exempted from military service under the Confederate Conscription Act of April 1862. However, as the military situation deteriorated, the number of exempted overseers was reduced, resulting in an acute shortage of plantation managers. Although various expe-dients were devised to combat this shortage, the paucity of skilled slave overseers contributed to demoralization on the home front and, consequently, was a sig-nificant factor in the defeat of the Confederacy.

SELECTED BIBLIOGRAPHY

John S. Bassett, *The Southern Plantation Overseer As Revealed in His Letters* (1925); Robert W. Fogel and Stanley L. Engerman, *Time on the Cross: The Economics of American Negro Slavery* (1974); Eugene D. Genovese, *Roll, Jordan, Roll: The World the Slaves Made* (1974); William K. Scarborough, *The Overseer: Plantation Management in the Old South* (1966, reprint ed., 1984); William K. Scarborough, "The Southern Plantation Overseer: A Re-evaluation," *Agricultural History*, 38 (1964), 13–20; and Kenneth M. Stampp, *The Peculiar Institution: Slavery in the Ante-Bellum South* (1956).

WILLIAM K. SCARBOROUGH

P

PACIFIC NORTHWEST, SLAVERY IN THE. Blacks arrived in the Pacific Northwest with the first white explorers and fur trappers. In August 1788 Marcus Lopez, a cabin boy aboard the *Lady Washington* of Captain Robert Gray, became the first black person to set foot on Oregon soil. Unfortunately, he was slain during an altercation between unfriendly Indians and the ship's crew. Sixteen years later another black, York of the Lewis and Clark expedition, passed through Oregon along the Columbia River. Over the next forty years numerous blacks traveled throughout the Oregon Country as trappers, servants, or explorers for the various British and American companies exploiting the fur resources of the region. Blacks also came with the exploring expeditions sponsored by the American government in the 1830s and 1840s, such as those led by Captain John C. Frémont and Lieutenant Charles Wilkes. But most blacks arrived in Oregon after crossing the plains with white families as servants or slaves. A majority of the fifty-eight blacks counted in the census of 1850 were listed as servants, laborers, or children living with white families.

Between 1840 and 1860, Afro-Americans never exceeded 1 percent of the total population of the Pacific Northwest. The question of slavery and free blacks,* however, dominated the political life of the region during that period. Proslavery forces* saw the Oregon Country as a chance to create a slave state, or at least a proslavery free state, in the newly settled lands of the Far West.* Two antislavery groups emerged in opposition to this force. One advocated a popular sovereignty approach while the other embraced abolitionism.* Neither the proslavery nor abolitionist interests ever succeeded in dominating the Pacific Northwest. Instead, the antislavery and antiblack views of popular sovereignty Democrats represented the majority viewpoint in the years prior to the Civil War.

Such sentiment reflected the origins of the adult whites who settled in the Oregon Country. Most of the pre–Civil War emigrants came from the Old Northwest, or the border states of Kentucky, Tennessee, and Missouri. Indeed, many had migrated west to escape the constant economic and political struggles with proslavery interests. They carried to their new homes a hatred of both slavery and blacks. When forming new governments in the Pacific Northwest, these settlers not only rejected slavery but sought to exclude or restrict free blacks as well.

In establishing a provisional government in 1843–1844, settlers in Oregon Country demonstrated their racial and social attitudes by adopting laws prohibiting slavery and involuntary servitude, restricting the franchise to free white males twenty-one years old, and excluding slaves or free blacks. Between 1845 and 1848 the provisional legislature dropped the exclusion law, probably because it proved impossible to enforce on a lightly populated frontier. However, fearing a potential alliance between Indians and blacks, in 1849 Oregon's new territorial legislature reenacted legislation prohibiting blacks and mulattoes from settling in the territory. The law exempted blacks and their offspring already residing in the territory. This exclusion act remained in force until accidentally repealed in 1854. The 1859 Oregon Constitution reinstated the ban on black migration and denied blacks voting rights.

Those blacks who came to Oregon either by their own free choice or as dependents of others were subjected to economic as well as political discrimination. Blacks were excluded from the benefits of the Donation Land Claim Act (1850), which permitted white settlers over twenty-one years of age and their wives to claim 640 acres if they arrived before December 1850 and half that amount if they came during the next three years. Still, a few black farmers persisted and even thrived. With white support, several blacks in both Oregon and Washington territories successfully petitioned their respective legislatures to confirm their land claims. Special acts also exempted individual blacks from Oregon's exclusion legislation. Court records indicate that judicial process expelled only one black from Oregon (1851) before statehood. Washington Territory never adopted exclusionary policies.

While slavery was prohibited by law in Oregon, evidence indicates that between 1850 and 1860 at least fourteen blacks clearly were slaves. Blacks resisted slavery in Oregon, and in the celebrated legal case of *Holmes v. Ford* (1853), Chief Justice George A. Williams of the Territorial Supreme Court declared that slavery could not exist in Oregon without specific legislation to create it. This case marked the last attempt to maintain slavery by judicial means. However, proslavery and antislavery groups openly debated whether slavery should be permitted in Oregon until voters in 1851 rejected a slavery clause in the proposed state constitution by a vote of 7,727 to 2,645. At the same time, the voters overwhelmingly approved a black exclusion clause for inclusion in the document. Although nullified by amendments to the federal constitution, the clause was not repealed until 1926.

By 1860, 154 blacks had settled in the Pacific Northwest, living in fourteen of nineteen Oregon counties and eight of nineteen counties in Washington Territory. Most were listed in the census as farmers, farm laborers, cooks, or barbers. They came from sixteen states and eight foreign countries. Black settlers braved the hardships of crossing the Great Plains or a long ocean voyage to build a new life on the frontier of the Pacific Northwest. Once there they encountered racial hostility and discrimination but established nonetheless a small but permanent black presence in the region.

SELECTED BIBILIOGRAPHY

Gordon Dodds, *Oregon: A Bicentennial History* (1977); Elizabeth McLagan, *A Peculiar Paradise: A History of Blacks in Oregon, 1778–1940* (1980); K. Keith Richard, "Unwelcome Settlers: Black and Mulatto Oregon Pioneers," *Oregon Historical Quarterly*, 84 (1983), 29–46, 173–205; and Quintard Taylor, "Slaves and Free Men: Blacks in the Oregon Country, 1840–1860," *Oregon Historical Quarterly*, 83 (1982), 153–170.

WILLIAM F. WILLINGHAM

PATERNALISM. Paternalism was an aspect of slaveholding that became salient in the South after about 1820. Its emergence coincided with increasingly militant defenses of the peculiar institution and with the elaboration of a growing body of proslavery theory.* The combination of paternalism and proslavery theory contributes to controversy about paternalism's meaning. An essential part of the new proslavery thought was its virulent racism, its definition of blacks as inherently and permanently inferior. Some theorists took this to the point of arguing that Negroes were a separate, and not fully human, species, a position apparently inconsistent with the concern and closeness implied by paternalism.

Paternalism also has emerged as a major concept used by historians and a key interpretive issue in the debate over the nature of master-slave relationships.* Disagreements among scholars over the meaning of paternalism may not be settled soon, because they reflect the variety and complexity of slavery within the South as well as the developing state of historical scholarship.

The meaning of paternalism—a concept drawn from family life—derives from the nature of family life among white Southerners during the generations before and contemporaneous with its emergence around 1820. The study of family relations is itself a developing field, and current research rests almost entirely upon a documentary record created by a small segment of the elite. But within that context, some major points are identifiable, including a transition from patriarchal families to a more intimate, affectionate, and child-centered style of family life. Nineteenth-century Southerners' understanding of paternalism derived from or was influenced by the distinction between patriarchal families on the one hand and more affectionate, paternalistic families on the other.

Originally, in the South's earliest colony, Virginia, neither patriarchal nor paternalistic relations were the rule. Instead, family life was shaped and disrupted by death. Due to high mortality, parental control loosened, the age at marriage dropped, and decision-making by the young increased. The death rate was so high that few nuclear families remained intact throughout the growth of a child, and grandparents were virtually unknown.

After about 1650, however, the period of extremely high mortality ended. From the late seventeenth to the middle of the eighteenth century, the patriarchal Southern family came into being. This pattern of family relations was based, as its name implied, on the preeminent authority of the husband and father, but a cluster of emotional realities gave it its distinctive flavor. Patriarchal families were highly ordered familial units that emphasized authority, self-restraint, and the performance of expected roles. Family members de-emphasized emotions and often hoped to avoid emotional displays. Extended family relations were quite important.

Recent studies agree that a shift to a more affectionate, child-centered, and nuclear family occurred in the latter half of the eighteenth century and the first half of the nineteenth century. Privatism reduced the importance of the extended family and put new emphasis on bonds of affection among parents and children who respected each other's individualism and autonomy. Family members expected more intense emotional relationships, and the family scene was more intimate, sentimental, and "modern" in its child-centeredness. This type of family furnished the connotations that informed antebellum Southerners' understanding of paternalism.

The causes of this shift remain uncertain but probably include a rising standard of living, greater amounts of leisure, growing literacy (especially among women), and the increased use of slave labor in the household. The use of house servants freed family members from tasks and may have made slaves the targets of discipline, in contrast to family members. Whatever the causes, this emerging paternalism was part of a wider transition that occurred in Northern society and West European nations as well. Some scholars regard the family patterns of the Northern and Southern elites as very similar. Paternalism thus signified a relationship between a superior and subordinates that was characterized by affection and closeness, concern for the welfare of individuals, and a benevolent supervision of growth and development. What relevance did this type of relation have to slavery?

The testimony of many antebellum slave owners and proslavery writers, as well as some influential historians, suggests that paternalism was very important in slaveholding. In the last few decades before the Civil War, many slave owners talked and wrote about their "family," black and white, and discussed their duties and obligations toward dependent slaves. A few Southern reformers pushed for greater religious instruction for the enslaved and for better legal protection of their families. These attitudes seem to have been more characteristic of old and wealthy families along the Atlantic seaboard rather than struggling owners or the newly wealthy of the Gulf states.

Proslavery theorists stressed that there was, in the South, concern for old and sick slaves, a concern bolstered by the identity between the slaves' physical welfare and the master's financial interests. Northern workers, by contrast, were alleged to be in a worse position, bound to their employers only by the cash nexus. Proslavery advocates also declared that the peculiar institution had uplifted and improved a savage, inferior, and helpless race.

Among historians, Willie Lee Rose has argued that there was a domestication of slavery during the nineteenth century, a softening of actual treatment that occurred simultaneously with the hardening of the legal structure. The chief exponent of the importance of paternalism, however, has been historian Eugene D. Genovese.

Genovese argued in *Roll, Jordan, Roll* (1974) that paternalism created "an organic relationship" and that a sense of "reciprocal duties" and "mutual obligations" in an organic relationship led slaves, though they tried to use paternalism to their advantage, to accept the paternalistic ethos and legitimize class rule. Though Genovese denied that masters were benevolent, as they claimed, he stated that paternalism "did encourage kindness and affection" and that there was "a genuine intimacy, not merely . . . black pretense." Paternalism, according to Genovese, created a "special sense of family" that "shaped southern culture . . . brought white and black together and welded them into one people with genuine elements of affection and intimacy." Paternalism thus was the planters' instrument of hegemony; it "created a tendency for the slaves to identify with a particular community through identification with its master" and "reduced the possibilities of their identification with each other as a class."

Other writers have disagreed with Genovese, seeing the coercion and exploitation of slavery as too salient to permit such feelings or judging racism to have been too strong and noxious to allow much intimacy. In 1979 Paul D. Escott argued that "masters and slaves lived in different worlds" and that "paternalism may have existed for white southerners primarily as a defense against outside criticism and as an argument that they were giving their bondsmen all the care that they required." Another historian, Jane Censer, concluded in 1984 that North Carolina's large planters "erected a barrier between themselves and their servants by focusing upon blacks as property." "Emotional distance between master and slave," she said, was the product of "planters' racism and slaves' chattel status."

It is distinctly possible that these differences may mirror, at least in part, real differences within the South. Some trends in scholarship have pointed toward significant regional variation, and systematic investigation of all slaveholders except the largest planters remains quite sketchy. Whether new research resolves these controversies quickly or not, paternalism seems certain to remain a major issue in studies of slavery.

SELECTED BIBLIOGRAPHY

John W. Blassingame, *The Slave Community: Plantation Life in the Antebellum South* (1972); Jane Turner Censer, *North Carolina Planters and Their Children, 1800–1860* (1984); Paul D. Escott, *Slavery Remembered: A Record of Twentieth-Century Slave Narratives* (1979); George M. Fredrickson, *The Black Image in the White Mind: The Debate on Afro-American Character and Destiny, 1817–1914* (1971); Eugene D. Genovese, *Roll, Jordan, Roll: The World the Slaves Made* (1974); Herbert G. Gutman, *The Black Family in Slavery and Freedom, 1750–1925* (1976); Willie Lee Rose, *Slavery and Freedom* (1982); and Daniel Blake Smith, *Inside the Great House: Planter Family Life in Eighteenth-Century Chesapeake Society* (1980).

PAUL D. ESCOTT

PATROLS, SLAVE. Wherever in New World colonial empires the growth of commercial agriculture led to concentration of servile labor, special institutional devices arose to maintain worker discipline and servile status. For this purpose, planters in the West Indies, Latin America, and Mexico, as well as in British North America, early resorted to bands of "searchers" or patrollers charged especially with preventing slaves from wandering from their owner's premises without leave, gathering in unauthorized assemblies, and possessing arms.

In England's continental colonies the South Carolina assembly led the way in 1690 by authorizing a patrol to enforce the colony's slave code. Virginia, Maryland, North Carolina, and Georgia soon followed. The patrols came to be thought essential to the slave system and thus were established in each new slave state, even in jurisdictions where slaves were few, as in Missouri (1825) and in Kansas Territory (1855).

At their origin and for decades afterward patrols were so closely linked with the militia system as to be virtually part of it. Typically, the commanding officer of the county militia was empowered to set the bounds for patrol districts and to appoint patrol companies from among the men under his command. But when in antebellum years the militia declined in significance, most state legislatures transferred the patrols to civil authority, typically to the justices of the peace or the county courts. With this shift in control the patrols lost most of the military attributes they once possessed and became in effect civilian police units. In reality this always had been their predominant character. Though patrols originated at a time when the English settlers faced military threats from Spain and thus especially feared slave unrest, their main function never had been to quell revolt. Instead, they protected the economic and social order by enforcing the slave codes.* Patrols were not responsible for suppressing actual uprisings.* Should these occur, the militia would be mobilized. Though legislatures from time to time changed the authorized size of patrols, they were in every instance small units. In Tennessee the number in each patrol usually was three; in Texas, three to five; in Georgia, seven; in Arkansas, up to ten.

In most states responsibility for patrol duty fell on slaveholder and nonslaveholder* without distinction. In Mississippi, however, legislation enacted in 1839 required the captain of a patrol to be a slaveholder, and in Texas one-half of the patrol had to own slaves. In Arkansas no citizen in a patrol district served more than four months until each slaveholder had served four months. By act of 1819 South Carolina exempted nonslaveholders over the age of forty-five from patrol duty. Alabama enacted a similar law in 1852. Georgia's legislature, like South Carolina's, required service from men and women slaveholders alike on the ground that all "ought to contribute to the Service and Security of that District wherein their interest lays." But in those states, as in most others, persons unwilling to serve might supply substitutes or else pay a penalty for not doing so. Apparently, many wealthy men (and, presumably, most women) took advantage of those provisions. The South Carolina planter Louis Manigault in the 1850s refused patrol duty, and in Georgia the statesman Robert Toombs regularly paid his fine for nonservice. Probably most patrollers were men whose economic status did not allow the luxury of hiring substitutes, or were men who welcomed such paid employment. The former slaves' impression that patrols commonly were made up of "poor whites" or nonslaveholders appears, then, to be accurate, and perhaps provides a source for the slaves' traditional scorn for "po-white trash."

The prominent position occupied by patrols in black folklore suggests that they performed their duties more systematically than often is supposed and that many slaves at some time encountered them. Slave parents threatened their errant children with visits by the "patterrollers," and oral tradition celebrated the triumphs of wily slaves in outwitting them. Frequent too were memories (substantiated by court records) of abuses suffered at their hands. At all times the large authority granted them was certain to bring resentment, and their right to search slave houses and to disperse slave gatherings easily could be productive of atrocity. The law empowered patrols to apprehend violators, determine their guilt, pronounce sentence, and inflict punishment on the spot—all without concurrence or review by any other authority. In most states and at most times patrols might administer ten lashes to those judged guilty, though in Arkansas twenty were allowed. Texas's original penalty of twenty lashes was cut to ten in 1856. Free blacks, over whom in most jurisdictions patrols also had authority, usually were taken before a justice of the peace for punishment.

Slave owners welcomed the patrollers' service in keeping the public roads free from wandering slaves and complained when they believed that duty was shirked, but some of them also hotly resented the patrols' occasional trespass on their premises in a search for weapons or to break up slave gatherings, and the overenthusiastic punishment they sometimes inflicted. But resentment could proceed in the other direction as well. Thus, the requirement of universal patrol service entered into the complaints offered by citizens of western Virginia during the Virginia legislature's slavery debates in 1831–1832,* and in Lincoln County, North Carolina, in 1825 eighty-eight citizens protested that they did not "wish to have anything to do as respects the government or discipline of the negroes."

The patrol system gave slaveless white men a degree of authority over blacks that they would not otherwise have experienced and enlisted them in support of an institution whose economic rewards largely eluded them. The tradition of racial power and, perhaps, of resentment thereby established outlived slavery and did not easily die. The Ku Klux Klan and the sundry other vigilante groups that in later years sought to maintain or reestablish white dominance had no legal basis; yet their roots lay deep in the Southern past. They were not created *de novo* by Southerners of the Reconstruction era.

SELECTED BIBLIOGRAPHY

Benjamin F. Callahan, "The North Carolina Slave Patrol" (M.A. thesis, University of North Carolina, 1973); Helen T. Catterall, ed., *Judicial Cases Concerning American Slavery and the Negro* (5 vols., 1926–1937); Stanley Feldstein, *Once a Slave: The Slave's View of Slavery* (1970); Gladys-Marie Fry, *Night Riders in Black Folk History* (1975); Howell M. Henry, *The Police Control of the Slave in South Carolina* (1914); Katherine Ann McGeachy, "The North Carolina Slave Code" (M.A. thesis, University of North Carolina, 1948); E. Russ Williams, Jr., ed., "Notes and Documents: Slave Patrol Ordinances of St. Tammany Parish, Louisiana, 1835–1838," *Louisiana History*, 13 (1972), 399–412; and Shirley Jo-Ann Yee, "The Origins of the Southern Slave Patrol System: South Carolina, 1690–1810" (M.A. thesis, Ohio State University, 1983).

MERTON L. DILLON

PERSONALITY, SLAVE. The term *slave personality* refers to the distinctive traits—including mental, emotional, and moral characteristics—that have been used to describe the temperament, demeanor, and behavior of American slaves. The existence and precise nature of the Afro-American slave personality has been the subject of considerable controversy, both during slavery and after. During the antebellum period proslavery apologists* frequently made assumptions about and assertions concerning slave character traits that served as ideological justifications for the institution of slavery. Moreover, debate over the relationship between slavery and personality has been one of the central issues in the surge of interest in American slavery by historians during the past quarter century.

During the slavery era, most whites perceived Africans as "primitive" and "uncivilized," the "natural" inferiors of Europeans. White observers attributed numerous personality traits to Africans and their New World descendants, and they interpreted these traits as innate, inherited, and inherent qualities. Specific traits, almost all of them negatively valued by whites, became linked together to form broad images of the slave personality in the mind of Southern whites. The frequency and pervasiveness with which different traits were emphasized during the antebellum period varied by region and in response to changes in demographic, political, economic, and cultural conditions of Southern life.

From a content analysis of the diaries of Southern slaveholders, Richard B. Erno has identified several images of the slave personality, each of which was used to justify slavery. He contends that these images were usually tacitly or subconsciously held and were only infrequently explicitly expressed; rather than a valid assessment of slave personality structure, they represented projections of the slaveholder's worldview.

Between 1800 and 1860 the dominant image of the slave was as Caliban, a "form of being that was neither animal nor wholly human." Caliban was essentially a beast of burden—submissive, servile, slothful, indolent, incompetent, and stupid. In his work habits he was perceived as a malingerer—lazy, shiftless, irresponsible, improvident, and inefficient—and therefore fit only for simple and menial tasks. The Caliban image was primarily a product of areas characterized by large plantation agriculture, a high proportion of unskilled slaves, and a relatively high ratio of blacks to whites in the general population.

Whereas the Caliban image emphasized the slave's submission and acquiescence to a subservient role, the Satan image, which was the second most widely held perception of slaves during the nineteenth century, demonstrated the slaveholder's ability to embrace conflicting images simultaneously. The Satan image reflected the prominent perception that slaves represented a "troublesome presence." At best, slaves were dissemblers—inherently untrustworthy, deceitful, deceptive, evasive, and prone to lying and stealing; at worst, they were impudent, insolent, recalcitrant, rebellious, and lascivious, representing a threat to the established social order. The Satan image, which appeared more prominently in the upper South in the early 1800s, spread after the 1830s to those areas, primarily in the lower South, with a higher percentage of blacks in the population.

A third image, although much less widely embraced by Southern slaveholders than either Caliban or Satan, was the comic slave, Sambo.* In this conception, slaves were portrayed as essentially childlike—carefree, playful, happy-go-lucky, clowning, foolishly imitative, and inherently musical. This image was restricted to the older, more urbanized areas of the South and to the border states.

The most positive images of slaves appeared toward the end of the antebellum period. Partly in response to abolitionist claims that blacks were dehumanized by the slave system, proslavery apologists contended that slavery performed a "civilizing" and training function. As a consequence three images—each personified as personal servants, rather than unskilled laborers—emerged: the noble and loyal Friday; the wise, intelligent, and nurturant mammy*; and the pious and long-suffering Uncle Tom. Each of these images appeared relatively infrequently and was restricted primarily to the Atlantic seaboard states.

The issue of slave personality became most explicitly articulated nearly a century after emancipation. In the most celebrated and provocative interpretation of slave personality, Stanley M. Elkins argued that the distinctive institutional arrangements of American slavery elicited a personality type—Sambo—that occurred only among American slaves. Elkins maintained that the image of a docile, submissive, infantile, childlike slave was not merely a stereotype advanced by defenders of slavery to justify their own interests, nor was it simply a projection of the worldview of American slaveholders. Rather, it represented a relatively valid description of the dominant slave psychological response to enslavement. According to Elkins, Sambo was an adaptive personality type, a response to and a product of the unique nature of American slavery.

However, Elkins did not argue that the psychological effects of the American slave system would be uniformly felt among all slaves. He hypothesized that the Sambo personality would be most frequently found among certain categories of slaves—those most vulnerable to the direct effects of the master's power and sanctions. In Elkins's model the Sambo personality would be found primarily among powerless field hands on large plantations and relatively infrequently among autonomous urban slaves who arranged their own employment. Thus, the basic question Elkins posed was whether occupying different roles in the slave system exacted differences in personality.

The issues Elkins raised concerning the psychological consequences of the American slave system on the enslaved came to define the boundaries of much of the debate over slavery during the 1960s and 1970s. The issue of slave personality became essentially a social psychological problem that focused ultimately on broader questions of how social structure, and, in particular, relative power or powerlessness affect psychological functioning.

The relationship between the slave's overt behavior and his or her underlying personality structure has been one of the major sources of dispute in the controversy over slave personality. Many critics have argued that any accommodation or conformity to white stereotypes by slaves was merely a superficial and situational adaptation and did not affect their "true" character. In other words, slaves adopted a highly sophisticated "stage presence," an ability to play a role to the satisfaction of the master while not fully internalizing the demeaning aspects of the role itself. Such critics deny that conformity to slave role prescriptions provided an accurate index of the psychological adjustment of the slave. In other words, slaves were not substantially psychologically affected by their subordinate position in the slave system. Thus, John W. Blassingame has argued that "the same range of personality types existed in the quarters as in the mansion."

Other critics have challenged Elkins's notion that the Sambo personality was idiosyncratic to American slavery. They contend that such demeaning stereotypes are an inevitable and universal concomitant of slavery. Orlando Patterson has noted that slave systems widely separated in time and space have produced remarkably similar stereotypes. Thus, the image of the slave as a "lying, cowardly, lazy buffoon devoid of courage and manliness" was prominent in the stereotypes of the " 'Graeculus' of ancient Rome, the 'Zandj' of medieval Iraq, the 'Quashee' of eighteenth-century Jamaica, the 'Sambo' of the U.S. South, and the 'Diimaajo' . . . of the Fulani." Patterson argues that such stereotypes of the slave represent rationalizations or projections of the superordinate class—a means of legitimating their interests and maintaining their dominant position in a system of class relations. Such stereotypes are "an ideological imperative of all systems of slavery."

Other interpretations agree with Patterson's that such demeaning stereotypes are a universal consequence of slavery, but they advance other explanations for their presence. Eugene D. Genovese has adopted a cultural interpretation to account for work habits typically attributed to slaves, contending that slave labor was not efficient and highly rationalized and, instead, reflected the traditional irregular rhythms and patterns of rural, premodern people. Similar to other preindustrial people, slaves worked hard, but they resisted regularity, routine, and regimentation. Their work habits, he writes, reflected a "set of attitudes toward time, work, and leisure which black people developed partly in Africa and partly in the slave quarters and which constituted a special case of a general pattern of behavior associated with preindustrial cultures." Genovese continues, "Preindustrial peoples knew all about hard work and discipline, but their standards were neither those of the factory nor those of the plantation, and were embedded in a radically different culture."

On the other hand, several writers have suggested a structural explanation to interpret the characteristics Elkins has associated with the Sambo personality. A structural interpretation considers such traits a behavioral response to enslavement, an inevitable consequence of slavery. If the distinctive feature of slavery is the "totality of the slave's powerlessness," one would anticipate that such powerlessness would elicit a similar psychological syndrome—what Genovese has characterized as a "slavish" personality—as a consequence of the relations between master and slave. M. I. Finley has noted that "a special slave psychology must have developed. . . . In order to survive as human beings, slaves had to adapt to their state of deracination by developing [distinctive] new psychological features . . . ." Therefore, although considerable variation occurred among different systems of slavery, from a structural perspective slavery by its very nature produces similar personality types.

A basic assumption of much of the controversy over slave personality was that slave psychic functioning was a dependent variable, a response to the kinds of slave systems to which slaves were exposed. In this model slaves were acted upon; they did not themselves initiate action. However, merely to analyze and describe the effects of oppression obscures the dynamic and creative responses of the enslaved. To analyze adequately the psychic damage exacted by a slave system, it is also necessary to investigate the creative mechanisms by which slaves survived. Slaves were not merely passive recipients of white demands and sanctions; they were able themselves subtly to influence the slave system and to adopt ways of dealing with its effects. In reaction to the power of the master, slaves developed a rich and varied cultural underlife, including music,* folklore,* and religion,* that enabled them to survive the potential psychic damage of the slave system.

SELECTED BIBLIOGRAPHY

John W. Blassingame, *The Slave Community: Plantation Life in the Antebellum South* (1972); Stanley M. Elkins, *Slavery: A Problem in American Institutional and Intellectual Life* (2nd rev. ed, 1968); Richard B. Erno, "Dominant Images of the Negro in the Antebellum South" (Ph.D. dissertation, University of Minnesota, 1961); M. I. Finley, "Slavery," in *International Encyclopedia of the Social Sciences*, 14 (1968), 307–313; Eugene D. Genovese, *Roll, Jordan, Roll: The World the Slaves Made* (1974); Ann J.

Lane, ed., *The Debate over Slavery: Stanley Elkins and His Critics* (1971); and Orlando Patterson, *Slavery and Social Death: A Comparative Study* (1982).

NORMAN R. YETMAN

PERSONAL LIBERTY LAWS. The abolition of slavery in the North left conflicting moral and legal systems* in the United States: one based upon the ownership of human beings (and the presumption that all blacks were slaves), and the other upon the assumption that all persons were free. As long as these two systems coexisted in a federal union, there was a crushing problem whenever a runaway passed from a slave-owning jurisdiction to a free one. The Constitution's fugitive slave clause provided for his or her return, but it did not clarify upon what principles, or who was responsible. In 1793 Congress enacted a fugitive law,* but questions remained, including what role the free states would play whenever someone within their jurisdictions who claimed to be free was also claimed as a slave.

Abolition, of course, had meant more than freeing individuals: it had meant eliminating rules of law based on slavery and substituting rules based upon the presumption of freedom. Northern states, beginning in the 1780s, enacted laws to protect free blacks* from being kidnapped as alleged slaves. These early personal liberty laws rested upon the presumption that all persons are free until proven otherwise by orderly legal process. This position undermined a right slave owners claimed, the right of recaption. This was a common-law right to recover one's property without going to law. One of the clearest rejections of this asserted right came in 1826 in Pennsylvania. This law was a compromise: it provided state procedures for the recovery of runaways,* but required putative owners to follow legal process. It was struck down in *Prigg v. Pennsylvania* (1842) by a fragmented U.S. Supreme Court. One point that was clear was that the Court held that slave owners possessed a federal right of recaption. At the same time it held that the states were not required to implement the guarantee in the Constitution, or to act under the federal law of 1793. Thereafter, a new category of personal liberty law appeared as a number of Northern states withdrew all state aid in the recovery process. This led to the Fugitive Slave Law of 1850* which, among other things, prohibited states from interfering whenever someone was claimed as a slave.

Throughout these years state habeas corpus and jury trials were used to protect free blacks, as well as to obstruct the recovery of actual fugitives. By the 1850s several states expressly provided by statute for these rights in cases involving alleged runaways. Because of the presumption of freedom, these laws, some argued, did not deal with fugitives but with free blacks, whose rights otherwise would be subordinated to the demands of slave owners. By the 1850s, moreover, some states became more aggressive when they provided state counsel to aid alleged fugitives.

Another challenge to the South in the mid-1850s came from Wisconsin. That state's court declared that the federal law was unconstitutional. The Supreme

Court rejected this in *Ableman v. Booth* (1859). Frustrations were high by the late 1850s; bills were even introduced in some states to repudiate the constitutional obligation. The effort to accommodate two moral and legal orders within the same federal union clearly had ended in failure.

SELECTED BIBLIOGRAPHY

Stanley W. Campbell, *The Slave Catchers: Enforcement of the Fugitive Slave Law, 1850–1860* (1968); Robert Cover, *Justice Accused: Antislavery and the Judicial Process* (1976); William R. Leslie, ''The Fugitive Slave Clause, 1787–1842: A Study in American Constitutional History and in the History of the Conflict of Laws'' (Ph.D. dissertation, University of Michigan, 1945); Thomas D. Morris, *Free Men All: The Personal Liberty Laws of the North, 1780–1861* (1974); and Norman L. Rosenberg, ''Personal Liberty Laws and Sectional Crisis: 1850–1861,'' *Civil War History*, 17 (1971), 25–44.

THOMAS D. MORRIS

PHILADELPHIA, PA, SLAVERY IN. Little is known about the African people who arrived in the Delaware Valley with the Swedes and Dutch in the mid-seventeenth century. However, with the arrival of William Penn, and the Quaker* ideals of his settlers, a debate opened which underlay black life in Philadelphia until 1780, when Pennsylvania became the first state to officially abolish slavery. There was some antislavery sentiment* as early as 1688, when the Germantown Friends Meeting issued ''A caution to Friends concerning the buying or keeping of Negroes''—the first such document in English-speaking America. Penn provided for the manumission of his own slaves upon his death, and through the first half of the eighteenth century, passionate Friends such as Ralph Sandiford, Benjamin Lay, John Woolman, and Anthony Benezet employed dramatic tactics to keep alive the issue of slavery's injustice. In 1758 the Philadelphia Yearly Meeting of Friends made official its proscription against its members holding slaves. On the other hand, throughout the eighteenth century many of the fortunes of Philadelphians—including Robert Morris, Thomas Willing, and other Quakers as well as non-Quakers—were the result of slave trade* and/or slave labors, and up until the Civil War, many Philadelphians maintained family and/or economic ties to the slave South.

Eighteenth-century newspaper advertisements show that slaves enhanced the Philadelphia area economy with such skills as spinning, dressmaking, ironworking, woodworking and medicine as well as cooking, field or farm work, and maritime occupations. A few slaves, such as Moses Williams, slave of Charles Willson Peale, used skills learned from their masters to buy their own freedom and make successful independent careers.

Early newspapers, legislation, and court records reveal that Pennsylvania's African-Americans also ran away and imposed their own styles of self-expression, economic activity, recreation, and religious worship. Comprising only about 7 percent of the city's population at the time of the American Revolution, Philadelphia's black people still managed, in the 1780s, to establish an independent group, the Free African Society, out of which grew several black churches and secular organizations, including Richard Allen's Bethel African Methodist Episcopal Church, the still-extant founding unit of a now worldwide black religious network. The efforts of such leaders were encouraged and supported by the "Pennsylvania Society for Promoting the Abolition of Slavery and the Relief of Free Negroes unlawfully held in Bondage," a largely Quaker group founded on the eve of the Revolution, and active through the mid-nineteenth century in purchasing slaves for the purpose of freeing them, as well as defending kidnapped free blacks and opposing legislation that might have banished free Afro-Americans from Pennsylvania.

As a result of the Quaker influence a few Philadelphia blacks—including Allen and James and Absalom Jones—found themselves free, educated and in possession of property by the end of the Revolution. Although the 1780 state manumission law provided only for gradual emancipation over several decades, in fact, by 1800, the overwhelming majority of Philadelphia's 4,000 Afro-Americans were no longer enslaved. Their freedom, however, was severely circumscribed, subject to local discrimination and the whim of kidnappers.

As the closest Northern city to the slave South, Philadelphia became a major recipient of fugitive slaves,* who often were aided by sympathetic black and white citizens. Philadelphia Afro-Americans were in the forefront of the antebellum abolitionist movement. In the 1790s they began to petition the federal government to abolish slavery. By the 1820s they were outspoken in their resistance to the return of free blacks to Africa, making the case that Afro-Americans had fought in the Revolution to secure American freedom, and therefore were entitled to a part of that freedom, and the exile of free black people would solidify the system of slavery by removing the slaves' free advocates. The 1820s and 1830s brought not only a rise in the city's black population (15,000 by 1840) but also an intensification of antislavery activity. The work of many black churches, and secular groups such as the all-black Vigilance Committee, served as a principal support for underground railroad* activity. Their work was augmented by the activities of such interracial groups as the Philadelphia Female Anti-Slavery Society (organized in 1833), the revitalized Pennsylvania Abolition Society, and the Convention of the Free People of Color (begun in 1830), each with its own strategy for attacking the institution of slavery, including petitioning legislatures, purchasing and freeing slaves, and organizing boycotts of slave-produced goods. Such groups, especially if they were interracial, aroused the ire of the sizable proslavery forces in Philadelphia. Antiabolitionist violence intensified with the burning of the abolitionists' new Pennsylvania Hall (1838) being only one of the most widely publicized of such incidents. Dramatic underground railroad escapes, such as that of Henry "Box" Brown (1854), stood in nervous contrast to the realities of slave catchers* who were aided by proslavery Philadelphians.

Prior to the 1830s few Philadelphia Afro-Americans had actually exercised their right to vote. However, the 1838 state constitutional convention specifically disfranchising Pennsylvania blacks was perceived by many blacks as the entrenchment of discrimination. Thereafter, a mood of despair coexisted with a frantic redoubling of abolitionist and self-development efforts. Black activists such as Octavius Catto, William Douglass, Jesse Glasgow, and Jacob White, while giving full support to the underground railroad efforts to aid escaped slaves, nevertheless found time to develop local debate and literary societies (e.g., the Library Company of Colored Persons [1837] and the Banneker Institute [1854]) and to organize intercity conventions to discuss strategy. Some of these groups, such as the Gilbert Lyceum (1841), included women as well as men, reflecting a trend among the black community to give serious attention to the contributions of women. Such groups stressed not only the need to boycott slave-produced products, but also the need to sharpen the mind by studying science and the humanities. While some of these groups were church-affiliated, many were secular, reflecting the industrial society's growing trend toward voluntary societies based on mutual interests. As most blacks were unable to compete in the capital-intensive industrial modernization, the voluntary intellectual association was one viable alternative to being completely excluded from the styles of the modernizing city.

When hope returned to black Philadelphia in the form of the Civil War,* black leaders launched an aggressive campaign to recruit Afro-American troops for the Union army.* Black activists and their advocates hoped thereby to demonstrate the worthiness of Afro-American citizens. In fact, however, discrimination and prejudice in Philadelphia continued far beyond the Civil War, despite the nominal success of the all-black Pennsylvania Equal Rights League in lobbying to have the state legislature officially restore the black vote (1871). And, as a legacy of this checkered history, the "City of Brotherly Love" has continued to maintain its early acquired reputation as an ambivalent sanctuary for blacks escaping Southern oppression.

SELECTED BIBLIOGRAPHY

Emma J. Lapsansky, "Since They Got Those Separate Churches: Afro-Americans and Racism in Jacksonian Philadelphia," *American Quarterly*, 32 (1980), 54–78; David McBride, "Black Protest against Racial Politics: Gardner, Hinton, and Their Memorial of 1838," *Pennsylvania History*, 46 (1979), 149–162; Gary B. Nash, "Slaves and Slaveowners in Colonial Philadelphia," *William and Mary Quarterly*, 3rd ser., 30 (1973), 223–256; Jean R. Soderlund, "Conscience, Interest, and Power: The Development of Quaker Opposition to Slavery in the Delaware Valley, 1688–1780" (Ph.D. dissertation, Temple University, 1982); and Richard R. Wright, *The Negro in Pennsylvania: A Study in Economic History* (1912, reprint ed., 1969).

EMMA J. LAPSANSKY

PHILLIPS, WENDELL (1811–1884). Wendell Phillips, born in Boston on 29 November 1811, was educated at Harvard (B.A., 1831, LL.B., 1834), and died in the same city on 11 July 1884. Soon after his marriage to radical abolitionist Ann Terry Greene in 1836, Phillips, too, embraced the cause of immediate black emancipation and came to dominate the leadership of the American Anti-Slavery Society by establishing himself as abolitionism's* foremost white rhetorician. His enormous skill and broad impact as an orator eventually earned him the title of "abolitionism's golden-trumpet." As a result, his impact in American political culture far transcended the formally organized abolitionist movement. From the 1840s onward he dominated the Northern lecture circuit, provoking broad hostility to slavery by speaking so eloquently against the institution, and for the national goal of racial equality. During the Civil War* and Reconstruction, he amplified on these demands, insisting that freed slaves take title to confiscated Confederate lands, have free public education, and receive full constitutional guarantees of civil and political equality. Seeking these ends, he also became a bitter critic first of Abraham Lincoln's,* then of Andrew Johnson's, Reconstruction policies and a leading proponent of "radical" Reconstruction.

Phillips's commitments to racial equality also involved him deeply in local and personal struggles. In Massachusetts, he allied with militant black leaders such as John Hinton and William Nell to oppose segregated public schools, transportation systems, and laws against miscegenation. He was instrumental in securing the 1846 *Roberts* decision outlawing segregated schools and in repealing state laws against racial intermarriage. His protests against these injustices naturally led him to resist all attempts by federal or state authorities to recapture fugitive slaves residing in his native Boston. Although the 1850 Fugitive Slave Law* provoked his most passionate resistance, he also took direct, nonviolent action to prevent the enforcement of its predecessor, the milder 1793 Fugitive Slave Law,* using his legal skills as well as his oratorical power to protect fugitives' rights and to call forth public resistance.

Phillips also employed his considerable private fortune to aid the needy, black and white alike. His private correspondence reflects a lifetime preoccupation with charitable giving and his willingness to put his legal skills and personal contacts at the disposal of the disadvantaged. By the end of his life, Phillips had divested himself of a fortune which had once ranked him among Massachusetts's ten wealthiest citizens. A black unwed mother, desperate for assistance; an illiterate fugitive slave anxious for education; an orphan of "mixed" background searching for adoption; an enterprising Negro craftsman soliciting capital—all provide examples of those who found Phillips a sensitive and generous sponsor.

Ann Greene Phillips, a housebound invalid, always collaborated closely with Wendell Phillips during his long and rich career. Grievously afflicted by rheumatoid arthritis, she spent most of her adulthood confined to a sickroom, usually attended by her famous husband. In long conversations she always exerted profound influences on Wendell Phillips's doctrines and choices as a reformer. But as their relationship deepened, both partners also began finding greater fulfillment by learning to live apart for weeks at a time. By the mid-1850s, this evolution had freed Wendell Phillips to tour the length and breadth of the North, establishing himself as a major force in the developing controversy over slavery. And, in the years following emancipation and Reconstruction, Ann Greene Phillips's continuing insistence on preserving her own independence further supported Wendell Phillips's ongoing career as an advocate of temperance, labor, and women's rights. She died, childless, in 1887, three years after her husband's passing.

SELECTED BIBLIOGRAPHY

Irving H. Bartlett, *Wendell Phillips: Brahmin Radical* (1961); Louis Filler, ed., *Wendell Phillips on Civil Rights and Freedom* (1965); Richard Hofstadter, "Wendell Phillips: The Patrician as Agitator," in Hofstadter, *The American Political Tradition* (1948); and James Brewer Stewart, *Liberty's Hero: Wendell Phillips* (1986).

JAMES BREWER STEWART

PHOTOGRAPHS. The possibility of photographic documentation of Afro-Americans in bondage was limited to a very short period. The process of photography dates from 1839, when the daguerreotype was invented in France. From that date until the passage of the Thirteenth Amendment in 1865, abolishing slavery, was barely a quarter of a century. The new invention reached the United States almost overnight. The phenomenal ability of the daguerreotype to reproduce likeness caused it to spread rapidly. The early commercial photographers made portraits of people under commission; the amateurs captured family, friends, or neighbors. Progress in the medium continued steadily, with the development of the calotype, the tintype, and the *carte de visite*, all before the Civil War.

Among the photographs that have survived, few are of slaves. Photographic evidence of the conditions of plantation life exists, particularly shots of slave quarters, cotton gins, and the Big House. During the Civil War, when photography was just beginning to emerge as a means of depicting social life, pictures of slaves in contraband camps* or as soldiers in the Union army* became available. But individual portraits of slaves as persons with their own unique identities and personalities are rare.

Slavery was abolished in the last of the Northern states, New York, in 1827, before photography was invented. No photographs of slaves in that region exist. In the South, while many daguerreotypists set up studios, it was highly unlikely that they could have had slaves as patrons. It is conceivable that some slave owners, for whatever reason, might have paid photographers to take pictures of their human property. The only such photographs to come to light are a set of fifteen nude studies made in the spring of 1850 by J. T. Zealy, a daguerreotypist in Columbia, South Carolina. These were not discovered until 1976 when they were found in an unused storage cabinet in Harvard's Peabody Museum of Archaeology and Ethnology. All but one of the fifteen depict slaves born in Africa, with each identified by name, by tribe or region from which they came, and by the plantation on which they labored.

Investigation by their discoverer, Elinor T. Reichlin, revealed these exceptional photographs were made at the request of the Harvard naturalist, Louis

Agassiz, to document his belief that blacks were a separate species, separately created. After he conducted field research on race at plantations near Columbia, a colleague arranged for Zealy to photograph the slaves Agassiz had examined, posing them nude to point up anatomical details. It was one of the earliest instances of the use of photography for scientific research. The theory advanced by Agassiz and others, used by defenders of slavery to bolster their belief in racial inequality, was soon discredited by Darwin's theory of evolution and modern anthropology, but the photographs survive as a rare example of a documented visual record of Afro-Americans in slavery.

Among the holdings of libraries, museums, and private collectors are scattered examples of slave photographs. Usually they were revealed as the by-product of manuscript research. (Thus far few scholars have searched explicitly for graphic documentation of slavery.) Even these few photographs are chiefly of runaway slaves or slaves liberated by advancing Union troops. The National Archives contain photos of contrabands, including some shown in their work clothes before enlisting, and then in uniform. The Library of Congress has many photographs of blacks in the Union army or navy, or working for the services as teamsters, cooks, or dock laborers. In the Metropolitan Museum of Art are the well-known photographs of some fifty slaves left behind on Edisto Island plantation when their master, James Hopkinson, fled South Carolina in 1862.

The originals of such photos have often disappeared. But engravings made from them can be found in the illustrated weeklies or in pamphlets and books and magazines of the period. The engraving and printing processes of that time could not reproduce photographs on ordinary paper. Photographs had to be converted into drawings and then into woodcuts before they could appear as pictures.

To give a few instances, in 1863 *Harper's Weekly* printed from photographs by M'Pherson and Oliver three engravings of Gordon, a runaway Mississippi slave who had come into the Union lines at Baton Rouge. The first shows Gordon in his torn and muddy clothing; the second with back bared to show the scars of whippings; and the third in uniform, with musket. Often, as in this case, the periodical credits the original photographer. The same weekly for 2 June 1860 ran engravings from photographs taken at Key West, showing the captured slaveship *Wildfire*, with many slaves crouched on deck.

Among the best-known photographs are an 1851 portrait of Caesar, once a slave in New York (now located at the New-York Historical Society), and one of Isaac Jefferson, formerly the slave of Thomas Jefferson (now located at the Alderman Library, University of Virginia). An engraving of Dred Scott, the Virginia-born slave who was the subject of the crucial Supreme Court decision of 1857, showing him with his wife and two daughters, appeared in *Leslie's Weekly* of 17 June 1857, made from a photograph by Fitzgibbon of St. Louis. The Valentine Museum, Richmond, Virginia, has a photograph of Gilbert Hunt, the heroic slave blacksmith, who died in 1863.

The Schomburg Center holds four *cartes de visite* of slave children in New Orleans, and the Kennedy Galleries in New York have a photograph of a slave nurse in Louisiana, holding her master's child. In the Blagdon Collection at Harvard's Houghton Library are two photographs of slaves sent to Wendell Phillips from the South. One is of Nonice Eilkinson, taken when she was seventy-eight. She had been born free in Santo Domingo and sold into slavery in Charleston at age eighteen. The other is of Richardson, a young female slave in Richmond, Virginia, shown with back scalded by her mistress.

In the Southern Historical Collection at the University of North Carolina at Chapel Hill there are some forty photographs of blacks, scattered in family or institutional papers. The Penn School Papers, for example, have about twenty images of slaves newly freed on St. Helena Island, South Carolina. In later years, of course, after emancipation, ex-slaves in the United States and Canada were frequently photographed, down through the 1930s when several elderly survivors were put on film by government photographers.

A few black photographers were active before the Civil War, in Boston, New York, Philadelphia, and Cincinnati, but no photographs by them of slaves have been found. Published works on the many aspects of slavery and on the Civil War often contain reproductions of photographs, mostly of ex-slaves.

SELECTED BIBLIOGRAPHY

Elinor Reichlin, "Faces of Slavery: A Historical Find," *American Heritage*, 28 (1977), 4–11.

MILTON MELTZER

PLANTATION MISTRESS. From the founding of the Southern colonies, white women on plantations were central to the growth and expansion of the region. In 1619 the Virginia House of Burgesses declared "in a newer plantation it is not known whether man or woman be the most necessary." Planters depended upon their wives to provide them with a string of heirs, to build up their stake in the New World. Colonial authorities also counted on the "civilizing" and "domesticating" influence of white women, which could transform rowdy frontier areas into gentrified plantation communities.

During the colonial era women had marginal roles in shaping the Southern colonies, but some plantation mistresses could and did transcend these limitations. The enterprising Eliza Lucas Pinckney certainly was not the average eighteenth-century plantation mistress, but evidence allows us to appreciate her many accomplishments. During her marriage to one of the largest planters in South Carolina, Pinckney demonstrated her talents at management, skills she had learned while overseeing her father's estates while he served as the governor of Antigua. Her experiments with the cultivation of indigo* led to the flourishing of this cash crop in the colony. In 1758 when she was widowed at the age of thirty-five, Pinckney became a formidable manager of several plantations while rearing her children. When she died in 1792 one of her great admirers, George

Washington, was a pallbearer. Pinckney's spirit and talents, which were out-standing in her own age, became more common for her daughter's generation.

When the American Revolution* erupted and the colonies broke trade relations with England during the 1770s, Southern plantations were forced into self-sufficiency. Planter wives were required to spin, weave, cultivate, and supply goods and services at an unprecedented rate, not only for their white family, but for the increasing number of slaves. The slave population increased dra-matically during the eighteenth century. The slave population in the Southern colonies, excluding Virginia, grew from 650 in 1685 to 31,000 in 1730 to 187,000 in 1775. This dramatic growth increased the burden of household man-agement for plantation mistresses, who were expected to provide for their slaves in four significant areas: food, shelter, clothing, and medical care. Although the quality of care varied from plantation to plantation and the degree to which each mistress provided for slave families depended upon slave contributions as well, planters increasingly relied upon their wives to oversee the important domestic spectrum of slave care.

Ironically, many mistresses were unprepared, both for increasing burdens and for the new responsibilities thrust upon them by the Revolutionary war. While their husbands waged fortunes and lives in the War for Independence, slave-holders' wives shouldered enormous responsibilities in keeping the plantation running. Many women, at a loss as to how to manage, turned to their female slaves for training; many mistresses learned how to spin and weave and even how to make clothing from black women on plantations. Although the daughters of Southern planters had been taught sewing in school or at home, they had busied themselves with stitching samplers and embroidering handkerchiefs. These ornamental aspects of their education did little to prepare them for the harsh realities of plantation life. Most girls within the planter class married at such a young age that they had very little preparation for their roles as wife and mother, and little experience at household or plantation management.

This syndrome was compounded by the great migration onto the frontier that followed the invention of the cotton gin* in 1793. Following this crucial de-velopment, the number of planters (roughly those who owned estates with twenty slaves or more) increased as it became more economically profitable to employ slaves to grow cotton.* The "new South" region—western Georgia, Alabama and Mississippi—boomed during this "Cotton Revolution." As the slave owners of the South extended their influence in the nation as a whole, as well as within their own region, the plantation mistress was not only an important contributor to the system, but she became a symbol of the entire culture. The plantation mistress was a distinctly important representation within the iconography of the Old South. She especially projected the image of grace and ease to which white Southerners aspired. Despite the rigors of her plantation chores, despite her dissatisfactions with the system that bound her to the plantation as securely as her husband's slaves, the planter wife stood as a living monument to slavery's success.

The private records of planter wives and daughters, mothers and sisters, suggest that women felt themselves unfairly subjected to isolation and household drudgery by their roles on plantations. Those planter wives whose sufferings are revealed in divorce records provide evidence of widespread abuse of women on Southern plantations. Not only were Southern wives expected to ignore gambling, excessive drinking and family violence, but planters could philander with their female slaves—if they managed their affairs discreetly—with few or no reprisals. As Mary Boykin Chesnut decried in her journal: "God forgive us, but ours is a monstrous system, a wrong and iniquity . . . a man who runs a hideous black harem with its consequences under the same roof with his lovely white wife, and his beautiful and accomplished daughters . . . holds his head as high and poses as a model of all human virtues to these poor women whom God and laws have given him." Although the extent to which this practice flourished remains a matter of debate, the fact of the double standard remains: both for race and gender. Plantation slavery limited women's power just as surely as it robbed slaves of theirs.

When the Civil War* erupted women were ill-prepared to cope with the rigors of war. Although mistresses might be able to run plantations in their husbands' absences, the prolonged stress of wartime burdens and unrelieved responsibilities eroded women's capabilities. By the second year of the war, shortages of staple goods created hardships, the mounting death toll spread fear and grief, and as the war dragged on, even women isolated on rural estates were forced to confront the crumbling of order, the slow descent into chaos. Most symbolic of this loss of control, slaves grew increasingly difficult for whites to manage. Almost all slave owners complained of droves of runaways.* Open defiance grew widespread and violence* among slaves was no longer rare, consequences mistresses faced with varying degrees of apprehension. The Civil War heightened the tensions, exacerbated the contradictions, and intensified the moral dilemmas that characterized the condition of the plantation mistress in slave society. The surrender of the Confederacy* did not resolve these problems for white women, but signified the recasting of complex social and political interactions for the plantation mistress and her world.

SELECTED BIBLIOGRAPHY

Lois Green Carr and Lorena S. Walsh, "The Planter's Wife: The Experience of White Women in Seventeenth-Century Maryland," *William and Mary Quarterly*, 3rd ser., 34 (1977), 542–571; Jane Turner Censer, "Smiling through Her Tears: Ante-Bellum Southern Women and Divorce," *American Journal of Legal History*, 25 (1981), 24–47; Catherine Clinton, *The Plantation Mistress: Woman's World in the Old South* (1982); David L. Coon, "Eliza Lucas Pinckney and the Reintroduction of Indigo Culture in South Carolina," *Journal of Southern History*, 42 (1976), 61–76; D. Harland Hagler, "The Ideal Woman in the Antebellum South: Lady or Farmwife?" *Journal of Southern History*, 46 (1980), 405–418; Suzanne D. Lebsock, "Radical Reconstruction and the Property Rights of Southern Women," *Journal of Southern History*, 43 (1977), 195–216; Anne

Firor Scott, *The Southern Lady: From Pedestal to Politics, 1830–1930* (1970); and Julia Cherry Spruill, *Women's Life and Work in the Southern Colonies* (1938).

CATHERINE CLINTON

PLANTATION SYSTEM. In its earliest usage, the term *plantation* referred to a plot of ground set with plants, particularly to the movement of plants from one place to another. With the English invasion of America in the seventeeth century it became a metaphor for colonization. Any colony, town, or farm was called a plantation, any colonist a planter. Gradually, the term *plantation* became a more specialized word, acquiring the meaning attached to it in the early nineteenth century: a large agricultural enterprise specializing in the production for sale of crops cultivated by gangs of laborers closely supervised by the planter or his agents.

Although plantations flourished in the British West Indies with the Barbadian sugar revolution of the 1640s, the modern plantation form made a late appearance on the North American mainland. Farms with more than a handful of workers were rare in the Chesapeake region during the seventeenth century or in the Carolinas before approximately 1720. With the rise of slavery along the tobacco* coast, and the rapid expansion of rice* culture in the Carolina low country, the plantation evolved as the dominant unit of production in the Southern colonies. By the eve of the American Revolution, a distinct "plantation belt" stretched along the coast from the Chesapeake Bay to the Georgia low country. That belt was not homogeneous but rather was interrupted by a mixed farming zone covering southeastern Virginia and much of North Carolina. Plantations were relatively small in the tobacco growing areas of Maryland and Virginia, where even great planters divided their operations into several "quarters," rarely employing more than a dozen laborers. Small farms worked without slave labor remained common in the Chesapeake, accounting for perhaps 35 percent of tobacco production as late as 1770. The rice and indigo* districts of the Carolina low country contained much larger plantations and fewer small farms.

The plantation unit of agriculture migrated westward in the nineteenth century with the expansion of cotton* cultivation. Indeed, the plantation led the movement of population and retained its original function as a major institution of settlement. By 1860, cotton had extended the old colonial plantation belt into a long, shallow arc beginning at the Chesapeake Bay in Maryland and swinging southward through the Virginia and North Carolina piedmont. It then widened to include the coastal and central regions of South Carolina and Georgia, before moving west across the Tennessee Valley and the black prairie regions of central Alabama. The western end of the belt was defined by the rich alluvial river basins of Mississippi, Louisiana, Arkansas, and east Texas. Sharp regional variations continued to characterize the plantation belt, while small farms worked by a few slaves or entirely by the farmers' family members remained important, especially in areas where tobacco and cotton predominated. Median slaveholdings ranged from approximately twenty-five slaves in the tobacco regions of Maryland, Virginia, and North Carolina, to thirty to fifty in most upland cotton regions. In the Sea-Island cotton and rice areas of Georgia and South Carolina, and in the sugar* parishes of Louisiana, median slaveholdings were significantly larger: an average of sixty and eighty slaves, respectively. There were several small areas in Louisiana, South Carolina, and Mississippi where most slaves lived on units with 125 to 175 blacks. Pockets of large-scale agriculture also existed outside of the main plantation districts, particularly in the tobacco counties of western Kentucky and on scattered general farms.

In 1860, 53 percent of the slaves in the South lived on plantations (defined as a unit with twenty or more slaves). That proportion reflects a substantial increase over 1790, when only 44 percent of the slaves lived on such large units. It is likely that the 1790 proportion prevailed as early as 1750, following a rapid rise in the beginning decades of the eighteenth century. Taking the period as a whole, perhaps 45 to 50 percent of the slaves in the American South lived on plantations, a proportion that would be much larger if extended to include blacks in regions where plantations dominated.

Several features of the plantation system held crucial implications for the slaves. Most important was the organization of work. Whether they used the task* or gang* systems (many planters employed both depending on the job at hand), planters forced slaves to work long and hard, often achieving an efficiency and intensity of labor in the production of cash crops that led some to call plantations "factories in the fields." Planters also insisted that the great bulk of their slaves work at the crop, excusing only the very young and old and the few with valued skills or privileged positions. A high proportion of the population thus was engaged in income-producing labor.

While labor in the staple crop was routinized and repetitive, considerable variety in plantation work existed nevertheless. Slaves often worked as jobbers when the main crop did not require attention (digging ditches, mending fences, tending farm animals), performing a nearly endless round of tasks to maintain the plantation. Furthermore, plantations were large enough to permit occupational specialization that allowed some slaves to escape the drudgery of field labor by working as supervisors, as craftsmen,* or as domestics. The occupational ladder was truncated, however, for many slaves who moved off the bottom rung did so for only part of their lives, when too young or old for fieldwork, and were forced into the fields at critical times in the crop cycle. Finally, planters pursued self-sufficiency, both as a buffer against market uncertainty and as a way of maximizing earnings from slaves by keeping them employed when cash crops required little attention. That strategy made plantations highly diversified enterprises producing a wide range of goods and services for internal use despite their concentration on a single cash crop, all the while increasing the variety of work slaves performed.

A second key feature of the plantation system was discipline, a subject still not fully understood. Discipline loomed as a major concern to planters. They believed that a regulated, orderly, hardworking labor force was central to successful plantation management. To obtain this, planters employed a mix of incentives and physical punishments, although in what proportions (a critical question for slaves) remains unknown. Certainly force was an ever-present threat, and the whip served as an appropriate symbol of plantation agriculture. Even so, many planters preferred nonviolent over violent means to attain their ends.

The size of the resident slave population represents a third important aspect of the plantation system. Large-scale units provided blacks with more opportunities for interaction with each other than was afforded on small farms. In this sense the plantation served as a cultural institution as well as an institution of settlement and production. Especially on the larger plantations, slaves were able to marry within the estate, build strong families,* construct deep, affectionate ties of kinship and friendship, and fashion a religion* based on Christianity but still attentive to their needs. All the while they developed a sense of community and solidarity that helped them cope with bondage. Seen from this perspective, the plantation system—while harsh and oppressive—played a key role in the elaboration of a distinct Afro-American culture.

Significantly, most of the great planters of the American South resided on their plantations. True, there were exceptions, and many planters withdrew to town for the social season or to vacation spots to escape the heat and disease of late summer. However, in contrast to the West Indies where absentee planters* who lived in London left their estates in the hands of resident overseers,* most Southern planters resided at home and managed their plantations. Although they spent a large share of their profits on imported luxuries, much of their income and entrepreneurial talent was employed locally, to the benefit of the domestic economy. Resident planters played a key role in defending slavery, in elaborating an ideology of paternalism,* and in regulating the lives of their slaves. And they provided the South with an indigenous ruling class. As a whole, plantation masters were a powerful and self-conscious group, fully capable of leading their region down the road to rebellion, to the establishment of a new nation, and to defeat in the Civil War.

The plantation system had a mixed impact on Southern economic development. In the short run it fostered high per capita incomes, although at heavy human cost. Planters captured scale economies in the production process, created a disciplined and efficient organization of labor, gained efficiencies in management and marketing, and forced blacks to work longer and harder then they would have done if free. Over the long haul, however, the plantation system inhibited the South's economic growth. For one thing, it blunted entrepreneurship—not only because it wasted the creativity of slaves—but because it channeled the activities of ambitious and able whites into building ever larger plantations rather than into innovative commercial and industrial ventures that might have diversified the region's economy. For another, the diversity of plantation operations discouraged the growth of specialized firms that might have employed the most advanced methods available to supply the goods and services produced by slaves in those times when the main crop did not require their attention. Finally, the great planters had little interest in improving the land, supporting education,* or promoting internal improvements. Investing heavily in bondsmen, planters generally lacked capital necessary to sponsor local development. Slave property, unlike real property, was not tied to a specific locality, and as a result, the South lacked an infrastructure diversified enough to support broad economic growth. The plantation system kept the South dependent on world demand for a few agricultural products. While demand stayed high, the South flourished. But when demand for the South's agricultural staples faltered, the weaknesses of the plantation system and the Southern economy were clearly revealed.

To be sure, the plantation system survived emancipation. But it was thoroughly transformed, as the great planters, labor lords before the Civil War,* became landlords who adjusted to the demands of newly freed blacks for greater control over their lives and conditions of work. The transition was not abrupt. There were several years of experimentation and struggle before the outlines of the new regime emerged clearly. Initially, ex-masters attempted to preserve the essentials of the plantation organization of labor with wage contracts. In the early years of Reconstruction many ex-slaves worked in gangs for yearly wages, housing, and food; lived in their former slave cabins; and were subjected to plantation discipline backed by the newly enacted black codes or other labor legislation. By the late 1860s the wage system declined for several reasons. Most important, the blacks complained that the new system resembled slavery too closely, and they insisted on arrangements that provided greater autonomy. They were successful in part because planters also found wage labor wanting. The limits on force that emancipation brought reduced the efficiency of gang labor, the need to pay workers competitive wages reduced profits, and the difficulties of retaining free workers often resulted in labor shortages at critical times in the production cycle. By 1870 tenancy, usually for shares although sometimes at fixed rents, dominated plantation agriculture. Share tenancy represented a compromise between ex-slaves and ex-masters. Freedmen* gained autonomy, control over family labor, and relief from plantation discipline and gang work. Planters retained some centralized supervisory control over plantation operations while forcing tenants to share the risks of staple agriculture.

The plantation system, then, survived the Civil War, but not without major changes. Planters still owned large tracts of land and usually operated a home farm with hired labor. They also had a voice in the production decisions of their tenants, especially those farming shares, and continued to capture scale economies from centralized management and marketing. However, self-sufficiency in food production disappeared and plantation handicrafts declined as small plots and credit arrangements forced tenants to concentrate heavily on cash crops. Further, planters showed more interest in internal improvements as their wealth now rested on land values closely tied to local development. Most important, tenants escaped the rigors of plantation discipline and the closely supervised and circumscribed lives of slaves as they moved out of the old quarters and onto family farms. Whites, however, still retained control of the South's farm acreage.

In this new form the plantation system flourished until the 1930s, when it began a sharp decline. New Deal farm policies struck the first blow with what has been called an "American enclosure movement." Shaped by powerful Southern politicians—who were often planters themselves—those policies encouraged the displacement of sharecroppers and tenants, the expansion of home farms, and a greater reliance on hired labor. Ironically, the planters wrote agricultural policy that finally undermined the plantation system and spelled the demise of an era in Southern history. The displacement of farm families led to dramatic changes in Southern agricultural life: migration out of the rural South, labor shortages, mechanization, and the transformation of great plantations, once worked on shares or cash rents, into highly mechanized large farms with little need for the descendants of slaves as day workers, sharecroppers, or tenants. By 1970 the plantation system, after shaping the lives of Southerners for nearly three centuries, was largely a memory, a nostalgic vision for some, a bitter legacy for many.

SELECTED BIBLIOGRAPHY

Ralph V. Anderson and Robert E. Gallman, "Slaves as Fixed Capital: Slave Labor and Southern Economic Development," *Journal of American History*, 64 (1977), 24–46; Lewis C. Gray, *History of Agriculture in the Southern United States to 1860* (2 vols., 1933); James Oakes, *The Ruling Race: A History of American Slaveholders* (1982); Roger L. Ransom and Richard Sutch, *One Kind of Freedom: The Economic Consequences of Emancipation* (1977); Edgar T. Thompson, *Plantation Societies, Race Relations, and the South: The Regimentation of Population* (1975); and Gavin Wright, *Old South, New South: Revolutions in the Southern Economy Since the Civil War* (1986).

RUSSELL R. MENARD

PREACHERS, SLAVE. "Three things," W. E. B. Du Bois wrote in *The Souls of Black Folk* (1903), "characterized this religion of the slave,—the Preacher, the Music, and the Frenzy. The Preacher is the most unique personality developed by the Negro on American soil." Slave preachers arose consequent to the evangelization of the African as early as the eighteenth century and despite attempts by white clergy and planters to control and regularize the Afro-American response to Christianity. Their number was legion, their functions multiple, their message powerful, and their task difficult. Slave preachers were easily the most important religious personalities among Southern blacks. "On almost every large plantation and in every neighborhood of small ones," journalist Frederick Law Olmsted observed in the early 1850s, "there is one man who has come to be considered the head or pastor of the local church." An ex-slave recalled, "My father would have church in dwelling houses and they had to whisper . . . sometimes they would have church at his house. That would be when they would want a real meetin' with some real preachin'."

Jupiter Hammon* (b. 1711), a slave on Long Island who is remembered as the first Afro-American to write and publish poetry, preached among fellow slaves during the revolutionary era. However, the slave preacher was predominantly a Southern phenomenon, coexisting at first alongside free black preachers who conducted itinerant and frequently independent ministries fostered by the egalitarian spirituality of the eighteenth-century evangelical movement in the South. From the 1740s through the early decades of the nineteenth century, the evangelicals reshaped the religious identity of the Old South by preaching an experiential faith, one that was predicated upon personal conversions among whites and blacks.

Prior to Nat Turner's insurrection* of 1831, Southern denominations, notably the Methodists* and Baptists,* encouraged the development of black preachers who would proclaim "de words o' wisdom" to fellow slaves. Men of natural eloquence, such as the famous "Black Harry" Hosier, a traveling companion of Methodist Bishop Francis Asbury, preached to biracial audiences with notable success. White evangelicals encouraged black preachers to set up their own congregations or societies. Afro-American Baptist slaves, such as David George and George Liele* of Silver Bluff, South Carolina, received ordination at the hands of white elders. White Christians sometimes purchased the freedom of a talented slave preacher so that he might more fully exercise his gifts among the unconverted, black and white alike. Methodists licensed slave preachers as deacons and exhorters, assistant clergy who tended to exercise full pastoral duties among fellow slaves because of the shortage of white missionaries willing to work among the concentrated plantation populations. Denominations which required an educated ministry, such as the Presbyterians,* Catholics,* and Episcopalians,* rarely credentialed or recognized illiterate slave preachers.

Many slave preachers functioned within the slave quarters, at the prayer meetings, and clandestine night sings, without official endorsement by a white denomination. These men—available evidence provides few examples of female slave preachers—established themselves on the basis of personal charisma and a "call" from God. Slaves remembered only as "Sampson," "Job," or "Caesar" became the natural leaders of "the invisible institution," the folk religion of the slave community. They competed with the practitioners of conjure, hoodoo,* and herbalism for the allegiance of the slave quarters but rarely dabbled themselves in these largely African-derived folk practices* of dealing with evil in daily life. A few slave preachers learned to read enough of the Bible to interpret it for themselves, but most gleaned their understanding of Christianity from living on the edges of white Christianity. After hearing white preachers, the slave preacher had to reinterpret the Gospel for his own people. Despite white efforts to dole out "safe" versions of biblical stories, the slaves took Christianity for themselves at the inspiration of slave preachers who encouraged them to "steal away to Jesus." The more astute white authorities recognized the risk in allowing independent black preaching, especially by slaves who claimed as a warrant their own conversions and visionary experiences.

Nat Turner was one such self-appointed preacher. In the wake of the Turner-led uprising in Southampton County in 1831, Virginia's governor claimed that "the most active incendiaries among us, in stirring up the spirit of revolt, have been the negro preachers.'' Thereafter most Southern states proscribed black preaching or sought to place it under white supervision. For example, Alabama passed a law in 1833 prohibiting slaves or free blacks from preaching unless at least five slave owners were present and the preacher had received authorization from some white denomination. Mississippi allowed a master to select one of his own slaves to preach on his plantation but required that at least two ''reputable'' whites be present and prohibited slaves from anywhere else from attending for fear of servile insurrection. From the 1830s on, white denominations generally refused to ordain slaves or license them to perform full pastoral functions. Exhorters could preach in the praise-houses and plantation chapels under the attentive eye of the master or his surrogate, the ''boss preacher,'' often a visiting white missionary. Charles C. Jones,* a Presbyterian leader of plantation missions, wrote that the black exhorter or deacon was to ''assist members in their Christian walk, by warnings, reproofs, and exhortations of a private nature, heal breaches; report cases of delinquency to the church; see that the children are taught their prayers, and that people attend worship; visit the sick and bury the dead.'' Henry Clay Bruce stated that, as a class, the black exhorters had little or no education ''but had a fair amount of brain, good memories, were fluent talkers, and [were] considered pious and truthful.''

Favored slaves might be selected, often from among the house servants,* to become ''watchmen'' over spiritual matters in the slave quarters and to exhort at approved worship services. Fellow slaves considered them privileged characters. One black exhorter, James Lindsay Smith, said of himself: ''I was very proud and loved to dress well, and all the young people used to make a great time over me. . . . '' He was allowed to possess a fine suit, a watch and chain, and even his own seal as a mark of his authority among fellow slaves. The favored slave preacher walked a tightrope between accommodation to the white power structure and acceptance in ''the invisible institution.'' An ex-slave from Florida recalled: ''The Pamell slaves had a Negro minister who could hold services any time he chose, so long as he did not interfere with the work of the other slaves. He was not obliged to do hard menial labors and went about the plantation all dressed up in a frock coat and store-bought shoes. He was more than a little conscious of this and was held in awe by the others.''

The illiterate plantation hand who demonstrated a gift for reflecting on the troubles and sorrows of fellow slaves and interpreting the spiritual realm emerged as the natural leader in the ''hush-arbor,'' or secretive religious meetings. Though described as bad characters by whites whose control over the quarters was threatened by their presence, these folk preachers established themselves as central figures in the rituals of slave worship—the shouting, singing, and ecstatic behavior. Many had learned the biblical stories by heart and could retell them with vivid imagery in extemporaneous exhortation with the result that their hearers were ''struck dead'' in the spirit. Certain individuals, such as John Jasper* of Virginia, the famous ''De Sun Do Move an' de Earth Am Square'' preacher, demonstrated such unusual religious gifts that they attracted white audiences as well as black. Though his stock sermon concerning Joshua's defeat of the Amorite kings while the "sun stood still" (Joshua 10:13) struck some white hearers as a burlesque on the Bible, Jasper impressed black and white alike with the rhetorical power and craft of the spoken word.

Black preaching evolved into a folk art. Slave preachers relied on the promptings of the "spirit" and drew from the reservoir of African call-and-response rituals as well as from the florid and emotional sermons of white camp meeting revivalists. The singsong style of slave preachers, replete with the dialect of the field hands, fostered a patois which developed as black English among rural Southern blacks and endured long after the Civil War. In dreams and visions, slave preachers looked into another world than that of the peculiar institution and heard another Gospel than that preached by whites. They were thus able to capture the imagination of their hearers and provide spiritual solace and support amidst the physical and psychological pressures of everyday life. As one ex-slave testified concerning biracial camp meetings, "mostly we had white preachers, but when we had a black preacher, that was heaven." An ex-slave from Mississippi said of Matthew Ewing: "He never learned no real readin' and writin' but he sure knowed his Bible and would hold his hand out and make like he was readin' and preach de purtiest preachin' you ever heard."

Slave preachers were, by force of circumstances, born to frustration. Only by subtle techniques were they able to preach resistance,* for to advocate servile insurrection openly was to invite the severest of consequences. White church authorities recognized that slave preachers would "become leaders in *fact*, whether they are made leaders by an *official act* of the societies in which they move or not." Slave preachers were closely watched and gagged, whipped, or worse if they strayed too far from the texts assigned to them. They could and did disguise talk of freedom in traditional Christian imagery and by implication passed judgment on whites who prayed with them on Sunday and beat them on Monday. One ex-slave remembered that a slave exhorter once got carried away and at the close of his sermon exclaimed: "Free indeed, free from hell, free from work, from the white folks, free from everything." Another ex-slave narrative relates: "A yellow man [mulatto] preached to us. She [the slave owner] had him preach how we was to obey our master and missy if we want to go to heaven, but when she wasn't there, he come out with straight preachin' from the Bible."

Ex-slave testimony also reveals that not a few slave preachers succumbed to becoming mouthpieces for their masters, hewing to the line advocated by most white missionaries, namely, that the essence of slave Christianity was to become better slaves. By and large, the slave community recognized such preaching for what it was and turned a deaf ear to crude attempts to rob them of the notion that they were God's chosen people, precious and redeemed, meant to be free, if not in this life, certainly in the next. Though escapist and otherwordly on the surface, such preaching helped to provide the slave community with a moral benchmark, an alternative worldview to that of slave drivers, masters, and hypocritical white Christians. Slave lay preachers, deacons, exhorters, and watchmen pointed to a transcendent order that called into question the legitimacy of all human institutions that robbed children of God of their essential dignity. At those critical junctures in life's passage—baptisms, weddings, and funerals— slave preachers provided the black community with ritual celebration and solace, necessary to the task of "keepin' on keepin' on" while awaiting the balancing of the divine scales of justice.

At ninety years of age, Jane Simpson, an ex-slave, recalled: "I used to hear old slaves pray and ask God when would de bottom rail be de top rail, and I wondered what on earth dey talkin' about. Dey was talkin' about when dey goin' to get from under bondage. Course I know now." When the year of Jubilee came and the slaves entered onto freedom's landscape, many of the plantation preachers, deacons, and exhorters were eager to learn to read the Bible and set up for themselves. Now they could openly proclaim all that was in their hearts. Known somewhat derisively as "contraband" preachers because they had been freed by Yankee troops during the Civil War, they vied for leadership with representatives from the Northern black denominations for control of the freed-men's churches. They formed the core of the clerical ranks of the numerous black Baptist associations and the Colored Methodist Episcopal denomination, organized in 1870 from among the ex-slaves formerly claimed by the Methodist Episcopal Church, South. With the passing of the freedmen's generation, the ranks of the old-time slave preachers thinned, but they bequeathed a heritage that has endured in Afro-American religion,* folk culture,* and literature.*

SELECTED BIBLIOGRAPHY

Eugene D. Genovese, *Roll, Jordan, Roll: The World the Slaves Made* (1974); Charles V. Hamilton, *The Black Preacher in America* (1972); Albert J. Raboteau, *Slave Religion: The "Invisible Institution" in the Antebellum South* (1978); and Milton C. Sernett, *Black Religion and American Evangelicalism: White Protestants, Plantation Missions, and the Flowering of Negro Christianity, 1787–1865* (1975).

MILTON C. SERNETT

PRESBYTERIAN CHURCH. Presbyterians were late arrivals in the American colonies and were strongest in the mid-Atlantic colonies where slavery was widespread. In the Southern colonies Presbyterian organization was weak, and the church found the institution of slavery well-established by the time it gained a foothold. Presbyterians adapted their theological outlook to their colonial social and cultural settings. After the American Revolution Presbyterians increased in numbers and influence in the coastal areas of the South and became part of the culture of slavery. In the North Presbyterians joined other Protestants in pushing for legislation to emancipate slaves by gradual means.

In the era of the American Revolution* a few Presbyterians opposed slavery, and some in the Northern states sought emancipation through state legislation. William Livingston, who served as governor of New Jersey during the Revolution, tried, unsuccessfully, to secure the passage of legislation to abolish slavery in New Jersey in 1778. In 1780 George Bryan, an Irish immigrant who became an influential Scotch-Irish leader in Pennsylvania, gained passage of a gradual emancipation bill in Pennsylvania. A Presbyterian clergyman, Samuel Miller, denounced slavery on the grounds that the principles of the Revolution, which were in harmony with the Word of God, made slavery unacceptable. The Reverend Jacob Green opposed slavery on theological grounds, and his church in New Jersey refused to admit slaveholders to church fellowship. David Rice, who worked among slaves in Virginia for twenty years, moved to Kentucky, where he tried, unsuccessfully, to secure a plan for the gradual emancipation of slaves in the state constitution.

In 1787 the Synod of New York and Philadelphia (then the highest American Presbyterian body) discussed demands for a sweeping condemnation of slavery but chose a more cautious approach. The Synod endorsed a program for the gradual abolition* of slavery, with provisions for educating slaves to prepare them for freedom. By the end of the eighteenth century the Presbyterian General Assembly followed a policy of condemning slavery in general terms, while permitting local governing bodies to apply these principles to local situations. In the Southern colonies/states in the eighteenth century, where slavery was a part of the established social order, local church bodies moved cautiously in opposing slavery, and sometimes silenced ministers who spoke out publicly against it.

Presbyterian efforts to evangelize slaves were limited because of the pressures of ministering to the influx of white immigrants in the eighteenth century. Samuel Davies, the pioneer Presbyterian missionary to Virginia, preached to slaves in connection with his work with their white masters. Davies stressed the missionary responsibility of Christians toward slaves, but conceded that while baptism brought spiritual liberty to the slave it did not free him from his earthly bondage. Missionary* efforts for slaves in the Southern colonies were limited, since most Presbyterians settled in the "backcountry" rather than in the lowlands where the slave system was strongest. Also, Presbyterians were cautious about revivalism, which proved to be an effective method of reaching blacks and whites. Some missionary efforts for slaves came from local white churches, like the Midway Church in Georgia which permitted free blacks and a slave owned by the church to preach to slaves attending services. The earliest black missionary commissioned by Presbyterians in the South was John Chavis,* who was appointed by the General Assembly in 1801. Until 1808 Chavis reported regularly to the Assembly on his work, but after 1831, when legal restrictions were placed on the activities of blacks, Chavis was barred from exercising his ministry.

A famous white missionary to slaves was Charles C. Jones,* who became interested in evangelizing blacks during a pastorate in Savannah, Georgia. Jones developed guidelines for this mission activity designed to keep it safely within the limits of the slave culture. The work was to be carried on by white missionaries who sympathized with slavery and could distinguish between the civil and the spiritual relationships of slaves. Instruction of slaves was to be conducted orally, and emotionalism, spirituals, and revival hymns were to be discouraged. Although Jones tried to ameliorate the conditions of slaves, he was convinced that the souls of black folk could be saved only within the institution of slavery. In spite of the efforts of Jones and others, like John B. Adger of Charleston, South Carolina, Presbyterians gained few slave converts. Black Presbyterians had to remain under white supervision with an inferior status in the life of the church, and they were barred from holding church office. Even the marriages* of slaves were not inviolable, since a husband and a wife could be sold separately, and such separation, in the eyes of the church, would dissolve the marriage. A few slaves were attracted to Presbyterianism by the promise of better status and greater opportunity for education. Other slaves, however, were alienated by the lack of equality in the church and the Presbyterian rejection of revival music and emotional appeals. Few slaves became Presbyterians.

The rise of sectionalism affected Presbyterians deeply, since they constituted a connectional church, with members in the South and in the North. The South developed a culture based upon the importance of slavery in its economic life, so that its social institutions, including the churches, were enlisted in its support. The rise of abolitionism in the North hardened the South's support of slavery, and brought pressure upon those holding moderate views to conform or to migrate. John D. Paxton of Virginia was ousted from his church in 1826 for insisting that slavery ought to be abolished before it destroyed the nation. In North Carolina some antislavery ministers were silenced, and others were forced to migrate to the North.

Some Presbyterians in the South became defenders* of the slave system. They argued that the Bible either sanctioned slavery or, at least, did not condemn it. Most stopped short of extremist views that blacks shared the curse of Ham, or were subhuman. One prominent apologist for slavery was James H. Thornwell. He asserted that the Bible accepted slavery, and thus, to reject slavery, was to reject the authority of the Bible. Thornwell also developed a doctrine of church and society, in which the church had the power to regulate personal morality, but not the power to shape society.

A number of Presbyterians tried to find a middle way in the slavery controversy, between abolitionists and proslavery advocates, by supporting the colonization* of free blacks* in Africa. Supporters of colonization stressed national and denominational unity against the divisive forces of sectionalism. Many Presbyterians were active in the American Colonization Society,* which lobbied for federal subsidies for the repatriation of freed slaves to Liberia. Their basic assumption was that blacks were racially inferior and could never be integrated into American society. Colonization was supported by such Presbyterians as Cortlandt Van Rensselaer, A. A. Alexander, John Hartwell Cocke, Robert J. Breckinridge, and J. Aspinwall Hodge. Colonization was opposed by abolitionists and by free blacks, including two black Presbyterian ministers, Samuel Cornish and Theodore Wright. One unintended result of the colonization movement was the founding of the Ashmun Institute (later Lincoln University) by Presbyterians to train blacks as missionaries to Africa.

Henry Highland Garnet, a black Presbyterian minister, was an early advocate of resistance to slavery, and J. W. C. Pennington, Samuel Cornish, and Theodore Wright were also active in the antislavery cause. White Presbyterian ministers also contributed to the struggle against slavery. James G. Birney,* a former slaveholder who was converted from the colonization cause to the abolition movement, spoke out on the basis of personal experience. Chillicothe (Ohio) Presbytery became a center of antislavery sentiment and regularly sent antislavery resolutions to the Presbyterian General Assembly. George Bourne, a radical critic of slavery, was forced out of the denomination by proslavery forces in Virginia. Another opponent of slavery, Elijah P. Lovejoy, a graduate of Princeton Seminary, died while defending his printing press against a mob, and thus became a martyr in the abolition cause.

A major schism in the Presbyterian church, the Old School–New School division of 1837, was a dispute over theological orthodoxy and cooperation with the Congregationalists in joint mission work. The division also involved differences over the church's role in dealing with slavery, although neither side was strongly antislavery. After the schism the Old School branch, which included many Southern churches, pursued a policy of silence on the slavery issue. A few Old School ministers, like Erasmus MacMaster and Thomas E. Thomas, voiced their opposition to slavery. When the Old School divided in 1861, it did so not on the issue of slavery, but over loyalty to the federal government. In spite of its more liberal views, the New School branch was slow to oppose slavery, fearing to offend its members in the South. In 1858 most of the New School churches in the South withdrew as a protest against the growing pressures against slaveholders in the denomination.

The struggle against slavery led to the withdrawal of a small group of Presbyterians who were impatient with their church's failure to bar slaveholders. In 1847 a number of small churches in the Midwest withdrew to form the Free Presbyterian church. Its membership was never large, and after the Civil War it dwindled away. The Reverend Joseph Gordon, an uncompromising opponent of slavery, was a prominent Free Presbyterian spokesman. Another minister of this church, the Reverend George Gordon, became an antislavery martyr when he was imprisoned for assisting in the rescue of a slave from the custody of a U.S. marshal. Although he was finally freed from prison, he died a short time later from the effects of his imprisonment. The smaller Presbyterian bodies, chiefly from the Scottish Covenanter tradition, were generally opposed to slavery. Homogeneous and small in size, they were able to discipline slaveholding members and thus free their churches from involvement with slavery.

SELECTED BIBLIOGRAPHY

Andrew E. Murray, *Presbyterians and the Negro—A History* (1966); H. Shelton Smith, *In His Image, But . . . Racism in Southern Religion, 1780–1910* (1972); P. J. Staudenraus, *The African Colonization Movement, 1816–1865* (1961); Ernest T. Thompson, *Presbyterians in the South, 1607–1972* (vols. 1 and 2, 1963, 1973); Louis B. Weeks, *Kentucky Presbyterians* (1983); and Gayraud Wilmore, *Black and Presbyterian: The Heritage of Hope* (1983).

ANDREW E. MURRAY

PRICES, SLAVE. Slaves were assets to their owners, with annual streams of incomes and costs. Several factors entered into the calculation of the price of a slave. These included the expected volume of output at each age and its market value (including, for the female, the value of offspring); the costs of consumption and supervision at each age; the life expectancy of a slave (as well as the expectation that slavery as a system would survive); and the rate of interest used to discount future values. No planters had all this detailed information, and expectations varied with political, social, and cultural factors. Nevertheless, the patterns of slave prices at a particular time and price changes over time, as well as contemporary discussions, indicate that planters did make calculations based upon their beliefs at the time of purchase or valuation.

Slave prices at any time were affected by a number of different considerations, including age, sex, color, skill, health, behavior, birthplace, and height. Over time, the prices of slaves varied with the changing prices expected for the output produced, as well as with changing productivity of slave labor, which was influenced by the availability of other factors of production, such as land and farm equipment.

A number of different sources contain information on the prices of slaves. Bills of sale in slave markets, probate inventories, plantation listings, newspapers, letters, and discussions of compensations to be paid for those executed for crimes are sources of slave prices. The most useful sources are generally the probate inventories and slave bills of sale, not only because they represent actual financial recordings, but because they frequently include detailed descriptions of each slave, making it possible to examine the price structure as well as to standardize comparisons over time.

The first major slave price series prepared for the United States, and one still widely used, was first published in 1918 by Ulrich B. Phillips, covering four areas of the South in the years 1795 to 1860. This has recently been supplemented by a series prepared from data on slave sales in New Orleans (the largest of the slave markets) for the period 1804 to 1862, by Laurence J. Kotlikoff. In addition, a large sample drawn from probate inventories by Robert W. Fogel and Stanley L. Engerman has been used to describe price changes over time as well as the structure of nineteenth-century slave prices, with particular attention to the relationship among age, sex, and price. The price series prepared by Phillips and by Kotlikoff provide the basic pattern of slave price change for the nineteenth century. For the eighteenth century various sources for British North America and West Africa have been brought together by Richard Bean.

The price of slaves varied over time, with a cyclical pattern of rise and fall, generally related to conditions in the market for slave-produced commodities. Prior to 1808 there was the possibility of importing slaves from Africa, but the United States required a relatively small part of the international slave trade.* Thus, the U.S. demand for slaves influenced the quantity of slaves received rather than the world price of slaves. For the eighteenth century, slave prices generally show a rising trend. Creole slaves were valued above those newly imported from Africa, for reasons of health and acculturation. Prices declined somewhat with the start of the Revolutionary war, but by the 1790s, even before the onset of the cotton* expansion, they had returned to earlier levels. In the nineteenth century the general course of slave prices was upward, with several sharp cyclical fluctuations. According to Kotlikoff, New Orleans prices in 1860 were more than twice those of 1810. Prime-age male prices in New Orleans rose to a high of about $1,250 in the cotton boom of the late 1830s and then, after falling to below one-half that level in the 1840s, rose to about $1,450 in the boom of the late 1850s. In general, as Phillips argued, slave prices varied with the state of the cotton market. Noteworthy is the sharp rise in slave prices in the 1850s indicating that (rightly or wrongly) planters at that time believed that the system would continue to remain profitable.

Some general patterns in the price structure for slaves appear to have persisted with the rise and fall in the overall level of slave prices. Male slaves generally sold at higher prices than did females. Males also tended to be given the more highly valued skilled occupations. Among field laborers* at prime-age, males were valued 10 to 20 percent more than were females, the differential not developing until the teen-ages and becoming larger at older ages. The value of the childbearing capacity accounted for approximately one-fifth of the value of a twenty-year-old female field hand. In general the values of infants were positive even though it would take many years for them to yield a positive surplus to their owners. Prices equal to one-half that of prime-age male field hands were reached at about age ten, and again at about age fifty. Female prices rose, relative to their peak, more rapidly than did male prices. Among field hands, the price of females tended to peak a few years before that of males (which was in the late twenties). At any time prices for slaves of similar age, sex, and skill were higher in the newer areas of the South. The movement of slaves from older to newer areas served to keep interregional prices in some agreement. The internal movement of slaves was greatest in those years of "cotton boom," in which slave prices were rising most rapidly.

Clearly the price patterns have important implications for understanding slavery. The price structure and the changes over time in response to changing economic and political conditions indicate that slave owners were concerned with the valuation of slaves. Calculations of the profitability of slavery,* as in the seminal work of Alfred H. Conrad and John R. Meyer, demonstrated that the prices of slaves were affected by the slave's ability to produce marketable output, and that the prices were consistent with their owners' earning "normal" profits. Moreover, the prices of slaves were above the costs of "producing" slaves, and this surplus increased over time, reaching peak levels in the 1850s. This sharp rise in slave prices indicates that, on economic grounds, slavery was becoming more valuable to planters on the eve of the Civil War.

SELECTED BIBLIOGRAPHY

Alfred H. Conrad and John R. Meyer, "The Economics of Slavery in the Ante-Bellum South," *Journal of Political Economy*, 66 (1958), 95–130; Robert W. Fogel and Stanley L. Engerman, *Time on the Cross: The Economics of American Negro Slavery* (1974); Laurence J. Kotlikoff, "The Structure of Slave Prices in New Orleans, 1804–1862," *Economic Inquiry*, 17 (1979), 496–518; Ulrich B. Phillips, *American Negro Slavery* (1918); and U.S. Department of Commerce, Bureau of the Census, *Historical Statistics of the United States, Colonial Times to 1970* (1975).

                                                                                        STANLEY L. ENGERMAN

PROFITABILITY OF SLAVERY. By the end of the seventeenth century, the New World tobacco* planter aristocracy had no doubts about the profitability of their huge tracts of land and gangs of slaves. A quarter-century later, however, conditions had changed. If some colonists, such as the Quakers,* had always attacked slavery on moral grounds, many American revolutionaries found slavery to be morally incompatible with their talk of liberty, equality, and freedom. Others, more concerned with economics than morals, also had doubts about slavery. Facing declining tobacco prices, deteriorating land, mounting debt, and competition from newly opened lands, they agreed with George Washington,* who in 1794 called slaves "a very troublesome species of property." Some advocated emancipation followed by colonization* to rid the new nation of an economic burden and an alien race. Yet, as Thomas Jefferson* noted in 1786, most Southerners opposed emancipation. Slaves could still produce profits on new lands, and many landowners in the older areas hoped that a rise in tobacco prices would restore the value of their slaves.

But it was cotton,* not tobacco, that ended whatever doubts remained about the value of slave labor. Cotton prices rose sharply as the demand of the growing textile industry outstripped traditional sources of supply. The South—with the climate* and soils that produced high-quality cotton, a location accessible to consuming markets in England and Europe, and Eli Whitney's cotton gin* to separate cheaply and efficiently the sticky seeds from the staple—quickly became the world's primary cotton producer. The rapidly expanding Cotton Kingdom breathed new life into what had once seemed to be a dying slave system. By the beginning of the nineteenth century sentiment among slave owners for emancipation had evaporated.

Criticism of slavery continued, of course. Abolitionists,* along with many others, termed the peculiar institution morally reprehensible, and Free Soilers opposed its expansion into new territories, fearing that slave owners would monopolize the best lands and prevent the spread of small farms. But these critics seldom condemned slavery as an unprofitable investment. Indeed, implicit in the moral condemnation of slavery was the view that slave owners derived their profits by depriving their workers of their freedom, by buying and selling them in the marketplace, and by forcing them to work hard and long by the vicious and unrelenting use of the lash. Such critics condemned not profits but the means by which slave owners earned them.

Some critics of slavery, such as Solon Robinson and Frederick Law Olmsted,* added an economic attack to their moral condemnation, noting that slave labor was less profitable than free labor, a view, ironically, that some Southerners accepted in the course of their ardent defense of slavery.* James Henry Hammond, owner of a large South Carolina plantation, for example, admitted that slave labor was less productive than free labor, but neither he nor other Southerners, such as political economists Jacob N. Cardozo and Thomas Roderick Dew who shared this opinion, found this reason enough to condemn the institution. On the contrary, they, along with other proslavery advocates, proclaimed that slavery economically benefited the South, the nation, the world, and even the slaves themselves. Slavery, they argued, transformed ignorant and inferior African savages into efficient workers who produced a crop that enriched the section and the nation and provided the raw material to clothe the world. According to these writers, slavery mitigated the class conflict endemic in a free labor society by uniting whites on the basis of race, by providing nonslaveholders with ample opportunities for social mobility through the purchase of slaves, and by shielding slaves, who were valuable property, from the privations that were so often the lot of the wage worker in the North.

When slavery's defenders conceded that slaves were not the most profitable investment available, they implied that high returns on investment were not their major concern. Indeed, they charged, many of slavery's benefits arose from the fact that most planters were not primarily motivated by profit maximization as were Yankee employers of free labor. The Alabamian Daniel Robinson Hundley, in his analysis of the *Social Relations in Our Southern States* (1860), roundly criticized the "Southern Yankees," those few planters who, unlike the "gentlemen," adopted the Northern practice of putting profits above all other considerations.

Not everyone agreed that the slave system was economically beneficial. Southerners such as Hinton Rowan Helper,* Daniel Reaves Goodloe, George Tucker, and Cassius M. Clay; Northerners such as Daniel Raymond and Frederick Law Olmsted; and foreigners such as the British political economist, J. E. Cairnes— all indicted slavery for causing Southern economic backwardness. Slavery, they argued, degraded labor, kept wages low, produced a shallow market, blocked industrial and commerical development, prevented the spread of scientific agriculture, absorbed capital that might have been available for other investments, discouraged immigration, and created an arrogant and menacing ruling class.

Thus, the antebellum dispute over the profitability of slavery centered almost exclusively on the economic effects of slavery and gave scant attention to the question of returns to slave owners on their investment. Critics and defenders alike agreed that slavery was more than a particular means to organize labor. It was the basis for a particular social system. By mid-century, Americans, Northerners and Southerners alike, defined and sharply contrasted the Northern free labor system and the Southern slave labor system.

Although slavery's defenders and its critics came to diametrically opposed conclusions, their arguments and the data used to support them were not always mutually exclusive. Ulrich B. Phillips, a Southerner squarely in the Progressive tradition, incorporated many of the arguments of both sides in his early twentieth-century studies of slavery, including *American Negro Slavery* (1918) and *Life and Labor in the Old South* (1929). Phillips noted that when the plantation system, an effective means to organize and supervise unskilled labor, became inseparable from slavery, a means to capitalize labor, the resulting slave system had pernicious economic effects. Because the planter had to buy his labor force, his wage bill, instead of being short-term operating capital as in a free labor system, became a long-term capital investment, absorbing capital resources that might otherwise have been available for investment in commerce, banking, manufacturing, and agricultural improvements. With so much capital tied up in labor, Phillips explained, Southerners had to turn to the North for credit, manufactured goods, shipping, and other services, thereby draining additional resources from the region and compounding the capital shortage. Unable to diversify its economy, the South remained poor, backward, and dependent upon the North.

The slave plantation, Phillips admitted, was an efficient unit of production and "a school constantly training and controlling pupils who were in a backward state of civilization." Rationally routinized tasks and strict supervision, combined with careful attention to the health and well-being of the slaves turned what Phillips deemed ignorant, unskilled laborers into productive workers. But success became an economic liability. If the plantation* was a school, the slave system prevented apt students from ever graduating. Because they were enslaved, efficient workers never could become independent farmers; because efficient production required closely supervised unskilled labor, planters had no incentive to teach skills to good workers or encourage ideas of independence among them; and because the plantations were more efficient than small farms, they drove small farmers out of the best lands.

Phillips thus combined those arguments of slavery's defenders that emphasized efficiency and good treatment of the slaves with those arguments of slavery's critics that emphasized the detrimental effects of slavery on Southern economic development. In addition, however, he raised the issue of the profitability of slavery as an investment, a matter largely ignored by antebellum disputants. Phillips argued that the capitalization of labor continually absorbed the slave owners' profits, a loss that increased as slave prices rose. By the end of the 1850s, he said, only the most efficiently supervised plantations on the best lands were profitable.

Slavery persisted, Phillips explained, despite its economic costs, because it was a necessary means to control an inferior and potentially dangerous race and because it was the basis for an attractive and popular social system. Thus, like slavery's antebellum supporters, Phillips suggested that profit maximization did not motivate the slave owners. Slavery, he wrote in 1918, "was less a business than a life; it made fewer fortunes than it made men."

Phillips's work was enormously influential. Supported during the 1920s and 1930s by studies of North Carolina, Georgia, Mississippi, and Alabama, Phillips's interpretation became so widely accepted during the first four decades of the twentieth century that it not only became what later critics dubbed the "traditional" interpretation, but it also set out the main themes that later historians, including Phillips's most ardent critics, continue to debate to this day.

Robert R. Russel and Lewis Cecil Gray were among the first of Phillips's critics. They questioned parts of Phillips's interpretation as early as the 1930s by denying that slavery was an unprofitable investment. They insisted that *because* slavery was so profitable, Southerners concentrated on staple crop production and refused to invest in manufacturing and commerce. During the 1940s others maintained that Phillips and his followers had miscalculated income and costs. These critics insisted that more accurate figures showed that planters indeed earned a good profit from their investment in slaves.

By the 1950s historians were completely rewriting the history of slavery and questioning virtually every aspect of traditional views, including the question of profits. Kenneth M. Stampp, in his major revisionist study *The Peculiar Institution* (1956), insisted that as a business, slavery was profitable for all "but the most hopelessly inefficient masters." Two years later, economists Alfred H. Conrad and John R. Meyer presented detailed statistics showing that planters' profits were as high as those derived from investments elsewhere in the nation. The South's comparative advantage lay in staple crop agriculture, they concluded; Southerners neglected manufacturing and commerce because land and slaves proved more profitable.

In finding slavery to be a profitable investment, the revisionists had not only reversed Phillips's calculations, they had also changed his emphasis. Phillips, like the antebellum critics and supporters of slavery, had concentrated on the effects of slavery as an economic system. The revisionists, on the other hand, had confined their analysis to returns on investment. Implicit in the revisionist argument was the assumption that slavery did not create a peculiar system, but was merely a peculiar institution within American capitalism. Planters, like profit-maximizing businessmen elsewhere in the nation, chose the most profitable investment available to them.

Robert W. Fogel and Stanley L. Engerman in their two-volume *Time on the Cross* (1974) made this assumption explicit and central in their analysis. But their revisionism went much further: they denied that the slave South was economically backward and stagnant. Drawing on the per capita income data assembled by Richard A. Easterlin, Fogel and Engerman argued that the region was not poor in comparison to the nation as a whole and, more important, the South's *rate of growth* did not lag behind that of the rest of the nation.

This changed the terms of the old profitability argument altogether. Where others had sought to explain Southern economic backwardness either by blaming or by exonerating slavery, Fogel and Engerman found the region's economy healthy and vigorous *because* of slavery, especially on the larger plantations where economies of scale proved possible. Southern planters were bourgeois businessmen of the highest order, they said, seeking and achieving profit maximization through the careful organization of production. Slaves in fact proved more efficient than free workers in the North because they could be worked more efficiently and at a greater intensity. Slave plantations, wrote Fogel and Engerman, were like "factories in the field." Significantly, the two economists returned the debate to the older issue of the profitability of slavery as a system rather than as a form of investment. They found slaves to be a profitable investment, but this was only an aspect of their larger argument that the economic system and the prevailing ideology in the South differed little from that of the North.

Eugene D. Genovese, a historian who was also concerned with the nature of the slave system, sharply disagreed. Slavery, he argued in a series of books (*The Political Economy of Slavery* [1965], *The World the Slaveholders Made* [1969], and *Roll, Jordan, Roll* [1974]), created a unique society and economy in the South. Part of the United States and a participant in the world market, the South had much in common with the North and the rest of the mid-nineteenth century Western capitalist world. But more important than similarities were differences arising from the absence of free labor. According to Genovese, slavery produced a prebourgeois or precapitalist society with its own class structure, ideology, and legal institutions.

Under this system slave owners became rich and powerful, dominating antebellum Southern society, subordinating merchants, bankers, and incipient manufacturers as they established their ideological hegemony in the South. Southern economic development—in contrast to growth in income—lagged, Genovese argued, because the dominant planters blocked it, fearing, with good reason, that development would undermine their ideological hegemony and eventually destroy the slave system they controlled. They realized that economic development would produce powerful new classes of industrialists and free workers who would clash with and ultimately overwhelm the planters. The slave owners had only to look to the North to see the dismal future that awaited them if they allowed economic development in their section.

In a sense, the profitability debate has come full circle, returning to the issues in the antebellum dispute. Both Fogel and Engerman and Genovese, despite the differences in their methods and conclusions, view the question as a matter of political economy just as the antebellum disputants did. When Phillips raised the matter of returns on investment, he opened a very different sort of debate. Scholars then argued over production costs, interest rates, risk levels, depreciation, and other accounting matters without being aware, it would seem, that by making such issues paramount they assumed that the return on investment was central to the debate. When the revisionists found profit rates to be high, they were convinced that they had found the source of the planters' behavior; they assumed that high profit rates meant that the planters were rational, bourgeois businessmen motivated by profit maximization. Only if Southerners continued to invest in an unprofitable enterprise would it appear that they were motivated by goals that modern economists term "irrational," and only then, it seems, would it be necessary to find a different motivation for behavior.

Fogel and Engerman, correctly recognizing that the question of the profitability of slavery is inextricably linked to the larger question of the nature of Southern society, attempted to describe the links and thereby to prove what others had assumed. Genovese, however, found different connections. Although he raised doubts about the work of Conrad and Meyer and others who contended that investment in slaves was profitable for the planters, Genovese insisted that profits were irrelevant, whatever their levels, because high profits in the bourgeois accounting sense were not the planters' primary goal. Thus, both Fogel and Engerman and Genovese in very different ways explicitly recognized that the profitability debate inevitably involves far more than economics and the measurement of profit and loss. It turns on matters of politics, class relations, and ideology.

Although the long dispute over the profitability of slavery remains unresolved, recent work has clarified the issues by making assumptions explicit and by suggesting new questions and new approaches to answer them. That the South was different or distinct is indisputable; how different and how distinct remains the central issue in the continuing debate over the profitability of slavery.

SELECTED BIBLIOGRAPHY

Paul A. David et al., *Reckoning with Slavery: A Critical Study in the Quantitative History of American Negro Slavery* (1976); Richard A. Easterlin, "Interregional Differences in Per Capita Income, Population, and Total Income, 1840–1850," in Conference on Research in Income and Wealth, *Trends in the American Economy in the Nineteenth Century*, Studies in Income and Wealth, vol. 24 (1960), 73–140; Ulrich B. Phillips, *The Slave Economy of the Old South: Selected Essays in Economic and Social History*, ed. by Eugene D. Genovese, (1968); Harold D. Woodman, "The Profitability of Slavery: A Historical Perennial," *Journal of Southern History*, 29 (1963), 303–325; and Harold D. Woodman, ed., *Slavery and the Southern Economy* (1966).

HAROLD D. WOODMAN

PROSLAVERY ARGUMENT. Defenses of slavery appeared in the American colonies nearly as early as the establishment of the peculiar institution itself. Curiously, one of the first lengthy and systematic proslavery tracts was published in Massachusetts, where in 1701 John Saffin defended human bondage as consistent with Calvinist theology. Although Northerners continued to write justifications for chattel servitude through the time of the Civil War, the defense of slavery, like the slave institution itself, became predominantly the interest of the South. By the late antebellum years, the proslavery tract was the most characteristic intellectual expression of the Southern states. Increasingly isolated within the nation and the world, the slave South felt compelled to articulate ever more elaborate vindications of its way of life in order to confront intensifying political and ideological attack. The defense of slavery thus attained its greatest sophistication and fullest expression in the last three decades before the Civil War. Although it demonstrated remarkable consistency from the seventeenth century on—and even continued to trace its origins to the Old Testament, Aristotle, and St. Augustine—proslavery thought became in the South of the 1830s an explicit and formalized ideology, seeking systematically to enumerate all possible foundations for human bondage.

The intensification of proslavery argumentation in the 1830s was a change of style and tone rather than of substance. Revolutionary* idealism had led Southerners temporarily to adopt an apologetic mien in regard to the institution, but this hardly masked their failure to take decisive steps for its abolition or transformation. As antislavery sentiment* grew in the North after the Missouri debates of 1818–1820, it was impossible any longer to disarm the free states by conceding slavery's shortcomings. As Thomas Dew's pathbreaking *Review of the Debate in the Virginia Legislature* (1832) made clear, Southerners could straddle the issue no longer. It was time, he insisted, for the South to acknowledge its commitment to its way of life and to come out strongly in slavery's defense.

Dew's essay inaugurated what antebellum Southerners themselves, like many historians after them, regarded as a new era in proslavery writings. Southerners who had previously taken the peculiar institution for granted needed in these newly perilous times to understand precisely *why* slavery was right and how its justice could best be demonstrated. Proslavery tracts thus tended to be directed less at the North, which now seemed beyond rational persuasion, than at Southerners in need of deepened understanding of the assumptions that underlay their civilization. Some modern scholars have argued that this essentially internal purpose for proslavery writings identifies the apologies as a means of dealing with the South's deep-seated guilt about its peculiar institution. But it is difficult to find the explicit introspective statements of remorse that would support such an interpretation. Slavery's defenders might criticize specific aspects of the system, acknowledging, for example, that cruel and oppressive masters did exist. But the essayists insisted that these failures were simply idiosyncracies within an overwhelmingly benevolent system.

Unsympathetic to the perfectionism embraced by many abolitionists, proslavery advocates recognized evils in slavery, as they were sure they would in any terrestrial system of society and government. All earthly arrangements, they believed, necessarily required men to cope as best they could with sin; it was the relative merits of social systems, their comparative success in dealing with inherent evil, that was relevant. But as the slavery controversy intensified, apologists tended to concentrate more exclusively on the positive aspects of the system.

The pragmatic tone of Dew's 1832 effort served as the inspiration for the inductive mode of almost all proslavery tracts thereafter. Rejecting the deductive principles of the Lockean contractual social theory that had influenced the Founding Fathers, Dew embraced the conservative organic view of social order that had been implicit in proslavery philosophy since its Aristotelian beginnings. Social institutions and arrangements evolved slowly over time, Dew insisted, and could not be beneficially altered by abrupt human intervention. Like the proslavery advocates who followed him, Dew called upon his readers to study society as it had existed through the ages and to derive social principles from these empirical observations. Theoretical notions of equality could not controvert the striking differences in men's capacities evident to any impartial observer. Idealized conceptions of justice—such as those of the abolitionists—could never serve as reliable bases for social organization.

Although Dew launched a new era in proslavery thinking, Southerners followed with significant numbers of similar tracts only after Northern abolitionists inundated the South with antislavery propaganda sent through the federal mails in 1835. In the next two and a half decades, nearly every Southerner of intellectual status or pretensions wrote a defense of human bondage, and the roster of slavery's apologists came to include individuals of such prominence as novelist William Gilmore Simms, college professors George Frederick Holmes and Nathaniel Beverley Tucker, and public figures William Harper, James D. B. De Bow, Edmund Ruffin, and James Henry Hammond.

The proslavery advocates, in their collective oeuvre, developed a comprehensive defense of the peculiar institution that invoked the most important sources of authority in their intellectual culture and associated slavery with the fundamental values of their civilization. Modern scholars have thus regarded proslavery thought chiefly as an index to the mind of the white South, and not as a source of information about slavery itself. Interpretations of proslavery argument have reflected differing understandings of prewar white Southern society, and historians have variously characterized the argument, like the Old South, as premodern or forward-looking, as fundamentally based either in hierarchal class assumptions or, by contrast, in the racial tenets of *herrenvolk* democracy and the guilt of would-be American egalitarianism. Beneath these historiographical differences, however, lies the shared notion that proslavery thought is a key to the essence of antebellum Southern society and culture.

A striking commonality in almost all Southern defenses of slavery is the effort of their authors to demonstrate that their arguments were consistent with wider systems of legitimation current in Western thought. Southerners hoped in the proslavery argument to provide the foundation for overcoming their growing intellectual isolation—and seeming aberration. The Bible served as the core of this defense. In the face of abolitionist claims that slavery violated the principles of Christianity, Southerners demonstrated with ever more elaborate detail that both the Old and the New Testament sanctioned human bondage. God's Chosen People had been slaveholders; Christ had made no attack on the institution; and his disciple Paul had been its active supporter.

But for an age increasingly enamored of natural science, biblical guidance was not enough. The accepted foundations for truth were changing in European and American thought, as intellectuals sought to apply the rigor of science to the study of society and morality, as well as of the natural world. The proslavery argument accordingly called not only upon divine revelation, the traditional source and arbiter of truth, but also sought to embrace the positivistic standards increasingly accepted for assessment of all social problems. Man could and must, these authors contended, determine his social and moral duties scientifically, through examination of God's will revealed in nature and history, A subspecies of general social thought, the defense of slavery assumed the methods and arguments of broader social theories and reflected an intellectual perspective that in these years first began to regard "social science" as a discrete and legitimate domain of human learning. Reverend Thornton Stringfellow would devise a proslavery theory meant to be at once "Scriptural and Statistical"; George Fitzhugh* would write a *Sociology for the South*; Henry Hughes's proslavery tract would appear in the guise of a *Treatise on Sociology*. But most advocates did not go so far. Sociology was not yet the academic discipline it has since become; moral science—from which sociology would later emerge—still remained the central framework for social analysis both North and South. Thus the mainstream of the proslavery argument endeavored to embed the peculiar institution within nineteenth-century moral philosophy, with its emphases on man's duties and its invocation of historical precedent as guide for future action.

From the time of Greece and Rome, slavery's defenders argued, human bondage had produced the world's greatest civilizations. The peculiar institution, they insisted, was not so very peculiar. In fact, the experience of the ages showed the fundamental principles of the American Revolution to be sadly misguided. Men had not been created equal and free, as Jefferson had asserted. Nature produced individuals strikingly unequal in both attributes and circumstances. "Scientific" truth thus prescribed a hierarchically structured society reproducing nature's orderly differentiations. Social organicism replaced concepts of natural law; the prestige of modern science served to legitimate tradition and conservatism in a manner that held implications far wider than the bounds of the slavery controversy.

Such an approach to social order stressed the importance of man's duties rather than his rights. And, for rhetorical purposes, it was often the duties of masters, rather than those of slaves, that apologists chose to emphasize. Within the organic community of slave society, they argued, the master could not ignore the obligation to care for his bondsman. The slave was better off, apologists claimed, than the Northern factory worker whose employer had no interest in his health or even his survival. Northern laborers had liberty only to starve. Every civilization needed what James Hammond dubbed a "mud-sill" class to do the menial labor of society. The Southern system of human bondage, proslavery tracts insisted, simply organized this interdependence and inequality in accordance with principles of morality and Christianity.

The humanitarian arrangements of slavery, the Southerners proclaimed, contrasted favorably with the avaricious materialism of the supposedly "free" society of the North. The proslavery argument asserted its opposition to the growing materialism of the age and offered the model of evangelical stewardship as the best representation of its labor system. The master was God's surrogate on earth; the South institutionalized the Christian duties of charity in the master and humility in the slave. The nineteenth century's concern with philanthropy, defenders of slavery argued, was most successfully realized in the South's system of human bondage. The truths of science, religion, and history united to offer proslavery Southerners ready support for their position.

But by the 1850s, challenges to the unity of proslavery ideology had begun to appear. In large part, these emerging rifts mirrored wider intellectual currents. Forms of knowledge and legitimation long assumed to be necessarily compatible were everywhere displaying disquieting contradictions. Most significant was an increasingly unavoidable conflict between the claims of science and those of the Scriptures. Rather than supporting the truths of biblical revelation, science seemed to many mid-century thinkers already a threat to the conclusions of other modes of knowledge.

But in the proslavery argument, as in patterns of American thought more generally, these inconsistencies were still largely dormant. Southerners defending slavery attempted to minimize the impact of philosophical contradictions in order to maintain the strength that derived from proslavery unity. By the end of the antebellum period, however, even those recognizing the necessity for consistency sometimes found it difficult to make their own views conform to the moral-philosophical mainstream of proslavery thought. The emergence of ethnology by the late 1840s as a recognized science of racial differences was to pose inevitable difficulties for the fundamentalist bases on which the proslavery movement had been built. On the other hand, scientific validation of Negro inferiority offered an alluring support to those favoring the social subordination of blacks in slavery. Yet theories that urged the existence of two permanently unequal and separate races of men challenged Genesis and its assertion that all humans were descended from a single set of common parents.

The dilemma implicit in this conflict of knowledge and values was neatly illustrated in the experience of Josiah Nott. A physician and a leading spokesman for racial science, he was anxious to de-emphasize challenges to religious orthodoxy, yet unable to contain his contempt for the clergy, whom he viewed as purveyors of false doctrines. While Nott proclaimed his devotion to revelation, he mercilessly attacked its clerical interpreters. Science and religion were consistent, he maintained, but ministers were clearly fallible and in challenging science misinterpreted the divine word.

For the most part, Nott's audience did not perceive his subtle distinction between anticlericalism and antireligionism. Nott provoked violent controversy, and clerical defenders of slavery moved to affirm the unity of the human race and of proslavery ideology by disproving his polygenist theories.

Many defenders of slavery, however, were happy to call upon the scientific prestige of ethnology while ignoring the logical difficulties it presented. Racial arguments had been a part of proslavery thought since its earliest manifestations in the colonial period. The impact of ethnology was chiefly to enlarge and systematize this facet of the argument and to offer a variety of skull measurements and geological and anthropological "facts" as incontrovertible evidence for the mainstream position. Nature was invoked to provide additional support for the moral justifications that remained the core of the proslavery argument.

Perhaps the source of greatest controversy within the Southern proslavery movement, however, was George Fitzhugh. The only Southerner vigorously to advocate slavery as the most desirable arrangement for white as well as black labor and the only apologist to transform the discussion of slavery into an attack on capital, Fitzhugh thoroughly enjoyed the intellectual notoriety his extremism won him. He stood largely apart from the effort of the mainstream proslavery argument to associate itself with basic values of Western civilization, and he was frequently criticized by other southern apologists. Yet Eugene Genovese has argued that Fitzhugh's ideas were a "logical outcome" of notions left unexplored in the more moderate proslavery tracts. Because Fitzhugh was extreme, he was able to articulate the unspoken—even unrecognized—assumptions on which proslavery rested, and, in Genovese's view, to confront the South with the inconsistencies inherent in maintaining a prebourgeois labor system in a capitalist-world cotton market and an increasingly modern nation. The paradoxes that the proslavery argument encountered and unwittingly exposed—conflicts of tradition and modernity, of human and material values, of science and religion— are but further evidence of the argument's relevance not just to the South, but to nineteenth-century American intellectual and social history more generally.

SELECTED BIBLIOGRAPHY

E. N. Elliott, ed., *Cotton Is King, and Pro-Slavery Arguments* (1860); Drew Gilpin Faust, ed., *The Ideology of Slavery: Proslavery Thought in the Antebellum South, 1830–1860* (1981); George M. Fredrickson, *The Black Image in the White Mind: The Debate on Afro-American Character and Destiny, 1817–1914* (1971); Eugene D. Genovese, *The World the Slaveholders Made: Two Essays in Interpretation* (1969); William Sumner Jenkins, *Pro-Slavery Thought in the Old South* (1935); *The Pro-Slavery Argument, As Maintained by the Most Distinguished Writers of the Southern States* (1852); and Larry E. Tise, "Proslavery Ideology: A Social and Intellectual History of the Defense of Slavery in America, 1790–1840" (Ph.D. dissertation, University of North Carolina, 1975).

DREW GILPIN FAUST

PROSSER, GABRIEL (1775?–1800). Gabriel Prosser, born roughly 1775–1777, was a slave coachman owned by Thomas Prosser of Henrico County, Virginia. Prosser led "Gabriel's Insurrection," the first of three great slave rebellions* in nineteenth-century America.

Beginning in mid-1800, Prosser and other slaves (including his wife and two brothers) began recruiting slaves for rebellion near Richmond. American-born and acculturated, these skilled, traveled, and knowledgeable slaves developed an elaborate plot. In August "General" Gabriel defeated Jack Bowler in an election for leader of the uprising. Quoting the Bible for support, Prosser pushed for immediate action.

The plotters fashioned and stockpiled weapons and agreed to converge on Richmond in three columns after killing whites in surrounding areas. One column would ignite diversionary fires along the waterfront while the others seized the treasury and armory, freed prisoners, and kidnapped Governor James Monroe. The rebels gathered on 30 August, but a severe rainstorm rendered streams impassable, and two slaves betrayed the plot to their master. Governor Monroe quickly mobilized white forces and captured and scattered the rebels before they could act. Prosser escaped and hid for about three weeks. Given refuge aboard a schooner by an antislavery Methodist ship captain, Prosser was betrayed by two slave crewmen (perhaps tempted by the $300 reward). Refusing to talk about the revolt, Prosser was tried, sentenced, and hanged on 7 October.

Gravely alarmed (the Haitian slave rebellion was but a recent memory), Virginia slaveholders hanged thirty-five rebels. They also stationed a permanent guard in Richmond that remained intact until the Civil War, restricted slave movements and manumission* procedures, and took greater interest in African colonization* schemes.

SELECTED BIBLIOGRAPHY

Virginius Dabney, *Richmond: The Story of a City* (1976); John F. Marszalek, "Battle for Freedom: Gabriel's Insurrection," *Negro History Bulletin*, 39 (1976), 540–543; Gerald W. Mullin, *Flight and Rebellion: Slave Resistance in Eighteenth-Century Virginia* (1972); and Michael Mullin, ed., *American Negro Slavery: A Documentary History* (1976).

RICHARD W. SLATTA

PUNISHMENTS. Slave punishments ran the gamut from grotesque public executions to mild embarrassment-intended punishments. Those of the seventeenth and eighteenth centuries were harsher than the slave punishments of the nineteenth century, but all periods had harsh punishments. Moreover, in the colonies, the slave codes of the Middle and Southern colonies were the harshest.

Constables, town marshals, and other public officials punished slaves who broke state and local codes,* while slaveholders punished those who broke plantation rules. Lawmakers devised penal codes based primarily upon physical punishment. The slaves' lowly state presented a challenge to lawmakers since the slaves could not own property and were in bondage, which militated against imposing fines or mandating imprisonment in noncapital cases. Accordingly, banishment, stocks, treadmills, branding, castration, ear cropping, and other mutilations—or some combination of these—were some of the punishments administered in noncapital cases; and burning, breaking on the wheel, decapitating, and hanging were administered in capital cases.

Colonial records are replete with instances of slaves being burned as punishment for the commission of a crime.* In 1741 the New York–East Jersey area was alarmed over an alleged slave conspiracy in New York City,* which resulted in two New Jersey slaves and eleven New York slaves being burned alive. In 1749 two slaves in Cambridge, Massachusetts, were hanged in chains, then burned for committing treason. In 1773 a North Carolina slave was burned alive for murdering a white man. Moreover, in colonial Williamsburg slaves found guilty of committing arson or of poisoning their masters were decapitated.

In Louisiana, six slaves who led an 1811 revolt were decapitated and their heads stuck along the banks of the Mississippi for several counties. Equally as barbarous were the laws of New York and other colonies/states that punished slaves convicted of capital offenses by breaking on the wheel, burning at the stake, and gibbeting in chains. The most common form of capital punishment, however, was hanging. Executions usually occurred in public, and the bodies, or what was left of the corpses, remained on public display for long periods.

Although a slave convicted of a noncapital offense may have been spared his life, he had no guarantee that his limbs would remain intact. Virginia punished slaves convicted of attempted rape of a white woman with castration. Ear cropping was a common sentence, but other kinds of mutilations were practiced. A habitual runaway,* for instance, was likely to have his foot cut off.

Branding served a dual purpose: to identify criminals and to deter crime. As early as 1640 a Virginia court sentenced a runaway slave to be branded in the cheek with the letter R. In Pennsylvania, thefts of greater than five pounds sterling were punished by whipping, branding on the forehead with a T, and deportation. In 1822 a Georgia slave convicted of burglary was given thirty-nine lashes each day for three days, his ears were cropped, and his right cheek was branded with a B.

Irons, deportation, and imprisonment were some of the other punishments administered in noncapital cases. Irons were bothersome, but some shackled slaves still managed to run away. The deported slave was viewed as an incorrigible who had to be removed from his family and state before other slaves came under his influence. Deportation created mental anguish for the slave forced to leave his or her mate, children, and other family members. Except in Louisiana, slaves were rarely sentenced to imprisonment. Slaves who were, however, did not live a life of ease away from plantation chores and the demanding slave regimen because conditions in jail were awful. Jails, usually dirty and foul smelling, were too hot in the summer and often so cold in winter prisoners suffered frostbite. Some jails had treadmills, a dreadful experience which usually was an effective deterrent to future criminal acts by those who had the experience of being subjected to one.

Punishments administered on plantations were similar to those meted out by the state in noncapital cases, but the volume and kinds of punishments handled privately far exceeded in number and often in violence those handled by the state. Slaves were even dismembered by their masters. As one ex-slave said:

"Iffen a nigger, was to be found what could write, den right straight dey would chop his forefinger offen dat hand what he write with."

It was generally accepted that slaves dreaded isolation, which prompted some slaveholders to build "nigger boxes," or calabooses, to detain fractious slaves after hours and on weekends. Some plantations had homemade stocks and pillories. For those many slave infractions not serious enough to require physical punishment, masters devised punishments which included refusing to issue passes on Saturday nights to visit relatives and next of kin; stopping allowance of tobacco; assigning harder tasks; making males wear dresses and wash clothes; exhibiting the offender on a scaffold with a red flannel cap on his head; assigning tasks as scavengers in the street, chained to each other; reducing the amount of weekly rations; demoting unfaithful domestics, foremen, and drivers to fieldwork; excluding fractious slaves from participating in Saturday night dances; assigning work on Sundays, holidays, and at night after the others had finished; and confiscating crops in the truck patches. Furthermore, one Maryland tobacco grower forced a slave to eat the worms he had failed to pick off tobacco leaves.

By the mid-nineteenth century most of the harsher punishments such as burning at the stake, breaking on the wheel, decapitation, branding, ear cropping, and other mutilations gradually disappeared from the penal codes and became rare on plantations. In some instances where a punishment was not discontinued, the crime associated with it became more serious. In the South, for example, castration was prescribed for attempted rape only, where formerly it was prescribed for running away, plotting insurrection, and other offenses. Privately inflicted castration did not disappear. Some masters still castrated slave rivals for coveted slave females, but these acts were no longer committed with impunity. In 1850 a Tennessee slaveholder was sent to jail for two years for castrating his slave. Branding did not disappear from the slave penal code of South Carolina until 1833. Occasionally after that year ear cropping was still prescribed in some felony cases. Alabama retained branding in its slave code of 1852, and this practice remained a part of the penal code of Mississippi. Even so, their codes were not as harsh as those of the colonial period, which suggests that punishment was less severe in the nineteenth century.

SELECTED BIBLIOGRAPHY

Eugene D. Genovese, *Roll, Jordan, Roll: The World the Slaves Made* (1974); Edgar J. McManus, *Black Bondage in the North* (1973); Willie Lee Rose, ed., *A Documentary History of Slavery in North America* (1976); Kenneth M. Stampp, *The Peculiar Institution: Slavery in the Ante-Bellum South* (1956); Richard C. Wade, *Slavery in the Cities: The South, 1820—1860* (1964); and Arthur Zilversmit, *The First Emancipation: The Abolition of Slavery in the North* (1967).

WHITTINGTON B. JOHNSON

Q

QUAKERS. The Society of Friends (Quakers) was the first religious institution to condemn slavery as morally evil and the first to require all its members to free their slaves. After the American Revolution, the Friends founded and participated in antislavery organizations* in Great Britain and the United States and, in several ways, defined Anglo-American criticism of slavery into the nineteenth century.

Friends initially encountered slavery in their missionary journeys to the New World, where slavery was an accepted local practice in the several British colonies they entered. Planters in the British West Indies and the Southern mainland colonies who converted to Quakerism in the late seventeenth century did not give up their slaves as a condition of conversion. Travelers then or later never mentioned that Quaker slaveholders treated their blacks more humanely than other Englishmen. George Fox (1624–1691), the founder and leader of the Friends, visited Barbados and the mainland in 1672–1673. Fox cautioned masters about cruelty, suggested that slaves receive religious instruction, and recommended freeing blacks after a period of service, but never condemned slavery per se.

The first Quaker known to have publicly questioned the morality of slavery was William Edmundson (1627–1712), a prominent Irish Quaker minister, who accompanied Fox to America and later returned again. In 1676 Edmundson sent letters to Friends in New England and Maryland contrasting Christian liberty, the Golden Rule, and the gentleness necessary to convert slaves with the covetousness that reduced a part of God's people to perpetual destitution and misery.

Pennsylvania was the site of a major sustained Quaker antislavery crusade. Friends controlled the government and constituted a majority of the population from 1682 until the 1720s, and their religious organization of monthly, quarterly, and yearly meetings set behavior norms for the entire colony. Those Friends with moral qualms about slavery took their ''concern'' to the meeting. In 1688 a few Dutch pietist Quakers from Germantown protested to their monthly meeting against slavery, racism, and the vile conditions in the slave trade. In 1693 an influential Quaker theologian, George Keith, published the first Quaker tract advocating abolition. After Keith left the Quakers because of religious differences, other Friends took up the cause of antislavery. In 1696, Philadelphia Yearly Meeting, the annual gathering of Friends from western New Jersey, Pennsylvania, and Delaware, suggested that Quakers not encourage the importing of slaves. Quakers arrived at decisions in their meetings by a consensual procedure that required the virtual unanimity of the members. The Yearly Meeting's recommendations, warning against the slave trade* but not slavery, suggest that there was opposition to stronger measures. The Meeting's weak language hindered neither the slave trade nor slavery. So Friends in Chester County remained dissatisfied and frequently placed slavery on the Yearly Meeting's agenda. Evidently no agreement could be reached, because Philadelphia Quakers wrote to London Yearly Meeting seeking advice. Both London and Philadelphia Friends agreed that Quakers were not to import nor buy and sell slaves. Those reformers who wished Pennsylvania to be a truly "free" land hoped that stopping the slave trade would also discourage slavery. The Pennsylvania Assembly in 1711 and 1712 attempted first to forbid slave importation and then to place a duty on each slave brought into the colony. The Crown vetoed both statutes. The Assembly made no further effort to use taxation as a way of hindering the growth of slavery.

In the formative period of Pennsylvania between 1681 and 1720 a few Quakers decided that their religious tenets required antislavery. Their reasoning did not sway the entire Yearly Meeting, but their arguments created the foundation upon which all later Friends relied. These early Quakers felt that slavery and pacifism were incompatible. Slavery rested upon force in the capture of blacks in Africa, in the Middle Passage to America, and in continual labor with no hope of freedom. Quakers rejected the notion that Africans taken captive in a "just war" deserved death but were spared and should be thankful for perpetual bondage. Friends were well aware that blacks did not like slavery and could revolt. An armed insurrection by blacks might require so much force to quell that it would be indistinguishable from a war. In addition, the power invested in a master and his family was not conducive to cultivating the quiet humility that Friends defined as necessary for a Christian life.

The official Quaker position on the slave trade after 1719 was a matter of caution, not discipline; that is, disregarding the meetings' counsel brought no penalty. In both New England and the Middle colonies, important members engaged in the slave trade and owned slaves. Quakers in Philadelphia and Newport had close relations with planters in the West Indies and the Southern colonies. Abolitionists who publicly attacked the Quaker involvement in the slave trade and slavery risked being disciplined by the meetings for endangering the unity of Friends. Still, an undercurrent of antislavery feelings continued, primarily among Friends who lived in rural areas.

Between 1720 and 1750 the antislavery cause slowly gained adherents, even though those who temporized could stop decisive action. During the 1730s Philadelphia Yearly Meeting debated whether its anti–slave trade stance should be expanded to forbid the purchase of a slave after importation. In 1743 this prohibition became official policy. The wills of Friends in Shrewsbury and Rahway, New Jersey, show that many Friends were not contented with the Yearly Meeting's waverings, for they began manumitting slaves in the 1730s. Some Friends had always refrained from owning slaves; the wills show something new: that the antislavery cause was now influencing slave owners to feel enough guilt that they did not wish to die and face God's judgment while owning blacks. Antislavery sentiments remained localized, since similar wills were not made by Chesterfield, New Jersey, or Philadelphia Friends. When Ralph Sandiford and Benjamin Lay, recent migrants to Pennsylvania, published in 1729 and 1737 searing attacks upon Quakers' hypocrisy in defending religious and political liberties while holding slaves, the Meeting denounced both for threatening the unity of Friends. The Meeting officially ignored the antislavery sentiments that motivated both men.

The rising tide of antislavery sentiment among reformers could not be indefinitely postponed by the conservative prosperous Quakers who served in the assembly and dominated the Yearly Meeting. The proslavery cause was weakened because wealthy Philadelphia merchants during the 1740s opted to purchase indentured servants* rather than slaves. The merchants' shift to white labor could have been caused by the plentiful supply of German immigrants, moral qualms about slavery, or economic considerations. Non-Quaker merchants continued to import and to use slaves.

During the 1750s a reform movement within the Society of Friends sought stricter oversight of members, strengthening of the peace testimony, withdrawal of members from political involvement, and a purification of members from holding slaves. John Woolman (1720–1772) especially symbolized the reform movement. Woolman was a minister, a man of deep sincerity and unquestioned integrity whose *Journal* records his awakening to the evils in slavery. Woolman's conversion to antislavery brought the issue before the Meeting in a fashion which neither threatened the unity of Friends nor attacked the individuals. But the movement for a change had to come from the entire body of Friends, because the Yearly Meeting made decisions by the clerk's ascertaining the corporate will of the members who in silent waiting sought direction from the Lord.

While the 1758 decision did nothing about Friends who already owned slaves, the new policies gave the imprimatur of the largest and most influential yearly meeting in America to those Friends elsewhere who opposed slavery. Traveling ministers spread the message, and within a few years Friends everywhere had been challenged to uphold the unity of Quakers by condemning the slave trade and slavery.

Anthony Benezet (1713–1784) made the parochial Quaker antislavery impulse interact with a more general revulsion against slavery that was emerging in England and France. Benezet's investigation of the effects of the slave trade upon traditional African cultures culminated in 1762 in the first English language history of West Africa; the book was expanded, modified, and published ten years later as *Some Historical Account of Guinea*. In the period before the Revolution Benezet reminded both Britons and colonists of the incompatibility of slavery with natural liberties and the rights of Englishmen. Picturing the noble black and idealizing the family ties in Africa, he drew upon the heightened emphasis on feelings and sympathy in late eighteenth-century romanticism to emphasize the sufferings caused by the slave trade. Benezet argued that the blacks' social and intellectual capabilities were equal with the whites' and any difference was due to environment.

He observed that slaves had supported masters for years, and so admonished the masters who emancipated their slaves to be responsible that the freedmen did not become public charges. If whites and blacks could not live together as equals, then lands should be set aside in the American West for blacks.

In rural New England and Nantucket the antislavery efforts of a few Friends had been rebuffed by merchants in Newport. Woolman's visit in 1760 prompted New England Yearly Meeting to bring its position into conformity with Philadelphia's, but antislavery Quakers in New England soon began agitating for additional measures. In 1770 New England recommended that all slaves should be freed, except the very young and old. Between 1772 and 1776 Friends in New England ceased to own slaves, and those who resisted were disowned.

Philadelphia Yearly Meeting began catching up to New England in 1772, first taking a survey of all members who owned slaves, and then, in 1773 and 1774, making owning slaves a disownable offense. Visiting committees had persuaded virtually all Friends to free their slaves by 1783; those who refused had been disowned.

Southern Quakers followed the promptings of Northern Friends. By the late 1760s, for example, members of Third Haven Monthly Meeting on the Eastern Shore of Maryland began freeing slaves. In 1772 Baltimore Yearly Meeting established committees to work with slaveholders, and in 1778 the monthly meetings began disowning those who refused to free blacks. Virginia Yearly Meeting in 1766 and North Carolina in 1768 denounced the slave trade, but laws against manumission* made the process of freeing slaves more difficult than in the Northern states. Virginia, for example, restricted manumissions until 1782. So while Virginia Yearly Meeting recommended freeing slaves in 1773, most emancipation occurred after 1782.

North Carolina Friends began freeing their slaves between 1775 and 1777, but the new state government reenslaved them and passed another antimanumission law in 1777. After Friends won a case in court showing the illegality of the state's action, the legislature overruled the court. Eventually, North Carolina Friends determined that the only way to free people was to vest title in the Yearly Meeting. Some of the slaves "owned" by the yearly meeting migrated, but others remained the nominal property of the Meeting for many years. In 1828 an English Friend estimated the North Carolina Friends had freed their slaves at a cost of £50,000. During the Revolution, Friends in the Northern and

Southern states alike demonstrated that they did not stop freedom at the color line.

Emancipation was not followed by attempts to convert blacks to Quakerism. Friends generally did not proselytize, and assumed that only white children with a "birth and education" among Quakers would accept the meetings' disciplined way of life. Sectarian isolationism and racial prejudice delayed Friends from allowing blacks to become full members until 1796. Even then, seating arrangements within meeting houses and cemeteries reserved special sections for blacks. Quakers treated blacks as an oppressed group deserving of paternalistic philanthropy.

During and after the Revolution* Friends took satisfaction in the actions of Northern states to restrict or end slavery, and they hoped for similar activities in the Southern states. Friends petitioned the states, the Confederation, and the federal government to end the slave trade. American and English Quakers cooperated in the movement against the slave trade, furnishing each other information to use in political debates. In 1783 the London Meeting for Sufferings created an official committee and an agency to disseminate information about slavery. London Quakers mobilized public opinion through petition campaigns, distributed antislavery literature to leading members of Parliament, and formed contacts with leading evangelical opponents of slavery including William Wilberforce, Granville Sharp, and Thomas Clarkson. In 1787 Friends joined these men to found the Society for Effecting the Abolition of the Slave Trade. English Quakers remained active in the agitation that resulted in Parliament's outlawing of the slave trade in 1807 and ending slavery in 1833.

In America Friends founded and constituted an overwhelming percentage of the membership in manumission societies in the North and South. In Philadelphia, which had a large free black population, James Pemberton, a wealthy Quaker merchant, served as clerk of the Meeting for Sufferings and president of the Abolition Society. The same Quakers dominated both organizations which worked together to guarantee the legal rights of blacks, to prevent freedmen from being reenslaved, to provide schools and apprenticeships for children, and to support financially the destitute aged and the building of black churches. The manumission societies searched for an adequate method of ending slavery in a way that jeopardized no Quaker testimonies. Friends preferred gradualism and moderate rhetoric without hatred of the slave owner and with compassion for the black because these methods, they believed, had influenced Northerners to free their slaves.

Between 1780 and 1810 Quakers in Virginia and North Carolina joined the general migration to the fertile lands in western Pennsylvania, central Ohio, and Indiana. The push to migrate was primarily economic, but a major attraction of the Northwest Territory* was the absence of slavery. The Quaker settlers in Ohio and Indiana provided a strong nucleus of antislavery sentiment and they strenuously resisted efforts to introduce slavery there.

Concentrating upon morality in confronting the evil of slavery seemed to some Friends to ignore the crucial issue of the economic advantage of slavery. A few Quakers organized the Free Produce Association, whose members pledged to use only goods produced by free labor. As a method of demonstrating commitment to the cause of antislavery, the free produce movement had some successes, but it never attracted a majority of Friends.

Slavery occasioned acute moral dilemmas for Friends wanting to obey the law yet unwilling to recognize the legal basis of the peculiar institution. The Philadelphia merchant-tailor Isaac Hopper (1771–1852), for example, mastered the intricacies of the laws concerning manumission, evidence, and slavery in order to serve as a defender of blacks, protesting their kidnapping and supporting those attempting to gain their freedom. Conservative Friends approved of the good Hopper did, but questioned whether Friends' support of fugitive slaves using legal technicalities was in keeping with Quaker attitudes towards honesty and the law. A series of schisms beginning in 1827 divided the Society of Friends and focused energies on problems within the Meeting, thereby weakening the role of Quakers in antislavery agitation. Supposed temporizing of Indiana Yearly Meeting over slavery occasioned a separation in 1842.

In popular memory, Quakers conducted the underground railroad.* Friends like Levi Coffin of Indiana, reported "president" of the underground railroad, and Thomas Garrett, of Wilmington, Delaware, helped thousands of blacks to freedom. Many Quakers, however, had no direct contact with fugitive slaves.* Undoubtedly, most Friends would have quietly aided fugitives rather than return them to slavery, but some members also recognized that helping a few runaways* did not seriously weaken the slave system while complicating the difficult task of persuading the South of the evil of the institution.

The Quaker tactics of sympathy with the Southerners' dilemma, understanding racial prejudices, and working through the political system did not stop the spread of slavery. In 1831 William Lloyd Garrison,* unhappy with the polite tactics and moderate language used by Quakers in manumission and colonization societies, founded *The Liberator* to advocate immediate emancipation. Garrison attracted a few Quaker supporters, including feminist Lucretia Mott and poet John G. Whittier, but his violent rhetoric and attacks upon the Constitution and the churches alienated others who saw the new methods as fostering hatred for the South rather than meaningful reform. Yearly meetings throughout America cautioned their members against participating in activities for good purposes, like abolition, which used divisive methods. New York meetings disowned Isaac Hopper and other radicals because of their association with attacks upon individual Friends made by other abolitionists associated with Garrison.

In the period from 1840 to 1860 Friends' meetings continued their traditional methods of antislavery. They protested the Mexican War,* supported personal liberty laws,* petitioned Congress to end slavery in the federal territories, and pressured the Pennsylvania legislature to nullify the fugitive slave law.* During the late 1850s the meetings seemed caught between their dread of disunion and their opposition to slavery. Still, when the war and emancipation came, Friends, who believed that all Americans bore the responsibility for the evils of slavery and owed compensation to blacks, willingly accepted a role to work with and for the newly freed men and women.

SELECTED BIBLIOGRAPHY

Roger Anstey, *The Atlantic Slave Trade and British Abolition, 1760–1810* (1975); Roger Bruns, ed., *Am I Not a Man and a Brother? The Antislavery Crusade of Revolutionary America, 1688–1788* (1977); David B. Davis, *The Problem of Slavery in the Age of Revolution, 1770–1823* (1975); Thomas Drake, *Quakers and Slavery in America* (1950); J. William Frost, "The Origins of the Quaker Crusade against Slavery: A Review of Recent Literature," *Quaker History*, 67 (1978), 42–58; J. William Frost, *The Quaker Origins of Antislavery* (1980); Nancy Slocum Hornick, "Anthony Benezet: Eighteenth-Century Social Critic, Educator and Abolitionist" (Ph.D. dissertation, University of Maryland, 1974); Sydney V. James, *A People among Peoples: Quaker Benevolence in Eighteenth-Century America* (1963); Jack Marietta, *The Reformation of American Quakerism, 1748–1783* (1984); Jean R. Soderlund, "Conscience, Interest, and Power: The Development of Quaker Opposition to Slavery in the Delaware Valley, 1688–1780" (Ph.D. dissertation, Temple University, 1982); and Stephen B. Weeks, *Southern Quakers and Slavery: A Study in Institutional History* (1896).

J. WILLIAM FROST

R

RACE. Race as a distinct concept for classifying people became prominent in nineteenth-century Europe and America through the work of investigators in the fledgling science of anthropology. In prior generations, European writers had associated *race* with the term *nation* to refer to persons sharing culture, biological descent, and presumably political destiny. The term was used vaguely to describe classes, like the nobility, or large cultural groups, like the Irish, who shared behavioral characteristics. European explorers and settlers believed that the Christian religion and European culture were superior to all others, and denigrated the moral codes of nonwhites. Where they discovered people with primitive material cultures like the natives of North America or the inhabitants of West African coastal villages, European writers might romanticize their simplicity, compared with the complexities of the more devious European commercial societies, but they often deplored the savagery of their warfare or puberty rites. British explorers associated blacks with the exotic new animals, especially anthropoid apes, which were discovered in West Africa, and fantasized about black and anthropoid sexual relations. Prior to the nineteenth century, however, the personalities of individuals within races or nations were presumed to be plastic, their mental faculties of roughly equal capacity, and their appearance, as well as the content of their culture, largely the consequence of climate and other environmental conditioning.

Just as the plantation agricultural system in the West Indies and the Chesapeake had preceded the importation of large numbers of Africans as slaves, so slavery as a legal status preceded the use of race as a justification for exploitation. Scholars do not know why only nonwhites were enslaved in the Americas. They do know that the Portuguese in the fifteenth century had acquired slaves in North and West Africa and utilized them extensively in agriculture near Lisbon. The Spanish in the sixteenth century had enslaved Indians as the "heathen" objects of conquest in a "just war" for the glory of king and pope. British settlers on Barbados and Jamaica and later in Virginia turned agricultural colonies into permanent settlements dominated by large units dependent on bound labor, but they had made do initially with white indentured servants.* By the 1680s planters on Barbados and Jamaica had turned to the international slave trade* in Africans for a surer labor supply. Planters in South Carolina from its founding in the 1680s and those in the Chesapeake by 1700 also turned to the slave trade for their work force. They also drafted codes* that identified Africans and their descendants with perpetual bondage. While slave traders and planters did not necessarily believe that Africans were innately inferior to Europeans, by lumping all blacks and their offspring, including children of mixed race, into one legal and social category, they moved a long way to denying the humanity of Afro-Americans.

The social conditioning surrounding slavery in North America reinforced the monolithic perception of people of African descent. In locales like Brazil and even Jamaica, where blacks greatly outnumbered whites through 1815, a demand for free skilled labor which might facilitate the marketing of commercial crops led to the substantial manumission of young people of mixed ancestry. A whole vocabulary to describe the various appearances of mixed African, native, and European ancestries contributed to a more complex perception of the social mix and a more individualized appreciation of people. The so-called mulatto escape hatch to freedom and identity in Brazil fulfilled an economic need and created a variety of social types. While descendants of Europeans were usually afforded higher social status than other persons, and Brazil later pursued a policy of ''whitening'' to attract European immigrants, social conflict did not assume stark racial outlines as it did in the United States.

The larger proportion of free whites in the United States and their new political power as popular democracy replaced aristocratic republicanism led to the increased use of racial thinking to justify, yet also to limit, both geographic expansion and slavery. The extension of America's cotton kingdom depended on the expropriation of native peoples and coincided with the conquest of Liberia* in West Africa to resettle disaffected ''free Negroes.'' The expulsion of the Southern Indian tribes was justified on the grounds that as inferior peoples they could not fully develop the land. But talk of conquering Mexico after 1846 was undermined by the fear that Southern whites would be inundated by free natives and ''mixed breeds.''

In the Southern states the possession of slaves provided the key measure of social mobility, while in the North slavery was seen as a threat to the economic opportunity of small landholders in the developing West. To justify the ownership of persons in an otherwise democratic society, slaveholders either pointed to biblical precedents or began to assert that blacks were less than human. In addition, most Southern states placed severe restrictions on free blacks, usually requiring that newly manumitted persons leave the state. Northern whites, promoting their own mobility, wished to exclude freed Negroes from their own states and from the West. Most Northern states from Pennsylvania westward either abolished or forbade slavery, but also prohibited free Negroes from entering, becoming citizens, or voting. Although sexual exploitation of slave women marked all slave societies, the marriage of whites to blacks was forbidden almost everywhere in the United States. The proliferation of racial stereotypes denigrating the intelligence and individuality of blacks in the popular theater and then in minstrelsy* by the 1840s further suggests how deeply racism pervaded American culture.

As a scientific ideology, racism emerged from the eighteenth-century speculation of writers like Benjamin Rush and Thomas Jefferson* and the taxonomy of Carolus Linnaeus into the formal theorizing of such nineteenth-century medical doctors as Charles Caldwell and Samuel G. Morton of Philadelphia and Josiah Nott of Mobile, and of the Swiss biologist and Harvard professor, Louis Agassiz. Jefferson simply speculated on the inherent inferiority of the "rational faculty" in Africans compared to the Europeans, while the popular South Carolina historian David Ramsay believed that blacks were uniquely and inherently capable of agricultural labor in tropical climates. Under the aegis of disinterested scientific experimentation, Morton and the French surgeon Paul Broca measured anthropoid and human skeletal remains which European and American explorers were submitting to new "natural history" museums. Morton fudged his data, comparing skull sizes by preselecting race as the basis for comparison and by ignoring the age, sex, and height of his specimens. His faulty statistical techniques and monocausal logic reinforced his presumption that Europeans had larger and therefore more complex brains than either native Americans or Africans. Agassiz, the most respected biologist in America, then concluded that Asians, native Americans, and Africans differed sufficiently in anatomical structure from Europeans to justify their separate origins and evolution.

In a culture nurtured on evangelical Protestantism, Agassiz's argument for separate creation, or "polygenesis," struck a less responsive chord than did biblical precedents for slavery. But Southern religious leaders rarely denied that blacks were innately inferior to whites. Secular writers like George Fitzhugh* justified slavery on archaic sociological grounds as a patriarchal system for organizing all lower classes; Fitzhugh, in fact, shifted to a racist defense of slavery* only when literature on the subject dramatically increased in the late 1850s.

Acceptance of a polygenesist, racialist interpretation of human differences did not lead necessarily either to a defense of slavery or to the acceptance of evolution as an inevitable process. Intense racialists like Hinton R. Helper* attacked slavery as an unnatural means of allowing privileged white planters to monopolize land and opportunity, and called for the elimination of slavery and of blacks. Horace Bushnell, though a Northern abolitionist, also accepted polygenesis, and like Helper saw slavery as an unnatural means of protecting blacks from direct competition with superior whites. He felt that abolition was necessary so that nature might eliminate inferior stock. For the balance of the nineteenth century much attention was paid to the census data on black population growth to see if blacks could survive in freedom. Likewise, native Americans were perceived to be a dying people, with most writers attributing their decline to genetic weakness rather than to the depredations of whites and the reservation and allotment policies of the federal government.

Other abolitionists like Harriet Beecher Stowe* accepted a form of romantic racialism, from which Stowe, at least, drew very different conclusions. Romantic racialism, which to some degree drew sustenance from eighteenth-century writings on native Americans, did not so much rank races as see in them unique essences which should be allowed to flourish so that humanity, conceived of as a social whole, might be enriched by cultural diversity. Stowe endowed her fictional blacks with qualities of gentleness, piety, and generosity missing in the commercial competition of Northern cities. Unlike Bushnell, she assumed that after slavery proper education would enable blacks to compete as farmers and skilled workers, though probably not in occupations which required substantial abstract thought.

Racialist thinking had a direct impact on how political leaders from Northern states dealt with blacks after emancipation. Those like Abraham Lincoln,* who never accepted the polygenesis argument, believed nevertheless that different races were best suited to different climates and could not share the same locales without the less-suited succumbing. Lincoln experimented unsuccessfully with black emigrant colonies in the Caribbean. Other Republicans* like Horace Greeley accepted the climatic theory of racial differentiation but did not care to assist the less-suited. Still others like Stowe, Samuel Chapman Armstrong of Hampton Institute, and Booker T. Washington,* while not speculating on the origins of races, assumed a relationship between mental and biological differences. But they felt that an enriched environment would improve the capacity of races to survive. They accepted the eighteenth-century theory of Chevalier de Lamarck that acquired characteristics (or learned behavior) could be internalized through the acquisition of an ''instinct,'' which could then be transmitted genetically to offspring. While the biological description of an ''instinct'' remained vague, Lamarckism as a general theory persisted in psychology and underlay the faith that the freedmen, despite temporary mental disabilities, could gradually be brought to a higher mental plane. Nevertheless, because the disabilities of the freedmen were believed to have a genetic source, the type of education provided had to suit their current capacities. The enthusiasm for mechanical rather than humanistic education for the freedmen and their offspring rested precisely on this racialist theory.

The popularity of racial ideologies grew dramatically in the late nineteenth and early twentieth centuries, perhaps because the abolition of slavery and then the admission of blacks to citizenship under the Fourteenth Amendment cast race relations into a political maelstrom. Racial theorizing came to justify a great spectrum of programs from intensive racial segregation and disfranchisement amidst lynchings and rioting, to a black cultural renaissance in a multiethnic urban world. Many Southern white politicians seized on the theories of Herbert Spencer, the British author who distorted the writings of Charles Darwin to interpret history as an inevitable competition between races. Darwin, on the basis of empirical research with birds and other animals, argued that species originated through a process of natural selection, so that those best suited to survive in a *specific* environment would pass on their characteristics to their offspring. Spencer then argued that societies were produced by genetically determined races, which could be easily graded from savage to barbarous to civilized. The most complex society had been produced by the most complex minds, which were monopolized by the race most fit to survive in *any* environment. Southern politicians then argued that Anglo-Saxons had produced the most complex societies and Africans the most primitive, and that inherently inferior blacks should not be allowed to contaminate white institutions.

By the 1880s black historians like George Washington Williams (and later William Ferris) joined the racial argument. They countered white supremacy by claiming Egypt as an African civilization and by emphasizing the sophistication of West African societies prior to Portuguese explorations. More sophisticated black writers like Alexander Crummell, Paul Dunbar, and W.E.B. Du Bois combined romantic racialist assertions of the superiority of certain black "instincts" with an environmentalist explanation of most black behavior. Du Bois argued, for example, that blacks had the same mental capacities as whites, but for instinctual reasons preferred compassion and humor to competition and cynicism. His sociological studies emphasized how similar social conditions like low income, limited education, or overcrowded housing produced the same behavior in poor whites as in poor blacks.

The decisive separation of the social from the biological (or the cultural from the racial) explanation of behavior came through the work of the anthropologist Franz Boas and his students between 1910 and 1930. In place of ranking societies within a deterministic, evolutionary, and hierarchal whole called "culture," they studied individual "cultures" as sophisticated, holistic constructs, each with its own integrity. By 1911 Boas concluded that "the mind of primitive man" had the same capacities for logical inference, aesthetic creativity, and moral judgment as did the minds of people in technologically advanced societies. His students like A. L. Kroeber, Melville Herskovits, and Margaret Mead rejected the notion that acquired behavior could be transmitted genetically or that members of a descent group shared "instincts." They verified through field research the earlier conclusion of W. E. B. Du Bois, that "race" represented a social loyalty rather than a biological affinity. The political uses to which the race concept has been put since 1930, unlike the case in the nineteenth century, have simply ignored or defied the findings of the contemporary biological and social sciences.

Despite the demonstration by anthropologists that the concept "race" lacked an empirical referent, shapers of policy in Europe, South Africa, and the United States have used it to defend a variety of preconceptions and interests. In Germany in the 1930s, Nazi theorists like Alfred Rosenberg counteracted the effects on the lower middle class of industrialization and defeat in World War I by deliberately rejecting scientific evidence in favor of a mystical "intuition." For Rosenberg and Hitler, race was an eternal and unitary entity embodied in the "blood" and expressed in a spirit or "mythos." History from the earliest human record should be seen as a conflict, with heroic and morally pure Nordics or Aryans (depicted as blue-eyed blonds with long heads), against bestial Africans and cunning "Syrians" (or Jews). Combining romantic racialism, conspiratorial anti-Semitism, and pagan brutality, the Nazis concocted an ideology to justify the extermination of tens of millions from the hereditarily "lower" races.

In the United States, the idea of race never received as deterministic a metahistorical rationale, because American theorists felt they had sufficient physical space to adjust racial tensions more pragmatically. Sociologists like E. A. Ross and armchair anthropologists like Lothrop Stoddard accepted a hereditarian explanation for the low social status of ethnic enclaves, but they also agreed with the historian Frederick Jackson Turner that the American frontier could forge self-reliance in some European immigrants. Turner himself, however, felt that groups like the Italians and Jews who clustered in cities had to be limited and controlled. Students of American blacks like Ulrich B. Phillips and Alfred Holt Stone reiterated the view that Africans were congenital savages and argued that only the reintroduction of the plantation system of agriculture under paternalistic white management in a warm climate could civilize blacks. By 1927, Stoddard proposed a policy of "Bi-racialism" which rationalized and sought to legitimate the patterns of segregation which were springing up throughout the country. His view that blacks had to be permanently segregated from public life was justified by Phillips's two massive volumes on slavery (*American Negro Slavery* [1918] and *Life and Labor in the Old South* [1929]), which provided the authoritative scholarly explanation of black behavior through the 1940s. Not until the publication of Gunnar Myrdal's *An American Dilemma* (1944), which exhaustively exposed the ideological biases of racial discrimination, and Kenneth M. Stampp's *The Peculiar Institution* (1956), which attacked Phillips's interpretation of slavery point for point, was racial determinism largely eliminated from the study of Afro-American slavery. The notion that blacks developed their own cultural norms within the system of plantation slavery, however, was not explored until the publication of studies by Eugene D. Genovese, John W. Blassingame, and others in the 1970s.

Hereditarian racialism was also projected more subtly through American public schools between 1918 and the 1970s via a battery of tests which purported to measure intelligence. The IQ tests were devised by the French psychologist Alfred Binet to identify slow learners so that new teaching techniques could improve their performance. But H. H. Goddard and Lewis M. Terman, the psychologists who brought the Binet test to America, believed that intelligence was hereditary, unitary, and easily measured. They hoped to identify pupils who performed well below age level so they might be institutionalized and prevented from having offspring. During World War I their colleague, R. M. Yerkes, convinced the U.S. Army to administer tests of intelligence to recruits so that a standard measure could be generated. The tests verified Yerkes's prejudice that East Europeans and blacks had lower mental ability than native-born whites, and his findings were subsequently cited in the early 1920s by successful proponents of immigration restriction. The National Origins Quota system (1924) set an annual limit to immigration (156,000), and allotted very small proportions to the countries of eastern and southern Europe. Asians and Africans were formally excluded. The system remained unchanged until 1965.

By the early 1940s, through internal criticism of the IQ tests, scholars like Ashley Montague demonstrated that they measured primarily acculturation rather than innate ability, and more importantly that intelligence was too complex to be measured by a series of simple tests. Combined with the work of Boas and his pupils, Montague demonstrated that intelligence could not be correlated with race and that race itself could not be correlated with specific genetic traits. He suggested that in scholarly discussions the term *ethnic group* should be substituted for race. Nevertheless, as late as the 1970s, the Harvard psychologist Arthur Jensen could reify intelligence as a measurable quality, and through dubious statistical artifacts claim causal relationships between racial groups and abstract intelligence.

SELECTED BIBLIOGRAPHY

Robert F. Berkhofer, Jr., *The White Man's Indian: Images of the American Indian from Columbus to the Present* (1978); Carl N. Degler, *Neither Black nor White: Slavery and Race Relations in Brazil and the United States* (1971); George M. Fredrickson, *The Black Image in the White Mind: The Debate on Afro-American Character and Destiny, 1817–1914* (1971); Stephen Jay Gould, *The Mismeasure of Man* (1981); Winthrop D. Jordan, *White over Black: American Attitudes toward the Negro, 1550–1812* (1968); George W. Stocking, Jr., *Race, Culture and Evolution: Essays in the History of Anthropology* (1968); and William Toll, *The Resurgence of Race: Black Social Theory from Reconstruction to the Pan-African Conferences* (1979).

WILLIAM TOLL

RAPIER, JAMES THOMAS (1837–1883). James T. Rapier was born in Florence, Alabama, on 13 November 1837, the fourth son of former slave John Rapier and his free Negro wife, Susan. He attended school in Nashville, Tennessee, living with his slave grandmother Sally Thomas (1840s), and in Buxton and Toronto, Canada (1856–1864). Returning to the South, he was elected to represent Lauderdale County at the 1867 Alabama Constitutional Convention. In 1870 he ran on the Republican ticket for secretary of state, but in an atmosphere of violence, he lost and the entire ticket went down to defeat. The next year he was appointed assessor of internal revenue (Montgomery District), the first Negro in the state to attain such a high patronage position. His superior ability as an administrator as well as his high standing among freedmen* resulted in his nomination as the Republican candidate for Congress in 1872 from the second district in Alabama. In a relatively peaceful campaign, Rapier was elected, receiving 54 percent of the votes. In December 1873, he took his seat in the forty-third Congress, where he supported legislation to improve the public schools in the South, and made an eloquent speech in behalf of civil rights.

Rapier lost two subsequent bids for Congress (1874 and 1876) and, as a result, turned his attention to farming and business. In 1878 he was appointed Alabama Collector of Internal Revenue for the second district. During the last five years of his life, he became increasingly embittered by the lack of improvement for blacks in the South. Having previously attempted to assist his brethren through the National Negro Labor Union (1869–1872) and its affiliate the Alabama Negro Labor Union (1871–1872), which he helped organize, Rapier now advised blacks to leave their native section and emigrate to the West. Before his dreams of emigration could be realized, however, he died of pulmonary tuberculosis in Montgomery, 31 May 1883, at the age of forty-five.

SELECTED BIBLIOGRAPHY

Loren Schweninger, *James T. Rapier and Reconstruction* (1978).

LOREN SCHWENINGER

RECREATION, SLAVE. To minimize problems and to guarantee a smooth-running plantation,* Southern slaveholders found it necessary to requite their slaves by granting them brief periods of leisure time. Slaves normally were given time off on Saturdays, Sundays, and during various holidays that their masters celebrated such as Easter, the Fourth of July, Thanksgiving, and Christmas. In addition, slaves often were able to realize additional leisure time simply by outmaneuvering their "unsuspecting" masters.

Slaves looked forward to the Christmas holidays with a great deal of anticipation. It was unquestionably the most joyous time of the year for the majority of slaves. The Christmas holidays usually lasted anywhere from two days to a week or more, depending on the disposition of the master and the condition of the crop. On many plantations the Christmas season lasted as long as the slaves could keep a log burning. If it was necessary for the slaves to labor during the Christmas holidays, most planters would make up for the celebrations their slaves missed by giving them time off later in the year. The planters in the sugar-making* regions of the Deep South frequently were compelled to compensate their slaves for Christmas holidays they had to forgo.

Slaves longed for Christmas and other holiday times not simply as periods free from labor but as times when slaves could be with one another. Holidays provided opportunities for bondsmen to participate in family* and community activities or merely party with their friends and relatives. Slave children* in particular relished these moments because it meant they could frolic with their parents and the other adult slaves—free from the continual surveillance of the planter and his family. The children loved to congregate outside of the cabins and listen to some "learned" old slave relate tales of Africa; gather around a blazing fire to dance and sing songs; accompany the more gamesome men on raccoon and possum hunts; travel with their family to a nearby plantation for a dance* or corn-shucking; or simply stay around the slave quarters and "cut capers" with the other children. Slave boys, and less frequently the girls, challenged members of their peer group to impromptu contests that would test their physical prowess. They delighted in seeing who could run the fastest, jump the highest, throw the farthest, swim the longest, and lift the heaviest objects. The ability to perform well in games and "athletic" contests usually guaranteed slave children the respect of their impressionable young playmates.

Dances were the most popular recreational pursuits engaged in by members of the slave quarter during social gatherings. Slaves apparently found European-style dances—reels, minuets, and schottishes—too sedate and formalized. Nevertheless, the slave narratives contain occasional references to these dances. The dances in the slave quarters, such as the "patting juba" and the "buzzard lope" performed in the isolated Sea Islands region off the coast of Georgia, closely resembled African dances in terms of method and style. They often were performed from a flexed, fluid, bodily position as opposed to the stiffly erect position of European dances. In their dances slaves often imitated and portrayed such animals as the buzzard, eagle, crow, and rabbit in realistic detail, placing great emphasis upon satire, improvisation, and freedom of individual expression. Slave dances tended to concentrate on movement outward from the pelvic region, gyrations that whites found despicable. Many slave dances were performed to a propulsive swinging rhythm animating the whole body.

When the slaves were not spending their leisure time dancing, they often were engaged in hunting or fishing* excursions. Slave men, and less frequently slave women, loved to roam the fields and streams of their home plantation in search of their favorite animal or fish. Hunting and fishing were ideal ways for slaves to supplement their rather monotonous diets. Slave fathers also gained a degree of status by adding delicacies to the family table. Often precluded by their masters from contributing to their families' material welfare, slave men relished the chance to hunt and fish for food. Slave men also must have enjoyed the camaraderie and parity of their fellow sportsmen. There was nothing quite like sitting around a blazing fire relating the tales of the phantom-like raccoon or the sixteen-foot catfish that got away. Slave men, furthermore, found these activities satisfying because they afforded them the opportunity to teach their older children the intricacies involved in hunting and fishing. There were few activities in the plantation community where slave fathers and sons could share in the excitement of common pursuits, and hunting and fishing satisfied an important need.

Advancing age or labor requirements rarely diminished the slaves' competitive spirit or love for the sporting activities they had engaged in as children. Slaves welcomed the opportunity to engage in very informal boat and horse races, or refresh themselves by swimming in nearby rivers or lakes. They also were particularly fond of gambling. The more peccant slave men placed bets on everything from dice and card games to local horse races and cockfights. Slaves experienced the problem of not having enough to bet with and the fear that the slaves of the more devout planters would be reprimanded for their gaming, but no matter the restrictions, gambling remained popular among the slaves. The temperament of their masters as well as the economic, social, and political conditions of their community proved important in determining the extent to which slaves were allowed to gamble. And like other recreational activities, the bondsmen found ways to transcend the various condemnations made against gambling and continued to place bets with a high degree of seriousness. To elude the eyes of their masters or a concerned white community, slaves often resorted to gambling in the woods or in some other secluded spot. Possessing little money with which to gamble, the bondsmen's stakes often consisted of particular objects to which they attached special importance.

Many of the slaves' recreational pursuits were linked closely with rural customs and were significantly influenced by the type of work done on the particular plantation. Corn shuckings, log rollings, hog killings, and quilting bees commonly were joyous occasions for members of the slave-quarter community. In an effort to increase the productivity of their slaves, planters frequently made these tasks grand social gatherings and normally included different material incentives, lavish dinners, and all-night partying. As a consequence, slaves looked forward to these herculean tasks because it gave them opportunities to socialize with friends and relatives. The chance to gamble with fellow slaves did much to efface the physical exertion that was required during these occasions and resulted in some of the most happy times of the year for the bondsmen and women.

Despite the oppression of the peculiar institution, slaves played and participated in a variety of recreational activities with a remarkable degree of intensity. The chance to frolic with neighboring slaves, opportunities to dance in their own particular style, freedom to roam the fields and woods in search of game, and the privilege of testing their physical strength were sources of fun and enjoyment for members of the slave quarters. Recreational activities enabled slaves to realize particular social needs that could not be accomplished in any other fashion. Their recreation helped to ensure the slaves' identity as individuals and as a community.

SELECTED BIBLIOGRAPHY

Fisk University, *Unwritten History of Slavery: Autobiographical Accounts of Negro Ex-Slaves* (1945); George P. Rawick, ed., *The American Slave: A Composite Autobiography* (19 vols., 1972); Ronnie C. Tyler and Lawrence R. Murphy, eds., *The Slave Narratives of Texas* (1974); and David K. Wiggins, "Sport and Popular Pastimes in the Plantation Community: The Slave Experience" (Ph.D. dissertation, University of Maryland, 1979).
                                                                                      DAVID K. WIGGINS

RECRUITMENT OF BLACK SOLDIERS. Black Americans have fought in every American war. The fundamental reason for their military use has been practical utility. Although denied membership in colonial militia, slaves nevertheless served in wars for North American empire, often as substitutes for their masters. At the start of the American Revolution,* there were black Sons of Liberty and black Minutemen until the Continental Congress, in the name of national unity, ordered their rejection. But manpower needs and British precedent soon dictated relaxation of that order. "The desperate need for troops and laborers," writes Ira Berlin, "forced both belligerents to muster blacks into their service with the promise of liberty." By the end of that war, some 5,000 black men had served in Continental and state forces.

In the republic's early years, blacks were almost totally excluded from militia units. Only in Louisiana, where their distinguished military service under the Spanish and French gave *gens de couleur* a place, did blacks serve as citizen soldiers. These "free men of color" fought under Andrew Jackson* at New Orleans in 1815, and subsequently maintained separate militia organizations up to the Civil War.* Generally, however, nineteenth-century Americans viewed war as "white men's business." The very presence of armed black men threatened slavery, provided a dangerous example to slaves and freemen alike, and denied the doctrine that a slave was not a man.

Events in the early months of the Civil War clarified that racial conviction. Secretary of War Simon Cameron rejected offers of black units, despite Frederick Douglass's* claims that slavery should be eradicated as a primary Union war aim. To do this, Douglass would "LET THE SLAVES AND FREE COLORED PEOPLE BE CALLED INTO SERVICE, AND FORMED INTO A LIBERATING ARMY, to march into the South and raise the banner of emancipation." Not until the war's second year, when manpower shortages developed, did Union leaders heed Douglass's advice.

Concerned for border state loyalty, and ever sensitive to white pride, Abraham Lincoln* opposed black recruitment until crises forced him to shift his ground and broaden his war aims. When he opened Union ranks to blacks after his Emancipation Proclamation* of 1 January 1863, Lincoln accepted the facts of military necessity. But black recruitment had begun months earlier. In the summer of 1862 Union troops enlisted slaves in South Carolina, Louisiana, and Kansas—all suffering from manpower shortages. General David Hunter began what by 1864 would become a "prodigious revolution" when he rounded up former slaves on Treasury Department plantations in South Carolina. His recruiting tactics—little better than impressment—attracted wide attention and forced the issue. General Benjamin F. Butler, commanding the Department of the Gulf, built on former Confederate militia units composed of "free men of color" and had mustered three regiments of "Native Guards" before the end of 1862. Meanwhile, Senator James H. Lane raised the First Kansas Colored Volunteer Infantry (later the 79th USCT). Before Lincoln had signed his great proclamation, five black regiments already had been mustered.

With Lincoln's blessing, and under War Department supervision, the movement to recruit slaves grew and spread in the spring of 1863. Recruitment followed a variety of patterns: Colonel James Montgomery went to South Carolina to raise a sister regiment for Hunter's pioneering unit (now commanded by Harvard abolitionist Thomas Wentworth Higginson). Colonel Daniel Ullman assembled a white cadre in New York to raise a black brigade in Louisiana. Simultaneously, General Nathaniel P. Banks added more regiments to his "Corps d'Afrique.'' Massachusetts and Rhode Island took the lead among Northern states to raise three regiments including the famous 54th Massachusetts Infantry. In March, Secretary of War Edwin M. Stanton sent Adjutant General Lorenzo Thomas to the Mississippi Valley to raise regiments among the contrabands there. In May, Stanton put the whole enterprise under War Department control by establishing the Bureau of Colored Troops. By the end of 1863 fifty black regiments had joined Lincoln's army. The number tripled by war's end, when 12 percent of the Union army consisted of U.S. Colored Troops.

General George H. Thomas concluded after the Battle of Nashville: "the question is settled; negroes will fight." Recruited by every Union state, 180,000 black men had, as Ben Butler put it, "with the bayonet . . . unlocked the iron-barred gates of prejudice, and opened new fields of freedom, liberty, and equality of right." Congress, in its 1866 army reorganization bill, set the capstone of revolution by authorizing black regiments as part of the regular army. Black Americans had won the right to fight, proved their manhood, and helped break their own chains.

SELECTED BIBLIOGRAPHY

Ira Berlin, *Slaves without Masters: The Free Negro in the Antebellum South* (1974); Ira Berlin et al., eds., *Freedom: A Documentary History of Emancipation, 1861–1867;* Series 2: *The Black Military Experience* (1982); Dudley Taylor Cornish, *The Sable Arm: Negro Troops in the Union Army, 1861–1865* (1956); Thomas Wentworth Higginson, *Army Life in a Black Regiment* (rev. ed., 1960); James M. McPherson, *The Negro's Civil War: How American Negroes Felt and Acted during the War for the Union* (1965); and Benjamin Quarles, *The Negro in the American Revolution* (1961).

                                                            DUDLEY T. CORNISH

RELIGION, SLAVE. The religion of the slaves provided its adherents with various intellectual, social, and spiritual needs. Slave religion helped to explain suffering, it offered resolutions to life's trials and contradictions, and it organized individual and social behavior. The slave's religion provided these benefits within the uniquely oppressive context of enslavement.

Except for a tiny minority of Catholics* and Muslims,* most African slaves brought with them the ethnic faith and practice now called "African Traditional Religion" (ATR). ATR existed as a separate and distinctive system in each African society, but shared a common worldview, including a universe united under (or within) a High God and supervised in great detail by a pantheon of deities and a host of lesser spirits. The ATR worldview further included close and extensive bonds of kinship that endured beyond the grave, elaborate public ceremonies for relating to deities and ancestors, and a reservoir of sacred power accessible through ritual magic for dealing with such practical concerns as decision making, maintaining health, and neutralizing enemies. ATR withstood the brutal Atlantic crossing and became most identifiable in the African slave religions of the Caribbean and South America. It also survived in North America, though not so visibly or strongly. Those who had been priests or other religious specialists in Africa played important religious roles among their fellow slaves in America.

Before 1750 North American slaves only gradually became aware of Protestant Christianity, the religion of the British colonists. Composed primarily of Anglicans,* Congregationalists,* and Presbyterians,* and secondarily of Quakers* (Society of Friends), Baptists,* and some others, colonial Protestants shared religious values that were, in many ways, far from those of the African tradition. Colonial Protestantism was monotheistic and aggressively antipolytheistic. It was opposed to sacred dance, holy objects, and most ritual, insisting, rather, on simple, generally passive worship (except for congregational singing). It also condemned magic, including charms and fetishes, although these things were used by Euro-Americans throughout the period of slavery.

The lack of convergence between the African and Christian traditions in the period before 1750 favored the retention of African traditions* among the slaves. In addition, the rate of slave importation increased dramatically in the eighteenth century, assuring that Africans for a time would predominate in the slave population. Most slaves were inclined, like other immigrants, to cling to the old ways as far and as long as possible in their new situation. Also, many African-born slaves had trouble recognizing Christianity as religion at all, so different was it from their own. In addition, their generally inadequate English limited their chances for understanding white religion even when their interest was aroused.

A lack of conversionist enthusiasm on the part of the whites served to protect African traditions during this period. Overworked or indolent ministers and religiously indifferent owners simply neglected to evangelize among the new slave populations. Other slave owners opposed missions to slaves, claiming that blacks did not have the mental or moral capacity for Christianity and that conversion would make the slaves impudent, insubordinate, and perhaps violently rebellious.

The small group of conversionist promoters—mainly Anglican bishops during this period—answered these objections and in the process created a new chapter in the Christian "theology of slavery." The main points of the theology of slavery were that God permitted Christians to hold Africans as slaves even after they had converted to Christianity; that Africans, though "stupid and barbaric," had mental and moral abilities sufficient to save their souls for heaven; that a Christian owner's duty obliged him to lead slaves to salvation; that Christian instruction could be tailored to the blacks' supposedly inferior abilities and their status as slaves by using special homilies and catechisms; and that their conversion in this manner made them more useful as slaves, not rebellious but diligent and loyal. This theology of slavery endured and grew throughout the era of enslavement whenever ministers wanted to promote the evangelization of slaves. Before 1750, despite a flurry of pro-conversion pamphlets and letters, few slaves heard even this proslavery gospel. Most of those who heard it rejected it.

Even though Christianity had little support among the slaves, they were unable to reconstruct African religion as a coherent system in North America. Though the African-born population was large, it was divided. Languages* were barely, if at all, mutually intelligible, and different calendars and customs had been observed. Also, African religion was intricately interwoven with the land and society of Africa, now irrevocably lost. Furthermore, in North America (in contrast to the Caribbean and South America) whites were proportionately more numerous, while farms and plantations usually were small and isolated. These demographic features* worked against ATR by preventing the formation of adequate communication networks among the slaves. In addition, slave owners and public authorities sometimes actively suppressed African traditions by forbidding special religious buildings, certain kinds of slave gatherings, and the use of drums.

Thus, the success of African Traditional Religion among slaves in the New World tropics was not repeated in North America. However, even though the African system disintegrated, it did not disappear. Fragments survived, especially those that could be nurtured secretly by individuals and small groups—certain beliefs, values, and ritual elements that served the needs of slaves in distinction from the needs of owners.

During the period between 1750 and 1800 English language skills increased among the slaves, which allowed for improved communication within the slave community and with whites as well. At the same time Christianity became both more accessible and more appealing to slaves, due to the rise and triumph of revivalism in Protestantism, especially in the South, and to the connection between Christianity and freedom popularized in the rhetoric of the American Revolution.*

The revival in the upper South during the quarter century after 1750, an outgrowth of the Great Awakening of 1739–1742, was itself succeeded by countless other periods of fervor in the following century throughout the slave states. Among the denominations revivalism favored the Methodists* (newly arrived in the 1760s) and the Baptists, raising them to preeminence in the nineteenth century, with the Presbyterians in third place.

Revivalism affected slave religion in several ways. First, it increased the general level of white religious commitment, so that some owners who had been opposed or merely negligent began allowing slaves to attend (or even conduct) services. Second, it introduced a new criterion of conversion: a definite experience of God's saving grace. Understanding and accepting doctrines, while still valued, were subordinate to the signs of God's work "in the heart." This experience crossed racial and social lines, for the mistress and her maid had equal access to it, and the field hand and his master had equal need for it. Here the slave could find a direct and independent link with God, forged in a self-authenticating experience. This made possible the slaves' claiming equality with or even superiority over those who held them in bondage. Third, revivalism changed the "style" of Protestantism. Services were held in the streets when church buildings became too small or too inhibiting. Congregations prayed extemporaneously, testified to their experiences, and encouraged the preachers with a spontaneous litany. People displayed the age-old signs of religious ecstasy. The Baptists initiated believers by immersion in the "living water" of streams and rivers. Slaves found an affinity for these and other revivalist practices, in some cases because they resembled African traditions.

In addition to revivalism, the religious rhetoric of the Revolution also affected slave religion. In supporting the Revolution, the colonists talked about the God-given right to "liberty," claiming that Britain was holding them in "slavery." Not many whites saw the connection between their cause and the enslavement of Africans, but a few did. For the first time outside the Society of Friends, some Christians placed slavery in the category of sin—"a very great and public sin"—and asserted that Africans too had the God-given right to liberty.

For the first time slaves could see the antislavery potential* of Christianity. After the war there was considerable antislavery sentiment, leading to gradual abolition in the North and to agitation and debate in the South. Southern antislavery convictions were most often expressed by certain Methodist, Baptist, and Presbyterian ministers, who were the very people most likely to influence the rising religious leaders among the slaves. The antislavery sentiment among Southern white Protestants was suppressed after 1800. But by that time a generation of black preachers had revealed to slaves the antislavery gospel of Jesus that the masters had so carefully concealed.

Under these favorable circumstances a growing number of slaves embraced Christianity during the last quarter of the eighteenth century. Black leaders— preachers,* exhorters, class leaders, and teachers—emerged, some approved by white ministers and others not. Some slaves formed organized churches; others practiced in informal congregations. In cities and large towns churches sometimes consisted of both slaves and free blacks. Many slaves worshiped in biracial congregations, but in other places whites were so hostile to black religious expression that slaves had to meet secretly.

The growth of Christianity among slaves did not exclude the memory or influence of Africa. Evidence suggests that most converts retained African elements in their religious practice. For these people, Christianity provided the large perspective on life, death, and destiny, while the African heritage provided concrete ways of dealing with everyday problems relating to health, interpersonal relations, and the natural world. Christian leaders and African practitioners complemented each other even while competing for the allegiance of their constituents. Both African and Christian traditions helped people defend themselves against the psychic assaults of enslavement. Africa was remembered as the place of freedom and the place of mysterious power. American-born slaves tended to view the native Africans as persons with special powers for coping with enslavement, such as the ability to fly or to avert whippings. At the same time,

Christianity in its antislavery version declared that the universe was controlled by a slavery-hating God who intended to liberate the slaves.

As the eighteenth century ended, Afro-American Christianity was an expanding, self-interpreting system. Enslaved Christians were in a position to extend their viewpoint in large gatherings or in families and small groups, openly or secretly, as circumstances required. Christianity was no longer a white religion. Slaves had discovered a Christianity with a friendly dark face, blended with the mysteries of Africa and turned to the well-being of the oppressed, bringing them power, comfort, and delight.

Between 1800 and 1860 expansion into the Old Southwest (Alabama and westward) and the rage to grow cotton set Southern planters on a new and prosperous road. The slave population grew to over four million by the end of the period, about 13 percent of the total population of the United States. Legal importation of slaves ceased in 1808, after which illegal traders brought in only about a thousand persons a year. As a result, fresh African influences upon slave religion decreased. In this period whites both restricted and encouraged slave religion. Because religious leaders led slave uprisings and conspiracies early in the century, Southern authorities placed more restrictions upon the activities of black preachers, prohibited unsupervised black religious meetings, and forbade teaching slaves to read and write. At the same time, a number of Southern ministers and slaveholders expressed a new interest in fostering the "right kind" of religion among the slaves, using camp meetings and plantation missions for the purpose.

Camp meetings were begun in 1800 by Presbyterians and exploited vigorously by Baptists and Methodists throughout the period. They were predominantly white rural revival meetings, a week or more long, designed to draw the westward-moving population into (or back into) the churches. Slaves often attended with their owners, and black preachers sometimes were active on these occasions. Southern camp meetings before the Civil War were the most expressive, ecstatic religious exercises in the Western world. Many slaves eagerly embraced Christianity at these gatherings, where they could respond aloud to the preacher, move their bodies, compose music spontaneously, and cry out as the divine power entered their hearts. That style of religion converged with both their African heritage and their predicament as slaves.

The plantation missions,* unlike the camp meetings, were aimed exclusively toward the slaves. Reaching full stride in the 1840s, the missions were promoted by a few dedicated clergymen, who emphasized that a Christian slave was a better slave and raised funds to send missionary ministers to remote plantations not easily reached by the regular ministry. The missionaries preached to the slaves, supervised the black leaders, and taught the planter's family to conduct Sunday schools for their slaves. The slaves of course did not like the messages that legitimized their enslavement and made docility a condition of their salvation. But there was plenty of opportunity for black Christians to teach another version of the Gospel "on the sly." The plantation missions brought new opportunities for frequent worship and instruction, drawing more slaves into the Christian orbit.

As a result of these activities, the Afro-American version of evangelical Protestantism pervaded the slave population. By the time of the Civil War perhaps 15 percent or more of adult slaves thought of themselves as attached to a Christian group, normally Baptist or Methodist. (The situation was similar among white Southerners.) In addition to these "believers" and the children under their influence, countless others were strongly drawn to Christianity, sharing its worship and values, even though they were not yet converted. Within this religious mainstream, running throughout the slave population, variations existed according to region, denomination, owner's attitudes, beliefs of influential black leaders, class structure among the slaves, and individual experience. For instance, Baptists insisted on immersion baptism while Methodists did not; some owners forbade religious meetings, while others encouraged them; African influence was stronger among field hands* (who generally had less contact with whites than did house servants* or craftsmen*) and along the Gulf Coast (where more smuggled Africans lived).

Outside the mainstream, but interacting with it in most cases, were variant and dissenting groups. First, there were a few Catholic slaves. Of the relatively few Catholic owners, some were unconcerned about religion among their slaves, while others deliberately allowed theirs to follow Protestant ways. But Catholicism was carefully promoted by some owners, notably French-speaking families in and around New Orleans and slave-owning religious orders in Maryland and Louisiana.

Among those who consciously rejected Christianity were a few Muslims. In West Africa Islam was often the religion of the ruling classes, so that some Muslim slaves had powerful social as well as religious reasons for keeping that faith. Occasionally, they even succeeded in transmitting it to their American-born children.

Numerically more important than Islam was the remnant of African Traditional Religion. The most respected representatives of the African traditions were the professional dispensers of the mysteries often called conjure or hoodoo (voodoo).* These people were called root doctors or other names. Their predecessors had worked among the slaves long before the rise of the black preachers. People sought them out in such urgent matters as preventing or healing diseases, enhancing affairs of the heart, and repelling or attacking enemies. They also counseled people by interpreting dreams and reading other signs of the future. For some people, conjure formed a defiant alternative to Christianity. On the other side, some Christians rejected conjure entirely as inconsistent with Christian practice. But in the middle were a great many Christian believers and aspirants who saw conjure as an acceptable and effective means of dealing with pressing difficulties.

The last important group of dissenters were the "sinners," so called not only by Christian believers but often—with a measure of pride—by themselves as well. Little is known about their religious lives except their dissent. They recoiled from certain Christian prohibitions, especially those against dancing and "worldly" music. (Christians had "spiritual" music and dancing, carefully distinguished from the other; indeed, spiritual dancing was not even called dancing, but "shouting.") They also regarded Christianity as the contemptible religion of the masters, whose slavery-supporting God was a fraud. Sinners and believers were closely intermingled in most places, displaying unity on some occasions but at other times carefully separating themselves from each other.

Despite the varieties and nuances of slave religion, it is possible to present a general picture of religious life, starting with the mysterious experience of conversion. This began with a period of anguish ("sin-sickness") regarding one's sinfulness and the prospect of death. Then at some point there was a sudden sense of relief: "the darkness vanished, light sprang up, . . . I felt alive in Christ." This was sometimes accompanied by a trancelike experience, which might include an elaborate vision. Then came a period of joy and inner harmony.

The two main settings for slave worship were open meetings, overseen by whites, and secret meetings at night. The lives of many slaves included both, and it is hard to generalize from the evidence about how they were related. There were cases where the slave owners were so hostile that all religious meetings had to be secret. It is a mistake to suppose that all such occasions were joyous and uninhibited. Often the precautions necessary for a secret meeting imposed such restraint on expression (hushed voices, constant lookout) that it must have seemed a poor expedient. On the other hand, some meetings with whites looking on were remarkably uninhibited. Of course slaves could not utter prayers and songs of freedom at such times. But clandestine instruction could establish hidden meanings for songs and spoken phrases, so that whites would not hear anything offensive. Secret or open, the meetings consisted of singing, praying, testifying, and—whenever appropriate persons were present—preaching or exhorting.

Slave's beliefs were intimately related to their enslavement. Jesus was the Messiah-King who would liberate them, as Moses had liberated the Israelites. And Jesus was also the Savior who would carry them to freedom in heaven. To the slaves' mind, the slaveholders' religion was hopelessly corrupt, for it countenanced slaveholding. The masters' hypocritical religion would not protect them from God's sure punishment: "Pharoah's army got drowned, O Mary don't you weep."

Meanwhile, the followers of God's true religion should live as God's children, that is, not as slaves. For many, this meant resistance* as a Christian duty: flight, sabotage, malingering, perhaps merely a tilt of the chin or a phrase in a prayer. The least of these could cost you the skin on your back. One should not romanticize the connection between religion and resistance. As Eugene D. Genovese comments, "Religious ideology invariably is politically ambiguous." Slave religion sometimes served the master's interest. But for many slaves religion fueled resistance, and resistance shaped religion.

Because many slave owners never stopped being afraid of slave religion, and even punishing slaves for the most innocuous religious exercises, the slaves came to believe that their religion harnessed greater forces on behalf of their dignity than their owners could command to humiliate them. Whether or not particular slaves resisted overtly, they could resist in their hearts, knowing that God intended them for freedom.

SELECTED BIBLIOGRAPHY

Olli Alho, *The Religion of the Slaves: A Study of the Religious Tradition and Behaviour of Plantation Slaves in the United States, 1830–1865* (1976); David T. Bailey, *Shadow of the Church: Southwestern Evangelical Religion and the Issue of Slavery, 1783–1860* (1985); John B. Boles, *Black Southerners, 1619–1869* (1983); Eugene D. Genovese, *Roll, Jordan, Roll: The World the Slaves Made* (1974); Lawrence W. Levine, *Black Culture and Black Consciousness: Afro-American Folk Thought from Slavery to Freedom* (1977); Donald G. Mathews, *Religion in the Old South* (1977); Albert J. Raboteau, *Slave Religion: The "Invisible Institution" in the Antebellum South* (1978); Lester B. Scherer, *Slavery and the Churches in Early America, 1619–1819* (1975); Milton C. Sernett, *Black Religion and American Evangelicalism: White Protestants, Plantation Missions, and the Flowering of Negro Christianity, 1787–1865* (1975); and Carter G. Woodson, *The History of the Negro Church* (3rd ed., 1972).

LESTER B. SCHERER

REPUBLICAN PARTY. Although formed in the midst of the slavery crisis that led to the Civil War, the Republican party was also born in an era when the reputation and condition of blacks in America were falling. That anomaly— a seeming rise in antislavery sentiment while white racism also was on the ascent—stands as one of the central problems for modern historians of the Republican party.

The origins of the Republican party lay indirectly in the history of the Liberty party, which in the presidential elections of 1840 and 1844 infused antislavery ideology into American politics. In 1848 the Free Soil party helped to defeat the Democratic candidate, Lewis Cass. Both parties opposed the spread of slavery into the territories. Drawing upon this background, the early Republican party was an antislavery party only briefly, when it was very small and in its infancy. In 1854 coalitions of Northern anti-Nebraska Democrats, "conscience" Whigs, Free Soilers, and old Liberty men, angered by the threat of slavery spreading into the territories because of the Kansas-Nebraska Act,* came together to form the Republican party. The exact site of the party's origins remains in dispute because the party grew from an almost spontaneous and simultaneous series of meetings, across the North, protesting the act. Opposition to slavery's extension became the glue binding the otherwise disparate elements together as the party rapidly matured.

Their number, however, was not large enough for serious national political contention until 1856, when violence in Kansas Territory and Preston Brooks's caning of Massachusetts Senator Charles Sumner outraged many Northerners.

Events that could be portrayed as Southern assaults on the rights of white men were necessary in order to make the new Republican party a major contender. Most recent authorities agree that the Republican party after 1856 was more an anti-Southern party than an antislavery one. Republican party orators stressed not the plight of enslaved blacks, but the arrogant violence and rule-or-ruin attitude of a tiny planter aristocracy—the so-called Slave Power conspiracy.

In 1856 western explorer John C. Frémont became the Republican party's first presidential nominee and ran on a platform that denounced slavery as a "relic of barbarism." The Republican party, however, advocated attacking slavery only in constitutionally legitimate ways. Before the Civil War the party was determined to stop the spread of slavery to the territories, in which, unlike the states, Congress had authority to define local institutions. In its early years rank-and-file Republicans knew no constitutional means to outlaw slavery where it already existed.

Although the Republicans lost the presidential election of 1856, party leaders quickly saw that they could win in 1860 by holding on to the gains of 1856 while winning victories in combinations of four key Northern states that Frémont had lost: Indiana, Illinois, New Jersey, and Pennsylvania. Doing so, however, required the strategy of broadening Republican appeal on issues beyond slavery. Specifically, the Republicans, drawing heavily on a free labor ideology, sought to capture ethnic voters in Northern urban areas and hoped to usher substantial numbers of anti-Catholic voters out of the Know-Nothing party into their ranks. The nomination of Abraham Lincoln* of Illinois, over the supposedly more "radical" William Henry Seward, as the party's presidential candidate in 1860, fit the Republican strategy of appealing to moderate voters in the key swing states. The party's 1860 platform was more moderate on the slavery question. Voting analysis of the 1860 election suggests that Republicans captured a substantial portion of former Know-Nothings, men for whom slavery had not been the key issue in 1856.

The Republican victory in the 1860 presidential election had the undesired and unanticipated consequence of provoking real secession, as South Carolina and six other Deep South states made good their threat to leave the Union if the "black Republicans" won. Even before assuming effective power in 1861, Republican leaders had to define the party's purpose and direction anew as the divided nation lumbered toward civil war. Southern secession and the resulting friction of war, as well as the sincere antislavery leadership of Lincoln, led the party in a more antislavery direction after 1861. By 1864 the platform of the Union party—the label under which the Republicans ran that year—included a plank advocating a constitutional amendment to end slavery in the United States forever. Even before that, however, the Republican party had long been the practical focus of antislavery efforts. The Democratic party* was, in many places and ways, essentially a party of white supremacy, and those abolitionists* who did vote cast Republican ballots almost to a man. In 1860 Lincoln received only about 40 percent of the popular vote, and the antislavery record of the Republicans was deemed unacceptable enough that in 1861 eleven states refused to remain aligned in the same nation with them.

SELECTED BIBLIOGRAPHY

Eric Foner, *Free Soil, Free Labor, Free Men: The Ideology of the Republican Party before the Civil War* (1970); and William E. Gienapp, *The Origins of the Republican Party, 1852–1856* (1987).

MARK E. NEELY, JR.

RESISTANCE, SLAVE. In the modern reinterpretation of slavery, considerable attention has been devoted to the subject of slave resistance. Earlier observers argued that such slave characteristics as clumsiness, slovenliness, listlessness, destructiveness, and inability to learn indicated racial inferiority. A nineteenth-century physician labeled such behavior a mental illness, *Dysaethesia Aethiopica*. Recent studies of slavery, however, attribute these observed characteristics to the slaves' defiant determination to resist slavery's worst manifestations and to make the institution as livable as possible. Slaves knew better than anyone else that, in a society where whites monopolized power, organized rebellions against slavery were doomed to failure. But they also recognized that they could take day-to-day action on an individual or small-group basis, engaging in what one historian has termed "personal or communal foot-dragging." Such resistance successfully thwarted the master's attempt to gain total control over their lives. They were indeed "a troublesome property," as Kenneth M. Stampp has said.

The extent and success of this day-to-day resistance depended upon the support of a strong and close-knit slave community. Despite white society's belief that slaves were nothing more than laborers, they were in fact part of an elaborate and well-defined social structure that gave them identity and sustained them in their silent protest. Laborers by day, they had other roles to play at night in the slave quarters—roles such as father, mother, husband, and wife—roles that provided a psychological lift from their demeaning daily labor. In the quarters, slaves expressed themselves with relative freedom from white interference. The family structure,* though subject to the master's whim, was nevertheless strong and compensated somewhat for the personal degradation slaves endured working in the field, house, or factory.

Religion* provided a similar support. By attending their own church, whether openly or in secret, slaves fashioned a Christianity that emphasized salvation for all peoples, slaves included, and promised rewards in the afterlife. In church, blacks assumed leadership roles and openly expressed feelings they otherwise had to suppress. Masters tried to use religion negatively to teach slaves obedience and duty; slaves used it positively as an affirmation of their self-worth and as a promise of future deliverance as a chosen people.

Their community provided slaves with the chance to be among their own people, to express themselves, to develop their own culture, and to have control over some portions of their own lives. These opportunities were limited and varied greatly, but the ability to be fathers or mothers, to worship in their own church, to take part in a communal holiday celebration, to use illicitly gathered gossip against the master—all helped to give bondsmen the strength and will to resist the dehumanizing aspects of their enslavement.

Specific forms of slave resistance varied as much as masters and slaves differed in their personalities and situations. The absence of a single slave personality* was, in fact, one of the frustrating facts of life for masters. Just when they thought they knew their slaves, the slaves responded in unexpected ways. How could the same individual be a compliant hard worker one day, a slow moving malingerer the next, a fugitive the third? The masters were unable to understand that slaves wore different masks at different times in their determination to grasp whatever power or leverage they could gain over their own lives. Many masters found such unpredictable behavior puzzling and troubling.

The essence of slavery was, of course, work, and, while there were urban* and industrial* slaves, most of the blacks toiled as field hands engaged in some sort of agricultural labor. The bondsmen worked hard not only because they were coerced to labor, but also because they realized that a plantation's economic failure would make their already meager existence even worse. Nevertheless, slaves tried to work at their own pace, resisting speedups, trying, as much as they could, to avoid being overworked. Some of the techniques they used were to feign illness or pregnancy, break or misplace tools, mistreat horses and mules, and fake ignorance so they would not have to learn any sophisticated tasks they wished to avoid. When the master or overseer* was not looking, slaves might hide among the rows of cotton plants and then load their bags with rocks or sand or wet cotton to camouflage their malingering. If an overseer tried to correct them too harshly, they might become clumsy and destroy crops rather than tend to them. Masters and overseers thought this kind of slave activity exasperating, and some masters responded by planting inferior crop strains, purchasing less efficient but more durable tools, and, in general, lowering agricultural expectations.

When such activity failed to ameliorate a condition slaves found oppressive, they might run away. Some proslavery theorists saw this tendency toward flight as yet another African mental disease, calling it *Drapetomania*. Unless slaves lived near free territory, or near a city where they could melt into an urban free black population, they knew that permanent escape was unlikely. Therefore, bondsmen were more likely to run off for a few days, perhaps to a nearby woods, and risk punishment upon their return. Other slaves listlessly joined in the pursuit and conspired to feed and hide a fugitive until they could pass word that it was safe to return. Only rarely did a large group of slaves attempt a mass escape or try to establish and maintain an extended independent existence. (Slaves who did attempt the latter course were called Maroons.*) On numerous occasions, however, groups of runaway slaves either attacked white slave patrollers* or tried to bribe them.

Sometimes slaves could neither effectively slow down their work nor successfully run away. Or they had specific grievances that caused them to want to strike back at the master especially hard. Then they turned to more surreptitious methods. Throughout the South, many slaveholders watched newly harvested crops go up in smoke or saw a building burn to the ground from unknown causes. This kind of slave resistance was so prevalent, or at least so widely suspected, that as early as 1740 South Carolina passed an antiarson law.

Thievery was another way slaves tried to make their condition more endurable. Many slaves did not believe stealing from the master was wrong, arguing, for example, that, when a slave illicitly ate the master's chicken, he or she was not stealing it. The master's chicken was simply becoming part of the master's slave and making the slave fatter and stronger to perform the master's work. Thus, the slave was actually helping the master. The only time slaves considered thievery to be wrong was when one slave stole from another. They were intolerant of this or any act of resistance that adversely affected the slave community.

Slaves generally saw nothing wrong in lying to protect themselves or others. Those who could write would also sometimes forge passes or other documents to hoodwink their enslavers. Whether verbally or in writing, such deception became an accepted weapon in the arsenal of slave resistance.

When slaves became desperate enough, they openly resisted their masters. Numerous examples illustrate slaves refusing to accept punishment and battling with the white man trying to administer it. Frederick Douglass,* for example, fought with a slave breaker, an individual specializing in reforming rebellious slaves. Douglass found that the white man desisted once he realized that his slave would resist any whipping. This experience exhilarated Douglass. "When a slave cannot be flogged," he concluded, "he is more than half free."

Such slave resistance was rarely successful, however, because most masters refused to tolerate it. Physically or verbally opposing a white man was dangerous, and running away, disrupting work patterns, and destroying or stealing property could result in similarly harsh punishment if detected. When such resistance was too dangerous, slaves employed more subtle ways to voice their opposition.

Slave masters consistently tried to eradicate African culture* from their slaves' memories, insisting repeatedly that slavery had rescued blacks from the barbarism of Africa and introduced them to the superior white civilization. Some slaves came to believe this propaganda, but the continued influence of Africanisms in the slave community indicated slave resistance to acculturation. Some slaves, for example, answered to an English name in the fields but used an African name* in the quarters. Sometimes they wore clothes* or wore their hair according to remembered and transmitted African styles. The slaves' lives were filled with remnants of African culture, and their gravestones, artwork, music, and architecture reflected this influence.

It was in music, dance,* and storytelling that slaves most expressed their African heritage and passed it along to their children. They played a wide variety of stringed and percussion musical instruments similar to those used in Africa.

Musical tempos were based on African rhythms, and the words expressed a defiance that whites failed to recognize as objectionable. Dances similarly were African-inspired and also expressed an exuberant affirmation of a self-worth and artistic creativity that masters insisted slaves did not possess.

Folktales served the same function. Slaves told stories with clear African origins about weak humans or animals who, through native cunning, often outsmarted their more powerful adversaries. Brer Rabbit and a slave named Old John were the major folk heroes who entertained and encouraged the slaves. Listening to these stories, slaves gained a fictional victory denied them in real life. Brer Rabbit repeatedly made the seemingly more powerful Brer Fox and Brer Bear look foolish. Stories of his activities encouraged the slaves to believe that their own resistance might not always be fruitless.

Slaves were constantly told that the master was their "white father," and they were his children. When an overseer proved to be particularly demanding, therefore, the slaves appealed to their "father" directly, or they planted suspicions about the overseer with him. Sometimes the master fired an overseer as a result of such slave tattling, or he intervened to soften some discipline. At the very least, any suspicion of the master toward the overseer worked to the slaves' benefit, weakening the white solidarity against the blacks and making efficient discipline more difficult.

When all else failed, slaves still had other means of resistance. Plantations often had conjurers, slaves with supposed supernatural powers. Particularly aggrieved slaves would appeal to the conjurer for a spell to punish an offending white. Because many whites also feared conjurers, these slaves held unusual power within their community. Their position told the slaves that not all whites were superior to all blacks. The conjurer was the only black person regularly able to frighten the normally dominant masters.

Sometimes circumstances became so oppressive that slaves received little satisfaction from their usual means of resistance. Then, in their despair, they turned on an oppressing white, or, in even further despair, turned on themselves. Slaves sometimes assaulted whites or murdered them, using guns, knives, clubs, and poison. Murder by poisoning was apparently so prevalent that, as early as 1748, Virginia passed a law prohibiting slaves from handling medicines.

Slaves also mutilated themselves to avoid work, punishment, or sale. They cut off fingers, hands, toes, or feet, and disfigured other parts of their bodies to make themselves less valuable slave property. Some slaves committed suicide to escape enslavement. There is even some evidence of parents murdering their children to keep them from having to live lives as chattels. Some newly captured slaves from Africa believed that death would cause them or their children to return home, a belief that provided additional incentive for suicide and infanticide.*

The resistance slaves offered to their enslavement was rarely open or violent confrontation. Rather, it was constant, steady pressure. The main goal of resistance was survival—to insure the most decent life possible within an intrinsically indecent institution. Slaves rarely were able to overcome the master's ultimate control over them, but they were able to prevent such control from becoming total. Slave resistance, flowing out of the slave's Afro-American culture, allowed an enslaved people to nurture the spark of freedom until it could burst into flame during the Civil War.

SELECTED BIBLIOGRAPHY

Raymond A. Bauer and Alice H. Bauer, "Day to Day Resistance to Slavery," *Journal of Negro History*, 27 (1942), 388–419; John W. Blassingame, *The Slave Community: Plantation Life in the Antebellum South* (rev. ed., 1979); John B. Boles, *Black Southerners, 1619–1869* (1983); Eugene D. Genovese, *Roll, Jordan, Roll: The World the Slaves Made* (1974); Leslie Howard Owens, *This Species of Property: Slave Life and Culture in the Old South* (1976); Kenneth M. Stampp, *The Peculiar Institution: Slavery in the Ante-Bellum South* (1956); and James Walvin, *Slavery and the Slave Trade: A Short Illustrated History* (1983).

JOHN F. MARSZALEK

REVOLTS, NORTH AMERICAN SLAVE. In North America Afro-American aspirations for freedom from slavery rarely found expression in collective uprisings. Although slave revolts occurred infrequently, the slaveholders' pervasive fear of such insurrection significantly shaped the public contours of black lives— both slave and free—from colonial times until emancipation. Since whites created most of the contemporary accounts of slave uprisings and conspiracies, historians have necessarily labored with severely restricted and often biased sources. It is impossible to know how many plans for freedom remained undetected conspiracies or how many tentative dreams of freedom grew into murderous conspiratorial plots. Within these limitations, however, certain patterns of revolt within North American slavery are apparent. These contrast in important ways with slave rebellions elsewhere in the New World.

Three distinctive types of slave revolts occurred in North America: systematic revolts, vandalistic revolts, and situational revolts. Carefully planned and organized, systematic revolts sought to establish autonomous black polities—differentiating functional tasks among rebels, mobilizing insurgents from several counties, and intending often the initial conquest of an urban center. In contrast, vandalistic revolts, aimed at the indiscriminate destruction of slaveholders and their property, lacked systematic preparation and were based on the expectation of mobilizing recruits during the revolt. Situational revolts involved groups of slaves seeking to escape from servitude either to a free area or from deportation to an area of more repressive servitude. Of the sixty-five North American slave revolts for which information exists, 19 percent were situational, 27 percent systematic, and 22 percent vandalistic. Information on the remaining 32 percent is insufficient to classify them as either systematic or vandalistic. Thus, approximately one-fifth of North American slave revolts can be classified as situational and four-fifths as systematic or vandalistic. While many vandalistic and situational revolts reached the implementation stage of insurrection, almost all systematic revolts were intercepted during the planning phase, causing slave-holders to characterize them as "conspiracies."

Whether regarded as conspiracy or insurrection, all three types of slave revolts occurred throughout the history of slavery and in all slave regions of North America. As the geographic provenance of slavery changed over time, so too did the location of slave revolts. In the colonial period, slave revolts occurred in the Northern colonies of New York and New Jersey as well as in the Southern colonies of Virginia, South Carolina, and Georgia. With the virtual disappearance of the slave system in the North, and its extension in the South during the revolutionary period (1776–1810), slave revolts originated only in Southern states such as Virginia, North Carolina, and Louisiana. During the first three decades of the nineteenth century, slave revolts occurred in the eastern seaboard slave states and in the border states. With the entrenchment of slavery in the Old Southwest in the 1840s and 1850s, slave revolts were recorded throughout the slave region from Virginia to Texas.

Although slave revolts occurred throughout the antebellum period and in every region of the South, the spatial clustering of revolts suggests certain societal factors that facilitated revolts. Slave revolts were concentrated in those areas characterized by large and impersonal plantation systems: the tobacco-growing* coastal counties of Virginia, the rice-growing* parishes of South Carolina, and the sugar cane* parishes of Louisiana. Such concentration of slave revolts discloses certain socioeconomic preconditions of slave revolts.

Slave revolts also clustered in areas near communication networks such as cities and rivers. As slaveholders understood well, propinquity to such communication networks provided slaves with access to cosmopolitan ideas and information. Fears of slave unrest were high during the American Revolution,* after the Haitian Revolution, and at other times of national and international crisis. At such times of social and political unrest, the slaveholders feared insurrection, and sometimes their fears were realized.

To develop into revolt, however, such preconditions required catalytic leadership. Although little information is available on black slave revolt leaders, the three best-known insurrectionists—Gabriel Prosser,* Denmark Vesey,* and Nat Turner*—each had held skilled occupational positions, had exposure to cosmopolitan ideas and experiences, and felt imbued with a sense of personal destiny. Each believed himself to be divinely inspired and sanctioned in his endeavor. Following capture, only Turner revealed aspects of his plans for achieving freedom.

Throughout the slavery period the North American slaveholders reacted consistently to slave revolts. Distinguishing between situational revolts and other types, they sought reprisals only against the immediate offenders in situational revolts. They responded, however, much more comprehensively to systematic and vandalistic revolts. Within the area of revolt, an initial period of panic among whites caused them to wreak vengeance upon innocent blacks as well as insurgents. During this period of mob panic and activity, white moderates within the area and outsiders who were not implicated indirectly in the revolt sometimes also suffered from mob violence. After such an initial period of response, a period of increased armed oppression ensued, aimed at reinforcing the threatened slave system. Finally, a third period of reaction followed in which legislative action was taken to prevent similar outbreaks. Although ameliorative measures such as colonization* schemes and proposals to reduce the oppressiveness of the slave system came under discussion during legislative debates, the invariable outcome of the legislative phase of response was the tightening of repressive laws against blacks—both slave and free.

In the wake of major slave revolts, a secondary response occurred outside the area of revolt. Fearing insurrection in their own neighborhoods, whites in other areas of the South initiated aspects of the three-phased revolt responses. Following Prosser's and Turner's rebellions, for example, repressive legislation against blacks—slave and free—was enacted in other parts of the slave South. Nevertheless, the actual threat Afro-American revolts posed to slavery—as some contemporary slaveholders acknowledged—never merited the exaggerated penalties they invoked against Afro-Americans within and outside revolt areas.

Among North American slave revolts, seven stand out either in scale or in notoriety: three systematic revolts and four vandalistic revolts. The systematic revolts took place in New York in 1712,* in Virginia in 1800, and in South Carolina in 1822. Of these three revolts only the one in colonial New York City reached the insurrection stage. In early January 1712, the conspirators, who were slaves of African birth, sealed their rebellious pact with a blood oath. This led to a mid-April insurrection during which the rebels burned buildings and wounded or killed sixteen whites.

Although the two other notable systematic revolts—Gabriel Prosser's 1800 revolt and Denmark Vesey's 1822 rebellion—never reached the insurrectionary phase, they are among the most celebrated North American conspiracies. Prototypical of systematic revolts, these conspiracies aimed to establish a Negro polity. Both Prosser and Vesey planned initially to gain control of a city, Richmond in 1800 and Charleston in 1822, thereafter probably intending to extend their hegemony over the surrounding areas. Prosser planned to spare certain sympathetic groups of whites and hoped for aid from poor whites and Indians. Vesey expected assistance from the West Indies and Africa. Led by skilled artisans—one a slave, the other a freeman—both conspiracies were betrayed by blacks more loyal to their masters than to their racial confreres. When the insurrectionary plots were discovered, Prosser and Vesey revealed little about their insurrectionary intentions before their executions.

The four great North American vandalistic revolts occurred in areas where blacks significantly outnumbered whites: on the Stono River in South Carolina in 1739, in the Pointe Coupée area of Louisiana in 1795 and 1811, and in Southampton County, Virginia, in 1831. The Stono Rebellion* began on a September Sunday when twenty slaves, many African-born, set out to kill whites. The insurrectionists first murdered two storekeepers from whose shop the rebels obtained ammunition and armaments. As the day progressed, the rebel group swelled to sixty before encountering armed resistance from local whites. The Stono Rebellion ultimately took the lives of sixty people—twenty-five whites and thirty-five blacks.

The Pointe Coupée conspiracy of 1795 took place in an area where blacks outnumbered whites by more than three to one. It led ultimately to the execution of twenty-five blacks with an equal number sentenced to hard labor for at least five years. Sixteen years later the largest insurrection in North America began in the same area. Led by a Santo Domingan mulatto slave, between 100 and 500 slaves marched toward New Orleans, destroying plantations and killing whites before succumbing to the superior force of the local militia. During the battle between insurgents and militia sixty-six rebels were killed. At the subsequent trial, twenty-two rebels were found guilty and later executed.

In Southampton County, Virginia, where blacks also outnumbered whites, Nat Turner long dreamt of an uprising in which every white person along the route from his master's plantation to Jerusalem, the nearest town, would be killed. In the summer of 1831, Turner and five co-conspirators set out to realize his dream. Acquiring recruits along the way, Turner's band of rebels swelled from six to sixty or seventy blacks at its height. More than fifty whites within a twenty-mile area were murdered before the local white pursuers destroyed Turner's rebellion.

These slave revolts share several qualities that underscore basic sociopolitical and demographic elements in North American slave revolts. All seven revolts occurred during periods of social dissension within the greater polity—the 1712 New York revolt during the aftermath of Leisler's rebellion, the Stono Rebellion during conflict between Spanish and British colonists, the Louisiana revolts amidst Spanish and French antagonisms, Prosser's revolt during a time of French and American conflict, Vesey's conspiracy after the Missouri debate, and Turner's insurrection during rumors of war between Britain and the United States. Such periods of social and political unrest created climates congenial for slave revolts. They revealed sociopolitical strain and instability within the ruling elite and suggested possibilities for social change. The five rural revolts also were located in areas where blacks significantly outnumbered whites. Such demographic imbalances necessarily implied not only greater social distance between slave owner and slave, but greater opportunity for interaction among blacks. Nevertheless, slave revolts, even if located in rural areas, had an urban orientation insofar as the capture of an urban center was often an initial rebel goal. The preconditions, then, for these slave revolts included ecological factors enhancing independent solidarity among blacks and those encouraging cosmopolitan interconnection between blacks and others.

The contrapuntal interplay between isolationist and cosmopolitan forces also is revealed in slave revolt leadership patterns. The men who led these revolts had experienced diverse sociocultural environments, performed skilled occupational tasks in service to whites, and had assumed leadership roles among blacks. The 1811 Louisiana revolt, for example, was led by a mulatto born in Saint-Domingue. Denmark Vesey was a well-traveled slave seaman who, after buying his freedom with lottery winnings, settled in Charleston as a carpenter. Many New York and Stono insurgents were born in Africa. Gabriel Prosser was a blacksmith and religious exhorter, Nat Turner was a foreman and exhorter, and the leader of the New York revolt was a skilled craftsman.

Each slave revolt leader not only chafed at the limitations on black status within the slave system, but developed the internal strength and charisma to transform his personal opposition into collective confrontation. In the New York, Prosser, Vesey, and Turner revolts, religious rituals served important bonding functions among conspirators. With such supernatural sanctions, black leaders and their followers felt empowered to confront the overwhelming force of the white elite.

In a comparative sense, the scale of North American revolts was smaller than elsewhere in the New World. Only the 1811 vandalistic revolt in Louisiana mobilized as many insurgents as smaller uprisings in the Caribbean and Latin America. Social preconditions for the mass revolts of Brazil, Jamaica, and other Latin American countries included large-scale impersonal plantation systems,* significant black majorities within the population, significant preponderances of men in the black population, large numbers of African-born blacks, and accessible runaway slave communities. In addition to such general preconditions, adverse economic conditions and charismatic leadership triggered insurrections. Although the North American slave system generally lacked the combination of social preconditions found elsewhere in the New World, North American revolts illustrate the force of such preconditions.

Although the white slaveholding society's overwhelming physical force ultimately doomed slave revolts to failure in the Americas, blacks everywhere resisted enslavement. Still, realism tempered resistance. Resistance took the form of collective opposition to the master class only where ecological conditions favored its success. Slave revolts thus erupted more often and with greater intensity in the Southern hemisphere than in the Northern. In North America, moreover, slave revolts occurred most frequently in sociocultural environments approximating those characterizing Latin American and Caribbean slavery.

SELECTED BIBLIOGRAPHY

Herbert Aptheker, *American Negro Slave Revolts* (rev. ed., 1963); Joseph C. Carroll, *Slave Insurrections in the United States, 1800–1865* (1938); Eugene D. Genovese, *From Rebellion to Revolution: Afro-American Slave Revolts in the Making of the Modern World* (1979); Thomas Wentworth Higginson, *Black Rebellion: A Selection from Travellers and Outlaws* (rev. ed., 1969); Jack D. L. Holmes, "The Abortive Slave Revolt at Pointe Coupée, Louisiana, 1795," *Louisiana History*, 11 (1970), 341–362; Marion D. de B. Kilson, "Towards Freedom: An Analysis of Slave Revolts in the United States," *Phylon*, 25 (1964), 175–187; John Lofton, *Denmark Vesey's Revolt: The Slave Plot That Lit a Fuse to Fort Sumter* (rev. ed., 1983); Stephen B. Oates, *The Fires of Jubilee: Nat Turner's Fierce Rebellion* (1975); Richard C. Wade, "The Vesey Plot: A Reconsideration,"

Journal of Southern History, 30 (1964), 143–161; and Harvey Wish, "American Slave Insurrections before 1861," *Journal of Negro History*, 28 (1937), 299–320.

MARION D. DE B. KILSON

RICE. By about 1725 rice culture had been successfully developed in the Charleston area of South Carolina. This occurred only after a long and costly period of experimentation by a group of Barbadian planters who came there to escape the saturation of the sugar industry in their home island. West African slaves imported into the colony in the early 1700s, too, brought technical knowledge of where and how to plant rice based on their previous experience with rice planting in their homelands. Another century would be spent, however, in search of suitable milling devices for threshing and polishing the rice. Rice planting expanded from South Carolina northward into North Carolina along the Cape Fear River in the 1730s and southward into Georgia along the Savannah, Ogeechee, and Altamaha rivers in the 1750s. A century later the "Rice Kingdom," when fully developed, consisted of about 100,000 planted acres (70,000 in South Carolina, 25,000 in Georgia, and 5,000 in North Carolina) along some seventeen rivers from the Cape Fear on the north to the St. Johns in northern Florida, with very small amounts of rice grown in Alabama, Mississippi, and Louisiana. The coming of the Civil War, which brought massive destruction to plantation facilities and the eventual emancipation of the slaves, dealt a staggering blow to the Southern rice industry. Indeed, no more than half of the planted acreage of the rice coast in 1860 ever revived in the postwar era.

Initially, rice was planted in inland swamps above the tidewater where ponds or dammed-up streams provided enough water to inundate small fields. By the 1750s, however, the technology was developed to use the ebb and flow of the tidal rivers to flood or drain the fields, thus removing rice planting to the tidal swamplands. The increased volume of water from the river tides enabled the planters to use this not only to nourish the rice plants, but also to kill grass and weeds. The accruing decreased labor needs increased the number of acres of rice the slave could grow from three to five. The amount of land available for tidal flooding was severely limited, for a stretch of only a few miles (generally five to twenty) along the lower reaches of the rivers above saltwater was sufficiently influenced by the tides to make that system practical. The shift from the inland swamps to the tidal swamplands, though, was very gradual, with the greater part coming years after the American Revolution.

The rice crop cycle began with the seed being sown in rows about fifteen inches apart (wide enough for the slaves to walk between while hoeing) in late March and April. The fields were flooded for about a week to enable the seed to sprout and then drained for hoeing. The remainder of the growing season saw alternate flooding and draining with several hoeings in between. During slack periods the slaves engaged in cultivating provision crops such as corn, peas, and potatoes, with most rice plantations producing the needed provisions for the work force. Harvest came in late August and September, with the threshing, polishing, and sale of the rice following in the fall and winter. Some planters in the Georgetown area and along the Savannah River used the innovative method of open planting. This involved planting seeds previously rolled in clay to keep them from floating when the field was flooded. The initial flooding was kept on about three times as long as when the seeds were covered, which gave the plants a faster start, reduced the number of hoeings, and generally brought better yields.

The rice industry represented dramatic extremes of agricultural techniques and equipment. The knowledge and skills used to flood the rice fields (generally four to five times during the season) and thresh and pound the rice required the hand of an expert, but most of the work in rice production was simple drudgery of the meanest form, performed under extremely unhealthy conditions. Because the slaves (unlike the whites) were largely able to develop immunity to the various fevers of the rice swamps, virtually all of the commercial crop was produced by slave labor. The implements used to break the soil, plant, cultivate, and harvest the rice were ancient and primitive. Not until the eve of the Civil War did plows begin to replace the hoe for breaking the ground. Yet no other crop, with the possible exception of sugar,* involved as large an investment of capital to provide suitable plantation facilities—extensive irrigation systems with large embankments to keep out the river waters, sizable drainage ditches, numerous trunks or sluice gates to control the various flows, and expensive mills to thresh and pound the rice. By the 1850s steam-powered threshing mills cost $8,000 and pounding mills, $20,000. As a result, only the largest plantations had threshing mills (most rice was threshed on large wooden floors by the slaves using hand flails), and even fewer had pounding mills, with most planters sending their rice for polishing to neighboring planters who specialized in milling, or more likely to the large commercial mills in Charleston and Savannah.

A successful rice plantation represented a considerable total investment, ranging from $50,000 to $500,000. Numerous slaves were essential, so the "Rice Coast" had the heaviest concentration of slaves anywhere in the South. By 1850 the slaveholdings on rice plantations averaged four times those on sugar estates, ten times those for cotton* and tobacco,* and forty times those on hemp* plantations. By 1860 there was even greater concentration, with the Rice Kingdom having twenty of the seventy-four estates that had 300 to 500 slaves, eight of the fourteen that had 500 to 1,000 slaves, and the only estate of more than 1,000 slaves in America. Rice planting was profitable only in quantity production; in 1859, accordingly, 96 percent of the commercial crop was produced on plantations yielding more than 100,000 pounds. For planters producing in this volume, the profits were about 10 percent of the capital investment. Thus, economics joined with geography in further restricting the industry to all but the wealthy few. In 1850 there were only 551 rice planters; by 1860 there would be even fewer planters, indictating considerable consolidation of holdings, sometimes by as much as 50 percent.

Most slaves on rice plantations were field hands* engaged in the production of the crop. However, each plantation had another group of slaves employed in nonfield pursuits. They consisted of animal raisers, baby keepers, barbers, blacksmiths, boatmen, bricklayers, butchers, butlers, carpenters, coachmen, cobblers, cooks, coopers, engineers, gardeners, gunkeepers, laundresses, lumbermen, maids, nurses, pantry minders, saltworkers, seamstresses, shoemakers, stock minders, tailors, tanners, tinsmiths, trunk minders, valets, waiters, and weavers. Many of these skilled slaves were trained to perform two or more of these particular trades and could also double as field hands during critical labor periods such as that of the harvest. A few slaves served in managerial positions. An occasional planter defied the slave codes and appointed a slave as black overseer.* However, the highest position most slaves could aspire to was that of driver,* or slave foreman, whose function it was to direct the day-to-day labor of the slaves and maintain discipline and decorum in the slave quarters. Rice plantations generally had a driver for each fifty slaves; however, there were a number of instances of plantations with one hundred or more slaves having only one driver.

Rice slaves experienced a more miserable form of labor in the mosquito- and snake-filled swamps and a more isolated existence than was the lot of slaves producing the other crops such as cotton and tobacco, yet enjoyed a greater degree of independence and generally a much shorter workday. Because the planter deserted the plantation during the malarial season from early May to the killing frosts of November, leaving only the overseer and slave drivers to control affairs there, a labor format was needed in which the slaves could largely direct themselves. In consequence, the task system was developed, providing for an assignment that the poorest workers could complete in eight or nine hours. In practice, however, most slaves finished their tasks by mid-afternoon as opposed to the dawn-to-dusk gang labor system used on most plantations, and could devote the rest of the day to working in their gardens, farming small tracts of rice of their own, looking after their livestock, or going hunting or fishing. By the 1840s all the tasks in rice planting had become standardized: for breaking the soil with the hoe, 1,500 square feet; for trenching, sowing, hoeing, or harvesting, a half acre; for digging canals and ditches, 600 cubic feet; and for threshing by the flail, 600 sheaves or twelve bushels of rice. Younger, elderly, or partially disabled slaves were required to do only three-quarters, a half, or one-fourth of a task, according to their ability. More than anything else, the task system kept lonely slaves from becoming restless and rebellious.

There was little interchange between rice slaves and those from the other plantations. Tobacco or cotton slaves would have difficulty acclimating to the isolated existence of the rice plantation and adjusting to the rice diet and the task system of labor. Thus, new hands on rice plantations were generally acquired from other rice plantations, where sales were necessitated by some planters overextending themselves, by the breakup of estates, or by slaves being too refractory to retain. The natural increase on rice plantations was normally about 5 percent. At the same time rice slaves would not adapt very easily to the gang labor system of the cotton, tobacco, or sugar plantation.

SELECTED BIBLIOGRAPHY

James M. Clifton, "The Rice Driver: His Role in Slave Management," *South Carolina Historical Magazine*, 82 (1981), 331–353; James M. Clifton, ed., *Life and Labor on Argyle Island: Letters and Documents of a Savannah River Rice Plantation, 1833–1867* (1978); J. Harold Easterby, ed., *The South Carolina Rice Plantation As Revealed in the Papers of Robert F. W. Allston* (1945); Duncan C. Heyward, *Seed from Madagascar* (1937); Albert V. House, "Labor Management Problems on Georgia Rice Plantations, 1840–1860," *Agricultural History*, 28 (1954), 149–155; Albert V. House, ed., *Planter Management and Capitalism in Ante-Bellum Georgia: The Journal of Hugh Fraser Grant, Ricegrower* (1954); Charles Joyner, *Down by the Riverside: A South Carolina Slave Community* (1984); Philip D. Morgan, "Work and Culture: The Task System and the World of Lowcountry Blacks, 1700 to 1880," *William and Mary Quarterly*, 3rd ser., 39 (1982), 563–599; and Julia Floyd Smith, *Slavery and Rice Culture in Low Country Georgia, 1750–1860* (1985).

JAMES M. CLIFTON

RICHMOND, VA, SLAVERY IN. Slavery in Richmond dated from before the founding of the city in 1737 by William Byrd, for he and his father had engaged in the trading of slaves and other commodities at the falls of the James since the 1670s. The new capital of revolutionary Virginia became the target of Gabriel's [Prosser] revolt* in 1800, and the site of the Virginia slavery debates in 1831–1832.*

Antebellum Richmond developed into a leading industrial center, its economic importance far out of proportion to its population. The nature of urban slavery,* and whether it weakened in cities, are controversial subjects, and perhaps nowhere more so than in Richmond. Slaves were a vital part of the labor force for the city's major industries,* as well as its busy transport facilities, and a slave chain gang even cleaned its streets. Richmond was the heart of the early tobacco* industry, with scores of factories. It had the world's largest flour mill, and a milling complex that equaled Baltimore's. It was the leading metalworking center in the South. Skilled slaves of both sexes and all ages were particularly important in the labor-intensive tobacco industry. At the Tredegar ironworks* Joseph R. Anderson pioneered the use of master slave craftsmen* in heavy industry. As a slave-trading market Richmond was second only to New Orleans. The profits of dozens of auctioneers exceeded those derived from flour mills and iron foundries.

Richmond's slave population increased from 4,387 in 1820 (36 percent of the total population), to 11,699 by 1860 (31 percent). The growing number of slaves who were allowed to hire* themselves, or were owned not by private individuals but by railroads and other large corporations, undeniably affected the texture of slavery in Richmond. A vigorous debate continues over how, and to what degree, such practices as boarding out and living out, corporate ownership and self-hiring changed slavery; and what effect the city, its industries, and urban surroundings had upon the slave family, black society, and race relations.

Richmond's slave community developed a complex and vigorous life of its own by 1860. Some postwar patterns, notably in the areas of black separatism and white-imposed segregation,* may be seen by the 1850s. The Civil War* disrupted this society, as the economy faltered and slaves were impressed for government service. Slaves built Richmond's defenses, and most of the nurses at Chimborazo Hospital were slaves. They filled important jobs in Confederate shops and armories. And slaves were still being sold, or bartered, as late as March 1865, when the first two companies of black troops regularly enlisted into Confederate service drilled on Richmond's streets.

Slavery died a hard death in the city its victims had helped to build. Indeed, one prominent trader tried and failed to get a coffle of his slaves aboard the train that carried Jefferson Davis out of the doomed Confederate capital. Freedom came on 3 April 1865. Today the old industries are gone and an interstate highway runs through the valley where slave pens once stood.

SELECTED BIBLIOGRAPHY

Ira Berlin, *Slaves without Masters: The Free Negro in the Antebellum South* (1974); James H. Brewer, *The Confederate Negro: Virginia's Craftsmen and Military Laborers, 1861–1865* (1969); Claudia Dale Goldin, *Urban Slavery in the American South, 1820–1860: A Quantitative History* (1976); Ronald L. Lewis, *Coal, Iron, and Slaves: Industrial Slavery in Maryland and Virginia, 1715–1865* (1979); John T. O'Brien, "Factory, Church, and Community: Blacks in Antebellum Richmond," *Journal of Southern History*, 44 (1978), 509–536; Marianne Sheldon, "Black-White Relations in Richmond, Virginia, 1782–1820," *Journal of Southern History* 45 (1979), 27–44; and Robert S. Starobin, *Industrial Slavery in the Old South* (1970).

MICHAEL B. CHESSON

RIVERBOATMEN. Almost from the beginning of slavery in North America, black slaves worked as riverboatmen, handling small boats in the Chesapeake region, introducing African boatways to South Carolina, and serving in military capacities on American rivers throughout the colonial era and during the American Revolution. Slaveholders worried about employing slaves on rivers, for the waterways provided avenues of escape for slaves and the slave riverboatmen gained knowledge about the countryside and its hideaways, information that might be turned against slaveholders during a slave revolt. The exigencies of moving staples to market, however, overrode planter fears about losing control over slaves plying skiffs, dugouts, rafts, or larger craft on the rivers. Slaves as riverboatmen remained ubiquitous but hardly noticed throughout the South.

Nowhere was the presence and importance of slave riverboatmen more profound than on the Mississippi River. As early as 1733 French officials were using Africans to row military bateaux between settlements of lower Louisiana. These slaves made excellent boatmen. They no doubt had civilian counterparts. Under Spain, Louisiana's population created a large demand for food staples, and the flatboat/keelboat era began in earnest. Blacks, slave and free, manned such boats in significant numbers. Frequently slaves were both cargo and crew, moving with owners to resettle or with dealers for resale. Sometimes escaped slaves became river pirates.

Flatboat commerce continued to employ slaves until emancipation. Simon Gray* and other slaves transported numerous flatboats of lumber and huge log rafts downriver. They enjoyed considerable responsibility, mobility, and economic opportunity. Gray even bossed white crews and handled large sums of cash. Despite his position, hard work and fevers wrecked his health.

Probably more blacks worked on steamboats than on other river craft; indeed, crews without blacks were rare. In personal services blacks functioned as waiters, cooks, maids, dishwashers, stewards, barbers, and musicians. From these ranks emerged such postwar leaders as P. B. S. Pinchback, Reconstruction governor of Louisiana, and R. R. Church, wealthy Memphis civic leader.

Roustabouts performed the heavy labor. In port or taking on fuel they did hurried, body-racking work. Underway, however, they enjoyed relative ease when not stoking the furnaces. Their storytelling and singing later became blues music.

Slaves also worked dredge-boats and snagboats. They tended ferries and maintained levees. Many joined the Union's Civil War fleets. Slave contributions to river transport were far-reaching but, ironically, are unsung.

SELECTED BIBLIOGRAPHY

Leland Baldwin, *The Keelboat Age on Western Waters* (1939); Lawrence Kinnaird, ed., *Spain in the Mississippi Valley, 1765–1794: Translations of the Materials from the Spanish Archives in the Bancroft Library*, (3 vols., 1946–1949); James M. McPherson, *The Negro's Civil War: How American Negroes Felt and Acted during the War for the Union* (1965); John Hebron Moore, "Simon Gray, Riverman: A Slave Who Was Almost Free," *Mississippi Valley Historical Review*, 49 (1962), 472–484; Nancy M. Surrey, *The Commerce of Louisiana during the French Regime, 1699–1763* (1916); and Reuben Gold Thwaites, ed., *Early Western Travels, 1748–1846*, (31 vols., 1907).

JOHN E. HARKINS

RUNAWAY SLAVES. Runaway slaves in the antebellum South were a constant irritant to slave owners, overseers,* employers, and law enforcement agencies responsible for their recovery. While never a large percentage of the slave population in any period before the Civil War, slaves, by running away, disrupted work routines on farms and plantations,* undermined discipline among slaves, and exasperated managers of households in both the countryside and the cities. The few bondsmen who successfully gained freedom by escaping to the North served to erode faith in the compact of union and contributed significantly to the sectional conflict. Much can be learned about the peculiar institution by examining the personal characteristics of the slaves who ran away, their motivations for absconding, and their destinations. Runaway slaves confronted almost insurmountable difficulties in their quest for freedom. They faced methods of recovery and a system of law that were designed to facilitate their recovery.

As given in runaway slave advertisements, the personal characteristics of runaways reveal interesting profiles that distinguish the fugitives from the general population of slaves. Far and away males constituted the great majority of runaways. Between 1804 and 1828, for example, the Richmond *Enquirer* advertised 1,253 runaway slaves. Of the slaves advertised by owners and employers, 1,054, or 84.1 percent, were males; 174, or 13.9 percent, were females; and 25, or 2 percent, were children. James Benson Sellers, in *Slavery in Alabama* (1964), found that, of 562 fugitives advertised between 1820 and 1860, 84.1 percent were males, and 15.4 percent were females. In *Roll, Jordan, Roll* (1974), Eugene D. Genovese reported that 82 percent of the runaways in North Carolina during the period 1850 to 1860 were men. In 1981 Judith Kelleher Schafer reported in the *Journal of Southern History* that 31.7 percent of the runaways advertised in New Orleans in 1850 were women.

The average ages for runaway slaves throughout the South remained consistent. In the Virginia sample, the average age was twenty-seven. Schafer reported that 66.6 percent of the runaway males in New Orleans were between fifteen and thirty-nine years of age. To run away and remain at large for an extended period of time required agility, ingenuity, and bravery. The runaway had to move about with extreme care because any white citizen in most slave states had the legal right to stop any Negro and demand to see his free pass. Commonly, the runaway was forced to "lay up" during the day and advance only at night. Unless aid was forthcoming from friends, the fugitive had to rely on his own wits to obtain food and shelter. Because many of the slave women* were already responsible for children, the rigor and danger of such an existence discouraged them from running away.

Of the 1,253 slaves advertised in the Richmond *Enquirer*, 297 were skilled workers. Forty different skills were reported, a large number in the building trades, including bricklayers, carpenters, stone masons, plasterers, cabinetmakers, and brickmakers. Many of the runaways were house servants, cooks, seamstresses, waiters, gardeners, and carriage drivers. Other skills included shoemakers, tanners, blacksmiths, wheelwrights, millwrights, stevedores, wagoners, mine workers, ironworkers, and watermen.

Such skilled slaves frequently hired out,* and were likely candidates for running away. One hundred forty-four of the slaves advertised in the Richmond *Enquirer* had fled from their employers. P. V. Daniel had hired the services of a slave calling himself John Brown, who was a "good house servant, ostler and driver, and a pretty good barber"; he could also read and write. One evening John obtained a pass to go to Richmond and had "not since been heard of." Nelson Patterson of Kanawha County hired John and Reuben from Thomas Logwood of Gloucester County. Patterson had "carried them" to Buckingham County to make salt.* Apparently the two slaves disliked the work and ran away. Commenting upon the value of hired slave labor, W. C. Beard, agent for the U.S. Arsenal at Richmond, wrote that he had hired three "good Negroes" from Lewis C. Tyler of Williamsburg. Having "woefully experienced Mr. Tyler's judgement of good negroes," he said, "I think it a duty to advise every person in the habit of hiring negroes, and who wishes to avoid losses and trouble," not to hire Tyler's Negroes, "two of which are noted robbers and runaways."

Bondsmen had diverse reasons for running away. Genovese argued that the fear of the whip "provided the single biggest provocation to running away." If one believes that slave owners understood why their slaves ran away, however, the evidence in the Virginia sample, supported by what Sellers found in Alabama, suggests that the most prevalent causes involved the breaking up of families and the fear of being "sold down the river." Alexander A. Campbell, for example, reported that Stephen "will no doubt make direct for Madison county, Mississippi Territory, as his wife was sold last fall to a gentleman who resides there." Gabriel ran away from Anny Duncan in Buckingham County because his wife lived in Louisa County. Billey Ross, owned by the Roanoke Navigation Company, ran off to Hanover County because he had a wife at Major Thomas Storkes's "in whose neighbourhood it is probable he is lurking." A frequent reason cited for running away was the fear of sale following the death of an owner.

Cruelty of masters and overseers ranked high among the reasons for running away. Several slaves were reported in runaway slave advertisements as having distinguishing scars caused by the whip. Samuel McCrary of Rockbridge County, Virginia, when describing his slave Aaron, stated that "on examining his back, it will be found very much scarred on account of whipping." Another owner described her slave Betsey as "a negro woman . . . [with] no scars recollected except one on the back of her neck, which appears to have been made by the lash of a whip." Sometimes the scars were caused by branding irons. Charles, only recently purchased by John Sanders, had been "lately branded on the left hand." Perhaps the most branded Negro in Virginia was another Charles, who belonged to Thomas Coleman of Lunenburg County. He had been branded on each cheek with the letter C, "pointing to his nose," and with the same letter in the middle of his forehead. Charles also had been branded in three places on his chest with the letter C, apparently the initial of his owner Thomas Coleman.

Although slave owners constantly complained about their runaway slaves, they exhibited surprisingly little concern for the return of their fugitive slaves.* Sellers reported that most Alabama runaways "were gone from one to four weeks." In Virginia, the average time lapse between running away and advertising in the newspapers was six weeks. In several instances the owners' statements suggest that they in fact knew where their slaves were hiding. But rather than go after the slaves themselves, they would offer a reward for the return of their slaves, or for having them placed in jail. Rewards during the period 1800 to 1830 ranged between $3 and $300. The latter figure, however, was exceedingly rare. In reality, the value of the slave strongly influenced the amount of the reward; highly skilled slaves obviously were more valuable and brought the highest rewards for their return. According to Sellers, after 1830 the average reward for runaways increased to about $25. The evidence in all of the slave states suggests that the great majority of runaway slaves returned of their own volition, or were captured and returned to their owners. Of the 1,253 slaves advertised in Virginia between 1804 and 1828, 294, or 23.4 percent, were captured and placed in jail. Only 2 percent had been charged with a criminal act. Those slaves who were placed in jail had to be claimed within one year or were commonly sold at auction. Moreover, during that year the jailer was authorized to hire the slave to an employer to recover the cost of maintaining him in jail.

Virginia owners reported that only 113, or 9 percent, of the slaves advertised were headed for freedom in the free states. Sellers found that of the 1,017 slaves who ran away in 1850, only thirty-two escaped to the free states. Where, then, did the bondsmen go when they ran away? Some slaves attempted to reestablish family ties* broken by the sale of members of their families. The evidence seems to suggest that a large majority of the slave runaways simply went home, back to the plantations or communities where they had been born and reared. In their opinion family and friends there would be more likely to offer support and protection. According to Charles S. Sydnor in *Slavery in Mississippi* (1933), and corroborated by Sellers, overseers frequently noted in their reports to owners that missing slaves had been seen "lurking" in the woods on the periphery of the plantations. Owners apparently believed that the slaves would return in their own good time. The runaway sometimes secured free papers and attempted to pass as a free Negro, but his chances of being caught were high. Throughout the South free blacks were registered with city and county officials. And if whites determined who furnished aid to the fugitive, the punishment was severe for both slave and accomplice. Few slaves actually ran away—not because they were satisfied with their plight, but because they feared the severity of the laws designed to curtail their flight and of their punishments.

SELECTED BIBLIOGRAPHY

Eugene D. Genovese, *Roll, Jordan, Roll: The World the Slaves Made* (1974); Michael P. Johnson, "Runaway Slaves and the Slave Communities in South Carolina, 1799–1830," *William and Mary Quarterly*, 3rd ser., 38 (1981), 418–441; Gerald W. Mullin, *Flight and Rebellion: Slave Resistance in Eighteenth-Century Virginia* (1972); Richmond *Enquirer*, September 1804-June 1828; Judith Kelleher Schafer, "New Orleans Slavery in 1850 As Seen in Advertisements," *Journal of Southern History*, 47 (1981), 33–56; James Benson Sellers, *Slavery in Alabama* (2nd ed., 1964); and Charles S. Sydnor, *Slavery in Mississippi* (1933).

STANLEY W. CAMPBELL

S

SALT INDUSTRY. From colonial times until settlement crossed the piedmont, imported foreign salt supplied America's domestic market. In the revolutionary era, however, western settlers discovered numerous salt springs. Below the Ohio River, slaves often worked at minor manufactories at these sites. By 1814 in the Ohio and Mississippi River drainage basins, the Great Kanawha River salt industry in western Virginia dominated all but the most isolated western markets. In this year, Kanawha salt production, resting largely on slave labor, doubled the output of any other state—640,000 bushels annually—and it steadily increased to 3,224,786 bushels in 1846.

In 1850 thirty-three Kanawha salt companies employed approximately 1,600 bondsmen. Allied industries used additional numbers. Individual salt firms possessed from 12 to 232 slaves. Of the 1,600 slaves who worked in the Kanawha furnaces, about 75 percent were male with 64 percent being between fifteen and thirty-nine years of age. Although the single male slave predominated, some slave family* units existed among the older and larger companies. Kanawha producers leased the majority of the whole number of slave workmen. The companies generally hired between 30 and 45 percent of their slave labor force, but some firms leased as many as 90 percent of their hands. The Kanawha slave economy relieved the declining eastern Virginia agricultural system that had surplus slaves for hire. The manufacturers used family relationships, contacts, and agents to comb eastern counties to fulfill their labor needs.

Slaves participated in all phases of salt manufacturing: as woodcutters and coalminers for furnace fuel; wheelers and haulers of coal inside and outside the mine; kettle tenders at furnaces; ash removers; engine tenders; salt lifters; packers; coopers; blacksmiths; and general laborers. A few bondsmen served as working foremen and slave women usually cooked for the work force. A routinized task system* of time and production measurement paced the continual, round-the-clock salt furnace operation. Production incentives, such as accumulated monetary rewards and store credit, molded a motivated, mostly compliant work force.

Kanawha slaves generally were well-clothed and adequately fed, and they had access to an unusual variety of consumer commodities stocked in salt company stores. Nevertheless, many occupations exposed the slaves to hazardous conditions: underground mining (which employed the majority of bondsmen); boiling brine water; moving machinery; and tending steam boilers that were prone to explode. The location of the salt industry on an interstate river afforded opportunities for possible escape and a passageway for five antebellum cholera epidemics. The common hire* system encouraged harsh treatment for slaves removed from the absentee owners'* eyes. Leased slaves normally dug coal, the most unskilled and dangerous position in the slave work force. Owned chattels tended to labor in safer, skilled occupations.

Kanawha saltmakers, not enjoying the option of an available pool of free whites, insisted that slave labor proved cheaper and more dependable than free labor. The saltmakers consistently paid high rents for slaves, costs that were elastic and that fluctuated with the prosperity of the enterprise. The success of Kanawha slavery answered questions about the profitability of slavery* posed both by contemporaries and by generations of historians. Indeed, slaves employed in the salt industry proved the efficiency of the peculiar institution in a factory environment and suggested slavery's potential value in extractive industries had it survived into the industrial age.

SELECTED BIBLIOGRAPHY

John A. Jakle, "Salt and the Initial Settlement of the Ohio Valley" (Ph.D. dissertation, Indiana University, 1967); Robert P. Multhauf, *Neptune's Gift: A History of Common Salt* (1978); John E. Stealey III, "The Salt Industry of the Great Kanawha Valley of Virginia: A Study in Ante-Bellum Internal Commerce" (Ph.D. dissertation, West Virginia University, 1970); and John E. Stealey III, "Slavery and the West Virginia Salt Industry," *Journal of Negro History*, 59 (1974), 105–131.

                                                              JOHN EDMUND STEALEY

SALZBURGERS. The Salzburgers were a group of pietistic Lutherans who emigrated from southeastern Germany to colonial Georgia between 1734 and 1741. Numerous authors have described these colonists as staunch supporters of James Oglethorpe's efforts to keep Georgia a slave-free province. Other scholars have observed slave-free social patterns in early German settlers in both Northern and Southern American colonies.

Recent work indicates that the Salzburgers were not culturally opposed to black slavery. Rather, they were concerned primarily with maintaining good relations with their sponsors and benefactors. The Salzburgers arrived in Georgia under English sponsorship, establishing the village of Ebenezer twenty-five miles northwest of Savannah. The new colonists used sixteen borrowed slaves in 1734, finding the "best" slaves "useful and faithful." The colony's London trustees enacted Georgia's slave ban in 1735 as a security matter, out of concern for the growing slave unrest in the Caribbean and South Carolina and to strengthen

Georgia's role as a buffer colony against the Spanish in Florida. The Salzburgers, dependent on the goodwill of Oglethorpe and, later, on the goodwill of the trustees, voiced support of the slave ban in terms echoing the official security rationale. Caught between factions in the proslavery agitation by other Georgia settlers in the 1740s, and with some defections by Ebenezer residents, the Salzburgers' leader and pastor Johann Martin Boltzius dropped opposition to slavery by 1748 and participated in drafting a proposed slave code in 1749. In 1751, a year after the trustees ended the slave ban, Boltzius wrote that slaves "are smart enough. . . . The benefit from their work is great, and their yearly upkeep costs very little. White servants do not easily do well in this free country . . . ." The Salzburgers had adapted to American conditions.

SELECTED BIBLIOGRAPHY

Richard Hofstadter, *America at 1750: A Social Portrait* (1971); George Fenwick Jones, *The Salzburger Saga: Religious Exiles and Other Germans along the Savannah* (1984); Klaus G. Loewald et al., "J. M. Boltzius Answers a Questionnaire on Carolina and Georgia, Part II," *William and Mary Quarterly*," 3rd ser., 15 (1958), 230–252; William L. Withuhn, "Salzburgers and Slavery: A Problem of Mentalité," *Georgia Historical Quarterly*, 68 (1984), 173–192; and Betty Wood, *Slavery in Colonial Georgia, 1730–1775* (1984).

WILLIAM L. WITHUHN

SAMBO. In name and stereotype, Sambo was a basic component in the racist construction of slavery. Stereotypes are primarily a form of social and psychological, and hence political, control; and the system of slavery rested heavily on the image of the Afro-American as a Sambo figure.

Of the various features ascribed to all dark-skinned persons by Caucasians in colonial North America, two were developed and flourished almost simultaneously: "Sambo" and the "savage." Although the images complemented each other, whites generally stressed the Sambo stereotype to minimize black hostility and maximize the slave's energies as worker and entertainer.

The term *Sambo* actually came into high prominence in the post–Civil War period, but it was used along with other similar given names during the slave period, including "Tambo," "Pompey," and "Sam." The use of a single name conveyed lesser status and, at times, comicality. Its origins were a fusion of a tribal African designation together with the Spanish and Portuguese word "Zambo," meaning bandied-legged monkey, and the English "Sam."

Name and image combined to convey a figure at once childish and buffoonish who was viewed as a natural comic. Sambo was thus perceived as being cheerful, optimistic, musical, ignorant—but always grinning. The figure was extremely active in Southern culture in drama, literature, folklore, and artifactual terms. Recognizing white perceptions, slaves used the role to their advantage in order to secure essential items denied to them, such as food, clothing, and work relief, and to avoid certain punishments.

Over time, Sambo became in fact an image unrivaled in American popular culture for being both the prodder and the butt of white humor.

SELECTED BIBLIOGRAPHY

John W. Blassingame, *The Slave Community: Plantation Life in the Antebellum South* (rev. ed., 1979); Joseph Boskin, *Sambo: The Rise and Demise of an American Jester* (1986); Stanley M. Elkins, *Slavery: A Problem in American Institutional and Intellectual Life* (2nd rev. ed., 1968); Winthrop D. Jordan, *White over Black: American Attitudes toward the Negro, 1550–1812* (1968); and Robert C. Toll, *Blacking Up: The Minstrel Show in Nineteenth-Century America* (1974).

JOSEPH BOSKIN

SAVANNAH, GA, SLAVERY IN. Steady growth and overall stability characterized slavery in Savannah from its legalization by the Georgia Trustees (1750) until the Civil War. Slave numbers increased from 821 in 1771 to 3,075 in 1820, both figures representing 41 percent of the community's population. By 1820 more than half of the city's households owned blacks. Savannah's commercial prominence during the antebellum period attracted thousands of white workingmen, many of them poor immigrants,* dropping the percentage of slaves to 35 and the percentage of families owning them to 33 by 1860. Yet Savannah counted 7,712 slaves at the end of the period, having added approximately 1,500 per decade after 1830. In absolute terms the number of slave owners was still rising in the 1850s, as was the number of large slaveholdings, and several hundred additional male bondsmen were being absorbed into skilled and unskilled occupations.

The problem of controlling mobile urban blacks was perennial, most antebellum legislation for the purpose in fact having its genesis decades earlier. Laws* passed by the Georgia Assembly in the colonial era to regulate the hire of town slaves and monitor their conduct in leisure hours were replaced by more comprehensive ordinances between 1787 and 1810, as the new city council contended with increased numbers of bondsmen and free blacks.* By 1810 free Negroes were subject to the same police regulations as slaves, and segregation* of blacks, regardless of legal status, in public facilities was common policy.

No less worrisome to authorities were black efforts to create a separate community life. While urban bondage militated against stable family life, before the end of the eighteenth century Savannah's fringe areas contained concentrations of slaves living in their own, illegally rented, shacks. Through the next several decades these rapidly growing neighborhoods, especially Yamacraw on the west side, were sanctuaries for runaway slaves* seeking family and friends, the location of underground schools operated by free blacks, and the scene of constant mingling of slaves and free blacks in homes, grog shops,* and the area's three African Baptist churches.*

Despite incessant violation of ordinances by slaves, considerations of profit usually encouraged loose law enforcement as well as legislation protective of the slave owner's investment. Laws restricting use of slave artisans, the first in 1758, were temporary and ineffectual, as were attempts to limit the practice of slaves hiring* their own time and paying wages to their owners. Prices for badges worn by hirelings remained constant after 1839, while taxes* on slaves, already modest, were actually reduced in 1849. Even tight controls over free Negro seamen while in port could be relaxed, as they were in 1854, in "the interests of commerce."

As during the American Revolution, wartime conditions after 1861 upset the equilibrium of Savannah's slave system. During the Civil War* the presence of increased numbers of bondsmen left to support themselves by financially pressed masters, as well as rural male slaves impressed to work on fortifications, accentuated problems of slave control. Blacks suffered privation but gained greater autonomy, and the proximity of Union armies* encouraged the ultimate act of rebellion—an escape to freedom.

SELECTED BIBLIOGRAPHY

William A. Byrne, Jr., "The Burden and Heat of the Day: Slavery and Servitude in Savannah, 1733–1865" (Ph.D. dissertation, Florida State University, 1979); William Grimes, *Life of William Grimes, the Runaway Slave, Brought Down to the Present Time* (1855); Richard H. Haunton, "Savannah in the 1850's" (Ph.D. dissertation, Emory University, 1968); Clarence L. Mohr, "Georgia Blacks during Secession and Civil War, 1859–1865" (Ph.D. dissertation, University of Georgia, 1975); Thomas R. Statom, Jr., "Negro Slavery in Eighteenth-Century Georgia" (Ph.D. dissertation, University of Alabama, 1982); and Betty Wood, *Slavery in Colonial Georgia, 1730–1775* (1984).

RICHARD HAUNTON

SEAMEN ACTS. In the wake of Denmark Vesey's abortive rebellion in December 1822, South Carolina's legislature passed a series of measures to prevent future uprisings. Among these, the state ordered that all free black seamen should be jailed while their vessels were in port. Their employers were liable for all costs of detention, and any sailor unredeemed by his employer would be sold into slavery. Over the next four decades, this law inspired similar legislation in Georgia (1829), North Carolina (1830–1831), Florida (1832), Alabama (1839, 1841), Louisiana (1842, 1859), and Texas (1856), although all states enforced the law only intermittently and often only under public pressure. Originally intended as a measure of "police regulation," the acts' import quickly escalated in the face of diplomatic complaints and court challenges to an assertion of state sovereignty.

This pattern of events was established early in South Carolina. After an initial wave of arrests, the law fell into disuse. But when British consular authorities and the federal courts asserted its illegality in 1823, influential Charlestonians, through the nascent South Carolina Association, demanded stricter implementation. Long after fears of insurrection had cooled, and in spite of the damage the seamen acts caused to commerce in their port cities, white Southerners defended the acts as a touchstone of state's rights, virtually daring outside interference. As Charleston lawyer James Louis Petigru admitted in 1851, "the unconstitutionality of the law would not stagger them at all. They would continue to enforce it, even after the Supreme Court had declared it void, & if it produced a collision the result would only [be] so much the more to their taste."

Direct assaults on the seamen acts proved fruitless. In South Carolina, appeals by the British consul, the Charleston Chamber of Commerce—even the state governor—failed to move the legislature to rescind its statute. In 1844 mobs in New Orleans and Charleston drove representatives of Massachusetts back north before they could initiate suits to test the law's constitutionality. Fearful of stirring up the hornet's nest of secession, and of weakening Southern support for the Democratic party,* federal officials promised action but achieved nothing throughout the period. In the 1850s, however, through a mixture of lobbying, bribery, and obsequiousness, the British consulate convinced Louisiana (1852), Georgia (1854), and South Carolina (1856) to rescind or modify their acts. In other states the law had already become a dead letter. By 1859, when John Brown's* raid resurrected Southern radicalism, the seamen acts were viewed as too mild and ineffective for revival. Wholesale expulsion or enslavement of Southern free blacks* became the new rallying cry.

SELECTED BIBLIOGRAPHY

Philip M. Hamer, "Great Britain, the United States, and the Negro Seamen Acts, 1822–1848," *Journal of Southern History*, 1 (1935), 3–28; Philip M. Hamer, "British Consuls and the Negro Seamen Acts, 1850–1860," *Journal of Southern History*, 1 (1935), 138–168; Howell M. Henry, *The Police Control of the Slave in South Carolina* (1914); and Alan F. January, "The South Carolina Association: An Agency for Race Control in Antebellum South Carolina," *South Carolina Historical Magazine*, 78 (1977), 191–201.
                                                            LAWRENCE T. MCDONNELL

SEASONING. By the latter half of the seventeenth century, the word *seasoning* had come into general usage in referring to the process by which a person became hardened or inured to a strange climate. The term came into use because of increased colonization and importation of slaves to the New World. A century later *seasoning* also was used in the West Indies to refer to the process by which slaves were oriented to the plantation system,* but its predominant meaning always was related to the development of immunities to diseases.

With the close of the African slave trade* to the United States in 1808, seasoning slaves in the West Indies before sending them to North American plantations no longer concerned American buyers and slaveholders. Indeed, the practice of acquiring "seasoned" slaves had already been altered by the mid-eighteenth century when slave traders brought Africans directly to the North American market.

Europeans in America believed that blacks possessed special immunities to the effects of a hot climate,* and this belief became a cornerstone of pseudo-scientific racism. Because Africans possessed greater acquired immunities to malaria and yellow fever than did Europeans, they tended to have a slightly higher survival rate in the tropics than did newly arrived Europeans. From the economic viewpoint of white planters, the price paid for a slave provided a sounder promise of future labor than did the cost of an indentured servant. As a result, blacks who had been "seasoned"—had survived the first attack of New World disease—commanded a higher price than others.

Because both malaria and yellow fever were Old World diseases, most colonies in the New World established legal requirements of quarantine. Typical of such measures was the passage of an act in the General Assembly of South Carolina in 1712 requiring that a health officer visit all vessels proposing to enter the colony to send their sick passengers to "pest houses" and to require a twenty-day quarantine period if anyone on board had died of a contagious disease during passage. The justification given for the measure was that "great numbers of the inhabitants of this Province have been destroyed by malignant, contagious diseases brought from Africa and other parts of America." In 1744 the law was changed to add a requirement that all Negroes imported to Charleston from Africa or elsewhere undergo ten days of quarantine on Sullivans Island in the harbor.

Some historians of the West Indies have referred to a period of three to six years in which slaves were seasoned. That form of seasoning, however, was more than a quarantine or weathering of disease. It referred to the whole process of acclimatization and acculturation that molded Africans into productive members of a plantation system. This usage represented a broader definition of the term *seasoning* than prevailed among slaveholders on the North American continent.

SELECTED BIBLIOGRAPHY

Mayo B. Crawford, "Diamond in Dirt Theory of Slavery: Seasoning the Female Slave," in Willa D. Johnson and Thomas L. Green, eds., *Perspectives on Afro-American Women* (1975); Philip D. Curtin, "Epidemiology and the Slave Trade," *Political Science Quarterly*, 83 (1968), 190–216; and Elizabeth Donnan, ed., *Documents Illustrative of the History of the Slave Trade to America* (4 vols., 1930–1935).

WILLIAM S. PRICE

SEGREGATION. Segregation, the elaborate system of laws, customs, and proprietary practices that defined in terms of physical distance the caste distinctions between white and black Americans, existed side by side with the institution of slavery primarily in the major cities of the antebellum South. Segregation developed long before the Civil War in several cities, North and South alike, with large black populations and correspondingly high white anxiety levels. Although house servants and field hands alike routinely were excluded from many activities and amenities, formal segregation did not coexist with the peculiar institution in the rural antebellum South. It would have been a needless nuisance, for slavery itself was the supreme segregator, defining racial roles and limiting black liberties with much greater clarity than a formal color line ever could do. Racial segregation spread into the rural South in a real sense only after Appomattox.

In many antebellum cities, however, the conditions were vastly different. Sizable communities of rather independent blacks, slave and free, combined with white nonslaveholders and transients to form a cosmopolitan society totally alien to the plantation tradition of rigid and personal racial control. White hostility to unwelcomed contacts with blacks in public places, combined with apprehension over the threat to white supremacy posed by interracial fraternization, resulted in the patchwork evolution of local segregation systems comprised of city ordinances, management policies, and unwritten arrangements. These varied somewhat from city to city, but antebellum urban blacks* usually were seated in separate galleries (known commonly as "nigger heavens") in churches and theaters, confined to separate and distinctly second-class areas on public conveyances and in hospitals and jails, and excluded altogether from white schools, hotels, saloons, restaurants, and cemeteries. In cities, North and South alike, vocations commonly were divided into white trades and "nigger jobs," though not to the extent that became common after emancipation. A major difference between the color lines in Northern and Southern cities was that residential or neighborhood segregation, enforced either by law or unwritten fiat, was common in the North and a rarity in the older cities of the South. Another vital distinction, although difficult to document, was that in the North the strongest motive for a color line appears to have been widespread white squeamishness over close personal contact with blacks. In Southern cities, however, the main impetus came from white apprehensions over the preservation of white supremacy and the desire to keep blacks "in their place" through public humiliation and ostracism.

Unlike their counterparts in Northern cities, the white residents of such Southern cities as New Orleans, Charleston, Savannah, Richmond, and Mobile not only worried about their local free black* communities but had to contend as well with large numbers of uncommonly independent and assertive slaves. As Samuel Walker, a Louisiana sugar planter, observed in his diary after a New Orleans visit: "Slavery is from its very nature eminently patriarchial and altogether agricultural. It does not thrive with master or slave when transplanted to cities." By their very nature, the larger Southern cities (especially New Orleans and Charleston) simply were too cosmopolitan, too anonymous, too rich in opportunities for interracial fraternization, and too dependent upon a high degree of flexibility in labor utilization to permit the effective personal control of slaves by masters that prevailed on farms and plantations. The most liberated of all city slaves were those "hired-out"* by their owners to other employers. Many of these bondsmen rented their own living quarters and enjoyed exclusive control of their free time, seeing their owners only at stipulated intervals to turn over a share of their earnings. The breakdown of white control was mirrored by a patent lack of deference and servility in the behavior of many city blacks, slave and free alike. They drank, gambled, fought, danced, and procreated with whites in the grog shops, back rooms, and secluded sheds that comprised the social "underworld" of every Southern city. The boldest blacks abused whites both physically and verbally.

As the traditional system of racial control broke down in the Southern cities, the burden of maintaining white supremacy fell increasingly to a public, visible color line that separated the races in municipal facilities and places of public accommodation. What may well have been the South's first Jim Crow law, a New Orleans city ordinance adopted in 1816 that forbade interracial seating in theaters and public exhibitions, merely formalized a long-standing proprietary policy in the city. Blacks in Savannah, Charleston, and Richmond were banned by statute from certain municipal gardens, grounds, promenades, and parks. New Orleans prohibited racially mixed balls in 1828, although the measure was widely ignored. In Charleston, Savannah, and Baltimore blacks were prohibited by statute from engaging in many crafts and trades. In other cities job segregation was achieved by unwritten consensus. Blacks were banned from white private and public schools, hotels, taverns, and restaurants throughout the urban South. Such public facilities as cemeteries, hospitals, poorhouses, and jails were also invariably segregated. Black prisoners in New Orleans even were required to wear uniforms of a different color than those worn by white convicts. Black riders on public conveyances also were segregated, though less often by statute than by proprietary practices. In New Orleans streetcars operated for blacks were designated by large black stars painted on the fronts and sides to eliminate confusion. During the 1850s, as sectional tensions mounted and white fears of slave conspiracies and insurrections escalated, Southern cities enacted new statutes to combat the most blatant forms of interracial fraternization. In New Orleans, for example, ordinances passed in 1856 and 1857 prohibited mixed gambling in grog shops and racially integrated whorehouses.

When slavery died in 1865, segregation soon became a key mechanism to preserve white supremacy throughout the entire South. After a period of testing during Reconstruction and for a decade afterward, state legislatures began enacting the segregation codes known as the Jim Crow laws. These essentially defined the black "place" in Southern society until the civil rights movement of the mid-twentieth century.

SELECTED BIBLIOGRAPHY

Roger A. Fischer, "Racial Segregation in Ante-Bellum New Orleans," *American Historical Review*, 74 (1969), 926–937; Leon F. Litwack, *North of Slavery: The Negro in the Free States, 1790–1860* (1961); and Richard C. Wade, *Slavery in the Cities: The South, 1820–1860* (1964).

ROGER A. FISCHER

SELF-PURCHASE. From the 1640s through the Civil War a small percentage of American slaves succeeded in buying their freedom. This action required permission from the master and entrepreneurship from the slave. In some cases it meant breaking the law. Self-purchase was a much safer route to liberty than flight or rebellion. On the master's side, the practice usually demonstrated both a weak commitment to proslavery* ideology and financial need. In 1956 historian Kenneth M. Stampp suspected that self-purchase arrangements most often involved skilled slaves in the cities of the upper South.

A variety of circumstances enabled a deal to be struck between master and slave. In one of the first self-purchases, around 1650, a Virginia slave's unwillingness to work well pressured his master into an agreement. Other bondsmen, like the preacher Richard Allen, won their owners' gratitude through valuable services. The Fugitive Slave Act of 1850* motivated some runaways, including Frederick Douglass,* to arrange their purchases from masters who were open to restitution. A number of owners simply wanted a short-term profit by selling freedom to their slaves. Others planned the process as steps to freedom for the slave. From the slave's point of view, the best financial arrangements were generous with terms that ended quickly. The worst were highly exploitative and lasted most of a slave's life. Payments usually occurred in installments and masters often charged interest.

To raise the money for self-purchase required persistence and ingenuity on the part of the slave. Technically slaves worked entirely for the benefit of their masters, but workdays usually ended at dusk and did not include Sundays (benevolent masters also excepted half of Saturday). Industrious slaves thus could gain earnings from working "overtime," performing odd jobs, or producing domestic and agricultural goods during their "free time." A few slaves received tips or incentive payments at their regular jobs. A number, mostly bondsmen with craft skills or business talents, contracted with their owners to hire themselves out and subsequently used their work time to gain access to more income. At least one slave, the controversial Denmark Vesey,* obtained the necessary funds to purchase himself by buying a winning lottery ticket. An approach available only to favored slaves and runaways* was public fund-raising. Many bondsmen, however, failed to raise enough money within a reasonable time. Those who tried had to exercise great thrift and guard their savings securely. An arbitrary master or unsympathetic heir all too easily could cancel fulfillment of the slave's dream. Unscrupulous masters even confiscated payments already made.

Local slave codes closely regulated self-purchase. Starting in the colonial period, Virginia, Delaware, and all of the New England colonies permitted contracts formalizing the terms of self-purchase. Louisiana and Tennessee later accepted the practice, while Maryland, North Carolina, and the District of Columbia rejected it. By the end of the eighteenth century nearly every state required a manumitting owner to post bond that the freedman would not become a public charge, thereby raising the self-purchase costs. By 1836 eight Southern states required that blacks leave the state upon manumission. Four states mandated legislative permission for each manumission, and Maryland disallowed all forms of slave liberation in 1860. By the outbreak of the Civil War nine states had prohibited slaves from hiring* their own work time, thereby trying to limit the opportunities for slaves to accumulate funds for self-purchase. At best, the practice of self-purchase was an anomaly in a slave society predicated on the absolute ownership of the slave by his master, and the inability of the slave to own property, even himself.

SELECTED BIBLIOGRAPHY

Herbert Aptheker, *To Be Free: Studies in American Negro History* (1948); John W. Blassingame, ed., *Slave Testimony: Two Centuries of Letters, Speeches, Interviews, and Autobiographies* (1977); Sumner E. Matison, "Manumission by Purchase," *Journal of Negro History*, 33 (1948), 146–167; Edmund S. Morgan, *American Slavery, American Freedom: The Ordeal of Colonial Virginia* (1975); and Kenneth M. Stampp, *The Peculiar Institution: Slavery in the Ante-Bellum South* (1956).

JOHN CIMPRICH

SEMINOLE WARS. Early in the eighteenth century slaves from the Southern colonies began to flee to Spanish Florida to escape their bondage. Once in the peninsula, they often obtained protection by becoming slaves of the Seminole Indians.* All Florida blacks—including a few free Negroes—were natural allies of the Indians because their African heritage, by no means forgotten, contained religious, ceremonial, governmental, and mythical similarities to the Seminole culture. Also, their lot as slaves under Indian masters was far better than as bondsmen of the whites. Bondage under the Seminoles more closely resembled feudal vassalage than chattel slavery. Finally, the Florida blacks hoped ultimately to attain independence, personal importance, and plunder by allying with the Indians.

By the second decade of the nineteenth century, the flow of escaped slaves southward to Florida from South Carolina and Georgia became entangled in international tensions between the United States and England and Spain. During the War of 1812* the British built a dirt fort armed with cannon on the Apalachicola River inside Spanish Florida, sixty miles from the U.S. border. At war's end, the British left the Indians to cope with the United States and runaway slaves,* renegades in American eyes, to garrison the Negro fort. Slaveholders in the United States considered the fort a menace to slavery, and implored the government to attack it, even though the fort stood on Spanish territory. On 27 July 1816 one lucky hot shot exploded the powder magazine, shattering the Negro fort and about 325 slaves with it. The Negro-Indian power in northern Florida, weakened already by heavy losses during the Patriot War of 1812–1813, was further damaged by this loss. Destruction of the fort, however, did not end the threat to slavery existing in the southeastern United States. Accordingly, Andrew Jackson,* at first on his authority as general, then with government sanction, made a second invasion of Spanish Florida in early 1818 in order to break the power of the nonwhite allies, a purpose that Spain could not accomplish.

Jackson's invasion, the beginning action of the First Seminole War, overran the Indian-Negro war parties and destroyed their towns and food supplies east as far as the Suwannee River. In the attempt to stop him, bands of blacks fought in separate units beside the Indians, but in vain. At the last battle, occurring in April 1818, a band of blacks fought a gallant rear guard action to give the noncombatants, both red and black, time to escape across the Suwannee. In characteristic fashion Jackson called his campaign a "Savage and Negro war."

After 1821, the year in which the United States took control of Florida, trouble between Indians and whites became continuous, much of it over slavery. Trouble enlarged into warfare in December 1835, the opening date for the Second Seminole War. Negroes of all classes knew that they had everything to lose and nothing to gain if the Americans conquered the Florida Indians. As a result, bands of red and black warriors fused to fight U.S. forces. Many army officers rated the blacks better fighters than their red allies. Black warriors were present in numbers in all major actions up to the Battle of Okeechobee, fought on 25 December 1837. General Thomas S. Jesup, commanding in Florida from early December 1836 to May 1838, recognized that white Floridians would not rest until all blacks, except slaves to white masters, were forced out of the peninsula. This was, he said, a Negro not an Indian war, and Jesup shaped his strategy accordingly to split the blacks away from their red allies. Finally, by March 1838, he had achieved that goal.

By then most of the black leaders who had been undyingly loyal to the red-black alliance had already been either killed or captured. Then, too, a significant number of runaways from American plantations had found life in the Florida swamp country unbearable, and surrendered to be returned to their white masters. The remaining Negroes began to see that the Indian cause was doomed, and that it was to their interest to ingratiate themselves with the foe. Moreover, when captured, leaders were given the choice between being guides or being hanged. Most chose to live and, knowing the terrain as well as the Indians, led army detachments into the ultimate retreats of the Seminoles. In the end these expeditions brought about the defeat of the red cause. Naturally, the Indians directed their fire at the turncoat guides. The Negroes, and only they, knew both English and Indian well enough to say at least approximately what was in the speeches made at meetings. Throughout the Second Seminole War they did the interpreting.

Because most of the fighting blacks were gone from Florida, killed or shipped out, by the time the Second Seminole War was formally declared to be at an end in August 1842, slavery no longer served as a primary cause of subsequent Indian-white trouble. Instead, relentless encroachment by whites into the Indians' range brought on the Third Seminole War, 1855–1858. There were probably no more than 120 warriors fighting back in this war, none of them black. The central story of red-black relations had been transferred to the West.* About 3,900 hostiles had been transplanted there from Florida since 1821, of whom 400 were black allies of the Indians.

SELECTED BIBLIOGRAPHY

Joshua R. Giddings, *The Exiles of Florida* (1858); John K. Mahon, *History of the Second Seminole War, 1835–1842* (1967); and Kenneth Wiggins Porter, *The Negro on the American Frontier* (1971).

JOHN K. MAHON

SLAVEHOLDERS, BLACK. From the beginning of slavery in colonial America a few blacks possessed slaves. As early as 1655, Anthony Johnson, a black farmer in Northampton County, Virginia, had not only secured his own freedom but acquired a slave named John Castor. In early Virginia, Pennsylvania, New York, and Massachusetts, free Negroes* became slave masters, but it was not until the postrevolutionary era—with its wave of emancipations in the South—that black slave owning became widespread.

Although only a small percentage of free Negroes ever owned other blacks, and though only a tiny proportion of those who did ever possessed more than a few slaves, by 1830, 3,775 free blacks in the United States (almost all of them in the Southern states) owned approximately 12,760 slaves. At this time the free black population stood at 182,070, probably representing 35,000 or 40,000 families. Thus, about one out of ten free black family heads owned at least one bondsman.

Some of them had purchased relatives, or friends, or family members, holding them in nominal bondage, because the laws* in many states, required newly freed blacks to emigrate from their native state or return to slavery. This type of ownership appeared commonly in some towns and cities.* Among the 753 free persons of color (mostly Creoles of color) who possessed slaves in New Orleans in 1830, four out of five owned fewer than five slaves. During the 1830s and 1840s, while constituting only a small fraction of the city's slaveholders, they filed nearly one-third of all emancipation petitions (501 of 1,553) recorded at the district court. Parents often sacrificed a life's work and savings to extricate their children from bondage, purchasing them from a white owner, and then holding pro forma ownership rather than seeking legal emancipation that could result in forced emigration.

Many black slaveholders, even those who owned only a few of their brethren, held slaves for economic reasons. They purchased slaves to assist them as skilled artisans or as farm laborers; sometimes they bought slaves for resale.

Those who owned large numbers of slaves, primarily in South Carolina and Louisiana, seemed to differ little from white slaveholders in their attitudes toward slavery and in their treatment of their chattel. They bought, sold, traded, mortgaged their blacks, and worked them long hours in the fields. In the Louisiana sugar parishes, black masters broke up families or purchased only young men to undertake the arduous labor required in the cane fields. "You might think, master, dat dy would be good to dar own nation; but dy is not," one black explained to Frederick Law Olmsted during the 1850s. "I'd rather be a servant to any man in de world, dan to a brack man."

Even those who had some compassion for their fellow blacks found it difficult to maintain a productive plantation without considering slaves primarily as property. Plaquemines Parish sugar planter Andrew Durnford,* a French-speaking Creole of color, allowed his slaves many privileges, but on a slave-buying trip to Richmond, Virginia, in 1835, he purchased only "likely" men and "likely" women. Similarly, Nicholas and Dominique Metoyer in Louisiana, James Pendarvis and Elias Collins in South Carolina, and Alfred Anderson in Virginia, all members of the planter class, differed little from their white neighbors in the treatment of their chattel.

These black slave owners represent some of the wealthiest free persons of color in the South. They owned large tracts of land, livestock, and farm machinery, and they boasted estates in excess of $10,000. In each state the richest free blacks came from the slave owning class: Zeno Chastang in Alabama; Anthony Odingsells in Georgia; Ciprien Ricard, Antoine Dubuclet, and Jean Baptiste Meullion in Louisiana; and William Ellison in South Carolina. On the eve of the Civil War, Ellison, who manufactured cotton gins and planted cotton in Stateburg, possessed wealth in excess of $60,000 and owned a total of sixty-three slaves. To protect such holdings, Ellison and others formed small, tightly knit communities, arranging for the marriage of their children to families of equal status, and isolating themselves as much as possible from other free blacks and whites. It was no accident that the Metoyer, Chastang, and Odingsells families established their homes and plantations on islands.

During the 1840s and 1850s the number of black slaveholders decreased substantially. This resulted in part from the attacks on free persons of color by whites, including restrictive laws and acts of violence. It stemmed also from the move of free blacks themselves, especially outside of Louisiana, away from slave-owning as a means of economic advancement. In South Carolina, for instance, the number of black slaveholders dropped from 450 in 1830, to 171 in 1860. As the data in the following table show, the number of slaves they owned also fell off considerably.

In values and attitudes, many Negro slave owners were not unlike white planters who believed that family lineage, gender, age, masculinity, and skin color (most free persons of color who owned slaves were mulattoes) mattered more than diligence and industry. They educated their children, either in schools especially established for that purpose, such as Romaine Verdun's private school in Saint Mary Parish, Louisiana, or with private tutors. They rejected the cultural values of the black slaves—their folktales and folk songs, fears and superstitions, conjurism and voodooism,* extended kinship patterns, and emotional Christianity. In Louisiana many black slaveholders joined the Catholic church,* while in other states they sometimes attended white Episcopal* or Presbyterian* churches. John Carruthers Stanley, a black Craven County, North Carolina, plantation owner and barber, for instance, was one of the original purchasers of pews (at the rear) in the white New Bern Presbyterian Church.

Table 1
Black Slave Owners in South Carolina, 1790–1860

	Negro Slave Owners	Slaves Owned	Average Number
1790	59	357	6
1800	45	414	9
1810	*	*	*
1820	230	1148	5
1830	450	2412	5
1840	454	2357	5
1850	297	1277	4
1860	171	766	4.5

* accurate data missing

Source: Larry Koger, *Black Slave Owners: Free Black Slave Masters in South Carolina, 1790–1860* (Jefferson, North Carolina, 1985), pp. 20–21.

During the Civil War,* black slave owners, like their white counterparts, suffered substantial financial setbacks. Not only did they lose their slave property—$215,000 in South Carolina and nearly $1,000,000 in Louisiana—but they seemed unable to cope with new conditions during the Reconstruction era. By the 1870s the vast majority, including some of the richest prewar blacks in the United States, had lost virtually everything. They also suffered from their loss of prestige and status. As Catherine Johnson, the daughter of a black slave owner in Mississippi, confessed in 1866: "It seems that the times grow harder instead of better and I do so dread poverty. And another thing, every body seems so changed, and most of all I grieve over the change that has taken place in My self. [T]o the present the past seems so Bright, so bright that I dare not call up its memories, for it makes me wretched to think that in reality I can never live them again, and I know that it is wrong but sometimes I long to die."

SELECTED BIBLIOGRAPHY

R. Halliburton, Jr., "Free Black Owners of Slaves: A Reappraisal of the Woodson Thesis," *South Carolina Historical Magazine*, 76 (1975), 129–142; Michael P. Johnson and James L. Roark, *Black Masters: A Free Family of Color in the Old South* (1984); Larry Koger, *Black Slaveowners: Free Black Slave Masters in South Carolina, 1790–1860* (1985); Gary B. Mills, *The Forgotten People: Cane River's Creoles of Color* (1977); David O. Whitten, *Andrew Durnford: A Black Sugar Planter in Antebellum Louisiana* (1981); and Carter G. Woodson, "Free Negro Owners of Slaves in the United States in 1830," *Journal of Negro History*, 9 (1924), 41–85.

LOREN SCHWENINGER

SLAVEHOLDERS, LARGE. What counted as a "large" slaveholding in the South is a relative judgment, though not an arbitrary one. Both historians and contemporaries have sought to describe a minority of large slaveholders numerous enough to possess distinctive interests and characteristics, yet not so numerous as to shade into the average. For the South as a whole, after the rise of the cotton economy,* the ownership of twenty slaves has been accepted as transforming a farmer into a planter. Given the expanded operation permitted by this number of slaves, and given the considerable capital necessary to acquire them, historians largely agree that owners of twenty or more slaves (12 percent of all slaveholders in 1860) appropriately are termed large slaveholders. In the Cotton Belt, however, where planters abounded, many historians have used fifty as the number of slaves qualifying an individual as a large holder. With these regional differences in mind, and in view of the difficulty in assigning a single number to represent a social group, the range from twenty to fifty seems an acceptable marker.

More important than numbers is the fact that agricultural wealth and its prospects, farming practices, and political power have adhered to large slaveholders since the beginning of the systematic importation of black slave labor. By the eighteenth century, every county in the Chesapeake where slavery was well established had its minority of large owners who almost invariably were those men with the most real property, the highest political office, and the most widespread public reputation. Although the particulars of their slave management and financial arrangements often are unclear at this remove, it is certain that slave ownership was soon the main route to wealth and that the large slaveholder was better equipped than his smaller counterpart to absorb the risks involved in owning men and women. The substantial owner was more likely to secure at least a modest profit* year after year despite demographic fluctuations in his labor force, and he could use his large force as capital as well as labor. Slavery rewarded bigness. It became conventional wisdom by the eighteenth century that a small slaveholder had to struggle to become a large one or be forever at the mercy of the accidents and death that could decimate his few hands.

It was the rise of the cotton empire that rationalized the ownership of large holdings and dispersed them throughout the South. It is also the cotton era that gave final definition to the large slaveholder as planter and as a regional influence on the social life of both races. As slavery moved south and west after 1800, it traced an arc from the Carolinas across Alabama and Mississippi to the river-rich counties of Louisiana. Along this arc clustered the large slaveholders, on whose plantations a significant number of Afro-Americans lived and worked. Throughout the decade of the 1850s, one-half of all slaves in the South lived on plantations of twenty or more. By 1860, in the cotton South, about 60 percent of all slaves lived on holdings of at least twenty, with fully one-third living on units of fifty or more. Such numbers of Afro-Americans in the hands of the large owners take on additional importance in that the percentage of all white families who owned slaves decreased from 36 percent in 1830 to 31 percent in 1850, falling to 25 percent by 1860. At the same time, the planter class increased from 10 percent of all slaveholders in 1850 to 12 percent a decade later. Thus, Afro-American experience under slavery increasingly was shaped by the characteristics of large slaveholdings.

Large slaveholders shared certain ways of organizing production, dividing up what needed to be done, and making the calculations necessary for economic gain. A large cotton-producing operation, sometimes spread over hundreds of acres at different sites, required consistent oversight, shrewd business judgment, and a network of supportive bankers, factors, and shippers as a hedge against the ravages of bad weather or recalcitrant slaves. Successful planters possessed all of these in some measure, and in this sense the large slaveholding was like other business enterprises. But this is not to suggest that most large slaveholdings were run like railroads. To the contrary, contemporary observers, including many nonplanters, frequently remarked upon the large slaveholders' fondness for their land, for their "home place," and for a traditional way of farming that did not always make the best economic sense. Contrasts were often drawn between the steady, time-conscious business class in the North and the more intuitive planter, not by any means to the planter's disadvantage. The large slaveholder frequently was admired for having both machine and garden, profitable business and agrarian ideals.

Most of them also were remarkable for living at home; owners esteemed their personal presence as fundamental to sound agricultural practice. Even the largest planters, on the Carolina-Georgia coast or along the lower Mississippi, generally made it a point to live within riding distance of their holdings. If absenteeism* occurred anywhere, it was in the Old Southwest during the 1820s, and even here a slaveholder who remained back home in Georgia would usually delegate a family member as his representative at the new place in Alabama. In part this was because most planters were compelled to rely on paid overseers* and slave drivers* for daily operations and wanted a trusted observer to keep tabs on them. The overseer on most large units was responsible for organizing workers into either the gang system or the task system. Most large plantations used a combination of both, and owners generally preferred the task system* (where each slave was given a specific job and could set the pace) for specialized work like equipment repair, and the gang system* (where slaves worked in larger, synchronized groups) for basic agricultural work. From the owner's point of view, the task system rewarded an individual slave's initiative, but required careful oversight; the gang system was more easily controlled, but in larger numbers slaves could coordinate work slowdowns and find other ways of thwarting all but the harshest drivers. Most large slaveholders expected about 60 percent of their workers to be "full hands," that is, the equivalents of able-bodied, adult males. But everyone who could worked in the fields, with men comprising the plow gang and women, and children of both sexes, making up the hoe gang.

The other division of labor characteristic of the large slaveholding was that of house servant* and field hand,* a division that on most establishments was not hard and fast. Most large owners, as soon as they were able, did purchase full-time cooks, yardmen, and sometimes skilled craftsmen and general maids. Well-to-do slaveholders might add a "mammy"* and a butler. But on most large plantations, because a work force could plant more than it could harvest, a slave working as a house servant during planting season would always be pressed into fieldwork during harvest time. Discussing such arrangements among themselves, privately and in agricultural journals, large slaveholders debated the different ways to divide a holding of twenty to fifty slaves most efficiently and also most suitably for the comfort of the master and his family. Difficulty with resistant or slow-working slaves was a constant topic, as was the need to appear remote enough to be the unquestioned judge in all matters, but accessible enough to strike some sort of personal bargain with slaves entrusted with crucial tasks. Some contemporaries (and histories) have observed that discipline was more severe on large units. But large or small, slaveholders ultimately disciplined by their own individual standards; personal factors more than the size of the holding accounted for the quality of slave life on a plantation. Certainly slaves themselves did not express any wish to be sold to small owners, the community and anonymity possible on large units perhaps making up for the routinized work and generalized discipline.

In terms of production, the increase in the number of all slaveholdings throughout the antebellum South by the 1820s of course paralleled the growth in European demand for cotton. The nearly ideal climate in the Deep South, along with the fact that the cultivation of cotton was neither technically difficult nor particularly expensive, made the crop profitable for small as well as large growers. Apparently, the yield for each worker (on flat, accessible land, a single slave could be expected to plant six to ten acres) was not significantly greater on large holdings. Indeed, in some instances, close supervision made a smaller farm more efficient, and in general cotton planting did not seem to offer much in the way of economies of scale. However, wealthier landowners tended to own more productive land, and they frequently enjoyed savings by buying in large volume, diversifying their crops, owning their own gins, and having the ability to finance their operation on credit when necessary. Moreover, larger plantations could meet their own needs for food and some equipment while devoting a larger percentage of their acreage to the staple crop. For these reasons, large slaveholders usually realized a higher profit per acre.

But the production of individual units is only one way to gauge the importance of the large slaveholding and its master, and it has been established that while large-scale cotton production certainly made fortunes for individuals, it had more ambiguous consequences for the region's economic and social life as a whole. This raises the issue of the large owner's influence over these circumstances. Some histories underscore the relatively small proportion of large slaveholders to all white Southerners, point out that landownership in most areas of the South increased during the antebellum era, and conclude that large slaveholders have been credited with too much economic influence in the region. More recent studies, however, show that it is slave ownership, not the ownership of land, that is the surest measure of Southern economic power, and that by itself the sheer number of small and nonslaveholders says little about their social situation and political leverage. Moreover, state and regional studies of the cotton South point to increasing concentration of slave ownership in the hands of large owners, especially on the eve of secession, and thus to increasing concentration of farm value and agricultural wealth generally. This shift, in view of the continuing surge in cotton production and the rise in slave prices,* tended to enhance the considerable economic sway of the large slaveholders.

This economic hegemony did not translate into a set formula for exercising authority with respect to less wealthy whites. But from the eighteenth century on, a certain pattern emerged which helped to bind the large owner to the small. First, whether in the Cotton Belt or not, all white farmers enjoyed a racial dominance and a free status which muted the frictions arising from differences in wealth and hubris. Second, mutual interests and even a shared outlook between Cotton Belt slaveholders of whatever size and nonslaveholders consisted of local political loyalties, kinship connections, traditions of patronage and common-use practices, and, not least, a wariness of outsiders. From its origins, slavery fostered real commonalities among all farmers whose reliance on the same crop, credit, cheap land, and racial vigilance set them apart from slaves and Yankees. At the height of slavery, few small farmers reflected on the ways in which the slave system was stunting the region's economy or shaping its social life. Instead, they were more likely to aspire to own more slaves themselves, and to look to the large owners for the political leadership and ideological formulations which the latter increasingly seized by the late 1840s. Even so, the ideology of states' rights and Southern white identity that led rich and poor together into war did not suffice to keep them in alliance after the war was lost and wealth and influence passed into new orbits.

SELECTED BIBLIOGRAPHY

John B. Boles, *Black Southerners, 1619–1869* (1983); Eugene D. Genovese, *Roll, Jordan, Roll: The World The Slaves Made* (1974); Steven Hahn, *The Roots of Southern Populism: Yeoman Farmers and the Transformation of the Georgia Upcounty, 1850–1890* (1983); Edmund S. Morgan, *American Slavery, American Freedom: The Ordeal of Colonial Virginia* (1975); Darrett B. Rutman and Anita H. Rutman, *A Place in Time: Middlesex County, Virginia, 1650–1750* (1984); Kenneth M. Stampp, *The Peculiar Institution: Slavery in the Ante-Bellum South* (1956); Ralph Wooster, *The People in Power: Court-house and Statehouse in the Lower South, 1850–1860* (1969); and Gavin Wright, *The Political Economy of the Cotton South: Households, Markets, and Wealth in the Nine-teenth Century* (1978).

STEVEN STOWE

SLAVEHOLDERS, SMALL. Masters but not planters, farmers but not yeo-men, the small slaveholders occupied a unique and perhaps strategic place in the social structure of the Old South. They owned slaves, and their political and economic interests reflected that much. Yet they were anything but the country gentlemen of Southern mythology. Feeling no instinctive ties to the wealthiest planters, they were more likely to exhibit a cultural affinity with slaveless yeo-men. Indeed, because the class barrier separating small slaveholders from yeomen farmers was so easily and frequently crossed, the two groups are often counted as one. This is a mistake. The political, economic, and historical implications of slave ownership were profound. The most important class lines in the white South were marked not by dollars and cents but by the ownership of specific forms of property and the social relations that each implied. The slaveholders should therefore be distinguished from the yeomen farmers who owned land but not slaves. Furthermore, small slaveholders and yeomen farmers generally lived in different areas of the South, and their lives were shaped by material conditions and historical circumstances that were distinct and often incompatible.

This was a pattern two centuries in the making. Small slaveholdings were a commonplace long before there was a secure and independent yeomanry, in part because slave farms could develop without stable white families while yeomen farms could not. The seventeenth-century Southern colonies were notoriously inhospitable to family life. A grossly unbalanced sex ratio, high infant mortality, and short life expectancy prevented white colonists from establishing economically viable and productive households for nearly a century after the first colonization of Virginia. But slavery and indentured servitude* freed masters from their reliance on the labor of their own families. They made permanent settlement possible long before the white population was able to reproduce itself naturally, long before the number of women equaled the number of men, long before whites lived enough years to organize large and stable families. To prosper in the seventeenth-century Chesapeake, a few servants or slaves were essential.

Even when white family life did stabilize in the eighteenth century, however, slave ownership was still necessary for the economic security of most white families at the time. As the slave economy expanded westward onto the piedmont plateau, for example, the proportion of squatters and slaveless farmers declined substantially. Some became slaveholders; others simply moved farther west. But slaveless farms were in the minority wherever slavery flourished. By the time settlement of an area was complete, between two-thirds and three-fourths of all farms were likely to have slaves. One reason for this was that slavery raised land values beyond the means of slaveless newcomers. In addition, slavery altered the social division of labor within the white community, reducing the number of artisans and craftsmen upon whom slaveless farmers depended. An independent, non–slave-owning yeomanry did not really emerge until the late eighteenth century, when western settlement reached mountainous areas too distant from the market to sustain profitable staple agriculture. From the seventeenth century onward, therefore, the ownership of a few slaves was apparently necessary for farmers who lived and worked in those areas most amenable to market-oriented agriculture. This pattern persisted in the Black Belt during the nineteenth century, where as many as 70 percent of the farms had slaves, but where the vast majority of slave farms were not plantations.

In their rights as masters, their ties to the market, and the ways they organized family life, small slaveholders often shared more with planters than they did with yeomen. However much their political and cultural sympathies distinguished them from the planters, small slaveholders could not escape the fact that their lives were significantly altered by their ownership of slaves. Slave ownership vested in every master a vast and terrible body of legal rights—the right to sell a human being, to sit in judgment of his or her "crimes," to break up a family, to brutalize a man or woman without fear of legal recrimination, to extract labor by force, to control and restrict the slave's ability to learn, to travel, to marry, and even to live. These rights were activated with the ownership of one slave; wealthy planters had no more of them than did small slaveholders.

Small or large, every slaveholder was a petty tyrant. This was not because masters consistently mistreated their slaves but because of the intrinsic inconsistency that followed from the master's virtually unchecked authority. By 1860 there were nearly 400,000 minor despotisms scattered across the South, but only a small proportion were ruled by large planters. On any one of them the clash of personalities between master and slave set the tone of daily life. But we do not yet know enough about slave culture* on small farms to make firm generalizations. Close supervision or an intimate working relationship with the owner of one or two slaves could make life miserable or even pleasant. A small master, like a large planter, could be an amiable partner or a violent drunkard.

The brutality of uncertainty stemmed from the distinctive nature of the master-slave relationship.* Small masters and large planters shared the difficult problem of motivating a work force that had little incentive other than the constant threat of violence to produce beyond the level necessary for subsistence. Slavery lacked the motivating force of the wage, the volition of the marriage vow, and the implicit promise of future independence that guided parent-child relations in free society. In this sense all slaveholders formed a single class, sharing a similar relationship to the means of production, unified by material interests that differed from, and sometimes clashed with, those of the slaveless yeomen as well as the slaves.

Slavery affected the way husbands, wives, and children lived with each other in the white household. Slaveless farmers relied extensively on the labor of their own families. They divided up work in clear patterns based on age and gender, and these patterns changed over time as the family grew and matured. The ownership of only a few slaves, perhaps even one, could subtly but profoundly alter these patterns. With slave labor readily available, the master's children could be sent to school more easily, and his wife could be relieved of some of her most difficult chores. As the children reached adulthood, slave labor could make it easier for parents to subsist and prosper without the help of their own offspring. Bound labor often replaced child labor in the life cycle of the slave-holding family,

Finally, slave ownership changed the way a master participated in the market economy. Even one slave cost a great deal of money to purchase and maintain. To own a slave was to be subject to periodic mortgage payments and yearly taxes that no slaveless farmer had to meet. Since slaveholders monopolized the most productive soils, even the taxes on their lands were higher than those of yeomen farmers. Black Belt communities often lacked a local class of artisans and craftsmen to provide essential goods to small slaveholders, while superior transportation facilities made it easier to purchase those goods from distant manufacturers. Thus, slaveholders needed more cash and were more dependent on merchants and creditors than were yeomen farmers. They were less able to fall back on subsistence farming during hard times. But economic insecurity was not necessarily unprofitable. The average slave produced at least twice as much as was necessary for his or her subsistence, making slave ownership a source of considerable profit* to masters for as long as the market in staples remained vibrant.

Despite cultural affinities, fluidity across class lines, and life-cycle patterns that drew small farmers into the slaveholding class, significant distinctions sep-arated masters from yeomen. But this does not mean that all slaveholders were identical. On the contrary, important cultural and political distinctions separated small slaveholders from wealthy planters. While half of all slaves lived on farms with twenty or more bondsmen, half of all masters owned five slaves or fewer. The typical master did not own the typical slave. Yet because there were so many small slaveholders, the master class included anywhere from one-quarter to one-half of all Southern white families. The sheer number of small slaveholders significantly altered the balance of social and political power in Southern white society. If the slaveholders were able to exercise disproportionate influence in a political system where all white men could vote, it was in part because so many white men were slaveholders.

Small slaveholders reflected both the diversity and homogeneity of Southern white society itself. They were often deeply religious, and were attracted to the same evangelical tradition that successfully incorporated slaves, women, and wealthy planters alike. Nine out of ten slaveholders were men. But included among them were the descendants of German, Scottish, French, and Spanish immigrants. Native Americans, Mexicans, and even free blacks* owned slaves— and only rarely in large numbers. Small slaveholders worked primarily as farmers, but they included a disproportionate number of Southern artisans, shopkeepers, and bureaucrats.

Small slaveholders were more likely to move west than were large planters. Indeed, demographic instability is a common theme in their biographies. Similarly, small masters were uniquely subject to the fluctuations of the staple economy, for while slave ownership tied them inextricably to the market, they lacked the wealth and resources to withstand the pressures of economic dislocation. Over the course of a typical small slaveholder's career, it may have been more common than not to move into and out of the master class.

Generalizing from their own historical circumstances, small slaveholders developed a quintessentially liberal ideology of social consensus, competitive individualism, and political pluralism. They never translated economic and demographic instability into the kind of anti-capitalist ideology that sometimes informed the politics of radical yeomen and artisans in nineteenth-century America. Nor were they noticeably impressed by the reactionary philippics that passed for intellectual discourse in some parts of the South. Instead, the slaveholders responded to the implicit and explicit threats emanating from the up-country, the low country, the slave quarters, and the North, by espousing principles drawn largely from the experience of the typical master. They consistently capitalized on the very instability that marked the life of the small slaveholders. Where economic and demographic instability disrupted the lives of thousands of families, slaveholding politicians boasted of the social fluidity that presumably gave every hardworking Southerner the chance to rise up the ladder of success. In the absence of aristocratic class barriers, the wealth of slavery was pronounced open to all who would pursue it.

Racism* became an essential element in the slaveholders' ideology precisely because it was the only politically acceptable justification for the social hierarchy. The preponderance of small slaveholders weakened the possibility of a broad-based antislavery movement within the South, while the presence of a politically active yeomanry prevented slaveholding politicians from retreating into a reactionary defense of Southern society. The slaveholders therefore sealed their call for social consensus by appealing to the racial solidarity of all white men.

But their very cries for unity exposed the sharp divisions that marked Southern society, divisions uniquely embodied in the conflicting impulses of the small slaveholders. They lacked the wealth that brought entrance into planter circles, yet they are best understood as members of a single slave-owning class. This dualism helps explain the nature and limits of planter power. Had the slaveholding class been limited to a tiny handful of reactionary planters, had those planters been able to capture and retain control of the machinery of Southern politics, a purely aristocratic defense of the status quo might have prevailed. But the slaveholding class was too large and small holdings too much the rule for that to happen. Small slaveholders often shared with the yeomanry a political heritage that pitted them against the conservatives, and *herrenvolk* democracy gave power to their numbers. The planters who did hold public office in the antebellum South therefore expressed the class interests of the slaveholders, the democratic inclinations of small farmers, and the racist ideology that held them together. In short, Southern politics revealed the significance of the small slaveholders.

SELECTED BIBLIOGRAPHY

Allan Kulikoff, *Tobacco and Slaves: The Development of Southern Cultures in the Chesapeake, 1680–1800* (1986); James Oakes, *The Ruling Race: A History of American Slaveholders* (1982); Kenneth M. Stampp, *The Peculiar Institution: Slavery in the Ante-Bellum South* (1956); J. Mills Thornton III, *Politics and Power in a Slave Society: Alabama, 1800–1860* (1978); and Gavin Wright, *The Political Economy of the Cotton South: Households, Markets, and Wealth in the Nineteenth Century* (1978).

JAMES OAKES

SLAVE TRADE, ATLANTIC. Colonial North America figured in the transatlantic slave trade late in the trade's history. Portuguese pioneers inaugurated the trade in the early sixteenth century, at first concentrating on South America and enjoying a virtual monopoly for a century or so. The Caribbean in time became a major market, supplied by Dutch, French, and English traders. North America never became a major market in the trade's history, nor did North American traders ever have a share amounting to more than one-fifth of the carrying trade. Even so, the trade profoundly shaped the demographic,* social, economic, and ethnic development of the United States.

Not until the 1730s did North America significantly import black laborers. The spread of staple agriculture, the problems of getting and keeping white labor, and a sharpening entrepreneurial spirit among British and colonial American merchants contributed to the shift from white to black workers. The years from 1730 to the outbreak of the American Revolution* saw a surge of imports, followed by a complete cessation during the war, and succeeded by heavy importation in the last years of the legal trade. The North American share of the total transatlantic slave importation appears to have been only about 6 percent. It is a striking fact that though black slave labor is often associated with cotton* cultivation, the bulk of the importation occurred well before the invention of the cotton gin,* with its encouragement of cotton growing. And the legal ban on importation occurred fourteen years after Eli Whitney invented his famous gin.

The chronological pattern, together with estimates of the volume of imports, is illustrated in Table 1.

Contrary to the widely publicized view that nearly all slaves came to the North American mainland from the Caribbean, the mass in fact came directly from Africa. For most of the slaves there was no "seasoning"* in the West Indies, no second uprooting and passage from the islands to the mainland. Numerous slaves entering the Middle colonies, and the first slaves imported to South Carolina, were brought from the West Indies. But from the late seventeenth century on most slaves arrived in North America directly from Africa, bringing their native culture with them. Purchasers often preferred Africans directly imported, believing the West Indies rid themselves of undesirables by selling them to the mainland. Negro duty laws enacted by the colonies favored African-born blacks by placing higher duties on imports from elsewhere.

It was, then, not the West Indies but West Africa that provided the primary source for the black migration. The littoral stretching from the Senegal River to southern Angola furnished most of the slaves. Perhaps one-fourth of the whole had lived in Angola, and a smaller proportion in the Bight of Biafra region. The Gold Coast, Senegambia, the Windward Coast, Sierra Leone, the Bight of Benin, and Mozambique-Madagascar—roughly in descending order—were homelands of most black migrants. Export-import records were very imperfect, often stating only "Africa" or "Guinea" as a ship's point of departure. One therefore must consider the matter of African origins with caution.

Though knowledge of African culture and geography was hazy, buyers displayed marked ethnic preferences in purchasing slaves. Broadly speaking buyers preferred slaves from the Windward and Gold Coasts and with less favor accepted laborers from other regions. Colonies varied in their preferences, particularly in the heavy-importing South. South Carolinians preferred slaves from Gambia, the Windward Coast, and Angola, and distrusted those from Calabar, who were thought to have a suicidal tendency, and from the Bight of Biafra. Describing a prospective importation, the Charleston slave merchant Henry Laurens wrote, "There must not be a Callabar amongst them. Gold Coast or Gambia's are best, next to them the Windward Coast are prefer'd to Angola's." In the Chesapeake region buyers preferred Gold Coast and Windward Coast blacks, accepted those from the Bight of Biafra, and disfavored those from Angola. Northern purchasers were less distinct in their preferences.

Slaves in Africa were procured by black merchants for sale to white buyers. Contrary to popular belief, as much as half of the slaves were not kidnapped, but rather captured in war. Conviction of crime, indebtedness, preexisting servitude or dependency accounted for another large proportion. Victims of kid-

Table 1
African Slave Imports into British North America and the United States,
Including Louisiana

1620–1700[1]		20,500
1701–1760[2]		188,600
1761–1770[3]		62,668
1771–1780[3]		14,902
1771–1790[3]		55,750
1791–1800[3]		79,041
1801–1810[4]		114,090
1761–1810[2]	Louisiana imports	10,200
1810–1870		51,000
Total		596,751

Sources:
1. Robert W. Fogel and Stanley L. Engerman, *Time on the Cross* (2 vols., 1974), 2:30.
2. Philip D. Curtin, *The Atlantic Slave Trade: A Census* (1969), 216.
3. Roger Anstey, "The Volume of the North-American Slave-Carrying Trade from Africa, 1761–1810," *Revue française d'histoire d'outre-mer*, 62 (1975), 63 n.75, revised by letter from Stanley L. Engerman to James A. Rawley, 26 September 1983, correcting Anstey's figures for 1801–1810.
4. Letter from Engerman to Rawley, 26 September 1983.

napping formed a small fraction of the whole. Black traders operated in diverse ways, sometimes having extended networks into the interior, sometimes using wares supplied by a white trader. Frequently, they left someone as a pawn or guarantee of return.

Although antebellum Southern defenders of slavery violently accused New Englanders of having been culpable of bringing blacks to the United States, by far the largest number of slaves—well over two-thirds—were sold by English traders. In the eighteenth century, England became the foremost slaving nation in the Atlantic world. From three of its ports—Liverpool, Bristol, and London—vessels ventured to Africa to buy slaves for sale in the Americas, of which North America was but a part. Enjoying a flourishing commerce with continental Europe and India, leading the world in industrialization, manning a large mercantile fleet and navy, and possessing a vast empire, England had great advantages over her rivals. It established trading posts in Africa, especially at Gambia and along the lower Guinea coast, where Cape Coast Castle ranked as one of the most substantial trading stations in Africa. Where the shore afforded few or dangerous harbors, English traders conducted their business from ships, sending boats or receiving Africans in canoes as a means of making exchanges.

To trade for slaves England exported great quantities of goods both of her own manufacture and of foreign origin. Cloth, including domestic woolens and Continental and Indian fabrics, was a major export. Colorful and cool, Indian cloths were highly favored by Africans. Metal wares, bars of iron, beads, spirits, and guns filled the holds of ships sailing from English ports.

American traders, lacking the commercial advantages of their English brethren, plied a different kind of trade. In the colonial era Americans of course had access to English trading posts. But in the period of independence the United States never established its own posts in Africa. And as a result, Americans continued to trade at English posts. Rum was the chief commodity Americans had to offer for slaves. So strong in proof that it had to be watered down, American rum was preferred above English rum for its strength and taste. Perhaps three quarters of the cargo valuations sent out from Rhode Island consisted of rum. Distilled from molasses obtained in the West Indies, rum formed a part of the notorious triangle trade. Though rum was indispensable to the American slave trade, modern research has shown that the triangular trade was not a mainstay of colonial commerce. Nor was the slave trade the major outlet for molasses. Housewives, using molasses for cooking, and householders making molasses beer for home consumption consumed far greater amounts of molasses.

The American trade differed from the British in other particulars as well. Americans tended to restrict their trading to certain areas in Africa, such as Senegambia, Sierra Leone, and the Gold Coast. Moreover, American ships had a smaller carrying capacity than British. A study of British and American vessels in the Gold Coast trade between 1755 and 1775 reveals a stark difference: British vessels averaged 273 slaves, American vessels 124 slaves. In these years 167 British vessels carried 45,593 slaves; 126 American vessels carried 15,565.

About 43 percent of the ships, then, transported only about 25 percent of the total.

Legend to the contrary, Massachusetts played only a small part in the American carrying trade. The center of the American enterprise was Rhode Island, too tiny to prosper in agriculture, but possessing a magnificent bay and a seafaring spirit. Nearly one thousand voyages to Africa can be documented as originating from Rhode Island, transporting in a period of a century over 100,000 Africans to the New World. The Rhode Island trade began in a very small way, rising in volume in the middle of the eighteenth century, ceasing during the American Revolution when Newport was occupied by the British. Its impact towered to a mighty pitch in the last fifteen years of the legal trade when nearly two-fifths of the whole were carried.

In the Middle colonies, New Yorkers actively plied the trade and a few Quakers* in Pennsylvania took part as well. Even though the Southern colonies and states were the great consumers of slaves, few Southern vessels were employed in the Atlantic slave trade. Only South Carolina sent substantial numbers of ships to Africa in quest of slave labor.

The long ocean voyage from Africa to America—the Middle Passage—is a stereotype of horror in the history of the Atlantic slave trade. The stereotype is marked by almost unexampled inhumanity—overcrowding of vessels, brutality of treatment, inadequate food and water, neglect of hygiene and medical care, and enormous mortality. Created by abolitionists,* the stereotype has elements of truth in it. At the same time modern scholarship has offered a different perspective.

To be sure, mortality was high on the slave ships, but death was often attributable to factors other than human callousness. Today's scholars stress the condition of slaves when they arrived at the port of embarkation and discern a relationship between health on departure and death on the crossing. Slaves brought from a long distance and in poor health before embarkation tended to have a higher death rate than others. In 1749–1751 the *Wolf*, owned by Philip Livingston and Sons of New York, bought 135 slaves in Africa. Of this cargo, 60 died or were sold before departure and 2 died during the crossing. The length of crossings also figured in the death rate: slaves carried on long or unexpectedly slow voyages suffered a high death rate. Arrival in America during winter weather could further add to losses. There were other factors as well: variations in ports, periods of time, and national patterns of the carriers. In general, losses dropped with the advance of the eighteenth century and appear to have risen in the period of illegal trade.

Dysentery, "fevers," measles, smallpox, and scurvy ranked among the leading killer diseases. Tropical medicine was of little efficacy in dealing with dysentery or the diseases* vaguely described as "fevers," or measles. The *Wolf*'s surgeon recorded his helplessness in treating an epidemic of measles. "There is scarce a day now passes without my being in the utmost anxiety." Occasionally surgeons treated smallpox with inoculation and scurvy with antiscorbutics. By the end of the eighteenth century the prevention of both diseases was substantially improved. Although British slavers often carried a ship's surgeon, the *Wolf* proved to be an exception. Ships' surgeons, always of varying quality, were induced to take good care of slaves by payment by the number of Africans they delivered in America in good health. Surgeons' duties included examining prospective purchases in Africa, treating slaves on shipboard, and preparing slaves for sale in America.

The notorious Middle Passage began with traumatic events in Africa: capture, sale, and incarceration in a pen or on shipboard. Olaudah Equiano,* chained with others on a slave ship, saw a large copper pot boiling and was convinced he and his fellows were to be eaten. "Overpowered with horror and anguish, I fell motionless on the deck and fainted," he wrote in his autobiography in 1789. Life on shipboard was routine, a monotony of confinement relieved by daily exercise and twice daily feeding. Male slaves usually were shackled on coming aboard, manacled together in pairs, left leg to right leg, left wrist to right wrist. The continuing use of shackles after departure from Africa depended upon the disposition of the captain. Usually shackles were removed for the daily exercises, sometimes all day, and sometimes until American shores were sighted.

Slaves customarily ate in groups of ten, clustered about a tub holding their food, each person equipped with a wooden spoon. English vessels offered horse beans boiled in lard as a staple of slave diet. Such fare was supplemented by rice carried from Europe or purchased in Africa along the Windward Coast. Meat was uncommon. Slaves from the Bight often were fed yams. North American slavers offered corn fried into cakes, boiled rice, and black-eyed peas. Water was the standard beverage. Wine, spirits, and tobacco were administered for medicinal purposes.

Torn from their homes, held in cramped quarters, lorded over by white-skinned masters, driven by anxiety and fear, slaves sometimes took their own lives by jumping overboard, preferring a watery death to the dread uncertainties of the future. Others rose in revolt, though in the American trade this occurred with less frequency than might be supposed. According to Jay Coughtry, in the Rhode Island trade only seventeen revolts occurred from 1730 to 1845, or one every four and one-half years. The incidence in the British trade was one about every other year.

Mortality losses have been exaggerated by abolitionists and popularizers. A close study of British losses in the period 1761 to 1791 by Roger Anstey found a figure ranging from 8.5 percent to 9.6 percent and dropping to 4 percent in the last ten years of the lawful trade. Whereas the abolitionist T. F. Buxton had imputed a loss of 17 percent in 1792, Anstey cut the figure to 8.4 percent. Varying from region to region in Africa, British losses in the years 1760–1807 appear to have been smaller than those of other nations. Figures for the trade conducted from North America are fragmentary, but a record of one hundred voyages made from 1752–1807 indicated a loss of 12 percent. The higher figure for North America may be attributable to the tendency to ply the ship rather than the faster shore trade and to slave in the distant regions of the lower Guinea Coast—factors making for long and often deadly incarceration on shipboard.

Present-day scholarship emphasizes epidemiology in explaining mortality in the slave trade. Changes in disease environments account for the high incidence of death among whites as well as blacks involved in the slave trade. Africa was "the white man's grave," conclude modern scholars, and a greater proportion of crewmen died than did slaves. The use of slave labor in tropical climates was promoted by the greater immunity of blacks than whites to common tropical diseases. Even so, blacks in considerable numbers fell victims to yellow fever and malaria in the New World.

Scholars no longer stress "tight packing" as an explanation of heavy slave mortality. A diagram of the huge slaver *Brookes*, depicting slaves packed like spoons in a drawer, was exploited by abolitionists to propagandize the horrors of the Middle Passage. Few ships were guilty of overcrowding in this manner, and many sailed from Africa with less than a full cargo. Recent studies have discounted any relationship between crowding and mortality. Time at sea, length of voyage, African region (the Bights of Benin and Biafra being particularly lethal), and duration of stay in embarkation port more accurately account for mortality.

By the end of the legal slaving era, significant changes had occurred that lessened mortality in the trade. Improvements in ship design created vessels made expressly for the trade. The use of copper sheathing quickened the voyage. Greater knowledge of tropical medicine, increasing use of ships' doctors, and better hygiene practices reduced the toll. Accumulation of experience in slaving played a part, as did the realization that slaves were a valuable and perishable commodity whose health was worth preserving.

In all some 600,000 slaves were imported into the present-day United States, representing a substantially higher figure than some previous estimates. This vast involuntary migration had a chronological as well as a geographical pattern. Few slaves were imported in the seventeenth century. The numerous Anglo-French wars of empire suspended trading. Heavy importation characterized less than three quarters of a century of American history. And almost one-third of the importation occurred in the last two decades of the lawful trade.

It was the staple-growing colonies that received the bulk of the imports. The special labor needs of the tobacco,* rice,* indigo,* and cotton growers account for this phenomenon. Each of these crops required many manual tasks performed over an extended growing season in a warm climate that entailed minimal expense for shelter and clothing. With the growth of plantation agriculture economics of scale was realized by ownership of labor.

The foremost slave-importing area of North America was the region from the Chesapeake to the Savannah River. By 1780 four states held 85 percent of all mainland slaves. Virginia, the first colony as well as the first to import blacks, with 220,582 had the largest slave population. South Carolina, with 97,000 slaves, came second. So dependent was South Carolina upon slave labor for the cultivation of rice and indigo that from early in the century it had a black majority. North Carolina, with 91,000, stood third, and Maryland, with 80,515, ranked fourth. Before the invention of the cotton gin, tobacco growing more than any other activity absorbed the energies of slaves. The fifth largest black population, astonishingly, was in New York, whose metropolis was a thriving center of the external slave trade and whose hinterland employed large numbers of slaves in agriculture, domestic service, and as artisans. Although Georgia had prohibited slavery until 1750, a change in policy and the spread of staple agriculture encouraged substantial importation. These factors fostered a fourfold increase in the black population there between 1780 and 1810.

Not the foreign slave trade alone but a phenomenal rate of natural increase accounts for the large growth in numbers of slaves. Virginia, which had virtually stopped importing slaves by 1780, saw an increase in numbers of blacks to a figure of 306,000 by 1810. By that date the seaboard slave states were supplying the Southern frontier with their surplus slaves.

Newport, Rhode Island, ranked as the major slaving port in North America. Here the Vernon brothers, Samuel and William, were among the most considerable traders, dispatching at least twenty-one slave voyages between 1754 and 1774. Owning their ships, lading them with rum, the Vernons favored the Gold Coast, particularly Anamabo, as the source of their cargoes. Within a few years after embarking upon the business they turned from dependence upon the West Indies as a market and developed a trade in Virginia and South Carolina. Though their business was suspended during the American Revolution, William returned to the trade as merchant, shipowner, and insurer, continuing well until the end of the century.

At Bristol, Rhode Island, the De Wolf family, numbering seven persons, were the most active merchants in the American trade in the years 1784–1807. Involved in eighty-five voyages, they alone accounted for one quarter of Rhode Island's participation in the slave trade of these years. One member, James, was involved in no less than thirty-one ventures, his vessels contributing heavily to the surge in importations in Charleston.

Henry Laurens, slave merchant, diplomat, and politician, figured significantly in South Carolina's slave trade. Laurens did not maintain his own ships but served as an agent, acting largely for English slave shippers. In this capacity he carried on a wide correspondence with shippers in London, Bristol, and Liverpool as well as with other agents in the Caribbean. Laurens greatly benefited from the mid-century boom in indigo production, and for a decade beginning in 1761 he and his partners handled many consignments. Early in his career he remitted the proceeds of his sales in rice and indigo, but by the 1750s, when bills of exchange became abundant, Laurens paid almost entirely in bills. While a commissioner at the Paris peace negotiations in 1782, Laurens confronted his "worthy friend," Richard Oswald, a London slave merchant for whom he had been an agent. Laurens succeeded in stipulating in the treaty "that the British troops should carry off no negroes or other American property." Though Laurens had earlier abandoned the slave trade, he later lamented that in doing so "I have given up many Thousands of pounds."

In spite of Laurens's remark, the slave trade appears to have been less profitable than popular writers have supposed. To be sure, some merchants became wealthy—the Vernons, the De Wolfs, Laurens, and others. But the trade was speculative, replete with hazards including mortality, weather, revolt, and adverse markets. "It is a lottery," exclaimed William Wilberforce, the British abolitionist. The best estimate of profits in the British trade from 1761 to 1810 is that profits averaged less than 10 percent of invested capital. Data to justify an estimate of the American trade's profitability have not yet been produced.

The suppression of the trade began as early as the revolutionary era. In 1776 the Continental Congress voted "That slaves not be imported into any of the thirteen United Colonies." State after state prohibited further importation. And although an attempt to nationalize prohibition in the Constitutional Convention failed, it was agreed the new government could not abolish the trade before 1808. Though there was a rush to import Africans in the last years, Congress with minor resistance, in contrast to the great parliamentary struggle in Britain and to the later congressional struggle over domestic slavery, prohibited the further importation of slaves in the United States after 1 January 1808.

SELECTED BIBLIOGRAPHY

Roger T. Anstey, "The Volume of the North American Slave-Carrying Trade from Africa, 1761–1810," *Revue Française d'Histoire d'Outre-Mer*, 62 (1975), 47–66; Jay Coughtry, *The Notorious Triangle: Rhode Island and the African Slave Trade, 1700–1807* (1981); Philip D. Curtin, *The Atlantic Slave Trade: A Census* (1969); Tommy Todd Hamm, "The American Slave Trade with Africa, 1620–1807" (Ph.D. dissertation, Indiana University, 1975); James A. Rawley, *The Transatlantic Slave Trade: A History* (1981); and Darold D. Wax, "A Philadelphia Surgeon on a Slaving Voyage to Africa, 1749–1751," *Pennsylvania Magazine of History and Biography*, 92 (1968), 465–493.

JAMES A. RAWLEY

SLAVE TRADE, DOMESTIC. The domestic slave trade developed as one of the most unsavory features of slavery in the antebellum South. During the first fifty years of the nineteenth century a substantial growth in the interstate slave trade occurred. This expansion was triggered largely by an increasing surplus of slaves in the upper South and a corresponding shortage of slaves in the newly settled areas of the Old Southwest. Once the trade had begun, it engendered not only a forced migration of a large number of people, but it also served indirectly to bring on the American Civil War.

Although slavery was a basic feature of eighteenth-century American society, professional slave traders handling the transfer and sale of slaves within the American colonies, and later the states, were not necessary because individual owners usually bought and sold their slaves directly. By 1802, however, the professional interstate slave trader's day had begun. Trading depots sprang up in border cities like Washington in the early nineteenth century to serve a small interstate trade. This new trade largely resulted from a shift (in the Chesapeake area in particular) away from tobacco* farming to wheat* cultivation. Since fewer slaves were needed in producing the latter crop, Maryland and Virginia planters now had excess hands whom they were willing to sell. In 1808 the new law ending the legal importation of slaves further benefited the position of the interstate traders by cutting off the foreign supply of slaves and thus making the domestic supply that much more important. In contrast, the War of 1812* served to dampen the trade. Following the conclusion of that war in 1815, the trade grew dramatically and continued with moderate fluctuations until the Civil War. The chief impetus for growth was the increasing demand for forced labor in the expanding cotton and sugar plantations of the Old Southwest.

Traders considered the four decades prior to the Civil War as their golden age. In terms of the numbers of slaves sold, the most important decade was the 1830s, followed by the 1820s, the 1850s, and finally the 1840s. A number of forces contributed to the erratic flow of slave sales, including fluctuations in the prices of goods produced by slave labor, such as cotton or tobacco; general economic depression; soil exhaustion and new concepts in scientific farming, especially in the upper South; and changing attitudes toward slavery and the interstate trade. Growing concern about the trade, reinforced by the pressures from the antislavery societies during the 1830s and 1840s, caused many owners in the border states to reconsider the merits of dealing with traders.

In the so-called golden age of trading, two groups of people emerged to dominate the interstate trade. They were the professional traders and the Southern planters who traveled through the upper South seeking chattels for their own use. The latter were pushed out of the trade by the early 1830s, but the patterns of operation for both groups were similar. The traders typically established themselves in large-sized and well-located cities and often hired part-time assistants to scour the countryside in search of slaves. Most traders advertised in the local newspapers. The ads frequently ran for months at a time, and occasionally several traders competed simultaneously. They generated a sense of optimism by offering to pay the highest prices possible for slaves. As occasional ads indicated, a single trader sought as many as 5,000 slaves in a single season. But aside from suggesting that a healthy market did exist, the ads revealed little about the realities of the trade.

Slave traders generally bought slaves individually or in small groups, often as a family. While some traders attempted to keep families together, this practice was not common. Major purchases, of thirty slaves or more for example, were infrequent and usually occurred when estates were being settled. Slave traders preferred to deal with young, marketable slaves ranging from ten to twenty-five years of age. Although male slaves purchased by traders were mostly in their twenties, the age of female slaves was more evenly distributed. In numbers, the males predominated by a 25-percent margin. This ratio was brought back into balance by a more even distribution of sexes in the shipments of the nontraders. Nevertheless, the practice created an excess number of female slaves in some parts of the upper South. Whether or not this practice was deliberate on the part of the local slave owners cannot be determined. If deliberate, the retention of the child-bearing element, the female slaves, might lend credence and statistical evidence to the charge of slave breeding.*

While Southern planters bought their charges after the harvest season, usually from October to May, the professional traders made their purchases the year round. Slave auctions served as convenient meeting places for buyers and sellers. In the border states regular auctions were held in such cities as Memphis, Louisville, Richmond, and Easton (in Maryland). There the trader competed with local buyers as well as other traders for the slaves. Travelers and curiosity seekers were also on hand, and, indeed, much of the graphic description of the slave sales came from the witnesses who attended these spectacles.

Once the slaves had been shipped to their destination, a second auction usually awaited them in such places as Natchez or New Orleans, the latter city having become the prime trading center of the Deep South. There records of all transactions were meticulously kept and preserved. These provide much of the data available in evaluating the financial costs of the trade.

The auction prices* of slaves depended on the slaves' value. Skilled craftsmen, for example, sold for twice as much money as ordinary field hands, but for only half as much as "fancy girls." Again, New Orleans enjoyed a reputation as a good market for such "choice stock," although the sales of women for this purpose, both public and private, occurred elsewhere as well.

Maintenance and shipment were important features of the slave trade. Slaves awaiting shipment were kept in jail spaces or in specially built pens until sufficient numbers were available for the move southward or westward. Major traders generally sent their cargoes by water, with New Orleans the chief destination. Some of the smaller traders and most of the planters preferred the overland routes and such smaller ports as Charleston, Savannah, and Mobile. By land, coffles marched westward to river ports on tributaries of the Mississippi and by steamboat to New Orleans, or they might move directly south by land to cities like Natchez. The water route was safer and more convenient. Groups numbering from 100 to 150 slaves were dispatched, often with the last space filled by slaves of the small traders.

The source of slaves in the auctions and in the private market came from several types of owners. Some slave owners entered the trade because they had surplus chattels or they found slavery no longer economically viable. Others deliberately sought a large profit in the interstate trade. Still others, as executors of wills, found the Southern market a convenient means of disposing of chattel property in settling an estate. Yet, for all those who were ready to sell, there were many who showed great hesitation. Hiring* a slave out on an annual basis or granting a slave his freedom was often a preferred alternative to selling him southward, particularly in the border states. Many who did sell slaves often stipulated that the slave could not be removed from the state. Under these circumstances the volume of interstate activity was somewhat reduced.

Such limitations naturally had an effect on the traders and their profits. The rather sharp price differentials that existed between the border states and the lower South suggested that money could be made in trading slaves. By the 1820s, for example, a slave who brought $350 in the Virginia market could be sold for $500 in New Orleans. By 1860 the comparative prices had moved to $1,100 and $1,500, respectively. With such margins for possible gains, the business of trading was considered to be a lucrative one, and a number of figures, such as William Williams and Isaac Franklin, both of Virginia, reportedly made fortunes in the business.

Although great success may have been true for a few, it was not the case for most traders. High overhead costs and many serious hazards in slave trading made the business somewhat precarious. Operating expenses included such items as sustenance for slaves awaiting shipment, local transportation charges, advertising and legal fees, commissions for local and New Orleans agents, losses due to illness or runaways, shipping costs southward, and implicit interest on money tied up in slaves until those slaves were sold. Such costs might be as much as $170 per slave, quite a large sum but not an uncommon one. If a trader cleared an average of $200 per slave, which was about normal for the best years of the 1820s, his real profit, after subtracting overhead costs, was only about $30 per slave. Because of the short-term operations of the small traders and their inability to control the major phases of the business, their endeavors probably led to limited profits. The major traders fared better, and nineteenth-century observers concluded that profits for the major traders ranged as high as 30 percent of the capital invested. Thus traders supposedly cleared somewhere between $15 and $60 per slave sold. The profits of Maryland's biggest trader, Austin Woolfolk, approached this latter figure, for he made perhaps $4,000 a year in the 1820s and 1830s, and approximately $50,000 for his entire trading career. Considering the amount of risk and the stigma attached to the business, such a modest degree of success is really not that impressive.

The price in terms of a trader's loss of reputation is harder to determine. In the eyes of articulate Southerners as well as critical antislavery Northerners, the trader was a hard-hearted "Southern Shylock" who performed a distasteful but economically important task for society. In general, those involved in slave-mongering were accepted only with reluctance throughout most of the South. Aristocratic polite society naturally shunned them. Businessmen and yeomen farmers were more ambivalent. A jury in Baltimore in 1829, for example, had little difficulty in finding the trader Austin Woolfolk guilty of assault in striking a citizen who had called him a wolf in sheep's clothing, but the jury also refused to award damages of more than one dollar. Interestingly, the same trader and his Virginia rival, Isaac Franklin, would be remembered by others for their "kindliness" and their "engaging and graceful manners."

Once a trader had established himself, it was typical, especially if he was a large trader, to dominate his geographic region for a number of years. The leading figure in Maryland and northern Virginia in the 1820s and early 1830s was Austin Woolfolk. He was succeeded by Hope Slatter and Joseph Donovan in the late 1830s and 1840s and then by John Denning and finally Bernard Campbell in the 1850s. Virginia's major traders were Isaac Franklin and John Armfield who created the famous firm of Franklin and Armfield, which in its heyday in the 1830s became the biggest trading firm of the antebellum South. By the 1840s they in turn were succeeded in that area by George Kephart, whose operations by contrast were much smaller. The chief traders in Kentucky and in South Carolina were Tarlton Arterburn and Norman Gadsden, respectively.

Whatever economic success the traders enjoyed was more than counterbalanced by the traumatic social upheaval that the slaves themselves experienced as a result of the interstate trade. The trade attacked the slaves' family unity.* As a consequence, slaves often reacted strongly to the threat or possibility of being sold south. In fact, the greatest temptation to run away usually occurred when a slave sensed that he was about to be sold. Furthermore, the fear of being sold was such that masters often used the threat of such a sale as a means of discipline. Because shipment southward usually meant a family parting that would be permanent, many slaves found it hard to bear the thought of separation, and there were a number of instances when a family member (usually a husband or a wife already free) would accompany or follow a spouse on the solemn journey southward. Nevertheless, accounts of travelers in the early 1830s who had visited slave pens to observe those awaiting shipment suggest that probably a large majority had quietly resigned themselves to their fate and that their spirits, outwardly at least, had not been wholly dampened by their plight. To what extent this picture reflected reality and to what extent this sense of resignation changed as the years passed to 1860 would be difficult to say. Evidence does suggest, however, that in border states like Maryland the slaves themselves were coming to believe that the condition of slavery, including the threat of sale southward, had grown less severe and that alternatives like freedom through African colonization* had clearly lost their former appeal.

Although it had always been known that the interstate trade was fairly extensive, it has been only since the 1970s that efforts have been made to quantify the exact level of trading activity. Historians writing in the 1920s noted that, according to the decennial census figures, the upper South had been losing sizable numbers of slaves and the Deep South had been gaining them. They attributed this shift in slave population to the interstate trade. Such deductive reasoning, however, has not withstood modern criticism. By a careful examination of statistical evidence—including bills of sale, slave manifest lists, records of overland shipment, and accounts of the migratory activities of planters moving from the border states—modern historians have reconstructed a truer picture of the degree of interstate trading.

From such material, historians can obtain two separate sets of statistics regarding black population shifts during slavery. First, in the thirty-year period prior to the Civil War, the upper South and Atlantic Coast South (Virginia, Maryland, Kentucky, Tennessee, and North and South Carolina) lost approximately 600,000 slaves in the movement to the Deep South and Old Southwest. This was a dramatically large total, and it created demographic* repercussions throughout the entire region. Second, although the interstate trade was an important part of this process, its role was nowhere nearly as great as many historians had assumed it to be. Studies of Maryland and Virginia trading suggest that the trader's share was, at the most, 20 to 25 percent of the total number of slaves who reached the Deep South and that it was the emigrating planter taking his slaves with him that made up the greatest bulk of that population movement. If this pattern of activity in Virginia and Maryland is as typical for the rest of the upper South (and there is no reason to believe that it should not be), then the contribution of the trader was an important force but not the dominant force in the nineteenth-century slave population shifts.

Nevertheless, because of the grimness associated with the forceful removal and shipment of large numbers of people against their will, the trade itself, in spite of its size, will always remain one of the ugliest chapters in the history of American slavery.

SELECTED BIBLIOGRAPHY

Frederic Bancroft, *Slave-Trading in the Old South* (1931); William Calderhead, "How Extensive Was the Border State Slave Trade? A New Look," *Civil War History*, 18 (1972), 42–55; William Calderhead, "The Role of the Professional Slave Trader in a Slave Economy: Austin Woolfolk, A Case Study," *Civil War History*, 23 (1977), 195–211; W. H. Collins, *The Domestic Slave Trade of the Southern States* (1904); Eugene D. Genovese, *Roll, Jordan, Roll: The World the Slaves Made* (1974); and Kenneth M. Stampp, *The Peculiar Institution: Slavery in the Ante-Bellum South* (1956).

WILLIAM L. CALDERHEAD

SMALLS, ROBERT (1839–1915). Robert Smalls was born a slave on John McKee's plantation in Beaufort, South Carolina, the son of Lydia, a slave, and most likely, Moses Goldsmith, a prominent Jewish merchant. He moved with his master to Charleston in 1851, where he was hired out* on a variety of tasks over the next decade. Through a number of such assignments along the city's waterfront, Smalls became an accomplished sailor and pilot.

When impressed into Confederate* service soon after Fort Sumter's fall, Smalls was assigned to the crew of the *Planter*, a transport steamer serving in the Charleston harbor. On 13 May 1862 he and eight black crew members stole the *Planter* from its dock. After picking up his wife, two children, and several other passengers, Smalls drove the ship out of the harbor, past five Confederate garrisons, and into the hands of the Union fleet blockading the coast. This feat, along with others almost as daring, earned Smalls a commission in the U.S. Navy as pilot and later captain of the *Planter* once it was refitted as a gunboat in 1863. Under his command in 1864–1865, the steamer provided food and other supplies to black refugees moving along the coast in the wake of General William T. Sherman's invasion of Georgia and South Carolina. Smalls continued to supply blacks after the war under the auspices of the Freedmen's Bureau.* Smalls's actions gained him an invitation to Washington in 1863, where he met with President Abraham Lincoln* and Secretary of War Edwin M. Stanton. Despite their reluctance to utilize Southern blacks in military service, Smalls convinced them to permit 5,000 South Carolina "contrabands"* to enlist in the Union army.

Smalls returned to Beaufort when his ship was decommissioned in 1866. His popularity among Sea-Island blacks led him to become one of the state's most influential black leaders during and after Reconstruction. In 1868 Smalls was elected to the state constitutional convention, serving in the state legislature, 1868–1874, and in the U.S. House of Representatives, 1875–1887. In 1889 Smalls was appointed customs collector for the port of Beaufort, a position he held until 1913, two years before his death.

SELECTED BIBLIOGRAPHY

Interview with Robert Smalls, 1863, in John W. Blassingame, ed., *Slave Testimony: Two Centuries of Letters, Speeches, Interviews, and Autobiographies* (1977); Okon Edet Uya, *From Slavery to Public Service: Robert Smalls, 1839–1915* (1971); and Joel Williamson, *After Slavery: The Negro in South Carolina, 1861–1877* (1965).

JOHN C. INSCOE

SOCIETY FOR THE PROPAGATION OF THE GOSPEL IN FOREIGN PARTS (SPG).

This private Anglican* missionary* organization was founded by Thomas Bray, commissary for the bishop of London, in 1701. Its goal was to spread Church of England congregations in North America. In 1703 the SPG sent its first missionary, Samuel Thomas, to South Carolina, where he reported the people were like "sheep without a shepard." By 1706 the SPG had adopted the conversion of blacks and Indians,* who were largely outside the regular structure of Anglican parishes, as its chief goal. Emphasizing education* and catechism, it opened schools throughout the colonies, most notably in New Jersey and the Carolinas, where the society purchased two black boys in 1747 to train as teachers. The established church's missionary wing accepted the institution of slavery, and even owned slaves on its West Indian plantations, but the SPG worked hard to persuade both masters and the colonial government to see that blacks were baptized and instructed in Anglicanism. These efforts aroused much suspicion on the part of slaveholders who feared that conversion might also make a slave free. In all, the SPG played an important part in spreading Anglicanism throughout the colonies among blacks as well as whites. Because its charter restricted the SPG's activities to "His Majesties' Dominions," the society ceased operating in the United States after independence, but remained the most significant Anglican missionary organization working with blacks in the British Empire.

SELECTED BIBLIOGRAPHY

Frank J. Klingberg, "The S.P.G. Program for Negroes in Colonial New York," *Historical Magazine of the Protestant Episcopal Church*, 8 (1939), 306–371; C. F. Pascoe, *Two*

Hundred Years of the S.P.G.: A Historical Account of the Society for the Propagation of the Gospel in Foreign Parts (1901); H. P. Thompson, *Into All Lands: The History of the Society for the Propagation of the Gospel in Foreign Parts, 1701–1950* (1951); John Van Horne, ed., *Religious Philanthropy and Colonial Slavery* (1986); and Faith Vibert, "The Society for the Propagation of the Gospel in Foreign Parts: Its Work for the Negroes in North America before 1783," *Journal of Negro History*, 18 (1933), 171–212.

CHARLES CARLTON

SOCIETY OF FRIENDS. *See* QUAKERS.

SONGS, SLAVE. Many characteristic elements of African song recurred in Afro-American slave songs. European traders and travelers in the early seventeenth century described African singing, which to them seemed exotic and unfamiliar. The music was typified by strong rhythms accompanied by bodily movement in which everyone participated. It was characterized by stamping, hand clapping, and other percussive devices that accented rhythm. Improvised words, frequently derisive or satiric in nature, and the ubiquitous call-and-response form also marked African, and Afro-American, songs. Song was commonly used to regulate the rate of work in rowing, grinding grain, and in the fields. Song also had a major role in religion,* public ceremonies, and other nonsecular aspects of life. Scholars disagree as to whether harmony was present, but the simultaneous sounding of more than one pitch was common. Vocal ornaments were frequently employed, and a strong, rasping voice quality was admired.

Ironically, the transmission of African song, dance,* and instruments* to the New World was encouraged by slaving captains who demanded that their captives sing and dance aboard ship. Slave singing first was reported in the West Indies and the North American mainland in the mid-seventeenth century. Dance and work songs were most common. Throughout the antebellum period many work songs and songs that accompanied dancing shared similar words. Besides the occupations that had been known in Africa, new forms of work in the New World—such as corn husking and engine firing—prompted slave songs.

The sacred songs of the slaves, the spirituals, whatever their African counterparts may have been, appeared after the slaves' gradual conversion to Christianity, a slow process. Some planters opposed the baptism of their slaves, believing that baptism might mean freedom or interfere with work. When planters permitted religious instruction, the Africans responded with enthusiasm. But the missionaries* sent from England were too few to minister to widely separated plantations* and to such a heterogeneous population. In the mid-eighteenth century, a few Presbyterian* ministers led by Samuel Davies of Hanover, Virginia, made special efforts to convert blacks. Davies reported his black converts' rapturous singing of psalms and hymns, "enough to bear away the whole congregation to heaven."

By the late eighteenth century black worshipers joined whites at frontier protracted meetings. This practice continued throughout the antebellum period, and
without question, the two races regularly worshiped and sang together in an
atmosphere highly charged with emotion. Songs, parts of songs, and ways of
singing were exchanged without the excited folk taking cognizance of derivation.
The call-and-response style of singing especially suited the service of the camp
meeting, where vast numbers of people required musical responses they could
learn on the spot. For whites, it recalled the practice of "lining out"—in which
a leader sang or read two lines of a hymn to the congregation who then repeated
them. This practice was followed in churches with illiterate members and in
congregations with too few books to go around. The camp meeting thus provided
an introduction for both groups to the sound and style of each other's singing.

The earliest reports of black religious song, distinct from European-style
psalms and hymns, date from the early nineteenth century, somewhat earlier
than the first organized program of missions to the slaves. These songs were not
written down until after the Civil War, but contemporary accounts described
musical elements that defied conventional musical notation then and now—notes
outside European scales, the so-called blue notes, glissandos, growls, polyrhythms, and the overlapping of leader and chorus in the call-and-response style.
All of these elements were characteristic of African musical forms and were
present in the slaves' sacred and secular songs.

Slave songs served various functions in the black community. They provided
comfort in time of sorrow, raised low spirits, passed the time during tedious
tasks, regulated the rate of work, heightened group feeling, and afforded psychological escape from unbearable conditions. Both sacred and secular songs
could fill these functions, but the bondsmen most valued the spirituals because
of the comfort and inspiration they provided.

The pervasive belief that the slaves shunned secular music and sang only
hymns was derived from the strict evangelical belief that all secular music was
sinful. Frontier sects expected their members to "put away the things of the
world," and their black members dutifully accepted this doctrine. Among religious slaves, sacred texts were used in work songs to replace secular words.
Along the Atlantic seaboard—from Richmond's tobacco factories to the boats
on the tidal rivers of the Sea Islands—work songs commonly contained religious
words.

Reports by travelers* before the Civil War of the singing of blacks usually
were vague, lacked musical detail, and frequently were condescending. Most
educated people of that time simply were unprepared to accept the music of
uneducated people on its own terms. Although the spirituals became widely
known in the South, they were still largely unknown in the North until wartime
conditions brought Northern whites into contact with plantation slaves. The first
spiritual to be published with its music was "Go Down, Moses," under the title
*The Song of the Contrabands "O Let My People Go," words and music obtained
through the Rev. L. C. Lockwood, Chaplain to the Contrabands at Fortress*

Monroe . . . (1862). Newspaper and magazine articles described the songs in more detail, but the first comprehensive collection was not published until 1867. *Slave Songs of the United States*, edited by William Francis Allen, Charles Pickard Ware, and Lucy McKim Garrison, included songs collected by persons stationed in the South during the war as newspapermen, army officers, missionaries, teachers, or agents of freedmen's aid societies or the Freedmen's Bureau. Very few of these collectors were professional musicians, and none of them knew much about non-European music. But all were capable of writing melodies in musical notation, and they were painfully aware that the music included elements that could not be transcribed in conventional notation. Fortunately, the three editors shared education, skills, and talents that made them as well qualified as any of their generation for the work of preserving a music they could not fully understand. Allen, Ware, and Garrison recognized slave songs as valuable, attractive, and eminently worth preserving from the hazards of time and historic change.

The public, however, was not ready to appreciate authentic folk music. Some reviews of *Slave Songs of the United States* were openly hostile, and even the most sympathetic critics stressed the curious aspects of the collection. They could not conceive that these songs were art worthy of appreciation. The volume sank into oblivion, all but forgotten until the 1930s when the folk song revival brought it the acclaim it deserved.

More successful in acquainting the public with the spirituals were the Fisk Jubilee Singers (1871), the Hampton Singers (1872), and other groups that toured the Northern states and Europe, singing versions designed for concert performance. These singers were only a few years removed from slavery, but many had already been trained in European music and its harmony. Their ears were more or less acclimated to the sound of European choral music and their versions of slave songs were somewhat removed from folk traditions. How much their versions diverged from the singing of slaves is still a matter of conjecture. The notated versions of their songs cannot be a reliable guide in such matters since so many elements of the performance style could not be transcribed. Moreover, the musicians who transcribed the songs varied in their experience with the folk tradition and in their sensitivity to it. Some felt no obligation to make accurate transcriptions even if that were possible. Yet these transcriptions were the only form in which the music could be preserved until the development of sound recording. The public acceptance of these transcriptions as the equivalent of the music as it was performed contributed to the growth of the theory that slave songs were based on earlier white originals, a theory once widely accepted in academic circles. When recordings made available the performances themselves, the public finally heard Afro-American slave music without the intermediation of transcribers and arrangers.

SELECTED BIBLIOGRAPHY

William Francis Allen, Charles Pickard Ware, and Lucy McKim Garrison, *Slave Songs of the United States* (1867); Harold Courlander, *Negro Folk Music, U.S.A.* (1963); Dena

J. Epstein, "A White Origin for the Black Spiritual? An Invalid Theory and How It Grew," *American Music*, 1 (1983), [53]–59; Dena J. Epstein, *Sinful Tunes and Spirituals: Black Folk Music to the Civil War* (1977); Lucy McKim [Garrison], "Songs of the Port Royal 'Contrabands,' " *Dwight's Journal of Music*, 21 (1862), 254–255; Thomas Wentworth Higginson, "Negro Spirituals," *Atlantic Monthly*, 19 (1867), 685–694; and Lawrence W. Levine, *Black Culture and Black Consciousness: Afro-American Folk Thought from Slavery to Freedom* (1977).

DENA J. EPSTEIN

SOURCE MATERIALS. Documentary source materials are the foundation upon which historians build their accounts of past events. Judicious treatment of these materials contributes to the soundness and staying power of an author's interpretation. Careless or biased handling of documentary sources invariably misleads readers and makes the writer vulnerable to criticism. Thus, the productive use of historical documents goes far beyond the marshaling of evidence to prove a favored thesis. The best, most convincing modern slavery studies not only are grounded in a wide variety of sources but also evidence an author's recognition of the ambiguities and other practical limitations inherent in each type of source material. Such works also reveal that certain documents within each category speak with more authority than others.

Source materials on slavery are as varied and as geographically dispersed as the individuals who have chronicled Southern history. In recent years, the archival collections most often visited by researchers in American slavery studies have included the Southern Historical Collection at the University of North Carolina, Chapel Hill; South Caroliniana Library of the University of South Carolina, Columbia; Alderman Library at the University of Virginia, Charlottesville; William R. Perkins Library of Duke University, Durham, North Carolina; Tulane University Library, New Orleans; Louisiana State University Library, Baton Rouge; Alabama Department of Archives and History, Montgomery; Mississippi Department of Archives and History, Jackson; Virginia State Library, Richmond; Georgia Historical Society, Savannah; South Carolina Historical Society, Charleston; and the Library of Congress, Washington, D.C.

Each of these repositories has its own unique focus, but even though a library's strength may lie in its regional specialization, its public document collection, or its holdings of correspondence in manuscript, most contain a much broader assortment of potentially valuable source materials. Increasingly, commercial and university presses are joining reprint and microform companies in making these resources more accessible to researchers.

Whether eyewitness or latter-day observer, professional or amateur historian, each writer who has written an account of the slave South has selected evidence from this pool of available data. Early historians of slavery often have been accused of racial bias. They also have been criticized for spreading their research net too narrowly and for their inability to spot obvious weaknesses in the types of documentary sources that they have employed. As a result, their views on

Southern slave economy, the master-slave relationship, and the slave personality have been extensively critiqued and, in some cases, discredited.

The gradual withdrawal of professional accreditation from the interpretive works of Georgia-born Yale University historian Ulrich B. Phillips is a classic example of this revisionist process. A dominant figure in the early twentieth-century movement to collect, preserve, and expand the scholarly use of plantation documents, town and county records, and manuscript census returns, Phillips worked to convince his Progressive era peers that histories grounded in these primary sources were preferable to the romanticized apologias of the immediate postbellum era. His success in this endeavor can be gauged by the long-standing influence of his *American Negro Slavery* (1918) and *Life and Labor in the Old South* (1929) as well as by the establishment and expansion of state archival programs throughout the South.

Nevertheless, Phillips's characterization of plantation records as "the most reliable source of knowledge" for the study of slavery did not long remain the definitive statement on the topic. Early black critics who scored the Georgian for mistrusting travelers' accounts* and "Negro sources," ignoring evidence of slave rebelliousness,* and relying too heavily upon the records of large planters* eventually were joined by white academicians who felt that Phillips's data were both inadequate and misleading. By the time of the modern civil rights movement, an increasing number of scholars had concluded that Phillips's portrayal fell short of providing a complete history of the slave institution.

Fortunately, Ulrich Phillips's favored documentary sources have not been abandoned by subsequent generations. The planters' diaries, account books, and correspondence remain key resources for reconstructing the daily routine of the slaveholders' world. Probate records, statute books, and census schedules continue to be mined for what they reveal about demographic and economic relationships in both the urban and rural, agricultural and industrial South. Even traditional "white" sources such as newspapers and agricultural periodicals have been put to new, innovative uses by historians studying slave management techniques, hiring and naming practices, and the characteristics of fugitives. Certainly, the history of Southern agriculture would be far more difficult to chart without such publications as *De Bow's Review, American Farmer, Southern Agriculturist, Farmer's Register, American Cotton Planter, Southern Cultivator,* and *Southern Planter.*

While rightfully refusing to relegate these materials to the historiographical dustbin, historians have become ever more inclusive in their approach to documentary source materials. Motivated by both utility and necessity during the turbulent 1960s, many writers recognized that the contemporary relevance of their works oftentimes was determined by the extent to which they supplemented traditional sources with Northern, and especially, Afro-American perspectives. To exclude the views of the antebellum traveler would betoken provincialism. To discredit the black viewpoint could subject the author to charges of racial bias.

Accounts written by travelers from the North, Great Britain, or various parts of Europe provide useful perspectives on slavery. During the immediate post-revolutionary period and continuing into the first three decades of the nineteenth century there emerged from the travel literature a heightened awareness of sectional differences and of the growing Southern reliance upon black slave labor. The number of visitors continued to increase during the 1840s and 1850s as steamships replaced the Atlantic sailing packet and railroads quickened the pace of travel from Northern cities southward. Some 150 visitors recorded and published their impressions of the South between 1846 and 1852 alone. In addition to the travel narrative format, a significant number of accounts were brought to press as components of personal memoirs and autobiographies, while others appeared in contemporary magazines and newspapers.

Historians who have used these materials in their studies of the slave South have done so in the belief that the views of outsiders provide a much-needed check upon native opinions and prejudices. Often, things too commonplace or too unpleasant for resident Southerners to mention were noticed, investigated, and thereby exposed by the travelers. On the other hand, the visitors' preconceptions about blacks, the South, and slavery sometimes distorted their writings. Unfamiliar with people of color and beset by the difficulties of obtaining a more complete view of the Southern countryside than that which could be seen from the deck of a steamer, from the parlors of an urban hotel, or from a hospitable slaveholder's veranda, only the most persistent, perceptive traveler could hope to leave an account that was unblemished by stereotypes.

Black-authored source materials useful to the study of slavery also contain qualities which require circumspection by modern-day historians. The use of Afro-American testimony* was long urged but seldom heeded until demands for a black perspective within a new American history written "from the bottom up" echoed through the academy. Only then were the autobiographies,* oral testimonies, and correspondence of slaves and their descendants thoroughly organized, critiqued, and found requisite in balancing the views of white planters and travelers.

More than 200 book-length autobiographies of former slaves were published in the United States and England between 1760 and 1967. Popular accounts, such as those of William Wells Brown,* Gustavus Vassa [Olaudah Equiano],* Josiah Henson,* Solomon Northup,* Moses Roper, and Frederick Douglass,* sold well in their day and constitute one of the chief forms of early Afro-American literary and historical expression. Many additional personal narratives may be found in contemporary journals, court proceedings, and church records. Significant collections of these materials are located in the Schomburg Center for Research in Black Culture, New York City, and in the libraries of Brown, Cornell, Harvard, and Howard universities. A number of recent microform and reprint series contain copies of the original works.

Like the more frequently cited reminiscences of planters and their kin that were produced in such large quantities after the Civil War, black autobiographies—especially those of antebellum vintage—often have been treated as biased apologias for partisan positions taken during the debate over slavery. In adapting the narratives to historical purposes, scholars must consider both the practical constraints of the genre and the white editor's frequently heavy-handed use of popular literary devices to heighten dramatic effect. Researchers also should realize that the black autobiographies underrepresent female slaves, overrepresent the upper South, and too often focus on the fugitive's flight from bondage while excluding descriptive commentary on the slave community's internal affairs. Despite these limitations of form and perspective, there is increasing professional agreement that most of the narratives are authentic, reliable accounts of slavery which can be independently corroborated. That so few were directly challenged by antebellum Southerners speaks well for their use as a documentary resource.

A second variety of Afro-American source material that has acquired new respectability is the oral history account. Just as Benjamin Drew's *The Refugee; or, The Narratives of Fugitive Slaves in Canada* (1856) and the interviews conducted by the American Freedmen's Inquiry Commission in 1863 foreshadowed later efforts to collect ex-slave testimony, oral history programs instituted during the 1920s and 1930s by John B. Cade of Southern University and by the staff of Fisk University's Social Science Institute paved the way for the more extensive Federal Writers' Project (FWP).* Between 1936 and 1938, FWP personnel interviewed some 2,200 ex-slaves in seventeen states. Their edited transcripts, accompanied by photographs of the elderly respondents, were deposited in the Rare Books Division of the Library of Congress in 1941. This 10,000-page, 3.5 million-word Slave Narrative Collection,* along with associated narrative materials from a variety of archival sources, has been made widely available by the publication of George P. Rawick's forty-one-volume *The American Slave: A Composite Autobiography* (1972–1979).

The ex-slaves' oral testimony is an important supplement to the black autobiographical accounts. These transcribed reminiscences are rich in folklore* and provide considerable insight into the social structure of the slave community. Women,* residents of the Deep South, and ''average'' individuals who neither fled bondage nor consciously sought to compile and publish their memoirs are better represented in the FWP collection than in the autobiographies.

Nevertheless, interpretive problems specific to the interviews must be considered. Poorly selected, leading questions, clumsy or skewed interpolations of transcripts, the respondents' lengthy separation in time from the events described, and a caste etiquette that limited the degree of candor possible between ex-slaves and a predominantly white group of interviewers all have served to check expansive claims for this variety of source material. Like the autobiographies, the narratives must be evaluated on an individual basis with constant attention given to social context and textual nuance.

In addition to the autobiographies and oral accounts, several additional categories of Afro-American source materials are likely to find increased use in future studies of slavery. Although not a common form of expression, personal

letters from bondsmen and former bondsmen to masters, family members, legislative bodies, or antislavery organizations provide insights into the master-slave
relationship, plantation work and authority patterns, black attitudes toward colonization, and the nature of black family ties. Like the more carefully preserved
correspondence of the slaveholders, these black-authored documents often contain candid expressions of the writer's most intimate thoughts. Nevertheless, the
letters vary considerably in credibility. Those directed to whites, dictated to an
amanuensis, or written expressly for use in the antislavery crusade must be used
with considerable care.

Future studies of the slave South also should benefit from both the methodologies and research findings of scholars working with material and folk culture.
Since historical archaeology* has been used to uncover precise data on the slave's
living quarters, diet, kitchen utensils, and items of personal adornment, it is
hoped that comparative studies of black and white material culture and the more
extensive evaluation of slave-produced craft items, tools, and musical instruments
will provide new insights into plantation social structure and the cross-pollination
of cultures. A representative collection of these items is housed in Charleston's
Old Slave Mart Museum and Library.

In like manner, folklorists, cultural anthropologists, ethnomusicologists, and
linguists offer fresh perspectives on slavery-related topics. Because written records do not always provide a complete or accurate picture of African and Afro-
American cultural life, the orally transmitted expressive culture of blacks needs
to be more solidly established as a historical resource. Although distorted by
time and the often careless manner in which these folk materials have been
handled by external observers, increased utilization of data on the slaves' secular
and religious music, on folk beliefs as expressed through tales, jokes, and proverbs, and on the process of creolization as it affects both linguistic and cultural
forms of expression would deepen our understanding of the slave community.

However bewildering and contradictory, this vast array of folk and material
culture data, along with relevant correspondence, oral histories, autobiographies,
plantation records, travel narratives, government documents, and contemporary
newspapers and periodicals serves as the modern historian's window on the slave
South. The extent to which each type of source material is accepted as valid
historical evidence continues to rest with the individual interpreter, but both
contemporary sensibilities and the historiographical lessons of the past encourage
a far greater inclusiveness and analytical sophistication in the use of these materials than that envisioned by earlier generations of slavery scholars.

SELECTED BIBLIOGRAPHY

John W. Blassingame, "Using the Testimony of Ex-Slaves: Approaches and Problems,"
Journal of Southern History, 41 (1975), 473–492; Frances Smith Foster, *Witnessing
Slavery: The Development of Ante-bellum Slave Narratives* (1979); Lawrence W. Levine,
"Slave Songs and Slave Consciousness: An Exploration in Neglected Sources," in Tamara
K. Hareven, ed., *Anonymous Americans: Explorations in Nineteenth-Century Social*

History (1971); George W. McDaniel, *Hearth & Home: Preserving a People's Culture* (1982); Gloria L. Main, "Probate Records as a Source for Early American History," *William and Mary Quarterly*, 3rd ser., 32 (1975), 89–99; Sterling Stuckey, "Through the Prism of Folklore: The Black Ethos in Slavery," *Massachusetts Review*, 9 (1968), 417–437; Mark Tushnet, "Approaches to the Study of the Law of Slavery," *Civil War History*, 25 (1979), 329–338; and Norman R. Yetman, "The Background of the Slave Narrative Collection," *American Quarterly*, 19 (1967), 534–553.

WILLIAM L. VAN DEBURG

SOUTH CAROLINA, SLAVERY IN. Slavery in South Carolina was a local institution that changed over time. Early in its history, Indian slavery,* black slavery, and white indentured servitude* existed side by side, but by the antebellum period black slavery predominated. These changes reflected important fluctuations in the importation of slaves from Africa. After the initial transfer of slavery and plantation models from Barbados, South Carolina slaveholders turned to Africa to supply their need for black slave labor. Few blacks, for example, were imported from the West Indies because South Carolinians suspected them of being the unwanted, the ailing, and the rebellious. The creolization process also brought changes over generations. At first brutal in form, slavery in South Carolina became more humane in its operation, although ironically there seemed to be more hope of emancipation in the colonial period and less in the antebellum period. The hopes of the American Revolution* for freedom withered amid the attack of the abolitionists.* On the eve of the Civil War a reenslavement crisis resulted because white laborers resented the competition of free black* workers. What finally fixed the institution on the state was not merely the need for labor but the profitability of the system, with its concomitant cultural ramifications. So embedded were these in the social fabric of South Carolina that they could only be dislodged by the havoc of the Civil War.

South Carolina was to be a staple-producing province. The articles of trade were in succession deerskins, cattle,* naval stores,* rice,* indigo,* and much later cotton.* There was need for a labor force. Indians as hunters and burden bearers were adequate for the trade in deerskins, but black slaves more quickly adapted to cattle herding and the naval stores industry and by the 1730s became absolutely necessary for the culture of rice.

But why black slaves? The example of Barbados was the prime model and the greatest influence. South Carolina's first settlers came by way of that island, and among those arriving in 1690 were the first black slaves. The first slave code of 1690 was adapted from the code of Barbados. The crucial determining factors, however, were climate, disease, and skills. Historian Peter H. Wood has shown that African slaves became indispensable because of their ability to exist in the hot humid climate,* their relative immunity to malarial fevers, and the skills that they brought with them, particularly herding cattle and planting rice. The blacks also were superb boatmen, acting as pilots and patroons in the intricate low-country estuaries. Indian slavery that resulted from the Indian wars reached its peak in 1724 and 1725, but the Indians were decimated by the diseases* transmitted by the Europeans and were not inured to the hard labor that the Africans could endure. By the time of the rice boom of the 1730s African slavery had become fixed upon South Carolina society, although a black majority had emerged there as early as 1708.

In the beginning the need was to wrest a profit from the land. There was not much time for thinking of whether slavery was right or wrong. Such conflicting doubts emerged out of the Great Awakening of 1740, which in South Carolina may have come as a distinct aftermath of the Stono Rebellion of 1739.* The ideas that would eventually destroy slavery percolated through American society with John Woolman and the Quakers* as early as the 1750s, though there was no intention on either side during the American Revolution to free the slaves as a result of victory. The slaves that the British took away during the Revolution (anywhere from 6,000 to 25,000 from South Carolina) were not given their freedom, but were taken mainly to the West Indies where they were sold into slavery again or put to work on land acquired by the American Loyalists.* Only a few, such as those who went to Nova Scotia, gained freedom, and then only with the financial aid of philanthropists in England who transported the blacks to the newly created territory of Sierra Leone.

In 1790 three Charleston free blacks petitioned the state legislature asking that they be recognized as citizens of South Carolina. The petition was denied. As late as 1857 the Supreme Court of the United States stated that free blacks were not citizens, proof of the ambiguous status of free blacks throughout the ante-bellum period. On the other hand, the founding fathers of South Carolina felt confident that slavery would come to an early end. They could not predict in 1787 the eventual growth and spread of the cotton culture. But they did at least take tentative steps to end the foreign slave trade* which by the Constitution* could and did end in 1808, a year which in one sense represents a great dividing line in the history of slavery. It cut the American black population off from Africa and forced a creolization that as early as the 1820s had produced uniquely black South Carolinians.

Each generation brought a different mind-set for the black slaves as well as for their white masters. Historian Herbert G. Gutman, in his study of the black family,* pointed out that each generation passed on to the next a sense of family and of place from which evolved a new Afro-American culture. Gutman's analysis of the births, baptisms, marriages,* and deaths of three generations of slaves on Santee River plantations revealed a culture capable of passing on its achievements and its accommodations to the next generation.

Historian Philip D. Morgan has described tendencies that seemed to be fracturing slavery in eighteenth-century Charleston. Opportunities existed for slaves in the urban center that were lacking in the countryside. There was a "measure of freedom involved in hiring and living out" that was highly valued by the slaves. Fishing* and butchering, portering and hauling, were trades dominated by slaves. A skilled slave could clear a profit of £250 in 1760. Even the loss of runaways* could be absorbed. According to Morgan, the "ability of slaves to enjoy a change of scene, visit a relative, or go underground probably siphoned off as much potential disorder as it created." Black women* outnumbered black men. Many thus lived beyond the constant observation of whites. Black potential resentment was deflected by their own communal outlets. Yet, in the end, these hard-won gains probably bound the blacks more completely to slavery. The apparent openness meant that there were differences among the blacks themselves—of color, of trade, of property, of origin, of arrival, and of freedom. This fragmentation, plus the fact that the blacks in Charleston were only a slight majority (not an overwhelming majority as in the country), meant that Charleston whites were less fearful, more certain of control in times of danger. Slavery was disintegrating in Charleston as the eighteenth century progressed, but ironically the very disintegration made it easier for slavery to exist in the city. Morgan concludes "that slavery in Charleston was more, not less, secure than it was in the surrounding countryside." But these eighteenth-century signs of a loosening of the grip of slavery were blocked by the appearance and spread of cotton.

It seemed that slavery would be cut off from its source and that it would be confined to the coastal regions where rice could be grown, but the introduction of cotton brought about the spread of slavery throughout the South. The black slaves taken to the Bahamas by Loyalists in the 1780s produced by the end of that decade a very profitable crop of sea-island cotton. Seeds and know-how were sent back to the Loyalists' friends and relations in South Carolina and Georgia. Abraham Eve invented a roller gin for the fine sea-island cotton that was used in the Bahamas and on the Sea Islands. Eli Whitney invented a saw-toothed gin in 1793 for the coarser, upland cotton. As a result, cotton culture swept into the interior, and the institution of black slavery followed.

Black slaves had appeared in the up-country as early as 1716, accompanying a military expedition sent against the Cherokees. By the 1760s slaves composed approximately 10 percent of the population. Many of these were undoubtedly runaways, individuals who could perhaps assume a new identity amid the turbulence of the frontier. In her analysis of gangs and banditti, historian Rachel Klein has proved their presence. More organized settlement of slaves into the interior came with Thomas Sumter's bounty scheme for raising troops—each recruit who signed up received a slave—and with Wade Hampton's spiriting of slaves from the low country amid the immediate post revolutionary chaos. The Regulator Movement of the 1760s had been designed not only to eliminate crime but also to find a labor force for the farmers who wanted to advance into the planter class. This transformation of farmer into planter proceeded with speed in the three decades after the Revolution. But it was not until the period 1800–1810 that slavery appeared in its mature form in the interior. The slave trade was reopened in 1803 and remained open until a federal law brought an end to the foreign slave trade on 1 January 1808. Some 45,000 slaves were introduced into South Carolina in these years and most of these undoubtedly found their way to the new up-country cotton plantations. While a white majority existed in the state in the 1790s, by the 1820s a black majority had returned once more. By then the black majorities of the coastal parishes reached 85 to 88 percent of the population. But black slavery had also spread throughout the state, except for the districts in the foothills of the mountains.

From the moment the slaves arrived in colonial South Carolina they yearned for freedom. While running away could not overturn the system, a concerted effort planned by slaves might have done so. Such concerted effort, however, could not arise until the slaves could communicate among themselves. They had come from different parts of Africa and spoke varying tongues. The rise of a pidgin language* among the slaves facilitated the Stono Rebellion of 1739, the first and perhaps the last actual slave uprising with a plan and a program. Although slaves were confined to plantations, there were constant opportunities for movement and communication: messages to be carried, boats to be navigated, militia duty to be performed, fighting to be done. In this fashion, Gullah*—a corruption of European tongues and African dialect—emerged by mid-century and provided the bondsmen a means to communicate their plot. The magnet in 1739 that drew the slaves of Colleton County was St. Augustine. A Spanish proclamation promised freedom to those bondsmen who reached Florida. Fort Moosa, a settlement outside the walls of St. Augustine, was a colony of free black settlers. Only quick action on the part of Lieutenant Governor William Bull suppressed the revolt.

The basic code* to regulate the slaves was adopted in 1740, a result of the Stono Rebellion. That code, which lasted in its fundamental principles until the end of slavery in 1865, defined the status of the slave. If black, the law assumed that the person was a slave; if Indian, it assumed the person was free unless there was proof of enslavement. The basic rights and privileges of both slave and free men were stated in that legislation. The code also established South Carolina's slave patrol system,* which also was to remain a fixture of South Carolina slavery until emancipation. At each muster of militia companies some men were selected for patrol duty until the next muster. They were instructed to ride through the country and challenge all slaves found off plantations. The patrollers could stop and inquire, search and seize, and even punish for violations. According to the 1740 code, slaves were to be tried in a court of justices and freeholders. No record of the trial was to be kept and punishment ensued immediately without any higher approval, unless the sentence was death.

The revolution in Santo Domingo, one of the reverberations of the French Revolution, had a profound impact upon the minds of both black and white South Carolinians. More refugees from Santo Domingo flocked into Charleston than into any other U.S. port. These included white families, mulatto families, and black slave families. The establishment of the black Republic of Haiti provided what white South Carolinians considered to be a dangerous example of a revolt. Consequently, in the mid-1790s Charlestonians adopted a series of city ordinances to control both mulattoes and black slaves. Segregation of the town theaters took place in 1795. Three years later the state legislature passed a law to control the movement of all blacks and free persons of color in and out of the state. In 1804 a city ordinance placed a curfew on free blacks in Charleston; in 1806 an ordinance stated that a white person had to be present when seven or more free blacks assembled. The state also made it far more difficult to emancipate a slave. A law of 1800 prevented manumission* by will or deed and required that a group of citizens certify that the freed person could support his or her family. Over the next two decades laws were tightened so that only the legislature could grant manumission. These city ordinances and state laws expressed the growing concern of whites to control the free black population, just as the 1740 code had been enacted to regulate the slaves.

It was during this period that Denmark Vesey,* a slave who labored as a sailor, won a lottery and bought his freedom. Having sailed in the West Indies, Vesey knew of the Haitian revolution. He also was aware of the pressure of the laws and ordinances upon his own people, as well as of the Missouri debates that had raised the question whether free blacks had the privileges and immunities of citizens as guaranteed in the U.S. Constitution. In June 1822 Vesey and his co-conspirators from Charleston and the surrounding countryside were ready to rise up in rebellion, but a slave loyal to his master betrayed the plot. Eventually Vesey and thirty-six other persons were executed. The conspirators presumably had planned to sail to Haiti once freedom had been won in South Carolina.

To counter this threat, and to prevent the flow of information through the port of Charleston into the local black community, in 1822 and 1823 the state legislature passed the Seamen Acts.* Under these laws free black sailors on vessels coming into the port were to be jailed while the vessel was docked. If the captain of the ship could not pay for the room and board of his sailors, the blacks could be sold into short-term slavery to pay for these services. The spirit of such laws contributed to the fear of reenslavement among Charleston's free black community. After June 1823 free blacks could no longer come and go, and each had to secure a white guardian to vouch for his reputation. To assure added police control of slaves and free blacks, a new guardhouse was built in Charleston in 1825. In 1842 this structure became the Citadel, a military college visibly representing the force and power of the white community.

South Carolinians also took steps to block the circulation of abolitionist literature, including David Walker's* inflammatory *Appeal* (1829) and William Lloyd Garrison's* newspaper, *The Liberator*. In 1835, for example, Charlestonians raided their city's post office to prevent distribution of antislavery publications. Several years earlier the level of intolerance was so great in Charleston that two prominent antislavery spokeswomen, Sarah and Angelina Grimké,* moved to Philadelphia to attack slavery at a safer distance. Great Britain's decision in 1833 to free the slaves in the West Indies added to the uneasiness and apprehensions of South Carolina slaveholders. In 1834 the state tightened its slave code, making it unlawful to teach blacks, free or slave, to read or write. As a result Thomas S. Bonneau was forced to close his famous school and one of his former pupils, Daniel A. Payne, who himself had established a school for blacks in Charleston, moved to the North. Amid this rigidifying climate, it was not surprising when John C. Calhoun* rose on the floor of the U.S. Senate in 1837 to declare that slavery was "a positive good."

In 1837 another influential South Carolinian, Chancellor William Harper, published his *Memoir on Slavery*. According to Harper, slavery lay at the core of all civilization. "If any thing can be predicated as universally true of uncultivated man, it is that he will not labor beyond what is absolutely necessary to maintain his existence." "He who has obtained the command of another's labor, first begins to accumulate and provide for the future, and the foundations of civilization are laid." Harper went on to challenge the statement in the Declaration of Independence* that all men were born free and equal. "Is it not palpably nearer the truth to say that no man was ever born free, and that no two men were ever born equal? Man is born in a state of the most helpless dependence on others." Harper's rationalizations went so far as to assert that "*Servitude* is the condition of civilization." "It is by the existence of slavery, exempting so large a portion of our citizens from the necessity of bodily labor, that we have a greater proportion than any other people, who have leisure for intellectual pursuits, and the means of attaining a liberal education." These thoughts were a long way from the professed egalitarianism of 1776 and help to explain the ideological underpinnings of slavery in the last two decades before the Civil War.

Although these dogmas strengthened the resolve of the planter class to maintain the peculiar institution, there also were attempts to make slavery less severe. Such contradictions and ironies were part and parcel of the human dimension of slavery. In 1820, for example, Governor Thomas Bennett urged the legislature to reform the slave code because, he said, slavery in the nineteenth century differed from the institution that had existed in the eighteenth century. In 1821 the legislature made the crime of murdering a slave punishable by death, thereby providing bondsmen protection previously denied them. When the court of appeals interpreted the law in 1834, the judge who delivered the opinion wrote: "This change I think made a most important alteration in the law of his [the slave's] personal protection. It in a criminal point of view elevated slaves from chattels personal to human beings in the peace of society." In 1834 the South Carolina legislature also prohibited the branding of slaves. The blacks themselves were partly responsible for the changes in South Carolina slave law and treatment. By the 1820s black South Carolinians had forged their own Afro-American society, with its own integrity, its own reason for being. The growing distance from Africa meant a greater reliance on things known in the New World, not remembered from the Old World. Though this distancing had been interrupted somewhat by the importation of some 45,000 slaves between 1803 and 1808, South Carolina slaves established their own unique slave community, a mix of Africanisms and characteristics unique to American experience. Circumstances required that these blacks live and labor among whites. As elsewhere, the day-to-day interaction of blacks and whites in slave society was characterized by varying degrees of stress and strain and give-and-take. Blacks, however, never were totally absent from the dynamics of decision making.

Black preachers* tended to provide both secular and religious leadership within the South Carolina slave community. By the late 1780s Francis Asbury had provided religious instruction to the slaves, but after the Vesey plot whites became increasingly concerned over the nature of this training. Nevertheless, planters invited Methodist* and Baptist* clergymen to preach to their slaves. On the largest plantations planters provided chapels with regular Sunday schools and church services for the bondsmen. Slave children* commonly were drilled in the catechism, while the adults were indoctrinated with the message of obedience to masters. The Christian message had a strong appeal to the slaves. The Methodist hymns were rapidly absorbed into African ritual songs,* dances,* and shouts. The belief in the second coming of Christ offered slaves a message of hope, a promise of salvation, of ultimate emancipation. Significantly, blacks transformed the radical evangelicalism of the late eighteenth century into their Afro-American faith, a creed that served them well for life after emancipation.

Changes in the use and organization of South Carolina's slave labor force also paved the way for self-assertion and later emancipation.* Early in the state's history slaves were called upon to perform brutal work—clearing stumps from swamps, building dikes, and digging ditches. By the early nineteenth century, however, except for the last rice frontier along the South Carolina side of the Savannah River, most of this work had been done. The same was true for the clearing of up-country lands. Even more crucial, though, was the development of the task system* on South Carolina's rice plantations. Some estimates indicate that by three o'clock in the afternoon many slaves had completed their assigned tasks for the day and thus could use the remaining daylight hours to raise and sell vegetables, to fish, to tend farm animals, or to relax. The task system enabled slaves to acquire private property, which occasionally passed from one generation to another. This represented a small but significant measure of freedom. The task system helped to prepare the slaves for freedom and shaped the market economy that flourished around Charleston and Savannah. In the up-country where the system of gang labor* was more common, these changes had far less impact. The task system permitted low-country slaves to carve out space and meaning for themselves. Their assertiveness represented yet another prelude to freedom.

Nowhere was the sense of independence more pronounced than in the case of South Carolina's free black community. Although few in number (1,801 in 1790 and 9,914 in 1860), their history reveals the contradictions inherent in the slave system. The story of William Ellison of Stateburg can stand in part for the story of South Carolina's free blacks. Ellison, the mulatto son of a Fairfield District planter, had been trained as a ginwright. Upon his emancipation in 1817, Ellison began manufacturing cotton gins* in Stateburg. Hard work and catering to the needs of his white neighbors enabled him to accumulate substantial amounts of land and slaves, eventually amassing a fortune worth about $100,000 in 1860.

Necessity forced Ellison and his family to identify more with whites than with blacks. The reenslavement crisis of 1859 highlighted their nervousness and emphasized the pervasive need for accommodation. Not surprisingly, the Ellisons supported the Confederates* during the Civil War.

As early as November 1861, with the invasion of Port Royal Sound by the Union navy, the world of South Carolina's masters, slaves, and free blacks began to be turned upside down. While the slaves were not immediately set free, steps were taken to secure land for them around Beaufort and other coastal areas. Planters who could not pay the federal government's direct tax on their lands had their property confiscated. This land then was sold, some to Northern philanthropists who wanted to put the former slaves to work, some to Northern speculators who were quite willing to use the former slaves as new wage slaves, and some to blacks who had managed to save some money. What was to emerge as a postwar black society in South Carolina had its roots in the eighteenth-century changes in Charleston slavery, the growth of a free black society, and the changing nature of slavery in the last thirty years of the antebellum period. So many of those who were to guide the freedmen* into the promised land came from within this black society. Indeed, the break that came with emancipation was neither as sharp nor as clear as a movement from slavery to freedom might imply.

SELECTED BIBLIOGRAPHY

Jack P. Greene, " 'Slavery or Independence': Some Reflections on the Relationship among Liberty, Black Bondage, and Equality in Revolutionary South Carolina," *South Carolina Historical Magazine*, 80 (1979), 187–232; Herbert G. Gutman, *The Black Family in Slavery and Freedom, 1750–1925* (1976); Thomas Holt, *Black over White: Negro Political Leadership in South Carolina during Reconstruction* (1977); Michael P. Johnson and James L. Roark, *Black Masters: A Free Family of Color in the Old South* (1984); Rachel Klein, "The Rise of the Planters in the South Carolina Backcountry, 1767–1808" (Ph.D. dissertation, Yale University, 1979); Philip D. Morgan, "Black Life in Eighteenth-Century Charleston," *Perspectives in American History*, n.s., 1 (1984), 187–232; Willie Lee Rose, *Rehearsal for Reconstruction: The Port Royal Experiment* (1964); and Peter H. Wood, *Black Majority: Negroes in Colonial South Carolina from 1670 through the Stono Rebellion* (1974).

                                                         GEORGE C. ROGERS, JR.

STEWARD, AUSTIN (ca. 1793–1865). Born a slave in Prince William County, Virginia, Austin Steward left the South very early in his life to accompany his master to western New York. Steward obtained his freedom at the age of twenty-two by taking advantage of a clause in New York State's gradual emancipation law that manumitted those slaves who had been hired out for additional work. Relocating to Rochester, New York, by the 1820s Steward had established himself as a prosperous grocer. Yet, Steward soon found himself drawn toward the antislavery crusade. In 1830 he attended the first National Negro Convention, in Philadelphia, where he was elected a vice president of the meeting. Because of his leadership capacities, Steward attracted the attention of the board of managers at the Wilberforce Settlement, a black communal experiment in Upper Canada (Ontario). Consequently, in 1832, Steward was recruited to Canada to assume the chairmanship of the board of Wilberforce, a position he held until 1837, at which time he returned to Rochester.

Steward's administration at Wilberforce was characterized by controversy, dissension, and the economic malfeasance of the settlement's agents. As a result, Wilberforce, like other black communities in Canada, met an early demise. After returning to New York, Steward opened a school for black children at Canandaigua and joined the antislavery lecture circuit as a Garrisonian abolitionist. In 1857 he published a narrative of his experiences in Canada and the United States, *Twenty-Two Years a Slave and Forty Years a Freeman*. Eight years later, at approximately the age of seventy-two, Steward died in Rochester.

SELECTED BIBLIOGRAPHY

William H. Pease and Jane H. Pease, *Black Utopia: Negro Communal Experiments in America* (1963); Jason H. Silverman, *Unwelcome Guests: Canada West's Response to American Fugitive Slaves, 1800–1865* (1985); Austin Steward, *Twenty-Two Years a Slave and Forty Years a Freeman* (1857); and Robin W. Winks, *The Blacks in Canada: A History* (1971).

JASON H. SILVERMAN

STILL, WILLIAM (1821–1902). William Still was a leader of underground railroad* operations in southeastern Pennsylvania from 1849 to 1861. His book, *The Underground Railroad* is the most detailed account of underground railroad operations produced in the nineteenth century.

Still was born in Burlington County, New Jersey. His father had purchased his freedom. His mother had twice fled slavery; on her second flight, she left two sons, Levin and Peter, in bondage. Still received little formal education; later an able writer and businessman, he was essentially self-taught.

Still came to Philadelphia in 1844. In 1847 he became a clerk at the Pennsylvania Anti-Slavery Society office. Within two years he was involved with the Vigilance Committee, responsible for underground railroad activities.

Still's home was always a safe refuge for fugitive slaves.* He was involved in many notable escape episodes, including those of Henry "Box" Brown, William and Ellen Craft,* and Jane Johnson. In 1851 Still warned the black community near Christiana, Philadelphia, of the arrival of fugitive slave hunters, resulting in the blacks' armed resistance in what became known as the Christiana riot.* In 1855 Still toured the fugitive slave settlements in lower Canada, writing positive accounts of their resettlement.

The most poignant episode of Still's career occurred in 1850. When interviewing a recent arrival from the South, Still realized that the fugitive was his long-lost brother, Peter. This episode inspired him to start a journal of his underground railroad activities, which became the principal source for his later book.

SELECTED BIBLIOGRAPHY

James P. Boyd, "William Still: His Life and Work to this Time," in William Still, *Still's Underground Rail Road Records* . . . (1886); and William Still, *The Underground Rail Road. A Record of Facts, Authentic Narratives, Letters, Etc.* (1872, 1879, 1886).

PHILIP LAPSANSKY

STONO REBELLION. The largest black uprising in colonial North America, the Stono Rebellion was part of a broader groundswell of resistance to English enslavement in the era of the Great Awakening. Among South Carolina's 56,000 inhabitants, blacks outnumbered whites almost two to one by 1739, and the proportion of recently imported slaves was at an all-time high. When the Spaniards in St. Augustine offered liberty to black fugitives, runaways* to Florida increased, and in February 1739 rumors circulated that enslaved South Carolinians were conspiring "to rise and forcibly make their way out of the Province."

On Sunday, 9 September 1739, hours after news reached Charleston of hostilities between England and Spain, twenty black persons broke into Hutchenson's store near the Stono River in St. Paul's Parish southwest of Charleston, seizing arms and executing two storekeepers. Led by a slave named Jemmy, the blacks marched southward to the beat of drums and cries of "Liberty," burning selected plantations, killing a score of whites, and adding over fifty new recruits to their cause. Had the rebels captured Lieutenant Governor William Bull I (as they almost did), or evaded pursuit for several days while their ranks swelled, this blow for freedom might have overturned South Carolina's slavery regime and altered American history.

Though a few of the slaves remained at large for months and even years, scores of blacks were captured and killed within a week. A contemporary account referred to them as "some shot, some hang'd, and some Gibbeted alive." In 1740 the white minority, its worst fears confirmed, moved quickly to reconsolidate its power by revising the slave code, curtailing African importations, and challenging the neighboring Spanish.

SELECTED BIBLIOGRAPHY

Daniel C. Littlefield, *Rice and Slaves: Ethnicity and the Slave Trade in Colonial South Carolina* (1981); Philip D. Morgan, "En Caroline Du Sud: Marronnage et Culture Servile," *Annales-Économies, Sociétés, Civilisations*, 37 (1982), 574–590; John T. TePaske, "The Fugitive Slave: Intercolonial Rivalry and Spanish Slave Policy, 1689–1764," in Samuel Proctor, ed., *Eighteenth-Century Florida and Its Borderlands* (1975);

Robert M. Weir, *Colonial South Carolina—A History* (1983); and Peter H. Wood, *Black Majority: Negroes in Colonial South Carolina from 1670 through the Stono Rebellion* (1974).

PETER H. WOOD

STOWE, HARRIET BEECHER (1811–1896). Harriet Beecher Stowe, a sibling within Lyman Beecher's family of New England preachers and teachers, was the mother of six when she wrote *Uncle Tom's Cabin; or, Life Among the Lowly*, the premiere antislavery novel of the antebellum period, in 1852. This romantic novel utilized the theme of redemption to create a literary parable for the national dilemma of slavery in the United States. The author's religious conscience, experience with the abolitionist community* of Lane Theological Seminary, and association with free blacks* and escaped slaves during her eighteen years in Cincinnati, Ohio, combined with the death of an infant son in 1849 and the passage of the Fugitive Slave Act in 1850* to produce the psychological and political context for her vision of Tom's death scene in February of 1851. In forty serial installments for the *National Era*, Stowe constructed the complete story of Tom's life. She drew upon the antislavery nonfiction of Lydia Maria Child, Theodore Weld,* Frederick Law Olmsted,* and the autobiographies of Frederick Douglass* and Lewis Clark for further details of the novel's scenes and character development. The novel's general popularity at home and abroad incited scathing criticism of the book from Southern critics, whereupon Stowe responded with a laboriously documented defense of its accuracy, *A Key to Uncle Tom's Cabin* (1853).

Stowe used her research for *A Key* in her second antislavery novel, *Dred. A Tale of the Dismal Swamp* (1856), which employed the 1831 Nat Turner rebellion* as its historical setting. All Stowe's antislavery writings challenged readers to confront slavery's existence within the republic as a moral issue. After the Civil War Stowe occasionally commemorated the passing of ardent abolitionists in magazine articles. Her tribute "Sojourner Truth, the Libyan Sibyl"* contributed to the preservation of black history and acknowledged black participation in the abolition movement. Over time, however, Stowe's fictional black characters, especially Tom, were debased by inaccurate dramatic interpretations into the demeaning racial stereotypes still enshrined in the popular conception of *Uncle Tom's Cabin*.

SELECTED BIBLIOGRAPHY

Charles Foster, *The Rungless Ladder: Harriet Beecher Stowe and New England Puritanism* (1954); Charles Edward Stowe, *Life of Harriet Beecher Stowe . . .* (1889); Harriet Beecher Stowe, *Uncle Tom's Cabin; or, Life Among the Lowly* [1852], edited with an introduction by Ann Douglas (1982); Harriet Beecher Stowe, *The Writings of Harriet*

Beecher Stowe (reprint ed., 1967); and Forrest Wilson, *Crusader in Crinoline: The Life of Harriet Beecher Stowe* (1941).

ANGELA HOWARD ZOPHY

SUGAR. The commercial sugar industry of the United States dates from the Louisiana Purchase. Only in southern Louisiana are soil and climatic* conditions sufficient to produce a sugar crop competitive with cotton.* Immigrants from troubled Caribbean sugar islands, who settled in Louisiana during the final decades of the eighteenth century, experimented with sugar cane cultivation and manufacture. The first successful crystallization of cane juice in 1795, credited to Étienne de Boré, initiated Louisiana's commercial sugar industry.

Although sugar cane had been cultivated and manufactured by African slaves on Caribbean islands for over a century, and small crops of cane were common on farms in the Southern mainland colonies of British North America, the mainland colonies had no commercial sugar cane industry. To develop fully, sugar cane requires a tropical climate. Only in limited parts of the southern United States is the growing season long enough to produce a cane that can be crushed for juice and then boiled into syrup—a common household sweetener and whiskey raw material in the early United States.

Sugar production in Louisiana has always suffered competitive disadvantages relative to tropical cultivation. The growing season in the limited area of southern Louisiana, where commercial cane is possible, is delineated by the first fall frosts and the final ones of spring. Sugar cane must be planted to profit from the earliest warm temperature, and must be harvested at the latest possible time. The cane begins to deteriorate with cutting and with freezing. Once cut, the crop demands immediate processing to maximize its sugar potential. Tropical growers have a year-round growing season. They cut cane at its maturity, not with arrival of frosts. Further, tropical planters can rely on ratoon crops, the regrowth of cane on old roots, for as long as twelve years. Louisiana planters rarely harvest more than three crops with a single planting. Cane itself is used for seed, so Louisiana growers sacrifice a far higher percentage of their cane for seed than their tropical competitors do.

Slavery represents yet another area in which North American cane sugar producers operated at an economic disadvantage vis-à-vis their tropical competitors. Most tropical producers enjoyed access to the international slave trade long after that commerce in humanity was closed to American planters. Many tropical sugar planters found it economically feasible to buy labor when it was needed and to disregard natural reproduction of enslaved Africans. American sugar planters operated within a legally closed market for chattel labor. The demand for slaves in an expanding American South combined with a market restricted to domestic Africans—Afro-Americans—to create speculation in slaves. American slave owners probably did not contemplate slave breeding* as such, but they were aware of the limitations of the market and the possibility of rising slave prices.* Maintaining slaves in family units provided a hedge against rises in slave prices that frequently rewarded a speculative profit. Such profits* were of particular importance to sugar planters because of the unfavorable competition in their industry.

The U.S. sugar industry has historically depended on a protective tariff for survival in a market that favors the more efficient tropical producers. When Louisiana became a part of the United States, her infant sugar industry inherited a tariff code established not for protection but for revenue. Soon, however, Louisiana successfully lobbied for governmental protection of her sugar industry from world markets.

Cane sugar cultivation and manufacture in the slave labor era was clustered about the rivers and bayous of southern Louisiana. Prospective planters of cane were attracted to lands (usually measured in arpents—one arpent, usually taken to be the Arpent de Paris, equals 0.84 of an acre) fronting a watercourse that could provide inexpensive access. If a complete manufacturing operation was to be established, heavy machinery and building materials had to be transported. The expense of hauling heavy loads overland precluded building on almost any but water-access sites. The transportation demands for marketing the manufactured sugar reinforced the preference for water-access plantations. Raw sugar was packed in hogsheads to weights around a thousand pounds each. Again, in a time of scarce and rude roads, a water route to market was an essential part of a sugar plantation.

The first work assigned slaves on a new sugar plantation was land clearing, levee construction, and ditch digging. The waterfront acres usually sloped gradually from the river to a swamp, an alluvium produced by centuries of overflows. The rich, damp soil was heavily forested. Clearing the land of the trees, and eventually the stumps as well, was a task of enormous proportions, a task carried out by slaves equipped with hand tools. Once cleared, the new planting area had to be drained by a complex grid of main ditches and cross ditches. Ditching was never completed: silt buildup could fill the system in a few years, so slaves cleaned and redug ditches regularly. Control of the watercourse demanded construction of earthen dikes at waterside, and at intervals between the river and the swamp. Most established planters sought backup protection from the river with a series of levees. If the main one broke and another held, some of the crop and land improvements could be salvaged.

Once the land was sufficiently cleared, ditched, and diked to support a crop, the slave force was put to plowing and planting seed cane. Although the cane itself required limited attention once planted, slaves enjoyed few slack days on a sugar plantation. Ditches and dikes demanded constant attention after initial construction was completed. Roads and bridges to facilitate travel on the place had to be built and maintained. Preparations for manufacturing the crop were also demanding tasks for slaves. Of these, cutting, hauling, and storing of firewood were perhaps the most exhausting. Production of a single hogshead of raw sugar required from two to three cords of dry wood. In addition to labor directly related to the sugar planting and manufacturing, slaves worked at building houses for the owner and for themselves. They also constructed the various factory outbuildings and barns.

At the harvest slaves chopped the cane and hauled it to the mill in small carts pulled by oxen, mules, or horses. Cane to be kept for seed had to be put up in mattresses—piles covered with leaves, waste, and dirt. In the factory (in most cases manufacturing was carried on at the plantation) the field slaves became factory hands. They fed fuel to steam engines that powered grinding mills (small plantations used horse-driven mills of small size), tended and fired kettles in which sugar syrup was boiled to crystallization (especially large sugar houses had steam-powered vacuum pans for boiling the syrup), and hauled the final product, raw sugar, to the purgery. In the purgery the wet, brown mass was deposited in hogsheads drilled to permit the molasses by-product to drain into a large catch basin for later reboiling or sale. The steam engine was usually operated by an engineer, and the sugar manufacturing was supervised by a professional sugar maker.

As sugar drained it was shoveled into hogsheads (frequently built on the plantation by a slave cooper) and stored or shipped to market. Once the entire crop was manufactured, slaves were accustomed to an annual break before work on the new crop got underway. After the break, slaves undertook to burn or plow under the trash from the harvested cane and prepare the land for the new crop. Ratoons required little attention beyond clearing away of waste and hoeing the soil. Seed that was exhausted, however, was plowed up and replaced with seed cane. Of course, ditches had to be cleaned, dikes repaired, and wood cut and hauled for the next run of the mill.

Routine life for a slave on a Louisiana sugar plantation was characterized by the heavy labor necessary to farm and manufacture sugar cane. Nature frequently interrupted that routine with hurricanes and high water or both. One great storm or flood could destroy in a few hours what thousands of slaves had labored to produce over the course of years. Then, after the storm or flood, the slaves were, without choice, put to clearing the debris and rebuilding.

The life of Afro-American slaves on sugar plantations was harsh compared with that of urban slaves* and those laboring to grow cotton or tobacco.* Only rice* plantations offered similarly harsh conditions. The sugar-producing slave lived in a rude hut with the bare essentials of life. He rarely had time or land space to grow his own food. His diet was made up largely of corn* and cheap cuts of pork. When time allowed, he might supplement his regular fare with fish from the river or bayou. Opportunities for escape to permanent freedom were all but nonexistent; nevertheless, plantation journals abound with tales of slave runaways.* Even in the face of certain capture and return, many slaves found the temporary respite from the heavy work of sugar planting worth the costs of escape. Slaves did the work of building the American sugar industry, but it would be difficult to argue that they received anything for their efforts.

SELECTED BIBLIOGRAPHY

Manuel Moreno Fraginals, *The Sugar Mill: The Socioeconomic Complex of Sugar in Cuba, 1760–1860* (1976); Lewis C. Gray, *History of Agriculture in the Southern United States to 1860* (2 vols., 1933); V. Alton Moody, "Slavery on Louisiana Sugar Plantations," *Louisiana Historical Quarterly*, 7 (1924), 191–301; Walter Prichard, "Routine on a Louisiana Sugar Plantation under the Slavery Regime," *Mississippi Valley Historical Review*, 14 (1927), 168–178; J. Carlyle Sitterson, *Sugar Country: The Cane Sugar Industry in the South, 1753–1950* (1953); David O. Whitten, *Andrew Durnford: A Black Sugar Planter in Antebellum Louisiana* (1981); and Whitten, "Sugar Slavery: A Profitability Model for Slave Investments in the Antebellum Louisiana Sugar Industry," *Louisiana Studies*, 12 (1973), 423–442.

DAVID O. WHITTEN

T

TASK SYSTEM. Under the form of labor organization known as the task system, slaves were assigned a certain amount of work for the day or perhaps the week. Upon completion of this work they were then "free" to use their time as they pleased. Unlike slaves working under the gang system* task laborers worked neither in unison nor under close supervision. Rather, they were accorded a measure of independence in their work. Provided the slaves could finish their tasks expeditiously, they might gain time for their own affairs.

Task systems were associated with many New World staples. Rice* and sea-island cotton* production in low-country South Carolina and Georgia generated an extensive and deeply rooted task system. The basic unit, the quarter-acre, became so ingrained in low-country life that ex-slaves in the twentieth century still thought in terms of it. In places as remote from one another as the forests of British Honduras, North Carolina, and Surinam, task work was the norm for enslaved timber workers. Each operation in the North Carolina turpentine work cycle, for instance, had its own task. In the British Caribbean, long-staple cotton, coffee, cocoa, pimento, and arrowroot were generally the preserve of task systems. On Jamaican coffee plantations, for example, land was laid off in task-acres—which were somewhat larger than statute acres—in order that more regular divisions could be allotted to the slave workers.

Tasking also made inroads into staple crops that traditionally had been worked by slaves organized into gangs. By the late eighteenth and early nineteenth centuries, for example, some sugar planters had introduced individual tasking into the cane-holing operation. By the 1820s and 1830s the task system had been adopted on many sugar estates in Trinidad, Demerara-Essequibo, and Berbice. Similarly, planters of tobacco* and short-staple cotton in the antebellum South were attracted to tasking. Picking cotton, husking corn, stripping and prizing tobacco were operations that lent themselves to individual tasks.

Several factors accounted for the association of certain staples or certain operations with tasking. The degree to which direct supervision was required by various crop cycles or by pivotal operations within crop cycles was one important factor. Where a crop was relatively hardy (as with rice) or where there was no particular urgency in the production cycle (as with the tending of pimentos or drawing off turpentine) a relaxed attitude toward supervision was possible, and individual tasking arrangements usually evolved. Related considerations were the practicability and costs of supervision and the facility with which the slave-holder or overseer could measure an individual laborer's output.

However onerous tasking was for some slaves, the system had a number of advantages from the laborers' point of view. It at least allowed the slave to apportion his own day, to work intensively in his task and then have the balance of his time. Many low-country slaves, for instance, could finish work as early as midday; turpentine workers in North Carolina often completed their weekly tasks by mid-afternoon on Friday. Once the daily or weekly task was complete, the slave could engage in his own pursuits. Indeed, low-country planters were, in the words of one contemporary, "very particular in never employing a negro, without his consent, after his task is finished, and agreeing with him for the payment which he is to receive." It is not surprising that this measure of freedom enhanced the self-esteem of task workers. Most tangibly, those who could finish their tasks early might grow crops and raise livestock* in their own time, thereby acquiring a modicum of property and a measure of control over their own lives.

SELECTED BIBLIOGRAPHY

Lewis C. Gray, *History of Agriculture in the Southern United States to 1860* (2 vols., 1933); B. W. Higman, *Slave Populations of the British Caribbean, 1807–1834* (1984); Philip D. Morgan, "Task and Gang Systems: The Organization of Labor on Plantations," in Stephen Innes, ed., *Work and Society in Colonial America: Essays in the New Labor History* (1987); and Philip D. Morgan, "Work and Culture: The Task System and the World of Lowcountry Blacks, 1700–1880," *William and Mary Quarterly*, 3rd ser., 39 (1982), 563–599.

PHILIP D. MORGAN

TAXATION OF SLAVES. Because slaves represented a major category of taxable property, the methods by which they were taxed were both varied and controversial. In the colonial period the earliest form of taxation was the import duty which was, for example, in Virginia, often the nominal fee imposed on all immigrants. But as the number of slave importations increased, colonies seized upon the duty as a source of revenue and significantly raised it. When in the eighteenth century slave revolts* created fears that too many slaves were being imported, duties were raised to prohibitive levels as a means to restrict importation. English authorities, however, generally disallowed these laws.

Banned during the American Revolution,* the slave trade* resumed in the 1780s, and the duty on slaves again became a major source of revenue, particularly in South Carolina. In the years before the 1808 prohibition on slave imports the Constitution* empowered Congress to levy a $10 tax on slave imports, but it never did so.

Internally, the poll tax constituted a major tax on slaves during the colonial period. At first this tax was uniform regardless of the age or sex of the slave and often equal to the poll on whites. But increasingly this tax was differentiated by age and sex so that the tax became more closely related to the slave's actual value.

The antebellum period saw a greater variety of taxes imposed on slave property. On the national level, slaves were taxed by their inclusion in the federal ratio. On the local level, state, county, and town governments assessed taxes on skilled slaves through licensing, and on the sale of slaves through brokerage fees and inventory taxes. Although the primary purpose of most of these levies was revenue, licensing fees frequently were aimed at regulating competition between free and slave labor. In the antebellum period state and local governments often replaced the poll tax with either a general property tax or an ad valorem tax. But whatever the method, slave taxation produced significant amounts of revenue for every Southern state. In Georgia in 1850, for example, it generated one-half of all property tax revenues. Slave taxation accounted for forty-six cents out of every dollar of tax revenue in Alabama in 1849.

Despite the fact that slave taxes generated much revenue, nonslaveholders consistently protested that slaves were undertaxed. This agitation was strongest in North Carolina and Virginia where a rigid poll tax structure was retained. Protest reached such a height in North Carolina in the 1860s that the state was forced to adopt ad valorem taxation to preserve wartime unity.

During the Civil War,* the tax burden on slave property increased substantially. The Confederate* government classified slaves as taxable property and subjected them to a war tax in August 1861. In 1864 the Richmond government assessed a 5 percent ad valorem tax against slaves. Impressment—a final form of taxation of slaves—granted the Confederacy the right to seize slaves for work in war industries or for the building of fortifications. Under the Impressment Act of 26 March 1863, the Confederacy paid slave owners $30 a month or some other agreed-upon wage, or in case of death, the full value of the bondsman.

Slave property having provided a major source of tax revenue throughout the antebellum period, its loss at the end of the Civil War mandated major changes in the tax structure of the South during Reconstruction.

SELECTED BIBLIOGRAPHY

Robert A. Becker, *Revolution, Reform, and the Politics of American Taxation, 1763–1783* (1980); Donald C. Butts, "A Challenge to Planter Rule: The Controversy over the Ad Valorem Taxation of Slaves in North Carolina: 1858–1862" (Ph.D. dissertation, Duke University, 1978); William Z. Ripley, *The Financial History of Virginia, 1609–1776* (1893); J. Mills Thornton III, *Politics and Power in a Slave Society: Alabama, 1800–1860* (1978); Richard C. Todd, *Confederate Finance* (1954); Peter Wallenstein, "From

Slave South to New South: Taxes and Spending in Georgia from 1850 Through Reconstruction'' (Ph.D. dissertation, Johns Hopkins University, 1973); and George R. Woolfolk, ''Taxes and Slavery in the Antebellum South,'' *Journal of Southern History*, 26 (1960), 180–200.

DONALD BUTTS

TENNESSEE, SLAVERY IN. Almost as if a biblical parallel were intended, the first slave on record as living in Tennessee had the name Abraham. In 1760 his master sent him to Charleston, South Carolina, for help when hostile Indians besieged Fort Loudoun, a trading post on the Little Tennessee River. Soon after, Tennessee's permanent settlers employed a few slaves in grain farming at Watauga. By 1779 about 10 percent of east Tennessee's taxpayers owned slaves, mostly in sets of three or fewer (the largest slaveholding was ten). Slaves accompanied the first explorers and settlers who entered middle Tennessee. Indians captured or killed some of them there and in east Tennessee during the skirmishing of the 1780s and 1790s. A few slaves boldly fled to the Indians in order to escape their masters.

As the frontier era passed, middle Tennessee slaves found themselves cultivating market crops of tobacco* and cotton.* Montgomery Bell began the use of Tennessee slaves in manufacturing at his ironworks downriver from Nashville. Although by 1800 slaves composed 25 percent of middle Tennessee's population, their percentage in east Tennessee was only 8 percent, lowering the statewide proportion of slaves to 13 percent. In 1818 the opening of west Tennessee greatly expanded the use of slaves in cotton and tobacco farming. The new region's slave population reached 13 percent by 1820 and 26 percent by 1830, pulling the statewide proportion up to 21 percent that year. The slave proportion of the population grew at a slower pace thereafter.

By 1830 Tennessee had a detailed slave code* that had evolved from that of its mother state, North Carolina. Provisions borrowed from the North Carolina code prohibited slaves from possessing guns, leaving the master's premises without a written pass, owning property, testifying against whites, being manumitted unless the county court ruled they had performed ''meritorious service,'' hiring* their own time, and selling goods without a master's permission. Whites could not encourage or aid a slave to run away. Counties hired patrollers* to enforce the code and held special courts to try slave violators.

In 1801 Tennessee replaced the ''meritorious service'' requirement for manumission* with the posting of a bond. The legislature in 1806 forbade assembling, seditious speech, and provocative language by slaves; responsibility for patrolling was transferred to the militia. During the next decade laws were passed prohibiting the importation of slaves into the state for sale (1812) and the sale of liquor to a slave without the master's approval (1813). Arson, burglary, and rape became capital crimes in 1819 exclusively when committed by blacks. In 1829 the legislature disbanded the separate slave courts and granted slaves jury trials.* In doing so, Tennessee was one of only five Southern states that permitted jury trials for bondsmen. In 1831 the hiring of patrollers by county courts was reinstated, and slaves were required to leave the state when manumitted. In the 1830s, in the wake of sharp attacks against slavery by immediatist abolitionists,* Tennessee tightened its slave controls: laws forbade advocating abolition, providing slaves with weapons, and permitting slaves to act in any way as if free. The revised 1834 state constitution banned abolition without the master's consent.

While Tennessee courts zealously protected the owners' property rights in cases involving dishonest sales, lynching, and capital crimes, they also gained distinction for fair treatment of slave defendants and plaintiffs. For example, the ruling in the 1846 case of *Ford v. Ford* proclaimed that "A slave is not in the condition of a horse. . . . He has mental capacities, and an immortal principle in his nature, that constitute him equal to his owner, but for the accidental position in which fortune has placed him."

Government officials did not enforce all provisions of the slave code with relentless rigidity. Permissive masters ignored many rules and apparently suffered nothing more than popular derision for subsisting "free negroes." Lenient masters seemed to be concentrated in particular localities, most notably Nashville. One slave, Bob Renfro, received manumission there in 1801 for the "meritorious service" of operating a popular tavern. Nashville always had some slaves, like Renfro, who hired their own time and otherwise lived as if free. In Maury County during the secession crisis a crusading prosecutor initiated cases against masters who let their slaves keep animals but gave up when the judge ordered merely nominal fines. Nevertheless, even in Nashville an insurrection scare or a petition with many signatures could tighten up law enforcement.

A series of insurrection scares began in the state during the 1830s, possibly as a response to renewed abolitionist activity in the North. These scares were localized, brief, and barely publicized. Most likely the alleged insurrections never took place at all, resulting from nothing more than unsubstantiated fears that were quickly dispelled.

Such disruptions actually were rare and by 1840 slavery was firmly entrenched in Tennessee society. The state's basic economic and social patterns by then had already become clear. The distribution of slave property generally corresponded with soil fertility, because better soil meant more commercial farming and a greater demand for labor. In mountainous east Tennessee slaves never exceeded 9 percent of the population. The bulk of the state's slaves lived in the other two regions, peaking in 1860 at 29 percent of middle Tennessee's population and 34 percent of west Tennessee's inhabitants. Even in those areas, however, slave populations remained low in such infertile localities as the Tennessee River valley and the Cumberland Plateau. In very few Tennessee counties did slaves ever make up the majority. In fact, among the fifteen slaveholding states Tennessee ranked tenth in the percentage of slaves (25 percent) in its whole population at the end of the antebellum period. Nonetheless, probably one-third of Tennessee's white families owned or hired slaves. Most masters held fewer than four, and none owned over 500 bondsmen.

The minority of slaves not in agriculture or industry worked in transportation and domestic service. Several turnpike companies staffed their repair gangs with slaves; steamboat and stevedore crews included them too. Domestic servants cooked, cleaned, sewed, and waited upon masters.

As property, slaves were commercial goods. Some owners, like Andrew Jackson,* speculated in slave sales, just as they did with horses and land. A few men, like the notorious John Murrell, profited from slave stealing. Commercial slave traders appeared in the state as early as 1790, and a handful of businessmen in Knoxville, Nashville, and Memphis came to specialize in this line of goods. Lively markets also existed in the seats of counties with large slave populations.

Masters employed the threat of selling troublesome slaves away from family and friends as one of the control devices. While in the White House President James K. Polk promised just such a fate for runaways in a letter read to the assembled slaves on one of his plantations. White Tennesseans rarely manumitted or educated slaves lest some blacks start questioning their bondage, though Tennessee was one of the few slaveholding states that never prohibited slave education.* During the 1830s and 1840s evangelicals—preaching obedience to slaves and paternalism* to masters—made major efforts to convert the state's slaves to Christianity. When allowing blacks to hold their own religious* meetings, whites demanded supervision for the religious instruction. Of course, the ultimate control device in slavery always was physical punishment. While state law guaranteed slaves a right to life and the necessities of life, it also excused masters from deaths resulting from "moderate correction."

Rural isolation and routine stand out as central experiences in the autobiographical* accounts of Tennessee slaves (the state had only a small number of urban* slaves). Parties and visits to town were special occasions. Church services were a regular source of intellectual and social stimulation for many bondsmen. Black members had either separate seating or separate services. A few churches established chapels exclusively for blacks, sometimes with a black preacher in charge.

Unbeknownst to whites another type of black church flourished within the slave community—underground, secret, religious meetings held by the slaves. A common theme in these covert services was the belief in imminent providential deliverance. Building upon Old Testament parallels and evangelical millennialism, slave preachers* argued that God opposed slavery and that He would soon liberate them and punish their masters. Not all slaves, however, considered this believable, nor were all bondsmen religious.

Tennessee slaves shared a common hostility toward the abuse they received at the hands of their masters. Physical punishment* particularly offended slaves. Louis Hughes, a house slave in Memphis, recalled that "after the first burst of tears, the feeling came over me that I was a man, and it was an outrage to treat me so—to keep me under the lash day after day." The other major complaint of slaves was the breakup of families.* Ex-slave George Knox remembered vividly how at age three he was placed on a Wilson County auction block, where his father had to hold him up because of his small size. Families also were shattered when a master moved, because many Tennessee slaves married* someone with a different owner. Abuses and grievances did not necessarily lead to action, however. Jermain Loguen felt "so habituated . . . to wrongs, that he met them without disappointment, and endured them without complaint."

When resistance* occurred, it took a number of forms. Louis Hughes secretly learned to read and write so as to gain access to forbidden information and to forge passes for himself. J. W. Lindsay successfully used threats to limit abuse: "they treated me pretty well," he recalled, "for the reason that I would not allow them to treat me any other way." Jack, a slave on President Polk's plantation, fought fiercely with his supervisor rather than succumb to the humiliation of captivity. The ultimate way out of slavery, of course, was to escape to the North, but distance made that very difficult for Tennessee bondsmen. The quick method was to hide on a northbound steamboat. The long way, adding weeks more to the trip, was to travel overland. The odds strongly leaned toward capture either way. Census officials reported only seventy successful runaways* from Tennessee in 1850 and just twenty-nine in 1860.

The tensions within Tennessee slavery increased during the 1850s. In 1854 the legislature moved to make manumission more difficult by conditioning it upon emigration to Liberia.* Further demonstrating their dedication to slavery, the next year the legislators lifted the ban on slave importation, a prohibition that had never been strictly enforced anyway. Close to the 1856 presidential election, the first campaign in which a Northern party critical of slavery made a strong showing, came Tennessee's most serious slave insurrection panic. Beginning in Fayette, the county with the largest proportion of slaves in its population, fear of slave revolt spread quickly through many other neighborhoods in west and middle Tennessee. Vigilantes hanged four slaves at Dover, a number of others were punished or arrested, and confessions were extorted through whipping. The mere purchase of a bugle by a Wilson County slave aroused grave suspicions among whites there. In his thorough study of the panic, historian Charles B. Dew concluded that except possibly for loose talk among a handful of slaves, no substance ever existed behind the widespread fears. Nevertheless, the scare motivated the city governments of Memphis and Nashville to prohibit slaves from preaching, receiving education, or being out after a curfew. Toward the end of the 1850s Tennessee's legislature mandated capital punishment for slaves conspiring to revolt and discussed reenslaving free blacks who refused to leave their state. Fear over slavery's security was on the rise as Tennessee and the rest of the nation drifted toward war.

Editorials and pamphlets clearly show that these fears led directly to Tennessee's decision in 1861 to secede from the Union and join the Confederacy.* During the Civil War* the Confederate state government created large home guard patrols to insure slave submissiveness, while the Confederate army helped to capture and return runaways. Slaves proved essential to Confederate operations in Tennessee, as a labor resource in the fields, in ironworks, and in military camps. They constructed the state's line of defensive fortifications, embankments that remained unfinished when the Union troops invaded in the winter of 1861–1862 because masters did not want their valuable property's health threatened by such hard work.

As Union armies proceeded to drive Confederates out of Tennessee, slavery's control system broke down. Though most slaves never left home, some interpreted the Confederacy's defeat as their long-expected providential deliverance. Others saw it simply as a practical opportunity to escape slavery and to advance themselves. Runaways first appeared at federal camps in 1861–1862, offering to help the invaders, only to be turned away by the Union troops. Some Northern officers returned slaves to masters. Gradually, however, the growing tide of fugitives* wore the army's resistance down, and the fugitives were put to work as military laborers. Other contrabands bypassed the army camps entirely en route to the occupied towns, where a labor shortage existed. Large black shanty-towns, the first black ghettos in Tennessee, quickly sprang up at these posts. The contrabands vigorously sought to gain paying jobs, reunite their families, secure an education, hold religious meetings without supervision, enter military service, and win the vote.

Such assertiveness pressured Union authorities to support change. Once the army began hiring black laborers, the establishment of refugee camps quickly ensued. The army supervised the work of the contrabands, who labored under contracts with local farmers and planters. Many black Tennesseans flocked to join the U.S. Colored Troops* once military enlistment of blacks began in 1863. Northern reformers distributed charitable donations among needy blacks and established schools for them.

Although Lincoln* excluded Tennessee from the force of the final Emancipation Proclamation* in January 1863, it nonetheless pushed the state's unionists to abolish slavery as they reconstructed local government. In August 1863, military governor Andrew Johnson began swaying public opinion in that direction. In September 1864 Johnson suspended Tennessee's slave code. Five months later a referendum approved an amendment to the state constitution to abolish slavery. Practically speaking, though, it took the state courts, the Union army, and the Freedmen's Bureau* the remainder of 1865 to liberate individuals forcibly kept enslaved by stubborn masters.

SELECTED BIBLIOGRAPHY

John Cimprich, *Slavery's End in Tennessee, 1861–1865* (1985); Louis Hughes, *Thirty Years a Slave, from Bondage to Freedom: The Institution of Slavery As Seen on the Plantation and in the Home of the Planter* (1897); George L. Knox, *Slave and Freeman: The Autobiography of George L. Knox* (1979); Lester C. Lamon, *Blacks in Tennessee, 1791–1970* (1981); Jermain W. Loguen, *The Rev. J. W. Loguen as a Slave and as a Freeman* (1859); and Chase C. Mooney, *Slavery in Tennessee* (1957).

JOHN CIMPRICH

TESTIMONY, SLAVE. Any statement by slaves or ex-slaves concerning their experiences in bondage or their perceptions of slavery may be considered slave testimony. The term encompasses sermons and public speeches, folktales and songs, published fiction, drama, and poetry. Statements of conviction and fact in lawsuits, petitions, apologies, and exhortations fit this category. Slave testimony includes the letters between family members enslaved in different states and the twentieth-century interviews of elderly persons some sixty years removed from slavery. Best known are the personal narratives* by former slaves. These range from the narratives of Job ben Solomon, kidnapped Senegalese merchant, whose letter in Arabic to his father set in motion his release from slavery in Maryland, to that of Solomon Northup,* a New York freeborn black, whose smuggled letter to his family revealed his enslavement in Louisiana. Among the other narratives are those of criminals, missionaries, sailors, merchants, and fugitive slaves. In short, slave testimony includes the panorama of personal attitudes and experiences witnessed by those who have been enslaved.

Their stories and songs reflect the slaves' worldview. From Anansi the spider to Brer Rabbit and John the slave, the folktales* instructed, motivated, and sustained the slave community. The spirituals were personal narratives that proclaimed not only religious convictions but referred to the entire slave experience. Slave songs* were the "grape-vine telegraph" by which news was passed and issues were discussed. Often they were coded messages used by fugitives such as Harriet Tubman* whose presence was advertised by "Steal Away" and "Go Down, Moses." Basic themes of faith, optimism, patience, weariness, and fighting prevailed in both the secular songs and the spirituals. These themes as well as the dominant motifs of escape correspond with those of written slave testimony.

Slave testimony includes that which is quoted in court documents, essays, journals, church records, and newspapers. Probably the earliest recorded testimony is a collection of pamphlets, court documents, and diaries spanning the years 1701–1710 and known as "Adam Negro's Tryall." Although Adam did not write this material, they evidence one man's fight for freedom and reveal some of his attitudes and experiences during and after slavery. Other records such as the 1655 Virginia court reports concerning Elizabeth Key's suit for freedom, the 1774 petition to Governor Thomas Gage by a group of Massachusetts slaves, the tombstone of John Jack, and the military papers of Casey, a fugitive slave, give witness to the attitudes and experiences of individual slaves.

The 1760 *Narrative of the Uncommon Sufferings, and Surprizing Deliverance of Briton Hammon, A Negro Man* is the earliest extant American slave autobiographical account. Some ex-slaves published works such as J. W. C. Pennington's *Text Book of the Origin and History, &c.&c. of Colored People* (1841), thus providing record of the slave scholars' version of history. Writings such as Phillis Wheatley's* letters and her *Poems on Various Subjects, Religious and Moral* (1773), Jupiter Hammon's* poems and his "Address to the Negroes of the State of New York" (1787), Thomas Cooper's *The African Pilgrim's Hymns* (1820), George Moses Horton's* *The Hope of Liberty* (1829), Frederick Douglass's* "The Heroic Slave" (1858), and William Wells Brown's* *Clotel* (1853) also reveal the lives and literary claims of a few privileged slaves.

More representative, perhaps, are the slave letters. Some were written to newspapers, but most were intended solely for relatives, friends, or former masters. They recount everyday details and speak candidly of the slaves' feelings and emotions. Some requested money or new clothes for a special occasion and in this way suggest ways in which slaves provided materially for one another. Since many of these letters were written directly from one slave to another, they are also evidence of the slaves' informal written language.

Though papers such as the *New York Times* and the Toronto *Globe* occasionally published slave interviews, most accounts were published in antislavery papers or in abolitionist anthologies. Typical of these collections are H. G. Adams's *God's Image in Ebony: Being a Series of Biographical Sketches, Facts, Anecdotes, Etc., Demonstrative of the Mental Powers and Intellectual Capacities of the Negro Race* (1854) and Benjamin Drew's *A North-Side View of Slavery. The Refugee: or, The Narratives of Fugitive Slaves in Canada. Related by Themselves, . . .* (1856).

Most personal histories were related by ex-slaves or fugitives. Some dictated their stories for public distribution. Others wrote their own. The poles of these testimonies are bondage and freedom. Those narratives which stressed the former slaves' achievements after freedom reveal by contrast the great waste of human potential that slavery effected. The most common antebellum testimonies were the slave narratives, those personal accounts by slaves and ex-slaves concerning their lives in bondage and their efforts to become free. Some, such as Olaudah Equiano's* *Narrative* (1789), recalled memories of Africa and spoke to the special problems of being enslaved in a foreign culture. Most were written, at least in part, as antislavery documents. Typical is Henry Bibb's* prefatory statement that says he wrote his narrative to expose the "sin and evils of slavery" and to "leave my humble testimony . . . to be read by succeeding generations when my body shall lie mouldering in the dust." Slave narratives such as these sometimes achieved best-seller status during the antebellum period. More than a hundred are extant, and many have been reprinted in recent years so that slave testimony lives on as an important genre in its own right and as an accessible historical record by the slaves themselves.

SELECTED BIBLIOGRAPHY

John W. Blassingame, ed., *Slave Testimony: Two Centuries of Letters, Speeches, Interviews, and Autobiographies* (1977); Frances Smith Foster, *Witnessing Slavery: The Development of Ante-Bellum Slave Narratives* (1979); John Lovell, Jr., *Black Song: The Forge and the Flame: The Story of How the Afro-American Spiritual Was Hammered Out* (1972); Charles H. Nichols, ed., *Black Men in Chains: Narratives by Escaped Slaves* (1972); Gilbert Osofsky, ed., *Puttin' on Ole Massa: The Slave Narratives of Henry Bibb, William Wells Brown, and Solomon Northup* (1969); and Robert S. Starobin, ed., *Blacks in Bondage: Letters of American Slaves* (1974).

FRANCES SMITH FOSTER

TEXAS, SLAVERY IN. American Negro slavery had a relatively brief history in Texas. The institution lasted fewer than fifty years in the Lone Star State, whereas in some areas of the Old South it existed for more than two centuries.

Texas had just a small fraction of the total slave population of the United States (less than 5 percent in 1860), and slavery spread over only the eastern two-fifths of the state before 1865. Emancipation ended the institution far short of full maturity in Texas.

The limited historical experience of Texas with slavery must be recognized, but at the same time, this fact should not obscure the vital role of black bondage during the antebellum years. Texas was settled primarily by Southerners, many of whom brought with them bondsmen and all aspects of slaveholding culture as it existed in their home states. By the 1850s black slaves constituted a sizable minority, approximately 30 percent, of the Lone Star State's population. Moreover, Texas was slavery's last frontier. The state's rich soil held much of the future of the peculiar institution, and Texans knew it. James S. Mayfield of Fayette County undoubtedly spoke for many when he said, during the constitutional convention of 1845, slavery "is the most important institution of our land."

There were virtually no black bondsmen in Spanish Texas, so slavery as an institution of significance in the area arrived with settlers from the United States. Anglo-Americans, some of whom owned slaves, settled along the upper Red River and in the San Augustine–Nacogdoches area between 1815 and 1820, but slavery as an officially recognized institution in Texas began first at Austin's colony in 1821. The original grant given Moses Austin by Spanish authorities made no mention of slaves, but when Stephen F. Austin was recognized as heir to his father's impresario contract later in 1821, it was agreed that settlers could receive eighty acres of land for each bondsman brought to Texas. Enough of Austin's original 300 families brought slaves with them that a census of his colony in 1825 showed 443 slaves in a total population of 1,800.

Texas began to receive Anglo-American settlers just as Mexico gained full independence from Spain, and it remained a part of the new Mexican nation until 1836. During that period, both the national government in Mexico City and the state government of Coahuila y Texas based in Saltillo often threatened to restrict or destroy the institution of slavery. Their efforts resulted in a tangle of constitutional provisions and decrees, two of which will serve as examples. First, the Mexican Constitutional Convention of 1824 issued a decree on July 13 of that year outlawing the foreign and domestic slave trade. American settlers took this to mean that the importation of slaves as merchandise was illegal but that bondsmen could still come in with migrating owners. The intent of the Mexican Convention is not clear, but the American interpretation stood. A second example of this attitude of Mexican authorities came in 1827–1828. The constitution of the state of Coahuila y Texas outlawed any further importation of slaves and decreed that all children born into servitude thereafter would be freed at birth. Americans in Texas protested, however, and the state government soon agreed that slaves could be bound by labor contracts and brought in as indentured servants. Before migrating to Texas, masters signed contracts with their slaves promising freedom upon entering Mexican territory. The slaves in turn agreed that they owed their masters compensation for the property loss of emancipation plus the costs of moving to Texas and annual maintenance costs once there. They promised to work for their masters until this obligation was met. The debt, of course, could never be paid in full, and slaves who came in under such labor contracts remained firmly in servitude. Their children, even those born in Texas, were bound by the same system.

Thus political authorities in Mexico from 1821 to 1836 were hostile to slavery but did not adopt any consistent or effective policy to prevent or destroy the institution in Texas. Even then, their negative stance worried slaveholders and possibly retarded the immigration of planters from the Old South. It was estimated in 1836 that Texas had a population, excluding Indians, of 38,470, approximately 5,000 of whom were slaves. This amounted to 13 percent of the total, probably a smaller proportion than slaves would have been under more favorable circumstances.

The Texas Revolution opened the way for rapid expansion on slavery's frontier. This is not to say that securing slavery was a major cause of the revolution against Mexico. There is little direct evidence that slavery had more than peripheral involvement in the general cultural conflict and specific political grievances that led the Americans to revolt. Nevertheless, as they fought for independence, Texans were careful to preserve and protect the peculiar institution. The constitution of 1836 provided that slaves would remain the property of their owners, that congress could not prohibit the immigration of slaveholders bringing their property, that slaves could be imported from the United States (although not from Africa), and that no free blacks could enter the republic without the approval of congress.

Given these protections, slavery expanded rapidly during the period of the republic. By the end of 1845, when Texas approved annexation by the United States, its population included at least 30,000 bondsmen. Statehood then further secured the position of slavery in Texas. The constitution of 1845 continued the protections offered under the republic, and British influence in favor of emancipation, a threat during the early 1840s, was removed. Under these circumstances, the growth of slavery was spectacular for the remainder of the antebellum period. The U.S. census of 1850 reported 58,161 slaves, 27.4 percent of the 212,592 people in Texas, and the census of 1860 enumerated 182,566 bondsmen, 30.2 percent of the total population. The number of slaves thus rose 213 percent during the last antebellum decade. Texas was the fastest growing slave state in the Union on the eve of the Civil War.

Texas received thousands of new slaves every year during the 1840s and 1850s. The majority migrated with their owners to the Lone Star State. Sizable numbers, however, came through the domestic slave trade.* They were bought in the older states and sold to new masters in Texas. New Orleans was the center of the Deep South slave trade, but there were dealers in Shreveport, Galveston, and Houston too who always had bondsmen for sale. Finally, a small proportion of Texas's slaves, perhaps as many as 2,000 between 1835 and 1865, came through the illegal African trade.*

Slave prices* inflated rapidly as the institution flourished in Texas. Data are scarce on the early years, but it appears that slaves, regardless of age, sex, or condition, cost on the average approximately $400 in Austin's colony. Prices remained in that range until the 1840s and then inflated rapidly. The average price rose from approximately $400 in 1850 to roughly $800 in 1860. On the eve of the Civil War, prime male field hands* aged eighteen to thirty cost on the average $1,200, and skilled slaves such as blacksmiths often were valued at $1,800 to $2,000. In comparison, good cotton land could be bought for as little as $6 an acre. Antebellum Texas was certainly land rich and labor poor.

Slavery grew most importantly along the rivers that offered the richest soil and relatively inexpensive transportation. The greatest concentration of large plantations was along the lower Brazos and Colorado rivers near the state's central Gulf Coast. Texas's largest planters, such as the brothers Robert and D. G. Mills who owned 344 slaves in 1860, had plantations in this area, and the population was as heavily slave as that of the Old South's famed Black Belt. The combined population of Brazoria, Matagorda, Fort Bend, and Wharton counties, for example, was 70 percent slave in 1860. Northeastern Texas counties with reasonably good access to the Red River also had numerous slaves. Harrison County, situated on the Louisiana border west of Shreveport, had more bondsmen in absolute numbers than any other county in the state in 1850 (6,213) and 1860 (8,784). North-central Texas, the area centering on Dallas, had fewer slaves than any other settled part of the state in 1860, but it contained much good cotton land and would have expanded rapidly once adequate transportation was provided. Slavery's frontier seemed to have vast potential in 1860; some Texans believed that their state would eventually employ two to four million bondsmen.

Black slavery came to Texas as a preeminently economic institution, a system of unfree labor used to produce cash crops for profit.* Cotton* and sugar* plantations would not have been possible without it, and the evidence is strong, although not everyone will agree, that slavery in Texas generally was profitable as an individual business investment. The rate of return from cotton production and the natural increase of the slaves in 1850 and 1860 was consistently 6 percent or higher and ranged up to 12 percent for large planters on the eve of the Civil War. Slavery as an individual business in antebellum Texas thus showed no sign of falling under its own economic weight. But its impact on the state's broad economic development is more uncertain. Certainly the institution promoted expansion of Texas's agricultural economy, providing most of the labor for a 600 percent increase in cotton production during the 1850s. On the other hand, it may have contributed to the fact that the Lone Star State, like the rest of the South, lagged behind the northern United States in commercialization and industrialization. Planters, as the individuals who had the capital necessary to diversify the economy, appear to have been generally satisfied with their position as agriculturalists. Most saw no compelling reason to risk money on commercial or industrial ventures. Moreover, approximately 30 percent of Texas's population, the slaves, were not free consumers, and markets were limited accordingly.

Economic modernization lagged in Texas for many reasons, including the state's comparative advantage in agriculture, but slavery may have been part of the cause.

Slavery was also a vital social institution in antebellum Texas. Only one in every four families owned slaves, but these slaveholders, especially the planters who held twenty or more bondsmen, constituted the state's wealthiest and most influential class. They stood at the top of the social ladder that most other Texans hoped to climb. Even among the Texas Germans whose antislavery sentiments were emphasized by Frederick Law Olmsted* and others, many appear to have been nonslaveholders* primarily due to economic circumstances rather than conviction. Slavery reflected basic racial views in Texas too. Most whites believed that blacks were inferior and wanted to be sure that they remained at the bottom of the social ladder. Slavery guaranteed this.

It has frequently been claimed that slavery in Texas was somehow "better" or "easier" than bondage elsewhere in the Old South. The merits of such an argument could be disputed endlessly, but there appear to have been no basic differences between the legal status, work requirements, disciplinary standards, and material conditions of Texas slaves and those elsewhere in the South. Bondsmen in the Lone Star State had the legal status of personal property, movable chattels that could be bought and sold, mortgaged, hired out, and bequeathed as an inheritance. They had no legally prescribed way out of slavery, no property rights, and no rights of marriage and the family. Slaves in Texas had every imaginable occupation. There were craftsmen,* house servants,* and herdsmen, for example, but the majority worked as field hands five days a week and half a day on Saturday. Bondsmen were subject to disciplinary action by their masters, protected only by constitutional provisions that they be treated "with humanity" and that punishment* not extend to the taking of life or limb. Whipping* was the most common form of punishment. Use of the lash obviously varied from owner to owner, and it is not possible to determine the proportion of Texas slaves who escaped whippings. It is clear, however, that every slave lived daily with the knowledge that he could be whipped at his master's discretion.

The material conditions of slave life in Texas could best be described as "adequate." Bondsmen had enough food, shelter, clothing, and medical care to work effectively, rear families, and have their own social and cultural life. There was, however, little comfort and no luxury. Texas slaves ate primarily corn* and pork, foods heavy in calories and limited nutritionally. But most also had sweet potatoes and garden vegetables to supplement their basic diets,* and many had wild game and fish as well. Some suffered from too limited or unvaried a food supply, but apparently this was not common. Slave families typically lived in log cabins with dirt floors and little or no furniture except beds attached to the walls. Clothing* was generally made of cheap, coarse materials; shoes were notoriously rough and ill-fitting. Slaves seem to have found their clothing more objectionable than their food or housing. Health care,* due primarily to limited medical knowledge, was seriously lacking for everyone in antebellum

Texas, white as well as black. Masters generally tried to protect their slaves' health; after all, bondsmen were valuable property. But most slaves had a harder daily life than whites and accordingly suffered more from diseases and injuries.

In spite of constant labor and material conditions that were generally adequate at best, slaves in Texas maintained a social life and culture* of their own. They were able to do this in part because of the unequal distribution of bondsmen among the Lone Star State's slaveholders. In both 1850 and 1860, a majority of slaves (71 percent in 1860) belonged to holders of ten or more bondsmen. By 1860, nearly half were owned by planters who held twenty or more. This meant that the "typical" slave lived with a relatively large number of his fellow bondsmen. Therefore, they could form family units, educate their children about the slave system, worship together, have their own songs and celebrations, and in general develop the beliefs and practices of a slave culture.

Families appear to have been the central institution in transmitting this culture. Many Texas slaves had their families disrupted when they moved from older Southern states, and all the threats to family stability such as sales and estate settlements remained even after they settled in new homes. Nevertheless, most bondsmen in Texas lived with at least some members of their immediate families. Together they shaped and shared a culture that helped give them the strength to endure.

Slaves in Texas exhibited a broad range of behavioral adjustments to the peculiar institution. Some were willing to resist directly by running away or plotting violent rebellion. The state's proximity to Mexico apparently offered special inducements to runaways.* Thousands succeeded in crossing the Rio Grande where they were given a reasonably hospitable reception by the Mexicans. Texas slaveholders complained bitterly and pressed the U.S. government during the 1850s to negotiate an extradition treaty with Mexico. They also threatened to take matters into their own hands along the border and had the state legislature pass laws offering special incentives for the capture of runaways. Regardless, however, of this concern and the loss of thousands of slaves, runaways to Mexico were not numerous enough to pose a serious threat to slavery in Texas at the close of the antebellum period.

Texas had no major slave rebellions. Perhaps the most significant attempt was a plot involving several hundred Colorado County slaves in 1856. According to the bondsmen who gave away the proposed insurrection, they hoped to fight their way to freedom in Mexico. Three slaves were hanged, and two hundred were whipped. During the summer of 1860, northern and eastern Texas were swept by a series of fires and water source poisonings which supposedly resulted from an abolitionist plot. Vigilantism took over, and a number of whites and blacks were hanged. It is by no means clear that a plot ever existed; if it did, it was far short of a slave uprising.

Runaways and rebels were thus a minority among Texas slaves. The same was true of the loyal servants, those slaves who formed emotional ties of trust with kindly or paternalistic masters and were faithful bondsmen. Most, it seems, took a clear-eyed view of the institution. They recognized the injustice of their position as human property and knew that kind treatment did nothing to change the institution's basics. Josephine Howard, a slave in Harrison County, stated this view succinctly when she noted that her master was not any "worser dan other white folks." At the same time, most bondsmen recognized all the controls such as slave patrols* that existed to preserve the system and saw the heavy price runaways and rebels paid when they failed. Their reaction was to offer only nonviolent resistance and seek to survive on the best terms possible. The majority were not revolutionaries determined to destroy slavery, but they did not surrender totally to their situation either. Most Texas slaves dreamed of freedom and adjusted their behavior in ways that allowed them to endure until deliverance came.

Slaveholders dominated antebellum Texas. They held a disproportionately large share of all forms of wealth, and although a numerical minority, they controlled a majority of important public offices at the local and state level. The benefits of ownership were obvious, but slavery was a troublesome institution in many ways too. Constant tension was inherent in the management of human property. And the drumfire of moral criticism from outside the South was also unsettling. Texas's slaveholders always stood ready to defend slavery, but they paid a price, albeit a smaller one than the bondsmen, for the institution.

The Civil War* did not disrupt slavery in Texas because Union forces did not invade any major slaveholding area. The occupation of Galveston in 1862–1863 drove many slaveholders from that city, and bondsmen were used in preparing coastal fortifications. Generally, however, slaves in the Texas interior continued to live and work as they had during the 1850s. In fact, the population increased notably, even doubling in some interior counties by 1864, as owners in other states "refugeed" their property away from battle areas to the more secure Southwest. A great many Texas slaves did come to understand during the war that they would be free if the South lost. They listened eagerly for war news, passed it around among themselves, and in some cases even discussed what they would do when freedom came.

Slavery formally ended in Texas on 19 June 1865 ("Juneteenth," as it became known among blacks) when General Gordon Granger arrived at Galveston with occupying Union forces and announced emancipation. It took time for this news to spread across the state, but slavery ended everywhere that summer. The emancipated slaves joyfully celebrated their dream of deliverance come true and then set about discovering what emancipation meant. Unfortunately, few Texans, black or white, were prepared for freedom.

SELECTED BIBLIOGRAPHY

Lester E. Bugbee, "Slavery in Early Texas," *Political Science Quarterly*, 13 (1898), 389–412 and 648–668; Abigail Curlee, "A Study of Texas Slave Plantations, 1822–1865" (Ph.D. dissertation, University of Texas, 1932); James Smallwood, "Blacks in Antebellum Texas: A Reappraisal," *Red River Valley Historical Review*, 2 (1975), 443–

466; Ronnie C. Tyler and Lawrence R. Murphy, eds., *The Slave Narratives of Texas* (1974); and George R. Woolfolk, "Cotton Capitalism and Slave Labor in Texas," *Southwestern Social Science Quarterly*, 27 (1956), 43–52.

RANDOLPH B. CAMPBELL

TEXTILE INDUSTRY. Textile manufacturers in the antebellum South employed slaves as workers from the earliest days of the industry until the end of slavery. They used slave labor when it was economically viable and advantageous to do so, and they generally found that slave labor was just as good as, if not better than, free labor.

Labor costs and the availability of an adequate supply of suitable workers were the primary determinants in decisions to employ or not employ slaves. Personal preference was a secondary consideration. Labor costs included either wages for free labor or the purchase price or hiring price for slave labor. There were maintenance costs also. For slaves, those costs included housing, food, and sometimes clothing and health care. For free labor, those costs might include erecting and operating a village.

The adequacy of the labor supply depended both upon the pool of workers a manufacturer could draw on and the size and kind of operation the manufacturer had. During the initial phase of the texile industry in the South, the 1790s to the 1830s, most manufacturers were planters/mill owners whose principal concern was their agricultural operations. They ran very small factories on their plantations where they used slaves who had little or no value as field hands,* primarily women* and children.* During slack seasons in farming, they sometimes expanded their factory force by using idle field hands.

By the 1840s the nature of the Southern textile industry had changed markedly. Mills had more spindles than earlier mills (at least 1,000 or more), usually had their own looms, sometimes ran their own dyeing operations, and generally employed thirty to forty workers. Instead of running mills as ancillaries to their plantations, mill owners expended most of their energies and time on factory operations. These operations had to have work forces which were better trained and more steady than mills of the earlier era. Here, slave labor—especially if the slaves were owned, not hired, by the manufacturer—offered real advantages to employers since turnover and absenteeism were severely restricted.

The widespread use of slaves in the Southern textile industry underscores these advantages and clearly demonstrates the ability of slave labor to perform well in the industry. Postbellum assertions that blacks could not do the work required of textile workers were based upon prejudice, not fact. Slaves worked in textile factories in Virginia, the Carolinas, Georgia, Florida, Alabama, Tennessee, and Mississippi. Their numbers did not, however, reach the "thousands" that one historian claimed. In fact, their numbers shrank markedly during the 1850s when the rising prices* of slaves and of raw cotton made hiring* or purchasing slaves for work in textile mills less advantageous financially. By 1860 few textile firms in the Southeast used slaves as workers, while those in the Old Southwest continued to rely heavily upon slave labor. Mills sometimes used only slaves and sometimes mixes of slaves and free blacks and whites. In at least one instance, in Columbus, Georgia, mill owners ceased using slaves to appease those in the community who denounced racial mixing, especially employing both blacks and white women. Racial mixing did not, however, seem to have evoked as strong a protest in the South as when slaves were used as artisans. This difference may indicate that white mill hands in the antebellum South had little status or political voice. At least one textile manufacturer, William Gregg, thought that the threatened or actual use of slaves in mills could serve as a means of controlling white workers.

Textile mill owners confronted problems in managing slave labor that were not unlike those confronted by employers of free labor. They offered the slave workers several incentives: extra pay for extra work, promotions to better positions in the mill, and free time. Moreover, a number of firms used slaves in family units. Employers in textiles, unlike those in iron* and coal, lumber,* or some urban services, could severely limit the physical mobility of their slave workers. They could not, however, offer mill work as an attractive alternative to fieldwork since mill work then was so arduous and even dangerous.

In textile mills slaves often behaved in ways not unlike those of other workers, bound or free. They malingered and stole. They ran off. They sabotaged their work and their workplace. The worst they did was commit arson, a danger to which textile factories were particularly subject. Within the walls of cotton mills in the South, slaves struggled to control their own lives even as they demonstrated convincingly that slavery and industrialization were not necessarily alien to each other.

SELECTED BIBLIOGRAPHY

Randall M. Miller, "The Fabric of Control: Slavery in the Antebellum Southern Textile Mills," *Business History Review*, 55 (1981), 471–490; Robert S. Starobin, *Industrial Slavery in the Old South* (1970); Allen H. Stokes, Jr., "Black and White Labor and the Development of the Southern Textile Industry, 1800–1920" (Ph.D. dissertation, University of South Carolina, 1977); Tom E. Terrill, "Eager Hands: Labor for Southern Textiles, 1850–1860," *Journal of Economic History*, 36 (1976), 84–99; and Gavin Wright, "Cheap Labor and Southern Textiles before 1880," *Journal of Economic History*, 39 (1979), 655–680.

TOM E. TERRILL

THIRTEENTH AMENDMENT. In the wake of Union military victories at Gettysburg and Vicksburg in 1863, which severely weakened the Confederacy and promised to fulfill Lincoln's Emancipation Proclamation* freeing slaves in rebel areas, the Republican party majority in Congress turned its attention to the elimination of slavery in law as well as in fact, and to the extension of civil rights to the freed people. On 14 December James M. Ashley (Ohio) introduced into the House of Representatives a proposition for a constitutional amendment to abolish slavery throughout the United States. One year later (January 1865) the proposal was adopted by both houses of Congress after protracted debates. Following ratification by twenty-seven states, the Thirteenth Amendment became part of the Constitution in December 1865. "Neither slavery nor involuntary servitude," ran the amendment, "except as a punishment for crime, whereof the party shall have been duly convicted, shall exist within the United States, or any place subject to their jurisdiction. Congress shall have power to enforce this article by appropriate legislation."

The simplicity of the amendment's language is deceptive, as a perusal of the voluminous record of the congressional debates makes clear. The proponents of the measure had clearly in mind a fourfold objective when they enacted the destruction of slavery: to abolish property rights in human beings and to strike off the shackles that bound them; to abolish all the "burdens and badges" of slavery that afflicted not only slaves in the South but free black people wherever they might live; to endow victims of discrimination on the grounds of color with equal rights under American law; and to extend the mantle of federal protection not only to black people but to any Americans who might in the future be branded with a stigma of inferiority and exposed to unequal treatment.

The Democratic minority, especially in the House of Representatives, vehemently opposed passage of the amendment. This measure, they said, would accomplish a huge transfer of power from the states to the federal government and would thus destroy the constitutional system. The amendment, its opponents said, would not amend the Constitution; it would revolutionize it.

The objectives of the Republican party* were indeed far-reaching. Republicans understood clearly enough that a "revolution in federalism" was necessary if they were to achieve their goals. In this respect authorization to enforce the amendment by "appropriate legislation" was no ordinary grant of power.

An authoritative statement with regard to the original meaning and thrust of the Thirteenth Amendment comes from the pen of John Marshall Harlan (1833–1911), associate justice of the U.S. Supreme Court, and himself a Kentucky slaveholder during the antebellum period. Harlan's analysis of the amendment was part of his dissenting opinion in the *Civil Rights Cases* (1883), in which the Supreme Court initiated the process of "burying" the wartime amendments and reducing them to dead letters. This dissent carries weight because it is a concise, accurate summation of the consensus reached by the Thirteenth Amendment's proponents during the congressional debates of 1864 and 1865.

The amendment, wrote Justice Harlan, went far beyond the abolition of chattel ownership, important though that was. One central purpose of the Thirteenth Amendment was to overturn and set aside the Supreme Court's decision in the infamous Dred Scott case* (1857). Speaking through Chief Justice Roger B. Taney, the Court had declared in that case that black people, whether slave or free, were an inferior race that could never be accepted as an integral part of the American community; they did not have, nor could they ever have, any rights which white people were bound to respect. Both North and South, said Taney, this was "an axiom of American politics," practiced by individuals, and built into the fabric of the nation's institutional life with the explicit purpose of maintaining and enforcing the inferior status of black people.

The Thirteenth Amendment, argued Justice Harlan, rejected Taney's "axiom" in terms that "are absolute and universal." The amendment required the elimination of all the badges and incidents of slavery denoting inferior status that had been imposed upon millions of people both North and South. The most odious of these were segregation, discrimination, and violence directed against people who bore a stigma and were stripped of human rights simply because their skin was black.

The Thirteenth Amendment was the first crucial step in elevating black people from the status of helots or slaves to citizens endowed with full rights under the protection of the sovereignty and laws of the United States. The amendment widened the sweep of the struggle for human rights that had been initiated by the American Revolution* but never carried to completion. It implied a new concept of paramount national citizenship that accomplished a radical change in the federal system. Freedom, a newly created national right, now came under the direct protection of the national government. Executive and judicial as well as legislative branches were now duty-bound to use their authority to protect the rights of black citizens.

Following the Compromise of 1877, which conceded the return of the South to white supremacist rule, the memory of the Thirteenth Amendment as a national charter of liberty faded. Historians came to view the amendment as an item in the constitutional record as archaic as the fugitive slave clause itself. But revival of black Southerners' struggle against segregation (1955–1965) stimulated the beginning of a reappraisal. In a landmark decision of 1968, *Jones v. Mayer*, the Supreme Court resurrected the Thirteenth Amendment and ruled that discrimination in the sale or leasing of property based solely upon the color of the purchaser's skin was a badge of slavery. "[W]hen," said Justice Potter Stewart for the Court, "racial discrimination herds men into ghettos and makes their ability to buy property turn on the color of their skin, then it too is a relic of slavery."

Jones v. Mayer pointed the way toward the recovery of the original purpose and intent of the Thirteenth Amendment. As interpreted by the Court in *Jones v. Mayer*, the amendment directed the federal government to aid the black community to eliminate urban ghettos with their slum housing, massive unemployment, and inadequate schools. These, said the Court, are badges of slavery which perpetuate second-class citizenship and the stigma of inferiority. As a result of the *Jones* decision, the Thirteenth Amendment has emerged in our own time as a universal charter of freedom and equality for all people in the United States.

SELECTED BIBLIOGRAPHY

G. Sidney Buchanan, *The Quest for Freedom: A Legal History of the Thirteenth Amendment* (1976); Arthur Kinoy, "The Constitutional Right to Negro Freedom," *Rutgers Law*

Review, 21 (1967), 387–441; Arthur Kinoy, "The Constitutional Right to Negro Freedom Revisited: Some First Thoughts on *Jones v. Alfred H. Mayer Company*," *Rutgers Law Review*, 22 (1968), 537–552; and John Anthony Scott, "Segregation as a Fundamental Aspect of Southern Race Relations, 1800–1860," *Journal of the Early Republic*, 4 (1984), 421–441.

ARTHUR KINOY
JOHN ANTHONY SCOTT

TOBACCO. When John Rolfe began his experiments with imported *Nicotiana tabacum* seed at Jamestown in 1612, Europeans had already acquired a taste for the Spanish variety of tobacco. The discovery that this milder tobacco could be successfully grown on the North American mainland and profitably sold in England was the most important economic event in the history of seventeenth-century Virginia, Maryland, and, to a lesser degree, North Carolina. By 1700 these three colonies produced roughly forty million pounds of tobacco annually.

White labor dominated seventeenth-century tobacco husbandry. In the early 1680s, for example, there were 15,000 white indentured servants in Virginia, but only 3,000 Negroes. Such a sizable impermanent labor force made large-scale farm operations exceptional. Beginning in the last decade of the century, however, black slaves were imported in large numbers as the tobacco culture expanded beyond the tidewater and into the piedmont. Black slaves soon replaced white servants as the major source of servile labor. By 1775 Virginia, Maryland, and North Carolina were exporting more than one hundred million pounds of tobacco annually. Blacks thus played an important role in the economic growth and development of these tobacco colonies in the eighteenth century. Although the tobacco industry was sharply curtailed during the American Revolution, prewar production levels returned by the early 1790s.

Several important developments occurred in the tobacco industry between the American Revolution and the Civil War: the geographical expansion of the crop as a commercial staple; the impact of different soil types that produced several distinct types of tobacco; the emergence of three different curing methods; and changes in the primary methods of consuming tobacco. The decline of tobacco culture in tidewater Virginia was accompanied by a comparable expansion into the piedmont areas of Virginia and North Carolina, and temporarily into South Carolina and Georgia. By 1800, as settlers moved from Virginia and North Carolina across the mountains, tobacco was emerging as an important commercial staple crop in Kentucky and Tennessee. During the next half-century Florida, Missouri, Ohio, Arkansas, Indiana, Wisconsin, Pennsylvania, New York, Connecticut, and Massachusetts began to produce tobacco commercially.

Throughout the colonial era tobacco was air-cured, though by the end of the period, small, open wood fires on the earthen floors of the tobacco barns were used to drive out excessive moisture and to hasten the curing process. Though both methods were carried across the mountains, by 1860 air-curing was more common than curing with fire. In the Virginia–North Carolina tobacco belt a third curing method evolved using charcoal instead of wood. Credit for the first curing of Bright tobacco using charcoal instead of wood rightfully belongs to Stephen, a young slave blacksmith and foreman on Abisha Slade's farm in Caswell County, North Carolina. In 1839, during the wood-curing of a barn of tobacco, the fire became almost extinguished; Stephen hurried to the charcoal pit and seized several charred butts of wood instead of wet logs and placed them on the dying embers. Application of the sudden drying heat from the charcoal produced a barnful of the brightest yellow tobacco ever seen. Although curing with charcoal soon became the most common method of curing Bright tobacco until after the Civil War, flue-curing systems were being developed and their use spread rapidly after the cessation of hostilities.

Until the Civil War, most tobacco was transported on rivers and canals. Negro slaves became experts at handling the hogsheads of tobacco, manning the river craft and canal boats, and providing many of the skilled services required on the tobacco plantation. Southern tobacco factories, located mainly in Virginia and North Carolina, employed slave labor almost exclusively. In 1860 52 percent of the blacks employed in the Virginia tobacco factories were slaves hired* from their owners. In the tobacco towns, especially in Richmond and Petersburg, Virginia, hired slaves received privileges more characteristic of free laborers. These slaves commonly were allowed to select their own employers and were supplied with money on a weekly basis, with which to obtain food and lodging. Hired tobacco slaves generally could come and go as they pleased and were assigned reasonable tasks. They received appreciable bonuses in cash for extra labor. Some Negroes outside the factory towns, such as Lunsford Lane of Raleigh, North Carolina, were also quite enterprising. Lane became a well-known local manufacturer of smoking tobacco favored by the state legislators. He earned enough to purchase his freedom in 1835.

As a rule, slaveholding in the tobacco regions of the South was less extensive, less formal, and more patriarchal than in cotton cultivation. The utilization of Negro foremen was also more common on the small farming units of the upper South than in the large plantation belts to the South. Ownership of one or two slaves provided tobacco farmers with an enormous advantage, oftentimes spelling the difference between mere subsistence and a cash income. Nor was it uncommon for small slaveholders to work in the tobacco fields alongside the blacks.

The Civil War brought several changes to the Southern tobacco belts. Due largely to the devastation of war, and the growing demand for a new variety of Burley tobacco, Kentucky replaced Virginia as the leading tobacco-growing state. The increased demand for smoking tobacco influenced the expansion of the Bright tobacco belt in the post–Civil War era. The end of slavery produced a change in the nature of the labor supply. Most ex-slaves who engaged in tobacco farming now did so as sharecroppers.

SELECTED BIBLIOGRAPHY

W. W. Garner, *The Production of Tobacco* (1951); Lewis C. Gray, *History of Agriculture in the Southern United States to 1860* (2 vols., 1933); Robert K. Heinmann, *Tobacco and Americans* (1960); G. Melvin Herndon, *William Tatham and the Culture of Tobacco* (1969); Allan Kulikoff, *Tobacco and Slaves: The Development of Southern Cultures in the Chesapeake, 1680–1800* (1986); Joseph C. Robert, *The Story of Tobacco in America* (1967); and Nannie May Tilley, *The Bright-Tobacco Industry, 1860–1929* (1948).

G. MELVIN HERNDON

TRAVEL ACCOUNTS. Between 1780 and 1860 visitors produced a remarkably voluminous body of travel accounts on slavery in the Old South. Coming from England, Europe, and the American North, the travelers represented diverse professions and occupations. Among them were missionaries,* land scouts, actors following the theatrical circuit, and scientists. Many were political theorists who wished to observe the workings of American democracy in the various sections of the United States. Some observers were patient, methodical, and persistent in searching for answers to their questions. Most, however, were satisfied to record conclusions drawn from casual street, roadside, and tavern-room and drawing-room conversations, cursory visits to farms and plantations, and wayside talks with planters.

Such hit-and-miss observations provided travelers with severely limited information on slavery and weaken the value of travel accounts as historical sources. Rarely did travelers actually observe slavery through day-to-day or season-to-season operation. Few viewed the peculiar institution from the perspective of the slave owner—his concern over the management, production, and marketing of staple crops, his fear of crop failures, his nagging uncertainties about the profitability and sociological and political future of slavery. In virtually no instance did a traveler conduct extensive conversations with the slaves themselves. And few travelers were adept at recording verbatim testimony from individuals they encountered in their travels.

Observations of slave life generally resulted from casual contacts with slaves—at roadsides, at ferry crossings, on steamboats, on streets, in lodging places, and at slave auctions. Frequently travelers judged the entire institution by isolated incidents they viewed or heard about. The most dependable evidence of the nature and impact of slavery in the South among the travelers' accounts are those in which the authors confirmed their observations with recognized statistical sources. In 1856 Henry Chase and Charles W. Sanborn published such a source, *The North and South: A Statistical View of the Conditions of the Free and Slave States.*

Most early travel accounts published before 1820, however, outlined a formula that appeared repeatedly in numerous later travel accounts. Visitors to the South in the late eighteenth and early nineteenth centuries generally agreed that slavery was an evil, an anachronism in a republican society. They found it difficult to reconcile the existence of slavery in the same region that had spawned such Enlightenment thinkers as Thomas Jefferson* and James Madison. Many foreign missionaries and Quakers* came to the South with rather firmly fixed negative opinions of slavery as an inhumane and socially immoral institution. In their travels they set out to confirm their prejudices.

In 1791, for example, Jacques Pierre Brissot de Warville published his three-volume *Nouveau Voyage dans les États Unis de l'America* in which he charged that slavery debauched eighteenth-century white Southerners. Another traveler, German surgeon Johann David Schoepf, made extensive observations of slavery in Virginia and North Carolina in *Reise durch einige der Mittlern und Südlichen Vereinigten Nord Staaten* . . . (1788). He recorded a wide range of impressions of slavery, including differing racial groups within the slave communities, different treatment accorded slave field hands and house servants, and the presence of talented slave artisans. On the whole, however, Schoepf damned slavery as an oppressive and exploitative system, one that forced whites to pass repressive curfew and patrol laws. In 1808 another foreign traveler, Methodist minister Thomas Coke (*Extracts of the Journals of the Late Rev. Thomas Coke, LL.D.* [1816]), barely escaped being mobbed on the Virginia–North Carolina border for espousing similar views.

Foreigners were struck by slavery's importance in a land supposedly devoted to freedom and liberty. Captain Thomas Hamilton (Cyril Thornton) raised this contradiction succinctly in *Men and Manners in America* (2 vols., 1833), when he asked: "But now when the United States of America have enjoyed upwards of a half century of almost unbroken prosperity, when their people, as they themselves declare, are the most moral, the most benevolent, the most enlightened in the world, we are surely entitled to demand, what have these people done to elevate the slave in the scale of moral and intellectual being, to prepare him for the enjoyment of those privileges to which, sooner or later, the coloured population *must* be admitted?" To his query, Hamilton responded: "NOTHING." He realized, however, that the abolition of slavery involved for the South numerous fears and tensions.

One traveler after another noted the ill effects slavery had upon the South. They blamed slavery for everything from the region's alleged low morality to its high level of illiteracy. Almost universally travelers faulted slavery for holding back the South's economy, by keeping its agriculture less diversified than farms of the free states. For example, those travelers who followed the "grand circuit" by way of the western rivers and Cincinnati identified in northern Kentucky the supposedly deleterious influences of slavery. They failed to realize, however, that few slaves resided there and that the natural forces of geology and geography had conditioned the land, not slavery.

Many travelers also recited instances of maltreatment and brutalities committed by the slaveholders, though few were able to describe such incidents firsthand. In 1828, for instance, Karl Postal (Charles Sealsfield) wrote in *The Americans as They Are, Described in a Tour Through the Valley of the Mississippi* that he

saw slave catchers returning to central Kentucky with three runaway slaves*
who had fled to Ohio. The wretched victims reportedly were led by ropes attached
to iron neck bands. The slaves were lashed with long whips in order to keep
them apace with trotting horses. Their backs were slashed and bloody. In *Remarks
During a Journey Through North America in the Years 1819, 1820, and 1821*
(1823) Adam Hodgson wrote that he had learned of harsh treatment of slaves
who had run away for being overworked by their master. Hodgson also mentioned
an instance when a slave woman had been burned to death for murdering her
master.

Few aspects of slavery stirred emotions more fervently among travelers than
the public auction of bondsmen. Many visitors to the South described slave sales
minutely, detailing how masters, auctioneers, and prospective purchasers had
fondled female slaves in what they termed a disgusting and socially unacceptable
manner. Travelers recorded the grievous wails of parents forcibly separated from
their children, and the cries of spouses who were separated by sale. English
merchant Robert Sutcliff (*Travels in Some Parts of North America, in the Years
1804, 1805, & 1806* [1811]), accused Richmond, Virginia, slaveholders of both
cohabiting freely with their female slaves and selling at auction their own flesh
and blood.

Travelers also criticized slavery by cataloging such institutional elements of
slave life as diet* and clothing.* Foreigners judged the coarse rations issued the
bondsmen fit more for animal consumption than for humans. Field hands were
said to be thinly clad, often working in a near naked state. Children up to a
certain age reportedly walked about unclothed. One or two travelers repeated
stories of naked slave children waiting on their masters' dining tables. Travelers
described such privileged slaves as house servants, however, as receiving special
food and clothing and generally presenting highly respectable appearances.

Again and again travelers to the South noted the fears and doubts that white
Southerners shared over slavery. The enslaved population, some travelers were
convinced, posed a constant threat to the South's peace of mind and safety. To
prove their point, some observers described acts of violence by slaves against
masters and overseers. Many commented on the Denmark Vesey conspiracy*
and Nat Turner insurrection,* remarking that even in the happiest plantation
situations, an incipient rebellion seethed beneath the apparent calm. In *Travels
in North America in the Years 1841–1842* (2 vols., 1845), the famous English
geologist Sir Charles Lyell stated the case succinctly when he wrote: "Many
proprietors live with their wives and children quite isolated in the midst of slaves,
so that the danger of any popular movement is appalling." Travelers to Charleston
in the wake of the 1822 Denmark Vesey scare described the city's elaborate
policing and jail systems. While in another coastal city, Savannah, Georgia,
Lyell noticed that his slave guide bore a pass that restricted him to certain streets
when he traveled after dark.

Landscape architect Frederick Law Olmsted* ranks as the best-known and
most influential of the Northern travelers who recorded their impressions of

slavery. In 1854 Olmsted visited the lower Mississippi Valley, the first of three trips below the Mason-Dixon line. Olmsted's views of the conditions of life of both whites and blacks varied sharply with those of visitors to the older coastal states. The picture of slavery that emerged in *A Journey in the Back Country in the Winter of 1853–1854* (1860) was harsher than that portrayed in his subsequent *Journey in the Seaboard Slave States in the Years 1853–1854* (2 vols., 1856). Olmsted criticized slavery, arguing that it stifled the training of skilled craftsmen and laborers, belittled free labor, debased self-respect, thwarted ambition, and withheld from human beings motives to develop their capabilities. In progressing through the South, Olmsted followed somewhat the paths of migration into the Old Southwest, though with excursions away from the beaten path. He traveled across almost every geographical and sociological segment of Southern slavery from Virginia to Louisiana. In no instance, however, did Olmsted linger long enough to view either the Southern economic system or slavery over a broad interval of time or scope or geography. In no case did he accumulate sufficient data on the scene to sustain his broad generalizations. The Southerner's fear of educating slaves, or training them in the more sophisticated or finished crafts, was at best degrading to everybody, he wrote. "Wherever the influence of slavery extends," Olmsted explained, "these occupations to which slaves are condemned are considered to belong to a lower *Caste* of the community and to degrade them."

Whereas Olmsted's travel accounts indicted slavery on economic grounds, other travelers subjected the institution to severe moral and social strictures. In 1849, for example, Scotch journalist Alex MacKay published the two-volume work *The Western World; or, Travels in the United States in 1846–1847*. MacKay devoted much of his observations to slavery's moral and political sides. In doing so he produced one of the most perceptive and incisive accounts of the peculiar institution as it existed in the 1840s. Commenting on the morality of slavery, MacKay wrote, "the peculiar position of the Southern States is this, that they [the whites] are afflicted with an evil which they fear to attempt the removal of; an evil already grown beyond their control, and increasing in magnitude every hour; an evil of which nothing but a social convulsion can rid them; which when it comes, as it assuredly will, may give rise to a political disposition of the continent as yet undreamed of . . . ."

Five years after MacKay's book appeared, the Reverend Nehemiah Adams, a Boston Congregationalist minister, visited the South when "the providence of God made it necessary for [him] to become for a while a stranger in a strange land." At the conclusion of his three-month visit, Adams wrote: "Let us adopt the principle that the South is competent to manage the subject of slavery, and straightway cease from offensive action." He predicted that continued abolitionist assaults on slavery might indeed force the South to abandon the Union. This in itself, Adams explained, would do nothing to ameliorate the lot of the slaves. Although antislavery in tone, Adams's comments on slavery were nonetheless remarkably fair. He attempted to view slavery as objectively as possible, examining the institution from several perspectives, including slave dress, physical care, conditions of labor, the domestic slave trade, slave home life, and religious training. In instances where he lacked firsthand observations, Adams solicited information from men whom he considered to be well-informed, such as Virginia Governor Henry A. Wise. Perhaps reflecting the influence of such influential Southerners, Adams judged Harriet Beecher Stowe's* book *Uncle Tom's Cabin* (1852) as grossly inaccurate. Stowe's harsh description of slave treatment clashed with Adams' personal observations.

Obviously, historians must use great care and caution when employing travel accounts as primary sources to document the slave experience. Many factors helped shape travelers' observations—the physical discomforts of travel, strange diet, indifferent lodging accommodations, the casualness with which Southerners passed on gossip to strangers, and the exceedingly fleeting nature of most of the observations. In addition, few of the travelers understood the impact that the emerging frontier had upon both slaves and masters. English travelers especially tended to compare institutions and social developments with those in contemporary Britain. Many of them arrived in the South with preconceptions of what they would find and never relinquished them. After the 1830s the views of British travelers were no doubt influenced by England's emancipation of the slaves. They naturally compared the conditions of slave life unfavorably with conditions of the recently freed black men and women of the British Empire.

Significantly, most travelers in the late antebellum period emphasized slavery's social, economic, and political deficiencies. They viewed the institution on moral grounds and faulted the slave owners for failing to educate their bondsmen, to grant them equal justice before the law, and to grant the blacks political representation. They criticized the harsh physical treatment meted out to the slaves and judged the domestic slave trade* the most egregious element of an undeniably heinous system. They underscored the paradox of slavery's presence in a political system that was built upon democracy. Some predicted that slavery would succumb to the competition of free labor; others prophesied that the peculiar institution would ultimately destroy the Union.

SELECTED BIBLIOGRAPHY

Max Berger, "American Slavery As Seen by British Travelers, 1836–1860," *Journal of Negro History*, 30 (1945), 181–202; Eugene H. Berwanger, *As They Saw Slavery* (1973); Thomas D. Clark, ed., *Travels in the Old South* (3 vols., 1956–1959); Lenworth Gunther, ed., *Black Image: European Eyewitness Accounts of Afro-American Life* (1978); David G. Hewett, "Slavery in the Old South: The British Travelers' Image, 1825–1860" (Ph.D. dissertation, Tulane University, 1968); Eugene L. Schwab and Jacqueline Bull, eds., *Travels in the Old South Selected from Periodicals of the Times* (2 vols., 1973); and Dana F. White and Victor A. Kramer, eds., *Olmsted South: Old South Critic/New South Planner* (1979).

THOMAS D. CLARK

TRIALS, SLAVE. Slave trials in the Old South varied substantially in formality, fairness, and punitive severity. Post–1970 scholarship on the legal history of American slavery has left intact or refined some earlier generalizations, advanced new ones, and reached no consensus about other issues. Three important generalizations remain largely intact. First, most "slave trials" were not formal trials. Rather, slave discipline occurred largely on the South's farms and plantations. Refinement of earlier views, however, indicates substantial penetration of formal law into the slave economy by the Jacksonian era, especially in Southern cities.

Second, lower court trials for misdemeanors generally used procedures defective relative to current American conceptions of due process. Most such trials were conducted by judges and slaveholders acting together as "judge-jurors," soon after the offense was detected, and without defense counsel. Recent scholarship, however, stresses interjurisdictional differences in felony procedures. Virginia (lacking provision for appeal to its highest court) and South Carolina (using magistrate and freeholder courts even in capital cases, but permitting appeal) offered the least protection for the slaves. North Carolina and Tennessee offered the most protection for the bondsmen, including rights to counsel, jury trial, and appeal.

Third, statutes regarding slave jurisprudence became more humane over time. Nothing in nineteenth-century Southern law approached the cruelty, for example, of the 1741 New York court that sentenced an insurrectionary slave "to be burned with a slow fire, that he may continue in torment for eight or ten hours . . . until he be dead." Nonetheless, Southern trends toward humanizing slave law lagged behind Northern legal reform, and remained subject to lynch-law breakdown and repressive severity, especially during insurrectionary scares.

Two new generalizations commanding reasonable consensus in post-1970 scholarship particularly merit notice. Many post-1800 Southern supreme courts declared concern for insisting upon fair procedures. Of 185 appeals between 1830 and 1860 taken by slaves to nine slave state supreme courts, 111 were successful. Also, regionwide verdicts about slave trial justice may be too gross to be very meaningful. On the one hand, Texas and Tennessee courts frequently leaned in favor of the slave. The Georgia court, on the other hand, was much less generous. Critical differences sprang from answers to a fundamental jurisprudential question. Were slaves protected only by positive statute, as the Georgia judiciary held? Or, were they also protected by the common law, as the North Carolina judiciary held?

At least two important lower court issues remain unresolved. How often were the innocent convicted? And what proportion of erroneous convictions were appealed?

There is scholarly disagreement concerning the mix of purposes behind, not statutory law, but rather judge-made law. The "neo-abolitionist" interpretation sees appellate decisions as "dependent variables," reflecting, and sufficiently explained by, the South's repressive internal and combative external political economy. This clashes with the other two principal views. Both the revisionist Marxist interpretation and the "neo-Whiggish" one argue that numerous judges did more than merely apply statutes, repress slaves with maximal force, and reflect "mirror-like" the judges' class interests. While they concur with each other in attributing greater autonomy to the legal system, they differ respecting the overall development of slave law. The Marxist view perceives a clearer evolution of Southern legal rules away from Northern and English legal systems. The "Neo-Whiggish" view stresses more both inter-slave-state differences and the individualism of different judges' behavior. It argues that struggles between liberalism and repression characterized Southern slave trials to the Civil War and that Southern law did not as a whole break clearly away from its anchorage in Anglo-American law.

SELECTED BIBLIOGRAPHY

Paul Finkelman, *An Imperfect Union: Slavery, Federalism, and Comity* (1981); Michael Stephen Hindus, *Prison and Plantation: Crime, Justice, and Authority in Massachusetts and South Carolina* (1980); Arthur Howington, "Not in the Condition of a Horse or an Ox," *Tennessee Historical Quarterly*, 34 (1975), 249–263; A. E. Keir Nash, "Fairness and Formalism in the Trials of Blacks in the State Supreme Courts of the Old South," *Virginia Law Review*, 54 (1970), 64–100; A. E. Keir Nash, "Reason of Slavery: Understanding the Judicial Role in the Peculiar Institution," *Vanderbilt Law Review*, 32 (1979), 7–218; and Mark V. Tushnet, *The American Law of Slavery, 1810–1860: Considerations of Humanity and Interest* (1981).

A. E. KEIR NASH

TRUTH, SOJOURNER (ca. 1797–1883). Named Isabella at her birth in Hurley, Ulster County, New York, Sojourner Truth was the daughter of James and Elizabeth, slaves of a wealthy Dutch farmer. Sold when about eleven, she worked on family farms in Ulster County. Unusually tall and strong, she was "better than a man," one master boasted, "for she will do a good family's washing in the night, and be ready in the morning to go into the field." Her industry did not prevent beatings or a forced marriage to Thomas, a fellow slave. Of her five children, four (Elizabeth, Hannah, Sophia, and Peter) survived infancy. In 1826, the year before New York State emancipated its slaves, she ran away from her owner with her infant daughter Sophia.

In New York City from 1829 to 1843, she supported herself by domestic work while searching for life's deeper meanings. A religious mystic, she took the name Sojourner Truth and set out to preach against sin, including the sin of slavery. Six feet tall, wearing a gray dress and white turban which accentuated her black skin, she became a commanding presence at antislavery and women's rights meetings. Her trenchant sayings and witty repartee, delivered in a deep, Dutch-accented voice, were widely reported. Teaching freedwomen in Washington, D.C., during the Civil War and finding jobs for them afterwards, she spent her last years crusading for black settlements on public lands in the West. She made her home in Battle Creek, Michigan, near her daughters and their families, until her death.

SELECTED BIBLIOGRAPHY

Jacqueline Bernard, *Journey toward Freedom: The Story of Sojourner Truth* (1967); Arthur H. Fauset, *Sojourner Truth* (1938); Olive Gilbert and Frances W. Titus, *Narrative of Sojourner Truth . . . drawn from Her Book of Life* (1878); and Hertha Pauli, *Her Name Was Sojourner Truth* (1962).

                                                                        DOROTHY STERLING

TUBMAN, HARRIET (ca. 1820–1913). Harriet Tubman was born in Dorchester County, Maryland, the daughter of Benjamin and Harriet Ross. She was hired out as baby nurse when aged five or six. When she was in her teens, an overseer struck her in the head; the blow caused spells of unconsciousness which persisted throughout her life. Despite the injury, she performed the heaviest tasks in the fields, plowing with an ox team and lifting huge barrels. In 1849, learning that she and her brothers were to be sold, she determined to run away. Five years earlier she had married John Tubman, a free black. When he refused to accompany her, she set out alone, traveling at night, hiding by day, until she reached Pennsylvania.

Working as a domestic, she financed periodic trips to the South to rescue family and friends. Using ingenious disguises, carrying infants and sometimes exhausted men, she made nineteen trips, freeing, she estimated, more than three hundred slaves. Illness prevented her from accompanying John Brown* to Harpers Ferry, but in 1862 she traveled to South Carolina to serve for three years as a spy, scout, and nurse for the Union army.*

In Auburn, New York, after the war, she supported her parents and other freed people, converting her residence into a Home for Indigent and Aged Negroes. In 1869, after learning of John Tubman's death, she married Nelson Davis, a war veteran. A suffragist and a founder, in 1896, of the National Association of Colored Women, she died in Auburn, where her home is still maintained by the AME Zion Church.

SELECTED BIBLIOGRAPHY

Sarah Bradford, *Harriet Tubman: The Moses of Her People* (1886); Earl Conrad, *Harriet Tubman: Negro Soldier and Abolitionist* (1942); Dorothy Sterling, *Freedom Train: The Story of Harriet Tubman* (1954); and Dorothy Sterling, ed., *We Are Your Sisters: Black Women in the Nineteenth Century* (1984).

                                                                        DOROTHY STERLING

TURNER, NAT (1800–1831). Organizer and leader of the most significant slave revolt* in the history of the United States, Nat Turner was born in Southampton County, Virginia. Initially the slave of Benjamin Turner, Nat achieved a high degree of literacy and learned the trade of carpentry. At an early age he became a figure greatly admired within the slave community because of his mechanical skills and popularity as a slave preacher.*

Though little is known with certainty about Nat's family, there is evidence that his father escaped from the Turner plantation and fled to the North during Nat's early childhood. In 1821 Nat himself absconded, returning after a month to the Turner farm. In 1822 he was sold to a neighboring planter, Thomas Moore. Six years later Nat had a religious vision informing him that he should lead in the struggle to liberate his people. His religious calling dominated Nat's mature years and served as a crucial element in motivating him to lead a slave revolt. Obsessed by this messianic impulse, Nat came to believe that his sole mission in life was to break the bonds of slavery.

In February 1831 Nat interpreted an eclipse of the sun as a sign from God that he should commence the insurrection, though the actual revolt would not occur until six months later. On 22 August Turner and five followers began their attack. Eventually their ranks swelled to possibly as many as eighty bondsmen. For almost two days Turner and his insurrectionists ravaged Southampton County, murdering between fifty-seven and sixty-five white men, women, and children. Whites quickly crushed the revolt although Nat, who hid in a cave, was not apprehended until 30 October. On 5 November Turner was tried and found guilty. He was hanged six days later.

Turner's revolt generated widespread hysteria among whites in Virginia and the South. Scores of blacks were murdered in Southampton County in the revolt's aftermath. Throughout the region blacks were arrested and executed. Whites who dared to intervene in the random execution of blacks, both free and slave, were themselves regarded as suspect by the white community. Turner's insurrection no doubt excited Virginia's Afro-American slave community. On the one hand, it represented direct action by blacks against their oppressors and fueled the incipient Northern antislavery movement. On the other hand, Turner's revolt symbolized the fear and unlimited power of the master class who used the insurrection as cause to intensify their proslavery appeals.* Significantly, Turner's revolt inspired white Virginians to debate the merits of slavery; some campaigned to abolish slavery from the state. Proponents of the emancipation movement included Governor John Floyd. Once this movement was defeated, however, proslavery forces moved swiftly to tighten controls on the state's slaves and free blacks.* Other states passed similar legislation.

Did Turner jeopardize the interests and well-being of his fellow slaves by openly challenging the system of slavery? Were those slaves who accommodated to slavery, gradually carving out a relatively autonomous living space for themselves, more significant revolutionaries than Turner? Unquestionably, Turner's revolt proved disastrous. It resulted in new levels of legal restraints on blacks and heightened racial oppression in the South. Nonetheless, Turner's violent resistance to slavery, even though accompanied by severe retaliation, reaped long-term benefits for blacks. It provided precisely the psychic energy that allowed slaves to accommodate to slavery, to retain their self-respect, and, ultimately, to break the chains that bound them.

SELECTED BIBLIOGRAPHY

Herbert Aptheker, *American Negro Slave Revolts* (1943); John Henrik Clarke, ed., *William Styron's Nat Turner: Ten Black Writers Respond* (1968); John B. Duff and Peter M. Mitchell, eds., *The Nat Turner Rebellion: The Historical Event and the Modern Controversy* (1971); Eugene D. Genovese, *From Rebellion to Revolution: Afro-American Slave Revolts in the Making of the Modern World* (1979); Stephen B. Oates, *The Fires of Jubilee: Nat Turner's Fierce Rebellion* (1975); Henry I. Tragle, ed., *The Southampton Slave Revolt of 1831: A Compilation of Source Material* (1971); and [Nat Turner], *The Confession, Trial, and Execution of Nat Turner; the Negro Insurrectionist: Also, a List of Persons Murdered in the Insurrection in Southampton County, Virginia, on the 21st and 22nd of August, 1831, with Introductory Remarks* (1881).

REGINALD BUTLER

U

UNDERGROUND RAILROAD. This loosely organized system provided aid in the form of shelter and transportation to fugitive slaves* traveling through Northern states, usually on their way to Canada. Organized largely by abolitionists* and their sympathizers, underground railroad activity formed the basis for a popular postwar legend replete with stories of exciting adventure, secret hiding places, and a special railroad nomenclature, including references to underground railroad "stations," "trainmen," and the "president of the line." The legend of the underground railroad described a highly organized institution with trunk lines running into the South and heroic deeds of abolitionists.

The legend resulted from exaggerated views of a busy operation and from inflated estimates of the actual number of escaped slaves. Unreliable census figures indicate that about a thousand slaves a year escaped from the South. There were probably twice that number. William Still,* black chairman of the Philadelphia Vigilance Committee, kept careful records of the fugitives going through that city and later published an important sourcebook. According to Still's records, about 5,000 fugitives passed through Philadelphia from 1852 to 1857.

The legend of the underground railroad was based partly on fact. Some abolitionists, like Levi Coffin of Cincinnati and Thomas Garrett of Wilmington, Delaware, devoted themselves to helping fugitives and gave a semblance of organization to the work in their locales. Most such efforts, however, were haphazard and makeshift, without a comprehensive system. To be sure, there were secrecy and some exciting rescues, such as the Oberlin-Wellington rescue in Ohio in 1858. Yet there were times when fugitive aid was open, even advertised, in antislavery publications. Abolitionism, always a minority position, gained considerable popularity in the North after the Civil War, when Northern communities boasted of their antislavery records and found such evidence of underground railroad benevolence. Homes of known abolitionists were reported to have been "stations" on the underground railroad, and one or two incidents of aiding runaway slaves* were cited as proof of a once active organization.

Part of the legend stemmed from the recollection, by blacks and abolitionists, of the vigilance committees that grew in importance after passage of the Fugitive Slave Act of 1850.* They offered food, temporary housing (usually in the black community), and sometimes transportation to fugitives passing through their communities. They also planned some well-publicized rescues of arrested fugitives. In 1851, for example, the Syracuse committee succeeded in rescuing Jerry Henry, an escaped slave. The Boston committee, however, failed in its efforts to free Anthony Burns, who was returned to slavery in 1854 under heavy military guard.

Those fugitive slaves who located the underground railroad did so by chance, and only after they had planned and carried out their own escapes and had completed the most dangerous part of the journey on their own. Except for such rare heroism as that of Harriet Tubman,* there was nothing resembling formal, systematic underground railroad activity in the South. Escaping bondsmen usually relied on their own resources, though they occasionally received assistance from other slaves and free blacks and even, at times, from sympathetic white Southerners. The legend, with its emphasis on the contributions of white abolitionists, seriously understates the heroism of blacks. In fact, in the legend blacks seldom are considered except as frightened "passengers," completely dependent on the assistance of whites. On the contrary, by the time black fugitives contacted white abolitionists they already had achieved the nearly impossible: escaping from their masters and making their way to the North. Frederick Douglass,* William Wells Brown,* Henry Bibb,* Anthony Burns,* William and Ellen Craft,* and countless others merit recognition as much as those white abolitionists who at times risked liberty and property to assist their escapes.

While secrecy proved essential for much underground railroad success—many times slaves were hidden or transported clandestinely to another location—abolitionists nevertheless were frequently quite open about their fugitive aid work. As early as 1844 a Chicago antislavery newspaper published a humorous cartoon, captioned "The Liberty Line," that described the workings of the underground railroad and provided the names of local "conductors." Levi Coffin's work never was a secret in Cincinnati, where his reputation for assisting fugitives was widespread. Secrecy became less important after 1850, as Northern public opinion against returning slaves to the South spread. Each rescue or attempted rescue received widespread notice in the abolition press, and the assault on the civil liberties of whites abetting fugitive slaves provided a useful propaganda weapon for the activists. Exhibiting fugitive slaves at antislavery gatherings became commonplace, and abolitionists often featured fugitive slave speakers. Frederick Douglass, however, the most famous fugitive slave, complained in his autobiography that the abolitionists' open mention of their activity aided the slaveholders, not the slaves. In the pre–Civil War editions of Douglass's narrative he refused to reveal his own escape tactic.

While abolitionists used the underground railroad to popularize their cause, Southern apologists attacked it as a system that violated the constitutional protection of private property. In 1850 a North Carolina congressman estimated that the South already had lost $15 million worth of property through abolitionist-inspired escapes. Trials for violating the Fugitive Slave Act of 1850 gave both sides of the controversy more propaganda ammunition. By 1855 the law had become a dead letter in many Northern states but a major bone of contention in the South.

The legend of the underground railroad took hold of the American psyche in the post–Civil War years. Northern newspapers glorified stories of antislavery and underground railroad activity, often relying for facts on interviews with relatives or acquaintances of the old abolitionists. Several leading abolitionists published their memoirs, which over time became source material for later histories of the underground railroad. Slave narratives,* however, such as William Still's *The Underground Railroad* (1872), were generally overlooked by whites. As a result, the significant contributions of blacks to the underground railroad received short shrift, and the entire movement was distorted almost beyond recognition. Without question, the underground railroad succeeded in assisting fugitive slaves to reach freedom. It was a far more complex and interesting system, however, than the oversimplified and self-serving legend would suggest.

SELECTED BIBLIOGRAPHY

Larry Gara, *The Liberty Line: The Legend of the Underground Railroad* (1961); Wilbur H. Siebert, *The Underground Railroad from Slavery to Freedom* (1898); and William Still, *The Underground Rail Road. A Record of Facts, Authentic Narratives, Letters, Etc.* (1872).

LARRY GARA

UNION ARMY. As Union forces captured the Confederacy's last citadels, Northerners recognized a profound irony. In 1861 Secretary of War Simon Cameron had declared that his department had "no intention at present to call into the service of the Government any colored soldiers." Yet four years later black soldiers were the first Union troops to enter both Charleston and Richmond. This dramatic transformation in policy began in 1862 when individual officers, such as James H. Lane in Kansas, John W. Phelps in Louisiana, and David Hunter in South Carolina, ignored the government's lily-white policy and recruited blacks without official sanction. The activities of these officers helped spur the Lincoln administration toward a policy of black recruitment,* although it moved cautiously, beset by fears that enlisting blacks might drive the border states into the Confederacy, alienate Southern Unionists, and fragment the North by enraging racists.

Despite these concerns, the government's intentions became obvious during the summer and fall of 1862. On 17 July Congress passed the Second Confiscation and Militia Acts, which authorized the president to employ black soldiers at his discretion. On 25 August Secretary of War Edwin M. Stanton (who had replaced

Cameron on 15 January 1862) authorized General Rufus Saxton, the superintendent of contrabands in the Department of the South, to arm and equip 5,000 former slaves, officially sanctioning the raising of black troops for the first time. Then on 1 January 1863 Lincoln signed the Emancipation Proclamation,* which endorsed the use of black soldiers.

The North's motives in converting a white man's war into a black man's war as well combined crass exploitation, a perception of military realities in a total war, and noble idealism. The Union army's manpower demands were seemingly insatiable, and as Lincoln wrote, "The colored population is the great *available* and yet *unavailed* of, force for restoring the Union." Since slavery supported the South's economy and social system (and hence its military effort), emancipation and utilizing blacks as soldiers were superb methods of economic and psychological warfare. Some Northerners also supported black enlistments for more altruistic reasons: letting black men don Union blue would give their race a claim to both freedom and equality.

The new policy took root during the first half of 1863. Initially, the War Department authorized state governors and enterprising citizens to enlist regiments, but this procedure was too haphazard and the government soon established a near monopoly over black recruiting. Stanton ordered Daniel Ullman to Louisiana to raise a black brigade, dispatched Edward A. Wild to North Carolina to recruit another black brigade, and in March sent Adjutant General Lorenzo Thomas to the Mississippi Valley to organize as many black regiments as possible. These officers achieved great success, and in May the War Department established the Bureau of Colored Troops to supervise recruitment nationwide.

From mid-1863 onward, black soldiers proved their worth on the battlefield, infusing new vigor into the Union war effort at a critical point when war weariness and defeatism afflicted a growing number of Northern whites. At Port Hudson (27 May 1863), Millikin's Bend (7 June 1863), and Fort Wagner (18 July 1863) blacks participated in their first large-scale engagements, dispelling the myth of black docility and cowardice. Thereafter, the combat role of black troops steadily increased.

Black troops achieved a splendid battlefield record despite enduring many inequities. The army, like slavery, was a white-dominated institution that embodied the pervasive racism of American society. Thus, black soldiers had to fight two wars, one for freedom and another for equality.

One serious inequity involved officership. Black troops served in segregated regiments except for the commissioned officers, almost all of whom were white. Reflecting racist skepticism about black leadership abilities and fearful of antagonizing white soldiers by appointing black officers, the North virtually excluded blacks from the ranks of commissioned officers, even in black regiments. Although many blacks served as noncommissioned officers, only about 100 received commissions. Most of these were prewar free blacks; none had been emancipated by the war. Moreover, approximately one-fourth of the black commissioned officers were chaplains and surgeons (who were outside the line of command), and another two-thirds of them served in the three regiments of Louisiana Native Guards. The Native Guard officers were free, light-skinned, educated, and propertied. Almost all the others—about a dozen men—received their commissions late in the war (or even after the war ended) when they had no opportunity to exercise an important line command.

The white officers in the initial black regiments were invariably dedicated abolitionists,* but the tremendous expansion of black units resulted in many officers who simply sought personal advancement. General-in-Chief Henry Wager Halleck, for example, advised his young friends to seek commissions in black regiments because "any officer who fights well with them will have rapid promotion—more rapid, I think, than if fighting with white troops. . . ." The promotion-seekers were often blatant racists who followed disciplinary practices similar to those of plantation masters and who sometimes alienated the men under their command to the brink of mutiny.

Another inequity concerned pay and bounties. The War Department originally promised blacks remuneration equal to that of whites, but the government soon revoked its pledge. Whether officers or privates, all blacks received $10 per month, *minus* $3 for clothing; white privates received $13 per month, *plus* clothing, while white officers were paid even more. The government also denied federal bounties to black troops. Many black soldiers felt betrayed by the government's broken promise, saw their wives and children confined in poorhouses, and wondered why, having done a soldier's duty, they could not receive a soldier's pay. Perceiving the issue as symbolic of the greater struggle for equality, black troops pushed hard for equal financial treatment. In mid-1864 Congress finally responded by granting blacks a federal bounty and by taking the initial steps that eventually resulted in equal pay for all black soldiers.

One of the army's most onerous discriminatory practices was that, compared to white soldiers, blacks did excessive fatigue duty. Wielding spades and axes for weeks on end lowered morale and sapped health, especially since blacks labored under two additional handicaps. They subsisted on an inappropriate diet (Southern blacks were used to pork and corn, but army rations were built around beef and wheat), and black regiments never had a sufficient number of surgeons. The unremitting labor, bad diet, and poor medical care resulted in an extremely high death rate from disease. About one in every twelve white soldiers, but roughly one out of every five black soldiers, died of disease. Constant fatigue duty also left little time or energy for military drill; consequently, when blacks entered battle they were often inadequately trained. In June 1864 Adjutant General Thomas ordered that black and white units should share fatigue duty proportionately. Unfortunately, some black troops continued to serve as military drudges since field commanders did not consistently enforce the order.

Finally, the Confederacy* refused to consider captured black soldiers as prisoners of war, and although the Lincoln administration enunciated a retaliatory policy to try to deter mistreatment, it never implemented the policy. Thus, the government failed to guarantee equal treatment for black prisoners, who faced the prospect of summary execution or enslavement at the hands of their Confederate captors.

By the end of the war approximately 179,000 blacks had served in the Union army. Although exact numbers will never be known, a reasonable estimate is that about 38,500 free black men and 140,500 freedmen fought for the North—and for the liberation of their race, for by 1863 the Union army had become a liberating army. Wherever the Union army smashed into the Confederacy, slavery disintegrated. The price of liberty was high as black soldiers suffered 68,178 casualties (of whom 2,751 died in action). Yet blacks were among the North's most patriotic soldiers, for they self-consciously viewed themselves as liberators. They knew that whites were not *giving* freedom to blacks. Black courage and determination were *earning* the slaves' freedom, and *earning* black people a right to full citizenship.

In light of their contribution to Union victory, many black troops faced the postwar era with optimism. But others were not so confident. Their wartime experiences with inequities in the army and the government's hesitant efforts to ensure equal treatment left some soldiers wary of the whites' commitment to justice. In the end the blacks' ambiguous view of the future mirrored the war's ambiguous result: freedom, but without equality.

SELECTED BIBLIOGRAPHY

Ira Berlin et al., eds., *Freedom: A Documentary History of Emancipation*, 2nd ser.: *The Black Military Experience* (1982); Dudley Taylor Cornish, *The Sable Arm: Negro Troops in the Union Army, 1861–1865* (1956); Morris J. MacGregor and Bernard C. Nalty, eds., *Blacks in the United States Armed Forces: Basic Documents*, vol. 2: *Civil War and Emancipation* (1977); James M. McPherson, *The Negro's Civil War: How American Negroes Felt and Acted during the War for the Union* (1965); Benjamin Quarles, *The Negro in the Civil War* (1953); U.S. Adjutant General's Office, *The Negro in the Military Service of the United States* (1968); and Bell I. Wiley, *Southern Negroes, 1861–1865* (1938).

PETER MASLOWSKI

UNITARIAN CHURCH.   The Unitarians in America primarily derive their origins from the liberal wing of the Congregational churches* of New England. In 1825 they assumed denominational form by founding the American Unitarian Association (AUA). By 1860 the Unitarians claimed over 200 churches, mostly clustered in eastern Massachusetts and centered in Boston.

The Unitarians found the South to be rocky ground for their liberal theology. Their solitary congregations in the slave states were located in St. Louis, Louisville, Nashville, Baltimore, Washington, Augusta, Charleston, Mobile, New Orleans, Richmond, Savannah, and Wheeling. By the late 1850s one-half of these congregations were either dying or dead. The degree of accommodation to slavery made by the Unitarians can be judged from a sampling of their Southern congregations.

In Charleston, the Unitarian minister, Samuel Gilman (1791–1858), and his wife, the author Caroline Gilman (1794–1888), owned slaves. Mrs. Gilman maintained that the slaves enjoyed health care, social security, and contented retirement that free white laborers could envy. Slaves were subjects, she wrote, of "little kingdoms" ruled with "wisdom and love." At least fifty communicants of the Charleston church were slaves, although Dr. Samuel Henry Dickson (1798–1872) of the congregation argued that Unitarianism suited only "those of superior station" and that "any Christian teaching" could satisfy "the poor ignorant slaves." To their credit the Gilmans educated their slaves and Dickson, as a slave owner, supported the intensely unpopular position that all legal impediments to teaching the slaves be repealed.

In New Orleans, the Unitarian minister, Theodore Clapp (1792–1886), owned several slaves. An enthusiastic apologist for slavery, he taught that God himself had established slavery as a means to raise the blacks from barbarism to Christianity. "The most enlightened philanthropists, with unlimited resources," Clapp explained, "could not provide a more salubrious existence for the slaves than they enjoyed in servitude."

In Savannah, a lay leader, Dr. Richard Arnold (1808–1876), kept the Unitarian church there alive through a succession of difficult times. Arnold was a professor, politician, and editor. He was also a slave owner, plantation physician, and a legal guardian of free blacks. Under his leadership, Unitarian slave owners were encouraged to bring their slaves to the church. Arnold viewed slavery as "the cornerstone" of the South's other institutions.

Twice Unitarians in the South saw their accommodation to slavery shaken. In 1840, a New England–born minister had to flee from the Unitarian pulpit in Mobile for preaching gradual emancipation. Two years later, a Southern-born minister found the pulpit in Savannah closed to him because of false rumors over his being an abolitionist.

Many of the most prominent Unitarian ministers in the North were sympathetic to the South and antiabolitionist. Powerful conservatives such as Orville Dewey (1794–1882), Ezra Stiles Gannett (1801–1871), Francis Parkman (1788–1852), and William Parsons Lunt (1805–1857) favored the colonization movement* and urged compliance with the Fugitive Slave Act of 1850.* They were opposed by such able abolitionist ministers as Samuel J. May (1797–1871), Samuel May, Jr. (1810–1899), and James Freeman Clarke (1810–1888). These ministers ultimately secured, with help from coreligionists in Great Britain and Ireland, antislavery resolutions from the AUA and the Unitarian Antislavery Protest of 1845. The many Unitarian ministers and lay persons who fought against slavery tended to do so as individuals rather than as representatives of their denomination. Antislavery opinion among them ranged the full spectrum, from the patient gradualist antislavery philosophy of the Unitarian patriarch William Ellery Channing (1780–1842), to the impatient immediate abolitionist activism of the Garrisonian matriarch Maria Weston Chapman (1806–1885).

SELECTED BIBLIOGRAPHY

Charles Richard Denton, "American Unitarians, 1830–1865: A Study of Religious Opinion on War, Slavery, and the Union" (Ph.D. dissertation, Michigan State University, 1969); Clarence Gohdes, "Some Notes on the Unitarian Church in the Ante-Bellum South: A Contribution to the History of Southern Liberalism," in David Kelly Jackson, ed., *American Studies in Honor of William Kenneth Boyd* (1940); Douglas C. Stange, "Abolitionism as Maleficence: Southern Unitarians versus 'Puritan Fanaticism'—1831– 1860," *Harvard Library Bulletin*, 26 (1978), 146–171; Douglas C. Stange, "Abolitionism as Treason: The Unitarian Elite Defends Law, Order, and the Union," *Harvard Library Bulletin*, 28 (1980), 152–170; Douglas C. Stange, *British Unitarians against American Slavery, 1833–1865* (1984); Douglas C. Stange, "From Treason to Antislavery Patriotism: Unitarian Conservatives and the Fugitive Slave Law," *Harvard Library Bulletin*, 25 (1977), 466–488; and Douglas C. Stange, *Patterns of Antislavery among American Unitarians, 1831–1860* (1977).

DOUGLAS C. STANGE

U.S. COLORED TROOPS. On 1 January 1863 President Abraham Lincoln* issued the Emancipation Proclamation* declaring free those slaves held in areas controlled by the Confederate States of America. Two years later, on 31 January 1865, Congress passed the Thirteenth Amendment freeing all slaves. In the meantime, black Americans played an important role in winning their own freedom through volunteer service in the U.S. Army.

Black Americans, both slave and free, had fought for the United States in the American Revolution* and free blacks* had fought in the War of 1812.* The institutionalization of slavery and the absence of a national emergency kept blacks out of the U.S. Army for the next forty-seven years. When the Civil War* began in 1861, the Lincoln administration opposed arming blacks in order to maintain the loyalty of the slaveholding states of the upper South. The War Department discouraged efforts to arm blacks until Congress authorized black regiments on 17 July 1862. While a few individual blacks had already enlisted in volunteer regiments, not until 27 September 1862 did the first black regiment, the First Louisiana Native Guard, composed largely of free blacks, gain muster into the U.S. Army. The First South Carolina regiment, mustered in on 31 January 1863, actively recruited slaves; as the number of black troops increased, so too did the percentage of former slaves.

By early 1863, a war for the Union had become transformed into a war against slavery, and the U.S. government actively encouraged black enlistments. By 1863 the War Department drastically needed bodies to fill the Union army's depleted ranks. Black regiments also provided opportunities for whites, especially noncommissioned officers, to serve as officers in black units. By the end of the war, the War Department counted 178,975 black soldiers (of 2,778,304 enlistments). Louisiana supplied the largest number of black troops, 24,052; Kentucky supplied the second largest number, 23,703.

Black troops originally organized as state regiments served under a bewildering array of names, including the Native Guards, Corps d'Afrique, and African

Descent. In 1864 most of the black units were renamed and renumbered as U.S. Colored Troops. Originally slated only for garrison and fatigue duty to release white troops for the field, black troops quickly proved their fighting abilities at Port Hudson (27 May 1863), Millikin's Bend (7 June 1863), and on many other battlefields. The army of General Ulysses S. Grant that besieged Petersburg in 1864 included two black divisions.

Black troops suffered originally from discrimination in pay, limited opportunities for advancement, and the distrust of white commanders. If captured, blacks risked massacre, as at Fort Pillow, Tennessee (12 April 1864), or sale into slavery. Yet free blacks and ex-slaves served willingly and bravely. Ironically, the fine record of black troops under white officers led the army to maintain this arrangement into the twentieth century. Military service aided many blacks in the transition from slavery to freedom, and their influence as veterans helped to shape U.S. policy toward civil rights, especially voting. White leaders came to realize that those who served as first-class soldiers ought not to be treated as second-class citizens.

SELECTED BIBLIOGRAPHY

Ira Berlin et al., eds., *Freedom: A Documentary History of Emancipation 1861–1867;* Series 2: *The Black Military Experience* (1982); Dudley Taylor Cornish, *The Sable Arm: Negro Troops in the Union Army, 1861–1865* (1956); Benjamin Quarles, *The Negro in the Civil War* (1953); George W. Williams, *A History of the Negro Troops in the War of the Rebellion 1861–1865* (1888); and Joseph T. Wilson, *The Black Phalanx: A History of the Negro Soldiers of the United States in the Wars of 1775–1812, 1861–'65* (1888).
                                                                    JOHN Y. SIMON

U.S. CONSTITUTION, SLAVERY AND THE. From the first day of the Constitutional Convention in 1787 to almost the last, slavery consumed an extraordinary amount of the delegates' time. Several times James Madison argued that the real differences between the states were due "principally from their having or not having slaves." Eventually a large number of delegates supported this position. Delegates argued vehemently over the place of slavery in the scheme of representation and over the continuation of the African slave trade.* Slavery also affected the debate over how the president would be chosen. The debate over the fugitive slave clause was short, but heated.

During the debates the delegates spoke frankly about the importance of slavery. In opposing the three-fifths clause, for example, Elbridge Gerry of Massachusetts protested, with much irony, that "Blacks are property, and are used to the southward as horses and cattle to the northwards; and why should their representation be increased to the southward on account of the number of slaves, than horses or oxen to the north?" Later, Gouverneur Morris of Pennsylvania concluded that the three-fifths clause "when fairly explained comes to this; that the inhabitant of Georgia and S.C. who goes to the Coast of Africa, and in defiance of the most sacred laws of humanity tears away his fellow creatures from their dearest connections & damns them to the most cruel bondages, shall have more votes in a Govt. instituted for the protections of the rights of mankind, than the Citizen of Pa or N. Jersey, who views with a laudible horror, so nefarious a practice.''

Southern delegates of course defended their institution. Pierce Butler of South Carolina asserted that ''The security the Southn. States want is that their negroes may not be taken from them which some gentlemen within or without doors, have a very good mind to do.'' Charles Pinckney, another South Carolinian, cited ancient Greece and Rome in asserting that slavery and the slave trade were ''justified by the example of all the world.'' His cousin, General Charles Cotesworth Pinckney, simply told the convention that a prohibition of the slave trade would be ''an exclusion of S. Carola from the Union'' because ''S. Carolina & Georgia cannot do without slaves.'' The threat that the Deep South states would not support the Constitution led many Northerners grudgingly to support the three-fifths and the slave importation clauses. The slave importation clause also gained critical Northern support after South Carolinians agreed to support the commerce clause.

Southerners opposed a popular election of the president partly because slaves could not vote, enabling the North to outvote the South. During the debates on this subject Hugh Williamson of North Carolina bluntly rejected popular election because, he said, ''slaves will have no suffrage.'' James Madison personally favored direct election of the president but ultimately supported the electoral college. Otherwise, he explained, the South ''could have no influence in the election on the score of the Negroes.''

Overall, the slave state delegations won considerable protection and power for their institution. Although the word *slavery* appears in the Constitution in only one place—the Thirteenth Amendment*—which abolished the institution, slavery was directly at issue in five clauses of the document drafted in Philadelphia.

The three-fifths clause provided for counting three-fifths of all slaves for the purposes of congressional representation. This clause also provided that if any ''direct tax'' was levied on the states it could only be imposed proportionally, according to population, and that only three-fifths of all slaves could be counted in assessing what each state's contribution would be. The three-fifths clause did not declare that slaves were three-fifths of a person. The clause resulted from a political compromise at the convention awarding the South extra strength in the House of Representatives and in the electoral college for its slave population.

The slave migration and importation clause prohibited Congress from banning the African slave trade before 1808, but did not require Congress to prohibit the trade after that date. This clause rivaled the three-fifths clause for the amount of vitriolic debate it stimulated at the convention. During the ratification process this clause led to more Anti-federalist opposition than any other slavery-related provision in the Constitution. Joshua Atherton of New Hampshire typified this opposition, opposing the Constitution because this clause would render all Americans "*consenters to*, and *partakers in*, the sin and guilt of this abominable traffic."

The capitation tax clause declared that any federal "capitation" or head tax had to take into account the three-fifths clause. This guaranteed that the South would pay proportionately less than the North if a head tax was imposed. A separate provision specifically prohibited any amendment to the slave migration and importation and capititation clauses before 1808.

The fugitive slave clause nullified any law or court decision that might have emancipated a runaway slave escaping into a free state. The clause further required that fugitive slaves* be "delivered up on Claim" of the owner. The clause failed, however, to indicate how it was to be enforced. Although this clause was the focus of more antebellum strife than any other connected with slavery, it was barely mentioned by Northerners during the ratification struggle. In the South, however, the fugitive slave clause was an important argument for ratification of the Constitution. For example, James Madison urged the Virginia ratifying convention to support the Constitution because the fugitive slave clause "secures us that property which we now possess." He noted that without the Constitution "if any slave elopes to any of those states where slaves are free, he becomes emancipated by their laws" because the free states were "uncharitable to one another in this respect." But the fugitive slave clause "was expressly inserted to enable owners of slaves to reclaim them." He reminded the delegates: "This is better security than any that now exists."

In addition to the five provisions directly protecting slavery, other clauses indirectly affected the institution. Some, such as the prohibitions on taxing exports, were clearly included in the Constitution to support the interests of slave owners. Others, such as the formula for the electoral college and the guarantee of federal support to "suppress insurrections," were written with slavery in mind, but were supported for other reasons as well. Finally, some clauses, such as the limitations on federal court jurisdiction, protected slavery in unexpected ways.

In addition to those clauses in the Constitution that protected slavery, a few clauses provided a two-edged sword that could have been used to attack slavery. Because slave owners or their allies controlled the federal government throughout most of the antebellum period, these clauses were never used to harm slavery. They were, however, sometimes used to help it. The commerce clause, for example, empowered Congress to regulate interstate commerce, including the slave trade between states. Congress might have prohibited the interstate slave trade under this clause. Another article gave Congress the power to regulate the national capital. Under this clause Congress might have prohibited slavery in the District of Columbia, but instead, Congress supported slavery in the District. The only exception to this was part of the Compromise of 1850* that banned the public sale of slaves in the District.

In the late antebellum period two clauses and one amendment appeared to be potential antislavery tools. One article required that every state maintain a "Republican form of government.'' Some abolitionists* argued that such a form of government precluded slavery. However, these abolitionists were never successful in convincing the Congress, the executive, or the courts that this was a proper interpretation of the clause. More successful were those opponents of slavery who argued that under another article slavery could be prohibited from the federal territories. This interpretation was adopted by Congress, which prohibited slavery in most of the western territories through the Missouri Compromise* of 1820. However, in *Dred Scott v. Sandford* (1857)* the Supreme Court declared that all federal laws prohibiting slavery in the territories were unconstitutional. Finally, some abolitionists argued that the Fifth Amendment required that slaves be set free because they were denied their liberty without due process of law. This interpretation of the amendment was never adopted by any branch of the national government. Ironically, in *Dred Scott v. Sandford* Chief Justice Roger B. Taney interpreted the Fifth Amendment's provision against taking property without due process of law to mean that Congress could not prohibit slavery in the territories.

More important than what the Constitution said about slavery was what it did not say. The Constitution created a limited form of government. The framers clearly intended to prevent the Congress from interfering with slavery where it existed. This proslavery aspect of the Constitution was underscored during the ratification debates by Charles Cotesworth Pinckney, who had been one of the ablest defenders of slavery in the Constitutional Convention. Pinckney proudly told his fellow South Carolinians, ''considering all circumstances, we have made the best terms for the security of this species of property it was in our power to make. We would have made better if we could; but on the whole, I do not think them bad.''

Pinckney was only one of many Southern Federalists to praise the Constitution for its support for slavery. Even those in the South who were wary of the Constitution nevertheless conceded it was sound on slavery. When the Antifederalist Patrick Henry warned that the Constitution threatened slavery, Edmund Randolph demanded to know ''*Where* is the part that has tendency to *the abolition of slavery?*'' He told the Virginia ratifying convention that no member of the Virginia delegation ''had *the smallest suspicion of the abolition of slavery.*''

Northern Federalists faced a more difficult challenge. They had to explain away the three-fifths clause and the slave importation clause. Some argued that the slave importation clause would lead to the end, not only of the slave trade, but of slavery as well. Thus, James Wilson told the Pennsylvania ratification convention that in only ''a few years, Congress will have power to exterminate slavery within our borders.'' Wilson's analysis was of course wrong. It was also rejected by many Northern Antifederalists. For example, ''Cato,'' who has been variously identified as George Clinton or Abraham Yates, opposed the Constitution at least in part because of both the slave trade provision and the three-fifths clause. Other Northerners thought that slavery was a threat to the security of the new nation. Slaves, after all, could not be counted on in a national emergency, and they might even aid America's enemies. Three Massachusetts Antifederalists complained in a newspaper that "this lust for slavery, [was] portentous of much evil in America" and in true Puritan fashion they predicted that "the cry of innocent blood" would eventually bring upon America "vengeance adequate to the enormity of the crime." Yet, despite some Northern opposition over slavery, the Constitution was ratified by each state.

In subsequent years the Supreme Court heard over 250 cases touching on slavery. In many of these slavery was only a tangential issue. In a few cases slavery was *the* issue, and national policy and American politics turned on the outcome of these cases. The areas in which constitutional adjudication affected slavery were the African slave trade, fugitive slaves, slaves in transit and commerce, and slavery in the territories.

In 1794 and again in 1800 Congress passed laws prohibiting American ships from participating in the African slave trade. In 1807 Congress passed legislation prohibiting the importation of slaves as of 1 January 1808, the earliest time allowed under the Constitution. This law was strengthened by statutes in 1818, 1819, and 1820.

The lower federal courts heard numerous cases under the various statutes regulating and prohibiting the importation of slaves. The courts consistently upheld the constitutionality of the federal prohibitions on the African slave trade. In *United States v. La Jeune Eugenie* (1822) Justice Joseph Story declared that the African slave trade was piracy in violation of all international law. That case, however, was decided in the circuit court and was not binding on the full Supreme Court. In *The Antelope* case (1825)* Chief Justice John Marshall rejected Story's position, and held that the slave trade was in fact recognized by international law.

The most important slave trade case to reach the Court was *United States v. The Amistad* (1841).* This case resolved the fate of thirty-nine slaves who had been illegally imported to Cuba from their native Africa. In 1839, while on a voyage from one part of Cuba to another, the Africans seized the ship and attempted to force the captain to sail back to Africa. Instead, the ship eventually landed in Connecticut, where the status of the African slaves came before the U.S. District Court and later before the Supreme Court. The cause of the Africans became a national issue. The case was ultimately argued by former President John Quincy Adams and Roger S. Baldwin, who later served as a governor and U.S. senator from Connecticut. In 1841 the Supreme Court ruled that the Africans had been illegally seized in their homeland and that they should be repatriated.

Throughout the 1850s the federal courts in a number of states heard cases involving the illegal African trade. Convictions, especially in the Deep South, were difficult to obtain. Although the statute of 1820 provided for a death penalty for slave traders, no trader was actually executed until after the Civil War began (*United States v. Gordon* [1861]). During the war a number of prosecutions for slave trading were successful.

The rendition of runaway slaves proved a more common and more complex constitutional problem. In 1793 Congress passed legislation facilitating the return of fugitive slaves. This statute gave jurisdiction to both the state courts and the federal courts to issue certificates of removal to allow masters to bring runaway slaves out of a free state and back to a slave state. The law provided a $500 penalty for anyone who aided a fugitive slave or impeded a master seeking to remove a fugitive slave from a free state. Federal courts heard few cases under this statute in the following four decades, but the state courts decided a number of important cases. In *Jack v. Martin* (1835) the New York courts ordered a fugitive slave returned to his owner. But in reaching this decision, the New York court specifically rejected the application of the law of 1793 to a state court claiming that Congress could not order a state to enforce a federal law. Nevertheless, the court declared it was obligated to act because the "right to reclaim" a fugitive was "secured . . . by the federal constitution."

By the mid-1830s most Northern states had passed statutes—generally known as personal liberty laws*—to protect free blacks. These laws also impeded the rendition of fugitive slaves, therefore placing the free states in direct opposition to the enforcement of the federal statute. *Prigg v. Pennsylvania* (1842) decided the validity of the 1793 law and the Northern personal liberty laws. In 1839 Edward Prigg, a professional slave catcher, was convicted of kidnapping in Pennsylvania for removing a slave from the state without following all the requirements of the Pennsylvania personal liberty law. This initiated the first U.S. Supreme Court case on fugitive slaves, *Prigg v. Pennsylvania*. In *Prigg* Justice Story held that the fugitive slave law of 1793 was constitutional; that state laws impeding the return of fugitive slaves were unconstitutional; that an owner could exercise a "right of self help" to capture a fugitive slave, provided the peace was not breached; and that although state officials *ought* to enforce the 1793 law, the Congress could not require that they do so. In a stinging concurrence, Chief Justice Taney agreed with the result (which overturned Prigg's kidnapping conviction) but attacked the notion that state officials could not be required to enforce the federal law. Taney argued that without the aid of state officials slave owners would be unable to recapture their runaway slaves.

Five years later, in *Jones v. Van Zandt* (1847), the Supreme Court strengthened the rights of masters by holding that a person could be held liable for damages to a slave owner for helping slaves escape, even if he had no actual notice that the people he aided were slaves. John Van Zandt gave a ride to a group of blacks he found walking along a road in Ohio. These blacks were Wharton Jones's slaves, and ultimately Jones, a Kentucky slave owner, won a judgment of $1,200. Van Zandt was represented in this case by two prominent antislavery lawyer/politicians, Salmon P. Chase of Ohio and William H. Seward of New York.

Although *Jones v. Van Zandt* strengthened the rights of slave owners, Southerners demanded a stronger fugitive slave law. This led to the Fugitive Slave Act of 1850,* which created a federally sponsored enforcement apparatus and provided harsh financial and criminal penalties for those who impeded the return of fugitive slaves. This law was upheld by the Supreme Court in *Ableman v. Booth* (1859). Sherman Booth, a Wisconsin abolitionist, had been convicted in federal court for violating the 1850 act by helping a fugitive slave escape. The Wisconsin Supreme Court declared that the 1850 law was unconstitutional, and ordered the federal marshal, S. V. Ableman, to release Booth. The U.S. Supreme Court reversed the Wisconsin court decision. In his opinion Chief Justice Taney completely rejected the state's rights position of the Wisconsin court, declaring that the Supreme Court was the final authority on questions of constitutionality.

The last major Supreme Court case involving fugitive slaves was *Kentucky v. Dennison* (1861). In that case the governor of Kentucky sought the extradition from Ohio of a free black accused of aiding slaves to escape from Kentucky to Ohio. Governor William Dennison of Ohio refused to approve the extradition. While the Supreme Court chastised the Ohio government for its refusal to fulfill its constitutional obligations, the Court nonetheless concluded that it lacked power to order the Ohio governor to act.

Unlike the slave runaway issue, the Supreme Court was never asked to decide the constitutionality of the domestic slave trade.* In a number of cases, however, the Court treated slaves as property and articles of commerce. In *Groves v. Slaughter* (1841), for example, it ruled that a provision of the Mississippi constitution prohibiting the importation of slaves as articles of commerce could not bar a slave trader from recovering the sale price for slaves sold into that state. With many thousands of dollars at issue the Court avoided the key commerce clause question by concluding that the Mississippi constitutional provision could not go into effect without a statute. In separate concurrences Justices Taney, John McLean, and Henry Baldwin asserted that states were free to prohibit the introduction of slaves into their jurisdiction.

An equally thorny constitutional problem involved the status of slaves brought into free jurisdictions. Most cases of this nature were settled in the state courts. Most Northern jurisdictions accepted the British precedent of *Somerset v. Stewart* (1772), which held that a slave became free the moment he or she entered a free state. The only exception to *Somerset* for Northern courts was for fugitive slaves, whose status was directly controlled by the Constitution. The *Somerset* case was adopted by free state courts in a series of decisions starting with *Commonwealth v. Aves* (Massachusetts, 1836) and ending with *Lemmon v. The People* (New York, 1860). Many Southern states adopted the *Somerset* precedent as well, but by the 1850s they had abandoned it.

The status of slaves in free jurisdictions reached the Supreme Court in two important cases. *Strader v. Graham* (1850) involved three slaves who had been allowed to visit Ohio and Indiana. A Kentucky court declared that these blacks remained slaves under Kentucky law. The Supreme Court upheld this position, asserting that states were free to decide for themselves the status of persons in their jurisdiction. In reaching this position the Court declared that by the 1850s the slavery prohibition in the Northwest Ordinance (1787)* was no longer in force, because all the territories in the Northwest had become states.

A similar question arose in *Dred Scott v. Sandford* (1857). In this controversial case, the slave Dred Scott had lived in both Illinois and the territory north of Missouri (present-day Minnesota), which was free under the Missouri Compromise of 1820. In declaring that Scott was still a slave Chief Justice Taney held that the Missouri Compromise was unconstitutional, because it denied Southerners their right to bring slaves into federal territories. Scott thus was not freed when his master took him to what had been considered "free" territory. In other parts of his opinion Taney essentially denied that blacks had any legal rights in the United States. This was the most blatantly proslavery decision written by the Supreme Court.

Such proslavery court decisions led the most radical wing of the abolitionist movement—the Garrisonians—to argue that the Constitution was a proslavery document. William Lloyd Garrison* called it a "covenant with death and an agreement with Hell." Part of this analysis was based on the understanding that the national government could not destroy slavery where it already existed. This view of the Constitution was echoed by proslavery theorists in the South and by mainstream politicians on both sides of the Mason-Dixon line. Thus, in his 1861 inaugural address Abraham Lincoln* asserted that he had "no lawful right" to "interfere with the institution of slavery in the States where it exists."

Only the secession of eleven slave states allowed the national government to interfere with slavery where it existed. This interference resulted because secession removed the South's veto power over legislation and constitutional amendments. With only the four border slave states remaining in the Union, the free states now had the political power to pass legislation affecting slavery in the states. Similarly, Lincoln justified the Emancipation Proclamation (1863)* as a war measure, which he issued in his capacity as commander-in-chief of the American military. Because the proclamation was a war measure, it was limited to those areas of the South that were still in a state of rebellion. Thus parts of the Confederacy* then under Union control, as well as the border states, were not affected by the proclamation.

Congress sought to remedy these defects in the proclamation by the adoption of the Thirteenth Amendment to the Constitution. The amendment, adopted in 1865, permanently ended slavery in the nation and precluded anyone from demanding compensation for the loss of slave property. This was also the first amendment that gave Congress specific power to enforce an alteration in the nature of the Constitution.

The intention of the framers of the Thirteenth Amendment remains unclear. At the very least it was designed permanently to end slavery, peonage, and all other forms of involuntary servitude in the nation. However, many supporters of the amendment believed it had in fact fully enfranchised the ex-slaves. This belief was based on the theory that it was impossible to have a republican form of government if a large percentage of the population was treated as second-class citizens. Because blacks were no longer slaves, many Republicans and abolitionists reasoned that they must be full-fledged citizens, with the same rights and privileges as whites. Under this theory the Congress adopted the Civil Rights Act of 1866. The Fourteenth and Fifteenth amendments were in part adopted to guarantee that the expansive interpretation of the Thirteenth Amendment would not be rejected by some future legislature or court.

Modern applications of the Thirteenth Amendment include prosecutions for the exploitation of rural farm workers, some urban workers, and even domestic servants in wealthy homes. More importantly, the Supreme Court has applied the Thirteenth Amendment to prohibit some forms of racial discrimination. In *Jones v. Alfred H. Mayer Co.* (1968), for example, the Court ruled that the refusal to sell houses to blacks constituted a "badge of slavery" and thus violated the Thirteenth Amendment. In upholding a ban on housing discrimination, the Court declared: "Surely Congress has the power under the Thirteenth Amendment rationally to determine what are the badges and the incidents of slavery, and the authority to translate that determination into effective legislation."

SELECTED BIBLIOGRAPHY

Don E. Fehrenbacher, *The Dred Scott Case: Its Significance in American Law and Politics* (1978); Paul Finkelman, *An Imperfect Union: Slavery, Federalism, and Comity* (1981); Harold M. Hyman and William M. Wiecek, *Equal Justice under Law: Constitutional Development, 1835–1875* (1982); Staughton Lynd, *Class Conflict, Slavery, and the United States Constitution* (1967); Thomas D. Morris, *Free Men All: The Personal Liberty Laws of the North, 1780–1861* (1974); Donald L. Robinson, *Slavery in the Structure of American Politics, 1765—1820* (1971); and William M. Wiecek, *The Sources of Antislavery Constitutionalism in America, 1760–1848* (1977).

PAUL FINKELMAN

URBAN SLAVERY. While slavery is almost universally thought of as—and, indeed, most commonly was—a plantation phenomenon, it should not be forgotten that the antebellum South had an urban dimension and that slaves, like other Southerners, lived in the cities and towns as well as in the countryside. There they worked, formed families, worshiped, and associated with other city residents of various color and condition. And there their daily lives were almost as much affected by the urban environment in which they lived as by the slave condition into which they were born.

Among the many things that we do not know about slavery is the exact size of the urban slave populations. Census takers were both casual and inconsistent in their recording of the slave residents in the towns. Sometimes they apparently recorded slaves living in urban places at the plantation residence of their owners; sometimes they recorded slaves residing in the countryside at the town residence of their owners; and often they would appear to have ignored slaves who did not live on the property of their owners or hirers. The collection of data is further complicated by the fact that the census data for many smaller cities were not always separated from the county data. Nevertheless, once the federal census began to be taken each decade, there are at least figures available that are probably roughly indicative of the numbers of slaves living in urban areas. For purposes of convenience the data presented in table 1 are confined to twenty of the larger Southern towns for the years 1800–1860. Most of the comments in this essay will conform to these same limits.

The number of slaves residing in a given city at a particular time is a figure of little importance or utility in determining the significance of that component of the city's population. For instance, there were about a hundred more slaves in Baltimore in 1850 than in 1800, but they constituted less than one-fiftieth of the city's population in the later year as compared to more than a tenth a half-century earlier. The figures given below, showing the relative sizes of the slave components of the populations of these twenty cities, are, in many respects, more revealing than the raw data.

Urban black populations did not have, even on the crudest bases, the same demographic characteristics as the white populations or, in some instances, the rural populations. For instance, both the free black* and the slave components were female-dominant while the white elements (both urban and rural) tended to be male-dominant, as did the rural slave populations. An extreme example is Baltimore in 1850, where the federal census of 1850 recorded 985 white females to each 1,000 white males; the comparable figures for the free black and slave components were 1,349 and 2,111, respectively. Moreover, the slave (and free black) populations in the cities tended to contain smaller percentages of children than the white element. Again, using Baltimore in 1850 as an example, 26 percent of the white, 24 percent of the free black, and 18 percent of the slave populations were under ten years of age.

Slavery had, of course, existed in the Northern states—and, naturally, cities—during the colonial and early national period. The Dutch West India Company had imported slaves into New Amsterdam within a few years of its establishment. Employed at first only for the benefit of the company, these blacks were soon leased, and later sold, to private citizens, and the majority of them were soon engaged in agricultural endeavors outside the town limits. The same patterns developed in most of the other Northern English colonies; generally the percentage of slaves was roughly the same in both the urban and the rural populations. A notable exception was Massachusetts, where the Boston population contained about four times the proportion of slaves as that in the colony as a whole. In New York—perhaps because of the early practices of the company—slaves were often hired* by their owners to nonslaveholders. This practice was probably common elsewhere, but there is less evidence in the other Northern towns.

Although slaves sometimes assisted skilled artisans (and doubtless in some cases became accomplished craftsmen*), they were mostly employed as carters, draymen, coachmen, and especially house servants.* In postrevolutionary New York the use of slaves persisted not because they were cheaper to maintain (which they were not) but primarily because of the prestige associated with the employment of black personal servants. During the third of a century after the end of the Revolution, as slavery was essentially eliminated from the area north

Table 1
Number of Slaves in Twenty Cities, 1800–1860

CITY	1800	1810	1820	1830	1840	1850	1860
Alexandria, D.C./Va.	875	1,488	1,435	1,261	1,074	1,061	1,386
Augusta, Ga.	1,017	1,321	n.a.	n.a.	2,989	5,718	3,663
Baltimore, Md.	2,843	3,713	4,357	4,120	3,199	2,946	2,218
Charleston, S. Car.	9,053	11,671	12,652	15,354	14,673	19,532	13,909
Fayetteville, N. Car.	626	n.a.	n.a.	1,070	1,414	1,542	1,519
Georgetown, D.C.	n.a.	1,162	1,526	1,176	785	725	577
Lexington, Ky.	439	1,526	1,641	2,065	2,483	n.a.	2,480
Louisville, Ky.	76	484	1,031	2,406	3,430	5,432	4,903
Mobile, Ala.	n.a.	n.a.	n.a.	1,169	3,869	6,803	7,587
Nashville, Tenn.	151	n.a.	n.a.	1,808	2,114	2,028	3,226
Natchez, Miss.	n.a.	459	654	n.a.	1,599	1,511	2,132
New Bern, N. Car.	1,298	n.a.	n.a.	1,766	1,583	1,927	2,383
New Orleans, La.	n.a.	5,961	7,355	14,469	23,448	17,011	13,385
Norfolk, Va.	2,724	3,825	3,261	3,756	3,769	4,295	3,284
Petersburg, Va.	1,487	2,173	2,428	2,850	3,636	4,728	5,680
Richmond, Va.	2,293	3,748	4,385	6,349	7,509	9,927	11,699
St. Louis, Mo.	301	n.a.	n.a.	n.a.	1,531	2,656	1,542
Savannah, Ga.	2,367	2,195	3,075	n.a.	4,694	6,231	7,712
Washington, D.C.	n.a.	1,437	1,945	2,330	1,713	2,113	1,774
Wilmington, N. Car.	1,125	n.a.	n.a.	n.a.	2,463	3,031	3,777

Table 2
Percentage of Slaves in the Populations of Twenty Cities, 1800–1860

CITY	1800	1810	1820	1830	1840	1850	1860
Alexandria, D.C./Va.	17.60	20.59	17.46	15.30	12.70	12.15	10.95
Augusta, Ga.	45.79	53.35	n.a.	n.a.	46.68	48.65	29.32
Baltimore, Md.	10.72	10.43	6.94	5.11	3.13	1.74	1.04
Charleston, S. Car.	48.09	47.23	51.06	50.69	50.15	45.44	34.32
Fayetteville, N. Car.	37.80	n.a.	n.a.	37.31	33.00	33.19	31.71
Georgetown, D. C.	n.a.	23.48	20.73	13.93	10.74	8.67	6.61
Lexington, Ky.	24.46	34.88	31.09	34.27	35.49	n.a.	26.05
Louisville, Ky.	21.17	35.67	25.70	23.27	16.17	12.58	7.21
Mobile, Ala.	n.a.	n.a.	n.a.	36.60	30.53	33.16	25.93
Nashville, Tenn.	43.77	n.a.	n.a.	32.48	30.51	19.95	18.99
Natchez, Miss.	n.a.	30.38	29.95	n.a.	33.31	34.08	32.24
New Bern, N. Car.	52.61	n.a.	n.a.	46.52	42.90	41.17	43.87
New Orleans, La.	n.a.	34.57	27.06	31.46	22.94	14.62	7.94
Norfolk, Va.	39.33	41.61	38.46	38.27	34.51	29.98	22.46
Petersburg, Va.	42.23	38.34	36.29	34.25	32.65	33.75	31.10
Richmond, Va.	39.97	38.50	36.33	39.53	37.26	36.01	30.86
St. Louis, Mo.	28.94	n.a.	n.a.	n.a.	9.30	3.41	0.96
Savannah, Ga.	46.00	42.09	40.87	n.a.	41.86	40.69	34.60
Washington, D. C.	n.a.	17.51	14.68	12.38	7.33	5.28	2.90
Wilmington, N. Car.	66.61	n.a.	n.a.	n.a.	51.92	41.73	39.54

of the Mason-Dixon line, the tendency was for slaves in the urban areas to be emancipated more rapidly than required by law. Slavery thus disappeared more rapidly in the larger Northern cities than in the countryside. For example, in 1800 slaves constituted 6.2 percent of the population of New York State but only 4.74 percent of that of New York City. The comparable figures were 0.8 percent in Pennsylvania and 0.13 percent in Philadelphia.

In the South the situation was more variable. Table 3 shows the percentage of slaves in 1800, 1830, and 1860 in the populations of ten Southern cities and of the states in which they are located.

Although in 1800 the percentages of slaves in the populations of several of the larger Southern cities (e.g., Charleston, Louisville, Richmond, Savannah, and probably St. Louis) were greater than that in the state (or territorial) population, by 1860 the reverse was true in each of these ten cities. Indeed, only in the populations of such smaller cities as Lexington, Kentucky, and New Bern and Wilmington, North Carolina, did heavier proportions of slaves reside than in the state populations as late as 1860. The reasons for this relative decline in the urban slave populations (indeed, actual declines in more than half of the cities listed in tables 1 and 2) is a matter of some dispute. Some would argue, with Frederick Douglass, that slavery does not like a dense population and that, ultimately, the decline of this inharmonious institution in the urban environment was inevitable. Others might suggest that the heightened antislavery agitation of the 1850s caused urban slaveholders to fear for the security of their property, and perhaps of their persons, in an area where slaves could more easily absorb the ideology and rhetoric associated with this agitation; they consequently transferred their bondsmen (by sale or otherwise) to more rural areas. Finally, the decline can be seen as simply the result of economic conditions—the rapidly escalating prices* paid for slaves represented a dramatic increase in the demand for agricultural labor in the sixth decade of the nineteenth century, which quite naturally pulled slaves out of the urban areas, where their employment was no longer economically rewarding. In this respect, it is notable that the only city in which the proportion of slaves in the population remained relatively stable was Richmond, where more slaves were employed in manufacturing activities* than in any other of the twenty cities here examined.

Many—perhaps even most—slaves worked for their owners, but in the cities slave hiring was certainly more prevalent than it was in rural areas. Many urbanites, including those of modest means, needed or wanted the labor that could most easily be supplied by slaves but were either reluctant or unable to invest the capital necessary to purchase bondsmen. Concomitantly, a fair number of urban slaveholders owned more slaves than they could profitably employ in their homes and business. Doubtless some of these individuals had purchased "excess" slaves as an investment. Moreover, it was rather common for men of some wealth, when distributing their property by will, to bequeath slaves to unmarried female relatives because such property yielded a good and reliable return and required little or no management. The circumstance that made slave

Table 3

Comparative Percentages of Slaves in Urban and State Populations

	1800		1830		1860	
	City	State	City	State	City	State
Baltimore, Md.	10.72	30.80	5.11	23.00	1.04	12.69
Charleston, S. Car.	48.09	42.20	50.69	54.20	34.32	57.19
Louisville, Ky.	21.17	18.20	23.27	24.00	7.21	19.51
Mobile, Ala.	n.a.	n.a.	36.60	37.90	25.93	45.12
Nashville, Tenn.	43.77	12.80	32.48	20.70	18.99	24.85
Natchez, Miss.	n.a.	39.40	n.a.	48.00	32.24	55.18
New Orleans, La.	n.a.	n.a.	31.46	50.80	7.94	46.95
Richmond, Va.	39.97	39.20	39.53	38.70	30.86	36.79
St. Louis, Mo.	28.94	n.a.	n.a.	17.80	0.96	9.72
Savannah, Ga.	46.00	36.60	n.a.	42.00	34.60	43.72

property desirable as either an investment or a legacy was the combination of the large and constant demand for slave labor, coupled with the practices associated with slave hiring that had developed in the cities in response to peculiarly urban conditions.

Slaves might be hired on any of several different contractual terms. The type of hiring that best fitted the theoretical aspects of the slave system—and was usually most satisfactory to slave owners—was an annual hiring contract. In this case the hirer leased the slave for a year—as a practical matter, often for fifty weeks from 1 January—and assumed responsibility for the slave's food, clothing, housing, and medical care, paying the owner a specified amount, either in a lump sum or, more frequently, monthly. On that basis many urban residents hired house servants; many hotels employed cooks, housemaids, and waiters; and many manufacturing firms secured workers, both skilled and unskilled.

But much of the work to be done in cities did not demand or, indeed, permit structuring by such long-term contracts. Many jobs required labor for only a month, or ten days, or a week, or a day. While it was entirely possible for slaveholders to make a large number of such short-term contracts, it was highly inconvenient for them to do so. Consequently, the practice early developed of permitting slaves to hire themselves in accordance with terms established by their owner, returning the hiring fee to the master, usually at the end of each day. Under these circumstances slaves might exercise one very slight element of freedom—by manipulation and evasion they could, within very narrow limits, make a choice of employers. The next deviant step in slave employment was more revolutionary in nature. Masters and slaves alike testified to the fact that slaves who had tasted the greater freedom of the urban environment almost always sought, at whatever price or risk, to extend the area of control over their own daily lives. "You couldn't pay me," said Charlotte, a Louisville slave, "to live at home if I could help myself." Masters, in turn, frequently wished to shed continuing daily responsibility for those of their slaves who were not serving them directly, and for whom they had not negotiated annual hires. Consequently, when slaves proposed new arrangements that served both the slaves' and the owners' purposes, they frequently found their masters amenable to a change. More and more urban slaves—though doubtless never more than a modest minority in any city—thus assumed responsibility for providing their own food,* clothing,* and housing,* in return for making agreed-upon payments to their owners at specified intervals. In this manner, these slaves achieved control of their employment (within the limits of their abilities and skills) and their employer, choice of residence (within the limits of their financial standing and the social mores of their community), and freedom from constant oversight by their masters.

Slaves who "hired their own time" and "found for themselves" (and the former term was normally used to embody the latter) might board with free black families, or join with other slaves in similar circumstances to rent a house and pool their food expenses, or rent separate quarters for themselves and their families. No adequate data exist to establish the extent of such "living out," but it was far from uncommon. Joseph Bancroft, who compiled the 1848 Savannah census, informed his readers that "the plan was adopted of enumerating the slave population in their places of abode, without recourse to owners." This course of action was decided upon, he said, because "under the system, so much in vogue at the present time, of permitting this class of our population to live in streets and lanes by themselves," such reports had "proved more reliable than . . . depending upon the owners for returns." In Charleston, moreover, the census of 1861 recorded literally hundreds of houses whose occupants were listed only as "slaves," and many other instances of slaves and free blacks residing in the same dwelling.

Under these circumstances skilled slaves could seek the most remunerative market for their labor or the products of their labor, and slaves who were unskilled might decide to engage in entrepreneurial activities* rather than seeking employment as common laborers. A slave might, for example, find it more profitable to cook and sell food items, or to catch and sell fish, or to rent (and perhaps eventually buy) a horse and cart and become a drayman. If their entrepreneurial activities were successful they might even employ other slaves to perform the services that they contracted to provide. While doubtless not common, such circumstances were at least sufficiently prevalent to cause the Charleston City Council to pass an ordinance regulating, but not prohibiting, the hiring of slaves by other slaves. Such slaves—or, as they were sometimes called, quasi-slaves or half-free blacks—had achieved a degree of independence and self-determination wholly incompatible with the traditional image of slavery.

For this degree of freedom, however, the slaves paid a price in addition to the hire returned to their owners. Owners could, in some measure, shield their slaves from the local authorities in the case of minor infractions, for Southern officials were reluctant to interpose the authority of the state between the master and the slave. Moreover, such slaves frequently resided in less healthful quarters and consumed less nutritious diets than would have been provided by their masters. A Washington observer wrote that their "place of repose is generally a cellar, the dampness of which is favorable to the propagation of contagion." It is worthy of note that between the 1820s and the middle of the nineteenth century, when "living out" was on the rise, the death rate among Baltimore's slaves rose from less than twenty per thousand to almost sixty per thousand, while the death rates for whites remained steady and that for free blacks probably declined slightly.

However employed—by their owners, by slave hirers, or by employers under terms negotiated by themselves—urban slaves frequently followed occupational pursuits radically different from those that were common on the plantations. Reliable and detailed information about slave employment patterns in the cities is not available, for neither federal census marshals nor directory compilers (those great sources of occupational data for the free population) inquired about or reported the jobs held by slaves. Still, visitors to the antebellum Southern cities reported that blacks—they frequently did not know whether they were bond or free—were highly visible in all the towns, both because of their absolute numbers and because they followed many diverse occupations. These sources show that blacks (and, probably, slaves) worked as factory operatives (especially in the iron and tobacco establishments in Richmond and other Virginia cities), carriage drivers, hotel servants, pastry cooks, market vendors, draymen, porters, carpenters, bricklayers, and stevedores. But such data are impressionistic and spotty. In 1848 local censuses were taken in Charleston and Savannah that at least attempted to address the question of occupational patterns. That of Savannah is almost useless in the matter of slave occupations, reporting only that 83 of perhaps 1,400 adult male slaves followed nonmenial occupations—doubtless a gross understatement. The Charleston census is more helpful, showing the occupations of almost 3,500 male and well over 3,800 female slaves. Just under 90 percent of the women and rather more than half of the men held personal service jobs—mostly as house servants—while another quarter of the males and almost a tenth of the females performed unskilled labor. But almost a sixth of the men were artisans; indeed, 40 of the 89 blacksmiths in the city were slaves. Slave artisans were almost as numerous as white artisans in Charleston. Although the slave employment pattern in that city in 1848 was not representative of all cities in this region throughout the antebellum period, these figures at least indicate the slave occupational diversity that existed in the urban South.

Aside from the potential freedoms that the city might offer to some slaves in residence, occupation, and owner oversight, there were some general freedoms that urban conditions made available to all slaves, even those working as servants in their master's house. One of these was the freedom to increase their range of associations. For a great variety of reasons urban house servants frequently left their owner's property, something that rarely happened in the rural, plantation environment. Carriage drivers not only transported members of the master's family to various places inside and outside the city, but were also dispatched to get friends or to bring bulky items to the master's house. Maids and other house servants went on a variety of errands, carrying messages and obtaining smaller items from various shops. Cooks, butlers, and majordomos went early every day to the markets to secure the provisions for the family's (and the slaves') meals. Such peregrinations brought these slaves into contact with a multitude of other blacks, slave and free, and opened to their view an enormously more complex society. They saw black schools, though, with rare exceptions before 1850 and almost none after that date, they could not attend them. They encountered black social organizations, most, but not all, of which were open only to free people of color. And they entered and were welcomed in black churches, where they not only found both a congregation and an order of worship more congenial to their desires and more attuned to their needs, but where they could participate in the management and governance of an institution. It was this widening of horizons in the urban setting that slaveholders found particularly threatening and that influenced many masters to remove their servants from this unsettling environment and send them back to their plantations.

Another gift of the city to the slave was anonymity. On the plantation or the farm or in small towns the slaves were known and were, therefore, in some measure accountable to every white that they met; they were under constant surveillance. But in the cities, though they might be almost constantly observed, actual surveillance scarcely existed because they were not, with rare exceptions, known as individuals. They were submerged in the mass of hundreds or, on occasion, thousands of blacks, slave and free, and because their names and those of their masters and, indeed, their slave status were unknown to more than a handful of whites, they had achieved without personal effort a significant degree of practical freedom. Consequently, the pass system of the plantation South, which was designed to limit the movement of slaves off their owners' property, utterly collapsed in the cities. The closest that the urban societies could come to regulating slave movement was the imposition of curfews that were applicable only to blacks. These laws* required that blacks be off the streets by a specified time, but although slaves were constantly seized for curfew violations, they could be, and often were, off their masters' property but still not in violation of curfew regulations if they were in the houses of other slaves or free blacks or in their own lodgings.

Other restraints imposed by ordinance reflected the collective will of white society to define permissible slave conduct. Some of these restraints applied to all blacks, some only to slaves. They were excluded from some parks or public grounds unless attending whites. They were prohibited from smoking cigars in public or carrying canes or purchasing liquor or selling farm produce. They could not gather in groups at night without the permission of the city government. They had to inform city officials of their place of residence and to be licensed if they hired their own time. They were required to assist in fighting fires and excluded from the vicinity of fires if they were not actively engaged in firefighting under white direction. Many of these ordinances were enforced only intermittently and, even then, inadequately, for the police and constabulary were few, largely untrained, usually corrupt, and almost always incompetent.

Punishments* meted out to urban slaves were generally less severe than on the plantations. Slaves were flogged by their masters and mistresses in town as well as in the countryside, and travelers commented with disgust upon the spectacle of whites brutally beating their bondsmen and women in their houses, in their yards, and occasionally on the streets. But for the very reason that such punishments attracted attention (and, often, condemnation), many masters were reluctant to apply the lash with the same degree of frequency and lack of concern as on the plantation. Here, as in many other areas of human activity, the cities provided institutional answers to problems dealt with in a more individual fashion in the rural regions. Slave owners might send their slaves to the city jail to be flogged or, on rare occasions, incarcerated. When urban masters proved somewhat reluctant to avail themselves of these services, authorities in Charleston, at least, bowed to their scruples and constructed a treadmill to provide noncorporal punishments to slaves of tender-hearted owners. The local press asserted that slaves hated the treadmill worse than the lash and voiced the hope that more masters of lazy and impudent bondsmen would make use of this public facility. For infractions of city ordinances, slaves were almost universally flogged unless their fines were paid by their owners; a few cities recognized realities by specifically providing that slaves might pay their own fines.

Thus, at that point where the institution of slavery and the multiple institutions that comprised nineteenth-century urbanism intersected, each institution was in some measure changed by the other. The most extensive modification, however, occurred in slavery as it reshaped itself to conform to the needs, demands, and opportunities of the urban environment. Slaves broadened their range of experiences, associated with a greater diversity of individuals and institutions, and formed new and different work practices and living circumstances. In the process many slaves acquired a greater measure of control over their own lives and took steps in the direction of freedom. Indeed, they became more nearly free. Whether these modifications of the generally accepted patterns of slave life represented the slow death of the South's peculiar institution in the urban environment or testified to the durability and flexibility of that institution, which enabled it to survive in and adapt to the least promising of circumstances, is a question the answer to which depends largely on one's own personal assessment. The reality of the change, and perhaps even its magnitude, are unquestionable.

SELECTED BIBLIOGRAPHY

Tommy L. Bogger, "The Slave and Free Black Community in Norfolk, 1775–1865" (Ph.D. dissertation, University of Virginia, 1976); William A. Byrne, Jr., "The Burden and Heat of the Day: Slavery and Servitude in Savannah, 1733–1865" (Ph.D. dissertation, Florida State University, 1979); E. Merton Coulter, "Slavery and Freedom in Athens, Georgia, 1860–1866," *Georgia Historical Quarterly*, 49 (1965), 264–293; Leonard P. Curry, *The Free Black in Urban America, 1800–1850: The Shadow of the Dream* (1981); Claudia Dale Goldin, *Urban Slavery in the American South, 1820–1860: A Quantitative History* (1976); Joyce D. Goodfriend, "Burghers and Blacks: The Evolution of a Slave Society at New Amsterdam," *New York History*, 59 (1978), 125–144; Lloyd A. Hunter, "Slavery in St. Louis, 1804–1860," *Bulletin of the Missouri Historical Society*, 30 (1974), 233–265; John S. Kendall, "New Orleans' 'Peculiar Institution,' " *Louisiana Historical Quarterly*, 23 (1940), 864–886; Mary L. O'Brien, "Slavery in Louisville during the Antebellum Period, 1820–1860" (M.A. thesis, University of Louisville, 1979); Maximilian Reichard, "Black and White on the Urban Frontier: The St. Louis Community in Transition, 1800–1830," *Bulletin of the Missouri Historical Society*, 33 (1976), 3–17; Robert C. Reinders, "Slavery in New Orleans in the Decade before the Civil War," *Mid-America*, 44 (1962), 211–221; William L. Richter, "Slavery in Baton Rouge, 1820–1860," *Louisiana History*, 10 (1969), 125–145; Marianne B. Sheldon, "Black-White Relations in Richmond, Virginia, 1782–1820," *Journal of Southern History*, 45 (1979), 27–44; and Richard C. Wade, *Slavery in the Cities: The South, 1820–1860* (1964).

LEONARD P. CURRY

V

VESEY, DENMARK (ca. 1767–1822). Born in Africa or Saint Thomas around 1767, Denmark Vesey spent much of his youth as a slave on the latter island, a Danish slave-trading center. During 1781 a Bermuda slave trader, Joseph Vesey, took him to Saint-Domingue where Denmark was sold to a sugar planter. Exposed to this harsh existence, the slave experienced epileptic fits and his master quickly returned him to Vesey. After two years on Vesey's slave ship in the Caribbean, the slave was taken to Charleston where his master established himself as a prosperous merchant. Denmark remained with Vesey, experiencing the relative freedom of an urban slave.* In 1800, however, Denmark won the East Bay Street lottery and purchased his freedom for $600.

Once free, Denmark became a carpenter, joining the approximately 1,000 other free blacks in Charleston. By 1822 he had accumulated $8,000 in property, considerable wealth for a free black. Despite his success, Denmark was distressed by the condition of other blacks, especially his seven wives and numerous children who remained slaves. He urged other blacks to resist white oppression, lashing out at those blacks who deferred. As Charleston's free black community grew to 3,600 by 1822, white hostility and repression increased.

Even earlier the literate, cosmopolitan Vesey had woven together several strands of thought that justified slave revolt.* These included the rights of man from the American Revolution,* armed resistance to whites from the Haitian Revolution of 1800, solidarity from his own African Methodist Episcopal church,* as well as traditional African charms and spells. In addition, Vesey capitalized on white disagreements during the congressional debates over the admission of Missouri to the Union in 1819 and 1820. Attempting to incite his followers, Vesey informed them that the Missouri Compromise of 1820* had actually freed the slaves, but that white Southerners refused to obey it. Approaching free blacks, as well as slaves who were fairly independent and trusted by the community, Vesey carefully chose his followers. Vesey's 1822 conspiracy, involving as many as 9,000 blacks and designed to take advantage of lax white security, included murder, arson, and Vesey's escape to Haiti.

Despite Vesey's careful preparations, one of his lieutenants ultimately failed him, recruiting a slave who reported the plot to his master. Although whites at first refused to credit the story, they increased security when other conspirators confessed. Vesey moved the date forward for his revolt from 15 July (Bastille Day) to 16 June, but whites prevented the revolt anyway, capturing and punishing the conspirators. Thirty-five blacks were hanged, including Vesey; thirty-seven were exiled.

Vesey's conspiracy left deep scars on South Carolina society. In an effort to control free blacks, the legislature passed the Seamen Acts* confining black sailors to jail while their ships were in port. Although the governor questioned the extent of the danger, Vesey's conspiracy also played a role in converting the defense of slavery from one emphasizing slavery as a necessary evil to one that defended slavery as a positive good. In addition, Vesey's plot contributed to further sectional difficulties. White South Carolinians never forgot that Vesey's hero was Rufus King, an antislavery spokesman during the Missouri debates. Some historians, notably William W. Freehling, consider Vesey's plot to have been a trigger to the nullification movement* in South Carolina in 1832.

SELECTED BIBLIOGRAPHY

William W. Freehling, *Prelude to Civil War: The Nullification Controversy in South Carolina, 1816–1836* (1965); Eugene D. Genovese, *From Rebellion to Revolution: Afro-American Slave Revolts in the Making of the Modern World* (1979); John Lofton, *Insurrection in South Carolina: The Turbulent World of Denmark Vesey* (1964); Robert S. Starobin, ed., *Denmark Vesey: The Slave Conspiracy of 1822* (1970); and Sterling Stuckey, "Remembering Denmark Vesey: Agitation or Insurrection?" *Negro Digest*, 15 (1966), 28–41.

ALICE E. REAGAN

VIOLENCE, SLAVE. Violence was intrinsic to the Afro-American slave experience from colonial times through emancipation. Slaves resisted authority by committing violent acts against whites and also engaged in violent behavior for reasons unrelated to, or only indirectly related to, their bondage. The average slave may have been a far cry from the latent Spartacus suggested by some authorities on the slave personality, but he or she certainly broke the mold of cringing Sambo hypothesized in Stanley Elkins's once controversial *Slavery: A Problem in American Institutional and Intellectual Life* (1959).

Because general slave uprisings only involved a minute percentage of the slaves who engaged in violent aggression against the master class, violent slave resistance* should be evaluated primarily in terms of individual acts of defiance. Though slave parents customarily inculcated obedience before white authority within the upbringing of their children,* they rarely advised abject submission. When sufficiently provoked by owners, overseers,* other whites, or blacks enforcing white rule (for example, fellow slaves who participated in the pursuit of fugitives*), some slaves responded with physical violence. Punishment,* particularly whippings,* triggered a high percentage of slave assaults on whites. All kinds of grievances, however, including anger about liberties taken by whites with black women,* provoked slave violence. Some individual acts of violence are best attributed to a smoldering resentment of bondage itself. Not long before his abortive 1800 revolt, Gabriel Prosser* bit off the ear of a white who had caught another black stealing a hog—an act most likely prompted by the kind of yearning for freedom that sparked his insurrection plot.

Brawls and criminal acts such as rape were a part of life within the slave community. Blacks fought, and sometimes murdered, over sexual jealousies, thefts, and an infinite variety of other provocations. In some instances, such behavior was instigated by whites; slave narratives and ex-slave interviews occasionally allude to sadistic owners and overseers who enjoyed the spectacle of slaves fighting among themselves to the point of even insisting upon it. Most masters, however, gave high priority to order as a virtue in labor management, and it was more common for owners to attempt to suppress, not foment, violent flare-ups between slaves.

There is no way to calculate how much the rhythm of intra-race aggression related to frustration over the inability of most blacks to strike effective blows against white authority, but the correlation can be presumed to be significant. Slaves, though sometimes elevating violent resisters such as Nat Turner* into folk heroes, nonetheless comprehended all too well that attacks on whites almost invariably brought severe retribution upon themselves and that they also risked jeopardizing the welfare of relatives and other slaves. Recent research has discovered a pattern of self-inflicted violence among Afro-American slaves, including suicide, infanticide,* and mutilation of one's own limbs. Many such instances can be attributed to slave impotence before the power of the master class. Certainly the American Civil War* revealed what could happen when the slaveholders' controls were relaxed. While Afro-Americans never exploded in the kind of general, violent orgy so feared by many Southern whites, they nevertheless destroyed enough property and committed sufficient numbers of assaults upon whites (including retaliatory whippings of former masters and overseers) to belie entirely prewar proslavery propaganda* that portrayed slaves as docile and content with their fate.

Warfare in America, from the colonial period through the Civil War, often legitimized black violence. In colonial times, for instance, slaves generally were excluded from the militia. Yet in struggles like South Carolina's Yamassee War (1715–1716) when insufficient white manpower seemed to spell impending defeat, white authorities proved themselves quite willing to arm blacks. Such pragmatism continued during the American Revolution,* when both the British and the American states used slaves in land and sea forces. Slaves also fought in later American wars, including the Civil War, when a high percentage of the approximately 180,000 black soldiers and sailors in Union military ranks were "contrabands"* and—after the Emancipation Proclamation*—former slaves. Even the Confederacy* resorted to arming slave soldiers in the waning moments of the war.

Afro-American slave violence remains a controversial topic. To establish that slaves in the American colonies, and then the United States, committed violent acts is not the same as to certify that they were as prone to violence as victims of other Western Hemisphere slave societies, not to mention slaves through the epochs. Some authorities, hypothesizing that slaves in the United States were less violent than other slave groups, credit evangelical Christianity with fostering "accommodationist" patterns among Afro-American slaves. They assert that the slaves, anticipating glory in the afterlife, repressed violent tendencies. Other scholars, however, have contended that the Second Great Awakening, with its egalitarian message of access to salvation for all, inspired slave resistance and accompanying violence. Intuitive logic suggests that antebellum Southern slaves, in particular, *should* have been violent; their masters' mores exalted dueling and other manifestations of an aggressive social code. According to this argument, such a violent white culture must have filtered down into the slave community at least to a limited degree.

Quantification offers some help regarding the problem of slave violence. Statistical data has been assembled, for example, that shows that in the Anderson and Spartanburg districts of South Carolina between 1818 and 1860, a much lower percentage of slave than white prosecutions in court concerned the crime of assault. But the applicability of such findings, since a high proportion of incidents of slave violence went unreported, is limited. Perhaps a more fruitful line of inquiry considers the social context of slave violence. How much did the presence of free black role models affect the likelihood of Afro-Americans' committing violent acts? Did different slave classes (plantation,* household,* urban,* factory,* etc.) channel their aggressive impulses in similar or disparate directions? In a monograph about slave resistance in eighteenth-century Virginia, historian Gerald W. Mullin demonstrated the potential for such an approach. According to Mullin, plantation slaves, particularly recent arrivals from Africa, tended toward spontaneous assaults against individual whites. Skilled, acculturated slaves, in contrast, inclined to more planned, freedom-oriented violence such as a general slave uprising. Much more, however, remains to be learned about Afro-American slave violence.

SELECTED BIBLIOGRAPHY

Dickson D. Bruce, Jr., *Violence and Culture in the Antebellum South* (1979); Helen H. T. Catterall, ed., *Judicial Cases Concerning American Slavery and the Negro* (5 vols., 1926–1937); Vincent Harding, *There Is a River: The Black Struggle for Freedom in America* (1981); Michael S. Hindus, "Black Justice under White Law: Criminal Prosecutions of Blacks in Antebellum South Carolina," *Journal of American History*, 63

(1976), 575–599; and Gerald W. Mullin, *Flight and Rebellion: Slave Resistance in Eighteenth-Century Virginia* (1972).

ROBERT E. MAY

VIRGINIA, SLAVERY IN. Virginia was the first permanent English colony in America, and the first to import African laborers. At the time of the American Revolution Virginia contained almost half the black population of the United States. As late as 1860, the Old Dominion still contained more slaves than any other state, and more free blacks* as well. Culturally similar to her neighbors, Maryland and North Carolina, Virginia grew from her Jamestown beginnings to encompass the enormous area that now also contains Kentucky, separated by mutual agreement in 1792, and West Virginia, separated with some hard feelings during the Civil War. Besides producing four of the first five presidents of the United States, Virginia produced two of America's three most famous black rebels: Gabriel Prosser* and Nat Turner.* Booker Taliaferro Washington* was born in Franklin County, Virginia, in 1856. The state eventually produced passionate proslavery advocates like Edmund Ruffin and George Fitzhugh,* but also produced many abolitionists,* such as the Tory Anglican Jonathan Boucher, the Presbyterian David Rice, and the Quaker Robert Pleasants. Virginia was startled and dismayed by John Brown's* invasion of 1859, but remained calmer about it than most other states. In the election of 1860 Virginia favored the Constitutional Union candidates, John Bell and Edward Everett, and was determined to stay in the Union if the federal government used only peaceful measures to persuade "erring sisters." But once the shooting began, Virginia joined the Confederate States of America, accepted the transfer of its capital to Richmond, and became the principal battleground of the war.

Virginia has received much ingenious attention as the place where American slavery began, but it did not really begin there at all. Like the English language, the Church of England (*see* Anglican church), and the commercial production of tobacco,* Afro-American slavery was an importation which, in time, took on distinctive local characteristics. In fact, black slaves could be found all over the commercial and colonial world of the Atlantic in the seventeenth century.

Though slavery had died out in northern Europe in the Middle Ages, it had persisted in the Mediterranean, and had increased there in the fifteenth and sixteenth centuries, partly because of the development of sugar production on Crete, Cyprus, and other islands. The rise to power of Spain and Portugal in the fifteenth century sent European traders out into the Atlantic, where Portugal developed a trade in black slaves from West Africa to the Iberian Peninsula, and to Atlantic islands like the Canaries, the Azores, the Cape Verdes, and the Madeiras. Finally, in league with Italian and Spanish merchants, Portugal supplied blacks to the New World. The Spanish especially needed them in their Caribbean colonies, where native laborers rapidly died out.

Table 1
White and Black Population in Early Virginia

Year	White	Black	Free Black
1625	1,204	23	*
1648	15,000	300	*
1671	38,000	2,000	*
1700	60,000	6,000	*
1715	72,500	23,000	*
1756	173,316	120,156	*
1782	296,852	270,762	3,000

* Records of occasional free blacks begin in the 1630s, but no one bothered to estimate the whole number of them before 1782. Many of the figures given here are estimates, but they give a cogent sense of the growth of Virginia population.

It remained for the Dutch, the world's premier navigators, traders, and manufacturers in the early seventeenth century, to establish their West Indies Company in 1621 and then introduce black slavery into the Caribbean for the purpose of intensive sugar cultivation and processing. A small country, the Netherlands sent out relatively few colonists; their empire consisted mainly of trading posts, not settlements. They were therefore pleased to sell slaves and machinery for the refining of sugar to the English settlers who had swarmed to tropical islands from 1625 onward. The Dutch were also pleased to buy English sugar and tobacco, and market them in Europe. This trade especially flourished in the 1640s, during the English Civil War. A triumphant Parliament tried to stop it by the Navigation Act of 1651 and the Anglo-Dutch War of 1652–1654. But then, in a sudden switch of foreign policy, the English resumed plundering the Spanish in the New World. Among their booty were thousands of blacks, and Jamaica, soon to become the most profitable of the British sugar islands. Only with the permanent establishment of the Royal Africa Company in 1672 did England become firmly established in the Atlantic slave trade, with bases in Africa, and a fleet regularly bringing hundreds, and then thousands, of blacks to the Americas each year. Gradually displacing the Portuguese (who, however, continued to supply their huge colony of Brazil) and the Dutch, the British became the world's leading slave trader for most of the eighteenth century, yielding that doubtful honor to the French around the time of the American Revolution.

The first blacks in Virginia arrived long before either England or her colonies were deeply involved in the slave trade or the rationalized use of slave labor to produce staple crops. Nevertheless, that earliest importation is worth reviewing, especially because it has been so widely misunderstood. In August 1619 a Dutch warship arrived at Point Comfort, several miles downstream from Jamestown, and right on Chesapeake Bay, where it unloaded "twenty and odd Negroes," according to John Rolfe. All subsequent accounts derive from Rolfe's letter to John Smith, who, writing in England, reduced the number to twenty. The Dutch ship unloaded its cargo at the dock of Abraham Piersey, probably the wealthiest man in Virginia at the time, and the one who owned the largest number of white *and black* laborers in 1625. The Dutch ship had an English pilot, "Mr. Marmaduke," and had been privateering in the West Indies along with the *Treasurer*, an old ship much employed between London, Bermuda, and Virginia. *Treasurer* proceeded to Bermuda, where she unloaded a cargo of sixteen blacks. The legend has been repeated endlessly that the first blacks in Virginia were "indentured servants,"* but there is no hint of this in the records. The legend grew up because the word *slave* did not appear in Virginia records until 1656, and statutes defining the status of blacks began to appear casually in the 1660s. The inference was then made that blacks, called servants, must have had approximately the same status as white indentured servants. Such reasoning failed to notice that Englishmen, in the early seventeenth century, used the word *servant* when they meant *slave* in our sense, and, indeed, white Southerners invariably used *servant* until 1865 and beyond. *Slave* entered the Southern vocabulary as a technical word in trade, law, and politics. As for statute law,* Virginia was quite casual about codification before 1705. The record of judicial law, on the other hand, amply proves the existence of slavery, especially after the creation of county courts around 1630. Surviving court records also prove that some of the earliest Virginia blacks were free, and a few were, indeed, indentured servants.

The black population of Virginia grew slowly for the first twenty years, when the chief source was robbing the Spanish. After 1640 blacks appeared in all the mainland colonies of North America as a consequence of their massive importation to the West Indies, and the rapidly developing trade of mainland colonies—especially New Netherland and New England—with the bustling sugar islands. A Virginia statute of 1660 promised to reduce the duties charged to the Dutch and other nations which brought them black slaves in exchange for their tobacco. The new series of Navigation Acts passed under Charles II rendered this invitation void, but it does prove that Virginians, far from being reluctant to acquire black labor, were positively eager for it.

Between 1660 and 1720 Virginia changed from a tobacco-exporting plantation economy primarily using white servants to one primarily using black slaves. Edmund S. Morgan has argued that this was the result of Bacon's Rebellion (1676), which he sees as an uprising of former white indentured servants against their rich and greedy former masters. My view, however, is that Virginia planters turned (very gradually) to black labor because the great and growing British

Table 2
The Slave Trade into Virginia

Before 1700	2,000–2,500
1700–1719	14,115
1720–1749	41,067
1750–1773	19,301
Total	76,473–76,973

commercial empire strongly encouraged them to do so. Under Charles II England conquered New Netherland and established New York. Almost simultaneously she created the colonies of New Jersey and the Carolinas, Pennsylvania following in 1682. Meanwhile, the British Caribbean continued to increase its output of sugar, a brisk trade with Africa developed, and the East India Company, followed by "private traders," extended its operations wonderfully in Asia. A cycle of world wars from 1689 to 1713 left the Netherlands exhausted, France firmly checked, and the British, soundly financed by the new Bank of England and now united with enterprising Scotland, dominant in the European world. Even with an unprecedented birthrate, England no longer had a surplus population to send off to colonial plantations.

Although no one ever forced a Virginian to buy African slaves, the British system made it very easy to do so in the eighteenth century, bringing choice young blacks directly to the shores of the James and York rivers, and accepting tobacco or extending credit for purchases. Perhaps there was an indirect element of coercion in this situation, for the planter without slaves was surely at a competitive disadvantage in colonial Virginia. But Virginia bought fewer and fewer slaves after 1750, and virtually none after 1773. This was partly the result of the new antislavery ideology, and partly the result of breaking off all trade with the British for political reasons. But it was also the result of black Virginians being prolific; ever since the 1720s natural increase had done more to increase the population than importations from Africa. On the eve of the American Revolution, upper-class Virginians were concerned about the overproduction of tobacco, the danger of a black majority, and the injustice of slavery. It is impossible to know how much weight each motive carried, but Virginia would have stopped the trade before independence had Britain allowed it, and Thomas Jefferson* undertook to shift all the blame for slavery to the mother country in his initial draft of the Declaration of Independence.* Shortly after the conclusion of the Revolutionary war, Virginians began their trans-Appalachian migration to Kentucky and elsewhere in the West and Southwest. Virginia became such a great supplier of blacks for the interstate slave trade* that abolitionists began accusing white Virginians of deliberately breeding* slaves for distant sale.

The social structure of Virginia in the eighteenth century has been widely misunderstood because of the otherwise valuable preservation or restoration of upper-class homes and colonial Williamsburg. It is very easy to suppose that it was divided among rich planters, ambitious overseers, black slaves, and poor whites. Of course all these classes were present, but the numerically largest class in late colonial and early national Virginia was a solid, stable, hardworking, churchgoing, literate middling class of planters who owned a few slaves and a few hundred acres of land. Over half the blacks belonged to such people, who rarely employed overseers, and often worked along with their servants. On the other hand, there were also great planters like "King" Carter and his descendants, the three generations of William Byrds, George Washington,* and Thomas Jefferson, who eventually numbered their blacks by the hundreds. Somewhere handy to their mansions, these magnates had small villages of Afro-Americans with well-developed kinship groups, and regular social gatherings. But these communities remained quite small; the great planters owned several discrete plantations, located in different parts of the province, rarely retaining more than thirty-five hands on each.

Planters who owned dozens or hundreds of blacks were typically second- or third-generation slaveholders; if they sent a group of blacks off to a remote plantation, the blacks were very likely to be Virginia-born and bred. Conversely, the Virginians most likely to buy new Africans, right off the boat, were first-generation slaveholders, building up a stock which would, after a few such purchases, become largely self-perpetuating for their descendants. The African newly arrived in Virginia was typically a child or youth between twelve and twenty-one years of age. Distributed singly or in groups of two or three among small-scale planters, most of them proved to be adept both at learning English and mastering their plantation chores. The transition from African to Virginian cultural characteristics was rapid both because of their youth and because of the practice of dispersing them widely among white Virginians and well-acculturated or Virginia-bred blacks.

This is not to say that no African traits survived in Virginia; unfortunately white Virginians were terrible ethnologists. The opportunity to learn from their African-born slaves was lost, except for a very few casual observations. In 1680 the Virginia Assembly passed a law forbidding the gathering of blacks at night for funerals. We may assume that these were African, not English, observances. In 1720 the assembly purchased the freedom of a black man to reward him for a herbal remedy of great value. In music* blacks displayed the eclecticism that has characterized them ever since, mastering European instruments and English tunes, but also improvising their own instruments and music as opportunities permitted.

Most waking hours were, of course, given to work. On large plantations, considerable specialization was possible: black coopers (tobacco demanded endless quantities of wooden casks), carpenters, stonemasons, bricklayers, hostlers, and smiths enriched their masters and improved civilization all over Virginia.

Those who lived on family farms had a more varied experience. On turning six or seven the black child would become a household helper; with more maturity and strength, the child would have outdoor work as a chief duty. As the household expanded, the mistress might keep one or two black women at cooking, gardening, dairying, spinning, and weaving. Similarly, if a planter of modest circumstances found that his black man was unusually effective at a trade—carpentry, for instance—he might find it more advantageous to hire him out to neighbors rather than employ him in setting, worming, topping, and curing tobacco leaves.

The long distances and extensive trade of Virginia required a large force of workers in transportation, and most of these were black. One could see them any day, floating tobacco casks down the river to the provincial warehouses that held them for ocean-going ships. They were sailors on the larger boats that crossed and recrossed Chesapeake Bay, and the still larger ones that ventured off to the West Indies. They could be seen as teamsters and coachmen, moving the goods and families of their masters over the wretched roads of the province. In normal years, Virginia produced a surplus of food; besides tending tobacco, blacks raised a variety of grains, vegetables, fruit trees, and livestock for their masters and on their own account. Sheep, horses, hogs, and cattle were typically the property of their masters, but they were usually permitted to keep their own poultry and eggs.

After independence, with the further growth of both Virginia and the United States, a distinction developed in Virginia between rural and urban slavery.* Black slaves, often hired out* from year to year by their masters, worked as wage laborers at canal and railroad building, in ironworks, and in shipyards. Although the laws of Virginia prescribed an elaborate system of passes, patrols, and curfews, the countervailing atmosphere of laissez-faire, reinforced by a great reluctance to spend money on the public good, left the black industrial worker with considerable freedom. This situation permitted, if it did not actually encourage, the formation of conspiracies. One such, vast in its ambition and possibly in its extent, was discovered in Richmond in 1800. Its ringleader, Gabriel Prosser, became one of the most famous black rebels in American history, though his rebellion never occurred. Prosser's ideas were based on the natural rights ideology of the American and French revolutions.

By contrast, Nat Turner, leader of a rebel band of sixty or more in remote Southampton County (near the border of North Carolina), was a preacher* driven by voices and visions. In August 1831, Turner's band killed fifty-five white Virginians, most of them women and children, before they were overwhelmed by superior force. When Virginia suffered major military invasions during the war for independence, and again during the war for Southern independence, blacks could be found on both sides. Thousands took advantage of the confusion to escape from bondage. The "loyalty" of most blacks to their Virginia masters between 1861 and 1865 remains a remarkable fact.

Table 3
Virginia Population, 1790–1860

Year	White	Slave	Free Colored
1790	442,117	292,627	12,866
1820	603,381	425,148	36,875
1840	740,968	448,988	49,481
1860	1,047,299	490,865	58,042

Note: The 1790 figures exclude Kentucky, but the figures for 1860 include West Virginia.

There were a number of distinct frontiers in the early history of Virginia. Settlement had reached the fall line by the time of Bacon's Rebellion, and the Blue Ridge by 1730. The 1740s saw settlers taking up the best lands in the Shenandoah Valley, and land speculators were looking beyond the mountains toward the Ohio Valley before 1750. White Virginians were mainly of the property-owning class. They almost always married and, health permitting, raised large enough families so that the white population doubled each generation. Far from being lazy, the typical Virginia slaveholder was a man or woman working not only for a comfortable and prosperous estate, but for land and slaves enough so that some of each could be bestowed on each son and daughter at the time of marriage. The practice of setting up young couples with estates comparable to those of their parents made for a very rapid westward expansion. And this produced a society quite different from the slave societies where rice, indigo, sugar, and eventually cotton were produced. In Virginia, blacks often grew up on plantations along with sons or daughters who would take them along when they set up plantations of their own. Such a move might be only a few miles away, but after the Revolution it might be to Kentucky, and, after the War of 1812, to Alabama or Mississippi. Whether they moved short or long distances, the life cycles of black Virginians were usually tied to those of the white people that owned them.

We know very little of the religious and philosophical views of the Africans brought to Virginia on the slave ships. A few, certainly, were Muslims.* The rest no doubt entertained a lively belief in the supernatural, and had experienced various rites and observances in Africa. By the end of the eighteenth century, however, the black people of Virginia were Christians in the sense that they lived in a province where virtually everyone in the owning classes professed Christianity and where major Christian holidays—especially Christmas and Easter—were celebrated with relief from work and extra rations. At least some clergy and laypersons of the Church of England worked seriously to convert blacks from the middle years of the seventeenth century. As early as the 1720s, a parson on the early settled Eastern Shore reported 300 black communicants in his parish. But the Church of England was unable to keep pace with either the growth of population or the advance of the frontier. Baptists,* Presbyterians,* and finally Methodists* became important in all sections of Virginia, and dominant in the West. Before 1865 blacks were obliged by law and custom to attend their master's churches; this is why, eventually, there were more black Baptists and Methodists than Presbyterians or Episcopalians.* There were far more white ones as well. Black field preachers appeared from time to time after the first Great Awakening, and the Presbyterians formally ordained an unusually gifted black, who preached to a white congregation. But Virginia outlawed black preachers after Nat Turner's rebellion.

Virginia's slavery took root when social stratification, not equality, was the rule in American and European society. It is therefore no insult to colonial blacks to point out that most of them accepted the social order in which they lived fatalistically. Acts of resistance* or escape were individual projects, or the efforts of small groups. Most blacks seem to have accepted their lot as cheerfully as they could. But the last twenty-five years of the eighteenth century made an enormous difference in attitudes. The white upper classes largely adopted the new dogmas of natural rights and universal equality, on the basis of which they proclaimed the right of revolution wherever human freedom was denied. At the same time a great religious revival became deeply intertwined with democratic ideals. Led by Quakers,* Methodists, and Baptists, but rapidly gaining adherents in every denomination and among upper-class skeptics, the antislavery movement took shape. By 1804 the states north of Maryland and Delaware had either completely abolished slavery or had firmly set it on a course of extinction. Although it has been largely forgotten, antislavery and pro-colonization voices remained strong and numerous in Virginia right down to 1865. There was no keeping these doctrines from blacks, especially when many white Virginians saw no reason to do so. Inevitably, a defensively proslavery party arose in Virginia, and it was responsible for many laws curtailing the liberties of free blacks and outlawing the education of slaves. But the number of free blacks continued to increase, and Virginians proved, overall, too liberal and individualistic to enforce the antieducation laws.

The case of Virginia is important for several reasons. It was in the Chesapeake region, with its tobacco and grain cropping, that black slavery first became fixed in North American society. Cotton did not figure either in its establishment or in its perpetuation into the nineteenth century. Africans came gradually, over the course of a century, and never outnumbered white Virginians except in a few lower counties along the James and York. Most blacks had strong and continuing ties to particular white families. Virginia suffered terribly during the Civil War and Reconstruction, and has hardly been free of racial problems since. Yet one has the sense that in the Old Dominion white and black alike take enough satisfaction simply in being Virginians that they do not allow other problems, however grave, to overwhelm them.

SELECTED BIBLIOGRAPHY

James C. Ballagh, *A History of Slavery in Virginia* (1902); James H. Brewer, *The Confederate Negro: Virginia's Craftsmen and Military Laborers, 1861–1865* (1969); Robert E. Brown and B. Katherine Brown, *Virginia, 1705–1786: Democracy or Aristocracy?* (1964); Wesley F. Craven, *White, Red, and Black: The Seventeenth-Century Virginian* (1971); Luther Porter Jackson, *Free Negro Labor and Property Holding in Virginia, 1830–1860* (1942); James H. Johnston, *Race Relations in Virginia and Miscegenation in the South, 1776–1860* (1970); Robert McColley, *Slavery and Jeffersonian Virginia* (rev. ed., 1973); Randall M. Miller, ed., *"Dear Master": Letters of a Slave Family* (1978); Edmund S. Morgan, *American Slavery, American Freedom: The Ordeal of Colonial Virginia* (1975); and Gerald W. Mullin, *Flight and Rebellion: Slave Resistance in Eighteenth-Century Virginia* (1972).

ROBERT MCCOLLEY

VIRGINIA SLAVERY DEBATE OF 1831–1832. On the night of 23 August 1831, Nat Turner* and his slave followers massacred fifty-five Virginia whites in the remote tidewater county of Southampton. This fiery slave insurrection so convulsed white society as to provoke unprecedented public debate on emancipation in the 1831–1832 Virginia legislature. For two weeks in January 1832, the House of Delegates debated slavery's fate in Virginia, then the nation's largest slaveholding state.

Historians of the antebellum South have long viewed the debate as a decisive watershed, the moment when Virginians renounced Jeffersonian antislavery principles* and endorsed the "perpetual good" proslavery philosophy of the Deep South. Close study of the debate reveals, however, that although the House rejected immediate emancipation legislation, a majority coalition of antislavery delegates proclaimed slavery an "evil" and pledged future emancipation once Virginia public opinion approved. Indeed, not even the staunchest opponents of legislative abolition advocated perpetual slavery in Virginia. Anticipating Thomas R. Dew, conservative legislators argued that urban-industrial growth would make slave labor increasingly unprofitable, prompting Virginia slave owners to sell surplus blacks to the cotton-sugar-rice states. The domestic slave trade* would thus gradually rid Virginia of slavery and blacks.

If Virginia's declaration of future emancipation kept antislavery tenets alive, the 1832 debate in no way resolved internal conflicts over slavery. Throughout the antebellum years, nonslaveholders'* demands for equal political representation, suffrage, and taxation challenged slavery's compatibility with majority rule. Always nonslaveholding and slaveholding whites sought to compromise, to postpone, this explosive issue. When Civil War* precluded further compromise, Virginia split apart and her predominantly nonslaveholding trans-Allegheny counties joined the Union as free-soil West Virginia.

SELECTED BIBLIOGRAPHY

Thomas Roderick Dew, *Review of the Debate in the Virginia Legislature of 1831–1832* (1832); Alison Goodyear Freehling, *Drift toward Dissolution: The Virginia Slavery Debate of 1831–1832* (1982); and Henry I. Tragle, ed., *The Southampton Slave Revolt of 1831: A Compilation of Source Material* (1971).

ALISON GOODYEAR FREEHLING

VOODOO. West Africans had a three-tiered pantheon that included one supreme deity, various ancestral gods, and numerous spirits that inhabited animate and inanimate objects. Among many of the slaves obtained by French traders the words *vodu* and *vodun* expressed the Africans' awe of these supernatural beings. In the New World the derivations *vaudou* and *voodoo* referred to black religious activities in French settlements—especially Saint-Domingue (Haiti), but also Martinique, Guadeloupe, and Louisiana. In these locales Afro-Americans blended their beliefs in the powerful spirit world with the Catholicism* of tolerant Frenchmen and the folklore* of other superstitious inhabitants. Voodoo became a religious cult whose adherents, also called voodoos, worshiped African gods syncretized with Catholic saints and were possessed by spirits invoked during mysterious rites. Voodoo also was a variety of folk medicine in which conjurers used charms and potions to work both good and evil.

The first evidence of voodoo in North America dates from 1782, when Louisiana's Spanish governor forbade further importation of slaves from Martinique because their voodoo practices threatened white colonists. In 1792 Spanish authorities extended this ban to slaves from Saint-Domingue, where a violent revolt challenged French authority. Some white refugees nevertheless managed to bring in their slaves from the French Antilles. Moreover, in 1809, the United States admitted a special group of Haitian refugees, including over 3,000 slaves and nearly as many free people of color. Significant voodoo activities soon developed in and around New Orleans where these immigrants settled.

Because voodoo rites were secretive and most participants were illiterate, minimal documentary evidence exists. However, occasional police and court records, several comments in the ex-slave narratives, infrequent newspaper articles, and scattered references in plantation papers indicate that voodoo ceremonies did occur. Voodoo rituals occurred at night, lit by flickering fires. Enthralling drum music induced dancing and singing around an altar decorated with fetishes. The leader, usually a woman called the queen, presented an animal such as a snake, chicken, or cat to the worshippers and sometimes sacrificed it. Aroused by the pulsating rhythms, dances, and chants, the voodoo spirit possessed the true believers with the frenzied paroxysms and ecstatic trances. Recent research has uncovered an underground black church, the "invisible institution," that existed throughout the antebellum South. Voodoo was a divergent form of this black religion* practiced in south Louisiana. It was most prevalent in permissive New Orleans, where police investigating unusual activities sometimes found voodoo groups of slaves, free coloreds, and whites, most of them females.

Slaveholders in south Louisiana occasionally discovered strange charms around slaves' necks, odd signs in doorways, and distraught blacks who believed that they suffered from a voodoo curse. All of these were manifestations of voodoo conjuring, a special variety of magical folk medicine common among many preliterate nineteenth-century Americans. Voodoo doctors earned money and prestige dispensing philters (*gris-gris*), predicting the future, and helping believers cast or remove spells. Gradually, they diluted African practices, as did root doctors throughout the country who adopted the labels *voodoo* or *hoodoo* in order to identify with the powers of the original cult.

SELECTED BIBLIOGRAPHY

Roger Bastide, *African Civilisations in the New World*, trans. by Peter Green (1971); Newbell Niles Puckett, *Folk Beliefs of the Southern Negro* (1926); Albert J. Raboteau, *Slave Religion: The "Invisible Institution" in the Antebellum South* (1978); and Blake Touchstone, "Voodoo in New Orleans," *Louisiana History*, 13 (1972), 371–386.

BLAKE TOUCHSTONE

W

WALKER, DAVID (1785–1830). The son of a free black woman and a slave father, David Walker was born in Wilmington, North Carolina, and, according to the law of his home state, assumed the free status of his mother. Able to travel throughout the South during his youth, Walker observed firsthand what he considered to be the horrors of the institution of slavery. His embitterment toward the South was intensified by ill-treatment suffered by his mother and the restrictions placed upon his father. Determined to leave the South, Walker first moved to Philadelphia where he became a devout follower of Richard Allen, the black bishop of the AME church. By 1825 Walker had moved to Boston, where he not only taught himself to read and write but also opened a clothing store.

In Boston Walker quickly involved himself in many of the local black anti-slavery activities. Upon its creation in Boston in 1826, Walker immediately became a vocal and vehement member of the anticolonizationist General Colored Association of Massachusetts. In an eloquent address to that organization in the winter of 1828, Walker urged free blacks to act collectively to undermine both the institution of slavery in the South and the recovery of fugitive slaves* in the North. The following year, 1829, Walker published the first of three editions of his pamphlet, *David Walker's Appeal, in Four Articles; Together with a Preamble to the Coloured Citizens of the World, But in Particular, and Very Expressly, to Those of the United States of America.*

The text of this pamphlet was a soundly reasoned, eloquent indictment against slavery. Walker implored all black people to rise in violent insurrection, if necessary, against their oppressors and their oppression. Yet Walker also preferred a gesture of Christian forgiveness, suggesting that peace and harmony would prevail should the slaveholders free their slaves voluntarily. The publication of the *Appeal* had far-reaching ramifications. Indeed, some historians have identified Walker as America's first significant black nationalistic ideologue. Within the text of the *Appeal* appear most of the major tenets of black nationalism: the belief that blacks must some day reside in their own nation; the conviction that blacks must provide their own leadership and defense; and the faith that blacks must play a messianic role. Walker's *Appeal* created such an outrage in the South that some state legislatures not only passed laws preventing its circulation, but also made it a crime punishable by death to introduce similar literature. Throughout the South a price was placed upon Walker's head as the *Appeal* became one of the most widely read and circulated books written by a black. Three months after the *Appeal* went into its third edition, in June 1830, Walker was found dead near his shop. Though never proven, it was rumored and widely held that he had been poisoned.

SELECTED BIBLIOGRAPHY

Herbert Aptheker, *"One Continual Cry": David Walker's Appeal to the Colored Citizens of The World, 1829–1830, Its Setting & Its Meaning, Together with the Full Text of the Third—and Last—Edition of the Appeal* (1965); Clement Eaton, "A Dangerous Pamphlet in the Old South," *Journal of Southern History*, 2 (1936), 323–334; Sterling Stuckey, *The Ideological Origins of Black Nationalism* (1972); and Charles M. Wiltse, ed., *David Walker's Appeal, in Four Articles; Together with a Preamble to the Coloured Citizens of the World, But in Particular, and Very Expressly, to Those of the United States of America* (1965).

JASON H. SILVERMAN

THE *WANDERER*. The *Wanderer* was the most notorious slave ship of the 1850s. Built in 1857 by a wealthy New York sportsman as a swift pleasure schooner, the *Wanderer* could reach twenty knots, a greater speed than most vessels of its day. In 1858 a group of Southern adventurers, headed by Charles A. L. Lamar of Savannah, purchased the *Wanderer* and dispatched her to Africa to obtain a cargo of slaves. In order to avoid capture by British or American naval squadrons patrolling for slavers, the *Wanderer* sailed for the announced destination of Saint Helena. In the Atlantic, the ship veered eastward and entered the Congo River. While the crew prepared to take on their human cargo of about 410 blacks, its officers secured the cooperation of the British on board the warship *Medusa* by lavishly entertaining them. When the *Wanderer* darted from the African coast, an American patrolling vessel made an attempt to stop her, but it could not match the speed of the slaver.

Six weeks later the *Wanderer* landed on remote and lonely Jekyll Island, sixty-five miles south of Savannah. Only about 170 imported Africans, most of whom were emaciated teenage boys, survived the terrible trauma of the Middle Passage. Under cover of darkness they were moved to distribution points along the coast and above Savannah.

Finally alerted to the *Wanderer's* nefarious business, local federal officials ordered the ship seized before she could sail again. They also arrested three of her crewmen and charged them with piracy. The incident attracted national attention when Lamar, the arrogant scion of a prominent Southern family, used Northern antislavery attacks to create local sympathy for his case. Secretary of the Treasury Howell Cobb, himself a Georgian, however, had the *Wanderer* condemned and sold at auction. At the sale Lamar regained control of the ship, partly by violence to stop the bidding against him. In the case of the crewmen, a federal jury returned a verdict of not guilty, though Justice James M. Wayne recommended conviction.

Although advocates for the reopening of the foreign slave trade seemingly received a victory in the *Wanderer* case, the publicity given to the episode led to stronger federal measures against the illegal traffic. The Civil War soon ended it forever. Ironically, during the war the *Wanderer* served as a Union gunboat. In 1871 its remarkable history ended when it went down off the coast of Cuba.

SELECTED BIBLIOGRAPHY

Warren S. Howard, *American Slavers and the Federal Law, 1837–1862* (1963); Alexander A. Lawrence, *James Moore Wayne, Southern Unionist* (1943); Ronald T. Takaki, *A Pro-Slavery Crusade: The Agitation to Reopen the African Slave Trade* (1971); Tom Henderson Wells, *The Slave Ship Wanderer* (1967); and Harvey Wish, "The Revival of the African Slave Trade in the United States, 1856–1860," *Mississippi Valley Historical Review*, 27 (1941), 569–588.

WILLIAM C. HARRIS

WAR OF 1812. The War of 1812 affected slavery in many ways, but the most immediate cause for anxiety was fear in the South of slave uprisings.* Even before the war, slave revolts in the West Indies were a continuing concern. The outbreak of war with England, along with the Creek Indian War, which became part of the general conflict, created a truly dangerous situation. Not only were many blacks fighting alongside the Indians,* but the British were encouraging slaves to join their forces.

The British commanders believed that support for the war came mostly from the South, and, therefore, sought to break the will of the South—and, so, America—by occupying New Orleans with black troops. Admiral Alexander Ingles Cochrane implemented such a plan by recruiting runaway slaves and by bringing 1,000 Jamaican black troops with the Louisiana expedition.

A unit composed of former slaves served with Admiral George Cockburn when he raided the Atlantic Coast. Another black unit of 500 men was established at Apalachicola on the Gulf Coast by Major Edward Nicolls of the Royal Marines. Both groups had cadres of West Indian black troops and the Royal Marines.

When the British evacuated the Gulf Coast at the end of the war, many black troops remained at the old British base at Prospect Bluff on the Apalachicola River, later known as Negro Fort. This fort was destroyed by Colonel Duncan Clinch on 27 July 1816, but black forces in Florida, along with their Seminole allies, long continued to resist American encroachment and to provide havens for runaway slaves.

In New York and several Northern states black troops were recruited and mustered in both black and mixed units. Some of them were slaves who were promised freedom in exchange for good service. Large numbers of black seamen also served in the navy and aboard privateers.

Although Southerners were reluctant to use black troops, Andrew Jackson* accepted the support of two battalions of free men of color in New Orleans. Jackson needed soldiers, and he did not want to insult the admirable units composed of free men of color who had always fought to defend Louisiana when it was under French or Spanish rule.

The free men of color fought well in the New Orleans campaign. The great assault on Jackson's line of 8 January 1815 did not cause many American casualties, but after the assault British sharpshooters fired on several groups of colored troops. In retaliation, a detachment commanded by Joseph Savary, a free black officer, attacked the British snipers and drove off or killed them. The Americans suffered fourteen casualties in actions after the British attack (thus the casualties do not appear on Jackson's report). In these late actions free men of color had more casualties than the entire American force on the east bank. Units from the colored Louisiana militia were also at forts St. Philip and St. Leon.

Although a number of slaves did join the British and/or the Indians, the much-feared slave revolt failed to materialize. The main long-range effect of the war on the institution of slavery was to open a vast new area to cotton culture* which, in turn, brought new slave states into the Union.

SELECTED BIBLIOGRAPHY

Daniel F. Littlefield, Jr., *Africans and Creeks: From the Colonial Period to the Civil War* (1979); Roland McConnell, *Negro Troops of Antebellum Louisiana: A History of the Battalion of Free Men of Color* (1968); Frank L. Owsley, Jr., *Struggle for the Gulf Borderlands: The Creek War and the Battle of New Orleans, 1812–1815* (1981); and Robert V. Remini, *Andrew Jackson and the Course of American Empire, 1767–1821* (1977).

FRANK L. OWSLEY

WASHINGTON, BOOKER TALIAFERRO (1856?–1915). The world's most famous Afro-American slave spent little of his life in slavery but almost all of it addressing the legacy of that institution. Born in the spring of 1856 to Jane Washington and an unknown but probably white father from the immediate neighborhood in Franklin County, Virginia, Washington spent his first eight years as a slave of James Burroughs, "a raw-boned yeoman, a dirt farmer of the Southern uplands." Restraints of slavery confronted him in many ways, from the absence of play* or decent clothing* and shelter, to the lack of access to schooling.* While Washington remembered bonds of affection between master and slave, he also recalled the contrast between his labor and the sloth of the master's children, the horrors of slave punishment* and the varieties of slave protest. Upon emancipation, Washington's mother took the family to Malden, West Virginia, to join her husband, who had earlier fled from slavery.

Washington owed his renown to having risen "up from slavery" and to his efforts at aiding that transition for slaves and their descendants. After securing his own education and teaching experience at Hampton Institute, he founded Tuskegee Institute in 1883. Industrial education became his program for full freedom for Southern black folk. He remained at the head of the institute until his death at the campus in 1915. Washington's influence spread far beyond Tuskegee, as his cultivation of white elites gave him power unparalleled among his black contemporaries. He was unable, however, to translate his personal prestige into an acceptance of black equality, a goal for which he worked largely in secret. Indeed, his autobiography's* interpretation of slavery, playing down its evils and attributing civilizing qualities to it, reinforced the reconciliation of the white North and South which came at the expense of black freedom.

SELECTED BIBLIOGRAPHY

Louis R. Harlan, *Booker T. Washington: The Making of a Black Leader, 1856–1901* (1972); Louis R. Harlan, *Booker T. Washington: The Wizard of Tuskegee, 1901–1915* (1983); Louis R. Harlan and Raymond W. Smock, eds., *The Booker T. Washington Papers* (13 vols., 1972–1984); Booker T. Washington, *Up from Slavery: An Autobiography* (1901); and Booker T. Washington, *The Story of My Life and Work* (1900).

WILBERT AHERN

WASHINGTON, GEORGE (1732–1799). George Washington—commander in chief of the Continental army, first president of the United States, and planter—made few public comments on slavery. Its ethical considerations concerned him very little before the American Revolution, when his views differed little from those of his Virginia neighbors. After the war his view of his role as a national leader precluded public involvement in the slavery question. However, his changing views on slavery and his relationship with his slaves can be traced from his voluminous instructions to his managers and from occasional observations in his private correspondence. By 1786 Washington owned several hundred slaves, acquired through inheritance, purchase, and through his marriage, which brought him the use of the so-called dower slaves.

As long as his slaves lived up to his exacting criteria that "my people be at their work as soon as it is light, work till it is dark, and be diligent while they are at it," Washington, motivated not only by humanitarianism but self-interest, was generally an enlightened master. Slaves were not worked when they were ill, and as a policy families were not separated by sale or purchase although they might work on different plantations. His ledgers and invoices indicate that medical advice was frequently sought for ailing slaves, housing was adequate, food was ample, and the slaves were well supplied with strong and substantial clothing.* In the prewar years punishment,* including whipping,* was meted out when Washington considered it merited, and he backed his overseers though he feared their brutality in his absence. Runaways* were pursued assiduously, and occasionally a recalcitrant slave was shipped off for sale in the West Indies. In the long run, however, Washington believed that he achieved better results "by watchfulness and admonition, than by severity," and it is clear that the Mount Vernon slaves did not hesitate to complain, frequently and usually successfully, when rations and living conditions did not meet their expectations.

During the time he could spend at home, Washington was his own manager and he knew his slaves well. Generally, he held a low opinion of their efficiency as a labor force. Slaves, he contended, worked only when closely supervised. He frequently commented disparagingly on their propensity toward theft, nightwalking, laziness, and irresponsibility, although he apparently considered these actions and attitudes inherent results of the system. The economic life of his plantations suffered from his conviction that slave labor precluded the use of the new agricultural methods and machinery that he had hoped to introduce.

During the American Revolution* Washington was forced for the first time to deal with slavery on a public basis. At the beginning of the war he was an outspoken critic of British plans to reward slave enlistments with freedom and was reluctant at first to enlist slaves into the Continental army, both because of the effect on other slaves and because of his belief in the inefficiency of slave labor. In time, however, his own desperate need for troops and the fact that several states had already enlisted slaves and free blacks led him finally to give very considerable support not only to the recruitment of slaves for army service with manumission at the end of their service, but to advocate strongly both their integration into regular Continental regiments and the formation of black corps in Southern states.

The rhetoric of the Revolution had its impact. Washington's postwar correspondence contains frequent references to his desire to see "some plan adopted, by which slavery in this country may be abolished" on a gradual basis and reveals his conviction that emancipation would come "at a period not remote." Although Washington considered some abolitionist plans in the 1790s "very mal-apropos," he found the institution itself increasingly repugnant for both moral and economic reasons. By the mid-1780s he virtually stopped buying or selling slaves, because "I am principled against this kind of traffic in human species," even though by the last years of his life the surplus of slaves was sapping the economic viability of Mount Vernon. He was also increasingly reluctant to resort to the stern measures of discipline he had used with his slaves before the war. At his death in 1799, his will stipulated that after his wife's death the slaves Washington had owned outright would be given their freedom, although any slaves preferring to remain at Mount Vernon because of age or disability would be cared for and a permanent fund established for their support.

SELECTED BIBLIOGRAPHY

John C. Fitzpatrick, ed., *The Writings of George Washington* (39 vols., 1931–1944); Douglas Southall Freeman, *George Washington* (7 vols., 1949–1957); and Donald Jackson and Dorothy Twohig, eds., *The Diaries of George Washington* (6 vols., 1976–1979).

DOROTHY TWOHIG

WEBSTER, DANIEL (1782–1852). Daniel Webster, as attorney, orator, political leader, and diplomat, championed American nationalism and earned a reputation as defender of the Union and critic of slavery. He served two terms in Congress from his native New Hampshire before moving to Massachusetts in 1816 to seek a larger stage for his talents. Reelection to Congress from Boston continued a political career that included several terms in the Senate; Webster also served as Secretary of State in two cabinets.

In Congress Webster forcefully advocated Northern interests. Beginning in 1819, when he argued on behalf of Congress's right to make the prohibition of slavery a condition for the admission of Missouri, or any new state, Webster was counted in the antislavery camp. In his powerful second reply to South Carolina Senator Robert Y. Hayne (January 1830), Webster described slavery as "one of the greatest evils, both moral and political," in American life. While he never retreated from this view, Webster acknowledged that the Constitution* gave the states exclusive control over slavery where it already was established. He realized that the Union could not survive continued agitation over slavery such as abolitionists* began in the 1830s.

This position served as the basis for Webster's last concerted political effort. With sectional tensions at a flash point in 1850, Webster spoke for compromise on all slavery-related issues. His famous "Seventh of March Speech" contributed to the compromise settlement that postponed civil war for a decade. When the war came, Webster's theme of "Liberty and Union" provided a rallying cry for the Northern war effort that commenced as a defense of the Union but gradually broadened to encompass a crusade against slavery.

SELECTED BIBLIOGRAPHY

Irving Bartlett, *Daniel Webster* (1978); Maurice G. Baxter, *One and Inseparable: Daniel Webster and the Union* (1984); Robert S. Dalzell, Jr., *Daniel Webster and the Trial of American Nationalism, 1843–1852* (1972); Claude M. Fuess, *Daniel Webster* (2 vols., 1930); and Charles M. Wiltse et al, eds., *The Papers of Daniel Webster* (11 vols. to date, 1974–).

MICHAEL BIRKNER

WELD, THEODORE DWIGHT (1803–1895). Theodore Dwight Weld was one of the great abolitionist* leaders of the 1830s. As orator, writer, and organizer, he brought countless thousands into the antislavery fold and inspired in his fellow reformers almost worshipful loyalty. Born in 1803 the son of a Connecticut minister, Weld and his family all assumed he would follow in his father's footsteps. Instead, he embraced the more romantic calling of an itinerant lecturer. After his conversion in 1827 at the hands of Charles Grandison Finney, he fused his oratorical talents and religious zeal to become Finney's indispensable revival lieutenant and a master advocate of temperance and other reform causes of the day.

In 1831 he was converted to the abolition cause. At the time he was student leader of the experimental Lane Seminary in Cincinnati, and there planned and held a series of evening talks about slavery known as the Lane Debates. In fact, the debates were simply a series of antislavery meetings, and the broaching of this sensitive issue brought upon Weld and his fellows the wrath of the board of trustees. In 1834 the board passed regulations that effectively curtailed the rights of students to engage in antislavery activity. In response Weld led a walkout. These so-called Lane Rebels soon became a nucleus for the antislavery movement in Ohio, Pennsylvania, and New York.

The Lane Rebellion brought Weld into antislavery prominence. For two years he traveled across Ohio, Pennsylvania, and New York State, gaining a reputation as the most revered and the most mobbed of antislavery orators. When his voice gave out in 1837, he took upon himself the task of creating a new roster of antislavery speakers and training them in both the substance and method of abolitionist agitation. At the training sessions in New York in 1837 and 1838, he met Sarah and Angelina Grimké,* two renegade sisters from South Carolina's slaveholding elite who had moved to the North and become antislavery speakers and writers. Weld and Angelina fell in love and were married in 1839, and the two sisters and Weld lived together for the rest of their lives. Almost immediately they began work on *American Slavery As It Is*, the most widely distributed and most influential of all American antislavery tracts. But marriage also restricted the public career of the Grimkés and, in the end, led to Weld's removal from the scene. Increasingly frustrated by the shortcomings of his colleagues and the implacability of proslavery enemies, he had come to find an alternative to reform in the cultivation of personal holiness and the promotion of good in individuals and families. He performed one last mission by helping the antislavery lobby in Washington, but in 1844 bade farewell to reform. He turned instead to the role of educator, and aside from a brief foray on the speaker's rostrum to support the Union cause during the Civil War, devoted the rest of his long life (he died in 1895) to experimental schools and other community-based projects.

SELECTED BIBLIOGRAPHY

Robert H. Abzug, *Passionate Liberator: Theodore Dwight Weld and the Dilemma of Reform* (1980); Gilbert Hobbs Barnes, *The Anti-Slavery Impulse, 1830–1844* (1933); and Gilbert Hobbs Barnes and Dwight L. Dumond, eds., *Letters of Theodore Dwight Weld, Angelina Grimké Weld, and Sarah Grimké* (2 vols., 1934).

ROBERT H. ABZUG

WEST, SLAVERY IN THE. The topic of black slavery on the trans-Mississippi Western frontier might, at first glance, hardly seem worthy of consideration. After all, the total number of blacks living west of the Mississippi River on the eve of the Civil War numbered a mere 5,500. Of that number, only a fraction, probably less than 1,000, were or had ever been slaves. The mere presence of involuntary servitude in the West, moreover, ran contrary to the prevalent image of an American frontier that Frederick Jackson Turner later celebrated as characterized by "individualism, economic equality, freedom to rise [and] democracy." In fact, American settlers, white and black, moving along this frontier from Iowa to the Pacific Coast, confronted the peculiar institution throughout the crucial period from 1830 to 1865. This slavery, in turn, affected Westerners, and Americans generally, in ways that transcended the relatively small number of blacks actually held in bondage.

Iowa, for example, was a trans-Mississippi frontier region where black slavery existed as early as the 1830s. This was the case despite the provisions of the Missouri Compromise* of 1820, which prohibited slavery in Iowa due to its location north of the line 36° 30'. According to historian Joel H. Silbey, "great support of slavery existed" in Iowa until about 1846 due to the large, early influx of white Southerners into the region.

Approximately 150 slaves were held in Iowa during the 1830s, not a large number, but worthy of note because their presence suggests a local tolerance for the peculiar institution. Both U.S. Senators, Augustus C. Dodge and George W. Jones, were listed as slaveholders following Iowa's 1846 ascension to statehood. Iowa's most famous slave, Dred Scott, resided in Davenport with his master, Dr. John Emerson, during the 1830s—two decades before the Supreme Court's famous decision denied him his freedom and humanity. As late as 1860, black slaves continued to be held in the Hawkeye State.

In addition to their tolerance for black slavery, citizens of Iowa enacted legislation restricting the actions of black residents, both slave and free. In 1839, for example, the Iowa Legislature enacted a law prohibiting the entry of individual free blacks* and mulattoes without a certificate of freedom and the posting of a $500 bond. Blacks also were prohibited from voting, belonging to the state militia, and intermarrying with whites. Iowa's two U.S. Senators gave strong backing to the federal Fugitive Slave Act of 1850,* a position that stood in sharp contrast to that of most other Northern senators. One Iowa newspaper characterized this measure as "the most important, equitable and just portion" of the Compromise of 1850. A year later, Iowa's legislature enacted a law completely prohibiting the migration of free blacks into the state.

Despite these restrictions, Iowa's black population increased threefold from 333 to 1069, during the decade of the 1850s. Much of this increase resulted from the influx of fugitive slaves* fleeing bondage in neighboring slave states, particularly Missouri. Many Iowans, particularly Quakers* living in the southern part of the state, opposed slavery and became the backbone of the underground railroad* there. In addition, by the 1850s, Iowans generally became less tolerant of black slavery as more and more settlers from nonslaveholding states emigrated into the Hawkeye State, displacing Southerners who had heretofore been dominant. But Iowa's ambivalent attitudes and practices regarding slavery and the treatment of blacks generally represented a pattern of behavior transposed to other parts of the trans-Mississippi frontier.

California was one such region. Prior to California's American settlement and annexation, blacks or people of mixed black-Mexican origins played a significant role, first under Spanish and later under Mexican rule. An estimated 20 percent of early California's settlers were black or had some African ancestry. Among the prominent individuals of mixed black-Mexican background was Pio Pico, the last governor of Mexican California. Black slavery itself had been abolished under Mexican law following that country's independence from Spain in 1821.

The Americanization of California in the wake of the gold rush brought changes. Black Americans joined whites in migrating to the gold fields. Over 2,200 black settlers had arrived in California by 1852. According to historian Rudolph M. Lapp, an estimated "200 to 300 black men and women" were held "in the mining country . . . as slaves . . . at any given time in the early 1850s." In all, there were "probably between five hundred and six hundred slaves involved in the gold rush." Black slaves also were held in parts of California outside the mining regions. Two dozen black slaves were brought into southern California by a group of Mormon* pioneers who settled at San Bernardino. Significantly, black slavery existed in California despite its statutory prohibition by California's state constitution and by the provisions of the Compromise of 1850.* Many of these slaves, however, arrived prior to the time that slavery was clearly prohibited under the provisions of the Compromise of 1850. Nevertheless, a large number of bondsmen were brought into California after that date by slaveholders aware of this prohibition but willing to gamble to realize a quick profit. They reasoned that a few years of lucky gold mining with slave labor could reap profits far exceeding those obtained by working an entire lifetime in Southern agriculture.

Slaves in California labored under diverse conditions. Although cases existed of individual slaveholders migrating to California with as many as twenty to thirty slaves, most bondsmen came in groups of two or three. The treatment of these blacks also varied, depending of course on their individual masters. In general, slavery in California appears to have been less severe than in the traditional slaveholding areas of the South. As Lapp notes, "the daily lives of blacks in California were probably very similar to that of the average white miner, with the exception of their servile status." These slaves, moreover, were frequently given the opportunity to purchase their freedom with profits earned in mining.* This emancipation-by-self-purchase* could involve the slave working for a stated period of time (during which the master would benefit from his labor) or the payment of a specified amount of gold dug. According to one scholar, California slaves spent a total of $750,000 to buy their freedom.

Black slavery in California continued largely due to a lack of adequate law enforcement—a common problem throughout the frontier West. In 1852 the state legislature enacted a fugitive slave law that gave some legal backing to California's peculiar institution. Under its provisions, slaves who had escaped into

California or who entered the state prior to statehood were considered fugitives and liable to arrest. In addition, whites who aided black fugitives were subject to a $500 fine and a prison sentence. Judges sympathetic to slaveholders interpreted this law in such a way as to allow slaveholders to bring blacks into the state, work them in the mines, and ultimately return to the South with both their profits and slaves.

Other antiblack measures also were enacted in California during the 1850s. California lawmakers, inspired by the earlier actions of their Iowa counterparts, passed laws prohibiting blacks from voting, belonging to the state militia, or testifying in court in cases involving whites. On three different occasions—in 1849, 1852, and 1857—legislation was proposed to prevent further black migration into the state. Although all three efforts failed, the rate of black migration into California leveled off by 1860 with a total of 4,086 blacks listed as living in the state. Indeed, by this time, California's black population was eclipsed by that of two other nonwhite minorities—the Chinese, numbering 35,000, and Latin Americans, totaling 50,000. Whites perceived these two groups as posing a greater threat than the relatively small black population, and Chinese and Latin Americans thus bore the brunt of white discrimination. This ultimately paved the way for improved treatment of black Californians.

Reflective of this trend, by the late 1850s California's slave population gradually withered away. This reduction was accomplished, in part, by the willingness of many California slaveholders to free their slaves, either voluntarily or under pressure from an increasingly militant black community. Free blacks, along with sympathetic whites, grew less willing to accept black slavery in their midst. By 1855, California's 1852 fugitive slave law was allowed to lapse. Also, the fallout from the 1858 Archy Lee fugitive slave case gave California slaveholders new cause for concern. Archy, a black slave, had been brought into California from Mississippi by his master, Charles A. Stovall, in 1857. Soon after arriving, Archy fled his bondage because Stovall decided to return to Mississippi. Stovall then sought legal redress. The California Supreme Court declared that legally Archy deserved his freedom. But it decreed that "since [Archy's] master was an inexperienced young man and not in good health and since this was the first case of its kind" Archy should be returned to Stovall and slavery. In the face of this controversial, convoluted decision, the aroused, angry, black population of San Francisco (where the case was tried), aided by sympathetic whites, helped Archy to regain his freedom. It therefore became obvious to Southern slaveholders contemplating migration to California that the security of their chattel property could no longer be guaranteed. Thus, by the late 1850s the influx of black slaves into California virtually ended, further hastening the disappearance of black slavery.

New Mexico, like California during the years immediately prior to its annexation to the United States, experienced a period of ambivalence on the question of black slavery. Under the terms of the Compromise of 1850, the question of black slavery was left to New Mexico residents according to popular sovereignty.

In New Mexico, as in California, black slavery had been prohibited by the Mexican government prior to the American takeover. But two other forms of human bondage had flourished during the Spanish and later Mexican periods. Indian* slavery, resting on custom rather than written law, dated from the seventeenth century. It resulted from warfare between Spanish-Mexican settlers and local Indian tribes or among the rival Indian tribes themselves. Captured Indians, usually children or adolescents, were bought and sold in much the same way as blacks on American slave markets. A healthy Indian boy or girl could bring $400. Although never recognized by statute, Indian slavery nonetheless continued to flourish in New Mexico following its annexation to the United States. By the 1860s, an estimated 1,500 to 3,000 Indian slaves were held in New Mexico.

Peonage, the other form of human bondage widespread throughout New Mexico, unlike Indian or black slavery, was not based on the sale or purchase of human beings, but on "contract between master and servant." Much like the system of indentured servitude in the American colonies prior to the Revolution, peons were bound to their masters by some form of indebtedness. Once the debt was discharged, the peon supposedly was released of his servile status. The statutes governing this system, however, favored the master and made it extremely difficult for the peon to discharge his obligation. As a result, he frequently found himself, and indeed his family, in perpetual servitude. Peonage received legal recognition in New Mexico under the Master and Servant Law enacted in 1851, thereby establishing Indian slavery and peonage as important labor systems in the territory. Indeed, as late as 1865, the family of New Mexico's Republican delegate to Congress, J. Francisco Chavez, held more peons and Indian slaves than any other individual in the territory.

Little support existed, however, for black slavery in New Mexico during the early territorial period. Though the 1850 census listed twenty-two blacks living in the territory, there were no slaves enumerated among them. The climate* and economic conditions within the territory were "entirely unsuited for [black] slave labor," explained Hugh N. Smith, New Mexico's territorial delegate to Congress in April 1850. According to Smith, "the country is cold . . . exceedingly mountainous" with its "general agricultural products [consisting of] wheat and corn." Then, alluding to the existing systems of Indian slavery and peonage, he noted, "Labor is exceedingly abundant and cheap. It may be hired for three or four dollars a month, in quantity quite sufficient for carrying on all the agriculture of the territory."

Although only a handful of free blacks lived in New Mexico, territorial lawmakers nevertheless insisted upon discriminatory legislation. Blacks were prohibited from voting and holding public office. In 1856, the territorial legislature passed a black exclusionary law similar to that in force in Iowa. This law forbade the further immigration of free blacks into New Mexico and required those currently living within the territory to post a $200 bond to ensure their good behavior. This law also prohibited marriages between Negroes and Caucasians.

In 1859 the status of blacks within New Mexico further deteriorated when the territorial legislature approved a measure legalizing black slavery. This "Act for the Protection of Slave Property" resembled the slave codes in force in the slaveholding South by defining and protecting the property rights of white masters. No slave was permitted to be away from his master's premises after sunset or before sunrise without a written pass. The theft of, or abetment in escape of, a slave was punishable by imprisonment from four to ten years and fines. The act further prohibited the arming of slaves except by the master's written consent and absolutely forbade the emancipation of slaves within the territory.

Why did New Mexico enact this measure so late in the antebellum period? First, despite what contemporaries believed were the natural limits of working slaves in the West, at least two prominent territorial officials held black slaves. Territorial Governor William Carr Lane and Chief Justice of the New Mexico Supreme Court Grafton Baker constituted a "respectable minority," undoubtedly anxious to have their slave property protected by law. The second driving force behind this statute was Miguel A. Otero, New Mexico's territorial delegate to Congress. Otero was motivated by both personal and political motives. During his first term in Congress, he had married a Southern woman and increasingly became identified with the social life of Southerners in Washington. These connections in turn affected his official interests. Resulting mainly from Otero's influence, a Southern clique of federal appointees controlled political affairs within New Mexico. The territorial governor, secretary, and editor of the territory's leading newspaper were all Southerners. On the eve of the Civil War, then, it appeared to observers that New Mexico had undergone a "complete conversion to Southern principles."

New Mexico, in legalizing black slavery, appeared to be following in the footsteps of its sister territory to the north, Utah, which in 1852 had adopted its own "Act in Relation to Service." Like New Mexico, Utah under the provision of the Compromise of 1850 had been allowed the option of popular sovereignty. Utah's "Act in Relation to Service" resulted from instructions by Brigham Young, territorial governor and Mormon church leader. Several factors motivated Young. Although the number of black slaves in Utah numbered less than 100 (out of a total black population of less than 200), slave owners ranked among Utah's most prominent church and community leaders. Abraham O. Smoot, the first mayor of Salt Lake City; Charles C. Rich, a Mormon Apostle; and William H. Hooper, Utah's delegate to Congress—like their counterparts in New Mexico—constituted a "respectable minority." Young also hoped to win new converts among Southern slaveholders who he hoped might be persuaded to migrate to Utah if their slave property were protected by law.

Young's proslavery action was motivated by another factor, perhaps the most important of all. This involved the impact of certain racist concepts that had their basis in Mormon beliefs. According to Mormon dogma, blacks were inherently inferior and therefore were fit subjects for involuntary servitude. Like other nineteenth-century biblical literalists, the Mormons ascribed the inferiority of black people to their alleged descent from the accursed lineage of Ham and Canaan—a lineage destined to be "servants of servants." In this spirit, and following the examples of Iowa and California, Young and other Utah territorial officials supported legislation that prohibited blacks from voting, holding public office, belonging to the territorial militia, and intermarrying with whites. Within the Mormon church itself, blacks were denied entry into its priesthood, a lay organization open to all other adult males regardless of race or ethnic origins. This ban continued until it was finally lifted in June 1978.

While black slavery gained legal recognition in both Utah and New Mexico during the 1850s, national attention on slavery's expansion into the territories was riveted on Kansas. Here proslavery settlers were attempting to establish the peculiar institution on a firm footing. Actually, the first slaves, 500 in all, entered what became known as Kansas in 1718. They were brought from Santo Domingo by Francis Renault to work in the lead mines near Pittsburg. Black slaves also were present at the early forts established in Kansas to protect trade routes to Santa Fe. After 1820, however, black slavery was outlawed in this region under the terms of the Missouri Compromise because it, like Iowa, was north of the line 36° 30′. This prohibition remained in force until the enactment of the Kansas-Nebraska Act* of 1854 that allowed local residents popular sovereignty.

Kansas, in the eyes of many, appeared promising as an arena for the use of black slave labor. For one thing, Kansas was bounded on three sides by regions where slavery flourished or was sanctioned by law—Missouri to the east, the Creek nation to the south (where 23,000 black slaves were held), and Utah to the west. Also, the climate and soil of Kansas initially appeared ideal for the production of hemp* and tobacco*—both products produced elsewhere with black slave labor. These products, moreover, could be sent down the Missouri River to St. Louis and from there down the Mississippi, thereby tying Kansas to the South economically. Many Southerners believed that some sort of unwritten compact among national leaders would make Kansas a slave state and keep neighboring Nebraska free.

By the early 1850s settlers from neighboring Missouri and other slave regions began to move into Kansas, some bringing their black slaves. In 1855 Kansas had 195 slaves and a year later "over 400," according to one estimate. These blacks were scattered throughout the territory. In 1855 the territorial legislature passed "An Act for the Protection of Slave Property." In describing the treatment of slaves in Kansas, historian Charles E. Cory noted that "the rigor and cruelty of slavery" evident in the South "was not present here." Instead, Kansas slaves were given "general kind treatment" and, according to Cory, "the slaves did very little work."

Northerners and antislavery advocates viewed the issue of slavery in Kansas differently. Their opposition to Southern efforts to turn Kansas into a slave state helped generate the violence associated with "Bleeding Kansas" and led to the formation of the Republican party,* a political organization opposed to slavery in Kansas and, initially, adverse to the extension of slavery into all western territories. Several factors favored the North in the contest over Kansas. For one thing, "the populous North," in the words of historian James A. Rawley, "possessed the greater opportunity to dispatch settlers into Kansas," whereas the South was hindered by "the cost and hazard of removing slaves to a territory where competition with free farmers might be keen." In addition, not all Missourians migrating to Kansas were potential slaveholders or even proslavery in their beliefs. Many were nonslaveholding small farmers who appeared willing to accept Kansas as a free state. Finally, the geography and climate of Kansas were not conducive to producing the great staple slave crops of cotton,* sugar,* or rice.* Observers noted that breadstuffs and livestock, the most likely crops to come out of this region, could be produced most cheaply by free labor. The climate of most of Kansas was generally subhumid, treeless, semiarid, and subject to scorching summers and harsh winters. Kansas stood in stark contrast to settled slaveholding regions to the east and south. Thus slaveholders desiring to move west found the relatively unsettled regions of Arkansas and Texas much more appealing.

It is not surprising, therefore, that by the late 1850s Kansas held few prospects as a slaveholding region. In fact, even among Kansas slaveholders themselves, the peculiar institution had a precarious existence. According to Cory, slaves were brought in "as a part of the proslavery propaganda—not for profit." These owners merely "wanted to establish the 'institution' " demonstrating "its physical existence here." Thus, when proslavery advocates lost in Kansas, slaveholders were quick to leave the region with their chattel property. By the time of the 1860 census, only two black slaves were listed as living in the entire territory. That same year, the Kansas legislature, just prior to securing statehood, implemented "An Act to Prohibit Slavery in Kansas" and repealed the Slave Code of 1855.

On the eve of the Civil War, then, the residents of Iowa, California, and Kansas had determined that black slavery was unsuitable to their respective states. Only in New Mexico and Utah did slavery enjoy respectability under territorial statutes. In Utah, Mormon religious beliefs, not economic necessity or widespread practice, lent support to slavery's legal status there. And in 1862, when Congress outlawed black slavery in all federal territories, Utah slaveholders quietly acquiesced. Officials in New Mexico acted even earlier, repealing the "Otero Slave Code" in 1861, following the outbreak of the Civil War and after pro-Union elements gained political control of New Mexico, ousting Miguel Otero and the pro-Southern clique previously in control of territorial politics.

Other parts of the trans-Mississippi West settled just before or during the Civil War also proved unsuitable to black slaveholding. Although a few slaves were found after 1859 in the Pikes Peak region of Colorado, and later in the Montana gold fields around Virginia City, their presence was noted more as a curiosity than as a precursor of future large-scale slaveholding in these regions. Confident that slavery was no longer an issue in the West, Republicans in 1860 felt safe in backing off from their long-standing position of absolute prohibition of slavery in all newly formed territories. Ironically, the Republicans now accepted the old popular sovereignty doctrine of Stephen Douglas* and his Democratic allies—allowing local residents to vote on the status of slavery as they pleased. In the end, it made little difference: residents of Nebraska, Nevada, Colorado, Dakota, Montana, and Arizona all approved statutes prohibiting slavery in their respective territories. Nevada achieved statehood in 1864 just in time to help reelect Abraham Lincoln* to a second term as president and to help ratify the Thirteenth Amendment,* forever outlawing black slavery in the United States.

SELECTED BIBLIOGRAPHY

Delilah L. Beasley, *The Negro Trail Blazers of California* (1919); Eugene W. Berwanger, *The Frontier against Slavery: Western Anti-Negro Prejudice and the Slavery Extension Controversy* (1967); Newell G. Bringhurst, *Saints, Slaves, and Blacks: The Changing Place of Black People within Mormonism* (1981); Charles E. Cory, "Slavery in Kansas," *Transactions of the Kansas State Historical Society*, 7 (1901–1902), 229–242; Lawrence B. deGraaf, "Recognition, Racism, and Reflections on the Writing of Western Black History," *Pacific Historical Review*, 44 (1975), 22–51; Loomis Morton Ganaway, *New Mexico and the Sectional Controversy, 1846–1861* (reprint ed., 1976); Charles D. Hart, "The Natural Limits of Slavery Expansion: Kansas-Nebraska, 1854," *Kansas Historical Quarterly*, 34 (1968), 32–50; Rudolph M. Lapp, *Blacks in Gold Rush California* (1977); James A. Rawley, *Race and Politics: "Bleeding Kansas" and the Coming of the Civil War* (1969); W. Sherman Savage, *Blacks in the West* (1976); and Joel H. Silbey, "Proslavery Sentiment in Iowa, 1838–1861," *Iowa Journal of History*, 55 (1957), 289–318.

                                                                        NEWELL G. BRINGHURST

WEST VIRGINIA, SLAVERY IN. Slavery never flourished in the western portion of Virginia that in 1863 became the new state of West Virginia. The inhospitable mountain environment concentrated the institution into four regions: Shenandoah, South Branch, Kanawha, and Greenbrier. Slavery, if not widespread, nevertheless strongly determined western Virginia's political destiny. From the American Revolution onward, slavery permeated every phase of Virginia's politics and supplied the basic source of the social, economic, and political grievances instrumental in the ultimate breakup of Virginia.

Quantitatively, in 1850 slavery in western Virginia attained its highest numerical level with 20,500 slaves, or 6.79 percent of a total population of 302,313. In 1860 the number of slaves declined to 4.88 percent of the aggregate population. In only seven western Virginia counties did the slave population in 1850 constitute more than 10 percent of the aggregate population, and these counties contained 70.77 percent of all slaves in the region. In 1850 Jefferson County had the largest number of slaves (4,341) in the Shenandoah Valley region; Hampshire County had the most slaves (1,433) in the South Branch region; Kanawha Salines County had the most slaves (3,140) in the Kanawha region; and Greenbrier County had the most slaves (1,317) in the Greenbrier region.

In the Shenandoah Valley, tidewater Virginians, migrating between 1768 and 1810, brought great numbers of slaves to carve plantations from ancestral lands often acquired from Fairfax proprietors. Slaves sometimes preceded the gentry to clear land and to construct houses. The transplanted tidewater aristocrats rapidly exploited the fertile, well-watered limestone soil that yielded bountiful harvests of wheat,* corn,* and livestock.* Gangs* of slaves under overseers* cleared the forest, rolled and skidded rocks from fields, broke rockbreaks, and split rails for fencing. They plowed the thousands of acres, harnessed the livestock, and reaped the crops. Performing all labor supporting the domestic establishment and the sometimes opulent life-style of their masters, slaves perfected numerous crafts; endlessly cut wood to fuel the huge houses; and raised, preserved, and cooked the food. Though the life-style was less extensive than in Berkeley and Jefferson counties, large slaveholders on the South Branch and on the limestone soil belt of Greenbrier and Monroe employed their chattels in similar ways. Obstacles to transportation caused their agricultural economy to be oriented largely toward livestock raising. Extensive land-clearing occupied slaves until the Civil War.

Throughout the trans-Allegheny, slaves labored in the domestic service of those who could afford them. Here, masters generally held slaves in small numbers and worked beside them on farms and in small manufactories engaged in blacksmithing, milling, and tanning. In the southwest below the Great Kanawha River, bondsmen joined their masters in labor-intensive tobacco culture.* The widespread industrial use* of slaves in the Great Kanawha salt industry* at Malden was exceptional.

Antislavery sentiment,* even in areas of slave concentration, persisted in western Virginia from colonial times. Germans, Quakers,* Methodists* of various types, and residents originating from New England had moral objections to slavery. Virginia's militia regulations and commitment to slavery tended to encourage the western migration of such people, but a sufficient minority remained to affect antebellum opinion. Western Virginians witnessed one of the cruelest scenes associated with the institution when slave traders drove coffles from eastern Virginia over their turnpikes to Deep South markets.

Eastern Virginia's continuous repression of western political equality and its contrived dominance of public policy to protect its "peculiar interest" galvanized western opinion on slavery. Western Virginians, the majority of whom had few moral objections to the institution and to whom Northern abolitionists were anathema, based their opposition on social, political, and economic realities. Since the Staunton Convention in 1816, western politicians had awaited political relief for underrepresentation and restricted franchise. The Constitutional Convention of 1829–1830 accepted the reactionary arguments of easterners who feared for the safety of their slave property in a democracy. The eastern counties retained legislative power, however, and the franchise remained severely restricted. Reapportionment was delayed until 1841, and it occurred only then with the approval of two-thirds of each legislative house. The Virginia legislative debates of 1831–1832* over gradual emancipation further exacerbated the fundamental sectional differences when the east favored a gag rule and the west opted for *post-nati* emancipation. The west won an illusory victory, securing a legislative statement rejecting the idea of perpetual slavery in Virginia, but eschewing practical and immediate action.

Western Virginia's disaffection continued unresolved and her citizens chafed under the imposed burden of what they charged was undemocratic government and retarded economic development, while neighboring states prospered and attracted her citizens. The 1847 pamphlet of Reverend Mr. Henry Ruffner, president of Washington College in Lexington and a Kanawha native, summarized western Virginian thoughts on slavery and signaled a proposed change in strategy in dealing with the problem. If eastern Virginians would never consent to statewide emancipation, stated Ruffner, perhaps gradual emancipation could be implemented west of the Blue Ridge Mountain range. Ruffner's *Address to the People of West Virginia* attacked slavery for depleting Virginia's white population, depressing its agricultural income as contrasted with Northern states, retarding its investment in manufacturing, and discouraging education.

The Constitutional Convention of 1850 wrestled with the same questions on slavery raised in 1829–1830. Different orators repeated identical arguments. Westerners won a partial victory by compromising on legislative apportionment: the west would control the house while the east would dominate the senate. Slave owners received a major concession that forbade taxation* of slaves under twelve years of age and limited the tax on other slaves to a sum not to exceed the amount charged on realty assessed at $300. Reapportionment was to occur in 1865 and every tenth year thereafter. Suffrage was extended to all white male adults, and most offices became elective.

The Civil War destabilized the bonds of control, affording West Virginia slaves de facto freedom and unlimited mobility. For those who could obtain employment, this disruption converted chattel slavery into wage and share systems of agriculture. For slaves who remained with their masters, especially in remote areas, the patterns of work continued as before. Fleeing slaves who remained in West Virginia tended to congregate in towns. Often free persons of color with established economic competence helped sustain them. In Clarksburg, Wheeling, Parkersburg, and other county seats, free and slave blacks practiced a wide diversity of trades and relied upon domestic service for support. In the Great Kanawha Valley, blacks continued to mine coal and manufacture salt.

In the Shenandoah Valley, many able-bodied male slaves fled to Northern lines and states. Some flocked to Harpers Ferry to labor for federal forces and to enlist in the Union army. While single black males often prospered, black families who stayed together frequently experienced great hardship. The feeble, women, and children created a refugee class. Many destitute, land-poor white families refused to sustain slave dependents without the labor of males. Some valley landowners encouraged the casual formation of black communities on their land, to retain labor in the vicinity. Even under these conditions, Northern missionaries* who traveled from tidewater Virginia commented on the relative well-being of Shenandoah Valley blacks.

Although slavery was fundamentally at the root of sectional grievances, state-makers attempted to ignore the issue in West Virginia's first constitutional convention. They feared antagonizing slave-owning westerners and jeopardizing the movement in Congress. Because the Emancipation Proclamation* never applied to the area, constitutional provisions regarding slavery were potentially controversial. Delegates Robert Hager and Gordon Battelle, both Methodist Episcopal clergymen, forced the convention to face the issue. Their resolutions against future slave importation and gradual emancipation caused the assembly to accept the free-soil idea in general while ignoring emancipation per se. Congressional opposition to the statehood bill, led by Charles Sumner and other abolitionists, moved Senator Waitman Thomas Willey of the Restored Government of Virginia to offer a gradual emancipation amendment. This provided that no new slaves were permitted in the state for permanent residence; children of slaves born in the state after 4 July 1863 would be free; slaves under ten years of age on that date would be free when they reached age twenty-one; and slaves over ten years of age and under age twenty-one on 4 July 1863 would become free when they reached twenty-five. Congress enacted the West Virginia Bill with the Willey Amendment, and President Abraham Lincoln* approved statehood upon the condition that the constitution be appropriately revised by the convention and ratified by a state referendum. The reconvened convention inserted the Willey Amendment into the constitution, but petitioned for congressional appropriations to compensate slave owners. Slavery legally continued in West Virginia until 3 February 1865, when the ratification process of the Thirteenth Amendment* spurred the legislature to abolish slavery by statute.

SELECTED BIBLIOGRAPHY

Alison Goodyear Freehling, *Drift toward Dissolution: The Virginia Slavery Debate of 1831–1832* (1982); George E. Moore, "Slavery as a Factor in the Formation of West Virginia," *West Virginia History*, 18 (1956), 5–89; John R. Sheeler, "The Negro in West Virginia before 1900" (Ph.D. dissertation, West Virginia University, 1954); John E. Stealey III, "The Freedmen's Bureau in West Virginia," *West Virginia History*, 39 (1978), 99–142; John E. Stealey III, "Slavery and the West Virginia Salt Industry," *Journal of Negro History*, 59 (1974), 105–131; and Edward M. Steel, Jr., "Black Monongalians: A Judicial View of Slavery and the Negro in Monongalia County, 1776–1865," *West Virginia History*, 34 (1973), 331–359.

JOHN EDMUND STEALEY

WHEAT. After its introduction in Virginia in 1607, wheat generally remained an unimportant crop in colonial North America because early plantation owners found tobacco* more profitable and because they encountered difficulties growing wheat and developing an export market. In 1657 Virginia offered a substantial prize to anyone who could produce and export a crop worth £500 sterling. But sending wheat to England at that time was likened to "sending sugar to Barbados."

During the seventeenth century it took two men eight weeks to plow and sow twenty acres, although it was said, somewhat contemptuously, one man alone could do the job if he "Dutch plowed." This horticultural method involved planting wheat in earthen mounds where it then was cultivated with a hoe. Significantly, black slaves readily adapted to this system, and it continued to be employed throughout the colonial era by small farmers and wherever labor was scarce. Sowing required as much as two bushels of seed per acre, and harvesting was done entirely by sickle. It took three men three weeks of arduous stoop labor to reap and shock twenty acres; only after the Revolutionary War did the scythe and cradle come into widespread use. A man with a flail could beat out a bushel per day, but often it was trodden out by oxen. If left too long unthreshed, the grain heads became weevilly.

By 1720 some tidewater plantations switched to wheat when tobacco prices fell. Many others eventually were forced to make the change when soils in the tobacco fields became exhausted. As settlement spread westward, farmers had more success growing wheat on piedmont soils, and by the middle of the eighteenth century, Maryland and Virginia competed in shipping grain to Europe when prices rose. Meanwhile, barreled bread became a popular export to the British West Indies where it was largely consumed by the wealthy.

Blacks themselves generally disliked wheat bread. Writing in the seventeenth century, a Virginia planter remarked that slaves who were forced to eat wheat "found themselves so weak that they begged of their Master to allow them Indian corn again, or they could not work." Thomas Jefferson,* however, encouraged Virginians to diversify their crops with wheat. It "feeds the labourers plentifully," he said, "requires from them only a moderate toil, except in the season of harvest, raises great numbers of animals for food and service, and diffuses plenty and happiness among the whole."

After the American Revolution, flour increasingly became an important export. Between 1831 and 1843, for example, an annual average of more than 80,400 barrels were sent to Cuba, 170,700 to Brazil, and 135,000 to the West Indies where emancipated slaves now chose to eat the wheat bread formerly reserved for their masters. Ironically, these increasing tonnages were shipped through Charleston and New Orleans where they were handled by Negro stevedores who continued to prefer their traditional maize bread.

Although there long had been two wheat crops—winter and spring—wheat generally was promoted as a winter crop that would not interfere with the harvest of maize or cotton.* This was an important consideration before the advent of mechanized equipment, especially on the smaller homesteads that commonly grew crops for mere subsistence. Diseases and insects posed serious problems for the cultivation of wheat in antebellum America. And, according to historian Lewis C. Gray, "Because of the prevailing belief in the lower South that the climate was not favorable to wheat and because of the superior economic advantages of cotton and corn, wheat was grown only for home consumption."

During the Civil War* wheat continued to be neglected in the South in an effort to grow more cotton. Considerable efforts were necessary to reestablish it late in the war and during Reconstruction. Not until railroads linked the prime Midwestern growing areas with the population centers of the East did wheat again become of major importance. By the 1870s, field-workers, black and white, were beginning to be replaced by a series of modern agricultural machines that changed wheat flour from a luxury to the most common of staples.

SELECTED BIBLIOGRAPHY

Philip A. Bruce, *Economic History of Virginia in the Seventeenth Century* (2 vols., 1895); J. D. B. De Bow, *The Industrial Resources of the Southern and Western States* (3 vols., 1853); and Lewis C. Gray, *History of Agriculture in the Southern United States to 1860* (2 vols., 1933).

ALAN K. CRAIG

WHEATLEY, PHILLIS (ca. 1754–1784). Though her parentage and place and date of birth are unknown, Phillis Wheatley, according to her purchaser and master, John Wheatley, "was brought from Africa to America in the Year 1761, between Seven and Eight Years of Age." Unlike most Africans sold into American slavery, she enjoyed a privileged childhood, quickly becoming a part of the Wheatley household. Within sixteen months after her arrival she had mastered the English language, becoming able to read "the most difficult Parts of the Sacred Writings." By 1772 her milieu had greatly expanded. Writing on the Boston scene, specific events, especially death, and religious themes, she demonstrated a familiarity with classical Latin poets and eighteenth-century English poets, notably Alexander Pope. A dominant influence was the Anglo-American religious and humanitarian world in which her mistress moved, inspired by the Great Awakening.

Her *Poems on Various Subjects, Religious and Moral* was published in London in 1773. *Poems* created an international sensation, less for the quality of the work than for the capacity of an African to produce it. It had been necessary to preface her book with an attestation by eminent Bostonians that it was the work of a Negro. Blacks for two centuries have been justly proud of her achievement, though in recent years some have criticized her for a lack of emphasis upon slavery and Africa.

Freed soon after her return from England, by 1778 she was thrust into a prejudiced world. An unhappy marriage, the deaths of her three children, and grinding poverty closed out the last decade of her life. She was buried in an unknown place.

SELECTED BIBLIOGRAPHY

Julian D. Mason, Jr., ed., *The Poems of Phillis Wheatley* (1966); James A. Rawley, "The World of Phillis Wheatley," *New England Quarterly*, 50 (1977), 666–677; and William H. Robinson, *Phillis Wheatley: A Bio-Bibliography* (1981).

JAMES A. RAWLEY

WHIPPING. Whipping became popular in the nineteenth century as the harsher punishments* of the seventeenth and eighteenth centuries were discarded. When the whip was used in those centuries, both free men and slaves felt its sting, and little, if any, regional differences existed in flogging slaves. Later, however, as slavery was confined to the South, whipping became a punishment that was largely restricted to slaves, both males and females, with the deeper South enacting harsher laws than those of the other slave states.

Few adult slaves had the good fortune to escape getting whipped during their lifetime. Sometimes the flogging was punishment for breaking a state code,* a local code, or a plantation regulation; sometimes it was administered on general principle. For instance, the last slave out of the cabin to the fields might receive a lashing. Some masters used the whip to break in a young slave and to break the spirit of an insubordinate older slave. An Alabama slaveholder declared that slaves had to be whipped until they showed "submission and penitence." Moreover, whites generally believed that "whipping was the only thing that would do a Negro any good."

It seems that everywhere the slave turned someone with a whip stood poised to beat him. The slaveholder, slaveholder's wife, overseer, and driver on the plantation; patrollers off the plantation; and jailers, constables, and other officials—all were authorized to whip slaves. Jailers and constables who carried out court sentences also whipped unruly slaves for slaveholders who were reluctant to whip their own. Breaking a state or local code resulted in sentences of from 20 to 100 lashes, depending upon the severity of the offense. A slave once received a sentence of 500 lashes, to be administered over several weeks.

Breaking plantation regulations resulted in fewer lashes, usually about fifteen, although the number could be much higher. But chances of breaking those regulations were much greater than those of violating public codes since plantation regulations covered a multitude of transgressions. Slaves, in a sense, constantly walked through a punishment tinderbox: the marvel is that any escaped getting burned.

Several instruments were used to administer whippings, but the most common were the rawhide whip (or cowhide whip), the leather strap, the cowhide paddle (or "hot paddle"), and the buckskin cracker whip. The rawhide whip caused lacerations; the others, allegedly, did not. These and other instruments were usually directed to the uncovered back of the slave who was immobilized during the whipping by being tied to a whipping post, a tree, stumps in the ground, or some other objects; or by being placed either in stocks or pillory.

The common practice was to administer the whippings publicly, this being the ultimate act of degradation. According to a slaveholder, "every Negro in this community regards a whipping in the market as the greatest disgrace which can befall them [sic]." This traumatic experience was exacerbated sometimes by rubbing salt in the raw flesh laid open by the flogging. A former slave recalled that his master would "chain a nigger up to whip em and rub salt and pepper on him, like he said 'to season him up.' " This treatment was reserved for obstreperous slaves.

Whipping became the most commonly used form of punishment because it conveyed the message with the least amount of negative ramifications. Accordingly, the whip became the badge of slaveholders' authority, through which slaveholders achieved the dreadful trio of *d*'s—discipline, deterrence, and degradation.

SELECTED BIBLIOGRAPHY

John Spencer Bassett, *The Southern Plantation Overseer As Revealed in His Letters* (1925); Kenneth M. Stampp, *The Peculiar Institution: Slavery in the Ante-Bellum South* (1956); Charles S. Sydnor, *Slavery in Mississippi* (1933); Richard C. Wade, *Slavery in the Cities: The South, 1820–1860* (1964); and Norman R. Yetman, ed., *Life under the Peculiar Institution: Selections From the Slave Narrative Collection* (1970).
                                                    WHITTINGTON B. JOHNSON

WOMEN, SLAVE. Slavery as a social system dominated the lives of Afro-American slave women, just as it did the lives of Afro-American slave men. But a combination of African traditions and American conditions ensured that the experience of Afro-American slave women also differed in certain important respects from that of their fathers, husbands, brothers, and sons. In theory, enslavement could desocialize and desexualize a slave woman as it could a slave man. Slavery could strip away the normal social and human relations that help to constitute any woman's sense of herself in the world. In practice, the theoretical atrocity occurred only in extreme cases. Normally, especially during the nineteenth century, slave women belonged to a community of slaves to which they contributed and that helped to shape their roles and identities as women.

African slave women started to arrive in the North American colonies in the seventeenth century along with slave men. But then, and throughout the eighteenth century, fewer slave women arrived than slave men, primarily because Africans held slave women at a premium and would not readily export them. The vast majority of African women who were transported by the Atlantic slave trade* had already been slaves in Africa. The Middle Passage threw slave women and their children* together with women and children of different kin and language* groups. Slave-ship captains normally divided the women and children from the men during the voyage, allowing the women more mobility. Some women used their relative freedom to assist revolts.* Occasionally others betrayed revolts in the hopes of bettering their situation through sexual relations with white men.

The experience of the slave ships crudely prefigured that which slave women would find in the New World. African slaves would build an Afro-American culture and slave community with peoples of different African backgrounds.* They would normally communicate with each other in languages other than their native tongues. They would slowly blend practices and beliefs of different West African peoples into a new Afro-American culture. Where possible—especially in the organization of labor—masters tended to separate slave men and slave women, to organize their slaves according to gender. Because all West African peoples also organized their societies according to gender, African slave women from different groups adapted to working with other women and began to re-establish a network for the preservation of women's special traditions and skills. Unavoidably, slave women's sexuality also always afforded them special forms of exploitation as well as special opportunities to improve their personal situation.

The unsettled conditions that prevailed during most of the eighteenth century clearly affected the experience of slave women, who remained less numerous than slave men. Disease* and brutal work conditions led to many women's pre-mature deaths, or to the deaths of their children. During this period, slave women participated actively in the establishment of maroon* (''outlier'') colonies and even sometimes emerged as leaders of revolts. The forms of their resistance,* including violence,* suggest that neither African nor American ''normal'' gender conventions fully governed their lives. But second-generation Creole slave women, especially in the Chesapeake and in South Carolina, began to emerge as the core of a distinct slave community and kin group. The gradual emergence of this community of slaves corresponded to the gradual consolidation of slavery as a social system in the Southern colonies and states. As the conditions of slavery and the sinews of the slave community became more clearly defined, slave women increasingly assumed a role as members of a gender group.

Slave women, as mothers, established the unique aspect of North American slave society: the growth of the slave population. By the close of the slave trade in 1808, slave women were bearing and rearing enough children to account for a steady increase. Their impressive record as reproducers derived in part from the growing coherence and stability of the slave community, including personal relations between women and men, and in part from the encouragement of the slaveholders. Slave women bore and reared children as members of a viable community. Had they not been able to establish some rewarding relations with men, had they not been able to rear a significant number of the children they bore, had they not been able to believe in some future, they would not likely have borne so many children or to have sustained the strong African commitment to the value of children.

Slave women's experience differed according to the size of the plantation on which they lived. As a rule, slave women and men were distributed equally among plantations of different sizes. Women, however, were less likely than men to be among the early migrants to the Cotton Belt and more likely to remain on the farms of Virginia. In general about 25 percent of female slaves lived on plantations of more than fifty slaves, and another 25 percent on plantations of twenty to fifty slaves. For these 50 percent and probably also for the majority of the other 50 percent, their gender played an important role in their daily experience.

The Southern farms and plantations on which most slave women lived con-sisted of households that contained within themselves the basic relations of production and reproduction. White male slaveholders presided over the pro-ductive and personal relations of these households, which they normally preferred to organize according to gender. These men assuredly did not treat slave women as they treated white women, but they did attribute some social significance to their being women. In particular, those who had enough slaves for work gangs* organized them according to gender. This division of labor by gender had no necessary implications for the kinds of labor slave women were assigned. As Sojourner Truth* bitterly claimed in her famous remarks to a Northern women's rights convention, slave women did hoe, and plow, and gather crops into barns. They also fenced, planted and picked cotton, dug potatoes, and did almost everything else common to mid-nineteenth-century agricultural production. Slave women, however, were less often assigned to plow. In general, among field hands,* gender specialization seems to have been a matter of organization of the labor force rather than one of gender-specific tasks.

House servants* and skilled workers, however, were assigned more rigidly gender-specific tasks. Almost without exception men served as drivers,* blacksmiths, carpenters, carters, coopers, bricklayers, engineers, millhands, stock minders, gardeners, stablemen, and watchmen. Women predominated as cooks, nurses, seamstresses, laundresses, housemaids, and midwives. Slaveholders trained their slaves for skilled occupations according to their own gender prejudices. To the extent that slave women specialized in particular kinds of labor, they did so in the manner of white women. Like white women, slave women were more likely than men to be restricted to the plantation household, less likely to be literate, and, above all, less likely to be offered any role that implied leadership.

Female house servants worked in close proximity with, and under the direction of, white women. House servants' tasks most closely followed the white division of labor by gender. Depending upon the size of the plantation, house servants would pursue more or less specialized tasks. On a large, low-country plantation, the female house servants might include one or more cooks, one or more maids, one or more nurses for children, one or more wet nurses, a seamstress, a laundress or two, and even weavers. A female servant might also oversee the infirmary, under the direction of the mistress. Training for work in the Big House could begin young. The nurses, frequently as young as ten, were responsible for minding the small white children. Wet nurses may have been less common, although they were numerous enough. But the functions of nurse and wet nurse were not always combined in a single figure known as "Mammy," or, more commonly, "Maum." Mammies* did exist, but frequently the wet nurses supplemented the mother's milk rather than replaced it. Typically, slave women doubled white women's functions whether as mammies or as cooks. Typically, white women tried to treat slave women as extensions of themselves. As a result, the sources must be read with care to determine whether a white woman is performing a specific task or having a slave woman perform it for her. The distinctions often only become clear at moments of conflict.

And moments of conflict abounded. Slave women notoriously tried the patience of their white mistresses, who might box their ears or even whip them, but who claimed to hate to manage them. Conversely, slaves and mistresses could share a real—if never really conflict-free—companionship in their domestic responsibilities. Both slave women and mistresses loved and lost their children. Slave women and mistresses both disliked housework. Slave cooks frequently knew more about their jobs than the young mistresses who commonly were snatched from a carefree girlhood to direct them. Slave women might also know more about medicinal herbs or birthing than their young mistresses. House slaves were more likely than field slaves to receive presents of cast-off clothing,* perhaps also more likely than field slaves to value the status that attached to such finery. In general, house slaves were especially exposed to the hegemony of their mistresses' culture and values and were especially well placed to resent and resist them. But, except possibly on the largest, caste-ridden plantations and town houses, female house slaves formed their closest ties with others in the slave community.

The conditions established by the slaveholders opened some avenues to slave women and closed others. Life within the plantation household permitted the development of strong bonds among women. Women worked together and shared much of daily experience with other women, including gossip, which constituted a primary form of socialization and censorship for the community as a whole. Through gossip, singing, shared work, and daily conversation, slave women perpetuated, transmitted, and transformed elements of African culture. Their vigorous oral culture filtered the particles of African experience and lore and adapted remnants of their various African traditions to their Afro-American present.

For slave women, even more than for slave men, the daily routine of work overlapped with the maintenance of the bonds of the slave community, especially with care of the young and the aged. Many women who could honestly or dishonestly claim pregnancy or illness related to reproduction worked lighter tasks. In the trash gang, for example, they would work with younger and older women and help to integrate diffuse social bonds into a daily routine. Whether through work, religious gatherings, or other possible informal women's associations, women shared a body of knowledge, especially of medicine, herbs, childbirth, and beliefs about womanhood.

Slave women, whether they worked in the Big House or in the fields, developed their own forms of resistance to slavery. As cooks, for example, slave women were especially likely to steal from their masters' kitchens or to poison members of the white family. All female house servants were well positioned to steal—even a gun—and to commit arson. As runaways,* slave women were likely to flee for a few days or a week to kin on a neighboring plantation, but less likely than men to escape to the North. And during the nineteenth century, slave women were absent from the leadership of the best organized revolts. In all these ways, the actions of slave women betrayed a combination of African influences and the conditions of life in Southern slave society.

By the high antebellum period, slave women's strong attitudes towards womanhood represented something new: a transformation and new synthesis of African legacies, white influences, and the specific material and political conditions of their lives. There is no reason to believe that they regarded sexuality either with indifference or guilt. There is good evidence, in fact, that slave mothers, fully cognizant of the dangers of their society, attempted to protect females in their teens from precocious sexual encounters with white or black men, although they did not regard the failure to protect that young sexuality as a special cause for guilt. Slave women never enjoyed the kind of control over their own sexuality that would have permitted them—or their men—to establish it as the principal standard of a woman's excellence, virtue, or selfhood. Nevertheless, female sexuality remained a matter of concern for slave women and men. The evidence comes from the violence that occasionally rent the slave community over questions of sexual loyalty. For slave women, sexuality could range from a primary source of exploitation to a token of love and loyalty for another. As slaves, they could hardly have afforded to tie their identities or souls to their sexuality. As members of a vigorous community that included an ideal of gender relations, they could hardly have afforded to dismiss it as irrelevant to community stability. The balance remained tricky in a world where the rape of a slave woman did not constitute a crime no matter who the perpetrator—where it did not constitute a crime against the woman or against any of her male kin, who had no legal right to protect or avenge her honor or theirs.

Some scholars have recently stressed slave women's freedom from the control of slave men as a foundation for slave women's self-reliance and sense of autonomy. Indeed, slavery did deprive slave men of all of the common attributes of male power. Because slave marriages had no status before the law, slave men had no rights over their women and children. They could be separated from spouse or children by their master with no recourse except personal pleas; they could not protect their wives from the sexual assault of white men; they did not support their wives, who worked at the will of the master; they did not provide for their children or their children's training. The legal incapacity of black men as husbands and fathers constituted the foundation for the slave woman's freedom from domestic domination. In fact, slave women frequently experienced an unusually harsh form of male dominance—wielded by their white masters rather than by the black men of their community and kinship.

African traditions and American conditions reinforced one particular aspect of slave women's identities: motherhood. All West African societies valued motherhood highly. North American slaveholders encouraged their female slaves to bear children. If slaveholders did not wax as sentimental about the motherhood of their slave women as they did about that of white women, nevertheless they valued it. And their female slaves fully exploited their masters' interest in reproduction. For if a master failed at least minimally to respect his slave woman's motherhood, she could retaliate with contraception, abortion, or infanticide.* Yet most slave women seem to have valued childbearing as central to their own identity and possible status. Slave women probably viewed menarche and pregnancy as more important rites of passage than the loss of virginity or marriage. The masters' attitudes towards gender organization gave slave women ample opportunity to induct younger women into the rites and values of womanhood, which they passed down among generations of women.

Slave women made the most of the African traditions that they perpetuated and the opportunities of life in a slave society to forge viable roles for themselves as women. The strength of their gender roles derived from the viability of the slave community that they did so much to help create and sustain. Although slavery offered slave women no positive model of identity, it nonetheless afforded them participation in the community of slaves and, as a result, solidified their identity as Afro-American women.

SELECTED BIBLIOGRAPHY

Robert W. Fogel and Stanley L. Engerman, *Time on the Cross: The Economics of American Negro Slavery* (2 vols., 1974); Eugene D. Genovese, *Roll, Jordan, Roll: The World the Slaves Made* (1974); George P. Rawick, ed., *The American Slave: A Composite Autobiography* (19 vols., 1972); Dorothy Sterling, ed., *We Are Your Sisters: Black Women in the Nineteenth Century* (1984); and Deborah Gray White, *Ar'n't I a Woman? Female Slaves in the Plantation South* (1985).

ELIZABETH FOX-GENOVESE

CHRONOLOGY OF AFRO-AMERICAN SLAVERY

1619	In August, "twenty and odd" blacks were sold at Jamestown, Virginia, as bound servants.
1621	The Dutch West India Company was organized.
1624	Slavery was introduced in New Netherland.
1642	Virginia passed a fugitive law fining those who harbored runaways.
1661	Virginia law revealed that some blacks were assumed to serve their masters for life.
1663	Maryland law provided life servitude for blacks.
1664	Maryland law declared that baptism had no effect on slave status.
1667	England passed the "Act to Regulate the Negroes on the British Plantations."
1670	An act passed in Virginia declared that "all servants not being Christian," imported by sea, were servants for life, the issue following the status of the mother.
1672	The Royal African Company was chartered and granted a monopoly on the English slave trade.
1681	An estimated 3,000 blacks resided in Virginia.
1682	Slavery was legally sanctioned in South Carolina.
1688	In April, Pennsylvania Quakers declared that slavery was contrary to Christian principles.
1696	In their Yearly Meeting, American Quakers admonished members against importing slaves.
1698	The Royal African Company lost its monopoly on the English slave trade.
1700	Slavery was legally sanctioned in Rhode Island and Pennsylvania.
1701	Thomas Bray founded the Society for the Propagation of the Gospel in Foreign Parts.
1704	Elias Neau established the Catechism School for Negroes at Trinity Church, New York City.

1705	Virginia's black code severely restrained the mobility of slaves and forbade miscegenation under heavy penalties.
1708	Virginia had 12,000 blacks in its population.
1712	In April, a slave revolt in New York City left nine whites dead and seven wounded. Twenty-five slaves were convicted and sentenced to death.
1717	Cotton Mather began an evening school for Indians and slaves.
1723	Virginia denied free Negroes the right to vote and discriminated against them in the levying of taxes.
1731	Royal instructions to governors forbade duties on slave importations.
1739	Three slave revolts broke out in South Carolina, the most serious occurring in September along the Stono River. Fatalities included thirty whites and forty-four blacks.
1740	In January, a Negro plot was uncovered in Charleston, South Carolina. Fifty blacks were hanged.
1741	In February, rumors spread in New York City that blacks and poor whites sought to seize control of the city. Eighteen blacks were hanged, thirteen were burned alive, and seventy were banished.
1749	The Georgia Trustees repealed their prohibition on the importation of slaves.
1755	Quakers excluded from their denomination all Friends who thereafter imported slaves.
1760	Jupiter Hammon published *Salvation by Christ with Penitential Cries.*
1770	Crispus Attucks, a runaway slave, was killed in the Boston Massacre.
1771	Slavery was abolished in England by judicial decision.
1773	Phillis Wheatley, a slave, published a book of poems.
1775	The first antislavery society in the United States was organized by the Quakers.
	Lord Dunmore, the British governor of Virginia, proposed to free male slaves who joined the British forces in resisting the American "patriots."
1776	Following the protest of Southern delegates to the Continental Congress, Thomas Jefferson's attack on the role of the crown in the slave trade was stricken from the Declaration of Independence.
	Jefferson proposed a plan for African colonization.
	The Continental Congress passed a resolution calling for an end to the importation of slaves. Between 1776 and 1781 5,000 slaves and free blacks served in the Continental army and navy.
1780	Pennsylvania passed a gradual abolition act.
1783	Maryland prohibited the slave trade.
	Slavery was abolished by judicial decision in Massachusetts.
1784	Connecticut and Rhode Island passed bills providing for the gradual abolition of slavery.

1785	The New York Society for Promoting Manumission, with John Jay as president, was established.
1787	The Northwest Ordinance excluded slavery from all land north of the Ohio River in the Northwest Territory.
	In October, Prince Hall and other Boston blacks petitioned the Massachusetts legislature for equal school facilities for blacks.
	Led by Richard Allen, Philadelphia blacks, forced from a white church, established their own congregation.
1790	The United States' black population included 59,557 free blacks and 697,624 slaves.
	America's first treaty with the Creek Indians contained a provision requiring the return of runaway slaves.
	In February, the Society of Friends presented the first petition to Congress for emancipation.
1793	Eli Whitney invented the cotton gin.
1794	Congress prohibited the slave trade to foreign ports and the outfitting of foreign slave-trade vessels in U.S. ports.
1795	The approximate price of a slave field hand was $300.
1797	Congress rejected the first recorded petition by American blacks.
1799	New York passed a bill providing for the gradual abolition of slavery.
1800	The Virginia Assembly passed the first of four pro-colonization resolutions.
	In August, Gabriel Prosser's Virginia slave revolt was discovered and suppressed.
1803	South Carolina opened the slave trade from South America and the West Indies.
1804	Ohio passed black laws that restricted the movement of free blacks.
	New Jersey passed a bill providing for the gradual abolition of slavery.
1806	Virginia required all slaves emancipated after 1 May to leave the state.
1807	Congress passed a law prohibiting the importation of slaves from Africa effective 1 January 1808.
1814	Two black battalions answered General Andrew Jackson's call to defend New Orleans against the British.
1815	Paul Cuffe, an affluent free black merchant, helped a group of blacks reach Africa.
1816	The American Colonization Society was established in Washington.
	U.S. Army troops entered Florida to destroy a fort occupied by escaped slaves.
1820	The Missouri Compromise admitted Missouri as a slave state but prohibited slavery in future states north of the 36° 30′ parallel.

In February, the U.S. Army forbade acceptance of blacks or mulattoes into the service.

1821   In January, Benjamin Lundy first published the *Genius of Universal Emancipation*.

1822   The American Colonization Society settled its first colony at Monrovia, Liberia, West Africa.

In May, Denmark Vesey's insurrection plot was uncovered in Charleston, South Carolina.

1826   Nashoba, a utopian community near Memphis, Tennessee, was established by Frances Wright for the training of blacks and their eventual resettlement beyond the United States.

1827   The *Freedom's Journal*, America's first black newspaper, was published in New York City.

1829   David Walker, a Boston free black, published *Walker's Appeal, in Four Articles*. He advocated militant resistance to slavery by blacks.

1831   The Mississippi Colonization Society established an African colony for black emigrants from that state.

In January, William Lloyd Garrison began publication of *The Liberator* in Boston.

In August, a slave rebellion broke out under the leadership of Nat Turner, a literate slave preacher, in Southampton County, Virginia. Turner and his followers killed fifty-seven whites. Turner was captured and hanged in Jerusalem, Virginia.

1831   During the winter session the Virginia Convention debated virtually every
–32   phase of the slavery question. Ultimately, a small majority defeated various proposals for emancipation.

1832   Prudence Crandall admitted a black girl to her school in Canterbury, Connecticut. Her school later was vandalized and demolished.

Students and faculty at Lane Theological Seminary in Cincinnati debated colonization and abolition. In May 1833 most of the students withdrew when the trustees ordered a halt to such discussion.

1833   The American Anti-Slavery Society was established in Philadelphia.

In August, the British government provided slaveholders in the West Indies £20,000,000 for the abolition of slavery.

1836   Congress introduced the "gag rule" to prevent the reading and circulation of antislavery petitions.

1837   In November, Elijah Lovejoy, a newspaper editor, was murdered in Alton, Illinois, by an antiabolition mob while defending his press.

1838   Frederick Douglass escaped from slavery in Maryland.

1839   Theodore Dwight Weld published *American Slavery As It Is*.

James G. Birney organized the Liberty party.

In July, a group of Africans led by Cinqué revolted, killed the captain, and seized their Spanish slave ship, *L'Amistad*, off the coast of Cuba.

1840   The American and Foreign Anti-Slavery Society, led by Theodore Dwight Weld, a non-Garrisonian abolitionist, broke with the Garrisonians over tactics and strategy.

1841   Slaves on board the *Creole*, en route from Richmond to New Orleans, captured control of the vessel and headed for Nassau.

1843   Great Britain and the United States agreed to patrol the West African coast in order to intercept ships engaged in the slave trade.

In February, the Massachusetts legislature repealed a 1786 law against interracial marriages.

1844   The Methodist church of the United States split over the issue of whether or not a bishop could hold slaves. White Southerners organized the Methodist Episcopal Church, South.

1845   The "gag rule" was rescinded in the House of Representatives.

1846   David Wilmot, a representative from Pennsylvania, proposed the exclusion of slavery from territory acquired from Mexico. Wilmot's proviso was defeated in the Senate.

1847   Frederick Douglass and Martin Delany began publication of the *North Star*, an abolitionist newspaper, in Rochester, New York.

1848   The Free-Soil party was organized in Buffalo, New York.

1850   The Compromise of 1850 admitted California to the Union as a free state; established New Mexico and Utah as territories under popular sovereignty; passed a more stringent fugitive slave law; and restricted the slave trade in the District of Columbia.

1851   Frederick Douglass split from William Lloyd Garrison over the tactics and strategy of the abolitionist movement.

1852   Harriet Beecher Stowe published *Uncle Tom's Cabin*.

The Pro-Slavery Argument was published by William Harper, Thomas R. Dew, James H. Hammond, and others.

1853   In July, delegates from several states established the National Council of Colored People in Rochester, New York, to encourage the mechanical training of blacks.

1854   The Kansas-Nebraska Act was passed, repealing the prohibition of the Missouri Compromise of slavery north of the 36° 30' line in federal territories. It allowed popular sovereignty in Kansas and Nebraska territories. As a result, the Republican party was created in opposition to the extension of slavery into the West.

George Fitzhugh published *Sociology for the South; or, The Failure of Free Society*.

In April, antislavery forces organized the New England Emigrant Aid Society to settle "free-soilers" in Kansas Territory.

In August, delegates from eleven states met in Cleveland, Ohio, to establish the National Emigration Convention of the Colored People.

1855   Frederick Douglass published *My Bondage and My Freedom*.

In April, racial segregation in Massachusetts schools was abolished by law.

1856   The Republican party was formally organized.

1857   The *Dred Scott v. Sanford* case declared that blacks were not citizens and that Congress had no power to exclude slavery from the territories. This rendered the Missouri Compromise unconstitutional.

1858   In June, while accepting the Republican nomination for senator from Illinois, Abraham Lincoln stated that "A house divided against itself cannot stand. I believe this government cannot endure permanently half *slave* and half *free*. I do not expect the Union to be *dissolved*. I do not expect the house to *fall*, but I do expect it will cease to be divided."

In his summer debates with Abraham Lincoln, Stephen A. Douglas alienated many of his Southern supporters.

1859   In October, John Brown raided the federal arsenal at Harpers Ferry, Virginia, to seize arms with which to free the slaves of the upper South.

1860   Of the more than eight million whites in the South, only 383,637 held slaves.

The approximate price of a slave field hand ranged between $1,200 and $1,800.

Skilled slave artisans were hired out at an average rate of between $500 and $600 per annum.

In a prenomination speech, Abraham Lincoln described slavery "as an evil not to be extended, but to be tolerated and protected only because of and so far as its actual presence among us makes that toleration and protection necessary."

In its presidential campaign, the Republican party opposed the extension of slavery into the western territories; the Democratic party supported the Dred Scott decision.

In December, President James Buchanan urged passage of constitutional amendments upholding the fugitive slave acts.

In December, South Carolina seceded from the Union, followed by the secession of six lower South states between 9 January and 1 February 1861.

1861   In his inaugural address, Confederate President Jefferson Davis endorsed slavery "as necessary to self-preservation."

In March, Alexander Stephens, vice president of the Confederacy, proclaimed that his new government "rests upon the great truth that the Negro is not equal to the white man, that slavery, subordination to the superior race, is a natural and normal condition . . . our new Government, is the first in the history of the world, based upon this great physical, philosophical, and moral truth."

In July, the U.S. Senate affirmed that "this war is not waged . . . for any purpose . . . of overthrowing or interfering with the rights or established institutions of . . . southern States."

Though black volunteers were officially rejected by the Union Army, by September blacks already had fought the Confederacy both on land and sea.

1862 Robert Smalls, a slave, commandeered a Confederate gunboat for the Union navy in Charleston Harbor.

In March, military commanders were forbidden to return fugitive slaves to their owners.

In April, Congress agreed to cooperate with any state adopting a plan of gradual emancipation and compensation.

In April, compensated emancipation for slaves in the District of Columbia became law.

In July, the Confiscation and Militia Acts authorized the president to employ "persons of African descent" in any way necessary, including as armed troops.

In August, President Lincoln met with prominent blacks, urging them to support colonization.

In September, President Lincoln issued the preliminary Emancipation Proclamation.

1863 In January, the Emancipation Proclamation declared free all slaves except those in states or parts of states that were not in rebellion.

In February, Representative Thaddeus Stevens's bill calling for 150,000 U.S. Colored Troops was passed in the House of Representatives.

In May, the War Department's General Order No. 143 placed control of black troops under the U.S. Colored Troops.

By July, thirty regiments of U.S. Colored Troops had been armed and equipped.

Whites exhibited antiblack sentiment in the New York City draft riots in July.

1864 Federal law enabled Northern states to recruit black soldiers in the South.

In April, roughly 300 blacks were massacred by Confederate troops at Fort Pillow, Tennessee.

In June, in its Army Appropriations Bill, Congress equalized the enlistment bounty for blacks and whites.

In July, the U.S. government entitled the families of black soldiers killed in the war to pensions.

1865 The Confederate States government authorized the filling of military quotas by using blacks. The number of slaves, however, was not to exceed 25 percent of the able-bodied male slave population between ages eighteen and forty-five. This last-ditch effort came too late to assist the Confederate war effort.

In December, the Thirteenth Amendment abolished slavery.

EDITORS AND CONTRIBUTORS

EDITORS

RANDALL M. MILLER is Professor of History and Director of American Studies at Saint Joseph's University in Philadelphia and also Editor of the *Pennsylvania Magazine of History & Biography*. He is the author or editor of ten books, including the award-winning *"Dear Master": Letters of a Slave Family* (1978). His most recent book is *Ethnic & Racial Images in American Film & Television* (1987). His articles have appeared in *American Heritage, Business History Review, Phylon, Southern Studies*, and elsewhere.

JOHN DAVID SMITH is Associate Professor of History at North Carolina State University. His books include *Window on the War: Frances Dallam Peter's Lexington Civil War Diary* (with William Cooper, Jr., 1976); *Black Slavery in the Americas: An Interdisciplinary Bibliography, 1865–1980* (2 vols., 1982); and *An Old Creed for the New South: Proslavery Ideology and Historiography, 1865–1918* (1985). His articles have appeared in *Civil War History, The Journal of Negro History, Phylon*, and numerous other scholarly journals.

CONTRIBUTORS

ROBERT H. ABZUG is Professor of History at the University of Texas at Austin.

WILBERT AHERN is Professor of History at the University of Minnesota, Morris.

CHARLES S. AIKEN is Professor of Geography at the University of Tennessee.

TERRY ALFORD is Professor of History at Northern Virginia Community College.

STEVEN E. ANDERS teaches history at the U.S. Army Quartermaster School in Virginia.

THOMAS F. ARMSTRONG is Professor of History and Dean of the College of Arts and Sciences at Georgia College.

DAVID T. BAILEY is Associate Professor of History at Michigan State University.

HUGH C. BAILEY is President of Valdosta State College.

WILLIAM L. BARNEY is Associate Professor of History at the University of North Carolina at Chapel Hill.

JOHN D. BARNWELL is enrolled at the Law School of the University of North Carolina at Chapel Hill.

DONNIE D. BELLAMY is Regents' Professor of History at Fort Valley State College.

ROBERT A. BENNETT is Professor of Old Testament at the Episcopal Divinity School, Cambridge, Massachusetts.

MICHAEL BIRKNER is Assistant Professor of History at Millersville University.

JOHN B. BOLES is Professor of History at Rice University and the Editor of the *Journal of Southern History*.

S. CHARLES BOLTON is Professor of History at the University of Arkansas at Little Rock.

F. N. BONEY is Professor of History at the University of Georgia.

JAMES C. BONNER was Professor Emeritus of History at Georgia College.

JOSEPH BOSKIN is Professor of History at Boston University.

MARY JO BRATTON is Associate Professor of History at East Carolina University.

NEWELL G. BRINGHURST is Instructor of History and Political Science at the College of the Sequoias.

JEFFREY P. BROWN is Assistant Professor of History at New Mexico State University.

MARTHA H. BROWN is Director of Libraries at Langston University.

SUZANNE AUSTIN BROWNE is Assistant Professor of History at the University of Delaware.

ORVILLE VERNON BURTON is Associate Professor of History at the University of Illinois.

JON BUTLER is Professor of American Studies at Yale University.

REGINALD BUTLER is Instructor of History at North Carolina State University.

DONALD BUTTS teaches history at Gordon Junior College, Georgia.

WILLIAM L. CALDERHEAD is Professor of History at the U.S. Naval Academy.

EDWARD D. C. CAMPBELL, JR., is Editor of *Virginia Cavalcade*.

RANDOLPH B. CAMPBELL is Professor of History at North Texas State University.

STANLEY W. CAMPBELL is Professor of History at Baylor University.

CHARLES CARLTON is Professor of History at North Carolina State University.

DAN T. CARTER is Professor of History at Emory University.

JUDITH WRAGG CHASE is Director of the Old Slave Mart Museum, Sullivans Island, South Carolina.

MICHAEL B. CHESSON is Associate Professor of History at the University of Massachusetts at Boston.

JAMES R. CHUMNEY is Associate Professor of History at Memphis State University.

PAUL A. CIMBALA is Assistant Professor of History at Fordham University.

JOHN CIMPRICH is Assistant Professor of History at Thomas More College.

THOMAS D. CLARK is Professor Emeritus of History at Indiana University.

JAMES M. CLIFTON teaches history at Southeastern Community College in North Carolina.

CATHERINE CLINTON is Assistant Professor of History at Harvard University.

CHERYLL ANN CODY is Assistant Professor of History at the University of Houston.

DUDLEY T. CORNISH is Professor Emeritus of History at Pittsburg State University.

JAY COUGHTRY is Associate Professor of History at the University of Nevada, Las Vegas.

JOAN WELLS COWARD is Associate Professor of History at Rutgers University, Camden.

ALAN K. CRAIG is Professor of Geography at Florida Atlantic University.

MICHAEL B. CRATON is Professor of History at the University of Waterloo.

JAMES E. CRISP is Assistant Professor of History at North Carolina State University.

JEFFREY J. CROW is Administrator of the Historical Publications Section, North Carolina Division of Archives & History.

ROBERT EMMETT CURRAN, S. J., is Associate Professor of History at Georgetown University.

LEONARD P. CURRY is Professor of History at the University of Louisville.

PATRICIA ROMERO CURTIN teaches in the Atlantic Studies Program at Johns Hopkins University.

W. HARRISON DANIEL is Professor of History at the University of Richmond.

THOMAS J. DAVIS is Professor of Afro-American Studies at the State University of New York at Buffalo.

DAVID M. DEAN is Professor of History at Frostburg State College.

J. L. DILLARD is Professor of Language at Northwestern State University of Louisiana.

MERTON L. DILLON is Professor of History at Ohio State University.

JAMES H. DORMON is Professor of History at the University of Southwestern Louisiana.

MICHAEL B. DOUGAN is Professor of History at Arkansas State University.

RICHARD B. DRAKE is Professor of History and Political Science at Berea College.

RICHARD DUNCAN is Associate Professor of History at Georgetown University.

JOHN EGERTON is a Nashville-based journalist.

WALTER EHRLICH is Professor of History at the University of Missouri, St. Louis.

JOHN A. EISTERHOLD is Associate Professor of History at the University of Tennessee, Martin.

LYNNE FAULEY EMERY teaches in the Health, Physical Education, Recreation and Dance Department at California State Polytechnic University, Pomona.

STANLEY L. ENGERMAN is Professor of Economics at the University of Rochester.

DENA J. EPSTEIN is the former Assistant Music Librarian at the University of Chicago.

PAUL D. ESCOTT is Professor of History at the University of North Carolina at Charlotte.

JAMES D. ESSIG was Assistant Professor of History at Western Maryland College.

WILLIAM McKEE EVANS is Professor of History at California State Polytechnic University, Pomona.

DREW GILPIN FAUST is Professor of American Civilization at the University of Pennsylvania.

THOMAS FIEHRER is Editor of *Plantation Society in the Americas*.

PAUL FINKELMAN is Associate Professor of History at the State University of New York at Binghamton.

ROY E. FINKENBINE is Associate Editor of *The Black Abolitionist Papers* at Florida State University.

ROGER A. FISCHER is Professor of History at the University of Minnesota, Duluth.

BETTY FLADELAND is Professor of History at Southern Illinois University, Carbondale.

FRANCES SMITH FOSTER is Professor of English and Comparative Literature at San Diego State University.

ELIZABETH FOX-GENOVESE is Professor of History at Emory University.

ALISON GOODYEAR FREEHLING is a historian, living in Sparks, Maryland.

LAWRENCE J. FRIEDMAN is Professor of History at Bowling Green State University.

J. WILLIAM FROST is Director of the Friends Historical Library at Swarthmore College.

DAVID W. GALENSON is Professor of Economics at the University of Chicago.

LARRY GARA is Professor of History at Wilmington College, Ohio.

EUGENE D. GENOVESE is Professor of Arts and Sciences at the University of Rochester.

LOUIS S. GERTEIS is Professor of History at the University of Missouri, St. Louis.

LAURENCE GLASCO is Associate Professor of History at the University of Pittsburgh.

WILLIAM B. GRAVELY is Professor of Religious Studies at the University of Denver.

JOHN D. W. GUICE is Professor of History at the University of Southern Mississippi.

STEVEN HAHN is Associate Professor of History at the University of California, San Diego.

ROBERT L. HALL is Assistant Professor of Afro-American Studies at the University of Maryland, Baltimore County.

HAROLD B. HANCOCK was Professor Emeritus of History at Otterbein College.

NICHOLAS P. HARDEMAN is Professor of History at California State University, Long Beach.

JOHN E. HARKINS is on the history faculty at the Memphis University School, Memphis, Tennessee.

DAVID E. HARRELL, JR., is Professor of History at the University of Alabama, Birmingham.

WILLIAM C. HARRIS is Professor of History at North Carolina State University.

WILLIAM G. HARTLEY teaches history at Brigham Young University.

RICHARD HAUNTON is Professor of History at Appalachian State University.

J. NOEL HEERMANCE teaches history at Lincoln University, Missouri.

DAVID J. HELLWIG is Professor of Interdisciplinary Studies at Saint Cloud State University.

G. MELVIN HERNDON is Professor of History at the University of Georgia.

SAM B. HILLIARD is Professor of Geography at Louisiana State University.

JERROLD HIRSCH is Assistant Professor of History at the University of the South.

SVEND E. HOLSOE is Associate Professor of Anthropology at the University of Delaware.

JAMES F. HOPKINS is Professor Emeritus of History at the University of Kentucky.

GOSSIE HAROLD HUDSON is Professor of History at Morgan State University and Editor of the *Negro History Bulletin*.

JOHN C. INSCOE is Associate Editor of the *Georgia Historical Quarterly*.

HARVEY H. JACKSON is Professor of History at Clayton State College.

ROBERT W. JOHANNSEN is Professor of History at the University of Illinois.

CLIFTON H. JOHNSON is Director of the Amistad Research Center in New Orleans.

KENNETH R. JOHNSON is Professor of History at the University of North Alabama.

MICHAEL P. JOHNSON is Professor of History at the University of California, Irvine.

WHITTINGTON B. JOHNSON is Associate Professor of History at the University of Miami.

HOWARD JONES is Professor of History at the University of Alabama.

TERRY G. JORDAN is Professor of Geography at the University of Texas at Austin.

WINTHROP D. JORDAN is Professor of History at the University of Mississippi.

DAVIS D. JOYCE is Associate Professor of History at East Central University, Oklahoma.

CHARLES JOYNER is Professor of History at the University of Alabama.

MARION KILSON is Academic Dean, Emmanuel College, Massachusetts.

ARTHUR KINOY is on the faculty at the School of Law, Rutgers University, Newark.

KENNETH F. KIPLE is Professor of History at Bowling Green State University.

JAMES C. KLOTTER is General Editor at the Kentucky Historical Society.

ALAN KRAUT is Professor of History at American University.

MARC W. KRUMAN is Associate Professor of History at Wayne State University.

ALLAN KULIKOFF is Assistant Professor of History at Northern Illinois University.

EMMA J. LAPSANSKY is Associate Professor of History at Temple University.

PHILIP LAPSANSKY is Research Librarian at the Library Company of Philadelphia.

J. STANLEY LEMONS is Professor of History at Rhode Island College.

GEORGE A. LEVESQUE is Associate Professor of African and Afro-American Studies at the State University of New York at Albany.

RONALD L. LEWIS is Professor of History at West Virginia University.

JOSEPH LOGSDON is Professor of History at the University of New Orleans.

MARION B. LUCAS is Professor of History at Western Kentucky University.

ROBERT MCCOLLEY is Professor of History at the University of Illinois.

GEORGE W. MCDANIEL is on the staff at the Atlanta Historical Society.

ARCHIE P. MCDONALD is Professor of History at Stephen F. Austin State University.

LAWRENCE T. MCDONNELL is a Fellow at the Centre for American Studies, University of Western Ontario.

ROBERT H. MCKENZIE is Associate Professor of Humanities and Public Policy at the University of Alabama.

JOHN R. MCKIVIGAN is Associate Editor of the *Frederick Douglass Papers* at Yale University.

EDGAR J. MCMANUS is Professor of History at Queens College, New York.

LINDA O. MCMURRY is Professor of History at North Carolina State University.

EDWARD MAGDOL taught at the State University of New York at Potsdam.

JOHN K. MAHON is Professor Emeritus of History at the University of Florida.

JOHN F. MARSZALEK is Professor of History at the Mississippi State University.

PETER MASLOWSKI is Professor of History at the University of Nebraska.

ROBERT E. MAY is Professor of History at Purdue University.

MILTON MELTZER is a historian and biographer, living in New York City.

RUSSELL R. MENARD is Professor of History at the University of Minnesota.

JOSEPH C. MILLER is Professor of History at the University of Virginia.

JOHN D. MILLIGAN is Professor of History at the State University of New York at Buffalo.

ELIZABETH SHOWN MILLS is Co-Editor of the *National Genealogical Society Quarterly*.

GARY B. MILLS is Professor of History at the University of Alabama.

CLARENCE L. MOHR is Associate Professor of History at Tulane University.

JOHN HEBRON MOORE is Professor of History at Florida State University.

CURTIS F. MORGAN, JR., is an editor at the Foreign Broadcast Information Service, Washington, D.C.

PHILIP D. MORGAN is Associate Professor of History at Florida State University.

THOMAS D. MORRIS is Professor of History at Portland State University.

ANDREW E. MURRAY is Professor of Religion at Lincoln University, Pennsylvania.

A. E. KEIR NASH is Professor of Political Science at the University of California, Santa Barbara.

MARK E. NEELY, JR., is Director of the Louis A. Warren Lincoln Library and Museum, Fort Wayne, Indiana.

FRANKLIN D. NICKELL is Associate Professor of History at Southeast Missouri State University.

JOHN T. NOONAN, JR., is Judge, Ninth Circuit, Court of Appeals and a member of the law faculty at the University of California, Berkeley.

JAMES OAKES is Professor of History at Northwestern University.

GAIL W. O'BRIEN is Associate Professor of History at North Carolina State University.

JOHN SOLOMON OTTO teaches in the American Studies department at the University of Maryland.

FRANK L. OWSLEY is Professor of History at Auburn University.

THEDA PERDUE is Professor of History at Clemson University.

PERCIVAL PERRY is Professor Emeritus of History at Wake Forest University.

LESLIE J. POLLARD is Chair, Division of Social Sciences and Business Administration at Paine College.

WILLIAM S. PRICE is Director of the North Carolina Division of Archives and History.

BENJAMIN QUARLES is Professor Emeritus of History at Morgan State University.

ROBERT E. QUIGLEY is Professor of History at Rosemont College.

DAVID C. RANKIN teaches in the history department at the University of California, Irvine.

JAMES A. RAWLEY is Professor of History at the University of Nebraska.

ALICE E. REAGAN is a doctoral candidate in history at the University of Maryland.

EDWIN S. REDKEY is Dean of Humanities, State University of New York at Purchase.

LARRY E. RIVERS is Director of the Division of Social and Behavioral Sciences at Florida A & M University.

HENRY S. ROBINSON teaches in the history department at Morgan State University.

GEORGE C. ROGERS, JR., is Professor Emeritus of History at the University of South Carolina.

CHARLES P. ROLAND is Alumni Professor of History at the University of Kentucky.

MARION ROYDHOUSE is Assistant Professor of History at the Philadelphia College of Textiles & Science.

TODD L. SAVITT is Professor of Medical Humanities at the School of Medicine, East Carolina University.

WILLIAM K. SCARBOROUGH is Professor of History at the University of Southern Mississippi.

LESTER B. SCHERER is Professor of History at Eastern Michigan University.

LOUIS D. SCHMIER is Professor of History at Valdosta State College.

PHILIP J. SCHWARZ is Associate Professor of History at Virginia Commonwealth University.

LOREN SCHWENINGER is Professor of History at the University of North Carolina at Greensboro.

JOHN ANTHONY SCOTT is on the faculty at the School of Law, Rutgers University, Newark.

MILTON C. SERNETT is Associate Professor of Afro-American Studies at Syracuse University.

ROBERT G. SHERER is Professor of History at Wiley College, Texas.

JOAN R. SHERMAN is Associate Professor of English at Rutgers University.

TOM W. SHICK taught Afro-American Studies at the University of Wisconsin.

JASON H. SILVERMAN is Associate Professor of History at Winthrop College.

JOHN Y. SIMON is Executive Director of the Ulysses S. Grant Association, Southern Illinois University, Carbondale.

J. CARLYLE SITTERSON is Professor Emeritus of History at the University of North Carolina at Chapel Hill.

KATHRYN KISH SKLAR is Professor of History at the University of California, Los Angeles.

RICHARD W. SLATTA is Associate Professor of History at North Carolina State University.

ELBERT B. SMITH is Professor of History at the University of Maryland.

JULIA FLOYD SMITH is Professor Emerita of History at Georgia Southern College.

DOUGLAS C. STANGE teaches in the Religious Studies department at Cleveland State University.

JOHN EDMUND STEALY is Professor of History at Shepherd College.

DOROTHY STERLING is a historian and biographer, living in South Wellfleet, Massachusetts.

PHILIP STERLING is a writer, living in South Wellfleet, Massachusetts.

JAMES BREWER STEWART is Professor of History at Macalaster College.

STEVEN STOWE is Assistant Professor of History at Indiana University.

RICHARD C. SUTCH is Professor of Economics at the University of California, Berkeley.

DANIEL E. SUTHERLAND is Professor of History at McNeese State University.

TOM E. TERRILL is Professor of History at the University of South Carolina.

EMORY M. THOMAS is Professor of History at the University of Georgia.

WILLIAM TOLL is a historian, living in Eugene, Oregon.

BLAKE TOUCHSTONE is Instructor of History at Tulane University.

MARK V. TUSHNET is on the law faculty, School of Law, Georgetown University.

DOROTHY TWOHIG is Associate Editor of the *Papers of George Washington* at the University of Virginia.

ROBERT TWOMBLY is Professor of History at the Graduate School of the City University of New York.

WILLIAM L. VAN DEBURG is Professor of Afro-American Studies at the University of Wisconsin.

JOHN MICHAEL VLACH is Associate Professor of American Studies at George Washington University.

CLARENCE E. WALKER is Associate Professor of History at the University of California, Davis.

JAMES W. ST.G. WALKER is Professor of History at the University of Waterloo.

JULIET E. K. WALKER is Associate Professor of History at the University of Illinois.

DAROLD D. WAX is Professor of History at Oregon State University.

DAVID O. WHITTEN is Professor of Economics at Auburn University.

DAVID K. WIGGINS is Associate Professor of Physical Education, Dance, and Leisure Studies at Kansas State University.

WILLIAM F. WILLINGHAM is a historian with the U.S. Army Corps of Engineers, Portland District.

CLYDE N. WILSON is Associate Professor of History at the University of South Carolina.

MAJOR L. WILSON is Professor of History at Memphis State University.

ROBIN W. WINKS is Professor of History at Yale University.

BERNARD W. WISHY is Professor of History at North Carolina State University.

WILLIAM L. WITHUHN is on the staff of the National Museum of American History, Smithsonian Institution.

PETER H. WOOD is Associate Professor of History at Duke University.

HAROLD D. WOODMAN is Professor of History at Purdue University.

GAVIN WRIGHT is Professor of Economics at Stanford University.

NORMAN R. YETMAN is Professor of Sociology at the University of Kansas.

ANGELA HOWARD ZOPHY is Assistant Professor of History at the University of Houston, Clear Lake.

INDEX

Boldface page numbers refer to complete articles.